MW01143800

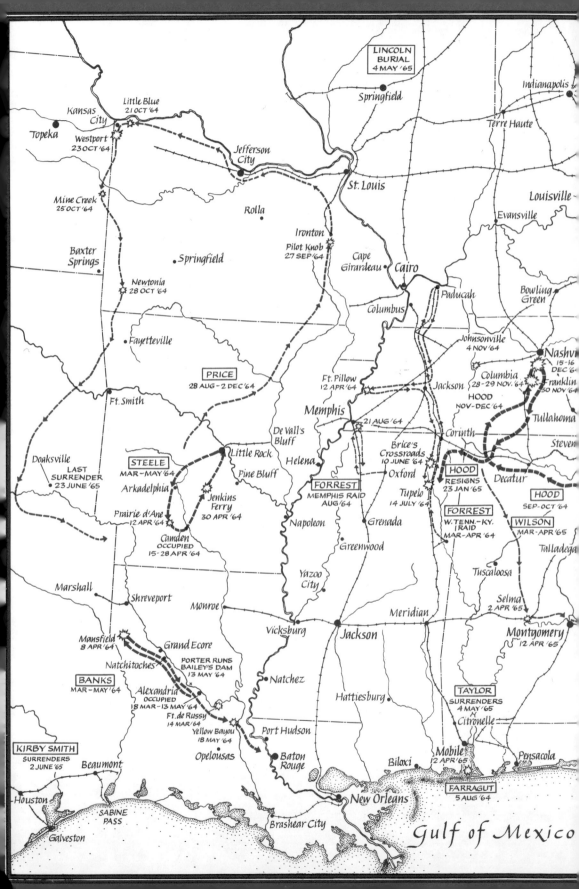

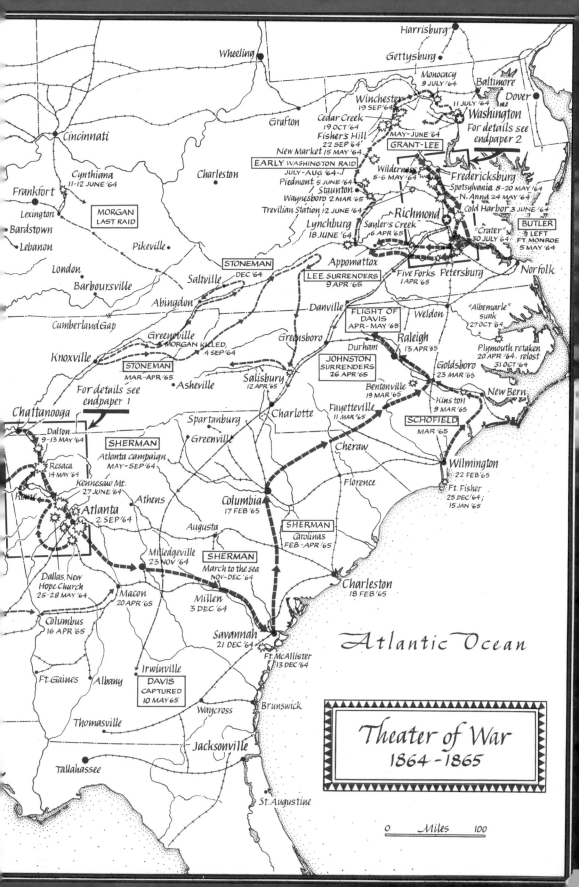

Harrisburg

Wheeling

Gettysburg

Baltimore

Monocacy
9 JULY '64

Dover

Winchester
19 SEP '64

11 JULY '64

Grafton

Cedar Creek
19 OCT '64

MAY–JUNE '64

Washington
For details see
endpaper 2

Cincinnati

Fisher's Hill
22 SEP '64

GRANT–LEE

Charleston

New Market 15 MAY '64

EARLY WASHINGTON RAID
JULY–AUG '64

Wilderness
5–6 MAY '64

Cynthiana
11–12 JUNE '64

Piedmont 5 JUNE '64

Fredericksburg

Frankfort

Staunton

Spotsylvania 8–20 MAY '64

Waynesboro 2 MAR '64

N. Anna 24 MAY '64

Lexington

MORGAN
LAST RAID

Trevilian Station 12 JUNE '64

Cold Harbor 3 JUNE '64

Bardstown

Lynchburg
18 JUNE '64

Sayler's Creek
6 APR '65

Richmond

"Crater"
30 JULY '64

BUTLER
LEFT
FT. MONROE
5 MAY '64

Lebanon

Pikeville

STONEMAN
DEC '64

Appomattox

Five Forks
1 APR '65

Petersburg

Norfolk

London

LEE SURRENDERS
9 APR '65

Danville

Weldon

"Albemarle"
sunk
27 OCT '64

Barboursville

Saltville

Abingdon

Cumberland Gap

Greeneville
MORGAN KILLED,
4 SEP '64

Greensboro

FLIGHT OF
DAVIS
APR–MAY '65

Raleigh
13 APR '65

Durham

Plymouth retaken
20 APR '64, relost
31 OCT '64

Knoxville

STONEMAN
MAR–APR '65

Asheville

Salisbury
12 APR '65

JOHNSTON
SURRENDERS
26 APR '65

Goldsboro
23 MAR '65

New Bern

For details see
endpaper 1

Spartanburg

Charlotte

Bentonville
19 MAR '65

Kinston
9 MAR '65

Fayetteville
11 MAR '65

SCHOFIELD
MAR '65

Chattanooga

Dalton
9–13 MAY '64

SHERMAN
Atlanta campaign
MAY–SEP '64

Greenville

Cheraw

Wilmington
22 FEB '65

Resaca
14 MAY '64

Kennesaw Mt.
27 JUNE '64

Florence

Ft. Fisher
25 DEC '64;
15 JAN '65

Rome

Athens

Columbia
17 FEB '65

Atlanta
2 SEP '64

Augusta

SHERMAN
Carolinas
FEB–APR '65

Dallas, New
Hope Church
25–28 MAY '64

Milledgeville
23 NOV '64

SHERMAN
March to the sea
NOV–DEC '64

Macon
20 APR '65

Millen
3 DEC '64

Charleston
18 FEB '65

Columbus
16 APR '65

Savannah
21 DEC '64

Atlantic Ocean

Ft. Gaines

Irwinville

Albany

DAVIS
CAPTURED
10 MAY 65

Ft. McAllister
13 DEC '64

Thomasville

Waycross

Brunswick

Jacksonville

Theater of War
1864–1865

Tallahassee

St. Augustine

0   Miles   100

THE CIVIL WAR-3

Although he now makes his home in Memphis, Tennessee, Shelby Foote comes from a long line of Mississippians. He was born in Greenville, Mississippi, and attended school there until he entered the University of North Carolina. During the Second World War, he served in Europe as a captain of field artillery. He has written six novels: *Tournament, Follow Me Down, Love in a Dry Season, Shiloh, Jordan County* and *September, September.* While writing *The Civil War: A Narrative* (Pimlico, 3 volumes) he was awarded three Guggenheim fellowships.

ALL THESE WERE HONOURED IN THEIR GENERATIONS

AND WERE THE GLORY OF THEIR TIMES

THERE BE OF THEM

THAT HAVE LEFT A NAME BEHIND THEM

THAT THEIR PRAISES MIGHT BE REPORTED

AND SOME THERE BE WHICH HAVE NO MEMORIAL

WHO ARE PERISHED AS THOUGH THEY HAD NEVER BEEN

AND ARE BECOME AS THOUGH THEY HAD NEVER BEEN BORN

AND THEIR CHILDREN AFTER THEM

BUT THESE WERE MERCIFUL MEN

WHOSE RIGHTEOUSNESS HATH NOT BEEN FORGOTTEN

WITH THEIR SEED SHALL CONTINUALLY REMAIN

A GOOD INHERITANCE

AND THEIR CHILDREN ARE WITHIN THE COVENANT

THEIR SEED STANDETH FAST

AND THEIR CHILDREN FOR THEIR SAKES

THEIR SEED SHALL REMAIN FOR EVER

AND THEIR GLORY SHALL NOT BE BLOTTED OUT

THEIR BODIES ARE BURIED IN PEACE

BUT THEIR NAME LIVETH FOR EVERMORE

Ecclesiasticus xliv

THE CIVIL WAR

A Narrative

3 Red River to Appomattox

SHELBY FOOTE

PIMLICO

PIMLICO

20 Vauxhall Bridge Road, London SW1V2SA

London Melbourne Sydney Auckland Johannesburg
and agencies throughout the world

First published in Great Britain by The Bodley Head
1991
Pimlico edition 1992
Reprinted 1993
© Shelby Foote 1958 and renewed by
Shelby Foote 1986

Printed and bound in the USA

ISBN 0-7126-9802-7 (volume 1)
0-7126-9807-8 (volume 2)
0-7126-9812-4 (volume 3)

CONTENTS

★ ✗ ☆

I

II

III

☆ I ☆

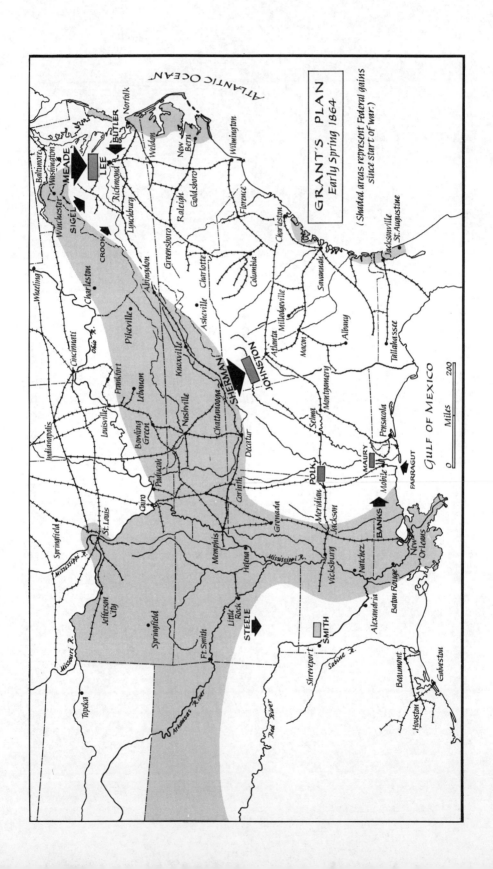

GRANT'S PLAN
Early Spring 1864

(Shaded areas represent Federal gains
since start of war.)

ATLANTIC OCEAN

GULF OF MEXICO

Miles

0   200

Another Grand Design

★ ✗ ☆

LATE AFTERNOON OF A RAW, GUSTY DAY
in early spring — March 8, a Tuesday, 1864 — the desk clerk at Willard's Hotel, two blocks down Pennsylvania Avenue from the White House, glanced up to find an officer accompanied by a boy of thirteen facing him across the polished oak of the registration counter and inquiring whether he could get a room. "A short, round-shouldered man in a very tarnished major general's uniform," he seemed to a bystanding witness to have "no gait, no station, no manner," to present instead, with his ill-fitting jacket cut full in the skirt and his high-crowned hat set level on his head, a somewhat threadbare, if not quite down-at-heels, conglomerate impression of "rough, light-brown whiskers, a blue eye, and rather a scrubby look withal . . . as if he was out of office and on half pay, with nothing to do but hang round the entry of Willard's, cigar in mouth." Discerning so much of this as he considered worth his time, together perhaps with the bystander's added observation that the applicant had "rather the look of a man who did, or once did, take a little too much to drink," the clerk was no more awed by the stranger's rank than he was attracted by his aspect. This was, after all, the best known hostelry in Washington. There had been by now close to five hundred Union generals, and of these the great majority, particularly among those who possessed what was defined as "station," had checked in and out of Willard's in the past three wartime years. In the course of its recent and rapid growth, under the management of a pair of Vermont brothers who gave it their name along with their concern, it had swallowed whole, together with much other adjacent real estate, a former Presbyterian church; the President-elect himself had stayed here through the ten days preceding his inauguration, making of its Parlor 6 a "little White House," and it was here, one dawn two years ago in one of its upper rooms, that Julia Ward Howe had written her "Battle Hymn of the Republic," the anthem for the crusade the new President had begun

to design as soon as he took office. Still, bright or tarnished, stars were stars; a certain respect was owed, if not to the man who wore them, then in any case to the rank they signified; the clerk replied at last that he would give him what he had, a small top-floor room, if that would do. It would, the other said, and when the register was given its practiced half-circle twirl he signed without delay. The desk clerk turned it back again, still maintaining the accustomed, condescending air he was about to lose in shock when he read what the weathered applicant had written: "U.S. Grant & Son — Galena, Illinois."

Whereupon (for such was the aura that had gathered about the name "Unconditional Surrender" Grant, hero of Donelson, conqueror of Vicksburg, deliverer of Chattanooga) there was an abrupt transformation, not only in the attitude of the clerk, whose eyes seemed to start from his head at the sight of the signature and who struck the bell with a force that brought on the double all the bellboys within earshot, but also in that of the idlers, the loungers roundabout the lobby, who soon learned the cause of the commotion in the vicinity of the desk. It was as if the prayers of the curious had been answered after the flesh. Here before them, in the person of this undistinguished-looking officer — forty-one years of age, five feet eight inches tall, and weighing just under a hundred and forty pounds in his scuffed boots and shabby clothes — was the man who, in the course of the past twenty-five months of a war in which the news had mostly been unwelcome from the Federal point of view, had captured two rebel armies, entire, and chased a third clean out of sight beyond the roll of the southern horizon. Now that he made a second visual assessment, more deliberate and above all more informed than the first, the bystander who formerly had seen only an "ordinary, scrubby-looking man, with a slightly seedy look," perceived that there was more to him than had been apparent before the authentication that came with the fixing of the name. The "blue eye" became "a clear blue eye," and the once stolid-seeming face took on "a look of resolution, as if he could not be trifled with."

Such, then, was the effect of the gathered aura. And yet there was a good deal more to it than fame, past or present. There was also anticipation, and of a particular national form. Just last week, on Leap Year Day, the President had signed a congressional act reviving the grade of lieutenant general, and Grant had been summoned east to receive in person his promotion, together with command of all the armies of the Union, which he was expected to lead at last to final victory over the forces that had threatened its destruction. Forgotten now was the small top-floor room his modesty had been willing to accept. Instead, the clerk obsequiously tendered the distinguished guest "the best in the house": meaning Parlor 6, where Abraham Lincoln himself had held court in the days preceding his inauguration, less than one week more than three years ago today.

Grant accepted this as he had the other, with neither eagerness nor protest, which caused a second witness to remark upon "his shy but manly bearing." Still another even saw virtue in the dead-level way he wore his hat. "He neither puts it on behind his ears, nor draws it over his eyes; much less does he cock it on one side, but sets it straight and very hard on his head." A fourth believed he detected something else beneath the general's "rough dignity" of surface. "He habitually wears an expression as if he had determined to drive his head through a brick wall, and was about to do it." Just now though, here in the close atmosphere of the lobby of Willard's — which a disgruntled Englishman complained was compounded, in about equal parts, of "heat, noise, dust, smoke, and expectoration" — what he mainly seemed to desire was an absence of fanfare.

But that was not to be. For a week now the town talk had been of his imminent arrival, and now that the talkers had him within actual reach they intended to make the most of him. Returning downstairs presently for dinner in the main dining room, and holding his son Fred by the hand as if for mutual reassurance, he managed to get as far as his table and even to order the meal before he was recognized by a gentleman from New Orleans who came over for a handshake. Then, as before, all hope of privacy ended. Word of his presence "spread from table to table," according to one who was there; "people got up and craned their necks in an anxious endeavor to see 'the coming man.'" This reached a climax when one of the watchers, unable to contain his enthusiasm, mounted a chair and called — prematurely, for the promotion had not yet been conferred — for "Three cheers for Lieutenant General Grant!" These were given "in the most tremendous manner" and were followed by a pounding that made the glasses and silverware dance on the tables, "in the midst of which General Grant, looking very much astonished and perhaps annoyed, rose to his feet, awkwardly rubbed his mustache with his napkin, bowed, and resumed his seat." For a time, good sense prevailed; "the general was allowed to eat in peace." But when he rose again and began to make his way out, once more with his son in tow, a Pennsylvania congressman took him in hand and began a round of introductions. "This was his first levee," the witness added; after which his retreat through the crowded lobby and up the staircase to his rooms was characterized by "most unsoldierly blushing."

Hard as this was on a man who valued his privacy and was discomfited by adulation, before the night was over he would find himself at storm center of an even worse ordeal. Word of his arrival having spread, he found on his return to Parlor 6 a special invitation to come by the White House, presumably for a conference with the Commander in Chief, whom he had never met although they both were from Illinois and were by now the two most famous men in the country.

If he had known that the President's weekly receptions were held on Tuesday evenings he would perhaps have postponed his call, but by the time he completed the short walk up the avenue to the gates of the executive mansion it was too late. He found himself being ushered up the steps, through the foyer, down a corridor, and finally into the brightly lighted East Room, where the reception was in full swing. The crowd, enlarged beyond the norm tonight by the news that he would be there, fell silent as he entered, then parted before him to disclose at the far end of the room the tall form of Abraham Lincoln, who watched him approach, then put out a long arm for a handshake. "I'm glad to see you, General," he said.

The crowd resumed its "stir and buzz"; there was a spattering of applause and even "a cheer or two," which struck Navy Secretary Gideon Welles as "rowdy and unseemly." Lincoln turned Grant over to Secretary of State William H. Seward for presentation to Mrs Lincoln, who took his arm for a turn round the room while her husband followed at a distance, apparently much amused by the general's reaction to being placed thus on display before a crowd that soon began to get somewhat out of hand, surging toward him, men and women alike, for a close-up look and a possible exchange of greetings. Grant "blushed like a schoolgirl," sweating heavily from embarrassment and the exertion of shaking the hands of those who managed to get nearest in the jam. "Stand up so we can all have a look at you!" someone cried from the rim of the crowd, and he obliged by stepping onto a red plush sofa, looking out over the mass of upturned faces whose eyes fairly shone with delight at being part of an authentic historical tableau. "It was the only real mob I ever saw in the White House," a journalist later wrote, describing how "people were caught up and whirled in the torrent which swept through the great East Room. Ladies suffered dire disaster in the crush and confusion; their laces were torn and crinolines mashed, and many got up on sofas, chairs, and tables to be out of harm's way or to get a better view of the spectacle. . . . For once at least the President of the United States was not the chief figure in the picture. The little, scared-looking man who stood on a crimson-covered sofa was the idol of the hour."

Rescued from this predicament — or, as the newsman put it, "smuggled out by friendly hands" — Grant presently found himself closeted in a smaller chamber, which in time he would learn to identify as the Blue Room, with the President and the Secretary of War, Edwin M. Stanton. Lincoln informed him that he would be given his lieutenant general's commission at a ceremony here next day and would be expected to reply to a short speech, "only four sentences in all, which I will read from my manuscript as an example which you may follow . . . as you are perhaps not so much accustomed to public speaking as I am." For guidance in preparing his reply, he gave him a copy of what he himself would say, together with two suggestions for remarks which he hoped the general would incorporate in his response: first, something that would "prevent or obviate any jealousy" on the part of the generals about to come under his command, and second, something that would put him "on as good terms as possible with the Army of the Potomac," to which he was a stranger. "If you see any objection to doing this," Lincoln added as a final sign of consideration for a man about to be cast in an unfamiliar role, "be under no restraint whatever in expressing that objection to the Secretary of War."

Grant expressed no objection, but as he returned to the hotel after midnight for his first sleep in Washington he was perhaps regretful that he had ever left the West, where life was at once less pushy and more informal, and convinced no doubt of the wisdom of his resolution to go back there at the first opportunity.

Returning next day to the White House for the ceremony that would correspond to a laying-on of hands, he brought with him his chief of staff and fellow townsman, Brigadier General John Rawlins, who had come east with him from Nashville in response to the presidential summons, and the thirteen-year-old Fred. Promptly at 1 o'clock, as scheduled, the Galena trio was shown into the presence of the President, the seven members of his Cabinet, his private secretary John Nicolay, and Major General Henry W. Halleck, the present general-in-chief, over whose head the man they had gathered to honor was about to be advanced. Facing Grant, Lincoln handed him the official document and read the speech of which he had given him a copy the night before. "General Grant: The nation's appreciation of what you have done and its reliance upon you for what remains to do in the existing great struggle are now presented with this commission, constituting you lieutenant general in the Army of the United States. With this high honor devolves upon you also a corresponding responsibility. As the country herein trusts you, so under God it will sustain you. I scarcely need to add that with what I here speak for the nation goes my own hearty personal concurrence." Brief as this was, Grant's response was briefer by seven words. He took from his coat pocket a half-sheet of notepaper covered with a hasty lead-pencil scrawl. Either the light was poor or else he had trouble reading his own writing. In any case he read it badly. "Mr President," he replied, groping and hesitant as he strained to decipher the words: "I accept this commission with gratitude for the high honor conferred. With the aid of the noble armies that have fought on so many fields, it will be my earnest endeavor not to disappoint your expectations. I feel the full weight of the responsibilities now devolving on me and know that if they are met it will be due to those armies, and above all to the favor of that Providence which leads both nations and men."

The surprise in this, to anyone aware of the Blue Room exchange the night before, was that the general had not incorporated either of the remarks the President recommended for inclusion in his acceptance speech. Nicolay, for one, thought that Grant, in an attempt to establish an independence none of his predecessors had enjoyed, had decided it would be wise to begin his career as general-in-chief by disregarding any suggestions from above. Lincoln himself, on the other hand, seemed not to notice the omission which his secretary considered, if not a downright act of insubordination, then in any case a snub.

Once the congratulations were over, the two leaders had a short talk that began with Grant asking what special service was required of him. The taking of Richmond, Lincoln said, adding wryly that the generals who had been told this in the past "had not been fortunate in their efforts in that direction." Did Grant think he could do it? Grant replied that he could if he had the troops, whereupon Lincoln assured him that he would have them. That ended their first strategy conference, such as it was, and Nicolay observed that nothing was said as to the route or method to be employed, the jump-off date, or the amount of time the operation would require. All Grant said was that he could take Richmond if he had the troops, and Lincoln had been willing to let it go at that; after which the general took his leave. He was going down to Virginia today, specifically to Brandy Station, headquarters of the Army of the Potomac, for a consultation with its commander as a prelude to the planning of his over-all campaign.

One thing remained to be done before he got aboard the train. No truly recognizable photograph had been made of him since the early days of the war, when his beard reached the middle buttons on his blouse, and he had agreed — perhaps without considering that he thus would lose the near-anonymity he had enjoyed among strangers up to now — to an appointment that would remedy the lack. Accompanied by Stanton, who proposed to go to the station to see him off, he rode from the White House, down Pennsylvania Avenue, to the intersection of Seventh Street, where the carriage stopped in front of Mathew Brady's Portrait Gallery. The photographer was waiting anxiously, and wasted no time in getting the general upstairs into what he called his "operating room," where he had four of his big cameras ready for action. It was past 4 o'clock by now and the light was failing; so while Grant took his place in a chair on which the cameras, their lenses two full feet in length and just under half a foot in diameter, were trained like a battery of siege guns, Brady sent an assistant up on the roof to draw back the shade from the skylight directly overhead. To his horror, the fellow stumbled, both feet crashing through the glass to let fall a shower of jagged shards around the general below. "It was a miracle that some of the pieces didn't strike him," the photographer later said. "And if one had, it would have been the end of Grant; for that glass was two inches thick." Still more surprising, in its way, was the general's reaction. He glanced up casually, with "a barely perceptible quiver of the nostril," then as casually back down, and that was all. This seemed to Brady "the most remarkable display of nerve I ever witnessed."

It was otherwise with Stanton, who appeared unstrung: not only for Grant's sake, as it turned out, but also for his own, though none of the splinters had landed anywhere near him. Grasping the photographer by the arm, he pulled him aside and sputtered excitedly, "Not a word about this, Brady, not a word! You must never breathe a word of what happened here today. . . . It would be impossible to convince the people that this was not an attempt at assassination!"

The train made good time from Alexandria, chuffing through Manassas and Warrenton Junction, on to Brandy, a distance of just under sixty miles; Grant arrived in a driving rain, soon after nightfall, to find that the Army of the Potomac, whatever its shortcomings in other respects — there was scarcely a place-name on the landscape that did not mark the scene of one or more of its defeats — knew how to greet a visitor in style. A regiment of Zouaves, snappy in red fezzes and baggy trousers, was drawn up to give him a salute on his arrival, despite the rain, and a headquarters band, happily unaware that Grant was tone-deaf — he once remarked that he only knew two tunes in all: "One was Yankee Doodle. The other wasn't" — played vigorous music by way of welcome as the army commander, Major General George G. Meade, emerged from his tent for a salute and a handshake. He and Grant, six years his junior and eight years behind him at West Point, had not met since the Mexican War, sixteen years ago, when they were lieutenants.

Tall and dour, professorial in appearance, with a hook nose, a gray-shot beard, glinting spectacles, and heavy pouches under his eyes, Meade was one of the problems that would have to be dealt with before other, larger problems could be tackled. Specifically, the question was whether to keep him where he was, a prima donna commander of a prima donna army, or remove him. His trouble, aside from a hair-trigger temper that kept his staff on edge and caused associates to refer to him, behind his back, as "a damned old goggle-eyed snapping turtle," was that he lacked the quality which Grant not only personified himself but also prized highest in a subordinate: the killer instinct. At Gettysburg eight months ago, after less than a week in command, Meade had defeated and driven the rebel invaders from his native Pennsylvania, but then, with his foe at bay on the near bank of a flooded, bridgeless river, had flinched from delivering the coup de grâce which Lincoln, for one, was convinced would have ended the war. Instead, the Confederates, low on ammunition and bled down to not much more than half their strength, had withdrawn unmolested across the rain-swollen Potomac to take up a new defensive position behind the Rapidan, where they still were. Meade had crossed in late November, with the intention of coming to grips with them in the wintry south-bank thickets, but then at the last minute had held his hand; had returned, in fact, ingloriously to the north bank, and ever since had seemed content to settle for the stalemate that resulted, despite practically unremittent prodding from the press and the politicians in his rear. Just last week he had been grilled by Congress's radical-dominated Joint Committee on the Conduct of the War, whose members for the most part, in admiration of his politics and his bluster, favored recalling Major General Joseph Hooker to the post he had lost to Meade on the eve of Gettysburg. Much bitterness had ensued between the Pennsylvanian and his critics; "My enemies," he called them in a letter this week to a kinsman, maintaining that they consisted "of certain politicians who wish me removed to restore Hooker; then of certain subordinates, whose military reputations are involved in the destruction of mine; finally, [of] a class of vultures who in Hooker's day preyed upon the army, and who sigh for a return of those glorious days."

This was accurate enough, as far as it went, but it seemed to Grant — as, indeed, it must have done to even a casual observer — that the trouble lay deeper, in the ranks of the army itself. Partly the reason was boredom, a lack of employment in the craft for which its members had been trained. "A winter in tents is monotonous," one officer complained. "Card playing, horse racing, and kindred amusements become stale when made a steady occupation." Moreover, Grant would have agreed with an assessment later made by a young West Pointer, a newcomer like himself to the eastern theater, that the trouble with the Army of the Potomac, predating both Meade and Hooker, was its "lack of springy formation and audacious, self-reliant initiative. This organic weakness was entirely due to not having had in its youth skillfully aggressive leadership. Its early commanders had dissipated war's best elixir by training it into a life of caution, and the evil of that schooling it had shown on more than one occasion."

Before coming down to Brandy, Grant had rather inclined to the belief that the removal of Meade was a prerequisite to correction of this state of mind in the army he commanded. But once the round of greetings and introductions had ended and the corps and division commanders had retired for the night, leaving the two men alone for a private conference, Meade showed Grant a side of himself that proved not only attractive but disarming. He began by saying that he supposed Grant would want to replace him with some general who had served with him before and was therefore familiar with his way of doing things: Major General William T. Sherman, for example, who had been Grant's mainstay in practically all of his campaigns to date. If so, Meade declared, he hoped there would be no hesitation on his account, since (as Grant paraphrased it afterwards) "the work before us was of such vast importance to the whole nation that the feeling or wishes of no one person should stand in the way of selecting the right men for all positions. For himself, he would serve to the best of his ability wherever placed." Grant was impressed. The offer, he said, gave him "even a more favorable opinion of Meade than did his great victory at Gettysburg," and he assured him, then and there, that he had "no thought of substituting anyone for him," least of all Sherman, who "could not be spared from the West." Now it was Meade who was impressed, and he said as much the following day in a letter to his wife. "I was much pleased with Grant," he wrote, "and most agreeably disappointed in his evidence of mind and character. You may rest assured he is not an ordinary man."

Mutual admiration on the part of the two leaders might be a good and healthy thing for all concerned, but the troops themselves, having paid in blood for the blasting of a number of overblown reputations in the drawn-out course of the war, were unconvinced and noncommittal. While this latest addition to the doleful list of their commanders was on his way eastward, they had engaged in some rather idle speculation as to his professional ability, and it did not seem to them that the mere addition of a third star to each of his shoulders would necessarily increase his military worth.

"Who's this Grant that's made a lieutenant general?"

"He's the hero of Vicksburg."

"Well, Vicksburg wasn't much of a fight. The rebs were out of rations and they had to surrender or starve. They had nothing but dead mules and dogs to eat, as I understand."

About the best thing they could say for him was that he was unlikely to be any worse than John Pope, who had also brought a western reputation east, only to lose it at Bull Run. "He cannot be weaker or more inefficient," a jaundiced New York veteran declared, "than the generals who have wasted the lives of our comrades during the past three years." For one thing, Grant was likely to find a good deal less room between bullets here in Virginia than he had found in the region of his fame. "If he's a fighter," another hard-case infantryman put it, "he can find all the fighting he wants." Then he arrived and some of them got a look at him. What they saw was scarcely reassuring.

"Well, what do you think?" one asked a friend, who replied thoughtfully, having studied the firm-set mouth and the level glance of the clear blue eyes:

"He looks as if he meant it."

Nodding agreement, the first allowed that they would find out for themselves before too long. Meanwhile he was willing to defer judgment, except as to looks. "He's a little 'un," he said.

Talk of Vicksburg brought on the inevitable comparison of western and eastern Confederates, with particular reference to the presence here in the Old Dominion of General Robert E. Lee, the South's first soldier. Grant could never have penned up Lee, as he had done John Pemberton, thereby forcing his surrender by starvation; Lee, they said, "would have broken out some way and foraged around for supplies." Thus the men. And Rawlins, as he moved among the officers on Meade's staff, found a similar respect for the southern commander, as if they took almost as great a pride in having opposed "Mars Robert" as the Virginian's tattered veterans took in serving under him. "Well, you never met Bobby Lee and his boys," they replied when Grant's chief of staff presumed to speak of victories in the West. "It would be quite different if you had." As for the campaign about to open here in the East, they seemed to expect nothing more than another version of the old story: advance and retreat, Grant or no Grant. They listened rather impatiently while Rawlins spoke of past successes, off on the far margin of the map. "That may be," they said. "But, mind you, Bobby Lee is just over the Rapidan."

In any case, whatever opinions had been formed or deferred, the new chieftain and his major eastern army had at least had a look at each other, and next morning, after a second conference at which both past and future campaigns in Virginia were discussed, Grant returned to the station and got aboard the train for Washington. Last night he had received a presidential telegram extending an invitation from Mrs Lincoln for him and Meade "to dine with us Saturday evening," and he had replied by wire that they were pleased to accept. Overnight, however, he changed his mind. Today was Friday, March 11, and he would be leaving at once for the West — but only for a visit of a week or ten days, in order to confer with Sherman and other commanders there; after which, despite his previous resolution to avoid the political snares so thickly strewn about the eastern theater, he would be returning here to stay. Paradoxically, now that he had seen them at first hand, it was just those snares that determined his decision. "When I got to Washington and saw the situation," he later explained, "it was plain that here was the point for the commanding general to be. No one else could, probably, resist the pressure that would be brought to bear upon him to desist from his own plans and pursue others."

Not that the adulation and the invasions of his privacy did not continue to go against his grain. They did indeed. Closeted that afternoon with the President at the White House, he complained that the past three days, in Washington and at Brandy, had been "rather the warmest campaign I have witnessed during the war." Lincoln could sympathize with this, but he was disappointed that the general would not stay on through tomorrow night for the banquet planned in his honor. "We can't excuse you," he protested. "Mrs Lincoln's dinner without you would be *Hamlet* with Hamlet left out." But Grant was firm. "I appreciate the honor Mrs Lincoln would do me," he said, "but time is very important now. And really, Mr Lincoln," he added frankly, "I have had enough of this show business."

He left that evening on a westbound train, with stops for inspection at several points along the way, and reached Nashville in time to keep a St Patrick's Day appointment with Sherman, whose troops were advanced beyond Chattanooga, into northwest Georgia, to confront the main western Confederate army under General Joseph E. Johnston, around Dalton. They traveled together by rail to Cincinnati, the voluble red-head, "tall, angular, and spare, as if his superabundant energy had consumed his flesh" — so an acquaintance saw him at the time — and the new lieutenant general, who had once been described as "a man who could be silent in several languages" and who now seemed doubly reticent by contrast with his talkative companion. In the Ohio city they left the cars and checked into a hotel for privacy and room to spread their maps. There they worked on a preliminary draft of the over-all campaign which Sherman defined long afterwards: "He was to go for Lee and I was to go for Joe Johnston. That was his plan."

That was what it basically was. That was what it came to, in the end. At the outset, however, the plan — which might better have been defined, at this stage, as a plan for a plan — was a good deal more complicated, involving a great many other forces that were thrown, or were intended to be thrown, into action against the South. Grant had under him more than half a million combat soldiers, "present for duty, equipped," about half of them in the ranks of six field armies, three in the East and three in the West, while the other half were scattered about the country in nineteen various departments, from New England to New Mexico and beyond. His notion was to pry as many as possible of the latter out of their garrisons, transfer them to the mobile forces in the field, and bring the resultant mass to bear in "a simultaneous movement all along the line." Long ago in Mexico, during a lull in the war, he had written home to the girl he later married: "If we have to fight, I would like to do it all at once and then make friends." Apparently he felt even more this way about it now that the enemy were his fellow countrymen. In any case, the plan as he evolved it seemed to indicate as much.

"From an early period of the rebellion," he said afterward, looking back, "I had been impressed with the idea that active and continuous operations of all the troops that could be brought into the field, regardless of season and weather, were necessary to a speedy termination of the war." The trouble from the outset, east and west, was that the Federal armies had "acted independently and without concert, like a balky team, no two ever pulling together, enabling the enemy to use to great advantage his interior lines of communication." It was this that had made possible several of the greatest Confederate triumphs, from First Bull Run to Chickamauga, where reinforcements from other rebel departments and even other theaters had tipped the tactical scale against the

Union. "I determined to stop this," Grant declared. Moreover, convinced as he was "that no peace could be had that would be stable and conducive to the happiness of the people, both North and South, until the military power of the rebellion was entirely broken," he held fast to his old guideline; he would work toward Unconditional Surrender. He had it very much in mind to destroy not only the means of resistance by his adversaries, but also the will. The Confederacy was not only to be defeated, it was to be defeated utterly, and not only in the field, where the battles were fought, but also on the home front, where the goods of war were produced. "War is cruelty," Sherman had said four months ago, in response to a southern matron's complaint that his men appeared hardhanded on occasion. "There is no use trying to reform it. The crueler it is, the sooner it will be over." Grant felt much the same way about the matter, and here at the start, in formulating his plan for achieving what he called "a speedy termination," he was determined to be guided by two principles of action: 1) "to use the greatest number of troops practicable," and 2) "to hammer continuously against the armed force of the enemy and his resources, until by mere attrition, if in no other way, there should be nothing left to him but an equal submission with the loyal section of our common country to the Constitution and the laws of the land."

To achieve the first of these, the concentration of fighting men on the actual firing line, he proposed that most of the troops now scattered along the Atlantic coast, in Florida, Georgia, and the Carolinas, be brought to Virginia for a convergent attack on Richmond and the army posted northward in its defense. All down the littoral, various forces of various sizes were attempting to make their way toward various objectives, few if any of them vital to Grant's main purpose. Accordingly, he prepared orders for abandoning all such efforts south of the James, along with as much of the region so far occupied as was not clearly needed to maintain or strengthen the naval blockade. The same would apply in the West, along the Mississippi River from New Orleans to Cairo, where the men thus gained were to be employed in a similar convergence upon Atlanta and the forces likewise posted in its defense. As for the troops held deep in the national rear, serving mainly by their numbers to justify the lofty rank of political or discredited generals assigned to duty there, Grant proposed to abolish some of these commands by merging superfluous departments, thus freeing the men for duty at the front. As for the generals themselves, useless as most of them were for combat purposes, he favored their outright dismissal, which would open the way for just that many promotions in the field. Though this last was rather a ticklish business, verging as it did on the political, he thought it altogether worth a try because of the added opportunities it would afford him to reward the ablest and bravest of his subordinate commanders, even before the fighting got under way, and thus incite the rest to follow their example. By such methods (though little came of the last; out of more than a hundred generals Grant recommended for removal, Lincoln let no more than a handful go, mindful as he had to be of the danger of making influential enemies with the presidential election less than nine months off) he would reduce the ratio of garrison to combat troops from one-to-one to one-to-two, which in itself was a considerable accomplishment, one that no previous general-in-chief, from Winfield Scott through George McClellan to Henry Halleck, had conceived to be possible even as a goal.

As for his method of employing that continuous hammering which he believed was the surest if not the only way to bring the South to her knees, the key would be found in orders presently issued to the commanders involved: "So far as practicable all the armies are to move together, and toward one common center." This was to be applied in two stages. West and East, there would be separate but simultaneous convergences upon respective goals, Atlanta and Richmond, by all the mobile forces within each theater; after which, the first to be successful in accomplishing that preliminary task — the reduction of the assigned objective, along with the defeat of the rebel army charged with its defense — would turn east or west, as the case might be, to join the other and thus be in on the kill, the "speedy termination" for which Grant had conceived his grand design. It was for this, the western half of it at least, that he had come to Tennessee to confer with Sherman, his successor in command of the largest of the three main armies in this and the enormous adjoining theater beyond the Mississippi.

There the commanders of the Departments of the Gulf and Arkansas, Major Generals Nathaniel P. Banks and Frederick Steele, were engaged in the opening phase of a campaign of which Grant disapproved and which they themselves had undertaken reluctantly on orders from Lincoln, issued through Halleck before Grant was given over-all command. Advancing on Shreveport by way of Red River, which would afford them gunboat support, they were charged with the invasion and conquest of East Texas, not because there was much of strategic importance there, but because of certain machinations by the French in Mexico, which Lincoln thought it best to block by the occupation of Texas, thus to prevent a possible link-up between the forces of Napoleon III and those of the Confederacy, with which that monarch was believed to be sympathetic. Grant opposed the plan, not because of its international implications, of which he knew little and understood less, but because of its interference with, or in any case its nonfurtherance of, his design for ending the rebellion by concentrating "the greatest number of troops practicable" against its military and manufacturing centers. None of these was in the Lone Star State, so far at least as he could see, or for that matter anywhere else in the Transmississippi, which he preferred to leave to the incidental attention of Steele alone, while

Banks moved eastward, across the Mississippi, to play a truly vital role in the drama now being cast. Yet here he was, not only moving in the opposite direction, but taking with him no less than 10,000 of Sherman's best soldiers, temporarily assigned by Halleck to assist him in seizing the Texas barrens. Grant found this close to intolerable, and though he could not directly countermand an order issued by authority of the Commander in Chief, he could at least set a limit to the extent of the penetration and, above all, to the amount of time allowed for the execution of the order, and thus ensure that Sherman would get his veterans back in time for the opening of the offensive in northwest Georgia. Accordingly, two days before Sherman joined him in Nashville on March 17, he wrote to Banks informing him that, while he regarded "the success of your present move as of great importance in reducing the number of troops necessary for protecting the navigation of the Mississippi River," he wanted him to "commence no move for the further acquisition of territory" beyond Shreveport, which, he emphasized, "should be taken as soon as possible," so that, leaving Steele to hold what had been won, he himself could return with his command to New Orleans in time for the eastward movement Grant had in mind for him to undertake in conjunction with Sherman's advance on Atlanta. Above all, Banks was told, if it appeared that Shreveport could not be taken before the end of April, he was to return Sherman's 10,000 veterans by the middle of that month, "even if it leads to the abandonment of the main object of your expedition."

Sherman's own instructions, as stated afterward by Grant in his final report, were quite simple and to the point. He was "to move against Johnston's army, to break it up, and go into the interior of the enemy's country as far as he could, inflicting all the damage he could upon their war resources." For the launching of this drive on the Confederate heartland — admittedly a large order — the Ohioan would have the largest army in the country, even without the troops regrettably detached to Banks across the way. It included, in fact, three separate armies combined into one, each of them under a major general. First, and largest, there was George Thomas's Army of the Cumberland, badly whipped six months ago at Chickamauga, under Major General William S. Rosecrans, but reinforced since by three divisions from Meade for the Chattanooga breakout under Thomas, which had thrown General Braxton Bragg back on Dalton and caused his replacement by Joe Johnston. Next there was the Army of the Tennessee, veterans of Donelson and Shiloh under Grant, of Vicksburg and Missionary Ridge under Sherman, now under James B. McPherson, who had been promoted to fill the vacancy created by Sherman's advancement to head the whole. Finally there was the Army of the Ohio, youngest and smallest of the three, takers of Knoxville and survivors of the siege that followed under Major General Ambrose Burnside, who was succeeded now by

John M. Schofield, lately transferred from guerilla-torn Missouri. Made up in all of twenty infantry and four cavalry divisions, these three armies comprised the Military Division of the Mississippi under Sherman, redoubtable "Uncle Billy" to the 120,000 often rowdy western veterans on its rolls. This was considerably better than twice the number reported to be with Johnston around Dalton, but the defenders had a reserve force of perhaps as many as 20,000 under Lieutenant General Leonidas Polk at Demopolis, Alabama, and Meridian, Mississippi, in position to be hastened by rail either to Mobile or Atlanta, whichever came under pressure in the offensive the North was expected to open before long.

That was where Banks came in; that was why Grant had been so insistent that the Massachusetts general finish up the Red River operation without delay, in order to get his army back to New Orleans for an eastward march with 35,000 soldiers against Mobile, which would also be attacked from the water side by Rear Admiral David G. Farragut, whose Gulf squadron would be strengthened by the addition of several of the ironclads now on station outside Charleston, where the naval attack had stalled and which, in any case, was no longer on the agenda of targets to be hit. This double danger to Mobile would draw Polk's reserve force southward from Meridian and Demopolis, away from Atlanta and any assistance it might otherwise have rendered Johnston in resisting Sherman's steamroller drive on Dalton and points south. Later, when Banks and Sherman had achieved their primary goals, the reduction of Mobile and Atlanta, they would combine at the latter place for a farther penetration, eastward to the Atlantic and Lee's rear, if Lee was still a factor in the struggle by that time. "All I would now add," Grant told Banks in a follow-up letter sent two weeks after the first, "is that you commence the concentration of your forces at once. Preserve a profound secrecy of what you intend doing, and start at the earliest possible moment."

Such, then, was the nature of the offensive Grant intended to launch in the West, with Sherman bearing the main tactical burden. Similarly in the East, in accordance with his general plan "to concentrate all the force possible against the Confederate armies in the field," he planned for Meade to move in a similar manner, similarly assisted by a diversionary attack on the enemy rear. But he wanted it made clear from the start that this was to be something more than just another "On to Richmond" drive, at least so far as Meade himself was concerned. "Lee's army will be your objective point," his instructions read. "Wherever Lee goes, there you will go also."

If past experience showed anything, it clearly showed that in Virginia almost anything could happen. Moreover, with Lee in opposition, that *anything* was likely to be disastrous from the Federal point of view. Four of the five offensives so far launched against him — those by McClellan, by Pope, by Burnside, by Hooker — had broken in blood and ended in headlong blue retreat, while the fifth — Meade's own, the previous fall — had managed nothing better than a stalemate; which last, in the light of Grant's views on the need for unrelenting pressure, was barely preferable to defeat. Numerical odds had favored the Union to small avail in those encounters, including Hooker's three-to-one advantage, yet that was a poor argument against continuing to make them as long as possible. Just now, as a result of the westward detachments in September, the Army of the Potomac was down to fewer than one hundred thousand men. By way of lengthening the odds, Grant proposed to bring unemployed Ambrose Burnside back east to head a corps of four newly raised divisions which would rendezvous at Annapolis, thus puzzling the enemy as to their eventual use, down the coast or in Virginia proper, until the time came for the Rapidan crossing, when they would move in support of the Army of the Potomac, raising its strength to beyond 120,000 effectives, distributed among fifteen infantry and three cavalry divisions.

Such assurance as this gave was by no means certain. Lee was foxy. No mere numerical advantage had served to fix him in position for slaughter in the past. But Grant had other provisions in mind for securing that result, involving the use of the other two eastern armies. In the West, the three mobile forces had three separate primary assignments: going for Johnston, taking Mobile, riding herd on Transmississippi rebels. In the East, all three were to have the same objective from the start.

Posted in defense of West Virginia and the Maryland-Pennsylvania frontier, the smallest of these three armies was commanded by Major General Franz Sigel; "I fights mit Sigel" was the proud boast of thousands of soldiers, German-born like himself, who had been drawn to the colors by his example. This force was not available for use elsewhere, since its left lay squarely athwart the northern entrance to the Shenandoah Valley, that classic avenue of Confederate invasion exploited so brilliantly two years ago by Stonewall Jackson, who had used it to play on Lincoln's fears, thereby contributing largely to the frustration of McClellan's drive on Richmond at a time when the van of his army could hear the hours struck by the city's public clocks. To Grant, however, the fact that Sigel's 26,000 troops were not considered withdrawable, lest another rebel general use the Valley approach to serve him as Stonewall had served Little Mac, did not mean that this force was not usable as part of the drive on the Virginia capital and the gray army charged with its defense. It seemed to him, rather, that a movement up the Valley by a major portion of Sigel's command would serve even better than an immobile guard, posted across its northern entrance — or exit — to deny it to the enemy as a channel of invasion. Elaborating on this, he directed that the advance was to be in two columns, one under Brigadier General George Crook, who would march west of the

Alleghenies for a rapid descent on the Virginia & Tennessee Railroad, along which vital supply line he would move eastward, tearing up track as he went, then north for a meeting near Staunton with Sigel himself, who would have led the other column directly up the Valley. There they would combine for a strike at Lee's flank while Meade engaged his front; or if by then Lee had fallen back on Richmond, as expected, they would join in the pursuit, by way of the Virginia Central — another vital supply line — to the gates of the city and beyond.

So much for the task assigned the second of the three Union armies in Virginia. The third, being larger, had a correspondingly larger assignment, with graver dangers and quite the highest prize of all awaiting the prompt fulfillment of its task.

One reason Grant expected Lee to fall back on Richmond in short order, before Sigel had time to get in position on his flank, was that he intended to oblige him to do so by launching a back-door attack on the capital, from across the James, at the same time Meade was effecting a crossing of the Rapidan, sixty-odd miles to the north. The commander of this third force would be Major General Benjamin F. Butler, who had won a reputation for deftness, along with the nickname "Spoons," in the course of his highly profitable occupation of New Orleans, all of last year and most of the year before. Much as Sigel had been commissioned to attract German-born patriots to the colors, Butler had been made a general to prove to Democrats — at whose Charleston convention in 1860 he had voted fifty-seven consecutive times to nominate Jefferson Davis for President of the United States — that the war was not exclusively a Republican affair; Grant did not select, he inherited him, political abilities and all. For the work at hand, the former Bay State senator would have some 35,000 effectives of all arms, about half of them to be brought up from Florida and South Carolina by the commander of the Department of the South, Major General Quincy A. Gillmore, while the other half would be drawn from Butler's own Department of Virginia and North Carolina. He was to have naval support in moving up the James from his initial base at Fortress Monroe, as well as for the landing at City Point. That would put him within easy reach of Petersburg, the southside railroad center only twenty miles from his true objective, Richmond, which he was then to seize by means of a sudden lunge across the river. Or if Lee had managed a quick fall-back in such strength as to prevent a crossing at that point, Butler, having severed the city's rail connections with the granaries to the south, would combine with Meade and Sigel, upstream or down, for the resultant siege of the capital and its eventual surrender.

If all went as intended in the three-way squeeze he had designed to achieve Lee's encompassment, Grant himself would be there to receive the gray commander's sword at the surrender ceremony. For by now he had decided not only that he would return to the East for the duration of the war, so as to be able to interpose between the Washing-ton politicians and the strategy they might attempt to subvert, but also that the most effective position from which to do this would be in close proximity to the headquarters of the Army of the Potomac. There were, indeed — in addition to the most obvious one, that being in the field would remove him from the constricting atmosphere of the District of Columbia and the disconcerting stares of over-curious civilians, in and out of government — several reasons for the decision: not the least of which was that Meade, in command of much the largest of the three armies in Virginia and charged with much the heaviest burden in the fighting, was outranked not only by Butler and Sigel, whose armies were assigned less arduous tasks, but also by Burnside, whose corps would move in his support and had to be more or less subject to his orders if he was to avoid delays that might prove disastrous. Although the problem could be ignored in the easier-going West — there Thomas, for instance, outranked Sherman, and McPherson was junior to several other major generals in all three armies — Easterners were notoriously touchy about such matters, and if a command crisis arose from the striking of personality sparks on the question of rank, Grant wanted to be there to settle it in person, as only he could do. If this resulted in some discomfort for Meade, whose style might be cramped and whose glory would no doubt be dimmed by the presence of a superior con-stantly peering over his shoulder and nudging his elbow, this was re-grettable, but not nearly as much so, certainly, as various other un-fortunate things that might happen without Grant there.

Besides, there was still another reason, perhaps of more importance than all the rest combined. For all its bleeding and dying these past three years, on a scale no other single army could approach, the paper-collar Army of the Potomac had precious few real victories to its credit. It had, in fact, in its confrontations with the adversary now awaiting its advance into the thickets on the south bank of the river it was about to cross, a well-founded and long-nurtured tradition of defeat. The correction for this, Grant believed, was the development of self-confidence, which seemed to him an outgrowth of aggressiveness, an eagerness to come to grips with the enemy and a habit of thinking of wounds it would inflict rather than of wounds it was likely to suffer. So far, this outlook had been characteristic not of eastern but of western armies; Grant hoped to effect, in person, a transference of this spirit which he had done so much to create in the past. Twenty months ago, it was true, John Pope had come east "to infuse a little western energy" into the flaccid ranks of the accident-prone divisions that came under his command in the short-lived Army of Virginia. Unfortunately, he had only contrived to lengthen by one (or two or three, if Cedar Mountain and Chantilly were included) the list of spectacular defeats;

his troops had wound up cowering in the Washington defenses — what was left of them after the thrashing Lee had administered, flank and rear. But Grant, despite this lamentable example, had much the same victory formula in mind. The difference was that he backed it up, as Pope had been unable to do, with an over-all plan, on a national scale, that embodied the spirit of the offensive.

Sherman, for one, believed he would succeed, although the severely compressed and beleaguered Confederacy still amounted, as Grant said, to "an empire in extent." He expected victory, not only because of the plan they had developed in part between them in the Cincinnati hotel room, but also because he believed that the struggle had entered a new phase, one that for the first time favored the forces of the Union, which at last had come of age, in a military sense, while those of the South were sliding past their prime. Or so at any rate it seemed to Sherman. "It was not until after both Gettysburg and Vicksburg that the war professionally began," he later declared. "Then our men had learned in the dearest school on earth the simple lesson of war . . . and it was then that we as professional soldiers could rightly be held to a just responsibility." Heartened by the prospect, he expressed his confidence to Grant before they parted: he to return to Nashville, the headquarters of his new command, and his friend and superior to Washington for a time, riding eastward past crowds that turned out to cheer him at every station along the way.

Nor was there any slackening of the adulation at the end of the line. "General Grant is all the rage," Sherman heard from his senator brother John the following week. "He is subjected to the disgusting but dangerous process of being lionized. He is followed by crowds, and is cheered everywhere." The senator was worried about the effect all this might have on the man at whom it was directed. "While he must despise the fickle fools who run after him, he, like most others, may be spoiled by this excess of flattery. He may be so elated as to forget the uncertain tenure upon which he holds and stakes his really well-earned laurels." Sherman, though he was pleased to note that his brother added: "He is plain and modest, and so far bears himself well," was quick to jump to his friend's defense, wherein he coupled praise with an admonition. "Grant is as good a leader as we can find," he replied. "He has honesty, simplicity of character, singleness of purpose, and no hope or claim to usurp civil power. His character, more than his genius, will reconcile armies and attach the people. Let him alone. Don't disgust him by flattery or importunity. Let him alone."

Let him alone, either then or later, was the one thing almost no one in Washington seemed willing to do; except Lincoln, who assured Grant that he intended to do just that, at least in a military sense. "The particulars of your plan I neither know nor seek to know," he was to tell him presently, on the eve of commitment, and even at their first interview, before the general left for Tennessee, he had told him (according to Grant's recollection of the exchange, years later) "that he had never professed to be a military man or to know how campaigns should be conducted ... but that procrastination on the part of commanders and the pressure from the people at the North and Congress, which was always with him, forced him to issue his series of 'Military Orders' — one, two, three, etc. He did not know but they were all wrong, and did know that some of them were. All he wanted or had ever wanted was someone who would take the responsibility and act, and call on him for all the assistance needed."

Welcome though this was to hear, Grant was no doubt aware that the President had said similar things to previous commanders (John C. Frémont, for example, whom he told: "I have given you carte blanche. You must use your own judgment, and do the best you can." Or McClellan, who quoted his assurances after Antietam: "General, you have saved the country. You must remain in command and carry us through to the end. I pledge myself to stand between you and harm") only to jerk the rug from under their feet a short time later, when their backs were turned; Lincoln had never been one to keep a promise any longer than he believed the good of the country was involved. However, in this case he supplemented his private with public remarks to the same effect. "Grant is the first *general* I have had," he was reported to be saying. "I am glad to find a man who can go ahead without me." To a friend who doubted that Grant should be given so free a rein, he replied: "Do you hire a man to do your work and then do it yourself?" To another, who remarked that he was looking well these days, he responded with an analogy. "Oh, yes, I feel better," he laughed, "for now I'm like the man who was blown up on a steamboat and said, on coming down, 'It makes no difference to me; I'm only a passenger.'"

Partly Lincoln's ebullience was the result of having learned, if not the particulars, then at any rate certain features of Grant's plan. Of its details, an intimate said later that they "were communicated only to Grant's most important or most trusted subordinates" — Meade, Butler, and Sigel, of course, along with Sherman and Banks. "To no others, except to members of his personal staff, did Grant impart a knowledge of his plans; and, even among these, there were some with whom he was reticent." The President and the Secretary of War were both excluded, though he was willing to discuss with them the principle to be applied in bringing "the greatest number of troops practicable" to bear against the forces in rebellion; for example, that the units charged with the occupation of captured territory and the prevention of rebel incursions into the North "could perform this service just as well by advancing as by remaining still, and by advancing they would compel the enemy to keep detachments to hold them back, or else lay his own territory open to invasion." Lincoln saw the point at once, having urged it often in the past, although with small success. "Those not skinning can hold a leg," he said. Grant, as the son of a tanner, knew that this had reference to hog-killing time in the West, where all hands were given a share in the work even though there were not enough skinning-knives to go round. He liked the expression so well, in fact, that he passed it along to Sherman the following week in a letter explaining Sigel's share in the Virginia campaign: "If Sigel can't skin himself he can hold a leg while someone else skins."

By that time he was in the field, where he enjoyed greater privacy in working on his plan for the distribution of knives to be used in flaying the South alive. Having returned to Washington on March 23, he established headquarters three days later at Culpeper, six miles beyond Brandy Station on the Orange & Alexandria Railroad, about midway between the Rappahannock and the Rapidan. This was the week of the vernal equinox; tomorrow was Easter Sunday. Yet a fifteen-inch snow had fallen that Tuesday and the land was still locked in the grip of winter, as if to mock the hope expressed to Sherman that the armies could launch their separate but concentric attacks by April 25. To the west, in plain view, the Blue Ridge Mountains bore on their peaks and slopes deep drifts of snow, which Grant had been told by old-timers hereabouts would have to have melted away before he could be sure that bad weather had gone for good and the roads would support his moving trains and guns. Down here on the flat at least its whiteness served to hide the scars inflicted by commanders North and South, who, as one observer remarked, "had led their armies up and down these fields and made the landscape desolate." Roundabout Culpeper, he added, "not a house nor a fence, not a tree was to be seen for miles, where once all had been cultivated farmland or richly wooded country. Here and there, a stack of chimneys or a broken cistern marked the site of a former homestead, but every other landmark had been destroyed. The very hills were stripped of their forest panoply, and a man could hardly recognize the haunts familiar to him in his childhood."

Although at present much of this was mercifully blanketed from sight, the worst of the scars no snow could hide, for they existed in men's minds and signified afflictions of the spirit, afflictions Grant would have to overcome before he could instill into the Army of the Potomac the self-confidence and aggressiveness which he considered prerequisite to the successful prosecution of its offensive against an adversary famed throughout the world as the embodiment of the qualities said to be lacking on the near side of the river that ran between the armies. Discouraging to his hopes for the inculcation of the spirit of the offensive, the very landmarks scattered about this fought-over section of Virginia served as doleful reminders of what such plans had come to in the past. Westward beyond the snow-clad Blue Ridge lay the Shenandoah Valley, where Banks and Frémont had been sorely drubbed and utterly confused, and northeastward, leading down this way, ran the course of the Buckland Races, in which the cavalry had been chased and taunted. Cedar Mountain loomed dead ahead; there Sigel, thrown forward by bristly Pope, had come a cropper, as Pope himself had done only three weeks later, emulating the woeful example of Irvin McDowell on the plains of Manassas, where the rebels feasted on his stores, forty miles back up the railroad. Downriver about half that distance, Burnside had suffered the throbbing pain and numbing indignity of the Fredericksburg blood-bath and the Mud March; while close at hand, just over the Rapidan, brooded the Wilderness, where Hooker had come to grief in a May riot of smoke-choked greenery and Meade had nearly done the same, inching forward through the ice-cramped woods a scant four months ago, except that he pulled back in time to avoid destruction. All these were painful memories to the veterans who had survived them and passed them on to recruits as a tradition of defeat — a tradition which Grant was seeking now, if not to erase (for it could never be erased; it was too much a part of history, kept alive in the pride of the butternut scarecrows over the river) then at any rate to overcome by locking it firmly in the past and replacing it with one of victory.

    In working thus at his plans for bringing that tradition into existence, here and elsewhere, he was assisted greatly by a command arrangement allowed for in the War Department order appointing him general-in-chief in place of Halleck, who was relieved "at his own re-quest" and made chief of staff, an office created to provide a channel of communication between Grant and his nineteen department heads, particularly in administrative matters. The work would be heavy for Old Brains, the glory slight; Hooker, who had feuded with him through-out his eastern tenure, sneered that his situation was like that of a man who married with the understanding that he would not sleep with his wife. But Halleck thereby freed Grant from the need for attending to a great many routine distractions. Instead of being snowed under by paperwork, the lieutenant general could give his full attention to strategic planning, and this he did. From time to time he would return to Washington for an overnight stay — primarily, it would seem, to visit Mrs Grant, who had joined him in Cincinnati for the ride back east — but mainly he kept to his desk in the field, poring over maps and blueing the air of his Culpeper headquarters with cigar smoke, much as he had done a year ago in the former ladies' cabin of the *Magnolia*, where he planned the campaign that took Vicksburg.

✻ 2 ✻

Of all these several component segments, each designed to contribute to Grant's over-all pattern for victory on a national scale, the first to go awry was the preliminary one — preliminary, that is, in the sense that it would have to be wound up before the more valid thrust at Mobile could begin — involving Banks and Steele in the far-off Transmississippi, hundreds of miles from the two vital centers around which would swirl the fighting that would determine the outcome of the war. It was the first because it had already begun to falter before Grant was in a position to exercise control. Moreover, once he was in such a position, as general-in-chief, his attempts along that line only served to increase the frustration which both subordinates, proceeding as it were against their hearts, had been feeling all along. Not that it mattered all that much, whatever he did or did not do, for the seeds of defeat had been planted in the conception. By then the only cure would have been to abandon the crop entirely; which would not do, since Lincoln himself, with a fretful sidelong glance at France's latter-day Napoleon, had had a hand in the sowing.

Promptly after the midsummer fall of Port Hudson opened the Mississippi to Union trade throughout its length, Halleck had taken the conquest of Texas as his prime concern in the western theater. It seemed to him the logical next step. Besides, he had always liked to keep things tidy in his rear, and every success achieved under his direction had been followed by a pause for just that purpose. After Donelson, after Corinth, after Vicksburg, he had dismembered the victorious blue force, dispersing its parts on various lateral or rearward assignments, with much attendant loss of momentum. Consequently, although it was here that the North had scored all but a handful of its triumphs in the field, the war in the West had consisted largely of starts and stops, with the result that a considerable portion of the Federal effort had been expended in overcoming prime inertia at the start of each campaign. And so it was to be in the present case, if Old Brains had his way. With the President's unquestioning approval — which, as usual, tended to make him rather imperious in manner and altogether intolerant of objections — Halleck had been urging the conquest of Texas on Banks, who had been opposed in the main to such a venture, so far at least as it involved his own participation. A former Massachusetts governor and Speaker of the national House of Representatives, he was, like most political appointees, concerned with building a military reputation on which to base his postwar bid for further political advancement. He had in fact his eye on the White House, and he preferred a more spectacular assignment, one nearer the center of the stage and attended with less risk, or in any case no more risk than seemed commensurate with the prize, which in his opinion this did not; Texas was undeniably vast, but it was also comparatively empty. He favored Mobile as a fitting objective by these standards, and had been saying so ever since the surrender of Port Hudson first gave him the feel of laurels on his brow. Halleck had stuck to Texas, however, and Halleck as general-in-chief had had his way.

　　Texas it was, although there still was considerable disagreement as to the best approach to the goal, aside from a general conviction that it could not be due west across the Sabine and the barrens, where, as one of Banks's staff remarked, there was "no water in the summer and fall, and plenty of water but no road in the winter and spring." Halleck favored an ascent of Red River, to Shreveport and beyond, which would allow for gunboat support and rapid transportation of supplies; but this had some of the same disadvantages as the direct crosscountry route, the Red being low on water all through fall and winter. While waiting for the spring rise, without which the river was unnavigable above Alexandria, barely one third of the distance up to Shreveport, Banks tried his hand at a third approach, the mounting of amphibious assaults against various points along the Lone Star coast. The first of these, at Sabine Pass in September, was bloodily repulsed; the navy lost two gunboats and their crews before admitting it could put no troops ashore at that point. So Banks revised his plan by reversing it, end for end. He managed an unsuspected landing near the mouth of the Rio Grande, occupied Brownsville unopposed, and began to work his way back east by way of Aransas Pass and Matagorda Bay. There he stopped. So far he had encountered no resistance, but just ahead lay Galveston, with Sabine Pass beyond, both of them scenes of past defeats which he would not risk repeating. All he had got for his pains was a couple of dusty border towns and several bedraggled miles of beach, amounting to little more in fact than a few pinpricks along one leathery flank of the Texas elephant. By now it was nearly spring, however, and time for him to get back onto what Halleck, in rather testy dispatches, had kept assuring him was the true path of conquest: up the Red, which soon was due for the annual rise that would convert it into an artery of invasion.

　　By now, too, as a result of closer inspection of the prize, Banks had somewhat revised his opinion as to the worth of the proposed campaign. Mobile was still what he ached for, but Mobile would have to wait. Meantime, a successful ascent of the Red, as a means of achieving the subjugation of East Texas, would not only add a feather to his military cap; it would also, by affording him and his army valuable training in the conduct of combined operations, serve as excellent preparation for better and more difficult things to come. Besides, study disclosed immediate advantages he had overlooked before. In addition to providing a bulwark against the machinations of the French in Mexico, the occupation of Shreveport would yield political as well as strategic fruits. First there was Lincoln's so-called Ten Percent plan, whereby a state would be permitted to return to the national fold as soon as ten percent of its voters affirmed their loyalty to the Union and its laws. With Shreveport firmly in Federal hands, Confederate threats would no longer deter the citizens of West Louisiana and South Arkansas from taking the oath required; Louisiana and Arkansas, grateful to the Administration which had granted them readmission, would cast their votes in the November election, thereby winning for the general who had made such action possible the gratitude of the man who, four years later, would exert a powerful influence in the choice of his successor. There, indeed, was a prize worth grasping. Moreover, the aforementioned strategic fruits of such a campaign had been greatly enlarged in the course of the fall and winter, occasioned by Steele's advance on Little Rock in September, which extended the Federal occupation down to the Arkansas River, bisecting the state along a line from Fort Smith to Napoleon, and posed a threat to Confederate installations farther south. Ordnance works at Camden and Arkadelphia had been shifted to Tyler and Marshall, Texas, where they now were back in production, as were others newly established at Houston and San Antonio. Cut off from the industrial East by the fall of Vicksburg, still-insurgent Transmississippians had striven in earnest to develop their own resources. Factories at Tyler, Houston, and Austin, together with one at Washington, Arkansas, were delivering 10,000 pairs of shoes a month to rebel quartermasters, and inmates of the Texas penitentiary at Huntsville were turning out more than a million yards of cotton and woolen cloth every month, to be made into gray or butternut uniforms for distribution to die-hard fighters in all three states of the region. Shreveport itself had become an industrial complex quite beyond anyone's dream a year ago, with foundries, shops, and laboratories for the production of guns and ammunition, without which not even the doughtiest grayback would constitute the semblance of a threat. If Banks could lay hands on Shreveport, then move on into the Lone Star vastness just beyond, the harvest would be heavy, both in matériel and glory. By late January, having considered all this, and more, he was so far in agreement with Halleck that he wired him: "The occupation of Shreveport will be to the country west of the Mississippi what that of Chattanooga is to the east. And as soon as this can be accomplished," he added, his enthusiasm waxing as he wrote, "the country west of Shreveport will be in condition for a movement into Texas."

Another persuasive factor there was, which in time would be reckoned the most influential of them all, though less perhaps on Banks himself than on various others, in and out of the army and navy, about to be involved in the campaign. This was cotton. Banks was intrigued by the notion that the proposed invasion not only could be carried out

on a self-supporting basis, financially speaking, but could result in
profits that would cover other, less lucrative efforts, such as the ones
about to be launched through the ravaged counties of northern Virginia
and across the red-clay hills and gullies of North Georgia. What was
more, he backed his calculations with experience. On his march up
Bayou Teche to Alexandria, in April of the year before, he had seized
an estimated $5,000,000 in contraband goods, including lumber, sugar
and salt, cattle and livestock, and cotton to the amount of 5000 bales.
This last represented nearly half the value of the spoils — and would
represent even more today, with the price in Boston soaring rapidly
toward two dollars a pound in greenbacks. Yet those 5000 bales collected
along the Teche were scarcely more than a dab compared to the number
awaiting seizure in plantation sheds along the Red and in the Texas
hinterland; Banks predicted that the campaign would produce between
200,000 and 300,000 bales. Even the lower of these two figures, at a
conservative estimate of $500 a bale, would bulge the Treasury with
no less than a hundred million dollars, which by itself would be enough
to run the whole war for two months. Nor was that all. In addition to
this direct financial gain, he would also put back into operation the
spindles lying idle in the mills of his native state, where he had got his
start as a bobbin boy and where the voters would someday turn out in
hordes to express their thanks for all he had done for them and the
nation in their time of trial. It was no wonder his enthusiasm rose with
every closer look at the political, strategic, and financial possibilities
of a campaign he formerly had thought not worth his time.

Perhaps the most persuasive factor of all, so far at least as Banks
was concerned, was that he secured Halleck's approval of a plan, worked
out between them, that assured the coöperation not only of Steele, who
would move south from Little Rock to the vicinity of Shreveport with
15,000 troops, but also of Sherman, who was to send 10,000 of his
veterans to Alexandria for a combination with the 20,000 Banks himself
would bring to that point by repeating last year's profitable march up
the Teche. Including a marine brigade and the crews of twenty-odd
warships under Rear Admiral David D. Porter, which were to serve
as escort for the transports bringing Sherman's men from Vicksburg
and thenceforth as an integral part of the command in its ascent of the
Red, this would give Banks a total strength of just under 50,000; which
he believed was sufficient, in itself, to guarantee success in the campaign.
His opponent, General Edmund Kirby Smith, commanding that vast,
five-state Transmississippi region already beginning to be known as
"Kirby-Smithdom," had not much more than half that many soldiers
in all of Arkansas, Louisiana, Texas, and the Indian Territory combined.
Such opposition as Smith might be able to offer the veteran 45,000-man
blue army and its hard-hitting 210-gun fleet, Banks was not unjustified

in believing, would only serve to swell the glory involved in the inevitable outcome.

Sherman himself was inclined to agree with this assessment, though he was aware (as Banks perhaps was not, having had little time for theoretic study) of Napoleon's dictum that the most difficult of all maneuvers was the combination of widely divided columns, regardless of their over-all numerical superiority, on a field of battle already occupied by an enemy who thus would be free, throughout the interim preceding their convergence, to strike at one or another of the approaching columns. His only regret, the red-haired general said when he came down to New Orleans in early March to confer with Banks about his share in the campaign, was that Grant had forbidden him to go along. He stayed two days, working out the arrangements for his troops to be at Alexandria in time for a meeting with Banks's column on the 17th — the same day, as it turned out, that he would meet with Grant in Nashville, though he did not know that yet — then steamed back upriver to Vicksburg, declining his host's invitation to stay over for the inauguration on March 5 of the recently elected Union-loyal governor of Louisiana, one Michael Hahn, a Bavaria-born lawyer and sugar planter who had opposed secession from the start. Despite the delay it would entail, Banks apparently felt obliged to remain for the ceremony — which was quite elaborate, one item on the program being a rendition of the "Anvil Chorus" in Lafayette Square by no less than a thousand singers, accompanied by all the bands of the army, while church bells pealed and cannon were fired in unison by electrical devices — then at last, after managing to get through another two weeks of attending to additional political and administrative matters, got aboard a steamboat for a fast ride up the Mississippi and the Red for the meeting at Alexandria with Sherman's men and his own, whose ascent of the Teche had been delayed by heavy going on roads made nearly bottomless by rain. Before leaving he had written to Halleck of the public reaction to the inaugural celebration, thousand-tongued chorus, electrically fired cannon, and all. "It is impossible to describe it with truth," he wrote. In the future, much the same thing would be said of the campaign he was about to give the benefit of his personal supervision.

It was March 24 by the time he reached Alexandria, one week late. Even so, he got there ahead of the men in his five divisions, who did not complete their slog up the Teche until next day. Plastered with mud and eight days behind schedule, they did not let the hard and tardy march depress their spirits, which were high. "The *soldier* is a queer fellow," a reporter who accompanied them wrote; "he is not at all like other white men. Tired, dusty, cold or hungry — no matter, he is always jolly. I find him, under the most adverse circumstances, shouting, singing, skylarking. There is no care or tire in him." Banks, for all the dignity he was careful to preserve, shared this skylark attitude when he arrived, and with good cause. The time spent waiting for him to show had been put to splendid use by Sherman's veterans, who had arrived on time, with one considerable victory already to their credit and another scored before the Massachusetts general joined them.

Three divisions under Brigadier General A. J. Smith, a Pennsylvania-born West Pointer, they had left Vicksburg on March 10 and gone ashore two days later at Simsport, just up the Atchafalaya from its confluence with the Red. While Porter's twenty-two heavily gunned warships — thirteen of them ironclads, accompanied by some forty transports and quartermaster boats — returned to the Red for a frontal attack on Fort De Russy, a once-abandoned but now reoccupied Confederate strongpoint about halfway up to Alexandria, the infantry crossed a lush, bayou-mazed prairie called Avoyelles to come upon the fortification from the rear. Such few rebels as they saw en route were quick to scamper out of reach, having no apparent stomach for a fight. By late afternoon of March 14 the bluecoats were in position for a mass assault, not only hearing the roar of Porter's guns, which showed that he too was in place on schedule, but also receiving a few of his heavy shells that overshot the fort. Just before sundown, at a cost of only 38 killed and wounded, they stormed and took it, along with its ten guns and its garrison of 300 bitter, shell-dazed men, who, according to a newsman with the attackers, "screamed in demoniac tones, even after our banners flaunted from their bastions and ramparts." This done, the victors got back aboard their transports for the thirty-mile ride to Alexandria: all, that is, but the men of one division, who stayed behind to raze the fort by tearing out and burning its wooden beams and leveling the earthworks, after which they gave it the finishing touch by blowing up the powder magazine.

They had received excellent schooling in such work under Sherman, especially on the recent expedition to Meridian, where, in Sherman's words, they had cut "a swath of desolation fifty miles broad across the State of Mississippi which the present generation will not forget." In such work they used sledges and crowbars more than rifles, and though it involved much vigorous exercise, it was not only a fine way of relaxing from the rigors of the Vicksburg siege, it was also a good deal safer, since their efforts were mainly directed against civilians. Moreover, this particular division had a commander, Brigadier General T. Kilby Smith, whose views along these lines coincided more or less with their own. "The inhabitants hereabouts are pretty tolerably frightened," the thirty-three-year-old former lawyer was presently to write home to his mother in Ohio. "Our western troops are tired of shilly shally, and this year they will deal their blows very heavily. Past kindnesses and forbearance has not been appreciated or understood; frequently ridiculed. The people now will be terribly scourged." Presumably such words had been passed down as well as out, for private residences had begun to burn in Simsport almost as soon as the transports ran out their gangplanks for the troops to go ashore, and their progress across the lovely Avoyelles Prairie was marked by the ruins of burnt-out houses, some with nothing to show they had been there except an unsupported chimney; "Sherman Monuments," these were called. Arcadians of the region, a gentle people with a heritage of freedom, many of whom had been pro-Union up to now, were indeed "terribly scourged." The pattern was set for the campaign, so far at least as the western troops — "Sherman's gorillas," they dubbed themselves — were concerned. Next would come the turn of the inhabitants of the piny uplands beyond Alexandria, although a correspondent of the St Louis *Republican* was already predicting that unless such practices were discouraged there was a danger of "our whole noble army degenerating into a band of cutthroats and robbers."

By way of proving their skill as fighters as well as burners, six regiments of gorilla-guerillas, accompanied by a brigade of Banks's cavalry that rode in ahead of his infantry, pressed on above Alexandria to Henderson's Hill, twenty miles up Bayou Rapides, on a forced reconnaissance which reached a climax on the night of March 21 with a surprise attack, through rain and hail and darkness, that captured a whole regiment of rebel cavalry, some 250 men and mounts, together with all four guns of a battery also caught off guard by the assault. Returning to base three days later, they paraded their captives before Banks, who had just arrived and was delighted to find that they had not wasted the time spent waiting for him and the rest of the five divisions they were supposed to reinforce. When these wound up their march next day, March 25, he had concentrated under his immediate command by far the most impressive display of military strength ever seen in the Transmississippi, on land or water. With ninety pieces of field artillery and considerably better than twice that number of heavier guns afloat, he had 30,000 effectives on hand, practically all of them seasoned campaigners, and was about to move up the Red for a conjunction near Shreveport with half that many more under Steele, who he now learned had left Little Rock two days ago, marching south-southwest toward the same objective. The outlook was auspicious, especially in light of the fact that his troops had already proved their superiority, first at Fort De Russy and again at Henderson's Hill, over such forces of the enemy as they had managed to trick or cower into remaining within their reach. But then next day, as he was about to order a resumption of the march, a high-ranking courier arrived with Grant's eleven-day-old letter of instructions from Nashville, written while waiting for Sherman to join him there.

This could not but give Banks pause, stipulating as it did that if he did not feel certain of taking Shreveport by the end of April he was to return A. J. Smith's command to Sherman by the middle of that month "for movements east of the Mississippi." Discouraging as this was in part — for it not only fixed him with a tighter schedule than he had felt obliged to follow when he set out, it also threatened him with the imminent loss of the three best divisions in his army — Banks took heart at something else the letter said. If the expedition was successful, he was to leave the holding of Shreveport and the line of the Red to Steele, while he himself returned to New Orleans for an advance on Mobile as part of the new general-in-chief's design for a spring offensive in the central theater. This was the assignment he had coveted all along, and though he was aware of the danger of being over-hasty in military matters, this went far toward reconciling him to the step-up in the tempo of his march. With Mobile to follow, more or less as a reward for past successes, he wanted this Red River business over and done with as soon as possible. Accordingly, he put his cavalry in motion that same day and followed it two days later with his infantry, while A. J. Smith's men got back aboard their transports to accompany the fleet. The immediate objective was Grand Ecore, sixty miles upstream or roughly half the total distance. His plan was to move rapidly to that point and to Natchitoches, four miles south of Grand Ecore and the river, after which would come the leap at Shreveport that would wind up the campaign.

Banks himself did not leave Alexandria until after April 1, having remained behind to supervise an election on that date, by such voters as had taken the loyalty oath, of delegates to a state convention whose task it would be to draw up a new constitution tying Louisiana more firmly to the Union. Meanwhile the troops had been making excellent progress, encountering nothing more than scattered resistance that was easily brushed aside. By the time of the April Fool election, both Natchitoches and Grand Ecore had been occupied by leading elements of the respective columns, one advancing by land, the other by water. This meant that the campaign was back on schedule, despite the delay at the start. So far all was well, except perhaps that the lack of opposition had resulted in a dwindling of public concern outside the immediate area of operations. "It is a remarkable fact," the New Orleans correspondent of the New York *Tribune* declared on April 2, "that this Red River expedition is not followed by that anxious interest and solicitude which has heretofore attended similar army movements. The success of our troops is looked upon as a matter of course, and the cotton speculators are the only people I can find who are nicely weighing probabilities and chances in connection with the expedition."

If anxious interest and solicitude were what he was seeking, he could have found them not only in the New Orleans cotton exchange but also up Red River, aboard the flagship of the fleet. Porter had already lost one of his prized vessels, the veteran *Conestoga*, sunk March 8 in a collision on the Mississippi while returning from Vicksburg with a heavy load of ammunition that took her to the bottom in four minutes. She was the eighth major warship the admiral had lost in the past sixteen months, and two of these had been captured and turned against him, at least for a time. What was worse, it had begun to seem to him that if he continued to go along with Banks he would be in danger of losing a great many more, not so much through enemy action — he had never been one to flinch from combat — as through an act of nature; or, rather, a non-act. The annual rise of the Red, which usually began around New Year's, had not thus far materialized. Perhaps it was merely late this year; but twice before, in 1846 and 1855, it had not occurred at all. That was a nine-year interval, and now that another nine years had elapsed, there were indications that if Porter got his boats above the mile-long falls and rapids at Alexandria, he might not be able to get them down again. If the river, instead of rising, took a drop, he would be left with the agonizing choice of blowing them up or having them fall into rebel hands, which would mean nothing less than the undoing of all the navy had accomplished in these past two years of war on the western waters. That was unthinkable, but he had boasted so often that he could take his fleet "wherever the sand was damp," the admiral now found it impossible to renege on his promise to stay with the army to the end of its upstream trek. After three days of tugging and bumping — during which time the river, to his alarm, began to dwindle, then rose slightly — he got his largest ironclad, *Eastport*, over the falls; after which he followed with a dozen lighter-draft gunboats and twenty transports laden with troops. "The water is quite a muddy red and looks anything but inviting," a sailor wrote in his diary as the column began its winding crawl to Grand Ecore. "The transports from the head belch out three bellowing whistles which is caught up by the next, and sometimes two or three vie in a euphonious concert much resembling the bellowing of cattle at the smell of blood."

So far, except for the considerable slaughter of pigs and chickens encountered on the march, the smell of blood had been little more than a figurative expression. Moreover, if Banks could judge by indications, the Confederates were either content to have it remain so, or else they were incapable of having it otherwise, knowing only too well that most of the blood that would be spilled would be their own. In any case, the one thing they had not done was fight, and as he boarded his headquarters boat at Alexandria for an upstream ride on the evening of April 2 — a nattily dressed man in his vigorous prime, two years short of fifty, wearing highly polished boots and chinking spurs, a light-blue overcoat, buckskin gauntlets elbow-high, a bell-crowned hat, and a neatly groomed mustache and brief imperial — he got off a dispatch to

Halleck expressing his confidence in "an immediate and successful issue" of the campaign, the end of which he believed was in plain view.

"Our troops now occupy Natchitoches," he informed Old Brains, "and we hope to be in Shreveport by the 10th of April. I do not fear concentration of the enemy at that point. My fear is that they may not be willing to meet us."

In the course of the past three years Lincoln had read other such dispatches, and all too often they had turned out to be prologues to disaster. Reading this one, when in time it reached Washington, he frowned and shook his head in disapproval.

"I am sorry to see this tone of confidence," he said. "The next news we shall hear from there will be of a defeat."

A defeat was what the Confederates had very much in mind for the invaders: especially Major General Richard Taylor, Kirby Smith's West Louisiana commander, who had crossed swords with Banks before, first in the Shenandoah Valley, two years ago, and then along the Teche the previous year. Tactically, the second of these confrontations had not been as brilliant as the first, in which Taylor, serving as one of Stonewall Jackson's ablest lieutenants, had helped to strip the former Bay State politician of so many well-stocked wagons that he had been nicknamed "Commissary" Banks; but the aptness of this nom-de-guerre had been redemonstrated last summer, west of New Orleans, when Taylor's surprise descent on Banks's forward supply base at Brashear City, yielding an estimated $2,000,000 in ordnance and other stores, helped immeasurably to equip the army he had been raising for the defense of his home state ever since his transfer from Virginia. A son of Zachary Taylor and brother of Jefferson Davis's first wife, now just past his thirty-eighth birthday, he was described by one of his soldiers as "a quiet, unassuming little fellow, but noisy on retreats, with a tendency to cuss mules and wagons which stall on the road."

This tendency had been given a free rein for the past three weeks, in the course of which he had been obliged to fall back nearly two hundred miles before an adversary he was convinced he could whip, if he could only manage to meet him on anything approaching equal terms. But there was the rub. With fewer than 7000 troops in the path of better than four times that number backed by the guns of the Union fleet, he had no choice except to continue his retreat, hard though it was to suffer without retaliation the vandalism of A. J. Smith's gorillas, not to mention such professional indignities as Fort De Russy and the loss of most of his cavalry at Henderson's Hill. His consolation was that he was falling back toward reinforcements, which Kirby Smith kept assuring him were on the way from Arkansas and Texas. However — as might have been expected of a young man who had served his war apprenticeship under the bloody-minded and highly time-conscious Stonewall — he chafed at the delay. On the last day of March, with his troops in motion for a concentration forty miles northwest of Natchitoches and less than half that distance from the Texas border, he sent an irate dispatch informing the department commander that his patience was near the snapping point. "Had I conceived for an instant that such astonishing delay would ensue before reinforcements reached me," he told Smith, "I would have fought a battle even against the heavy odds. It would have been better to lose the state after a defeat than to surrender it without a fight. The fairest and richest portion of the Confederacy is now a waste. Louisiana may well know her destiny. Her children are exiles; her labor system is destroyed. Expecting every hour to receive the promised reinforcements, I did not feel justified in hazarding a general engagement with my little army. I shall never cease to regret my error."

"Hydrocephalus at Shreveport produced atrophy elsewhere," he afterwards protested, complaining acidly that while his superior "displayed much ardor in the establishment of bureaux, and on a scale proportioned rather to the extent of his territory than to the smallness of his force," Smith neglected the more vital task of resisting blue aggression in the field. In thus indulging his fondness for classical allusion, while at the same time venting his spleen, Yale man Taylor was not altogether fair to a West-Point-trained commander who by now had spent a hectic year being responsible for a region the size of western Europe, much of it trackless and practically none of it self-sustaining, at any rate in a military sense, at the time he assumed his manifold duties. Not the least of these was the establishment of those bureaus of supply and communication scorned by Taylor but made altogether necessary by the loss, within four months of Smith's arrival, of all practical connection with the more prosperous half of his country lying east of the Mississippi. In short, he had been involved in a year-long strategic and logistic nightmare. If at times he seemed to vacillate in the face of danger, that was to a large extent because of the scantiness of his resources, both in manpower and equipment, in contrast to those of an adversary whose own were apparently limitless and who could move against him, more or less at will, by land and water. Missouri had been lost before he got there. Then had come the subtraction of the northern half of Arkansas, suffered while pinprick lodgments were being made along the lower coast of Texas. Now it turned out that all this had been by way of preparation for a simultaneous advance by two blue columns under Steele and Banks, converging respectively from the north and east upon his headquarters at Shreveport and containing between them more veteran troops than he had in his entire five-state department, including guerillas and recruits. If he was jumpy it was small wonder, no matter how resentful Richard Taylor might feel at being obliged to backtrack, across the width of his beloved home state, before the menace of a force four times his own.

Warned early of the double-pronged threat to his headquarters and supply base — the fall of which would mean the loss, not only of Louisiana and what remained of Arkansas, but also of much that lay beyond — Smith decided to meet the nearer and larger danger first: meaning Banks. He would hit him with all the strength he could muster, then turn and do the same to Steele when he came up. Accordingly, he alerted his Texas commander, Major General John B. Magruder, to prepare his entire force, garrisons excluded, for a march to support Taylor. In Arkansas, Lieutenant General Theophilus Holmes was given similar instructions, except that he was to retain his cavalry for use against Steele's column, slowing it down as best he could until such time as Taylor had disposed of Banks and was free to come in turn to his assistance. These alerting orders were issued in late February, before either enemy force had been assembled. In early March, though neither Federal column had yet set out, Magruder was told to put his men in motion. They amounted in all to some 2500 horsemen, combined in a division under Brigadier General Thomas Green, and left Magruder with only about the same number for the defense of all of Texas: a situation the Virginian considered not unlike the one he had faced two years ago, on the York-James peninsula, when he found himself standing with one brigade in the path of McClellan's huge blue juggernaut. Meanwhile Holmes, whose deafness was only one of the symptoms of his superannuation, had been relieved at his own request and succeeded by Major General Sterling Price, his second in command; Price was told to put his alerted troops — two small divisions of infantry under Brigadier General T. J. Churchill, with a combined strength of 4500 effectives — on the march for Shreveport. These were the reinforcements Taylor had been expecting all the time he was fading back across the width of Louisiana, protesting hotly at their nonarrival.

Green's progress was necessarily slow across the barrens and the Sabine, but Churchill's was impeded by Smith himself. By now the Transmississippi chieftain had begun to suspect that he had hoisted himself onto the horns of a dilemma: as indeed he had, since he thought he had. Having attended boldly to the threat posed by Banks, he feared that he had erred in leaving Price too little strength to hinder Steele, who might be able to descend on Shreveport before Taylor could dispose of Banks and come to its defense. Taking council of his fears, which were enlarged by information that Steele had set out from Little Rock on March 23, Smith held Churchill for a time at headquarters, so as to be able to use him in either direction, north or south, depending on whether the need was greater in Arkansas or Louisiana, then finally, in response to Taylor's increasingly strident dispatches, ordered Churchill to move south to Keatchie, a hamlet roughly midway between Shreveport and Taylor's latest point of concentration, just southeast of Mansfield. He had known what to do, but he had been so hesitant to do it that he had wound up not knowing what to do after all.

Dick Taylor had not helped with his hard-breathing threats to gamble everything on a single long-odds strike, provoked by desperation and congenital impatience. "When Green joins me, I repeat," he notified headquarters, "I shall fight a battle for Louisiana, be the forces of the enemy what they may." Horrified, Smith urged caution. "A general engagement should not be risked without hopes of success," he warned, reminding his impetuous lieutenant that rashness "would be fatal to the whole cause and to the department. Our role must be a defensive policy." Moreover, such resolution as he had managed so far to maintain, regarding his plan for meeting the two-pronged Federal menace, was grievously shaken by Taylor's expressed opinion that Steele, a "bold, ardent, vigorous" professional, might constitute a graver danger, despite his reported disparity in numbers, than the amateur Banks, who was "cold, timid, [and] easily foiled." Smith continued to waver under the suspicion that he had chosen the wrong man to tackle first. Finally on April 5, alarmed by news that Steele was making rapid progress, and in fact had completed nearly half his southward march by crossing the Little Missouri River the day before, he decided to ride down to Mansfield for a conference with Taylor. His intention was to revise his plan by reversing it. He would concentrate everything first against Steele, rather than in front of Banks, even if this meant standing a siege at Shreveport or retreating into Texas, where — it now occurred to him, as a further persuasive argument for postponing the showdown — a defeat would be more disastrous for the invaders.

Taylor was dismayed by his chief's vacillation. Asked for his advice three days ago he had been quick to give it. "Action, prompt, vigorous action, is required," he replied. "While we are deliberating the enemy is marching. King James lost three kingdoms for a mass. We may lose three states without a battle." He still felt that way about it, and he said so, face to face with Smith at Mansfield on the morning of April 6. Smith heard him out, a mild-mannered Floridian just under forty, outwardly unperturbed by the short-tempered Taylor, but left that afternoon to return to his headquarters, still gripped inwardly by indecision. Taylor, though he had been reinforced that day by Green, whose arrival raised his strength to 9000 effectives, still had been given no definite instructions. Churchill's 4500 were at Keatchie, twenty miles away, but when or whether they would be released to him he did not know. All Smith had said was that he would inform him as soon as he made up his mind — the one thing he seemed incapable of doing. Taylor apparently decided, then and there, that if anything was going to be done in this direction he would have to accomplish it on his own. And that was what he did, beginning the following day, except that he had considerable help from his opponent, who presented him with a tactical opportunity he did not feel he could neglect, with or without the approval of his superior, forty miles away in Shreveport.

Banks came on boldly, still exuding confidence as he prepared at Natchitoches and Grand Ecore for the final stage of his ascent of the Red. Alexandria lay sixty miles behind him, Shreveport only sixty miles ahead. The first half of this 120-mile stretch had been covered in five days of easy marching, and he planned to cover the second half in less.

Such frets as he had encountered up to now came not from the rebels, who he was convinced wanted no part of a hand-to-hand encounter, but from internal complications. For one thing, smallpox had broken out in the Marine Brigade, with the result that it was returned to Vicksburg and Kilby Smith's division took over the pleasant duty of "escorting" — that is, riding with — the fleet. The loss of these 3000 marines, who had not been included in his original calculations anyhow, was largely offset by the arrival of the 1500-man Corps d'Afrique, composed of Negro volunteers who had proved their combat worth to doubters at Port Hudson the year before.

Another complication was not so easily dismissed, however, for it had to do with money: meaning cotton. Banks had been getting very little of this because of Porter, who had been getting a great deal of it indeed — all, in fact, that came within his 210-gun reach. Unlike the army, which seized and turned over rebel cotton to the government as contraband of war, the navy defined cotton as subject to seizure more or less as if it was an authentic high-seas prize, the proceeds of which were to be divided among the officers and crew of the vessel that confiscated it, the only stipulation being that the bales had to have been the property of the Confederate government. Very little of it was, of course, but that did not cramp Porter or his sailors. They simply stenciled "C.S.A." on each captured bale, then drew a line through the still-wet letters and stenciled "U.S.N." below. When an army colonel remarked that the result signified "Cotton Stealing Association of the United States Navy," the admiral laughed as loud as anyone, if not louder, in proportion to his lion's share of the proceeds as commander of the fleet. This would not have been so bad, in itself; Banks, though punctiliously honest, had grown more or less accustomed to such practices by others, in the service as in politics. The trouble was that the upriver planters, hearing of Porter's activities below, began to burn their cotton rather than have it fall into his hands. By the time the civilian speculators, who had accompanied the army from New Orleans and were prepared to pay the going backwoods price for the hoarded staple, arrived in the wake of the gunboats, bearing trade permits signed by Chase and even Lincoln, there was nothing left for them to buy, either cheap or dear, for resale to the hungry mills of New England. Moreover, they directed their resentment less at Porter, who after all was doing nothing they would not have done in his place, than at Banks, who they believed had lured them up this winding rust-colored river only to dash their hopes by failing to deliver even a fraction of what he had encouraged them to expect. By the time they reached Alexandria it was evident there was nothing to be gained by going farther; Banks made it official by ordering their return. They had no choice except to obey, but they were bitter as only men could be who had been wounded in their wallets. "When General Banks sent them all back to Alexandria, without their sheaves," a staff officer later wrote, "they returned to New Orleans furious against him and mouthing calumnies."

It was of course no good thing, militarily or politically, for a man to have such enemies in his rear, but at least he was rid of a frock-coated clan who, he complained, had "harassed the soul out of me." And though they would be quick to fix the blame on him in case of a mishap, let alone an outright failure, Banks was more confident than ever that nothing of the kind was going to happen. It was not going to happen because there would be no tactical occasion for it to happen; Taylor simply would not risk a probable defeat. After reviewing his troops at Natchitoches on April 4 — a frequent practice which always brought him pleasure and tended to enlarge his self-respect — the former Bay State governor said as much in a letter to his wife. "The enemy retreats before us," he informed her, "and will not fight a battle this side of Shreveport if then."

When two days later — April 6: the second anniversary of Shiloh — he set out on the final leg of his advance, his route and order of march demonstrated, even more forcefully than his letters to Halleck and Mrs Banks had done, the extent of his conviction that the rebels would not dare to stand and fight before he reached his goal. At Grand Ecore the land and water columns diverged for the first time in the campaign, the former taking an inland road that curved west, then northwest, through the villages of Pleasant Hill and Mansfield, and finally northeast, back toward the Red, for a meeting with the fleet abreast of Springfield Landing, roughly two thirds of the way to Shreveport, which they then would capture by a joint attack. Banks chose this route either because he did not know there was a road along the river (there was, and a good one) or else because he thought the inland road, leading as it did through piny highlands, would make for better progress. If this last was what he had in mind, he was mistaken in that too. According to one of the marchers, a heavy rain soon made the single narrow road "more like a broad, deep, red-colored ditch than anything else." Heavy-footed, sometimes ankle-deep in mire, they cursed him as they slogged: particularly A. J. Smith's Westerners, who by now had acquired a scathing contempt for the former Massachusetts politician and the men of his five divisions, mainly Easterners from New York and New England. Paper-collar dudes, they called them, and referred with grins to the general himself, whose lack of military training and acumen was common gossip around their campfires, as "Napoleon P. Banks" or, even more scornfully, "Mr Banks."

Nor was the poor condition of the road itself the worst of the disadvantages an inland march involved. Beyond Natchitoches, in addition to being deprived of the support of Porter's heavy guns, the westering column would encounter few streams or wells, which would make for thirsty going, and little or nothing in the way of food or feed. One look at the sparsely settled region back from the river convinced a newsman that "such a thing as subsisting an army in a country like this could only be achieved when men and horses can be induced to live on pine trees and resin." Fortunately — at least from the subsistence point of view — Banks had brought along a great many wagons, no fewer in fact than a thousand, which assured that his soldiers would suffer no shortage of bacon or hardtack or coffee while crossing the barrens, although Smith's gorillas, whom Sherman had accustomed to traveling light, were so unappreciative as to sneer that they were loaded with iron bedsteads, feather bolsters, and other such creature comforts for the city-bred dandies under his command. That was of course false, or in any case a gross exaggeration, but it was altogether true that those thousand wagons and their teams did at once decrease the speed and greatly increase the length of the column: the more so because of the way they were distributed along it, with an eye for accessibility rather than for delivering or receiving an attack. Up front was a division of cavalry, followed by its train of 300 wagons. Next came the three remaining infantry divisions (the fourth had been left on guard at Alexandria, charged with unloading and reloading supply boats in order to get them over the low-water falls and rapids) of the two corps that had slogged up the Teche under Major General William B. Franklin, top man in the West Point class of 1843, in which he had finished twenty places above his classmate U. S. Grant, and a veteran of hard fighting in Virginia. Close behind them came their train of 700 wagons, with the Corps d'Afrique as escort. A. J. Smith's two remaining divisions (the third, Kilby Smith's, was taking it easy aboard transports, ascending Red River with the fleet) brought up the rear. However, so slow was the progress, so wretched the road, and so strung-out the column by the accordion action of all those interspersed mules and wagons, it was not until the following morning that Smith's jeering veterans lurched into motion out of Grand Ecore. By then the column measured no less than twenty miles from head to tail: a hard day's march under better conditions, by far, than here prevailed.

That was April 7, and before it was over Banks had cause to

suspect that he had erred in his estimate of the enemy's intention. Three miles beyond Pleasant Hill by midafternoon of this second day out, the cavalry encountered mounted graybacks who, for once, did not scamper at the threat of contact. Instead, to the dismay of the Federal horsemen, they set spur to their mounts, some half a dozen regiments or more, and charged with a wild Texas yell. The bluecoats broke, then rallied on their reserves; whereupon the rebels fell back, as before. That was about all there was to it; but the cavalry commander, Brigadier General Albert Lee, a thirty-year-old former Kansas lawyer, began to reflect intently on the disadvantages of his situation, particularly with regard to those 300 wagons directly in his rear, between him and the nearest infantry support. Several times already he had asked Franklin to let him shift his train back down the column, combining it with the infantry's, but Franklin had declined; let the cavalry look after its own train, he said. Now that the rebs were showing signs of fight, Lee made the same request again, with a further plea for infantry reinforcements, and received the same reply to both requests. In fact, when the young cavalryman tried to make camp near sunset, six miles beyond Pleasant Hill, Franklin sent word for him to push on four miles farther, train and all, so that the infantry would have plenty of room to clear the town next morning. Lee obeyed, though with increased misgivings, and was brought to a halt at nightfall, just short of his objective, Carroll's Mill, where he found gray riders once more drawn up in a strong position directly across his front, midway between Pleasant Hill and Mansfield.

Depressed by the notion of what was likely to result if he was struck by superior numbers on the march next day, he repeated his plea for reinforcements to Colonel John S. Clark, one of Banks's aides, who came forward that night to see how things were going. The colonel, agreeing that things were not going well, or in any case that the danger Lee foresaw was possible, rode back to present the cavalryman's request to Franklin in person, only to have him refuse it as flatly as before. So Clark returned to Pleasant Hill, where headquarters had been established that afternoon, for a conference with the army commander. Banks agreed that caution was in order, overruled Franklin, and directed him to send a brigade of infantry to reinforce the cavalry by daybreak. Franklin did so, though it went against his grain, and when Lee started forward next morning at sunrise he was pleased to find the rebel horsemen once more fading back from contact after each long-range exchange of shots, apparently intimidated by the steely glint of bayonets down the column, which signified that the front-riding cavalry now had close-up infantry support.

This continued for half a dozen miles: quick spatters of small-arms fire, followed by sudden gray withdrawals. It was hard for Lee to tell whether the Johnnies were really afraid of him or only pretending to be, in order to lure him on. Then the head of the column emerged from the dense pine woods to find itself on the rim of a large clearing, half a mile deep and half again as wide, with a broad, low hill in the center, on whose crest he saw a line of butternut skirmishers. He halted, brought his infantry to the front, and sent them forward, text-book style. The gray pickets gave ground before the massed advance, but when Lee rode up to the crest of the hill down whose opposite slope the rebs had scrambled for safety, he found his worst fears realized. There below him, in the woods along the far edge of the clearing, stretched a Confederate line of battle: not merely cavalry now, he saw, but infantry too, in heavy files, with artillery mixed in.

It was Taylor, and it was here, within twenty miles of the Texas border — only that bit short of having retreated across the entire width of his home state, leaving its people to the by no means tender mercy of the self-styled "gorillas" in his wake — that he was determined to make his stand. Last night, on his own initiative, he had sent Churchill word to march at dawn from Keatchie, twenty miles away; after which (but no sooner than the sun was four hours high, lest there be time for his order to be countermanded) he got off a note to Kirby Smith at Shreveport, saying laconically of Banks: "I consider this as favorable a point to engage him at as any other."

Sabine Crossroads, the place was called, three miles short of Mansfield, where four roads forked. One led east, allowing the Federals a chance to effect an early junction with their fleet; another branched northwest to Keatchie, which would place them in the path of the reinforcements moving toward him; while the other two ran generally north along parallel routes, giving the invaders a straight shot at Shreveport. Once they were where those four roads came together, free to choose whichever fit their fancy, Taylor's hope of blocking them would be gone, along with his chance to catch them out from under the umbrella protection of their heavy naval guns, strung out on a narrow, ditchlike road in a single, wagon-choked column. Moreover, in considering the tactical opportunity Banks was thus affording him, he had more in mind than a mere defensive stand, whatever numerical odds he might encounter. Like his old mentor in the Shenandoah Valley, he hoped to inflict what Stonewall had sometimes called "a speedy blow" or, more often, "a terrible wound."

Accordingly, while Tom Green and his Texans continued the harassment they had begun in earnest three miles this side of Pleasant Hill, Taylor chose his field of fight and began to make his preparations, including the summoning of the two infantry divisions then at Keatchie. The two already with him, under Major General J. G. Walker and Brigadier General Alfred Mouton, were ordered to return at first light, from Mansfield back to Sabine Crossroads, where they would take position along the near edge of the clearing, respectively on the right and left of the road that crossed the low hill just ahead. Cavalry under Brigadier Generals Hamilton Bee and James Major would guard the flanks, and a four-gun battery, posted astride the road, would stiffen the center. In Mansfield itself, by way of further preparation, private houses were selected and put in order for use as hospitals, and surplus wagons were sent rearward to clear the streets. Taylor was leaving as little as possible to chance, though he was also prepared to seize upon anything chance offered in the way of tactical opportunities; Green's troopers, for example, the most experienced and dependable body of men in his command, were to be employed wherever they seemed likely to prove most useful in that regard when they arrived. This force of 9000 infantry, cavalry, and artillery would be increased to 13,500 when Churchill got there, and though Taylor would not enjoy a numerical superiority even then — there were 20,000 blue effectives in the twenty-mile-long column toiling toward him — he intended to make up for that with the sheer fury of his attack, which he would design to make the most of his intimate knowledge of the ground, having chosen it with just that aim in mind. Nor was terrain the only advantage on which he based his belief that he would win when it came to shooting. "My confidence of success in the impending engagement was inspired by accurate knowledge of the Federal movements," he later wrote, adding that he was encouraged as well by previous acquaintance with "the character of their commander, General Banks, whose measure had been taken in the Virginia campaigns of 1862 and since."

By midmorning, April 8, he had established the line of battle the blue cavalry commander found confronting him when he topped the hill at midday. Young Lee sent back at once for additional reinforcements, meantime getting his batteries into positions from which to probe the gray defenses. A long-range artillery duel ensued, in the course of which Banks arrived in person for a look at the situation. He was undismayed. In fact, this was precisely what he had said he wanted on the day he set out from Grand Ecore: "The main force of the enemy was at last accounts in the vicinity of Mansfield, on the stage road between Natchitoches and Shreveport, and the major general commanding desires to force him to give battle, if possible, before he can concentrate behind the fortifications of Shreveport or effect a retreat westerly into Texas." Warned now by Lee that, in his opinion, "we must fall back immediately, or we must be heavily reinforced," Banks told him to hold what he had; he himself would "hurry up the infantry." That took time, partly because the cavalry train had two or three miles of the road blocked, but about 3.30 the other brigade of Franklin's lead division arrived to join the first. Hard on its heels came a courier with instructions for Lee to advance immediately on Mansfield. Shocked — for the town was three miles beyond the enemy line of battle, and he estimated that the rebels "must have some 15,000 or 20,000 men there; four or five times as many as I had" — the young cavalryman rode in search of Banks, who confirmed the validity of the order. Paraphrasing his protest, Lee said later: "I told him we could not advance ten minutes without a general engagement, in which we would be most gloriously flogged, and I did not want to do it." Given pause by this, although he was unwilling to abandon the attack, the army commander at any rate agreed to postpone it until another division of Franklin's infantry arrived, and he sent a staffer back to see that it was hurried forward with a minimum of delay.

Dick Taylor had bided his time up to now, but only by the hardest. Though he affected the unbuttoned, rather languid combat style of his father, Old Rough-and-Ready, sitting his horse with one leg thrown across the pommel of his saddle while casually smoking a cigar, he was anxious to force the issue. At one point, around 2 o'clock, when he believed he saw bluecoats massing for an attack on his left, he shifted one of Walker's brigades to Mouton and one of Bee's regiments to Major, but aside from this he did little except watch for an opening that would justify going over to the offensive before Churchill arrived from Keatchie. Meantime the Union buildup continued, although toward no apparent climax; Banks seemed unwilling to throw the punch that would invite the counterblow Taylor was eager to deliver. Finally, just after 4 o'clock, with a scant three hours of daylight still remaining, he decided to wait no longer. Mouton, on the strengthened left, was told to go forward.

He did so, promptly: "like a cyclone," one blue defender later said, while another described the charging graybacks as "infuriated demons." Mouton was among the first to fall, thirty-five years old, a West-Point-trained Shiloh veteran, son of the Creole governor who had helped to vote Louisiana out of the Union. His senior brigadier, Camille Armand Jules Marie, Prince de Polignac — "Polecat" to his Louisianians and Texans, who were unable to pronounce the royal name of the young Crimea veteran with the dapper beard and spike mustache — took over and pressed the uphill charge. His unleashed soldiers struck and broke the Federal right, routing two of the regiments there, and turned three captured guns on the fugitives as they fled. Taylor, observing the success of this while it was still in midcareer, sent word for Walker and Bee to go in, too: which they did, with similar results on the right, while Green threw his Texans into the melee on the left, exploiting on horseback the confusion Mouton and Polignac had begun on foot. All down the line, as the gray chargers emerged from the pine woods into the clearing to strike at both ends of the confused blue line, the high-throated rebel yell rang out.

Some on the opposite side did what they could to stay the rout. "Try to think you're dead and buried," a Massachusetts colonel told his men, "and you will have no fear." Either they did not try it at all, or else they tried and found it did not work; in any case, they ran and kept on running. Apparently it was the abruptness of the assault that made it so demoralizing, and this applied as much to those in the rear as to those up front. "Suddenly," a journalist on Banks's staff would recall, "there was a rush, a shout, the crashing of trees, the breaking down of rails, the rush and scamper of men. It was as sudden as though a thunderbolt had fallen among us, and set the pines on fire. I turned to my companion to inquire the reason of this extraordinary proceeding, but before he had the chance to reply, we found ourselves swallowed up, as it were, in a hissing, seething, bubbling whirlpool of agitated men." Franklin was among them by then, having brought his second division up the hill in time for it to join the rout and add to the lengthening casualty list, which would include some 1500 captives and about half that many killed and wounded. One of these last was Franklin himself, who was struck by a bullet in the shin and lost his horse, then took off rearward on a borrowed mount to brace his third division for the shock about to come. Banks too was intimately involved in the confusion, and like Franklin he did what he could, which was not much. Removing his hat for easy recognition, he shouted to the skulkers running past him on the road: "Form a line here! I know you will not desert me." He knew wrong. "Hoo!" they cried, and kept running. So he drew his sword and waved it about; but that worked no better. By then the fleeing troops had become what one of them afterwards called "a disorganized mob of screaming, sobbing, hysterical, pale, terror-stricken men."

Taylor was intent on completing his triumph by pressing the pursuit. Near sundown there was an interruption by a courier who arrived from Shreveport with a letter Kirby Smith had written that morning, urging caution. "A general engagement now could not be given with our full force," he advised. "Reinforcements are moving up — not very large, it is true. . . . Let me know as soon as you are convinced that a general advance is being made and I will come to the front." Taylor scanned it hastily, then looked up smiling. "Too late, sir," he said. "The battle is won." However, he took time to get off a dispatch announcing the victory to his chief, so far as it had been accomplished up to now. "Will report again at the close of the action," he ended the message. "Churchill's troops were not up in time to take part [but] will be fresh in the morning. I shall push the enemy to the utmost."

He did not wait for morning; Jackson-style, he made full use of the hour of daylight still remaining, though the going was as rough for him as it was for the retreating Federals. Panicky teamsters, unable to turn around on the narrow road, had unhitched their mules for a mounted getaway and left the wagons behind as a barricade against pursuit, their bare tongues extended at all angles to trip the unwary. One result of this was the denial of the road to such guns as had avoided capture up to then; Taylor took no less than twenty of them in all, along with ten times as many wagons, some with and some without their teams, but all loaded. Meantime Franklin was putting his third division, which was as large as the other two combined, into a stout defensive position along a ridge just back from a creek in a ravine about four miles from Sabine Crossroads. The pursuers came up raggedly, attacked piecemeal in the dusk, and were repulsed. Taylor knew it was time to call a halt, but not quite yet if his men were to have water for the night; so he contented himself with driving the blue pickets back to their ridge and taking possession of the creek in the ravine. There he stopped, intending to renew the pressure in the morning, and the firing died away in the darkness, giving place to a silence broken only by the wounded crying for water and by the scavengers, back up the road, reveling on the good things found in the captured Yankee train.

As one of his own generals had predicted at the outset, to his face, Banks had been "most gloriously flogged." Out of 12,000 Federals engaged, 2235 had been killed, wounded, or captured, while Taylor, with 9000, had lost less than half as many. Nor was that the worst of it, by any means. In addition to twenty guns and two hundred wagons, Banks had also lost time — the one thing he could least afford to lose if he was to occupy Shreveport and get Sherman's soldiers back to him on schedule. And to make matters worse, caught as he was without water for his parched troops on the ridge, he must lose still more time by retreating still farther to reach another stream and another stout position in which to defend himself from the blood-thirsty graybacks, whom he could hear feasting on their spoils, back up the road, and who obviously intended to have another go at him tomorrow, probably at daylight. Even if he could stay here all night without water, it was doubtful whether A. J. Smith's two divisions, camped a dozen miles away at Pleasant Hill, could arrive in time for a share in the defense. A council of war advised the obvious, and the withdrawal got under way at 10 o'clock. By midnight all the survivors were on the march in a bedraggled column made up largely of stragglers blown loose from their commands, "men without hats or coats, men without guns or accoutrements, cavalrymen without horses and artillerymen without cannon, wounded men bleeding and crying at every step, men begrimed with smoke and powder, all in a state of fear and frenzy."

One among them saw them so, yet supposed in his extreme distress that Banks was the most dejected man of all. He had left Grand Ecore expecting to be in Shreveport within four days, yet here he was, marching in the opposite direction into the dawn of that fourth day. As he rode among his trudging men it must have begun to occur to him that a great deal more than the van of his army had been wrecked at Sabine Crossroads. Any general who could not capture Shreveport with the odds as much in his favor as these had been was not likely to be given the chance to take Mobile. And without that feather in his cap, his chances of occupying the White House were considerably diminished, if not abolished, especially when he recalled the scapegoat hunt that invariably followed every failure such as the one in which he was now involved. Who that scapegoat was likely to be, he knew only too well; perhaps he even had time to regret the cotton speculators he had sent back to New Orleans "without their sheaves," and who were there now, "mouthing calumnies." He was indeed dejected by the time he drew near Pleasant Hill, having failed to spot a good defensive position anywhere along the road, though it may well have improved his outlook to find A. J. Smith's hard fighters already disposed for battle and looking determined. "If it comes to the worst," an Iowa colonel had told his troops when he called them out at 2 o'clock that morning to give them news of the defeat a dozen miles away, "I ask of you to show yourselves to be men."

They showed that, and more, when Taylor came up eleven hours later, hard on the trail of the dejected bluecoats he had whipped the day before, and after a two-hour rest halt, required by Churchill's road-worn Arkansans and Missourians, flung his reinforced victors forward with orders for them to "rely on the bayonet, as we had neither time nor ammunition to waste."

This was bravely said, but it was far from easily done. Taking heart from the stalwart look of Sherman's veterans, Banks had spent the morning hours preparing to defend the low, open, house-dotted plateau known felicitously as Pleasant Hill. During this time, according to a newsman, the area "had the appearance of a parade ground on a holiday, regiments marching to the right, regiments marching to the left, batteries being moved and shifted." Near the center of all this activity, in the yard of a house affording a panoramic view of the line thus being drawn, the journalist observed "a small cluster of gentlemen to whom all this phantasmagoria had the meaning of life and death, and power, and fame." It was Banks, surrounded by his chief lieutenants. He wore his light blue overcoat buttoned high against the April chill, and he passed the time "strolling up and down, occasionally conversing with a member of his staff or returning the salute of a passing subaltern." Franklin was there, limping on his wounded leg, his manner calm except for an occasional nervous tug at his whiskers, and so were A. J. Smith, sunlight glinting on his spectacles, and Brigadier General Charles P. Stone, who, after six months of confinement in army prisons and nine of unemployment, had been militarily resurrected by Banks as his chief of staff, thus giving the West Pointer a chance to dispel the cloud of suspicion that had gathered about his head and caused his arrest following Ball's Bluff, where he was accused of having treasonably exposed his men to slaughter. Not yet forty, "a quiet, retiring man who is regarded, by the few that know him, as one of the finest soldiers of our time," Stone sat on a rail fence, smoking cigarettes — a modern touch; cigarettes would continue to be rare and exotic until well into the following decade — and seemed to the reporter "more interested in the puffs of smoke that curled around him than in the noise and bustle that filled the air."

Gradually the noise and bustle died away as the various outfits settled down in their assigned positions and the day wore on and grew warmer. The genial cluster of uniformed gentlemen began to seem to the newsman "a rather tedious party," and apparently they themselves were of much the same opinion. Having done all they could in the way of preparation, the gold braid wearers had nothing to do now but wait, and while they did so they milled about rather aimlessly; "group after group formed and melted away," the reporter noted, "and re-formed and discussed the battle of the evening before, and the latest news and gossip of New Orleans, and wondered when another mail would come."

Whatever tedium his lieutenants might be experiencing, Banks had felt his confidence rise steadily with the sun. By noon, when the generals broke for lunch, he had convinced himself there would be no serious fighting today, and afterward, digesting the excellent meal while the sun swung past the overhead and began its long decline, he took such heart that he began to think of recovering the initiative and thereby repairing the damage his reputation had suffered yesterday. Surely Grant and Lincoln would forgive him for being a little behind schedule if he emerged from these piny highlands with a substantial victory in his grasp. He would go back over to the offensive; he would redeem his failure; he would salvage his career. Though his train was already well on its way to Grand Ecore — what was left of it, at any rate — he made up his mind to resume the advance on Shreveport, and he got off a message saying as much to Porter. "I intend to return this evening on the same road with General Franklin's and General A. J. Smith's commands," he informed the admiral. Today was Saturday, and he added that he expected "to be in communication with the transports of General Kilby Smith and the gunboats at Springfield Landing on Sunday evening or Monday forenoon."

Once more he was wrong in a prediction, but this time it was not for lack of a tactical success. Aware that the Federals were braced for an attack from straight ahead, Taylor took his time about deploying for an end-on strike by Churchill, designed to crumple and roll up the Union left while Walker held in front; Green meantime would probe and feint at the enemy right, working his way around it in order to cut off the expected blue retreat to Grand Ecore, and Polignac would be in reserve, since his division had suffered two thirds of the casualties yesterday, though he would of course be committed when the time was ripe. It was close to 5 o'clock before Churchill, having roused his men from their two-hour rest, had marched them into position in the woods due west of the unsuspecting Federal left.

He then went forward with much of the fury Mouton had shown the day before, provoking similar consternation in the Union ranks. To one defender, "the air seemed all alive with the sounds of various projectiles." These ranged, he said, "from the spiteful, cat-like spit of the buckshot, the *pouf* of the old-fashioned musket ball and the *pee-ee-zing* of the minie bullet, to the roar of the ordinary shell and the *whoot-er whoot-er* of the Whitworth 'mortar-pestle'; while the shrieks of wounded men and horses and the yells of the apparently victorious rebels added to the uproar." Back up the Mansfield road, Green and Walker chimed in with their guns, contributing new tones to the concert, and now that the assailed enemy flank had begun to crumble, they put their troops in motion, mounted and dismounted, against the right and center. Churchill kept up the pressure, gathering prisoners by the score as Franklin's unstrung men fled eastward across the open ground of the plateau. Determined to make up for having missed it, the Arkansans and Missourians were intent on restaging yesterday's blue rout, about which they had heard so much since their arrival from Keatchie the night before, in time to share in the pursuit but not the glory.

A. J. Smith's two divisions had not been at Sabine Crossroads either, but they too were very much in the thick of things at Pleasant Hill: as Churchill's elated attackers soon found out. Smith had seen the flank give way, the graybacks whooping in pursuit of Franklin's rattled soldiers, who by now were in flight through the village behind their line, and had sent a reserve brigade in that direction on the double, soon following it with other units which he pulled out of his portion of the line to meet the graver threat. Attempting a wide left wheel, which would enable them to assault the Federal center from the rear and in mass, the cheering rebels at the extremity of the pivot were caught end-on by the advancing blue brigade, freezing the cheers in their throats and bringing them to a huddled, stumbling halt. They wavered, lashed by sheets of fire, and then gave way, not in a single rush but in fragments, as regiment after regiment came unhinged. They made one stand, in a heavy growth of cane along a creekbank they had passed on their way in, but Smith's Westerners came after them with a roar, delivering point-blank volleys and finally closing with clubbed muskets; whereupon the gray withdrawal, already touched with panic, degenerated abruptly into a rout. Now it was the Federals doing the whooping and the crowing, and the Confederates doing the running, as the counterattack grew into a grand right wheel, pivoting irresistibly on the retaken village of Pleasant Hill, so recently overrun by gray attackers.

Taylor saw and tried to forestall the sudden reverse, but Walker had just been carried from the field with a bullet in his groin, Green was intent on maneuvering to cut off the expected blue retreat, and Polignac could not come up through the gathering dusk in time for anything more than a try at discouraging the exultant pursuit. This he managed to do, holding a line two miles from the scene of the break, while the other three divisions fell back another four miles to the nearest water. The battle was over and Taylor had lost it, along with three guns abandoned when his flankers were themselves outflanked and thrown into sudden retreat. With some 12,500 men engaged, the Confederates had suffered a total of 1626 casualties, while the Federals, with about the same number on the field, had lost 1369. Though it was by no means as great as yesterday's, when fortune had smiled on the other side and blood had flowed more freely, Banks knew whom to thank for this disparity, along with much else. When the firing stopped and the rebels had passed out of sight in the pines and darkness, he rode over to A. J. Smith and took him gratefully by the hand. "God bless you, General," he said. "You have saved the army."

Tremendously set up by the sudden conversion of near-certain defeat to absolute victory, he was more anxious than ever to get back on the track to Shreveport, and he not only said as much to Smith while shaking his hand; he also sent a message instructing Albert Lee, who was riding escort, to turn the wagon train around and come back to Pleasant Hill. However, when he returned to headquarters to confer with Franklin and two of his brigadiers, William H. Emory and William Dwight — both had commanded divisions under Banks for more than a year, and both had always given him dependable advice — he found all three West Pointers opposed to resuming the offensive, especially in the precipitous manner he proposed. Franklin and Emory favored an eastward march across Bayou Pierre to Blair's Landing on the Red, there to reunite with Kilby Smith, secure a safe supply line, and regain the protection of the fleet, whereas Dwight urged a return to Grand Ecore for the same purpose. This last was much the safest course, and Banks, his enthusiasm quenched by this dash of cold water from the high-ranking trio of professionals, decided to adopt it. Orders went out for an immediate resumption of the retreat.

When word of this reached A. J. Smith he went at once to protest what seemed to him a loss of backbone. Banks refused to reconsider his decision, citing his lack of supplies, his loss in the past two days of just over 3600 men, and the advice of all his other generals. Smith then asked for time at least to bury his dead and finish gathering up his wounded, but Banks declined that too. Furious, the bespectacled Pennsylvanian, his gray-streaked whiskers bristling with indignation, went to Franklin, whom he found enjoying a cup of coffee, and proposed that, as second in command, he put Banks in arrest and take charge of the army for a rapid advance on Shreveport. Franklin stirred and sipped his coffee, nursed his injured shin, and said quietly: "Smith, don't you know this is mutiny?" That ended the protest, if not the anger. In the small hours after midnight, leaving their non-walking wounded behind — the train had left that morning with all the wagons: including through some mixup, those containing the army's medical supplies — the weary bluecoats formed ranks and slogged away from the scene of their victory, down the road to Grand Ecore.

Ten miles in the opposite direction, up the Mansfield road at Carroll's Mill, Taylor was wakened from his badly needed sleep at 10 o'clock that night by Kirby Smith, who had learned of the Sabine Crossroads fight at 4 o'clock that morning and left Shreveport at once to join his army in the field, only to find at the end of his sixty-mile horseback ride that still a second unauthorized battle had been fought. What was worse, even though this one had been lost, Taylor seemed intent on provoking a third — with any number of others to follow, so long as his blood was up and anything blue remained within his reach. It was more or less clear to Smith by now that if the Louisianian was left to his own devices he would use up the army entirely, leaving him nothing with which to defend his Transmississippi headquarters and supply base from an amphibious assault by Porter, whose gunboats and gorilla-laden transports were at Loggy Bayou, within pouncing distance of Shreveport, and/or an overland attack by Steele, whose troops had crossed the Little Missouri five days ago, brushing Price's horsemen casually aside, and by now might well be closer to their goal than its supposed defenders were at Carroll's Mill. Informed of this, Taylor increased his chief's dismay by proposing to ignore that double threat in order to keep the heat on Banks; both Porter and Steele would withdraw of their own accord, he argued, as soon as they learned that the main Federal column had pulled back. Smith would not hear of taking such a risk, even though Taylor kept insisting that, with Banks on the run and Porter likely to be stranded by low water, "we had but to strike vigorously to capture or destroy both." Finally the department commander ended the discussion with a peremptory order for the infantry to take up the march for Shreveport the following day. If the danger there was as slight as Taylor claimed, he could return and try his hand at the destruction he had in mind downriver.

The result next morning was a rather unusual tactical situation wherein two armies, having met and fought, retreated in opposite directions from the field for which they had presumably been contending. It was made even more unusual, perhaps, by the fact that the victors were unhappier than the losers, and this was especially true of the two commanders. Disgruntled though Taylor was at having been overruled by his superior, Banks was put through the worse ordeal of being sneered at by his military inferiors, all the way down to the privates in the ranks. Taking their cue from Franklin, who avoided such blame as came his way by letting it be known that he would never have recommended a withdrawal if the army had had a competent general at its head, even regimental commanders looked askance at Banks as he rode by them, doubling the column. The men themselves did more than exchange sly glances. Angry because some four hundred of their wounded comrades had been left behind to be nursed and imprisoned by the rebels, they began the march in a mutinous frame of mind, muttering imprecations. But presently the company clowns took over. After the manner of all soldiers everywhere, in all ages, they began to ridicule their plight and mock at the man who had caused it, inventing new words for old songs which they chanted as they slogged. For example, in remembrance of Bull Run:

> *In eighteen hundred and sixty-one*
> *We all skedaddled to Washington.*
> *In eighteen hundred and sixty-four*
> *We all skedaddled to Grand Ecore.*
> *Napoleon P. Banks!*

This last — "Napoleon P. Banks!" — was shouted for good measure as the general rode past, and recurred as a refrain in all the parodies they sang. Nor were such high jinks limited, as before, to A. J. Smith's irreverent gorillas. Banks's own men, whom he had commanded at Port Hudson and through the easy-living months in New Orleans, took up the songs and bawled them as he passed along the roadside, trailing a kite tail of smirking officers from his staff.

Fortunately, they had nothing worse to contend with, in the way of opposition on the march, than butternut cavalry which mainly limited its attention to stragglers until near the end of the second day, April 11, when it made a cut-and-slash attack that drove the rear brigade into Grand Ecore on the run. Once there, their prime concern was to protect themselves from the vengeful Taylor, who was reported to be hard on their heels with 25,000 effectives. They themselves would not have that many on hand until Franklin's fourth division came up the Red from Alexandria and A. J. Smith's third division returned from Loggy Bayou with the fleet, whose heavy guns they presently heard booming in the distance, apparently involved in some kind of trouble far upstream. Meantime they kept busy constructing a semicircular line of intrenchments around the landward side of the high-sited village on its bluff. They worked hard and well, incorporating the trunks and tops of large trees which they felled for use as breastworks and abatis. Not only did they require no urging from their officers in this work; they kept at it after they were told that they could stop.

"You don't need any protection. We can whip them easily here," Franklin chided a detail of diggers as he rode on a tour of inspection.

But they remembered Sabine Crossroads and the hilltop they had lost to a savage rebel charge: the result, they now believed, of having trusted their security to generals like this one. They kept digging.

"We have been defeated once," a spokesman replied, leaning on his shovel, "and we think we will look out for ourselves."

In point of fact they were by no means in such danger as they feared. Far from closing on their heels, Taylor's four divisions of infantry were fifty muddy miles away at Mansfield, marched there against his wishes in order to have them within supporting distance of Shreveport. And even when it turned out that the withdrawal had been unnecessary because his prediction was fulfilled — Steele veered from his southwest course on April 12 for an eastward strike at Camden, which would put him as far from Shreveport as he had been when he crossed the Little Missouri a week ago, and Porter not only ventured no farther up the Red, he was even now bumping his way downstream in an effort to rejoin Banks — Taylor constituted no real threat to the Federals intrenched at Grand Ecore, even though he was free at last to move against them, since he had by then a good deal less than one fourth the number of soldiers his adversary believed he was about to use in an all-out assault on the blufftop citadel. Convinced by captured dispatches that Banks would soon be obliged to withdraw if he was to get Sherman's troops across the Mississippi within the little time remaining, Kirby Smith believed there would be small profit in pursuing him through a region exhausted of supplies. Instead, he decided to go in person after Steele, who was still a threat, and for this purpose he took from Taylor not only Churchill's Arkansans and Missourians, who had been lent to help in stopping Banks, but also Walker's Texans, who would now return the favor by helping to stop Steele. That left the Louisiana commander with barely 5000 men in all: Polignac's infantry, bled down to fewer than 2000 effectives, and Green's cavalry, which numbered only a little above 3000, including a small brigade that had just arrived. In any case, however few they were, on April 14 he started them southward for Grand Ecore, where the bluecoats had obligingly penned themselves up, as if in a stockyard, awaiting slaughter.

Taylor himself went up to Shreveport next day, on the outside chance that he could persuade his chief to countermand the orders which he believed would deprive him of a golden opportunity. "Should the remainder of Banks' army escape me I shall deserve to wear a fool's cap for a helmet," he had said the week before, but now that his force had been reduced by more than half he was less confident of the outcome: especially when he learned that Tom Green, while attempting to add to the problems of the Union fleet in its withdrawal down the still-falling Red, had been killed two days ago in an exchange of fire with the gunboats at Blair's Landing, twenty miles above Grand Ecore. A veteran of the Texas war for independence, the Mexican War, the horrendous New Mexico expedition of early 1862, and the retaking of Galveston, the fifty-year-old Hero of Valverde had been Taylor's most dependable lieutenant in last year's fighting on the Teche and the Atchafalaya, as well as in the campaign still in progress down the Red. His loss was nearly as heavy a blow as the loss of the three divisions about to set out for Arkansas, and caused Taylor to redouble his efforts to have them returned while there was still a chance to overtake and destroy the invaders of Louisiana, afloat and ashore. But Kirby Smith was not to be dissuaded; Steele was the major danger now, and he intended to go after him in strength. "Should you move below and Steele's small column push on and accomplish what Banks has failed in, and destroy our shops at Jefferson and Marshall," he told Taylor, "we will not only be disgraced, but irreparably deprived of our means and resources."

Accordingly, he left Shreveport on April 16, taking Walker and Churchill with him. Taylor stayed on for two more days, arranging for the shipment of supplies, and then set out on the 19th to join what he called "my little force near Grand Ecore." He was still hopeful that the Federals could be bagged, despite the disparity in numbers, and he counted on using deception to that end. Compelled, as he said, "to eke out the lion's skin with the fox's hide," he had instructed his unit commanders to keep Banks on edge, and deceived as to their strength, "by sending drummers to beat calls, lighting campfires, blowing bugles, and rolling empty wagons over fence rails."

All this they had done, and more, with such effect that when Taylor dismounted near Grand Ecore on the evening of April 21, ending his ninety-mile ride, he found that the Federals had begun to pull out of the place that afternoon. The head of their column was already beyond Natchitoches, slogging south in an apparent attempt to take up a safer position at Alexandria, if not to get away entirely. Determined not to permit this, Taylor set about planning how to intercept the retiring bluecoats and, if possible, bring them to battle, although they outnumbered him five to one, exclusive of their heavily gunned flotilla. Their march was down the narrow "island" lying between Cane River and the Red, and it was his hope to force them into a strung-out halt that would give him a chance to go to work on them piecemeal. With this in mind, he sent Bee's brigade of cavalry on a fast ride south to Monett's Ferry, forty miles away at the far end of the island, with instructions to block the crossing of the Cane at that point, so that the rest of his troops could be thrown upon some vulnerable segment of the blue column stalled between there and Natchitoches. This was an ambitious undertaking for some 5000 men opposed by 25,000, but Taylor undertook it gladly, anticipating the Cannae he had been seeking all along.

Banks anticipated much the same thing, and moved rapidly to avoid it if he could. He was by now, as a result of the strain of the past ten days, about as edgy as even Taylor could have wished, and this edginess had been provoked by more than the various nerve-jangling ruses those "22,000 to 25,000" graybacks had been practicing in the woods beyond his semicircular line. For one, there was a growing sense of failure. He still had spasms and flickers of hope, during which he planned to go back over to the offensive, but these grew fewer and weaker as the days wore on, until finally they stopped. For another, he had found waiting for him at Grand Ecore a message from Sherman, notifying him that his lease on A. J. Smith's three divisions had expired and ordering their immediate return. This could be ignored or counter-manded because of the exigencies of the situation, which plainly would permit no such detachment; but a few days later, on April 18, he re-ceived from Grant a follow-up letter of instructions that had for him, in his present hemmed-in state, a sound of hollow mockery not so easily dismissed. Written at the end of March, it set forth in some detail the procedure he was to follow, once Shreveport had been taken, in moving without delay against Mobile. "You cannot start too soon," the letter ended. "All I would now add is that you commence the concentration of your force at once. Preserve a profound secrecy of what you intend doing, and start at the earliest possible moment."

That was perhaps the cruelest blow; Grant had written as if in fervid haste, lest time be wasted between the fall of Shreveport, ap-parently expected momentarily, and the arrival of his letter urging Banks to be quick in taking the road to glory, which led from Shreveport to the White House, by way of Mobile, Atlanta, and Richmond. Contrast-ing what was with what might have been — for the road's only en-trance, for him, was Shreveport, and he could not get there to take it — the former Bay State governor was correspondingly depressed. He relieved his spleen to some degree, however, with a pair of summary dismissals. One was of Stone, his chief of staff (Stone took no further part in the war, though afterwards he served the Khedive of Egypt in the same capacity for thirteen years, with the rank of lieutenant general, and then returned to act as chief engineer in the construction of the pedestal for the Statue of Liberty); Banks let him go because he found him "very weak," and the same might have been said of young Albert Lee, whom he relieved of duty as cavalry commander and sent back to New Orleans, although not without regret. He testified later that Lee had been "active, willing, and brave," if not skillful, and had "suffered, more or less unjustly, as all of us did, for being connected with that affair."

Such administrative corrections had little effect on a tactical situa-tion which seemed to be growing increasingly grim as the rebels out in the brush continued to beat drums, build a myriad of campfires, blow bugles, and bring up what sounded like thousands of wagonloads of supplies and ammunition. For what purpose all this was being done Banks could only guess, but with every passing hour he was brought closer to the inevitable conclusion that if he could not go forward, as was obviously the case, then he would do well not to postpone going back. This applied most of all to Porter's gunboats, for the river was still falling: was already down, in fact, to half the seven-foot depth required to float them over the double falls at Alexandria. The thing to do was get back there as soon as possible, before the river took another perverse drop, for a close-up look at what was reported to be an impossible situation. So the admiral advised, although the temptation was strong to remain where he was, under the friendly bluff at Grand Ecore, his recent trip to Loggy Bayou having given him all too graphic a preview of what to expect in the course of his return to the Mississippi, down those more than three hundred winding miles of the Red. "It is easy to die here, and there are many ways of doing it," a sailor diarist had observed en route. In addition to the more or less normal dangers involved in descending a swift and crooked river at the speed required to maintain steerage — staved-in bows, unshipped rudders, broken wheels, and punctured hulls, all brought on by collisions with other boats, with underwater snags, with the iron-hard red clay bottom — there were the rebels to contend with, fast-firing marksmen who shot at passing or stalled vessels from hidden positions along both banks. At Blair's Landing, for example, where Tom Green was killed by a blast of canister, the fleet was exposed to what one veteran skipper called "the heaviest and most concentrated fire of musketry I have ever witnessed." As a result of this and other such nightmare encounters at places with names like Campti and Coushatta Chute, the thirty-boat flotilla got back from its ten-day upstream excursion sadly altered in appearance: especially the vessels loaded with Kilby Smith's gorillas, to which the butternut riflemen and cannoneers had given their particular attention. "The sides of some of the transports are half shot away," a soldier noted in his diary on April 15, after watching them come in, "and their smoke-stacks look like huge pepper boxes."

Porter recommended an immediate return to Alexandria, but Banks was not quite ready to make so frank an admission of defeat. That took him another four days, two of which he used to compose a letter to Grant, explaining that his retrograde movement from Mansfield had been due more to a shortage of water and the nonarrival of Steele than to resistance by the enemy — though he added, rather ingeniously, that the stubborn quality of the latter had proved the campaign to be "of greater importance than was generally anticipated at its commencement," and asked therefore that he be allowed to continue it beyond schedule, but only a bit, since "immediate success, with a concentration of our forces, is within our reach." Knowing Grant's low tolerance for failure, however skillfully disguised, he did not have much hope that his request would be granted, and he had even less hope, in case it was, that he would be continued in command. At the end of the four days (April 19: the day Taylor set out on his ninety-mile ride from Shreveport) Banks issued orders for a withdrawal to Alexandria. It got underway two days later, after A. J. Smith moved out and occupied Natchitoches, from which point he would cover the retreat by protecting the flanks of the column as it passed, then follow to serve as rear guard on the long march down the "island" between the two rivers, Cane and Red.

Whatever shortcomings the invaders had shown in the past forty days, they demonstrated conclusively, in the course of the next two, that their ability to cover ground at a fairly dazzling rate of speed not only had not been impaired, but in fact had been considerably improved by the events of the past two weeks. The march began at 5 o'clock in the afternoon, and by the time the tail of the column left Grand Ecore at 3 o'clock next morning, April 22, the men at the head were twenty miles away, taking their first rest while waiting for the others to close up. Before nightfall, the entire command had cleared Cloutierville, thirty-two miles from the starting point. Not even then was the blistering pace relaxed; Banks had learned that the rebels intended to contest his crossing of the Cane at Monett's Ferry, another dozen miles southeast, and he pressed on, determined to get off this jungly island and past the last natural obstacle between him and Alexandria, where he would recover the protection of the fleet and his army could once more break out its shovels and throw up dirt between itself and the danger of assault.

So far, its performance had been highly commendable from the logistics point of view; nor had it permitted haste to interfere unduly with the exercise of its various other talents. A. J. Smith's irrepressible campaigners, while holding off pursuers with one hand, so to speak, still found time for more than their usual quota of vandalism and destruction with the other. Grand Ecore had gone up in flames at the outset, along with the surplus goods the army left behind; then Natchitoches, whose old-world French and Spanish charm had been admired by many of its blue-clad visitors, was put to the torch as a farewell gesture. Gray cavalry came up in time to turn fire-fighters and save the latter place, as well as Cloutierville the following day, far down the island. But Smith's troops made up for this double disappointment with the amount of damage they inflicted on barns and houses along the road between the two, including even the cabins of the Negroes who turned out to welcome them. "At night the burning buildings mark our pathway," a marcher recorded. "As far as the eye can reach, we see in front new fires breaking out, and in the rear the dying embers tell the tale of war."

Close in their rear with Polignac, while his cavalry harassed their flanks and rode hard to get into position in their front, Taylor was finding it "difficult to restrain one's inclination to punish the ruffians engaged in this work." He meant that the prisoners were a temptation in that regard — blue-clad stragglers picked up along the roadside, blown and blistered or drunk on looted whiskey, unable to hold the pace Banks was setting them in his eagerness to attain the safety Alexandria would afford — but there was also the temptation for the pursuers to strike before the tactical iron was hot. Too quick a blow, delivered before the Federals had been brought to a disjointed halt on unfavorable terrain, would merely hasten their march and inflict only superficial damage, not to mention that it would be likely to disclose the smallness of Taylor's command; whereas if he waited till their path was blocked he might be able to bag the lot by tricking them (much as Bedford Forrest had tricked Abel Streight, about this time last year in Alabama) into surrendering to the "superior force" Banks believed was breathing down his neck. However, the Lousianian soon had cause to regret that he had stayed his hand, forgoing a leaner in hope of a fatter prize. Brigadier General Richard Arnold, Lee's replacement as chief of the Union cavalry — a thirty-six-year-old West Pointer, son of a former governor of Rhode Island and descendant of a distinguished New England family that included the notorious Benedict — had come upon Bee's dismounted brigade in a stout defensive position overlooking, from the opposite bank, the approaches to the Cane at Monett's Ferry. Instead of attempting the suicidal attack Bee expected, head-on down the road, Arnold located an upstream crossing for the infantry to use while he kept up a show of force in front and probed industriously below, as if in search of another crossing a couple of miles downriver, to attract Bee's attention in that direction.

It was neatly done. Emory's division, coming up at the head of the Federal main body on the morning of April 23, crossed the river two miles above the ferry and struck in force at the upstream rebel flank, while a second arriving division added its weight to the frontal demonstration and the downstream feint. This last was so well carried out, indeed, that Bee — a Charleston-born adoptive Texan whose younger brother had given T. J. Jackson his nom-de-guerre at First Manassas, but who himself had been a desk soldier until the present campaign — believed he was swamped on the right as well as the left, though in fact he had managed to inflict rather heavy casualties on the attackers from upstream. "The critical moment had come," he later reported; "the position turned on both flanks and a large force close in front ready to spring on the center." He counted himself fortunate to get away — "in good order at a walk," he noted — with a loss of "about 50 men and 1 artillery wagon . . . while the enemy lost full 400 killed and wounded," and he complained that, with fewer than 2000 men in all, he had been expected to block the path of "an army of 25,000 marching at their leisure on the main road to Alexandria." Yet that was exactly what had been expected of him, and Taylor was no more inclined to be charitable in such cases than was the man Bee's brother had caused to be nicknamed Stonewall. The fact remained that Banks had made his getaway, avoiding the destruction planned for him, and Bee had let the escape hatch be slammed ajar with a loss to himself of only "about 50 men and 1 artillery wagon." Nor was the disparity of losses any mitigation of the offense. "He displayed great personal gallantry, but no generalship," Taylor said of the South Carolinian, and ordered his removal from command.

Into the clear at last, though greatly relieved to be out of a jungle whose gloom seemed made for ambuscades, Banks did not slacken the pace for his foot-sore troops. He was still not half way to his goal, and he covered the last fifty miles with something of the hard-breathing urgency of a long-distance runner entering the stretch and catching sight of the tape drawn taut across the finish line, ready to be breasted. All through what was left of that day and the next, molested by nothing worse than small clusters of Confederate horse taking pot shots at the column from off in the pines, he kept going hard and fast, his over-all casualties now increased to about 4000, more than half of them captured or missing in battle and on the march. On the third day, April 25 — the fifth since he left Grand Ecore — the lead division slogged into Alexandria, followed next day by the others. There they promptly got to work with their shovels, heaving dirt, despite the recovered protection of Porter's fleet: what was left of it, at any rate, after an equally strenuous five days of fighting rebels and the river.

The admiral had suffered woes beyond a landman's comprehension, including the loss of his finest ironclad, the 700-ton *Eastport*. Sunk by a torpedo eight miles below Grand Ecore, she was patched and raised with the help of two pump boats hastily summoned upriver, and continued on her way — only to ground again in the shallow water forty miles below. Porter unshipped her four 9-inch guns, along with her other four 50- and 100-pounder Dahlgren and Parrott rifles, loading them onto a flat behind the light-draft gunboat *Cricket*, and thus got her afloat; at least for a time. She had only gone a few more miles, bumping bottom as she went, when she ran full tilt into a pile of snags, and there she stuck and settled. After three days' work by her crew and skipper, Lieutenant Commander Ledyard Phelps, who could not bear to lose "the pride of the western waters," Porter, having observed that such efforts to haul her off only made her stick the harder, gave orders for her destruction. A ton and a half of powder was distributed about her machinery and hold. When the electrical detonator failed to work, Phelps himself, in accordance with the tradition requiring the captain to be the last to abandon ship, applied a "slow match," then went over the side and into a waiting launch. The match was almost not slow enough, however. When the *Eastport* blew, Phelps was only a short way off and barely avoided being crushed by one of the dory-sized fragments from the 280-foot iron hull that came hurtling down and raised huge red geysers all around the launch.

Porter had a double reason for ordering the ironclad's destruction. One was that further delay seemed likely to cost him not only the *Eastport* — which, in point of fact, had been Confederate at the outset, captured uncompleted up the Tennessee River near the Mississippi town

that gave her her name, just after the fall of Fort Henry in early 1862 —
but his other boats as well. While the attempted salvage work was in
progress, enemy marksmen were gathering on both hostile banks of the
river and adding to his discomfort by sniping at the flotilla. Small-arms
fire, though deadly enough, was only part of the danger; for presently,
emboldened by the absence of the infantry escort now on the march with
Banks, they brought up batteries of horse artillery and opened fire from
masked positions. So intense and accurate was this, Porter lost one of his
unarmored pump boats that afternoon and the other the following morning, together with all but five of about 175 Negroes, mostly fieldhands
taken aboard from surrounding plantations, who were scalded to death
by steam from a punctured boiler. The gunboats *Juliet* and *Fort Hindman*
lost 22 men between them in the course of the downstream run, along
with their stacks and most of their upper works. Hardest hit of all,
though, was the *Cricket*, now serving as the flagship. Rounding a bend,
she came upon a rebel battery cleverly sited atop a bluff, and took 38
hits within the five minutes she was exposed to its plunging fire. Out of
her crew of fifty, 31 were casualties, including a dozen killed. "Every
shot [went] through and through us, clearing all our decks in a moment,"
according to the admiral, who had to take the wheel himself when he
ran up to the pilot house and found the helmsman badly wounded.

This was the firing the soldiers heard at the end of their long
march from Grand Ecore, and when Porter reached Alexandria next
morning, April 27, he saw at close range the validity of his other reason
for having abandoned the deep-draft ironclad far upstream: which was
that, even if he had managed to get her this far down, he would not have
been able to get her one mile farther. The Red had dwindled by now to
a depth of three feet four inches over the falls — two inches less than
half the draft of his heavier gunboats — and there still was no sign that
the river was going to rise at all this spring, if indeed it ever stopped
falling. In fact, it was becoming more evident every day that the fate of
the *Eastport* was likely to be the fate of every warship in the fleet; that
is, if they were to be kept out of enemy hands. And now there was
added to the admiral's woes, as if this last was not enough, the apprehension that he was about to be left on his own by the army. Banks
came aboard the badly shot-up *Cricket* with a ten-day-old letter just
arrived from the general-in-chief, peremptorily ordering him to desist
from any activity that might cause him to be "detained one day after the
1st of May in commencing your movement east of the Mississippi." Today was Wednesday; May Day was Sunday, barely four days off. "No
matter what you may have in contemplation," Grant had added by way
of emphasis, "commence your concentration, to be followed without
delay by your advance on Mobile."

Knowing how eager the Massachusetts general was to engage in
the very campaign Grant's letter not only authorized but *ordered* him

to undertake at once, Porter had a nightmare vision of the fleet — or anyhow the dozen vessels trapped above the falls — being left stranded high and dry, unprotected from heavy-caliber snipers or highly explosive underwater devices, its fate restricted to a choice between capture and self-destruction. If the former was unthinkable, involving as it well might do the loss of all the navy had won in the past two years on western rivers, the latter choice was only a bit less so, since either would mean professional ruin for the admiral himself. Partly his apprehension was based on his contempt for Banks, which encouraged him to think the worst of the one-time politician, especially in regard to his feeling any obligation to a man who he knew despised him, who was of a rival and often high-handed branch of the service, and whom he could protect only by disregarding a direct order from a superior famed for sternness in such matters.

But in this the admiral did the general wrong. Banks quickly made it clear that he had no more intention of abandoning the navy here at Alexandria than he had had at Grand Ecore the week before, and for much the same reasons. One was that it was not his way, no matter what Porter might think of him, to desert an associate in distress. Another was that he still had nearly a hundred downriver miles to go before he would be out of the Red River country, and he wanted naval protection all the way. Still another, which would require the navy's continued support even more, was that he had not completely given up the notion that he could retrieve his reputation in the region where he had lost it. Whether he would get that chance depended on Grant's reply to the letter sent ten days ago from Grand Ecore, suggesting a return to the recently abandoned upriver offensive, provided he could secure "a concentration of our forces." That meant Steele, who was long since overdue, but about whose progress Banks knew little except for a disconcerting rumor that the Arkansas commander had turned aside from his southwest march on Shreveport for an eastward lunge at Camden, 165 air-line miles due north of Alexandria and almost twice that far by the few roads.

Meantime, while waiting to hear again from Grant and finally from Steele, Banks and Porter — despite their mutual distaste for striking, even figuratively, so intimate an attitude — put their heads together in an attempt to solve the apparently insoluble problem of how to get armored gunboats, drawing seven feet of water, down a still-falling river whose rocky bottom was in places only three feet four inches below its russet surface.

★ ★ ★

Steele had been at Camden, just as Kirby Smith had been informed and Banks had chanced to hear. In fact, he had been there for the past twelve days, penned up like his supposed partner at Grand Ecore, behind intrenchments. But he was there no longer. He had pulled out during the small hours of this same April 27 — headed not for the Red, as Banks expected and Smith intended to prevent, but back toward Little Rock, the headquarters he had left five weeks ago today. In the course of the first three of these he had crossed the Saline, the Ouachita, the Little Missouri, then the Ouachita once more, along with a number of lesser streams in a region as wet as the upper Red was dry; now he was hard on the march for the Saline again, fifty air-line miles to the north, hoping to put that river between him and his pursuers, a superior force dead bent on his destruction, and thus bring an end to what a Saint Louis newsman would presently call "a campaign of forty days in which nothing has been gained but defeat, hard blows, and poor fare."

Although he seemed on the face of it to have done even worse than Banks — who, in all conscience, had done poorly enough by almost any standards, not excluding Pleasant Hill, which amounted to little more than a pause in his flight before inferior numbers — it could at least be said of Steele, by way of extenuation, that he had never had a moment's belief that anything good was going to come of an undertaking he had protested being involved in from the start. Unlike the former Massachusetts governor, whose inveterate optimism was inclined to feed on straws, he had not been lured by cotton or dazzled by stars in a political firmament which for him did not exist. Yet he had certain other disadvantages. For one, while Banks merely believed he was outnumbered, Steele actually was outnumbered, at any rate in the final stage, when Kirby Smith came after him with all but a handful of the infantry Dick Taylor had used to drive the larger Federal column pell-mell down the Red, ironclads and all. The Arkansas commander's losses, though so far only half as great as those in Louisiana, stood a dismal chance of being considerably greater in the end. Banks had lost some 4000 men to date, but at least he had found sanctuary within the Alexandria intrenchments: whereas Steele, in northward flight for Little Rock with hordes of exultant graybacks hot on his trail across the hundred miles of intervening hinterland, was in grievous danger of losing about three times that many, the only limit being that that was all he had. Still, for whatever consolation it was worth, the outcome could scarcely be direr than he had predicted in response to Halleck's original suggestion that he move on Shreveport in coöperation with Banks's ascent of the Red. He could only do so, he wired back, "against my own judgment and that of the best-informed people here. The roads are most if not quite impracticable; the country is destitute of provision." Moreover, he added, if he marched south the butternut guerillas were likely to hold carnival in North Arkansas and Southwest Missouri, with predictable results. "If they should form in my rear in considerable force I should be obliged to fall back to save my depots, &c." He thought it best not to go at all, in any case not in earnest. A feint at Arkadelphia or

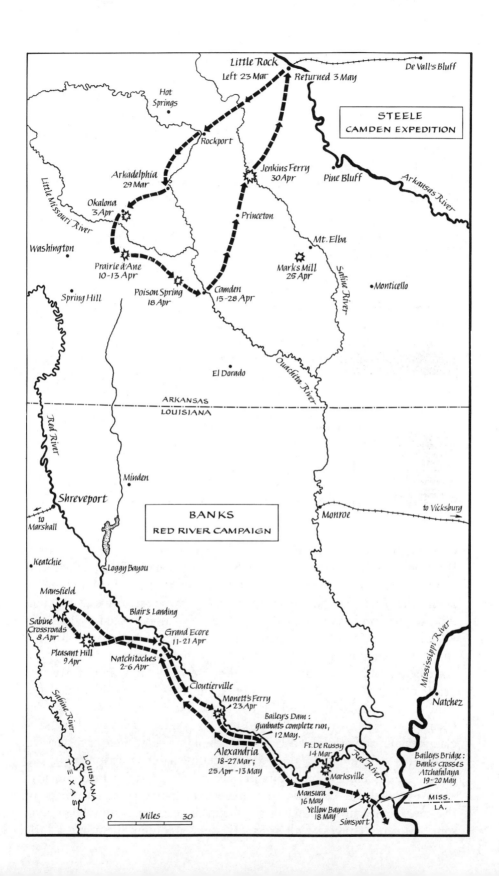

De Vall's Bluff

Little Rock
Left 23 Mar   Returned 3 May

STEELE
CAMDEN EXPEDITION

Hot
Springs

Rockport

Arkadelphia
29 Mar

Jenkins Ferry
30 Apr

Pine Bluff

Arkansas River

Little Missouri River

Okalona
3 Apr

Princeton

Mt. Elba

Washington

Prairie d'Ane
10-13 Apr

Poison Spring
18 Apr

Camden
15-28 Apr

Marks Mill
25 Apr

Monticello

Saline River

Spring Hill

El Dorado

Ouachita River

ARKANSAS
LOUISIANA

Red River

Minden

Shreveport

to
Marshall

BANKS
RED RIVER CAMPAIGN

Monroe

to Vicksburg

Keatchie

Loggy Bayou

Mississippi River

Mansfield

Blair's Landing

Sabine
Crossroads
8 Apr

Grand Ecore
11-21 Apr

Pleasant Hill
9 Apr

Natchitoches
2-6 Apr

Cloutierville

Monett's Ferry
23 Apr

Natchez

Sabine River

Bailey's Dam:
gunboats complete run,
12 May

LOUISIANA

T E X A S

Alexandria
18-27 Mar;
25 Apr -13 May

Ft. De Russy
14 Mar

Red River

Bailey's Bridge:
Banks crosses
Atchafalaya
19-20 May

Marksville

Mansura
16 May
Yellow Bayou
18 May
Simsport

MISS.
LA.

0   Miles   30

Hot Springs was the most he could recommend as a means of discouraging a rebel concentration against Banks, and having said as much — this was March 12, ten days past the time Old Brains had wanted him to set out southward — he remained at Little Rock, awaiting a reply. It came within three days, but not from Washington and not from Halleck. A brief telegram signed *U. S. Grant Lieutenant General* arrived from Nashville on March 15: "Move your force in full coöperation with General N. P. Banks' attack on Shreveport. A mere demonstration will not be sufficient."

That was that. Grant might or might not approve of this Transmississippi undertaking, conceived before his appointment as director of the nation's military effort, but it was clear he wanted it over and done with in the shortest possible time, and it was equally clear that to achieve this he intended to employ his accustomed method of bringing everything available to bear: including Steele. Accordingly, the Arkansas commander wasted no more energy on appeals which might have influenced Halleck but would obviously — as he knew from past experience, first as a classmate at West Point, then as a division commander in the Vicksburg campaign — do nothing but anger the new general-in-chief and probably bring on his own dismissal. Rather, he spent the next eight days preparing to move (an election of delegates to a constitutional convention, requiring the presence of his troops as poll watchers to protect the reconverted "loyal" ten percent of the state's voters from as many of the irreconcilable ninety percent as were not already in the field with Price, had been held the day before, March 14, with predictably satisfactory results) and then on March 23, midway through Holy Week, he set out.

Originally he had intended to proceed due south down the Ouachita, by way of Monroe, for a meeting with Banks at Alexandria. By now, though, it was too late for that; Alexandria had been taken, and he would scarcely be helping Banks by making him wait for him that far down the Red. So he chose instead to march southwest, through Arkadelphia and Washington to reach the upper Red, which he would then descend for a combination, near Shreveport, with the amphibious column moving northwest up that river toward that goal. An epicure and a sportsman, a breeder and racer of horses, forty-five years old, high-voiced and dandified in dress — "a velvet-collared esthete," one observer called him — Fred Steele was rumored by his enemies to live in the style of an Oriental prince, surrounded by silk-clad servants and pedigreed lapdogs, although this alleged limp-wristed aspect was considerably at odds with a lifetime habit of blasphemy, a full if silky beard, and a combat infantry record going back to the Mexican War, in which he had won two brevets for gallantry as an officer of the line. He had under him, for service in the campaign now beginning, some 14,000 effectives of all arms. Of these, a column including a little more than half — 5000 infantry and artillery, 3000 cavalry — left Little Rock under his immediate supervision, while another containing 4000 — the so-called Frontier Division, in occupation of Indian territory — marched from Fort Smith under Brigadier General John M. Thayer, who had orders to join the main body at Arkadelphia by April 1. A third force of about 2000, mostly cavalry and therefore highly mobile, was based on Pine Bluff, with instructions to divert attention in that direction, away from the column on the march to the southwest, and keep a close watch on the rebel garrison at Camden, one of the places where Sterling Price had had his headquarters since his loss of all the northern portion of the state in the fall of the previous year.

A warm-up march of nine miles on the first day flexed muscles used but scantly during months of easy duty. But next morning — Holy Thursday, and the weather remained clear — the men turned out of their blankets in the chill pre-dawn to find themselves involved in the full panoply of war. "Bugles rang out as we had never heard them before," an Iowa soldier would recall. "If an enemy had been in hearing distance, he must have thought we were at least a hundred thousand men, to raise such a wide-spread din." On the near bank of the Saline River by nightfall, still with no evidence that a single rebel was within earshot, they were informed that they would be on half-rations for the balance of the march. Digesting this as best they could, they woke to find it raining, which made for a hard Good Friday on soft roads. The same was true the next day and the next, Easter Sunday, when they crossed the Ouachita. The going was slow, especially across the frequent bottoms, which had to be corduroyed to get the wagons through. They did not reach Arkadelphia until March 29, having covered only seventy miles in a solid week of marching.

The worst of it, though, was that there was no sign at the rendez-vous of the column from Fort Smith, and no word of its whereabouts came back from scouts sent out to find it. A three-day wait, while welcome as a rest, reduced the dwindling supply of food and forage in the trains, and still there was no message from Thayer, whose division was known to have left Fort Smith two days before the main body left Little Rock. The earth might have swallowed him up: or the rebels, none of whom seemed to be lurking in this direction. On April 1, after three days of marking time and further depleting his supplies, Steele decided he could wait no longer. He ordered the southwest march resumed down the old military road that led to Washington, thirty miles beyond the Little Missouri, which lay twenty-five miles ahead. On that day — April Fools' — the marchers encountered their first opposition, in the form of slashing attacks by mounted graybacks who struck them flank and rear.

They encountered only cavalry because that was all Price had to send against them. His two small divisions of infantry, summoned to

Louisiana to help Taylor go for Banks, had reached Kirby Smith at Shreveport on the day Steele set out from Little Rock with the same goal in mind; so that, however much this might benefit him tactically by reducing the type and number of troops he would encounter on his march through Arkansas, the Federal commander had no sooner gotten started than he failed in his main purpose, which was to keep the Transmississippi Confederates from ganging up on Banks. In any case, having accomplished this much without the firing of a shot, Price was left with only five brigades of cavalry, some 5000 effectives in all, badly scattered about the state. Two of these, combined in a division under Brigadier General James Fagan, were stationed east of the Saline to counter a possible Union advance from Pine Bluff, while two of the remaining three were posted at Camden, on the lower Ouachita, and the third was just west of Washington, on the upper Red. These three were under Brigadier General John S. Marmaduke and contained about 3200 troopers, veterans of many fights and raids, particularly those in Brigadier General J. O. Shelby's brigade, hard-bitten Missourians who asked for nothing better than a chance to come to grips with the bluecoats on the march. Two more brigades were said to be on the way from Indian Territory under Brigadier General Samuel B. Maxey, freed by Thayer's withdrawal to Fort Smith for his share in the Arkansas offensive, but Price had no way of knowing when they would arrive. "Retard the enemy's advance," Smith urged him in an Easter dispatch. "Operate on their communications if practicable. Time is everything with us." This aggressiveness was somewhat modified, however, by a warning not unlike the ones that were stretching Taylor's patience thin at the same time: "Do not risk a general action unless with advantage to yourself. You fall back toward reinforcements." Accordingly, Price held Fagan where he was, shielding Camden from attack by the bristly Pine Bluff garrison, and turned Marmaduke loose on Steele with instructions to deal as roughly with him as the disparity in numbers would allow. Marmaduke ordered a concentration of two brigades in the path of the Federal advance, intending to give ground as slowly as conditions would permit, while the third brigade — Jo Shelby's — set out on a circuitous march to get into position to harass the flanks and rear of the enemy slogging through Arkadelphia. Which Shelby did: beginning with the slashing attack he launched on All Fools' Day against just those tender parts of the blue column.

Steele came on, skirmishing front and rear, still not knowing what had become of Thayer or whether his division still existed. Sizeable clashes at Hollywood, a few miles out of Arkadelphia, and then next day at Spoonville and Antoine, along Terre Noir Creek, cost him more in time than they did in men. Time was what he could least afford, however, obliged as he was to balance his consumption of rations against his dwindling supply, already reduced by about three fourths though he was still a good deal short of halfway to his goal. On April 3, while the head of the column moved into the valley of the Little Missouri, diverging from the Washington road to secure a crossing at Elkin's Ferry, off to the south, Marmaduke launched a concerted attack on the main body, back at Okolona. Steele had to call a halt to fight him off, losing still more time and consuming still more rations. At this rate, he perceived, he was never going to make it; Shreveport might as well have been on the Gulf of Mexico or the back side of the moon. Still he pressed on, and next day, having secured a bridgehead at the ferry, he began to cross the river, still under attack from several directions. Then on April 6, with most of his men across, word came from Thayer. He had been delayed by poor roads; he had had to change his route; he would arrive from Hot Springs in a day or two or three. Steele cursed, shrill-voiced and blasphemous, and kept his troops at work corduroying the soggy bottoms for the passage of his and Thayer's trains. Finally, on April 9 — one day short of three weeks on the march — the Frontier Division came up and began to cross the Little Missouri. For Steele and his men, marking time on the south bank, the meeting with the frontiersmen was a let-down. "While we lay here," one recorded in disgust, "the long-looked-for and much-talked-of reinforcement of 'Thayer's command' arrived, from Fort Smith. A nondescript style of reinforcement it was too, numbering almost every kind of soldier, including Indians, and accompanied by multitudinous vehicles, of all descriptions, which had been picked up along the roads."

Worst of all, from Steele's point of view, though the buggies and carriages and buckboards were heavily loaded with plunder, they had little in them in the way of food. What Thayer had mainly brought him was another 4000 mouths to feed, reducing still further any chance Steele had of getting to Shreveport before he starved. There was nothing for it, he decided, but to send back word to department headquarters for a train to be made up and dispatched to him at once, "using, if necessary, every wagon and mule at Little Rock," with a thirty-day supply of "one-half rations of hard bread, one-quarter rations of bacon, and full rations of salt and coffee for 15,000 men." Whether he could survive in the barrens surrounding Elkin's Ferry until the supplies arrived, and whether they had any chance of getting through the rebel-infested region he had just traversed with so much fret, Steele did not know. Nor did he intend to find out, on either count. "Leaving here," he informed his adjutant in Little Rock, thereby giving the destination for the train, "I shall proceed directly to Camden with the whole force."

Nothing Confederate was any longer there to dispute its seizure; Price had evaluated Camden and joined Marmaduke two days ago, bringing Fagan's two brigades along to get in on the action. That raised the total to half a dozen gray brigades, one of Maxey's having ridden in the day before from Indian Territory, so that Price now had about half as many troops as Steele and Thayer, who had 12,000 between them. The Virginia-born former Missouri governor, white-haired in his middle fifties and weighing close to three hundred pounds, mild-mannered despite his imposing bulk and much beloved by his soldiers — although he and they had won no solid victory since Wilson's Creek and Lexington, back in the early days of the war in his home state — had intended to use all six brigades to contest a crossing at Elkin's Ferry; but when he arrived to find the Federals established in their bridgehead he revised his plan to take advantage of a line of shallow earthworks already dug along the near side of the Prairie d'Ane, a gently rolling stretch of meadowland affording his horsemen an excellent field for maneuver, five to ten miles back from the river and about midway between Arkadelphia and Spring Hill. The latter place he now thought was Steele's immediate objective, and the earthworks blocked the way there.

Preliminary skirmishing continued through April 8 and 9 (Banks had left Natchitoches two days before, and while Thayer was crossing the Little Missouri the Louisiana commander was falling back from Sabine Crossroads and Pleasant Hill) and then on April 10 Steele moved against Price across the undulating prairie. All morning and into the late afternoon (while Banks was intrenching feverishly at Grand Ecore and Tom Green was riding toward Blair's Landing, where he would encounter Porter and the naval gun that killed him) the skirmishing continued, gradually building almost to battle proportions — including a noisy exchange of long-range artillery fire which accomplished little except to demoralize a pet bear named Postlewait, the mascot of a rebel battery — until it faded and died away. The following day was much the same, long blue lines of skirmishers moving forward only to recede, and so was the next. On April 13 Maxey's other brigade arrived, Choctaw riders led by Colonel Tandy Walker, eager to use their scalping knives on Thayer's men, who had been despoiling their homes for the past year out in the Territory. But that was not to be: at least not yet. Under cover of these impressive demonstrations, it soon developed, Steele had been preparing, not for a mass assault, but for a withdrawal, a tangential march due east to Camden, forty miles away.

It was neatly done, and in the course of it Steele's soldiers gave a good account of themselves. Left holding the bag on the Prairie d'Ane, Price sent Marmaduke on a cross-country ride to block the road ahead, while Fagan and Maxey set out to overtake the bluecoats who had camped the night before on Terre Rouge Creek, well to the east. Both gray forces were able to get in position for their work, front and rear, but neither had the strength to carry it out. Thayer, whose division served as rear guard, managed to hold off his attackers through a two-day running fight, and German-born Brigadier General Frederich Salomon, commanding the advance division, repulsed Marmaduke in a hotly contested two-hour engagement, fourteen miles from Camden, on the morning of April 15. Just before dark of that same day Steele's lead brigade marched into the town, followed that night and next morning by all the others. While the Federals got to work improving the Confederate-dug intrenchments, semicircular in design and anchored at both ends to the Ouachita, above and below, Price came up and made a leisurely investment of the place. Steele was besieged: besieged by greatly inferior numbers: *self*-besieged, so to speak. Rare as this was in military annals, the situation was not unlike the one that obtained at the same time at Grand Ecore, 125 air-line miles to the south, with the difference that Steele had only a two-to-one advantage, while Banks had better than twice that.

Another difference, far more stringent and constricting, was that the Louisiana Federals had a fleet to bring supplies up the river they were based on, whereas those in Arkansas had to depend on foraging expeditions, highly vulnerable to ambush and assault by the enemy waiting just outside their lines for just such opportunities. Steele had managed to get his wagons through, but there was little in them that was edible. "Our supplies were nearly exhausted, and so was the country," he wrote Halleck on April 17, explaining his perpendicular divergence. "We were obliged to forage from five to fifteen miles on either side of the road to keep our stock alive." The same was true at Camden, however, and next day he received a double shock, half of which provided a graphic demonstration of the risk attendant on venturing outside his fortifications, although the only alternative was starvation. Fifteen miles out the Washington road there was a settlement with an ominous name: Poison Spring. Returning from a successful hunt for food in that direction, a train of 198 heavily loaded wagons, escorted by a mixed command of 1100 infantry, cavalry, and artillery with four guns, was jumped by Marmaduke and Maxey, who had better than 3000 troops between them. The slaughter was heavy, the rebel success almost complete. All four guns were taken, together with 170 of the wagons and their teams, the rest being burned. According to one of the captors, the train was "laden with corn, bacon, stolen bed quilts, women's and children's clothing, hogs, geese, and all the *et ceteras* of unscrupulous plunder." This helped to explain the heavy losses of the escort, nearly one third of whom were killed or captured by the infuriated attackers: particularly by Tandy Walker's Choctaws, who whooped with delight at finding the 1st Kansas (Colored) to their front. This was one of Thayer's outfits, well known for its ransack activities in the past, and the troopers unsheathed their knives for bloody work. According to the regimental commander, the high death rate among his casualties, 117 out of 182, was due to the fact that a number of the wounded were "murdered on the spot" by the vengeful red men. Confederate losses totaled 115, many of them only slightly hurt. The Federals lost 301, mostly killed or missing, plus all their guns and wagons.

By the time the survivors came stumbling back from Poison Spring that afternoon, Steele had been profoundly shaken by the other half of the double shock to his nervous system. It had been given him by a scout sent out the week before to get some news of Banks. Returning with word that the Louisiana commander had been thrown into reverse, first at Sabine Crossroads and then again at Pleasant Hill, the messenger reported that he had left him at Grand Ecore, three days back, though where he might be now he did not know. Steele was quick to perceive the dangers of noncoöperation, now that they were directed at himself. If his supposed partner were to pull out, every rebel in the Transmississippi would be free to concentrate against Camden and its hungry garrison, with results no doubt as grisly as those at Poison Spring this morning. He thought this over for four days, wincing at the prospect — which was in fact more likely than he yet knew; Banks left Grand Ecore on the third of these days, beginning another withdrawal, this time to Alexandria, another ninety miles downriver — and then appealed to his superiors not to allow him to be swamped and slaughtered because an adjoining commander lost his army or his nerve. "Although I believe we can beat Price," he protested, "I do not expect to meet successfully the whole force which Kirby Smith could send against me, if Banks should let him go."

Next day, April 23, he heard at last from Banks himself, who proposed, in a dispatch written a week ago at Grand Ecore, before he decided to withdraw farther down the river, that Steele march south at once to join him on the Red for a resumption of the advance upriver. "If you can join us on this line," Banks told him, "I am confident we can move to Shreveport without material delay, and that we shall have an opportunity of destroying the only organized rebel army west of the Mississippi."

Steele wanted no part of such an operation, and frankly said as much that same day in his reply. "Owing to contingencies," he wrote, "it is impossible for me to say definitely that I will join you at any point on Red River within a given time." Among the contingencies, he was careful to say, was Price's army, which was not only highly "organized," whatever Banks might imply to the contrary, but had recently been "very much encouraged by an order of General E. K. Smith, detailing his success against your command." He wished Banks well in whatever he might undertake of an offensive nature down in Louisiana, but as for himself, he had his hands full where he was; "I desire to coöperate with you in the best manner possible, at the same time covering Arkansas until Shreveport shall be ours." Moreover, he informed the man he held responsible for a large part of the woes he now saw looming, "We have been receiving yesterday and today rumors of reinforcements sent by Kirby Smith to Price at this point, and of a contemplated attack. It is said that 8000 infantry have arrived." Interrupted by the jar of guns, he set his pen aside to look into the cause of the disturbance, then took it up again with something of the perverse satisfaction of a prophet watching his gloomiest fears materialize in fact. "They have just opened upon my outposts with artillery," he continued. "This may be to get as near our lines as possible tonight, preparatory to a general attack tomorrow morning."

He was wrong about the attack next morning. Rather than a prelude to assault, the boom of guns was part of a design to frighten him into retreat. But he was altogether right about the rebel reinforcements and his adversary's intention to make bloody use of them. Kirby Smith had arrived three days ago from Shreveport, accompanied by three divisions of infantry flushed with pride for their recent victory over Banks, and he had it in mind to bag the Camden garrison entirely: in which case, he said later, "the prize would have been the Arkansas Valley and the fortifications of Little Rock," to be used in turn, quite possibly, as a base from which to recover the offensive in Missouri. Before this ambitious program for reversing the tide of war could be placed in execution, however, Steele would have to be disposed of, and Smith had no intention of trying to do so by attacking him in his intrenchments, either at Camden or at Little Rock. He preferred to catch him out in the open, between the two, after frightening or forcing him into attempting a retreat across the intervening barrens, where the blue column could be intercepted and cut to pieces by the now superior gray force. The infantry-artillery demonstration of April 23 having resulted only in causing the Federals to button themselves more tightly in their works, Smith intensified his efforts to smoke them out by disrupting their supply lines, particularly those beyond the Ouachita, which Price had not felt strong enough to threaten up to now. Accordingly, while the Camden demonstration was in progress, Fagan crossed the river at Eldorado Landing, twenty miles downstream, with instructions to use his division, reinforced to a strength of more than 3000 by the addition of Shelby's brigade, to strike at logistical targets along the Saline and the Arkansas, as well as along the roads that ran between and across them, from Little Rock and Pine Bluff, down to Camden. The result was not long in coming, and when it came it was as decisive, on a larger scale, as the rout at Poison Spring.

Crossing the Ouachita on the morning of April 24, Fagan was informed by Shelby's scouts, who had ridden ahead, that a large train, heavily guarded, had left Camden two days ago, sent by Steele to Pine Bluff for supplies. Determined to intercept the Federals before they got across the Saline at Mount Elba, he led his troopers on a forced march of forty-five miles to halt at midnight near Marks Mill, where the road he had taken from Eldorado Landing joined the one connecting Camden and Pine Bluff, five miles short of the river. He was pleased to learn that the blue train, delayed by muddy going on cut-up roads, had made camp at nightfall on the near side of Moro Bottom, a few miles to the west, and he was also pleased to hear that the prize was quite as plump as he had hoped: 240 government wagons, together with a number of other vehicles belonging to "cotton speculators, refugees, sutlers, and other army followers," escorted by three regiments of infantry, one of cavalry, and a six-gun battery — in effect, a rein-forced brigade, whose strength of 1440 effectives was less than half his own. Anticipating a larger reward than Marmaduke and Maxey had won at Poison Spring, a week ago tomorrow, Fagan instructed Shelby to use his Missourians to block the road between Marks Mill and Mount Elba, thus to prevent an escape across the Saline, and posted his other brigades near Marks Mill itself, with orders to assail the flank and rear of the slow-grinding column as soon as it came up next morning.

It came up shortly after dawn and the action went as planned, except for a more determined resistance by the Iowa, Ohio, and Indiana infantrymen than had been expected. Alarmed by the sudden attack, they panicked, then rallied and counterattacked. Fagan used his superior numbers with skill, however, and after about four hours of hard fighting, some of it hand to hand — especially when Shelby came back and forced the issue; "I determined to charge them first, last, and all the time," he later reported — the blue regiments surrendered one by one, in different quarters of the field. "Less than 150 of the brigade escaped from the conflict," the Federal commander admitted, "the balance, including the wounded, being made prisoners." Himself among them, these totaled 1300, excluding the civilian hangers-on, whose captured vehicles brought the haul to more than 300 wagons, together with their teams. All were taken, along with the six guns and the four regimental standards, and Fagan, whose own loss of more than 300 killed and wounded testified to the savagery of the fighting, rode off northward, mindful of Kirby Smith's instructions for him to maneuver in the region between Camden and Little Rock, not only in order to continue his depredations, but also in order to be in position to intercept the retreat of Steele, which was expected any day now.

Even so, it came sooner than either side had anticipated before hearing of Fagan's coup. Informed of the disaster that night by the handful of fugitives who made it back to Camden from Marks Mill, Steele called an immediate council of war to ponder what had better be done to meet this latest crisis. The choice seemed limited to starvation, surrender, or flight. Without exception, his chief subordinates — Salomon, Thayer, and Brigadier General Eugene Carr, his cavalry commander — advised the last, and after a day of feverish preparations, including the destruction of such goods as there was no room for in the depleted train, issued what scant rations were left to his alerted troops, which in some cases consisted of two crackers of hardtack and half a pint of cornmeal, together with a warning that this was likely to be all they would get until they had covered a considerable portion of the hundred-mile trek to Little Rock. All day (while Porter was blowing up the *Eastport* and Banks was getting resettled in Alexandria, which the tail of his column had reached that morning) they worked from dawn to dark to complete their preparations for departure, loading wagons, rolling packs, destroying unneeded equipment with a minimum of noise and smoke, lest the rebels in their camps across the way become aware that they were leaving. By way of adding to the deception, and thereby lengthening the head start, drums beat a noisy tattoo at 8 o'clock, followed an hour later by taps, which was sounded on a far-carrying bass drum. Meantime the loaded wagons were rolling slowly across the Ouachita on the pontoon bridge. By midnight all were over and the infantry followed, breaking step to muffle the hollow sound of their crossing. In the small hours of April 27, with Camden lying silent and empty behind them, dark except for a few scattered lamps left burning to encourage the illusion that the army was still there, the engineers silently took up the bridge, knowing that it would be needed when and if they reached the Saline, then hurried after the column, which had been halted several miles beyond the river to give the troops some rest for the ordeal that lay ahead.

Back at Camden, the Confederates did not discover until well after sunrise that they were besieging an empty town. It was midmorning before they marched in, and even then the infantry could not take out after the departed garrison until some way was found for them to cross the bridgeless Ouachita. While Marmaduke's troopers were swimming their mounts across, and Maxey's were preparing for an unexpected return to Indian Territory in response to a report of a threatened invasion from Missouri — Kirby Smith made them a speech of thanks for their Arkansas service before they set out on their long ride home — Price began the construction of a "floating bridge," to be used in ferrying Churchill's and Walker's three divisions over the swollen river. Building and then using the raft, which had a limited capacity, was an all-afternoon, all-night affair; it was daylight, April 28, before the pursuit began in earnest. As a result of the loss of Maxey and the recent detachment of Fagan, who had done excellent work at Marks Mill but now was somewhere off to the north and west, unaware that Camden had been evacuated or that a race to the death was in progress in his rear, Smith was down to about 10,000 effectives. Although this amounted to nothing like the preponderance he might have enjoyed, he pressed them hard in the wake of the fleeing Federals — whose trail was marked by abandoned equipment, including personal effects, foundered mules, and wagons buried axle-deep in mud — knowing only too well that if he did not overtake them before they crossed the Saline he might as well give up hope of coming to grips with them anywhere short of Little Rock; which meant, in effect, that he would not be able to come to grips with them at all, since there they would have the advantage of intrenchments and could summon reinforcements from other departments roundabout.

Steele was down to roughly the same number of troops as Smith, having suffered 2000 casualties in the past month without inflicting half as many. What was worse, his men had been on short rations all this time, which tended to make them trembly in the legs and short on endurance. However, he had not only gained them a full day's head start in the race for the Arkansas capital, he had also managed to coax or prod them into making good time on the way there. Shortly after noon on this second day out of Camden, the head of the column reached the town of Princeton, in whose streets his rear guard bivouacked that night, two thirds of the distance to the Saline, which in turn was halfway to his goal. He had chosen this nearly barren route to Little Rock, rather than the more accustomed one through Pine Bluff, in order to avoid the Moro swamps, where the train that fell to Fagan had been so grievously delayed; but presently, as rain began to patter on the marchers and the road, he began to doubt that he had chosen wisely. The mud deepened, slowing the pace of his soldiers as they slogged along in the ankle-twisting ruts of the wagons up ahead, and the rain came down harder every hour. Before nightfall, rebel troopers — Marmaduke's amphibious horsemen — were shooting and slashing at the bedraggled tail of the column. By that time, though, the van had reached the Saline at Jenkins Ferry, and the engineers were getting their pontoons launched and linked and floored, while other details worked at corduroying the two-mile long approach across the bottoms giving down upon the river, beyond which there stretched another just as long and just as mean. Such labor was too heavy for troops in their condition, faint for sleep as well as food. While they strained at cutting and placing timbers, Steele's chief engineer afterwards reported, "wagons settled to the axles and mules floundered about without a resting place for their feet." After dark, he added, the work continued by the light of fires, and "every exertion [was] made to push the impedimenta across before daylight, it being evident that the enemy was in force in our rear. But we failed. The rain came down in torrents, putting out many of the fires, the men became exhausted, and both they and the animals sank down in the mud and mire, wherever they were, to seek a few hours' repose."

It was here, in this "sea of mud," as the engineer called it, that fleers and pursuers — blue and gray, though both would be dun before the thing was over — fought the Battle of Jenkins Ferry, a miry nightmare of confusion and fatigue. This last applied as much to one side as the other; for if the Confederates had no foundered mules and ship-wrecked wagons to haul along or strain at, they had to make a faster march, with fewer halts, in order to overcome the substantial Union lead. North of Princeton by nightfall, they took a four-hour rest, then moved out again at midnight. By 7.30 next morning, April 30, the lead brigade had come up to where Marmaduke's dismounted troopers were skirmishing with blue infantry posted astride the road leading down to the ferry, two miles in its rear. Price committed his troops as fast as they arrived, first Churchill's own and then its companion division, led by Brigadier General Mosby Parsons. They made little headway, for the Federals were crouched behind stout log breastworks, in a position whose access was restricted on the left and right by Toxie Creek and an impenetrable swamp. Moreover, this narrow, alley-like approach not only afforded the charging infantry no cover, it was for the most part slathered over with a spongy, knee-deep layer of mud and brim-full pools of standing water. Their only protection was a blanket of fog, thickened presently by gunsmoke, which lay so heavily over the field that marksmen had to stoop to take aim under it or else do their shooting blind. In point of fact, however, this was more of an advantage for the defenders, who were already lying low, than it was for the attackers toiling heavy-footed toward them through the mire. Besides, fog stopped no bullets: as the rebels soon found out, encountering fire that was no less murderous for being blind. They fell back, abandoning three guns in the process, and failed to recover them when Price, after giving the blown attackers time to catch their breath, ordered the assault renewed.

Kirby Smith was on the field by then, coming up with Walker, who insisted on remaining with his men despite his unhealed Louisiana wound, suffered three weeks ago today at Pleasant Hill. Committed just after Churchill and Parsons were thrown back the second time, his Texans attacked with such fury and persistence that all three of their brigade commanders were wounded, two of them mortally. But they did no better, in the end, than the Arkansans and Missourians had done before them. The bluecoats were unshaken behind their breastworks, apparently ready to welcome another attempt to budge them, although the Confederates were not disposed to try it, having lost no fewer than 1000 casualties in the effort, as compared to about 700 for the defenders, including stragglers who had fallen by the wayside on the three-day march from Camden. It was past noon; the last Federal wagon had passed over the river an hour ago, escorted by the cavalry, and now the infantry followed, unmolested by the former owners of the three captured guns they took along. Once on the far side of the Saline, they cut the bridge loose from the south bank and set it afire, partly because they had no further use for it, having no more rivers to cross, and partly because their mules were too weary to haul it. Bridgeless, the rebels could do nothing but let them go, even if they had been of a mind to stop them; which they no longer were, having tried.

Fagan came up soon afterward from over near Arkadelphia, where he had gone for supplies after proceeding north, then west and south, from the scene of his coup five days ago at Marks Mill, less than thirty miles downstream from the battle fought today. Though he made good time on his thirty-four-mile ride from the Ouachita to the Saline, which began at dawn when he learned that Steele was on the march for Little Rock by way of Jenkins Ferry, he not only arrived too late for his 3000 troopers to have a share in the fighting, he was also on the wrong side of the river for them to undertake pursuit. Kirby Smith saw in his failure to intercept and impede the Federals one of the might-have-beens of the war, saying later that if Fagan had "thrown himself on the enemy's front on his march from Camden, Steele would have been brought to battle and his command utterly destroyed long before he reached the Saline." Dismissing this, however, as "one of those accidents which are likely to befall the best of officers," the even-tempered Floridian was more inclined to count his gains than to bemoan lost opportunities. He had, after all, frustrated both Union attempts to seize his Shreveport base and drive him from his department, and though Banks at Alexandria was still to be reckoned with as a menace, the Arkansas column was no longer even the semblance of a threat, at least for the present, to the region it had set out forty days ago to conquer. At a cost to himself of about 2000 casualties, a good portion of whom had already returned to his ranks, Smith had inflicted nearly 3000, two thirds of them killed or captured and therefore permanent subtractions. Losing three guns he had taken ten, all told, in a campaign that had cost the invaders 635 wagons surrendered or destroyed, according to the Federal quartermaster's own report, along with no less than 2500 mules. The list of captured matériel was long, including weapons of all types, complete with ammunition, not to mention sutler goods, rare medical supplies, and enough horses to mount a brigade of cavalry. But the major gain, as Smith himself declared, was that he had "succeeded in driving Steele from the valley of the Ouachita . . . and left myself free to move my entire force to the support of Taylor."

That was clearly the next order of business. With one prong of the two-pronged Union offensive — Steele — now definitely snapped off, it was time to attend to the other — Banks — already severely bent. After giving the divisions of Churchill, Parsons, and Walker two days of badly needed rest, Smith issued orders on May 3 for them to return at once to Camden and proceed from there "by the most direct route to Louisiana."

Steele's men returned on the same day to Little Rock near exhaustion, having found the going even more arduous on the north side of the Saline than on the south. Partly this was because they were one day hungrier and one battle wearier, but it was also because the mud was deeper and timber scarce. As a result of this shortage of corduroy material, they had a much harder time trying to keep the wagons rolling. When one stuck beyond redemption, as many did, it was burned to keep it from falling into rebel hands, and when teams grew too weak to be led, as many did, they were set free: all of which added greatly to the army's loss of equipment and supplies. From dawn of May Day to 4 a.m. the next, out of the soggy bottoms at last, the infantry slogged in a daze that was intensified that night by the lurid flicker of roadside fires the cavalry had kindled to light their way through the darkness. "A strange, wild time," one marcher was to term it, recalling that hardtack sold for two dollars a cracker, while in one instance two were swapped for a silver watch. Late the second afternoon a shout went up from the head of the column, announcing that a train had come out from the capital with provisions. They made camp for the night, wolfing their rations before turning in, and were off again at sunrise. When the fortifications of Little Rock came into sight, around midmorning of May 3, they halted to dress their tattered ranks and thus present as decent an appearance as they could manage, then proceeded into town, giving a prominent place in the column to the three captured guns that were all they had to show, in the way of trophies, for their forty-two days of campaigning.

"The Camden Expedition," Steele called the unhappy affair, as if Shreveport had never been part of his calculations. But the men themselves, being rather in agreement with the Saint Louis journalist that all they had gained for their pains was "defeat, hard blows, and poor fare," were not deceived. They had failed to reach their assigned objective, whatever their silky-whiskered commander might claim to the contrary, and they knew only too well what the failure had cost them: not to mention what it might cost Banks, who seemed likely to lose a great deal more, now that Steele had left the rebels free to shift their full attention to matters in Louisiana.

★   ★   ★

All would now depend on speed in that direction: speed for the three divisions on the way to Taylor, speed for him in bringing them to bear, and speed for Banks and Porter in solving, before that happened, the problem of how to get ten gunboats, some of which drew seven feet of water, down and past a mile-long stretch of river less than half that deep. It was in that sense a race, with the odds very much in favor of the Confederates. So far at least as the concentration went, they had only to do in Louisiana what they had just finished doing in

Arkansas; whereas the Federals were confronted with a problem that seemed, on the face of it, insoluble. Yet by now, before they even knew that Steele had backtracked and a race was therefore on, the blue commanders had found a way to win it. Or in any case they had found a man who believed he knew a way to win it, if they would only let him try.

On April 29 — while Marmaduke was closing on Steele near Jenkins Ferry and opening the action that would swell to battle proportions tomorrow morning — Lieutenant Colonel Joseph Bailey, Franklin's chief of engineers, came to Banks with a plan for raising the level of the river by installing, above Alexandria, a system of wing dams that would constrict and thereby deepen the channel leading down to and over the falls. A former Northwest lumberman, thirty-nine years old this week, he had used such methods to get logs down sluggish Wisconsin streams, and he was convinced they would work here, too, on a larger scale and for a larger purpose. "I wish I was as sure of heaven as I am that I can save the fleet," he said. Banks needed little persuading, not only because he was desperate enough by now to try almost anything, but also because the young engineer had demonstrated his ability along those lines the previous summer at Port Hudson, where he had salvaged, by damming a shallow creek to float them free, a pair of transports the rebels had left lying on their sides in the mud. The general took him that evening to present his plan to Porter. Contemplating the loss of his gunboats and the wreck of his career, the admiral was in an unaccustomed state of dejection; "This fatal campaign has upset everything," he had recently complained to Wells in a dispatch designed to prepare the Secretary for darker ones to follow. His first reaction to Bailey's proposal was to scoff at it. "If damning would get the fleet off, we would have been afloat long ago," he broke in, brightening a bit at this evidence that his sense of humor, such as it was, was still in working order. When it was explained to him further that the navy would have little to do but stand by and watch the army sweat and strain, he declared that he was willing on those terms. Accordingly, Banks issued orders on the last day of April for the thing to be tried, and Bailey, given 3000 soldiers to use as he saw fit in getting it done, put them to work without delay on May Day morning.

His plan was to construct above the lower falls, where the Red was 758 feet wide, a pair of wing dams, each extending about three hundred feet out into the river, then sink high-sided barges filled with brick across the remaining gap. The north bank dam was to be formed of large trees laid with the current, their branches interlocked and their trunks cross-tied with heavy timbers on the downstream side; while the one on the south bank, where trees were scarce, would consist of huge cribs, pushed out and sunk and anchored in place with rubble of all kinds. Most of the left-bank work was done by a Maine regiment of highly skilled axmen and loggers, the rest being left to three regiments of New Yorkers, experienced in tearing down old buildings — one was the military academy of which Sherman had been superintendent just before the war — for bricks and stone, to be used to hold the sunken cribs and barges in position against the force of the nine-knot current. They worked day and night, under a broiling sun and by the light of bonfires, much of the time up to their necks in the swift, rust-colored water.

At the outset they provoked more jeers than cheers from the sailors and off-duty soldiers looking on, but as the ends of the two dams drew closer together, day by day and hour by hour, interest mounted and skepticism lessened among the spectators on the gunboats and both banks, who now began to tell each other that Bailey's notion might just be practicable, after all. The sailors, especially those aboard the "teakettles," as the ironclads were called, were pleased to be afforded this diversion, now that rising temperatures had added physical discomfort to their boredom. "During the day," an officer recorded, "the iron on the decks would get so hot that the hand could barely rest upon it. At night, sleep was impossible. The decks were kept wetted down, and the men lay on them, getting, toward the morning hours when the hulls had cooled down, such sleep as could be secured." Nor were excursions ashore of much help in this regard, involving, as they sometimes did, another form of torture which southern women, then and later, were adept at inflicting. "Saw quite a number of ladies from Pine Village opposite Alexandria," a sailor wrote in his diary after one such visit. "Two in particular were out on display promenade, one of whom had a beautiful black squirrel which ran all over her, up her dress sleeves and under her lace cape into her bosom, with a familiarity that made me envy the little favorite and sent a thrill that did not feel very bad through all the little veins in my body."

Still, being bored or titillated, painful though they were in their different ways, was better than getting shot at: as a good many soldiers and sailors could testify from experience while the dams were being built. If Taylor lacked the strength to interfere with the work going on behind the Federal intrenchments, he could at least make life hectic for the troops who manned them, and he could do considerably worse to those who ventured outside them, on foot or afloat. On the day Bailey started construction, the transport *Emma* was captured at David's Ferry, thirty miles below Alexandria, her captain and crew looking on as prisoners while the rebels burned her. Three days later another, the *City Belle*, was served in much the same fashion a few miles farther down, this time with a 700-man Ohio regiment aboard. More than a third of the soldiers were captured — 276 by Taylor's count — while the rest went over the side, escaped ashore, and eventually made their way back through the lines. Next day, May 5, saw the gravest loss of all. The transport *Warner*, escorted by the gunboats *Covington* and *Signal* while taking another regiment of Ohioans downriver to begin their reënlistment furloughs, came under fire from a masked battery as she rounded a bend near the mouth of Dunn's Bayou. Disabled by an unlucky shot in her rudder, she spun with the current, absorbing heavy punishment from riflemen posted along the high south bank, and when the two warships tried to come to her assistance by bringing their seventeen guns to bear on the rebel four, they were given the same treatment in short order. *Covington,* hulled repeatedly, went aground and was set afire by her skipper, who got away into the woods with 32 of his crew of 74, leaving the rest to the mercy of the gray marksmen who by then were at work on *Signal.* They cut her up so badly that the captain, prevented from destroying her by the fact that there was no time for removing the wounded, struck his colors and surrendered his 54 survivors, together with some 125 killed and wounded left strewn about the decks of the *Warner* when she and they were abandoned by her crew and their fellow soldiers. That brought the total for the past five days to better than 600 amphibious Federals killed or captured, together with three transports and two gunboats, at a cost to the Confederates of little more than the ammunition they expended. Worst of all, from the point of view of the soldiers and sailors cooped up in Alexandria or marooned above the falls, the Red was emphatically closed to Union shipping. They had to subsist on what they had, which by now was very little, or starve; or leave.

Along with everyone else in blue, Banks preferred the last of these three alternatives, although it appeared about as unlikely as the first. At this stage, the choice seemed narrowed to the second — starvation — which was scarcely a choice at all. As of May Day, he computed that he could subsist his army for three weeks on half-rations out of what he had on hand. That might or might not be enough, depending on whether the work begun on the dams that day could be completed within that span, but there seemed little doubt, at best, that he would lose his train for lack of animals to haul the wagons. Forage was so short already that Taylor was complaining, and exulting, that the horses he captured were little more than skeletons. Pitiable as they were, he intended to be still harder on them in the immediate future, as a means of being harder on the men who rode or drove them. On May 7, after claiming that his downstream successes near Dunn's Bayou had converted the lower Red, formerly a broad Federal highway of invasion, into "a *mare clausum,*" he reported to Kirby Smith: "Forage and subsistence of every kind have been removed beyond the enemy's reach. Rigid orders are given to destroy everything useful that can fall into his hands. We will play the game the Russians played in the retreat from Moscow."

So he intended, gazing all the while back over his shoulder for some sign of the approach of the troops from Arkansas, without whom he lacked the strength to come to earnest grips with the beleaguered Unionists. All he could do was pray that they would arrive before the bluecoats started the downstream march that would increase the distance his reinforcements would have to cover before they could be brought to bear.

In point of fact, the race was closer than he knew. Faith had replaced skepticism in the attitude of the watchers at the dam site. "Before God, what won't the Yankees do next!" a gray-haired contraband cried in amazement at his first sight of the week-old work in progress, now rapidly nearing completion. Crews of the largest of the ten warships above the falls, having caught the spirit of the workers in the water, were busy lightening their vessels by stripping off side armor, which they dumped in a five-fathom hole upstream to keep it out of rebel hands, and unloading such heavy materials as commandeered cotton, anchors, chains, ammunition, and most of the guns, which — all but eleven old 32-pounders, spiked and sunk, like the iron plating, to forestall salvage — were to be carted below on wagons for reloading in deep water beyond the falls. By the following day, May 8, the river had risen enough to allow three of the lighter-draft boats, the tinclad *Fort Hindman* and the broad-bottomed monitors *Osage* and *Neosho*, to pass the upper falls and take station just above the dam, awaiting the further rise that would enable them to make their run. That would not take long, apparently, for now that the dam was finished and the rubble-laden barges sunk to plug the gap between the wings, the river was rising so swiftly that it deepened more than a foot between sunset and midnight, increasing the midstream depth to a full six feet. Another foot would do it, the engineers said. As the depth increased, however, so did the speed of the current and the resultant pressure on the dam, which mounted in ratio to both. Banks, for one, began to fear that the whole affair would be swept away in short order. Arriving for an inspection by the light of bonfires late that night, he sent Porter a message expressing hope that the flotilla would be ready to move down at a moment's notice, since it seemed to him unlikely that the dam, already trembling under the weight of all that water, could survive past dawn.

He was wrong by about one hour. It held all night, then blew at 5.30 next morning when two of the barges shifted, first tentatively, then with a rush, and went with the boom and froth of current through the re-created gap.

Porter was on the scene. He had paid Banks's warning no mind last evening, but now that its validity was being demonstrated so cataclysmically, he reacted in a hurry by leaping astride a horse for a fast ride upstream to order the boats above the upper falls to start their run before the water, rushing Niagara-like between the unplugged wings of the dam, fell too low for them to try it. All but *Lexington*, the oldest vessel with the fleet — one of the three original "timberclads," she was a veteran of practically all the river fights since Belmont, where Grant got his start, and had harassed the Confederates trying to get some sleep in the captured Federal camps after the first day's fight at Shiloh — were unready for action of any kind, moored to bank with their steam down and all but their anchor watches taking it easy about the decks. *Lexington* got under way at once, passing scantly over the rocks of the upper falls, and headed straight for the 66-foot opening between the two remaining barges. The admiral, one of the thousands of soldiers and sailors who lined both banks of the Red to watch her go, later reported her progress and the reaction, afloat and ashore: "She entered the gap with a full head of steam on, pitched down the roaring current, made two or three spasmodic rolls, hung for a moment on the rocks below, and then was swept into deep water by the current and rounded to, safely into the bank. Thirty thousand voices rose in one deafening cheer, and universal joy seemed to pervade the face of every man present."

Encouraged by *Lexington*'s example, the skippers of the three boats that had crossed the upper falls the previous day decided to try their hand at completing the run before the mass of water drained away and left them stranded in the shallows of the rapids. *Neosho* led off, advancing bravely under a full head of steam. At the last minute, however, just as she was about to enter the gorge, the pilot lost his nerve and signaled for the engine to be stopped. It was, but not the monitor herself. She went with the sucking rush of the current, out of control; her low hull plunged from sight beneath the spume as she went into the gap, careening through at an angle so steep it was nearly a dive, and struck bottom with an iron clang, loud against the bated silence on both banks; then reappeared at last below, taking cheers from the watchers and water through the hole the stones had punched along her keel. This last was slight and soon repaired — a small price to pay for deliverance from a month's captivity, not to mention the risk of self-destruction or surrender. The other two warships, *Osage* and *Hindman*, made it through in a more conservative style, with less excitement for the troops on shore but also with less damage to themselves. Four boats were now below the double falls, assured of freedom and continuing careers in their old allegiance. But the remaining six were trapped as completely as before, the water having fallen too low for them to cross the upper falls by the time they got up steam enough to risk the run.

Banks was more or less unstrung by the fulfillment of his prediction that the dam was about to go. He foresaw indefinite postponement of the departure which just last night had seemed so near, and he was correspondingly cast down, having seen the effects of starvation only too clearly last summer at Port Hudson when the scarecrow garrison lined up for surrender. "We have exhausted the country," he told Porter that afternoon, "and with the march that is before us it will be perilous to remain more than another day."

The admiral, perhaps because he had put less faith in the dam as a means of deliverance, reacted less despairingly to the mishap. After all, he had saved four of his boats already — four less than he had feared he well might lose — and he believed he could save the other half dozen as well, if the army would only stand fast until the dam could be replugged. But there was the rub. Banks, in his depression, was giving what seemed to Porter signs that he was about to pull out, bag and baggage, workers and all, and leave the stranded warships to the mercy of butternut marksmen who had demonstrated at Dunn's Bayou, four days ago, their skill at naval demolition when there was no army stand-ing by to hold them off. On May 11, when Banks displayed further jumpiness by sending a staff officer to complain that the navy seemed unmindful of the need for utmost haste, Porter did what he could to calm him down. "Now, General," he replied soothingly, "I really see nothing that should make us despond. You have a fine army, and I shall have a strong fleet of gunboats to drive away an inferior force in our front." Up to now, he artfully pointed out, the press had been highly critical of the conduct of the campaign; but think what a glorious finish the salvation of the flotilla would afford the journalists for the stories yet to be filed. And having thus appealed to the former governor's political sensibilities, the admiral closed with an exhortation designed to stiffen his resolution. "I hope, Sir, you will not let anything divert you from the attempt to get these vessels all through safely, even if we have to stay here and eat mule meat."

No blue-clad soldier or sailor had yet been reduced to such a diet; nor would one be here, though Banks was quick to reply that he had no intention of leaving the navy in the lurch. The reason again was Bailey, who once more solved a difficult engineering problem in short order. Instead of attempting to plug the swift-running gap between the still-intact wings of the dam just above the lower falls, he decided instead to construct another at the upper falls, similar to the first, and thus not try any longer to sustain the weight of all that water with one dam. It was done with such dispatch, his thousand-man detail being thoroughly ex-perienced in such work by now, that within three days — that is, before sunset of the day Porter urged Banks to stand by him "even if we have to stay here and eat mule meat" — three more vessels completed their runs down the mile-long rapids and over the two sets of falls. These were the veteran Eads gunboats *Mound City, Pittsburg,* and *Carondolet.* Next day, May 12, the remaining three — the armored steamer *Chillicothe,* the fourth Eads gunboat *Louisville,* and finally the third monitor *Ozark,* successor to the *Eastport* as the pride of the river fleet — did the same. The admiral and his precious warships were delivered, thanks to Bailey, to whom he presented, as a personal gift, a $700 sword. The engineer also received, as tokens of appreciation, a $1600 silver vase from the navy, a vote of thanks from Congress, and in time a two-step promotion to brigadier general. None of this was a whit too much, according to Porter, who said of the former Wisconsin logger in his report: "Words are inadequate to express the admiration I feel for the abilities of Lieutenant Colonel Bailey. This is without doubt the best engineering feat ever performed. Under the best circumstances a private company would not have completed this work under one year, and to an ordinary mind the whole thing would have appeared an utter impossibility."

He might have added that his own mind seemed to fit in that category, since he had prejudged the attempt in just that way. But for the present, steaming down the lower Red, where the going was deep and easy because of backwater from the swollen Mississippi, he was altogether occupied with savoring his freedom, his narrow delivery from ruin. "I am clear of my troubles," he wrote home to his mother that week, though he was not so far clear of them that he forgot to add: "I have had a hard and anxious time of it."

So had Banks had a hard and anxious time of it, and so was he still, along with the slogging troops under his command. Leaving Alexandria on May 13, the day after Porter completed his run, they had another sixty hostile miles to cover before they would return to their starting point, Simsport on the Atchafalaya, where Sherman's men had opened the campaign, just one day more than two full months ago. In point of fact, except as a location on the map, the town no longer existed; A. J. Smith's gorillas had burned it at the outset. And now, looking back over their shoulders as they set out, they had a similar satisfaction — similar not only to Simsport, but also to Grand Ecore, three weeks ago, as well as to a number of lesser hamlets in their path, before and since — of seeing Alexandria aflame. It burned briskly under a long, wind-tattered plume of greasy smoke, while over the levee and down by the bank of the river, as one Federal would recall, "thousands of people, mostly women, children, and old men, were wringing their hands as they stood by the little piles of what was left of all their worldly possessions." They had been driven there by the sudden press of heat from a score of fires that quickly merged after starting simultaneously with the help of a mixture of turpentine and camphene, which the soldiers slopped on houses and stores with mops and brooms. Experience had greatly improved their incendiary technique. "Hurrah, boys! This looks like war!" Smith shouted by way of encouragement as he rode through the streets, rounding up his men for departure.

They had their usual assignment as rear guard, the post of honor on retreat, while the Easterners took the lead. Banks rode with the more congenial troops up front, commanded now by Emory; Franklin, after recommending that his chief engineer's proposal for saving the fleet be tried, had left on May Day, still fretted by his shin wound, which seemed to require more skilled attention than the Transmississippi doctors were able to furnish, and by disgust and bitterness at having been prominently connected with still another large-scale defeat. Banks of course had that fret too, without the red-badge distraction of a physical injury, but he felt better, all in all, than he had done at any time in the past horrendous month. For one thing, the salvation of the flotilla had given journalists the upbeat ending Porter had dangled as bait for prolonging the army's stay in Alexandria, and for another his casualties had been replaced, before the end of April, by reinforcements who arrived from Pass Cavallo, Texas, under Major General John A. McClernand, resurrected from his Grant-enforced retirement in Springfield, Illinois, and put in command of the lower Texas coast by his old friend and fellow townsman Abraham Lincoln. That brought the army's total strength to 31,000 effectives up the Red, more than Banks had had directly under him so far in the campaign. Even though there was no compensation for the loss of twenty guns, two hundred wagons, and something over a thousand mules, this added strength brought added confidence; which, aside from military skill, had been the thing most lacking at headquarters since the crossroads confrontation short of Mansfield, five weeks ago today. Moreover, there was the relief of having the end at last in sight, whatever disappointments had occurred along the way, and of discovering that Taylor, for all his bluster in the course of the Alexandria siege, seemed considerably less a menace now that the cooped-up bluecoats were out in the open, inviting the attack he formerly had seemed anxious but now seemed strangely reluctant to deliver.

At any rate that appeared to be the case throughout the first three days of the march downriver. Crossing the Choctaw Bayou swamps on the second day out of smouldering Alexandria, the Federals occupied Marksville on the evening of the third. That was May 15; they had covered forty miles by then, molested by nothing worse than grayback cavalry, which failed in its attempts to get at the wagons drawn by scarecrow mules, and were a good two thirds of their way to the sanctuary a crossing of the Atchafalaya would afford them. Banks tempered his optimism, however, by reminding himself that the tactical situation resembled the one that had obtained, or had seemed to obtain, on the march from Natchitoches to within three miles of Mansfield, where it ended in disarray. The resemblance was altogether too close for comfort, let alone for premature self-congratulation; Taylor might well be planning a repeat of that performance at another crossroads, somewhere up ahead. And sure enough, advancing next morning across the Avoyelles Prairie, five miles south of Marksville, Banks found the Confederates disposed in force athwart his path, much as they had been at Sabine Crossroads, except that here the terrain was open and gave him a sobering view of what he faced. Their line of battle extending east and west of the village of Mansura, they had thirty-odd pieces of artillery — more than half of them had been his own, up to the time of the previous confrontation just short of Mansfield, which this one so uncomfortably resembled — unlimbered and ready to take him under fire as soon as he ventured within range. Their numbers in infantry and cavalry were hard to estimate, masked as their center was by the town, but Banks did not decline the challenge. He shook out his skirmishers, put his own guns in position — as many of the remaining seventy, in any case, as he could find room for on the three-mile width of prairie — formed his infantry for attack with cavalry posted neatly on both flanks, and then went forward, blue flags rippling in the breeze.

The result, as the troops began to move and the guns to growl, was enough to make observers in both armies, each of which had a full view of the other, catch their breath in admiration. Advancing across the lush and level prairie — "smooth as a billiard table," Taylor was to say of it in his report — the Union host was "resplendent in steel and brass," according to one of its members, a Connecticut infantryman who afterward tried his hand at a word sketch of the scene, including "miles of lines and columns; the cavalry gliding over the ground in the distance with a delicate, nimble lightness of innumerable twinkling feet; a few batteries enveloped in smoke and incessantly thundering, others dashing swiftly to salient positions; division and corps commanders with their staff officers clustering about them, watching through their glasses the hostile army; couriers riding swiftly from wing to wing; everywhere the beautiful silken flags; and the scene ever changing with the involutions and evolutions of the vast host." It was, in short, that seldom-encountered thing, picture-book war — which it also resembled, as events developed, in its paucity of bloodshed. Though the armies remained in approximate confrontation for four hours, the action was practically limited to artillery exchanges, since neither commander seemed willing to venture within point-blank range of the other's guns. When at last Banks brought A. J. Smith's Westerners forward for an attack on the rebel left, Taylor withdrew in that direction, south and west, and the Federals resumed their march to the south and east, through Mansura, then on to Bayou de Glaise, on whose banks they stopped for the night. Next day, May 17, after skirmishing warmly with enemy horsemen on both sides of Moreauville, they pushed on to Yellow Bayou, within five miles of Simsport and the Atchafalaya, which would shield them from further pursuit once they were across it.

If Banks had known the extent of the odds in his favor, he not only would have been less surprised at the sidelong rebel withdrawal from Mansura, he would also have been considerably less concerned for the safety of his army, which in fact enjoyed a five-to-one numerical advantage over the force attempting to waylay and impede it. Taylor fairly ached for some sign of the three divisions on the march from Arkansas; to no avail. "Like 'Sister Ann' from her watch tower," he was to write, "day after day we strained our eyes to see the dust of our approaching comrades. . . . Vain, indeed, were our hopes. The commander of the 'Trans-Mississippi Department' had the power to destroy the last hope of the Confederate cause, and exercised it with all the success of Bazaine at Metz. 'The affairs of mice and men aft gang aglee,' from sheer stupidity and pig-headed obstinacy." And lest his meaning be clouded by his fondness for religious and historical allusions and poetic misquotations, he made the charge specific and identified by name the man he held responsible for his woes: "From first to last, General Kirby Smith seemed determined to throw a protecting shield around the Federal army and fleet."

This bitterness would grow; would in time become obsessive. But for the present the Louisiana general directed most of his attention to a search for some way, despite the odds, to inflict more vengeful damage on the spoilers of his homeland before they fled beyond his reach. The side-step at Mansura, allowing them to press on south and east, had been as necessary as it was painful; for if Taylor was to preserve his little army for future use, he could not afford to take on the blue host without a tactical advantage totally lacking on the open prairie. Then next day he received, as if from Providence, what he believed might be the chance for which he prayed. Pushing on through Moreauville, the Federal main body reached Yellow Bayou only to learn from its scouts, who had ridden ahead, that backwater from the Mississippi had swollen the Atchafalaya to a width too great for spanning by all the pontoons the engineers had on hand. Without a bridge, the crossing would be at best a slow affair, involving the use of transports as ferries. Penned up with its back to the river, as it had been at Grand Ecore and Alexandria, the blue mass would grow more vulnerable as it shrank, regiment by regiment, until at last a gray assault could be launched against the remnant — perhaps with the help, by then, of the slow-moving troops from Arkansas — extracting payment in blood for the vandalism of the past nine weeks. Taylor brightened at the prospect, and next morning, May 18, moved his infantry up to join his cavalry on Yellow Bayou, intending to advance from there and establish a semicircular, close-up line of intrenchments from which to observe the dwindling Union army, held under siege amid the ashes of what had once been Simsport.

Looking out across the unbridgeable 600-yard expanse of the Atchafalaya, a swollen barrier to the safety his army could only attain by reaching the far side, Banks foresaw an outcome all too similar to the one his adversary was moving to effect. Still, his despair was not so deep as to keep him from doing all he could to ward it off. When he was informed, around midmorning, that Taylor had moved up to

Yellow Bayou, close in his rear, he instructed A. J. Smith to counter-march and drive him back. Smith returned to the Bayou, crossed three brigades, and pitched without delay into the rebel skirmish line, throwing it back on the main body, which then attacked and drove him back in turn. It went that way for a couple of hours, first one side gaining ground and then the other — each had about 5000 men engaged — until at last the underbrush caught fire and both withdrew in opposite directions, choked and scorched, from the crackling barricade of smoke and flame. That ended the action. Unresolved and indecisive as it was, Smith's gorillas once more had proved their worth as fighters as well as burners, losing about 350 to inflict a total of 608 casualties on Taylor.

Nothing daunted, the Louisianian prepared to return to the offensive next day, May 19. But that was not to be. The back-and-forth engagement on the west side of Yellow Bayou turned out to be the last of the campaign — for the simple reason that presently no blue-clad troops remained within his reach. Banks by then had bridged the unbridgeable Atchafalaya.

Once more the *deus ex machina* was Joe Bailey. Handed the problem by Banks, the engineering colonel promptly solved it by mooring all the available riverboats and transports side by side across the near-half-mile width of the stream, like oversized pontoons, and bolting them together with timbers which then served as stringers for planks laid crosswise on them to form a roadbed. Soon after midday, though the varying heights of the boats on which it rested gave it something of the crazy, up-and-down aspect of a roller coaster, Banks had the bridge he needed to reach the sanctuary beyond the river. The wagon train began to cross at once, followed that night by the guns and ambulances; next morning, May 20, the troops themselves were marched across and the makeshift bridge dismantled in their rear. Two days later — a solid month past the time when they had been scheduled to rejoin Sherman in far-off Georgia — Smith's three divisions filed back aboard their transports and set out for Vicksburg. Banks meantime was as full of praise for Bailey, here on the Atchafalaya, as Porter had been the week before, back up the Red. "This work was not of the same magnitude, but was as important to the army as the dam at Alexandria was to the navy," he said of the improvised bridge in his final report, and repeated his recommendation that the former logger be promoted to brigadier as a reward for his resourcefulness under pressure.

Another upbeat flourish had been provided, but so had additions been made to the list of casualties — more than fifteen hundred of them, all told, since the return to Alexandria in late April. Army losses for the campaign now stood at 5245 killed, wounded, and missing, and to this were added some three hundred naval casualties, suffered in the course of the subtraction from the flotilla of an ironclad, two tinclads, three transports, a pair of pump boats, and 28 guns of various calibers, captured or spiked and abandoned up the Red. This Federal total of about 5500 exceeded by well over a thousand the Confederate total of 4275. Losses in matériel were of course even more disproportionate, not only because the rebels had lost much less in battle, but also because they had had a great deal less to lose: aside, that is, from civilian property, the destruction of which, if included, would doubtless swing the balance the other way. But perhaps the greatest contrast lay in what a member of Banks's official family called "the great and bitter crop of quarrels" raised in the northern ranks by what he referred to as "this unhappy campaign." If on the Confederate side there were arguments in the scramble to divide the glory, on the Union side there were hotter ones involved in the distribution of the blame. Looking back over the events of the past seventy days, the staffer noted that feelings had been severely ruffled and several lofty reputations quite undone. "Franklin quitted the department in disgust," he recalled; "Stone was replaced by Dwight as chief of staff, and Lee as chief of cavalry by Arnold; A. J. Smith departed more in anger than in sorrow; while between the admiral and the general commanding, recriminations were exchanged in language well up to the limits of 'parliamentary' privilege."

Now still another illustrious name was added to the list: Banks's own. Not that he was relieved outright or shunted into obscurity, as so many others had been in the doleful course of the past six weeks. This was an election year, and too much rode on the outcome for the authorities to risk alienating a man with as many votes as the one-time Speaker of the House controlled. Lincoln and Halleck put their heads together and came up with the answer. Major General Edward R. S. Canby, a forty-six-year-old Kentucky-born West Pointer, had come east after the New Mexico campaign of 1862, in which he had managed to save the Far West for the Union, and had since been involved in administrative matters, including the reëstablishment of law and order in New York after the draft riots of 1863. In all these positions his outstanding characteristic had been his prudence, a rare quality nowadays in the Transmississippi; Lincoln and Halleck, with Grant's concurrence — Canby had been another of his classmates at the Point — decided to send him there to supply it, not as Banks's replacement, but rather as his superior, by placing him in charge of the newly created "Military Division of West Mississippi," which stretched from Missouri to the Gulf and from Florida to Texas. Banks's unquestioned abilities as an administrator, honest amid corruption, were thus preserved for the government's use, along with his political support, while his military ineptness was set aside by depriving him of any further independence — or, as it turned out, service — in the field.

Canby was waiting for him with the necessary papers at Simsport, and accompanied him on the final leg of the retreat, another hundred miles downriver to Donaldsonville, where the campaign formally ended on May 26, seventy-five days after its start and more than a month beyond its scheduled finish. An Iowa soldier wrote in his diary that Banks looked "dejected and worn" at that stage, and small wonder. More had ended and more had been lost, for him, than the campaign. The former governor, whose reduction of Port Hudson had opened the Mississippi to northern trade throughout its length, was now the mere desk-bound head of a subdepartment in an organization commanded by a man almost two years his junior in age and three full years behind him in date of rank. That came hard, but that was by no means the worst of it for Banks, who was taunted not only by the thought of what he had lost but also by the thought of what he had failed to gain. Mobile might someday be attacked and taken, but not by him, and along with much else that had gone with the winds of war — including all those hundreds of thousands of bales of cotton, which were to have put the national effort on a pay-as-you-go basis, but which instead had tainted it with scandal — were his hopes for the highest political office. All that had ended up the Red. He not only had been defeated by his enemies up that river, he had been oversloughed by his superiors on his return: "a fit sequel," the Saint Louis *Republican* asserted, "to a scheme conceived in politics and brought forth in iniquity."

If contention was less widespread on the Confederate side, where there was more credit than blame to be divided, such contention as there was only flared the higher on that account. Taylor's distress in reaction to his fear that the Federals were going to escape — the result, he claimed, of "sheer stupidity and pig-headed obstinacy" on the part of the high command at Shreveport — was mild compared to the frustration he felt when the bluecoats did in fact improvise an Atchafalaya crossing before the arrival of the Arkansas reinforcements enabled him to exact the retribution he felt they owed. Though his pride in his outnumbered army was as boundless as his contempt for the invaders ("Long will the accursed race remember the great river of Texas and Louisiana," he said of the latter in a congratulatory order he issued to his troops on May 23. "The characteristic hue of its turbid waters has a darker tinge from the liberal admixture of Yankee blood. The cruel alligator and the ravenous garfish wax fat on rich food, and our native vulture holds high revelry over many a festering corpse") his wrath had mounted with each passing day of the unimpeded blue retreat. Moving up to Yellow Bayou five days ago, he had taken time to communicate his chagrin at having been obliged to step aside, just when he had the vandals within his grasp, for lack of strength to stand his ground at Mansura. "I feel bitterly about this," he protested in a dispatch to Kirby Smith's adjutant, "because my army has been robbed of the just measure of its glory and the country of the most brilliant and complete success of the war."

The further it receded into the past, the more "brilliant and complete" that missed victory became. Indeed, within a week or so, Taylor had come to believe that his superior's military ineptness, which had obliged him to forgo a certain triumph, might well have cost the South its one best chance to win its independence. What was more, he said as much to Kirby Smith himself on June 5, in a letter combining indignation and despair. "In truth," he wrote, quite as if he had a corner on that rare commodity, "the campaign as a whole has been a hideous failure. The fruits of Mansfield have turned to dust and ashes. Louisiana, from Natchitoches to the Gulf, is a howling wilderness and her people are starving. Arkansas is probably as great a sufferer. In both States abolition conventions are sitting to overthrow their system of labor. The remains of Banks' army have already gone to join Grant or Sherman, and may turn the scale against our overmatched brethren in Virginia and Georgia." What made the hot-tempered Louisianian angriest was the contrast between this and the situation that might have obtained if his chief had not rejected his advice on how to go about disposing of the invaders, which he was certain would have led to their destruction and the reversal of the tide of war. "The roads to Saint Louis and New Orleans should now be open to us. Your strategy has riveted the fetters on both." The more he wrote — and he wrote at length, including a full critique of the campaign, with emphasis on the mismanagement of events beyond his reach, both here and in Arkansas — the angrier he grew: until finally, as he drew to a close, his wrath approached incandescence. "The same regard for duty which led me to throw myself between you and popular indignation, and quietly take the blame for your errors," he wound up, "compels me to tell you the truth, however objectionable to you. The grave errors you have committed in the recent campaign may be repeated if the unhappy consequences are not kept before you. After the desire to serve my country, I have none more ardent than to be relieved from longer serving under your command."

Thus Taylor, whose rage had made him as blind to the virtues of others as he was perceptive of their faults. To refer to the just-ended campaign as "a hideous failure," simply because it had not yielded all that he had hoped for, was to overlook its fruits, which in fact were far from slight. Inflicting more than 8000 casualties on Steele and Banks, at a cost to Price and Taylor of 6500, Smith had captured or caused the destruction of 57 pieces of artillery, nearly half of them naval, along with about a thousand wagons, most of them loaded with valuable supplies, and more than 3500 mules and horses. This was a considerable tactical haul, by almost any standards, and yet the strategic gains were even greater. Despite the hot-tempered Louisianian's claim to the contrary, the campaign had cost Sherman the use of 10,000 veterans in North Georgia; which meant that he moved with that many fewer against Joe Johnston, while Johnston's own army was enlarged by nearly twice that number because the upset of Banks' schedule had ruled out an early movement against Mobile, leaving Polk free to shift from Demopolis toward Dalton with some 20,000 troops who otherwise would have been drawn in the opposite direction by the threat to coastal Alabama. The greatest effect of the campaign up Red River thus was felt in northern Georgia, where a net difference of 30,000 men was registered in favor of the defenders of Atlanta. If the South was going to lose the war, then this would no doubt prolong the conflict. On the other hand, this might just narrow the long odds enough for the South to win it.

That of course remained to be seen. In the meantime, there was nothing Kirby Smith could do, despite his disinclination in such matters, but act on Taylor's insubordinate letter. Appointing Walker as his successor, he ordered him to Natchitoches, there to await instructions from their superiors, and forwarded the correspondence to Richmond with a covering letter to his friend the President. The good of the service required that he or Taylor be removed from command, the mild-mannered Floridian declared, adding that if Davis thought it best — as he well might do; Smith freely acknowledged the Louisianian's "merits as a soldier" — "I will willingly, with no feeling of envy or abatement of interest in the service of my country, turn over my arduous duties and responsibilities to a successor."

It made a sorry end, this falling-out by the victors, after all the glory that had been garnered up the Red and on the Saline; Dick Taylor was afterwards far from proud of his conduct in the quarrel, and set it down as the result of overwork and nervous strain. For the present, though, he was not unhappy to be reunited with his wife and children in Natchitoches, the lovely old French-Spanish town he recently had saved from Sherman's burners, there to await the judgment of his presidential brother-in-law.

✗ 3 ✗

Davis had troubles enough by then, and differences enough to attempt to compose, without the added problem of trying to heal this latest split between two of his friends, one of whom was among the nation's ranking field commanders, responsible for the conduct of affairs in the largest of all its military departments, while the other was his first wife's younger brother. Down in Georgia, for example, on March 10 — the day A. J. Smith's gorillas left Vicksburg, beginning the ten-week campaign that would take them up and down Red River, and the day before Grant left Washington for the meeting with Sherman in Nashville, where they would begin to plan the campaign designed to bring Georgia to its knees and the Confederacy to extinction — Governor Joseph E.

Brown addressed the state legislature, which he had called into special session to hear some things he had to say on the subject of the war. What he had to say, in essence, was that the war had been a failure. This was not only because it was now to be waged on his doorstep, so to speak, but also because, as he saw it, the authorities in Richmond had abandoned the principles embodied in the Declaration of Independence, including "all self-government and the sovereignty of the States."

Brown's solution, as set forth in his address, was for the Confederacy to dissolve itself into its components, thus calling a halt to discord and bloodshed: after which, in an atmosphere of peace and fellowship, a convention of northern and southern governors would assemble at Baltimore or Memphis, Montreal or the Bermuda Islands, and each state, North as well as South, would "determine for herself what shall be her future connection, and who her future allies." In other words, he would stop and start anew, this time without taking so many wrong turnings in the pursuit of happiness along the path that led to independence. Brown was careful, in the course of his speech, not to propose that Georgia rejoin the Union. That would have amounted to outright treason. He proposed, rather, that the Union rejoin Georgia, and he favored "negotiation" as the means of achieving this end. "In a crisis like the present," he maintained, "Statesmanship is ever more important than Generalship. Generals can never stop a war, though it may last twenty years till one has been able to conquer the other. Statesmen terminate wars by negotiation."

Praised for its acumen or condemned as disloyal, the address pleased some of its hearers and outraged others, depending largely on their predilections. Politically, an observer remarked, "Georgia was rent asunder." Among the governor's firmest supporters, though he was not in Milledgeville to hear him, was Alexander H. Stephens, Vice President of the Confederacy. Stephens not only gave the speech his full approval — as well he might; "I advised it from stem to stern," he admitted privately — but arrived in person six days later from Liberty Hall, his estate at nearby Crawfordville, to reinforce it with one of his own, twice as long and twice as bitter, in which he lashed out at the national authorities for their betrayal of the secessionist cause by adopting conscription and suspending the writ of habeas corpus. "Better, in my judgment," he declared, "that Richmond should fall and that the enemy's armies should sweep our whole country from the Potomac to the Gulf than that our people should submissively yield to one of these edicts." A small, pale-faced man with burning eyes and a shrill voice, weighing less than a hundred pounds in the voluminous overcoat he wore against the chill he felt in all but the hottest weather, he spoke for three full hours, in the course of which he sustained at several points a critic's charge that his alarm "had long ago vaulted into the hysterical." Where personal freedom was concerned Stephens rejected all arguments as to expediency. "Away with the idea of getting our independence first, and looking after liberty afterward!" he cried. "Our liberties, once lost, may be lost forever." If he had to be ruled by a despot, he said darkly, he preferred that it be a northern one, and he closed on a dramatic note, quite as if he expected to be clapped in arrest by government agents as soon as he came down off the rostrum. "I do not know that I shall ever address you again, or see you again," he told the legislators filling the chamber, row on row, from wall to wall. "As for myself," he added by way of farewell—though he knew, as Patrick Henry had not known before him, that the authority he assailed would not dare call him to account—"give me liberty as secured in the Constitution, amongst which is the sovereignty of Georgia, or give me death!"

He proceeded not to the dungeon he had seemed to predict, but back to Liberty Hall, where he continued to fulminate, in letters and interviews, against the government of which he was nominally a part and the man whose place he would take in case of death or the impeachment he appeared to recommend. Reproached by a constituent for having "allowed your antipathy to Davis to mislead your judgment," Stephens denied that he harbored any such enmity in his bosom. "I have regarded him as a man of good intentions," he replied, "weak and vacillating, petulant, peevish, obstinate but not firm." Having gone so far, however, he then revoked the disclaimer by adding: "Am now beginning to doubt his good intentions." Meantime, back in Milledgeville, Brown's managers were steering through the legislature a double set of resolutions introduced by Little Aleck's younger brother Linton, one condemning the Richmond authorities for having overriden the Constitution, the other defining Georgia's terms for peace as a return, North and South, to the "principles of 1776." This took three days; the governor had to threaten to hold the legislators in special session "indefinitely" in order to ram the resolutions through; then on March 19 they passed them and were permitted to adjourn. Brown had his and the Vice President's addresses printed in full, together with Linton Stephens's resolutions, and distributed copies to all the Georgia soldiers in the armies of Lee and Johnston.

Stephens and Brown were two of the more unpleasant facts of Confederate life that had to be faced in Richmond by officials trying to get on with a long-odds war amid runaway inflation and spreading disaffection. Others were nearer at hand. In North Carolina, for example — that "vale of humility," a native called the state, "nestled between two humps of pride," Virginia and South Carolina — the yearning for peace had grown in ratio to a general disenchantment with "glory," of which the war, according to Governor Zebulon Vance, had afforded the Old North State too meager a share. Less bitter than Joe Brown—of whom a fellow Georgian was saying this spring,

"Wherever you meet a growling, complaining, sore-headed man, hostile to the government and denunciatory of its measures and policy, or a croaking, despondent dyspeptic who sees no hope for the country, but, whipped himself, is trying to make everybody else feel as badly as himself, you will invariably find a friend, admirer, and defender of Governor Brown" — Vance was an unrelenting critic of the ways things were done or left undone at Richmond, and his correspondence was heavy with complaints, made directly to the President, that Carolinians were constantly being slighted in the distribution of promotions and appointments. Late in March, Davis lost patience and sought to break off the exchange, protesting that Vance had "so far infringed the proprieties of official intercourse as to preclude the possibility of reply. In order that I may not again be subjected to the necessity of making so unpleasant a remark, I must beg that a correspondence so unprofitable in its character, and which was not initiated by me, may here end, and that your future communications be restricted to such matters as may require official action." But Vance, a self-made man from old Buncombe County, had long since learned the political value of persistence; he was not so easily restrained. Scarcely a mail arrived from Raleigh that did not include a protest by the governor that some worthy Tarheel had been snubbed or overlooked in the passing out of favors, military as well as civil. Davis could only read and sigh, thankful at least that Vance kept his distance, even though it was not so great as the distance Brown and Stephens kept.

That was by no means the case with Edward A. Pollard, who was not only very much at hand as associate editor of the Richmond *Examiner,* but also took the trouble to let the authorities know it daily. He often seemed to despise the Confederacy to its roots, and seldom relaxed in his efforts to impale its chief executive on what was agreed to be the sharpest pen in the journalistic South. Invective was his specialty, and when he got on his favorite subject — Jefferson Davis — he sometimes raised this specialty to an art. "Serene upon the frigid heights of infallible egotism," the Kentucky-born Mississippian was "affable, kind, and subservient to his enemies" but "haughty, austere, and unbending to his friends," and though he assumed "the superior dignity of a satrap," he was in fact, behind the rigid mask, "an amalgam of malice and mediocrity." Future historians of various persuasions were to take their cue from this carving-up of a man on his wrong side; it was small wonder that Pollard, who spoke with the gadfly rancor of Thersites, found many who nodded in gleeful agreement as they read his jabs and jibes. They read him, in this fourth and gloomiest spring of a war they had begun to believe they could not win, to find relief from a frustration which grew, like his own, in ratio to the dwindling of their hopes.

Thoroughly familiar with the American proclivity for blaming national woes on the national leader, Davis had engaged in the practice too often himself not to expect it to be turned against him. He viewed it as an occupational hazard, one that more or less went with his job, and he spoke of it as a man might speak of any natural phenomenon — gravity, say, or atmospheric pressure — which could not be abolished simply because it bore within it the seeds of possible disaster. "Opposition in any form can only disturb me inasmuch as it may endanger the public welfare," he had said. Moreover, no one could sympathize more with the people who felt this fourth-spring frustration, for no one was in a position to know as well how soundly based the feeling was. Such blame as he attached to men like Stephens and Brown and Pollard was not for entertaining, but rather for giving vent to their defeatist conclusions, since by so doing they betrayed their high positions, converting them to rostrums for the spreading of despair, and did indeed "endanger the public welfare." As for the frustration itself, Davis not only sympathized with, he shared it. However much he might condemn those who gave way under pressure, he knew only too well how great that pressure was: especially for those who saw the problem, as he did, from within. Wherever he looked he perceived that the Confederacy's efforts to "conquer a peace" were doomed to failure. And this applied most obviously to the three most obvious fields for aggressive endeavor, whereby the South might attempt to force its will upon its mortal adversary: 1) by entering upon negotiations with representatives from the North to obtain acceptable peace terms, 2) by mounting and sustaining a military offensive which would end with the imposition of such terms, or 3) by securing the foreign recognition and assistance which would afford the moral and physical strength now lacking to achieve the other two.

As for the first of these, Davis had pointed out the difficulty, if not the impossibility, of pursuing this line of endeavor three months ago in response to a letter from Governor Vance, in which the Carolinian urged that attempts be made to negotiate with the enemy, not only because such an expression of willingness on the part of the South to stop shooting and start talking would "convince the humblest of our citizens . . . that the government is tender of their lives and happiness, and would not prolong their sufferings unnecessarily one moment," but also because the rejection by the North of such an offer would "tend greatly to strengthen and intensify the war feeling [of our people] and will rally all classes to a more cordial support of the government." Davis replied that while such results were highly desirable, "insuperable objections" stood in the way of their being achieved. One was that, by the simple northern device of refusing to confer with "rebel" envoys, all such offers — except to the extent that they were "received as proof that we are ready for submission" — had been rejected out of hand. He himself had seldom neglected an opportunity, in his public addresses and messages to Congress, to inform the enemy and the world that "All we ask is to be let alone." Nothing had come of this, in or out of official channels, and it was becoming increasingly clear that to continue such efforts was "to invite insult and contumely, and to subject ourselves to indignity, without the slightest chance of being listened to."

Suppose, though, that they did somehow manage to break through the barrier of silence. What would that do, Davis asked, but confront them with another barrier, still more "insuperable" than the first? "It is with Lincoln alone that we could confer," he reminded Vance, "and his own partisans at the North avow unequivocally that his purpose in his message and proclamation [of Amnesty and Reconstruction] was to shut out all hope that he would *ever* treat with us, on *any* terms." The northern President himself had made this clear and certain, according to Davis. "Have we not been apprised by that despot that we can only expect his gracious pardon by emancipating all our slaves, swearing obedience to him and his proclamation, and becoming in point of fact the slaves of our own Negroes?" In the light of this, he asked further, "can there be in North Carolina one citizen so fallen beneath the dignity of his ancestors as to accept or enter into conference on the basis of these terms? That there are a few traitors in the state who would be willing to betray their fellow citizens to such a degraded condition, in hope of being rewarded for their treachery by an escape from the common doom, may be true. But I do not believe that the vilest wretch would accept such terms for himself."

Having gone so far — for the letter was a long one, written in the days before he sought to break off corresponding with the Tarheel governor — Davis then proceeded to the inevitable conclusion that peace, if it was to come at all, would have to be won by force of arms. "To obtain the sole terms to which you or I could listen," he told Vance, "this struggle must continue until the enemy is beaten out of his vain confidence in our subjugation. Then and not till then will it be possible to treat of peace."

That brought him to the second, and much the bloodiest, of his three aggressive choices: the launching of an offensive that would not stop short of the table across which peace terms would be dictated to an enemy obliged to accept them as a condition of survival in defeat. Pleasant though this was to contemplate as a fitting end to slaughter and privation, it amounted to little more than an exercise in the realm of fantasy. If three blood-drenched years of war, and three aborted invasions of the North, had taught anything, they had taught that, however the conflict was going to end, it was not going to end this way. Davis, for one, never stopped hoping that it might, and even now was urging a course of action on Joe Johnston, down in Georgia, designed to bring about just such a closing scene. That the general declined to march all-out against the Union center was not surprising; Johnston had always

bridled at cut-and-slash urgings or suggestions, and in this case, outnumbered and outgunned as he was, he protested with ample cause.
Nor was he the only one to demonstrate reluctance. "Our role must be
a defensive policy," Kirby Smith was warning his impetuous lieutenants
out in the Transmississippi; while nearer at hand, and weightiest by far
in that regard, the nation's ranking field commander was tendering
much the same advice to his superior in Richmond. The most aggressive
of all the Confederate military chieftains — indeed, one of the most
aggressive soldiers of all time, of whom a subordinate had declared,
quite accurately, on the occasion of his appointment to head the
Virginia army, just under two years ago: "His name might be Audacity.
He will take more chances, and take them quicker, than any other
general in this country, North or South" — R. E. Lee had taken care,
well before the occasion could arise, to forestall even the suggestion
that he attempt another large-scale offensive when the present "mud
truce" ended in the East. Back in early February, in response to a
presidential request for counsel, he said flatly: "We are not in a condition, and never have been, in my opinion, to invade the enemy's country
with a prospect of permanent benefit."

There Davis had it. For though Lee added characteristically that
he hoped, by a limited show of force, to "alarm and embarrass [the
enemy] to some extent, and thus prevent his undertaking anything of
magnitude against us," this was no real modification of his implied
opinion that past efforts to end the war on northern soil — his own two,
which had broken in blood along Sharpsburg ridge and across the
stony fields of Gettysburg, as well as Bragg's, which had gone into reverse at Perryville — had been errors of judgment, serving, if for
nothing else, to demonstrate the folly of any attempt at repetition of
them. Such a statement, from such a source, was practically irrefutable,
especially since it was echoed by the commanders of the other two major
theaters, Smith and Johnston. The war, if it was to be won at all by
southern arms, would have to be won on southern ground.

Third and last of these choices, the securing of foreign recognition
and assistance, had long been the cherished hope of Confederate statesmen: especially Davis, who had uttered scarcely a public word through
the first twenty months of the war that did not look toward intervention
by one or another of the European powers. However, as time wore on
it became clearer that nothing was going to come of such efforts and
expectations — Russia had been pro-Union from the start, and France,
whatever her true desires might be, could not act without England,
where the Liberals in power took their cue from voters who were predominantly anti-slavery and therefore, in accordance with Lincoln's
persuasions, anti-Confederate — the southern President, smarting under
the snubs his unacknowledged envoys suffered, grew increasingly petulant and less guarded in his reaction. Fifteen months ago, addressing his

home-state legislature on the first of his western journeys to revive confidence and bolster morale, he lost patience for the first time in public. " 'Put not your trust in princes,' " he advised, "and rest not your hopes on foreign nations. This war is ours; we must fight it out ourselves." The applause this drew, plus the growing conviction that nothing any Confederate said or did had any effect whatever on the outcome in Europe, encouraged further remarks along this line. Nor was his reaction limited to remarks. In June of 1863, with Lee on the march for Gettysburg and Vicksburg soon to fall, the exequatur of the British consul at Richmond was revoked. The presence of such consuls had long been irksome, not only because they sought to interfere in such matters as the conscription of British nationals and the collection of British debts, but also because they were accredited to a foreign power, the United States, rather than to the country in which they operated, the Confederate States, whose very existence their government denied except as a "belligerent." The strain increased. In August, James M. Mason, the still unreceived ambassador to England, was told to consider his mission at an end, and before the following month was out he gave up his London residence and removed the diplomatic archives to Paris. In October the final strings were cut. Declaring their continued presence at Charleston, Savannah, and Mobile "an unwarranted assumption of jurisdiction," as well as "an offensive encroachment," Davis expelled all British consular agents from the South.

In Paris, Mason found the position of his fellow ambassador, John Slidell, highly enviable at first glance. Fluent in New Orleans French, the urbane Louisianian had practically free — though, alas, unofficial — access to Napoleon and Eugénie, both of whom were sympathetic to his cause; or so they kept assuring him, although nothing tangible in the way of help had so far proceeded from their concern. In many ways, the situation in Paris was more frustrating than the one in London, where Mason's non-reception at least had not built up hopes that came to nothing every time. By now, as a result of such recurrent disappointments, Slidell had become convinced that he was being led along for some purpose he could not fathom, but which he suspected would be of little benefit, in the end, either to him personally or to the government he represented. Disenchanted with the postcard Emperor, he was turning bitter in his attitude toward his job. "I find it very difficult to keep my temper amidst all this double dealing," he informed his friend and chief, Secretary of State Judah P. Benjamin. In point of fact, his experiences at court seemed to have jaundiced him entirely, for he added, by way of general observation: "This is a rascally world, and it is most hard to say who can be trusted."

What it came down to, in the end as in the beginning, whether Slidell was right or wrong about Napoleon and his motives, was that France could not act without England. And now, as the war moved into its fourth critical spring, Davis could not resist lodging a protest which, in effect, burned the last bridge that might have led to a rapprochement with that all-important power. The trouble stemmed from British acceptance of evidence supplied by U.S. Ambassador Charles Francis Adams that certain warships under construction by the Lairds of Liverpool, ostensibly for the Viceroy of Egypt, were in fact to be sold to the Confederacy, which intended to use these powerful steam rams to shatter the Union blockade. "It would be superfluous in me to point out to your lordship that this is war," Adams informed Foreign Secretary Lord John Russell. It was indeed superfluous, since Russell, already alarmed by Seward's tail-twisting threats along that line, had previously taken steps to prevent delivery of the vessels by detaining them. That was in September, six months ago, and as if this was not enough to placate Seward there arrived in Richmond on April 1 — not through regular diplomatic channels, but by special courier under a flag of truce, as between belligerents — a message for Jefferson Davis from Lord Richard Lyons, the British minister in Washington, containing an extract from a dispatch lately sent by Russell protesting "against the efforts of the authorities of the so-called Confederate States to build war vessels within Her Majesty's dominions to be employed against the Government of the United States."

Davis bristled. Hard as this governmental decision was to take — for the matter was still in litigation in the British courts, and he hoped for a favorable outcome there — the phrase "so-called" cut deeper, adding insult to injury as it did. Never one to accept a slight, let alone a snub, the Mississippian summoned his secretary and dictated a third-person reply. "The President desires me to say to your Lordship, that . . . it would be inconsistent with the dignity of the position he fills, as Chief Magistrate of a nation comprising a population of more than twelve millions, occupying a territory many times larger than the United Kingdom . . . to allow the attempt of Earl Russell to ignore the actual existence of the Confederate States, and to contumeliously style them 'so-called,' to pass without a protest and a remonstrance. The President, therefore, does protest and remonstrate against this studied insult, and he instructs me to say that in future any document in which it may be repeated will be returned unanswered and unnoticed." Lyons had not used diplomatic channels for delivery of his message; Davis, stung in his national pride, did not use diplomacy at all in his response. Warming as he dictated, he termed British neutrality "a cover for treacherous, malignant hostility," and closed with an icy pretense of indifference. "As for the specious arguments on the subject of the rams . . . while those questions are still before the highest legal tribune of the kingdom . . . the President himself will not condescend to notice them." The signature read, "Burton N. Harrison, Private Secretary."

Such satisfaction as Davis got from thus berating the Foreign

Secretary for his government's "persistent persecution of the Confederate States at the beck and bidding of officers of the United States" was small recompense for the knowledge that the South, engaged in what its people liked to think of as the Second American Revolution, would have no help from Europe in its struggle for independence. And what made this especially bitter to accept was a general historical agreement that in the original Revolution, with the Colonists in much the same position the Confederates were in now — unable, on the face of it, either to enforce or to negotiate a peace — such help had made the difference between victory and defeat. "This war is ours; we must fight it out ourselves," Davis had warned, by way of prelude to a year of hard reverses, and though the words were bravely spoken and loudly applauded at the time, there was sadness in the afterthought of what they meant in terms of the lengthening odds against success or even survival. Militarily, the handwriting on the wall was all too clear. In late November, within five months of the staggering midsummer news from Gettysburg and Vicksburg that Lee's army had been crippled and Pemberton's abolished, Bragg's army was flung bodily off Lookout Mountain and Missionary Ridge, impregnable though both positions had been said to be, and harried southward into Georgia. With these defeats in mind, it was no wonder that every Sunday at Saint Paul's in Richmond — the obvious goal of the huge offensive the North was about to launch as a follow-up of its triumphs, east and west, over the three main armies on which the Confederacy had depended for existence — the congregation recited the Litany with special fervor when it reached the words, "From battle and murder, and from sudden death, good Lord, deliver us."

The good Lord might, at that. For though military logic showed that the South could not win an offensive war, fought beyond the Potomac or the Ohio, there was still a chance that it could win a defensive one, fought on its own territory. It could win, in short, because the North could lose. In his letter to Vance, defining the conditions for peace under "the sole terms to which you or I could listen," Davis had not simply declared that the enemy must be beaten, period. He had said that the enemy must be "beaten out of his vain confidence in our subjugation," which was quite another thing. What he was saying was that for the North, committed by necessity to achieving an unconditional surrender, to settle for anything less than total conquest would amount to giving the South the victory by default. Lincoln knew this as well as Davis did, of course, and was not likely to coöperate in the dismemberment he had pledged himself to prevent. Yet the whole say-so would not be Lincoln's. Beyond the looming figure of the northern leader were the northern soldiers, and behind them were the northern people. If either became discouraged enough, soldiers or civilians, the war would end on terms not only acceptable but welcome to the South. The problem was how to get at them, beyond the loom of their leader, in order to influence their outlook and their choice. Davis saw cause for hope in both directions — tactical on one hand, political on the other — if certain requirements could be met.

Paradoxically, the tactical hope resulted from past Confederate defeats. Davis saw in every loss of mere territory — Nashville and Middle Tennessee, New Orleans, even Vicksburg and the Mississippi and the amputation of all that lay beyond — a corresponding gain, not only because what had been lost no longer required a dispersal of the country's limited strength for its protection, but also because the resultant contraction allowed a more compact defense of what remained. What remained now was the heartland, an 800-mile-wide triangle roughly defined by lines connecting Richmond, Savannah, and Mobile. Agriculturally and industrially, as well as geographically, this was the irreducible hard core of the nation, containing within it the resources and facilities to support a war of infinite length and intensity, so long as it and its people's will to fight remained intact. How long that would have to be, not in theory but in fact, depended on the validity of the companion political hope, according to which it would only be until November — specifically, the first Tuesday after the first Monday in that month — or, at worst, until early the following March — specifically, Inauguration Day. For this was a presidential election year in the North. The northern people, restrained by an iron hand these past three years, would finally have the chance to speak their minds on the question of war or peace, and the southern leader did not doubt that if his tactical hope was fulfilled — if no great Union victory, worth the agony to the army and the sorrow on the home front, was scored within that eight-month span by the blue drive on the heartland — his political hope would be fulfilled in turn. Weary of profitless bloodshed, the northern people would vote to end the war by turning Lincoln out of office and replacing him with a man who preferred to see half the nation depart in peace, as the saying went, rather than to continue the aimless destruction the two halves would have been visiting on each other for nearly three years. That was the prospect Davis had referred to, four months ago, when he declared in his State of the Nation address, opening the fourth session of Congress: "We now know that the only reliable hope for peace is in the vigor of our resistance, while the cessation of hostility [on the part of our adversaries] is only to be expected from the pressure of their necessities."

In brief, the problem between now and November was how to add to the North's war weariness, already believed to be substantial in certain regions where Copperheads were rampant, without at the same time increasing the South's disconsolation beyond the point of no return. This might or might not be possible, in light of the long odds, but in any case the prerequisite was that the northern people were to be denied the tonic of a large-scale victory within the triangular confines of the secessionist heartland — especially a tonic of the spirit-lifting kind that had come with the celebration of such victories as Vicksburg and Missionary Ridge, which had seemed to show beyond denial that a blue army could rout or capture a gray one as the result of a confrontation wherein Federal generalship was up to the standard set by the Confederates in the first two years of the war. Moreover, the general who had designed and directed both of those triumphs was now in over-all command of the Union forces, presumably chafing for the mud truce to end so he could get his armies headed south. Given the conditions that obtained in regard to numbers and equipment, plus the lightweight boxer's need for yielding ground in order to stay free to bob and weave and thus avoid a slugging match with his heavyweight opponent, there were bound to be southern losses and northern gains in the months immediately ahead; but that was not in itself a ruinous concession by the South, provided the losses and gains could be kept respectively minor and high-priced. In fact, such losses would serve admirably to drive home to the North the point that the prize was by no means worth the effort. The object was to make each gain so costly in blood and tears that the expense would be clearly disproportionate to the profit — if not in the judgment of the Federal high command, whose political or professional survival depended on continuing the conflict, then at any rate in the minds of those who would be casting their ballots in November, many of whom had an intensely personal interest in the casualty lists, future as well as past, and who might therefore be persuaded that their survival, unlike their leaders', depended on bringing the conflict to a close. Thus the South would be waging war not only on its own terrain (an advantage from which it had profited largely in the past) but also in the minds of northern voters who would be going to the polls, under what Davis termed "the pressure of their necessities" some seven months from now, to register a decision as to whether sustaining Lincoln's resolution that the rebels not be allowed to depart in peace was worth the continuing loss of their blue-clad sons and brothers and nephews and grandsons down in Georgia and Virginia.

Time and time alone would provide the answer to the question of survival; Patrick Henry's "liberty or death" applied quite literally to Confederate hopes and fears, which had between them no middle ground a man could stand on, patriot or traitor. Give or take a week or two, depending on the weather, the six months that would follow the end of large-scale inactivity in Georgia and Virginia, where the major forces lay mud-bound in their camps, would decide the issue, since Lincoln's appeal on that all-important Tuesday in November was likely to be in ratio to the progress of his soldiers in the field. Meantime, though, while the outsized armies on both sides took their ease and prepared as best they could for the shock to come, lesser forces had not been idle, east or west. And for the most part, when the military balance sheet was struck, the result of these out-of-season confrontations was encouraging to the hopes of the South for continuing its resistance to the superior weight the North could bring to bear.

Of these several upbeat Confederate successes — for though it was by far the most remote (Shreveport and Richmond were a thousand air-line miles apart; communication between them was necessarily slow and at best uncertain) it was not only the largest in numbers engaged, it was also achieved against the longest odds — the most encouraging was Kirby Smith's frustration of the double-pronged offensive designed by the Federals for completion of their conquest of the Transmississippi. All through the last half of March and the first half of April, the news from Louisiana and Arkansas had been gloomy; Banks and Steele appeared unstoppable in their respective penetrations, across the width and down the length of those two states, with Texas obviously next on the inexorable blue list. Then came word of Mansfield and Pleasant Hill, of Prairie d'Ane and Poison Spring; Steele and Banks were in full retreat from Price and Taylor, and Porter's dreaded ironclads were in flight from probable capture or destruction, bumping their bottoms as they scurried down the Red. It was incredible, and Camden and Jenkins Ferry, like Mansura and Yellow Bayou, only added to the glory and the uplift when news of them reached Richmond across those thousand embattled air-line miles. Other successes had preceded this, and others were to follow. Down in Florida, for example, an all-out Union effort to return that scantly defended state to its old allegiance, in accordance with Lincoln's recent proclamation, had been thrown into sudden reverse by Brigadier General Joseph Finegan's decisive late-February victory at Olustee, which drove the disarrayed invaders all the way back to the banks of the Saint Johns River. About the same time, westward in Mississippi, Sherman was slogging practically unopposed from Vicksburg to Meridian, where he was to be joined by a heavy cavalry column from Memphis for a hundred-mile extension of the march to Selma, a major industrial center whose destruction would do much to weaken the South's ability to sustain its armies in the field. This went by the board, however, when he learned that no cavalry column was any longer moving toward him; Nathan Bedford Forrest, lately promoted to major general with authority to raise a cavalry force of his own in the region the blue troopers would traverse, had whipped them soundly at Okolona, despite their two-to-one numerical advantage, and sent them staggering back to Memphis, part afoot and the rest on mounts so winded that two thirds of them were presently judged unfit for service. Sherman, left marking time, had to be content with wrecking what he held. "Meridian, with its depots, storehouses, arsenals, hospitals, offices, hotels, and cantonments, no longer exists," he reported as his wreckers, having done their worst, fell in for the march back to Vicksburg. But Selma still existed, together with all that Sherman listed and still more — including its vital cannon foundry, which, thanks to Forrest and his green command, continued to forge the heavy-caliber guns that would tear the ranks of other columns of invasion in other quarters of the South. Similarly the following week, as March came in, a raid by 3500 horsemen under Brigadier General Judson Kilpatrick, intended to achieve the liberation of an equal number of prisoners held in Richmond, was turned back at the city limits by old men and boys, home guardsmen serving worn-out artillery pieces long since replaced by new ones, captured or manufactured, in the batteries with Lee on the Rapidan. Soon regular graybacks arrived from there, overtaking the raiders who had slipped past them two nights ago, and harried the survivors into the Union lines, well down the York-James peninsula. Like March itself, Kilpatrick (called "Kill Cavalry" now) had come in like a lion and gone out like a lamb, and Richmonders were proud of their scratch resistance in the emergency that prevailed until the regulars came up.

Olustee and Okolona, like the improvised action that marked the limit of Kilpatrick's penetration, were primarily defensive victories, counterpunches landed solidly in response to Federal leads. But now, between mid-March and mid-April, there followed two exploits that were even more encouraging to Confederate hopes, though admittedly on a limited scale, because they proved that the South could still defy the lengthening odds by mounting and being successful in offensive operations. One was eastern, necessarily amphibious since it occurred in the region giving down upon the North Carolina sounds, while the other was western, staged throughout the length of the critical geographical corridor that lay between the Tennessee River and the Mississippi and extended all the way north to Kentucky's upper border, the Ohio, whose waters no uniformed Confederate had gazed upon since John Morgan's troopers crossed it, ten months ago, on the ill-fated raid from which the colorful brigadier himself had returned only by breaking out of prison.

Forrest, in command of what he called "the Cavalry Department of West Tennessee and North Mississippi," had never stopped thinking of this river-bound, 100-mile-wide, 200-mile-long stretch of land as belonging to him, particularly as a recruiting area, although all of it lay well beyond the Union lines and had done so in fact for nearly two years now. For him, as for most of his men — North Mississippians, West Tennesseans, and Kentuckians — the region was home, and he and they looked forward to returning there, if only on a visit. Indeed, he had already done so twice since it passed into northern hands, once at the beginning and once at the end of the year just past, and now he was going back for the third time. Accordingly, after disposing of Sherman's troopers by chasing them pell-mell into Memphis, he reorganized his own, grown to a strength of about 5000 and seasoned by their recent victory, into two divisions, commanded by Brigadier Generals Abraham Buford and James R. Chalmers, and set out northward with one of them — Buford's — on March 15 from his headquarters at Columbus, Mississippi. There were, he said, some 3000 recruits still available in West Tennessee, and he intended to have them, along with much else that was there in the way of horses and equipment which now were U.S. Army property.

　　　The alarm went out at once to Federal garrisons in all three states bordering the Mississippi south of the Ohio; Forrest was much feared, his unorthodox methods and slashing attacks, often delivered in utter disregard of the odds and the tactics manuals, having led one blue opponent to protest that he was "constantly doing the unexpected at all times and places." Nor did all the complaints have their origin beyond the enemy lines. Some Southerners had their objections, too, although these were primarily social. A former Memphis alderman and planter, a self-made millionaire before the war, the forty-two-year-old Forrest had not only been "in trade"; the trade had been in slaves. And though some Southerners might fight for the peculiar institution, or send their sons to fight for its preservation, they would not willingly associate with others who made, or once had made, a living from it. "The dog's dead," a young Mississippi aristocrat wrote in his diary this winter. "Finally we are under N. Bedford Forrest. . . . I must express my distaste to being commanded by a man having no pretension to gentility — a negro trader, gambler — an ambitious man, careless of the lives of his men so long as preferment be *en prospectu*. Forrest may be, and no doubt is, the best cavalry officer in the West, but I object to a tyrannical, hot-headed vulgarian's commanding me."

　　　In Jackson, Tennessee, on March 20 — presumably with the disgruntled young grandee in tow — Forrest sent word for Chalmers to take up the march, feinting at Memphis en route to add to the confusion in his rear, and detached a regiment to move against Union City, up in the northwest corner of the state. This was the 7th Tennessee Cavalry, Confederate, and by coincidence the town was garrisoned by the 7th Tennessee Cavalry, Union, whose surrender was accomplished in short order four days later, March 24, by a pretense of overwhelming strength, including the use of wheeled logs in place of guns (actually, there were fewer troops outside than there were inside, while the outer 7th had no guns at all) and a blood-curdling note, sent forward under a flag of truce, which ended: "If you persist in defense, you must take the consequences. N. B. Forrest, Major General, Commanding." The Union colonel decided not to persist. Instead he surrendered his 481 men, together with 300 horses and a quantity of arms and stores — all, as the colonel who had signed the general's name declared, "almost without the loss of blood or the smell of powder." Sending his prisoners south, where Chalmers was bristling as if on the verge of clattering into

Memphis, he rode hard to catch up with the main column, which Forrest had led northward through Trenton two days ago, then across the Kentucky line near Fulton, to descend on Paducah in the early afternoon of the following day, March 25, having covered the final muddy hundred miles in fifty hours.

Paducah, strategically located at the confluence of the Tennessee and the Ohio, was an important Union supply base, and it was supplies the general was after, not the garrison, which retired posthaste into a stoutly fortified earthwork supported by two gunboats patrolling the river in its rear. While sending in his usual demand for an unconditional surrender — "If you surrender you shall be treated as prisoners of war, but if I have to storm your works you may expect no quarter" — Forrest put his troopers to work on the unprotected depot, gleaning what he later reported to be "a large amount of clothing, several hundred horses, and a large lot of medical stores," along with about fifty prisoners who had not made it into the fort before the gates were shut. Inside, the blue commander declined to capitulate despite continued threats and demonstrations, including one all-out attack that was launched by a Kentucky regiment whose colonel, a native of Paducah, disobeyed restraining orders, apparently in an excess of pride and joy at being home again, and led a charge in which he and some two dozen of his men were killed or wounded. These were the only Confederate casualties, although the town itself was badly damaged by shells thrown into it from the gunboats and the fort. At midnight, having gathered up everything portable and destroyed much that was not — a government steamboat found in dry dock, for example, and a number of bales of precious cotton awaiting shipment on the landing — Forrest withdrew in the direction from which he had appeared, eight hours before. At Mayfield, a dozen miles southwest, he halted to give his captives a head start south and to furlough his three Kentucky regiments, with instructions to go to their nearby homes for a week, there to secure new clothes and mounts, at the end of which time they would reassemble at Trenton, fifty miles south of the Tennessee line. This they did, on schedule and to a man, many of them accompanied by recruits, fellow Kentuckians anxious for service under "the Wizard of the Saddle," as Forrest was beginning to be called.

He was by then in Jackson, planning another strike before he ended what was afterward referred to as his "occupation" of West Tennessee. His losses so far, including those of Chalmers, who had been skirmishing much of the time near Memphis, amounted to 15 killed and 42 wounded, as compared to Federal losses of 79 killed, 102 wounded, and 612 captured. This was a clear gain, but there was more. While planning a sudden enlargement of these figures, he did not neglect the normal intelligence-gathering duties of cavalry on the prowl. In fact, from his vantage point well within the enemy lines — even as Grant was at work on the details in Washington, Cincinnati, Culpeper, and else-where — Forrest not only saw through the latest Union "grand design" for the conquest of the South, he also recommended a method by which he believed it could be frustrated, if not shattered, at least in the western theater. "I am of the opinion," he wrote Joe Johnston on April 6, "that everything available is being concentrated against General Lee and yourself. Am also of opinion that if all the cavalry in this and your own department could be moved against Nashville that the enemy's com-munication could be broken up." What would come of this plea that he be turned loose on Sherman's life line remained to be seen. For the pres-ent, however, he had a lesser blow in mind, one that he had mentioned two days earlier in a report to Polk, whereby he intended to mount and equip his growing number of recruits: "There is a Federal force of 500 or 600 at Fort Pillow which I shall attend to in a day or two, as they have horses and supplies which we need."

Fort Pillow, established originally by the Confederates atop a bluff overlooking the Mississippi forty miles above Memphis, had been in enemy hands for nearly two years, ever since the evacuation of Corinth following Shiloh, and was garrisoned by a force of about 550. Half were Negroes, former slaves who had volunteered for service in the army that freed them in the course of its occupation of the plantations they had worked on, while the other half were Union-loyal whites; "Tennes-see Tories" and "Homemade Yankees," their since-departed neighbors, many of whom now rode with Forrest, contemptuously styled the latter. This was the place and these were the men Forrest had said he would "attend to," and accordingly, by way of creating a diversion, he sent Buford with one brigade to menace Columbus and ride back into Paducah, where newspapers were boasting that he had overlooked 140 fine government horses kept hidden in an old rolling mill throughout the recent raid. Buford's instructions were to get those horses and, in the process, draw the enemy's attention northward, away from Pillow, which would be attacked by his other brigade and one from Chalmers, who was told to come along and take command of both — 1500 men in all — for the march, which got under way on April 10, and the invest-ment, which began at daylight two days later. Northward, on the Mississippi and the Ohio, Buford carried out his assignment to the letter, detaching a couple of companies to menace Columbus while he rode with the main body into Paducah at noon on April 14. There, as before, the defenders fell back to their fortified position, and the raiders gath-ered up the horses they had missed three weeks ago. Returning south across the Tennessee line next day, they found that Chalmers too had carried out his assignment to the letter: so zealously so, in fact, that he and his men and Forrest, who was in over-all command, were already being widely accused of having committed *the* atrocity of the war. "The Fort Pillow Massacre," it was called, then and thereafter, in the North.

Arriving at dawn of April 12 Chalmers had the fort invested by the time Forrest came up at midmorning and took over. Pillow's original trace, some two miles long and an average 600 yards in depth, had been reduced to about half that by the Confederates before their evacuation, and now the Federals had contracted it still farther into a single earthwork, 125 yards in length, perched on the lip of the bluff and surrounded on three sides by a ditch six feet deep and twelve feet wide. Parapets four feet thick at the top and eight feet tall added greatly to the sense of security when the defenders were driven in from their outer line of rifle pits, although they presently found a drawback to this massiveness which the attackers were quick to exploit. "The width or thickness of the works across the top," a rebel captain afterwards explained, "prevented the garrison from firing down on us, as it could only be done by mounting and exposing themselves to the unerring fire of our sharpshooters, posted behind stumps and logs on all the neighboring hills." Their six guns were similarly disadvantaged, since the cannoneers could not depress them enough to fire at the attackers at close range. "So far as safety was concerned," the captain summed up, "we were as well fortified as they were; the only difference was that they were on one side and we were on the other of the same fortification." In partial compensation, the Federals had a gunboat in support, which flung a total of 282 rounds of shell, shrapnel, and canister at the dodging graybacks in the course of the fight. Also, there was the reassuring thought of what half a dozen double-shotted guns could do in the way of execution if any mass of rebels tried to scale those high dirt walls and poke their heads above that flat-topped parapet.

Forrest was thinking of that too, of course, but he did not let it deter him any more than he did the loss of three horses shot from under him in the course of the five hours he spent maneuvering for a closer hug and waiting for the arrival of his ammunition train to refill the nearly empty cartridge boxes of his rapid-firing troopers. Shortly after 3 o'clock the train arrived, and the general sent forward under a flag of truce his usual grisly ultimatum. "Should my demand be refused," the note closed, "I cannot be responsible for the fate of your command." By way of reply, the Union commander requested "one hour for consultation with my officers and the officers of the gunboat." But Forrest by now had spotted a steamer "apparently crowded with troops" approaching, as well as "the smoke of three other boats ascending the river." Believing that the Federals were stalling for time in which to gain reinforcements and additional naval support, he replied that he would give them twenty minutes and no more; "If at the expiration of that time the fort is not surrendered, I shall assault it." Either because he considered this a bluff, or else because he believed an assault was bound to fail — his soldiers, white and black, apparently were of the same conviction, for they had been taunting the rebels gleefully and profanely from the parapets throughout the cease-fire that attended the exchange — the Union commander replied succinctly, "I will not surrender." Forrest had no sooner read the note than he turned to his bugler and had him sound the charge.

The assault was brief and furious, practically bloodless up to a point, and proceeded according to plan. While the sharpshooters back on the hillsides kept up a harassing fire that skimmed the parapet, the first wave of attackers rushed forward, leaped into the slippery six-foot ditch, and crouched in the mud at the bottom, presenting their backs to the men of the second wave, who thus were able to use them as stepping-blocks to gain the narrow ledge between the ditch and the embankment just beyond, then lean down and hoist their first-wave comrades up beside them. It was as neatly done as if it had been rehearsed for weeks, and in all this time not a shot had been fired except from the hillsides and around on the flanks, where Forrest had other marksmen at work on the gunboat. "Shoot at everything blue betwixt wind and water," he had told them: with the result that the vessel, which had closed to canister range, kept its ports tight shut to protect its gunners and took no part in attempting a repulse. By now the attackers were all on the narrow ledge, holding their unfired weapons at the ready and keeping their heads well down while the hillside snipers continued to kick dirt on the parapet, across whose width, although the graybacks were only a few feet away, flattened against the opposite side of the earthwork, no member of the garrison could fire without exposing two thirds of his body to instant perforation. At a signal, the sharpshooters held their fire and the men on the ledge went up and over the embankment, emptying their pistols and rifles into the blue mass of defenders, who fought briefly against panic, then broke rearward for a race to the landing at the foot of the bluff, where they had been told that the gunboat, in the unlikely event of a rebel breakthrough, would cover their withdrawal by pumping grape and canister into the ranks of their pursuers.

It did not work out that way, not only because the gunboat was shut up turtle-tight and took no part in the action, but also because the graybacks were too close on their heels for the naval gunners to have been able to fire without hitting their own men, even if they had tried. Flailed from the rear by heavy downhill volleys, the running bluecoats next were struck in the flanks by the troopers who had been shooting at the gunboat. Some kept going, right on into the river, where a number drowned and the swimmers became targets for marksmen on the bluff. Others, dropping their guns in terror, ran back toward the Confederates with their hands up, and of these some were spared as prisoners, while others were shot down in the act of surrender. "No quarter! No quarter!" was being shouted at several points, and this was thought by some to be at Forrest's command, since he had predicted and even threatened that what was happening would happen. But the fact was, he had done and was doing all he could to end it, having ordered the firing stopped as soon as he saw his troopers swarm into the fort, even though its flag was still flying and a good part of the garrison was still trying to get away. He and others managed to put an end to the killing and sort out the captives, wounded and unwounded. Out of a total Federal force of 557, no less than 63 percent had been killed or wounded, and of these about two thirds — 221, or forty percent of the whole — had been killed. Forrest himself lost 14 killed and 86 wounded. Before nightfall, having seen to the burial of the dead by the survivors, he gathered up his spoils, including the six pieces of artillery, and moved off with 226 prisoners, twenty of whom were men so lightly wounded they could walk. Next morning he sent his adjutant, accompanied by a captured Union captain, back to signal another gunboat — which had resumed the shelling of the woods around the fort, unaware that there was no longer anything Confederate there to shoot at, only Federals — to put in, under a flag of truce, and take the more seriously wounded aboard for treatment downriver in Memphis. That ended the Fort Pillow operation.

But not the talk, the cultivated reaction which quickly mounted to a pitch of outraged intensity unsurpassed until "the Rape of Belgium" fifty years later, when propaganda methods were much improved by wider and faster means of disseminating "eyewitness" accounts of such "atrocities," true or false. Within six days a congressional committee — strictly speaking, a subcommittee of the feared and ruthless Joint Committee on the Conduct of the War — left Washington for Tennessee, having been appointed to gather "testimony in regard to the massacre at Fort Pillow," and within another three days was taking depositions from survivors, along with other interested parties, which resulted in a voluminous printed report that the rebels had engaged in "indiscriminate slaughter" of men, women, and children, white and black, and afterwards had not only set barracks and tents afire, roasting the wounded in their beds, but had also "buried some of the living with the dead," despite their piteous cries for mercy while dirt was being shoveled on their faces. "Many other instances of equally atrocious cruelty might be enumerated," the report concluded, "but your committee feels compelled to refrain from giving here more of the heart-sickening details." Southerners might protest that the document was "a tissue of lies from end to end," as indeed it largely was, but they could scarcely argue with the casualty figures, which indicated strongly that unnecessary killing had occurred, although it was in fact the opposite of "indiscriminate." For example, of the 262 Negro members of the garrison, only 58 — just over twenty percent — were marched away as prisoners; while of the 295 whites, 168 — just under sixty percent — were taken. The rest were either dead or in no shape for walking. Here was discrimination with a vengeance, as well as support for a Confederate sergeant's testimony, given in a letter written home within a week of the affair, describing how "the poor, deluded negroes would run up to our men, fall upon their knees and with uplifted hands scream for mercy, but were ordered to their feet and then shot down." This was not to say that Forrest himself had not done all he could, first to prevent and then to end the unnecessary bloodshed. He had, and perhaps the strongest evidence of his forbearance came not from his friends but from his enemies of the highest rank. Within three days of the fall of the fort, when news of the "massacre" reached Washington, Lincoln told Stanton to investigate without delay "the alleged butchery of our troops." Stanton passed the word to Grant, who wired Sherman that same day: "If our men have been murdered after capture, retaliation must be resorted to promptly." Sherman undertook the investigation, as ordered, but made no such recommendation: proof in itself that none was justified, since no one doubted that otherwise, with Sherman in charge, retaliation would have been as prompt as even Grant could have desired.

As for Forrest, his mind was soon on other things, including the removal of his spoils and a stepped-up enforcement of the conscription laws throughout West Tennessee. His recruiting methods were as rigorous as they were thorough. "Sweep the country, bringing in every man between the ages of eighteen and forty-five," he told his agents. "Take no excuse, neither allow conscripts to go home for clothes or anything else; their friends can send them." Haste was required, for before he got back to Jackson, two days after Pillow fell, he received a dispatch from Polk directing him to return promptly to Okolona, where his two divisions would combine with those under Major General Stephen D. Lee, Polk's chief of cavalry in the Department of Mississippi, Alabama, and East Louisiana, to meet an anticipated raid-in-force from Middle Tennessee, southward through Decatur, Alabama. Forrest replied that the order would of course be complied with, though in his opinion "no such raid will be made from Decatur or any point west of there." Events were to prove him right in this, but even if such a raid had been intended he believed that the best way to turn it back was by striking deep in its rear. He still had his eye on Sherman's life line. He wanted to hit it, and he wanted to hit it hard. This time, however, he presented his views not only to Polk and Johnston, who seemed unwilling or unable to act on them, but also to Jefferson Davis, addressing him directly. Stephen Lee had about 7000 cavalry, and he himself was approaching that strength by now. "With our forces united," he wrote Davis on April 15, "a move could be made into Middle Tennessee and Kentucky which would create a diversion of the enemy's forces and enable us to break up his plans." It was Sherman he meant — specifically, the long rail supply line reaching down from Louisville on the Ohio, through Nashville on the Cumberland, to Chattanooga on the Tennessee. That was a lot of track, and Forrest had long since shown what he could do to a railroad when he turned his troopers loose on one in earnest. More-over, he assured the Commander in Chief lest the plan be considered an impractical hare-brained escapade like the one on which John Morgan had come to grief last summer, "such an expedition, managed with prudence and executed with rapidity, can be safely made."

Whatever merit there was in the proposal, for the present at least the authorities in Richmond were more interested in a project closer at hand, involving an attempt to recover the North Carolina coastal region, which got under way in earnest that same week, two days after Forrest wrote his letter. A Tarheel brigade under a native North Caro-linian, Brigadier General Robert Hoke, had been detached from the Army of Northern Virginia to undertake the job in coöperation with an ironclad ram that had been under construction for the past year in a cornfield at Edwards Ferry, two thirds of the way up the Roanoke River to Weldon. General Braxton Bragg, assigned as the President's chief military adviser after his removal from command of the Army of Tennessee, had conceived the plan, secured the troops, and worked out the details, beginning with an amphibious assault on Plymouth at the point where the Roanoke flowed into Albemarle Sound. Occupied for more than two years by the Federals, who had fortified it stoutly, the town would have to be attacked by water as well as by land, since other-wise the heavy guns of the Union fleet, on station in support of the place, would drive the attackers out about as soon as they got in. Bragg had much confidence in Hoke, who was given large discretion after a detailed briefing on this opening phase of the campaign — a veteran, though not yet twenty-seven, he had fought with distinction in all the major eastern engagements from Big Bethel through Chancellorsville, where he was severely wounded — as well as in the ironclad successor to the *Virginia* and the *Arkansas*, both of glorious memory.

Christened *Albemarle*, she was launched from the riverside corn-field in which she had been built, mostly by local carpenters and black-smiths, and set off downstream on the day she was commissioned, April 17, en route to her maiden engagement. Sheathed in two layers of two-inch iron and mounting a pair of 6.4-inch Brooke rifles pivoted fore and aft to fire through alternate portholes, she was just over 150 feet in length, 34 feet in the beam, and drew 9 feet of water. Because of the numerous twists and turns in the river this far up — which, incidentally, had served to protect her from interference by Federal gunboats during her construction — she set out stern-foremost, dragging a heavy chain from her bow to steer by. Fitters were still at work on her armor and machinery, and portable forges were brought along for emergency re-pairs. They soon were needed, first when the main driveshaft wrenched loose from its coupling, late that night, and next when the rudderhead broke off, early the following morning. Three miles from Plymouth the second night, and ten hours behind schedule because of time-out for repairs, she was stopped by reports that the river ahead was obstructed by hulks which the enemy, hearing rumors that the *Albemarle* was approaching completion, had sunk in the channel to tear out her bottom in case she ventured down. Aboard as a volunteer aide to her skipper, Commander James W. Cooke — another Tarheel and a veteran of more than thirty years in the old navy — was her builder, Gilbert Elliott, a native of nearby Elizabeth City, where he had learned his craft in his grandfather's shipyard. Elliott set out in the darkness in a small boat with a pilot and two men, taking a long pole for soundings, and presently returned to report that, thanks to the unusually high stage of the river this spring, "it was practicable to pass the obstructions provided the boat was kept in the middle of the stream."

Cooke by then had turned the ram around and cleared for action. He had no contact with Hoke ashore, but on being informed that a sporadic attack had been in progress against Plymouth most of the day and up until 9 o'clock that night, when the skirmishers withdrew — presumably because of the nonarrival of the *Albemarle*, without whose help the town could not be held under the frown of a quartet of gunboats just inside the mouth of the river — he weighed anchor and stood down to engage. It was close to 4 o'clock in the morning, April 19, when he passed safely over the sunken hulks, taking a few harmless heavy-caliber shots from the fort as he went by, and came in sight of the four Union warships. Warned of his approach, they were prepared to receive him. The two largest, *Miami* and *Southfield* — big, double-ended side-wheel steamers of a novel design, with rudders fore and aft for quick reversals — were lashed together, but not too tightly, in accordance with a plan to catch the *Albemarle* between them, thus making her useless as a ram, while they tossed explosives down her stack. Cooke avoided this by steering close to the south bank, then turning hard aport as he drew nearly abreast of the shackled gunboats, presenting his long, tapered bow to the nearer of the two. Both opened on him with solids at close range, bringing as many of their dozen guns into play as could be brought to bear, but with no more effect than if the shots had been tennis balls, except that they left spoon-shaped dents in the armor when they bounced. Closing fast, with the force of the current added to her thrust, the ironclad put her snout ten feet into *Southfield*'s flank, penetrating all the way to her fireroom, but then had trouble withdrawing it from so deep a wound. The two hung joined, the ram taking water into her forward port because of the weight of the rapidly sinking gunboat: seeing which, the captain of the *Miami* ran to one of his 9-inch Dahlgrens, depressed it quickly, and fired three explosive shells pointblank at the rebel monster. All three shattered against the iron casement, a scant twenty feet away. Pieces of the third, which was fired with a short fuse, flew back from the target and knocked down most of the gun crew, including the captain, who lay dead with the jagged fragments stuck deep in his chest and face.

Albemarle's captain was backing his engines hard to free the ram of the weight on her bow, but by the time he managed to do so, the *Miami* — called the "Miasma" by her crew, who had found duty aboard her boring up to now — cut loose from the sinking *Southfield* and ran with all her speed for open water. Followed out into Albemarle Sound by the other two gunboats, which had observed the action at long range, she wanted no more of a fight with an adversary impervious to shot and shell alike. Cooke attempted a brief pursuit, then broke off when he saw that it was fruitless, mainly because his engines were getting almost no draft through his badly shot-up smokestack, and turned back to give his full attention to the fort. Now it was the Federals' turn to learn what it was like to try to hold the place while under attack from the river as well as the land.

They found it hard indeed. Delaying only long enough to patch up his riddled stack and get in touch with the Confederates ashore, Cooke steamed back past Plymouth that afternoon and opened on the fort in conjunction with Hoke, whose batteries were skillfully disposed for converging fire and whose infantry returned to within small-arms range of the Federal ramparts. The result was altogether harrowing for the defenders, caught thus as it were between the devil and the deep blue sea, the landward attackers and the *Albemarle*, both of which kept up the pressure until well after sunset and resumed it at daylight with even greater fury. "This terrible fire had to be endured without reply, as no man could live at the guns," the fort's commander was to report. "The breast-height was struck by solid shot on every side, fragments of shell sought almost every interior angle of the work, the whole extent of the parapet was swept by musketry, and men were killed and wounded even on the banquette slope. . . . This condition of affairs could not be long endured without a reckless sacrifice of life; no relief could be expected, and in compliance with the earnest desire of every officer I consented to hoist a white flag, and at 10 a.m. of April 20 I had the mortification of surrendering my post to the enemy with all it contained." This included 2834 soldiers, thirty guns, and a large haul of supplies, all secured at a cost to the attackers of less than 300 casualties, only one of whom was naval, a seaman hit by a pistol ball while the *Albemarle* had her snout in the sinking *Southfield*. "Heaven has crowned our efforts with success," a presidential aide-observer wired Davis, who replied directly to Hoke: "Accept my thanks and congratulations for the brilliant success which has attended your attack and capture of Plymouth. You are promoted to be a major general from that date."

Young Hoke was the hero of the hour, together with Cooke and the *Albemarle*, all down the eastern seaboard, and Bragg — though his basic planning went unnoticed amid the general praise for Hoke and Cooke — was hard at work, now that the ram had reversed the naval advantage, projecting exploits of a similar nature for the immediate future.

It was this the Federals feared. Unable to get an ironclad through any of the shallow inlets into Pamlico Sound, and with no time left in which to build one there, they saw no way to stop the apparently invulnerable, new-hatched monster before it returned the whole region to Confederate control. "The ram will probably come down to Roanoke Island, Washington, and New Bern," the district commander, Major General John J. Peck, informed his department chief, Ben Butler, on the day Plymouth fell. "Unless we are immediately and heavily reinforced, both by the army and navy, North Carolina is inevitably lost." Butler shared the alarm, although belatedly. Two months earlier, when the navy had asked him to send troops up the Roanoke to destroy the rebel vessel on its stocks, he had replied: "I don't believe in the ironclad," and even now, in passing on to Halleck the news that the fort had been reduced in part by the guns of the nonexistent warship, he declined to accept a fraction of the blame, which he declared was all the navy's for having left the garrison's water flank exposed. "Perhaps this is intended as a diversion," he ended blandly. "Any instructions?"

In point of fact, New Bern was next on the *Albemarle*'s list, once she finished off the gunboats skittishly awaiting her emergence into the Sound from which she took her name, and Hoke was told to prepare for this, rather than for an early return to the Army of Northern Virginia, despite that army's commander's pleas that he and his brigade were needed to help meet the attack that was soon to be launched across the Rapidan. Whatever disappointment this might involve for Lee, outnumbered two to one by the bluecoats on the north side of the river, Plymouth made a fine addition to the list of late winter and early spring victories which the President was compiling for inclusion in the message he was preparing for delivery to Congress when it convened next week in Richmond.

"Recent events of the war are highly creditable to our troops," he wrote, "exhibiting energy and vigilance combined with the habitual gallantry which they have taught us to expect on all occasions. We have been cheered by important and valuable successes in Florida, northern Mississippi, western Tennessee and Kentucky, western Louisiana, and eastern North Carolina, reflecting the highest honor on the skill and conduct of our commanders and on the incomparable soldiers whom it is their privilege to lead. . . . The armies in northern Georgia and in northern Virginia," he added, by way of compensation for the fact that there had been no such recent, gloom-dispelling triumphs in either of those regions, "still oppose with unshaken front a formidable barrier to the progress of the invader, and our generals, armies, and people are animated by cheerful confidence."

So he would say, and so Congress would be pleased to hear. But there were things he left unmentioned because to air them — involving, as they did, plans untried and expectations unfulfilled — would serve to deepen, rather than relieve, the nation's gloom regarding one of the two main armies on which it depended for survival. Davis's disappointment was not in Lee, who was fairly immobilized by the fact that a solid third of the Army of Northern Virginia had been detached for the past seven months; it was in Johnston, who had been given command of the Army of Tennessee with the understanding, at least on the part of the Richmond authorities, that he would go over to the offensive in an attempt to recover East and Middle Tennessee, lost by his predecessor in the course of the bloody, erratic, year-long retreat from Murfreesboro to Dalton. "You are desired to have all things in readiness at the earliest practicable moment for the movement indicated," the transplanted Virginian was reminded in early March. "The season is at hand and the time seems propitious."

Plans for such an offensive were quite explicit. Union forces now preparing at Chattanooga and Knoxville for a spring advance were dependent on uninterrupted communication with Nashville; if this supply line could be severed, both would be obliged to abandon what they held, with much attendant disruption of their plans. In line with this, Richmond's proposal was that Johnston be reinforced by Polk for a shift northeast to Kingston, forty miles west of Knoxville, where he would be joined by two divisions under Lieutenant General James Longstreet, detached from Lee and wintering near Greeneville, for an advance across the Tennessee River with a combined strength of more than 70,000 men. By such a move, the authorities assured him, "Knoxville [would be] isolated and Chattanooga threatened, with barely a possibility for the enemy to unite. Should he not then offer you battle outside of his entrenched lines, a rapid move across the mountains from Kingston to Sparta (a very practicable and easy route) would place you with a formidable army in a country full of resources, where it is supposed, with a good supply of ammunition, you may be entirely self-sustaining, and it is confidently believed that such a move would necessitate the withdrawal of the enemy to the line of the Cumberland." Bragg was the author of these suggestions, and he wrote from experience. In essence, they called for a repetition of the movement he himself had made soon after he assumed command of the army in the summer of 1862, whereby the western seat of war was shifted, practically overnight and practically without bloodshed, from Mississippi to North Georgia and from there all the way north to Kentucky. The Federals then had been obliged to give up, at least for a season, their designs on Chattanooga, and Bragg was of the opinion that if Johnston would only profit by his example the same results could be obtained in regard to their designs on Atlanta — provided, of course, that he advanced before his adversaries did. "To accomplish this," he was re-reminded in mid-March, "it is proposed that you move as soon as your means and force can be collected."

Johnston had many objections to the plan. Time had probably run out; he lacked supplies, as well as the mules and wagons needed to haul them; the Federals, in greatly superior numbers, would combine and jump him as soon as he got started, obliging him to fight at a disadvantage and with nothing to do, in case of defeat, but scatter his troops in the mountains. What he preferred, he told Bragg on March 18, was to stand where he was, letting the bluecoats crack their skulls against his works, then follow them up when they retreated. Meantime, he urged, the proffered reinforcements under Longstreet should be sent to him at Dalton for a share in the defensive battle, rather than have them wait in idleness to join him on the march. Bragg's reply, three days later, was curt and stiff: "Your dispatch . . . does not indicate an acceptance of the plan proposed. The troops can only be drawn from other points for an advance. Upon your decision of that point further action must depend." Alarmed at this evidence that he would not be reinforced on his own terms, Johnston was quick to assert that he had been misunderstood. "I expressly accept taking offensive," he wired back. "Only differ with you as to details. I assume that the enemy will be prepared for an advance before we are and will make it to our advantage. Therefore, I propose as necessary both for offensive and defensive to assemble our troops here immediately. Other preparations for advance are going on."

For two weeks there was no reply to this. The answer, when it came on April 7, was in a dispatch addressed not to Johnston but to Longstreet, who was told to prepare his two divisions for an immediate return to Virginia. Johnston was depressed by this lack of confidence, and outraged by reports that he had declined to move against the enemy. "I learn that it is given out," he wrote to a senator friend whose son was on his staff, "that it has been proposed to me to take the offensive with a large army & that I refused. Don't believe any such story." Besides, he said, after outlining his objections to the plan he had rejected, Lee's army, not his, was the one that should have been ordered to advance. "It would have been much easier to take the offensive (excuse such frequent use of that expression) in Va. than here," he wrote, basing his statement on the erroneous double claim that Lee's army was not only larger than his but also had a smaller blue army to its front. However, he was not greatly surprised at the way things had gone. The authorities in Richmond — Davis himself, Secretary of War James A. Seddon, and now Bragg, his erstwhile friend — had about as low an opinion of him, apparently, as he had of them;

which was low indeed. His consolation was in his men. "If this army thought of me and felt toward me as some of our high civil functionaries do," he closed his letter, "it would be necessary for me to leave the military service. But thank heaven, it is my true friend."

It was true the army was his friend; no general on either side, not even R. E. Lee or George McClellan, had more affection from the soldiers he commanded. "He was loved, respected, admired; yea, almost worshipped by his troops," a Tennessee veteran was to say. Richmond had taken this quality into account in sending him to Dalton to repair the shattered morale of an army which had recently been thrown off Missionary Ridge and chased southward into Georgia by the opponent it faced there now. And in this he had succeeded. "He restored the soldier's pride; he brought the manhood back to the private's bosom," the same veteran declared. The drawback, according to those who had advised against his appointment, was that he was too defensive-minded for the tactical part of his assignment. He had only assumed the offensive once in the whole course of the war, and that had been at Seven Pines, which might well seem to him the exception that proved the unwisdom of attacking, since all it had got him was the wound that had cost him the command he most preferred, now held by Lee, and a subsequent transfer to the less congenial West. Those who had opposed his appointment in December, on grounds that he would never go forward as intended, were quick to point out now in April that their prediction had been fulfilled. In fact, they said, if he continued to follow his accustomed pattern of behavior, he would be likely to fall back from Dalton at the first bristly gesture by the Federals in his front. Davis and Seddon, who had favored his appointment — primarily, it was true, because no one could think of another candidate for the job — were obliged to admit the strength of this, as evidence of what to expect, and so was Bragg after his exchanges with the general, by letter and wire, throughout the latter part of February and the first two thirds of March. It was then, on the heels of this admission by Davis and Seddon and Bragg, that the summons went to Longstreet for a quick return to Lee. They had given up on Johnston, who would neither go forward nor refuse to go forward, and who they knew from past experience (in northern Virginia, down on the York-James peninsula, outside beleaguered Vicksburg, and back in the piny woods of Mississippi) would wind up doing exactly as he pleased in any case. He always had. He always would. The only decision left was whether to keep him — and the fact was, they had no one to put in his place. So they kept him. And in keeping him, however regretfully, they committed the Army of Tennessee to the defensive and gave up all hope for a slash at the Union center as a means of disrupting at the outset the latest Grand Design for their subjugation.

Lee was committed to the defensive, too, though not by inclination or from choice. "At present my hands are tied," he confessed in a mid-April letter to Bragg. "If I was able to move . . . the enemy might be driven from the Rappahannock and obliged to look to the safety of his own capital instead of the assault upon ours." As it was, he added, writing from the stripped region about Orange where his infantry was camped, "I cannot even draw to me the cavalry or artillery of the army, and the season has arrived when I may be attacked any day."

It was a question of subsistence for mounts and men. Scarcely a tree in the district wore its bark below the point to which a horse could lift its mouth, and few of the few animals on hand were fit for rigorous service; "Fully one half of them were incapable of getting up a gallop," a cavalry officer complained, "a trembling trot being their fastest gait." Conditions were nearly as bad for the leaned-down soldiers. Though Davis himself had managed to get hold of 90,000 pounds of meat for shipment to the Rapidan during a critical, near-starvation period that winter, this did not go far with troops whose usual daily ration comprised four ounces of bacon or salt pork, often rancid, and a scant pint of rough-ground corn meal. Sprouting grass was a help to the horses this rainy April, but hunger was still a condition of existence for the men. This pained Lee, who did not like to add to other people's troubles by recounting his own, into making a formal complaint to the President, coupled with the strongest warning he had given at any time in the twenty-two months since he assumed command: "My anxiety on the subject of provisions for the army is so great that I cannot refrain from expressing it to Your Excellency. I cannot see how we can operate with our present supplies. Any derangement in their arrival or disaster to the railroad would render it impossible for me to keep the army together, and might force a retreat into North Carolina."

That too was in mid-April — April 12 — one week after he had alerted the army to prepare for a Union crossing, any day now, of the river to its front. On that same April 5, having pored over information received from scouts, northern papers, and citizens beyond the Rapidan, he gave Davis his estimate of the situation. "The movements and reports of the enemy may be intended to mislead us, and should therefore be carefully observed," he wrote. "But all the information that reaches me goes to strengthen the belief that Genl Grant is preparing to move against Richmond." This was as far as he went at the time; he said nothing of his new opponent's probable route (or routes) or schedule. Three days later, however, he wrote of receiving two more reports from reliable scouts, in which "the general impression was that the great battle would take place on the Rapidan, and that the Federal army would advance as soon as the weather is settled." Continuing to study all the evidence he could gather — including much, of course, that was false or merely worthless — he arrived within another week at a considerably more detailed estimate, and he passed this too along to

Davis, saying: "We shall have to glean troops from every quarter to oppose the apparent combination of the enemy."

He expected three attacks, all to be delivered simultaneously from three directions: 1) a main assault across the Rapidan, more or less against his front, 2) a diversionary advance up the Shenandoah Valley, off his western flank, and 3) a rear attack, up the James, to menace Richmond from the east and south. To meet this last, he proposed that General P. G. T. Beauregard be shifted from his present command at Charleston, which Lee believed was no longer on the list of Union objectives, and brought to Petersburg or Weldon to take charge of the defense of southside Richmond. The Valley threat he would leave for the time being to Major General John C. Breckinridge, who had a small command in the Department of Southwest Virginia. As for the main effort, the blue lunge across the Rapidan, he kept that as the continuing exclusive concern of the Army of Northern Virginia. Recent news that Longstreet would soon be coming back with two of his three divisions, after seven months in Georgia and Tennessee, made Lee yearn for a return to the old days and the old method of dealing with such a threat as he faced now. "If Richmond could be held secure against the attack from the east," he told the President on April 15, "I would propose that I draw Longstreet to me and move right against the enemy on the Rappahannock. Should God give us a crowning victory there, all their plans would be dissipated, and their troops now collecting on the waters of the Chesapeake would be recalled to the defense of Washington." Having said as much, however, he returned to such realities as the scarcity of food for his men and horses, then closed on a note of ominous regret: "But to make this move I must have provisions and forage. I am not yet able to call to me the cavalry or artillery. If I am obliged to retire from this line, either by a flank movement of the enemy or the want of supplies, great injury will befall us."

On April 18 he ordered all surplus baggage sent to the rear, a sort of ultimate alert well understood by the troops to mean that fighting might begin at any time. Still Grant did not move. Lee's impatience mounted during the following week — in the course of which Breckinridge was warned to brace for action in the Valley and Beauregard, in compliance with orders from Richmond, reached Weldon to assume command of the region between the James and Cape Fear rivers — though he acknowledged that the gain was worth the strain, if only because the half-starved horses thus were allowed more time to graze in peace on the new-sprung grass. "The advance of the Army of the Potomac seems to be delayed for some reason," he wrote Davis on April 25. "It appears to be prepared for movement, but is probably waiting for its coöperative columns." He closed with an invitation for the President to visit the army, "if the enemy remains quiet and the weather favorable," by way of affording himself a diversion from the daily grind in Richmond. Davis declined, under pressure of business; Congress would convene next week, for one thing. But four days later Lee enjoyed a diversion of his own.

Longstreet's two divisions had arrived at last from Tennessee and were in camp around Gordonsville, nine miles south of army head-quarters at Orange. Lee did not know whether Meade would cross the Rapidan on his left or right, taking John Pope's intended route down the Orange & Alexandria Railroad or Joe Hooker's through the Wilder-ness. He rather thought (and certainly hoped) it would be the latter, but since he lacked solid evidence to that effect he kept Longstreet's hard-hitting veterans off to his left rear, in case the bluecoats came that way. On April 29 he rode down to review them for the first time in nearly eight months, which was how long it had been since they left the Old Dominion to supply Bragg's Sunday punch at Chickamauga. They were turned out in their ragged best, leather patched, metal polished, their shot-torn regimental colors newly stitched with the names of unfamiliar western battles, and when Lee drew rein before them, removing his hat in salute, the color bearers shook their flags like mad and the troops responded with an all-out rebel yell that reverber-ated from all the surrounding hills, causing the gray-haired general's eyes to brim with tears. "The effect was as of a military sacrament," an artillerist later wrote. Lee wept, another veteran explained, because "he felt that we were again to do his bidding." Deep Southerners or Westerners to a man — South Carolinians and Georgians, Alabamians and Mississippians, Arkansans and Texans — there was not a Virginian among them, and yet it was as if they had come home. A First Corps chaplain riding with the staff turned to a colonel as the yell went up and Lee sat there astride his gray horse Traveller, uncovered in salute, and asked: "Does it not make the general proud to see how these men love him?" The colonel shook his head. "Not proud," he said. "It awes him."

Awed or proud — no doubt with something of both, despite the staffer's protest — Lee felt his impatience mount still faster next day, back at Orange, when he got word that a four-division corps under Ambrose Burnside, formerly encamped at Annapolis and thought to be intended for service down the coast, had passed through Centerville two days ago and had by now reached Rappahannock Station, from which position it could move in direct support of the Army of the Potomac. Perhaps it was for this that Grant had been waiting to put his three-pronged war machine in motion. As for Meade, Lee informed Davis on this final day in April, "Our scouts report that the engineer troops, pontoon trains, and all the cavalry of Meade's army have been advanced south of the Rappahannock.... Everything indicates a concentrated attack on this front." His faith was in God and in the "incomparable infantry" of the Army of Northern Virginia, but now as he awaited the onslaught of the blue juggernaut whose numbers were roughly twice his own, he displayed more urgency of manner than those closest to him had ever seen him show on his own ground. Evidence of an early assault continued to accumulate, and still the Federal tents remained unstruck beyond the Rapidan. Lee's aggressive instinct, held in check by hard necessity, broke its bounds at last. "Colonel," he told a member of his staff, "we have got to whip them; we must whip them!" Apparently that was the high point of his impatience, for having said as much he paused, then added with a smile of amused relief: "It has already made me better to think of it."

Lee's confidence was based on past performance, against odds as long and sometimes longer, and Davis too drew reassurance from that source, having just completed his third full year of playing Hezekiah to Lincoln's Sennacherib. Whatever frets he had about developments out in Georgia, here in the Old Dominion at least the Confederacy had won for itself the military admiration of the world. Six blue comanders, in all their majesty and might — Irvin McDowell and George McClellan, John Pope and Ambrose Burnside, Joseph Hooker and George Meade — had mounted half a dozen well-sustained offensives, each designed to achieve the reduction of Richmond in short order, and all six had been turned back in various states of disarray. Now there was Grant, who seemed to many only a seventh name to be added to the list of discomfited eastern opponents. "If I mistake not," a young officer on Lee's staff wrote home on hearing of the elevation of this latest transfer from an inferior western school, "[Grant] will shortly come to grief if he attempts to repeat the tactics in Virginia which proved so successful in Mississippi." There were dissenters: Longstreet, for example, who had been Grant's friend at the Academy and a groomsman at his wedding — and who had fought, moreover, in a theater where Grant was in command. "We must make up our minds to get into line of battle and to stay there," Old Peter had told his visitors at Gordonsville the day before, "for that man will fight us every day and every hour till the end of the war." But for the most part there was general agreement that what had been done six times before (four of them, and the last four at that, more or less on this same Rapidan-Rappahannock line) could be done again by Lee, whose army was a rapier in his hand. If Grant was a fighter, as Longstreet said, there would be nothing unusual in that. One of the worst-defeated of the six had been known as "Fighting Joe," and the one who had been given the soundest drubbing of them all — the "miscreant" Pope — had also arrived with western laurels on his brow and a reputation for coming to savage grips with whatever tried to stand in his path of conquest.

Besides, what was called for now was not necessarily the outright defeat or even repulse of the invaders, east or west. What was called for, Davis could remind himself, was a six-month holding action which

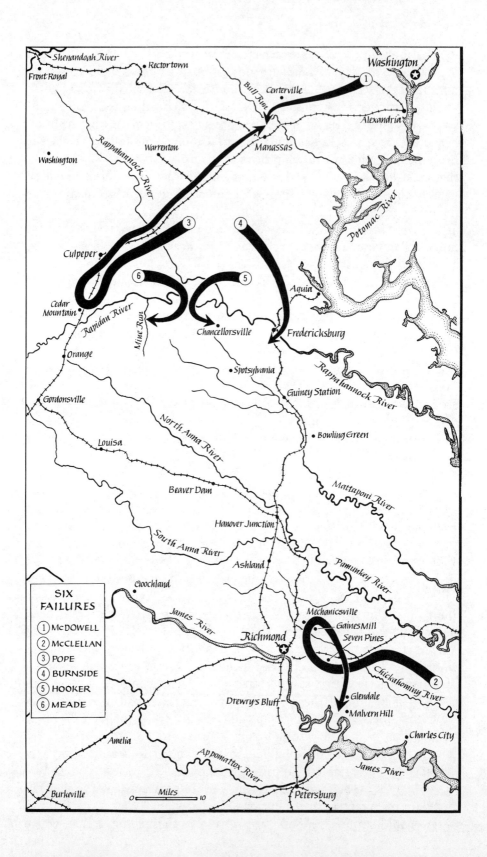

Washington
Shenandoah River
Rectortown
Front Royal
Bull Run
Centerville
①
Washington
⋆
Alexandria
Warrenton
Manassas
Washington
Rappahannock River
③
④
Culpeper
⑥
⑤
Aquia
Cedar
Mountain
Rapidan River
Mine Run
Chancellorsville
Fredericksburg
Orange
Spotsylvania
Rappahannock River
Gordonsville
Guiney Station
North Anna River
Louisa
Bowling Green
Beaver Dam
Mattaponi River
Hanover Junction
South Anna River
Ashland
Pamunkey River
Goochland
Mechanicsville
Gaines Mill
James River
Seven Pines
Richmond
Chickahominy River
②
Drewry's Bluff
Glendale
Malvern Hill
Amelia
Charles City
Appomattox River
James River
Burkeville
Petersburg

SIX
FAILURES
① McDOWELL
② McCLELLAN
③ POPE
④ BURNSIDE
⑤ HOOKER
⑥ MEADE

Miles
0   10

would allow them no appreciable gain except at a price that would be regarded as prohibitive, in money and blood, by voters who would be making their early-November choice between peace and war. In light of this, a head-down fighter like Grant might serve the South's purpose far better than would an over-all commander who was inclined to count his casualties and take counsel of his fears. Not that Davis abandoned all hope for a repetition of what had happened in the past to opponents who had come in roaring and gone out bleating; he hoped for it profoundly, and not without cause. Don Carlos Buell and William S. Rosecrans were western examples to match the six discomfited in Virginia, and Sherman had shown himself to have many of the qualities that made Grant an ideal opponent at this juncture. In some ways, now that the notion of an offensive against the Union center had been abandoned as a gambit, Joe Johnston seemed an excellent choice as a foil for the red-haired Ohioan, whose impulsiveness might expose him to the kind of damage his government could least afford on the eve of its quadrennial election. By way of further encouragement, Davis had only to consider more recent successes, scored east and west by Kirby Smith, Finegan, Forrest, and Hoke, for proof that the South could still stand up to combinations designed for its destruction, and could also carry the war to the enemy when the opportunity came. Just as Banks and Steele had been driven back across the Atchafalaya and the Saline — not only against the numerical odds, but also, as it were, against the tactics manuals — so might Sherman and Grant be driven back across the Tennessee and the Rappahannock. Like many brave men, before and since, Davis had found that when a difficulty amounted to an impossibility, the best course to pursue was one that did not take the impossibility into account. That was what he had meant all along when he said, "I cultivate hope and patience, and trust to the blunders of our enemy and the gallantry of our troops for ultimate success."

For the most part this attitude was shared by the people of Richmond. In fact, among the party-goers and the well-to-do — they had to be that; a dollar in gold was worth more than thirty in Confederate paper, while calico and coffee were $10 a yard and pound, eggs $2 a dozen, and cornfield beans were selling at $60 a bushel — there had never been a social season as lively as the one now drawing to a close. "Starvation parties" were all the rage, along with charades and taffy pulls, although they seemed to one diarist to have a quality of desperation about them, as if the guests were aware that these revels, honoring "Major This, or Colonel That, or Captain T'other," would be the last. In February Lincoln had issued a draft call for 500,000 men — more than the Confederacy could muster in all its camps between the Rappahannock and the Rio Grande — and then in March had upped the ante by calling for "200,000 more." All the South could do, by way of response, was lower and raise the conscription age limits to seventeen and fifty, robbing thus the cradle and the grave, as some complained, or as Davis put it, in regard to the half-grown boys about to be drafted and thrown into the line, "grinding the seed corn of the nation." Meanwhile U. S. Grant, "a bull-headed Suvarov," was poised on the semicircular horizon, about to lurch into motion from three directions, and in Richmond, his known goal, the revelry continued. "There seems to be for the first time," the diarist noted, "a resolute determination to enjoy the brief hour, and never look beyond the day."

Elsewhere about the country it was apparently much the same; a young man just back from Mobile reported that he had attended sixteen weddings and twenty-seven teas within the brief span of his visit. He did not add that he had found the gayety forced in that direction, but to a Richmond belle, looking back a decade later on this fourth and liveliest of the capital's wartime springs, the underlying sense of doom had been altogether inescapable. "In all our parties and pleasurings," she would recall, "there seemed to lurk a foreshadowing, as in the Greek plays where the gloomy end is ever kept in sight."

✗ 4 ✗

Grant was angered throughout April by increasingly glum reports of developments out in the Transmississippi, which in effect snapped off one prong of his spiky offensive before it could even be launched. "Banks, by his failure," he complained to Halleck, "has absorbed 10,000 veteran troops that should now be with Sherman, and 30,000 of his own that should have been moving toward Mobile; and this without accomplishing any good result." Nor was that the worst of it. Even more exasperating, from a somewhat different point of view, was the knowledge that Johnston now would not only have no worries about his rear and his supply lines to the Gulf, but would also be able to summon to the defense of North Georgia reinforcements who otherwise would have been occupied with the defense of South Alabama. Banks and Steele, as co-directors of the Louisiana-Arkansas fiasco, had disarranged the Grand Design at the outset; or as a friend of Grant's, after repeating his complaint that "30,000 men were rendered useless during six of the most important months of the military year," was to put it in a later appraisal of the situation, "The great combination of campaigns was inaugurated with disaster."

By way of insuring against such blunders here in the East, Grant contented himself with sending explicit and detailed instructions to Franz Sigel, who had received a military education in his native Germany, regarding the projected movement up the Shenandoah Valley and down the Virginia Central Railroad. But he went in person, soon after his return from Tennessee, to confer with the altogether nonpro-

fessional Ben Butler, whom he had never met and with whom he had
had no correspondence as to his share in the three-pronged convergence
on Lee and Richmond. Arriving on April 1 at Fortress Monroe, the
Massachusetts general's headquarters at the tip of the York-James
peninsula, he decided that a good way to size up the former Bay State
politician would be to invite his views on the part he thought he ought
to play in the campaign scheduled to open within four weeks. Butler
promptly gave them, and Grant was pleased, as he said later, to find
that "they were very much such as I intended to direct"; that is, an
amphibious movement up James River for a landing at City Point, eight
miles northeast of Petersburg, the hub of Virginia's life-sustaining rail
connections with the Carolinas and Georgia, and a fast northward
march of twenty miles for a knock at the back door of the Confederate
capital while Meade, so to speak, was climbing the front steps and
Sigel was coming in through the side yard. This augured well. Still,
gratifying as it was to find his military judgment confirmed in advance
by the man who was charged with carrying out this portion of the
plan it had produced, Grant did not neglect to give Butler, before he
got back aboard the boat next morning for the return up Chesapeake
Bay, written instructions as to what would be expected of him when
jump-off time came round. "When you are notified to move," he told
him, "take City Point with as much force as possible. Fortify, or rather
intrench, at once, and concentrate all your troops for the field there as
rapidly as you can." He added that, though "from City Point directions cannot be given at this time for your future movements," Butler
was to bear in mind "that Richmond is to be your objective point, and
that there is to be coöperation between your force and the Army of the
Potomac."

The latter, being charged with the main effort, was of course
Grant's main concern, and when he returned to Culpeper next day he
found it in the throes of an unwelcome top-to-bottom reorganization.
Designed to achieve the double purpose of tightening the chain of command and of weeding out certain generals who had proved themselves
incompetent or unlucky, the shakeup involved the consolidation of a
number of large units. Indeed, there was no unit above the size of a
brigade that was unaffected by the change. Two of the five corps were
broken up and distributed among the remaining three, while the same
was done with four of the fifteen infantry divisions, leaving eleven. The
result was painful to men in outfits which thus were abolished or in
any case lost their identity in the shuffle. Cast among strangers they felt
rejected, disowned, orphaned. They felt resentful at having been can-
nibalized, stung in their unit pride that theirs had been the organizations
selected for such a fate, and they voiced their resentment to all who
would listen. "The enemies of our country have, in times past, assailed
[this division] in vain," one dispossessed commander protested, "and

now it dissolves by action of our own friends." Although the recommendation had been made by Meade before Grant left Tennessee, the soldiers put the blame on the new general-in-chief, since the order of approval came down from Washington just two weeks after his arrival. By way of registering their complaint, at the first large-scale review Grant held after his return from Fortress Monroe in early April the men of one absorbed outfit wore their old corps badge on the crown of their caps, as usual, and — as he could see as soon as they swung past him — pinned the new one to the seat of their trousers.

He took no apparent offense at this, having other, more pressing matters on his mind. One was numbers. However well the chain of command was tightened, however ruthlessly high-ranking incompetents were purged, the army would be able to do little effective fighting, especially of the steam-roller kind Grant favored, unless its ranks were full and reserves were ample. And there was the rub. As spring advanced, the army moved closer to the time when it might lose the very cream of its membership, the men who had come forward on hearing that Sumter had been fired on, back in the pre-draft spring of 1861, and had learned since then, in what Sherman termed "the dearest school on earth," what it meant and what it took to be a soldier. Such veterans, survivors of many a hard-fought field, were scarcely replaceable. They were in fact not only the backbone, they were the body of the army, constituting roughly half the total combat force. Now their three-year enlistments were about to expire, and if they did not reënlist the army was apt to melt away, like the snow on the crest of the Blue Ridge, along with the volunteer organizations whose rolls they filled. Nor was this true only of the Army of the Potomac. Of the 956 volunteer infantry regiments in all the armies of the Union, 455 — nearly half — were scheduled to leave the service before the end of summer, while of the 158 volunteer batteries of artillery, 81 — more than half — would presently be free to head for home: unless, that is, enough of their members reënlisted to justify continuing their existence. By way of encouraging such commitments, the government offered certain inducements designed to make a combined appeal to greed and pride. These included, in the former category, a $400 bounty (to be increased by the amount his home town and county, or rather the civilians who had remained there for whatever reasons, were willing to put up) and a thirty-day furlough. As for pride, a man who reënlisted was to be classified as a "volunteer veteran" and was authorized to wear on his sleeve a special identifying chevron, a certificate of undeniable cold-blood valor. To these was added, as an appeal to *unit* pride, the guarantee that any regiment in which as many as three fourths of the troops "shipped over" would retain its numerical designation and its organizational status.

This last was perhaps the most effective of the lot: especially when regimental commanders, anxious to hold their outfits together as a prerequisite for holding onto their rank, carried the process down to the company level, where a man's deepest loyalties lay. Any company that attained its quota was encouraged to parade through the regimental camps, fifes shrieking and drums throbbing, while onlookers cheered and tossed their caps. Such enthusiasm was contagious, and the pressure grew heavier on holdouts in ratio to the nearness of the goal, until at last reluctance amounted to disloyalty, not only to comrades already committed, who stood in danger of being scattered among strangers, but also to the regiment, which would die a shameful death without its quota of reënlisted volunteers. "So you see I am sold again," one such wrote home, explaining that he had been swept off his feet by a fervor as strong as the spirit that makes a man be "born again" at a church revival. Not that the bounty and the prospect of a trip home, sporting the just-earned chevron, were not attractive. They were indeed, and especially together; $400, a tempted veteran pointed out, "seemed to be about the right amount for spending-money while on a furlough." Besides, regional supplements often raised the sum to more than a thousand dollars: a respectable nest egg, and enough for the down payment on a farm or a small business, once the fighting ended. Until then, after three years of life in the service, home was likely to be no great fun anyhow, except on a visit — and even that had its limitations, according to some who had been there and found that it fell considerably short of their expectations. "I almost wish myself back in the army," a furloughed soldier, barely a week after his departure, wrote to a comrade still in camp. "Everything seems to be so lonesome here. There is nothing going on that is new." In any case, as a result of these several attractions and persuasions, by mid-April no less that 136,000 veterans had signed on for another three years or the duration of the war.

Most of these were in the West, where the troops expected an early victory and were determined to be in on the kill; "fierce-fighting western men," one of their generals called them, "in for work and in for the war." In the Army of the Potomac the result was less spectacular; 26,767 veterans reënlisted — about half as many as signed up for another three years under Sherman, and also about half as many as were up for discharge. This meant that about the same number would soon be going home, dropped as emphatically from the army roster as if each man had stopped a rebel bullet. They would have to be replaced, and mainly this would be done by the conscripts and substitutes who now were arriving as a result of Lincoln's February call. Whatever they meant to Grant and Meade, for whom they were merely numbers on a fatted strength report, to the men they joined they were a mixed blessing at best. At worst, they were considerably less. "Such another depraved, vice-hardened and desperate set of human beings never before disgraced an army," an outraged New Englander complained. Partly this was the result of rising wages, which made enlistment a greater sacrifice than ever, and partly it was because the outsized bounties had created a new breed of soldier: the bounty jumper. "Thieves, pick-pockets, and vagabonds would enlist," a later observer remarked, "take whatever bounty was paid in cash, desert when opportunity offered, change their names, go to another district or state, reënlist, collect another bounty, desert again, and go on playing the same trick until they were caught." One nimble New Yorker confessed to having made thirty-two such "jumps" before he wound up in the Albany peniten-tiary, while another New England veteran recorded that no less than half the recruits in his regiment received in one large draft had so quickly forgotten their assumed names, on the trip down to the Rap-pahannock, that they could not answer roll call when they got there. What was more, the delivery system was far from efficient. Out of a shipment of 625 recruits intended for a distinguished New Hampshire regiment, 137 deserted en route and another 118 managed to do the same within a week of their arrival — 36 to the rear, 82 into the Con-federate lines — leaving a residue of 370, who were either the most patriotic or else the least resourceful of the lot. Across the way, on the south bank of the Rapidan, rebel pickets put up a placard: "Head-quarters, 5th New Hampshire Volunteers. RECRUITS WANTED." In much the same vein, they sent over a mock-formal message inquiring when they could expect to receive the regimental colors.

Something else this latest influx of draftees brought into the Rappahannock camps that was more disturbing than the rising desertion rate. Though few in numbers, compared to the men already there, the newcomers effected a disproportionate influence on certain aspects of soldier life. "They never tired of relating the mysterious uses to which a 'jimmy' could be put by a man of nerve," a startled veteran would recall, "and how easy it was to crack a bank or filch a purse." Such talents did not go unexercised, so far at least as the limited field allowed; nothing anyone owned was safe that was not nailed down, and there were more ways than one to skin a cat or fleece a sheep. With all that crisp new bounty money injected into the economy, gambling increased hugely and so did the stakes. According to one awed observer, "Thousands of dollars would change hands in one day's playing, and there were many ugly fights engaged in, caused by their cheating each other at cards." Outraged by what he called "this business of filling up a decent regiment with the outscourings of humanity," another veteran infantryman recorded that "the more we thought of it, the more discontented we became. We longed for a quiet night, and when day came we longed to be away from these ruffians." The result was a necessary tightening of restrictions, in and out of drill hours and applicable to all. That came hard. "No pleasure or privilege for the boys in camp any more," a volunteer lamented, "for the hard lines and severe military discipline apply with a rigidness never before applied." Old-timers yearned for a return to the easy-going life they once had groused about, and they blamed its loss, illogically or not, on Grant, whom they saw as a newcomer like all those unwelcome others, though in fact the change had begun before he had any notion, let alone intention, of coming east to assume command of all the armies.

More logically — quite accurately, in fact — they put the blame on him for another change which was going to have an even more baleful effect on the lives of thousands of men now in his charge. In mid-April, in a further attempt to lengthen his numerical advantage over the forces in rebellion, Grant put an official end to the three-year-old practice of exchanging Federal and Confederate prisoners of war. Whatever its shortcomings from a humanitarian point of view, militarily the decision was a sound one. Not only did a man-for-man exchange favor the side on which a man was a larger fraction of the whcle, but in this case there was also the added dividend that, in ending such a disadvantageous arrangement, the Union would be burdening its food-poor adversary with a mounting number of hungry mouths to feed. Just how much prolonged misery this was likely to cause, Grant's own troops knew only too well, either from having been captured in the days when they could be exchanged, or from awareness of what the daily food allowance consisted in the camps across the river. It was hard enough on the rebels, whose stomachs had long since shrunk to fit their rations, but for men accustomed to eating all they could hold ("Our men are generally overloaded, fed, and clad," their chief quartermaster was protesting even now, "which detracts from their marching capacity and induces straggling") such deprivation would amount to downright torture. Moreover, the prospect was further clouded by the knowledge that it had been devised by their own commander, the same man they accused of having foisted the detested reorganization upon them, as well as of having polluted their camps with rowdy gangs of thugs.

One further thing Grant did, however, that went far toward making up for the unpopularity of those other changes that followed hard on his arrival. This was to reach into the back areas of the war, especially into the fortifications around the capital, and pluck thousands of easy-living soldiers from their cushy jobs for reassignment to duty in the field. Individually and in groups, stripped of their plumes and fire-gilt buttons, they came down to the Rappahannock in a somewhat bewildered condition, if not in a state of downright shock, and the troops already there were glad to welcome them with cheers and jeers. The warmest welcome went to regiments of heavy artillery, prised out of their snug barracks, issued Springfields, and converted overnight into congeries of unblooded rifle companies; "Heavy Infantry," the veterans called them, or just "Heavies." The shocking thing about such regiments, aside from their greenness, was their size. Popular with volunteers in search of easy duty and security from wounds, several of them

had as many as 1800 men apiece. "What division is this?" a Massachusetts soldier asked when one of them marched in, his own regiment
being down to 207 effectives at the time. Other conversions were
applauded about as lustily. Parade-ground cavalry units, for example,
were suddenly unhorsed, handed muskets in place of carbines, and told
that they would henceforth go afoot. "Where are your horses?" a heavy
infantryman inquired of a dismounted cavalry outfit that came slogging
into camp soon after his own regiment arrived. "Gone to fetch your
heavy guns," one of the former troopers snapped. Teamsters too were
subject to such abrupt indignity, and many of them were similarly converted and accoutered, as a result of an order reducing transportation
to one wagon per brigade. "You needn't laugh at me," a transmuted
teamster called to a braying mule in a passing train. "You may be in the
ranks yourself before Grant gets through with the army."

In point of fact, now that they had time to look him over and
examine the results of some of the changes he introduced, the men had
begun to see that, whatever else he might do, in or out of combat, he
clearly meant business, and they found they liked the notion of this.
Some high-ranking officers, particularly the starch-collared regulars
among them, might have doubts about the new general-in-chief (an
old-line colonel of artillery, for instance, wrote home that he found
him "stumpy, unmilitary, slouchy and western-looking; very ordinary,
in fact") but the troops themselves, according to an enlisted diarist,
would "look with awe at Grant's silent figure" whenever he rode out
on inspection, which was often. They liked his reticence, his disregard
of mere trappings, his eye for the essential. He was seldom cheered,
except by greenhorn outfits trying to make points, but he seemed not
to care or even notice. "Grant wants soldiers, not yawpers," a veteran
observed approvingly. What was more, his success in prising the heavies
out of the Washington fortifications was good evidence that he had the
confidence of the authorities there — something most of his predecessors had lacked, to their discomfort and the resultant discomfort of the
army in their charge. This was seen as an excellent sign, as well as a
source of present satisfaction. There was also a solidity about him that
was welcome after service under a series of commanders who had shown
a tendency, and sometimes more than a tendency, to fly asunder under
pressure. A New Englander put it simplest: "We all felt at last that
the boss had arrived." Grant returned the compliment in kind. "The
Army of the Potomac is in splendid condition and evidently feels like
whipping somebody," he informed Halleck on April 26, one month after
establishing headquarters at Culpeper: adding, "I feel much better with
this command than I did before seeing it."

He had good cause to feel so, even though by now he was already
one day past the date he had set for the simultaneous jump-off, east and
west. Numerically, as a result of those various recruitment stratagems

in the army and on the home front, he was in better shape than anyone had dared to hope, particularly on the Rappahannock. After Burnside shifted his corps into position for closeup support of Meade, Grant had 122,146 infantry, cavalry, and artillery effectives on hand for the main-effort crossing of the Rapidan. This figure included only the troops who were "present for duty, equipped"; another 24,602 were on extra duty, sick, or in arrest, bringing the total to just under 147,000. Even at the lower figure, and leaving Butler and Sigel out of account, he had about twice as many effectives as Lee, who had 61,953 of all arms. In Georgia, moreover, the ratio was roughly the same. Sherman had 119,898, including men on reënlistment furloughs, while Johnston had 63,949, including Polk, who would be free to join him once the pressure was on and the Union strategy was disclosed. Just when that would be, east and west, depended in part on the method by which this pressure was to be applied; that is, on the tactical details of the strategy Grant and Sherman had worked out between them, six weeks ago, in the Cincinnati hotel room. Grant was willing to leave the working out of such details to his red-haired friend, as far as they were to be applied in the West. In the East, however, he had made the matter his prime concern ever since he had set up headquarters in the field.

From Culpeper, there in the toppled V of the rivers, and from the peak of nearby Stony Mountain, where an observation post had been established for surveillance of the landscape roundabout, he could give the problem informed attention. South of the V, disposed on a front of nearly twenty miles along the right bank of the river, from Mine Run upstream to Rapidan Station and beyond, Lee and his army lay in wait under cover of intrenchments they had spent the past six months improving. The problem was how to get at him: or, more precisely, how to get around him and then at him, since a frontal assault, across the river and against those earthworks, would amount to downright folly, if not suicide en masse. Once the blue army was on his flank or in his rear, however, with nothing substantial between itself and Richmond, Lee would be obliged to come out of his works for the showdown battle Meade had been told to seek. This being so, the question was reduced to whether to move around his right flank or his left, east or west of that twenty-mile line of intrenchments. Much could be said for the latter course. The country was more open in that direction, affording the attackers plenty of room for bringing all of their superior force to bear, and there was also the prospect of gobbling up what was left of the Orange & Alexandria Railroad, down to Gordonsville, and then moving onto the Virginia Central, converting them into a supply line leading back to the Potomac, while denying their use to the defenders. All this was good, so far as it went, but there were two considerable drawbacks. One was that the rebels would wreck the railroad as they withdrew, requiring the pursuers to rebuild it and then keep it rebuilt despite attempts by regular and irregular grayback cavalry to re-wreck it. To guard against this would require the crippling detachment of fighting men from the front to the rear in ever-increasing numbers, all the way back to the Rappahannock, since even a temporary break might prove disastrous, dependent as the army would be on that single line for everything it needed, including food for 56,500 horses and mules and better than twice that many soldiers. The other drawback was that a movement around Lee's west flank would uncover the direct approach to Washington. In some ways this was a greater disadvantage than the other; Lincoln was notoriously touchy in regard to the safety of his capital, and every commander who had neglected to remember this had found himself in trouble as a result. So far, since the advent of the new general-in-chief, the President had maintained a hands-off attitude toward all things military, for which Grant was altogether thankful, but that attitude might not extend to the point of seeing Washington endangered, even in theory, especially now that the surrounding fortifications had been stripped of their outsized regiments. Between them, these two drawbacks — one having to do with supply difficulties, the other having to do with Lincoln — fairly well ruled out a movement around the Confederate left. Grant shifted his attention to the region beyond Lee's right: more specifically, to the country between Mine Run and the confluence of the rivers, fifteen miles east of Stony Mountain and about ten miles this side of Fredericksburg.

That way, the march would be shorter, Washington would be covered from dead ahead, and the supply problem would be solved by ready access to navigable streams on the outer flank, affording rapid, all-weather connection with well-stocked depots in the rear and requiring no more than minimal protection. Here too there was a drawback, however, one that was personally familiar to every soldier who had served for as long as half a year in the eastern theater. The Wilderness, it was called: a forbidding region, some dozen miles wide and eight miles deep, which the army would enter as soon as it crossed that stretch of the Rapidan immediately east of Lee's right flank, a leafy tangle extending from just beyond Mine Run to just beyond Chancellorsville. Joe Hooker, for one, could testify to the pitfalls hidden in that jungle of stunted oak and pine, and so could the present commander of the army that had come to grief in its depths, chief among them being that the force on the defensive had the advantage of silent concealment — an advantage the butternut veterans had used so well, five months ago, that Meade still considered himself lucky to have got back out of there alive. Conversely, the blue army's main advantage, its preponderance in men and guns, would scarcely matter if it was brought to battle there; numbers counted for little in those thickets, except to increase the claustrophobia and the panic that came from being shot at from close quarters by a foe you could not see, and artillery had to fire blind or not at all. As a drawback, this could hardly be overrated; but Grant believed he saw a way to avoid it. The answer was speed. If the troops moved fast enough, and began their march after nightfall screened the crossing from the rebel lookout station on Clark's Mountain across the way, they could get through the Wilderness and gain the open country just beyond it, where there was plenty of room for maneuver, before Lee had time to interfere. Moreover, this belief was founded on experience. Both Meade and Hooker, who had crossed by the same fords Grant intended to use now — Ely's and Germanna — had spent two full days on the far side of the river before they came to grips with anything substantial, and in both cases, what was more, they had done so as part of their plans: Meade by moving directly against the enemy at Mine Run, Hooker by calling a halt at Chancellorsville and inviting the enemy to attack him. Grant had no intention of doing either of these things. He intended to bull right through, covering those eight vine-choked miles in the shortest possible time — certainly less than two full days — and thus be out in the open, where Lee would have nothing better than a choice between attacking or being attacked. Either would suit Grant's purpose admirably, once he had his troops on ground where their superior numbers and equipment could be brought to bear and thus decide the issue in accordance with the odds.

By way of assuring speed on the projected march, or in any case a touch of the hard-driving ruthlessness that would be needed to obtain it, he had already made one important change in the makeup of the arm of the service that would lead the way across the Rapidan and down the roads beyond. In conference with Lincoln and Halleck, soon after his return from Tennessee and before he established headquarters in the field, he had expressed his dissatisfaction with cavalry operations in the eastern theater. What was needed, he said, was "a thorough leader." Various candidates for the post were mentioned and discarded, until Halleck came up with the answer. "How would Sheridan do?" he asked. This was Major General Philip H. Sheridan, then in command of an infantry division under Thomas near Chattanooga. His only experience with cavalry had been a five-week term as colonel of a Michigan regiment after Shiloh, nearly two years ago, and he had not only never served in Virginia, he had never even been over the ground in peacetime, so great was his dislike of all things southern. But Grant thought he would do just fine in command of the eastern army's three divisions of 13,000 troopers. "The very man I want," he said, and Sheridan was sent for. He arrived in early April, checked into Willard's, and went at once to the White House, much as Grant had done the month before. The interview was marred, however, when the President brought up the familiar jest: "Who ever saw a dead cavalryman?" Sheridan was not amused. If he had his way, there were going to be a great many dead cavalrymen lying around, Union as well as Confederate. Back at Willard's with friends, he said as much, and more. "I'm going to take the cavalry away from the bobtailed brigadier generals," he vowed. "They must do without their escorts. I intend to make the cavalry an arm of the service."

He was different, and he brought something different and hard into the army he now joined. "Smash 'em up, smash 'em up!" he would say as he toured the camps, smacking his palm with his fist for emphasis, and then ride off on his big hard-galloping horse, a bullet-headed little man with close-cropped hair and a black mustache and imperial, bandy-legged, long in the arms, all Irish but with a Mongol look to his face and form, as if something had gone strangely wrong somewhere down the line in Ireland. Just turned thirty-three, he was five feet five inches tall and he weighed 115 pounds with his spurs on; "one of those long-armed fellows with short legs," Lincoln remarked of him, "that can scratch his shins without having to stoop over." Mounted, he looked about as tall and burly as the next man, so that when he got down from his horse his slightness came as a shock. "The officer you brought on from the West is rather a little fellow to handle your cavalry," someone observed at headquarters, soon after Sheridan reported for duty. Grant took a pull at his cigar, perhaps remembering Missionary Ridge. "You'll find him big enough for the purpose before we get through with him," he said. And in point of fact, the undersized, Ohio-raised West Pointer held much the same views on war as his chief, who was Ohio born and had finished West Point ten years earlier, also standing about two thirds of the way down in his class. Those views, complementing Sheridan's even more succinct "Smash 'em up, smash 'em up!" could be stated quite briefly, a staff physician found out about this time. They were sitting around, idle after a hard day's work, and the doctor asked the general-in-chief for a definition of the art of war. Grant turned the matter over in his mind — no doubt preparing to quote Jomini or some other highly regarded authority, his listeners thought — and then replied, as if in confirmation of what his friend Longstreet was telling Lee's staff about now, across the way: "Find out where your enemy is. Get at him as soon as you can, and strike him as hard as you can. And keep moving on."

That was to be the method, and by now he had also arrived at the date on which it would begin to be applied. April 27 — the day after he told Halleck, "I feel much better with this command" — was his forty-second birthday; a year ago today, at Hard Times, Louisiana, he had braced his western army for the crossing of the greatest river of them all, the Mississippi, and the opening of the final stage in the campaign that took Vicksburg. It was therefore a fitting day for fixing the date for what would be the greatest jump-off of them all, east or west, east *and* west. Burnside by now was in motion from Annapolis, charged with replacing Meade's troops on guard along the railroad between Manassas and the Rappahannock, and Meade was free to concentrate his whole force in the V of the two rivers. Today was Wednesday. Allowing a full week for the completion of all this, together with final preparations for crossing the Rapidan at designated fords, Grant set the date for Wednesday next: May 4. Notice of this was sent at once to Meade and Burnside, as well as to Sigel and Butler, at Winchester and Fort Monroe, and to Sherman in North Georgia, who would pass the word to subordinates already poised for the leap at Dalton. This was nine days later than the tentative date Grant had set in early April, but he saw in the delay a double gain. Not only would it afford more time for preparation, which should help to eliminate oversights and confusion; it would also allow the Wilderness roads just that much additional time to dry, an important factor in consideration of the need for speed in getting out of that briery snare in the shortest possible time.

As for getting out of Washington — also a highly desirable thing, from a personal point of view — Grant had done that, for good, the previous Sunday. Except for the chance they gave him to be with his wife, his brief visits there had brought him little pleasure and much strain. The public adulation had increased, and with it the discomfort, including a flood of letters requesting his autograph (he had found a way to cut down on these, however; "I don't get as many as I did when I answered them," he said dryly) and a great deal of staring whenever he ventured out, which he seldom did unless it was unavoidable, as it was for example in getting from the station to Willard's and back. Observing his "peculiar aloofness," a protective garment he wore against the stares, one witness remarked that "he walked through a crowd as though solitary." On his last morning there, having taken breakfast in the hotel dining room before leaving to catch the train for Virginia, he was spotted by a reporter as he came out into the lobby. "He gets over the ground queerly," the journalist informed a friend that night. "He does not march, nor quite walk, but pitches along as if the next step would bring him on his nose. But his face looks firm and hard, and his eye is clear and resolute, and he is certainly natural, and clear of all appearance of self-consciousness." On the theory that this might be his last chance for some time, the reporter presumed to intercept him with a question: "I suppose, General, you don't mean to breakfast again until the war is over?" — "Not here I don't," Grant said, and went on out.

Nothing he had said or written, in conference or in correspondence with Lincoln or Halleck or anyone else, had given any estimate as to how much time the campaign about to open would require before it achieved what he called "the first great object," which was "to get possession of Lee's army." His preliminary instructions to Meade, for instance — "Lee's army will be your objective point.

Wherever Lee goes, there you will go also" — had been dated April
9; but whether the result so much desired would be attained within
a year, or more, or considerably less, or not at all, remained to be seen.
No one was more concerned with the specific timing than Lincoln, who
would face a fight for survival in November, a fight he had good cause
to believe he would lose unless the voters' confidence was lifted within
the next six months by a substantial military accomplishment, rather
than lowered by the lack of one to compensate for the lengthening
casualty lists. And yet, despite the anxiety and strain — so well had he
learned his lesson in the course of having shared in the planning, and
often in the prosecution, of half a dozen failed offensives here in the
East in the past three bloody years — he maintained his hands-off attitude, even to the extent of not asking his new general-in-chief for an
informal guess at the schedule, east or west. It was as if, having tried
interference to the limit of his ability, he now was determined to try
abstention to the same extent. He had learned patience, and something
more; he had learned submission. "I attempt no compliment to my own
sagacity," he recently had told a Kentucky friend in a letter he knew
would be published. "I claim not to have controlled events, but confess
plainly that events have controlled me."

In line with this, as if to underscore his hands-off intention while
at the same time giving assurance of continuing support, he sent Grant
a farewell note on the last day of April, four days before the big offensive was to begin.

> Lieutenant General Grant:
>
> Not expecting to see you again before the spring campaign
> opens, I wish to express in this way my entire satisfaction with what
> you have done up to this time, so far as I understand it. The particulars
> of your plan I neither know nor seek to know. You are vigilant and
> self-reliant; and, pleased with this, I wish not to obtrude any con-
> straints or restraints upon you. While I am very anxious that any
> great disaster or capture of our men in great numbers shall be avoided,
> I know these points are less likely to escape your attention than they
> would be mine. If there is anything wanting which is within my
> power to give, do not fail to let me know it. And now, with a brave
> army and a just cause, may God sustain you.
>
> Yours very truly,
> A. LINCOLN.

Next day — May Day — Grant "acknowledged with pride" the
President's "very kind letter" as soon as it reached him at Culpeper.
"It will be my earnest endeavor that you and the country shall not be
disappointed," he wrote, and added, by way of returning the compliments paid him: "Since the promotion which placed me in command of
all the armies, and in view of the great responsibility and importance of
success, I have been astonished at the readiness with which everything

asked for has been yielded, without even an explanation being asked. Should my success be less than I desire and expect, the least I can say is, the fault is not with you."

And having said as much he turned his attention back to matters at hand. Two nights from now, in the small hours of Wednesday morning, the army would be moving down to the river for a crossing.

★ ★ ★

Braced as best he could manage for the blow he knew was coming, though he did not know just when or where it would land, Jefferson Davis had cause to be grateful for the apparent delay beyond the final day of April, which arrived without bringing word to Richmond that the Union drive had opened from any direction, east or west. Not only did this afford him time for additional preparations, such as getting a few more soldiers up to Lee or down to Beauregard; it also seemed to mean that he and his country would emerge unscathed from what had been in the past, for them, the cruelest month. Although he was by no means superstitious, the pattern was too plain to be denied. In April of 1861 the war itself had begun when Lincoln maneuvered him into opening fire on Sumter. Next year it had brought the death of his friend and idol, Albert Sidney Johnston, together with defeat in the half-won battle of Shiloh. Last year, in that same unlucky month, Grant and Hooker had launched the two offensives that cost the Confederacy the knee-buckling double loss of Vicksburg and Stonewall Jackson. However, this fourth April seemed about to be proved the exception to the rule. Militarily, so far as actual contact was concerned, the news from all three major theaters — from Louisiana and Arkansas, out in the Transmississippi, from Fort Pillow in the West, and from Plymouth, here in the East — had been nothing but good all month. If Davis, on the last morning in April, having walked the four blocks from the White House to his office adjoining Capitol Square and found no unduly woeful dispatch on his desk, paused to congratulate himself and his country on their delivery from the jinx, it would not have been without apparent justification. Yet he would have been wrong, horribly wrong. Before the day was over he would be struck the heaviest personal blow of the war: just such a blow as his adversary Lincoln had been struck, twenty-six months ago, in that other White House up in Washington.

He worked all morning, partly on administrative matters, which critics saw as consuming a disproportionate share of his time, and partly on intelligence reports — they made for difficult sifting, since different commanders predicted different objectives for the overdue Union offensive, generally in hair-raising proximity to their headquarters — then broke for lunch, which his wife brought on a tray from home to tempt his meager appetite. Before the dishes could be set in front of him, however, a house servant came running with news that Joe, their five-year-old, third of the four children who ranged in age from nine to three, had fallen from a high rear balcony onto the brick-paved court-yard thirty feet below. They hurried there to find him unconscious. Both legs were broken and his skull was fractured, apparently the result of having climbed a plank some carpenters had left resting against the balustrade when they quit for the noonday meal. He died soon after his mother reached him, and the house was filled with the screams of his Irish nurse, hysterical with sorrow and guilt from having let him out of her sight. His brother Jeff, two years older, had been the one to find him lying crumpled on the bricks. "I have said all the prayers I know how," he told a neighbor who came upon him kneeling there beside his dying brother, "but God will not wake Joe."

Under the first shock of her loss, the emotional impact of which was all the greater because she was seven months pregnant, Varina Davis was nearly as bad off as the nurse. But the most heartbreaking sight of all, Burton Harrison thought, was the father's "terrible self-control," which denied him the relief of tears. Little Joe had been his favorite, the child on whom he had "set his hope," according to his wife. Each night the boy had said his prayers at his father's knee, and often he had come in the early morning to be taken up into the big bed. Davis retired to his White House study, determined to go on with his work as an antidote to thinking of these things, and Mrs Davis joined him there as soon as she recovered from her initial shock. Presently a courier arrived with a dispatch from Lee. Davis took it, stared at it for a long minute, then turned to his wife with a stricken expression on his face. "Did you tell me what was in it?" he asked. Grief had paralyzed his mind, she saw, and her husband realized this too when he tried to compose his answer. "I must have this day with my little son," he cried, and moved blindly out of the room and up the stairs. Visitors heard him up there in the bedroom, pacing back and forth and saying over and over as he did so: "Not mine, O Lord, but thine." Meantime the boy was laid out in a casket, also in one of the upper rooms. His nurse lay flat on the floor alongside him, keening, while across the hall the father paced and paced the night away. "Not mine, O Lord, but thine," he kept saying, distracted by his grief.

All night the mourners came and went, cabinet members, high-ranking army and navy officers, dignitaries in town for the convening of Congress two days later, and yet the tall gray stucco house had an aspect of desolation, at once eerie and garish. Every room was brightly lighted, gas jets flaring, and the windows stood open on all three stories, their curtains moving in and out as the night breeze rose and fell. Next afternoon — May Day: Sunday — the funeral procession wound its way up the steep flank of Oregon Hill to Hollywood Cemetery, where many illustrious Confederates lay buried. Although Joe had been too young for school, having just turned five in April, more than a thousand schoolchildren followed the hearse, each bearing a sprig of evergreen or a spray of early flowers which they let fall on the hillside plot as they filed past. Standing by the open grave, Davis and his wife were a study in contrast. Heavy with the child she would bear in June, she wore black, including a veil, and her tall figure drooped beneath the burden of her grief, while her husband, twenty years her senior at fifty-five, yet lithe of form and erect as one of the monuments stark against the sky behind him, wore his accustomed suit of homespun gray. Down below, the swollen James purled and foamed around its rocks and islands, and now for the first time, as they watched him stand uncovered in the sunlight beside the grave of the son on whom he had set his hope, people saw that Davis, acquainted increasingly with sorrow in his private as in his public life, had begun to look his age and more. The words "vibrant" and "boyish," so often used by journalists and others to describe their impression of him, no longer applied. Streaks of gray were in his hair, unnoticed until now, and the blind left eye looked blinder in this light.

There was no evidence of this, however, in his message of greeting to the newly elected Second Congress when it convened the following day on Capitol Hill. Though the words were read by the clerk, in accordance with custom, their tone of quiet reliance and not-so-quiet defiance was altogether characteristic of their author. "When our independence, by the valor and fortitude of our people, shall have been won against all the hostile influences combined against us, and can no longer be ignored by open foes or professed neutrals, this war will have left with its proud memories a record of many wrongs which it may not misbecome us to forgive, [as well as] some for which we may not properly forbear from demanding redress. In the meantime, it is enough for us to know that every avenue of negotiation is closed against us, that our enemy is making renewed and strenuous efforts for our destruction, and that the sole resource for us, as a people secure in the justice of our cause and holding our liberties to be more precious than all other earthly possessions, is to combine and apply every available element of power for their defense and preservation." By way of proof that such a course of action could be effective against the odds, he was pleased to review the triumphs scored in all three major theaters since the previous Congress adjourned: after which he passed at once to the expected peroration, assuring his hearers that, just as they were on God's side, so was God on theirs. "Let us then, while resolute in devoting all our energies to securing the realization of the bright auspices which encourage us, not forget that our humble and most grateful thanks are due to Him without whose guidance and protecting care all human efforts are of no avail, and to whose interposition are due the manifold successes with which we have been cheered."

Just over sixty air-line miles northwest of the chamber in which the clerk droned through the presidential message, Lee was meeting with his chief infantry lieutenants atop Clark's Mountain, immediately north-east of the point where the railroad crossed the Rapidan north of Orange. He had called them together, his three corps and eight division com-manders, to make certain that each had a good inclusive look at the terrain for which they would be fighting as soon as Grant made the move that Lee by now was convinced he had in mind. Not that most of them had not fought there before; they had, except for Longstreet and his two subordinates, who had missed both Chancellorsville and Mine Run; but the panoramic view from here, some six or seven hundred feet above the low-lying country roundabout, presented all the ad-vantages of a living map unrolled at their feet for their inspection and instruction, and as such — lovely, even breath-taking in its sweep and grandeur, a never-ending carpet with all the vivid greens of advancing spring commingled in its texture — would serve, as nothing else could do, to fix the over-all character of the landscape in their minds.

For the most part — though their youth was disguised, in all but two heavily mustached cases, by beards in a variety of styles, from full-shovel to Vandyke — they were men in their prime, early-middle-aged at worst. Longstreet was forty-three, and the other two corps com-manders, Lieutenant Generals Richard S. Ewell and A. P. Hill, were respectively four years older and five years younger, while the division commanders averaged barely forty, including one who was forty-eight; "Old Allegheny," he was called, as if he vied in ancientness with the mountains beyond the Blue Ridge. Aside from him, Lee at fifty-seven was ten years older than any other general on the hilltop, and like Davis, despite the vigor of his movements, the quick brown eyes in his high-colored face, and the stalwart resolution of his bearing, he had begun to show his age. His hair, which had gone from brown to iron gray in the first year of the war, was now quite white along his temples, and the same was true of his beard, which he wore clipped somewhat closer now than formerly, as if in preparation for long-term fighting. The past winter had been a hard one for him, racking his body with frequent attacks that were diagnosed as lumbago, and though his health improved with warming weather, the opening months of spring had been even harder to endure, not only because they brought much rain, which tended to oppress him, but also because it galled his aggressive nature to be obliged to wait, as he fretfully complained, "on the time and place of the enemy's choosing" for battle. Just over twenty months ago, after less than three months in command of the newly-assembled army with which he had whipped McClellan back from the outskirts of

Richmond, he had stood on this same mountaintop and watched Pope's blue host file northward out of the trap he had laid for it there in the V of the rivers, and he had said to Longstreet then: "General, we little thought that the enemy would turn his back upon us thus early in the campaign." It was different now. Grant he knew would move, not north across the Rappahannock, but south across the Rapidan, and all Lee could do was prepare to meet him with whatever skill and savagery were required to drive him back: which, in part, was why he had brought his ranking subordinates up here for a detailed look at the terrain on which he planned to do just that. Believing as he did that an outnumbered army should be light on its feet and supple in the hands of its commander, his custom was to give his lieutenants a great deal of latitude in combat, and he wanted to make certain that they were equipped, geographically at least, to exercise with judgment the initiative he encouraged them to seize whenever they were on their own — as, in fact, every unit commander, gray or blue, was likely to be in that tangled country down below, especially in the thickets that lay like pale green smoke over that portion called the Wilderness, stretching eastward beyond Mine Run.

The Rapidan flowed to their right, practically at their feet as they stood looking north toward Culpeper, the hilltop town ten miles away, where A. P. Hill had been born and raised and where Grant now had his headquarters. Another ten miles farther on, hazy in the distance, the dark green line of the Rappahannock crooked southeast to its junction with the nearer river, twenty miles due east of the domed crest of Clark's Mountain, and then on out of sight toward Fredericksburg, still another ten miles beyond the roll of the horizon. All this lay before and below the assembled Confederates, who could also see the conical tents and white-topped wagons clustered and scattered in and about the camps Meade's army had pitched in the arms of the stream-bound V whose open end was crossed by the twin threads of the railroad glinting silver in the sunlight. There was a good deal of activity in those camps today, as indeed there had been the day before, a Sunday, but the generals on the mountain gave their closest attention to the gray-green expanse of the Wilderness, particularly its northern rim, as defined by the meandering Rapidan; Hooker and Meade had both crossed there in launching the two most recent Union offensives, and Lee believed that Grant would do the same, even to the extent of using the same fords, Ely's and Germanna, four and ten miles respectively from the junction of the rivers. He not only believed it, he said it. Apparently that was another reason he had brought his lieutenants up here: to say it and to show them as he spoke. Suddenly, without preamble or explanation, he raised one gauntleted hand and pointed specifically at the six-mile stretch of the Rapidan that flowed between the two points where the Federals twice had thrown their pontoon bridges in preparation for all-out assaults on the Army of Northern Virginia. "Grant will cross by one of these fords," he said.

Deliberately spoken, the words had the sound of a divination, now and even more so in the future, when they were fulfilled and his hearers passed them down as an instance of Lee's ability to read an opponent's mind. However, though this faculty was real enough on the face of it, having been demonstrated repeatedly in most of his campaigns, it was based on nothing occult or extrasensory, as many of his admirers liked to claim, but rather on a careful analysis of such information as came to hand in the normal course of events — from enemy newspapers closely scanned, from scouts and spies and friendly civilians who made it through the Yankee lines, from loquacious deserters and tight-mouthed prisoners tripped by skillful interrogation — plus a highly developed intelligence procedure, by which he was able not only to put himself in the other man's position, but also to *become* that man, so to speak, in making a choice among the opportunities the situation seemed to afford him for accomplishing the destruction of the Army of Northern Virginia. Like other artists in other lines of endeavor, Lee produced by hard labor, midnight oil, and infinite pains what seemed possible only by uncluttered inspiration. Quite the opposite of uncanny, his method was in fact so canny that it frequently produced results which only an apparent wizard could achieve. The Clark's Mountain prediction was a case in point. Lee had spent a major part of his time for the past two months — ever since Grant's arrival and elevation, in early March — at work on the problem of just what his new adversary was going to do, and for the past two weeks — ever since April 18, when he ordered all surplus baggage sent to the rear — he had given the matter his practically undivided attention: with the result that, after a process of selection and rejection much like Grant's across the way, he had come up with what he believed was the answer. Grant would cross the Rapidan by Ely's Ford or Germanna Ford, and having done so he either would turn west for an attack on the Confederate right flank, as Meade had done in November, or else he would do as Hooker had intended to do, a year ago this week, and maneuver for a battle in the open, where he could bring his superior numbers to bear. Which of these two courses the Federal commander meant to adopt once he was across the river did not really matter to Lee, since he did not intend to give him a chance to do either. Lee's plan was to let him cross, then hit him there in the Wilderness with everything he had, taking advantage of every equalizing impediment the terrain afforded, in order to whip him as thoroughly as possible in the shortest possible time, and thus drive him, badly cut up, back across the Rapidan. He did not say all this today, however. He merely said that Grant would cross by one of those fords on the rim of the Wilderness, and then he mounted Traveller and led the way back down the mountain.

Nor did he act, just yet, on the contingent decision he had reached. Only today, in fact, he had instructed Longstreet to shift one of his two divisions northwest of Gordonsville, in order to have it in a better position to meet the challenge Grant would pose if he attempted a move around the Confederate left, in the opposite direction from the one predicted. Lacking definite confirmation of what was after all no more than a theoretical opinion, an educated guess, Lee could not commit his army to a large-scale counteraction of a movement which there was even an outside chance the enemy might not make; he had to leave a sizeable margin for error, including total error. That night, however, the signal station on Clark's Mountain reported observing moving lights in the Federal camps, and next morning — May 3: Tuesday — there were reports of heavy clouds of dust, stirred up by columns marching here and there, and smoke in unusual volume, as if the bluecoats were engaged in the last-minute destruction of camp equipment and personal belongings for which they would have no use when they moved out.

All day this heightened activity continued, past sundown and into the night. Presently the signalmen blinked a message to army headquarters that long columns of troops were passing in front of campfires down there on the far bank of the Rapidan. Headquarters responded with a question: Was the movement west or east, upstream in Hill's direction on the left or downstream in Ewell's direction on the right? The signal station was in visual communication with both corps commanders, as well as with Lee, but it could find no answer to the question. All that could be seen across the way was the winking of campfires as files of men passed in front of them. There was no way of telling, from this, whether the troops were moving upstream or down, to the left or to the right. By now it was close to midnight; May 4 would be dawning within five hours. Lee decided to act at last on yesterday's prediction, and sent word accordingly for the signalmen to flash a message to the corps on the right, down toward Mine Run: "General Ewell, have your command ready to move at daylight."

The Forty Days

★ ✗ ☆

GRANT CAME AS LEE HAD SAID HE WOULD, only more so, crossing the Rapidan not merely by "one of those fords," Ely's or Germanna, but by both — and, presently, by still another for good measure. Sheridan's new-shod cavalry led the way, splashing across the shallows in the darkness soon after midnight, May 4, and while the engineers got to work in the waist-deep water, throwing a pair of wood and canvas pontoon bridges at each of the two fords, the troopers established bridgeheads on the enemy side of the river at both points and sent out patrols to explore the narrow, jungle-flanked, moonless roads tunneling southward through the Wilderness. Near the head of one column the horsemen got to talking as they felt their way toward Chancellorsville, a name depressing to the spirits of any Federal who had been there with Joe Hooker just a year ago this week. One of the group, anticipating a quick pink-yellow stab of flame and a humming, bone-thwacking bullet from every shadow up ahead, remarked uneasily that he had never supposed "the army went hunting around in the night for Johnnies in this way."

"We're stealing a march on old man Lee," a veteran explained.

They thought this over, remembering the loom of Clark's Mountain and the rebel lookout station on its peak, and before long someone put the thought into words. "Lee will miss us in the morning."

"Yes, and then watch out," another veteran declared. "He'll come tearing down this way ready for a fight."

Though all agreed that this would certainly be in character, Lee did no such thing: at least not yet. Morning came and the crossing progressed smoothly in their rear, including the installation of still a fifth bridge at Culpeper Mine Ford, two miles above Ely's, to speed the passage of the army train, the laggard, highly vulnerable element to which all the others, mounted or afoot, had to conform for its protection on the march. Slow-creaking and heavily loaded with ten days' subsistence for nearly 150,000 men and ten days' grain for better than 56,000 mules and horses (strung out along a single road, if any such had been available, this monster train would have covered the sixty-odd miles from the Rapidan to Richmond without a break from head to tail) the wagons passed over the two lower fords in the wake of Major General Winfield S. Hancock's II Corps, the largest of Meade's three, which crossed at Ely's in the darkness and began to make camp at Chancellorsville, five miles from the river, before noon. The brevity of the march was necessary if the combat units were to provide continuous protection for the road-jammed train, but the men, slogging along under packs about as heavy-laden as the wagons in their rear, were thankful for the early halt; they carried, as directed in the carefully worded order, "50 rounds of ammunition upon the person, three days' full rations in their haversacks, [and] three days' bread and short rations in their knapsacks." At Germanna, meantime, Major General Gouverneur K. Warren's V Corps crossed and marched six miles southeast to Wilderness Tavern, near the intersection of the Germanna Plank Road and the Orange-Fredericksburg Turnpike, where it made camp in the early afternoon, five miles west of Hancock, leaving room behind for Major General John Sedgwick's VI Corps to bed down beside the road, between the tavern and the river, well before sundown. Grant was pleased, when he reached the upper ford about midday and clattered over with his staff, to note that the passage of the Rapidan was being accomplished in excellent order, strictly according to schedule, and without a suggestion of enemy interference. "This I regarded as a great success," he later reported, because "it removed from my mind the most serious apprehensions I had entertained, that of crossing the river in the face of an active, large, well-appointed, and ably-commanded army."

Gratified by the evidence that he had indeed stolen a march on old man Lee, he got off a wire at 1.15 to Burnside at Rappahannock Station, instructing him to bring his IX Corps down to Germanna without delay. Another went to Halleck, back in Washington: "The crossing of the Rapidan effected. Forty-eight hours now will demonstrate whether the enemy intends giving battle this side of Richmond. Telegraph Butler that we have crossed." This done, he rode on a short distance and established headquarters beside the road, near a deserted house whose front porch afforded him and his military family a shaded, airy position from which to observe his soldiers on the march. He was dressed uncharacteristically in full regimentals, including his sword and sash and even a pair of brown cotton-thread gloves, three stars glinting impressively on each shoulder of his best frock coat. What was more, his manner was as expansive as his trappings — a reaction, apparently, to his sudden release from concern that he might be attacked with his army astride the river. As he sat there smoking and swapping remarks with his associates, a newspaper correspondent approached and asked the question not even

Lincoln had put to him in the past two months. How long was it going to take him to reach Richmond?

Grant not only expressed no resentment at the reporter's inquisitive presumption; he even answered him. "I will agree to be there in about four days," he said, to the astonishment of the newsman and his staff. Then he added: "That is, if General Lee becomes a party to the agreement. But if he objects, the trip will undoubtedly be prolonged."

Laughter increased the pervasive feeling of well-being and relief, and orders soon were distributed for tomorrow's march, which had been prepared beforehand for release if all went well: as, indeed, all had. One change there was, however, occasioned by a report that Sheridan received that afternoon. Chagrined at encountering none of Major General J. E. B. Stuart's highly touted butternut troopers in the course of his probe of the Wilderness south of the two fords, he learned that this was because they were assembled near Fredericksburg for a grand review next day at Hamilton's Crossing, a dozen miles to the east, and he asked permission to take two of his three divisions in that direction at first light in order to get among them, smash them up, and thus abolish at the outset of the campaign one of the problems that would have to be solved before its finish. Grant was willing, and so was Meade, though more reluctantly, being hidebound in his notion as to the primary duty of cavalry on a march through enemy country. In any case, the army would still have one of its mounted divisions for such work, and that seemed ample, especially if tomorrow's advance required no more of the blue outriders than today's had done. For one thing, since the train would not complete its crossing of the Rapidan before late tomorrow afternoon, and would thus require that the three infantry corps hold back and keep well closed up for its protection, the marches were to be about as brief. Hancock would move south and west, first to Todd's Tavern and then to Shady Grove Church, down on the Catharpin Road, extending his right toward Parker's Store on the Orange Plank Road, which was to be Warren's stopping point. Warren in turn would extend his right toward Wilderness Tavern, his present position astride the Orange Turnpike, which Sedgwick would occupy tomorrow, leaving one division on guard at Germanna Ford until Burnside's lead division arrived. Despite their brevity (Hancock had nine miles to cover, Warren and Sedgwick barely half that) all marches were to begin at 5 o'clock promptly, which was sunup. Upon reaching their designated objectives, Wilderness Tavern, Parker's Store, and Shady Grove Church — each commanding a major road coming in from the west, where Lee presumably still was unless he had already taken alarm and fallen back southward — all units were to prepare at once for getting under way as promptly the following day, Friday the 6th, which would take them out of the Wilderness and into the open country beyond, in position for coming to grips with the Confederates on terrain that would favor the army superior in numbers.

Forty-eight hours would tell the story, Grant had informed Halleck early that afternoon, and all the indications were that the story would have an ending that was happy from the Federal point of view. Careful planning seemed to have paid off handsomely. Not only were his "most serious apprehensions" — that he would be jumped while astride the Rapidan — behind him, but his second greatest worry — that he would have to fight in the blind tangle of the Wilderness — was all but behind him, too. "Enemy moving infantry and trains toward Verdiersville," the signal station on Stony Mountain informed him at 3 p.m. "Two brigades gone from this front. Camps on Clark's Mountain breaking up. Battery still in position behind Dr Morton's house, and infantry pickets on the river." That had far more the sound of preparations for a withdrawal than for an attack, and there seemed to be little of urgency in the Confederate reaction, such as it was. Grant could turn in for a good night's sleep in a much less fretful state of mind than the one in which he had lain down the night before, while poised for the crossing which now was complete except for a couple of thousand more wagons and Burnside's corps, whose arrival would give him a combat strength of 122,000 effectives on the rebel side of the river: an army which, arrayed for battle, two ranks deep, with one third of its units held rearward in reserve, would extend for twenty-five miles from flank to flank. That was roughly twice as many troops as Lee could muster of all arms. Grant was not only willing, he was altogether anxious to take him on at the earliest possible moment, preferably out in the open, where he could bring his superior ordnance to bear, or if not there then here in this green maze of vines and briers and stunted oaks and pines, if the opportunity offered and that was what it came to. He turned in early and apparently slept well.

That was not the case with a good many of the men who were bivouacked in this haunted woodland by his orders. Unlike him, they had been here before, and the memory was painful. In the fields around Wilderness Tavern, it was afterwards recalled — including the one just east of the deserted, ramshackle tavern itself, where Stonewall Jackson's maimed left arm was buried — there was little or no singing round the campfires, the usual pastime after a not-too-hard day's march, and there was even a tendency to avoid the accustomed small talk. This was due, one soldier declared, to "a sense of ominous dread which many of us found it almost impossible to shake off." There was, in fact, much about the present situation that was remindful of the one a year ago, when all ranks had engaged in a carnival of self-congratulation on the results of careful planning and stout marching; "The rebel army is now the legitimate property of the Army of the Potomac," Hooker had announced on that other May Day, just before he came to grief, suffering better than 17,000 casualties before he managed to scurry out of this scrub oak jungle and back across the Rappahannock, beyond the reach of a gray army barely one third the size of his own. Grant, they knew, was no such spouter, but they remembered Fighting Joe and other even more unpleasant things, such as brush fires set by bursting shells, in which men with broken backs and bullet-shattered legs had been roasted alive before the stretcher bearers could get at them. Even recruits could see the danger. "These woods will surely be burned if we fight here," one said when they first called a halt that afternoon.

Over near Chancellorsville, where the whippoorwills began calling plaintively soon after sunset, now as then, the mood was much the same. The fighting had been heaviest around here last year, and there still were many signs of it, including skeletons in rotted blue, washed partly out of their shallow graves by the rains of the past winter. No one but the devil himself would choose such ground for a field of battle, veterans said; the devil and old man Lee. In an artillery park near the ruin of the Chancellor mansion, which had burned to its brick foundations on the second day of conflict, a visiting infantryman looked glumly at a weathered skull that stared back with empty sockets, grinning a lipless grin. He prodded it with his boot, then turned to his comrades — saying "you" and "you," not "we" and "us," for every soldier is superstitious about foretelling his own death, having seen such words come true too many times — and delivered himself of a prediction. "This is what you are all coming to," he told them, "and some of you will start toward it tomorrow."

In point of fact, the conversion of the blue invaders into skeletons was just the kind of grisly work Lee had in mind, and he was moving toward it, even now, with everything he had. Grant had taken care, in his assignment of objectives for the following day, to see that each of the three main roads coming in from the west would be covered by a corps of infantry; for though logic and the evidence, such as it was, tended to indicate that his adversary was in the process of falling back to a strong defensive position athwart his path — probably on the banks of the North Anna, twenty miles to the south — there was a chance that the old fox might mass his troops for an attack, down one or another of those roads, in an attempt to strike while the Union army was strung out in the Wilderness. The truth was, Lee was coming by all three, a corps on each.

Ewell, alerted the night before, would march eastward on the Orange Turnpike, nearest the river, while Hill took the Orange Plank Road, which paralleled the turnpike at a distance that varied from one to three miles until the two converged, just short of Chancellorsville, twenty-five miles away; Longstreet, down around Gordonsville, had a greater distance to travel and would make a later start, having to call in his troops from the far-left positions they had been obliged to hold until Grant was committed to the upstream movement with all his force. Ewell, with three divisions, began his march at 9 o'clock. Hill reached Orange before noon, left one division there to guard the nearby Rapidan crossings, and had his other two in motion on the plank road shortly afterwards, the army commander riding with him near the head of the column. Since the troops on the turnpike had a three-hour head start and a straighter route, Ewell was told to regulate his speed by that of Hill. Longstreet then was notified by courier to set out with his two divisions, crossing the North Anna by Brock's Bridge, due east of Gordonsville, then turning north to strike the Catharpin Road at Richard's Shop, from which point his march would parallel those of the other two corps, on his left between him and the Rapidan. Lee's plan, though he announced no details yet, was to get within reach of the Federals as soon as possible, bring them to a Wilderness-hampered halt with Hill and Ewell, then launch an all-out hip-and-thigh assault with all three corps, as soon as Longstreet came up on the right.

Ewell stopped for the night at Locust Grove, a couple of miles into the Wilderness beyond Mine Run. Clustered about their skillet wagons for supper, the men of his three divisions had no such reaction to their surroundings as the men of Warren's four divisions were experiencing around Wilderness Tavern, five miles up the pike, or those of Hancock's four at Chancellorsville, another five miles east. Outnumbered as usual on the eve of contact, and having fought here against odds as long and longer, the butternut veterans understood that the cramped, leaf-screened terrain would work to their advantage, now as before, and their bivouacs hummed with banter and small talk as they bedded down, after ravening their rations, to rest for the shock they knew was likely to come tomorrow. Five miles southwest on the plank road, and still five miles short of the western limits of the Wilderness, it was much the same with the men of Hill's two divisions, rolled in their blankets and sleeping under the stars. At sundown he had called a halt at Verdiers-ville, eleven miles beyond Orange and nine from Parker's Store; "My Dearsville," Hill's troops dubbed the hamlet. Here Lee had had his headquarters during the Mine Run confrontation last November, and his tent was pitched, tonight as then, in a field beside the road. Soon there began to come to its flap a series of couriers bearing dispatches from all quarters of Virginia — dispatches which in turn bore out, to the letter, predictions he had been making for the past month as to the nature of the offensive the Federals now had launched.

Of these, the most alarming came from the President himself. A blue force, estimated at 30,000 of all arms and said to be commanded by Ben Butler, was unloading from transports at City Point and Bermuda Hundred, on the south bank of the James less than twenty miles from

Richmond, in position to break its vital rail connections with Petersburg and points south, if not indeed to come swarming across its bridges and into its streets in a matter of hours, since the capital had scarcely one tenth that many troops for its defense. "With these facts and your previous knowledge," Davis wired, demonstrating his accustomed calmness under pressure, as well as his abiding trust in Lee, "you can estimate the condition of things here, and decide how far your own movements should be influenced thereby." Lee's decision was not to allow his movements to be influenced at all by this development. He would continue to concentrate on meeting the threat to his immediate front, he informed Davis, and leave Butler to Beauregard, who had been ordered to proceed at once from Weldon to confront the southside invaders with such troops as he could muster in his newly formed department. Lee's reaction to a second grievous danger, reported from out in the Shendandoah Valley, was much the same. Warned that a force of undetermined strength under Sigel had begun an advance up the Valley in conjunction with another movement west of the Alleghenies, he replied with a wire instructing Breckinridge to assume "general direction of affairs" beyond the Blue Ridge. "I trust you will drive the enemy back," he told him. This done, he put both dangers — one to his rear, the other to his flank, and both to his lines of supply and communication — out of his mind, at least for the present, in order to give his undivided attention to the problem at hand: specifically, how best to deal with Meade's blue host, which had crossed the Rapidan bent on his destruction, but which was camped for the present across his front in the green toils of the Wilderness.

That the Federals had called at least a temporary halt, instead of pressing ahead on a night march to escape those toils and oblige him to race southward for a meeting in the open, was welcome news indeed, received in a series of messages Jeb Stuart kept sending to Verdiersville from shortly after dark until near midnight, when he apparently decided that the time had come to give his short-winded animals some rest. Abandoning his plans for the Hamilton's Crossing review next day, the cavalry leader was bringing his spruced-up troopers westward along the southern fringes of the Wilderness in order to get in position by morning on the right front of the army, there to protect its open flank and reconnoiter the enemy advance when it resumed. That too was welcome news, ensuring a continuous stream of intelligence, such as only cavalry could gather, and providing a resilient cushion against shock. Welcome, too, was a late-evening dispatch from Longstreet informing headquarters that he had crossed Brock's Bridge and would camp there tonight, on the near bank of the North Anna; he expected to reach Richard's Shop by noon tomorrow, nine miles from Shady Grove Church and twelve from Todd's Tavern. This meant that he most likely would be able to move into his assigned position, up the Catharpin Road, by nightfall, in plenty of time for launching the all-hands attack at first light Friday, after

Ewell and Hill made contact tomorrow and set the bluecoats up for the assault designed to drive them back across the river they had crossed today. Accordingly, Lee had his adjutant notify Ewell that he was to move out early in the morning, continuing his march up the turnpike in order to menace the Union flank if Grant kept heading south. If he veered east, toward Fredericksburg, Ewell was to pursue him and fall upon his rear; or if he turned this way, Ewell was to take up a strong defensive position and hold him there in the tangled brush until Hill and Longstreet came up on the right, at which point they would all three go over to the offensive in accordance with Lee's plan. In any case, the adjutant added, "the General's desire is to bring him to battle as soon now as possible."

At breakfast next morning between dawn and sunup Lee was in excellent spirits, refreshed by four or five hours of sleep and encouraged by a follow-up message, just in from Stuart, that the three Federal corps had in fact spent the whole night in their Wilderness camps. He expressed his satisfaction at this evidence that all was working as he hoped, as well as at information that a brigade of Ewell's, detached for guard duty at Hanover Junction, would be rejoining no later than tomorrow. Together with last-minute piecemeal reinforcements sent from Richmond during the past week, this would give him an over-all strength of nearly 65,000 men in his eight divisions of infantry and three of cavalry. Four brigades were still detached (Hoke's, in North Carolina, and three with Major General George E. Pickett, comprising Longstreet's third division, still convalescing in southside Virginia from its brief, horrific experience on the third day at Gettysburg, ten months back) but Lee regretted this less than he might have done except for a miscalculation that contributed to the boldness of his plan for the annihilation or quick repulse of the enemy in the thickets up ahead. He estimated the combined strength of Meade and Burnside at not more than 75,000 men, and therefore assumed — quite erroneously, since the Federals, with considerably better than half again that many troops, had in fact almost twice the number Lee could muster — that he was about to fight against the shortest odds he had faced at any time since he assumed command of the Army of Northern Virginia, two victory-crowded years ago next month. Rising from breakfast he mounted Traveller and gave A. P. Hill the word to resume his march up the plank road, first across the "Poison Fields," as the leached-out mining region west of the Wilderness was called, and then into the briery hug of the jungle where he intended to come to grips with the invaders who, Stuart reported, seemed unaware of his presence on their flank.

Beyond the moldering six-months-old intrenchments around the headwaters of Mine Run, a couple of miles out of Verdiersville, this unawareness ended with a spatter of fire from a detachment of Union cavalry armed with seven-shot carbines. They were few in number,

apparently, and easily driven back (Stuart had arrived by now, resplendent in his red-lined cape, to attend to this by fanning his horsemen
out on the right and front) but word was certainly on the way to Grant
that graybacks were approaching Parker's Store in strength. Moreover,
a staff officer arrived from Ewell about this time to report that he had
sighted heavy columns of bluecoats crossing the Wilderness Tavern
intersection, two miles ahead on the Germanna Plank Road, perpendicular to the turnpike. It stood to reason that if Ewell could see the enemy,
so could the enemy see him; Grant would be forewarned in that direction, too. Lee repeated his instructions that the Second Corps, continuing to regulate its march by that of the Third, was to move on and make
contact, but added that he preferred not to "bring on a general engagement" until Longstreet came up. Hill was deep in the Wilderness
by then, out of touch with Ewell as a result of a widening divergence,
beyond Verdiersville, of the plank road from the turnpike, which was

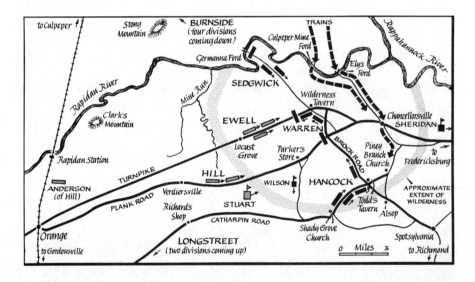

almost three miles away by the time he reached Parker's Store at noon. At
this point, still riding near the head of Hill's two-division column, Lee
heard a rising clatter of rifle fire from the left front. Obviously there was
fighting on the turnpike, and from the sound of it, filtered through three
miles of brush and branches, the engagement was indeed "general,"
mounting to a quick crescendo like the rapid tearing of canvas, though
it lacked the deeper, rumbling tones artillery gave a battle at that distance.
    Mindful of Lee's admonition not to "bring on a general engage-
ment," Ewell had deployed his lead division when he got within a couple
of miles of the Union-held crossroad, then brought up the second for
close support on both sides of the pike, warning the two commanders —
Major Generals Edward Johnson and Robert Rodes, who at forty-eight
and thirty-five were the oldest and youngest infantry division command-

ers in the army — "not to allow themselves to become involved, but to fall back slowly if pressed." So he later reported, but the words had little application when the time came, as it did all too soon: especially for the men of Johnson's lead brigade, Virginians under Brigadier General John M. Jones, who caught the initial and overwhelming impact of a whole blue division that came hurtling at them, as if out of nowhere, through brush and vines that limited vision to less than sixty feet in any direction. Caught thus, they found it as impossible to "fall back slowly" as they had to avoid becoming "involved." Losing Jones, who was killed by an early volley from the dense wave of attackers, they broke and fled, spreading panic through the ranks of an Alabama brigade Rodes had posted in their rear. Ewell, so close to the front that the attack exploded practically in his face, whirled his horse and raced back to bring help from his third division, Major General Jubal Early's, which had kept to the road in order to come up fast in an emergency such as the one that was now at hand. In the lead was Brigadier General John B. Gordon's brigade, Georgians who had a reputation for aggressiveness on short notice.

"General Gordon!" Ewell cried, his dragoon mustache bristling and his prominent eyes bulging as he checked his mount with a hard pull on the reins, "the day depends on you!"

"These men will save it, sir," Gordon replied, partly for the benefit of the troops themselves, who had come crowding up, as was their custom at such times, to hear what the brass had to say.

Going at once from march to attack formation, he advanced one regiment unsupported in a countercharge straight up the pike, while the rest deployed to go in on the right. On the left, two of Johnson's three intact brigades reacted by clawing their way through the brush toward the sound of firing, and Rodes's four did likewise, including the Alabamians who had been rattled by the flight of the Virginians through their ranks. As suddenly as it had risen, the tide of battle turned, and for the former attackers, overlapped on both flanks and savagely assailed from dead ahead by the screaming Georgians, the outcome was even more disastrous. Now it was their turn to backtrack, losing heavily in the process — though not as heavily as two other blue divisions, coming up in sequence on the left and groping blindly for the flank they had been told to support but could not find. Struck before they could form for attack or defense, they were driven eastward in confusion, suffering grievously in killed and wounded and losing several hundred prisoners, many of whom fled unknowingly into the rebel lines, bereft of all sense of direction in that maze of vines and brambles. It was, as one veteran said, a conflict "no man saw or could see"; "A battle of invisibles with invisibles," another called it. "As for fighting," a third declared, "it was simply bushwhacking on a grand scale, in brush where all formation beyond that of regiments or companies was soon lost and where such a thing as a consistent line of battle on either side was impossible."

The pattern of Wilderness fighting had been set, and one of its principal elements was panic, which came easily and spread rapidly on terrain that had all the claustral qualities of a landscape in a nightmare, with a variety of background sounds that ranged from a foreboding silence, so dense that a man was likely to jump six feet at the snap of a twig, to a veritable cataract of noise, referred to by a participant as "the most terrific musketry firing ever heard on the American continent."

Ewell, still mindful of Lee's admonition, did not pursue beyond the point at which the fight had opened, just under two miles west of the crossroad. It was 3 o'clock by now, and he could tell himself, quite truthfully, that he had done all that was asked of him and more, inflicting much heavier casualties than he suffered and fixing the enemy there in the tangled depths of the Wilderness. He put his men to work intrenching a line that extended about a mile to the left and a mile to the right of the turnpike, and after hauling off two guns he had captured in the course of his counterattack, he settled down to wait for tomorrow, when Longstreet would be up and the army would go over to the offensive. Fighting continued on a lesser scale all afternoon and into the evening, and though he lost two more brigade commanders — Brigadier Generals Leroy Stafford of Louisiana and John Pegram of Virginia, the former mortally wounded and the latter shot in the leg — Ewell had no doubt that he would be able to hold his newly fortified position, no matter what the Yankees sent against him.

There was no such assurance down on the plank road, three miles south, where a separate battle swelled to a sudden and furious climax at about the time the disjointed contest on the pike began to wane. For Hill, whose two divisions were struck by a much heavier and far better coördinated attack than the one that had been launched against Ewell's three, there was no waning; there was hard, stand-up fighting from the moment of earnest contact, around 4 o'clock, until darkness and exhaustion persuaded the troops of both sides to rest on their arms, where they then were, for a resumption at first light tomorrow of a struggle that had been touch-and-go for the past four hours. His two divisions, commanded by Major Generals Henry Heth and Cadmus Wilcox, had continued their march beyond Parker's Store to within a mile of the Brock Road, on which the Union infantry was known to be moving south, when stiffened resistance brought the head of the gray column to a halt. Heth formed for battle astride the road, and Lee — taking over for Hill, who was sick today, as he had been at Gettysburg — set up headquarters in a roadside clearing near the farmhouse of a widow named Tapp. He had no sooner dismounted to confer with Stuart and Hill, who had stayed with his men despite his disability, than a platoon of blue-clad skirmishers walked into the clearing from behind a stand of pines in its northeast corner, rifles at the ready. Apparently as startled as the high-ranking Confederates were by the sudden confrontation, the Federals faded back into the pines instead of opening fire or advancing to make the capture that would have changed the course of the war. However thankful Lee was for this deliverance from the hands of the bluecoats, their presence served to emphasize the dangerous possibility of an enemy plunge, whether on purpose or by accident, into the heavily wooded gap which the divergence of the two routes had created between Hill, down here on the plank road, and Ewell, whose battle was still in full swing on the turnpike. Accordingly, Lee sent word for Wilcox to extend Hill's left by moving his division northward into the brush beyond the clearing, thus to forestall a penetration of the gap, while Heth resumed his eastward advance to develop the strength of the blue force in his front. Though he still intended to withhold delivery of his main effort until Longstreet was on hand, the southern commander's hope was that Heth would be able to carry the Brock Road intersection, less than a mile away, as an effective means of bringing the Union army to a severed, panicky halt in the very depths of the Wilderness, half a dozen miles from open ground in any direction.

It was now past 3 o'clock. A note went at once to Heth asking whether, in his judgment, he could seize the intersection without bringing on a "general engagement." Heth replied that the enemy seemed to be there in strength; he could not tell how much an attack would spread the action, but he was willing to give the thing a try if that was what was wanted. While Lee was turning this over in his mind, back at the Widow Tapp's, a sudden uproar from the immediate front — louder, even, than the one that had exploded in Ewell's face, four hours ago — informed him that the decision had been taken out of his hands. Unsupported by Wilcox, who had moved off to the left, Heth was under heavy, all-out assault from dead ahead.

Both attacks — the one against Ewell, up on the turnpike, and the present one down the plank road against Hill — were the result of a deliberate decision by Grant, whose self-confidence and natural combativeness had not been lessened by the enlargement of his responsibilities and who was determined, moreover, not to yield the tactical initiative to an opponent with a reputation for making the most of it on all occasions. If this meant the abandonment of his original intention to get into, through, and out of the Wilderness in the shortest possible time, then that just had to be. His primary talent had always been instinctive, highly improvisatorial at its best, and though there was little about him that could be described as Napoleonic, he trusted, like Napoleon, in his star. The overriding fact, as Grant saw it, was that the rebels were there in the tangled brush, somewhere off to the west, and he was determined to hit them. He was determined, in Sheridan's phrase, to smash them up at every opportunity.

Meade began it, quite on his own. Shortly after 7 o'clock that morning, by which time the leading elements of all three corps had been two hours on the march, he was notified by Warren that the commander of his rear division, preparing to head south from Wilderness Tavern, had sighted a heavy butternut column moving toward him on the turnpike, two or three miles west of the Germanna Plank Road intersection. Reacting fast, Meade ordered Warren to bring his other three divisions back to their starting point and advance his whole corps down the pike, in order to confront and, if possible, destroy the rebel force. He believed that it amounted to no more than a division, "left here to fool us," he told Warren, "while they concentrate and prepare a position toward the North Anna," and he saw in the situation an opportunity to effect a considerable subtraction from Lee's army before coming to earnest grips with the rest of it in the open country to the south. With time to spare and the train still grinding slowly down the crowded roads to the east, he could afford a brief delay, especially one that held the promise of so rich a prize. In any case, with his exterior flank so threatened by a force of undetermined strength, he believed the decision was tactically sound; for, as he told Grant in a note informing him of the order for Warren to countermarch and attack, "until this movement of the enemy is developed, the march of the corps must be suspended."

Arriving shortly afterward for a meeting near the tavern, in whose yard Meade was conferring with Warren, Grant not only indorsed his chief lieutenant's aggressive reaction to the news that there were rebels on his flank; he also enlarged upon it, in a characteristic manner, with words that applied not only here but elsewhere. "If any opportunity presents itself for pitching into a part of Lee's army," he told him, "do so without giving time for disposition." In accordance with this policy — which might be described as: "Hit now. Worry later" — when word was brought that another gray force had been spotted marching eastward on the plank road, down around Parker's Store, Hancock too was given orders to backtrack. Instead of continuing down the Catharpin Road to Shady Grove Church, his previous objective, he would turn right when he reached Todd's Tavern and take the Brock Road north to its intersection with the road on which this second rebel column was advancing. Similarly, now that the plot had thickened, Sedgwick was told to send one division to join Warren's turnpike attack and another down the Brock Road to the intersection Hancock had been assigned to cover. His third division would remain on guard at Germanna Ford until Burnside's arrival, expected by midday, when it too would come down and get in on the action — whichever, if either, fight was still in progress by that time — leaving Burnside's four divisions as an available reserve, to be on call if they were needed. Thus Grant, though he still had no specific information as to the size or composition of either rebel column approaching his open flank, was determined to strike them both with everything he had.

While couriers went pounding off to deliver these several messages, Grant and Meade rode a short way down the pike, a bit under half a mile beyond a boggy little stream called Wilderness Run, and turned off into the southwest quadrant of the Germanna Plank Road intersection, where there was a meadow adjoined by a farmhouse belonging to a family named Lacy. Headquarters tents were being pitched there, in accordance with the change in plans, and the two generals dismounted and climbed a knoll on the far side of the field. Grant took a seat on a convenient stump, lighted another of the twenty cigars he distributed among the various pockets of his uniform at the start of every day, and sat calmly, an imperturbable figure wreathed in tobacco smoke, waiting for the attack to be launched beyond the heavy screen of brush at the rim of the clearing. Time dragged, the sun edging slowly toward meridian, and presently he took a penknife out of his trouser pocket, picked up a stick, and started to whittle. Snagged by the blade, the fingertips of his thread gloves began to fray, until at last they were ruined. He took them off, unbuttoned his coat because of the increasing heat, and resumed his whittling. At noon, or a little after, a sudden clatter of stepped-up rifle fire announced that the action had finally opened about one mile down the turnpike.

At first it was difficult to tell how the thing was going. The clatter moved westward, diminished briefly, as if it had paused for breath, then swelled louder than ever and rolled back east for another pause: after which a similar uproar came from the left front, subsided, and then was repeated. Along the limited horizon, west and southwest, the trees began leaking smoke along a line that seemed to conform in general to the one from which the initial attack had been launched an hour ago. All that was clear, so far, was that little or nothing had been gained, although it was fairly certain by now that there were a good many more graybacks out there in the brush than Meade had supposed at the outset. Grant kept whittling.

Presently details filtered rearward, brought to the Lacy meadow by dispatch bearers on lathered horses. Complying with Grant's instructions, relayed by Meade, that he was to give no "time for disposition," Warren had told Brigadier General Charles Griffin, the commander of what had been his rear but now was his lead division, not to wait for word from the heads of the three divisions assigned to support him on the flanks — Brigadier General Horatio G. Wright of Sedgwick's corps, on the march down from Germanna to go in on his right, and Brigadier Generals James S. Wadsworth and Samuel W. Crawford of his own corps, who were countermarching to come up on his left — but to pitch right into the Confederates, hard and fast, as soon as he got his troops in line astride the pike, trusting that the others would be there in time to furnish whatever assistance he might need. That was what he did; but he did so, as it turned out, unsupported in the crisis that resulted. Wright did not arrive for a full two hours, having gotten lost in the woods about as soon as he left the road, and Wadsworth and Crawford only came up in time to get badly mauled themselves, floundering around in the brush as if they were involved in a gigantic and altogether murderous game of blindman's bluff: as indeed they were — particularly Wadsworth, a Hudson River grandee who, at fifty-six, was nine years older than any other division commander in the army. Just now he was feeling the weight of all those years. Trying to navigate by compass in that leafy sea of green, he got badly turned around and drifted northward so that his naked left was exposed to a sudden descent by Gordon's screaming Georgians, who tore into it so savagely that the whole division fell back in disorder, the men crying "Flanked! We're flanked!" as they ran. Crawford caught it even worse from the rallied Alabamians when he came up, groping blind after he lost touch with the navigating Wadsworth. A former army surgeon who had been on duty at Fort Sumter when it fell, he was thirty-four, the next-to-youngest of Meade's division commanders, but he looked considerably older after three years of combat, including a bad wound taken at Antietam. "A tall, chesty, glowering man, with heavy eyes, a big nose, and bushy whiskers," he habitually wore what one of his soldiers described as "a turn-out-the-guard expression." His expression just now, however, was one of outrage. His division had once been Meade's own, made up entirely of Pennsylvanians, and Crawford was outraged at the heavy and useless losses he had suffered, including one veteran regiment captured practically intact when it fled in the wrong direction and found itself surrounded by grinning rebel scarecrows when it stumbled to a halt.

Unquestionably though, to judge by individual reaction, the most outraged man on the field today was Griffin. A hard-case West Pointer and a veteran of the Mexican War at thirty-eight, he was much admired by his men, including a brigade of regulars who had followed him through a lot of fighting over the past two years. An old line artilleryman, he was especially furious at the loss of a section of guns which had to be abandoned down the turnpike when his flanks were overlapped and his troops fell back to avoid being swamped by no less than seven Confederate brigades. The blame, as he saw it, lay with the commanders who had failed to come up on his left and right, and as soon as he managed to stabilize the line his three brigades had fallen back to, he got on his horse and galloped off to protest to Meade in person. Crossing the headquarters meadow, he dismounted and stalked up the knoll at the far side, fuming and cursing as he came. Meade heard him out and did what he could to soothe him, although with small success.

The air was full of God-damns. Finally, relieved by at least having vented his spleen, Griffin went back down the knoll, remounted his horse, and rode off to rejoin his division on the firing line. Grant, who had stopped whittling for the first time while the tirade was in progress, got up from his stump and walked over to Meade. He had not quite caught Griffin's name, but he had never been one to put up with out-of-channels insubordination, even in the easier-going West. "Who is this General Gregg?" he asked. "You ought to put him under arrest." Meade, whose extreme irascibility was masked today by an unaccustomed calm, turned to Grant with the same gentleness he had shown the angry brigadier. "His name's Griffin, not Gregg," he said, "and that's only his way of talking." In grizzled contrast to his younger chief, and towering a full head above him, Meade leaned forward as he spoke and buttoned up Grant's coat for him, as if in concern that he might catch cold after being overheated. Grant went back to his stump and his whittling.

By then it was close to 3 o'clock. Off to the south, although the sound of it did not get through until Warren's had died down, the second battle had been shaping up for the past hour. All that was there at the start was Brigadier General George W. Getty's division of Sedgwick's corps, which had come down from Germanna before midday to take over from a hard-pressed regiment of cavalry the task of delaying the progress of the second Confederate force, in position astride the plank road about half a mile from the Brock Road intersection, while Hancock came up from Todd's Tavern on a march that was much impeded by V Corps artillery, which had halted to await developments. Hancock arrived at 2 o'clock, riding at the head of his four-division column, and when Getty informed him that the graybacks to his front were commanded by the ever-aggressive A. P. Hill and that he might have to fall back at any moment under increasing pressure from such a savage fighter, thus uncovering the crossroad whose loss would cut the army in two and expose its train to capture or destruction, Hancock ignored Grant's instructions to forgo time-consuming preparations and instead put his troops to work improvising crude log breastworks along the road in rear of the position, north and south of the plank road intersection, thus to provide them with something on which to rally in case they were repulsed. Peremptory orders for an immediate advance put an end to this at about 3.30. Leaving Brigadier Generals Francis Barlow's and John Gibbon's divisions posted well down the Brock Road to guard against an attack from the southwest — he had been warned that Longstreet's corps was on the march, somewhere off in that direction, though it was not expected to arrive until tomorrow — Hancock put Major General David Birney's and Brigadier General Gershom Mott's divisions in line on the right and left of Getty's and sent them forward with orders to drive the enemy back on

Parker's Store, three miles from the vital crossroad in their rear, and thus abolish, for once and for all, this threat to the safe passage of the army through the Wilderness, together with its train. It was just past 4 o'clock by then, and on second thought, by way of giving more weight to the blow, he had Gibbon send two of his three brigades to stiffen the center of the attack which had now begun to roll.

It did not roll far, even though at this stage all that blocked the path of these 25,000 attackers was a single gray division with fewer than 7500 in its ranks. Advancing through the tangled brush, the Federals delivered blind volleys of musketry that lopped the saplings at breast height, all across their front, and made it nearly impossible, so heavy and continuous was the fire, for any standing defender to survive. The trouble was that scarcely a Confederate was standing.

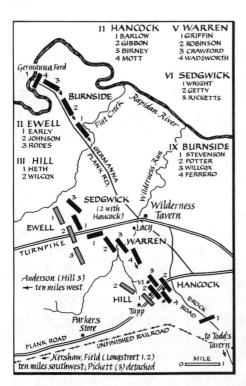

While waiting for a reply to his offer to go forward, if that was what Lee wanted, Heth — like Hancock, who was similarly engaged at the same time, half a mile away on the Brock Road — had had his men dig in and lie low along the slight, densely wooded ridge on which they had halted when the blue resistance stiffened. Prone beneath solid-seeming sheets of lead that slashed the leaves and clipped the breast-high branches, the troops along the ridge replied with volleys of their own. Not only were these as heavy as the ones the front-rank Federals were throwing; they were also a good deal more deadly. Caught thus, erect and unprotected by anything more substantial than smoke and foliage, the attackers suffered cruelly from a foe they could not see. Mott's division, bogged shoetop-deep in a swamp on the left, directly in front of the ridge, broke and ran from that first decimating fire, as did other outfits all along the line. Whole companies, whole regiments fell back in shock and panic, some of them all the way to the log defenses they had built an hour ago. There they were met, individually and collectively, with a curt demand from provost guards with leveled bayonets: "Show blood!" Those who could not show it were hoicked back into line alongside the troops who had not bolted, who were still in position, up there in

the bullet-whipped brush, firing blind — "by earsight," it was called —
in the general direction of the rebels lying prone in comparative safety
on their ridge, pumping volley after horrendous volley into the blue
mass down in the boggy swale to their immediate front.

Hancock, a hard hitter, never hit harder than he did here in the
Wilderness today, despite confounding difficulties of terrain far better
suited for defense (once the shock of surprise had been dispelled) than
for attack. A second assault was mounted and delivered, then a third
and a fourth, all with the disadvantage of trying to maintain alignment, as well as a precarious sense of direction, while attacking veterans
who had only to lie low and fire as rapidly as they could load their overheated rifles. Up at army headquarters, where there was full awareness
of the importance of keeping the Brock Road clear for travel, Meade had
Warren send Wadsworth's division south, across the mile-wide gap
between him and Hancock, with instructions to strike the left flank
of the rebels, fixed in position by headlong pressure from the front.
Hancock meantime was doing all he could to increase that pressure,
having added two of Barlow's four brigades to the struggle. This gave
him close to 30,000 men in his attack force, even after the deduction
of casualties, which were heavy and getting heavier by the minute,
including Brigadier General Alexander Hays, a lifelong friend of
Grant's and one of the heroes of Gettysburg, killed at the head of his
brigade in Birney's division. However, Lee by then had recalled Wilcox
from his attempt to link up with Ewell and close the gap across the
center. He came back fast and went in hard, supporting Heth just as
his flank was about to crumble. This doubled the number of defenders and reduced the odds from three- to two-to-one. Even so, the
issue could not have remained much longer in doubt, except that gathering darkness finally ended the contest. It dwindled by common consent,
then flared up momentarily as Wadsworth finally arrived in the twilight after thrashing around in the brush on a three-hour search for the
battle raging furiously one mile to the south. When he came up, in
position at last to wreck the interior rebel flank, Lee had no reserves
to throw in his path except a single Alabama battalion of 125 men, de-
dailed to guard the host of prisoners who had been streaming rearward
ever since the fight began. The Alabamians formed a widespread
skirmish line, leaving the prisoners to the care of a handful of wounded,
and went in yelling for all they were worth, quite as if they had an army
at their backs. Wadsworth stumbled to a halt, apparently convinced
that his jungle-foundered soldiers were about to be swamped by superior
numbers, and hastily took up a stout defensive position on Hancock's
right as night came down.

While both sides turned to attend to such of their wounded as
they could reach — lucky ones, these, compared to others caught between the lines, calling for help that could not come because the slight-

est movement drew instant volleys from troops made panicky by fear of a night attack at such close quarters, or trapped by fires that sprang up and spread rapidly when the night breeze rose and fanned the sparks in the dry leaves to flames — Grant went to his headquarters tent in the Lacy meadow to study reports of what had happened today and to make plans for what he wanted to happen tomorrow. He would, of course, continue the offensive on both fronts, though his best chance for a breakthrough seemed to lie with Hancock, who reported that he would have made one today if darkness had not ended the battle an hour too soon. Sedgwick, joined late in the day by his third division under Brigadier General James B. Ricketts, would remain in position on the right of the northern sector, with Warren, minus Wadsworth, on the left. These five divisions had attacked again near sunset, but with no greater success than before; Ewell, buttoned up tight in his intrenchments, would not budge. Tomorrow's attack in this sector would be made primarily to prevent him from sending reinforcements down to Hill, who was to be hit with everything Hancock could lay hands on: his own four divisions, plus one from each of the other three corps, including Burnside's, which had been arriving all afternoon, too late for today's fight but in plenty of time for tomorrow's. In addition to sending one division to Hancock, Burnside would leave another on guard at Germanna Ford and march the other two down the Germanna Plank Road tonight, turning off, south of the turnpike intersection, to move west through the woods for a plunge into the gap between Warren's left and Hancock's right and a drive against Hill's interior flank, which he would assail by turning south again, as soon as he was well into the gap between the two Confederate corps. Such was Grant's victory formula, compounded tonight for application tomorrow.

Jump-off time, he said, would be at first light, 4 o'clock. Sedgwick and Warren, with five divisions, would attack and pin down Ewell, while Hancock and Burnside, with nine divisions, were overrunning Hill — and Longstreet too, if he arrived by then and was put into that portion of the line. All that was known just now was that he was on the march, somewhere off to the south and west; Hancock was warned to be on the lookout for him on the far left, in case Lee tried something foxy in that direction, though Grant was as usual a good deal more intent on what he had in mind to do to the enemy than he was on what the enemy might or might not do to him. Meade was in full agreement with these orders, as indeed he had been with all orders from the start, except that he suggested that the jump-off be advanced an hour to sunrise, 5 o'clock, so that the troops commanders would have a little daylight time in which to get their men in line for the assault. Grant considered this briefly, then agreed, and the two turned in, along with their staffs, to get some sleep for the hard day coming up.

.   .   .

Lee too was planning an offensive for tomorrow, and he intended, moreover, to launch it in the same region Grant had chosen as the scene of his main effort: in the vicinity of the plank road intersection. This involved a revision, not of purpose — the Virginian had counted, all along, on going over to the offensive as soon as his whole army was at hand — but of method. Formerly Longstreet had been told to proceed up the Catharpin Road to Todd's Tavern, a position from which he could turn the Union left, but the daylong need for closing the tactically dangerous gap between Hill and Ewell now provoked a change of plans, whereby Old Peter would shift from the Catharpin to the Plank Road and come up, not on Hill's right, but in his rear; Little Powell then could sidle northward to connect with Ewell, thus abolishing the gap, while Longstreet took over his position and prepared to launch, with his own two divisions and Hill's third, a dawn attack designed to crumple Grant's left flank, roll it up, and in conjunction with Hill and Ewell, who would advance in turn against the Federals to their front, fling the blue invaders back across the Rapidan. Accordingly, around 7 o'clock, while Hill's battle was still raging and the outcome was in doubt, Lee sent Longstreet word of the change in objectives, together with a guide to insure against going astray on the cross-country night march he would have to make in order to get from one road to the other. A message went at the same time to Major General Richard Anderson, commander of Hill's third division, which had moved from Orange to Verdiersville today, instructing him to continue his march up the plank road beyond Parker's Store tonight, in order to be with Longstreet in plenty of time for the attack at first light tomorrow.

Heth and Wilcox — who could testify to the all-too-probable truth of Hancock's claim, across the way, that another hour of daylight would have given him the breakthrough he had been seeking — were pleased to learn from Hill that Longstreet and Anderson would be up tonight to relieve their fought-out men. Whether Lee had revised his previous estimate of the enemy strength or not, Little Powell was convinced that his 15,000 veterans had taken on upwards of 40,000 bluecoats in the Wilderness today, and he had little patience with the concern of his two division commanders about the tangled condition of their lines, which had come so close to buckling under repeated assaults that, in the words of one witness, "they were like a worm fence, at every angle." Heth went to Hill and told him flatly: "A skirmish line could drive my division and Wilcox's, situated as we now are." He proposed that a new line be drawn, just in rear of their present disordered position, for them to fall back on before morning, when, as he predicted, "we shall certainly be attacked." Little Powell would not hear of this, partly because such a move would have meant abandoning many of the wounded and also because it would rob his soldiers of their hard-earned rest. "Longstreet will be up in a few hours," he said. "He will form in your front. . . . The men have been marching and fighting all day and are tired. I don't wish them disturbed." Heth went back to his troops, but soon returned with Wilcox, who joined him in the proposal that both divisions be withdrawn to a new line. Hill repeated that he wanted the men to get their sleep between now and midnight, when Longstreet was expected. They went away, but Heth, whose heart was heavy with foreboding, came back for still a third time to renew the argument. This vexed Hill, whose own sleep was being interrupted now. "Damn it, Heth," he said angrily, "I don't want to hear any more about it. The men shall not be disturbed." Heth retired for good this time, though it was already after midnight and Longstreet was obviously behind schedule. 1 o'clock, 2 o'clock, 3 o'clock passed, and still there was no news that Old Peter was approaching. Not long before dawn, the two division commanders sent for a battalion of corps engineers to come forward with picks and shovels in a belated attempt to complete the neglected intrenchments before they were overrun by the blue attackers Heth was convinced would come with the sun, if not sooner.

Back at the Tapp farm, Lee had known since 10 o'clock that the First Corps would not be up till daylight at the earliest. The young cavalry officer who had ridden down to the Catharpin Road with instructions for the change in routes, Major Henry McClellan of Stuart's staff, had also been charged with giving Longstreet's lead division verbal orders to press on without delay, thereby assuring an early arrival in Hill's rear. He left about 7 and returned three hours later, highly indignant, to report to Lee that the commander of that division, Major General Charles W. Field, a West Pointer and a stickler for regulations — he had lately been promoted and appointed to his post, having served in Richmond as superintendent of the Bureau of Conscription since the loss of a leg at Second Manassas, twenty months ago — flatly declined to accept from a stray cavalryman possibly garbled verbal orders that were in contradiction to the ones he had received from his corps commander, which were that he was to rest his men at Richard's Shop until 1 o'clock in the morning. Then and not until then, he said stiffly, would the march be resumed. This meant that Old Peter's leading elements could scarcely arrive before sunup, since the distance from Richard's Shop was about a dozen miles, two or three of them over rugged terrain, across fields, through woods, and by roundabout lanes connecting the two main roads; but Lee seemed oddly unperturbed. When McClellan offered to ride back with written orders which Field would have no choice except to obey, the Virginian declined with a shake of his gray head. "No, Major," he said calmly. "It is now past 10 o'clock, and by the time you could return to General Field and he could put his division in motion, it would be 1 o'clock. At that hour he will move."

Lee returned to his tent for more paper work, including an 11 o'clock dispatch informing the Secretary of War of what had occurred since Grant's crossing of the Rapidan the day before — "By the blessing of God," he wrote of today's hard fight, "we maintained our position against every effort until night, when the contest closed" — then turned in for another four or five hours of sleep before rising to face what might well be disaster.

He did not mention the possibility of disaster or its cause, either to Seddon in Richmond or to Hill, whose troops were sleeping helter-skelter in the brush, in whatever random positions they had occupied when darkness ended the fighting and they fell asleep on their arms, many of them too weary to eat the scant rations sent up later in the evening. Perhaps, like Little Powell, Lee reasoned that rest would do more for them than would fretting about a situation they could do but little to repair in the few hours of darkness that remained. In any case, he left them and their commander undisturbed until dawn began to filter through the thickets and a popping of rifles, like individual handclaps, warned that another day of battle had begun: May 6. Exposed by daylight to this picket fire, the engineers dropped their picks and shovels, which they had had small chance to use, and scuttled rearward. Within an hour, sharply at 5 o'clock as the sun was rising, this intermittent racket merged and grew in abrupt intensity to a steady clatter, described by one observer as "the noise of a boy running with a stick pressed against a paling fence, faster and faster until it swelled into a continuous rattling roar." The Federals were attacking in greater strength than yesterday, along and down both sides of the plank road, and after a brief resistance the two Confederate divisions did just what Heth had said they would do. They broke. Though they did not scatter in panic or drop their rifles, still they made for the rear, more or less in a body, some among them firing as they went. "The men seemed to fall back upon a deliberate conviction that it was impossible to hold the ground and, of course, foolish to attempt it," one among them later wrote by way of explanation, adding rather philosophically: "It was mortifying, but it was only what every veteran has experienced."

Up on Ewell's front the dug-in troops held firm under assault, but Sedgwick and Warren were accomplishing all that was asked of them by keeping him from sending reinforcements down to the far end of the line. Such flaw as there was in the execution of Grant's plan was in the center. Burnside, ordered to penetrate the rebel gap and descend on Hill's interior flank, had gotten himself and his two divisions lost as soon as he left the road last night and struck out through the brush; he was somewhere rearward now, behind the space between Warren and Hancock, disoriented and wandering in circles while the conflict raged, first to his right, then his left, sometimes front and sometimes rear. Hancock was furious at this dereliction. Shouting to be heard above the din on the plank road, he told one of Meade's staff officers that if those missing 10,000 men could be added to the pressure being exerted, "we could smash A. P. Hill all to pieces!" In point of fact, he seemed well on the way to doing it anyhow. Except for the troops with Barlow, whose division had been reunited down the Brock Road to guard against a possible flank attack, he had all the men assigned to the main effort massed and in motion, flushing graybacks as they went. Forty years old, "a tall, soldierly man with light brown hair and a military jaw," he had what the staffer described as "the massive features and the heavy folds round the eye that often mark a man of ability." Elated by the propitious opening of that portion of the battle in his charge, he made a handsome figure on horseback, and his elation grew as the attack continued. Just ahead was the Tapp clearing, and beyond it the white tops of wagons parked in the Confederate rear. "We are driving them, sir!" Hancock called proudly to the staff man. "Tell General Meade we are driving them most beautifully."

Lee was there in the clearing, doing all he could to stiffen what little was left of Hill's resistance, and so had Longstreet himself been there, momentarily at least, when the blue assault was launched. He came riding up just before sunrise, a mile or two in advance of his column, the head of which had reached Parker's Store by then, and Hill's chief of staff crossed the Tapp farmyard to welcome him as he turned off the road. "Ah, General, we have been looking for you since 12 o'clock last night. We expect to be attacked at any moment, and are not in any shape to resist." Unaccustomed to being reproached by unstrung colonels, however valid their anxiety, Old Peter looked sternly down at him. "My troops are not up," he said. "I've ridden ahead —" At this point the sudden clatter of Hancock's attack erupted out in the brush, and Longstreet, without waiting to learn more of what had happened, whirled his horse and galloped back to hurry his two divisions forward. So Lee at least knew that the First Corps would soon be up. His problem, after sending his adjutant to order the wagon train prepared for withdrawal, was to hang on till these reinforcements got there, probably within the hour, to shore up Hill's fast-crumbling line. Presently, though, this began to look like more than he could manage; Wilcox and Heth, overlapped on both flanks, gave ground rapidly before a solid mass of attackers, and skulkers began to drift rearward across the clearing, singly and in groups, some of them turning to fire from time to time at their pursuers, while others seemed only intent on escape. Their number increased, until finally Lee saw a whole brigade in full retreat. Moreover, this was not just any brigade; it was Brigadier General Samuel McGowan's brigade of South Carolinians, Wilcox's best and one of the finest in the army.

"My God, General McGowan!" Lee exclaimed from horseback,

breasting the flood of fugitives. "Is this splendid brigade of yours running like a flock of geese?"

"General, these men are not whipped," McGowan answered, stung in his pride by this public rebuke. "They only want a place to form and they will fight as well as they ever did."

But there was the rub. All that was left by now for them to form on was a battalion of Third Corps artillery, four batteries under twenty-eight-year-old Lieutenant Colonel William Poague, lined up along the west side of the clearing which afforded one of the Wilderness's few real fields of fire. The cannoneers stood to their loaded pieces, waiting for Hill's infantry to fall back far enough to give them a chance to shoot at the bluecoats in pursuit. However, there was no time for this; Poague, with Lee's approval, had his guns open at what was already point-blank range, shaving the heads of the Confederate retreaters in order to throw their anti-personnel rounds into the enemy ranks. This took quick effect, particularly near the road, where the Federals tended to bunch up. Flailed by double-shotted grape and canister, they paused and began to look for cover: seeing which, the cannoneers stepped up their rate of fire. Lee remained mounted alongside Poague, who kept his men at their work — "getting the starch out of our shirts," they called it — without infantry support. This could not continue long before they would be overrun, but meantime they were making the most of it. Smoke from the guns drifted back, sparkling in the early-morning sunlight, and presently Lee saw through its rearward swirls a cluster of men running toward him, carrying their rifles at the ready and shouldering Hill's fugitives aside.

"Who are you, my boys?" he cried as they came up in rear of the line of bucking guns.

"Texas boys!" they yelled, gathering now in larger numbers, and Lee knew them: Hood's Texans, his old-time shock troops, now under Brigadier General John Gregg — the lead brigade of Field's division. Longstreet was up at last.

"Hurrah for Texas!" Lee shouted. He took off his wide-brimmed hat and waved it. "Hurrah for Texas!"

No one had ever seen him act this way before, either on or off the field of battle. And presently, when the guns ceased their fuming and the Texans started forward, they saw something else they had never seen: something that froze the cheers in their throats and brought them to a halt. When Gregg gave the order, "Attention, Texas Brigade! The eyes of General Lee are upon you. Forward...march!" Lee rose in his stirrups and lifted his hat. "Texans always move them," he declared. They cheered as they stepped out between the guns. "I would charge hell itself for that old man," a veteran said fervently. Then they saw the one thing that could stop them. Lee had spurred Traveller forward on their heels; he intended to go in with them, across the field and after the bluecoats in the brush. They slacked their pace and left off cheering. "Lee to the rear!" began to be heard along the line, and some of them addressed him directly: "Go back, General Lee, go back. We won't go unless you go back." He was among them now, flushed with excitement, his eyes fixed on the woods ahead. They stopped, and when an attempt by Gregg to head him off had no effect, a sergeant reached out and took hold of Traveller's rein, bringing the animal to a halt. "Lee to the rear! Lee to the rear!" the men were shouting. But his blood was up; he did not seem to hear them, or even to know that he and they were no longer in motion. At this point a staff colonel intervened. "General, you've been looking for General Longstreet. There he is, over yonder." Lee looked and saw, at the far end of the field, the man he called his war horse. For the first time since he cleared the line of guns he seemed to become aware that he was involved in something larger than a charge. Responding to the colonel's suggestion, he turned Traveller's head and rode in that direction. On the way he passed in rear of Brigadier General Evander Law's Alabama brigade, about to move out on the left. "What troops are these?" he asked, and on being told he called to them: "God bless the Alabamians!" They went forward with a whoop, alongside the Texans, who were whooping too. "I thought him at that moment the grandest specimen of manhood I ever beheld," one among them later wrote. "He looked as though he ought to have been, and was, the monarch of the world."

Longstreet yielded to no man in his admiration for Lee, yet his admiration never amounted to idolatry, especially if idolatry included a willingness to put up with tactical interference. Seeing him thus "off his balance," he later wrote, he informed him with jocular bluntness, as soon as he came up, "that his line would be recovered in an hour if he would permit me to handle the troops, but if my services were not needed I would like to ride to some place of safety, as it was not quite comfortable where we were." Lee complied by retiring westward a short distance with his staff officers, who no doubt were glad to get him out of there, and Old Peter kept his word, here and on the opposite side of the plank road as well.

There his other division had been put in line by its commander, Brigadier General Joseph Kershaw, whose Georgians, South Carolinians, and Mississippians hooted cruelly when Heth's badly shaken troops fell back through their ranks. "Do you belong to Lee's army?" they jeered, seeing their old comrades thus for the first time in eight months. "You don't look like the men we left here. You're worse than Bragg's men!" Taking over, they stalled Hancock's advance on this side of the road, while Field was doing the same across the way. Then the two divisions went forward together against the Federals, who were wearier and a good deal more disorganized than they had known until they were brought to a halt, first by Poague's four rapid-firing batteries and then by 10,000 newly committed rebels whose appearance was as sudden as if they had dropped out of the sky. Still, the going was rough for the First Corps, most of whose members had never fought in the region west of Fredericksburg before. Some brigades lost heavily, including the Texans, who went in boasting that they had "put General Lee under arrest and sent him to the rear." A captured private from the brigade expressed its collective opinion when his captors asked him what he thought of this Battle of the Wilderness. "Battle be damned," he said hotly. "It aint no battle, it's a worse riot than Chickamauga! At Chickamauga there was at least a rear, but here there aint neither front nor rear. It's all a damned mess! And our two armies aint nothing but howling mobs."

Before 10 o'clock, despite the various impediments of terrain and the refusal by most of Hancock's men to panic under pressure, Longstreet fulfilled his promise to recover the line that had begun to be lost at sunrise. Halting there, within half a mile of the Brock Road, he proceeded to consolidate the position, reinforced presently by Anderson, whose division arrived while the First Corps was advancing and moved up in its support. Hill meantime had rallied his other two divisions and swung them northward, in accordance with Lee's orders, to plug the gap that had yawned since yesterday between him and Ewell. Finding it unexploited by the Federals, whose own gap had been enlarged by Longstreet — Law's whooping Alabamians had struck and scattered Wadsworth's ill-starred division on Hancock's right, driving the remnant west and north, all the way to the Lacy meadow, and Burnside was still on his circuitous tour of the brush — Hill's men, willingly and hurriedly, did what they had failed to do the night before. They intrenched. Lee's line was now a continuous one, reasonably compact, and he had all his troops on hand at last, including Ewell's detached brigade, which arrived at midmorning from Hanover. The time had come for him to go over to the all-out offensive he had planned to launch as soon as he managed to bring Grant to a standstill in the thickets — as he now had done.

"There was a lull all along the line," a regimental commander later said of this period during which reconnaissance parties went out and came back and last-minute instructions were delivered: adding, "It was the ominous silence that precedes the tornado."

Tactically, Grant was in far worse shape than he or anyone else in the Lacy meadow seemed to know. In addition to the unmanned gap across his center, he had both flanks in the air. No blue army had ever remained long in any such attitude, here in Virginia, without suffering grievously at the hands of Lee for having been so neglectful or inept; Hooker, for example, had left only one flank open, but his discomfiture had been complete. Now the same treatment might well be in store for Grant, on practically that same ground just one year later.

Headquarters had been more or less in a turmoil for the past two hours, ever since Hancock's attack went into reverse. First, there was the matter of Burnside's nonarrival, which not only reduced the intended strength of the main effort but also left it unsupported on the right, exposing Wadsworth to the catastrophe that ensued. In point of fact, after all that had happened yesterday, the aging New Yorker — a brigadier since shortly after First Bull Run, military governor of the District of Columbia during the tenure of McClellan, whom he had helped to frustrate, and an unsuccessful candidate for governor of his home state on the Republican ticket in '62, the year of the Democratic sweep — had seemed to suspect from the start that today would be no better. He was feeling his years, and he told an aide he thought perhaps he ought to turn the command of his division over to someone else and go to the rear. As it was, however, he stayed and managed, today as yesterday, to lose his sense of direction in the course of the attack and came crowding down on the units to his left, creating a jam on the near side of the plank road and thereby adding to the effectiveness of Poague's fire from the Tapp farmyard, as well as to the confusion that prevailed when Law assailed his unprotected right. One of his three brigades disintegrated without more ado, and Wadsworth, in an attempt to keep the other two from doing likewise, appealed to them from horseback to stand firm; whereupon he was hit in the back of the head and fell to the ground with a bullet in his brain. His troops ran off and left him, pursued by the rebels, who gathered him up and took him back to one of their aid stations. (He died there two days later, having been stared at by a great many of his enemies, who came for a look at a man reputed to possess "more wealth than the treasury of the Confederate government." Rich men were not unusual in the armies of the South, where the West Point tradition was strong in leading families and no $300 commutation fee could secure exemption from conscription, but were rarely encountered on the other side, particularly on the firing line.) Meantime the fallen general's troops continued their flight all the way to the Lacy meadow, as if they expected to find sanctuary there with Grant, who sat on his accustomed stump atop the knoll, still whittling, still wreathed in cigar smoke. Headquarters was alarmed by their sudden appearance, even though they did not seem to be pursued, and presently, when long-range shots began to fall in the vicinity, an anxious staffer, fearful that the meadow was about to be overrun, suggested that it would be prudent to shift the command post rearward. Grant stopped whittling. "It strikes me it would be better to order up some artillery and defend the present location," he said quietly. This was done, although there was nothing the gunners could see in the way of targets, and Hancock bolstered what remained of Wadsworth's division by sending reinforcements over from the left.

On the right, Sedgwick and Warren had suffered heavy losses in carrying out their instructions to keep attacking Ewell's intrenchments and thus prevent his sending reinforcements down to Hill. This they had done, and in doing it they had kept him on the defensive. But if they assumed from this that he would remain so, or that Sedgwick's outer flank was secure because it was covered by Flat Creek, they would be disabused before nightfall; Gordon, whose brigade was on the left, was trying even now to get permission from his superiors to turn the Federal flank, which he insisted was wide open to such a maneuver, having scouted it himself. So far, Ewell and Early had declined to let him try it, being convinced that Burnside's corps was posted rearward in support. Obviously, Sedgwick's immunity from attack, based as it was on this misconception by Gordon's superiors, was going to last no longer than Burnside remained unaccounted for in the Union order of battle. Once he found his way up to the firing line and was identified, Ewell and Early would have to abandon their objection to Gordon's proposal and unleash him, with results that were likely to be spectacular if Sedgwick's dispositions were as faulty as the Georgian claimed to have seen with his own eyes.

Just now, however — for Burnside, having spent the past five hours out of pocket, was to spend another three in the same fashion, lost to friend and foe alike, before he managed to get where he belonged — the gravest danger was on the opposite flank, which was also exposed to being turned or struck end-on. This was due to a combination of misconceptions, based on erroneous information from headquarters. Hancock had kept Barlow in position down the Brock Road all this time, yesterday and today, in expectation that Longstreet would arrive from that direction. Instead he had come up the plank road, converting Hill's near rout into a counteroffensive; but Hancock still held Barlow where he was, outside the action, because only two of Old Peter's divisions, Field's and Kershaw's, had so far been identified. The third, Pickett's — reported to have been with Longstreet at Gordonsville, though in fact it was south of Richmond — might be maneuvering for an attack up the Brock Road, perhaps in conjunction with Anderson's division of Hill's corps, which had also not yet been accounted for. So Barlow was kept where he was, a mile and a half from the plank road intersection, to guard against a tangential strike by these 10,000 missing rebels. Meantime, evidence had accumulated to support the belief that they were already at hand, including one frantic eyewitness report that they were advancing in mass up the Brock Road. This was a case of mistaken identity; the advancing mass turned out to be a herd of Federal convalescents, marching from

Chancellorsville to rejoin the army by Hancock's roundabout route. No sooner was this mistake discovered, however, than heavy firing was heard from down around Todd's Tavern, where the Brock and Catharpin roads intersected, less than three miles from Barlow's outpost on the Union left. The assumption was that the cavalry must have encountered Pickett's column, coming up from the Catharpin Road, and was doing what it could to hold him off while Barlow got ready to receive him. This was partly correct and partly wrong. It was cavalry, right enough, but that was all it was. The blue troopers were shooting, not at Pickett (who was perhaps of greater service to his country here today, though he was not within sixty miles of the battle, than he had been ten months ago at Gettysburg, leading the charge that would be known forever after by his name) but at Stuart. Sheridan had served Grant poorly yesterday by plunging eastward, with two thirds of the army's cavalry, into the vacuum Stuart had left around Fredericksburg when he moved westward to take position on Lee's right. Still intent on closing with the graybacks, more for the purpose of destroying them than of finding out what was happening in their rear, Sheridan's horsemen made such a racket with their rapid-firing carbines that Barlow thought a large-scale action was in progress, though in fact it was nothing more than an unprofitable skirmish, which did not result in the slightest penetration of the cavalry screen Stuart kept tightly drawn to prevent his adversary from catching even a glimpse of the preparations now being made for attack, four miles northwest. As it was, Barlow was so impressed by the uproar down around Todd's Tavern that he called urgently for reinforcements to help him meet what he was convinced was coming, and Hancock obliged by sending him two brigades from the main body, which by then was back on the line it had left at sunrise.

Hancock had his hands full where he was, holding Longstreet west of the Brock Road, immediately north and south of the plank road intersection. For better than five hours now, advancing and retreating, the fighting had been as heavy as any he had ever seen, and so too had his casualties and the expenditure of ammunition. Drummer boys were pressed into unfamiliar service as stretcher bearers, and when they got to the rear with their anguished burdens, the stretchers were loaded with boxes of cartridges for the return to the firing line, so that, as one reporter wrote, "the struggle shall not cease for want of ball and powder." Involved as he was in the direction of all this, blinded by thickets and appealed to simultaneously from the left and right — Barlow was convinced that he was about to be hit by Pickett, and Wadsworth's division, adjacent to the unmanned gap across the army's center, had just come apart at the seams — Hancock was apparently too busy to notice that the contraction of his front in the vicinity of the crossroad, resulting from his losses and the withdrawal of four brigades to meet the reported dangers on the far left and the right, had widened to about a mile the brush-choked interval between the main body and Barlow's outpost position down the road. Consequently, though he was reasonably well protected against a flank attack by Pickett, who wasn't there, he was not protected at all from one by Longstreet, who was. His immediate left — as Gordon was saying of Sedgwick's right, four miles away — was wide open to either a turning movement or an end-on strike.

Then came the lull, a half-hour breathing space. Hancock spent it shoring up his line against an expected renewal of Longstreet's frontal effort to drive him back from the vital crossroad. Atop the knoll in the Lacy meadow, Grant, with a hole in his center and both flanks in the air, continued to whittle. Then, around 11 o'clock, the storm broke. Within minutes of the opening shots, according to Meade's chief of staff, the uproar of the rebel attack "approached the sublime."

"Longstreet, always grand in battle, never shone as he did here," a First Corps artillerist said of the general in his conduct of this morning's fighting on the right. Within three hours of his arrival he introduced tactics into a battle which, up to then, had been little more than a twenty-hour slugging match, with first one side then the other surging forward through the brush, only to fall back when momentum was lost and the enemy took his turn at going over to the offensive. All attacks had been frontal except for chance encounters, when some confused unit — a regiment or a brigade or, as in Wadsworth's case, a division — got turned around, usually in the course of an advance through blinding thickets, and exposed a naked flank to being torn. Now Old Peter, who was always at his calmest when the conflict roared its loudest, undertook to serve a Federal corps, reinforced to a strength of seven divisions, in that same tearing fashion.

Lee had ordered the army's chief engineer, Major General Martin L. Smith, to report to Longstreet at about the time the Federals began to yield the ground they had won from Hill. Sent out to reconnoiter the Union left, Smith — a forty-four-year-old New-York-born West Pointer whose most distinguished service to his adopted country up to now had been at Vicksburg, where he not only laid out and supervised the construction of its hilly defenses, but also commanded one of the divisions that manned them under siege — returned at 10 o'clock to report that he had found Hancock's flank wide open to attack from within the mile-wide gap that yawned between his main body and Barlow's outpost. Moreover, an unfinished and unmapped railroad, work on which had been abandoned when the war began, afforded an ideal covered approach to that vulnerable point; troops could be massed in the brush-screened cut, just where the roadbed made a turn southeast, perpendicular to the unguarded flank a briery quarter mile away.

Old Peter's eyes lighted up at the news, but he was no more inclined to be precipitate here than he had been at Second Manassas when a similar opportunity arose. He summoned his young chief of staff, Lieutenant Colonel G. Moxley Sorrel, instructed him to take charge of a force made up of three brigades, one from each of the three divisions at hand, and conduct them to the designated point for the attack. Knowing how likely such maneuvers were to become disorganized under the influence of exuberance, he stressed the need for careful preparation. "Form a good line," he told him, "and then move, your right pushed forward and turning as much as possible to the left." Characteristically, before sending him on his way, he added in true First Corps style: "Hit hard when you start, but don't start until you have everything ready."

Sorrel assembled the three brigades, headed by Brigadier Generals William Wofford, G. T. Anderson, and William Mahone, respectively from Kershaw's, Field's, and Richard Anderson's divisions, and just as he was about to move out, Colonel John M. Stone of Heth's division, in position on Longstreet's left, requested permission to add the weight of his Mississippi brigade to the blow about to be struck. Hill and Heth were willing, and that made four brigades from as many divisions, a pair each from two corps, not one of them under a professional soldier and all in charge of a young staff officer who never before had commanded troops in action. Sorrel was a former bank clerk, twenty-six years old, intensely ambitious and strikingly handsome, a Georgian like his chief, though of French not Dutch extraction. As he set out, leading this force of about 5000 into the railway cut, then eastward through its leafy tunnel to the bend where they would mass for the attack, he knew that his great hour had come and he was determined to make the most of it, for his own and his country's sake. Old Peter, who had a great affection for him dating back to First Manassas, watched him disappear in the woods, then settled back to wait for the uproar that would signal the launching of the flank assault. He kept his remaining eleven brigades in position astride the plank road, maintaining frontal contact and preparing to increase the pressure when the time came. Already he was planning a larger turning movement to follow the one about to start. Once Hancock's line had been rolled up, the fronts of the other two Confederate corps would be uncovered in rapid sequence; Hill's two divisions would join the grand left wheel, and Ewell's three would drive straight ahead, cutting the Federals off from the fords by which they had crossed the Rapidan. Obliged to fall back on Fredericksburg, Grant's army would be cut to pieces, train and all, as it jammed the narrow Wilderness trails and scattered in the brush. Anticipation made the wait seem long, though in fact it was quite brief. At 11 o'clock, within half an hour of his setting out, Sorrel's attack exploded on the Union left and began to roll northward, clattering across the right front of the Confederate position. Longstreet ordered his main body forward simultaneously to exploit and enlarge the panic already evident in the enemy ranks.

The end-on blow was as successful as even Sorrel had dared to hope it would be. Struck without preamble by a horde of rapid-firing rebels who came screaming through what up to then had been a curtain of peaceful green, the first blue unit — a brigade that had just been withdrawn from the line to catch its breath while the lull was on — disintegrated on contact, its members taking off in all directions to escape the sudden onslaught, and though others reacted differently, having at least had a semblance of warning that something horrendous was headed in their direction from the left, the result was much the same in the end, as unit after unit, finding itself under simultaneous fire from the front and flank, sought to achieve a similar deliverance from fury. Consternation in such cases was followed by a strangely deliberate acceptance of the military facts of life, the difference being that they reacted, not as individuals, but as a group seeking safety in numbers. A man from one of Gibbon's brigades reported that the first he knew of a flank attack was when he saw troops from Mott's division, on his left, trudging rearward in a body. At first, so deliberate was their step, so oddly sullen their expression, he could not make out what was happening. "[They] did not seem to me demoralized in manner," he declared, "nor did they present the appearance of soldiers moving under orders, but rather of a throng of armed men returning dissatisfied from a muster." The best explanation another observer could give was that "a large number of troops were about to leave the service," and apparently they were doing all they could to leave it alive. One thing at least was clear to a staff officer who watched them slogging rearward, oblivious to pleas and threats alike. "They had fought all they meant to fight for the present," he said, "and there was an end to it." Hancock himself put it simplest, in a statement years later to Longstreet: "You rolled me up like a wet blanket."

Elation on the Confederate side was correspondingly great, and it too was a sort of mass reaction. Here, the cheering troops perceived as soon as the flank attack began to roll, was another Chancellorsville in the making. Moreover, they were aware of the highly encouraging difference that, instead of launching their turning movement with a scant two hours of daylight left for its exploitation, as Jackson's men had done, they now had a substantial eight or nine such hours: enough, surely, to complete the destruction already under way. Not that they wasted time, simply because so much of it was available; Sorrel had carried out his orders with speed and precision. Wofford and Mahone were abreast in front, respectively on the left and right, supported by G. T. Anderson and Stone, whose added pressure shattered what little resistance was encountered or by-passed in the course of the advance.

Within less than an hour they had driven northward all the way to the plank road; some of Wofford's Georgians, in fact, plunged eagerly across it, intent on the chase, though Mahone's Virginians called a halt at that point, in accordance with instructions. When Sorrel rode up he found the plank road unobstructed all the way to its intersection with the Brock Road, where the displaced and rattled Federals were taking shelter behind the breastworks Hancock had had them build the day before. From the opposite direction he saw Longstreet and his staff riding toward him on the plank road, accompanied by several unit commanders to whom the burly lieutenant general was apparently giving directions for the follow-up assault. They made up a sizeable cavalcade, and Sorrel could see from their manner, their gestures and expressions as they rode, that they shared the exuberance he was feeling at the success of his first experience as a leader of men in battle.

Their high spirits were voiced by Brigadier General Micah Jenkins, the twenty-eight-year-old commander of a brigade in Field's division, who had just been informed that his troops would play a major role in the follow-up attack. "I am happy," the young South Carolina aristocrat told Longstreet, excited by the prospect of enlarging the gains already made. "I have felt despair for the cause for some months, but now I am relieved, and feel assured that we will put the enemy back across the Rapidan before night." When Sorrel came up Jenkins embraced and congratulated him warmly. "We will smash them now," he said.

Old Peter thought so, too. Engineer Smith had returned from a second reconnaissance of the Union left to report that a second turning movement, designed to flank the rallying bluecoats out of their breastworks along the Brock Road, was altogether as feasible as the first. Just then, however, as the cavalcade continued its ride east to within musket range of the Brock Road intersection, there was a sudden spatter of fire from the woods to the right front; some of Mahone's men were shooting at some of Wofford's, having mistaken them for Federals when they came hurrying back across the plank road to take their proper place in line. Aggressive as always, Longstreet whirled his horse in that direction, apparently intending to stop the undisciplined firing. Others followed his example — including Joe Kershaw, who had ridden forward to confer with Wofford on the condition of his detached brigade — and were met by a heavier volley from the Virginians in the woods. Four men were hit: a courier and a staff captain, both of whom were killed instantly, Micah Jenkins, who died a few hours later with a bullet in his brain, and Longstreet. "Friends! They are *friends!*" Kershaw shouted in a voice that rang above the clatter and the groans, and almost at once Mahone's veterans ceased firing and hurried out of the woods to express their regret for what had happened.

By then solicitous hands were helping the wounded lieutenant general to dismount. Hit solidly by a bullet that passed through the base of his neck and lodged in his right shoulder, he had been lifted straight up by the impact and had come down hard, his right arm hanging useless, though he managed to stay in the saddle, bleeding heavily, until his companions were there to ease him to the ground, the upper part of his body propped against the trunk of a roadside tree. Exultation turned to dismay as word spread rapidly through the Wilderness that Old Peter had been hit. All down the line, men's thoughts were more than ever of Chancellorsville, but with the bitter irony of remembering that Jackson too had been shot by his own soldiers, less than four miles up the road through these same woods, at the climax of a successful flank attack. As for Longstreet, his thoughts were neither on the past nor on the present, despite his pain. His concern was for the immediate future, the follow-up assault that would complete his victory. Field being the ranking division commander present in the corps, Longstreet blew the bloody foam from his mouth to say to Sorrel: "Tell General Field to take command, and move forward with the whole force and gain the Brock Road." Soon his staff physician was there to tend his wounds, and when Lee arrived he told him, in such detail as his shaken vocal cords allowed, of his plan for turning the Federals out of their new position. By now a stretcher had been brought. He was lifted onto it, his hat placed over his face to shield his eyes, and carried back down the plank road to a waiting ambulance. On the way, when he heard troops by the roadside saying, "He is dead. They are only telling us he is wounded," he raised his hat from his face with his usable hand. The answering cheers, he declared long afterward, served to ease his pain somewhat on the jolting rearward journey.

A wandering artillery major, on a fruitless search for a decent gun position, came up just as the ambulance moved off. Later he wrote of what he saw and felt. Members of the general's staff, "literally bowed down with grief," were all around the vehicle; "One, I remember, stood upon the rear step of the ambulance, seeming to desire to be as near him as possible. All of them were in tears." The doctor had said that Longstreet's wounds were not necessarily fatal, but they recalled that the prognosis had been even more favorable in Jackson's case right up to the day he died, a year ago next week. Though he had never really liked Old Peter, the artillerist wanted to see for himself what his condition was. For one thing, the procession's resemblance to a funeral cortege lent credence to a rumor that the general was dead. "I rode up to the ambulance and looked in. They had taken off Longstreet's hat and coat and boots. The blood had paled out of his face and its somewhat gross aspect was gone. I noticed how white and dome-like his great forehead looked and, with scarcely less reverent admiration, how spotless white his socks and his fine gauze undervest, save where the black red gore from his breast and shoulder had stained it. While I gazed at his massive frame, lying so still except when it rocked inertly with the lurch of the vehicle, his eyelids frayed apart till I could see a delicate line of blue between them, and then he very quietly moved his unwounded arm and, with his thumb and two fingers, carefully lifted the saturated undershirt from his chest, holding it up a moment, and heaved a deep sigh. He is not dead, I said to myself, and he is calm and entirely master of the situation. He is both greater and more attractive than I have heretofore thought him."

Back up the road, at the scene of the wounding, Field was doing what he could to carry out his orders to "take command, and move forward." But this was by no means as easy a task as Longstreet seemed to think. Other disruptive accidents, like the one that had just cost the corps its chief, were apt to follow if the main body, still in line astride the plank road, and Sorrel's flankers, drawn up facing it, were left to fight with their fronts at right angles. Lee ordered a postponement of the follow-up assault until the lines were readjusted. This was done, although the process was a slow one. Not only was the confusion greater than had been thought, it had also been increased by the loss of Jenkins and Old Peter. Four mortal hours, from noon to 4 o'clock, were required to get the troops untangled and into satisfactory positions for attack, and when they went forward at 4.15 they found that Hancock, too, had made good use of the time afforded for adjustments. He had strengthened his breastworks, brought up reinforcements, and posted a secondary line in support of the first. Worst of all (or best, depending on the point of view) he had shored up and realigned

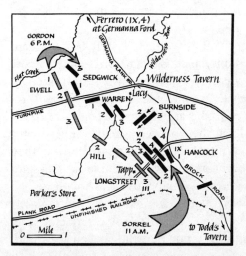

his outer flank, which the attackers found no longer dangling in the air. At a couple of points the Confederates achieved a penetration — one, where the log breastworks caught fire, forcing the defenders to abandon them, and Jenkins's Carolinians came leaping through the flames, intent on avenging the fall of their young brigadier — but in both cases supporting troops came up and restored the line by driving them out again: proof, if any such was needed, that seven divisions, snug behind breastworks and with both flanks secure (Burnside had come up at last, midway through the four-hour lull, and gone into position on Hancock's right) were not to be driven, or even budged, by three divisions attacking head-on through bullet-flailed brush. An hour of such fighting was quite enough to show that nothing more was going to be accomplished here. It was time — indeed, almost past time — to look elsewhere: meaning in Ewell's direction, up on the opposite flank.

All day, though he had had no chance to go in person, Lee had been sending messages to the Second Corps, urging an offensive in that quarter to relieve the pressure on the First or, if that was impracticable, the detachment of reinforcements to strengthen the offensive on the right. Invariably Ewell had replied that he could do neither. There was no fit opening for an attack; he needed all his troops to maintain his position astride the turnpike. When Lee arrived at 5.30 asking, "Cannot something be done on this flank?" Ewell said again that he believed it would be unwise to assault the Federals in their intrenchments, and he was supported in this by Early, who was at corps headquarters when Lee rode up. Gordon was also there, intending to renew his daylong plea that he be unleashed, and when his two superiors finished protesting that there was nothing to be done, he presumed to appeal to the army commander himself for permission to strike at the enemy flank, which he insisted had been wide open to attack for more than eight hours now. Ewell and Early repeated their objections, based on the conviction that Burnside was posted in Sedgwick's rear to forestall such a move. Lee, who knew that Burnside was in front of Hill, wasted no more time on reproaches, although, as Gordon later wrote, "his silence and grim looks . . . revealed his thoughts almost as plainly as words could have done." He simply ordered the attack to be made at once.

It was launched at straight-up 6 o'clock, and within the limitations of the little daylight time remaining — sunset came at 6.50 and darkness followed quickly in the thickets of the Wilderness — it was altogether as successful as Gordon, for the past nine hours, had been telling Ewell and Early it would be. With the support of the brigade that had arrived that morning from Hanover, North Carolinians under twenty-seven-year-old Brigadier General Robert D. Johnston, the Georgians struck and scattered Ricketts's unwary flank brigade and captured its commander, Brigadier General Truman Seymour. Seymour had led a division in the ill-starred Florida campaign, and after being whipped at Olustee had returned to Virginia to head a brigade whose members were known in both armies as "Milroy's weary boys," a description applied two years ago, after Stonewall Jackson gave them the run-around in the Shenandoah Valley, and confirmed last year when Ewell encountered them near Winchester on his way to Gettysburg. Weary or not, they broke badly again today and spread panic through the rest of the division, as well as through part of Wright's division, which was next in line and which also had a brigade commander scooped up by the rebels in the confusion. This was Brigadier General Alexander Shaler, a Connecticut-born New Yorker whose capture was especially welcome because he had recently been in charge of the prison for Confederate officers on Johnson's Island in Sandusky Bay, where winters were cold and blankets few; now he would get a taste of prison life from the inside, looking out, instead of from the outside, looking in. Seymour and Shaler, for all their lofty rank, were only two among some 600 Federals taken captive in the attack, while about as many more were killed or wounded, bringing Sedgwick's total loss to well over a thousand in one hour. Gordon himself lost only about fifty in the course of what his men referred to, ever afterwards, as their "finest frolic." The blue right flank was "rolled up" for more than a mile before dusk put an end to the advance and obliged the Georgians and Carolinians, who by then had plunged all the way to the Germanna Plank Road, to pull back with their prisoners, their booty from the over-run camps, and their conviction that an earlier attack, in Gordon's word's, "would have resulted in a decided disaster to the whole right wing of General Grant's army, if not in its entire disorganization."

Lee was inclined to think so, too, especially if the attack on this flank, against Sedgwick, had been delivered at the same time as Longstreet's against Hancock, on the other; in which case the indications were that Grant would have been overwhelmed and routed, not merely discomfited and bled down another one percent. An earlier visit to the left by the army commander would no doubt have resulted in an earlier attack, but Lee had come as soon as he felt he could leave the critical right, where the contest had been touch-and-go since sunrise. The trouble was that he could not be everywhere at once, despite the need for him to do just that. Although this impossible need had grown more pressing ever since the death of Stonewall Jackson, today it had become downright acute. Longstreet's departure left his corps in the hands of a newly promoted major general who had been with it less than three months, none of the time in combat, and whose deskbound year in Richmond seemed to have made him utterly inflexible at a time when flexibility was among the highest virtues. Hill's failing health, worse today than yesterday, and likely to be still worse tomorrow, obviously required him to take a sick leave that would deprive the army, however briefly, of the most aggressive of its corps commanders. It was harder, even, to think of Lee without A. P. Hill than it was to think of him without Longstreet, for Hill had never been detached. As for Ewell, although by ordinary standards he had done well today and yesterday, holding his own against the odds, he seemed incapable of doing one whit more than was required by specific orders; Ewell in the Wilderness, unable to bring himself to unleash Gordon despite repeated pleas from headquarters that *something* be attempted in that direction, was disturbingly like Ewell at Gettysburg, where his indecisiveness had cost the army its one best chance for a quick victory in what, instead, turned out to be a bloody three-day battle that ended in retreat.... All this might well have been heavy on Lee's mind as he rode southward, three miles through the twilight, to the Tapp farm. He was faced, at this most critical juncture, with a crisis of command: a crisis that would have to be resolved if the Army of Northern Virginia — at the close of only the second day of fighting, in what promised to be the longest and grimmest of its campaigns — was to survive the continuing confrontation, here in the depths of the Wilderness, with an enemy force roughly twice its size, superbly equipped, and still in possession of the main artery leading southeast, through the thickets and beyond into open country, where the tactical odds would lengthen and the capital itself would be in danger of being taken, either by sudden assault or inexorable maneuver.

All around him, as he dismounted in front of his tent in the Tapp farmyard, was confusion. East and north, out in the jungle where the battle had raged for two incredibly savage days, the moans of the wounded, blue and gray, were heightened to screams of terror when a brisk wind sprang up, shortly after dark, and fanned random smouldering embers into flames that spread faster through the underbrush than an injured man could crawl. Dead pines, their sap long dried to rosin, burned like twenty-foot torches, and the low clouds took on an eerie yellow cast, as if they reflected the glow from molten sulphur on the floor of hell. The roar of wind-whipped flames through crackling brush was punctuated from time to time by a clatter resembling the sudden clash of pickets, as groups of disabled men from both sides, huddled together against a common danger, were engulfed by the inferno and the paper-wrapped charges in their pockets or cartridge boxes caught fire and exploded. While stretcher bearers and volunteers did what they could to rescue all the wounded they could reach, others along the Confederate line of battle — including those Third Corps veterans who had thought they were too tired for such exertion the night before — worked hard to strengthen their defenses for a renewal of the contest at first light tomorrow. They expected it, and so did their commander. Less soundly beaten, tactically, and with no greater losses, Hooker had pulled back across the river. But neither Lee nor his soldiers thought it likely that Grant would do what Fighting Joe had done; at least not yet. Judging their new opponent by his western reputation, as well as by his aggressive performance over the past two days, they believed he would stay and fight.

Next to a retreat, which he did not expect, Lee preferred a Federal attack, and that was what he had his men prepare for. If Grant was to be beaten further, to and beyond the point at which he would have no choice except to pull back across the river, it would have to come as the result of a bloody, morale-shattering repulse. In any case, the next move was up to the invader. Today's abortive follow-up assault by the First Corps, launched after the long delay occasioned in part by the fall of its commander, had shown only too clearly that the Confederates, whatever their successes when they caught the enemy off balance, lacked the strength to drive an opponent who was not only twice their size but was also braced for the shock in well-prepared intrenchments — and there could be no doubt that the Federals were as hard at work on their defenses, left and right and center, as the gray-backs were on their side of the line. Obliged as he was, now that all chances for surprise had been exhausted, to rule out a resumption of the offensive by his badly outnumbered army, Lee's decision not to attack amounted to a surrender of the initiative. This was a dangerous procedure against an adversary as nimble as Grant had shown himself to be in the campaign that brought Vicksburg under siege, but Lee had no choice. His hope, as he turned in for the night, was that Grant, despite his freedom to maneuver, would continue to forget his Vicksburg method and hold instead to the pattern of headlong assault he had followed so far in Virginia. That might lead to his repulse, and another repulse, if decisive enough, might lead to his destruction. The alternative for Lee, who had no such freedom to maneuver, was stalemate and defeat.

This second day of battle in the Wilderness had been Grant's hardest since the opening day at Shiloh, where his army and his reputation had also been threatened with destruction. Here as there, however — so long, at least, as the fighting was in progress — he bore the strain unruffled and "gave his orders calmly and coherently," one witness noted, "without any external sign of undue tension or agitation." Internally, a brief sequel was to show, he was a good deal more upset than he appeared, but outwardly, as he continued to sit on his stump atop the knoll in the Lacy meadow, smoking and whittling the critical hours away, he seemed altogether imperturbable. When word came, shortly before noon, that Hancock's flank had been turned and the left half of his army was in imminent danger of being routed, his re-action was to send more troops in that direction, together with additional supplies of ammunition, followed at 3 o'clock by orders for a counterattack to be launched at 6 to recover the lost ground and assure the holding of the Brock Road leading south. As it turned out, Hancock was himself assaulted a second time, nearly two hours before that, and had to use up so much of the ammunition in repelling the attack that not enough was left for compliance with the order. Besides, Grant by then was faced with an even graver crisis on his right. Sedgwick too had been flanked and was being routed, he was told, by a rebel force that had penetrated all the way to the Germanna Plank Road, cutting the army off from its nearest escape hatch back across the Rapidan.

Meade was a steadying influence, in this case as in others. "Nonsense," he snorted when a pair of flustered staffers came riding in from the crumpled flank after sundown to report that all was lost in that direction, including all hope of deliverance from the trap the rebels had sprung on Sedgwick and were about to enlarge in order to snap up everything in blue. "Nonsense! If they have broken our lines they can do nothing more tonight." He had confidence in John Sedgwick, the least excitable of his corps commanders, and he showed it by sending reinforcements from the center to help shore up the tottered right. Grant approved, of course, and had an even stronger reaction to an officer of higher rank who came crying that this second flank assault meant the end of the northern army unless it found some way to get out from under the blow about to fall. "This is a crisis that cannot be looked upon too seriously," he declared. "I know Lee's methods well by past experience. He will throw his whole army between us and the Rapidan, and cut us off completely from our communications." Grant was not a curser, but his patience had run out. He got up from the stump, took the cigar out of his mouth, and turned on this latest in the series of prophets of doom and idolators of his opponent. "Oh, I am heartily tired of hearing about what *Lee* is going to do," he said testily. "Some of you always seem to think he is suddenly going to turn a double somersault and land in our rear and on both our flanks at the same time. Go back to your command and try to think what we are going to do ourselves, instead of what *Lee* is going to do."

Further reports of havoc on the right were received with the same firmness, the same quick rejection of all notions of defeat, although — as Rawlins told a friend who rode over to headquarters to see him later that evening — "the coming of officer after officer with additional details soon made it apparent that the general was confronted by the greatest crisis in his life." By nightfall, however, Meade's assessment was confirmed; Sedgwick established a new and stronger line, half a mile south and east of the one he had lost to Gordon's flankers, who withdrew in the twilight from their position astride the road leading back to Germanna Ford. Then, and not until then, did the general-in-chief show the full effect of the strain he had been under, all this day and most of the day before. He broke. Yet even this was done with a degree of circumspection and detachment highly characteristic of the man. Not only was his personal collapse resisted until after the damage to both flanks had been repaired and the tactical danger had passed; it also occurred in the privacy of his quarters, rather than in the presence of his staff or gossip-hungry visitors. "When all proper measures had been taken," Rawlins confided, "Grant went into his tent, threw him-

self face downward on his cot, and gave way to the greatest emotion."
He wept, and though the chief of staff, who followed him into the tent,
declared that he had "never before seen him so deeply moved" and
that "nothing could be more certain than that he was stirred to the
very depths of his soul," he also observed that Grant gave way to the
strain "without uttering any word of doubt or discouragement." Another witness, a captain attached to Meade's headquarters — Charles F.
Adams, Jr, son and namesake of the ambassador — put it stronger. "I
never saw a man so agitated in my life," he said.

However violent the breakdown, the giving way to hysteria at this
point, it appeared that Grant wept more from the relief of tension
(after all, both flanks were well shored up by then) than out of continuing desperation. In any case it was soon over. When Rawlins's friend,
Brigadier General James H. Wilson — a friend of Grant's as well,
formerly a member of his military family and recently appointed by
him to command one of Sheridan's cavalry divisions — reached headquarters about 9 o'clock, less than an hour after the collapse Rawlins
presently described, he found the general "surrounded by his staff in
a state of perfect composure," as if nothing at all had happened. And
in fact nothing had: nothing that mattered, anyhow. Unlike Hooker,
who broke inside as a result of similar frustrations, Grant broke outside,
and then only in the privacy of his tent. He cracked, but the crack
healed so quickly that it had no effect whatever on the military
situation, then or later. Whereas Hooker had reacted by falling back
across the river, such a course was no more in Grant's mind now than
it had been that morning, before sunup, when he was accosted by a
journalist who was about to leave for Washington to file a story on the
first day's fighting. Asked if he had any message for the authorities
there, Grant, whose usual procedure was to hold off sending word of
his progress in battle until the news was good, thought it over briefly,
then replied: "If you see the President, tell him, from me, that, whatever happens, there will be no turning back."

Late that evening another journalist, New York *Herald* correspondent Sylvanus Cadwallader, was reassured to find that Grant
still felt that way about the matter, despite the tactical disappointments
of the day just past. Seated on opposite sides of a smouldering headquarters campfire, these two — the reporter because he was too depressed for sleep, and the general, he presumed, for the same reason —
were the last to turn in for the night. Formerly of the Chicago *Times*,
Cadwallader had been with Grant for nearly two years now, through
the greatest of his triumphs, as well as through a two-day drunk up
the Yazoo last summer, and for the first time, here in the Wilderness
tonight, he began, as he said afterward, "to question the grounds of
my faith in him. . . . We had waged two days of murderous battle, and
had but little to show for it. Judged by comparative losses, it had been

disastrous to the Union cause. We had been compelled by General Lee to fight him on a field of his own choosing, with the certainty of losing at least two men to his one, until he could be dislodged and driven from his vantage ground. [Yet] we had gained scarcely a rod of the battle-field at the close of the two days' contest." He wondered, as a result of this disconsolate review of the situation, whether he had followed Grant all this long way, through the conquest of Vicksburg and the deliverance of Chattanooga, only "to record his defeat and overthrow" when he came up against Lee in the Virginia thickets. Musing thus beside the dying embers of the campfire, he looked across its low glow at the lieutenant general, who seemed to be musing too. "His hat was drawn down over his face, the high collar of an old blue army overcoat turned up above his ears, one leg crossed over the other knee, eyes on the ashes in front." Only the fitful crossing and recrossing of his legs indicated that he was not asleep, and Cadwallader supposed that the general's thoughts were as gloomy as his own — until at last Grant spoke and disabused him of the notion. He began what the reporter termed "a pleasant chatty conversation upon indifferent subjects," none of which had anything to do with the fighting today or yesterday. As he got up from his chair to go to bed, however, he spoke briefly of "the sharp work General Lee had been giving us for a couple of days," then turned and went into his tent to get some sleep. That was all. But now that Cadwallader realized that the general had not been sharing them, he found that all his gloomy thoughts were gone. Grant opposed by Lee in Virginia, he perceived, was the same Grant he had known in Mississippi and Tennessee, where Pemberton and Bragg had been defeated. "It was the grandest mental sunburst of my life," he declared years later, looking back on the effect this abrupt realization had had on his state of mind from that time forward. "I had suddenly emerged from the slough of despond, to the solid bedrock of unwavering faith."

In the course of the next twenty hours or so — May 7 now, a Saturday — the whole army experienced a like sequence of reactions, from utter doubt to mental sunburst. Reconnaissance parties, working their way along and across the charred, smoky corridors last night's fires had left, found the rebels "fidgety and quick to shoot" but content, it seemed, to stay tightly buttoned up in the breastworks they had built or improved since yesterday. Lee preferred receiving to delivering an attack, and Grant apparently felt the same, since he issued no orders directing that one be made. For this the troops were duly thankful, especially those who had had a close-up look at the enemy lines, but they were also puzzled. The Federal choice seemed limited to attack or retreat, and they had not thought that Grant, despite the drubbing he had received these past two days, would give up quite this early. Still, word soon came that the pontoon bridges had been taken up at Germanna and relaid at Ely's Ford to hasten the passage of the ambulance train with the wounded, who were to be sent by rail to Washington. This meant that a withdrawal of the army, whether by that route or through Fredericksburg, would have to proceed by way of Chancellorsville, the hub where roads from the south and west converged to continue north and east. Swiftly now the conviction grew that everything blue would be headed in that direction after sundown. Sure enough, such guns as had found positions for direct support of the infantry — including those on the knoll in the Lacy meadow — were limbered and started rearward that afternoon, obviously to avoid jamming the roads that night, and in this the men saw confirmation of their worst judgments and suspicions. Grant, for all his western bulldog reputation, was merely another Pope, another Hooker, at best another Meade. They had been through this before; they recognized the signs. "Most of us thought it was another Chancellorsville," a Massachusetts infantryman would remember, while a Pennsylvania cavalryman recorded that his comrades used a homlier term to describe the predicted movement. They called it "another skedaddle."

If the Chancellorsville parallel was obvious — both battles had been waged in the same thicket, so to speak, between the same two armies, at the same time of year, and against the same Confederate commander — it was also, at this stage, disturbingly apt. By every tactical standard, although the earlier contest was often held up as a model of Federal ineptitude, the second was even worse-fought than the first. Hooker had had one flank turned; Grant had both. Hooker had achieved at least a measure of surprise in the opening stage of his campaign; Grant achieved none. Indeed, the latter had been surprised himself, while on a march designed to avoid battle on the very ground where this one raged for two horrendous days, not only without profit to the invaders, but also at a cost so disproportionate that it emphasized the wisdom of his original intention to avoid a confrontation on this terrain. Moreover, it was in the three-way assessment of casualties, Hooker's and Lee's, along with his own, that the comparison became least flattering. Grant lost 17,666 killed and wounded, captured and missing — about four hundred more than Hooker — while Lee, whose victory a year ago had cost him nearly 13,000 casualties, was losing a scant 7800, considerably fewer than half the number he inflicted. Here the comparison tended to break down, however, because for anything like comparable losses, North and South, it was necessary to go back to Fredericksburg, the most one-sided of all the large-scale Confederate triumphs. In plain fact, up to the point of obliging Grant to throw in the sponge and pull back across the river, Lee had never beaten an adversary so soundly as he had beaten this one in the course of the past two days.

What it all boiled down to was that Grant was whipped, and soundly whipped, if he would only admit it by retreating: which in turn was only a way of saying that he had not been whipped at all. "Whatever happens, there will be no turning back," he had said, and he would hold to that. The midafternoon displacement of the guns deployed along the Union line of battle was in preparation for a march, just as the troops assumed, but not in the direction they supposed. No more willing to accept a stalemate than he was to accept defeat, he would shift his ground, and in doing so he would hold to the offensive; he would move, not north toward Washington, but south toward Richmond, obliging Lee to conform if he was to protect the capital in his rear. Grant thus clung to the initiative Lee surrendered when he had exhausted all his chances for surprise. Now it was Grant's turn to try again for a surprise, and he planned accordingly.

The objective was Spotsylvania Courthouse, less than a dozen miles down the Brock Road from the turnpike intersection. With an early start, to be made as soon as darkness screened the movement from the rebels in their works across the way, it was not too much to expect that the leading elements would be in position there by dawn, plying shovels and swinging axes in the construction of fortifications which Lee, when he caught up at last, would be obliged to storm, even if the storming meant the destruction of his army, because they would stand between him and the capital whose protection was his prime concern. Warren would have the lead and would go all the way tonight, marching down the Brock Road across the rear of Hancock, who would fall in behind, once Warren had passed, and stop at Todd's Tavern, where he would guard the rear and slow the progress of the rebels if they attempted to follow by this route. Sedgwick would move east on the turnpike to Chancellorsville, then south by the road past Piney Branch Church to its junction with the Brock Road at Alsop, between Todd's Tavern and Spotsylvania, close in Warren's rear and also within supporting distance of Hancock. Burnside would follow Sedgwick after taking the plank road to Chancellorsville, but would call a halt at Piney Branch Church to protect the trains and the reserve artillery, which were to assemble at that point. Sheridan's troopers would probe the darkness in advance of both columns, and he was directed to patrol the western flank in strength, in order "to keep the corps commanders advised in time of the approach of the enemy." Warren and Sedgwick would move out at 8.30, Hancock and Burnside as soon thereafter as the roads were clear. The emphasis was on silence and speed, both highly desirable factors in a maneuver designed to outfox old man Lee.

Meade issued the march order at 3 o'clock, in compliance with earlier instructions from Grant, and when the guns pulled out soon afterward, taking a five-hour lead to clear the roads for the infantry that night, the troops along the line of battle drew their conclusions and went on exchanging occasional long-range shots with the graybacks while awaiting their turn to join what they were convinced was a retreat. Soon after dark the expected orders came; Warren's and Sedgwick's veterans slung their packs, fell in quietly on the Brock Road and the turnpike, and set out. To the surprise of the V Corps men, the march was south, in rear of Hancock's portion of the line. At first they thought that this was done to get them onto the plank road, leading east to Chancellorsville, but when they slogged past the intersection they knew that what they were headed for was not the Rapidan or the Rappahannock, but another battle somewhere south, beyond the unsuspecting rebel flank. Formerly glum, the column now began to buzz with talk. Packs were lighter; the step quickened; spirits rose with the growing realization that they were stealing another march on old man Lee. Then came cheers, as a group on horseback — "Give way, give way to the right," one of the riders kept calling to the soldiers on the road — doubled the column at a fast walk, equipment jingling. In the lead was Grant, a vague, stoop-shouldered figure, undersized-looking on Cincinnati, the largest of his mounts; the other horsemen were his staff. Cincinnati pranced and sidled, tossing his head at the sudden cheering, and the general, who had his hands full getting the big animal quieted down, told his companions to pass the word for the cheers to stop, lest they give the movement away to the Confederates sleeping behind their breastworks in the woods half a mile to the west. The cheering stopped, but not the buzz of excitement, the elation men felt at seeing their commander take the lead in an advance they had supposed was a retreat. They stepped out smartly; Todd's Tavern was just ahead, a little beyond the midway point on the march to Spotsylvania.

Up on the turnpike, where Sedgwick's troops were marching, the glad reaction was delayed until the head of the column had covered the gloomy half dozen miles to Chancellorsville. "The men seemed aged," a cannoneer noted as he watched them slog past a roadside artillery park. Weary from two days of savage fighting and two nights of practically no sleep, dejected by the notion that they were adding still another to the long list of retreats the army had made in the past three years, they plodded heavy-footed and heavy-hearted, scuffing their shoes in the dust on the pike leading eastward. Beyond Chancellorsville, just ahead, the road forked. A turn to the left, which they expected, meant recrossing the river at Ely's Ford, probably to undergo another reorganization under another new commander who would lead them, in the fullness of time, into another battle that would end in another retreat; that was the all-too-familiar pattern, so endless in repetition that at times it seemed a full account of the army's activities in the Old Dominion could be spanned in four short words, "Bull Run: da capo." But now a murmur, swelling rapidly to a chatter, began to move back down the column from its head, and presently each man could see for himself that the turn, beyond the ruins of the Chancellor mansion, had been to the right. They were headed south, not north; they were advancing, not retreating; Grant was giving them another go at Lee. And though on sober second thought a man might be of at least two minds about this, as a welcome or a dread thing to be facing, the immediate reaction was elation. There were cheers and even a few tossed caps, and long afterwards men were to say that, for them, this had been the high point of the war.

"Our spirits rose," one among them would recall. "We marched free. The men begin to sing. . . . That night we were happy."

✗ 2 ✗

Lee was marching too, by then, having divined once more his adversary's intention. That morning, after riding the length of his Wilderness line and finding it strangely quiet — in contrast, that is, to the fury of the past two days, when better than 25,000 men had been shot or captured, blue and gray, along that four-mile stretch of tangled woodland — he drew rein on the far left to talk with Gordon, who supposed from Grant's lack of aggressiveness that he was about to retreat. "Grant is not going to retreat," Lee told him. "He will move his army to Spotsylvania." Surprised, the Georgian asked if there was any evidence that the Federals were moving in that direction. "Not at all, not at all," Lee said as he turned Traveller's head to ride back down the line. "But that is the next point at which the armies will meet. Spotsylvania is now General Grant's best strategic point."

There was, as he said, no indication that Grant was moving, but there was at least negative evidence that when he did move — as obviously he would have to do, in lieu of assaulting the Wilderness intrenchments, before he used up the supplies in his train — it would not be back across the Rapidan; Ewell had sent word, shortly after sunup, that the Federals were dismantling their pontoon bridges at Germanna, and though Ely's Ford was still available it seemed unlikely that they would give up either if they intended to retire to the north bank. That left Fredericksburg as a possible escape route, and in fact there were reports from cavalry scouts that wagon traffic was heavy in that direction. But there was also a report from Stuart, waiting for Lee when he got back to the Widow Tapp's, that the Union cavalry had returned to Todd's Tavern this morning, in strength enough to drive the Confederate horsemen out and hold the place against all efforts to retake it. Todd's Tavern was down the Brock Road, midway between Grant's present position and Spotsylvania, which lay in the angle between the Richmond, Fredericksburg & Potomac and the Virginia Central railroads and offered an excellent approach to Hanover Junction, where the two lines crossed en route to Richmond from the north and west, both of them vital to the subsistence of Lee's army. Spotsylvania then, as Lee told Gordon, was his adversary's "best strategic point," if what he wanted was either to steal the lead in a race for Richmond or to take up a stout defensive position which Lee would be obliged to attack, whatever the tactical disadvantages, not only because it would sever his lines of supply, but also because it lay between him and the capital whose protection was his primary concern.

As evidence, this was far from conclusive, but it was persuasive enough to cause him to summon Brigadier General William N. Pendleton, the fifty-four-year-old former Episcopal rector who served as his chief of artillery, and instruct him to begin at once the cutting of a road through the woods, due south from the army's right flank on the Orange Plank Road, down to Shady Grove Church on the Catharpin Road — the midpoint for Lee, as Todd's Tavern, which was also on the Catharpin Road, was for Grant — to be used as soon as the first hard evidence reached headquarters that his opponent had taken, or was about to take, the first step in the race for Spotsylvania. The new road, if it was finished in time, would shorten the march by doing away with the need to backtrack down the plank road to Parker's Store before turning south; but this was small comfort alongside the knowledge that Grant even then would have a shorter route, a better road to travel all the way, and the advantage of deciding when the race would begin or whether, indeed, it would be run at all.

Another, and possibly greater, disadvantage lay in the fact that the lead corps on the march would be the First, since its position was on the right and therefore closest to the objective. Normally — as in the case of the movement into the Wilderness earlier this week — one or both of the other two corps, composed for the most part of Jackson's famed "foot cavalry," sought out the foe or rounded his flank to set him up for the Sunday punch methodical Old Peter would deliver when he came up in turn. Moreover, the corps was now to be commanded by a general, forty-two-year-old Richard Anderson, whose reputation had never been one for dash or fire and whose performance over the past year under Hill had been undistinguished at best, while at worst it had been a good deal less than that. At Gettysburg, for example, the kindest thing that could be said of the easy-going South Carolinian's lack of aggressiveness was that it had been due to sloth. His earlier record, made in the days when he commanded first a brigade and then a division under Longstreet, had been better, and this was Lee's main reason, together with the consideration that he was the senior major general with the army, for giving the post to him instead of Early, whom Lee otherwise preferred. A former member of the corps, which Early was not — Field was of recent appointment and Kershaw was still a brigadier — Anderson would be welcomed back by the officers and men of the two divisions he would command, while his Third Corps division would pass into the capable hands of Mahone, the army's senior brigadier. Yet this was perhaps the greatest of all gambles, the appointment of genial, un-inspired Dick Anderson to replace his most dependable lieutenant at a time when dash and fire, both of which were conspicuous by their absence from his record, seemed likely to be the decisive factors in a contest that would begin at any moment and had Richmond for the prize. The fact that Lee was more or less obliged to take that gamble was one measure of the extent to which attrition was wearing down the army in his charge.

That afternoon he saw that still another such change was in the offing. Riding his line for the second time that day, he stopped off at Third Corps headquarters, which had been set up in a deserted house about midway between the plank road and the turnpike, and found A. P. Hill looking paler and sicker than ever. Though red-bearded Little Powell was unwilling to relinquish command at this critical juncture, it was evident that he soon would be obliged to do so. This meant that, once more — with Anderson transferred and Heth and Wilcox in-sufficiently seasoned — a temporary successor would have to be found outside a corps whose regular chief was incapacitated. In this case, how-ever, the problem was simplified by having been faced beforehand, although in another connection; Jubal Early, runner-up as a candidate for command of the First Corps, would be brought in from the Second to lead the Third, at least until Hill recovered from the ailment he would not yet admit was grave enough to require him to step down. One dividend of this arrangement, similar to the one that had given Ander-son's division to Mahone, was that Early's division could pass to Gordon, for whom Lee felt a growing admiration because of his performance yesterday. Lee's conversation with Little Powell was interrupted about 4 o'clock by a staff colonel who came down from the attic of the house, where he had established an observation post by ripping some shingles from the roof, to report on something he had seen with the aid of a powerful marine glass trained on what he believed was Grant's head-quarters, a bit under two miles across the way. A number of heavy guns, held in reserve there all through the fighting, had just pulled out and headed south down the Brock Road, toward the Confederate right.

Though Grant's dead were still thickly strewn in the woods in front of his line, along with a few surviving wounded, and though none of the blue infantry had yet shown any sign of preparing for a shift, Lee took this limited artillery displacement as the first step in the race for Spotsylvania, which lay in the direction the guns had gone. Accordingly, he returned at once to the Tapp farm and issued orders for Anderson to march that night, taking Pendleton's just-cut southward trace through the woods to Shady Grove Church, then eastward across the Po River to Spotsylvania, which he was to hold against all comers: provided, of

course, that he got there first. The new corps commander's instructions
were for him to withdraw his two divisions from their present lines
as soon as darkness masked the movement from the enemy, then give the
troops a few hours' rest and sleep before setting out, at 3 o'clock in the
morning, on the race for the objective a dozen miles away. Ewell and
Hill were told to follow, in that order, as soon as they judged that the
situation in their front would justify withdrawal.

In accordance with these instructions, Anderson pulled back about
9 o'clock, but finding no suitable rest area in the immediate rear — fires
had sprung up again in the smouldering brush, fanned alive, as on the
past two nights, by the early evening breeze — he set out at once, down
Pendleton's trace, with the intention of making a bivouac farther south,
outside the smoky battle zone, in which the men could get some rest
between then and 3 a.m., the designated hour for the start of the march.
He had not gone far, however, before he abandoned the notion of
making any considerable halt at all. For one thing, there simply was no
usable stopping place this side of Shady Grove, down along the fringes
of the Wilderness, and for another the condition of the newly built
"road," stump-pocked and cluttered with fallen trunks and limbs, was
so miserable that the rate of march along it in the dark could scarcely
be much better than a mile-an-hour crawl. He perceived that if he was
to win the race for Spotsylvania he would need every minute of the
four or five hours he would gain by keeping moving instead of halting
in accordance with Lee's order; so he kept moving. Eager to do well on
his first assignment as a corps commander, Anderson here rendered Lee
and the Confederacy the greatest service of his career.

Jeb Stuart too had one of his great days, perhaps his finest, although
the action promised little of the glory he had chased in former times.
His three cavalry divisions, under Major Generals Wade Hampton,
Fitzhugh Lee, and W. H. F. Lee — the first was a wealthy South
Carolina planter-sportsman, fifteen years older at forty-six than his
cinnamon-bearded chief, while the second and third, Virginians both,
were respectively the commanding general's twenty-eight-year-old
nephew and twenty-seven-year-old son — were scattered about the
landscape to undertake the double task of protecting the Confederate
march and impeding that of the Federals. There were six brigades, two
in each division. Stuart assigned half of these to accompany the gray
column, shielding its flank and clearing its front, while the other three
moved out ahead to block and bedevil the bluecoats who were slogging
southeast on a parallel route, a couple of densely wooded miles away.
Brigadier General Thomas Rosser, detached from Hampton, led his
brigade directly to Spotsylvania, under instructions to hold the place,
if possible, until Anderson arrived. Fitz Lee meantime turned northwest,
up the Brock Road, to give his full attention to the Federals moving
down it: two brigades of mounted men opposing a four-division corps

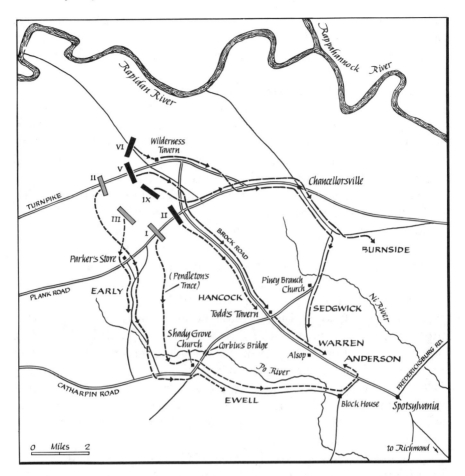

of infantry preceded by a cavalry division half again larger than his own. Near Todd's Tavern he put his troopers to work in the darkness, felling trees to obstruct the road as they withdrew. This gave the blue marchers almost as hard a time as their opponents were having on the crude trace across the way, and presently they had an added problem the Confederates did not have. When daylight began to filter through the thickets, the graybacks began to take potshots at the head and flanks of the Federal column, bringing it to a stumbling halt from time to time while details moved cautiously forward to flush the rebel marksmen out of their ambuscades. This continued, down past Alsop, to within two miles of Spotsylvania. There at last, beyond the fringes of the Wilderness and on comparatively open ground where he could bring his horse artillery into play, Fitz Lee had his dismounted men pile fence rails for a barricade and get down behind it, there in the dust of the road and the grass of the adjoining fields, for a last-ditch fight while couriers set out to bring Anderson cross-country to join in the defense. So far it had been cavalry against cavalry, and Fitz had managed to hold his own, despite the Union advantage of numbers and rapid-fire weapons. Sooner or later, however, the blue troopers would be replaced by infantry, brought forward Grant-style in a solid mass to overlap and overrun his flimsy breastwork. Unless Anderson came up fast and first, there would be nothing substantial between the Federals and Spotsylvania; Grant would have won the race whose prize was Richmond.

The sun by then was an hour high, and Anderson's two divisions, having covered nine miles on their all-night march out of the Wilderness, were ending an hour-long breakfast halt in the open fields, half a mile short of the Po and within about three miles of their objective. Sustained and heartened by the meal, such as it was — a frizzled chunk of fatty bacon, a piece of hardtack warmed and softened in the grease, and a cup of "coffee" boiled from roasted peanuts: poor fare, by any ordinary standards, but quite as much as they were accustomed to (and considerably more, in any case, than Warren's road-worn men received across the way) — the troops resumed their eastward march across the Po. Kershaw's division had the lead. About halfway to Spotsylvania, as he drew near a peculiar roadside dwelling built of squared logs and referred to locally as the Block House, he was met by a cavalry courier urging speed in the final heat of the race; Fitz Lee needed help, and he needed it quick. Fortified by the meager Sunday breakfast, the two front brigades quickened their step and hurried a mile northward, across the fields, to where the dismounted troopers were making their last-ditch stand on the Brock Road. "Run for our rail piles!" a cavalryman shouted as the men of the leading regiment came up. "The Federal infantry will reach them first if you don't run!"

They did run, and barely made it. Crouching behind the hastily improvised works, they opened fire on the advancing bluecoats at a range of sixty yards and blasted them back, at least for the moment. Thanks to Lee and Anderson, as well as to Stuart and Fitzhugh Lee — not to mention their own stout legs — they had won the race, although by a margin of less than a minute.

Whether it would stay won was another matter. Apparently not; for while the Federal infantry, recovering from the shock of having encountered more than cavalry in defense of the stacked rails, was massing for a heavier assault, Stuart sent word that Rosser's brigade had been driven out of Spotsylvania by a division of blue troopers who came surging down the road from Fredericksburg. Calm despite this evidence that the race had been lost after all, Anderson rerouted Kershaw's other two brigades, instructing them to proceed at once to the courthouse and fling the Federals out before they had time to intrench or bring in reinforcements. Field's division was coming up by now, and Anderson got the men into line on Kershaw's left, just in time to repulse a second and much heavier attack, which otherwise would have turned his western flank. No sooner had this been done than word came from the south that the blue horsemen had withdrawn from Spotsylvania of their own accord, apparently in the belief that they were escaping from a trap. Anderson at once summoned Kershaw's two detached brigades to rejoin him, leaving the defense of the town to Stuart, who by now had brought Fitz Lee down to help Rosser prevent a return by the rapid-firing Federals, in case they got their nerve back. Kershaw's men came hurrying up the Brock Road in time to extend his right and share in the repulse of a still heavier third assault by the Union infantry. This time, though they were punished even more cruelly in the course of their advance across the open fields and down the road, the bluecoats did not scatter or fall back as far as they had done before; they took up a semicircular position, just beyond easy rifle range of the defenders, and began to intrench.

This last was something the Confederates had been doing all along. Familiar enough with Grant's method by now to expect that at least one more all-out attack would be made on their line before the Union commander would be satisfied that it could not be shattered, they worked with picks and shovels and axes, bayonets and frying pans, tin cups and anything else that came to hand, improving and extending the fence-rail "works" they had inherited from Fitz Lee. By the time the sun swung past the overhead and the third assault had been repulsed, the artillery-studded defenses, extending about one mile west and half a mile east of the Brock Road, roughly a mile and a half from Spotsylvania, had grown as formidable as if they had been occupied for days. Across the way, however, in the woods and fields beyond the line the Federals were at work on, more blue troops were coming up and massing south of Alsop, obviously in preparation for a fourth assault, to be launched with greater numbers and on a broader front. Anderson's two divisions had fought Warren's four to a standstill, but now that Sedgwick's three were being added to the weight that Grant could bring to bear, the odds seemed overwhelming. About 2.30 the commanding general arrived, having ridden across the Po ahead of Ewell, whose corps by now was passing Shady Grove Church, a good two hours from the field of fight. Informed of the situation, Lee sent word for Ewell to hasten his march. This was no easy thing to ask of men who were trudging wearily through heat that was more like June than May, but fortunately the weather seemed to be having an even more lethargic effect on the Federals, who, unlike Ewell, had been marching all the previous night. It was 5 o'clock before they completed their leaden-legged dispositions and started forward. By then, Ewell's lead division had arrived and gone into position on Anderson's right, in time to block the attack on that flank and assist in driving the bluecoats back upon their works. It was smartly done, and that ended the fighting for the day.

Lee turned in early, rounding out a busy, fateful Sunday. Rising at 3 o'clock next morning — May 9; just one week ago today, although it seemed a great deal longer, he had stood on Clark's Mountain, extended a gauntleted hand, and told his assembled generals: "Grant will cross by one of those fords" — he wired the President of his success in frustrating the designs of the Army of the Potomac by winning the race for Spotsylvania: "We have succeeded so far in keeping on the front flank of that army, and impeding its progress, without a general engagement, which I will not bring on unless a favorable opportunity offers, or as a last resort. Every attack made upon us has been repelled and considerable damage done to the enemy." He expected the attacks to be renewed today, but he had little doubt of being able to withstand them, so long as the Federals held to the headlong methods they had favored on three of the past four days. A. P. Hill's corps, under Early — Hill had broken down at last, too sick to mount a horse, though he insisted on riding along in an ambulance in order to be with his men — was on the march even now, under instructions to come up on Ewell's right. With his army united and intrenched, dispositions complete and both flanks snug, Lee feared nothing the blue force could do, at least on this front, and he said as much in the telegram this morning. "With the blessing of God," he told Davis, "I trust we shall be able to prevent General Grant from reaching Richmond."

On the Union side, the trouble the leading elements had encountered in losing the race for Spotsylvania was compounded, in about equal parts, of weariness and Sheridan. Or perhaps it just came down to a prevalent loss of temper; weariness made tempers short, and Sheridan's was short enough already. In any case, after the elation that came with finding they were advancing, not retreating, the troops settled down to an ill-regulated march — stop and go, but mostly stop — that soon became what one of Sedgwick's men described as "a medley of phantasmagoria." Down on the Brock Road, tunneling southeast through the blackness, Warren's dust-choked marchers had it worse, for though the total distance was less, their progress was jerkier, mainly because of the cavalry up front, which seemed not only to have no definite notion of where it was going, but also to be in no hurry whatever to get there. One delay of about an hour, for example, was occasioned by an all-out fistfight between two cavalry regiments, one composed of veterans who effected a forcible exchange of their run-down horses for the well-groomed mounts of the other, made up of recruits who were not so green as to take such treatment without protest, even though the protest accomplished nothing except a prolongation of the delay. All this was short of Todd's Tavern, the midpoint of the march, where the real jam-up began.

Sheridan, like Stuart except that he began the campaign with 13,000 sabers, as compared to the Confederate 8500, had three divisions in his charge. One of these, James Wilson's, he ordered to move roundabout by the Fredericksburg road to Spotsylvania, while the other two, under Brigadier Generals Alfred Torbert and David Gregg, moved out in front of Warren's infantry to block the crossings of the Po before the rebels got there. So he intended. As all too often happened, however, someone failed to get the word — in this case, two someones: Gregg and Torbert. Reaching Todd's Tavern around midnight, Meade and his escort found the infantry column stalled and the crossroad jammed with Gregg's troopers, held up in turn by Torbert's, who were waiting for orders on the road beyond. Neither had been told what to do, and neither was doing anything at all. Meade got them moving by telling Gregg to proceed down the Catharpin Road toward Corbin's Bridge, where he would cover the wooded approaches from Parker's Store, and Torbert (or rather his senior brigadier, Wesley Merritt; Torbert was sick tonight) to remain on the Brock Road, clearing the way to Spotsylvania for the infantry and sending one brigade to the Block House, where it would stand in the path of any rebels on the march from Shady Grove. After issuing these instructions Meade sent word of them to Sheridan, wherever he might be, and rode back to get Warren on the move again. By now it was past 1 a.m. and the going was even slower than before. Up ahead, in the woods beyond the tavern, Merritt's troopers found the narrow road obstructed and enemy horsemen taking shots at them, out of the darkness, when they dismounted by lantern light to drag the just-felled timber from their path. This got worse as the march continued, especially for the infantry, with sudden starts and stops, races to close the resultant gaps, and long waits for the column to lurch into motion, segment by jangled segment. The first glimmers of daylight, so fervently hoped for in the gloom, only made things worse by improving the marksmanship of the snipers in the brush. Just before sunup Sheridan himself came pounding onto the scene on his big black horse. Fuming at Meade's highhanded "interference," which seemed to him to have exposed the cavalry to piecemeal destruction by scattering it about the countryside, he sent word for Wilson to withdraw at once from Spotsylvania, lest he be trapped there without adequate support when the rebel infantry arrived. Meantime the dismounted graybacks continued to snipe at the head of the column, toppling riders from their saddles. Beyond Alsop, within two miles of the courthouse — where, for all he knew, Wilson was being cut to pieces by superior numbers before he could pull out — Sheridan was galled even more by having to call on Warren's infantry to come forward with their bayonets and pry Fitz Lee's stubborn troopers out of their fence-rail barricade, which had proved too formidable for Merritt's frazzled cavalry to storm.

Chafed by the delays and aggravations, Warren was determined, now that Sheridan had his horsemen out of the way, to settle the issue before the defenders had time to strengthen their position on the low ridge just ahead, barely a mile and a half from the objective of his disjointed nightlong march. He told Brigadier General John C. Robinson, whose division had the lead, to attack as fast as his men could make it down the road. Weary, outdone, and unfed as they were, wobbly on their legs for lack of sleep, this wasn't very fast; but it was fast enough, as the thing developed, to accomplish their destruction in short order.

Robinson, a large, hairy New Yorker with an outsized beard and shaggy brows, a crusty manner, and a solid reputation earned in practically all of the major eastern battles, was at forty-seven Wadsworth's successor as the oldest division commander in the army. He studied the terrain, peering briefly out across a shallow valley, scarped along its bottom and lightly timbered, then up the gentle slope on its far side to where the graybacks crouched behind the fence rails they had stacked along the thickly wooded crest, about a quarter mile away. The scene had a certain bucolic charm, particularly by contrast with the smothering hug of the Wilderness, but Robinson found the situation tactically unpromising and he said as much to Warren, asking for time to bring up his three strung-out brigades and mass them before launching the assault. Warren said no, there was nothing across the way but dismounted cavalry; go in now, with the brigade at hand, and go in hard. This Robinson did, as hard at least as his winded men could manage after crossing the gullied valley and wheezing up the incline, only to have the rebel line explode in their faces, a scant sixty yards away. In quality and volume — a sudden, heavy bank of flame-stabbed smoke, jetting up and out, and a rattling clatter much too loud for carbines — the fire left no doubt that the line was occupied, not by cavalry, as the attackers had been informed when they set out, but by infantry who met them with massed volleys and blasted them back down the slope, a good deal faster than they had climbed it on their way to the explosion.

Nor was that the worst of the affair. By now the second brigade, four regiments of Maryland troops whose enlistments were to expire before the month was out, had come up and begun its descent into the valley, coincident with the arrival of Anderson's corps artillery on the ridge ahead. Startled to find the first wave of attackers in retreat from momentary contact with the rebels, the second was caught and churned up fearfully by a deluge of projectiles. The Marylanders broke, scrambling rearward in a race with the comrades they had intended to support. Dismayed and angered, Robinson hurried forward to rally them in person, but went down with a bullet through one knee. His third brigade fared no better, being struck in the flank and scattered by a savage counterattack, launched about as soon as it came up. This brought the casualty total to just under 1200 killed and wounded in less than an hour, while as many more were fugitives and stragglers, captured or otherwise unaccounted for. Robinson's knee wound cost him his leg, which was taken off that night. He was out of the war for keeps. And so, as another result of this brief engagement, was his division. It was disbanded next day, the remnants of its three cut-up brigades being distributed among the other divisions of the corps. Demoralized or not, these reinforcements were badly needed by all three, for they had suffered cruelly in the wake of Robinson's fiasco; Anderson's second division had arrived by then to strengthen the rebel line against the Federals, who were committed division by division, as fast as they came up, and division by division were repulsed. By the time Meade arrived, around midday, Warren had done his worst. He had to admit that he could not get over or around the Confederate intrenchments with what was left of his corps. Meade told him to hold what he had, then summoned Sedgwick from his reserve position, north of Alsop, to add the weight of his three divisions to the attack.

This took time — five hours, in all; Sedgwick's men were weary too — but the interim was livened, at any rate for the gossip-hungry clerks and staff, by a personality clash. Sheridan dropped by army headquarters, still fuming about last night's "interference," and Meade, losing his famous temper at last, retorted hotly that the cavalry had been doing less than had been expected of it ever since the campaign opened. That the charge was true did not make it any more acceptable to Sheridan, who replied, bristling, that he considered the remark a calculated insult. Meade recovered his balance for a moment. "I didn't mean that," he said earnestly, placing one hand on the cavalryman's shoulder in a conciliatory gesture. Sheridan stepped back out of reach ("All the Hotspur in his nature was aroused," a staff observer later wrote) and continued his protest. If the cavalry had done less than had been hoped for, he declared, it was not his fault, but Meade's; Meade had countermanded his orders, interfered with his tactical dispositions, and worst of all had kept his troopers hobbled by assigning them such unprofitable and distractive tasks as guarding the slow-plodding trains and providing escorts for the brass. If results were what Meade wanted, he should let the cavalry function as it was meant to function — on its own, as a compact hard-hitting body. Give him a free rein, Sheridan said, and he would tackle Jeb Stuart on his own ground, deep in the Confederate rear, and whip him out of his boots. The argument continued, both men getting madder by the minute, until Meade at last decided there was only one way to resolve their differences. He went to Grant.

Three days ago, the general-in-chief's reaction to a similar confrontation had been decisive. "You ought to put him under arrest," he had said of the riled-up Griffin. Today though, having heard Meade out, he seemed more amused than angered: especially by the bandy-legged cavalryman's reported claim that he would whip Jeb Stuart out of his boots if Meade would only turn him loose. "Did Sheridan say that?" he asked. Meade nodded. "Well," Grant said, "he generally knows what he's talking about. Let him start right out and do it."

Meade, having thus been taught the difference between eastern and western insubordination, returned to his own headquarters and issued the order; Sheridan would take off next morning, with all three of his divisions, on a maneuver designed to provoke Stuart into hand-to-hand combat by threatening the capital in his rear. Meantime Sedgwick was coming up. By 5 o'clock he had his three divisions in line alongside what was left of Warren's four, and all seven went forward, more or less together, in a final attempt to turn the day's disjointed fighting into a Union victory by taking possession of Spotsylvania, a mile and a half beyond the rebel works. It failed, as the earlier attacks had failed, because Lee again managed to get enough of his veterans — in this case, Ewell's lead division — up to the critical point in time to prevent a breakthrough. His losses had been light today, while Meade's had been comparatively heavy. "The ground was new to everyone, and the troops were tired," Meade's chief of staff explained.

For Grant, who smoked as he watched the sunset repulse, the day had been a grievous disappointment. Not only had he failed to pass Lee's front, but the resultant tactical situation in which he now found himself seemed to favor the defensive at least as much as had been the case in the one he abandoned, just last night, in the belief that it offered him little or no chance to achieve the Cannae he was seeking. Moreover, though he said that he left the Wilderness because he saw no profit in assaulting the works Lee's men had thrown up in the brush, the fortifications here were even more formidable, laid out on dominant ground between unfordable rivers, and getting stronger by the hour. Still smoking, he looked out across the shallow valley where so many of Warren's men had fallen — tousled rag-doll shapes becoming indistinguishable as the daylight faded into dusk — then turned, as imperturbable as ever, and rode back to his tent, there to make a study of the situation, based on such information as had been gathered.

Today's reconnaissance (for that was all it came to, in the end) had been costly, and next morning it grew more so, although nothing so patently wasteful as a repetition of yesterday's headlong approach to the problem was attempted. While Hancock and Burnside were on the march, summoned to come up on the right and left, Warren and Sedgwick limited their activities to improving their intrenchments and making a cautious investigation of the Confederate position. Restricted in scope by the absence of the cavalry, which had taken off soon after sunrise to challenge Stuart, this last was a gingerly business at best. Rebel marksmen, equipped with imported Whitworth rifles mounting telescopic sights, were quick to draw a bead on anything blue that moved, especially if it had a glint of brass about the shoulders. Moreover, in addition to this lack of respect for rank, they seemed to have none for the supposed reduction of accuracy by distance, with the result that there was a good deal of ducking and dodging on the Union side, even though the range was sometimes as great as half a mile. This not only interfered with work, it was also thought to be detrimental to discipline and morale. John Sedgwick looked at it that way, for one, and reproved his troops for flinching from a danger so remote. "What? Men dodging this way for single bullets?" he exclaimed when he saw one outfit react in such a manner to a far-off sniper. "What will you do when they open fire along the whole line? I am ashamed of you. They couldn't hit an elephant at this distance." The soldiers wanted to believe him, partly because they admired him so — "Uncle John," they called him with affection — but the flesh, being thus exposed, was weak; they continued to flinch at the crack of the sharpshooter's rifle, even though it was a good 800 yards away, and at the quick, unnerving whiplash of near misses, which seemed to part the hair of every man at once. "I'm ashamed of you, dodging that way," Sedgwick said again, laughing, and repeated: "They couldn't hit an elephant at this distance." Next time the glass-sighted Whitworth cracked, a couple of minutes later, Sedgwick's chief of staff was startled to see the fifty-year-old general stiffen, as if in profound surprise, and slowly turn his head to show blood spurting from a half-inch hole just under his left eye. He pitched forward, taking the unbraced colonel down with him, and though the doctors did what they could to help, they could not staunch or even slow the steady spurt of blood from the neat new hole beside his cheekbone. He smiled strangely, as if to acknowledge the dark humor of what had turned out to be his last remark, and did not speak again. Within a few minutes he was dead.

Sudden as it was, his death was a knee-buckling shock to the men of his corps, who had made him the best-loved general in the army. Besides, when corps commanders started toppling, alive one minute and dead the next, struck down as if by a bolt of blue-sky lightning, who was safe? All down the line, from brigadiers to privates, spirits were heavy with intimations of mortality. Sorrowfully, the staff carried his body back to army headquarters and laid it in a bower of evergreens beside the road, there to receive the salute of passing troops till nightfall, when he began the journey north to Cornwall Hollow, his home in the Connecticut Berkshires. Nor was the grieving limited to those who had served under him, or even under the same flag today; R. E. Lee, across the way, was saddened by this final news of his old friend. Meade wept, and Grant himself was stunned when he heard that Sedgwick had been hit. "Is he really dead?" he asked. Later, after characterizing the fallen general as one who "was never at fault when serious work was to be done," he told his staff that Sedgwick's loss was worse for him than the loss of a whole division. For the present, though, he found it hard to accept the fact that he was gone. "Is he really dead?" he asked again.

One fact was clear, in any case, and this was that a great many men of various ranks, now alive, were likely to be dead before long if they were ordered to overrun the intrenchments to their front. Formidable as these works had seemed at sundown, they were downright awesome this morning after an unmolested night of labor by the troops who manned them. Studded with guns at critical points throughout its convex three-mile length, Lee's Spotsylvania line was constructed, Meade's chief of staff declared, "in a manner unknown to European warfare, and, indeed, in a manner new to warfare in this country." Actually, it was not so much the novelty of the individual engineering techniques that made this log-and-dirt barrier so forbidding; it was the combination of them into a single construction of interlocking parts, the canny use of natural features of the terrain, and the speed with which the butternut veterans, familiar by now with the fury of Grant's assaults, had accomplished their intricate task. Traverses zigzagged to provide cover against enfilade fire from artillery, and head logs, chocked a few inches above the hard-packed spoil on the enemy side of the trench, afforded riflemen a protected slit through which they could take unruffled aim at whatever came their way. Where there were woods in front of the line, the trees were slashed to deny concealment for two hundred yards or more, and wherever the ground was open or insufficiently obstructed, timber barricades called abatis were installed within easy rifle range, bristling with sharpened sticks to entangle or slow the attackers while the defenders, more or less at their leisure, picked them off. For Grant, the prospect was altogether grim. To assault seemed suicidal, and yet to do nothing was militarily unsound, since a stalemate under such circumstances might well allow Lee to detach troops for operations against Butler or Sigel, back near Richmond or out in the Shenandoah Valley. On the other hand, to maneuver him out of position again by swinging wide around one of his flanks would amount to nothing more than a postponement of the inevitable showdown, which in that case would occur in closer proximity to his capital and would probably result in his being reinforced by units from the garrison charged with its ultimate defense. Grant pondered these three alternatives, unwelcome as they were, until about midday, when Burnside, coming up on the left, provided information which suggested a fourth alternative, more acceptable than the others. While making his far-out eastern swing across Ni River, the ruff-whiskered general reported, he had encountered Confederate infantry, and though he had not had much trouble driving them off, it seemed to him that they might be the leading element of a detached force of considerable strength, engaged in a deep penetration of the Federal left rear for a strike at the army's Fredericksburg supply base.

Burnside could scarcely be classed as a skilled assessor of enemy intentions, but in the absence of Sheridan's cavalry, which might otherwise have been sent out to confirm or refute the validity of the report, Grant accepted the information at face value, partly on grounds that such a move would be altogether in character for Lee. By now, after the buffeting he had taken in the course of the past five days, the old fox must be groping rather desperately in his bag of tricks for some such table-turning maneuver as the one he had devised, under similar circumstances, when he sent Jackson wide around Pope's flank for a strike at the supply base in his rear, compelling that hapless commander to abandon his position in short order. Grant's reaction was equally characteristic, and quite different. Instead of allowing concern for his base to deflect him from his purpose, he saw in this supposed development a chance to strike from an unexpected direction while his opponent's attention was distracted and his army was divided. Hancock, who had come up on the right, was instructed to detach one division, as a possible reinforcement for Burnside, and proceed westward with the other three for an upstream crossing of the Po. A fast march down the opposite bank — first south, to reach the road from Shady Grove, then eastward along it to the bridge one mile west of the Block House — would put him in position for a second crossing, well below the point where the rebel flank was anchored, and a sudden descent on Lee's left rear. At worst, this should bring the Confederates out of their intrenchments by obliging them to turn and meet the unexpected threat; while at best, assailed as they would be from two directions, north and south, it would result in their destruction. In any case that was the plan, devised in reaction to Burnside's report, and Grant considered it well worth a try, especially since the ablest of his surviving corps commanders was charged with its execution.

Hancock crossed upstream that afternoon, putting in three pontoon bridges, and encountered only sporadic opposition from butternut horsemen on the prowl. Even so, he had not reached the Shady Grove Road, leading eastward to the downstream point where he was to make the crossing that would land him in Lee's rear, before darkness obliged all three divisions to call a halt in the woods on the south bank. An early start next morning — Tuesday, May 10 — brought the head of the column within easy reach of Blockhouse Bridge by sunup. To Hancock's surprise, there on the opposite bank, fortifications had been thrown up overnight and were occupied in considerable strength, bristling with guns trained expectantly on the bridge and its approaches. Once more, with the help of his hard-working cavalry, Lee had forestalled a maneuver designed to discomfit or destroy him; Hancock could only regret that he had not waited until this morning to make his upstream crossing, in which case he would not have afforded the rebels a full night to work on their plans for his reception. Not much given to spilt-milk thinking, he devised an alternate crossing, half a mile downriver, and got one division in motion at once, intending to follow with the other two, when a courier arrived from Meade with instructions for a quick return by two of his divisions to their former position in line on the right of Warren. He himself was to come back with them, the message directed, to take charge of his and Warren's corps for an all-out frontal attack on the Confederate intrenchments at 5 o'clock that afternoon.... Hancock scarcely knew what to make of this sudden change of plans. By now, one brigade of the advance division was across the river; he had only to follow with the other two divisions and Lee's flank would be turned; instead of which, apparently, Meade intended to revert to a direct assault, Fredericksburg style, on fortifications that were admittedly the most formidable ever constructed by an army in the field. Still, orders were orders, comprehensible or not. Recalling the crossed brigade, lest it be gobbled up in the bridgehead it was holding, he left his lead division behind, with instructions to continue what had now become no more than a demonstration, and set out at once with the other two to recross the Po by the three bridges they had installed with such high hopes the day before.

Back on the main front, to which Hancock was returning, Grant had ordered the change in plans as a result of Lee's failure to sustain Burnside's assessment that he had detached a major portion of his army for a strike at the Union supply base. In point of fact, what the IX Corps had encountered on its approach march, down across the Ni the day before, had not been infantry at all, but more of Stuart's ubiquitous cavalry, dismounted as skirmishers to delay the Federal concentration; Burnside had simply been mistaken, here as elsewhere in his career, and Grant decided that if Lee had not divided his army, it would be unwise for him to divide his own, particularly if this involved detaching Hancock, his most dependable lieutenant, who would be needed to help meet whatever crisis Lee had it in mind to precipitate, not in theory but in fact. Accordingly, he had had Meade summon Hancock back to his former position alongside Warren, who had also contributed to the decision by informing his superiors that, despite his failure yesterday, he believed he could score a breakthrough today if he was properly supported. It was true, the attack would be made against what seemed to be the most impregnable part of the rebel line, but when Warren declared that he had examined it carefully and believed it could be broken, Grant was altogether willing to give him the chance to prove his claim. Hancock would come up on his right, and Sedgwick's corps was already posted on his left; at 5 o'clock they would all go forward together, and if Warren's judgment proved sound, Lee's defenses would be pierced, his position overrun, and his army shattered. Richmond then would be Grant's for the taking, which in turn would mean that the war was approximately over, all but the incidental task of picking up the pieces.

It did not work out that way for a variety of reasons. Like Sheridan two days ago, Warren was anxious to accomplish something solid that would cancel his poor showing up to now, and this apparently made him oversanguine in his assessment of the chances for a break-through, as well as overeager to get started. Faulty judgment thus laid the groundwork for a failure which impatience served to enlarge. Around 3.30, with Sedgwick's corps alerted on his left and one of Hancock's divisions back in position on his right, he decided that to wait another hour and a half for jump-off time, as scheduled, would be to risk losing the opportunity he believed he saw. Or perhaps he acted out of knowledge that Hancock, when he came up on the right, would take command by virtue of his rank. In any case he appealed to Grant, through Meade, for permission to attack at once. Always ready to encourage aggressiveness, Grant was willing, and Warren — who had put on his dress uniform that morning, evidently for the purpose of making a good appearance on what he hoped would be his finest day since Gettysburg — went forward, around 4 o'clock; into chaos. Exposed in the slashings and snagged by the abatis, his troops were badly cut up, their ranks thrown into disorder by artillery and rifle fire from the flanks and dead ahead. Some among the bravest pressed on to within point-blank range of the rebel works, and a few even made it to the crest of the parapet. But that was all; there was no penetration anywhere along the line. Warren kept trying, only to have the process repeated. He was deeply discouraged at seeing his hopes break in blood on the rim of the intrenchments, even though Grant and Meade were not: not so deeply, at any rate, that it caused them to discontinue the effort to score a breakthrough here today. When Hancock arrived soon after 5 o'clock with his other division, back at last from his overnight excursion on the far side of the Po, he was ordered to resume the attack at 6.30, taking charge of all the troops on the right, his own and Warren's.

Elsewhere along the concave Union line, north and northwest of Spotsylvania, results had been no better up to now. Posted astride the Fredericksburg Road to block the movement Lee failed to make, Burnside had scarcely been engaged; his only consequential loss today was the commander of his lead division, Brigadier General T. G. Stevenson, a young Bostonian of high promise, who was killed instantly, much as Sedgwick had been the day before, by a long-range sniper. Sedgwick's corps, headed now by Horatio Wright, who was also a Connecticut-born professional, had made no more of a dent in the enemy defenses than Warren's corps had done, but a close-up look at the rebel works had given one brigade commander a notion of how to go about making a good deal more than a dent.

This was Colonel Emory Upton, a twenty-four-year-old New Yorker who had graduated from West Point less than a month after Sumter and since then, aside from a brief, unhappy period as a drill instructor of volunteers, had served with distinction in all the army's battles, winning five promotions along the way. Strong on theory, as well as action, Upton returned from a personal examination of the Confederate fortifications to report to his division chief, Wright's successor Brigadier General David Russell, that he believed he knew a way to score a breakthrough in short order. His notion was that the troops should attack on a narrow front, four lines deep, without pausing to fire until a limited penetration had been achieved; whereupon the first line would fan out left and right to widen the breach and the second would plunge straight ahead to deepen it, supported by the third and fourth, which would form the reserve and be called upon, as needed, in any or all of the three directions. Russell liked the plan and took Upton to see the corps commander, who liked it too. In fact, Wright liked it so well that he not only gave the young colonel twelve regiments to use in the attack, but also arranged to have a full division standing by to exploit whatever success was gained. Speed and precision being the main elements, together with a clear distribution of duties, Upton took the dozen unit commanders forward to the line of departure, along the edge of a dense belt of pines 200 yards from the rebel works, and indicated to each of them just what was expected of him. The point selected for assault was about midway down the western face of a salient which Ewell's corps had occupied to deny the Federals possession of some high ground where they might otherwise have posted batteries to enfilade this central portion of Lee's line, the two wings of which slanted sharply back from the salient or "angle," as it was called. Rebel guns were thick in there, thicker than anywhere else along the line, but it was Upton's plan to get among them fast and overwhelm the crews before they had much chance to use them. Having explained all this to the individual leaders, and shown them their objectives on the map and on the ground, he told them to bring their regiments forward, one at a time to avoid attracting attention to the buildup, and post them under cover for the assault, which was set for 6 o'clock, one hour before sunset and two before dark.

At ten minutes past the appointed time, having waited for the pre-arranged bombardment to die down, Upton gave the signal and the column started forward with a cheer, three regiments in each of its four lines. Almost at once the rebel guns took up the challenge, blasting away at the mass of bluecoats running toward them across the field, but despite the delay involved in breaking through the tangled abatis, set up about midway between the woods and the intrenchments, men of all three leading regiments were mounting the parapet within five minutes of the jump-off. These first arrivers were shot or bayonetted or clubbed back — Upton later reported that at this stage the defenders "absolutely refused to yield the ground" — but as others came up, the weight of numbers began to tell. Presently there was hand-to-hand fighting in the trenches, which broke off when the second wave of attackers arrived and the badly outweighed Confederates turned and ran for their secondary defenses, just under 200 yards in their rear. Many did not make it, being captured or shot down. Meantime the first Federal line had fanned out left and right, widening the gap, and the reserves were surging forward to support the second in its continued penetration. So far, everything had worked precisely as Upton had planned; the rebel line was broken. Whether the break would be extended, or even remain — Confederate reinforcements were coming in fast by then from other parts of the salient — depended now on the division Wright had given the assignment of exploiting just such a success as had been gained.

This was not one of his own divisions, but the one that had been detached from Hancock when he crossed the Po the day before. Originally intended for support of the IX Corps, it had been attached to Wright when the threat to Burnside turned out to be nonexistent, and Wright had given its commander, Gershom Mott, instructions to support Upton by advancing simultaneously on the apex of the "angle," thus to divert the attention of the defenders away from the main effort, midway down the western face of the salient; after which he was to move fast to consolidate, and if possible enlarge, whatever gains had been scored in that direction. As it turned out, he was only too successful, both for his own sake and for Upton's, in carrying out the first half of this assignment. Forming his two brigades in full view of the objective, half a mile away, Mott did such a thorough job of attracting the attention of the rebels (particularly the gunners, who had crowded into that narrow space no fewer than 22 pieces of artillery with which to take him under fire across half a mile of open ground) that his division was knocked to pieces within minutes. Already badly shaken by their Wilderness experience, the troops milled about briefly under this pounding, some of them attempting ineffectively to return the fire with their outranged rifles, then scuttled backward in confusion, seeking cover and concealment. Staff officers, sent out to search for them that evening, found them deep in the rearward woods, huddled in groups about their regimental flags and boiling coffee to help them recover from the shock. Like Robinson's division, which had gone out of existence as a result of its misadventure two days ago, Mott's too would presently be abolished, the remnant of its two brigades being assigned three days afterward to another division in Hancock's corps.

But that was later. A more immediate consequence of the rout was that Upton's breakthrough went for nothing, not only because he was left without support, but also because the defenders now were free to concentrate all their attention and strength on healing the breach. This they were quick to do, obliging Upton to fight his way out of the rebel lines with much of the fervor and urgency he had displayed while fighting his way in. Darkness, gathering fast after sundown, was a help in the disengagement; all twelve regiments made it back to their own lines, having suffered about one thousand casualties. That was also about the number they inflicted, mostly in the form of prisoners taken in the initial rush and escorted into the Federal lines before the counterattack obliged their captors to follow in their wake. Far on the right, Hancock's attack, deferred till sunset, was repulsed at about the same time, as decisively as Warren's had been earlier, and Burnside continued his pointless vigil on the left. Night came down as the fighting ended. Men sat around campfires and discussed the events of the day, which provoked much blame of Mott and praise for Upton. Across the way, notes faint in the distance and filtered through the trees, a Confederate band lent an eerie touch to the scene by playing "Nearer, My God, to Thee," but this was offset to some extent, or anyhow balanced, when a Union band responded with the "Dead March" from *Saul*.

One of Upton's warmest admirers was the general-in-chief, who rewarded him with a battlefield promotion — subject, of course, to Washington approval — "for gallant and meritorious services." Much encouraged by the young colonel's tactical contribution, which he saw as the key to Lee's undoing if the maneuver could be repeated on a larger scale and properly supported, Grant was in high spirits. A head-quarters orderly saw him talking to Meade about the prospect that night with unaccustomed animation, puffing rapidly on a cigar. "A brigade today," he was saying; "we'll try a corps tomorrow."

Thinking it over he realized however that tomorrow would be too soon. One trouble with today's attack was that it had been launched with not enough daylight left for its full exploitation; dawn would be a much better time in that regard, and the preceding darkness would help to conceal the massing of large bodies of troops within charging distance of the rebel works. So Grant, having ruled out tomorrow, de-cided that the assault would be delivered at first light on the following day, May 12 — which would also give him plenty of time for briefing all commanders, high and low, and an unhurried movement of units, large and small, into their designated jump-off areas. Given the method, the tactical execution was fairly obvious. Hancock would be shifted from the far right to the center, where he would be in charge of the main effort, and he would make it with his whole corps, against the very point that Mott had failed to hit today, the apex of the "angle," the military theory being that the tip of a salient was hard to defend because fire from the lines slanting back from that forward point could not converge on a force advancing from dead ahead. It was true, this theory had not applied too well on that same ground today; Mott had been wrecked before he got within reach of the objective. But Hancock's assault would be delivered Upton-style, without pauses for alignment or for firing, and if it worked as well for him as it had worked for Upton, his men would be up to the enemy works, and maybe over them, before the defenders had time to offer much resistance. Moreover this attack, unlike the one today, would be heavily supported. Burnside, off on the left, would move up close tomorrow night and launch a simultaneous assault next morning against the salient's eastern face, while Wright and Warren kept up the pressure on the right and the far right. Further details could be worked out next day, when the formal order was drawn up. In any case, after Upton's demonstration late today, a Tuesday, Grant had little doubt that Lee's defenses would be breached on Thursday and that careful planning would see to it that the breach was enlarged to victory proportions. He went to bed in a better frame of mind than he had done on any of the other five nights since May 4, when his army completed its crossing of the Rapidan unopposed.

That his mood was still the same on Wednesday, hopeful and determined, was demonstrated shortly after breakfast by his response to a request from a distinguished visitor, U. S. Representative Elihu B. Washburne of Illinois, that he give him some word of encouragement to take back to Washington with him. Grant's congressional guardian angel from the outset of the war, Washburne had spent the past week at headquarters, where, incongruous in somber civilian broadcloth amid the panoply of the staff, he had been something of a puzzle to the troops; they could not figure who or what he was, until a wit explained that the general, with his usual concern for the eventualities, had brought his private undertaker along on the campaign. Now that he was returning to his duties at the capital, the congressman told Grant as they stood outside the latter's tent to say goodbye, it might be a good idea to relieve the anxiety of the President and the Secretary of War by sending them some word on the progress of the fighting here in Virginia. "I know they would be greatly gratified," Washburne said, "if I could carry a message from you giving what encouragement you can as to the situation." Grant looked doubtful. He was aware that anything of the kind would be released to the public, and he did not want to be hurt, as others before him had been hurt, by the boomerang effect of overoptimistic statements. Pleased though he was with his progress so far, he replied, he knew that the road ahead was a long one and he was therefore "anxious not to say anything just now that might hold out false hopes to the people." He hesitated, then added: "However, I will write a letter to Halleck, as I generally communicate through him, giving the general situation, and you can take it with you." He stepped inside the tent, sat down at his field desk, and after heading a sheet of paper, "Near Spottsylvania C. H., May 11, 1864 — 8.30 a.m.," scribbled a couple of hundred words, puffing away at his cigar as he wrote. "We have now ended our sixth day of very hard fighting," he informed Halleck. "The result up to this time is much in our favor. But our losses have been heavy, as well as those of the enemy.... I am now sending back to Belle Plain all my wagons for a fresh supply of provisions and ammunition, and purpose to fight it out on this line if it takes all summer. . . . I am satisfied the enemy are very shaky, and are only kept up to the mark by the greatest exertions on the part of their officers and by keeping them intrenched in every position they take."

When he finished he had a clerk make a fair copy, which he then signed and folded and gave to Washburne, along with a farewell handshake, before returning to work on his plans for tomorrow's dawn assault. Staff officers read the retained draft of the letter, one afterwards recalled, without finding in it anything unusual or "epigrammatic" until a few days later, when the New York papers reached camp with excerpts from it splashed across their front pages in large headlines — particularly a phrase or sentence which someone, either the copyist here or another at the far end, polished up a bit: "I propose to fight it out on this line if it takes all summer." That caught the attention of the editors, and through them the public, with a force unequaled by anything Grant had said or written since the Unconditional Surrender note at Donelson, more than two years ago. "I propose to move immediately upon your works" had passed into history as a watchword signifying Federal determination to press for total victory over the forces in rebellion, and so too, now, did "I propose to fight it out on this line if it takes all summer."

Grant's assessment of the Confederates as "very shaky" indicated that he had not really believed it would take "all summer" to settle the issue at hand that Wednesday morning, north of Spotsylvania. By mid-afternoon — coincident with a sudden change in the weather, brought on by a light drizzle of rain that dropped the temperature from the unseasonable high it had been holding for the past few days — the field order for tomorrow's attack was being distributed to the commanders of all four corps. Already in close proximity to the enemy along their respective portions of the line, Warren and Wright would remain more or less where they were, and Burnside had only a limited adjustment to make. It was otherwise with Hancock, who had to shift three of his divisions into position with the fourth, Mott's, which by now, although considerably diminished and dejected, had been reassembled just in rear of the area where it had begun its ill-fated advance the day before. The division he had left beyond the Po when he returned with the other two, in accordance with orders from Meade, had also recrossed the river after a clash with a rebel force Lee sent over from his right, and in this rear-guard action the division had had to leave behind a gun that, in the haste of the withdrawal, got wedged so tightly between two trees that it could not be freed. Hancock took this hard, the more so because it was the only piece of artillery the II Corps had ever lost in battle, and he was determined to get full revenge tomorrow.

Just now, though, he had his hands full getting his troops into position for the attack at first light, which the almanac said would come at 4 a.m. The march began at dusk, along a narrow road soon churned to mud by a pelting rain that seemed to be getting harder by the hour. It was midnight before the head of the column reached the jump-off area and the four divisions, three of them wet and cold from their rainy march, started forming in the dripping woods. This too was a difficult business, for more reasons than the unpleasantness of the weather or the loss of sleep and lack of food. Here on reconnaissance earlier that day, unable to see far or clearly through the steely curtain of rain, Hancock had tried to get Mott's disheartened men to drive the enemy pickets back so he could get a look at the objective; but little or nothing came of the attempt — they had too vivid a memory of what those 22 guns up there had done to them the day before — with the result that his examination of the apex of the "angle," along with most of the intervening ground across which he would charge, had practically been limited to what he could learn from the map. And so it was to-night, in the rain and darkness. The best Hancock could do was give his division commanders a compass bearing, derived from the map by drawing a line connecting a house in their rear with a house in the approximate center of the rebel salient, and tell them to move in that direction when they received his order to advance.

Four o'clock came, but not daylight; the almanac had not taken the rain or fog into account. Finally at 4.30, though there still was scarcely a glimmer of light from what the compass showed to be the east, word came for the lead division to go forward, followed closely by the other three.

Fearing the worst as they stumbled forward through fog so dense that it held back the dawn, Hancock and his soldiers were in better luck than they had any way of knowing. For one thing, those 22 guns assigned to defend the apex of the salient up ahead, which they expected to start roaring at any moment, tearing their close-packed ranks with shot and shell within seconds of hearing a picket give the alarm, were by no means the threat they had been two days ago, when they all but demolished one of these four divisions attempting this same thing on this same ground. They were in fact no threat at all. They were not there. They had been withdrawn the night before, as the result of an overdue error by Lee, whose intelligence machinery, after a week of smooth if not uncanny functioning, had finally slipped a cog.

Reports of activity beyond the Union lines had been coming in from various sources all the previous afternoon. A lookout perched in the belfry of a Spotsylvania church, which commanded a view of the roads in rear of the enemy left, informed headquarters of what seemed to be a large-scale withdrawal in that direction, and this was confirmed between 4 and 5 o'clock by two messages from Lee's cavalryman son, whose division — left behind by Stuart when he took out after Sheridan, two days ago, with three of his six brigades — was probing for information in that direction. Heavy trains were in motion for Fredericksburg, young Lee declared, and Federal wounded were being taken across the Rappahannock in large numbers to Belle Plain, eight miles beyond on the Potomac. "There is evidently a general move going on," he notified his father. Here as in the Wilderness, the southern commander was alert to the danger of having his opponent steal a march on him, and here as there he was prepared to react on the basis of information less than conclusive or even substantial. Such activity in Grant's left rear could mean that, having found the Spotsylvania confrontation unprofitable and restrictive, he had one of two strategic shifts in mind: 1) a limited retreat to Fredericksburg, where he would consolidate his forces and better cover his supply line for a subsequent advance by land or water, or 2) another swing around the Confederate right, to interpose his army between Lee and Richmond. From Lee's point of view, though a similar endeavor had failed four days ago, the latter was the more dangerous maneuver, one that he simply could not afford to have succeed. In this case, however, he believed from the evidence that what Grant was about to attempt was a withdrawal to the Rappahannock line, and he wanted to prevent this — or, more strictly speaking, take advantage of it — almost as much as he did the other. In conversation with two of his generals about an hour before sundown he told why.

It began as a discussion of Grant's worth as a tactician. Lee was visiting Harry Heth's headquarters, on the far right near the courthouse, as was A. P. Hill, up and about but still not well enough to return to duty, when a staff officer happened to remark that, in slaughtering his troops by assaulting earthworks, the Union commander was little better than a butcher. Lee did not agree. "I think General Grant has managed his affairs remarkably well up to the present time," he said quietly. Then he turned to Heth and told him what he had come for. "My opinion is the enemy are preparing to retreat tonight to Fredericksburg. I wish you to have everything in readiness to pull out at a moment's notice, but do not disturb your artillery till you commence moving. We must attack those people if they retreat."

Hill spoke up, pale but impetuous as always. "General Lee, let them continue to attack our breastworks. We can stand that very well."

The talk was then of casualties, and though no one knew the actual number of the fallen on either side (Grant in fact had lost about 7000 men by now in front of Spotsylvania, while Lee was losing barely one third that many) all expressed their satisfaction with the present position, which they were convinced they could maintain longer than the Federals could afford to keep assaulting it. Lee rose to go; "We must attack those people if they retreat," he had declared, and in parting he explained what he meant by that. "This army cannot stand a siege," he said. "We must end this business on the battlefield, not in a fortified place."

From there he rode in the rain to the center, where Ewell had disposed his three divisions to defend the salient, one along its eastern face and the apex, another along its western face, where Upton had scored an abortive breakthrough yesterday, and the third in reserve, posted rearward under instructions to move quickly in support of any stricken point along the inverted U of the intrenched perimeter. Dubbed the "Mule Shoe" by its defenders in description of its shape, the position was a little under a mile in depth and about two thirds as wide, heavily wooded for the most part and crisscrossed by a few narrow, winding roads. Because of this last, which would make removal of the guns a difficult business in the dark and the deepening mud, Lee told Ewell to get the batteries that were posted in the forward portion of the salient withdrawn before nightfall, in order to avoid delaying pursuit of the Federals when word arrived that their retreat was under way. It was close to sunset now, and while Ewell got to work on this Lee rode to First Corps headquarters on the left. After giving Anderson the instructions he had earlier given Heth — to be ready to pull out at a moment's notice, but to leave his artillery in position until then — the gray commander returned to his tent to get what sleep he could between then and 3.30, his usual rising time at this critical stage of the campaign.

Within the salient, as night wore on and the rain came down harder, a feeling of uneasiness, which began with the departure of the guns, pervaded the bivouacs and trenches. At first it was vague — "a nameless something in the air," one soldier was to call it, looking back — but after midnight it grew less so, particularly for the men who held the "toe" of the shoe-shaped line and were closest to the enemy position. A sort of rumble, slow but steady, came from the saturated darkness out in front; some likened it to the muffled thunder of a waterfall, others to the grinding of a powerful machine. Veterans who heard it, over and under the pelting of the rain, identified it as the sound of troops in motion by the thousands. Either a retreat was under way, as Lee had said, or else a heavy attack was in the making. If it was the latter, there was difficulty in telling whether the enemy was moving to the left or right, for a strike at Anderson or Early, or massing for another assault on the Mule Shoe. One of Edward Johnson's brigade commanders, Brigadier General George H. Steuart, a Maryland-born West Pointer, went out to his picket line for a closer investigation. He had not listened long before he decided that the Federals not only were preparing an attack, but were aiming it at him. His next thought was of the gun pits standing empty along his portion of the works, and he went at once to Johnson to urge the prompt return of his artillery, parked since sundown back near Spotsylvania. Old Allegheny passed the request to

Ewell, who approved it. All 22 of the withdrawn guns would be back in position by 2 o'clock, he said.

When the appointed time had come, but not the guns, Steuart's anxiety mounted. After waiting another hour he went again to Johnson, who had a staff officer make the round of the brigades with orders for the troops to turn out and check the condition of their rifles, while another rode back to inform Ewell that the artillery had not arrived as promised. All this time, that muffled grinding sound continued in the outer darkness. Shortly before 4.30, just as the fog began to lift a bit, Johnson was relieved to learn that the missing guns were returning up the road from the base of the salient. Before they came in sight, however, the sound out front in the paling darkness rose in volume and intensity, drawing nearer, until it became the unmistakable tramp of a marching host. From a distance of about 300 yards a mighty cheer went up — the deep-chested roar of charging Federals, as distinguished from the high-throated scream that was known as the rebel yell — and heavy masses of blue infantry, close-packed and a-bristle with bayonets glinting steely in the dawn, broke through the fog directly in front of the apex of the salient. Alerted, the Confederates rose and gave the attackers point-blank volleys. In some cases the fire was effective, while in others it was not, depending on whether unit commanders had acted on the warning to have their men draw the dampened charges from their rifles and reload. Not that it mattered tactically; for whether their losses were high or low, the various elements of the dense blue mass surged up and over the parapet, into the trenches. Johnson, who was sometimes called "Old Clubby" because of the stout hickory stick he used as a cane to favor the leg he had been shot in, two years back, limped about amid the confusion and implored his troops to keep fighting, despite the odds; the guns would soon be up to settle the issue, he told them, and for a moment it seemed to be true. The lead battery unlimbered, there in the toe of the Mule Shoe, and managed to get off one round each from two of the pieces. But that was all. "Stop firing that gun!" the cannoneers heard someone shout as they prepared to reload, and looked around to find scores of rifles leveled at them by hard-eyed Federals who had broken the gray line. They raised their hands. Others were less fortunate, taking fire from all directions before they knew the place had been overrun. "Where shall I point the gun?" a rattled corporal asked a badly wounded lieutenant. "At the Yankees," he replied with his last breath. But the two rounds already gotten off were all that were fired before all but two of the 22 guns were surrendered, most of them still in limber on the road.

Lee was breakfasting by lantern light when the rapid-fire clatter erupted in the Mule Shoe to inform him that the enemy, far from retreating, was launching an assault upon his center, which he had stripped of guns the night before. From the volume of sound he knew the attack was a heavy one, and presently, when he mounted Traveller to ride in that direction, he saw at first hand that, so far at least, it had also been successful. Fugitives fled past him, streaming rearward, with and without their weapons. "Hold on!" he cried, removing his hat so they would know him. "Your comrades need your services. Stop, men!" Some stopped and some kept running

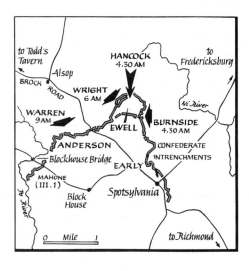

past him with a wild look in their eyes. "Shame on you men; shame on you!" he called after them in his deep voice. "Go back to your regiments." As he drew near the base of the salient he met an officer from Edward Johnson's staff riding to bring him word of what had happened up ahead. Pouring in through a quick break just east of the apex, which was held by Stonewall Jackson's old Manassas brigade, the Federals had fanned out rapidly, left and right, to come upon the adjoining brigades from the flank and rear. Johnson himself had been taken, after being surrounded and very nearly shot because he would not stop hobbling about, brandishing his hickory club and calling for his troops to rally, even though a whole company of bluecoats had their rifles trained on him. Steuart too was a prisoner, along with a number of his soldiers, and the Stonewall Brigade had surrendered practically en masse when the enemy came up in its rear and blocked the possibility of escape. In all, no less than half of Johnson's 5000-man division had been shot or captured in the first half hour of fighting, along with twenty guns and well over half of the regimental flags.

That was the worst of it. On the credit side, Lee was presently to learn, Rodes's division, by "refusing" its flank adjoining the break at the apex, was holding fast to the western face of the salient, and Wilcox had managed to do the same on the right, where Early's line joined Ewell's, even though an attack of nearly equal strength had been made against that point by Burnside at about the same time Hancock struck. This meant that, up to now at any rate, the breakthrough was laterally contained. Whether it could also be contained in depth was another matter, and it was to this that Lee gave his immediate attention. "Ride with me to General Gordon," he told the orphaned staff man, and continued to spur Traveller toward the open end of the Mule Shoe, where Gordon's division had been posted with instructions to support Rodes or Johnson in such a crisis as the one at hand.

Gordon had already begun to meet the situation by sending one of his three brigades forward on a wide front, the men deployed as skirmishers to blunt the Federal penetration, and was preparing to counterattack with the other two, his own Georgians and Pegram's Virginians, when Lee rode up. "What do you want me to do, General?" Gordon asked. Lee wanted him to do just what he was doing, and said so, knowing only too well that unless the Union drive was stopped his army would be cut in half. Gordon saluted and returned to the work at hand. However, as he was about to give the signal to go forward he looked back and saw that Lee, faced with a crisis as grave as the one six days ago in the Wilderness, was responding in the same fashion here at Spotsylvania. Still with his hat off, he had ridden to a position near the center of the line, between the two brigades, with the obvious intention of taking part in the charge. Horrified — for he knew how great the danger was, even here near the base of the salient, having just had his coat twitched by a stray bullet out of the woods he was about to enter — the young brigadier wheeled his horse and rode back to confront his gray-haired chief. "General Lee, this is no place for you," he told him. "Go back, General; we will drive them back." Soldiers from both brigades began to gather about the two horsemen for a better view, and Gordon spoke louder, wanting them to reinforce his plea. "These men are Virginians and Georgians. They have never failed you. They never will. Will you, boys?" The answer was prompt and vociferous. "No! No!" "General Lee to the rear; Lee to the rear!" "We'll drive them back for you, General!" Lee kept looking straight ahead, apparently determined not to be put off, until a tall Virginia sergeant took the matter into his own hands by grabbing Traveller's rein, jerking his head around, and leading him rearward through the cheering ranks.

Behind him Lee heard Gordon's voice ring out above the roar of battle, which grew louder as the breakthrough deepened: "Forward! Guide right!" And while the Virginians and Georgians crashed into the woods to come to grips with the attackers, as they had promised they would do, the southern commander resumed his higher duties. Of these, the most immediate was to find some means of strengthening the counterattack now being launched, and in this connection his first thought was of the fugitives, the troops blown loose from their units when the forward part of the salient went. "Collect together the men of Johnson's division and report to General Gordon," he told the orphaned staffer. That would help, though probably not enough. He thought then of Mahone's division, detached from Early two days ago to meet the threat from across the Po at Blockhouse Bridge, and sent word for Mahone to leave one brigade in the newly dug intrenchments there, protecting his flank, and move at once with the other three to reinforce Gordon's effort to restore the integrity of his broken center.

In point of fact Gordon was already doing remarkably well on his own, first by stemming, then by reversing the flow of the blue flood down the salient. His success in this unequal contest — in effect, a matching of three brigades against four divisions — was due in part to the fury of his assault, inspired by Lee, and in part to the assistance given by the hard-core remnant of Johnson's division, as well as by the troops from the adjoining divisions of Rodes and Wilcox, whose interior flanks hooked onto the wings of his line as he advanced. All this helped; but perhaps the greatest help came from the Federals themselves, who by then were in no condition, tactically or otherwise, to offer sustained resistance to what Gordon threw at them. Boiling over the works and onto unfamiliar ground, a maze of trenches and traverses, thickly wooded in spots and cluttered with prisoners and debris, they scarcely knew which way to turn in order to make the most of the breakthrough they had scored with such comparative ease and speed. The impetus at this point came mainly from the rear, as more and more of Hancock's men continued to pour into the salient; eventually there were close to 20,000 of them in an area less than half a mile square, with such resultant jumbling of their ranks that what had been meant to be a smoothly functioning military formation quickly degenerated into a close-packed mob, some of whose members were so tightly wedged against their fellows that, like muscle-bound athletes, they could not lift their arms to use their weapons. It was at this discordant stage that Gordon struck, and the effect of his fire on the men in that hampered mass of blue was appalling. A bullet could scarcely miss its mark, or if it did it struck another quite as vital. Turning to breast the pressure from the rear, where there was little knowledge of what was going on up front, they broke as best they could, a stumbling herd, and fled back up the salient to gain the protection of the intrenchments they had crossed on their way in. Gordon's troops came after them, screaming and firing as they ran.

Down the eastern face of the salient, the critical point being near its base, where Ewell's line joined Early's, Burnside had attacked at about the same time Hancock did; but there was less confusion here, on both sides, for the simple reason that there had been no penetration. Recoiling, the three blue divisions — made up of greener, less determined men than the veterans under Meade — found what cover they could, within range of the rebel works, and contented themselves with firing at whatever showed above the parapet. This gave Wilcox so little trouble that he was free to assist in Gordon's counterattack, thus helping to keep Hancock off his flank. Across the way, down the western face of the salient, Rodes was able to do the same, for the even simpler reason that he had not been hit at all; not yet. But then at 6 o'clock, with Hancock's attackers tamped firmly back into the toe of the Mule Shoe, Wright struck. He came up hard, with everything he had, against that portion of Rodes's front where Upton had scored the original breakthrough, two days back. Rodes managed to prevent a repetition of that archetypical success, though only by the hardest. Much of the fighting was hand-to-hand, across the works, but Wright's attack, like Hancock's, was muscle-bound, hampered by its bulk; he too had close to 20,000 men and he was mindful of Grant's concern that he bring the weight of every one of them to bear. Rodes kept his badly outnumbered division in position, but he knew that the line might go with a rush at any moment under all that pressure. Accordingly, he sent word to Lee that if he was to prevent a second breakthrough — potentially even more dangerous than the first, since it would put the attackers in rear of practically every Confederate in the salient — he must have reinforcements, and have them quick.

They were already on the way from Blockhouse Bridge. Sent for earlier to strengthen Gordon's counterattack, the three brigades from Mahone's division could be used instead to shore up Rodes; provided of course that they came up in time. Impatient at their nonarrival, Lee rode westward in rear of Anderson's position — which had not been attacked, so far, but was under fire from Warren's long-range artillery — to meet them and save time by redirecting their march to the hard-pressed west face of the salient, where the Federals were hammering at the works. Presently he came upon the lead brigade, Carnot Posey's Mississippians, now under Brigadier General Nathaniel Harris, a thirty-year-old former Vicksburg lawyer. Lee rode alongside Harris, giving instructions, and the Union gunners, spotting the column in brisk motion across the way, lengthened their ranges to bring it under fire. They concentrated mainly on the horsemen at its head, with the result that Lee had to give all his attention to Traveller, who began to rear wildly amid a flurry of plunging shot and bursting shell. Lee kept his seat, doing what he could to calm the animal, but Traveller kept rearing. It was well he did; for as he went back on his hind legs, boxing the air with his forehoofs, a solid shot, which otherwise would have killed or maimed both horse and rider, passed directly under his belly. Horrified, the Mississippians began to yell: "Go back, General! Go back! For God's sake, go back!" They tried to get between him and the exploding shells, urging him to hurry out of range, but Lee was in no more of a mind to retire from this fourth Lee-to-the-rear tableau than he had been to quit the other three. His blood was up, now as before; anxiety was on him. At last he said, "If you will promise me to drive those people from our works, I will go back." The soldiers cheered and, while Lee watched admiringly, took up the march at a faster rate, joining Rodes in time to prevent a breakthrough which one of his brigadiers had just warned him was only minutes away.

Now, however, this second phase of the contest, which ended with the approximate restoration of Lee's line, merged into the third, a struggle even fiercer than the two that had gone before. Tamped back into the toe of the Mule Shoe, Hancock's troops found cover by recrossing the log parapet and taking shelter behind it. There they stayed and there they fought, sometimes at arm's length, much as Wright's men were doing on their right, down the western face of the salient, where the region of Upton's abortive penetration acquired a new name: The Bloody Angle. The term had been used before, in other battles elsewhere in the war, but there was no doubt forever after, at least on the part of those who fought there, that here was where the appellation best applied. It soon became apparent to both sides that what they were involved in now was not only fiercer than what had gone before, today, but was in fact more horrendous than what had gone before, ever. This was grimmer than the Wilderness — a way of saying that it was worse than anything at all — not so much in bloodshed, although blood was shed in plenty, as in concentrated terror. These were the red hours of the conflict, hours no man who survived them would forget, even in his sleep, forever after. Fighting thus at arm's length across that parapet, they were caught up in a waking nightmare, although they were mercifully spared the knowledge, at the outset, that it was to last for another sixteen unrelenting hours. "All day long it was one continuous assault," a Pennsylvanian would recall. But in truth it was as much a defense as it was an attack, on either side, and the two were simultaneous. Neither victory nor defeat was any longer a factor in the struggle. Men simply fought to keep on fighting, and not so much on instinct as on pure adrenalin. Slaughter became an end in itself, unrelated to issues or objectives, as if it had nothing whatever to do with the war. Troops were killed by thrusts and stabs through chinks in the log barricade, while others were harpooned by bayonetted rifles flung javelin-style across it. Sometimes in this extremity even the instinct for self-preservation went by the board. From point to point, some wrought-up soldier would leap up on the parapet and fire down into the opposite mass of blue or gray, then continue this with loaded rifles passed up by comrades until he was shot down and another wrought-up soldier took his place. Rain fell, slacked, fell again in sheets, drenching the fighters and turning the floor of their slaughter pen to slime. Down in the trenches, dead and wounded men were trampled out of sight in the blood-splotched mud by those who staggered up to take their posts along the works, until they too were dropped or forced to retire because their weapons became so powder-fouled from rapid firing that they could not be loaded to fire again. High though the casualties were along this portion of the line, they would have been much higher if there had been time or room for taking aim. As it was, the largely unaimed fire — particularly heavy from the Federal side, where men were stacked up twenty deep in places — passed over the heads of the Confederates to destroy a whole grove of trees within the salient;

some, including an oak nearly two feet in diameter, were actually felled by the chipping bullets, which, to the amazement of a Vermont brigadier, continued their work until the fallen trunks and limbs "were cut to pieces and whipped into basket-stuff." One of Wright's officers, fighting in the Bloody Angle, tried afterwards to sum up what he had lived through. "I never expect to be believed when I tell of what I saw of the horrors of Spotsylvania," he wrote, "because I should be loath to believe it myself were the cases reversed."

Warren's infantry moved out at last, shortly after 9 o'clock, in a full-scale assault on the Confederate left, but this was broken up so effectively by Anderson's artillery and massed small-arms fire that not a Federal reached the works along this portion of the line. Severely hurt, the attackers recoiled and did not venture out again, permitting Lee to detach a brigade from each of the two First Corps divisions as reinforcements for Ewell in the Mule Shoe. They were sorely needed. It was noon by then and men were falling there from nervous exhaustion as well as from wounds. Veterans who had survived the worst this war afforded, up to now, went through the motions of combat after the manner of blank-faced automatons, as if what they were involved in had driven them beyond madness into imbecility; they fought by the numbers, unrecognizant of comrades in the ultimate loneliness of a horror as profoundly isolating in its effect as bone pain, nausea, or prolonged orgasm, their vacant eyes unlighted by anger or even dulled by fear. There were exceptions. One man, for example, stopped fighting to plunder an abandoned knapsack, and finding clean clothes in it, stripped off his butternut rags to exchange them for the laundered finery, underwear and all, then returned cheerfully to the grisly work at hand, apparently refreshed. But for the most part they had that look, well known to experienced officers of the line, of troops whose numbness under pressure might give way at any moment to utter panic, an abrupt collapse of all resistance. Unit commanders began to send word to superiors that the men were near their limits of endurance, but the answer was always the same: Hold on longer, a little longer, until a new line of intrenchments, under construction across the base of the salient by Martin Smith's engineers, could be completed to provide shelter for the troops when they withdrew. So they kept fighting, albeit mechanically, up in the blood-drenched toe of the Mule Shoe and down its western shank, and Hancock and Wright kept battering, although they too had most of the same problems with regard to keeping their larger masses of men involved in the meat-grinder action along those two portions of the line.

Sunset, twilight, and the following darkness brought no slackening of the struggle; 9 o'clock came, then 10, and then 11; "Not yet" was still the answer to urgent requests for permission to retire to the line being drawn across the gorge of the salient, half a mile in rear of the apex which had been under bloody contention for the past eighteen hours. Finally, at midnight, word arrived and was passed along the zigzag curve of trenches — defined against the moonless blackness by the wink and glare of muzzle flashes, fitful stabs of pinkish yellow stitching their pattern back and forth across the parapet — for a piecemeal disengagement to begin. Unit by unit, so stealthily that they were not detected, the weary graybacks stumbled rearward through the bullet-tattered woods to where the new line had been dug. It was close to dawn before the last of them completed their somnambulistic withdrawal and took up their position in the works near the Brock Road. Daybreak showed the abandoned salient held only by corpses, the sodden trenches yawning empty save for these and other shattered remnants of the all-day battle. Still hugging the outward face of the log barricade, the Federals did not cross it even now that the defenders had departed, and the Confederates were glad that this was so. Exhausted, out of contact at last, blue and gray alike slept on their arms in the mud where they lay, oblivious to the pelting rain. Lee had preserved the integrity of his position, but at a cruel cost, having had nearly 3000 of his hard-core veterans captured and a somewhat larger number killed or wounded. Grant had lost as many, if not more; 6820 was the subsequent Federal count for this one day, a figure almost as great as the total for the three preceding days, when the Confederates lost fewer than one third as many. The gray army, fighting for the most part behind intrenchments, had managed to maintain its one-for-two ratio of casualties suffered and inflicted since the start of the campaign. But that was by no means the whole story of comparable attrition, which, as it applied to the men of highest rank on the two rosters, was just the other way around. Eight days of combat had cost the Army of Northern Virginia better than one third of its corps, division, and brigade commanders — 20 out of 57, killed or captured or severely wounded — while its adversary was losing barely half as many, 10 out of 69. And presently word arrived that still another Confederate general was to be added to the doleful list, one whose loss might prove the hardest to bear of them all, since his absence in the past had left the army and its famed commander groping blind.

Soon after the blue assault was launched, on the morning of May 12, Lee received a telegram informing him of the mishap, which had occurred within ten miles of Richmond the afternoon before. "Gentlemen, we have very bad news," he announced to a group around him; "General Stuart has been mortally wounded. A most valuable and able officer — " He paused, as if in search of further words for a formal statement, but then gave up and merely added in a shaken voice: "He never brought me a piece of false information." His sorrow was commensurate with his personal affection for, and his military debt to, the stricken horseman. Still, throughout the long day's fight at Spotsylvania, he kept hoping that somehow Jeb would pull through this crisis, as he had escaped so many other dangers over the past three years. Late that night, however, shortly before the withdrawal to the line still under construction across the base of the embattled salient, a second message came; Stuart was gone. Lee put his hands over his face to conceal his emotion. Presently he retired to his tent to master his grief, and when one of the dead cavalryman's staff officers arrived to tell him of Jeb's last minutes, back in Richmond, he remarked: "I can scarcely think of him without weeping."

★ ★ ★

Directed by Grant, through Meade, to "cut loose from the Army of the Potomac, pass around Lee's army, and attack his cavalry and communications," Sheridan was determined not only to make the most of the opportunity, which came his way as a result of the high-tempered clash at headquarters earlier that same Sunday, May 8, but also to do so in a style that was in keeping with his claim that, left to the devices he had been urging all along, he could whip Jeb Stuart out of his boots. "We are going out to fight Stuart's cavalry in consequence of a suggestion from me," he told his three division commanders that evening, and he added, by way of emphasizing the highly personal nature of the challenge as he saw it: "In view of my recent representations to General Meade I shall expect nothing but success."

His method of assuring this was demonstrated at first light next morning, back near Fredericksburg, when the march began down the Telegraph Road, the main-traveled artery to Richmond. Riding four abreast, accompanied by all 32 of their guns and such forage and ordnance wagons as were needed, the 12,000 blue troopers comprised a column thirteen miles in length. They moved not at a run or trot, and not by separate, converging routes — both of which had been standard procedure on raids in the past — but at a walk and in a single inspissated column, compact as a fist clenched for striking on short notice. Not much concerned with deception, and even less with speed, Sheridan's dependence was on power, the ability of his three combined divisions to ride through or over whatever got in their path. Previous raiders had sought to avoid the fast-moving rebel horsemen, lest they be delayed or thwarted in their attempt to reach their assigned objectives; but Sheridan's objective, so to speak, was just such a confrontation. He defined the raid as "a challenge to Stuart for a cavalry duel behind Lee's lines, in his own country," and the more there were of the gray riders when the showdown was at hand, the better he would like it, since that would mean there were more to be "smashed up." His confidence was in numbers and the superiority of his horses and equipment: as was shown within an hour of the outset, when the head of the column ran into brisk fire from an enemy outpost line and stopped to ponder the situation. Little Phil, as his troopers had taken to calling him, came riding up and asked what was the matter. Skirmishers, he was told — apparently in strength. "Cavalry or infantry?" he demanded, and on being informed that they were cavalry, barked impatiently: "Keep moving, boys. We're going on through. There isn't cavalry enough in all the Southern Confederacy to stop us."

Southward the march led down across the Ni, the Po, the Ta, and around the mazy sources of the Mat — four streams that combined to contribute their waters and their names to the Mattaponi — until, well in the rear of Lee's far right, the column turned off the Telegraph Road and headed southwest for Chilesburg and the North Anna, three miles beyond which lay Beaver Dam Station, Lee's advance supply base on the Virginia Central Railroad. Stores of all kinds were collected there, drawn from the Carolinas and the Shenandoah Valley; Sheridan planned to "go through" them in the course of his move on Stuart and the Confederate capital itself, which he would approach by the front door, if it came within his reach, while Ben Butler's infantry was knocking at the back. Torbert's division, still under Wesley Merritt, had the lead, followed by Gregg and Wilson. Progress was steady all day long, mainly because Sheridan refused to be distracted, whether by threats or the rumor of threats, which were frequent, front and rear. When a rebel brigade launched an attack on his rear guard south of the Ta, for example, he simply detached one of Gregg's brigades as a reinforcement and kept the main body moving at the deliberate pace he had set at the start, on the far side of the Ni. Just before dusk the North Anna came in sight; Merritt crossed with his three brigades while the other two divisions went into camp on the near bank. Before long, the sky was aglow in the direction Merritt had moved and the night breeze was fragrant with the aroma of burning bacon, wafted northward all the way from Beaver Dam.

Much of the burning — close to a million rations of meat and better than half a million of bread, along with Lee's entire reserve of medical stores — had been done by the depot guards themselves, who fired the sheds to keep their contents out of the hands of the raiders. First on the scene was the brigade of twenty-four-year-old Brigadier General George A. Custer, Michiganders as skilled in wrecking as they were in fighting. They added more than a hundred railway cars to the conflagration, as well as two locomotives — one fourth of all the Virginia Central had in operation at the time — and for lagniappe freed 378 Union soldiers, captured in the Wilderness and en route to prison camps. After the excitement of all this, the horsemen bedded down for a few hours' sleep by the fitful light of the fading embers of the station, and were roused before dawn to get to work on the railroad track. Ten miles in all were torn up, together with the telegraph wires and poles that ran beside it, before the whooping troopers fell back into column to resume their march. Like their comrades on the north bank, they were well rested despite their overnight carnival of destruction, having slept in one large bivouac that required few sentinels, rather than in scattered groups requiring many. Reconsolidated, the three divisions proceeded again at an energy-saving walk, a road-wide dusty blue serpent more than a dozen miles long and crawling inexorably south. So leisurely, so unperturbed was this horseback saunter through the springtime greenness of Virginia — except of course for those engaged in the rear-guard fret of fending off the rebels snapping persistently at their heels — that the raiders had to remind themselves from time to time that they were deep in enemy country, out for blood.

By late afternoon (Tuesday, May 10: Upton was massing for his abortive penetration of Ewell's works, thirty air-line miles due north) the head of the column reached Ground Squirrel Bridge on the South Anna, and there in the grassy fields beside the river, well over halfway to Richmond, Sheridan called a halt for the night. He might have kept on; today's march had been a good deal shorter than yesterday's and there were still a couple of daylight hours left; but this was an excellent place to feed and water his mounts and rest his men. Besides, he not only was in no hurry, he also reasoned that Stuart by now, as he said later, was "urging his horses to the death so as to get in between Richmond and our column," and he preferred it so.

He wanted Jeb to win the race, since only in that way would it end in the confrontation he was seeking.

Stuart had accepted the gambit and was proceeding much as Sheridan supposed: with one exception. Unlike his opponent, who had stripped the Federal army of practically every horseman he could lay hands on, the southern cavalry commander had resisted the temptation to jump this latest adversary with everything he had, and instead of leaving Lee to grope as blind as Grant was going to be for the next week or two, had taken up the pursuit with only three of his six brigades, some 4500 sabers opposing 12,000 engaged in what might turn out to be an attempt to seize the scantly defended capital already menaced by Butler's army from the far side of the James. One factor in this decision to forgo a better chance at personal laurels was that he could not know, until the Yankees cleared Beaver Dam on the morning of the second day, whether their intention was to keep on riding south for Richmond or turn north for a strike at Spotslyvania from the rear, in which case Lee of course would need all the help he could get, especially from his cavalry. As a result of this limiting decision, made at the outset, Stuart knew as well as Sheridan did that, in light of the numerical odds prevailing, the confrontation could have only one result if it was head-on; Sheridan — whose three well-mounted divisions were equipped with rapid-fire carbines, whereas the three gray brigades were armed with single-shot muzzle loaders and mounted on crowbait horses — would ride right over him. Stuart's solution, in considering this dilemma, was not to avoid the confrontation, despite the likelihood that it would be disastrous on those terms, but rather to arrange for it to be something other than head-on and to get what assistance he could from the Richmond garrison, scant as it was, when the march of the two columns intersected in the vicinity of the threatened capital.

Whatever he lacked in comparative strength — even at the outset of the raid, before his underfed, short-winded horses started breaking down from the strain of the chase — there was at least no diminution of his accustomed vigilance and vigor. Pressing close in rear of the outsized blue formation with one of Fitz Lee's brigades, he sent for Fitz and his other brigade, as well as Brigadier General James B. Gordon's brigade of W. H. F. Lee's division, and with these three took up the pursuit in earnest, first down the Telegraph Road, then southeast to the North Anna, beyond which, as night came down, he saw to his distress the spreading reflection of the flames at Beaver Dam, where a three-week supply of food went up in smoke while the men for whom it had been intended went hungry in the Spotsylvania woods. In just one day, by this one blow, Sheridan had accomplished more than any of his predecessors had managed to do in the past three years. What was worse, with Richmond not much farther south than he had come already, he seemed likely to accomplish a great deal more, unless Stuart found some way to check or divert him. Up to now, the grayjackets had been limited to attacks on the Union rear, since to have doubled the blue column for a strike at its head would have left the raiders free to turn for an unmolested dash against the rear of Lee's intrenchments. By next morning, though, with all the enemy horsemen over the North Anna, proceeding south past the charred base they had destroyed the night before, Stuart was free at least of that restriction; he could give his full attention to covering Richmond, since that now seemed without much doubt to be the Federal objective. Accordingly, he told Gordon to keep his brigade of North Carolinians close on the tail of the blue column, impeding it all he could, while Fitz Lee and his two Virginia brigades, under Brigadier Generals Lunsford Lomax and Williams Wickham, rode east along the Virginia Central to regain the Telegraph Road, just this side of Hanover Junction, and hurry down it to take up a position in which to intercept the raiders before they got to Richmond. A message went to Braxton Bragg, informing him of the danger to the capital in his charge. Stuart hoped to be reinforced from the city's garrison in time for the confrontation on its outskirts, but if Sheridan brushed past him, he told Bragg, "I will certainly move in his rear and do what I can."

So much for intention; execution, he knew, would be a larger order. However, before setting out to catch up with Fitz, Jeb took advantage of an opportunity Sheridan had unwittingly given him to call on his wife Flora and their two children, who were visiting on a plantation near Beaver Dam Station, thought until yesterday to be a place of safety from the Yankees. She came out to meet him on the front steps of the house, and though he did not take the time to dismount, he at least had the satisfaction of leaning down from the saddle to kiss her hello and goodbye before continuing on his way. The parting had a somber effect on the normally jovial cavalier. So many goodbyes by so many soldiers had turned out to be last goodbyes in the course of the past three years, and today was the anniversary, moreover, of the death of his great and good friend Stonewall Jackson. Stuart rode in silence for a time before he spoke to his only companion, a staff major, on a theme he seldom touched. He did not expect to survive the war, he said, and he did not want to live anyhow if the South went down in defeat.

Sheridan's calculation that his adversary would be "urging his horses to the death so as to get in between Richmond and our column" was nearly confirmed quite literally that night. Tireless himself, Jeb was not inclined to have much patience with tiredness in others. "We must substitute *esprit* for numbers," he had declared in the early days of the war, adding in partial explanation, not only of his exuberant fox-hunt manner, but also for the gaudy uniform — red-lined cape, bright yellow sash, black ostrich plume, and golden spurs — he wore with such flamboyance, on and off the field of battle: "I strive to inculcate in my men the spirit of the chase." Overtaking Fitz Lee soon after dark near Hanover Junction, he learned from Gordon, who sent a courier cross country, that the Federals had made an early halt that afternoon at Ground Squirrel Bridge on the South Anna. This was within twenty miles of Richmond, five miles closer than Stuart himself was at the time;

Jeb was all for pushing ahead on an all-night march, until Fitz persuaded him that unless he stopped to feed and rest his weary mounts he would arrive with no more than a handful of troopers, the remainder having been left behind to clutter the road with broken-down horses. Stuart relented, on condition that Fitz would have his men back in the saddle by 1 a.m., but rode on himself for another few miles before he lay down by the roadside to get a little sleep. Up and off again before the dawn of May 11 — unaware, of course, that this was to be his last day in the field — he crossed the South Anna at sunrise and passed the farm where he had bivouacked, one month less than two years ago tomorrow night, on the eve of his first "ride around McClellan," the exploit that had made his name a household word. Nearing Ashland, four miles south on the Richmond, Fredericksburg & Potomac, he found that a brigade of raiders, detached from the main column, had struck the place the night before, burning a locomotive and a train of cars, along with several government warehouses, while tearing up six miles of track. Stuart quickened his pace at this evidence of what might be in store for Richmond, fifteen miles away, unless he managed to head the marauders off or force them into retreat by pitching into their rear while they were attacking the works that ringed the city. Today as yesterday, however, a staff officer who rode with him found him inclined to speak of personal rather than of military matters. "He was more quiet than usual, softer and more communicative," the staffer observed, believing, as he later wrote, that Jeb somehow felt "the shadow of the near future already upon him."

Informed by another courier from Gordon that the Federal main body had resumed its march from Ground Squirrel Bridge this morning on the Mountain Road from Louisa, Jeb found his problem as to the choice of an interceptive position more or less solved before he got there. Less than half a mile below the junction of the Mountain and Telegraph roads, which came together to form Brook Turnpike, a macadamized thoroughfare running the last six miles into Richmond, was an abandoned stagecoach inn called Yellow Tavern, paintless now, made derelict by progress, and set amid rolling, sparsely wooded fields of grass and grain. Stuart arrived at 8 o'clock, ahead of his troops, and after sending word to Bragg that he had won the race, proceeded at once to plan his dispositions. Sporadic firing up the Mountain Road confirmed that Gordon still was snapping terrierlike at the heels of the Union column, as instructed, and gave warning that Fitz Lee not only had no time to spare in getting ready to receive it, but also could expect no reinforcements from Bragg on such brief notice. Stuart's decision was to compromise between taking up a frontal and a flank position, since the former would invite the powerful enemy force to run right over him, while the latter would afford him little more than a chance to pepper the blue troopers as they galloped past him, bound for Richmond. He had Fitz put Wickham on the right, one mile north of Yellow Tavern, facing south into the V of the converging roads, and Lomax on the left, his left advanced so that the two brigades came together at an angle, presenting a concave front which allowed a concentration of fire upon whatever moved against them down the western arm of the V. By 10 o'clock these dispositions were completed; Stuart had his men in line, dismounted except for a single regiment, the 1st Virginia, which he held in reserve to be hurried wherever it was needed most. Within another hour the enemy too had come up and was massing for attack.

This was approximately what Sheridan had been wanting all along, and now that he had it he took care to make the most of it. Richmond lay just ahead, the prize of prizes, but he was in no hurry; Richmond would still be there tonight and tomorrow, whereas Stuart, with his reputation for hairbreadth extractions, might skedaddle. From noon until about 2 o'clock he reconnoitered the Confederate position, probing here and there to test its strength, then settled down in earnest, using one brigade to hold off Gordon in his rear, two more to block the turnpike escape route, and the remaining four against Fitz Lee, whom he outnumbered two-to-one in men and three-to-one in guns. For another two hours the fight was hot, sometimes hand to hand at critical points. By 4 o'clock Sheridan had found what he believed was the key to Lee's undoing, and orders went for Merritt to press the issue on the right, crumpling Lomax to fling him back on Wickham, after which the whole line would move forward to exploit the resultant confusion. Merritt passed the order on to Custer, who promptly attacked with two regiments mounted and the other two on foot as skirmishers, striking hard for the left of the rebel line just north of Yellow Tavern.

Stuart was there, having sensed the point of greatest danger from his command post near the center. A conspicuous target in his silk-lined cape and nodding plume, he laughed at an aide's protest that he was exposing himself unnecessarily. "I don't reckon there is any danger," he replied. For three years this had apparently been true for him, although his clothes had been slit repeatedly by twittering bullets and he once had half of his mustache clipped off by a stray round. Moreover, he was encouraged by a dispatch from Bragg expressing the opinion that he could hold the Richmond works with his 4000 local defense troops and the help of three brigades of regulars he had ordered to join him from the far side of the James, provided the raiders could be delayed long enough for these reinforcements to make it across the river. Jeb figured there had been time for that already, and once again was proudly conscious of having carried out a difficult assignment, though he was determined to gain still more by way of allowing a margin for error. Arriving on the far left as the two Michigan regiments thundered past in a charge on a section of guns just up the line, he drew his big nine-shot LeMatt revolver and fired at the blue horsemen going by. They took the guns, scattering the cannoneers, but soon came tumbling back, some mounted and some unhorsed by a counterattack from the 1st Virginia, which Fitz Lee threw at them. Stuart had ridden forward to a fence, putting his horse's head across it between two of his butter-nut soldiers in order to get as close as possible to the bluecoats coming back. "Steady, men, steady!" he shouted, still firing his silver-chased pistol at the enemy beyond the fence. "Give it to them!" Instead, it was they who gave it to him: one of them anyhow. A dismounted private, trotting past with his revolver drawn — John A. Huff of the 5th Michigan, who had served a two-year hitch in a sharpshooter outfit, winning a prize as the best marksman in his regiment, then returned home and reënlisted under Custer, apparently out of boredom, though at forty-five he was old for that branch of the service — took time to fire, almost casually in passing, at the red-bearded officer thirty feet away. Jeb's head dropped suddenly forward, so that his plumed hat fell off, and he clapped one hand to his right side. "General, are you hit?" one of the men alongside him cried as the blue trooper ran off down the fence line, pistol smoking from the fire of that one unlucky shot. "I'm afraid I am," Stuart replied calmly when the question was asked again. "But don't worry, boys," he told the distressed soldiers gathering rapidly around him; "Fitz will do as well for you as I have done."

They got him off his horse and did what they could to make him comfortable while waiting for an ambulance. Fitz Lee came riding fast when he heard of the wound, but Jeb sent him back at once to take charge of the field. "Go ahead, Fitz, old fellow," he said. "I know you'll do what is right." Then the ambulance came and they lifted him into it, obviously in pain. Just as it started rearward a portion of the line gave way and a number of flustered gray troopers made off across the field. "Go back!" Stuart called after them, sitting up in his indignation despite the wrench to his hurt side. "Go back and do your duty, as I have done mine, and our country will be safe. Go back, go back!" Then he added, though in different words, what he had told the staff major yesterday about not wanting to survive the South's defeat: "I'd rather die than be whipped!" Presently a surgeon and other members of his staff overtook the mule-drawn ambulance and stopped it, out of range of the Federals, for an examination of the wound. While his blood-stained sash was being removed and his bullet-torn jacket opened, Stuart turned to Lieutenant Walter Hullihen, a staff favorite, and addressed him by his nickname: "Honeybun, how do I look in the face?" Hullihen lied — for his chief was clearly in shock and getting weaker by the minute. "You are looking all right, General," he replied. "You will be all right." Jeb mused on the words, as if in doubt, knowing only too well what lay in store for a gut-shot man. "Well, I don't know how this will turn out," he said at last, "but if it is God's will that I shall die I am ready."

By now the doctor had completed his examination and ordered the ambulance to move on. He believed there was little chance for the general's survival, but he wanted to get him to Richmond, and expert medical attention, as soon as possible. An eighteen-year-old private followed the vehicle for a time on horseback, looking in under the hood at the anguished Stuart until it picked up speed and pulled away. "The last thing I saw of him," the boy trooper later wrote, "he was lying flat on his back in the ambulance, the mules running at a terrific pace, and he was being jolted most unmercifully. He opened his eyes and looked at me, and shook his head from side to side as much as to say, 'It's all over with me.' He had folded arms and a look of resignation."

Fitz Lee by then had restored his line, and Sheridan, after prodding it here and there for another hour, decided the time had come to move on after all. Shadows were lengthening fast; moreover he had inter-cepted a rebel dispatch urging Bragg to send substantial reinforcements. So he broke off what he called "this obstinate contest" north of Yellow Tavern, and pushed on down Brook Turnpike, through the outer works of Richmond, to within earshot of the alarm bells tolling frantically in the gathering darkness. This was the route Kilpatrick had taken ten weeks ago, only to call a halt when he came under fire from the fortifica-tions, and Little Phil had a similar reaction when he drew near the inter-mediate line of defense, three miles from Capitol Square. "It is possible that I might have captured the city of Richmond by assault," he would report to Meade, "but the want of knowledge of your operations and those of General Butler, and the facility with which the enemy could throw in troops, made me abandon the attempt." His personal inclination was to plunge on down the pike, over the earthworks and into the streets of the town, though he knew he lacked the strength to stay there long; "the greatest temptation of my life," he later called the prospect, looking back. "I should have been the hero of the hour. I could have gone in and burned and killed right and left. But I had learned this thing: that our men knew what they were about. . . . They would have followed me, but they would have known as well as I that the sacrifice was for no permanent advantage."

Forbearance came hard, but he soon had other matters on his mind. Withdrawal, under present circumstances, called for perhaps more daring, and certainly more skill, then did staying where he was or going in. Gordon was still clawing at his rear on Brook Turnpike, and Fitz Lee was somewhere off in the darkness, hovering on his flank; Bragg, for all he knew, had summoned any number of reinforcements from beyond the James, and presently the confusion was compounded by a howling wind- and rainstorm (the one that was giving Hancock so much trouble, out on its fringes, on the night march into position for his dawn assault on the toe of Ewell's Mule Shoe) so severe that the steeple of old St John's Church, on the opposite side of Richmond, was blown away. Sheridan turned eastward, headed for Meadow Bridge on the Chickahominy, which he intended to cross at that point, putting the river between him and his pursuers, and then recross, well downstream, to find sanctuary within Butler's lines, as had been prearranged, at Haxall's Landing on the James. In addition to the rain-lashed darkness, which made any sense of direction hard to maintain, the march was complicated by the presence of land mines in his path; "torpedoes," they were called, buried artillery projectiles equipped with trip wires, and the first one encountered killed a number of horses and wounded several men. Sheridan had an answer to that, however. Bringing a couple of dozen prisoners forward to the head of the column, he made them "get down on their knees, feel for the wires in the darkness, follow them up and unearth the shells." Despite the delay he reached Meadow Bridge at daylight: only to find that the rebels had set it afire the night before to prevent his getaway. At the same time he discovered this, Bragg's infantry came up in his rear and Fitz Lee's vengeance-minded troopers descended whooping on his flank.

He faced Wilson and Gregg about to meet the double challenge, and gave Merritt the task of repairing the bridge for a crossing. Fortunately, last night's rain had put the fire out before the stringers and ties burned through; a new floor could be improvised from fence rails. While these were being collected and put in place, the two divisions fighting rearward gave a good account of themselves, having acquired by now some of the foxhunt jauntiness formerly limited to their gray-clad adversaries. For example, when instructed by Sheridan to "hold your position at all hazards while I arrange to withdraw the corps to the north side of the river," James Wilson made a jocular reply. "Our hair is badly entangled in [the enemy's] fingers and our nose firmly inserted in his mouth. We shall, therefore, hold on here till something breaks." Nothing broke; not in the blue ranks anyhow, though James Gordon was mortally wounded on the other side, shot from his horse while leading a charge by his brigade. Merritt finished his repair work in short order and the three divisions withdrew, without heavy losses, to camp for the night down the left bank of the Chickahominy, near the old Gaines Mill battlefield. Proceeding by easy marches they rode past other scenes from the Seven Days, including Malvern Hill, to Haxall's Landing, which they reached on May 14. The raid was over, all but the return, and Sheridan was greatly pleased with the results, not only because of the specific damage accomplished at Beaver Dam and Ashland, but also because of other damage, no less grave for being more difficult to assess. At a cost of 625 killed and wounded and missing, he had freed nearly 400 Union prisoners and brought them with him into Butler's lines, along with some 300 captive rebels. How many of the enemy he had killed or wounded in the course of the raid he could not say, but he knew at least of one whose loss to Lee and the Confederacy was well-nigh immeasurable. The killing of Jeb Stuart at Yellow Tavern, he declared, "inflicted a blow from which entire recovery was impossible."

After three days' rest with Butler he was off to rejoin Grant. The northward march was uneventful except for a rather spectacular demonstration, staged while crossing the high railroad bridge over Pamunkey River, of the indestructibility of the army pack mule. Falling from a height of thirty feet, one of these creatures — watched in amazement by a regiment of troopers whose colonel recorded the incident in his memoirs — "turned a somersault, struck an abutment, disappeared under water, came up, and swam ashore without disturbing his pack." On May 24 the three divisions rejoined the army they had left, two weeks and one day ago, near Spotsylvania.

Stuart by then had been eleven days in his grave, not far from the church that lost its steeple in the windstorm on the night he arrived from Yellow Tavern. After six mortal hours of being jounced on rutted country roads because the ambulance had to take a roundabout route to avoid the raiders on the turnpike, he reached his wife's sister's house on Grace Street at 11 o'clock that evening, and there, attended by four of Richmond's leading physicians through another twenty hours of suffering, he made what was called "a good death" — a matter of considerable importance in those days, from the historical as well as the religious point of view. After sending word of his condition to his wife at Beaver Dam, in hope that she and the children would reach him before the end, he gave instructions for the disposition of his few belongings, including his spurs and various horses. "My sword I leave to my son," the impromptu will concluded. The night was a hard one, with stretches of delirium, but toward morning he seemed to improve; an aide reported him "calm and composed, in the full possession of his mind." Shortly after sunrise on May 12, when the rumble of guns was heard from the north, he asked what it meant, and on being told that part of the capital garrison had gone out to work with the cavalry in an attempt to trap the raiders at Meadow Bridge: "God grant that they may be successful," he said fervently, then turned his head aside and returned with a sigh to the matter at hand: "But I must be prepared for another world." Later that morning the President arrived to sit briefly at his bedside. "General, how do you feel?" he asked, taking the cavalryman's hand. "Easy; but willing to die," Jeb said, "if God and my country think I have fulfilled my destiny and done my duty."

Davis could scarcely believe the thirty-one-year-old Virginian was near death; he seemed, he said afterward, "so calm, and physically so strong." But one of the doctors, seeing the Chief Executive out, told him there was no chance for Stuart's recovery. The bullet had pierced his abdomen, causing heavy internal bleeding, and probably his liver and stomach as well; "mortification" — peritonitis — had set in, and he was not likely to see another dawn. That afternoon Jeb himself was told as much. "Can I last the night?" he asked, realizing that his wife might not arrive before tomorrow because of the damage to the railroad north of Richmond, and received the doctor's answer: "I'm afraid the end is near." Stuart nodded. "I am resigned, if it be God's will," he said. "I would like to see my wife. But God's will be done." Near sunset he asked a clergyman to lead in the singing of "Rock of Ages," and it was painful to see the effort he made to join the slow chorus of the hymn. "I am going fast now, I am resigned; God's will be done," he murmured. That was shortly after 7 o'clock, and within another half hour he was dead.

Flora Stuart and the children did not arrive until four hours later, but were with him in plenty of time for the funeral next day at St James Church and the burial in Hollywood Cemetery. There was no military escort; the home guard was in the field and Lee could spare no soldiers from the Spotsylvania line. Davis and Bragg were there, along with other government dignitaries, but Fitz Lee's troopers were still out after Sheridan, down the Peninsula. Such were the last rites for the man John Sedgwick, dead himself for four days now, had called "the greatest cavalry officer ever foaled in America."

★ ★ ★

"His achievements form a conspicuous part of the history of this army, with which his name and services will be forever associated," Lee was presently to declare in a general order mourning the fallen Jeb. This was the hardest loss he had had to bear since the death of Jackson, and coupled as it was with the disablement of Longstreet, the indisposition of A. P. Hill, and the increasing evidence that one-legged Ewell would never fulfill the expectations which had attended his appointment as Stonewall's successor, there was cause for despair in the Confederate army, near exhaustion from its twenty-hour struggle for the Mule Shoe. Fortunately, as if in respectful observation of Stuart's funeral fifty miles away in Richmond, the following day was one of rest. For the next two days, and into a third, rain fell steadily — "as if Heaven were trying to wash up the blood as fast as the civilized barbarians were spilling it," a South Carolina sergeant of artillery observed. Such killing as there was was mostly done at long range, by cannoneers and snipers on both sides. There was little actual fighting, only a lumbering shift by the Union army, east and south. Lee conformed to cover Spotsylvania, extending his right southward, beyond the courthouse, to the crossing of the Po. The blue maneuver seemed quite purposeless, not at all like Grant; Lee was puzzled. Unable to make out what the Federals were up to, if anything, he remarked sadly to a companion: "Ah, Major, if my poor friend Stuart were here I should know all about what those people are doing."

Grant was not as quiescent as he seemed; anyhow he hadn't meant to be. During the day of rest from his exertions of May 12 he considered what to do to break the stalemate his headlong efforts had produced. A move around Lee's left would draw the old fox into open country, but in the absence of Sheridan's troopers Grant would be at a disadvantage, maneuvering blind against a foe who still had half his cavalry on hand. His decision, then, was to strike the enemy right by shifting Warren from his own right to his left on a night march that would end in a surprise attack at first light, May 14; Wright would follow to extend the envelopment which, if successful, would turn Lee out of his Spotsylvania works and expose him to destruction when he retreated. Orders to effect this were issued before the day of rest was over; but all that came of them was lumbering confusion and the loss of many tempers. Floundering through roadless mud, rain-whipped under-brush, and swollen creeks, the V Corps did not reach its jump-off position on the Fredericksburg Road until 6 a.m., two hours behind schedule, and had to spend the rest of the day collecting the thousands of mud-caked stragglers left exhausted in its wake. The attack had to be called off, and instead there followed another day of rest.

This time it was Wright who had a notion. The Confederates having conformed to the Union movement by shifting Anderson to their right, Wright suggested that a sudden reversal of last night's march — left to right, instead of right to left — would provide a capital op-portunity for a breakthrough on the rebel left, which had been thinned to furnish troops for the extension of the line down to Snell's Bridge on the Po. Grant liked and enlarged the plan to include Hancock, setting dawn of May 18 as the time of attack. Reoccupying the aban-doned Mule Shoe in the darkness of the preceding night, Hancock and Wright were to assault the new works across its base, while Burnside made a diversionary effort on their left and Warren stood by to join them once the fortifications were overrun. That gave two full days for getting ready; Grant wanted the thing done right, despite the mud. Moreover, on the first of these two days the rain left off, letting the roads begin to dry, and the second — May 17 — hastened the drying process with a sun as hot as summer. Everything went smoothly and on schedule: up to the point at which the six divisions moved into the Mule Shoe in the darkness, under instructions to take up positions for the 4 a.m. assault. So much time was spent occupying and moving through the first and second lines of the original intrenchments, undefended though they were, that it was 8 o'clock before the troops were in position to make the surprise attack that should have been launched four hours ago, at the first blush of dawn.

It would not have been a surprise in any case, even if the attackers had stayed on schedule. Rebel cavalry scouts, undistracted by the blue troopers taking their rest at Haxall's Landing, and lookouts in the Spotsylvania belfry, surveying the Union rear with glasses, had reported the countermovement yesterday. That left only the question of just where on the left the blow was going to land, and this in turn was answered by Ewell's outpost pickets, who came back in the night to announce that the assault would be delivered from the Mule Shoe. At first the defenders could not credit their luck; this must be a feint, designed to cover the main effort elsewhere. An artillery major, whose battalion had lost eight of its twelve guns in the dawn assault six days ago, reported later that he and his cannoneers "could not believe a serious attempt would be made to assail such a line as Ewell had, in open day, at such a distance," but he added that "when it was found that a real assault was to be made, it was welcomed by the Confederates as a chance to pay off old scores." Pay them off they did, and with a vengeance, from the muzzles of 29 guns commanding the gorge of the abandoned salient and the shell-ripped woods beyond, first with round shot, then with case and canister as the Federals pressed forward "in successive lines, apparently several brigades deep, well aligned and steady, without bands, but with flags flying, a most magnificent and thrilling sight, covering Ewell's whole front as far as could be seen." The conclusion was foregone, but the gunners made the most of their opportunity while it lasted. Double-timing over the mangled corpses of the fallen, the attackers managed to reach the abatis at scattered points, only to find the fire unendurable at that range. They fell back with heavy losses and the worst wounds of the campaign, and when they reëntered the woods they had emerged from such a short time back, the guns fell silent, not out of mercy, but simply to save ammunition in case the attack was resumed. It was not. "We found the enemy so strongly intrenched," Meade admitted in a letter to his wife, "that even Grant thought it useless to knock our heads against a brick wall, and directed a suspension." By 10 o'clock the one-sided carnage was over, and nowhere along the line had the opposing infantry come to grips. "This attack fairly illustrates the immense power of artillery well handled," Ewell's chief of artillery said proudly.

Perhaps by now, if not earlier, Grant had learned the error of his statement to Halleck, a week ago today: "I am satisfied the enemy are very shaky." By now perhaps he also had discovered the basis for what had seemed to him the overexaltation of Lee by many high-ranking Federals, who had not agreed with their new general-in-chief that the Virginian would be likely to fall back in haste from the Rapidan when he found the blue army on his flank. "Lee is not retreating," Colonel Theodore Lyman of Meade's staff wrote home that night. "He is a brave and skillful soldier and will fight while he has a division or a day's rations left." As for the troops who served the gray commander, wretchedly fed and clad though they were, Lyman considered them anything but shaky. "These rebels are not half starved," he added. "A more sinewy, tawny, formidable-looking set of men could not be. In education they are certainly inferior to our native-born people, but they are usually very quick-witted, and they know enough to handle weapons with terrible effect. Their great characteristic is their stoical manliness. They never beg or whimper or complain, but look you straight in the face with as little animosity as if they had never heard a gun fired." Indeed, at this stage of the contest, there was a good deal more disaffection in the Union than there was in the Confederate ranks. "We fought here. We charged there. We accomplished nothing," a blue artillerist complained, while a disgruntled infantryman protested specifically, in the wake of this second Mule Shoe fiasco, that the army was being mishandled from the top. The Wilderness had been "a soldier's battle," he said, in which no one could see what he was doing anyhow. "The enlisted men did not expect much generalship to be shown. All they expected was to have battle-torn portions of the line fed with fresh troops. There was no chance for a display of military talent." But that was not the case at Spotsylvania, he went on. "Here the Confederates are strongly in-trenched, and it was the duty of our generals to know the strength of the works before they launched the army against them." He was bitter, and the bitterness was spreading: not without cause. There was a saying in the army, "A man likes to get the worth of his life if he gives it," and the survivors here could not see that their fallen comrades, shot down in close-packed masses flung off-schedule against impregnable intrench-ments, had gotten the smallest fraction of the worth of theirs.

Whatever else he saw (or failed to see; he was admittedly not much given to engaging in hindsighted introspection) Grant saw clearly enough that something else he had said in the week-old letter to Halleck was going to have to be revised, despite the wide publicity it had re-ceived in the newspaper version: "I propose to fight it out on this line if it takes all summer." Stalemate was little better than defeat, in his opinion, and yet — having assaulted headlong twice, without appreciable success, and tried in vain to turn both enemy flanks — that seemed the best he could do in this location. Ten May days were a long way short of "all summer," yet they sufficed to show that he had nothing to gain from continuing the contest on "this line." So he decided, quite simply, to abandon it: not, of course, by retreating (retreat never entered his mind) but by shifting his weight once more with a wide swing around Lee's right, in the hope once more that he would catch him napping. Still without his cavalry to serve as a screen for the movement and keep him informed of his adversary's reaction — although it was true Sheri-dan had failed him in both offices before — he decided to try a different method of achieving Lee's destruction. He would mousetrap him.

Hancock was to be the bait. Grant's plan, as set forth in orders issued next morning, May 19, was for the II Corps to march that night to the Richmond, Fredericksburg & Potomac Railroad, six miles east, then down it on the far side of the Mattaponi River to Milford Station,

well beyond Lee's flank and deep in his right rear. Lee could be expected
to try to overtake and destroy Hancock, and this would mean that he
would be exposed to the same treatment by Grant, who would give
Hancock about a twenty-mile head start before moving out with the
other three corps for a leap at the gray army whose attention would be
fixed on the bright lure dangling off its flank, beyond the Mattaponi.
That was the plan, and there was about it a certain poetic justice, since it
was a fairly faithful reproduction of what Lee himself had done to Pope
on the plains of Manassas — except that he had lacked the strength to
follow it through to the Cannae he was seeking, whereas Grant did not,
having just received about half of the more than 30,000 reinforcements
sent from Washington over a ten-day period starting four days ago. By
way of preparation for the move, he shifted Burnside around to the far
left on May 18, returned Wright to his former position alongside
Warren, and placed Hancock in reserve beyond the Ni, ready to take
off promptly the following night on the march designed to lure Lee out
of his Spotsylvania intrenchments and into open country, where he
would be exposed to slaughter.

First, though, there was a delay involving bloodshed. On the day
whose close was scheduled to see Hancock set out eastward, Lee lashed
out at the denuded Federal right.

Alert to the possibility that Grant might steal a march on him, the
Confederate commander, on receiving word that morning that the
Federals had resumed their ponderous sidle to his right, ordered Ewell,
who held the left, to test the validity of the report by making a demonstration to his front. Though he was down to about 6000 effectives —
considerably less than half his infantry strength two weeks ago, when he
opened the fight in the Wilderness — Ewell, feeling perky as a result of
his easy repulse of yesterday's assault, asked if he might avoid the risk
of a costly frontal attack, in case the Yankees were still there, by conducting a flank operation. Lee was willing, and Ewell took off shortly
after noon on a reconnaissance in force around the end of the empty-
looking — and, as it turned out, empty — Union works. Accompanied
by Hampton's two brigades of cavalry, he carried only six of his guns
along because of the spongy condition of the roads, and even these he
sent back when he reached the Ni, about 3 o'clock, and found the mud
too deep for them to make it over, although Hampton managed to get
his four lighter pieces across by doubling the teams. So far, Old Bald
Head had encountered nothing blue; but presently, he reported, less than
a mile beyond the river, on his own in what had been the Federal right
rear, "I came upon the enemy prepared to meet me."

What he "came upon" was Warren's flank division, posted beyond
the Ni as a covering force for Hancock, whose corps was getting ready
to take off eastward after sundown. Responding to orders from headquarters to reinforce Warren instead, Hancock sent his largest division

first — a new one, just arrived the day before from Washington, under Brigadier General Robert Tyler — and followed with Birney's three bled-down brigades. Tyler had been a heavy artilleryman until recently, and so had all his men, except that, unlike him, they had seen no combat up to now. Their reception by the Army of the Potomac was unkind, to say the least. In addition to the usual taunts — "Why, dearest, did you leave your earthworks behind you?" — they were greeted by the veterans, who were returning from their botched and bloody assault down the Mule Shoe, with a gruesome demonstration of what was likely to happen to infantry in battle. "This is what you'll catch up yonder," the wounded told them, displaying shattered arms and other injuries Ewell's batteries had inflicted at close range. One roadside group had a mangled corpse which they kept covered with a blanket until one of the oversized greenhorn regiments drew abreast, and then they would uncover it with a flourish. The heavies had been singing as they marched, perhaps to keep their courage up, but they fell silent under the impact of this confrontation with what was left of a man who had been where they were headed. As it happened, the attack was suspended before they were committed. That was yesterday, however. This was today, and they were about to discover at first hand what combat meant.

Ewell, having found what he came looking for — or, to put the case more critically, having blundered into what he had been in search of — would have been glad to withdraw without bloodshed, but the bluecoats gave him no choice except to fight, not only at a numerical disadvantage, but also without guns to take up the challenge from the many turned against him. The resultant two-hour struggle, which began about 5.30, might well have completed the destruction of Lee's Second Corps if Wade Hampton had not managed to post his rapid-firing battery of horse artillery where it could hold the enemy off while Ewell fell back across the Ni and returned under cover of darkness to his intrenchments, minus another 900 of his men. The Federals lost a good deal more — 1535 killed or wounded or missing, most of them Tyler's — but at least they could claim a victory, having remained in control of the field and taken no less than 472 prisoners. A larger gain was the admission of the heavies to full membership in the army that had greeted them with jeers the day before. They had made up in staunchness, even veterans agreed, for what they lacked in skill. "Well, they got a little mixed and didn't fight very tactically," one of their officers replied to a question from a correspondent, "but they fought confounded plucky."

This last was good news for Grant, who was going to have to depend increasingly on such replacements in the weeks ahead. Three days ago, on May 16, with 12,000 of his cavalry away, his strength was down to 56,124 effectives — less than half the number he had mustered when he crossed the Rapidan, twelve days before. About 35,000 of the absent were battle casualties, lost in the Wilderness and here at Spotsylvania. Another 4000-odd had fallen sick and been sent to Washington hospitals to recover or to die. The rest, a substantial 14,000, were deserters or men whose enlistments had expired, members of the first of the thirty-six regiments scheduled for discharge when their time was up in May and June. There was, therefore, much encouragement for Grant in this May 19 evidence that he could count on the heavies, as well as on the newly drafted troops among them, for staunchness during the critical period in which they learned their bloody trade and became, in their turn, veterans more or less like the men who had jeered at them on their arrival but now would jeer no more. In any case, he depended on them to lend their weight to whatever blows he decided to throw, and he did not let his heavy losses for the past two weeks, on and off the field of battle, deter him from his purpose, which was to whip the rebel army in the process of maneuvering it back on Richmond. Today's affair amounted to no more than an interruption, a twenty-four-hour delay. He would move out tomorrow night, as planned: with one exception, one revision prompted by Ewell's sortie across the Ni that afternoon, which apparently served to remind Grant just how bloody-minded Bobby Lee could be. Instead of sending Hancock well in advance of the other three corps, to be dangled as bait on the east bank of the Mattaponi, he decided to move at a much closer interval, lest the bait be gobbled before the rest of the army came up in support. Accordingly, orders were sent, not only to Hancock, but also to Warren, Wright, and Burnside, that the march to Milford Station would begin tomorrow night, May 20, and would be conducted with all possible secrecy — in the hope, once more, of stealing a march on old man Lee.

But no amount of secrecy could hide what Lee already knew as a result of Ewell's rather heavy-handed investigation of the Union dispositions in his front. Grant had stripped his right for another shift in the opposite direction, and Lee prepared for another interception, alerting all three of his corps commanders to be ready to march at the tap of a drum. Despite such precaution, the enemy would of course move first; yet Lee had little fear that he would lose the pending race, whenever it began. He had chosen Hanover Junction as his point of concentration just beyond the North Anna, at the crossing of the two critical rail lines back to Richmond. From there he believed he would be able to parry any thrust the Federals were likely to attempt, and this time — unlike the last, in the sprint for Spotsylvania — he would have the advantage of the interior route of march, traveling the chord of the arc his adversary's movement would necessarily describe. His confidence, in this as in much else, was based on the events of the past two weeks; especially on a comparison of losses. Though he did not know the precise figures, even for his own army, let alone Grant's — the latter had suffered a total of 36,065 casualties (17,666 in the Wilderness, 18,399 at Spotsylvania) while Lee was losing barely half as many (just under 8000 in the Wilderness, just over 10,000 at Spotsylvania) — he knew that Grant's were disproportionately heavy. No opponent, so far, had been able to sustain such losses without removal from command or frustration of his plans by Washington; nor, he hoped, would this one, despite his known tenacity and his reported unconcern for costs. Lee's confidence was in himself and in his men. "With the blessing of God, I trust we shall be able to prevent General Grant from reaching Richmond," he had told the President ten days ago, and that trust had been confirmed. Moreover, though it was true the contemplated shift to Hanover Junction would mean giving up half the region between his present position and the capital in his rear, the line of the North Anna was one of great natural strength, highly dangerous for an army attempting to cross it, as Grant's would do, in the face of determined resistance. Besides, he was presently to remind Davis, "[Grant's] difficulties will be increased as he advances, and ours diminished."

One reason for this — in addition, that is, to the advantageous lengthening and shortening of their respective lines of supply and communication, vulnerable to attack by raiders and tedious to maintain — was that Lee would be moving toward the first reinforcements he had been able to count on, or even contemplate with any real degree of hope, since the opening of Grant's triple-pronged offensive. The reason he could count on them now was that two of the Federal prongs had, in effect, been snapped off short in the course of the past week. Breckinridge, out in the Shenandoah Valley, and Beauregard, on the far side of the James, had scored tactical successes which served not only to neutralize or abolish the separate threats from those directions by Franz Sigel and Ben Butler, but also to convert at least a part of each of those two outnumbered and hard-pressed Confederate forces into reserves, available for rapid shipment by rail to the Army of Northern Virginia from the south and west; which, incidentally, was still another reason for Lee's choice of Hanover Junction, where the two lines met and crossed from Richmond and the Valley, as his point of concentration after leaving Spotsylvania. By May 20, with the evidence getting heavier by the hour that the Federals in his immediate front were about to begin their march around his right, Lee called on both victorious commanders — Breckinridge by orders wired directly, since he was already under his command, and Beauregard by means of an urgent request to the War Department — to hasten the departure for Hanover Junction of every soldier they could spare from those two fronts.

It was well that he specified haste, for the signs of Grant's imminent departure continued to multiply all day. By nightfall Lee was so convinced that the Federals were about to march that he decided to begin his own next morning. Accordingly, he sent instructions for Ewell, whose corps would peel off from the left in order to lead the movement south, to start at daylight unless he saw an opening for a strike at the enemy rear. Old Bald Head, finding no such opportunity, stepped off at 4 a.m. May 21 — a scant six hours, events would show, after Hancock started out across the way.

✗ 3 ✗

Sigel's offensive, like his chief's, was subdivided into three columns of penetration, each with a different preliminary objective to be attained before all three combined for a linkup with Grant's main body in front of Richmond. His own main body, consisting of about 8000 of all arms, would march the length of the Shenandoah Valley, from Winchester to Staunton, where he would strike the Virginia Central Railroad. Crook meantime, with roughly the same number, would move west of the Valley, southward in two columns, one of about 6000 infantry under his personal direction, the other of about 2000 cavalry under Brigadier General W. W. Averell, against the Virginia & Tennessee. Crook's objective was Dublin Station and the nearby railway bridge across New River, Averell's the salt works and lead mines at Saltville and Wytheville, a day's ride west of Dublin: from which point the two would proceed east along the Virginia & Tennessee to Salem, tearing up track as they went, and then turn north, through Lexington, for a hookup with Sigel at Staunton and, subsequently, with Meade somewhere east or southeast along the Virginia Central, which was to be given the same hardhanded treatment as the reunited 16,000 moved along it to be in on the kill when Lee was brought to bay.

Crook's being the more lucrative assignment, at least in the opening stage of the campaign — salt and lead were rare necessities in the Confederacy, and the intended double blow at Saltville and Wytheville would go far toward making them rarer — Sigel started first, on April 30, hoping to draw attention and troops away from the region beyond the Alleghenies. It worked. By the time Crook's infantry set out from Gauley Bridge on May 2, beginning the rugged trek from the Kanawha, southward up the left bank of New River to Dublin Station, a roundabout distance of more than a hundred miles, the rebel department commander was busy stripping Southwest Virginia of its few defenders in order to get them aboard trains for rapid shipment to Staunton and a fast march northward, down the turnpike, to challenge Sigel's bid for control of the wheat-rich Shenandoah Valley. Within another three days, when Averell's mounted column began its parallel march on May 5 from Logan Courthouse, fifty miles southwest of Gauley Bridge, the Confederate shift was well under way. Crook made good time, considering the nature of the terrain. At Shannon's Bridge by sunset of May 8, only seven miles from Dublin, he learned that a rebel force was lying in wait for him two miles ahead on a wooded spur of Cloyd's Mountain.

A fork-bearded West Pointer, Ohio born and thirty-five years old, a veteran of Antietam and Chickamauga, he rode ahead next morning to look the position over — and found it strong. "They may whip us," he said as he lowered his binoculars, "but I guess not."

He guessed right. The Confederate force of about 3000, part militia and home guards, commanded by Brigadier General Albert Jenkins, a former Charleston lawyer in what was now called West Virginia, was routed by a charge in which one of Crook's brigade commanders, Colonel Rutherford B. Hayes, made a showing that stood him in good stead when he ran for President twelve years later. Jenkins was wounded and taken, along with two of his three guns and many rifles dropped by his green troops when they fled; Union surgeons removed his mangled arm and gave him such care as they had time for, but he died the following week, thirty-three years old and still a captive. His losses at Cloyd's Mountain numbered 538, the Federals' 643. Crook, overcome by excitement and exhaustion — he had hurried about the contested field with his waterproof boots full of water from crossing a creek — fell to the ground in a faint as soon as he saw that the battle was won, but revived in time, attended by his staff, to order an immediate advance on Dublin and the Virginia & Tennessee Railroad, five miles ahead. Arriving before dark, he put his men to work firing and wrecking the depot installations, along with a large accumulation of military stores, and set out at first light next morning, May 10, to destroy the 400-foot wooden railway bridge across New River, eight miles east. By midday it was burning briskly, and soon afterwards it collapsed with a great hiss of steam into the river. "A fine scene it was," Hayes noted in his diary.

Having thus carried out his preliminary assignment — marching and fighting and wrecking, all three boldly and with skill — Crook now had only to wait for Averell to join him and continue the movement as planned, east along the railroad to Salem, then north through Lexington for the meeting with Sigel at Staunton. Yet he did neither. He not only declined to wait for the cavalry column, he also declined to press on eastward in accordance with his orders. Instead he decided to return at once to West Virginia: specifically to Meadow Bluff, on the Greenbrier River near Lewisburg, where he could draw supplies from Gauley Bridge, his starting point some fifty miles northwest. His reason, as he gave it two weeks later in his report, was that "I saw [at the Dublin telegraph office] dispatches from Richmond stating that General Grant had been repulsed and was retreating, which determined me to move to Lewisburg as rapidly as possible." Isolated as he was, and accepting the rebel claim at face value, he feared that Lee would send troops west by rail from Orange to cut him off and up, and under pressure of this fear he bolted for the fastness of the mountains. Not even the arrival of outriders from Averell, bringing word that the troopers had found

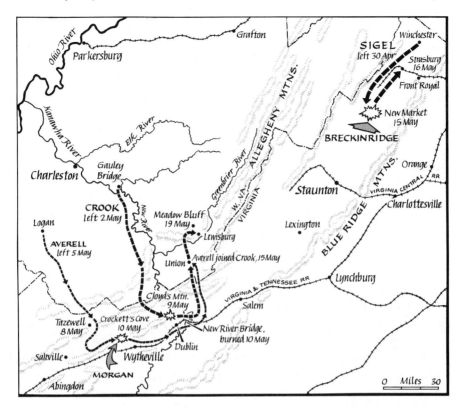

Saltville too well guarded for attack but that the column was moving on Wytheville even now, deterred Crook from making as quick a getaway as he could manage. He simply replied that Averell was to do his best to carry out the instructions he himself had just discarded, and took off northward, well beyond New River, which he crossed upstream and down. He made good time. It was five days later, May 15, before the cavalry overtook him at Union, eight miles beyond the West Virginia line.

Averell had a harrowing tale to tell: one that was unrelieved, moreover, by any such tactical victory as Cloyd's Mountain or any such gaudy feat as the demolition of New River Bridge. He had raided in this direction before, with conspicuous success, including the burning of Salem in December, but that had been done against next to no opposition. This time there was not only a considerable force in opposition — as he was told when he reached Tazewell on May 8, just this side of the state line — it was also commanded by John Morgan, who was known to be hungry for revenge for the indignities he had suffered in the Ohio Penitentiary during the four months preceding his year-end breakout. Now he was back in the field at last, having been rejoined by about 750 of his "terrible men," survivors of the disastrous July raid through Indiana and Ohio, and was posted at Abingdon to work with local units in defense of a department including portions of Southwest

Virginia and East Tennessee. At Tazewell Averell learned that the famed Kentuckian had shifted his headquarters and his troops to Saltville when he got word that a blue column was headed that way. What his strength was Averell did not know; he estimated it at 4500, better than twice his own. Consequently, he decided to forgo the scheduled destruction of the salt works, vital though they were to the Confederacy's efforts to feed its armies, and to strike instead directly at Wytheville and the lead mines, leaving Morgan holding the bag at Saltville. He feinted in that direction on May 9, then swung east, riding hard to give the rebels the slip. He thought he had succeeded until, approaching Wytheville the following afternoon, he found Morgan drawn up to meet him at a place called Crockett's Cove.

The position was admirably suited for defense, but that was not what Morgan had in mind. Fuming because the approach of the enemy column had delayed a projected return to his native Bluegrass, he charged and struck and kept on charging and striking the rattled Federals, who thus were afforded no chance to discover that they were not outnumbered. "My men fought magnificently, driving them from hill to hill," he wrote his wife that night. "It was certainly the greatest sight I ever witnessed to see a handful of men driving such masses before them. Averell fought his men elegantly, tried time and time again to get them to charge, but our boys gave them no time to form." This was Morgan's first engagement since the late-November jailbreak and he made the most of it until darkness ended the running fight, four miles east of Wytheville. He turned back then for Abingdon, to resume his plans for another "ride" into Kentucky, and Averell, minus 114 of his troopers, limped eastward to Dublin and beyond, where the railroad bridge had toppled hissing into New River that afternoon. Informed by his outriders that Crook had shied off into the mountains, he forded the river and tore up another ten miles of track and culverts before turning north to overtake his chief at Union on May 15. Hungry because supplies were low, and lashed by heavy rains, the reunited column spent two days getting over the swollen Greenbrier, then trudged upstream to Meadow Bluff, May 19, on the verge of exhaustion.

Crook's infantry had been seventeen days on the march from Gauley Bridge, the last eight without a regular issue of rations, and had crossed seventeen mountain ranges, each a bit steeper, it seemed, than the one before. They had accomplished little, aside from incidental damage to the railroad and the destruction of the New River bridge, but Crook was reassured to learn at Meadow Bluff that his superior, the major general commanding the department, had accomplished even less in the Shenandoah Valley. In fact, it now developed, the wide-swinging western column had been quite right not to press on east and north to Staunton, as instructed, since Sigel had covered barely half the distance from Winchester to that point, marching deliberately up the Valley

Pike, before he was obliged to turn and flee back down it, pursued by the victors of the battle that had defined the limit of his penetration.

It was Breckinridge's doing, and he did it on his own. Hearing from Lee in early May, while the Army of Northern Virginia was on its way to the confrontation with Grant in the thickets south of the Rapidan, that he was to assume "general direction of affairs" beyond the Blue Ridge, the former U.S. Vice President, electoral runner-up to Lincoln in the presidential race of 1860, continued his efforts to collect all movable troops in Southwest Virginia for a meeting with Sigel in the Valley. "I trust you will drive the enemy back," Lee had told him, and the tall, handsome Kentuckian, forty-three years old, with lustrous eyes, a ponderous brow, and the drooped mustache of a Sicilian brigand, was determined to do just that. Accordingly, he left the defense of the western reaches of his department to Jenkins and Morgan, scant though their resources would be in event of an attack, and set out for Staunton at once, by rail, with two veteran brigades of infantry totaling just under 2500 men. North of there, and hard at work observing and impeding Federal progress south of Winchester, was Brigadier General John D. Imboden, whose 1500 cavalry were all that would stand in Sigel's path until Breckinridge arrived. The Kentuckian reached Staunton on May 12 and set off promptly down the turnpike for New Market, forty miles away, where Imboden was skirmishing with advance elements of the blue main body, still a dozen miles to the north. Including these butternut troopers, Breckinridge would go into battle with close to 5000 of all arms: a figure he attained by mustering all the militia round-about — 750 at the most — and by summoning from Lexington the cadet corps of the Virginia Military Institute, 247 strong, all under conscription age and commanded by one of their professors, who later recalled that although Breckinridge said he hoped to keep these fifteen-, sixteen-, and seventeen-year-olds in reserve through the bloodiest part of the fighting (thus to avoid what Jefferson Davis had referred to as "grinding the seed corn of the nation") he added in all honesty that, "should occasion require it, he would use them very freely."

Occasion was likely to require it. Pleased that he had succeeded in drawing the rebels north and east, away from the now vulnerable installations in Southwest Virginia, Sigel was intent on completing his preliminary assignment by winning control of the Shenandoah Valley before the wheat in its fields was ripe for grinding into flour to feed Lee's army. This would entail whipping the gray force gathering to meet him, and he marched south with that welcome task in mind, anticipating his first victory since Pea Ridge, out in Arkansas more than two years ago, for which he had been made a major general. All the battles he had been involved in since that time, however slightly, had been defeats — Second Bull Run and Fredericksburg were examples — with the result that his demonstrations of military competence had been limited to the conduct of retreats. A book soldier, academy-trained in his native Germany, which he had fled in his mid-twenties after serving as Minister of War in the revolution of 1848, he was anxious to win the glory he had prepared for, though he did not let ambition make him rash. Advancing from Winchester, up the turnpike that led ninety miles to Staunton, he moved with skill and proper deliberation. There were mishaps, such as the loss of 464 men in a cavalry regiment surprised and captured by Imboden while on outpost duty beyond Front Royal, May 11, but Sigel knew how to accept such incidental reverses without distraction, even though this one, combined with the need for detaching troops to guard his lengthening supply line, reduced his combat strength to roughly 6500 of all arms. Past Strasburg by then, he kept his mind on the job ahead and continued his march up the pike to Mount Jackson, terminus of the Manassas Gap Railroad, on May 14. This was only seven miles from New Market, occupation of which would give him control of the single road across Massanutton Mountain and thus secure his left flank practically all the rest of the way to Staunton. He had sent his cavalry ahead to seize the crossing of the north fork of the Shenandoah River, two miles south of Mount Jackson, and when they arrived that afternoon they were taken under fire by a rebel battery posted on a height just over a mile beyond the bridge. They settled down to a brisk artillery exchange, preparing to force a crossing, but Sigel — perhaps recalling what had happened three days ago, when nearly 500 other troopers had been gobbled up near Front Royal — sent word that he preferred to wait until the infantry came up next morning, when all arms would combine to do the thing in style.

Breckinridge was within earshot of the cannonade. Just arrived from Staunton with his two brigades, plus the VMI cadets, he was taking a late afternoon dinner with Imboden at Lacy Springs, a dozen miles to the south, and when he heard the guns begin to rumble he told the cavalryman to return at once to New Market, hold the crossing of the North Fork till dark if possible, then fall back to a position just this side of the town, where he would join him before daybreak. Imboden, with Sigel's coöperation, carried out these instructions to the letter. Awakened at dawn by the arrival of the infantry — Sunday, May 15 — he assisted in getting the troops in line for what was intended to be a defensive battle. But when sunrise gave a clear view of the field, Breckinridge studied it carefully through his glasses and changed his mind. Sigel's men had crossed the river at first light to take up a position astride the turnpike north of town, and the Kentuckian apparently liked the looks of what he saw. "We can attack and whip them here," he said. "I'll do it."

And did. While the Confederates were adjusting their dispositions for attack, the guns on both sides — 28 of them Union, opposed by half as many firing north — began exchanging long-range shots across the rooftops of the town. This continued for an hour, at the end of which the gray line started forward, one brigade on the right, the other on the left, with a regiment of dismounted cavalry between them on the pike, supported by the cadets whose spruce uniforms had resulted in their being greeted with cat-calls by veterans on the march; "Katydids," they called them. Imboden struck first with a horseback charge through some woods on the right, and the infantry went forward through the town, cheered by citizens who came running out to meet them. On the far side, they scattered the blue pickets, then went for the main line. Sigel disengaged skillfully and fell back half a mile, disposing his troops on high ground to the left and right of a hillock on which a six-gun battery was slamming rapid-fire shots into the ranks of the advancing rebels. Spotting this as the key to the position, Breckinridge ordered the dismounted troopers to charge and take it, supported by the cadets; which they did, though only by the hardest, not only because of heavy fire from the well-served artillery, but also because of a gully to their front, less than two hundred yards from the fuming line of guns and floored with what turned out to be calf-deep mud. Moreover, as the movement progressed, it was the troopers who were in support. Lighter, more agile, and above all more ardent, the cadets made better time across the soft-bottomed depression, and though they were hit repeatedly with point-blank canister, they soon were among the cannoneers, having suffered better than twenty percent casualties in the charge: 8 killed and 46 wounded. Slathered with clay and stained by smoke, many of them barefoot, having lost their shoes and socks in the mud of the gully, the survivors were scarcely recognizable as yesterday's dapper Katydids. But they carried the position. "A wild yell went up," Imboden would remember, "when a cadet mounted a caisson and waved the Institute flag in triumph over it."

Sigel was in his element. Lean-faced and eager, not yet forty, his lank hair brushed dramatically back to bring out his sharp features and brief chin beard, he maintained an icy, steel-eyed posture under fire, but betrayed his inner excitement by snapping his fingers disdainfully at shellbursts as he rode about, barking orders at his staff. Unfortunately, he barked them in German, which resulted in some confusion: as, for example, when he directed that two companies of a West Virginia regiment move up to protect the six-gun battery under attack by the cadets. "To my surprise," he later protested, "there was no disposition to advance. In fact, in spite of entreaties and reproaches, the men could not be moved an inch!" And when the rest of the gray line surged forward to take advantage of the respite gained by the boy soldiers, there was nothing Sigel could do but attempt another displacement, and this he did, as skillfully as he had performed the first, though at a considerably higher cost. By now he was back on the knoll from which the rebel horse artillery had challenged his crossing of the river yesterday, four

miles north of town. He held on there, through a lull occasioned by the
need for refilling the cartridge boxes of the attackers, and when they
came on again he fell back across the North Fork, burning the bridge
behind him. Secure from pursuit, at least for the present, he intended
to stand his ground despite heavy losses (831 killed and wounded and
missing, as compared to the enemy's 577) but decided a better course
would be to retire to Mount Jackson, where he could rest and refit
before resuming his interrupted southward march. He got there around
7 o'clock that evening, took up a stout position, and remained in it
about two hours before concluding that the wisest course, after all,
would be to return to Strasburg, another twenty miles back down the
pike. A night march got him there the following afternoon, and after
one more trifling readjustment — rearward across Cedar Creek next
morning, May 17, to make camp on the heights he had left a week
ago — he finished his long withdrawal from the unfortunate field of
New Market and began making incisive preparations for a return.

But that was not to be; not for Sigel at any rate. Stymied at
Spotsylvania, Grant was growing impatient at having heard nothing of
or from his director of operations beyond the Blue Ridge. "Cannot
General Sigel go up Shenandoah Valley to Staunton?" he wired Halleck,
who replied that, far from advancing, Sigel was "already in full retreat.
... If you expect anything from him you will be mistaken," Halleck
added. "He will do nothing but run. He never did anything else."
Grant was furious: about as much so as he was with Banks, whose Red
River fiasco came to an end that same week. Four days later, on May 21,
Franz Sigel was relieved of his over-all command.

Lee on the other hand was delighted with his lieutenant's conduct
of affairs in that direction, and was quick to express his gratitude. "I
offer you the thanks of this army for the victory over General Sigel,"
he wired Breckinridge on the morning after the battle. "Press him down
the Valley, and if practicable follow him into Maryland." This last was
in line with the suggestion he had made to Stonewall Jackson, two years
ago today, at the outset of the campaign that had frightened the Washington authorities into withholding troops from McClellan's drive on
Richmond, and he hoped that it might have the same effect on Grant's
more energetic effort. In any event, New Market had saved the wheat
crop in what was called "the bread basket of Virginia," and even if
Breckinridge lacked the strength to undertake a crossing of the Potomac,
it at least freed a portion of his command to reinforce the army north
of Richmond. Lee, in a follow-up telegram that same day, left the decision to the general on the scene. "If you can follow Sigel into Maryland, you will do more good than by joining us," he wired. "[But] if
you cannot, and your command is not otherwise needed in the Valley
or in your department, I desire you to prepare to join me."

Breckinridge answered next morning that he preferred the latter course. He would move, he said, with 2500 men. Anticipating the shift from Spotsylvania, Lee replied: "Proceed with infantry to Hanover Junction by railroad. Cavalry, if available, can march."

★　★　★

That was on May 17, the day when news of a greater victory, together with the promise of much heavier reinforcements, was relayed to Lee from Beauregard, twelve days into a campaign that began with every prospect of a Union triumph, south of the James, and ended quite the other way around. Indeed, nothing could better illustrate the abruptness with which fortune's frown and smile were interchangeable than the contrast between the elation of Richmond's citizens on that date and the gloom that had descended on May 5, when they learned from downstream lookouts that an amphibious column ten miles long, containing no less than two hundred enemy vessels, was steaming up the river that laved the city's doorstep. Loaded at Yorktown the day before — while Grant was crossing the Rapidan — the armada had rounded the tip of the York-James peninsula in the night, and now, with the morning sun glinting brilliant on the water — and Grant and Lee locked in savage combat, eighty miles to the north — it was proceeding up the broad, shining reaches of the James.

Five ironclads led the way and other warships were interspersed along the line of transports, a motley array of converted ferries, tugs and coasters, barges and canal boats, whose decks were blue with 30,000 soldiers, all proud to be playing a role in what seemed to one of them "some grand national pageant." What was more, they had a commander who knew how to supply the epitomizing gesture. Riding in the lead, Ben Butler brought his headquarters boat about, struck a pose on the hurricane deck, and steamed back down the line. As he sped past each transport, past the soldiers gaping from its rail, he swung his hat in a wide vertical arc toward the west and lurched his bulky torso in that direction, indicating their upstream goal and emphasizing his belief that nothing could stop them from reaching it in short order. Unaware that within two weeks he and they were to wind up caged — or, as his superior was to put it, "corked" — they cheered him wildly from ship after ship as he went by, then cheered again, even more wildly, as he turned and churned back up the line, still waving his hat and lunging his body toward Richmond.

After dropping one division off at City Point, within nine miles of Petersburg, the flotilla proceeded north, past the adjoining mouth of the Appomattox River, and debarked the other five divisions at Bermuda Hundred, a plantation landing eighteen crow-flight miles from the rebel capital. Ashore, as afloat, the gesticulating Butler rode with the van, and close up he was even stranger-looking than he had been when viewed across the water; "the strangest sight on a horse you ever

saw," one witness thought, attempting a word portrait of the former
Massachusetts senator who shared with Banks, though he was more than
a year his junior at forty-five, the distinction of being the U.S. Army's
ranking active major general. "With his head set immediately on a
stout, shapeless body, his very squinting eyes, and a set of legs and arms
that look as if made for somebody else and hastily glued to him by
mistake, he presents a combination of Victor Emmanuel, Aesop, and
Richard III, which is very confusing to the mind. Add to this a horse
with a kind of rapid, ambling trot that shakes about the arms, legs, etc.
till you don't feel quite sure whether it is a centaur or what it is, and
you have a picture of this celebrated General."

Despite the neckless, bloated look, the oddly assorted members,
and the disconcerting squint of his mismatched eyes, Butler was all
business here today. Mindful of Grant's injunction that he was to "use
every exertion to secure footing as far up the south side of the river as
you can, and as soon as you can," he landed the bulk of his army just
short of the first of the half dozen looping bends or "curls" of the James,

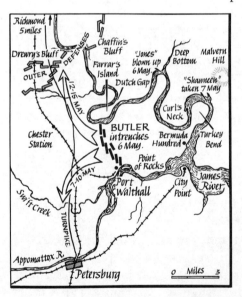

where the Confederates had
heavy-caliber guns sited high on
the steep bluffs to discourage
efforts to approach the city by
water, and next morning he began to comply with another item
in his instructions: "Fortify, or
rather intrench, at once, and concentrate all your troops for the
field there as rapidly as you can."
Five miles west of Bermuda
Hundred, between Farrar's Island and Port Walthall, the
James and the Appomattox were
less than four miles apart. By
intrenching this line he would
be safe from a frontal attack,
while the rivers secured his flanks and rear. It was true, the Bermuda debarkation required a crossing of the Appomattox to reach either City
Point or Petersburg, but this was better, Butler reasoned — bearing in
mind Grant's double-barreled admonition "that Richmond is to be your
objective point, and that there is to be coöperation between your force and
the Army of the Potomac" — than having to cross it in order to reach the
fattest and probably best-defended prize of all. By sundown of May 6, his
first full day ashore, he not only had completed the preliminary intrenchment of the line connecting the bends of the two rivers, he also had
sent a brigade of infantry another two or three miles west to look into
the possibility of cutting the railroad between Petersburg and Richmond,

which in turn afforded the rebel defenders their only rail connection with the Carolinas and the reinforcements they no doubt were calling for, even now, in their distress at his appearance on their doorstep.

Encouraged by a report from the brigadier who conducted the reconnaissance (he had run into spirited resistance on the turnpike, half a mile short of the railroad, but nothing that could not be brushed aside, he thought, by a more substantial force) Butler decided next morning to go for the railroad in strength, then turn southward down it to knock out Petersburg and thus assure that his rear would be unmolested when he swung north to deal with Richmond. While the others kept busy with axes and spades, improving the earthworks protecting their base from attack, four of the fourteen brigades in the two corps, each of which had three divisions, moved out to attend to this preamble to the main effort: three from Gillmore and one from Major General W. F. Smith, whose third division had debarked at City Point and was still there, despite his protest that it "might as well have been back in Fort Monroe." The march was along the spur track from Port Walthall, and their initial objective was its junction with the trunk line, three miles west. As they approached it around midday, a spatter of fire from the skirmishers out front informed them that the junction — grandly styled Port Walthall Junction, though all it contained was a run-down depot and a couple of dilapidated shacks — was defended. The four brigades came up in turn to add their weight to the pressure being exerted, but the rebels either were there in heavy numbers or else they were determined not to yield, whatever the odds. This continued for two hours, in the course of which the Federals managed to overlap one gray flank and tear up about a quarter mile of track on the main line. But that was all. At 4 o'clock, having suffered 289 casualties, Butler decided to pull back behind his fortifications and return in greater strength tomorrow; or, as it turned out, the day after.

Both good and bad news awaited him, back on Bermuda Neck. The bad was from the navy, which had sent a squadron out the day before to investigate an account by a runaway slave that the Confederates had torpedoes planted thickly in the James, especially in the vicinity of Deep Bottom, a dozen miles up the winding river from Bermuda Hundred. It was all too true: as the crew of the big double-ender *Commodore Jones* found out, about 2 o'clock that afternoon. A 2000-pound torpedo, sunk there some months ago and connected by wires to galvanic batteries on the bank, "exploded directly under the ship with terrible effect, causing her destruction instantly." So her captain later reported from a bed in the Norfolk Naval Hospital. Another witness, less disconcerted because he was less involved, being aboard another gunboat, went into more detail. "It seemed as if the bottom of the river was torn up and blown through the vessel itself," he wrote. "The *Jones* was lifted almost entirely clear of the water, and she burst in the air like an exploding firecracker. She was in small pieces when she struck the water again." For days, bodies and parts of bodies floated up and were fished out of the James; the death toll was finally put at 69. Just now, though, the problem of how to keep the same thing from happening over and over again was solved by the capture of two men caught lurking in the brush where the batteries were cached. They had triggered the explosion, and what was more they had helped to plant other such charges up ahead. They refused to talk, however, until one of them was placed in the bow of the lead vessel and the squadron continued its upstream probe: whereupon, in the words of an interrogator, he "signified his willingness to tell all."

That more or less solved the problem of torpedoes (in any case, of the ones already planted; future sowings were of course another matter) but next day, about the time the four brigades began their skirmish down the spur track from Port Walthall, the navy was given a violent reminder that older dangers, familiar to sailors long before any-one thought of exploding powder under water, still threatened the exist-ence of the fleet. U.S.S. *Shawneen*, a 180-ton sidewheel gunboat on patrol at Turkey Bend, dropped anchor under the loom of Malvern Hill to give her crew time out for the midday meal, only to have it interrupted when a masked battery and four companies of Confederate infantry opened fire from the north bank, peppering the decks with bullets and puncturing the steam drum. While most of the crew went over the side to keep from being scalded, *Shawneen*'s captain ordered her colors struck to save the lives of the injured still aboard. Ceasing fire, the rebel colonel in command sent out a boat to remove survivors and blow the vessel up; "which was effectively done," he reported, "consigning all to the wind and waves."

Such was the bad news — bad for Butler because it meant that the navy, having lost two ships in as many days, was likely to be reluctant to give him the slam-bang close support he would want when he moved against or beyond the high-sited batteries on Chaffin's and Drewry's bluffs, fortified works flanking the last tortuous upstream bend of the river below Richmond, both of them integral parts of the hard-shell outer defenses he would have to pierce if he was to put the hug on the rebel capital. The good news came from his cavalry, two brigades com-bined in a 3000-man division under Brigadier General August Kautz, a thirty-six-year-old German-born West Pointer. Off on his own while the rest of the army was steaming up the James, Kautz rode due west out of Suffolk on May 5 for a strike at the Petersburg & Weldon Rail-road, damage to which would go far toward delaying the arrival of enemy reinforcements from the Carolinas. Encountering little opposi-tion he did his work in a slashing style: first at Stony Creek on May 7, where he burned the hundred-foot railway bridge twenty miles south of Petersburg, and then next day at the Nottoway River, another five miles down the line, where he put the torch to a second bridge, twice as long, before turning north to rejoin the army two days later at City Point. Encouraged by news of the first of these two burnings, which reached him on May 8, Butler spent that day in camp, secure behind his Bermuda Neck intrenchments, putting the final touches to his plans for a movement against Petersburg next morning, much heavier than the one that had taken him only as far as Port Walthall Junction the day before.

This time he got a solid half of his infantry in motion, 14,000 in all. Smith, on the left, again ran into fire as he approached the Junction and called on Gillmore, who had advanced by then to Chester Station unopposed, to come down and join the fight. Gillmore did, although regretfully, having just begun to rip up track and tear down telegraph wire along the turnpike. But when the two corps began to maneuver in accordance with a scheme for bagging the force at the Junction, the graybacks slipped from between them and scuttled south. Pursuing, the Federals found the Confederate main body dug in behind unfordable Swift Creek, three miles north of Petersburg, which in turn lay beyond the unfordable Appomattox. When Butler came up to observe their fruitless exchange of long-range shots with the enemy on the far side of the creek, Gillmore and Smith informed him that Petersburg couldn't be taken from this direction. The thing to do, they said, was return at once to Bermuda Neck and lay a pontoon bridge across the Appomattox at Point of Rocks, which would permit an attack on Petersburg from the east. Fuming at this after-the-fact advice from the two professionals, Butler replied testily that he had no intention of building a bridge for West Pointers to retreat across as soon as things got sticky, and Smith later declared that he found this remark "of such a character as to check voluntary advice during the remainder of the campaign."

Tempers got no better overnight. Contemplating the situation next morning, with the uncrossable creek still before him, Butler decided that Petersburg was of little importance anyhow, now that Kautz had burned two bridges on the railroad in its rear. Accordingly, he ordered everyone back to Bermuda Neck, there to regroup for an advance to be made on Richmond as soon as he got his plans worked out. They returned the following day, May 11, filing in through gaps in the intrenchments around noon, and Butler retired to his tent to think things over for a while.

If he was bitter, so were his lieutenants, contrasting what had been so boldly projected with what had been so timidly and erratically performed. In Smith's opinion, based on what he had seen in the past six unprofitable days, the army commander was "as helpless as a child on the field of battle and as visionary as an opium eater in council." Butler returned the compliment in kind, including Gillmore in the indictment. Both generals, he said, "agreed upon but one thing and that was how they could thwart and interfere with me," while, to make matters worse, neither of them "really desired that the other should succeed." Feeling his reputation threatened (in the North, that is; in the South he was already known as "Beast" Butler, hanger of patriots, insulter of women) he had written to Stanton two nights ago, from the near bank of Swift Creek, reviewing his progress to date and placing it in the best possible light, even though this involved a rather ingenuous reinterpretation of his share in Grant's over-all design for the crushing of Lee and the taking of Richmond.

"We can hold out against the whole of Lee's army," he informed the Secretary, and he added for good measure: "General Grant will not be troubled with any further reinforcements to Lee from Beauregard's force."

Lee of course had no intention of attacking Butler, who was not even in his department, and though it was true he wanted reinforcements from any source whatever, he certainly expected none from the general opposing the southside threat, since, at the outset at least, that unfortunate commander — George Pickett, of Gettysburg fame — had practically no troops to fight with, let alone detach. He had, in all, fewer than 750 of all arms to stand in the path of the 30,000 Federals debarking at Bermuda Hundred and City Point, nine miles respectively from Drewry's Bluff and his district headquarters at Petersburg, whose garrisons were included in the total that showed him facing odds of forty-to-one or longer. Beauregard, sixty-five miles to the south at Weldon, which he had reached two weeks ago to assume command of the newly created Department of North Carolina and Southern Virginia, replied to an urgent summons from Richmond on May 5 that he was "indisposed," too ill to take the field. Three brigades were en route from his old command at Charleston; he would do his utmost to speed them northward, so long at least as the railroad stayed in operation, and would come up in person as soon as he felt well enough to travel. In the meantime, though, he left it to Pickett to improvise as best he could a defense against the host ascending the James.

Pickett himself was not even supposed to be there, having received orders the day before to proceed by rail to Hanover Junction and there await the arrival of his four brigades — two of which were now with Hoke in the movement against New Bern, down the coast, while the other two were with Major General Robert Ransom, charged with defending Richmond north of the James — for a reunion with Lee's army, then on its way eastward into the Wilderness to challenge Grant's advance. The long-haired Virginian looked forward to returning to duty under Longstreet, whose guidance he had missed these past eight months on detached service. Warned of the landings downriver today, however, he stayed to meet the threat to the near vacuum between the James and the Appomattox, although he was to regret profoundly, in the course of the next five days, that he had not caught an earlier northbound train. Those five days, May 5–10, were an unrelenting nightmare, illuminated from time to time by flashes of incredible luck which then were seen to have served perversely, not to resolve, but rather to prolong the strain on his jangled nerves. Fortunately, two regiments from the first of the three promised brigades from Charleston reached Petersburg on the morning of May 6, and Pickett got these 600 Carolinians up the turnpike in time to delay the advance of the brigade Butler sent probing for the railroad. They managed this, though only by the hardest, and just as they were about to be overrun they were reinforced by a brigade sent down from Richmond: Tennesseans who had arrived that morning under Brigadier General Bushrod Johnson, the first of two western outfits summoned east to replace Pickett's two brigades in the capital defenses. Johnson was a heavy hitter, as he had shown by spearheading the Chickamauga breakthrough, and his attack drove the reconnoitering Federals back on the line of intrenchments constructed that day across Bermuda Neck. Pickett told Johnson to dig in along the pike, and then — reinforced by the rest of the Charleston brigade, which came up after midnight to lift his strength to about 3000 — settled down to wait, as best his tormented nerves would permit, for what tomorrow was going to bring.

What tomorrow brought was Butler's four-brigade attack, 6000 strong, and news that Kautz had burned the bridge over Stony Creek, cutting off hope for the early arrival of more troops from the south. One reinforcement Pickett did receive, however, and this was Major General D. H. Hill, famed for a ferocity in battle rivaling that of his late brother-in-law Stonewall Jackson. His caustic tongue having cost him lofty posts in both of the Confederacy's main armies — together with a promotion to lieutenant general, withdrawn when he fell out with Bragg after Chickamauga — Hill had offered his services to Beauregard as an aide-de-camp, and Beauregard sent him at once to Petersburg to see if Pickett thought he could be of any help. Pickett did indeed think so, and put the rank-waiving North Carolinian in charge of the two brigades in position up the turnpike. Hill handled them so skillfully in the action today around Port Walthall Junction, losing 184 to inflict 289 casualties on a force twice the size of his own, that Butler pulled back, more or less baffled, and spent what was left of that day and all of the next, May 8, brooding behind his Bermuda Neck intrenchments.

Greatly relieved by this turn of events, Pickett experienced a mixed reaction to news that Hoke's projected attack on New Bern had been a failure, due to the nonarrival of the *Albemarle*, which had retired up the Roanoke River on May 5 after a three-hour fight with seven Union gunboats in the Sound from which the ironclad took her name. She had inflicted severe damage on her challengers and suffered little herself, except to her riddled stack, but the engagement had proved her so unwieldy that her skipper decided there was no hope of steaming down into Pamlico Sound to repeat at New Bern the victory she had helped to win two weeks ago at Plymouth. This meant that, without the support of the ram, Hoke's scheduled attack had to be called off: which in turn freed him and his five brigades, including the two from Pickett, for use elsewhere. Nowhere were they needed worse than at Petersburg, and Pickett was pleased to learn that they were to join him there by rail from Goldsboro — though when they would arrive was even more doubtful now than it had been the day before, word having just come in that Kautz had burned a second railway bridge, this one across the Nottoway, twice the length of the first and therefore likely to require about twice the time to replace.

Offsetting this last, there was good news from above. While Hill was making his fight for the Junction, the second western brigade reached Richmond — Alabamians under Brigadier General Archibald Gracie, another Chickamauga hero — and was sent across the James by Ransom, who not only followed in person but also brought along Pickett's other pair of brigades and posted all three in the works around Drewry's Bluff, bracing them for a stand in case the Federals turned in that direction. This addition of 4500 troops, combined with Pickett's remnant and the two brigades with Hill, increased the strength of the southside force to about 8000, roughly one third the number Butler had on Bermuda Neck. Pickett was greatly encouraged by this reduction of the odds — and so, apparently, was Beauregard, who wired from Weldon on May 8: "The water has improved my health." Whether the cause was the water or the buildup (not to mention the strangely hesitant performance by Pickett's opponent, who seemed to be groping his way piecemeal toward eventual destruction) the Louisiana general announced that he soon would be well enough to come to Petersburg and lift the awesome burden of responsibility from the district commander's shoulders.

By then Butler had ended his spell of brooding, and next morning he came on again, this time with half his army, only to pull up short on the north bank of Swift Creek, whose presence he seemed not to have suspected until now. Beauregard arrived the following day, May 10, in time to watch the baffled Army of the James — so Butler styled it — fade back once more from approximate contact and set out rearward to find sanctuary within its fortifications. Coming fast behind him on the railroad were seven veteran brigades of infantry, Hoke's five from Goldsboro and two more from Charleston. All reached Petersburg by nightfall, having marched across the five-mile gap between the Nottoway and Stony Creek, where they got aboard waiting cars for the last twenty miles of their ride. Pickett's five days were up at last, and rather as if the strain had been what kept him rigid, after all, he collapsed and took to his bed with a nervous exhaustion vaguely diagnosed as "fever." To replace him, Beauregard summoned Major General W. H. C. Whiting from Wilmington, and turned at once to the task of organizing the twelve brigades now south of the James into four divisions. Their combined strength was just under 20,000: enough, he thought, to deal with Ben Butler for once and for all by going over to the offensive, provided of course that the Beast could be lured from behind his intrenchments and out from between the two rivers protecting his flanks.

Butler complied, two days later, by moving northward against the works around Drewry's Bluff, apparently having decided to go for Richmond after all. Beauregard had anticipated this by sending Hoke with seven brigades to join Ransom, and now he prepared to follow and take command in person, leaving Whiting to hold Petersburg with the other two brigades of infantry, plus one of cavalry just come up from North Carolina. Arriving at 3 a.m. May 14, after taking a roundabout route to avoid capture, he found that the Federals had driven the defenders from some of the outworks, south and west of Drewry's, and now were consolidating their gains, obviously in preparation for an all-out assault that would open the way to Richmond. The high-spirited Creole, with his big sad bloodhound eyes and his hair brushed forward in lovelocks over his temples, did not quail before this menace; he welcomed it as a chance to catch Butler off balance and drop him with a counterpunch.

Though it came at a rather awkward time, Ransom having detached two brigades two days ago to help fend off Sheridan, whose troopers had broken through the outer defenses north of the capital, Beauregard had a plan involving Grand Strategy which he hoped would provide him with all the soldiers needed to dispose of the threat to Richmond, not only from the south, but from the north as well: not only of Butler, that is, but also of Grant. For three years now the Hero of Sumter had specialized in providing on short notice various blueprints for total victory, simple in concept, large in scale, and characterized by daring. This one was no exception. In essence, the plan was for Lee to fall back on the capital, avoiding all but rear-guard actions in the process, then send Beauregard 10,000 of his veterans, together with Ransom's two detached brigades, as reinforcements to be used in cutting Butler off from his base and accomplishing his destruction; after which, Old Bory subsequently explained, "I would then move to attack Grant on his left flank and rear, while Lee attacked him in front." He added that he not only "felt sure of defeating Grant," but was convinced that such a stroke would "probably open the way to Washington, where we might dictate *Peace! !*"

Thus Beauregard — at 3 o'clock in the morning. Wasting no time by putting the plan on paper, he outlined it verbally for a colonel on his staff and sent him at once to Richmond with instructions to pass it on without delay to the Commander in Chief. Davis was unavailable at that hour, but Bragg was not. Having heard the proposal, he dressed and rode to Drewry's for a conference with its author. Old Bory was waiting, and launched into a fervent plea for action. "Bragg," he said, "circumstances have thrown the fate of the Confederacy in your hands and mine. Let us play our parts boldly and fearlessly. Issue those orders and I'll carry them out to the best of my ability. I'll guarantee success!" Though noncommittal, the grim-faced military adviser listened to further details of the plan and returned to the capital, having promised to lay the facts before the President as soon as possible. This he did: along with his objections, which were stringent.

Not only did the scheme ignore the loss of the Shenandoah Valley and the Virginia Central Railroad, he declared, but "the retreat of General Lee, a distance of sixty miles, from the immediate front of a superior force with no less than 8000 of the enemy's cavalry between him and the Chickahominy . . . at least endangered the safety of his army if it did not involve its destruction." Moreover, he said, such a concentration of troops beyond the James was quite unnecessary; Beauregard already had a force "ample for the purpose of crushing that under Butler, if promptly and vigorously used." Davis agreed that the plan was neither practical not requisite, and in courtesy to the Louisiana general, as well as out of concern for his touchy pride, he rode to Drewry's Bluff to tell him so in person, in the gentlest possible terms.

Beauregard's spirits drooped; but only momentarily. They rebounded at the President's assurance that Ransom's two brigades, having wound up their pursuit of Sheridan, would be ordered back across the James for a share in the attack, and Old Bory, savoring the prospect of belaboring the Beast who had tyrannized New Orleans, set to work devising a plan for assailing him, first frontally, to put him in a state of shock, and then on the flanks and rear, so that, being "thus environed by three walls of fire, [Butler] could have no resource against substantial capture or destruction, except in an attempt at partial and hazardous escape westward, away from his base, trains, or supplies." To accomplish this consummation, his first intention was to assemble all twelve infantry brigades at Drewry's for the assault, but then he decided that, instead of waiting for the troops to arrive from Petersburg by a roundabout march to avoid the Federals on the turnpike, he would have Whiting move up to Port Walthall Junction and pitch into their rear when he heard the guns announce the opening of the attack on their front by the other ten brigades, four each under Hoke and Ransom and two in a reserve division under Brigadier General Alfred Colquitt, who commanded one of the three brigades from Charleston. Notifying

Whiting by messenger and the other three division chiefs in person, he set dawn of May 16 as the jump-off hour.

That gave them a full day to get ready, if Butler would only coöperate by remaining where he was. He did just that, though more from ineptness than by design; an attack planned for that day had to be called off when it turned out that he had provided so well for the defense of his newly won position that there were no troops left for the offensive. Butler was not greatly disturbed by this development, apparently having become inured to the fact that fumbling brought delay. For one thing, he had done well these past three days — especially by contrast with the preceding seven — and had encountered only token opposition in occupying the outworks around Drewry's. So had his cavalry, which he unleashed again when he left Bermuda Neck; Kautz had struck the Richmond & Danville two days ago, wrecking switches and culverts, and by now was astride the Southside line, tearing up sections of track. Back on the James, moreover, though the river was too shallow for the ironclads to proceed beyond City Point, the navy had been persuaded to lend a hand by pushing a few lighter-draft gunboats up to Chaffin's for a duel with the batteries on that bluff. All this should give the rebels plenty to fret about for the next day or two, Butler reasoned; by which time he would be ready to hit them in earnest.

His two corps commanders, while considering themselves honorbarred from tendering any more "voluntary advice," were by no means as confident that the Confederates would be willing to abide a waiting game. Smith, in fact — called "Baldy" from his cadet days when his hair began to thin, though he protested unavailingly nowadays that he still had more of it than did many who addressed him by this unwanted sobriquet — was so disturbed by what he took to be signs of a pending assault on his position that he spent a good part of May 15, a Sunday, scavenging rebel telegraph wire along the turnpike and stringing it from stumps and bushes across his front, low to the ground to trip the unwary; "a devilish contrivance none but a Yankee could devise," Richmond papers were presently to say of this innovation which Burnside had found useful in his defense of Knoxville six months before. Smith hoped it would serve as well here on Butler's right, though he ran out of wire before he reached his flank brigade, nearest the James. He and Gillmore each had two divisions on line; his third was still at City Point, completely out of things, and one of Gillmore's was posted in reserve, back down the pike. The night was dark, soggy with intermittent rain and a heavy fog that seemed to thicken with Monday's dawn, providing a curtain through which — true to Baldy's uncommunicated prediction — the graybacks came screaming and shooting and, as it turned out, tripping over the low-strung wire across much of the Federal right front, where the blow first fell.

Along those hampered portions of the line, Smith was to say, the attackers were "slaughtered like partridges." But unfortunately, as the next phase of the fight would show, there was no wire in front of Gillmore's two divisions on the left; nor was there any in front of the brigade on the far right, where Beauregard was intent on unhinging the Union line, severing its connection with the river, and setting it up for the envelopment designed, as he said, "to separate Butler from his base and capture his whole army, if possible." Struck and scattered, the flank brigade lost five stands of colors and more than 400 prisoners, including its commander, and though the adjoining brigades and Smith's other division stood fast behind their wire, inflicting heavy casualties on Ransom, Gillmore's divisions gave ground rapidly before an advance by Hoke, also losing one of their brigade commanders, along with a good many lesser captives and five guns. Confusion followed on both sides, due to the fog and the disjointed condition of the lines. Beauregard threw Colquitt in to plug the gap that developed between Hoke and Ransom, and Gillmore got his reserve division up in time to stiffen the resistance his troops were able to offer after falling back. By 10 o'clock, after five hours of fighting, the battle had reached the pendulous climax Old Bory intended for Whiting to resolve when he came up in the Union rear, as scheduled, to administer with his two brigades the rap that would shatter the blue mass into westward-fleeing fragments, ready to be gathered up by the brigade of saber-swinging troopers he was bringing with him, up the railroad from the Junction. Two hours ago, a lull in the fighting had allowed the sound of firing to come through from the south. It grew, then died away, which was taken to mean that Whiting had met with slight resistance and would soon be up. Since then, nothing had been heard from him, though Beauregard sent out couriers to find him somewhere down the pike, all bearing the same message: "Press on and press over everything in your front, and the day will be complete."

None of the couriers found him, for the simple yet scarcely credible reason that he was not there to be found. Not only was he not advancing, as ordered, from Port Walthall Junction; he had fallen back in a state of near collapse at the first threat of opposition, despite the protests of subordinates and Harvey Hill, who had reverted to his role of volunteer aide. A brilliant engineer, whose talent had made Wilmington's Fort Fisher the Confederacy's stoutest bastion and who had attained at West Point the highest scholastic average any cadet had ever scored, the forty-year-old Mississippian was cursed with an imagination that conjured up lurid pictures of all the bloody consequences incaution might bring on. Intelligence could be a liability when it took this form in a military man, and Chase Whiting was a case in point for the argument that a touch of stolidity, even stupidity, might be a useful component in the makeup of a field commander. In any event, wrought-up as he was from the strain of the past two lonely days at Petersburg, which he was convinced was about to be attacked by the superior blue force at City Point, he went into something resembling a trance when he encountered sporadic resistance on the turnpike beyond Swift Creek, and ordered a precipitate return to the south bank. Dismayed, the two brigade chiefs had no choice except to obey, and Hill, though he retired from Whiting's presence in disgust, later defended him from rumors that he had been drunk or under the influence of narcotics. Whiting himself had a simpler explanation, which he gave after the return to Petersburg that evening. Berated by the two brigadiers, who could not restrain their anger at having been denied a share in the battle today, he turned the command over to Hill, "deeming that harmony of action was to be preferred to any personal consideration, and feeling at the time — as, indeed, I had felt for twenty-four hours — physically unfit for action."

Up at Drewry's, the truth as to what was happening below lay well outside the realm of speculation. Expecting Whiting to appear at any moment on the far side of the field, Beauregard abstained from attempting a costly frontal assault, which might or might not be successful, to accomplish what he believed could be done at next to no cost by pressure from the rear. Jefferson Davis, who could seldom resist attending a battle whose guns were roaring within earshot, rode down from Richmond to share in the mystery and the waiting. "Ah, at last!" he said with a smile, shortly before 2 o'clock, when a burst of firing was heard from the direction of Whiting's supposed advance. It died away and did not recur, however, and Beauregard regretfully concluded that it had been produced by a cavalry skirmish, not by an infantry attack. After another two hours of fruitless waiting and increased resistance, the Creole general would report, "I reluctantly abandoned so much of my plan as contemplated more than a vigorous pursuit of Butler and driving him to his fortified base.... I therefore put the army in position for the night, and sent instructions to Whiting to join our right at the railroad in the morning."

As it turned out, no "driving" was needed; Butler drove himself. Badly confused by the events of the day — he had lost 4160 killed, wounded, or missing, including two brigade commanders and 1386 other prisoners, as compared to Beauregard's total of 2506 in those three categories — he ordered a nighttime withdrawal to Bermuda Neck. "The troops having been on incessant duty for five days, three of which were in a rainstorm," he informed Washington, quite as if no battle had been fought, "I retired at leisure to within my own lines." Once back there, within the sheltering arms of the two rivers, he busied himself with strengthening his three-mile line of intrenchments, followed by the victorious Confederates, who came up next morning and began digging a three-mile line of their own, studded with guns confronting those in the Union works. Thus, after two weeks of fitful confusion, in the course of which the Federals suffered just under 6000 casualties to inflict about half as many, a stalemate was achieved; Beauregard could not get onto Bermuda Neck, but neither could Butler get off it. The Beast was caged.

Richmonders exulted in the thought of cock-eyed Butler snarling behind bars, but Grant employed a different simile to describe the outcome of his well-laid plan for obliging Lee to fall back, in haste and probable disarray, to protect the threatened capital in his rear. Angered by the news from Bermuda Hundred, which reached him hard on the heels of equally woeful accounts of what had happened to Banks and Sigel, up the Red and at New Market, he borrowed a phrase from a staff engineer whom he sent to look into the tactical situation beyond the James. Butler's army, he presently reported, "was as completely shut off from further operations directly against Richmond as if it had been in a bottle strongly corked."

As for Beauregard the corker, though he was proud of his victory and its outcome, he was by no means content. "We could and should have done more," he said. "We could and should have captured Butler's entire army." Believing that this could still be done, he returned to his former proposal that he and Lee collaborate in disposing of the enemies before them, except that this time he reversed the order of their destruction. "The crisis demands prompt and decisive action," he notified Bragg on the night of May 18, outlining a plan whereby he would detach 15,000 troops for a flank attack on Grant while Lee pulled back to the Chickahominy. Once Grant was whipped, then Lee would reinforce Beauregard for attending to Butler in much the same fashion. Admittedly the odds were long, but Old Bory considered the prize well worth the gamble, especially by contrast with what was likely to result from not trying at all. "Without such concentration," he declared, "nothing decisive can be effected, and the picture presented is one of ultimate starvation."

Davis agreed that the future seemed bleak, but he could not see that Beauregard's plan, which reached his desk the following morning, was one that would make it rosy. All the previous objections still obtained, particularly the danger to Lee in falling back before a superior blue army reported to be receiving heavy reinforcements almost daily, while he himself got none, and it was to this problem that Davis gave his attention in returning the rejected plan to Bragg. "If 15,000 men can be spared for the flank movement," he noted, "certainly 10,000 may be sent to reinforce General Lee." This was not at all what Old Bory had had in mind, since it denied him anything more than a subservient role in Richmond's further deliverance from peril. He protested for all he was worth, and not entirely without success. Not 10,000, but 6000 were ordered detached that day, May 20, from the force that manned the intrenchments confronting and corking the bluecoats on Bermuda Neck. Pickett's four brigades, plus one of the three sent up from Charleston in the course of the past week — all five had been scheduled to do so anyhow, before Butler's appearance up the James — left next day to join or rejoin the Army of Northern Virginia.

✗ 4 ✗

Lee never liked the notion of abandoning any part of the Old Dominion to its foes, but in this case, setting out from Spotsylvania on May 21 to intercept another crablike Union sidle around his right, he not only was moving toward 8500 reinforcements, he also believed he was about to avail himself of his best chance, so far, to "end this business on the battlefield, not in a fortified place." With the two armies in motion, on more or less parallel routes, almost anything could happen, and he was exhilarated, as always, by the prospect. Best of all, though, he looked forward to the confrontation likely to follow on the line of the North Anna, a couple of miles this side of Hanover Junction, where the troops from Breckinridge and Beauregard had been told to join him in time to strengthen the attack he hoped to launch while Grant was astride the deep-banked river. Moreover, with his army holding the inside track, there was little of the strain there had been two weeks ago in the breakneck race for Spotsylvania; Ewell, whose corps had been withdrawn across the Po at dawn, had barely 25 miles to go on the main-traveled Telegraph Road, while Hancock, whose starting point was the north bank of the Ni, had 34 roundabout miles to cover, by inferior roads and without the customary mass of rapid-firing blue troopers to clear and screen his front. This meant that Lee could avoid exhausting his men on the march and still have plenty of time, at its end, for preparing the ground on which he would stand to deliver the blow he had in mind.

Ewell set off down the Telegraph Road at noon, Anderson four hours later. While Lee waited beside the Po, preparing to follow, A. P. Hill reported himself fit for duty. Despite his pallor, which seemed to deny his claim of recovery, Lee at once restored him to command, with instructions to hold his corps in position till well after nightfall unless the last of the departing Federals pulled out before that time, and sent Early ahead to resume charge of his division under Ewell. He himself left at 8 o'clock that evening. "Come, gentlemen," he told his staff, and turned Traveller's head southward in the twilight.

Two thirds of the way to Hanover Junction, having ridden past Anderson's marchers under the flooding light of a full moon, he took a two-hour rest beside Polecat Creek — which contributed its waters, but fortunately not its name, to the Mattaponi — and reached the North Anna soon after 8 o'clock next morning, about the same time the head of Ewell's column passed over and began filing into position along the south bank, covering Chesterfield Bridge, by which it had crossed, and the railroad span half a mile below, both of which were also protected by bridgeheads set up on the other side. When Anderson arrived at noon, his two divisions extended the line a mile and a half upstream to Ox Ford, the only point along this stretch of river where the right bank was higher than the left. Army headquarters was established in the southwest quadrant of the crossing of the Virginia Central and the Richmond, Fredericksburg & Potomac; Grant was reported to be marching down the latter. Breckinridge was waiting at Hanover Junction with his two brigades, as ordered, and was given a position in line between Anderson and Ewell. Pickett's division was also there (but not its ringleted commander, who was still convalescing from the strain he had been under, south of the James); Lee assigned it temporarily to Hill, who would arrive tomorrow to extend the line a couple of miles beyond Ox Ford, in case the bluecoats tried a flanking movement from that direction when they came up. For the present, Lee required no digging to be done, partly because he did not know for sure that Grant would attempt a crossing here when he found the graybacks once more in his path, intrenched or not, and also because he wanted to give his soldiers the leisure to enjoy their first full day out of contact with the enemy since the meeting engagement in the Wilderness, seventeen bloody days ago.

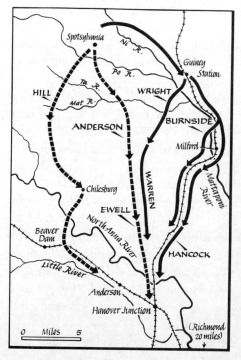

Hill arrived the following morning, May 23, coming in from the west shortly before the midday appearance of the Federals from the north. His approach was by the Virginia Central, since he had crossed the North Anna near Beaver Dam by a longer westerly route to guard the wagon train, and Lee had him rest his three divisions, with Pickett's as a fourth, under cover of some woods around Anderson Station, three miles short of Hanover Junction. While the last of his men were filing in to drop their packs in the shade of the trees, the first enemy columns came into sight beyond the river, heavy blue streams flowing sluggishly down the Telegraph Road and the tracks of the R.F.&P. Greeted by guns emplaced on high ground overlooking Ox Ford, they paused, then resumed their flow as the Union batteries took up the challenge. Short of the ford and the two bridgeheads, they stopped again and engaged the outpost rebels in the kind of long-range firefight known to veterans as a "squabble." Lee was watching with suppressed excitement, foreseeing his chance at another Fredericksburg if Grant would only continue to do as he so much hoped he would, when news arrived from the far left that another Union column was about to force a crossing beyond Jericho Mills, three or four miles above. Hill was available to counter such an upstream threat, but Lee decided to look into it in person before disturbing Little Powell's road-worn troops. Still weary from his all-night ride two nights ago, and feeling the first twinges of an intestinal disorder, he went in a borrowed carriage to the point that was said to be menaced and studied carefully with his binoculars some bluecoats in a skirt of woods across the river. He took his time, then turned at last to a courier he had brought along. "Go back and tell A. P. Hill to leave his men in camp," he said. "This is nothing but a feint. The enemy is preparing to cross below."

He was both right and wrong in this assessment: right in a lesser, wrong in a larger sense: as he discovered when he got back to headquarters, late that afternoon, and heard the uproar of a sizeable engagement on the far left, in the upstream region he had just returned from. Warren had his whole corps there and by 4.30 had completed a crossing of the river, not at the point where Lee had reconnoitered, but at nearby Jericho Mills — which was in fact "below," as Lee had predicted, but a good deal less so than he apparently had expected. Learning that the Federals had crossed and were advancing southward through the woods in unknown strength, Hill sent Wilcox up to meet them and Heth to follow in support if needed. The action opened briskly, on a promising note. Wilcox, by the luck of the draw, struck Wadsworth's depleted division, now under Brigadier General Lysander Cutler, and drove it back in panic on the other two divisions. At this point, however, things began to go badly for the attackers, who seemed to have forgotten, in the course of more than two weeks of defensive combat, how to function on the offensive. Confused by their quick success, they fought disjointedly when they moved forward to complete the Union rout. Struck in turn, they backpedaled and fell into confusion, glad to make their escape under cover of the woods and a furious rainstorm that broke over them at sundown to end the fighting before Heth arrived to join it. They had lost 642 men in the engagement, veterans who would be sorely missed in battles still to come, and had gained nothing more than the infliction of an equal number of casualties on an enemy who could far better afford the loss.

In any case, here was the first definite indication that Grant intended to attack Lee where he was, rather than continue his march downriver in search of an uncontested crossing, and presently there was another such indication, quite as definite, near the opposite end of the line. Under cover of the rainstorm that ended the Jericho Mills affair at sunset, Hancock launched a sudden two-brigade assault on the Chesterfield bridgehead, which was taken so quickly that the defenders not only had no time to fire the wooden structure in their rear, but also lost more than a hundred of their number killed or captured before they could scramble back across.

This was a small price to pay for the disclosure that the Federals were preparing to attack both Confederate wings tomorrow, above and below Ox Ford. On the off chance that it might be a ruse, employed by Grant to screen another sidle, Lee alerted Anderson to be ready for a downstream march next morning. At the same time, though — before turning in for such badly needed sleep as his cramped bowels would permit — he began devising a trap, the design for which was based on personal reconnaissance of the ground and careful study of the map, for Grant's reception if that general acted on the larger probability that he would hold to the plan whose beginnings had just been disclosed, upstream and down, for a widespread double attack on the gray army fanned out along the south bank of the river to his front.

That was just what the northern commander had in mind, and his confidence that he could bring it off, following up the double attack with a double envelopment, was shared by all around and under him, from major generals down to drummer boys and teamsters. Leaving Spotsylvania on May 21, however, after sixteen unrelenting, unavailing days of combat (waged at an average cost of 2300 casualties a day, as compared to Lee's 1100) the blue marchers had been discouraged by this second tacit admission that, despite their advantage in numbers and equipment and supplies, whenever the tactical situation was reduced to a direct confrontation, face to face, it was they and not their ragged, underfed adversaries who broke off the contest and shifted ground for another try, with the same disheartening result.

"Now what is the reason that we cannot walk straight through them with our far superior numbers?" a Michigan soldier asked, and after ruling out individual skill as a factor in the equation — "We fight as good as they" — came up with two possible answers: "They must understand the country better, or there is a screw loose somewhere in the machinery of our army."

Presently though, moving southeast, then south, and then south-southwest through a region so far untouched by war, with well-tended crops along the road and plenty of fence rails available for campfires at the end of each day's march, they perceived once more that the shift was not only sideways but forward. It was Lee, not Grant, who was yielding ground, and sooner or later — sooner, at this rate, for the march to the North Anna was better than twice the length of the one two weeks ago, out of the Wilderness — the southern commander would have none left to yield. Then would come the showdown, the last battle: which, after all, was the only one that counted in the long run, the only one they really had to win to win the war. And steadily, as this conviction grew, so did their confidence in themselves and the man who led them. A Massachusetts regiment, having crossed the Mattaponi on the morning of May 23, was slogging down the railroad, past a siding, and saw Grant, in his now tarnished uniform, perched on a flatcar gnawing a ham bone. When the New Englanders gave him a cheer he responded with a casual wave of the bone, which he then went back to. They liked that in him. It seemed to them that this singleness of purpose, this refusal to be distracted, was as characteristic of his way of fighting as it was of his way of eating. He was giving Lee the kind of attention he gave the ham bone, and it seemed to them that the result might be the same, just ahead on the North Anna — or if not there, then somewhere else this side of Richmond, where Lee would finally run out of space for backing up.

Grant believed the showdown would come here; anyhow he acted on that premise when he came within sight of the river around midday. Warren having taken the lead by turning south at Guiney Station, eight miles short of Milford, he sent him upstream to Jericho Mills and kept Hancock, who followed close behind, marching straight ahead to confront the rebels defending Chesterfield Bridge and the railroad span below. He had hoped that Lee would venture after him for an all-out scrap in the open country south and east of the Mattaponi, but since the old fox had declined the challenge there was nothing for Grant to do, as he saw it, but go for Lee where he now was. As for turning back, he had just finished making this practically impossible by closing down his Belle Plain base on the Potomac, severing all connection with that river except by sea, and opening another at nearby Port Royal on the Rappahannock. If Lee eluded him here on the North Anna he was prepared to leapfrog his base southward again when he took up the pursuit, thus keeping his supply line short and easily defended. But he did not intend to be eluded; he intended to fix the rebel army where it was by striking both of its flanks at once and moving around them to gain its rear; in which case, disadvantaged though the defenders would be, as to position as well as numbers, Lee would have no choice except to fight the showdown battle his adversary was seeking.

Soon after sunset Grant was pleased to learn that all was going well upstream and down. Warren, having crossed unmolested at

Jericho Mills, had repulsed a savage attempt by A. P. Hill to drive him back across the river. He was intrenching now, as a precaution, and would press on south and east tomorrow, to strike and turn the rebel left. Hancock too was ready for full offensive action, having seized the approaches to Chesterfield Bridge by driving off or capturing the hundred or so graybacks attempting to hold it. He would cross at first light, under instructions to serve the enemy right in much the same fashion. Burnside and Wright would be up by then, and they too would have a share in the attack, Burnside by crossing at Ox Ford to exert pressure against the center, thereby helping to fix the defenders in position, and Wright by crossing in Warren's wake to extend his right and make certain that rebel flank was overlapped and overwhelmed.

Such were the orders, and Grant turned in for a good night's sleep, with high hopes for tomorrow. These were encouraged, first thing next morning, May 24, by reports from the left and right. Hancock crossed dry-shod, unopposed, as did Wright upstream at Jericho Mills, following Warren, who encountered only token opposition when he proceeded southeast down the Virginia Central Railroad and the south bank of the river. While Burnside moved into position for a lunge across Ox Ford, good news came from Sheridan that he would be rejoining today, winding up his fifteen-day excursion down to Richmond and the James; Grant was pleased to have him back, along with his 11,000-odd troopers, presumably to undertake the welcome task of gathering up Lee's fugitives at the climax of the movement now in progress. Meantime, awaiting developments across the way, the general-in-chief attended to certain administrative and strategic details, the first of which was the incorporation of the IX Corps into the Army of the Potomac, thus ending the arrangement whereby Burnside, out of deference to his rank, had been kept awkwardly independent of Meade so far in the campaign.

Two other matters he also attended to in the course of the day, both having to do with rectifying, as best he could, the recent setbacks his diversionary efforts had suffered out in the Shenandoah Valley and down on Bermuda Neck. Sigel's successor, Major General David Hunter, was given specific instructions to accomplish all that Sigel had failed to do, and more; that is, to march up the Valley to Staunton, proceed across the Blue Ridge to Charlottesville, and continue from there southwest to Lynchburg, living off the country all the way. As for Butler, though there was no serious thought of removing him from command despite his ineptness, Grant now viewed his bottled army as a reservoir from which idle soldiers could be drawn for active service with the army still in motion under Meade. Accordingly, he was ordered to load a solid half of his infantry aboard transports — under Baldy Smith, whom Grant admired — for immediate shipment, down the James and up the York, to the Army of the Potomac. These 15,000 added reinforcements might or might not be useful, depending on what came of the maneuver now in progress across the North Anna.

Reports from there were beginning to be mixed and somewhat puzzling, not so much because of what was happening, but rather because of so much that was not. First off, finding Ox Ford covered by massed batteries frowning down from the high ground just across the way, Burnside felt obliged to state that any attempt to force a crossing at that point would result in nothing better than a bloodying of the water. Grant saw for himself that this was all too true, and accordingly changed the ruff-whiskered general's orders to avoid a profitless repulse. Leaving one division to keep up a demonstration against the ford, which in fact would serve his purpose about as well, Burnside was told to send his other two divisions — his fourth was still detached, guarding supply trains — upstream and down, to strengthen the attacks on the rebel left and right. But there was where the puzzlement came in. Neither Hancock nor Warren, who by now had been joined by Wright, had met with even a fraction of the resistance they had expected to encounter in the course of their advance. Enemy pickets did little more than fire and fall back at the slightest pressure, they reported. Except for the presence of these few graybacks, together with those in plain view on the high ground opposite Ox Ford, Lee's army might have vanished into quicksand. They found this strange, and proceeded with caution, scarcely knowing what to expect.

All Grant could do, under the circumstances, was approve the caution and advise a continuation of the advance, southeast from the right and southwest from the left. Sooner or later, he felt certain, Hancock and Warren would come upon the rebels lurking somewhere between them, over there, and grind them up as if between two millstones.

Lee rose early, despite a difficult night, and rode again in the borrowed carriage to visit A. P. Hill near Anderson Station. There he learned the details of yesterday's botched attack on Warren, made piecemeal by a single gray division, when a concerted blow by all the available four would have taken full advantage of the original blue confusion to wreck a solid quarter of Grant's army. Contrasting what might have been with what now was — Warren smashed, with Warren advancing southeast through the woods — Lee turned on Little Powell. "Why did you not do as Jackson would have done," he fumed: "thrown your whole force upon those people and driven them back?"

Red-bearded Little Powell had fallen out rather spectacularly, at one time or another, with every other superior he had ever had, including Longstreet and the general whose spirit was being invoked; but he held onto his temper now, rebuked though he was in the presence of his staff, and accepted from Lee, without protest, what he would never have taken from any other man. For one thing, he was aware of the justice of the charge, and for another he could see that Lee was not himself. Unaccustomed to illness, the gray commander had lost his balance under pressure of his intestinal complaint, and lashed out at Little Powell in an attempt to relieve the strain.

None of this was evident, however, when he moved on to the question of how to deal with the advancing Federals. This had to do with the preparation of the topographical trap he had devised the night before; Ewell and Anderson were already at work on their share of it on the right and in the center, down the railroad east of Hanover Junction and along the river in the vicinity of Ox Ford.

The North Anna was no more defensible here at close range than the Rappahannock had been at Fredericksburg, for the same reason that the opposite bank, being higher, permitted the superior Union batteries to dominate the position — all, that is, but a brief stretch of the south bank overlooking Ox Ford and extending about half a mile below. Here the Confederate batteries had the advantage, and here Lee found the answer to his problem: not of how to prevent a crossing, which was practically impossible anywhere else along the line, but of how to deal with the Federals once they were on his side of the river. He would hold this stretch of high ground with half of Anderson's corps, strongly

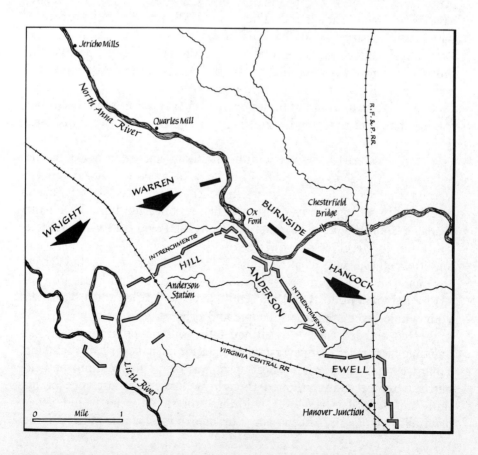

supported by artillery, and pull the other half, along with all of Ewell's, back on a line running southeast to Hanover Junction, just east of which there was swampy ground to cover this new right flank. Similarly, Hill would occupy a line extending southwest from Ox Ford to a convenient northward loop of Little River, just west of Anderson Station. Intrenched throughout its five-mile length, this inverted V, its apex to the north and both flanks securely anchored, would provide compact protection for Lee's army, either wing of which could be reinforced at a moment's notice from the other. Best of all, though, it not only afforded superb facilities for defense; it also gave him an excellent springboard for attack. By stripping one arm of the V to a minimum needed for holding off the enemy on that side, he could mass his troops along the other arm for an attack on that isolated wing of the blue army: *which* wing did not matter, since either would have to cross the river twice in order to reinforce the other, and would therefore not be likely to arrive in time to do anything more than share in the disaster. Here was something for Grant to ponder, when and if he saw it. But the hope was that he wouldn't see it until it blew up in his face.

Leaving Hill to get started on the intrenchment of the western arm, Lee rode back to his headquarters to await developments that would determine which Union wing he would assault. Ewell and Anderson, with Breckinridge still between them, were hard at work, the former having been reinforced by the fifth of the five brigades sent up from Richmond. So skillful were the men by now at this labor, which they formerly had despised as unfit for a white man to perform, that by midday formidable earthworks, complete with slashings and abatis, had risen where none had been six hours before. This augured well for the springing of the trap, once the bluecoats came within snapping distance of its jaws. While Lee waited, however, his intestinal complaint grew worse, and though he tried to attend to administrative matters as a distraction, they only served to heighten his irascibility. The result was fairly predictable. "I have just told the old man he is not fit to command this army!" a flustered aide protested as he emerged from the tent where he had been given a dressing-down by Lee.

Before long it was obvious that the charge, though highly irreverent, was true. Even the general himself had to admit it by taking to his cot, betrayed by his entrails on the verge of the crisis he hoped to resolve by defeating, with a single well-planned attack, the foe who had maneuvered him rearward across forty miles of his beloved Virginia in the past twenty days. If Lee could not deliver the blow, then no one could. It was too late to send for Beauregard, and none of his three ranking lieutenants — one-legged Ewell, who was also nearing physical collapse, or sickly Hill, who had shown only the day before that he was in no condition for larger duties, or lackluster Anderson, who had

been less than three weeks in command of anything more than a division
— seemed capable of exploiting the present opportunity, which would
vanish as soon as the Federals spotted the danger and reacted, either
by intrenching or by pulling back across the river for a crossing
farther down, beyond reach of the trap that had been installed for their
undoing. Time was passing all too fast, and the chance, once gone,
might never recur. Lee on his cot broke out vehemently against this
deprivation of the victory he felt slipping from his grasp.

"We must strike them a blow," he kept saying. "We must never
let them pass us again. We must strike them a blow!"

Betrayed from within, he raged against fate — and rightly; for
before the day was over his worst fears were realized. Hancock, nudging down from his crossing at Chesterfield Bridge, and Warren and
Wright, skirmishing fitfully all the way from Jericho Mills, came at
last upon what the old gray fox had devised for their destruction.
Not only were the works about as formidable as the ones they had
assaulted with little success at Spotsylvania, but the rebels were still at
work with picks and shovels, adding traverses at critical points to avoid
exposure to enfilade fire. Moreover, the blue generals were not long
in perceiving that such fortifications might have an offensive as well
as a defensive use. They took a good hard look and went into a frenzy
of digging, east and west, throwing up intrenchments of their own
against the attack they believed might come at any moment from either
arm of Lee's inverted V. And while they dug they sent headquarters
word of the situation, best described years later by Evander Law, commander of one of the three Alabama brigades in the works ahead:
"Grant found himself in what may be called a military dilemma. He
had cut his army in two by running it upon the point of a wedge. He
could not break the point, which rested upon the river, and the attempt
to force it out of place by striking on its sides must of necessity be
made without much concert of action between the two wings of his
army, neither of which could reinforce the other without crossing the
river twice; while his opponent could readily transfer his troops, as
needed, from one wing to the other, across the narrow space between
them."

This was no more apparent to Law, then or later, than it presently
was to Grant, who quickly sent down orders canceling the attack. It
was apparent, too, that as soon as a withdrawal could be effected without heavy losses, the thing to do was get back out of there. Meantime,
the digging progressed and dirt continued to fly. Fortunately the
graybacks seemed content with such long-range killing as their snipers
and artillery could manage, but this did little to relieve the feeling on
the Union side that they had once more been outgeneraled. This was
their twentieth day of contact, and the showdown was no closer within
their reach than at the outset. Dejection was taking its toll, along with the

profitless wear and tear of the past three weeks. "The men in the ranks did not look as they did when they entered the Wilderness," one among them would recall. "Their uniforms were now torn, ragged, and stained with mud; the men had grown thin and haggard. The experience of those twenty days seemed to have added twenty years to their age."

All night they stayed there, and all next day and the following night, still digging, while Grant pondered the situation. He had never liked the notion of backing away from any predicament, most of which he had found would resolve themselves if he held on long enough for the enemy's troubles, whether he knew what they were or not, to be enlarged by time and idleness to unbearable proportions; in which case, he had also found, it was his adversary who got jumpy and pulled back, leaving the field to him. That was not likely to happen here, although Lee's headquarters had been shifted three miles down the R.F.& P. from Hanover Junction, on his doctor's orders to provide a more restful atmosphere for the still ailing general. Fretful and regretful though he was that his well-laid trap had gone unsprung, Lee looked now to the future and the chance to devise another that would not fail. "If I can get one more pull at him," he said of Grant this morning, "I will defeat him."

But that was not likely to happen here either. On May 26, their second day of confronting the Confederates with a divided army, the Federals put on the kind of show that generally preceded a withdrawal and a shift. There were demonstrations along the river and both arms of the fortified V, together with an upstream probe by a full division of cavalry, as if for a crossing in that direction: a likely course for Grant to follow, Lee believed, since it would keep him on the direct route to Richmond and at the same time deprive Lee of the use of the Virginia Central, his only rail connection with the Shenandoah Valley, which not only provided most of the food his army ate but was also his classic route for a counteroffensive designed to frighten the Washington authorities out of their military wits, as he had done twice already to bring about the calling-off or the recall of invasions by Hooker and McClellan, last year and the year before. Though he preferred a downstream Union sidle, which he hoped would eventually put Grant in much the same position as the one that had brought Little Mac to grief two years ago, astride "the confounded Chickahominy," Lee followed his usual intelligence procedure of assuming that his adversary would do what he himself would have done in his place. For that reason, as well as the evidence of the cavalry demonstration, he thought the shift would be upstream, for a crossing beyond his left.

He was wrong: as he found out next morning, in plenty of time to rectify his error with a rapid southward march, still on the chord of the arc the Federals were traveling. Grant had pulled back under cover of darkness and set off down — not up — the North Anna, which combined with the South Anna, five miles southeast of Hanover Junction, to become the Pamunkey. The Pamunkey in turn combined with the Mattaponi to become the York, another forty miles below, but Grant marched only about one third of this distance down the left bank for a crossing at Hanovertown, which put him within fifteen miles of Richmond, ten miles closer than he had been on the North Anna. That was not his only reason for preferring to repeat his accustomed sidle to the left, around Lee's right; he would also be keeping in close touch with his supply base, leapfrogging it south once more as he moved in that direction. As for leaving the Virginia Central in Confederate control, he counted on Hunter to conquer the Valley, now that Breckinridge had departed, and thereby deny its use to Lee even as a source of supplies, let alone as a possible avenue of invasion. Besides, he saw the outcome of this latest confrontation not as a repulse — which in fact it was, with far-reaching effects, despite its comparative bloodlessness (he had suffered only 1973 casualties, and Lee less than half that number) — but rather as conclusive proof that the opposing army had lost its fabled sting. If the rebels would not fight him there on the North Anna, with all the advantage they had secured through Lee's admitted engineering skill, they apparently were in no condition to fight him anywhere at all. Knowing nothing of Lee's debility, he assigned its results to the deterioration of the force his adversary commanded.

"Lee's army is really whipped," he informed Halleck on the day he set out down the Pamunkey. "The prisoners we now take show it, and the action of his army shows it unmistakably. A battle with them outside of intrenchments cannot be had. Our men feel that they have gained the *morale* over the enemy, and attack him with confidence. I may be mistaken," he summed up, "but I feel that our success over Lee's army is already assured."

Grant's march was in two columns, of two corps each, along the left bank of the Pamunkey; Warren and Burnside crossed at Hanovertown, Wright and Hancock four miles short of there. Preceded by Sheridan's troopers, who had little to do on the way down but brush off prowling scouts, all four corps passed over on pontoon bridges between noon and midnight, May 28, and though they were delayed by a rackety seven-hour cavalry fight near Haw's Shop, three miles beyond the river, by nightfall of the following day the whole army had pushed south and west to Totopotomoy Creek, which had its beginnings above Atlee, a station on the Virginia Central about midway between the James and the South Anna, and flowed sluggishly eastward a dozen miles to join the Pamunkey just below Hanovertown. Weary from better than forty miles of marching — southeast for two days, then southwest for another — the Federals approached the marsh-fringed creek at last, within ten miles of Richmond, only to find Lee drawn up to meet them on the opposite bank, guns emplaced and all three corps arrayed for battle.

He had been there two days waiting for Grant to make a commitment. Before sundown of May 27, whose dawn showed the enemy gone from the North Anna, he had covered the eighteen miles from Hanover Junction to Atlee, where he took up a position from which he could block a variety of approaches by the wide-ranging bluecoats, either around the headwaters of the Totopotomoy, which would put them back astride the vital railroad north of Richmond, or down across the creek for a five-mile sprint to the Chickahominy and a quick descent on the capital only four miles beyond. Still obliged by his intestinal disorder to continue using the borrowed carriage, he rode in the lead with Ewell's corps — but not with its com-

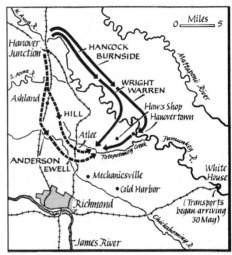

mander, who made the trip in an ambulance, racked by the same malady that afflicted Lee. Ewell was so much worse next day that he had to yield his place to Early and accept a sick leave of indefinite length; which meant that the army now had two of its three corps, four of its nine infantry divisions, and sixteen of its thirty-five original brigades under men who had not led them at the start of the campaign. Warned that elements of the Union host were across the Pamunkey at Hanovertown, Lee sent Hampton and Fitzhugh Lee to Haw's Shop to discover whether the crossing included infantry — and, if so, where it was headed. Unless he knew that, he could not move out to meet the invaders, lest they slip around one of his flanks for a lunge at Richmond from the north or the northeast.

The result was the largest cavalry engagement since Brandy Station, just under a year ago. After seven hours of savage combat, mounted and dismounted, with heavy losses on both sides — especially in a green South Carolina brigade whose troopers arrived in time for a share in a fight that converted the survivors into veterans overnight — Fitz and Hampton were obliged to give ground, but not before they had driven Sheridan's horsemen back on their supports and taken prisoners from both the V and VI Corps, which gave Lee at least half the information he was seeking. Grant's infantry was indeed over the

Pamunkey, already beyond Haw's Shop, and next day it began working its way south and west along the north bank of the Totopotomoy, still without disclosing whether it intended to cross or round the creek.

Fixed in position east of Atlee until he knew the answer, the southern commander by now had received 10,000 reinforcements. This amounted to about half his losses so far in the campaign: whereas Grant had received some 40,000, roughly the number he had lost in battle. Such disproportionate attrition could have but one result, and Lee implied as much that afternoon to Jefferson Davis, who rode out from the capital to see him for the first time since the opening of the Federal offensive. Further reinforcements would have to come from south of the James, of course, and the President was doubtful that any could be spared from there; Beauregard had been protesting all week that his force — which he had regrouped into two divisions, under Robert Hoke and Bushrod Johnson, and which he kept reminding the Commander in Chief was all that kept Butler's still-bottled army from making a sudden breakout and a dash for the back door of Richmond — had been bled down to, maybe past, the danger point. Davis made it fairly clear, before he left, that the question of detaching more troops from beyond the James would depend to a large extent on the judgment of the commander of that department. That evening Beauregard himself appeared at Atlee for a conference, the upshot of which was that, while he sympathized with Lee in all his troubles, he could not see that they were any larger than his own. As for evidence advanced by Lee that Butler was sending men to Grant, the dapper Creole admitted that perhaps 4000 had left Bermuda Hundred aboard transports in the past few days, but he stressed the claim that a substantial 24,000 still remained to pop the cork he was trying to hold in place with only half as many troops. "My force is so small at present," he had told Davis earlier today, "that to divide it for the purpose of reinforcing Lee would jeopardize the safety of the part left to guard my lines, and would greatly endanger Richmond itself." The most he would agree to was a further study of the situation on his front, and with that he departed to return there, leaving Lee no better off, even in prospect, than he had been when the rather baffling conference began.

Next morning, May 30, Grant pressed down closer along the Totopotomoy, massing opposite Anderson in the center and overlapping Early on the right; Hill, on the left, had only cavalry in his front. That seemed to rule out the Virginia Central as the enemy objective, and presently this view was strengthened by reports that two of the four blue corps had crossed downstream and were taking up a position on the near bank, facing west. Lee believed he saw now what the Federals were up to, and also how to head them off: "After fortifying this line they will probably make another move by their left flank over toward the Chickahominy. This is just a repetition of their former movements. It can only be arrested by striking at once at that part of their force which has crossed the Totopotomoy."

These words were included in a message instructing Anderson to support Early, whose corps, being on that flank, would lead the attack designed to discourage this latest sidle around the Confederate right to gain the Old Church Road, which led down across Beaver Dam Creek to Mechanicsville, where the Seven Days had opened in flame and blood. But even if he was successful in dealing with the immediate threat to Richmond from this line, Lee saw a larger danger looming. Beyond the Chickahominy lay the James, where McClellan had found sanctuary after the holocaust of Malvern Hill. Fortunately, the Washington authorities had not seen fit to sustain him in his position on the north bank of that river, nor to approve his proposal that he cross it for a movement against Richmond from the south, astride its lines of supply from Georgia and the Carolinas. Grant was no Little Mac, however, and the high command might well have learned a lesson from what had followed its failure to sustain his predecessor. In speaking to Early, who was preparing to attack at midday, Lee did not say, as he had said to Anderson, that the Federal threat must be "arrested"; he said, rather, that the Federals themselves must be destroyed. Otherwise the contest would come down to what he wanted to avoid, the loss of all freedom to maneuver.

"We must destroy this army of Grant's before he gets to James River," he told Early. "If he gets there it will become a siege, and then it will be a mere question of time."

Unfortunately, Early came closer to wrecking his newly inherited corps than he did to destroying even a portion of Grant's army. Repeating Hill's error at Jericho Mills, he attacked with one division and failed to bring the other two up promptly to exploit the initial success. Counterattacked from Bethesda Church, his objective on the Old Church Road, he barely managed to hold his ground, and Anderson only arrived in time for a share in the defensive action. Lee rebuked neither of them for the botched performance, in part because they were busy intrenching their new line, which at least forestalled an advance down the ridge between Beaver Dam and Totopotomoy creeks, and in part because of a report that reached him about the time it became apparent that the attack had failed — a report so alarming in its implications that it took precedence over his other dire concerns. Grant's new supply base was at White House Landing, fifteen miles down the Pamunkey from Hanovertown; Lee now received word that substantial reinforcements, identified as Smith's whole corps from Butler's army, were unloading there from transports which had left Bermuda

Hundred yesterday for an overnight trip down the James and up the York.

Grievous though it was to learn that he soon would be facing still a fifth blue corps with his embattled three, the danger here was more than numerical. From his debarkation point at White House, Smith was free to march due west, unhindered, to a position beyond Grant's left (to Cold Harbor, for example, a vital crossroads three miles southeast of Bethesda Church, where the Union line was anchored south of the Totopotomoy after standing firm against Early's mismanaged assault) and thus extend it beyond the reach of Lee's already thin-stretched right for a rapid swing around that flank and a leap across the Chickahominy. Convinced that this was what Grant had in mind, because it was what he would have attempted in his place, Lee first did what he could to meet the threat with what he had on hand in that direction: meaning cavalry. He sent Fitz Lee instructions to take up a position at Cold Harbor and hang on there until he was reinforced, hopefully by morning.

As things now stood, such reinforcements could not come from Hill or Anderson or Early, whose withdrawal from any part of the line would open the way for Grant to move on Atlee or Mechanicsville. They could come from only one source, beyond the James, and Lee had no time to spare for going through regular channels to procure them. Abandoning protocol he telegraphed an urgent request directly to Beauregard for every man he could spare, and when the Creole replied at sunset that the War Department would have to decide "when and what troops to order from here," Lee appealed by wire to the President in Richmond: "General Beauregard says the Department must determine what troops to send.... The result of this delay will be disaster. Butler's troops (Smith's corps) will be with Grant tomorrow. Hoke's division, at least, should be with me by light tomorrow."

It was unlike Lee to use the unequivocal word "disaster," and because it was unlike him it got immediate results. Davis promptly instructed Bragg to send Beauregard a peremptory order detaching Hoke's division for shipment by rail to Lee without delay, and before midnight Lee was informed that every effort was being made to get Hoke and his four brigades north of the Chickahominy by morning.

Once more it was as if Lee had sat in on his adversary's councils or even paid him a visit inside his head. Dissatisfied with the Totopotomoy confrontation (as well he might be; it had cost him another 2013 killed and wounded and missing, first at Haw's Shop and then along the mazy fringes of the creek, with no gain except the infliction of about an equal number of casualties) Grant by now had decided to try another sidle: a brief one, this time, aimed at just the crossroad Lee predicted he would head for.

The choice of Cold Harbor was natural enough. It was there —
well clear of the toils of the Totopotomoy, but not quite into those of the
treacherous Chickahominy — that the roads from Bethesda Church and
White House Landing came together, enabling him to extend his left
for a meeting with Baldy Smith, whose corps was debarking fifteen miles
due east. Depending more on celerity than surprise, which seemed to
be unobtainable here in Virginia anyhow, Grant counted on a rapid
concentration at that point for a concerted drive up the left bank of
the Chickahominy, one that would strike the assembling rebels before
they got set to resist it and would pen them up for capture or destruction
with their backs to Powhite Creek, less than two miles west, or Beaver
Dam Creek, another three miles upstream; after which he would
cross the river with all five corps, either below Mechanicsville or beyond
at Meadow Bridge, for a quick descent on Richmond. Accordingly,
while Lee was instructing his nephew Fitz to hold Cold Harbor against
all comers, Grant sent word for Sheridan to seize and hang onto that
vital hub until Wright, crossing in rear of Hancock on the Totopotomoy
and then in rear of Burnside and Warren at Bethesda Church, arrived
for a meeting with Smith at the end of his march from White House.
The result next day, May 31, was another all-out cavalry engagement.

This too was a nearly all-day fight, with no infantry involved on
either side till after sunset. Beauregard's bridling reaction to Lee's request for troops had delayed Hoke's departure so effectively that his
lead brigade did not unload at Meadow Bridge until near midday, and
consequently did not complete its eight-mile hike down the north bank
of the Chickahominy until dusk was gathering on the scene of Fitz
Lee's long-drawn-out defense of the crossroad his uncle had asked him
to hold. As for the Federals, there was no infantry in the attacking
columns even then. Concerned with keeping his withdrawal secret in
order to give him a decent head start in the shift to the southeast,
Grant instructed Wright to wait for nightfall before he set out on a
march that was necessarily roundabout, through Haw's Shop, since there
was no direct road available down across the Totopotomoy; he would
arrive tomorrow morning at the soonest. Smith's delay was for other
reasons, mostly involving slip-ups on Grant's staff. His original orders,
issued when he embarked two days ago at Bermuda Hundred, called for
a march from White House, up the south bank of the Pamunkey to
New Castle, and from there to a position supporting the main effort
on the Totopotomoy. Since then, Grant's plans had changed, but not
Smith's orders, which were forgotten in all the flurry of preparation
for the latest sidle. Completing his White House debarkation by midafternoon, May 31, Smith struck out northwestward, at a tangent to
his intended route due west. Though he called a halt that night near
Old Church, two miles short of his assigned objective, to send a wire requesting clarification from headquarters — it seemed to him he was

moving into a military vacuum — the reply came back, after some delay, that his orders stood: he was to continue his march to New Castle. This he did, getting farther and farther at every step from the scene of the daylong engagement, now six miles in his left rear, which Sheridan had had to fight alone.

Little Phil frequently preferred it thus, so long at least as what opposed him was cavalry on its own. That was the case here, but he found it difficult to budge or even get at the graybacks, who declined to fight him in the smash-up style he favored. Instead, when he came within a mile of the crossroads about midday, with Torbert's three brigades — Torbert himself, up from his sickbed, had returned to duty the week before — he discovered Fitz Lee's two brigades dismounted and crouched behind fence-rail breastworks, which gave them the advantage of taking aim from an unjogged platform, with little exposure to the rapid-firing weapons of the horsemen galloping toward them. In their rear was Cold Harbor, a name of British derivation signifying an inn that afforded overnight lodging without hot food, adopted here because of the settlement's main feature, a frame tavern set in a triangular grove of trees at the intersection of five roads coming in from all round the compass. Charges by Merritt and Custer were repulsed before they could be pressed home, and as the afternoon wore on it became evident that standard cavalry tactics would not serve; Sheridan had Torbert dismount his men and work them forward, troop by troop, while their fellows provided covering fire to make the defenders keep their heads down. Swarming over the dusty fields and through the brush, pumping lead from their stubby carbines, the blue troopers in their tight-fitting trousers, bobtail jackets, and short-billed kepis looked to one observer "as though they had been especially equipped for crawling through knotholes."

It was a slow and costly business, involving much risk and a good many wounds. Giving up on Baldy Smith after a patrol returned from a fruitless eastward search for some sign of his 15,000-man corps, Sheridan sent for Gregg to come down from Bethesda Church and add his two brigades to the effort being exerted, but the sun was down behind the trees along Powhite Creek by the time the courier rode off with the summons. As it turned out, such reinforcements as reached the field before full dark were Confederate, and infantry at that.

Hard-pressed by the agile blue troopers, who were about within range for a mass charge through the gathering dusk, Fitz Lee's men looked over their shoulders and, seeing Hoke's lead brigade moving toward them up the road past the triangular grove of trees, decided the time had come to fall back on these overdue supports. They did so, only to find that the startled foot soldiers fell back too. Hot and tired from their dusty trek down the Chickahominy, and softened by two weeks of inactivity in the southside trenches, they joined what they took to be

— and what now became — a general retreat, to and through Cold
Harbor; which their pursuers seized and occupied, rounding up some
fifty laggard graybacks in the process. Sheridan's elation over his
sudden victory was modified considerably, however, when he learned
from these captives that three more brigades of infantry would soon
be up to join the one he had scattered. He decided, despite the arrival
of Gregg's division hard on the heels of the rout, that his wisest course
would be to pull back from the tavern crossroads before he was overrun. "I do not feel able to hold this place," he notified Meade as the
withdrawal got under way. "With the heavy odds against me here,
I do not think it prudent to hold on."

Meade thought otherwise, and so did Grant, in view of the
sidle now in progress and the intended concentration there; Cold
Harbor was to be reoccupied and "held at all hazards," they replied.
Little Phil reversed his march, disposed his two divisions about the
southwest quadrant of the crossroads, and had the dismounted troopers
get to work in the darkness, throwing up temporary breastworks to
provide them with cover for meeting the attack he expected would
come with the dawn, if not sooner.

It would come with the dawn, and the odds would be even heavier
than Sheridan had feared when he pulled back, saying, "I do not think
it prudent to hold on." Lee was about to go over to the offensive.
What was more, in preparation for bloodier work to follow, he intended to begin with the retaking of the ground the troopers stood on.

Far from being discouraged by his nephew's report that the crossroads had been seized by Sheridan, he saw in this development confirmation of his suspicion that Grant had another sidle in progress, that Cold
Harbor was his intended point of concentration, and that so far he had
nothing there but cavalry; which meant that his infantry was still in
motion in that direction, strung out on roads converging from the north
and east, and might therefore be defeated in detail as it came up —
provided, of course, that Lee could get there first with a force substantial enough to inflict the damage he had in mind. He thought he
could. Hoke's division was assembling there already, and this was only
a fraction of what had become available now that Grant had tipped
his hand. Formerly fixed in position east of Atlee by the danger that the
Federals would round the headwaters of the Totopotomoy to turn
his left, Lee was now free to draw troops from there for use on the
opposite flank. His choice was Anderson, whose strength was up to
three divisions for the first time in the campaign, Pickett having rejoined him on the march from Hanover Junction. Both the Third and
the Second corps had had their turns at offensive action, Hill eight
days ago on the North Anna and Early here at Bethesda Church the
day before, and both had failed. Now the First — Old Peter's de-

pendables, who had rolled up the blue flank in the Wilderness and won the hairbreadth race for Spotsylvania — would have its turn. Anderson was told to pull back from his position on the Totopotomoy, leaving Little Powell to fill the gap, and make a night march down below Cold Harbor to join Hoke, who was placed under his command for the attack, first on Sheridan, to get possession of the crossroads shortly after dawn, and then on the other Union columns as they arrived from the east and north.

Though he still had not recovered sufficiently from his illness to resume direction of tactical operations, Lee advanced his headquarters to Shady Grove Church, a couple of miles southeast of Atlee Station, to be at least that much nearer the scene of tomorrow's action. Two years ago this evening, riding back from the confused field of Seven Pines — less than ten miles from where he would camp tonight — he had been informed by the President that he would replace the fallen Johnston, and next day he had assumed command of the Army of Northern Virginia. As he retired to his tent in the churchyard tonight to sleep out the final hours of this bloodiest May in American history, he had cause for hope that he would celebrate tomorrow's anniversary with an offensive victory as glorious as the one he had begun to plan on that night two years ago, when McClellan's vast blue host hovered within even easier reach of Richmond than Grant's did now.

There was no occasion for any such celebration on the hot first day of June, only a sorry repetition of the ineptness which had led Grant to believe that the fight had gone out of Lee's army. Anderson moved promptly enough, pulling Kershaw's division out of line in plenty of time for the march across Early's rear and into position on Hoke's left before daylight. His notion was to knock Sheridan back from the crossroads with a dawn attack by these two divisions, then continue the operation when the other two arrived. But a notion was all it remained. Kershaw went forward on schedule, giving his old brigade the lead, and that was when the trouble began and the offensive ended. Colonel Lawrence Keitt, a forty-year-old former congressman, had brought his green but handsomely uniformed regiment up from South Carolina the week before, and by virtue of his seniority over the other colonels took command of the brigade. Long on rank but short on combat experience, he went into his first attack in the gallant style of 1861, leading the way on a spirited gray charger; only to be killed by the first rattling clatter of semiautomatic fire from the two divisions of cavalry in the breastworks just ahead.

That was what had been expected by seasoned observers, who saw in Keitt's display only "inexperience and want of self control," but the reaction among his troops, recently uprooted from two years of languid garrison life in their home state, was something else. When they saw the colonel get toppled from his saddle — transformed, in the wink of an eye, from a saber-waving cynosure into a mangled corpse — they broke for the rear in what a dismayed artillerist called "the most abject rout ever committed by men in Confederate uniform." Nor was that the worst of the shame. "Some were so scared they could not run, but groveled on the ground trying to burrow into the earth." Veteran regiments on their flanks were obliged to give way too; the advance dissolved in panic, unredeemed by Hoke, who had not moved at all. First the brigade and then the division as a whole pulled out of range of the fast-firing Union carbines. Kershaw got the fallback stopped and even attempted to mount another attack, but it went no better. By the time Pickett and Field came up to form on Kershaw's left, around mid-morning, so had Wright arrived with his three divisions in relief of Sheridan, who retired with pride from the defense of what he called "our little works."

They did not stay little long; Wright's men got busy with picks and shovels, deepening and extending them north and south to cover the western approaches to Cold Harbor. Smith's wandering corps slogged wearily into position alongside Wright that afternoon, reaching up to connect with Warren, whose four divisions occupied two miles of line below the Old Church Road, beyond which Burnside anchored the northern flank to the south bank of the Totopotomoy. That left only Hancock's corps and Sheridan's third division north of the creek; Grant sent word for Hancock to withdraw at nightfall for a march to the far left, where Torbert and Gregg were patrolling a boggy two-mile extension of the line down to the Chickahominy. He was instructed to come up in time to take part in a dawn assault that would be launched by all five corps.

Grant's decision to make such an attack was arrived at by a process of elimination. This was coffin corner; another sidle would involve him in the toils of the Chickahominy, and even if he cleared them intact he would find himself confronted, when he swung back west, by Richmond's permanent defenses. He would, in short, be mounting a siege, which at this stage he wanted as little as Lee did, since it represented the stalemate he had avoided from the start. His decision, then, despite the shocks and throes of the past four weeks — the stunning repulse in the green riot of the Wilderness and the unrelieved horror of Spotsylvania, which together had cost him a solid third of the infantry that crossed the Rapidan, and the close call on the North Anna, where incaution had nearly cost him the other two thirds, along with his reinforcements — was to attack the old fox where he was, or anyhow where he would be tomorrow morning. If this was coffin corner for Grant, it was something worse for Lee, whose back was to the wall of his capital and who would have neither time nor space for recovery if even a limited breakthrough could be scored. Grant kept his mind on that agreeable possibility, and when Meade suggested that something might be done with what was left of today, by way of improving tomorrow's chances, he was altogether willing.

Meade proposed a preliminary effort, restricted to the southern half of his present line, to give Wright and Smith a closer hug on the rebel works along their front and better jump-off positions from which to launch their share of the all-out dawn assault. That was how it came about that Anderson, whose four divisions were busy intrenching three miles of line, north and south of a road leading due east to Cold Harbor, was struck by a six-division attack, shortly after 5 o'clock, which not only disposed of any vestigial intention to resume his boggled offensive, but also came close to driving him from his uncompleted works. Pickett and Field held firm under pressure, but a break quickly developed between Hoke's left, where a brigade gave way in panic, and Kershaw's right. Anderson detached a brigade from Pickett to heal the breach, and by sunset the line was approximately restored. Yet the fact remained that, at a moderate price in casualties — moderate, that is, as such things went in this campaign: about 1000 for Smith, 1200 for Wright — Meade had secured the jump-off positions he wanted for tomorrow. Anderson's losses had been light, consisting mainly of stragglers captured when Hoke's left gave way, but he saw only too clearly what might come of this. "Reinforcements are necessary to enable us to hold this position," he notified Lee that night.

This message, conveying Anderson's doubts that he could hold the ground he had been ordered to advance from, put a dispiriting end to an anniversary which had dawned with high hopes that it would close with the celebration of an offensive victory. For the third time in nine days, a corps commander had shown himself incapable of mounting a sustained attack, even under favorable circumstances.

One thing common to all three attempts, in addition to failure, was that neither Lee nor his "poor Stuart" had taken part in them first hand. Jeb of course was gone for good, three weeks in his grave, and Lee was still in no condition for personal conduct of operations in the field; but that did not mean that the ailing general would not keep to his task of devising plans for the frustration of the invaders of his country and his state. Foiled in his efforts to go over to the offensive, he would continue to improvise a defensive in which, so far, he had managed to inflict casualties in ratio to the odds he faced at the opening of the campaign. In this connection he had already moved to meet Anderson's needs before they were expressed, ordering Breckinridge to take up a position on Hoke's right tonight, and now he followed through with instructions that would add Hill's three divisions to the line tomorrow, one on the left of Early and two on the right beyond Breckinridge, tying those flanks respectively to the Totopotomoy and the Chickahominy. All this would take time, however — first for marching, then for digging — and Grant was bristling aggressively all along the seven miles of Confederate front when the sun came up on the second day of June.

Fortunately, despite the flurry, there was no attack; Lee had plenty of time to look to the extension and improvement of his line. Mounting Traveller for the first time in ten days, he rode down to Mechanicsville, where he found Breckinridge and his two brigades enjoying a leisurely breakfast, midway through their march to the far right. He got the distinguished Kentuckian back on the road again and then resumed his ride, eastward past Walnut Grove Church to his new headquarters beyond Gaines Mill, a mile and a half due west of Union-held Cold Harbor and about the same distance northwest of the scene of his first victory, scored two years ago this month, when Hood and Law broke Fitz-John Porter's line on Turkey Hill, now also Union-held. Mindful of the importance of that feature of the terrain, Lee had Breckinridge go forward, about 3 o'clock that afternoon, and with the assistance of one of Hill's divisions, which had just come up, drive a brigade of bluecoats off its slopes, thus affording his artillery a position from which to dominate the Chickahominy bottoms on the right. Simultaneously on the left, Early's corps and Hill's remaining division felt out the Federal installations above Old Church Road, on toward the Totopotomoy, and after brushing aside a sizeable body of skir- mishers, who yielded stubbornly, confronted the main enemy works northwest and north of Bethesda Church.

While these two adjustments were being made at opposite ends of the long line, a heavy rain began to fall, first in big individual drops, pocking the dust like buckshot scattered broadcast, and then in a steady downpour that turned the dust to mud. The discomfort was minor on both sides, compared to the relief from heat and glare and the dis- traction from waiting to receive or deliver the attack both knew was soon to be made, if not today then certainly tomorrow.

Rain often had a depressing effect on Lee, perhaps because it reminded him of the drenched fiasco his first campaign had been, out in western Virginia in the fall of 1861; but not now; now he valued it as a factor that would make for muddy going when the Federals moved against him. Back at his headquarters, near the ruins of Dr William Gaines's once imposing four-story gristmill on Powhite Creek — Sheri- dan's troopers had burned it when they passed this way two weeks ago, returning from the raid that killed Jeb Stuart — the southern com- mander kept to his tent, still queasy from his ten-day illness, reading the day's reports while rain drummed on the canvas overhead. He had done all he could to get all the troops he could muster into line. "Send to the field hospitals," he had told his chief lieutenants in a circular issued the last day of May, "and have every man capable of performing the duties of a soldier returned to his command." Such efforts, combined with those of Davis, who had summoned reinforcements from as far away as Florida in the course of the past two weeks, had brought his strength back up to nearly 60,000. Grant had about 110,000 across the way, but Lee feared the odds no more here than he had done elsewhere. In fact he feared them less; for, thanks to Grant's forbearance today — whatever its cause — he had had plenty of time to dispose his army as he chose. Having done so, he was content to leave the rest to God and the steady valor of his troops, whose defensive skill had by now become instinctive.

This last applied in particular to the use they made of terrain within their interlocking sectors. Whether the ground was flat or hilly, bare or wooded, firm or boggy — and it was all those things from point to various point along the line from Pole Green Church to Grapevine Bridge — they never used it more skillfully than here. Occupying their assigned positions with a view to affording themselves only so much protection as would not interfere with the delivery of a maximum of firepower, they flowed onto and into the landscape as if in response to a natural law, like water seeking its own level. The result, once they were settled in, was by no means as imposing as the fortifications they had thrown up three weeks ago at Spotsylvania or last week on the North Anna. But that too was part of the design. No such works were needed here and they knew it, having installed them with concern that they not appear so formidable as to discourage all hope of success in the minds of the Federal planners across the way. Crouched in the dripping blackness after sundown, with both flanks securely anchored on rising streams and Richmond scarcely ten miles in their rear, the defenders asked for nothing better, in the way of reward for their craftsmanship and labor, than that their adversaries would advance into the meshed and overlapping fields of fire they had established, unit by unit, along their seven miles of front.

They were about to get their wish. Indeed, they would have gotten it at dawn today — ten hours before they completed their concentration and were in any condition to receive it — except that Hancock's three divisions had not arrived on the Union left until about 6.30, two hours late and in no shape for fighting, tired and hungry as they were from their grueling all-night march. Grant accepted the delay as unavoidable, and rescheduled the attack for 5 o'clock that afternoon. That would do about as well, he seemed to think. But then, as the jump-off hour drew near, the rebs went into action on both flanks, seizing Turkey Hill and driving the outpost skirmishers back on their works above Bethesda Church. This called for some changes in the stand-by orders, and Grant, still unruffled, postponed the attack once more until 4.30 next morning. After all, all he wanted was a breakthrough, almost anywhere along those six or seven miles of enemy line; he could see that a hot supper and a good night's rest would add to the strength and steadiness of the men when they went forward.

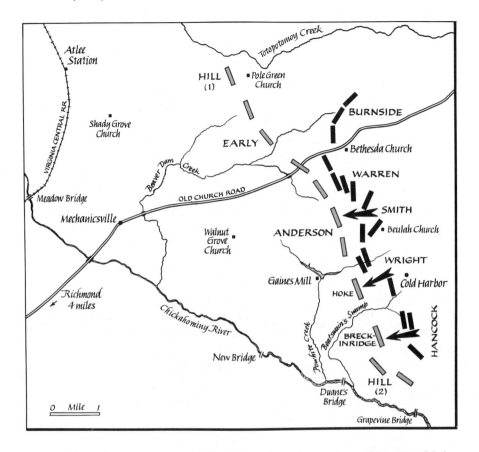

Aside from a general directive that the main effort would be made by the three corps on the left, where the opposing works were close together as a result of yesterday's preliminary effort, tactics seemed to have gone by the board, at least on the upper levels of command. Neither Grant nor Meade, or for that matter any member of their two staffs, had reconnoitered any part of the Confederate position; nor had either of them organized the attack itself in any considerable detail, including the establishment of such lateral communications as might be needed to assure coöperation between units. Apparently they assumed that all such incidental problems had been covered by a sentence in Meade's circular postponing the late-afternoon attack till dawn: "Corps commanders will employ the interim in making examinations of the ground on their front and perfecting the arrangements for the assault." New as he was to procedure in the Army of the Potomac, Baldy Smith — "aghast," he later wrote, "at the reception of such an order, which proved conclusively the utter absence of any military plan" — sent a note to Wright, who was on his left, "asking him to let me know what was to be his plan of attack, that I might conform to it, and thus have two corps acting in unison." Wright's reply was simply that he was "going to pitch in": which left Smith as much in the dark as before, and even more aghast. Grant, in short, was proceeding here at Cold Harbor as if he subscribed quite literally to the words he had written Halleck from the North Anna, a week ago today: "I feel that our success over Lee's army is already assured."

Up on the line, that was by no means the feeling prevalent among the troops who were charged with carrying out the orders contrived to bring about the result expected at headquarters. Unlike their rearward superiors, they had been uncomfortably close to the rebel works all day and knew only too well what was likely to come of any effort to assault them, let alone such a slipshod one as this. Their reaction was observed by Lieutenant Colonel Horace Porter, a young West Pointer, formerly an aide to McClellan and now serving Grant in the same capacity. Passing through the camps that rainy evening, he later wrote, "I noticed that many of the soldiers had taken off their coats and seemed to be engaged in sewing up rents in them." He thought this strange, at such a time, but when he looked closer he "found that the men were calmly writing their names and home addresses on slips of paper and pinning them on the backs of their coats, so that their bodies might be recognized and their fate made known to their families at home."

Some went even further in their gloom. A blood-stained diary, salvaged from the pocket of a dead man later picked up on the field, had this grisly final entry: "June 3. Cold Harbor. I was killed."

They came with the dawn and they came pounding, three blue corps with better than 60,000 effectives, striking for three points along the center and right center of the rebel line, which had fewer men defending its whole length than now were assaulting half of it. Advancing with a deep-throated roar — "Huzzah! Huzzah!" a Confederate thought they were yelling — the attackers saw black slouch hats sprout abruptly from the empty-looking trenches up ahead, and then the works broke into flame. A heavy bank of smoke rolled out, alive with muzzle flashes, and the air was suddenly full of screaming lead. "It seemed more like a volcanic blast than a battle," one Federal later said, "and was just about as destructive."

Dire as their expectations had been the night before, they perceived now for the first time the profoundly intricate nature of the deadfall Lee had devised for their undoing. Never before, in this or perhaps in any other war, had so large a body of troops been exposed to such a concentration of firepower; "It had the fury of the Wilderness musketry, with the thunders of the Gettysburg artillery superadded," an awed cannoneer observed from his point of vantage in the Union rear. And now, too, the committed victims saw the inadequacy of Grant's preparation in calling for a three-pronged assault, directed against three vague and widely spaced objectives. Smith on the right was enfiladed from his outer flank, as was Hancock on the left, and Wright, advancing between them with a gap on either side, found both of his flanks exposed at once to an even crueler flailing. What was worse, the closer the attackers got to the concave rebel line, the more this crossfire was intensified and the more likely an individual was to be chosen as a simultaneous target by several marksmen in the works ahead. "I could see the dust fog out of a man's clothing in two or three places where as many balls would strike him at the same moment," a defender was to say.

Under such conditions, losses tended to occur in ratio to the success of various units in closing the range. Barlow's division for example, leading Hancock's charge against Lee's right, struck a lightly defended stretch of boggy ground in Breckinridge's front and plunged on through to the main line, which buckled under sudden pressure from the cheering bluecoats. Barlow, not yet thirty — "attired in a flannel checked shirt, a threadbare pair of trousers, and an old blue kepi," he looked to a staff observer "like a highly independent mounted news-boy" — was elated to think he had scored the breakthrough Grant had called for. But his elation was short-lived. Attached to one of Hill's divisions on the adjoining slope of Turkey Hill, Joseph Finegan, who had arrived that week with two Florida battalions and been put in charge of a scratch brigade, counterattacked without waiting to be prompted and quickly restored the line, demonstrating here in Virginia the savagery he had shown at Olustee, three months ago in his home state. Barlow's men were ousted, losing heavily in the process, and it was much the same with others up the line. Though nowhere else was there a penetration, even a temporary one, wherever the range became point-blank the attack dissolved in horror; the attackers huddled together, like sheep caught in a hailstorm, and milled about distractedly in search of what little cover the terrain afforded. "They halted and began to dodge, lie down, and recoil," a watching grayback would remember, while another noted that "the dead and dying lay in front of the Confederate line in triangles, of which the apexes were the bravest men who came nearest to the breastworks under that withering, deadly fire."

The attack, now broken, had lasted just eight minutes. So brief was its duration, and so abrupt its finish, that some among the defenders had trouble crediting the fact that it had ended, while others could scarcely believe it had begun; not in earnest, at any rate. One of Hoke's brigadiers, whose troops were holding a portion of the objective assigned to Wright, square in the center of the three-corps Federal effort, afterwards testified that he "was not aware at any time of any serious assault having been given."

Part of the reason for this was the lightness of Confederate losses, especially as compared to those inflicted, although these last were not known to have been anything like as heavy as they were until the smoke began to clear. An Alabama colonel, whose regiment had three men killed and five wounded, peered out through rifts in the drifting smoke along his front, where Smith had attacked with close-packed ranks, and saw to his amazement that "the dead covered more than five acres of ground about as thickly as they could be laid." Eventually the doleful tally showed that while Lee was losing something under 1500, killed and wounded in the course of the day, Grant lost better than 7000, most of them in the course of those first eight minutes.

The attack had ended, but neither by Grant's intention nor with his consent. No sooner had the Union effort slackened than orders came for it to be renewed, and when Wright protested that he could accomplish nothing unless Hancock and Smith moved forward to protect his flanks, he was informed that they had filed the same complaint about his lack of progress in the center, which left them equally exposed. Faced with this dilemma, headquarters instructed each of the corps commanders to go forward on his own, without regard for what the others might be doing.

Up on the line, such instructions had a quality of madness, and a colonel on Wright's staff did not hesitate to say so. "To move that army farther, except by regular approaches," he declared, "was a simple and absolute impossibility, known to be such by every officer and man of the three corps engaged." Here too was a dilemma, and here too a simple answer was forthcoming. When the order to resume the attack was repeated, unit commanders responded in the same fashion by having their troops step up their rate of fire from the positions where they lay.

It went on like that all morning. Dodging shells and bullets, which continued to fall abundantly, dispatch bearers crept forward with instructions for the assault to be renewed. The firing, most of it skyward, would swell up and then subside, until another messenger arrived with another order and the process was repeated, the men lying prone and digging in, as best they could in such cramped positions, to provide themselves with a little cover between blind volleys. Finally, an order headed 1.30 came down to all three corps, eight minutes less than nine hours after it had been placed in execution: "For the present all further offensive operations will be suspended."

Over near Gaines Mill, with occasional long-range Federal projectiles landing in the clearing where his headquarters tent was pitched, Lee had spent an anxious half hour awaiting the return of couriers sent to bring him word of the outcome of the rackety assault, which opened full-voiced on the right, down near the Chickahominy, and roared quickly to a sustained climax, northward to the Totopotomoy. For all he knew, the Union infantry might get there first to announce a breakthrough half a mile east of the shell-pocked meadow overlooking the ruined mill. Mercifully, though, the wait was brief. Shortly after sunrise the couriers began returning on lathered horses, and their reports varied only in degrees of exultation. "Tell General Lee it is the same all along my front," A. P. Hill had said, pointing to where the limits of the enemy advance were marked by windrows of the dead and dying. Confederate losses were low; incredibly low, it seemed. Hoke, as an extreme example, reported that so far, though the ground directly in front of his intrenchments was literally blue with fallen attackers, he had not lost a single man in his division. In Anderson's corps, Law was hit in the head by a stray bullet that was to take him away from his brigade for good, and Breckinridge, after ending Barlow's costly short-term penetration, was badly shaken up when his horse, struck by a solid shot, collapsed between his knees. No other high-ranking defender received so much as a scratch or a bruise throughout the length of the gray line. By midmorning, with the close-up Union effort reduced to blind volleys of musketry fired prone in response to orders for a resumption of the attack, it was clear that Lee had won what a staff colonel was to call "perhaps the easiest victory ever granted to Confederate arms by the folly of Federal commanders."

Back in Richmond, although fighting had raged even closer to the city throughout five of the Seven Days, two years ago, citizens had been jolted awake that morning by the loudest firing they had ever heard. Windows rattled with the coming of dawn and kept on rattling past midday, one apprehensive listener declared, "as if whole divisions were firing at a word of command."

No one could say, at that range, who was getting the worst and who the best of it. Before noon, as a result, distinguished visitors began arriving at Lee's headquarters in search of firsthand information. Among them was Postmaster General John H. Reagan, who brought two lawyer friends along to help find out how the battle was going. Lee told them it was going well, up to now at least, and when they wondered if the artillery wasn't unusually active here today, the general said it was, but he added, with a gesture toward the contending lines, where the drumfire of a hundred thousand rifles sounded to Reagan like the tearing of a sheet: "It is that that kills men."

What reserves did he have on hand, they asked, in case Grant managed a breakthrough at some point along his front?

"Not a regiment," Lee replied, "and that has been my condition ever since the fighting commenced on the Rappahannock. If I shorten my lines to provide a reserve, he will turn me. If I weaken my lines to provide a reserve, he will break them."

Thinking this over, the three civilians decided it was time to leave, and in the course of their ride back to the capital they met the President coming out. Today was his fifty-sixth birthday. He had spent the morning, despite the magnetic clatter of the batteries at Cold Harbor, with his three children and his wife, who was soon to be delivered of their sixth; but after lunch, unable any longer to resist the pull of guns that had been roaring for nine hours, he called for his horse and set out on the nine-mile ride to army headquarters. There he found the situation much as it had been described in a 1 o'clock dispatch ("So far every attack has been repulsed," Lee wired) except that by now the Federals had abandoned all pretense of resuming the assault. The staff atmosphere, there in the clearing above Gaines Mill, was one of elation over a victory in the making, if not in fact over one already achieved. Returning to Richmond soon after dark, Davis was pleased to read a message Seddon had just received from Lee in summary of the daylong battle, which now had ended with his army intact and Grant's considerably diminished. "Our loss today has been small," the general wrote, "and our success, under the blessing of God, all that we could expect."

Beyond the lines where Lee's men rested from their exertions, and beyond the intervening space where the dead had begun to spoil in the heat and the wounded cried for help that did not come, the repulsed survivors brooded on the outcome of a solid month of fighting. This was the thirtieth day since the two armies first made contact in the Wilderness, and Union losses were swelling toward an average of 2000 men a day. Some days it was less, some days more, and some days — this one, for example — it was far more, usually as the result of a high-level miscalculation or downright blunder. Even Grant was infected by the gloom into which his troops were plunged by today's addition to the list of headlong tactical failures. "I regret this assault more than any one I ever ordered," he told his staff that evening. Uncharacteristic as it was, the remark made for a certain awkwardness in the group, as if he had sought to relieve his anguish with a scream. "Subsequently the matter was seldom referred to in a conversation," a junior staffer was to state.

Others were less reticent. "I think Grant has had his eyes opened," Meade wrote home, not without a measure of grim satisfaction, "and is willing to admit now that Virginia and Lee's army is not Tennessee and Bragg's army."

According to some observers, such an admission was a necessity if the campaign was to continue. James Wilson, riding over for a visit, found that several members of Grant's official family, including Rawlins, "feared that the policy of direct and continuous attack, if persisted in, would ultimately so decimate and discourage the rank and file that they could not be induced to face the enemy at all. Certain it is," the cavalryman added, "that the 'smash-'em-up' policy was abandoned about that time and was never again favored at headquarters." This would indeed be welcome news, if it was true, but just now the army was in no shape to take much note of anything except its weariness and depletion. A line colonel, stunned and grimy from not having had a full night's sleep or a change of clothes since May 5, found himself in no condition to write more than a few bleak lines in a family letter. "I can only tell my wife I am alive and well," he said; "I am too stupid for any use."

In the past month the Army of the Potomac, under Grant, had lost no less than half as many men as it had lost in the previous three years under McDowell, McClellan, Pope, Burnside, Hooker, and Meade on his own. Death had become a commonplace, though learning to live with it produced a cumulative strain. High-strung Gouverneur Warren, whose four bled-down divisions had fewer troops in them by now than Wright's or Hancock's three, broke out tonight in sudden expostulation to a friend: "For thirty days it has been one funeral procession past me, and it has been too much!" Criticism was mounting, not only against Grant, who had planned — or, strictly speaking, failed to plan — today's attack, but also against those immediately below him on the military ladder. "I am disgusted with the generalship displayed," young Emory Upton wrote his sister on the morning after the battle. "Our men have, in many cases, been foolishly and wantonly slaughtered." Next day, continuing the letter, he went further in fixing the blame. "Our loss was very heavy, and to no purpose. . . . Some of our corps commanders are not fit to be corporals. Lazy and indolent, they will not even ride along their lines; yet, without hesitancy, they will order us to attack the enemy, no matter what their position or numbers. Twenty thousand of our killed and wounded should today be in our ranks."

Horror was added to bitterness by the suffering of the wounded, still trapped between the lines, and the pervasive stench of the dead, still unburied after two sultry nights and the better part of a third day under the fierce June sun. "A deserter says Grant intends to *stink* Lee out of his position, if nothing else will suffice," a Richmond diarist noted, but a Federal staff colonel had a different explanation: "An impression prevails in the popular mind, and with some reason perhaps, that a commander who sends a flag of truce asking permission to bury his dead and bring in his wounded has lost the field of battle. Hence the resistance upon our part to ask a flag of truce."

No more willing to give that impression here in Virginia than he had been a year ago in Mississippi, following the repulse of his two assaults on the Vicksburg fortifications, the Union general held off doing anything to relieve either the stench or the drawn-out agony of his fallen soldiers until the afternoon of June 5, and even then he could not bring himself to make a forthright request for the necessary Confederate acquiescence. "It is reported to me," he then wrote Lee, "that there are wounded men, probably of both armies, now lying exposed and suffering between the lines." His suggestion was that each side be permitted to send out unarmed litter bearers to take up its casualties when no action was in progress, and he closed by saying that "any other method equally fair to both parties you may propose for meeting the end desired will be accepted by me." But Lee, who had no wounded out there, was not letting his adversary off that easy. "I fear that such an arrangement will lead to misunderstanding and difficulty," he replied. "I propose therefore, instead, that when either party desires to remove their dead or wounded a flag of truce be sent, as is customary. It will always afford me pleasure to comply with such a request as far as circumstances will permit."

Thus admonished, Grant took another night to think the matter over — a night in which the cries of the injured, who now had been three days without water or relief from pain, sank to a mewling — and tried a somewhat different tack, as if he were yielding, not without magnanimity, to an urgent plea from a disadvantaged opponent. "Your communication of yesterday is received," he wrote. "I will send immediately, as you propose, to collect the dead and wounded between the lines of the two armies, and will also instruct that you be allowed to do the same." Not so, Lee answered for a second time, and after expressing "regret to find that I did not make myself understood in my communication," proceeded to make it clear that if what Grant wanted was a cease-fire he would have to come right out and ask for it, not informally, as between two men with a common problem, but "by a flag of truce in the usual way." Grant put on as good a face as he could manage in winding up this curious exchange. "The knowledge that wounded men are now suffering from want of attention," he responded, "compels me to ask a suspension of hostilities for sufficient time to collect them in; say two hours."

By the time Lee's formal consent came back across the lines, however, the sun was down on the fourth day of exposure for the wounded and even the mewling had reached an end. Going out next morning, June 7, search parties found only two men alive out of all the Federal thousands who had fallen in the June 3 assault; the rest had either died or made it back under fire, alone or retrieved by comrades in the darkness. At the end of the truce — which had to be extended to give the burial details time to roll up the long blue carpet of festering corpses — Grant fired a parting verbal shot in concluding his white-flag skirmish with Lee: "Regretting that all my efforts for alleviating the sufferings of wounded men left upon the battlefield have been rendered nugatory, I remain, &c., U. S. Grant, Lieutenant General."

Lee made no reply to this, no doubt feeling that none was called for, and not even the northern commander's own troops were taken in by a blame-shifting pretense which did little more than show their chief at his worst. They could discount the Copperhead charge that he was a butcher, "a bull-headed Suvarov," since his methods so far had at least kept the rebels on the defensive while his own army moved forward more than sixty air-line miles. But this was something else, this sacrifice of brave men for no apparent purpose except to salve his rankled pride. Worst of all, they saw in the agony of their comrades, left to die amid the corpses on a field already lost, a preview of much agony to come, when they themselves would be left to whimper through days of pain while their leader composed notes in defense of conduct which, so far as they could see, had been indefensible from the start.

There was that, and there was the heat and thirst, the burning sun, the crowded trenches, and always the snipers, deadly at close range. "I hated sharpshooters, both Confederate and Union," a blue artillerist would recall, "and I was always glad to see them killed." Because of them, rations and ammunition had to be lugged forward along shallow parallels that followed a roundabout zigzag course and wore a man down to feeling like some unholy cross between a pack mule and a snake. "In some instances," another observer wrote, "where regiments whose terms of service had expired were ordered home, they had to leave the field crawling on hands and knees through trenches to the rear." That was a crowning indignity, that a man had to crouch to leave the war, at a time when he wanted to crow and shout, and that even then he might be killed on his way out. Devoured by lice and redbugs, which held carnival in the filthy rags they wore for clothes and burrowed into flesh that had not been washed for more than a month, the men turned snappish, not only among themselves but toward their officers as well. Tempers flared as the conviction grew that they were doing no earthly good in their present position, yet they saw no way to change it without abandoning their drive on Richmond, a scant ten miles away. At a cost of more than 50,000 casualties, Grant had landed them in coffin corner — and it did not help to recall, as a few surviving veterans could do, that McClellan had attained more or less the same position, two years ago, at practically no cost at all.

One who could remember that was Meade, the "damned old goggle-eyed snapping turtle" who had contributed a minor miracle to the campaign by holding onto his famous hair-trigger temper through a month of tribulations and frustrations. But now, in the wake of Cold Harbor, he lost it: lost it, moreover, in much the spectacular manner which those who knew him best had been expecting all along.

Baldy Smith was the first to see it coming. Two days after the triple-pronged assault was shattered, and with thousands of his soldiers lying dead or dying in front of his works, Meade paid Smith a routine visit, in the course of which the Vermonter asked him bluntly how he "came to give such an order for battle as that of the 2d." According to Baldy, Meade's reply was "that he had worked out every plan for every move from the crossing of the Rapidan onward, that the papers were full of the doings of *Grant's* army, and that he was tired of it and was determined to let General Grant plan his own battles." The result, once Grant had been left to his own devices, was the compounded misery out there between the lines. Smith saw from this reaction what was coming of the buildup of resentment, and two days later it came.

While the burial details were at work out front at last, Meade glanced through a hometown newspaper, a five-day-old copy of the

Philadelphia *Inquirer,* and his eye was caught by a paragraph that referred to him as being "entitled to great credit for the magnificent movements of the army since we left Brandy, for they have been directed by him. In battle he puts troops in action and controls their movements; in a word, he commands the army. General Grant is here only because he deems the present campaign the vital one of the war, and wishes to decide on the spot all questions that would be referred to him as general-in-chief." This was gratifying enough, but then the Pennsylvanian moved on to the following paragraph, the one that brought on the foreseen explosion. "History will record, but newspapers cannot, that on one eventful night during the present campaign Grant's presence saved the army, and the nation too; not that General Meade was on the point of committing a blunder unwittingly, but his devotion to his country made him loth to risk her last army on what he deemed a chance. Grant assumed the responsibility, and we are still on to Richmond."

Meade reacted fast. Though the piece was unsigned, he had the *Inquirer* correspondent — one Edward Crapsey — brought to his tent, confronted him with the article, and when the reporter admitted that he had written it, demanded to know the source of his remarks. Crapsey rather lamely cited "the talk of the camp," to the effect that after the second day of battle in the Wilderness, with both flanks turned and his center battered, only Grant had wanted to keep moving south. Enraged by the repetition of this "base and wicked lie," Meade placed the offender in arrest and had his adjutant draw up a general order directing that he "be put without the lines [of the army] and not permitted to return." The provost marshal was charged with the execution of the order next morning, June 8, and he carried it out in style. Wearing on his breast and back large placards lettered LIBELER OF THE PRESS, Crapsey was mounted face-rearward on a mule and paraded through the camps to the accompaniment of the "Rogue's March," after which he was less ceremoniously expelled. "The commanding general trusts that this example will deter others from committing like offenses," Meade's order read, "and he takes this occasion to notify the representatives of the public press that . . . he will not hesitate to punish with the utmost rigor all [such] instances."

Whatever he might have "trusted," the outcome was that Meade now had two wars on his hands, one with the rebels in his front, the other with "the representatives of the public press" in his immediate rear. Making his way to Washington, Crapsey recounted his woes to newspaper friends, who were unanimous in condemning the general for thus "wreaking his personal vengeance on an obscure friendless civilian." What was more, their publishers backed them up; Meade, one said, was "as leprous with moral cowardice as the brute that kicks a helpless cripple on the street, or beats his wife at home." By way of retaliation for what they called "this elaborate insult," they agreed that his name would never be mentioned in dispatches except in connection with a defeat, and they held to this for the next six months or more, with the result that another casualty was added to the long Cold Harbor list, a victim of journalistic strangulation.

Eleven months ago, the Gettysburg victor had been seen as a sure winner in some future presidential election; but not now. Now and for the rest of the year, a reporter noted privately, "Meade was quite as much unknown, by any correspondence from the army, as any dead hero of antiquity."

★ ★ ★

Meade had his woes, but so it seemed did everyone around him, high or low, in the wake of a battle whose decisive action was over in eight holocaustic minutes. Not only had it been lost, and quickly lost; it had been lost, the losers now perceived, before it began. Despite the distraction of wounds that smarted all the more from having been self-inflicted, so to speak, this made for a certain amount of bitter intro-spection at all levels, including the top. A colonel on Lee's staff, coupling quotes from Grant and Hamlet — admittedly an improbable combina-tion — remarked that the Union commander's resolution "to fight it out on this line if it takes all summer" seemed, at this stage, to be "sicklied o'er with the pale cast of thought."

It was in fact, all quips aside, a time for taking stock. Beyond the knowledge that attrition was a knife that cut both ways, Grant had accepted from the outset, as a condition of the tournament, the proba-bility that the knife would slice deeper into the ranks of the attacker; but how much deeper he hadn't known, till now. For twenty-nine days he had been losing about two men to Lee's one, and if this was hard, it was at any rate in proportion to the size of the two armies. Then came the thirtieth day, Cold Harbor, and his loss was five to one, a figure made even more doleful by the prospect that future losses were likely to be as painfully disproportionate if he tried the same thing again in this same region. Lodged as he was in coffin corner, it was no wonder if the cast of his thought was sicklied o'er, along with the thoughts of those around him, staff or line; Rawlins and Upton, for example. Moreover, the effect of that month of losses was cumulative, like the expenses of a spender on a spree, and during the lull which now ensued the bill came due. Halleck sent him what amounted to a declaration of bankruptcy, or in any case a warning that his credit was about to be cut off. On June 7, while the burial details were at work and Meade was berating Crapsey in his tent, Old Brains served notice from Washington that the bottom of the manpower barrel was in sight: "I inclose a list of troops forwarded from this department to the Army of the Potomac since the campaign opened — 48,265 men. I shall send you a few regiments more, when all resources will be exhausted till another draft is made."

These were hard lines, coming as they did at this disappointing juncture in the campaign. Just as the addition of Smith's 15,000 from the Army of the James had not made up for the number who departed from Meade's army because their enlistments had expired or they had broken down physically under the thirty-day strain, so too was Halleck's figure, even with the inclusion of those "few regiments more," considerably short of the number who had been shot or captured in the course of the month-long drive from the Rapidan to the Chickahominy. This would make for restrictions, which in turn seemed likely to require a change in style. Up to the present, Grant had been living as it were on interest, replacing his fallen veterans with conscripts, but from now until another of Lincoln's "calls" had been responded to, and the drafted troops approximately trained for use in the field, he would be living on principal. Formerly replaceable on short notice, a man hit now would be simply one man less, a flat subtraction from the dwindling mass. The law of diminishing utility thus obtained, and though Grant no doubt would find it cramping, if not prohibitive in its effect on his previous method of sailing headlong into whatever got in his path, it afforded in any case a gleam of hope for those around and under him. Some members of his staff had expressed the fear that any attempt to repeat the army's latest effort, here between the Totopotomoy and the Chickahominy, would render it unfit for future use. Now they could stop worrying; at least about that. Grant had no intention of provoking another Cold Harbor and they knew it, not only because they had heard him express regret that he had tried such a thing in the first place, but also because they knew that he could no longer afford it, even if he changed his mind.

One possible source of reinforcements was the remnant of Butler's army, still tightly corked in its bottle on the far side of the James and doing no earthly good except for keeping Beauregard's even smaller remnant from joining Lee. However, as a result of his casualties during the corking operation and the subsequent detachment of Smith, the cock-eyed general was down to about 10,000 men, scarcely enough to warrant the trouble of getting them on and off transports and certainly not enough to make any significant change in the situation north of the Chickahominy. Besides, Grant's mind was turning now toward a use for them in the region where they were. He still thought his plan for a diversionary effort south of the James had been a good one; aside, that is, from the designation of Butler as the man to carry it out. If a real soldier, a professional rather than an all-thumbs amateur, had been in over-all command — Baldy Smith, for example — Richmond might not have fallen by now, but at least it would have been cut off from Georgia and the Carolinas by the occupation of the Petersburg rail hub, and its citizens would be tightening their belts another notch or two to relieve far greater pangs of hunger than they were feeling with their supply lines open to the south. Grant's notion was to reinforce Butler for a breakout from Bermuda Neck, due west to Walthall Junction, or a sidle across the Appomattox for a quick descent on Petersburg. Smith's corps would go, he and his men being familiar with the southside terrain, and possibly a corps or two from Meade. In fact, the more Grant thought about it, there in the stench and dust around Cold Harbor, the more he was persuaded that the thing to do was send Meade's whole army, not only to assure the success of the operation beyond the James, but also to resolve what was fast becoming a stalemate, here on the north bank of the Chickahominy, and remove the troops from the scene of their most disheartening repulse.

Halleck was against it before he even learned the details. He preferred the slower but less risky investment of the Confederate capital from the north, which would not expose the army to the danger of being caught astride the James and would have the added virtue of covering Washington if Lee reverted to his practice of disrupting Union strategy with a strike across the Potomac. But Grant had had quite enough of maneuvering in that region.

"My idea from the start has been to beat Lee's army, if possible, north of Richmond," he admitted in a letter to the chief of staff on June 5, the day he opened negotiations for the burial of his dead, but he saw now that "without a greater sacrifice of human life than I am willing to make, all cannot be accomplished that I had designed." Then he told just what it was he had in mind. "I will continue to hold substantially to the ground now occupied by the Army of the Potomac, taking advantage of any favorable circumstance that may present itself, until the cavalry can be sent to destroy the Virginia Central Railroad from about Beaver Dam for some 25 or 30 miles west. When this is effected, I will move the army to the south side of James River." Cut off from supplies from the north and south, Lee would have no choice except to stay inside his capital and starve, abandon it to his foe, or come out and fight for it in the open. Grant had no doubt about the outcome if his adversary, as seemed likely from past usage, chose the third of these alternatives and tried to stage another Seven Days. "The feeling of the two armies now seems to be that the rebels can protect themselves only by strong intrenchments," he closed his letter, "while our army is not only confident of protecting itself without intrenchments, but can beat and drive the enemy whenever and wherever he can be found without this protection."

Then suddenly things began to happen fast. He learned that night that while he had been writing to Halleck, outlining his plan without committing himself to a schedule, Sigel's successor David Hunter had scored a victory out in the Shenandoah Valley that would shorten considerably the time Grant had thought he would have to devote to smashing Richmond's northwestern supply line. Disdaining the combinations his predecessor had favored — and which, it could be seen now,

had contributed to the failure of that segment of the grand design for
Lee's defeat — Hunter had simply notified Crook and Averell that he
was heading south, up the Valley pike, and that they were to join him
as soon as they could make it across the Alleghenies from their camp
on the Greenbrier River. He set out from Cedar Creek on May 26, five
days after taking command of the troops whipped at New Market the
week before, and at the end of a ten-day hike up the turnpike, which he
interrupted from time to time to demolish a gristmill, burn a barn, or
drive off butternut horsemen trying to scout the column at long range,
he reached the village of Piedmont, eleven miles short of Staunton, and
found the rebels drawn up in his path, guns booming. Attacking forthwith he wrecked and scattered what turned out to be three scratch
brigades, all that were left to defend the region after Breckinridge departed. His reward, gained at a cost of less than 500 killed and
wounded, included more than 1000 prisoners, a solid fifth of the force
that had opposed him; the body of Brigadier General William E. Jones,
abandoned on the field by the fugitives he had commanded until he was
shot; and Staunton. Hunter occupied the town next day, his two divisions marching unopposed down streets no blue-clad troops had trod
before. Two days later, on June 8, having torn up the railroad west of
town as they approached, Crook and Averell arrived from West
Virginia to assist in the consumption and destruction of commissary and
ordnance stores collected at Staunton for shipment to Lee's army. With
his strength thus doubled to 18,000, Hunter promptly took up the march
for Lynchburg, another important depot of supplies, located where
the Virginia & Tennessee Railroad branched east to form the Southside
and the Orange & Alexandria; after which he intended to strike northeast for Charlottesville, where he would get back astride the Virginia
Central and move down it to join Grant near Richmond, twisting rails
and burning crossties as he went.

Again he was moving toward reinforcements, this time of the
doughtiest kind. Grant had no sooner learned of Hunter's coup at Piedmont than he decided to proceed at once with the opening phase of the
plan he had outlined that day for Halleck. He sent for Sheridan
and gave him orders to take off at dawn of June 7, westward around
Lee's north flank, for a link-up with Hunter near Charlottesville; he was
to lend the help of his hard-handed troopers in wrecking the Virginia
Central on his way back and, if necessary, fight off any graybacks,
mounted or dismounted, who might try to interfere. In this connection
Grant conferred next day with Meade, explaining the ticklish necessity
of keeping enough pressure on Lee to discourage him from sending any
part of his army against Sheridan or Hunter, yet not so much pressure
that Lee would fall back to the permanent fortifications in his rear, whose
strength might also permit such a detachment of troops for the protection of the vital rail supply route from the Shenandoah Valley. (This

was also why Grant, in addition to his habitual disinclination in such matters, had not wanted to risk encouraging his opponent by making a forthright request for permission to bury his dead and bring in the wounded suffering in his front.) At the same time, Meade was instructed to start work on a second line of intrenchments, just in rear of his present works, stout enough to be held by a skeleton force if Lee attacked while the army was in the early stages of its withdrawal across the Chicka-hominy, down beyond White Oak Swamp, to and across the James.

One thing more Grant did while Sheridan was preparing to take off next morning, and that was to call in two of his aides, Horace Porter and another young lieutenant colonel, Cyrus Comstock, who was also a West Pointer and a trained engineer. Both were familiar with the region to be traversed, having served under McClellan in the course of that general's "change of base" two years ago, and Grant had a double mission for them: one as carriers of instructions for Butler at Bermuda Hundred, the other as selectors of a site for what promised to be the longest pontoon bridge in American military history. "Explain the con-templated movement fully to General Butler," he told them, "and see that the necessary precautions are made by him to render his position secure against any attack from Lee's forces while the Army of the Potomac is making its movement." That was their first assignment, and the second, involving engineering skill, followed close behind. "You will then select the best point on the river for the crossing."

They left, and the following day — with Sheridan's troopers gone before dawn, the burial squads at their grisly task out front, and Meade in a snit over Crapsey's piece in the *Inquirer* — Grant got to work, while awaiting the outcome of his preliminary arrangements, on logistic details of the projected shift. He did so, however, over the continuing objec-tions of the chief of staff. Halleck had been against a southside campaign two years ago, when McClellan pled so fervently for permission to undertake what Grant was about to do, and he still was as much opposed as ever, believing that such a maneuver was practically an invitation for Lee to cross the Potomac. The old fox had already crossed it twice with-out success, it was true, but the third time might prove to be the charm that won him Washington, especially now that Grant, having stripped its forts of soldiers, proposed to leave it strategically uncovered.

Old Brains continued thus to take counsel of his fears; but not Grant, whose mind was quite made up. "We can defend Washington best," he informed Halleck, putting an end to discussion of the matter, "by keeping Lee so occupied that he cannot detach enough troops to capture it. I shall prepare at once to move across James River."

Grant being Grant, and Halleck having long since lost the veto, that was that. The Union commander was soon to find, however, that his effort to keep Lee so occupied with the close-up defense of Richmond that he would not feel able to send any considerable part of his outnumbered force against Hunter or Sheridan had failed. Learning on June 6 of Jones's defeat at Piedmont and Hunter's rapid occupation of Staunton, Lee sent at once for Breckinridge and informed him that he and his two brigades would be leaving next morning for Lynchburg to prevent the capture of that important railroad junction by the bluecoats they had whipped three weeks ago under Sigel, a hundred miles to the north. Instructed to combine his 2100 veterans with the Piedmont fugitives for this purpose, the Kentuckian left on schedule, determined to repeat his New Market triumph, although he would be facing longer odds and was personally in a near-invalid condition as a result of having his horse collapse on him four days ago.

With Grant likely to resume his hammering at any moment, here at Cold Harbor or elsewhere along a semicircular arc from Atlee Station down to Chaffin's Bluff — all within ten miles of Capitol Square — even so minor a reduction in strength as this detachment of two brigades was a risky business for Lee, no matter how urgent the need. Yet before the day was over he was warned of another threat which called for a second detachment, larger and more critical than the first. Sheridan, he learned from outpost scouts, had taken off before dawn with two of his divisions, about the same time Breckinridge left Richmond, headed west by rail for Lynchburg. The bandy-legged cavalryman's march was north, across the Pamunkey; he made camp that night on the near bank of the Mattaponi, and next morning — June 8 — he was reported moving west. Lee reasoned that the blue horsemen intended to effect a junction with Hunter on this or the far side of the Blue Ridge, somewhere along the Virginia Central, which they would obstruct while waiting for him to join them for the return march. If Sheridan was to be thwarted it would have to be done by a force as mobile as his own, and though Lee found it hard to deprive himself of a single trooper at a time when his adversary was no doubt contemplating another sidle, he sent Hampton orders to set out next morning, with his own and Fitzhugh Lee's divisions, to intercept the raiders before they reached either Hunter or the railroad.

Yet this too, as it turned out, was a day that brought unwelcome news of the need for still another reduction of the outnumbered army in its trenches near Cold Harbor. Crook and Averell, Lee was informed, had joined Hunter that morning in Staunton, doubling his strength beyond anything Breckinridge, with less than a third as many troops — including the Piedmont fugitives, once he managed to round them up — could be expected to confront, much less defeat. Obviously he would have to be reinforced; but how? Then came the notion Halleck was even now warning Grant that his proposed maneuver would invite from Lee, who had a way of making a virtue of necessity. Hunter's strength was put at 20,000, and it was clear that if he was to be stopped it would have to be done by two or three divisions, available only — if at all — from the Confederate main body. Such a decrease in the force confronting Grant, merely for the sake of blocking Hunter, seemed little short of suicidal. But how would it be if a sizeable detachment could be used offensively, as a means not only of reclaiming the Shenandoah Valley and covering the supply lines leading to it, but also of threatening Washington by crossing the Potomac? Twice before, a dispersion of force, made in the face of odds as long or longer, had relieved the pressure on Richmond by playing on the fears of the Union high command. McClellan and Hooker had been recalled to protect the menaced capital in their rear; so might Grant be summoned back to meet a similar threat. Impossible though it seemed at this fitful juncture, such a maneuver was never really out of Lee's mind, and it was especially attractive now that rumors had begun to fly that Grant was designing a shift to the James, perhaps for a link-up with Butler on the other side. "If he gets there it will become a siege," Lee had told Early the week before, "and then it will be a mere question of time."

Hampton had no sooner taken off next morning, riding the chord of Sheridan's arc to intercept him, than an alarm from beyond the James lent credence to the rumor that the Federals were preparing a new effort in that direction, or in any case an improved resumption of the old one. Butler, crossing a portion of his command from Bermuda Neck by a pontoon bridge he had thrown across the Appomattox near Port Walthall, launched a dawn attack on the Petersburg intrenchments, four miles south. Beauregard, down to fewer than 8000 troops by now, managed to contain and repulse this cavalry-infantry assault because of the strength of the works and the valiance of the men who occupied them, mostly under- and over-aged members of a militia battalion, reinforced for the crisis by volunteers from the city hospital and the county jail. In the resultant "Battle of the Patients and the Penitents," as it came to be called, these inexperienced defenders — inspired by a local Negro band whose vigorous playing gave the attackers the impression that the works were heavily manned — held their own long enough for gray-jacket cavalry to arrive from the main line, beyond the Appomattox, and drive the bluecoats off. It was over by midafternoon, a near thing at best, and Beauregard, though proud of what had been achieved, warned that he could not be expected to repeat the performance unless the troops he had sent Lee were restored to him. Moreover, he told the War Department, they had better be returned at once, since in his opinion today's attack presaged a much larger one soon to come.

"This movement must be a reconnaissance connected with Grant's future operations," he wired Bragg while the fight was still in progress, and presently he added, by way of emphasizing the risk: "Without the troops sent to General Lee I will have to elect between abandoning lines on Bermuda Neck and those of Petersburg. Please give me the views of the Government on the subject."

Presented thus with a choice between losing Richmond to assault or by starvation, Bragg could only reply that the mercurial Creole was to do what he could to hold both positions, while he himself conferred with Davis, who authorized the return of Gracie's brigade from the capital defenses, and with Lee, who agreed to alert Hoke's division for a crossing at Drewry's in case another southside attack developed. Mainly, though, the Virginian saw this abortive maneuver of Butler's as a feint, designed to distract his attention from more serious threats presented by more dependable Union commanders on the north side of the James: by Meade, who might even now be bracing his army for another all-out lunge, here at Cold Harbor or elsewhere along the Richmond-hugging arc: by Hunter, who was evidently about to resume his march from Staunton, with either Lynchburg or Charlottesville as his intermediate goal, preparatory to a combination with Meade: or by Sheridan, who was in motion between the other two, probably with the intention of descending on the Virginia Central before linking up with Hunter for a return march that would complete the destruction of that vital supply line. Despite a rather superfluous warning from the President, who added his voice to Bragg's — "The indications are that Grant, despairing of a direct attack, is now seeking to embarrass you by flank movements" — Lee could not see that the thing to do, at this critical juncture, was weaken his army below the present danger point for the sake of relieving Beauregard's fears as to what Butler might or might not be up to, down on the far side of the James. Until Grant's intentions became clearer, and until he could see what came of the two detachments already made — Breckinridge, two days ago, and Hampton just this morning — Lee preferred to hold what he had, and hope that others, elsewhere, would measure up to his expectations.

Wade Hampton, whose assignment to lead the two-division column in pursuit of Sheridan was the nearest Lee had come to designating a successor to the fallen Stuart, was intent on fulfilling his share of the army commander's hopes, not so much because of a desire for fame or an ache for glory — "I pray for peace," he would presently say in a letter to his sister, having won the coveted post by demonstrating his fitness for it in the current operation; "I would not give peace for all the military glory of Bonaparte" — as because of a habitual determination to accomplish what was required of him, in this as in other phases of a life of privileged responsibility. He wore no plume, no red-lined cape, and a minimum of braid, preferring a flat-brimmed brown felt hat and a plain gray jacket of civilian cut. His manner, while friendly, was grave, and though he was perhaps the richest man in the South, his spurs were brass, not gold. A Virginia trooper noted another difference between the Carolinian and his predecessor as chief of cavalry, which was that, whereas Jeb had "sometimes seemed to have a delight in trying to discharge his mission with the smallest possible number of men, Hampton believed in superiority of force and exerted himself to concentrate all the men he could at the point of contact."

Superiority of force would not be possible short of the point of contact in this case; for though both mounted columns were composed of two divisions containing a total of five brigades, Sheridan had 8000 troopers, compared to Hampton's 5000, and four batteries of horse artillery opposing three. One advantage the gray riders had, however, and this was that they traveled lighter, with fewer impediments to slow them down. The Federals had a train of 125 supply wagons and ambulances, as well as a herd of beef to butcher on the march, while all the Confederates had was an issue of three-day rations, consisting of half a pound of bacon and a pound and a half of hardtack, carried on the person, along with a sack of horse corn slung from the pommel of each saddle. Another advantage, although no one could be sure of it beforehand, was that Lee had been right about Sheridan's objective; Hampton had a much shorter distance to travel, northwest from Atlee, across the South Anna, in order to get there first. This he did, despite the blue column's two-day head start in setting out on its roundabout route from Cold Harbor, first north across the Pamunkey, then west through Chilesburg, up the left bank of the North Anna for a crossing short of Gordonsville and a quick descent, as ordered, on the Virginia Central between that place and Louisa Courthouse, a dozen miles down the track. Shortly after sunrise, June 11, within about three miles of his objective at the outset of his fifth day on the go, Sheridan ran into fire from rebel skirmishers, who, he now found, had arrived the previous evening and had rested from their two-day ride within earshot of the bugles that called his troopers to horse this morning.

Hampton was not only there, he was attacking in accordance with plans made the night before, after learning that he had won the race for the stretch of railroad Sheridan had in mind to wreck. His own division, with three brigades, was to advance northeast from Trevilian Station, eight miles short of Gordonsville and half that distance above Louisa, where Fitz Lee, having bivouacked his two brigades nearby, was to set out north at daybreak for a convergence upon Sheridan's camp, five miles away. Each division had a convenient road to move on, and Hampton at least was unhindered on the approach march. Hearing firing off to the east, which he took to be Fitz brushing pickets from his path, he sent his lead brigade forward, dismounted, and made contact with the Federals, driving them rapidly back on their supports, who resisted stubbornly even when hit by a second brigade. Hampton withheld full commitment, waiting for Lee to come up and strike the defenders flank and rear. At this point, however, a sudden clatter from the south informed him that his own rear had been struck. By what, and how, he did not wait to learn. Disengaging with all possible speed, and pursued now by the enemy he had driven, he withdrew to find a host of blue marauders laying claim to his headquarters and the 800 horses left behind when he dismounted his lead brigade for the sunrise attack. He attacked again, this time rearward, and what had been a battle became a melee.

The marauders were members of Custer's brigade, one of Torbert's three. While the other two were holding fast under pressure from Hampton, Gregg's division had got the jump on Fitz and driven him back toward Louisa, enabling the Michiganders to slip between the converging gray columns for a penetration deep into Hampton's rear, near Trevilian. Yet they had no sooner begun to gather the fruits of their boldness — the 800 riderless horses, several ordnance wagons, and a couple of guns being held there in reserve — than they were hit, simultaneously from the north and east, by three hornet-mad rebel brigades, two of them Hampton's and one Lee's. Custer not only had to abandon what he had won; he also lost much that he brought with him, including a considerable number of troopers shot or captured, his headquarters wagon containing all his records and spare clothes, and his Negro cook Eliza, known to the soldiers as "the Queen of Sheba" because she usually rode in a dilapidated family carriage the yellow-haired general had commandeered for her professional use and comfort. Shaken, he fell back to the station and held on grimly against the odds, while Torbert fought his way down with the other two brigades and Gregg continued to slug it out with Fitz. The result was about as bewildering to one side as to the other, and was to be even more confusing to future students attempting to reconcile conflicting reports of the action. The Confederates at last pulled back, Hampton toward Gordonsville and Lee in the opposite direction. Sheridan did not pursue, west or east, but contented himself with holding the four miles of track between Trevilian and Louisa. It was a gloomy night for the Federals, especially those in Custer's brigade, which had lost heavily today; but their dejection was relieved, just before sunup, by the reappearance of the Queen of Sheba, grinning broadly and lugging along the gaudy young general's personal valise, which she had managed to bring with her when she stole out of the rebel lines and into her own.

Sheridan was far from pleased with the development of events. After a night of fitful sleep, with graybacks hovering east and west — about to be joined, for all he knew, by reinforcements from both directions, infantry by rail and cavalry on horseback — he put Gregg to work with sledges and crowbars on the four-mile stretch of track and prepared to enlarge his present limits of destruction, first by driving Hampton back on Gordonsville, eight miles northwest, and then by thrusting him aside to clear the way for the scheduled meeting with

Hunter, another twenty miles up the line at Charlottesville. It was past noon, however, before he got Torbert deployed for action; by which time Fitz Lee had joined Hampton, coming roundabout from Louisa, and the two divisions were dug in just above Trevilian, blocking both the Virginia Central and the turnpike leading west. Repeated and costly dismounted assaults failed to budge the rebels, snug in their works, and after nightfall, Gregg having done all the damage he could to the railroad within the cramped limits of the Federal occupation, Sheridan decided to abandon both his position and his mission.

Under cover of darkness he withdrew across the North Anna and took up the return march, retracing the route that had brought him to the unhappy confrontation at Trevilian. He pulled back, he said, because his supplies and munitions were low and there was no word from Hunter, either at Charlottesville or elsewhere, as to their intended combination. In any case, having spent four days on the march out, he took nine to make it back to White House Landing, his ambulances overloaded with wounded and his horses distressed at being reduced to a diet of bearded wheat. Meantime, the limited damage Gregg had done the railroad was repaired so promptly by work gangs that Virginia Central trains were back on schedule before Sheridan reached the Pamunkey and recrossed it under the protection of gunboats whose heavy-caliber frown kept the still-hovering butternut cavalry at bay. Hampton had lost nearly 1100 men in the course of the raid; Sheridan reckoned his own loss at about 800, though a more accurate revision put the figure at 1516, considerably better than twice the number he had lost on the Richmond raid the month before.

R. E. Lee of course was pleased to learn that Little Phil had been disposed of as a threat to his main supply route from the Shenandoah Valley: so pleased, indeed, that he at last named Hampton, rather than his nephew Fitz, as his new chief of cavalry. But word of Sheridan's repulse came in the wake of news of a fateful development, out beyond the Blue Ridge, which not only presented a more substantial menace to the newly delivered supply line, but also served notice that, even if the railroad escaped seizure, there would be little in the way of supplies available for shipment from the region, either to Richmond or to any other point in the shrinking Confederacy. The news was that David Hunter, his strength doubled by the arrival of Crook two days before, had resumed his march up the Valley on June 10. Leaving Breckinridge holding the bag at Rockfish Gap, where the Virginia Central passed through the mountains east of Staunton — the Kentuckian had shifted there from Lynchburg to block the western approach to Charlottesville, which he thought was next on the Union list — Hunter struck out south, not east, and by noon of the day the cavalry battle opened near Trevilian Station, eighty air-line miles away, reached Lexington and took under fire, from across North River, the crenelated turrets and ramparts of V.M.I., whose cadets had shared in the defeat of his predecessor four weeks ago. Marching in, flags flying, he completed his work of destruction, next day and the day after, by putting the torch to what was left of the Institute and turning his soldiers loose on the town to plunder a number of private homes and the library of Washington College. For good measure, after a visit to Stonewall Jackson's grave — perhaps to make certain the famed rebel had not come bursting out of it in his wrath — Hunter ordered the residence of Former Governor John Letcher burned, as he later reported, in retaliation for its absent owner's having issued "a violent and inflammatory proclamation . . . inciting the population of the country to rise and wage guerrilla warfare on my troops."

Such hard-handedness toward civilians was remindful of John Pope, of whom Lee had said: "He ought to be suppressed," and then had proceeded to do just that by dividing his army, confronted near Richmond by a superior force, and sending part of it north and west, under the one-time V.M.I. professor now buried in outraged Lexington, against the fire-breathing secondary invader attempting a descent on his left flank and rear. Close though the resemblance was between the situations then and now, there were also differences, none of them advantageous from the Confederate point of view. One was that Jackson, Lee's right arm, was no longer available to carry out the suppression, and another was the present depleted condition of the Army of Northern Virginia, which had lost in the past forty days a solid forty percent of the strength it had enjoyed at the beginning of the campaign. Its casualties totaled about 27,000, and though it had inflicted a precisely tabulated 54,929 — a number greater than all its original infantry and artillery combined — the forty percent figure, unlike Grant's forty-five percent, applied at the higher levels of rank as well as at the lower. Of the 58 general officers in command of troops on the eve of conflict, back in early May, no less than 23 had fallen in battle, eight of them killed, thirteen gravely wounded, and two captured. Nor was the distribution of these casualties, high and low, by any means even throughout the three corps. Hardest hit of all was the Second: just the one Lee had in mind to detach, since it contained, as a nucleus, the survivors of Jackson's old Army of the Valley and was therefore more familiar than the others with the region Hunter was laying waste. Not only had the corps commander been replaced, but so had the leaders of two of the three divisions, while of the twelve original brigade commanders only one remained at his post, two having been promoted and the other nine shot or captured. At Spotsylvania the corps had lost the equivalent of a full division, and this contributed largely to the reduction, by half, of its outset strength of just over 17,000. There now were barely 8000 infantry in its ranks, distributed through three divisions with only three brigades in each, all but one under leaders new to their responsibilities.

These were drawbacks not to be ignored in reaching a decision; but neither was the need for dealing promptly with Hunter to be passed over. From his current position at Lexington he would no doubt cross the Blue Ridge, marching southeast against Lynchburg or northeast against Charlottesville. One would be about as bad as the other, so far as Richmond was concerned, and there was also the possibility that the wide-ranging Hunter might move against them both, in that order. At Lynchburg, just under a hundred miles due west of the captial, he would be in a position to wreck not only the Southside Railroad but also the James River Canal, both vital to the subsistence of Richmond's citizens and its armies, while at Charlottesville he would be back astride the Virginia Central, which he would destroy, with or without Sheridan's help, on the march to join Grant or come down on Lee's flank. Reduced to those terms, the problem solved itself, insofar at least as they applied to reaching a decision. Like Pope, Hunter would have to be "suppressed," or anyhow stopped and, if possible, driven back. Lee's mind was quite made up. Moreover, there was the persuasive chance that in moving against the despoilers of Lexington he would be killing two birds with one stone. If, after disposing of the bluecoats out in the Valley, the gray column then moved down it, to and across the Potomac to threaten Washington from the rear, still larger benefits might accrue. There was small chance, at this late stage, that Grant's whole force would be recalled — as McClellan's had been — from the gates of Richmond, but it was altogether possible that he would be required to detach part of it for the closeup defense of his capital; or else, in desperation to avoid that, he might be provoked into launching another ill-considered Cold Harbor assault, there or elsewhere, in an attempt to settle the issue overnight. In either event, Lee reasoned, his adversary would be reduced enough for the Army of Northern Virginia to launch an all-out assault of its own: hopefully one that would be as productive as the Seven Days offensive, but in any case one that would be conducted with all the fighting skill his soldiers had acquired in their many victories since that grim beginning under his command.

His decision reached — June 12, a Sunday; the horseback fight was into its second day at Trevilian Station, and Hunter was putting the torch to Governor Letcher's house in Lexington — Lee sent for Jubal Early to talk over with him the nature of his mission. Tall despite an arthritic stoop, a bachelor at forty-seven, dour of face, with a scraggly beard and a habit of profanity, this fellow Virginian and West Pointer was admittedly no Stonewall; but who was? No other corps commander since the fall of Longstreet had done any better on the offensive, and though this was surely the faintest of praise — since, conversely, it could also be said that none had done any worse — the only really black mark against him was his failure, in conjunction with Ewell on the second day in the Wilderness, to take prompt advantage of Gordon's report that Sedgwick's flank was open to attack. No such opportunities must be missed if he was to succeed against the odds that lay before him, first in the Valley and then beyond the Potomac. Tactful as always, Lee made this clear in giving Early verbal instructions for setting out next morning, before daylight, with all three of his divisions and two battalions of artillery. Following as it did the detachment of Breckinridge, with whom he would combine to cover Charlottesville and Lynchburg, Early's departure would deprive Lee of nearly a fourth of his infantry; yet, even with the inclusion of the Piedmont fugitives, the gray force would not be up to Hunter's present strength. Victory would have to be won by superior generalship, by celerity, stealth, and an absolute dedication to the offensive: in short, by the application of principles dear to the commander of the erstwhile Army of the Valley, which was now to be resurrected under Early.

In written orders, sent that night while the Second Corps veterans were preparing feverishly and happily to be gone with the dawn, these hopes were repeated, together with specific instructions for the march. It would be northwest, like Hampton's four days earlier, for a link-up with Breckinridge near Rockfish Gap and a quick descent on Hunter before he reached Lynchburg. After that, if all went well, would come the northward march against a new old adversary, Abraham Lincoln — and, through Lincoln and his fears, against U. S. Grant, who presumably would still be knocking at the gates of Richmond, a hundred miles away.

Grant might still be knocking when the time came, but if so it would be at the back gate, not the front. Under cover of the darkness that would obscure Early's departure, north and west, the Army of the Potomac had begun its withdrawal, east and south, from its works around Cold Harbor for the crossing of the James. Moreover, if all went as intended, here and elsewhere, the issue would have been settled — so far, as least, as Richmond was concerned — well before any rebel detachment, of whatever size, had time to reach the Potomac, much less cross it to threaten Washington. With Sheridan astride the Virginia Central and Hunter about to wreck both the Southside Railroad and the James River Canal at Lynchburg (Grant did not know that Sheridan was being driven off that evening, any more than he knew that Lee was sending Early next morning to do the same to Hunter) Federal seizure of the Petersburg rail hub would cut all but one of the gray capital's major supply lines, the Richmond & Danville, which had only been extended down to Greensboro, North Carolina, the month before. No single route, let alone one as limited as this, could supply the city's needs, including subsistence for its defenders; Lee, more than ever, would be obliged to evacuate his capital or come out from behind his intrenchments for a fight in the open, and Grant did not believe that the Confederacy could survive what would follow the adoption of either course.

He had bided his time, anticipating solutions, and when they came he moved swiftly. When the two aides, Porter and Comstock, returned from their reconnaissance that Sunday morning to report that they had found a good site for the pontoon bridge across the James, ten miles downriver from City Point and just beyond Charles City Courthouse, he evidenced some measure of the strain he had been under this past week. "While listening to our report," Porter would recall, "Grant showed the only nervousness he ever manifested in my presence. After smoking his cigar vigorously for some minutes, he removed it from his mouth, put it on the table, and allowed it to go out; then relighted it, gave a few puffs, and laid it aside again. We could hardly get the words out of our mouths fast enough to suit him, and the numerous questions he asked were uttered with much greater rapidity than usual." This was a different Grant from the stolid, twig-whittling commander of the past six weeks. It was, as the next few days would show, the Grant of the Vicksburg campaign, fast on the march, sudden in striking, and above all quick to improvise amid rapidly developing events. "At the close of the interview," Porter wrote, still amazed years later at the transformation in his chief, "he informed us that he would begin the movement that night."

It began, in point of fact, that afternoon, when Grant and Meade and their two staffs proceeded down the north bank of the Chickahominy, past Dispatch Station on the defunct York River Railroad, to make camp for the night beside a clump of catalpa trees in the yard of a farmhouse near Long Bridge, where two of the five corps were to cross the river, ten miles downstream from the present Union left. The bridge was out, but Wilson's cavalry splashed across the shallows, just after sundown, and got to work throwing a pontoon span to be used by Warren, who began his march in the twilight and was over the river by midnight. Hancock and Wright meantime fell back to the newly dug second line, under orders to hold it at all costs, in case Lee got wind of the withdrawal and launched a night attack. Smith and Burnside simultaneously marched rearward from their positions on the right, the latter turning south beyond the railroad for a crossing of the Chickahominy at Jones Bridge, five miles below Long Bridge, and Smith continuing east to White House Landing, where transports were waiting to give his troops a fast, restful trip down the York and up the James to Bermuda Hundred. Satisfied that Lee had no overnight interference in mind, Hancock and Wright pulled out after midnight to follow Warren and Burnside, respectively, over Long and Jones bridges. Once across, three of the four corps would march hard for Charles City and the James, but Warren was instructed to turn west and take up a defensive position near Riddell's Shop in support of Wilson's troopers, who would

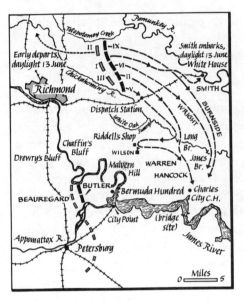

patrol the region between White
Oak Swamp and Malvern Hill
in case Lee, having missed his
chance tonight, tried to strike
tomorrow at the blue army in
motion across his front. Like
Wright and Hancock earlier,
once he was convinced that Lee
had been outfoxed, Warren
would take up the march for
Charles City and the crossing of
the James.

Intricate as these various
interdependent movements were,
they had been worked out in
accordance with the required
logistics of allotted time and road
space. All went smoothly. Despite the heat of the night and the choking
dust stirred up by more than a hundred thousand pairs of shoes, the men
stepped out smartly in the darkness, glad to be leaving a dismal field
where they had buried so many comrades after so much purposeless
suffering. Occupied as they had been with improving their intrenchments, right up to the hour they got orders to withdraw, they took it as
an excellent sign that their departure had been preceded by no rumor
that a shift was being considered, since what came as a surprise to them
was likely to be even more of one to the johnnies across the way, including Old Man Lee. "It was not now the custom," one veteran observed
approvingly, "to inform the rank and file, and the newspapers and the
enemy, of intended movements." He and others like him in those several
widespread dusty columns could remember another nighttime withdrawal from that same field, just two weeks short of two full years ago,
and though Cold Harbor was in itself an even more horrendous experience than Gaines Mill, the feeling now was different, and altogether
better. Now as then the march was south, away from the scene of a defeat; but they felt now — as they had not done then, while trudging
some of these same James-bound roads — that they were moving toward
a victory, even Victory itself.

Grant thought so, too, and on sounder ground, knowing, as they
did not, what he had devised for the undoing of the rebels on the far
side of the river. Smith, whose corps was familiar with the terrain down
there, would arrive first, being steam-propelled, and after going ashore
at Bermuda Hundred would repeat the maneuver Butler had rehearsed
four days ago, across the Appomattox, when his Petersburg reconnais-
sance-in-strength was stalled by green militia, convicts, convalescents,
and Negro bandsmen. That was not likely to happen this time, for

three reasons. One was that Baldy would be in charge of the advance, not the nonprofessional Butler, and Grant had already explained to his fellow West Pointer the importance of striking hard and fast. Another was that this attack would not only be made in much greater strength than the other, but would also be launched with the advantage of knowing the layout of the Petersburg defenses. The third reason was that, if there was any delay in the quick reduction of the place, Hancock — whose three divisions, in the lead on the march from Cold Harbor, would be ferried across the James to save time while the 2100-foot pontoon bridge was being assembled — would soon be down to add the weight of the hardest-hitting corps in Meade's army to the pressure Smith was exerting. As for the others, Burnside, Warren, and Wright would be arriving in that order behind Hancock and could be used as then seemed best: probably for a breakout westward from Bermuda Neck, dislodging Beauregard's cork, and a turning movement against Drewry's Bluff, which would block the path of any reinforcements Lee might try to send to Petersburg when he found what Grant had been up to all this time.

Members of the two staffs — Grant's and Meade's — shared the sanguine expectations of their chiefs, at least to the extent that they were privy to the plan, and their confidence grew as the day wore on and they rode south, doubling the columns of guns and men on the dusty roads. All the signs were that the army had indeed stolen a march on Lee, whose cavalry, unable to penetrate Wilson's screen below the Chickahominy, could give him no inkling of what was in progress east of Riddell's Shop, near which Warren's four divisions remained in position without firing a shot all afternoon, so effectively did the blue troopers perform, and then resumed their roundabout hike for the James. By that time the head of Hancock's column had come within sight of the broad, shining river, its choppy little waves as bright as polished hatchets in the sunlight.

Transports and gunboats were riding at anchor, all with steam up for the crossing, and army engineers were at work assembling their pontoons for the nearly half-mile span by which the other three corps would cross, tomorrow and the next day. An officer on Meade's staff observed Hancock's troops slogging down to Wilcox Landing just before sunset, hot and tired from their thirty-mile overnight march, their faded, sweat-splotched uniforms in tatters from forty days of combat, and was struck by the thought that, so far as these hard-bitten veterans were concerned, "the more they serve, the less they look like soldiers and the more they resemble day laborers who have bought second-hand military clothes." Then he watched them react with suspicion and puzzled dislike, much as he himself had done earlier, to their first sight of the neatly turned-out sailors and the engineers in uniforms of dark unweathered blue, until at last they saw, as he had seen, what it was that was so wrong about these strangers. They were clean — clean as visitors from some dirtless planet — and Grant's men, after six weeks on the go, shooting and being shot at, with neither the water nor the time for bathing, had become mistrustful of anyone not as grimy as themselves.

Yet despite the grime and the suspicion that went with it, despite the added weariness and the fret that over the past six weeks they had suffered three separate 18,000-man subtractions from their ranks — first in the Wilderness, then at Spotsylvania, and last on the North Anna, Totopotomoy Creek, and the Chickahominy — their spirits were even higher near the end of the Jamesward trek than at the outset: not only from being on the move again, away from the stench and snipers at Cold Harbor, but also because they could see what had begun to come of this latest sidle. Though they knew nothing of what lay ahead, on the far side of the shining river, they trusted Grant to make the most of the fact that they had given Lee the slip the night before and stolen a march on him today.

They had indeed done both those things, and were now in a position to do more. The first Lee had known of their departure was at sunup — two hours after Early withdrew his three divisions and set out for the Shenandoah Valley — when messengers reached head-quarters, back near Gaines Mill, with reports that the Yankees were gone from their works around Cold Harbor. Advancing scouts un-covered a second line of intrenchments, newly dug and intricately fashioned as if for permanent occupation, but these too were deserted, as were the woods and fields a mile and more beyond. June 13, which was to have been the fortieth day of contact for the two armies, turned out to be a day of practically no contact at all; Grant was gone, vanished with his blue-clad throng, perhaps toward the lower stretches of the Chickahominy, more likely to a new base on the James from which to mount a new advance on Richmond, either by crossing the river for a back-door attack or else by moving up its near bank for an all-out assault on the capital fortifications.

Whichever it was, Lee warned the government of this latest threat and moved to meet it, shifting south to put what was left of his army in position below White Oak Swamp, where he would block the eastern approaches to the city and also be closer to Drewry's for a crossing in case the blow was aimed at Beauregard. While his son's two thin-spread cavalry brigades — all that were left since Hampton and Fitz Lee took out after Sheridan four days ago — probed unsuccessfully at rapid-firing masses of Federal horsemen coming down the Long Bridge Road toward Riddell's Shop, he posted Hill's corps in their support, athwart the field of the Seven Days fight at Glendale, and Anderson's off to the right, reaching down to Malvern Hill, which the cavalry then occupied as a post of observation, although nothing of much interest could be seen from there except a good deal of apparently purposeless activity by Union gunboats at Deep Bottom, down below. Lee's ranks were so gravely thinned by Early's departure that he might have been expected to recall him while there still was time; but when the President inquired that afternoon whether this might not be the wisest course, Lee replied, rather laconically, that he did not think so. At the end of the Forty Days, as at the beginning, he remained the gambler he had always been, the believer that the weaker force must take the longer chances.

"I do not know that the necessity for his presence today is greater than it was yesterday," he said of Early. "His troops would make us more secure here, but success in the Valley would relieve our difficulties that at present press heavily upon us."

Those first four words, "I do not know," were the crux of the matter. All the prisoners taken so far today had been cavalry, which left him with nothing but guesses as to the whereabouts of the Union infantry and artillery, all hundred thousand of them. Most likely they were in motion for the James, but whether Grant intended for them to cross it or advance up the north bank Lee could not tell; nor could he act, for fear of being decoyed out of position, until he secured more or less definite information as to which course his adversary had taken or would take. Either way, the defense of Richmond had come down to a siege, the thing he had tried hardest to avoid. "This army cannot stand a siege," he had told Little Powell a month ago, just as Beauregard, one week later, had warned Bragg: "The picture presented is one of ultimate starvation."

Red Clay Minuet

★ ✗ ☆

AIR-LINE, THE HUNDRED-MILE DISTANCE
from Chattanooga to Atlanta was the same as that from Washington to
Richmond, and so were the respective sizes of the armies, which in each
paired case gave the Union commander a roughly two-to-one numerical
advantage. But there for the most part the resemblance stopped. Meade
and Sherman (or for that matter Grant and Sherman, since that was what
it came to) were as different from each other as were Lee and Johnston,
two very different men indeed, and so too — despite the fact that down
in Georgia, as in Virginia, the rivers mainly ran athwart the projected
lines of advance and retreat — was the terrain, flat or gently rolling in
the East, but mountainous in the West and therefore eminently defensible, at any rate in theory, although few of the place-names strewn
about the map had been connected with much bloodshed since the era
when settlers ousted the aborigines. In point of fact, harking back to
those massacre days, Sherman had something similar in mind for the
Confederates to his front, military and civilian. "If the North design
to conquer the South," he had written home two years ago, "we must
begin at Kentucky and reconquer the country from there as we did
from the Indians."

Now that he faced completion of that massive undertaking, he
was in what he liked to call "high feather." Instructed by Grant "to
move against Johnston's army, break it up, and get into the interior of
the enemy's country as far as you can, inflicting all the damage you can
against their war resources," the red-haired Ohioan, by way of showing
how well he understood his task, replied in paraphrase: "I am to knock
Jos. Johnston, and to do as much damage to the resources of the enemy
as possible."

By way of help in carrying out this project he would have an
advantage, a man-made facility available neither to his flintlock-carrying
predecessors nor to his cohorts in the East: namely, a rapid-transit all-

weather supply line in the form of a railroad, the Western & Atlantic, running all the way to Atlanta — provided, of course, he could put and keep it in shape while nudging Johnston backward; for the rebels would surely wreck it in their wake, and almost as surely would strike at it with cavalry in his rear as he advanced. With this in mind, he made the training of rail repair gangs an integral part of his preparations, including daily workouts as rigorous and precise as the drill required of gun crews, and elevated gandy dancers to a combat status as high as that of riflemen or cannoneers. The same precaution was taken with regard to the much longer line extending rearward from Chattanooga, up through Middle Tennessee and across Kentucky to Louisville, his main supply base on the Ohio. Practically all of this more than three hundred miles of highly frangible track was subject to strikes by grayback troopers from adjoining departments, hard-handed horsemen schooled in destruction by John Morgan and Bedford Forrest, and though Sherman planned to keep these slashers occupied by making adjunctive trouble for them in their own back yards, he also hoped to forestall or reduce the delays that were likely to attend such depredations, in case the raiders broke out anyhow, by turning Nashville into what an amazed staff brigadier presently described as "one vast storehouse — warehouses covering city blocks, one a quarter of a mile long; stables by the ten and twenty acres, repair shops by the fieldful." Also of help in reducing the supply problem would be a certain amount of belt-tightening by the troops, whose divisional trains, in accordance with Sherman's orders, would carry only "five days' bacon, twenty days' bread, and thirty days' salt, sugar, and coffee; nothing else but arms and ammunition." The main thing, as the commanding general saw it, was to keep moving: and this applied as much to rearward personnel as it did to the men up front. "I'm going to move on Joe Johnston the day Grant telegraphs me he is going to hit Bobby Lee," he told a quartermaster officer. "And if you don't have my army supplied, and keep it supplied, we'll eat your mules up, sir; eat your mules up!" Having passed before through un-fought-over regions of the South — recently, for example, on a march across the midriff of Mississippi, from Vicksburg to Meridian and back — he was aware of another resource which he did not intend to neglect. "Georgia has a million of inhabitants," he wrote Grant. "If they can live, we should not starve."

Thus Sherman; a violent-talking man whose bite at times measured up to his bark, and whose commitment was to total war. "I believe in fighting in a double sense," he said this spring, "first to gain physical results and next to inspire respect on which to build up our nation's power." Tecumseh or "Cump" to his family, he was Uncle Billy to his soldiers, one of whom called him "the most American-looking man I ever saw; tall and lank, not very erect, with hair like thatch, which he rubs up with his hands, a rusty beard trimmed close, a wrinkled face, sharp, prominent red nose, small, bright eyes, coarse red hands; black felt hat slouched over the eyes, dirty dickey with the points wilted down, black old-fashioned stock, brown field officer's coat with high collar and no shoulder straps, muddy trowsers and one spur. He carries his hands in his pockets, is very awkward in his gait and motions, talks continually and with immense rapidity." Such intensity often brought on a reaction in observers, including this one. "At his departure I felt it a relief, and experienced almost an exhaustion after the excitement of his vigorous presence."

All this, moreover, was by way of diversion, a spare-time release of superabundant energy from an organism described by another associate as "boiling over with ideas, crammed full of feeling, discussing every subject and pronouncing on all." His main concern for the past two months, as Grant's western heir, had been how to get at or around Johnston's army, posted thirty miles southeast of Chattanooga for the past five months, in occupation of Dalton and the wide, hilly valley of the Oostanaula, which extended southward forty-odd miles to the Etowah and southwestward about the same distance to Rome, where the two rivers combined to form the Coosa. The immediate tactical problem was Rocky Face Ridge, a steep, knife-edge bastion twenty miles long, rimming the upper valley on the west to cover Dalton and the railroad, which after piercing the ridge at Mill Creek Gap, one third of the way down, ran south and east for another hundred miles, through Resaca and Kingston, Allatoona and Marietta, on across the Chattahoochee to Atlanta, Johnston's base and Sherman's goal in the campaign about to open, here in North Georgia, in conjunction with Meade's plunge across the Rapidan, six hundred crow-flight miles to the northeast. Unlike Meade — thanks to Banks, holed up by now in Alexandria after his defeat at Sabine Crossroads — Sherman would not have the supposed advantage of diversionary attacks on the enemy flank or rear by troops from other departments, such as Sigel and Butler had been told to make. Whatever was going to be accomplished in the way of driving or maneuvering Johnston from his position along that ridge would have to be done by the men on hand. And though it was true that at present the Federals enjoyed a better than two-to-one numerical advantage (Johnston had just under 45,000 of all arms, with 138 guns, while Sherman had just over 110,000, with 254) the prospect was anything but pleasing. For one thing — thanks again to Banks, who was in no position to discourage, let alone interfere with, anything the Confederates might take it in mind to do on this side of the Mississippi River — Johnston had another 19,000 effectives and 50 guns, down in Alabama under Polk, presumably ready to join him at the first sign of danger, whereas Sherman could only look forward to receiving about 10,000 due back next month from reenlistment furloughs. That still would leave him roughly a two-to-one advantage, but this by no means assured victory in assailing a position such as the one the rebels occupied, just ahead on Rocky Face Ridge.

Johnston, while successfully resisting Richmond's efforts to nudge him forward across the Tennessee, had spent the past four months preparing to resist the pending Union effort to prod him backward across the Chattahoochee. His two infantry corps, commanded by Lieutenant Generals William J. Hardee and John Bell Hood, each with about 20,000 men, were disposed along the northern half of the ridge, charged with giving particular attention to defending Mill Creek Gap, four miles northwest of Dalton, and Dug Gap, a second notch in the knife edge, five miles south. From the north end of this fortified position, Major General Joseph Wheeler's 5000 cavalry extended the line eastward to give warning in case the Federals tried to descend on Dalton by rounding the upper end of the ridge for a southward strike down the Oostanaula valley, where the ground was far less rugged and less easy to defend.

Sherman had no intention of moving in that direction, however, since to do so would uncover his base at Chattanooga: which brought him, regrettably, back to the dilemma of having to challenge the rebs in their apparently unassailable position, dead ahead on Rocky Face Ridge, securely intrenched and with high-sited guns ready-laid to blast the life out of whatever moved against them, in whatever strength. Moreover, as if nature had not done enough for him already, Johnston's engineers had lengthened the odds against the attackers by clogging the culverts of the railway ramp on the near side of the ridge, thus converting Mill Creek into an artificial lake across the rear of the gap that bore its name. Natives had a grislier designation; Buzzard Roost, they called the desolate notch through which the railroad wound its way. But Sherman, when at last he got a look at the rocky, high-walled gorge, catching glints of sunlight on the guns emplaced for its defense, pronounced it nothing less than "the terrible door of death," a term which would apply about as well to Dug Gap, just below.

George Thomas, who had felt out the gray defenses back in February, as a diversion intended to discourage Johnston from sending reinforcements to Polk while Sherman marched on Meridian, came up with the suggestion that, while McPherson and Schofield took over the position he now held in front of Ringgold, confronting the Rocky Face intrenchments, he take his four-corps Army of the Cumberland down the west side of the ridge to its far end, then press on eastward through unguarded Snake Creek Gap for a descent on the railroad near Resaca, fifteen miles in Johnston's rear. At best, this would expose the Confederates to a mauling when they fell back to protect their life line, as they would be obliged to do; while at worst, even if they somehow managed to avoid encirclement, it would turn them out of their all-but-impregnable position between Chattanooga and Dalton and thus convert the present stalemate, which favored the defenders, into a war of maneuver, which would favor the side with the greater number of troops and guns. Sherman, though the result his lieutenant promised was all he hoped for, rejected the proposal for two reasons. Thomas's command, twice the size of McPherson's and Schofield's combined, comprised a solid two thirds of the Federal total; secrecy would surely be lost in withdrawing so large a force and moving it such a distance, first across the enemy's front, then round his flank — and without secrecy, Sherman was convinced, it would be dangerous in the extreme to divide his army in the presence of so wily an adversary as the distinguished Virginian he faced. That was the first reason. The second was Thomas himself, the plodding, imperturbable Rock of Chickamauga. His specialty was staunchness, not celerity, the quality most needed in the movement he proposed.

But then, having dismissed the project as impractical when examined from that angle, Sherman shifted his point of view and experienced a surge of joy not unlike that of a poet revising the rejected draft of a poem he now perceives will become the jewel of his collection. Celerity, presumed to be lacking in Thomas, was McPherson's hallmark, and the size of his command — just under 25,000, as compared to Thomas's more than 70,000 — seemed about right for the job. Moreover, there would be no need for a withdrawal from the immediate presence of a vigilant opponent; McPherson's two corps, not yet on line, could march south from Chattanooga, under cover of Taylor's Ridge, then swing east through Ship's Gap and Villanow to make a sudden descent on Resaca, by way of Snake Creek Gap, for the cutting of Johnston's life line before the Virginian even knew he was threatened from that direction, his attention having been focused all the while on Thomas, active in his front, and on Schofield, who would feint with his 13,000-man Army of the Ohio against the opposite flank, which lay in the path of his march down the railroad from Knoxville. Thus Sherman set the pattern for the campaign about to open in North Georgia, a pattern that would utilize Thomas's outsized command — which contained more infantry and cavalry than all of Johnston's army, including the troops in Alabama under Polk — as the holding force, fixing the enemy in place, while McPherson and Schofield probed or rounded his flank or flanks to prise or chevy him out of position and expose him to being assailed on the march, or in any case to being struck before he had time to do much digging, anywhere between Dalton and Atlanta.

Sherman was delighted at the prospect, now that it loomed, and he also took a chauvinistic pleasure in the fact that such an arrangement gave the stellar role to McPherson, his favorite as well as Grant's, and the Army of the Tennessee, which had been his own and, up till Vicksburg, Grant's. Grant would approve, he knew when he wrote him of the plan, and as soon as that approval came down he passed the word to his three lieutenants. They would be in position no later than May 3, troops alerted for the jump-off next day, coincidental with Meade's crossing of the Rapidan.

And so it was. Detraining on schedule at Cleveland, where the East Tennessee & Georgia, coming down from Knoxville, branched to connect with Chattanooga and Dalton, both just under thirty miles away, Schofield prepared to march his army — in reality a corps, with three divisions of infantry and one of cavalry — southward along the left fork of the railroad to Red Clay, the state-line hamlet from which he was to launch his disconcerting strike at Johnston's right, down the valley east of Rocky Face. Thomas was poised beyond Ringgold, prepared to confront the defenders on the ridge and hold them in position there by pressing hard against Buzzard Roost and Dug Gap, threatening a breakthrough at both places. McPherson meantime had moved down to Lee & Gordon's Mill, at the south end of Chickamauga battlefield, which gave him a twelve-mile leg on the roundabout march to Resaca and the Oostanaula crossing. On May 4, in accordance with orders, all three began their separate movements designed to "knock Jos. Johnston." Sherman rode with Thomas in the center, but his hopes were with McPherson; "my whiplash," he called the Army of the Tennessee.

Despite the setbacks the rebels had suffered East and West in the past year, hard fighting lay ahead and Sherman knew it. "No amount of poverty or adversity seems to shake their faith," he marveled; "niggers gone, wealth and luxury gone, money worthless, starvation in view ... yet I see no sign of let up — some few deserters, plenty tired of war, but the masses determined to fight it out." What they needed was more violent persuasion, he believed, and he was prepared to give it in full measure. "All that has gone before is mere skirmishing," he wrote his wife on setting forth.

Mere skirmishing was all it came to in the course of the next two days — the horrendous span of the Wilderness conflict, up in Virginia, where Lee and Meade lost better than 25,000 men between them — while Thomas felt his way forward along the Western & Atlantic and Schofield trudged down the other railroad to Red Clay, which took its name from the salmon-colored soil, powdery in dry weather and a torment to the nostrils of men on the march, but quick to turn as slippery as grease, newcomers would soon discover, under the influence of even the briefest shower.

There was no hurry at this stage of the game, both commanders having been told to give McPherson plenty of time on his roundabout march. On the third day out, the Cumberlanders ran into their first substantial opposition at Tunnel Hill, where the railroad went underground before emerging for its plunge through the gap in the ridge, two miles beyond. The rebs had set up a fortified outpost here, and

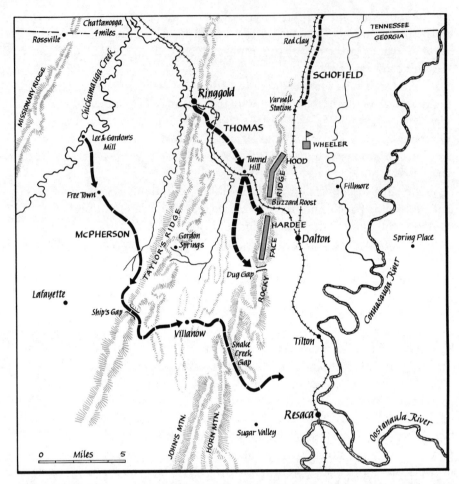

Thomas had to attack with a whole corps next day, May 7, in order to
drive them back on their main line, dug in along the steep west slope
of Rocky Face Ridge, above Buzzard Roost and below it down to Dug
Gap, five miles south. While this success — so complete, indeed, that
the Confederate rear guard had no time to damage the tunnel before
retreating — was being followed up, preparatory to coming to grips
in earnest with the defenders on their ridge, Schofield crossed the
Georgia line and pressed on for Varnell Station, his initial objective, a
little less than midway between Red Clay and Dalton. Harassed by
small bodies of gray horsemen, he moved slowly, that day and the
next, and then on May 9 detached a brigade of cavalry to brush these
gadflies from his path. It was a mistake. Wheeler's troopers, fading back,
drew the blue riders out of contact with the main body, then turned
and, with a sudden, unexpected slash, killed or captured some 150 of
them, including the colonel in command, and drove the remainder headlong from the field.

　　Sherman was no more upset by this than he was by Thomas's
lack of progress on the near side of the intervening ridge. Three full-

scale assaults the day before, and another five today — mainly against Mill Creek Gap, but also against Dug Gap, down the line — had met with failure in varying degrees. Two of the uphill attacks, in fact, had managed to put blue troops on the actual crest, within clear sight of Dalton, but they stayed there no longer than it took the defenders to counterattack and drive them back downhill. If anything, this was better than he had expected them to do: especially after his first hard look at what he described as "the terrible door of death that Johnston had prepared for them in the Buzzard Roost." Thomas and Schofield were charged with attracting and holding the attention of the rebels in their respective fronts, and this they had surely done. Sherman's main concern and hopes were still with McPherson, far off beyond the mountains to the south. What one observer called his "electric alertness," while following the progress of the fighting down the railroad below Ringgold, was probably due more to anxiety about his protégé, from whom he had heard nothing in the past three days, than it was to any expectation of victory in Thomas's contest on Rocky Face or Schofield's around Varnell Station, half a dozen miles across the way. Believing strongly in McPherson's military judgment and acumen, he had given him full discretion in conducting the movement designed to outfox Johnston; but he knew only too well that in war few things were certain, least of all the safety of a column deep in the enemy rear, no matter how capably led.

Then all, or nearly all, his worries vanished, giving way to jubilation and high feather. Taking an early supper near Tunnel Hill late that afternoon, May 9, he was delighted to receive a courier bearing McPherson's first dispatch, written that morning when he emerged from Snake Creek Gap after rounding the far end of Rocky Face Ridge. He was within five miles of Resaca, he reported, and pressing on, with nothing to contest his progress but a scattered handful of butternut horsemen, flushed out of the brush on the west side of the gap. Sherman boiled over with elation at the news, for it meant that by now McPherson's guns most likely had destroyed the bridges across the Oostanaula, thereby cutting the Confederates at Dalton off from all supplies and reinforcements south of that critical point; in which case they would have no choice except to turn and flee, and when they did he would come down hard and heavy on their rear, while McPherson stood firm in their front, astride the railroad.

Exultant, he banged the table so emphatically with his fist that the supper dishes did a rattling dance. "I've got Joe Johnston dead!" he cried.

He very nearly did; very nearly; except that Johnston, taking alarm at the first sign of his advance, had moved to forestall him without even suspecting what he was up to, out there beyond the screening

ridges to the west and south. The bluecoats had no sooner stirred
from their camps, May 4, than the southern commander renewed his
plea to Richmond for reinforcements from Polk, even if they amounted
to no more than a single division. "I urge you to send [these troops]
at once to Rome, and put them at my disposal till the enemy can be
met," he wired Bragg. Bragg replied, promptly for once, with orders
for Polk to do as Johnston asked. Moreover, Jefferson Davis (in still
another instance of that "presidential interference" with which his
critics often charged him) enlarged the order by telegraphing instructions for his friend the bishop-general to go along in person and
take with him not only the one requested division, but also "any other
available force at your command." Polk had three divisions of infantry
and one of cavalry, a total of 19,000 men. His decision was to hold
none of them back except a garrison of about 2000 for Selma. After
getting the first division on the road to Rome, where boxcars were being collected to speed this advance contingent down the branch line,
east to Kingston, then northward up the Western & Atlantic to join
Johnston around Dalton, he prepared to follow with the rest next day
for a share in the task of keeping the Yankees out of Atlanta and the
heartland.

    That was how it came about that Sherman's "whiplash" lost its
sting. For while Polk was en route from Demopolis — first by rail,
through Selma and Talladega, to Blue Mountain, the end of the line,
and then on foot the rest of the way, seventy rugged miles cross-
country to Rome — a brigade of about 2000 men under Brigadier
General James Cantey was summoned from Mobile to join him there
and thus complete what would constitute a third corps for the Army
of Tennessee, roughly equal in strength to each of the other two. Traveling all the way by rail, through Montgomery and Atlanta, Cantey
reached Rome on May 5, but was shifted two days later to Resaca,
clearing the way for Polk's arrival, placing him closer to Dalton in case
he was needed sooner, and incidentally doubling the strength of the
small garrison in the intrenchments Johnston had had constructed
there to cover the critical Oostanaula crossing. Two mornings later,
on May 9, after pausing only long enough to send the message that
would cause Sherman to set the supper dishes dancing, McPherson
pressed on across Sugar Valley, still driving the handful of butternut
cavalry before him, and at midday, within a mile of Resaca, came
under heavy infantry fire from a line of intrenchments, anchored on
the south to the Oostanaula and curving west and north of the town.

    There were only about 4000 Confederates in the works; but Mc-
Pherson did not know that, and in any case this was about 4000 more
than he expected. He felt out the defenses, found them stout, and
decided that under the circumstances, unsupported as he was, deep in
the rear of an enemy twice his size, his wisest course was to exercise

the discretion his orders afforded him and return to Snake Creek Gap, where his 25,000 would be safe from attack by whatever forces Johnston had sent or was sending to meet this no-longer-secret threat to the rebel life line. He was back in the gap by nightfall, and there, with both flanks covered, his front intrenched, and his rear out of reach of the enemy east of the ridge, he lay coiled in compact security — like a snake, ready to strike, or a whip laid away in a cubbyhole, unused.

When Johnston learned that evening of the sudden appearance of bluecoats in his rear he reacted by ordering Hood to move at once with three divisions, one from his own and two from Hardee's corps, to help Cantey meet any renewal of the threat. Hood did so, but when he reconnoitered west of Resaca next afternoon and reported McPherson still immured in Snake Creek Gap, Johnston interpreted the movement as a feint designed to draw his attention away from the main Union effort to turn or overrun the northern half of Rocky Face Ridge. Accordingly, he told Hood to come back to his former position but to drop Hardee's two divisions off at Tilton, a station on the railroad between Dalton and Resaca, from which they could move swiftly to meet a crisis in either direction. Meantime Hardee, stripped of half his corps, had been puzzled by the relative inactivity of Thomas, who, after three days of obstinate hammering, had finally slackened his effort to break through the two gaps. "I am only uneasy about my right," the Georgia-born West Pointer said, "and won't be uneasy about that when Hood returns." All the same, finding himself "unable to decide what the Yankees are endeavoring to accomplish," he began to suspect that they were up to something not in Johnston's calculations.

And so, by now, did Johnston himself. Polk had reached Rome today with his lead division and was sending it on to Resaca ahead of the others, which were close behind. This gave Johnston considerably more security at both places, but still he wondered at the easing of the pressure against one end of the ridge while McPherson took up a position off the other end. He began to suspect that Sherman might be moving more than McPherson, perhaps in the same direction and even farther, for a crossing of the river deep in his rear. Next morning, May 11, he gave Wheeler orders to send some horsemen around the north end of Rocky Face, if possible, for a probe at the flank of the Federals in position there. "Try to ascertain where their left rests," he told him, "and whether they are in motion toward the Oostanaula."

Altogether aware of Sherman's advantage, that with close to twice the number of troops he could apply immobilizing pressure in front while rounding or striking one or both Confederate flanks, Johnston had to count on luck as well as skill in maneuvering his opponent into committing some tactical gaffe that would expose the superior blue army, or anyhow some vital portion of it, to destruction. Such an opportunity, if it came, could scarcely occur except while that army was in motion, and for this reason — plus the fact that it had always been his style, his inclination, even back in the Old Dominion, around Manassas or down on the York-James peninsula — the Virginian was prepared from the outset to relinquish almost any position, no matter how strong, if by so doing he could encourage his adversary, on taking up the pursuit, to commit the blunder that might lead to his undoing. The odds against this were long, he knew, but so were the odds he faced. Moreover, he would be falling back toward reinforcements, even if they amounted to no more than Governor Brown's kid-glove militia, and would be shortening his supply line while the enemy's grew longer and more vulnerable. He also took encouragement from the belief that Sherman —who, after all, had been relieved of duty, back in the first year of the war, under suspicion of insanity — was high-strung, erratic in the extreme, and reported to be enamored of long-chance experiments, both tactical and strategic. These were qualities much to be desired in an opponent at this juncture. The trouble was that Johnston himself, with far less margin for error, had to rely on subordinates quite as erratic and a good deal more temperamental. "If I were President," he confided to a friend soon after taking over the faction-riddled Army of Tennessee, which had just been driven from Missionary Ridge after eighteen months under Braxton Bragg, "I'd distribute the generals of this army over the Confederacy."

In point of fact, that was precisely what R. E. Lee had been doing with some of those subordinates who failed or displeased or failed to please him in the course of the past two years; but Johnston, less in harmony with the authorities in Richmond, mainly had to make do with what he had. Fortunately, this wholesale condemnation did not include the leaders immediately below him on the military ladder. Highly dependable if not brilliant in the discharge of their duties, Polk and Hardee had been corps commanders ever since Shiloh, and Hood, though young and new to both his post and the army — he was thirty-two and had been made a lieutenant general at the time of his transfer from Longstreet, just three months ago, whereas Polk and Hardee, fifty-eight and thirty-eight respectively, had held that rank ever since it was created in the fall of '62 — was a fighter any chief would be glad to have at his disposal when victory swung in the balance and an extra measure of savagery was called for.

While he thus was counting his blessings and woes — and incidentally, such was the diminution of blue pressure against the gaps, admonishing some impetuous artillerists on Rocky Face Ridge for firing at targets not worth their ammunition — he sent word for Polk to proceed at once from Rome to Resaca, where he would assume command "and make the proper dispositions to defend the passage of the river and our communications." Johnston also took the occasion to suggest "the immediate movement of Forrest [who had been left

behind for the defense of North Mississippi] into Middle Tennessee."
Quite as desirous of cutting Sherman's life line as Sherman was of
cutting his, he added that he was "fully persuaded" that Forrest, rested
by now from his raid on Paducah and the reduction of Fort Pillow,
"would meet no force there that could resist him." What might come
of this he did not know; such a decision, involving the abandonment of
a portion of the President's home state to Yankee depredations, was up
to Richmond. But as evidence accumulated in Dalton that some kind of
movement was in progress on the other side of Rocky Face, Johnston
took the precaution of shifting another of Hardee's divisions south of
Dug Gap, to a position with a road in its rear leading down into Sugar
Valley. Late in the day Wheeler returned from his probe of the Union
left with confirmation of the wisdom of such precautions. Beyond the
ridge, the Federals were "moving everything" to their right, though
whether they were massing near Dug Gap for a renewal of their try
for a breakthrough there, or were heading for Snake Creek Gap to join
McPherson for an attack on Resaca, or had it in mind to slog on past
both gateways for a crossing of the Oostanaula farther down, no one
could say. In any case Johnston saw that if it turned out to be either
of the last two choices he could not long remain where he now was; he
would certainly have to fall back no later than tomorrow. The question
was whether he would end his withdrawal on this or the far side of the
river fifteen miles in his rear.

That evening he was encouraged by a visit and some welcome
news from Polk, who had encountered Hood at Resaca and returned
with him to Dalton for a conference with their chief. The good news
was that his second division had reached Rome today, was already on
its way by rail to join the first in the Resaca intrenchments, and would
soon be followed by the other two, expected at Rome tomorrow. Johnston shook his old friend warmly by the hand; they had been cadets
together at West Point thirty-five years ago. "How can I thank you?"
he said with feeling. "I asked for a division, but you have come yourself and brought me your army."

Polk flushed with pleasure at the praise, and after the council of
war had ended, around midnight, took part in another exchange which
gave him even greater pleasure than the first. On the train ride up to
Dalton, Hood had confided that he wished to be baptized and received
into the Church, and now that army business was out of the way the
churchman was glad to oblige. Episcopal Bishop of Louisiana for twenty
years before the war, he often remarked that he looked forward to returning to his priestly calling as soon as the fighting was over and independence had been won. Meantime he seldom neglected a chance, such as
this, to work for the salvation of any soul. The two repaired to the
young general's quarters, accompanied by members of their staffs, and
there by candlelight Polk performed the baptismal rites, using a tin

washpan for a font. Then came the confirmation. Because of the mutilations Hood had suffered at Chickamauga and Gettysburg, where he had lost a leg and the use of one arm, the bishop absolved the candidate from kneeling, as was customary, suggesting instead that he remain seated for the ceremony. But Hood would have none of this. If he could not kneel, and he could not, he would stand. And thus it was that, leaning on his crutches, the big tawny-bearded Kentuckian was received into the fold. "Defend, O Lord, this thy child with thy heavenly grace," the bishop intoned, his hand upon the bowed head before him, "that he may continue thine forever, and daily increase in thy Holy Spirit more and more, until he come unto thy everlasting kingdom."

Despite the lateness of the hour, Polk returned that night to Resaca, charged with holding the place on his own until such time as the rest of the now three-corps army joined him. He was unlikely to be alone for long, however; Johnston's mind was about made up. Next morning, as evidence of a full-scale Union sidle continued to mount, he decided to evacuate Dalton — or, more accurately, to complete the evacuation, since nearly half of his army, exclusive of Polk, was already south of the town in any case — as soon as the night was dark enough to mask his withdrawal from the covering ridge.

He would do so, what was more, with small regret. "The position had little to recommend it," he afterwards explained. "At Dalton the Federal army, even if beaten, would have had a secure place of refuge at Chattanooga, while our only place of safety was Atlanta, a hundred miles off with three rivers intervening.... I therefore decided to remain on the defensive." His mind, it would seem from this subsequent outline of his strategic intentions, was already on the third of those three rivers. "Fighting under cover," he went on, "we would have trifling losses compared with those inflicted. Moreover, due to its lengthening lines the numerical superiority of the Federal army would be reduced daily so that we might hope to cope with it on equal terms beyond the Chattahoochee, where defeat would be its destruction."

This did not mean that he did not hope to inflict a defeat on the enemy in the course of his hundred-mile withdrawal. He did hope for it, despite the odds, either as the result of breaking the railroad deep in Sherman's rear, which would oblige the blue host to retire, or else as the result of catching his adversary in a tactical blunder that would expose him to piecemeal destruction somewhere down the line: maybe even within the next couple of days near Resaca, Johnston's intended first stop, on the near bank of the Oostanaula, first of the three rivers in his rear.

That was his destination now, and by sunrise next morning — Friday the 13th — not a Confederate was left on the northern half of Rocky Face Ridge or in Dalton itself. Johnston was off on what an opposing general called "one of his clean retreats."

★ ★ ★

Sherman by now was on the verge of completing the movement that prompted Johnston's pull-out. Vexed by the news that his protégé had flinched from pressing the attack that was to have crowned his roundabout march to the outskirts of Resaca — news that hit all the harder by arriving close on the heels of the first report that the objective was practically within McPherson's grasp — the northern commander felt terribly let down. "Such an opportunity does not occur twice in a single life," he lamented, although he was quick to admit that his fellow Ohioan had been "perfectly justified" by his discretionary orders. "I regret beyond measure that you did not break the railroad, however little," he replied next morning, "but I suppose it was impossible."

He rather suspected that he should have used a larger force on the flanking operation, as Thomas originally suggested, and he planned to follow through by doing so now, all out. Leaving one corps of infantry and a cavalry division to continue the demonstration in front of "the terrible door of death," thereby covering Chattanooga and holding the Confederate main body in position around Dalton, he would march the rest of Thomas's army and all of Schofield's down the valley west of Rocky Face Ridge, on around its lower end, to join McPherson for a massive lunge at Resaca, the railroad that ran through it, and the vital river crossing in its rear. Johnston then would be cut off from his base, with no choice except to scatter or give battle: which in either case, as Sherman saw it, would result in his defeat. There was of course an outside chance that Johnston, who would have the advantage of moving a shorter distance over superior roads, might fall rapidly back on Resaca, while the rest of the blue army was en route, and turn on the force holed up in Snake Creek Gap; but that had been considered and taken care of, more or less, beforehand. "Should he attack you," Sherman told McPherson at the close of the dispatch informing him of his measureless regret and his new plan, "fight him to the last and I will get to you."

This was a good deal easier said, and planned, than done. Close to 70,000 troops had to be disengaged from contact with an enemy mainly on high ground, which made secrecy all the more difficult to maintain, and put in motion on narrow, meandering roads. A day was needed to get ready, then better than two more for the march. It was late afternoon of the fourth day, Friday the 13th, before the three commands were consolidated and put into attack formations, west of Resaca, for the contemplated lunge. By then the sun was too far down for anything more than a bit of preliminary skirmishing, including a crossroads cavalry clash in which Judson Kilpatrick and Joe Wheeler — West Pointers both, the former four months into and the latter four months short of his twenty-eighth year — took each other's measure. Kilpatrick was unhorsed by a stray bullet on this unlucky day, and though friendly troopers managed to lug him off the field before the graybacks could get at him, he would be out of action for some weeks.

Regrettable as this was, the loss of time on the cramped approach march down the valley was even more so. McPherson, Thomas, and Schofield were on hand and in line of battle by sundown, within gun range of the rebel works, but Johnston was there ahead of them with all three of his corps, Hood and Hardee having completed their retrograde movement from Dalton before noon. Increased in strength by nearly one third with the addition of Polk's corps to their army, they occupied skillfully laid-out intrenchments that ran in a long convex line from the Oostanaula, downstream from Resaca on their left, to the near bank of a tributary river, the Connasauga, on their right beyond the railroad north of town.

Sherman was neither daunted nor discouraged by his loss of the race for Resaca; Johnston was there, inviting attack with his back to the river, and the redhead planned to oblige him. "I will press him all that is possible," he wired Halleck. "Weather fine and troops in fine order. All is working well." Informed that Grant had emerged from the Wilderness and now was mauling Lee at Spotsylvania, he added, still in the pep-talk vein: "Let us keep the ball rolling."

It rolled, but only a short distance in the course of the daylong fight; Johnston's engineers had given him all he asked in the way of protection for his men. McPherson, on the right — goaded no doubt by Sherman's reproach when they met in Snake Creek Gap the day before: "Well, Mac, you missed the opportunity of your life" — scored what little gain there was by driving Polk's forward elements from some high ground west of the town. Elsewhere along the four-mile curve of the rebel works, the ball either stopped or rebounded. Thomas made no headway in the center, and Schofield took a beating on the left, beyond the railroad, when the Confederates in his front launched a sudden attack that drove him back nearly half a mile as the day ended. This came about as the result of Johnston's calculation that McPherson's success against his left, down near the Oostanaula, must mean that Sherman was concentrating most of his strength in that direction. Accordingly, while Bishop Polk, informally clad in an old hunting shirt and a slouch hat, stiffened his resistance to limit the enemy gains in his front, and Hardee continued to stand fast in the center, wearing by contrast a new dove-gray uniform with fire-gilt buttons and a white cravat, Johnston sent word for Hood to test the Union left for the weakness he suspected. This Hood did, with good results which might have been much better if darkness had not put an end to his pursuit.

Johnston, highly pleased, ordered a renewal of the attack at first light next morning.

He had been in excellent spirits all that day, riding from point to point along the line, at his jaunty best "in a light or mole colored hat, with a black feather in it." A Tennessee private, seeing him thus, recalled the scene years later. A small man, neatly turned out and genial in manner, fluffy white side-whiskers framing the wedge-shaped face with its trim mustache and grizzled chin beard — "like the pictures you see hung upon the walls," the veteran was to write — Johnston sat his horse, head cocked to catch the swell of gunfire, left and right and center, where Polk and Hood and Hardee were defending the works his foresight had provided. Scattered whoops of recognition prompted the rest of the troops in the passing column of Tennesseans, "and the very ground seems to shake with cheers. Old Joe smiles as blandly as a modest maid, raises his hat in acknowledgement, makes a polite bow, and rides toward the firing."

This brightened outlook persisted into the night, but darkened progressively in reaction to the arrival, in all too rapid sequence, of three unwelcome intelligence reports. While visiting Hood on the right he learned that the Union corps left at Dalton had completed its march down the railroad this evening to reinforce Schofield, and riding westward to confer with Polk he found McPherson had brought artillery onto the high ground lost today, with the result that long-range shells were able to reach both the railway and turnpike bridges close in his rear. Endangering as it did his line of retreat, this gave him pause indeed. He instructed his staff engineer to throw a pontoon bridge a mile above the permanent spans, beyond reach of the Yankee guns, and start at once to build a road leading down to it on the near bank and away from it on the other. Sensitive as always to such threats to his flanks or rear, he countermanded Hood's instructions for tomorrow and told him to return instead to the position from which he had launched his attack this afternoon. Presently, with the arrival of the third unwelcome bit of news, he had cause for greater alarm and even greater caution. Cavalry scouts reported that enemy units of considerable strength had crossed the Oostanaula several miles downstream, where a deep eastward bend of the river brought them within easy reach of the Western & Atlantic. Johnston reacted swiftly to this threat to the railroad and his line of retreat by ordering the immediate detachment of Major General W. H. T. Walker's division from Hardee for a night march to the reported point of crossing, there to contest any further advance by the Federals while the rest of the army prepared for a quick withdrawal across the river, either to reinforce Walker or outstrip the blue column which by then might have overwhelmed him.

Morning brought a renewal of Federal pressure all along the line, quite as if there had been no reduction for a sidle. Johnston held his ground, awaiting developments, and shortly after noon received a dispatch from Walker informing him that the report of a downstream crossing was untrue. By then the pressure against Resaca had somewhat diminished, and Johnston decided to go back to his plan for a renewal of the attack by Hood, who promptly returned to the position he had won the day before. A battery, pushed well to the front to support the jump-off, opened prematurely and was replied to so effectively, by infantry and counterbattery fire, that the cannoneers had to abandon all four guns, left mute and unattended between the lines. This did not augur well for the success of Hood's assault, but as he was about to go forward in all-out earnest, a message came from the army commander, once more canceling the attack and instructing the three lieutenant generals to attend a council of war that evening at his headquarters.

There they learned the reason for this second change of plans. A follow-up dispatch from Walker reported the bluecoats over the downstream Oostanaula after all, and Johnston had decided to give up Resaca. The council had not been called for a discussion of his decision, but rather for the assignment of routes on the march to meet this threat to the army's life line; Polk and Hardee would use the turnpike and railway spans, despite the danger of long-range interdictory fire, and Hood the new-laid pontoon bridge.

All went as planned, or nearly so, including heavy volleys of musketry by front-line units at midnight to cover the withdrawal of iron-tired artillery and supply vehicles. Rear guards took up the pontoons and loaded them onto wagons for use in crossing other rivers, farther south, and the railroad bridge was set afire to burn till it fell hissing into the Oostanaula. Through some administrative oversight — not unlike the one at Tunnel Hill a week ago, which left the railway tunnel unobstructed — in the last-minute confusion, as dawn was breaking, the turnpike bridge was overlooked and left standing, fit for use by the pursuers. All that was really lost in the way of army property, however, was the four-gun Confederate battery abandoned between Hood's and Schofield's lines that afternoon. This came hard for the young Kentucky-born West Pointer, who had a great deal of pride in such matters (in time he would take it even harder, since they turned out to be the only guns Johnston lost in the whole course of the campaign) but who consoled himself, as best he could, by pointing out "that they were four old iron pieces, not worth the sacrifice of the life of even one man."

Sherman pressed on after the retiring Confederates, hoping to catch up with them before they had time to develop still another stout position in which to receive him, and continued simultaneously two flanking operations he had set in motion two days ago, both involving only cavalry at the outset. Kilpatrick's division, minus its wounded leader, had been sent five miles downriver on May 14 to install a pair of pontoon bridges at Lay's Ferry, and Sherman had followed this up yesterday by detaching Brigadier General Thomas Sweeny's infantry division from McPherson to march down and cross the river at that point, along with Kilpatrick's troopers, in order to menace Johnston's rear; which Sweeny had done with such success that the graybacks were now in full retreat. At the same time, a wider, deeper, and potentially even more profitable thrust was launched by sending another of Thomas's mounted divisions, under Brigadier General Kenner Garrard, far down the right bank of the Oostanaula to threaten and if possible enter Rome, wrecking its factories and iron works and taking over the branch-line railroad leading east along the north bank of the Etowah to Kingston, on the Western & Atlantic, better than twenty miles below Resaca. Now that Johnston was falling back, Sherman decided to beef up this deeper probe by sending Brigadier General Jefferson C. Davis's division of Cumberlanders to follow the cavalry and take part in the raid on Rome and the eastward strike at Kingston.

The red-haired commander was leaving no card unplayed in his eagerness to come to grips with his skittish opponent, and he scoffed at the notion, advanced by several members of his staff, that Johnston was falling back quite willingly, in accordance with a plan to draw his pursuers southward to their destruction. "Had he remained in Dalton another hour, it would have been his total defeat," Sherman insisted, "and he only evacuated Resaca because his safety demanded it." As for the disappointment some critics expressed at his failure, so far, to bring the wily Virginian to all-or-nothing battle — particularly before Polk arrived from Alabama, in the interim between Dalton and Resaca, to shorten the long numerical odds — he countered that, while he shared the regret that he had not managed to do this, he also saw a clear advantage in the way the campaign had developed up to now. "Of course I was disappointed not to have crippled his army more at that particular stage of the game," he later wrote; "but, as it resulted, these rapid successes gave us the initiative, and the usual impulse of a conquering army."

Determined to make the most of that conquering impulse, he devised a pursuit combining speed with other tactical advantages. While Thomas struck out down the railroad, hard in the wake of the fleeing enemy, McPherson was instructed to proceed at once to Lay's Ferry for a crossing that would place him well to the right on the march south, in position to make another rapid flanking movement as soon as the rebels called a halt or were brought to one by pressure against their rear, and Schofield was told to do the same in the opposite direction, crossing upstream from Resaca at Field's Ferry for a march well to the east, in case it developed that the enemy right was the

flank that should be turned. This not only increased the celerity of
the pursuit by not funneling all the Federal troops down one crowded
road; it also assured that when the time came for fighting, all three
component armies would be ready for action in their accustomed
roles, Thomas's as the holding force and McPherson's and Schofield's
as flankers. Moreover, to bring all three into better numerical balance
and lessen the traffic on the turnpike, Sherman detached Hooker's
three divisions from Thomas and sent them off to the left with Scho-

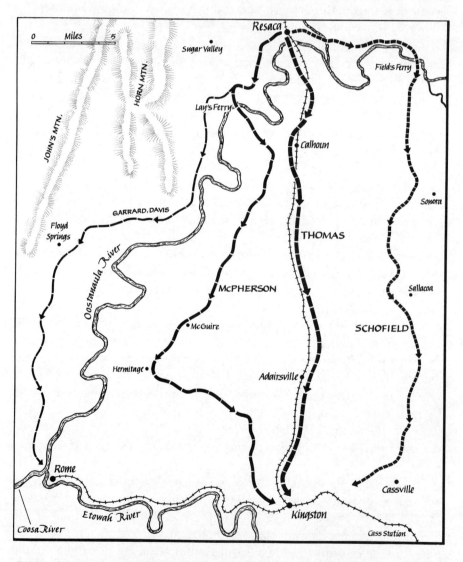

field, whose strength thus was raised to more than 30,000 while Thomas's
was reduced to about 40,000, three other divisions, including two of
cavalry, having already been detached for the raid on Rome, still in
progress down the Oostanaula, and the preliminary crossing at Lay's
Ferry, where Sweeny's division rejoined McPherson, together with

Kilpatrick's troopers, who fanned out frontward to provide a screen for the column west of the railroad.

The first day's march, May 16, ended at Calhoun, where Sherman thought it likely that Johnston would make a stand, six miles down the track from Resaca, but before he could call in either of the lateral columns, which were also over the river by then, the Confederate rear guard pulled out southward in the darkness, headed apparently for Adairsville, ten miles down the line. There was heavier skirmishing there next day near sundown, but dawn of May 18 showed the graybacks gone again. Schofield by now was in the vicinity of Sallacoa and McPherson at McGuire, hamlets respectively half a dozen miles east and west of Adairsville; Sherman, riding with Thomas in the center, held to this spread-eagle formation as he took up the march for Kingston, another ten miles down the Western & Atlantic. He felt certain that Johnston would dig in there, on the near bank of the Etowah, and he wanted to get at him before he had much chance to get set for the shock.

Spirits were high in all three columns of pursuit, not only because the rebs were on the run, having been turned out of two practically impregnable positions in less than two weeks, but also because well-drilled rail repair gangs — helped considerably, it was true, by the enemy's rattled negligence in failing to obstruct the tunnel short of Buzzard Roost — had functioned with such efficiency that even the troops out front, in the process of covering better than half the distance from Chattanooga to Atlanta, had scarcely missed a meal along the way. "The rapidity with which the badly broken railroad was repaired seemed miraculous," Major General O. O. Howard, one of Thomas's corps commanders, later noted. "We had hardly left Dalton before trains with ammunition and other supplies arrived. While our skirmishing was going on at Calhoun, the locomotive whistle sounded in Resaca. The telegraphers were nearly as rapid: the lines were in order to Adairsville on the morning of the 18th. While we were breaking up the state arsenal at Adairsville, caring for the wounded, and bringing in Confederate prisoners, word was telegraphed from Resaca that bacon, hard bread, and coffee were already there at our service."

All this had been accomplished, moreover, at a cost of fewer than 4000 casualties, and not only was this figure much lower than had been anticipated, it was also — despite the supposed high price entailed in attacking prepared defenses — not much larger than the enemy total, which included a number of lightly wounded men who had to be left behind and thus became permanent losses, as captives, whereas a Union soldier, left behind under similar circumstances, could be patched up and returned to duty, sometimes overnight. It was no wonder then, with success achieved at so low a cost and without the sacrifice of creature comforts, that spirits were high and the outcome of the expected Kingston confrontation seemed foregone. What was more, as the three main widespread columns prepared for a convergence at that point — forty air-line miles from Tunnel Hill, scene of the opening clash eleven days ago — word came that a prize even more valuable than the state arsenal at Adairsville had fallen into the hands of the invaders. That same morning, May 18, Rome fell undefended to Davis and Garrard, who soon would be working their way east along the branch-line railroad to rejoin the Army of the Cumberland.

Rome with its factories and iron works, so important to the rebel cause, was a strategic plum worth giving thanks for, but tactically the railroad was a prize worth even more, since practically all of Johnston's reinforcements had reached him by that route. Now it was closed, except to Federal use, and Sherman — still with Thomas, who was engaged in what Howard called "a running skirmish" down the Western & Atlantic with troops from Hardee's corps, which apparently had been given the rear-guard post of honor on the Confederate retreat — had 100,000 effectives converging as fast as their legs could carry them toward Kingston, where reports indicated that Johnston had at last been brought to bay with his back to the Etowah River.

For once, by dint of hard marching on rural roads and steady pressure on the rebel rear, execution matched conception; the convergence would be effected by midday tomorrow, May 19, on schedule and with each of the three component armies in its assigned position for the final thrust, Schofield left, McPherson right, and Thomas center. The trouble was that Sherman, for all the speed and precision of his approach, was converging on a vacuum. Johnston was not at Kingston; he was at Cassville, five miles east, preparing to spring an ambush that would eliminate, or at any rate badly mangle, a solid third of the blue force whose commander had at last afforded him the opportunity he had been awaiting ever since the campaign opened, two weeks and better than forty miles ago.

Leaving Resaca, two days back, he had intended to make a stand at Calhoun, provided he could find a suitable position — athwart a rather narrow valley, say, which would afford protection for his flanks and thus oblige the Federals to come at him head-on, their numerical advantage canceled by the limited width of front — but when reconnaissance revealed none he moved on that night, hoping to find what he was seeking near Adairsville the following day, May 17. He did not. He did, however, receive a telegraphic dispatch and some cavalry reports which together had the double effect of lifting his spirits and enabling him to arrive at a plan for stopping the blue army in its tracks. Stephen Lee, left in charge of the adjoining department when Polk departed for Georgia, responded to Johnston's week-old request by announcing that Forrest, with 3500 picked horsemen and two batteries of artillery, would set out within three days for an attack on Sherman's lines of supply and communication up in Middle Tennessee. This was welcome news, indeed, and Johnston called a council of war that evening to pass it on to his corps commanders, along with their respective assignments for carrying out his table-turning plan.

Intelligence reports from Wheeler made it clear that Sherman's pursuit was in three columns, widely spaced, and now that Johnston had decided to continue his march toward the Etowah, he saw in this a rare opportunity to deal with one of those isolated segments before it could call on either of the other two for help. From Adairsville, railroad and turnpike ran due south to Kingston; Hardee would continue on that route, skirmishing as he went, to draw Thomas after him and encourage the impression that he was guarding the rear of the other two corps as they moved ahead of him, down the tracks and pike, for a stand at Kingston. But that was by no means to be the case. Polk and Hood would march instead by a road leading east of south to Cassville, a village about two miles on this side of the Western & Atlantic, which swung due east at Kingston, five miles west. The advantage was that Schofield, reinforced to 30,000, would pass near there on his way to the convergence Sherman would surely order when he became convinced that the graybacks intended to call a halt at Kingston. With Thomas five miles off, McPherson perhaps ten, and Hardee in position to delay their eastward advance along the railroad, Hood and Polk should have ample time to dispose of Schofield before the other two could reach him. With any luck, all three gray corps could then combine to take on Thomas and strike at McPherson when he came up in turn. Dealt with piecemeal, all three Union armies might be destroyed in short order, or anyhow crippled and brought to a stumbling halt; which would serve about as well, since they soon would get the news that Forrest had severed their life line, up in Tennessee. That would leave them no choice except starvation or retreat. Either way, the campaign would be over and the world once more would stand amazed at still another Confederate triumph against overwhelming odds.

Eager though they were to take up their divergent marches, which were to end with a long-deferred return to the offensive, all three corps commanders went with their chief to his tent, where Polk donned his surplice and stood in front of an improvised altar, preparing to fulfill a request Mrs Johnston had made in a letter written two days ago. She wanted the bishop to do for her husband what he had done for Hood the week before; "lead my soldier nearer to God. General Johnston has never been baptised. It is the dearest wish of my heart that he should be, and that you should perform the ceremony." Once more with candlelight glinting on the brass and gold lace of the uniforms of candidate and witnesses, the rite of baptism was performed, after which the group dispersed to prepare for the execution of the plan designed to reverse the tide of war in North Georgia.

Hardee took up his march, southward down the railroad, and with the dawn resumed his "running skirmish" with Thomas, who continued to press hard upon his rear. Meantime the other two corps set out on the road for Cassville, Hood in front with orders to occupy a position tonight from which to strike at the left of Schofield's column next morning, while Polk attacked the front; Hardee would join them from Kingston, later in the day, so that all three could then turn on Thomas and McPherson, simultaneously or in sequence, when they came up in response to Schofield's cries for help. Unwelcome news from Stephen Lee reached Johnston in the course of the approach march, to the effect that a heavy enemy movement out of Memphis had obliged him to postpone Forrest's raid on Sherman's life line. Offsetting this somewhat, however, there was a report from Richmond that the Federals had acknowledged the so-far loss of 45,000 men in Virginia, thirty-one of them generals, and this gave rise to the airing of a theory by some members of Johnston's staff that Sherman's intention was to maneuver his adversary south of the Etowah, then call a halt and hurry reinforcements to the bled-down Army of the Potomac. Johnston put no stock in such talk; he remained intent on the prospect of giving Sherman so much trouble, on this side of the Etowah, that he soon would be seeking assistance, not sending it either to Meade or to Banks, whose fight at Yellow Bayou today was the last on his costly, disheartened retreat down Red River.

Nightfall found the divided Confederate army in position: Hardee at Kingston, prepared to turn east, and Hood and Polk at Cassville, their ambush laid. Johnston's spirits were as high as Sherman's across the way, and on far sounder grounds. Some measure of the Virginian's confidence and martial elation came through in a general order he composed that night and had read at the head of each regiment next morning, May 19:

> Soldiers of the Army of Tennessee:
>   You have displayed the highest qualities of the soldier—firmness in combat, patience under toil. By your courage and skill you have repulsed every assault of the enemy. By marches by day and marches by night you have defeated every attempt upon your communications. Your communications are secured. You will now turn and march to meet his advancing columns. Fully confiding in the conduct of the officers, the courage of the soldiers, I lead you to battle. We may confidently trust that the Almighty Father will still reward the patriots' toils and the patriots' banners. Cheered by the success of our brothers in Virginia and beyond the Mississippi, our efforts

will equal theirs. Strengthened by His support, these efforts will be crowned with the like glories.

J. E. JOHNSTON,
General.

Despite the weariness resulting from three days and four nights of marches broken only by rearward skirmishes and fitful snatches of road-side sleep — not to mention the cumulative depression that went with having abandoned better than forty miles of highly defensible terrain without so much as a single fight that attained the dignity of a full-scale battle — the reaction on all levels to the reading of this order, from regimental commanders down to drummer boys, was quite as ecstatic as even its author could have wished.

Among those officers who were better informed on current events, mainly through having read such newspapers as were available in camp and on the march, there lately had been growing an anxiety that the good effect of the news from Louisiana and Virginia, which had raised the price of gold on the New York market to 210, would be impaired by the apparently irreversible retreat of the Confederates in North Georgia. Now though, with the word that they were going over to the offensive, their anxiety was relieved and their hope soared, anticipating a still greater drop in the pocketbook barometer that best measured northern greed and fears. As for the men in the ranks, though their faith in Old Joe had never wavered, their spirits took an even higher bounce as they stood and heard the order read to them this morning. "I never saw troops happier or more certain of success," one private would recall. "A sort of grand halo illuminated every soldier's face. . . . We were going to whip and rout the Yankees."

Johnston apparently shared this conviction that the Yankees would be whipped and routed: especially as it applied to Schofield, who was reported to be advancing heedlessly into the trap about to be sprung northwest of Cassville. At 10.20, hearing from Hardee that Thomas was moving in strength on Kingston and soon would be too heavily committed to effect a rapid disengagement, he sent his chief of staff, Brigadier General W. W. Mackall — who had served Bragg, his West Point classmate, in the same capacity — to tell Polk and Hood "to make quick work" of their combined lunge at Schofield, so that they would be ready to turn without delay on Thomas, when he came up in Hardee's wake, for the second phase of the Confederate offensive. With accustomed caution, Johnston added to Hood's instructions a warning that, in launching his flank attack, he was not to undertake "too wide a movement," lest he lose contact with Polk on his left, which not only might leave Schofield an escape hatch, but also would delay the consolidation of all three corps for the follow-up strike at Thomas and McPherson.

Such a warning was altogether superfluous, the staffer found when he encountered Hood near Cassville. Not only had the Kentuckian moved out before Mackall got there; by now he was moving back again, feverishly preparing to take up a defensive position in which to resist attack by a blue column reported to be advancing on a road in his right rear, skirmishers deployed and guns booming.

Mackall sent word of this surprise development to Johnston, who flatly declined to credit the report. "It can't be," he said. He did not believe the Federals were there because none of Polk's cavalry had encountered them this morning while reconnoitering in that direction. (In point of fact, they had not been there earlier this morning, and it was entirely accidental that they were there at all. A nomadic fragment from Major General Daniel Butterfield's division, Hooker's corps, they had missed a turning, lost their way, and wound up deep in Hood's right rear, some five miles east of their comrades trudging south on the far side of Cassville.) All the same, though Johnston did not believe in their existence — then, any more than he did ten years later, when he declared: "The report upon which General Hood acted was manifestly untrue" — he took no chances. Having rejected the evidence, he proceeded to act upon it. "If that's so," he said, examining the situation on a map, "General Hood will have to fall back at once."

Accordingly, when Mackall presently returned, he sent him riding again to Polk and Hood with orders canceling their attack. Once more, as had been its custom for the past two weeks, the army would take up a stout defensive position and there await developments: meaning Sherman.

Johnston quickly found what he was seeking along a wooded ridge immediately southeast of Cassville, overlooking the town and the "broad, open, elevated valley" in which it lay. Hood and Polk fell back to there, followed prudently by Schofield, who by now had notified Sherman of the snare he had so narrowly avoided, and Hardee came up that afternoon to take position on their left, closely pursued by Thomas and McPherson, the latter having closed the gap between him and the Cumberlanders in the course of the daylong skirmish, first north, then east of Kingston. Before sundown the guns of both armies were banging away at each other, arching their shots above the hill-cradled streets and rooftops of the village. Despite the dismay of the townspeople at this harrowing turn of events ("Consternation of citizens," a staff lieutenant jotted in his diary; "many flee, leaving all; some take away few effects, some remain between hostile fires") Johnston was greatly pleased with his new position, later referring to it as "the best I saw occupied during the war."

Polk and Hood did not agree with this assessment, and they said as much that evening when they came to headquarters for the council of war to which they had been summoned. Protesting that Union batteries enfiladed that portion of the ridge where their lines joined, they liked the position so little, in fact, that both wanted to leave it at the earliest possible moment. The army had no choice, they said, except to schedule a dawn attack, on the chance of beating Sherman to the punch, or else to fall back tonight across the Etowah. Johnston did not want to do either: certainly not attack the reunited Federals with no better promise of success than the tactical situation seemed to him to afford. Hardee, who arrived at this point in the discussion, sided altogether with his chief, hoping like him that Sherman would oblige them tomorrow by exposing his superior numbers to severe and sudden curtailment by advancing them head-on across that broad, open valley to challenge the defenders on the wooded ridge.

Johnston ended by deciding to retreat. He did so, he explained later, not because he agreed with Hood and Polk that the position had its drawbacks, but "in the belief that the confidence of the commanders of two of the three corps of the army, of their inability to resist the enemy, would inevitably be communicated to their troops, and produce that inability."

The fall-back to the Etowah that night, though Sherman made no attempt to interfere, was by far the most disruptive of the campaign. "All hurried off without regard to order," the young staff diarist recorded. "Reach Cartersville before day, troops come in after day. General Johnston comes up — all hurried over bridges; great confusion caused by mixing trains and by trains which crossed first parking at river's edge and others winding around wrong roads."

Much of the mixup was a manifestation of the army's chagrin at the two-step disappointment it had suffered, first in the cancellation of the attack, which came hard on the heels of the reading of Old Joe's "I lead you to battle" address — "I could not restrain my tears when I found we could not strike," Mackall confessed in a home letter — and then in the directive, which came down that night, for a resumption of the southward march. "Change of line not understood but thought all right," the diarist put it, "but night retreat after issuing general order impaired confidence; great alarm in country round. Troops think no stand to be made north of Chattahoochee, where supply train is sent." Civilians north and immediately south of the Etowah reacted to their abandonment much as the people of Cassville had done the day before, milling about like ants in an upset ant hill. Johnston put the blame, or anyhow most of it, on Hood, and so did members of his staff, including the diarist, who wrote: "One lieutenant general talks about attack and not giving ground, publicly, and quietly urges retreat."

By way of consolation for its woes, the disgruntled army could see for itself the strength of its new position near Allatoona, four miles down the Western & Atlantic from the river. Here, beginning the day of their arrival, May 20, Johnston had his soldiers throw up breastworks commanding the deep, narrow gorge through which the railroad snaked its way, his flanks protected, left and right, by Pumpkin Vine and Allatoona creeks. Fifteen miles to the south, his new supply base was Marietta, just beyond Kennesaw Mountain, about midway between the Etowah and the Chattahoochee, last of the three main rivers between Chattanooga and Atlanta.

Allatoona Pass, as the gorge through this spur of the Appalachians was called, was a still more "terrible door of death" than Buzzard Roost had been, some sixty miles to the north. Paradoxically, though, it was precisely in this abundance of natural strength that the strategic weakness of the position lay. Sherman would be even less apt to call for a main effort here than he had been at Rocky Face Ridge. His solution, now as then, would most likely be to try another sidle — and there was always the danger that, sooner or later, one or another of these complicated flank maneuvers would succeed in accomplishing its purpose of placing the superior blue army squarely between the Confederates and Atlanta; in which case Johnston would have no choice except to attack the Federals where they were, intrenched and waiting, or scatter into the surrounding hills. Either course would mean the loss not only of the campaign (meaning Atlanta) but also of the army, whether by destruction or disintegration, the difference being that one would be somewhat less sudden than the other. All Johnston could do, in the way of attempting to forestall such a calamity, was alert Wheeler to be on the lookout for the first sign of another sidle, up or down the Etowah. He felt sure that one was pending, but he could not move to thwart it until he knew its direction, right or left.

One other thing he could attempt, however, and that was to protect himself from his detractors, in some measure at least, by putting his performance in the best possible light for his Richmond superiors, with emphasis on his desire for coming to grips with his pursuer. Since this latest retreat had no doubt set his critics' teeth on edge, he no sooner crossed the Etowah than he got off a wire to the President explaining the cancellation of the "general attack" he had ordered yesterday: "While the officer charged with the lead was advancing he was deceived by a false report that a heavy column of the enemy had turned our right and was close upon him, and took a defensive position. When the mistake was discovered it was too late to resume the movement." Despite this disappointment, which had obliged him to continue the withdrawal, he pointed out that he had "kept near [Sherman] to prevent his detaching to Virginia, as you directed, and have repulsed every attack he has made."

Next day, May 21, the army having spent the night improving its position near Allatoona, still with no sign of what the Federals were up to, he followed through with another message along similar lines. "In the last six days the enemy has pressed us back to this point, thirty-two miles," he conceded, but he assured Davis that, all this time, "I have earnestly sought an opportunity to strike." The trouble was that Sherman, by constantly extending his right as he moved down the railroad, had obliged the defenders to give ground no less constantly, and then, "by fortifying the moment he halted," had also "made an assault upon his superior forces too hazardous." Without committing himself to anything specific — as, indeed, he could scarcely be expected to do, under the circumstances outlined here — Johnston wanted the Commander in Chief to know that he was in full agreement as to the need for going over to the offensive at the earliest possible moment. Meantime, despite the discouragements generally involved in making a lengthy retrograde movement, he was pleased to report that the slightness of his losses from straggling or desertion showed that the army was in good shape for such exertions as he might presently require.

The answer came not from Davis — not just yet — but from Bragg, who combined good news with bad and wound up with a flourish that seemed to indicate that the Georgia commander perhaps had oversold his case. Another brigade of infantry from Mobile and a regiment of South Carolina cavalry were on their way to join him, but these were the last the government would be sending.

"From the high condition in which your army is reported," the message ended, "we confidently rely on a brilliant success."

★ ★ ★

Johnston's concern, lest the very strength of his Allatoona position deprive him of the quick defensive victory he felt certain he would score if his adversary could only be persuaded to attack him there, was better founded than he knew. Two decades back, as a young artillery lieutenant on detached duty at Marietta with the inspector general, Sherman "rode or walked, exploring creeks, valleys, hills" in the surrounding region, while his less energetic comrades "spent their leisure Sundays reading novels, card-playing, or sleeping." Now this seemingly useless pastime stood him in good stead. "Twenty years later the thing that helped me to win battles in Georgia was my perfect knowledge of the country. I knew more of Georgia than the rebels did." In the course of his rambles, sketch pad in hand, he had spent several days investigating some Indian mounds on the south bank of the Etowah, just north of the gorge where Johnston was intrenched, and "I therefore knew that the Allatoona Pass was very strong, would be hard to force, and resolved not even to attempt it, but to turn the position."

First, though, he would call a halt, a brief time-out from war; the combat troops would take a welcome three-day rest ("to replenish and fit up," he explained to Halleck) while Colonel W. W. Wright and his 2000 nimble rail repairmen, having rebuilt the Resaca bridge in jig time, put the Western & Atlantic back in operation down to Kingston.

"The dead were buried, the sick and wounded were made more comfortable, and everybody got his mail and wrote letters," one appreciative
officer would recall. Then on May 23, with twenty days' rations in his
wagons, Sherman was ready to cut loose from the railroad and strike out
cross-country with everything he had.

His preliminary objective on this all-out flanking operation was
Dallas, a road-hub settlement just under twenty miles west of Marietta
and about the same distance southwest of Allatoona, where Johnston
would be left holding the bag unless he pulled back in time to meet this
massive threat to his new supply base, fifteen miles down the track in
his rear. As usual, Thomas would take the direct central route, south
from Kingston through Euharlee and Stilesboro, while Schofield
marched on his left, by way of Burnt Hickory, and McPherson swung
well to the right, through Van Wert, to approach Dallas from the west.
The march would be a rigorous one, Sherman knew from previous ex-
ploration, "as the country was very obscure, mostly in a state of nature,
densely wooded and with few roads." It might take longer than he

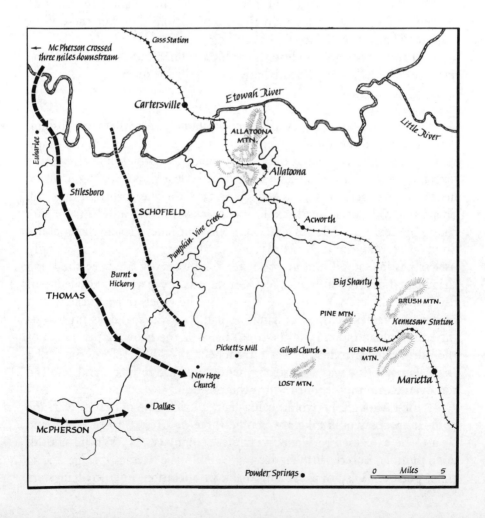

planned: in which case, he told Halleck, his twenty-day rations could
be stretched to thirty. But he was not inclined to worry much as he set
out from Kingston, riding with Thomas across the Etowah; "the
Rubicon of Georgia," he called that river in a dispatch sent just after
he gave the jump-off signal. "We are now all in motion like a vast hive
of bees," he declared, fairly buzzing with pleasure at being once more
on the go, "and expect to swarm along the Chattahoochee in five days."

So he said. But when Schofield captured a lone gray rider at
Burnt Hickory next day and found on him a dispatch which showed
Johnston already reacting to this latest turning movement, Sherman not
only knew that secrecy had gone by the board, along with all hope
for a substantial head start in the projected five-day sprint for the
Chattahoochee; he also perceived that "it accordingly became necessary
to use great caution, lest some of the minor columns should fall into
ambush," as Schofield had so nearly done, four days ago, near Cassville.

Caution was indeed called for, he found out the following morning, May 25, when Thomas pressed down in advance of the other two
armies for a crossing of Pumpkin Vine Creek. Hooker had the lead,
driving butternut cavalry pickets over a bridge which they set on fire
just as the first of his three divisions came in sight. He doused the flames,
double-timed across, and continued his pursuit of the skittery horsemen.
Four miles northeast of Dallas, near a Methodist meeting-house called
New Hope Church, he came under fire from a mass of rebel infantry
whose march he had apparently interrupted. With soldierly instinct, and
as if determined to justify his nom de guerre, Fighting Joe shook out a
line of skirmishers and attacked with his lead division, commanded by
Brigadier General John W. Geary, a six-foot six-inch Pennsylvanian
who had been San Francisco's first mayor and a territorial governor of
Kansas. A colonel in the Mexican War before he was thirty, he now was
forty-four and had seen much fighting, East and West, including
Chancellorsville and Gettysburg, Wauhatchie and Chattanooga, but in
none of these had he and his men found harder work than was required
of them in the next three hours around New Hope Church, which the
attackers ever afterwards referred to as the "Hell Hole."

What Geary struck, and promptly rebounded from, was Hood.
His corps had been last of the three to leave Allatoona the day before,
when Johnston, warned by Wheeler that Sherman was off on another
sidle, marched southwest up the near bank of Pumpkin Vine Creek to
intercept him around Dallas. Hardee was there now, with Polk in position on his right to connect with Hood near New Hope Church; so that
what Hooker had encountered was not a mere segment of Johnston's
army on the march, as he first thought, but the entire right wing of that
army, already beginning to scratch out intrenchments in expectation of
his arrival hard on the heels of the cavalry pickets fading back before
him through what Sherman called "the obscurity of the ambushed

country." Undaunted by the truth, which he began to suspect as soon as Geary was flung back, Hooker brought up his other two divisions, led by Butterfield and Brigadier General Alpheus Williams, massed them on a front no wider than Geary had spanned alone, and sent them forward, closely packed, against the rebel center. As a result, Major General Alexander P. Stewart's division caught the brunt of the all-out blue attack, some 20,000 strong. Known to his soldiers as "Old Straight," the nickname he had acquired while teaching mathematics at West Point and at Cumberland University in his home state of Tennessee, Stewart was forty-two and a veteran of all the army's battles, a strict disciplinarian much admired by his men, who gave him today all he asked of them, and more: especially the artillerists, whose guns were advantageously sited to exact a heavy toll from the charging bluecoats. Hooker's three divisions could make no headway against this one, despite two hours of trying without pause. Hood's other two divisions, under Major Generals Thomas Hindman and Carter Stevenson, had little to do on the left and right of the sector being assaulted, but when Johnston himself, alarmed by the desperate nature of the struggle, sent to ask Stewart if he needed reinforcements, the Tennessean replied calmly: "My own troops will hold the position."

Still another hour of such fighting remained, and it was this third hour, even more than the previous two, that prompted the Hell Hole description of the scene. Thunder rumbled and lightning crackled from a huge black cloud that gathered above the crossroad, dwarfing the boom of guns and the flicker of muzzle flashes, then loosed its torrential burden with all the abruptness of a water-filled bag split open, drenching men already wet with sweat from heat and exertion, whether prone behind log barricades or scrambling through bullet- and rain-whipped brush. "No more persistent attack or determined resistance was anywhere made," Stewart was to report with impartial praise. Thunderstorm and fighting came to a simultaneous end as the cloud blew off and the sun went down in a glory of red and purple beyond Dallas and the mountains to the west. Hooker put his casualties at 1665 killed or wounded, but the Confederates, knowing his reputation for understating his own losses while overestimating those of his opponent, were convinced the figure was much too low, since they themselves, fighting mostly behind cover, had lost nearly half that many in the course of the three-hour contest.

Darkness made the going hard for the rest of Thomas's army, coming up in the center, as well as for the other two, closing in on the left and right. "All was hurry and confusion," a Kentucky Federal recorded in his diary, "nearly everyone swearing at the top of his voice." Sherman would later recall that he "slept on the ground, without cover, alongside of a log, [and] got little sleep," but Schofield had worse luck. Swept off his horse by a low-hanging branch while combing the moonless woods in search of Sherman's bivouac, he was hurt by the fall

and would be out of action for several days; leadership of his Army of
the Ohio passed temporarily to Brigadier General Jacob Cox, the senior
division commander. McPherson made it nearly to Dallas by daylight,
coming in from the west to find Hardee securely intrenched there,
as were Polk and Hood to the northeast.

Sherman probed cautiously at the five-mile rebel line, all that day
and part of the next, but found no weakness he considered would
justify attack. Accordingly, by midmorning of the second day of un-
productive probing, May 27, he decided to turn Johnston's right with
a strike at Pickett's Mill, two miles beyond the Hell Hole Hooker had
failed to take two days ago. This time Howard drew the assignment, and
presently all three of his divisions were in position, massed for assault
in case there was serious opposition.

There was indeed, and "serious" was by no means too strong a
description of what he was about to encounter in the way of resistance.
Suspecting that the Federals would attempt some such maneuver, John-
ston the day before had instructed Hardee to shift one of his divisions
from the far left to a position beyond Hood's right: specifically, to
Pickett's Mill. It was Howard's ill fortune — as it had been Sherman's,
on Missionary Ridge six months ago, and Hooker's, two days later at
Ringgold Gap — that the division posted in his path was Major General
Patrick Cleburne's, by common agreement the best in Johnston's army.
Before emigrating to become a lawyer in Helena, Arkansas, Irish-born
Cleburne had done a three-year hitch in Her Majesty's 41st Regiment
of Foot, an experience that stood the former corporal in good stead
when it came to training his division of Arkansans, Texans, Mississippians,
and Tennesseans. Except under specific orders, which sometimes had
to be repeated, he and his men had never given up a piece of ground
assigned to their defense; nor did they do so here today at Pickett's Mill.
One-armed Howard gave the lead to his fellow West Pointer, Brigadier
General Thomas Wood — whose abrupt, inadvertent withdrawal under
orders at Chickamauga had created the "chasm" through which Longstreet plunged to defeat Rosecrans. Wood had his division in place by
early afternoon, formed six ranks deep for an end-on strike at the rebel
flank, wherever it might be. He moved out, floundered about for a
couple of hours in the heavy brush, then paused for some badly needed
rest, having sighted the newly turned earth of fresh intrenchments
through the trees. It was 4.30 by the time he got his three brigades in
motion again, still in a compact formation of two lines each, and what
turned out to be a three-hour fight, with an equally horrendous nighttime epilogue added for good measure, began almost at once.

His repulse was as complete as it was sudden. Ahead through the
trees, as the close-packed blue infantry came on, the head-logs of the
newly dug rebel intrenchments seemed to burst into flame, and a long,
low cloud of smoke boiled up and out, billowing as it grew, lighted from

within by the pinkish yellow blink and stab of muzzle flashes; Cleburne's emphasis on rapid-fire marksmanship in training produced a clatter as continuous as the uproar in a 5000-man boiler factory and an incidence of casualties that matched the stepped-up rate of fire. Wood's division fell apart, transformed abruptly from a compact mass into huddled clusters groping for cover in such low ground as the field afforded. "Under these circumstances," Howard reported, "it became evident that the assault had failed." He brought up reinforcements from Major General John M. Palmer's adjoining corps, as well as from Schofield's army, which was posted in reserve here on the Union left, and did what he could "to bring off the wounded and to prevent a successful sally of the enemy from his works." Darkness helped in both these efforts, but not much. At 10 o'clock, in a rare night action, Cleburne threw Brigadier General Hiram Granbury's Texas brigade into a charge that swept through a ravine where a number of fugitives from the attack had taken refuge, capturing all that were left alive when it was over. Howard's losses in Wood's division alone were 1457 killed, wounded, or captured. Cleburne's were 448, although Howard thought them higher in advancing a claim that "the enemy suffered immensely in the action, and regarded it as the severest attack made during this eventful campaign."

Now it was Johnston's turn to try his hand at what Sherman had been attempting all along. Reasoning that if his adversary was thus extending his left he might also have weakened his right, the Virginian told Hardee to test the Federal defenses around Dallas next morning. Hardee did, passing the word for Major General William Bate to make a probing attack with his division. Bate's repulse, though not as bloody, was as complete as Wood's had been the day before, at the far end of the line. He lost close to 400 men, half of them from the dwindling "Orphan" brigade of Kentuckians under Brigadier General Joseph Lewis, successor to Mrs Lincoln's brother-in-law, Ben Hardin Helm, who had fallen at Chickamauga.

All Bate got for his pains was the knowledge that McPherson was still around Dallas, apparently in undiminished strength — although the fact was he had been under orders to pull out for a march beyond New Hope Church and was about to leave when the rebel attack exploded against his works. Having fought it off, with fewer than half the casualties he inflicted, he notified Sherman and held his ground, awaiting instructions.

Meantime Johnston convened a council of war, at which Hood proposed that his corps be shifted eastward, beyond Cleburne, for an attack on the Union left, to be taken up in sequence by the other two corps with strikes at the right and center. Johnston liked the plan and issued the necessary orders, stipulating that Polk and Hardee would go forward when they heard Hood's artillery begin to roar. They waited past dawn and through sunup, May 29, poised for assault, heads cocked to catch the boom of guns that did not come. What came instead, around midmorning, was a note from Hood informing Johnston that he had found a newly arrived blue division intrenched in his path, perpendicular to the line he had scouted the day before. Finding it "inexpedient" to advance under these conditions, he had halted and now awaited new instructions. Johnston promptly canceled the offensive, directing instead that the army give all its attention to improving its defenses.

McPherson, Thomas, and Schofield were doing the same across the way, each on his own initiative, with the result that both lines grew more formidable than any seen so far in the campaign. Quick to improvise intrenchments — "The rebs must carry their breastworks with them," Federals were saying, marveling at the speed with which their adversaries could establish field fortifications, while the Confederates returned the compliment by remarking that "Sherman's men march with a rifle in one hand and a spade in the other" — blue and gray alike had become adept at the art of making any position well-nigh impregnable within a couple of days. While some troops hastily scratched and scooped out a ditch with bayonets and wooden shovels, canteen halves and fingers, others felled trees to provide timber for the dirt-and-log revetment, atop which a head log would rest on poles extending rearward across the trench to keep it from falling on the defenders in case it was struck by a shell while they were firing through the slit along its bottom between the skid poles. Other trees out front were cut so that their tops fell toward the enemy, their interlaced branches providing an entanglement to discourage assault, and if there was time for more methodical work, sharpened stakes were set in holes bored in logs and these too were placed to delay or impale attackers; *chevaux-de-frise* was the engineers' term for these spiky devices, which Westerners on both sides called "sheep racks." Whatever their name, they were cruelly effective and contributed largely to the invulnerability of the occupants of the trenches, taking it easy under the shade of blankets laid over the works to shield them from the sun. Taking it easy, that is, in a relative sense; for the snipers were sharp-eyed, quick to shoot from dawn to dusk, and the pickets on both sides were fearfully trigger-happy from dusk to dawn; Thomas alone was expending 200,000 rounds of small-arms ammunition daily.

May now ended, and as June came in, two days after Bate's repulse by McPherson helped to offset the subtractions Hooker and Howard had undergone in their assaults on Stewart and Cleburne, both commanders could take a backward look at what the four-week "running skirmish," uninterrupted by anything approaching either the dignity or the carnage of a full-scale battle, had cost them. Sherman's loss throughout the month of May was 9299, including nearly two thousand killed and missing; Johnston's, less precisely tabulated, was about 8500, three thousand of them captured or otherwise missing, left behind on his retrograde movement from Dalton to Dallas. Not even the larger of the two was a shudder-provoking figure at this stage of the war — particularly in comparison with the one being registered simultaneously in Virginia, where Meade was losing men at the rate of 2000 a day and would lose three times that many tomorrow, within less than twenty minutes, at Cold Harbor — but Sherman was getting edgy, all the same, over his inability to come to grips with his opponent on any terms except those that would clearly involve self-slaughter.

This he declined, around New Hope Church, as he had done before, wherever the Confederates called a halt to invite attack on their intrenchments. Instead, he continued to extend his left flank eastward toward the Western & Atlantic, obliging Johnston to conform by extending his right to keep him from slipping past it.

He was eager to get back astride the railroad, since two of his mounted divisions — Garrard's, which had rejoined from Rome, and another led by Major General George Stoneman, former chief of cavalry in the Army of the Potomac, under Hooker, now filling that position in Schofield's Army of the Ohio — had seized lightly held Allatoona Pass that morning, June 1, clearing the way for Sherman's rail repair gangs to extend his all-weather supply line across the Etowah, down to Acworth and beyond. Though Acworth was within ten miles of New Hope Church, the going would be rough, not only because of the rugged nature of the terrain and the probable interference of the rebels, but also because on the day Allatoona fell the rain began to fall as well: no brief tumultuous spring thunderstorm, such as had drenched the Hell Hole fighters, stopping about as abruptly as it started, but rather the slow, steady, apparently endless downpour of a dripping Georgia June. "Rain! Rain!! Rain!!!" an entry in a soggy diary read a few days later. This was as much of a strain on the spirits of men as it was on the backs and legs of mules who lugged ration and ammunition wagons through soupy troughs of wet red clay that once had passed for roads. "These were the hardest times the army experienced," Howard was to say, looking back. "It rained continuously for seventeen days; the roads, becoming as broad as the fields, were a series of quagmires." Mosquitoes stung and thrived, along with something new that bit and burrowed: redbugs, *Eutrombicula alfreddugesi* — chiggers. "Chigres are big, and red as blood," an Illinois private wrote. "They will crawl through any cloth and bite worse than fleas, and poison the flesh very badly. Many of the boys anoint their bodies with bacon rines which chigres can't go. Salt water bathing would cure them but salt is too scarce to use on human flesh."

Salt was not the only scarcity. Cut loose from their bountiful rail supply line, and with little chance to forage on their own, the troops had to live mainly on hardtack and bacon. Men began to come down with the symptoms of scurvy, "black-mouthed, loose-toothed fellows" who went on the roam in search of wild onions or anything green and fit to eat, though with small success in this barren, up-and-down backwoods region, miles off the main track. It was, as Howard said, a difficult time for everyone concerned, including Sherman.

Then on the night of June 4, the sounds of withdrawal muffled by the drumming of the rain, Johnston gave him the slip again. Morning showed the Confederates gone, and though some of his soldiers cheered "the nocturnal departure of the rebellious gentlemen," Sherman himself was far from pleased: especially when he received reports of their new position, which seemed, on the face of it, about as strong as any they had occupied in the past four weeks. Hardee held the left, on Lost Mountain and at Gilgal Church, Polk the center, from Pine Mountain to the Western & Atlantic, six miles below Acworth, and Hood the right, across the railroad, along the base of Brush Mountain. Cavalry covered and extended the flanks, Wheeler eastward, beyond Hood, and Brigadier General William H. Jackson's division, which had come with Polk from Alabama, westward beyond Hardee. Kennesaw Mountain, a commanding height, was two miles in the rear, handy in case another fallback was required, and Marietta about the same distance beyond its crest, which was less than twenty air-line miles from the heart of Atlanta.

By the following day, June 6, the three Union armies were again in confrontation with their foe, Thomas in the center, Schofield on the right, and McPherson on the left, astride the railroad at Big Shanty, a little more than midway between Allatoona and Marietta. Three days later Major General Francis P. Blair, Junior — brother of Lincoln's Postmaster General and a close friend of Sherman's — rejoined McPherson, bringing the 10,000 men of his corps back from their reënlistment furloughs and, incidentally, more than making up for the combat losses in all three armies up to now. By June 11 the hard-working railroad crews had the track repaired all the way to Big Shanty, and the troops, back on full rations and fairly well rested from their recent excursion through the wilds, felt much better.

"If we get to Atlanta in a week, all right," one veteran wrote home. "If it takes two months you won't hear this army grumbling."

Sherman was inclined to be less patient at this point. Though he was pleased that his latest sidle had accomplished its main purpose by obliging the rebels to give up impregnable Allatoona Pass, he was disappointed that it had not taken him all the way to the Chattahoochee (as he had predicted it would do, within five days) instead of fifteen rugged miles short of that river, with Johnston dug in across his front and able to look down his throat, so to speak, from the high ground up ahead. Obviously, if the graybacks were to be dislodged at something less than an altogether grievous price in casualties, this called for another sidle. Yet Sherman did not much like the notion of setting out on still another roundabout march away from the railroad: mainly, no doubt, because the last one had cost him more than he had planned for, both in morale and blood. In fact, before he crossed the Etowah and started his swing around Dallas, his losses had actually been lower than his adversary's, but now, as a result of the repulses he had suffered at New Hope Church and Pickett's Mill, they were nearly a thousand higher. Moreover, it seemed to him that his practice of avoiding pitched battle, wherever the terrain appeared unfavorable, had tended to make his soldiers unaggressive, timid in the face of possible ambush, and flinchy when confronted by intrenchments. Schofield, recovered by now from his horseback fall the week before, accounted for the reaction somewhat differently, seeing the nonprofessional volunteers and draftees as men who brought to army life, and to war itself, the practicality they had learned as civilians with the need for earning a living in the peacetime world outside. "The veteran American soldier fights very much as he has been accustomed to work his farm or run his sawmill," the young West Pointer declared. "He wants to see a fair prospect that it is going to pay."

That might be; Sherman yielded to no man in his admiration for and his understanding of the western volunteer. Still it seemed to him that all three armies were in danger of losing their fighting edge, if indeed they had not already lost it, and he put most of the blame on their commanders. Even McPherson, protégé or not, had begun to receive tart messages complaining of his slowness on the march. As for Schofield, he had come a long way from measuring up to expectations, and Sherman did not hesitate to say so. But Thomas, who had direct charge of two thirds of all the Federals in North Georgia, was the main object of the redhead's impatience and downright scorn.

"My chief source of trouble is with the Army of the Cumberland," Sherman informed Grant by telegraph this week. "A fresh furrow in a plowed field will stop the whole column and all begin to intrench. I have again and again tried to impress on Thomas that we must assail and not defend; we are on the offensive, and yet it seems that the whole Army of the Cumberland is so habituated to be[ing] on the defensive that from its commander down to its lowest private I cannot get it out of their heads."

He turned snappish in reaction to the delays and disadvantages involved in fighting what he called "a big Indian war" against an opponent whose army remained elusively intact and who, as Sherman complained in a letter to his brother in Washington, could "fight or fall back, as he pleases. The future is uncertain," he wound up gloomily, "but I will do all that is possible."

Aside from another unwanted sidle on muddy roads, not much seemed possible just now except to keep up the pressure, dead ahead, in hope that something would give. Nothing did. Johnston had contracted, somewhat retired, and thereby strengthened his line of defense, pulling Hardee in around Gilgal Church and Hood behind Noonday Creek, astride the railroad; Lost and Brush mountains were left to the protection of the cavalry, and Polk reinforced the center, on call to help cover not only the Western & Atlantic but also the wagon roads between Acworth and Marietta.

For outpost and observation purposes, a brigade from Bate's division remained on Pine Mountain, occupying what had become a salient when the line was readjusted in its rear. Called Pine Top by the natives, it was not so much a mountain as it was an overgrown hill, detached from the others roundabout and bristled atop with pine trees. Steepest on its northern face, it afforded a fine view of all three Federal armies and thus was well worth holding onto; Johnston had posted two batteries on its crest to help defend it, including one from South Carolina commanded by Lieutenant René Beauregard, the Creole general's son. Hardee was apprehensive, however, that both troops and guns were too far in advance of the main position for support to reach them before they were gobbled up by a sudden blue assault, and he asked his chief to go with him next morning, June 14, to judge in person the risk to which the salient was exposed.

Johnston agreed and the two set out on horseback as arranged, accompanied by their staffs and also by Polk, who wanted to come along for a look at the country from the hilltop. The rain had slackened and a cool breeze made the ride and the climb up the south slope a pleasant interlude, although Johnston had not gone far before he agreed that Hardee's fears were well founded; he told him to withdraw Bate's brigade and the two batteries after nightfall. Reaching the crest, however, he decided to avail himself of this last chance to study the enemy position from Pine Top, despite a warning that a battery of rifled Parrott guns, about half a mile in front, had been firing with deadly accuracy all morning at anyone who exposed himself to view. Sure enough, the three generals had no sooner mounted the parapet and begun adjusting their binoculars than they were greeted by a bursting shell.

Sherman himself, riding out on a line inspection down below, had seen them, although without personal recognition at that range, and had taken offense at their presumption. "How saucy they are," he said, and he turned to Howard, who held this portion of the front, and told him to have one of his batteries throw a few shots in their direction to "make 'em take cover." He rode on, and Howard passed the word to Battery I, 1st Ohio Light Artillery, whose commander, Captain Hubert Dilger, had already acted on the order before it reached him.

Dilger was something of a character, well known throughout the army, partly because of the way he dressed, immaculate in a white

shirt with rolled sleeves, highly polished top boots, and doeskin trousers
— hence the nickname "Leatherbreeches" — and partly because of his
habit of taking his guns so close to the front in battle that one general
had proposed to equip them with bayonets. On leave from the Prussian
army, in which he was also an artillerist, he had been visiting New York
in 1861 and had joined the Army of the Potomac, fighting in all its
battles through Gettysburg before coming west with Hooker to join
the Army of the Cumberland. Perhaps because he spoke with a heavy
German accent, he trained his crews to respond to hand claps, rather
than voice commands, and had won such admiration as an expert, famed
for the rapidity and precision of his fire, that he was allowed to function
largely on his own, roving about as a sort of free lance and posting his
battery wherever he judged it could do the most good. Today he was
within half a mile of Pine Top, and when he saw the cluster of saucy
Confederates mount the parapet on its crest he ran forward to one of
his rifled Parrotts, sighted it carefully, then stepped back. "Shust teeckle
them fellers," he told the cannoneer on the lanyard, and clapped his
hands.

That was the first shot, a near miss. Johnston gave the order to disperse, and all three generals and their staffs had begun to do so when
a second projectile landed even closer.

Hardee and Johnston moved briskly, heading for shelter behind
the crest of the hill, but Polk, a portly figure apparently mindful of his
dignity, walked off slowly by himself, hands clasped behind his back
as if in deep thought. Just then the third shell came shrieking; Dilger
had been quick to find the range. It struck the churchly warrior squarely
in the side, passing through his left arm and his body and his right arm
before emerging to explode against a tree. Johnston and Hardee turned
and hurried back through other shell-bursts to kneel beside the quivering
corpse of the bishop general. "My dear, dear friend," Hardee groaned,
tears falling. Johnston too was weeping as he laid his hand upon the
dead man's head. "We have lost much," he said, and presently added:
"I would rather anything but this."

An ambulance, summoned by wigwag from the Pine Top signal
station, brought Polk's mangled remains down off the mountain that
afternoon, followed that night, in accordance with Johnston's evacuation order, by the men of the two batteries and the infantry brigade,
who filed down in a long column not unlike a funeral cortege. Indeed,
the whole army mourned the fifty-eight-year-old bishop's passing; he
had been with it from the outset, before Shiloh, and at one time or
another had commanded nearly every soldier in its ranks. There were,
of course, those who doubted that his clerical qualities justified his
elevation to the leadership of a corps. "Thus died a gentleman and a
high Church dignitary," one of his division commanders wrote. "As a
soldier he was more theoretical than practical." Though there was

truth in this, it overlooked the contribution he made to the army's moral tone, which was one of the factors that enabled it to survive hardships, defeats, retreats, and Bragg. Northerners might express outrage that a man of the cloth, West Point graduate or not, should take up the sword of rebellion; Southerners took his action as strong evidence that the Lord was on their side, and they on His. That was part of what Jefferson Davis meant when he later referred to his old friend's death as "an irrepairable loss" and said that the country had sustained no heavier blow since the fall of Sidney Johnston and Stonewall Jackson.

One service Polk's maiming performed, at any rate, and that was to break up the pattern of Sherman's incipient depression. He had small use for the clergy anyhow, as a class, let alone this one who had joined in the current unholy attempt to dissolve the finest government the world had ever known, and when the news reached his headquarters at Big Shanty that afternoon — Federal signalmen decoded a wigwag appeal from atop Pine Mountain: "Send an ambulance for General Polk's body" — he took it as a sign that things were going better than he had thought. Sure enough, morning showed the enemy gone from the troublesome salient opposite his center. The rain had resumed its drumming on his tent, still further increasing the depth of the mud on all the roads, but Sherman did not let that keep his rising spirits from taking another mercurial jump. Ordering Thomas to close the gap in front while McPherson and Schofield stepped up the pressure on the flanks, he rode out to see it done and returned much pleased with the events of the past two days. Though he was careful, then and down the years, to deny the rumor that it was he, not Leatherbreeches Dilger, who had laid with his own hands the gun that sniped the militant churchman off of Pine Top, he was delighted with the result produced on this fortieth day of his campaign to "knock Jos. Johnston."

"We killed Bishop Polk yesterday," he wired Halleck, once more in high feather, "and made good progress today."

✗ 2 ✗

Not that, in his revived ebullience, he had dismissed all fear for what he called "that single stem of railroad 473 miles long," back through Nashville and Bowling Green, hurdling rivers and burrowing under mountains to reach his base on the Ohio; "Taxed [as it was] to its utmost to supply our daily wants," Sherman said flatly that without it "the Atlanta campaign was an impossibility." It was as much on his mind as ever, along with the two famed raiders who threatened its unbroken operation. "Thus far we have been well supplied, and I hope it will continue," he wrote his wife this week from Big Shanty, "though

I expect to hear every day of Forrest breaking into Tennessee from some quarter. John Morgan is in Kentucky, but I attach little importance to him or his raid. Forrest is a more dangerous man."

Even as he wrote, events were proving him right in both assessments. Morgan, after his victory at Crockett's Cove in the second week of May, reverted to his plan for a return to his homeland, which had been interrupted by the need for keeping Averell away from the salt works and lead mines in the Department of Southwest Virginia. His application for permission to make the raid had been turned down by the Richmond authorities, on the grounds that he was needed where he was, but he did not let that stop him now any more than he had done ten months ago, when he set out on the "ride" that landed him in the Ohio Penitentiary. Besides, having just learned that Brigadier General Stephen Burbridge, Union commander of the District of Kentucky, and a subordinate, Brigadier General Edward Hobson, were even then assembling troops in separate camps for a march across the Cumberlands to visit on Saltville and Wytheville the destruction Averell had failed to accomplish, Morgan believed he now had a more persuasive argument in favor of a quick return to the Bluegrass. Their combined forces were better than twice the size of his own, which amounted to fewer than 3000 men, and he was convinced that the only way to stop them was to distract them before they got started. "This information has determined me to move at once into the State of Kentucky," he informed the War Department on the last day of the month, "and thus divert the plans of the enemy by initiating a movement within his lines."

Forestalling another refusal, he set out that same day. By the time the message reached Richmond, two days later — "A most unfortunate withdrawal of forces from an important position at a very critical moment," Bragg indorsed it, and Seddon added: "Unfortunately, I see no remedy for this movement now" — Morgan was through Pound Gap and back on the soil of his native state.

That was June 2. It took him another five days to complete the rugged 150-mile trek across the mountains to within sight of the Bluegrass, and then on the morning of June 8 he approached the town of Mount Sterling, a day's ride west of Lexington. His strength was 2700 men, less than a third of them veterans from his old command, while another third were unmounted recruits for whom he hoped to find horses and equipment in the stock-rich country up ahead. A beginning was made at Mount Sterling, which he surrounded and captured, along with 380 Federals posted there to guard a large accumulation of supplies, including some badly needed boots.

While the prisoners were being paroled and Morgan was preparing to move on, looters began to break into shops, plunder homes, and even rough up citizens to relieve them of watches and wallets. "It was a general robbery," one merchant later protested, and though officers did what they could to stop the pillage, the undisciplined recruits, many of whom had spent the past two years avoiding conscription and stealing to make a living while on the run, were so far beyond control that some even drew pistols on women to rob them of their jewelry — an outrage the blood-thirstiest guerilla in Missouri had not perpetrated up to now. Confederates had mostly been greeted joyously on previous raids through this section of Kentucky, of which Morgan himself was a boasted product, but they were not likely to be welcome in the future, if indeed there was to be a future for them. A sort of climax was reached when a group of townspeople called indignantly on Morgan to show him an order, issued over the name of one of his brigade commanders, demanding immediate delivery of all the money in the local bank, under penalty of having "every house in the place" put to the torch; $72,000 in gold and greenbacks had been handed over. Morgan paled and turned to the colonel in question, who pronounced the signature a forgery and asked who had presented it. A light-haired officer with a blond beard and a German accent, he was told. Surgeon R. R. Goode answered that description, but when he was sent for he did not appear. He was missing — and remained so, though afterwards he was rumored to be living high in his native Germany.

Morgan could afford no time for an investigation, however desirable one was to clear his name, and set out without further delay for Lexington, his home town just over thirty miles away, leaving the foot-sore, horseless troopers behind to complete the distribution and destruction of the captured stores before taking up the march to join him.

Only about half of them ever did, the rest being killed or captured as the result of a miscalculation. "There will be nothing in the state to retard our progress except a few scattered provost guards," Morgan had predicted on setting out, and this opinion had been bolstered by reports from scouts that the heavy Union column under Burbridge, unaware of what was in progress across the way, had begun its eastward march toward the Cumberlands just before the Confederates emerged from them, headed west. Morgan's announced purpose was to oblige the blue invaders to turn back, but he had not thought they would react with anything like the speed they did. When Burbridge learned at Prestonburg that his adversary had passed him en route, by way of Pound Gap to the south, he not only countermarched promptly; he did so with such celerity that he was on the outskirts of Mount Sterling before daylight, June 9, and launched a dawn attack that caught the scantly picketed gray recruits so completely by surprise that many of them, still groggy from their excesses of the previous day and night, were shot before they could struggle out of their blankets. The survivors — about 450 of the original 800 — managed to fall back through the town and down the road to the west, thankful that the Federals were too worn by their hard return march to pursue.

Morgan was halfway to Lexington when he found out what had happened, and though his first reaction was to turn back and counter-attack with his whole command, on second thought (Burbridge had about twice as many men, well supported by artillery, and Morgan had been able to bring no guns across the mountains) he decided to wait for what was left of the horseless brigade to join him, then continue on to his home town. He approached it that night, made camp astride the pike, and rode in next morning to find, along with much else in the way of supplies and equipment, enough horses in its several government stables to mount all of his still-dismounted men and replace the animals broken down by the long march from Virginia.

Despite this valid military gain, June 10 was another stain on the reputation the raid had been designed, in part, to burnish. "Though the stay of Morgan's command in Lexington was brief, embracing but a few hours," the local paper reported next day, "he made good use of his time — as many empty shelves and pockets will testify." Once more looters took over, and this time veterans joined the pillage. Another bank was robbed, though more forthrightly than the one two days ago; the celebrants simply put a pistol to the cashier's head and made him open the vault, from which they took $10,000. Several buildings were set afire and whiskey stores were stripped, with the result that a good many troopers, too drunk to stay on a horse, had to be loaded into wagons for the ride to Cynthiana, thirty miles north-east. Morgan had learned there were supplies and a 500-man garrison there, and he was determined to have or destroy them both.

He marched by way of Georgetown to arrive next day, demand-ing surrender. This was declined, at first, but then accepted after a house-to-house fight in which, Morgan informed Richmond, "I was forced to burn a large portion of the town." Before he could enjoy the fruits of victory, lookouts spotted a blue column, 1200 strong, approaching from the east. It was Hobson; he too had turned back, well short of the Virginia line, on hearing from Burbridge that the raiders were in his rear. Headed for Lexington, he marched hard for Cynthiana when he saw the smoke and heard the firing. As it turned out, he was marching to join the surrender. Morgan threw two brigades directly at him and circled around to gain his rear with the other. This being done, Hobson was left with no choice except to be slaughtered or lay down his arms. He chose the latter course; which was doubly sweet for Morgan, Hobson having been widely praised for his share in the capture, near Buffington on the north bank of the Ohio River last July, of about half of Morgan's "terrible men," including the raider's second in command and two of his brothers, whom he later joined in prison as a felon. Now with Hobson himself a captive the tables were turned.

Proud of this latest exploit — as well he might be; he now had more prisoners than troopers — Morgan refused to be alarmed when scouts rode in at nightfall to report that Burbridge, having learned of his appearance at Cynthiana, was on the way from Mount Sterling with close to 5000 men. That was three times the strength of the Confederates, who were down to about 1400, half their original force, as a result of casualties, stragglers, and detachments sent out to mislead the numerous Union garrisons roundabout. Even more serious, perhaps, was a shortage of cartridges for the Enfield rifles his raiders favored so much that they declined to exchange them for captured Springfields, even though there was plenty of ammunition for the latter. But Morgan's mind was quite made up. Determined to give his weary men a good night's rest, he announced to his brigade commanders that he would meet the bluecoats next morning on ground of his own choosing, two miles south of town, and whip them as he had whipped Hobson today, whatever the odds. When one colonel protested that Burbridge was too strong to be fought without full cartridge boxes, the Alabama-born Kentuckian replied curtly: "It is my order that you hold your position at all hazard. We can whip him with empty guns."

Preceding another victory, the words would have had a defiant, martial ring, fit for the books and altogether in keeping with his earlier career; but followed as they were by a defeat, they took on the sound not of bravery, but of bravado. Burbridge attacked at dawn, June 12, and though Morgan was prevented from employing his accustomed flanking tactics by the need for putting all his men in line, he managed to stem the assault successfully until the shout, "Out of ammunition!" came from the right and was taken up next by the center, then the left. "Our whole command was soon forced back into the streets of the town, routed and demoralized," one raider would recall. "The confusion was indescribable. . . . There was much shooting, swearing, and yelling. Some from sheer mortification were crying."

Morgan did what he could to accomplish an orderly withdrawal, but what was left of his force by now had been split in two, with the halves presently blasted into fragments, some men fleeing southwest across the Sinking River to Leesburg, others northeast to Augusta. Many, caught on foot, surrendered; others were shot down. Not over half escaped, including their leader. "While falling back on the town," the same trooper wrote, "I saw General Morgan, on his step-trotting roan, going toward the Augusta road. He was skimming along at an easy pace, looking up at our broken lines and — softly whistling. I was glad to see him getting away, for had he been captured he would doubtless have fared badly."

He fared badly enough as it was. Back in Virginia before the month was out — minus half his troopers, even after all the stragglers had come in by various routes across the mountains, and considerably better than half his reputation — he put the raid in the best light he could manage in composing his report, stressing the frustration of Burbridge's expedition against the salt works and lead mines, the capture and parole of almost as many soldiers as he took with him, the procurement of nearly a thousand horses for men afoot and the exchange of roughly the same number of broken-down mounts for fresh ones, the destruction of "about 2,000,000$ worth of U.S. Govt. property," and the disruption of Federal recruitment in central and eastern Kentucky. All this was much; but it was not enough, in the minds of his Richmond superiors, to offset his unauthorized departure in the first place, the misbehavior of his raiders wherever they went, and his second-day defeats at Mount Sterling and Cynthiana. Moreover, he now faced all his old problems, with only about half as many troops, and the confirmed displeasure, if not the downright enmity, of the Confederate War Department. It was fairly clear, in any case, that John Morgan had taken his last "ride," that his beloved home state had seen its last of him and his terrible men.

Sherman was pleased, but hardly surprised, by Morgan's failure. Indeed, aside from having work crews standing by to make quick repairs in case the Kentuckian broke through to damage the railroad below Louisville, he feared him so little that he had scarcely planned for his coming beyond warning local commanders to be on the lookout. The other raider was another matter. After telling his wife, "Forrest is a more dangerous man," the red-haired Ohioan added: "I am in hopes that an expedition sent out from Memphis about the first of June will give him full employment."

It certainly should have done at least that, preceded as it was by a top-to-bottom shakeup of department personnel, beginning with Major General Stephen Hurlbut, commander of the District of West Tennessee. A Shiloh veteran and prewar Republican politician, Hurlbut had high-placed friends — Lincoln himself had made him a brigadier within a month of Sumter — but Sherman, far from satisfied with the "marked timidity" of his attempts to keep Forrest out of the region this past year, replaced him, less than a week after the fall of Fort Pillow, with Major General Cadwallader C. Washburn, who also had lofty Washington connections, including his brother Elihu, Grant's congressional guardian angel. Washburn had shown aggressiveness at Vicksburg, and Sherman chose him for that quality, which he encouraged by sending him a new chief of cavalry who shared it, Brigadier General Samuel D. Sturgis.

Seasoned by combat in Missouri as well as in Virginia (where he had contributed at least one famous quotation to the annals of this war: "I don't care for John Pope one pinch of owl dung") Sturgis had graduated from West Point alongside Stonewall Jackson and George McClellan. That he was more akin militarily to the former than to the latter was demonstrated by the manner in which he took hold on arrival in late April. Forrest by then was returning to North Mississippi from his raid to the Ohio; Sturgis pursued him as far as Ripley, seventy-five miles southeast of Memphis, before turning back for lack of subsistence for his 6400-man column. "I regret very much that I could not have the pleasure of bringing you his hair," he wrote Sherman on his return to Tennessee, "but he is too great a plunderer to fight anything like an equal force, and we have to be satisfied with driving him from the state. He may turn on your communications ... I rather think he will, but see no way to prevent it from this point and with this force."

In part — the remark about Forrest's hair, for example — this had a true aggressive ring, confirming the choice of Sturgis for the post he filled, but Sherman did not enjoy being told there was no way to keep the raider off his life line. His Georgia campaign had opened by then, and the farther he got from his starting point (Dalton to Resaca; across the Oostanaula to Kingston; then finally over the Etowah for the roundhouse swing through Dallas) the more vital that supply line became, and the more exposed it was to depredation. Concerned lest Forrest give Washburn the slip, he wired orders for the West Tennessee commander to launch "a threatening movement from Memphis," south-east into Mississippi, to prevent Forrest "from swinging over against my communications" in North Georgia or Middle Tennessee. Sturgis was to have charge of the expedition, but Washburn himself saw to the preparations, taking two full weeks to make certain nothing was omitted that might be needed, either in men or supplies or equipment. "The force sent out was in complete order," he later reported, "and consisted of some of our best troops. They were ordered to go in the lightest possible marching order, and to take only wagons for commissary stores and ammunition. They had a supply for twenty days. I saw to it personally that they lacked nothing to insure a successful campaign. The number of troops deemed necessary by General Sherman, as he telegraphed me, was 6000, but I sent 8000."

He sent in fact 8300: three brigades of infantry, totaling 5000, under Colonel William L. McMillen, the senior field officer in the district, and two of cavalry, totaling 3300, led by Brigadier General Benjamin Grierson, who had come into prominence a year ago with the 600-mile raid that distracted Vicksburg's defenders while Grant was beginning the final phase of the campaign that accomplished its surrender. In over-all charge of the two divisions, Sturgis also had 22 guns, of various calibers, and 250 wagons loaded with the twenty-day supply of food and ammunition. Grierson's troopers were equipped with repeating carbines of the latest model, which would give them a big advantage in firepower over their butternut opponents, and part at least of McMillen's command was armed with a zeal beyond the normal, one of his brigades being made up of Negro soldiers who had taken an oath to avenge Fort Pillow by showing Forrest's troops no quarter. "In case of an action in which they are successful," Hurlbut had stated on the eve of his depaiture, "it will be nearly impracticable to restrain them from retaliation." Now they and their white comrades, mounted and afoot, were on the march toward a confrontation with the man from whom they had sworn to exact vengeance.

They left Memphis on June 1, and as they set out from Collierville next day the rain began to fall, drenching men and horses and drowning fields and roads, much as it was doing 300 miles away in Georgia. Here, as there, the result was slow going, especially for the wagons lurching hub-deep through the mud. Five days of slogging about seven miles a day brought the marchers as far as Salem, a North Mississippi hamlet whose only historical distinction was that it had been Bedford Forrest's boyhood home. A disencumbered flying column of 400 troopers was detached there for a forty-mile ride due east to strike the Mobile & Ohio at Rienzi, a dozen miles below Corinth, in hopes that breaking the railroad at that point would delay the concentration, somewhere down the line, of the Confederates who no doubt by now had begun to gather in the path of the main column. Another three days of heavy-footed plodding, through June 8, covered another twenty miles of the nearly bottomless road to Ripley, where Sturgis had turned back from his pursuit of the plunderer a month ago.

Discouraged by the slowness of his march, as well as by the thought of all those graybacks probably gathering up ahead, he was inclined toward doing the same thing tomorrow, and that night he held a conference with his division commanders to get their views on the matter. Grierson felt much as his chief did. Delay had most likely enabled the rebs "to concentrate an overwhelming force against us," and he was impressed as well by "the utter hopelessness of saving our train or artillery in case of defeat." McMillen, on the other hand, declared that he "would rather go on and meet the enemy, even if we should be whipped, than to return again to Memphis without having met them." The key word here was *again*, Sturgis having turned back at this same point the month before. He thought it over and decided, on balance, that "it would be ruinous on all sides" — not least, it would seem, to the aggressive reputation that had won him his present post — "to return again without first meeting the enemy."

"Under these circumstances, and with a sad foreboding of the consequences," he afterwards summed up, "I determined to move forward, keeping my force as compact as possible and ready for action at all times."

His fears were better founded than he knew, although he was completely wrong about the odds he thought he faced. The Confederates were indeed preparing to oppose him, but it could scarcely be with an "overwhelming force," since the number of men available to the defenders was barely more than half as many as were in the blue column toiling toward them through the rain. On the day Sturgis left Memphis, June 1, Forrest had left Tupelo with 2200 troopers and six guns, bound at last for Middle Tennessee and a descent on Sherman's life line below Nashville. He was in North Alabama on June 3, preparing to cross the Tennessee River, when an urgent message from Stephen Lee summoned him back to meet Sturgis's newly developed threat to the department Lee had inherited from Polk. Forrest returned to Tupelo on June 5, the day the Federals reached his boyhood home fifty miles northwest. Uncertain whether they were headed for Corinth or Tupelo — the 400-man flying column, detached that day for the strike at Rienzi, contributed to the confusion — Lee told Forrest to dispose his men along the M. & O. between those two towns, ready to move in either direction, while he himself did what he could to get hold of more troops to help ward off the 8300-man blow, wherever it might land. His notion was that, if the enemy moved southward, the cavalry should retire toward Okolona, about twenty miles below Tupelo, in order to protect the Black Prairie region just beyond, where most of the subsistence for his department was grown and processed, and also to draw Sturgis as far as possible from his base of supplies and place of refuge in Memphis before giving him battle with whatever reinforcements had been rounded up by then. Lee made it clear before they parted, however, that Forrest was left to his own devices as to what should be done in the meantime, and Forrest took full advantage of the discretion thus allowed him.

He had at the time some 4300 troopers within reach: 2800 in Colonel Tyree Bell's brigade, which was part of Abraham Buford's division, and about 750 in each of two small brigades under Colonels Hylan Lyon and Edmund Rucker. While waiting for Sturgis to show his hand, Forrest spent the next two days posting these commands in accordance with Lee's instructions to cover both Tupelo and Corinth. Bell, with considerably better than half the available force, was sent to Rienzi, which he reached in time to drive off the 400 detached bluecoats before they did any serious damage to the railroad. Rucker and Lyon, with 1500 between them, moved to Booneville, nine miles south of Rienzi, accompanied by Captain John Morton's two four-gun batteries, all the artillery on hand. Forrest was there on June 8 when he received word that Sturgis was at Ripley, twenty miles away, and when he learned next morning that the mud-slathered Union column was continuing southeast, there was no longer any doubt that it was headed not for Corinth but for Tupelo, twelve miles below Guntown, a station on the M. & O. at the end of the road down which Sturgis was marching. A brigade remnant of 500 men under Colonel William A. Johnson arrived that day from Alabama, raising Forrest's strength to 4800. That was all he was likely to have for several days, but he figured it was enough for what he had in mind. He told Johnson to rest his troopers near Baldwyn, twenty miles down the track from Booneville, having decided to hit Sturgis, and hit him hard, before he got to Guntown.

In fact, he had already chosen his field of fight, twenty miles from Ripley and six miles short of the railroad — a timber-laced low plateau where the Ripley-Guntown road, on which the Federals were moving southeast, was intersected at nearly right angles by one from Booneville that ran southwest to Pontotoc — and when he learned that evening that Sturgis had called an overnight halt at Stubbs Farm, nine miles from the intended point of contact, his plan was complete. Orders went out to all units that night, June 9, and the march began before dawn next morning. Forrest led the way with his hundred-man escort company and Lyon's small Kentucky brigade; Rucker and Bell were to follow, along with Morton's guns, and Johnson would come in from the east. The result, that day, was the battle variously celebrated as Guntown, Tishomingo Creek, or Brice's Crossroads.

The enemy had close to a two-to-one advantage in men, as well as nearly three times as many guns, but Forrest believed that boldness and the nature of the terrain, which he knew well, would make up for the numerical odds he faced. "I know they greatly outnumber the troops I have at hand," he told Rucker, who rode with him in advance of his brigade, "but the road along which they will march is narrow and muddy; they will make slow progress. The country is densely wooded and the undergrowth so heavy that when we strike them they will not know how few men we have."

His companion might have pointed out, but did not, that the road they themselves were on — called the Wire Road because in early days, before the railroad, the telegraph line to New Orleans had run along it — was as muddy and as narrow as the one across the way. Moreover, all the Federals were within nine miles of the objective, while aside from Johnson's 500 Alabamians, seven miles away at Baldwyn, all the Confederates had twice as far to go or farther; Lyon, Rucker, and Morton had eighteen miles to cover, and Bell just over twenty-five. Forrest had thought of that as well, however, and here too he saw compensating factors, not only in the marching ability of his troopers, but also in the contrasting effect of the weather on their blue-clad adversaries. The rain had stopped and the rising sun gave promise that the day would be a scorcher.

"Their cavalry will move out ahead of their infantry," he explained, "and should reach the crossroads three hours in advance. We can whip their cavalry in that time. As soon as the fight opens they will send back to have the infantry hurried in. It is going to be hot as hell, and coming on the run for five or six miles, their infantry will be so tired out we will ride right over them."

Aside from the temperature estimate, which was open to question in the absence of any thermometer readings from hell, Rucker was to discover that this was practically a blow-by-blow account of what would follow; but the general quickly returned to present matters. "I want everything to move up as soon as possible," he said. "I will go ahead with Lyon and the escort and open the fight."

Sturgis rose at Stubbs Farm in a better frame of mind, encouraged by the letup of the rain and the prospect that a couple of days of mid-June heat would bake the roads dry, down through Tupelo and beyond. The flying column had returned from Rienzi the night before, and though their mounts were badly jaded the 400 troopers were doubly welcome as replacements for about the same number of "sick and worn-out men" he started back toward Memphis this morning in forty of the wagons his two divisions had eaten empty in the past nine days. These ailing bluecoats would miss a signal experience this hot June 10 at Brice's Crossroads, nine miles down the Guntown road, but their commander — round-faced and rather plump, Pennsylvania-born and a former Indian fighter, with a thick shock of curly hair, a trim mustache, and an abbreviated chin beard, he would be forty-two years old tomorrow: Forrest's age — did not know that, yet. All he knew, for the present, was "that it was impossible to gain any accurate or reliable information of the enemy and that it behooved us to move and act constantly as though in his presence."

This last, however, was precisely what he failed to do. Despite his previous resolution "to move forward, keeping my force as compact as possible and ready for action at all times," compassion for his weary foot soldiers led him to give them an extra couple of hours in camp to dry their clothes and get themselves in order for another hard day's march. Grierson and his troopers rode off for Guntown at 5.30 but McMillen's lead brigade did not set out till 7 o'clock, thus giving Forrest a full measure of the time he estimated he would need to "whip their cavalry" before the infantry "hurried up."

His plan, whose execution today would advance his growing reputation as "the Wizard of the Saddle," was for a battle in three stages: 1) holding attack, 2) main effort, and 3) pursuit. But Sturgis, riding with McMillen at the head of the infantry column, knew nothing of this — not even that Forrest was nearby — until shortly after 10 o'clock, when a courier from Grierson came pounding back with news that the cavalry was hotly engaged, some five miles down the road, with a superior hostile force; he had, he said, "an advantageous position," and could hold it "if the infantry was brought up promptly." Leaving orders for McMillen to proceed "as rapidly as possible without distressing the troops," Sturgis galloped ahead to examine the situation at first hand.

It did not look at all good from the rear, where a nearly mile-long causeway across a stretch of flooded bottomland led to and from a narrow bridge over Tishomingo Creek; "artillery and ambulances and led horses jammed the road," he observed, and when he reached Brice's about noon, another mile and a half toward Guntown, he found the cavalry hard pressed, fighting dismounted amid "considerable confusion." One brigade commander declared flatly that he "would have to fall back unless he received some support," while the other, according to Sturgis, was "almost demanding to be relieved." Grierson was more stalwart. Though the rebels were there "in large numbers, with double lines of skirmishers and heavy supports," he was proud to report that he and his rapid-firing troopers had "succeeded in holding our own and repulsing with great slaughter three distinct and desperate charges." The sun by now was past the overhead. How much longer he could hang on he did not say, but it could scarcely be for long unless he was reinforced, heavily and soon, by men from the infantry column toiling toward him through the mud and heat. Sturgis reacted promptly. With no further mention of concern about "distressing the troops," he sent word for McMillen to hurry his three brigades forward and save the day. "Make all haste," he told him, and followed this with a second urgent message: "Lose no time in coming up."

Grierson was wrong in almost everything he said, and Sturgis was fatally wrong in accepting his estimate of the situation. Those three "desperate charges," for example, had simply been feints, made by Forrest — a great believer in what he called "bulge" — to disguise the fact that his troopers, dismounted and fed piecemeal into the brush-screened line as soon as they came up, were badly outnumbered by those in the two blue brigades, who overlapped him on both flanks and had six pieces of horse artillery in action, unopposed, and four more in reserve. He opened the fight, as he had said he would do, by attacking with Lyon astride the Wire Road, then put Rucker and Johnson in on the left and right, when they arrived, for a second and a third attack to keep the Federals off balance while waiting for Morton's guns and the rest of his command to complete their marches from Booneville and Rienzi. "Tell Bell to move up fast and fetch all he's got," he told a staff major, who rode back to deliver the message.

It was just past 1 o'clock when this last and largest of his brigades came onto the field, close behind Morton; by which time, true to his schedule, Forrest had the enemy cavalry whipped.

Convinced, as he said then and later, that he had been "overwhelmed by numbers," Grierson was asking to have his division taken out of line, "as it was exhausted and well-nigh out of ammunition" for its rapid-firing carbines. McMillen rode up to the crossroads at that point, in advance of his lead brigade, and was dismayed to find that "everything was going to the devil as fast as it possibly could." Like Sturgis earlier, he threw caution to the winds. Though many of his troops had already collapsed from heat exhaustion on the hurried approach march, and though all were blown and in great distress from the savage midday, mid-June Mississippi sun, he sent peremptory orders for his two front brigades to come up on the double quick and restore the crumbling cavalry line before the rebels overran it.

They were hurrying to destruction, and hurrying needlessly at that; for just as they came into position, every bit as "tired out" as Forrest had predicted, a lull fell over the crossroad. It was brief, however, and lasted only long enough for the Confederate commander, now that all his troops were on the field, to mount and launch his first real assault of the day. Giving direction of the three brigades on the right to Buford, a Kentucky-born West Pointer two years his senior in age, he went in person to confer with Bell, whose newly arrived brigade comprised the left. This done, he came back to the right, checking his line along the way. In shirtsleeves because of the heat, with his coat laid over the pommel of his saddle, he "looked the very God of War," one soldier would remember, and as he rode among them on his big sorrel horse, saber in hand, he spoke to the dismounted troopers lying about for some rest in the blackjack thickets. "Get up, men," he told them. "I have ordered Bell to charge on the left. When you hear his guns, and the bugle sounds, every man must charge, and we will give them hell." Other things he said, then and later, went unrecorded. "I notice some writers on Forrest say he seldom cursed," one watcher was to recall. "Well, the fellow who writes that way was not where the 7th Tennessee was that day.... He would curse, then praise and then threaten to shoot us himself, if we were so afraid the Yankees might hit us."

Drawing rein at Morton's position, Forrest told him to double-shot four of his guns with canister and join the charge when the bugle sounded, then keep pace with the front rank as it advanced. Afterwards, the young artillerist, who had celebrated his twenty-first birthday on the field of Chickamauga, told his chief: "You scared me pretty badly when you pushed me up so close to their infantry and left me without protection. I was afraid they might take my guns." Forrest laughed. "Well, artillery is made to be captured," he said, "and I wanted to see them take yours."

But that was after the third stage ended, two days later; now the second, the main effort, was just beginning, and there was a grim struggle, much of it hand to hand, before the contest reached the climactic point at which Forrest judged the time had come to go all-out. Returning to the left, where he believed the resistance would be stiffest, he put an end to the thirty-minute lull by starting Bell's advance up the Guntown road. McMillen's second brigade was posted there, sturdy men from Indiana, Illinois, and Minnesota who, winded though they were from their sprint to reach the field, not only broke the gray attack but launched one of their own, throwing the Tennesseans into such confusion that Forrest had to dismount his escort troopers and lead them into the breach, firing pistols, to stop what had the makings of disaster. Over on the right, Buford too was finding the enemy stubborn, and had all he could do to keep up the pressure along his front. Finally, though, the pressure told. Orders came from Forrest — who fought this, as he did all his battles, "by ear" — that the time had come to "hit 'em on the ee-end." It was past 4 o'clock by now, and simultaneous attacks, around the flanks and into the rear of the Union left and right, made the whole blue line waver and cave in, first slowly, then with a rush.

"The retreat or rout began," in Forrest's words, or as Sturgis put it: "Order gave way to confusion and confusion to panic. . . . Everywhere the army now drifted toward the rear, and was soon altogether beyond control."

Fleeing past the two-story Brice house at the crossroads, the fugitives sought shelter back up the road they had run down, four hours ago, to reach the battle that now was lost. But conditions there were in some ways worse than those in what had been the front: especially along the causeway through the Tishomingo bottoms and on the railless bridge across the creek, the narrow spout of the funnel-shaped host of panicked men, who, as Sturgis said, "came crowding in like an avalanche from the battlefield." Morton's batteries had the range, and their execution was increased by the addition of four Federal guns, captured with their ammunition. Presently a wagon overturned on the high bridge and others quickly piled up behind it, creating what a retreating colonel described as "one indiscriminate mass of artillery, caissons, ambulances, and broken, disordered troops." Some escaped by leaping into the creek, swollen neck-deep by the rains, and wading to the opposite bank. But there was no safety there either. Though Sturgis had hoped to form a new line on the far side of the stream, the rebels were crossing so close in his rear that every attempt to make a stand only brought on a new stampede. The only thing that slowed the whooping graybacks was the sight of abandoned wagons, loaded with what one hungry pursuer called "fresh, crisp hardtack and nice, thin side bacon." They would pause for plunder, wolf it down, and then come on for more.

This continued, well past sundown, to within three miles of last night's bivouac, where there was another and still worse stretch of miry road across one of the headwater prongs of the Hatchie River. It was night now and the going was hard, one officer noted, "in consequence of abandoned vehicles, drowned and dying horses and mules, and the depth of the mud." Despairing of getting what was left of his shipwrecked train through this morass, Sturgis went on to Stubbs Farm, where he was approached before midnight by Colonel Edward Bouton, whose Negro brigade had served as train guard during the battle and had therefore suffered less than the other two infantry commands had done.

"General, for God's sake don't let us give up so," he exclaimed.

But Sturgis, quite unstrung, was at his wit's end. "What can we do?" he said, not really asking.

Bouton wanted ammunition with which to hold Forrest in check, on the far side of the bottoms, while the remaining guns and wagons were being snaked across to more solid ground beyond. Sturgis was too far in despair, however, to consider this or any other proposal involving resistance. Besides, he had no ammunition to give.

"For God's sake," he broke out, distraught by the events of this longest day in his life and the prospect of a sad birthday tomorrow, "if Mr Forrest will let me alone, I will let him alone! You have done all you could, and more than was expected. . . . Now all you can do is to save yourselves."

Mr Forrest, as Sturgis so respectfully styled the man he had said a month ago was "too great a plunderer to fight anything like an equal force," had no intention of letting him alone so long as there was profit to be gained from pressing the chase. Heaving the wreckage off the Tishomingo bridge and into the creek, along with the dead and dying animals, he continued to crowd the rear of the retreating bluecoats. "Keep the skeer on 'em," he told his troopers, remounted now, and they did just that, past sunset and on into twilight and full night. "[Sturgis] attempted the destruction of his wagons, loaded with ammunition and bacon," Forrest would report, "but so closely was he pursued that many of them were saved without injury, although the road was lighted for some distance." Furious at this incendiary treatment of property he considered his already, he came upon a group of his soldiers who had paused, still mounted, to watch the flames. "Don't you see the damned Yankees are burning my wagons?" he roared. "Get off your horses and throw the burning beds off." Much toasted hard-tack and broiled bacon was saved that way, until finally, some time after 8 o'clock, "It being dark and my men and horses requiring rest" — they did indeed, having been on the go, marching and fighting, for better than sixteen hours — "I threw out an advance to follow slowly and cautiously after the enemy, and ordered the command to halt, feed, and rest."

By 1 a.m. he had his troopers back in the saddle and hard on the equipment-littered trail. Within two hours they reached the Hatchie bottoms, where they came upon the richest haul of all. Despite Bouton's plea, Sturgis had ordered everything movable to proceed that night to Stubbs Farm and beyond, abandoning what was left of his train, all his non-walking wounded, and another 14 guns, all that remained of the original 22 except for four small mountain howitzers that had seen no action anyhow. This brought Forrest's total acquisition to 18 guns, 176 wagons, 1500 rifles, 300,000 rounds of small-arms ammunition, and much else. He himself lost nothing, and though he had 492 killed and wounded in the battle — a figure larger in proportion than the 617 casualties he inflicted — his capture of more than 1600 men on the retreat brought the Federal loss to 2240, nearly five times his own. Many of the enemy, especially from Bouton's brigade, which had the misfortune to bring up the rear and suffered heavily in the process, were picked up here in the Hatchie bottoms. A Tennessee sergeant later recalled the scene. "Somewhere between midnight and day, we came to a wide slough or creek bottom; it was miry and truly the slough of despair and despond to the Yanks. Their artillery and wagons which had heretofore escaped capture were now bogged down and had to be abandoned. This slough was near kneedeep in mud and water, with logs lying here and there. On top of every log were Yanks perched as close as they could be, for there were more Yanks than logs." They put him in mind "of chickens at roost," he said, but added: "We who were in front were ordered to pay no attention to prisoners. Those in the rear would look after that."

Four miles short of Ripley at dawn, the pursuers came upon a rear-guard remnant, which Forrest said "made only a feeble and in-effectual resistance." He drove its members back on the town, where they were reinforced and rallied briefly, only to scatter when attacked. "From this place," Forrest's report continued, "the enemy offered no organized resistance, but retreated in the most complete disorder, throw-ing away guns, clothing, and everything calculated to impede his flight." Beyond Ripley he left the direct pursuit to Buford and swung onto a roundabout adjoining road with Bell's brigade, intending to cut the Federals off at Salem. But that was a miscalculation. Buford pressed them so hard the interception failed; the blue column cleared the hamlet before Forrest got there around sundown. He called off the chase at that point and turned back to scour the woods and brush for fugitives, gather up his spoils, and give his men and mounts some rest from their famous victory, which would be studied down the years, in war colleges here and abroad, as an example of what a numerically inferior force could accomplish once it got what its commander called "the bulge" on an opponent, even one twice its size.

There was no rest, though, for Sturgis and his men, who continued to flee in their ignorance that they were no longer pursued except by rumors of graybacks hovering on their flank. "On we went, and ever on," a weary colonel was to write, "marching all that day and all that interminable [second] night. Until half past ten the next morning, when we reached Collierville and the railroad, reinforcements and supplies, we marched, marched, marched, without rest, without sleep, without food." At any rate they made excellent time. The march down had taken more than a week, but the one back took only a night and a day and a night. In Collierville that morning (June 12; Morgan's troopers were scattering from Cynthiana, 300 miles northeastward in Kentucky) the wait for the train that would take them on to the outskirts of Memphis, seventeen miles away, was in some ways even harder than the 90-mile forced march had been. Relieved of a measure of their fright, they now knew in their bones how tired they were and how thoroughly they had been whipped. An Ohio regimental commander reported that, in the course of their wait beside the railroad track, his troops "became so stiffened as to require assistance to enable them to walk. Some of them, too foot-sore to stand upon their feet, crawled upon their hands and knees to the cars."

Sturgis's hurts were mainly professional, being inflicted on his career. Back in Memphis, amid rumors that he had been drunk on the field — a conclusion apparently reached by way of the premise that no sober man could be so roundly trounced — he put the disaster in the best light he could manage. Winding up his official report with "regret that I find myself called upon to record a defeat," he added: "Yet there is some consolation in knowing that the army fought nobly while it did fight, and only yielded to overwhelming numbers." Just over 8000 troops had been thrown into a rout and driven headlong for nearly a hundred miles by just under 5000, but he persisted in claiming (and even believing, so persuasive were Forrest's tactics) that the odds had been the other way around, and longer. "The strength of the enemy is variously estimated by my most intelligent officers at from 15,000 to 20,000 men."

So he said; but vainly, so far as concerned the salvation of his career. For him, the war ended at Brice's Crossroads. Despite the board's finding no substance in the charge that he had been drunk, either in battle or on the birthday retreat, Sturgis spent the rest of the conflict on the sidelines, awaiting orders that did not come. Disconsolate as he was, he only shared what those who had served under him were feeling. Though in time their aching muscles would find relief and their wounds would heal, the inward scars of their drubbing would remain. "It is the fate of war that one or the other side should suffer defeat," a cavalry major who survived the battle was to write, more than twenty years later. "But here there was more. The men were cowed, and there pressed upon them a sense of bitter humiliation, which rankles after nearly a quarter of a century has passed."

Sherman was disappointed, of course, but he was also inclined to give Sturgis credit for having achieved his "chief object," which had been "to hold Forrest there [in Mississippi] and keep him off our [rail] road." There was truth in a participating colonel's observation that the expedition had been "sent out as a tub to Forrest's whale," and though the price turned out to be high, both in men and equipment, it was by no means exorbitant, considering the alternative. Learning that the raider had been in North Alabama, poised for a strike across the Tennessee River before Sturgis lured him back, the red-haired Ohioan wired the district commander instructions designed to discourage a return: "You may send notice to Florence that if Forrest invades Tennessee from that direction, the town will be burned, and if it occurs you will remove the inhabitants north of the Ohio River, and burn the town" — adding, as if by afterthought: "and Tuscumbia also."

He would send both places up in smoke, along with much else, if it would help to keep "that devil Forrest" off his life line. But that was only an interim deterrent. He had it in mind to follow through, as soon as possible, with a second expedition into northern Mississippi, stronger and better led, to profit by the shortcomings of the first. "Forrest is the very devil," he declared, "and I think has got some of our troops under cower." He proposed to correct this in short order. A. J. Smith's three divisions were on their way back from service up Red River with Banks, hard-handed veterans whose commanders had been closely observed by Sherman in the course of the fighting last year around Vicksburg. He had intended either to bring them to Georgia as reinforcements or else to send them against Mobile; but now, he notified Washington, he had what he considered a better, or in any case a more urgent, use for them. "I will order them to make up a force and go out and follow Forrest to the death, if it costs 10,000 lives and breaks the Treasury. There will never be peace in Tennessee till Forrest is dead."

★ ★ ★

Up in Washington, news of Morgan's defeat was about as welcome as that of Forrest's victory was irksome, although neither of these side shows of the main event provided much more than a brief diversion from the prevalent fret over Grant and Sherman — what their progress against Lee and Johnston meant, if anything, and above all what it was costing them in casualties per mile. These two, between them, would win or lose, if not the war, then in any event the election in November; which perhaps was the same thing. The Democrats would convene in August to nominate a candidate who would run on the issue of ending the conflict by declaring peace, whatever accommodations might be required by their late fellow countrymen down South, and it was generally agreed that the Republicans could not survive a prolongation of the bloody three-year stalemate through the five months between now and the election.

Lincoln had declared himself "only a passenger" on the juggernaut of war, but his hand was still on the tiller of the ship of state and he intended to keep it there if he could. Public attention was mainly fixed on the fighting in Virginia, where the casualties had been awesome from the start, and he tried to offset the civilian reaction by stressing his admiration for Grant's refusal to be distracted by the bloodshed and by recommending that his listeners do likewise. "I think, without knowing the particulars of the plans of General Grant, that what has been accomplished is of more importance than at first appears," he told a crowd that came to serenade him on hearing that the Army of the Potomac had resumed its southward march after two days of cataclysmic battle in the Wilderness. "I believe I know — and am especially grateful to know — that General Grant has not been jostled in his purposes, that he has made all his points, and today he is on his line as he purposed before he moved.... I commend you to keep yourselves in the same tranquil mood that is characteristic of that brave and loyal man."

Tranquillity was easier to prescribe than to attain. Hemmed in as he was by cares from all directions, including the importunities of incessant office seekers — "Too many pigs for the tits," he said wryly — Lincoln found the sight of the wounded, returning in their thousands from where he had sent them to get hit, a heavy burden on his spirit. "Look yonder at those poor fellows," he said one day when a long line of ambulances creaked past his halted carriage. "I cannot bear it. This suffering, this loss of life is dreadful." It was during this dark time that a White House visitor watched him pace the dawn-gray corridors in his nightshirt and long wrapper, hands clasped behind his back, head bent low, and with black rings under his eyes from loss of sleep.

By no means all the strain was of a purely military nature. While it was true that some events which normally would have awakened a sharp sense of national loss were muted by the uproar of the guns — the death of Nathaniel Hawthorne, for example, was barely noted amid the excitement over Grant's shift from Spotsylvania to the North Anna — others were so closely tied to the conflict that they stood out in stark relief against its glare. One was the so-called Gold Hoax, perpetrated on May 18, the day before Hawthorne died, by Joseph Howard, the journalist who three years ago had written of Lincoln's furtive passage through Baltimore in a "Scotch cap and long military cloak" to avoid assassination on the way to his inauguration. At 4 a.m. that morning Howard distributed anonymously to all the New York papers a bogus proclamation, complete with the forged signature of the President, fixing May 26 "as a day of fasting, humiliation and prayer," and calling for an additional draft of 400,000 men required by "the situation in Virginia, the disaster at Red River, the delay at Charleston, and the general state of the country."

Defeat, it seemed from the doleful tone of the document, was just around the corner. Only two papers, the *New York World* and the *Journal of Commerce*, were on the street with the story before the forgery was detected; bulletins of denial promptly quashed its effect on the gold market, defeating the scheme. With Lincoln's approval, Stanton moved swiftly in reprisal, padlocking the offices of both papers and clapping their editors into military arrest, along with Howard, who was soon sniffed out. Within three days the editors were released and their papers resumed publication; even Howard was freed within about three months, on the plea that he was "the only spotted child of a large family" and had been guilty of nothing worse than "the hope of making some *money*." No real harm was done, except to increase the public's impression of Stanton — and, inferentially, his chief — as a tyrant, an enemy of free speech and the press. One witness declared, however, that the affair "angered Lincoln more than almost any other occurrence of the war period." His ire was aroused in part by the fact that the country's reaction to the bogus proclamation obliged him to defer issuing an order he had prepared only the day before, calling, in far less doleful words, for the draft of 300,000 additional troops.

They were likely to be needed sooner, not later, at the rate men were falling in Grant's attempt to overrun Lee and Sherman's to outflank Johnston. And on top of these losses, before the month was out, there occurred a hemispheric provocation that seemed likely to bring on a second war, this one with a foreign power: France. Following up his occupation of Mexico City a year ago, purportedly to collect a national debt, Napoleon III landed his puppet Maximilian, whom he had persuaded to assume the title of Emperor of Mexico, at Vera Cruz, May 28; the Austrian archduke and his wife Charlotte were on their way to the capital, where they would reign over an empire designed to stand, with the help of still more French soldiers than the 35,000 already sent, as a bulwark against Anglo-Saxon expansion in Central and South America. This continued defiance of the Monroe Doctrine was hard for Lincoln to abide, but not so hard that he did not manage to do so, deferring action until he could afford to give it his full attention, preferably with a reunited country at his back; "One war at a time" was as much his policy now as it had been on the occasion of his near confrontation with England over the *Trent* affair, more than two years ago.

Besides, a domestic concern of a far more urgent nature than any posed by the latter day Napoleon — specifically, the double-barreled problem of getting renominated and reëlected — was hard upon him at the time. Three days after Maximilian stepped ashore at Vera Cruz, the radicals of Lincoln's own party, aware that they lacked the strength to dominate the regular Republican convention at Baltimore on June 7, called a convention of their own in Cleveland on May 31, one week earlier, and by acclamation nominated John C. Frémont as their candidate for President in the November election.

For some time Jacobinic disaffection had been growing, especially among New England abolitionists and German-born extremists in Missouri, who resented Lincoln's "manifest tendency toward temporary expedients," and complained bitterly that he had *"words* for the ultras and *acts* for the more conservative." Now their opposition had taken this form; they were out in the open, determined to bring him down. Frémont, the party's first presidential candidate in 1856 — he had polled a respectable 1,300,000 votes, as compared to James Buchanan's 1,800,000 — accepted the nomination "with a view to prevent the misfortune of [Lincoln's] reëlection," which he said "would be fatal to the country." Glad to be back in the public eye, after nearly two years of promoting railroads in New York State, the Pathfinder looked forward to a vigorous campaign. The trouble was that his most influential backers had to avoid giving him open support, for fear of committing political suicide, and this had been evident at the convention in Ohio, which one critic described as a "magnificent fizzle," attended mainly by "disappointed contractors, sore-head governors, and Copperheads."

Thousands had been expected, but only about four hundred showed up. Informed of this, Lincoln reached for the Bible on his desk, thumbed briefly through I Samuel until he found what he was seeking, then read it out: *And every one that was in distress, and every one that was in debt, and every one that was discontented, gathered themselves unto him; and he became a captain over them: and there were with him about four hundred men.*

A joke had its uses, particularly as therapy for a spirit as gloomy by nature as this one, but the million-odd votes Frémont might poll in November were no laughing matter. Before then, there would probably be ways to lure the Jacobins back into the fold. Some piece of radical legislation hanging fire in Congress for lack of Executive pressure, say, could be put through; or the scalp of some Administration stalwart they had singled out as an enemy could be yielded up. Meantime, however, the thing to do, if possible, was to solidify what was left of the party and broaden its base to attract outsiders, meaning those hard-war Democrats who would be repelled by the peace plank their leaders were sure to include in the platform at their Chicago convention in late August, nearly three months after the Republicans gathered next week in Baltimore.

Lincoln of course did not attend, despite the proximity to Washington; nor did David Davis, his manager at the convention four years ago and now a Supreme Court justice. Not since Andrew Jackson's reëlection, thirty-two years ago, had any man been chosen to serve a second term as President, although several had tried and failed to get renominated and Van Buren had even succeeded, only to be defeated at the polls. But Davis foresaw no difficulty requiring his considerable talent for maneuver, so far as the place at the top of the ticket was concerned, and he was right; there was no real opposition, only some wistful talk about "the salutary one-term principle," and no trouble. On the first ballot, Missouri's delegates rocked the boat a bit by casting their 22 votes for Grant, but switched when all the other 484 went to Lincoln, whose nomination thus was made unanimous. This done, the convention was free to turn to the business of solidification and broadening; which could be done, at least in part — so it was hoped — by the selection of the right man to replace Vice President Hannibal Hamlin, who not only lacked luster but also had sided with the radicals on most of the whipsaw issues before Congress.

A beginning had been made in this regard, first by changing the name of the party to National Union, which helped to reduce the onus of sectionalism, and then by adopting a platform that had, as one observer put it, "a radical flavor but no Radical planks." Appealing for unity in continuing the national effort to put down the rebellion, it called for the extirpation of slavery as the root cause of the war, promised to visit upon all rebels and traitors "the punishment due to their crimes," thanked soldiers and civilians alike for their sacrifices over the past three years, and wound up by favoring the encouragement of immigration and the construction of a transcontinental railroad. Now came the vice-presidential nomination, and though Lincoln kept aloof from the contest, not wanting to anger the friends of disappointed candidates — "Convention must judge for itself," he indorsed a letter requesting a statement of his wishes as to the contest for second place on the ticket — he had confidants on the scene, including his secretary Nicolay and Henry J. Raymond, editor of the friendly *New York Times* and chairman of the platform committee. When Raymond saw to it that the name of Andrew Johnson, former senator and now military governor of Tennessee, was presented at a critical juncture, scarcely anyone failed to see that here was the best possible way of strengthening the ticket by giving simultaneous recognition to the claims of loyal men from the South, especially the border states, as well as to War Democrats all across the land. Johnson was both, and with an outburst of enthusiasm so vociferous that one delegate later testified that he "involuntarily looked up to see if the roof were lifted," his nomination too was made unanimous.

Lincoln learned informally of the outcome that afternoon, when he happened to walk over to the War Department and was congratulated as he entered the telegraph office. "What! Am I renominated?" he exclaimed, smiling, and when the operator showed him a confirming telegram his first thought was of his wife: "Send it over to the Madam. She will be more interested than I am."

He perhaps wanted to brace her for things to come, and they were not long in coming. Next day the *New York World*, back on the streets after being shut down for its unwitting share in the Gold Hoax three weeks ago, served notice that this was to be the bitterest of campaigns. Commenting on the nominations of Lincoln and Johnson — who like his running mate was a self-made man, having started out as a tailor before he studied law and entered politics — the *World* clucked its tongue over the come-down the national tone had suffered with the selection by the opposition party of this ungracious pair of candidates for the two most honored posts in all the land. "The age of statesmen is gone," the lead editorial lamented; "the age of rail-splitters and tailors, of buffoons, boors, and fanatics, has succeeded. . . . In a crisis of the most appalling magnitude, requiring statesmanship of the highest order, the country is asked to consider the claims of two ignorant, boorish, third-rate backwoods lawyers, for the highest situations in the government. Such nominations, in such a conjecture, are an insult to the common-sense of the people. God save the Republic!"

Lincoln hoped God would, but he was modest in his judgment of why he had been chosen to compete again for the task of serving as God's chief helper in the search for that salvation. "I do not allow myself to suppose that [the delegates] have concluded to decide that I am either the greatest or best man in America," he replied to formal congratulations which presently followed, "but rather they have concluded it is not best to swap horses while crossing the river, and have further concluded that I am not so poor a horse that they might not make a botch of it in trying to swap."

Renomination was only the first, and much the lower, of the two formal hurdles to be cleared if he was to retain his post. The second was reëlection, and that would be a far more difficult matter, requiring not only a great deal of skill in maneuvering his way along the thorny path of politics — skill, that is, such as he had just shown while skimming the first hurdle — but also a great deal of ability on the part of his hand-picked commanders in the field. In short, they would have to convince the public that he and they could win the war; otherwise, neither he nor the war would continue. Up to now, whatever admiration he might express for their refusal to be "jostled," their progress had been made at a price the voters were likely to find excessive, particularly if they were obliged to continue paying it over the course of the next five months. Even as the delegates converged on Baltimore, Grant was engaged in the grisly and belated task of burying his dead at Cold Harbor — a position McClellan had reached two years ago, the opposition press was pointing out, with the loss of less than a tenth as many soldiers — and Sherman, after his fruitless roundhouse swing through Dallas, was just getting back astride the railroad at Big Shanty, having also suffered checks about as abrupt, though not as bloody, along the way at New Hope Church and Pickett's Mill. As a result, in his continuing attempt to bolster national morale, Lincoln was reduced to the necessity of making what he could of such minor victories as Cynthiana, which at least disposed of John Morgan for a season, more or less.

That was on the Sunday ending the week of the Republican convention, and one week later there occurred another side-show triumph which more or less disposed of another Confederate raider; one even more famous, or infamous, than Morgan.

★   ★   ★

Sunday, June 12; U.S.S. *Kearsarge*, a thousand-ton sloop named for one of New Hampshire's rugged mountains, was anchored off the Dutch coast, in the mouth of the River Scheldt near Flushing, when her skipper, Captain John A. Winslow, received word from his government's minister in Paris that the Confederate cruiser *Alabama*, which had eluded him throughout a year-long search of European waters, had steamed into Cherbourg the day before to discharge prisoners, take on coal, and perhaps refit. If he hurried, the telegram said, she might still be there when he arrived.

Winslow hurried. Firing a gun to recall his men on shore, he had the *Kearsarge* under weigh within two hours. Two days later he entered Cherbourg harbor, three hundred miles to the west, and there "lying at anchor in the roads" was the rebel vessel, just as he had prayed she would be. He stopped engines and lay to, looking her over and being in turn looked over; which done, he left to assume a position in the English Channel, beyond the three-mile limit required by international law, for intercepting her when she ventured out. He took precautions against a sudden night attack, knowing the enemy to be tricky, but his principal fear was that the raider might slip past him in the dark and thus avoid the fate he had in mind for her.

He need not have worried on that score, he discovered next day when the American vice consul sent him a message just received from the skipper of the *Alabama:* "My intention is to fight the *Kearsarge* as soon as I can make the necessary arrangements. I hope these will not detain me more than until tomorrow evening, or after the morrow morning at furthest. I beg she will not depart before I am ready to go out. . . . I have the honor to be, respectfully, your obedient servant, *R. Semmes*, Captain."

Winslow made no reply to this except to maintain station beyond the breakwater; which, after all, was answer enough, and spared him moreover the loss of dignity involved in exchanging cards, as it were, with a "pirate" who by now had captured, burned, or ransomed 83 U.S. merchant vessels, worth more than five million dollars, and sunk the heavier gunboat *Hatteras* in short order. Raphael Semmes, for his part, gave all his attention to trimming ship, drilling his gun crews, and otherwise preparing to meet the challenge extended by the *Kearsarge* when she steamed into the harbor, looked him over from stem to stern, then turned with the same cool insolence and steamed back out again to await his response, if any, to the insult. "The combat will no doubt be contested and obstinate," he wrote in his journal that night, "but the two ships are so evenly matched that I do not feel at liberty to decline it. God defend the right, and have mercy upon the souls of those who fall, as many of us must."

Fame aside — for Winslow had none whatever, and the *Kearsarge* had never been within gunshot of a foe; whereas Semmes and the *Alabama* were better known around the world than any other sailor or vessel afloat — the two warships and their captains were indeed quite evenly matched. Messmates for a time in the Mexican War, both men were southern-born, the Confederate in Maryland, Winslow farther south in North Carolina; Semmes was fifty-five, his opponent less than two years younger, and both had close to forty years of naval service, having received appointments as midshipmen in their middle teens. Alike as they were in their histories up to the outbreak of the current war, they were altogether different in looks. Winslow, going blind in his right eye, was rather heavy-set and balding, with a compensating ruff of gray-shot whiskers round his jaw, while Semmes was tall and slender, with a full head of hair, a tuft of beard at his lower lip, and a fantastical mustache twisted to needle points beyond the outline of his face; "Old Beeswax," his men called him.

Conversely, it was not in their histories, which were about as mutually different as could be, but in their physical attributes that the two ships were alike. Both were three-masted and steam-propelled, just over two hundred feet in length and a thousand tons in weight. *Kearsarge* had a complement of 163, *Alabama* about a dozen less. The Federal carried seven guns, the Confederate eight — though this implied advantage was deceptive, mainly because of a pair of 11-inch Dahlgrens mounted on pivots along the center line of the *Kearsarge*, which, combined with the 32-pounders on each flank, enabled her to throw a 365-pound broadside, port or starboard. *Alabama*'s heaviest guns were an 8-inch smoothbore and a 7-inch Blakely rifle, also pivot-mounted, so that, in combination with three 32-pounders on each flank, her broadside came to 264 pounds, a hundred less than her adversary's. Two other disadvantages she had, both possibly dire. One was the state of her ammunition, which had not been replenished since she was commissioned, nearly two years ago; percussion caps had lately been failing to explode the shells, whose powder had been weakened by exposure to various climates on most of the seven seas. The other disadvantage had to do with the vessel's maneuverability and speed. Entering Cherbourg harbor, Semmes declared, she was like "the weary foxhound, limping back after a long chase, footsore and longing for quiet and repose." He had intended to put her in dry dock and give all aboard a two-month holiday; her bottom, badly fouled, needed scraping and recoppering, and her boilers had begun to leak at the seams. *Kearsarge*, on the other hand, though nine months older, had been refitted only three months ago and was in trim shape for the contest. Semmes, however, had confidence in his crew, which he affectionately referred to as "a precious set of rascals," his Blakely rifle, which not only had more range but also provided greater accuracy than did Winslow's outsized Dahlgrens, and his luck, which had never failed him yet.

Concern for this last but by no means least of the things in which he put his trust caused him to defer the promised action three days beyond the "morrow morning at furthest" he had fixed in his Wednesday note begging Winslow not to depart. He wanted to fight on Sunday, considering that his lucky day. It was a Sunday when he ran the *Sumter*, his first raider, past the Union gauntlet below New Orleans, out of the mouth of the Mississippi and into the Gulf of Mexico to begin his career as the scourge of Yankee commerce; a Sunday off the Azores, back in August '62, when he christened the *Alabama*, and a Sunday when he sank the *Hatteras*, as well as many of the other prizes he had taken in the course of the past three years.

His crew found the waiting hard, being anxious for the duel and the shore leave that would follow, but Semmes and his officers kept them busy. They cleaned and oiled the guns and other weapons, including cutlasses and pikes, sorted powder and shot from the magazines and laid them out in relays, took down the light spars, disposed of top hamper, and stoppered the standing rigging. They polished brasswork and holystoned the decks as for a ball, and while they worked they roared out a chantey a British seaman composed for the occasion:

> *We're homeward bound, homeward bound,*
> *And soon shall stand on English ground.*
> *But ere that English land we see*
> *We first must fight the Kearsargee!*

Such work continued through Saturday, June 18, when Semmes, aware that "the issue of combat is always uncertain," put ashore four sacks containing 4700 gold sovereigns, the ransom bonds of ten ships he had released for lack of space for their crews aboard the *Alabama*, and the large collection of chronometers taken from his victims, which he periodically wound by way of keeping tally or counting coup. After notifying the port authorities that he would be steaming out next morning, he went ashore for Mass, then came back and turned in early as an example for his officers and men, who did so too, despite many invitations to dine that night in Cherbourg with admirers.

Sunday dawned bright and nearly cloudless, cool for June, with a calm sea and a mild westerly breeze to clear the battle smoke away. After a leisurely breakfast, the crew weighed anchor at 9.45 and headed out, cheered by crowds along the mole and in the upper windows of houses affording a view of the Channel and the *Kearsarge*, still on station beyond the breakwater. News of the impending duel had been in all the papers for the past three days and excursion trains had brought so many spectators from Paris and other cities that there was no room left in the hotels; many sportsmen-excursionists had slept on the docks, as if at the entrance to a stadium on the night before a game between archrivals. They fluttered handkerchiefs and cheered, some waving small Confederate flags hawked by vendors along with spyglasses and camp stools. "Vivent les Confederates!" they cried, looking down at the trim and polished raider, all of whose sailors were dressed in their Sunday best except the gun crews, who were stripped to the waist, like athletes indeed, and stood about on decks that had been sanded to keep them from slipping in their blood when the contest opened. "Vivent les Confederates!" the crowd shrilled, flourishing its home-team pennants triumphantly when the *Kearsarge*, seeing the *Alabama* emerge from around the western end of the breakwater, turned suddenly and steamed away northeastward, as if in unpremeditated flight.

Semmes knew better: knew, indeed, that this maneuver signified that his adversary meant to give him the fight-to-a-finish he was seeking. Engaged in reading the Sunday service when a yardarm watchman sang out the warning, "She's coming out and she's headed straight for us!" Winslow closed the prayer book, ordered the drum to beat to quarters, and brought his ship about in a run for bluer water, his intention being to lure the rebel well beyond the three-mile limit, inside which she could take sanctuary in case she was disabled. This applied as well to the *Kearsarge*, of course, but Winslow was thinking of punishment he would inflict, rather than of damage he might suffer; his aim was not just to cripple, but to kill.

The warning had been given at 10.20; at 10.40, some seven miles out, he once more came about and bore down on the *Alabama*, just over two miles away, wanting to bring his two big Dahlgrens within range of his adversary.

Semmes held his course, closing fast. Resplendent in a new gray uniform, long-skirted and with a triple row of bright brass buttons down the breast, epaulets and polished sword making three fierce glints of sunlight, he had had all hands piped aft as soon as he cleared the breakwater, then mounted a gun carriage to deliver his first speech since setting out from the Azores. "Officers and seamen of the *Alabama!*" he declaimed, pale but calm behind the fantastical mustache whose spike-tips quivered as he spoke. "You have, at length, another opportunity of meeting the enemy — the first that has been presented to you since you sank the *Hatteras....* The name of your ship has become a household word wherever civilization extends. Shall that name be tarnished by defeat? The thing is impossible! Remember that you are in the English Channel, the theater of so much of the naval glory of our race, and that the eyes of all Europe are at this moment upon you. The flag that floats over you is that of a young Republic who bids defiance to her enemies, whenever and wherever found; show the world that you know how to uphold it. Go to your quarters!" Having said as much, he set the example, while the crew still cheered, by taking station on the horseblock abreast the mizzenmast, a vantage point from which he could see and be seen by the enemy throughout the fight to come.

Watch in hand, he waited until there was barely a mile between the two ships bearing down on each other, then at 10.57 turned to his executive, Lieutenant John Kell, a six-foot two-inch Georgian who, like himself, was a veteran of the old navy: "Are you ready, Mr Kell?" Kell said he was. "Then you may open fire at once, sir."

The Blakely roared. Its 100-pound shell raised a sudden geyser, well short of the target, and was followed within two minutes by another, which, overcorrected, went screaming through the Federal's rigging. By now the other guns had joined, but their shots too were high, fired without proper calculation of the reduction of space between the rapidly closing vessels. Not until the range was down to half a mile did Winslow return fire, sheering to bring his starboard battery to bear. All the shots fell short, but Semmes had to port his helm sharply to keep from being raked astern. He succeeded, though at the cost of having *Kearsarge* close the range. As the Confederate swung back to starboard, Winslow followed suit and the two warships began to describe a circle, steaming clockwise around a common center and firing at each other across the half-mile diameter.

Alabama drew first blood with a shell that exploded on the Union quarterdeck and knocked out three of the after Dahlgren's crew. Then came what Semmes had prayed for, ashore at church last night. A shell from the Blakely struck and lodged itself in the sternpost of the *Kearsarge.* But as he watched through his telescope, awaiting the explosion that would signal the end of the enemy vessel — "Splendid! Splendid!" he exclaimed from his perch on the horseblock — the long moment passed with no sign of smoke or flame in that vital spot. The projectile, a dud, accomplished nothing except to make the helmsman's job a little harder by binding the rudder, which was already set to starboard anyhow. *Alabama*'s gunners kept hard at it, firing fast while straining for another, luckier hit.

Winslow's gunnery was methodical by contrast, and a good deal more effective; he would get off a total of 173 shots in the course of the engagement, only about half as many as Semmes, but the accuracy in both cases, a tally of hits and misses would show, was in inverse ratio to the rate of fire. As the two sloops continued their wheeling fight, churning along in one another's wake, a three-knot current bore them westward so that they described a series of overlapping circles, each a little tighter than the one before, with the result that the range was constantly shortened, from half a mile on the first circle, down to little more than a quarter-mile on the seventh, which turned out to be the last.

From the outset, once the blue crews got on target, the damage inflicted by the 11-inchers was prodigious; *Alabama* was repeatedly hit and hulled by the 135½-pound shells aimed at her waterline by the Dahlgrens, in accordance with Winslow's orders, while the 32-pounders swept her decks. The combined effect was devastating: as for example when a projectile breached the 8-inch smoothbore's port, disemboweling the first man it struck, then plunging on to mangle eighteen others when it blew. Survivors and replacements cleared away the wounded and heaved the corpses overboard, but resumption of fire had to wait for a shovel to be used to scrape up the slippery gobs of flesh and splinters of bone; only then, with the deck re-sanded, could the crew secure a proper footing for its work. Meantime, Semmes had seen the most discouraging thing he had encountered since the shot lodged in the enemy sternpost failed to explode. Observing that shells of all sizes were bouncing ineffectively off the Federal's sides, like so many tennis balls, he told Kell to switch to solids for better penetration. Yet these too either splintered or rebounded, and it was not until after the battle that he found out that the cause lay in anything more than the weakened condition of his powder. *Kearsarge* was armored along her midriff with 120 fathoms of sheet chain, suspended from her scuppers to below her waterline, bolted down and boxed out of sight with one-inch planking. Indignant at the belated disclosure that his adversary was "iron-clad," Semmes protested that this violation of the code duello had produced an unfair fight. "It was the same thing as if two men were to go out and fight a duel, and one of them, unknown to the other, were to put on a suit of mail under his outer garment."

However true or false the analogy — and Old Beeswax, one of the trickiest skippers ever to prowl the sea lanes, was scarcely in a position to protest the use of a stratagem that had been common in all navies ever since Farragut employed it, more than two years ago, to run past the forts below New Orleans — the *Alabama*, with all her timbers aquiver from the pounding being inflicted by the *Kearsarge*, was clearly nearing the end of her career. Semmes, nicked in the right hand by a fragment of shell as the raider went into her seventh circle, had a quartermaster bind up the wound and rig a sling, never leaving his perch on the horseblock. From there he could see better than anyone the damage being done his ship and the ineffectiveness of his return fire. This seventh circle must be the last. The only course left was to attempt a run for safety. Accordingly, he told the exec: "Mr Kell, as soon as our head points to the French coast in our circuit of action, shift your guns to port and make all sail for the coast."

Kell tried, but Winslow quickly interposed the *Kearsarge*, slamming in shots from dead ahead and at a shorter range than ever. At this point the *Alabama*'s chief engineer came topside to report that his fires were being flooded by rising water from holes the Dahlgrens were blasting in the hull. "Go below, Mr Kell," Semmes said grimly, "and see how long the ship can float."

The Georgian went, and on his way through the wardroom saw a sight he would never forget. Assistant Surgeon David Llewellyn, a Briton and the only non-Southerner among the two dozen officers aboard, stood poised alongside where his operating table and patient had been until an 11-inch solid crashed through the adjoining bulkhead, snatching table, wounded seaman, and all his instruments from under the ministering hand of the doctor, who stood there, abruptly alone, with a dazed expression of horror and disbelief. Kell continued down to the engine room, where he saw through the steam from her drowned fires that the ship could scarcely remain afloat another ten minutes. He picked his way back up, through the wreckage and past the still-dazed surgeon, to report to the captain that the *Alabama*'s ordeal was nearly over.

"Then sir," Semmes replied, "cease firing, shorten sail, and haul down the colors. It will never do in this nineteenth century for us to go down, and the decks covered with our gallant wounded."

Across the water, less than 500 yards away, Winslow saw the rebel flag come down, but being, as he later explained, "uncertain whether Captain Semmes was using some ruse," called out to his gun crews: "He's playing a trick on us. Give him another broadside." They did just that, adding to the carnage on *Alabama*'s bloody, ripped-up decks with every gun that could be brought to bear; whereupon a white flag was run up from the stern. "Cease firing!" Winslow cried at last.

Through his telescope he observed on board the sinking raider a pantomime that called up within him, in rapid sequence, mixed emotions of pity, mistrust, sympathy, and resentment. Settling fast, with only a thread of smoke from her riddled stack, the *Alabama* had lost headway; Semmes, though still on his horseblock, obviously had given

the order to abandon ship. While some of the crew milled about in confusion, engaging Winslow's pity by their plight — which, after all,
might have been his own if the 100-pound shell lodged in his sternpost
had not turned out to be a dud — others aroused his mistrust by piling
into a dinghy and shoving off, apparently in an attempt to avoid capture.
This was disproved, however, when the dinghy made for the *Kearsarge*
and he saw, when it came within hailing distance, that it was filled
with wounded men, including a master's mate who shouted up a request
that boats be sent to rescue survivors gone over the side and thrashing
about in the water.

Winslow had only two boats not smashed in the course of the
fight, but he ordered them lowered without further delay and gave
permission, moreover, for the rebel dinghy to be used as well, once
the wounded had been unloaded. Obviously, though, these three small
boats would not hold all the men in the water; so he called through his
speaking trumpet to a nearby English pleasure yacht whose owner had
sailed out of Cherbourg that morning for a closeup view of the duel:
"For God's sake, do what you can to save them!" The yacht responded
promptly, and as she did so Winslow turned his telescope back to the
final scene of the tableau being enacted on *Alabama*'s canted deck.

The rebel skipper by now had descended from his perch, and he
and another officer, a large, heavily bearded man — John Kell — began
to undress for their leap into the Channel. The big man stripped to his
underwear, but Semmes, apparently mindful of his dignity, retained
his trousers and waistcoat. He seemed to part reluctantly with his sword.
After unbuckling it rather awkwardly with his unhurt left hand, he
held it above his head for a long moment, flashing brightly in the noonday sunlight, before he did the thing that brought Winslow's resentment to a boil. He flung it whirling and glinting into the sea, thereby
making impossible the ceremony of handing it over to his vanquisher.
Winslow could scarcely expect him to bring it along while he swam
one-handed across four hundred yards of choppy water to the *Kearsarge*
to surrender, but it seemed to the Federal captain that his adversary
took a spiteful pleasure in this gesture which deprived him of a customary right.

Semmes followed Kell and his sword into the Channel, and the
two men struck out as best they could, the former clutching a life
preserver, the latter a wooden grating, to avoid the suction that might
pull them under when the *Alabama* sank. She was filling fast now, air
gurgling, hissing, chuckling under her punctured decks while the sea
poured in through rents in her hull. Her stern awash, her prow was
lifting, and suddenly it rose higher as her guns, still hot from battle,
tore loose from their lashings and slid aft. The breeze freshening, she
recovered a little headway with her sails, and as she moved she left behind her a broad ribbon of flotsam, broken spars and bodies, bits of

tackle and other gear. Fifty yards off, Semmes turned to watch her die. Backward she went, beginning her long downward slide, anchors swinging wildly in the air below her bow; the main-topmast, split by a solid in the fight, went by the board when she paused, nearly vertical; then she was gone, the Channel boiling greenly for a time to mark the place where she had been.

It was 12.24, just under ninety minutes since she fired her first shot at the *Kearsarge*. For all his grief, Semmes was glad in at least one sense that she was on the forty-fathom bottom with his sword. "A noble Roman once stabbed his daughter, rather than she should be polluted by the foul embrace of a tyrant," he later wrote. "It was with a similar feeling that Kell and I saw the *Alabama* go down. We had buried her as we had christened her, and she was safe from the polluting touch of the hated Yankee!"

By now the trim British yacht *Deerhound* — whose captain-owner John Lancaster, a wealthy industrialist on vacation with his family, had had her built up the Clyde by the Lairds two years ago, at the same time they were at work on the sloop that became the *Alabama* — was within reach of the crewmen bobbing amid the whitecaps. She lowered her boats and began fishing them out, including Semmes and Kell and Marine Lieutenant Beckett Howell (Varina Davis's younger brother) but not Dr Llewellyn; a nonswimmer, he had drowned. Forty-two men were saved in all by the *Deerhound* in response to Winslow's plea; another dozen by the captains of two French pilot boats, who needed no urging; while seventy more were taken and made captive aboard the *Kearsarge*. Semmes himself might have been among these last except for Kell's quick thinking. Exhausted, the Confederate skipper was laid "as if dead" on the sternsheets of one of *Deerhound*'s boats when the *Kearsarge* cutter came alongside. "Have you seen Captain Semmes?" a blue-clad officer asked sharply. Kell, who had put on a *Deerhound* crewman's cap and taken an oar to complete the disguise, had a ready answer. "Captain Semmes is drowned," he said, to the Federal's apparent satisfaction. Aboard the yacht, after the shipwrecked men had been given hot coffee and shots of rum to counter the chill and exhaustion, Lancaster put the question: "Where shall I land you?" This time it was Semmes who had the answer that meant salvation. "I am now under English colors," he said, "and the sooner you put me, with my officers and men, on English soil the better."

Well before nightfall the *Deerhound* put in at Southampton, where, news of the battle having preceded them, Semmes and his men were given a welcome as hearty as if they had won; "A set of first-rate fellows," the London *Times* pronounced them. As soon as he had rested from his ordeal, the Maryland-born Alabamian used the gold left at Cherbourg to pay off the survivors and send allotments to the nearest kin of the nine men killed in action and twelve drowned. He was banqueted by admirers, including officers of the Royal Navy, who united to present him with an elegant, gold-mounted sword, engraved along the blade to signify that it was a replacement for the one he had flung into the Channel after his "engagement off Cherbourg with a chain-plated ship of superior power, armament, and crew." However, when Confederate officials tendered him a new command with which to continue the record begun aboard the *Sumter*, he declined, needing time to absorb the shock of his "impossible" defeat. Though he was promoted to rear admiral and eventually made his way, via Cuba and Mexico, back to the Confederacy (none of whose ports the *Alabama* ever touched) he had done all he would do afloat. Other raiders would continue to strike at Yankee shipping around the globe, but not Raphael Semmes. "I considered my career upon the high seas closed by the loss of my ship," he later explained.

As for Winslow, he too was being lionized by now as the man who had abolished in single combat the myth that the *Alabama* was invincible. After clearing his decks and assembling the crew for thanks-giving prayers — which helped to ease his dudgeon at having seen the British yachtsman make off with his prize of prizes, Semmes — he steamed into Cherbourg, flags aflutter from every mast of the *Kearsarge*, and was promptly surrounded by boatloads of people out to greet the ship whose victorious crew had somehow been transformed into the home team.

Her casualties were limited to the three men hit early in the duel, one of whom died a few days later; *Alabama*'s came to 43, just under half of them drowned or killed in action. Once he had paroled his pris-oners and patched up superficial damage, Winslow went to Paris to consult a specialist about his failing eye, only to learn that he had waited too long for treatment to be of any use. A victory banquet, tendered by patriotic fellow countrymen in the French capital, helped to dispel the medical gloom of the occasion, and a letter from Gideon Welles was even more effective in that regard. "I congratulate you," the Secretary wrote, "on your good fortune in meeting the *Alabama*, which had so long avoided the fastest ships and some of the most vigilant and intelli-gent officers of the service, and for the ability displayed in the contest you have the thanks of the Department.... The battle was so brief, the victory so decisive, and the comparative results so striking that the country will be reminded of the brilliant actions of our infant Navy, which have been repeated and illustrated in the engagement."

Presently this was followed, upon the President's recommendation, by a vote of thanks from Congress and a promotion to date from June 19. Commodore Winslow returned to the United States by the end of the year, and while the *Kearsarge* was being refitted in the Boston Navy Yard carpenters removed a section of her sternpost, still with the 100-pound dud embedded in the oak, and boxed it for shipment to

Washington, the Commander in Chief having expressed a desire to see for himself what a close call the ship and all aboard had had on that famous Sunday, six miles out in the English Channel, when she sank the *Alabama*.

Lincoln was indeed glad to learn that the most famed of rebel raiders had been struck from the list of woes to be endured until the war had run its course. Lately, though, he had begun to perceive that while striving to keep up national morale he would also have to deal with national impatience, which mounted with every indication, true or false, that the end might not be far off. Earlier that week, on June 14 — the day Bishop Polk was cannon-sniped on Pine Top and Grant began crossing the James — he had confessed to a friendly newsman that the country's tendency to "expect too much at once" was, for him, a matter of considerable private anxiety: "I wish, when you write or speak to people, you would do all you can to correct the impression that the war in Virginia will end right off and victoriously. . . . As God is my judge, I shall be satisfied if we are over with the fight in Virginia within a year. I hope we shall be 'happily disappointed,' as the saying is; but I am afraid not. I am afraid not."

This was something new, this concern lest the public, in its ebullience, demand an end to the war before it was won, and Lincoln bore down to counteract it two days later, nine days after his renomination, when he went to attend and address a sanitary fair in Philadelphia. "It is a pertinent question often asked in the mind privately, and from one to the other: When is the war to end? Surely I feel as deep an interest in this question as anyone can, but I do not wish to name a day, or month, or a year when it is to end. I do not wish to run any risk of seeing the time come, without our being ready for the end, and for fear of disappointment because the time had come and not the end. We accepted this war for an object, a worthy object, and the war will end when that object is attained. Under God, I hope it never will until that time."

Cheers went up at this, and he pressed on to warn his hearers that the approach of victory might call for more, not fewer sacrifices. "If I shall discover that General Grant and the noble officers and men under him can be greatly facilitated in their work by a sudden pouring forward of men and assistance, will you give them to me?"

"Yes! Yes!" the crowd roared, catching fire.

"Then I say, stand ready," Lincoln told the upturned faces about the rostrum, as well as those that would be downturned over tomorrow's newspapers all across the land, "for I am watching for the chance."

✗ 3 ✗

Now that Johnston had relinquished Pine Top, retiring down its rear-ward slope with the corpse of Bishop Polk, Sherman followed close on his heels, determined to keep up the pressure which, so far, had gained him eighty of the critical hundred air-line miles between Chattanooga and Atlanta, his base and his objective. He did so with caution, however, being confronted on the left and right by the loom of Brush and Lost mountains, both occupied by butternut marksmen who asked nothing more, in the way of compensation for their pains, than one quick glimpse down their rifle barrels at blue-clad soldiers moving toward them, within range and without cover. "We cannot risk the heavy loss of an assault at this distance from our base," the red-haired Ohioan had wired Halleck on the day before Polk's mangling. But on June 16, two days after that event, he changed his mind and began to consider trying what he had said he could not risk. "I am now inclined to feign on both flanks and assault the center," he told Old Brains. "It may cost us dear, but in results would surpass any attempt to pass around."

Presently, though, he changed his mind again — or, more strictly speaking, had it changed for him by Johnston, who gave him the slip the following night with another of his "clean retreats." This one was not so much an outright withdrawal, however, as it was a rectification, an adjustment whereby the foxy Confederate not only shortened his rather extended line but also shored up the sagging center Sherman had planned to assault. Turning loose of the high ground on his flanks, he fell back to Kennesaw Mountain, two miles in rear of the abandoned Pine Top salient. Polk's corps — temporarily under Major General W. W. Loring, the senior division commander — was posted there, dug in along its northern face, with Hood on the right, astride the Western & Atlantic, and Hardee on the left, denying the Federals access to Marietta by blocking the roads coming in from Dallas and Burnt Hickory. Johnston's line, which had been concave after he gave up Pine Top, was now convex, and its center, which had been its weakest element when Sherman contemplated launching a headlong strike, was now its stoutest part. In point of fact, the graybacks had occupied no stronger position in the course of their six-week retreat.

"Kennesaw Mountain is, I should think, about 700 feet high," an Illinois major wrote home in reaction to his first sight of this for-bidding piece of geography reared up in the army's path, "and consists of two points or peaks, separated by a narrow gorge running across the top. The mountain itself is entirely separated from all mountain ranges, and swells up like a great bulb from the plain." Sherman too was im-pressed and given pause by what he called "the bold and striking twin mountain." Rebel signalmen were at work on its two bulbous peaks, both of which were "crowned with batteries," while "the spurs were alive with men busy felling trees, digging pits, and preparing for the grand struggle impending." As he stood and looked, awe gave way to determination. "The scene was enchanting; too beautiful to be disturbed by the harsh clamor of war," he was to say, years later; "but the Chattahoochee lay beyond, and I had to reach it."

He had to reach it; but how? In an attempt to find some easier means than a headlong assault, which seemed foredoomed, he brought up his guns and began to pound away at the fortified slopes of the mountain, hoping to fix the enemy in position there while he probed both flanks of the rebel line in search of a way around it, one that would enable him to menace the railroad in Johnston's rear and thus provoke him into abandoning his present all-but-impregnable position, as he had done so many others in the course of his long retreat, rather than risk a fight whose loss would mean the severance of his supply line. The result was a series of skirmishes, some of which attained the dignity of engagements, first at Gilgal Church, where the graybacks fought a holding action to cover their withdrawal, and then along Mud and Nose (or Noyes) creeks, both of which had to be crossed if Sherman was to turn the rebel left for a strike at Marietta, Johnston's base, two miles back of Kennesaw, or at Smyrna Station, another four miles down the railroad. While Schofield, reinforced by Hooker, was doing all he could in that direction, McPherson, strengthened by Blair's return the week before, was feeling out the Confederate right, but with little success, being under the guns and surveillance of the enemy on the taller of Kennesaw's two peaks. Thomas meantime kept up the pressure dead ahead, firing so many rounds from his massed batteries — he had 130 guns in all: half a dozen more than McPherson and Schofield combined — that his soldiers, watching the bombardment from dug-in positions on the flat, began to tell each other that Uncle Billy was determined to take the double-crested mountain in their front, or else "fill it full of old iron."

For three days this continued, neither Thomas nor McPherson achieving much with their pounding and probing, and then on June 22, having proceeded well to the south around Kennesaw's western flank, Schofield too was brought to a sudden halt.

It happened at a place called Culp's (or Kolb's) Farm, four miles southwest of Marietta on the road from Powder Springs, and it came about because Johnston, in reaction to Sherman's continuing effort to reach around his left, had issued instructions the night before for Hood, whose intrenchments on the right would be occupied temporarily by Wheeler's dismounted troopers, to march at daylight across the rear of Kennesaw and go into position beyond Hardee on the far left, south of the mountain's western flank, in order to block the Federal turning movement. Hood did this, and more. Within a mile of his objective by midday, he encountered troops from Schofield's corps advancing up the Powder Springs Road, and with soldierly instinct, but without taking time for reconnaissance, attacked at once.

Assuming he had the flankers outflanked, he figured that a prompt assault would "roll them up," drive them back with heavy casualties, and abolish this threat to Johnston's lifeline. The result was heavy casualties, all right, though not for Schofield, who had taken the precaution of having his and Hooker's men dig in while awaiting reports from patrols sent out to find the best route up the valley of Olley's Creek for a strike at the Western & Atlantic above Smyrna, three miles across the way. Hood drove these forward elements rapidly back, giving chase with the two divisions on hand, but at Culp's Farm the pursuers came unexpectedly upon the enemy main body, stoutly intrenched, and were bloodily repulsed. A second assault, launched near sundown, only added to the carnage; Stevenson's division alone lost more than 800 men, and Hindman's brought the total to better than 1000. Schofield and Hooker, whose soldiers did their fighting behind earthworks for a change, suffered less than a third that many casualties in breaking the two attacks. Then at nightfall, while the graybacks dug in too along the line where the fighting stopped, Schofield and Hood sent word to their superiors at Big Shanty and Marietta of what had happened.

Johnston's anger at this loss of a thousand badly needed veterans, once more as a result of Hood's impetuosity, was exceeded by Sherman's when he received an out-of-channels dispatch that evening from Hooker, proudly reporting that he had "repulsed two heavy attacks" and calling urgently for reinforcements before he was overrun. "Three entire corps are in front of us," he added by way of lending weight to his proud cry for help. "Hooker must be mistaken; Johnston's army has only three corps," Sherman noted in passing the message along to Thomas, who, knowing only too well that Hardee and Loring were still in position to his and McPherson's front, replied rather mildly: "I look upon this as something of a stampede." Sherman agreed and next morning, still miffed, rode down to Culp's Farm in a pouring rain to tell Fighting Joe he wanted no more of his boasts and misrepresentations. In reaction, Hooker went into a month-long pout; or, as his superior later put it, "From that time he began to sulk."

This would have its consequences for all concerned; but the fact was, Sherman's anger had its source in something far more irksome than Hooker's inability to avoid exaggeration. Daylight showed the graybacks intrenched across Schofield's front. This meant that the army had gone as far as it could go in that direction without turning loose of its supply line, already under threat from rebel horsemen, and the drowned condition of the roads precluded any movement on them so long as the rain continued.

Confronted thus with the probability of a stalemate — which was not only undesirable on its own account, here in Georgia, but might also give Richmond the chance to reinforce Lee's hard-pressed Virginia army from Johnston's, biding its time north of the Chattahoochee — Sherman reverted to his notion, expressed a week ago, "to feign on both flanks and assault the center." The trouble was that the center now was Kennesaw Mountain, and Kennesaw seemed unassailable. But there, perhaps, was just the factor that might augur best; an attacker would greatly increase his chance for success by striking where the blow was least expected. Besides, continued probes by McPherson today showed that Loring's corps had been extended eastward to include a portion of the works abandoned yesterday by Hood when he set out westward to counter Schofield's flanking threat. That march, with its extension of the Confederate left while Loring spread out to cover the right, stretched Johnston's line to a width of about eight miles, exclusive of the cavalry on his flanks. It must be quite thin somewhere, and that somewhere was likely to be dead ahead on Kennesaw, whose frown alone was enough to discourage assault. So Sherman reasoned, at any rate, in his search for some way to avoid a stalemate. Moreover, he explained afterwards, he conferred with his three army commanders, "and we all agreed that we could not with prudence stretch out any more, and therefore there was no alternative but to attack 'fortified lines,' a thing carefully avoided up to that time."

Such a change in tactics, abruptly sprung, would also serve to increase the element of surprise, which figured largely in Sherman's calculations. But the outlook remained grim, if not downright awesome. "The whole country is one vast fort," he informed Halleck on June 23. "Johnston must have full fifty miles of connected trenches, with abatis and finished batteries.... Our lines are now in close contact and the fighting incessant, with a good deal of artillery. As fast as we gain one position, the enemy has another all ready."

These were minor adjustments, permitting no more than a closer look at the honeycombed slopes of the mountain up ahead, and a closer look only magnified the original impression of impregnability. One-armed Howard, studying the rebel line from a position well to the front, pronounced it "stronger in artificial contrivances and natural features than the cemetery at Gettysburg," which he had helped to hold despite Lee's all-out efforts to oust him. But Sherman refused to be distracted, let alone dissuaded. Determined, as he had told Grant the week before, to "inspire motion into a large, ponderous and slow, by habit, army," he believed that his soldiers, weary of roundabout marches that never quite managed to bring the enemy to bay, needed the stimulus the pending assault would provide, even if most of the blood that was shed turned out to be their own — and he was concerned, as well, lest Johnston's habitual caution, which had led him to give up so many stout positions in the course of the past seven weeks, should be replaced by a conviction that the Federals would never attack him once he was snugly intrenched. Both of these things counted heavily in the redhead's calculations, as did the promise of all that would be gained if the attack was anything like as successful as the one up Missionary Ridge, seven months ago, by many of these same men against many of these same opponents, with the difference that there had been no unfordable Chattahoochee in the rebel rear on that occasion.

Other factors there were, too, no less persuasive because Sherman himself — defined by Walt Whitman as "a bit of stern open air made up in the image of a man" — was perhaps not even aware of their influence on him. For one, the Union army in Virginia was not only doing most of the bleeding in the double-pronged offensive, it was also getting most of the headlines, and despite his dislike of journalists, and indeed of the press in general, he could see that his troops would be heartened by a more equitable distribution of praise, such as the overrunning of Kennesaw would secure. Moreover, back in Nashville and Chattanooga, while preparing for the campaign, he had learned that certain observers snidely characterized him as "not a fighting general." He dismissed the charge without exactly denying it, saying: "Fighting is the least part of a general's work. The battle will fight itself." Still, the imputation rankled, containing as it did some grains of truth, and he welcomed the opportunity, now at hand, to refute it for once and for all. On June 24 he issued a special field order directing his army commanders to "make full reconnaissances and preparations to attack the enemy in force on the 27th instant, at 8 a.m. precisely."

That left two full days for getting set; Sherman, having decided to be rash, had also decided to go about it methodically, even meticulously, so as to minimize the cost if the breakthrough failed. For one thing, he would limit the weight of his assault to less than a fifth of the troops on hand, and for another, despite its regrettable but inevitable detraction from the element of surprise, the jump-off would be preceded by an hour-long bombardment from every gun that could be brought to bear on the critical objectives. Of these there were two, main and secondary, neither of them, properly speaking, on the mountain that would give the battle its name, although the secondary effort, assigned to McPherson, would be made against — and, if successful, across — the gently rolling southwest slope of the lower of the two peaks, called Little Kennesaw to distinguish it from Big Kennesaw, the taller and more massive portion of the mountain to the east, overlooking the slow curve of the Western & Atlantic on that flank. This attack would be launched astride the Burnt Hickory Road, simultaneously with Thomas's main effort, along and to the right of the Dallas Road, one mile south; both commanders would assault with two divisions,

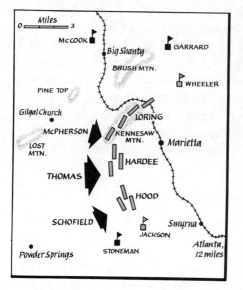

their others standing by to exploit whatever progress was achieved. Schofield and Hooker would feint on the far right, Garrard's cavalry on the left, all at the same prearranged hour, hard on the heels of the softening-up artillery bombardment, so as to prevent Johnston from knowing which part of his line to reinforce from any other, or from his reserves if he had them, before it was swamped. "At the time of the general attack," the special order ended, foreseeing a happy outcome to the rashness so meticulously prescribed, "the skirmishers at the base of Kennesaw will take advantage of it to gain, if possible, the summit and hold it. Each attacking column will endeavor to break a single point of the enemy's line, and make a secure lodgment beyond, and be prepared for following it up toward Marietta and the railroad in case of success."

Throughout that two-day interim, although few along the eight-mile curve of intrenchments knew what they were waiting or getting set for — "All commanders will maintain reserve and secrecy even from their staff officers," the field order had cautioned — fire fights, picket clashes, and sudden cannonades would break into flame from point to point, then subside into sputters and die away, sporadic, inconclusive, and productive of little more than speculation. Whether off on the flanks or crouched near the critical center, men listened and wondered, unable to find a pattern to the action. The crash of guns would come from somewhere up or down the line, an Indiana soldier would recall, "then the hurrahing, sometimes the shrill, boyish rebel yell, sometimes the loud, full-voiced, deep-toned, far-sounding chorus of northern men; then again the roar of cannon, the rattle of musketry and the awful suspense to the listeners. If, as the noise grew feebler, we caught the welcome cheer, answering shouts ran along. But if the far-off rebel yell told of our comrades' repulse, the silence could be felt."

Across the way, within the horseshoe curve of works containing Kennesaw and Marietta, the reaction was much the same, but in reverse. No one there could discern a pattern either, including the men of Major Generals Samuel French's and Benjamin Cheatham's divisions of Loring's and Hardee's corps, respectively astride the Burnt Hickory and Dallas roads, up which the two Union assaults were to be delivered on Monday morning, June 27, one week past the summer solstice.

The rain left off on Sunday and the sun came up in a cloudless sky next morning at 4.40 to begin its work of drying the red clay roads, the sodden fields and breathless woods. By the time it was three hours high the day was hot and steamy with the promise of much greater heat to come. Twenty minutes later, precisely at 8 o'clock and without preamble, 200-odd Union cannon roared into action, pounding away at the rebel line on the mountainside and across the flats beyond. Crouched in their pits and ditches, jarred and shaken about by the sudden hurtle of metal exploding over and around them, the defenders marveled at the volume and intensity of the fire, which was to them still another manifestation of Yankee ingenuity and wealth. "Hell has broke loose in Georgia, sure enough!" one grayback shouted amid shellbursts, and as the bombardment continued, sustained by an apparently inexhaustible supply of ammunition, they began to snatch down the blankets pegged for shade across the open tops of their trenches, preparing for what they knew would come when the guns let up. Finally, close to 9 o'clock, the uproar reached a spasmodic end; the cannoneers stepped back from their pieces, panting, and the blue infantry started forward in two clotted masses, about a mile apart, to assail the Confederate center.

For a time they advanced in relative security, protected by the intervening woods and the butternut pickets trotting back to join their comrades along the main line of resistance. Then the attackers emerged into brilliant sunlight, silhouetted against the bright green backdrop of trees, and the rebel headlogs seemed to burst spontaneously into flame along their bottoms, all up and down that portion of the line. Sam French, whose left-flank division of Loring's corps was challenged first on Little Kennesaw's lower slopes, said later that the rattle and flash of musketry, combined with the deep-voiced boom of guns whose crews had held their fire till now, produced "a roar as constant as Niagara and as sharp as the crash of thunder with lightning in the eye."

Such was the fury of the sound that accompanied McPherson's attack, launched astride the Burnt Hickory Road by Brigadier General Morgan Smith, whose division was reinforced for the effort by a brigade from another division in Major General John A. Logan's corps. Sound and fury were all it came to, however, in the end. In the course of their plunge across a rocky, brush-choked gully, unexpectedly encountered in rear of the line abandoned by the gray pickets, 563 of the 4000 attackers fell before they could get to grips with the defenders intrenched on the far side. At one point "within about thirty feet of the enemy's main line," Smith reported, they came close; but there, receiving the full blast of massed rifles, they "staggered and sought cover as best they could behind logs and rocks." Stalled ("It was almost sure death to take your face out of the dust," one prone Federal declared, while another expressed a somewhat less gloomy view of the consequences, saying: "It was only necessary to expose a hand to procure a furlough") they were no longer much of a threat to French, who turned his high-sited batteries a quarter circle to the left and added the weight of the metal to Hardee's resistance, a mile away, astride and beyond the Dallas Road.

There Thomas was making a sturdier bid for a breakthrough, and Cheatham's division had all it could do to keep from being overrun by nearly twice as many Federals as French had had to deal with. "They seemed to walk up and take death as coolly as if they were automatic or wooden men," one defender was to say of these troops from two divisions under Jeff Davis and Brigadier General John Newton, respectively of Palmer's and Howard's corps.

Two of Cheatham's four brigades were posted where Hardee's line bent sharply to the south, creating a somewhat isolated salient, and it was here at the hinge, known thereafter as the Dead Angle, that Thomas struck. "The least flicker on our part would have been sure death to all," a Tennessee private who helped to hold it later declared. "We could not be reinforced on account of our position, and we had to stand up to the rack, fodder or no fodder." They did stand up, inflicting in the process — with the help of French's guns and Cleburne, whose marksmen brought their rifles to bear from up the line — a total of 654 casualties on Newton and 824 on Davis, both of whom notified their superiors that they hoped they could hang on where they were, if that was what was wanted, but that there was no further hope of carrying the position. Howard put it strongest, some time later, looking back. "Our losses in this assault were heavy indeed," he wrote, "and our gain was nothing. We realized now, as never before, the futility of direct assault upon intrenched lines already well prepared and well manned." Thomas agreed, sending word around 11 o'clock for those who could fall back to do so at once, while those who could not were to dig in where they were and wait for darkness.

The sudden resultant drop in the intensity of the fighting came none too soon for the defenders of the Angle, one of whom was to testify that he fired no less than 120 rounds in the course of the repulse. "My gun became so hot that frequently the powder would flash before I could ram home the ball," he said, adding: "When the Yankees fell back and the firing ceased, I never saw so many broken down and exhausted men in my life. I was sick as a horse, and as wet with blood and sweat as I could be, and many of our men were vomiting with excessive fatigue, overexhaustion, and sunstroke; our tongues were parched and cracked for water, and our faces blackened with powder and smoke, and our dead and wounded were piled indiscriminately in the trenches."

Cheatham's loss came to 195, French's to 186; between them, they had shot down 2041 of the 12,000 Federals thrown against their works. Other losses, elsewhere in Loring's and Hardee's corps, as well as in Hood's, which had been skirmishing with Schofield all the while, brought the Confederate total to 552. Sherman put his at 2500 — a figure Johnston vowed was a good deal less than half the true one — but later revised it upward to "about 3000."

Even so, and despite the shock of the sudden double repulse, he had been willing to drive it still higher at the time. From Signal Hill, his command post on the left, he could see that McPherson had shot his wad, and word had come from Schofield that little could be done on the far right. That left Thomas, the Rock of Chickamauga. He too had been checked, losing two of his best brigade commanders in the process, but he might be willing to try again for a repetition of what he had achieved on Missionary Ridge despite conditions even more unfavorable. "McPherson and Schofield are at a deadlock," Sherman wired him at 1.30. "Do you think you can carry any part of the enemy's line to-day? . . . I will order the assault if you think you can succeed at any point." Thomas replied: "We have already lost heavily today without gaining any material advantage. One or two more such assaults would use up this army."

He recommended a change to siege methods, the digging of saps for a guarded approach. But Sherman, wanting no part of such a time-consuming business, preferred to maneuver the rebels out of position, as before. Encouraged by the let-up of the rain and the fast-drying condition of the roads, he telegraphed Thomas that evening: "Are you willing to risk [a] move on Fulton, cutting loose from our railroad?" Fulton was two miles beyond Smyrna Station, within three miles of the Chattahoochee and about ten miles in Johnston's rear; Sherman proposed to move by the right flank "with the whole army." Thomas considered the venture highly risky, exposing as it would the Union life line to Confederate seizure while the wheeling movement was in progress; but in any case, he replied before turning in for the night, "I think it de-cidedly better than butting against breastworks twelve feet thick and strongly abatised."

While waiting for the roads to finish drying Sherman worked on plans for his newest sidle and, eventually, on securing a truce for the burial of the unfortunates who had fallen in the double-pronged repulse. Undaunted — at least on paper — he took the offensive in defending his decision to strike at the rebel center, even though all it had got him was a lengthened casualty list. "The assault I made was no mistake; I had to do it," he wired Halleck, explaining that after nearly eight weeks of gingerly skirmishing, all the time conforming to a pattern about as precise as if he and Johnston were partners in a classic minuet, Federals and Confederates alike "had settled down into the conviction that the assault of lines formed no part of my game." Now that both sides knew better, having seen the dance pattern broken as if with a meat ax, he expected to find his adversary "much more cautious." That was his gain, as he saw it, and he continued to pursue this line of consolation. "Failure as it was, and for which I assume the entire responsibility," he would assert in his formal report of the lost battle, "I yet claim it produced good fruit, as it demonstrated to General Johnston that I would assault, and that boldly."

Earlier, while smoke still hung about the field and the wounded mewled for help between the lines, he had reminded Thomas: "Our loss is small compared with some of those in the East. It should not in the least discourage us. At times assaults are necessary and inevitable." However, his most forthright statement with regard to losses was reserved for his wife, to whom he wrote two days after the Kennesaw repulse. " I begin to regard the death and mangling of a couple of thousand men as a small affair, a kind of morning dash," he told her, adding: "It may be well that we become hardened. . . . The worst of the war is not yet begun."

That might well be, though there could be no denying that for a considerable number of his soldiers — young and old, recruits and veterans alike — the best was over, along with the worst. Their interment was a grisly thing to watch. "I get sick now when I happen to think about it," a Confederate wrote years later, remembering the June 30 burial armistice that was asked and granted "not for any respect either army had for the dead, but to get rid of the sickening stench." Although three days of festering midsummer Georgia heat had made the handling of the corpses a repugnant task, he recalled that Yankee ingenuity once more had measured up to the occasion. "Long and deep trenches were dug, and hooks made from bayonets crooked for the purpose, and all the dead were dragged and thrown pell mell into these trenches. Nothing was allowed to be taken off the dead, and finely dressed officers, with gold watch chains dangling over their vests, were thrown into the ditches. During the whole day both armies were hard at work, burying the Federal dead."

Thus June ended, bringing with it another pause for a backward look at the casualty count in each of the two armies. In both cases these were lower than they had been the month before, and they were similar in another way as well. Just as New Hope Church and Pickett's Mill, engagements fought near the bottom of the previous calendar leaf, had reversed the May tally, raising Sherman's losses above Johnston's, which had been higher than his opponent's before the clashes around Dallas, so now did Kennesaw Mountain reverse the count for June, which had been lower for the Union up till then. Sherman's loss for the past month was 7500, Johnston's around 6000. This brought their respective totals for the whole campaign to just under 17,000 and just over 14,000. Roughly speaking, to put it another way, one out of every four Confederates had been shot or captured, as compared to one out of seven Federals.

In time, when the guns had cooled and approximate figures from both sides became available in books, Sherman would take great pride in this reversal of the anticipated ratio of losses between attacker and defender (as well he might: especially in reviewing a campaign fought on ground as unfavorable to the offensive as North Georgia was, against an adversary he admired as much as he did Joe Johnston) but just now there was the war to get on with, the wheeling movement he had designed to flank the rebels off their impregnable mountain and back across the only remaining river between them and his goal, Atlanta. By July 1 the roads were baked about hard enough for marching; the sidle began next day.

Garrard's dismounted troopers replaced the infantry in the trenches astride the Western & Atlantic, blocking a possible track-breaking sortie by the graybacks on that flank, and McPherson set out across Thomas's rear to join Schofield for a lunge around Hood's left the following day. If successful, this would not only sever Johnston's life line, it would also oblige him to fight without the protection of intrenchments when he fell back, through Marietta and Smyrna, to where the flankers would be waiting around Fulton, three miles short of the Chattahoochee and better than 50,000 strong. McPherson thus was given a chance to redeem his Resaca performance by repeating it without flaws, although Sherman's expectations were by no means as great as they had been eight weeks ago, some eighty miles back up the railroad. Warned by lookouts high on Kennesaw, which afforded a panoramic view of the country for miles and miles around, Johnston would probably choose to give up his present position rather than risk the consequences of fighting simultaneously front and rear, with a force about as large as his own in each direction. Anticipating this reaction the night before, Sherman told Garrard and Thomas to advance their pickets at daylight, July 3, and determine whether the Kennesaw trenches were occupied or abandoned; whether Johnston had chosen to stand his ground, despite the menace to his life line, or fall back, as he had always done in the face of such a threat.

On Signal Hill before dawn next morning, while the skirmishers were groping their way forward through the brush, Sherman waited impatiently for the light to grow enough to permit the use of a large telescope he had had mounted on a tripod and trained on the double-humped bulk of Kennesaw, looming blacker than the starless sky beyond it. Presently the sun broke clear and he saw, through the high-powered glass, "some of our pickets crawling up the hill cautiously. Soon they stood upon the very top, and I could see their movements as they ran along the crest."

Not a shot had been fired; the works were empty; the rebels had pulled out southward in the night.

The red-haired Ohioan caught fire at the notion that now they were out in the open, somewhere between the abandoned mountain and the river ten miles in its rear — his for the taking, so to speak, if he could overhaul them with his superior numbers before they reached whatever sanctuary their commander had it in mind to fortify. "In a minute I roused my staff, and started them off with orders in every direction for a pursuit by every possible road, hoping to catch Johnston in the confusion of retreat, especially at the crossing of the Chattahoochee River." Thomas could be depended on to descend at once on Marietta, but what was needed most just now, if the pursuers were to overcome whatever head start the Confederates might have gained, was cavalry. Sherman told Garrard to get his three brigades remounted and ride hard to bring the enemy to bay, short of the Chattahoochee, while McPherson and Schofield caught up to close in for the kill.

Events moved fast now, but not fast enough for Sherman. Without waiting for Garrard, he rode ahead with a small escort, around the eastern flank of the mountain and on into Marietta, nestled in its rear. He got there by 8.30 and was pleased to find that, although the graybacks had made a clean getaway with all their stores and had torn up several miles of railroad to the south, Thomas already had soldiers in the town. As the minutes ticked off, however, and no troopers appeared, his impatience mounted. "Where's Gar'd?" he began to storm. "Where's Gar'd? Where in hell's Gar'd?" Finally the cavalryman — a fellow Ohioan, seven years his junior in age and eleven years behind him at West Point — arrived, explaining that it had taken time to bring his horses forward and get his men into column on the road. Dissatisfied to find still more time being wasted on excuses, Sherman yelled at him: "Get out of here quick!" Garrard was flustered. Transferred from the East on the eve of the present campaign, he was not yet accustomed to being addressed in this manner. "What shall I do?" he asked, and his red-haired chief barked angrily: "Don't make a damned bit of difference so you get out of here and go for the rebs."

Despite such urgency it was midafternoon before contact was reëstablished near Smyrna, five miles down the line, and reconnaissance used up the daylight needed for mounting an assault. Fortified in advance for ready occupation, its flanks protected east and west by Rottenwood and Nickajack creeks, the rebel position astride the railroad, midway between Marietta and the river crossing five miles in its rear, obviously called for caution if the Federals were to avoid blundering into a bloody repulse. Sherman was convinced, however, that his adversary had occupied it only in hope of delaying the blue pursuit, and he said as much in a message to Thomas near sundown: "The more I reflect the more I know Johnston's halt is to save time to cross his material and men. No general, such as he, would invite battle with the Chattahoochee behind him. . . . I know you appreciate the situation. We will never have such a chance again, and I want you to impress on Hooker, Howard, and Palmer the importance of the most intense energy of attack tonight and in the morning. . . . Press with vehemence at any cost of life and material. Every inch of line should be felt and the moment there is a give, pursuit should be made."

But there was no give, and no pursuit. In fact there was no attack. Vehemence yielded to prudence next morning — July 4: the first anniversary of Vicksburg's fall, Lee's retreat from Gettysburg, and Holmes's drubbing at Helena — when Sherman found the works in his front still a-bristle with bayonets and Johnston apparently desirous of nothing so much as he was of a blue assault that would permit a repetition of what had happened on the slopes of Little Kennesaw a week ago today.

On second thought, the Ohioan cancelled his sundown instructions to Thomas, which had called for "the most intense energy of action," and reverted instead to his time-tested method of attempting to maneuver, rather than knock, the graybacks out of fortifications established in his path. While the Cumberlanders kept up a noisy demonstration in front, banging away with all their guns as if in celebration of the Fourth, McPherson set out on another of his whiplash marches, down the near bank of Nickajack Creek, to threaten the Confederate left rear. Darkness fell before his troops were in position, and the following sunrise proved Sherman right after all. The Smyrna works yawned empty; the rebs once more had stolen away in the night. Eager as ever to catch them amid the confusion that always attended a river crossing, the northern commander took off fast, making excellent time on a march of about three miles; which ended unexpectedly, within two miles of the Chattahoochee, when he came upon Johnston, just beyond Vining Station, in occupation of what Sherman frankly called "the best line of field intrenchments I have ever seen."

Looking back on the experience, years later — mindful no doubt of what he had said, two nights before, about his adversary's unwillingness to "invite battle with the Chattahoochee behind him" — he expanded the compliment: "No officer or soldier who ever served under me will question the generalship of Joseph E. Johnston. His retreats were timely, in good order, and he left nothing behind."

One exhilarating gain there was at any rate, available from the crest of a hill inclosed by a loop of the railroad as it approached the Chattahoochee beyond Vining's. "Mine eyes have beheld the promised land," an Illinois major wrote home to his wife. "The 'domes and minarets and spires' of Atlanta are glittering in the sunlight before us, only eight miles distant." Sherman and Thomas were both on the hilltop for a Pisgah view of the prize beyond the river, and though the

Union-loyal Virginian took it calmly, as always — to look at his deep-set eyes and massive brow, a newsman declared, "made one feel as if he were gazing into the mouth of a cannon; and the cannon said nothing" — the volatile Ohioan, as usual, let his exhilaration show. "Stepping nervously about, his eyes sparkling and his face aglow, casting a single glance at Atlanta, another at the river, and a dozen at the surrounding valley," he seemed to the major to be studying the rebel dispositions in order to "see where he could best cross the river, how best he could flank them."

Clearly this would take some doing: Johnston once more had chosen well. Faced with the problem of defending a stream whose low south bank was dominated by high ground on the side which a crossing would leave in enemy control, he had intrenched in advance a six-mile line along the north bank, above and below the critical railroad span. With this and five other bridges at his back — a pair for each of his three corps — he could withdraw quickly in case of a break-through, left or right, or counterattack without delay if the Federals were repulsed. His wagons were already over the river, parked in safety beyond a secondary line of south-bank works, preconstructed for instant occupation if needed, and so was his cavalry, posted up-stream and down to guard against probes in either direction. Sherman, after a look at these canny dispositions from the Vining's hilltop, wired Halleck that he would have to "study the case a little" before proceeding. He foresaw delays and he wanted Washington braced for the disappointment they would bring.

"I am now far ahead of my railroad and telegraph, and want them to catch up," he explained; "[I] may be here some days. Atlanta is in plain view, nine miles distant.... The extent of the enemy's parallels already taken is wonderful, and much of the same sort confronts us yet, and is seen beyond the Chattahoochee."

Still, he was not long in deciding that he "could easily practice on that ground to better advantage our former tactics of intrenching a moiety in [Johnston's] front, and with the rest of our army cross the river [above or below] and threaten either his rear or the city of Atlanta itself." Accordingly, while repair gangs were hard at work restoring the railroad down to Vining's, he confronted the north-bank rebel *tête-du-pont* (as he called it) with the forces of Thomas and McPherson, posted Schofield rearward in reserve, under instructions to be ready to march at a moment's notice, and sent a division of cavalry in each direction, upstream and down, in search of a likely point or points for crossing.

Stoneman, who led the downriver column, found all the bridges destroyed and their sites covered by horse artillery on the opposite bank. Although Garrard, who rode all the way to Roswell, nearly twenty miles above, had no better luck with regard to bridges, in other respects he was fortunate indeed. Roswell was a manufacturing center; or it had been, anyhow, until Garrard's troopers put in a hard day's work with sledges and torches, wrecking and burning. One problem there was, of a somewhat diplomatic nature, but not for long. He came upon a cotton mill running full tilt, still turning out gray cloth for the rebel armies; a French flag flew above it and the Gallic owner claimed immunity from damage or interference on the grounds that he was not only not a Confederate but was of foreign allegiance. Feeling rather beyond his depth in international waters, the cavalryman referred the claim to Sherman, who reacted with predictable indignation. "Such nonsense cannot deceive me," he wired Halleck, a specialist in such matters. "I take it a neutral is no better than one of our own citizens." And to Garrard went instructions to proceed against the foreign-owned mill as he had done against the others. As for the Frenchman himself, Sherman was specific as to how he might be dealt with. "Should you, under the impulse of natural anger, natural at contemplating such perfidy, hang the wretch," he told Garrard, "I approve the act beforehand."

But there was neither a hanging nor another burning; Garrard let the Frenchman go and tore down his mill to provide material for rebuilding the nearby bridge, destroyed the week before. This took three days, which allowed plenty of time for one of McPherson's corps to arrive for a crossing on July 10, dry-shod and without rebel opposition, Schofield having crossed two days earlier, about midway between Roswell and the Confederate right at Pace's Ferry, and driven the butternut vedettes away from their picket posts on the south bank. Sherman thus had been quick to solve the Chattahoochee problem, and Johnston's stand with his back to the river was correspondingly brief. Much of the credit went to Stoneman, whose downriver excursion had drawn the enemy's attention in that direction, but most of it went to Schofield, who showed for the first time in the campaign what he could accomplish when left to his own devices.

Ordered to carry out an upstream crossing, the New-York-born West Pointer — he had been a schoolteacher and a surveyor on the western plains by the time he was seventeen, and even now, though balding fast, was two years less than twice that age — arrived at daylight, July 8, reconnoitered briefly, and decided to cross where Soap Creek emptied into the river, seven miles below Roswell, the opposite bank being held at that point by a light force of gray cavalry, apparently not over-vigilant and equipped with only one gun. Silently he brought up his batteries, screened by brush along the north bank, and loaded infantry assault teams into pontoon floats launched well back from the creek mouth. "At the appointed time," he later reported, "the artillery was pushed quickly into position and opened fire, a line of battle advanced, rapidly firing, to the river bank, while the batteaux, loaded with men, were pulled down the creek and across the river.... The astonished rebels fired a single shot from their single gun, delivered a few random discharges of musketry, and fled, leaving their piece of artillery in our possession. The crossing was secured without the loss of a man." By dawn of July 9, the pontoon bridge having been installed the night before, "two divisions occupied a secure tête-de-pont a mile in depth, giving ample room for the *debouché* of the whole army."

Johnston reacted to Schofield's upstream crossing as expected, and with all his accustomed stealth and skill. Destroying or dismantling the six bridges in his wake — and, incidentally, provoking Sherman's one uncomplimentary postwar comment on the quality of his generalship throughout the long campaign: "I have always thought Johnston neglected his opportunity there, for he had lain comparatively idle while we got control of both banks of the river above him" — he withdrew his main body across the Chattahoochee that night, and after temporarily occupying the south-bank works, prepared in advance for just such an emergency, continued the pull-back the following day, July 10, to a line in rear of Peachtree Creek, apparently prompted by concern that if he took up a position any closer to the river the Federals might cut in behind him and seize the city. In any case he now was less than five miles from the heart of Atlanta.

Grateful though Sherman was for this development, which meant that he would be able to cross this last of North Georgia's three broad rivers without a battle that had seemed likely to prove costly both in casualties and time, he once more found himself confronted with the problem that had loomed with every major gain: What now? — meaning *how?* Should he swing left or right, upstream or down, for the accustomed flanking effort, or bull straight ahead for an end-all strike at an opponent whose back was at last to the gates of the city in his charge, with little room for maneuver unless he chose to give it up without a fight?

While the red-haired general pondered and pored over maps and reports, his troops moved up to the unguarded Chattahoochee, anticipating their first leisurely bath in ten weeks. Admiration for their commander had grown with every tactical leap or sidestep, and now it reached a climax in which almost anything seemed possible. "Charley," one dusty infantry man told a comrade as they approached this last natural barrier and saw smoke rising from the buildings along its banks, "I believe Sherman has set the river on fire." Nor was the wonder limited to wearers of the blue. A butternut prisoner, conducted rearward past exuberant Federals in their tens of thousands, was so impressed by their multitude that he said to his captors: "Sherman ought to get on a high hill and command, 'Attention! Kingdoms by the right wheel!'" The general, in point of fact, was squatting naked in the

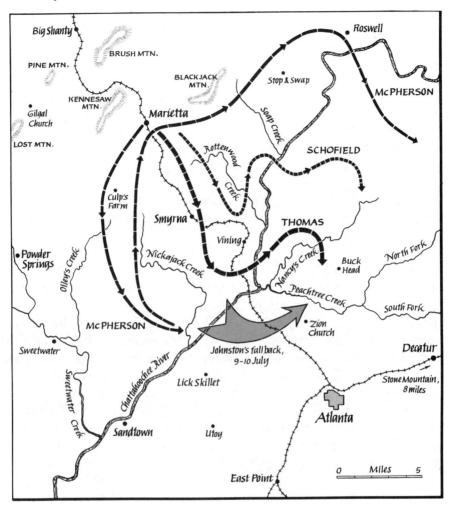

Big Shanty

BRUSH MTN.

PINE MTN.

BLACKJACK MTN.

KENNESAW MTN.

Gilgal Church

LOST MTN.

Marietta

Roswell

Stop & Swap

McPHERSON

Soap Creek

Rottenwood Creek

SCHOFIELD

Culp's Farm

Smyrna

Vining

THOMAS

Nancy's Creek

Buck Head

North Fork

Powder Springs

Olley's Creek

Nickajack Creek

Peachtree Creek

South Fork

McPHERSON

Zion Church

Decatur

Sweetwater

Chattahoochee River

Johnston's fall back, 9–10 July

Stone Mountain, 8 miles

Sweetwater Creek

Lick Skillet

Sandtown

Utoy

Atlanta

East Point

0   Miles   5

Chattahoochee at the time, discussing the temperature of the water with a teamster who admired him from the bank, while all around them other soldiers lolled neck deep in the river, soaking away the grime of more than a hundred red-clay miles of marching and fighting and the caked sweat of seventy days of exertion and fear, or else whooped and splashed in pure delight at having nothing else to do.

But not for long. After the brief time-out for his dip in the Chattahoochee, Sherman returned to his maps and reports, designing the next, and he hoped final, move in the campaign to whip Joe Johnston and take Atlanta. With the two-weeks-old repulse at Kennesaw fresh in mind, he quickly rejected the notion of mounting an all-out frontal attack on the Confederates dug in behind Peachtree Creek — attractive though that would be as a slam-bang finish, if successful — and reverted instead to his accustomed practice of operating on or around one of the enemy flanks.

Mostly, before, he had moved by his right, in a series of mirror images, so to speak, of Grant's leftward sidles in Virginia; but in this case the choice was by no means simple. It was true, a downstream crossing would not only give him ground that favored the offensive (the south-bank creeks, below, ran into the Chattahoochee at right angles, affording Johnston no perpendicular ridges to defend but many to cross in changing position to meet the challenge, while permitting Sherman to advance on the city by moving up the ravines, unhindered in front and sheltered on the flanks); it would also place him in rear of his objective from the outset, within easy striking distance of the railroads leading southwest through Montgomery to Mobile and south-east through Macon to Savannah, without which Atlanta could not long survive a siege. An upstream crossing, on the other hand, would give the advantage of terrain to the defenders; for there the creeks ran more or less parallel to the Chattahoochee, presenting Sherman with ridges to cross while advancing and Johnston with ravines to shelter his army while shifting to meet the threat. Geography clearly favored a downriver flanking operation. Yet there was a good deal more to the problem than geography per se. For one thing, there was the risk of exposing the all-important Union supply line to depredations, and this would be a far greater danger if the crossing was made below the railroad bridge. Just above there, after receiving the waters of Peach-tree Creek, the Chattahoochee swerved northward (on the map, that is; the flow, of course, was south) and ran alongside the Western & Atlantic all the way beyond Vining Station, the newly established Federal railhead and supply dump, which would be within easy reach not only of rebel cavalry but also of rebel infantry, launched across the nearby river on a track-breaking sortie that could scarcely be blocked if most of the blue army moved below. This gave Sherman pause, as well it might, and so did something else. Recent dispatches from Grant indicated that their previous concern, lest Johnston reinforce Lee for a blow at Meade, was now reversed; Lee's current problem, Grant explained, was not how he could get more troops, but rather how he could feed the ones he had, and under such circumstances it was not unlikely that he might detach a sizeable portion of them for service in far-off Georgia, just as he had done the year before, on the eve of Chickamauga. If he did so, they would come by rail: specifically, by way of Augusta on the Georgia Railroad, the one line into Atlanta that would not be threatened, let alone broken, if Sherman crossed downriver to close in on the city from the west.

Thus to define the problem was to solve it, so far at least as the choice of directions was concerned: Sherman decided to break the pattern of his campaign and move by the left, crossing the river well upstream for a preliminary strike at the Georgia Railroad. Schofield in fact had already begun the movement three days ago, when his improvised amphibious assault teams emerged from the mouth of

Soap Creek to surprise the rebel pickets across the way, and Sherman had followed through by sending one of McPherson's corps to join Garrard at Roswell, seven miles beyond Schofield. On July 13, having reached a firm decision the night before, he continued the buildup by ordering McPherson to take his second corps upriver and reinforce the first, leaving the third in position on Thomas's right to maintain the downstream feint until Stoneman got back from the ride designed to mislead Johnston still further into thinking that the Federals were about to cross below.

"All is well," Sherman wired Halleck next day. "I have now accumulated stores at Allatoona and Marietta, both fortified and garrisoned points. Have also three places at which to cross the Chatta-hoochee in our possession, and only await General Stoneman's return from a trip down the river, to cross the army in force and move on Atlanta."

Stoneman got back the following night and McPherson's third corps set out for Roswell next morning, July 15. Reunited, the whip-lash Army of the Tennessee would thus be on the rim of what Sherman described as "a general right wheel," designed to roll down on the city from the north and east, with Schofield about midway out the twelve-mile radius and Thomas holding the hub, or pivot, to confront and fix the Confederate main body in position for the crunch. McPherson would cross the river and march south to strike the railroad near Stone Mountain, six miles east of Decatur, Schofield's preliminary objective, about the same distance east of Atlanta. The two commands would then advance westward in tandem along the right-of-way, tearing up track as they went, and link up with Thomas for the final push that would assail Johnston along his front, outflank him on his right, and drive him back through the streets of the city in his rear.

"Each army will form a unit and connect with its neighbor by a line of pickets," the warning order read. "Should the enemy assume the offensive at any point, which is not expected until we reach below Peachtree Creek, the neighboring army will at once assist the one attacked.... A week's work after crossing the Chattahoochee should determine the first object aimed at, viz, the possession of the [Georgia Rail]road east of Decatur, or of Atlanta itself."

July 17 was the jump-off date, a Sunday, and everything went as ordered for all three armies involved in the grand wheel. Crossing with Schofield in the center, Sherman grew concerned, as usual, about what was happening out of sight: particularly in Thomas's direction, where the going was likely to be slow. "Feel down strong to Peach Tree and see what is there," he urged the Virginian. "A vigorous demonstration should be made, and caution your commanders not to exhibit any of the signs of a halt or pause." Next morning he rode over to check on the progress of the Cumberlanders, and found them crossing Nancy's

Creek on schedule to descend on Buckhead, a crossroads hamlet where Thomas would set up headquarters before sundown, within a mile of Peachtree Creek and its intrenched defenders.

"I am fully aware of the necessity of making the most of time," Sherman wired Halleck, "and shall keep things moving." Accordingly, he kept prodding Thomas: "I would like you to get to Buckhead early today and then to feel down strong on Atlanta," meantime fretting about McPherson's progress on the far left: "I want that railroad as quick as possible and the weather seems too good to be wasted."

Informed after nightfall that both Schofield and McPherson had reached their objectives and would begin their wrecking marches westward along the railroad at daybreak, Sherman exulted: as well he might, having accomplished within two days what he had predicted would require "a week's work after crossing the Chattahoochee." He had control of the Georgia Railroad from Stone Mountain through Decatur, and now, secure against reinforcements sped from Virginia by Lee, he was out to take Atlanta by bringing his combinations to bear on its outflanked defenders. The question was whether Johnston would stand, as he had done at Kennesaw, or skedaddle, as he had done everywhere else in the course of the seventy-seven-day campaign.

Riding out to confer on the matter with Thomas next morning, July 19, the red-haired Ohioan encountered an answer of sorts in a copy of yesterday's newspaper, brought out of the semi-beleaguered city by a spy. Johnston, it seemed, would neither stand nor skedaddle. "At this critical moment," Sherman later put it, looking back, "the Confederate Government rendered us most valuable service."

✗ 4 ✗

In Atlanta, all this time, there had been growing consternation as Sherman's "worse than vandal hordes" bore down on the city, preceded by a stream of refugees in wagons and on foot, mostly old men and boys, below or beyond the conscription limits of seventeen and fifty-two, and "yellow-faced women and their daughters in long-slatted sun-bonnets and faded calico," who had fled their upcountry farms and hamlets at the approach of the blue outriders. City parks were no longer parks; they bloomed instead with gray-white clusters of hospital tents, where the reek of disinfectants competed with the morbid stench of gangrene, and both combined to rival the predominant smell of horses. Trains chuffed into the station, day and night, loaded with sick and wounded soldiers, many of them dying, many dead before they got there. "Embalming: Free from Odor of Infection," signs proclaimed, soliciting business, and Bohnefield's Coffin Shop on Luckie Street had more orders than it could fill. "Give us this day our daily bread," the Second Baptist minister had taken as his text the previous Sunday, when news came that Marietta had been abandoned in still another retreat. And before the dawn of another sabbath, so quickly did things move at this late stage of the campaign, word arrived that the gray army had retired across the Chattahoochee, burning in its rear the bridges spanning the last natural barrier between Atlanta and destruction. "Stay a few days longer," a member of Hardee's staff advised a family he joined in town that afternoon for Sunday dinner. "I think we will hold this place at least a week."

They did not take the colonel's advice, but left next morning, scrambling with others like themselves for places on a southbound train. Places were hard to get now, for the military had commandeered most of the cars for removal of the wounded, along with all government stores and the vital machinery taken from outlying mills and factories, a salvage project assigned by Johnston to a high-ranking volunteer aide, Major General Mansfield Lovell, who presumably was experienced in such matters, having given up New Orleans two years back. Atlanta had not expected to share the fate of the Crescent City, but as the fighting grew nearer, week by week, the possibility seemed less and less remote, until finally even diehards had to admit that it had developed into a probability. Loyal admirers of Old Joe — including an editor who maintained, even now, that his reputation had "grown with every backward step" — were hard put to defend the general from charges that he intended to give up the city without a fight. For the most part, he retained the confidence and above all the devotion of his soldiers, but there were those who questioned his Fabian strategy, which they saw as leading only to one end: especially after he turned loose of Kennesaw and fell back to the Chattahoochee.

"There was not an officer or man in this Army who ever dreamed of Johnston falling back this far," a young artillery lieutenant, whose home in Atlanta was then only seven miles in his rear, wrote his mother from the north bank of that river, "or ever doubted he would attack when the proper time came. But I think he has been woefully outgeneraled and has made a losing bargain."

Official concern had been growing proportionately as the Union forces closed down on Atlanta. "This place is to the Confederacy as important as the heart is to the body. We must hold it," Joe Brown wrote Jefferson Davis in late June, appealing for strategic diversions and substantial reinforcements to help Johnston avert what seemed certain to happen without them. The governor was in touch with other prominent men throughout the South, and he urged them to use their influence on the President to this end.

His chief hope was in a fellow Georgian, Senator Benjamin Hill, who occupied the unusual position of being the friend of both Davis and Johnston, a relationship they could scarcely be said to enjoy in reference to each other. Brown's hope was that Hill could serve as a go-between, if not to bring the two leaders together, then in any case to improve communications — particularly at the far end of the line, where Brown believed the messages were having the greater difficulty in getting through. He suggested that the senator write at once to the Commander in Chief, urging a more sympathetic response to the general's pleas now that the crisis was at hand. Hill said he would do better than that; "Time is too precious and letters are too inadequate"; he would go to Richmond and talk with Davis face to face. First, though, he thought it best to confer with Johnston for a clearer understanding of the hopes and plans he then would pass along. Accordingly, he rode up to the general's headquarters at Marietta next morning, July 1, and had what he later called a "free conversation" along these lines with the Virginian.

Reviewing the situation, Johnston declared that his principal aim, up to now, had been to defeat Sherman by obliging him to attack Confederate intrenchments, but after the limited effort which had been so decisively repulsed, four days ago at Kennesaw, he doubted that his adversary could be persuaded to try the thing again. As for himself, he certainly had no intention of wasting his outnumbered veterans in any such attempt. All he could do with his present force, he said, was block the direct path to Atlanta, thus delaying another Union advance until such time as Sherman again compelled his retreat by "ditching round his flank." Aside from the long-odds chance that the enemy mass would expose itself to piecemeal destruction by dividing into segments he could leap at, one by one, he saw but a single hope for reversing the blue tide, which even then was lapping the flanks of Kennesaw and would otherwise in time no doubt roll down to the Chattahoochee and beyond. This was that 5000 cavalry be thrown without delay against Sherman's life line up in Tennessee, either by Forrest or John Morgan; in which case, Johnston said, the Federals would have to accept battle on his terms — that is, attack him in his intrenchments — or else retreat to avoid starvation. Asked why he did not use his own cavalry for such a profitable venture, the general replied that all his horsemen were needed where they were. Observing that "I must go to Richmond, and Morgan must go from Virginia or Forrest from Mississippi, and this will take some time," Hill expressed some doubt whether either body of gray cavalry could reach the Federal rear before the Federals reached Atlanta. "How long can you hold Sherman north of the Chattahoochee River?" he pointedly asked Johnston, who replied somewhat evasively that the bluecoats had covered less than a dozen southward miles in the past month, shifting their ground from around New Hope Church to Kennesaw Mountain, where they had made no progress at all in the past two weeks; Hill could figure for himself, the general said, how long it would take them to reach the river at this rate.

Hill calculated, accordingly, that the Confederates could remain north of the Chattahoochee "at least fifty-four days, and perhaps sixty."

Johnston assented, but not Hood, who though present throughout the interview had held his peace till now. He disagreed, saying: "Mr Hill, when we leave our present line, we will, in my judgment, cross the Chattahoochee River very rapidly." Johnston turned on the tall blond Texan, who was twenty-four years his junior in age, as well as in length of service. "What makes you think that?" he asked, and Hood replied: "Because this line of Kennesaw is the strongest line we can get in this country. If we surrender this to Sherman he can reconnoiter from its summit the whole country between here and Atlanta, and there is no such line of defense in the distance." Johnston demurred. "I differ with your conclusion," he said. "I admit this is a strong line of defense, but I have two more strong lines between this and the river, from which I can hold Sherman a long time."

Hill took his leave, pleased to learn that two more stout positions had been prepared for the army to defend before it retired across the Chattahoochee, some fifty-four to sixty days in the future, according to his Johnston-approved calculations, or in any case "a long time" from now. Delayed by personal matters, he took a train for Virginia before the end of the following week, passing en route a group of public men proceeding by rail on a mission similar to his own, except that the two were headed in opposite directions toward diametric goals. Hill was going from Atlanta to Richmond in hope of impressing Johnston's views on Davis, while they were going from Richmond to Atlanta in hope of impressing Davis's views on Johnston. Congressmen all, they had been delegated by their colleagues, as friends of the general, to warn him that his conduct of the Georgia campaign was under heavy attack in the capital and to urge him to disarm these rearward critics by taking aggressive action against the enemy in his front.

Reaching Atlanta on the evening of July 8 they proceeded next morning to army headquarters for a conference with Johnston, who by then had fallen back through Smyrna, the first of his two stout positions south of Kennesaw, to his bridgehead on the north bank of the Chattahoochee, which was his second. The Virginian received them graciously, heard them out, and replied, alas, as if they had been dispatched for irksome purposes by the President himself: "You may tell Mr Davis that it would be folly for me under the circumstances to risk a decisive engagement. My plan is to draw Sherman further and further from his base in the hope of weakening him and by cutting his army in two. That is my only hope of defeating him."

There was silence at this until one delegate, a Missourian, remarked that what was required, both for the country's sake and the general's own, was for him to strike the Yankees "a crushing blow," and then went on — tactlessly, but apparently in hope of jogging

Johnston into action — to say that lately he had heard the President quoted to the effect that "if he were in your place he could whip Sherman now." The general was jogged into action, all right, but not of the kind intended. He bridled and did not try to hide his scorn.

"Yes," he said icily, "I know Mr Davis thinks he can do a great many things other men would hesitate to attempt. For instance, he tried to do what God failed to do. He tried to make a soldier of Braxton Bragg, and you know the result. It couldn't be done."

This might have wound up the matter then and there, to no one's satisfaction, but a courier arrived at that point with news of a development to which Johnston's response provided the conference with an upbeat ending. Schofield had effected a south-bank lodgment yesterday, seven miles upriver, the courier reported, and this morning he had continued the crossing with what appeared to be most, if not all, of his command. . . . If the general's visitors expected him to react with dismay to this information that he had been flanked, they were agreeably disappointed. Pointing out that Sherman had thus divided his army, north and south of the deep-running Chattahoochee, Johnston declared that the time at last had come to strike and "whip him in detail."

The delegates returned to Atlanta expecting to hear before nightfall the roar of guns that would signal the launching of the attack. It did not come, either then or the following morning, July 10, when all that broke the sabbath stillness was the peal of church bells, summoning the city's dwindling population to pray for a deliverance which Johnston himself seemed less and less willing to attempt.

Bells were tolling that Sunday morning in Richmond, too, when Benjamin Hill stepped off the train from Georgia. He went straight to his hotel and stayed there only long enough to wash up before going to the White House for the appointment he had secured by wiring ahead. Having, as he said, "repelled the idea that any influence with the President was needed, if the facts were as General Johnston reported them," the senator was convinced that all the situation required was for him to relay the general's requests to Davis; "I did not doubt he would act promptly."

He was ushered without delay into the Chief Executive's residential office, and as he advanced across the white rug that was said to provoke temerity in the breasts of men who called in unscraped boots, the Mississippian rose to greet him with a geniality that matched the Virginia general's own, nine days ago in Marietta. Davis heard him out, his smile fading when Hill spoke of Morgan and Forrest as presumably lying more or less idle in Southwest Virginia and North Mississippi. As for Morgan, he replied, it was true that he was where Johnston said he was, having just returned, sadly depleted, from just such an expedition as Johnston recommended, whipped and in no condition for anything more than an attempt to pull his few survivors together for operations necessarily weeks in the future. Forrest too was unavailable, Davis said, although for different reasons. Having disposed of Sturgis at Brice's Crossroads in mid-June, he now was engaged in opposing a 15,000-man Union force that had left Memphis two weeks ago under A. J. Smith, bound either for Georgia to reinforce Sherman, in front or in rear of Atlanta, or for Mobile in conjunction with an even larger blue column reported to be on the march from New Orleans under Canby; he not only could not be spared for the proposed raid into Middle Tennessee, but his superior, Polk's successor Stephen Lee, was protesting hotly — as Johnston had only recently been informed — that he needed "his troops now with Johnston more than the latter can need Forrest."

Hill's hopes, which had been so high on the ride east, declined rapidly while he listened to this double-barreled refutation of the "facts" behind them. But presently they took an even sharper drop when Davis paused and asked: "How long did you understand General Johnston to say he could hold Sherman north of the Chattahoochee River?" Fifty-four to sixty days, the senator replied; whereupon Davis took up and read to him a telegraphic dispatch received just before his arrival. It was from Johnston and it announced that, a part of Sherman's army having crossed upriver two days ago, several miles beyond his right, he had begun his withdrawal across the Chattahoochee last night and completed it this morning.... Hill retired in some confusion, which was increased next day when the Secretary of War called on him "to reduce my interview with General Johnston to writing, for the use of the Cabinet."

He perceived now that his trip to Richmond, designed to help the Atlanta commander, had resulted instead in furnishing the general's Confederate foes with ammunition they could use in urging his removal from command. Three days later, after taking a still closer look at the attitude of those in high positions at the capital, he wired Johnston by way of warning: "You must do the work with your present force. For God's sake do it."

Just as the pressure had been greater, so now was Johnston's time even shorter than Hill knew — unless, that is, the general was somehow able to follow his friend's advice and "do the work." Atlanta, with its rolling mill and foundries, its munition plants and factories, its vital rail connections and vast store of military supplies, was the combined workshop and warehouse of the Confederate West, and as Sherman closed down upon it, Davis later wrote, the threat of its loss "produced intense anxiety far and wide. From many quarters, including such as had most urged his assignment, came delegations, petitions, and letters," insisting that the present army commander be replaced by one who would fight to save the city, not abandon it to the fate which Johnston seemed to consider unavoidable without outside help. "The clamor for his removal commenced immediately after it became known that the army had fallen back from Dalton," Davis added, "and it gathered volume with each remove toward Atlanta."

Nowhere was this clamor more vociferous than at meetings of the cabinet, not one of whose six members was by now in favor of keeping the Virginia general at his Georgia post. Some had advised against sending him there in the first place: including the Secretary of State, who afterwards told why. "From a close observation of his career," the shrewd-minded Benjamin declared, "I became persuaded that his nervous dread of losing a battle would prevent at all times his ability to cope with an enemy of nearly equal strength, and that opportunities would thus constantly be lost which under other commanders would open a plain path to victory." Still, those who had opposed his selection were not nearly so strident in their demands for his removal, at this stage, as were those who had been his supporters at the outset. The Secretary of War, for example, explained that, having made "a great mistake" seven months ago, "he desired to do all he could, even at this late date, to atone for it."

Davis resisted — now as in the case of that other Johnston, two and a half years ago, after Donelson and on the eve of Shiloh — both the public and the private clamor for the general's removal; Seddon later revealed that though "the whole Cabinet concurred in advising and even urging" the change, the President moved toward a decision "slowly and not without much hesitation, misgiving and, even to the last, reluctance." His concern was for Atlanta, for what it contained and for what it represented, not only in the minds of his own people, but also in the minds of the people of the North, who would be voting in November whether to sustain their present hard-war leader or replace him with one who might be willing, in the name of peace, to let the South depart in independence. A military professional, Davis knew only too well, as he put the case, "how serious it was to change commanders in the presence of the enemy," and he told Senator Hill flatly, in the course of their Sunday conference at the White House, that he "would not do it if he could have any assurance that General Johnston would not surrender Atlanta without a battle."

In this connection, he had sent his chief military adviser, Braxton Bragg, to determine at first hand, if possible, what the intentions of the western commander were. Bragg had left the previous day, July 9, but before he reached Atlanta — a three-day trip, as it turned out — the War Department received from Johnston himself, on July 11, a telegram which seemed to some to answer only too clearly the question as to the city's impending fate: "I strongly recommend the distribution of the U.S. prisoners, now at Andersonville, immediately."

Andersonville, a prisoner-of-war camp for enlisted personnel, established that spring near Americus, Georgia, and already badly crowded as a result of the northern decision to discontinue the exchange of prisoners, was more than a hundred miles due south of Atlanta. That distance, combined with the use of the word "immediately," gave occasion for alarm. For though Davis knew that what mainly caused Johnston to recommend the camp's evacuation was fear that Sherman, finding it within present cavalry range, might send out a flying column to liberate its 30,000 Federal captives — and thus create, as if by a sowing of dragon teeth, a ferocious new blue army deep in the Confederate rear — still, following hard as it did on the heels of news that Atlanta's defenders had retired in haste across the Chattahoochee, the telegram was an alarming indication of the direction in which Johnston's mind had turned now that Sherman was about to leap the last natural barrier in his path. For the first time since the clamor for the Virginian's removal began, two months ago, Davis agreed that his relief seemed necessary, and he said as much next day in a cipher telegram asking R. E. Lee's advice in choosing a successor: "General Johnston has failed and there are strong indications that he will abandon Atlanta. . . . It seems necessary to remove him at once. Who should succeed him? What think you of Hood for the position?"

Lee replied, also by wire and in cipher: "I regret the fact stated. It is a bad time to relieve the commander of an army situated as that of Tenne. We may lose Atlanta and the army too. Hood is a bold fighter. I am doubtful as to other qualities necessary." That evening he expanded these words of caution and regret in a follow-up letter. "It is a grievous thing," he said of the impending change. "Still if necessary it ought to be done. I know nothing of the necessity. I had hoped that Johnston was strong enough to deliver battle." As for the choice of his former star brigade and division chief as his old friend's successor out in Georgia, second thoughts had not diminished his reservations. "Hood is a good commander, very industrious on the battlefield, careless off, and I have had no opportunity of judging his action when the whole responsibility rested upon him. I have a high opinion of his gallantry, earnestness, and zeal." Further than this Lee would not go, either in praise or detraction, but he added suggestively: "General Hardee has more experience in managing an army. May God give you wisdom to decide in this momentous matter."

A series of telegrams and letters from Bragg, who reached Atlanta next morning, July 13, confirmed the need for early action, either by Johnston or the government. "Indications seem to favor an entire evacuation of this place," he wired Davis on arrival, and followed with a second gloomy message a few hours later, still without having ridden out to the general's headquarters in the field: "Our army is sadly depleted, and now reports 10,000 less than the return of the 10th June. I find but little encouraging." Two days later he was able to report more fully on conditions, having paid two calls on Johnston in the meantime. "He has not sought my advice, and it was not volunteered," Bragg wired. "I cannot learn that he has any more plan for the future than he has had in the past. It is expected that he will await the enemy on a line some three miles from here, and the impression prevails that he is now more inclined to fight. . . . The morale of our army is still reported good."

In a letter sent by courier to Richmond that same day he went more fully into this and other matters bearing on the issue. Johnston's apparent intention, now as always, Bragg declared, was to "await the enemy's approach and be governed, as heretofore, by the development in our front." What was likely to follow could be predicted by reviewing what had happened under similar circumstances at Dalton, Resaca, Cassville, and Marietta — or, indeed, by observing what had happened in and around Atlanta just this week; "All valuable stores and machinery have been removed, and most of the citizens able to go have left with their effects. . . . Position, numbers, and morale are now with the enemy." Which said, Bragg moved on to the problem of choosing a successor to the general who had brought the army to this pass. Hardee had disqualified himself, not only because he had declined the post seven months ago (and thereby brought on Johnston) but also because he had "generally favored the retiring policy" of his chief. Alexander Stewart, who had been promoted to lieutenant general and given command of Polk's corps on the retreat to the Chattahoochee, was too green for larger duties yet, despite the commendable savagery he had displayed at New Hope Church. That left Hood, who had "been in favor of giving battle" all the way from Dalton and who, in fact — aside, that is, from the peculiar circumstances that prevailed at Cassville — had done just that whenever he was on his own. By way of evidence that this was so, Bragg included a letter he had received from the young Texan the day before, expressing regret that the army had "failed to give battle to the enemy many miles north of our present position."

"If any change is made," Bragg concluded, "Lieutenant General Hood would give unlimited satisfaction." Then, as if aware of the misgiving Lee had expressed three days ago, he added: "Do not understand me as proposing him as a man of genius, or a great general, but as far better in the present emergency than any one we have available."

Davis agreed that Hood was the man for the post, if its present occupant had to be replaced, but he would not act without giving Johnston one last chance to commit himself to a fight to save Atlanta, in which case he would keep him where he was. Accordingly, in a wire next day, July 16, he put the case to the general in no uncertain terms: "I wish to hear from you as to present situation, and your plan of operations so specifically as will enable me to anticipate events."

Johnston felt no more alarm at this than he had done at Hill's

"For God's sake do it" telegram, received the day before. Busy with
tactical matters, he did not take the time or trouble to outline for the
Commander in Chief what he afterwards claimed was his plan for the
overthrow of the blue host in his front: which — as he would set it
forth some ten years later, after the guns had cooled but not the
controversy — was to engage the enemy "on terms of advantage"
while they were divided by Peachtree Creek. If this did not work he
planned to hold the intrenchments overlooking the creek with 5000
state militia, lately sent him by Governor Brown, "and leisurely fall
back with the Confederate troops into the town and, when the Federal
army approached, march out with the three corps against one of its
flanks." If this was successful, the bluecoats would be driven back
against the unfordable Chattahoochee and cut to pieces before they
could recross; if not, "the Confederate army had a near and secure place
of refuge in Atlanta, which it could hold forever, and so win the
campaign." So he later said — "forever" — but not now. Now he
merely responded, as before, that he would have to be governed by
circumstances; circumstances which it was clear would be of Sherman's
making. "As the enemy has double our number, we must be on the
defensive," he replied to Davis's request for specific information. "My
plan of operations must, therefore, depend on that of the enemy. It
is mainly to watch for an opportunity to fight to advantage. We are
trying to put Atlanta in condition to hold it for a day or two by the
Georgia militia, that army movements may be freer and wider."

On the defensive. A day or two. The Georgia militia. Freer and
wider movements.... Johnston would later maintain that just as he
was about to deliver the blow that would "win the campaign," and
which he had had in mind all along, his sword was wrenched from his
grasp by the Richmond authorities; but the fact was, he signed his own
warrant of dismissal when he put his hand to this telegram declaring,
more clearly than anything else it said, that he had no plan involving
a battle to save Atlanta.

Word came next morning — July 17, another Sunday — that
Sherman's whole army was over the Chattahoochee, apparently engaged
in an outsized turning movement designed to close down on the city
from the north and east. After nightfall Johnston was at his headquarters three miles out the Marietta Road, conferring with his chief
engineer about work on the Atlanta fortifications, when a message for
him from Adjutant General Samuel Cooper clicked off the telegraph
receiver:

> Lieutenant General J. B. Hood has been commissioned to the
> temporary rank of General under the late law of Congress. I am
> directed by the Secretary of War to inform you that as you have
> failed to arrest the advance of the enemy to the vicinity of Atlanta,

far in the interior of Georgia, and express no confidence that you can defeat or repel him, you are hereby relieved from the command of the Army and Department of Tennessee, which you will immediately turn over to General Hood.

Old Joe spent most of the rest of the night in the throes of composition, preparing first a farewell address, in which he expressed his affection for the troops who had served under him, and then a response to his superiors, in which he managed to vent a measure of the resentment aroused by the backhand slap they had taken at him in the order for his removal. "I cannot leave this noble army," he told its members, "without expressing my admiration of the high military qualities it has displayed. A long and arduous campaign has made conspicuous every soldierly virtue, endurance of toil, obedience to orders, brilliant courage. The enemy has never attacked but to be repulsed and severely punished. You, soldiers, have never argued but from your courage, and never counted your foes. No longer your leader, I will still watch your career, and will rejoice in your victories. To one and all I offer assurances of my friendship, and bid an affectionate farewell."

The other document was briefer, if no less emotional under its surface of ice. "Your dispatch of yesterday received and obeyed," it began, and passed at once to a refutation of the charges made in the dismissal order: "Sherman's army is much stronger compared with that of Tennessee than Grant's compared with that of Northern Virginia. Yet the enemy has been compelled to advance much more slowly to the vicinity of Atlanta than to that of Richmond and Petersburg, and has penetrated deeper into Virginia than into Georgia." Then at the end came the stinger. "Confident language by a military commander is not usually regarded as evidence of competency. J. E. Johnston."

Hood too got little if any sleep after he received at 11 p.m. the War Department telegram which, he said, "so astounded and overwhelmed" him that he "remained in deep thought throughout the night." He had in fact much to ponder, including a follow-up wire from Seddon: "You are charged with a great trust. You will, I know, test to the utmost your capacities to discharge it. Be wary no less than bold. . . . God be with you." His appointment was plainly an endorsement of the aggressive views he had been propounding all the way south from the Tennessee line, and he was clearly expected to translate them into action. But he perceived that to do so here on the flat terrain south of the Chattahoochee, with his back to the gates of the city in his care, was a far more difficult undertaking than it would have been in the rugged country Johnston had traversed in the course of his long retreat from Dalton. "We may lose Atlanta and the army too," Lee had warned Davis five days ago, and though Hood had not seen the message, he was altogether aware of the danger pointed out — as well as of his own shortcomings, which Lee had by no means listed in full.

For one, there was his youth. He had just last month turned thirty-three, the crucifixion age, which made him not only younger than any of his infantry corps or division commanders, but also a solid ten years younger than the average among them. Then too there was his physical condition; Gettysburg had cost him the use of his left arm, paralyzed by a fragment of bursting shell as he charged the Devil's Den, and at Chickamauga his right leg had been amputated so close to the hip that from then on he had to be strapped in the saddle to ride a horse. Worst of all, though, was the timing of the change now ordered by the War Department. Sherman's final lunge at Atlanta was in full career, and only Johnston knew what plans had been made, if any, to meet and survive the shock. Certainly Hood knew nothing of them, except as they applied to the disposition of his corps on the Confederate right, astride the Georgia Railroad. Emerging at last from the brown study into which the telegram had plunged him, the blond, Kentucky-born Texan came out of his tent before dawn, mounted his horse with the help of an orderly, and set out for Johnston's headquarters near the far end of the line.

On the way there, about sunrise, he encountered Stewart on the way there too. Old Straight, who had led a division under Hood until his recent promotion to head the corps that had been temporarily under Loring, was also disturbed by the untimely change. He proposed that they unite with Hardee "in an effort to prevail on General Johnston to withhold the order and retain command of the army until the impending battle has been fought." Hood readily agreed, and they rode on together.

At headquarters, where a candle flickered atop a barrel with the telegram beside it, Johnston received them courteously, but when Hood appealed to him to "pocket that dispatch, leave me in command of my corps, and fight the battle for Atlanta," the Virginian would have no part of such an irregular procedure. He was off the hook and he intended to stay off. "Gentlemen, I am a soldier," he said. "A soldier's first duty is to obey." So that was that.

Or perhaps not. Hardee having arrived by now, the three lieutenant generals dispatched a joint telegram to the President requesting that he postpone the transfer of command "until the fate of Atlanta is decided."

Davis's answer was not long in coming, and it was a flat No: "A change of commanders, under existing circumstances, was regarded as so objectionable that I only accepted it as the alternative of continuing a policy which had proved so disastrous.... The order has been executed, and I cannot suspend it without making the case worse than it was before the order was issued."

Hood made one last try, returning to plead a second time, "for the good of the country," that Johnston "pocket the correspondence" and remain in command, "as Sherman was at the very gates of the city." Old Joe again declined: whereupon Hood launched into a personal appeal, referring to "the great embarrassment of the position in which I had been placed." Not only was he in the dark ᵃs to such plans as had been made for meeting the enemy now bearing down on Atlanta and its defenders, he did not even know where the other two corps of the army were posted. "With all the earnestness of which man is capable," Hood later wrote, "I besought him, if he would under no circumstances retain command and fight the battle for Atlanta, to at least remain with me and give me the benefit of his counsel whilst I determined the issue." Touched at last, and "with tears of emotion gathering in his eyes," Johnston assured his young successor that, after a necessary ride into Atlanta, he would return that evening and help him all he could. So he said. According to Hood, however, "he not only failed to comply with his promise, but, without a word of explanation or apology, left that evening for Macon, Georgia."

There was some fear, according to a number of observers, that the men in the ranks "would throw down their muskets and quit" when they learned of the transfer of command: not so much from distrust of Hood, who at this stage was little more than a damaged figurehead to most of them, as because of their "love for and confidence in Johnston," who many said "had been grievously wronged" by his superiors in Richmond. "A universal gloom seemed cast over the army," a lieutenant on Hood's own staff declared, and a Tennessee private — a veteran who remembered Bragg and the aftermath of Missionary Ridge — later told why the news was received with so much sorrow and resentment: "Old Joe Johnston had taken command of the Army of Tennessee when it was crushed and broken, at a time when no other man on earth could have united it. He found it in rags and tatters, hungry and broken-hearted, the morale of the men gone, their manhood vanished to the winds, their pride a thing of the past. Through his instrumentality and skillful manipulation, all these had been restored.... Farewell, old fellow!" he cried, breaking into an apostrophe of remembered grief as he approached the end of this "saddest chapter" of the war; "We privates loved you because you made us love ourselves."

Not all who felt that way about the Virginia general had to say goodbye from such a distance, either of time or space. Between the reading of his farewell address that Monday morning and his actual departure for Macon that afternoon, several units passed his head-quarters on their way up to the lines on Peachtree Creek, and thereby got the chance to demonstrate their affection in his presence. A Georgia regiment happened to march out the Marietta Road, for example, and the colonel left a record of how he and his men reacted to what they thought would be their last look at their former commander, who came out of the house and stood by the gate to watch them pass. "We lifted our hats. There was no cheering. We simply passed silently, our heads uncovered. Some of the officers broke ranks and grasped his hand, as the tears poured down their cheeks."

Higher up the ladder of rank, the reaction was scarcely less emotional. Hardee, upset at having someone more than a year his junior in grade promoted over his head, promptly asked to be relieved, complaining that the President — who in the end persuaded him to withdraw his application for a transfer — was "attempting to create the impression that in declining the command [six months ago] at Dalton, I declined it for all future time." He doubted Hood's ability to fill the position to which he had been elevated, and others felt, as one of them put it, that the appointment was an "egregious blunder." Sam French called at headquarters that evening to assure the new commander of his full coöperation, but did not fail to add, with his usual forthrightness, that he regretted the change. "Although he took my hand and thanked me," he later said of Hood, "I was ever afterwards impressed with the belief that he never forgave me for what I said." Still others, aware of the reason behind the shift, foresaw hard fighting and had mixed opinions concerning the fate of Atlanta, as well as their own. Undoubtedly, Hood being Hood, they were about to go over to the offensive; Pat Cleburne, for one, believed that this was likely to take them far — in miles, at any rate. "We are going to carry the war to Africa," he predicted, "but I fear we will not be as successful as Scipio was."

Across the way, on the far side of Peachtree Creek and eastward out the Georgia Railroad, the reaction among Federals of rank was not dissimilar, so far as expectation of a step-up in the scale of fighting went, when it became known next day that the Confederates, in Lincoln's current campaign phrase, had "swapped horses in midstream."

McPherson and Schofield had been West Point classmates of Hood's, standing first and seventh respectively in a class of fifty-two, while he stood forty-fourth — ten places below even Sheridan, who had been held back a year for misconduct. Schofield in fact had been his roommate, and by coaching him in mathematics, which gave the Kentucky cadet a great deal of trouble, had managed to keep his military career from ending in academic failure and dismissal. "I came very near thinking once or twice that perhaps I had made a mistake," the Illinois general would remark in later years, though for the present he simply warned his chief: "He'll hit you like hell, now, before you know it." McPherson agreed, and so did Thomas, under whom Hood had served five years ago in Texas. But perhaps the most convincing testimony as to this new opponent's boldness came from a Union-loyal fellow Kentuckian who had watched him play old-army poker. "I seed Hood bet $2500," this witness declared, "with nary a pair in his hand."

Warned from all sides that his adversary was "bold even to rashness, and courageous in the extreme," Sherman took the precaution of advising his unit commanders to keep their troops "always prepared for battle in any shape."

Not that he regretted the predicted shift in rebel tactics. His casualties would undoubtedly mount, but there was plenty of room for taking up the slack that was evident from a comparison of Union losses, east and west. In the eleven weeks of his campaign against Johnston and Atlanta, he had lost fewer men than Meade had lost in the two-day Wilderness battle that opened his drive on Lee and Richmond. Besides, as Sherman saw it, the heavier the casualties were — provided, of course, that they could be kept in ratio, Federal and Confederate — the sooner the fighting would end with him in occupation of his goal. That was what he meant, in part, when he wrote home the following week: "I confess I was pleased at the change."

CHAPTER X

War Is Cruelty . . .

★ ✗ ☆

EASTWARD, WITH LEE AT LAST OUT-FOXED, the blue tide ran swift and steady, apparently inexorable as it surged toward the gates of the capital close in his rear. But then, at the full, the outlying Richmond bulwarks held; Beauregard, as he had been wont to do from the outset — first at Sumter, three years back, then again two years ago at Corinth, and once more last year in Charleston harbor — made the most of still another "finest hour" by holding Petersburg against the longest odds ever faced by a major commander on either side in this lengthening, long-odds war.

Grant's crossing of James River went like clockwork, and the clock itself was enormous. Preceded in the withdrawal by Baldy Smith, whose corps took ship at White House Landing on June 13 for the roundabout journey to rejoin Butler at Bermuda Hundred, Hancock reached Wilcox Landing by noon of the following day, completing a thirty-mile hike from Cold Harbor to the north bank of the James, and began at once the ferrying operation that would put his corps on Windmill Point, across the way, by dawn of June 15. While he crossed, the engineers got to work on the pontoon bridge, two miles downriver, by which the other three corps of the Army of the Potomac were to march in order to reinforce Smith and Hancock in their convergence on Petersburg, the rail hub whose loss, combined with the loss of the Virginia Central — Hunter and Sheridan were presumed to be moving down that critical Shendandoah Valley supply line even now — would mean that Richmond's defenders, north as well as south of the James, would have to abandon the city for lack of subsistence, or else choose between starvation and surrender. In high spirits at the prospect, Grant was delighted to recover the mobility that had characterized the opening of the final phase of his Vicksburg campaign, which the current operation so much resembled. Now as then, he was crossing a river miles downstream from his objective in order to sever its lines of supply and come upon it from the rear. Whether it crumpled under a sudden assault, as he intended, or crumbled under a siege, which he hoped to avoid, the result would be the same; Richmond was doomed, if he could only achieve here in Virginia the concert of action he had enjoyed last year in Mississippi.

By way of ensuring that this would obtain, he did not tarry long on the north bank of the James, which he reached on the morning of June 14 to find the head of Hancock's column arriving and the engineers already hard at work corduroying approaches to the bridge the pontoniers would presently throw across the nearly half-mile width of river to Windmill Point. Instead, wanting to make certain that Butler understood his part in the double-pronged maneuver, Grant got aboard a steamer for a fast ride up to Bermuda Hundred and a conference with the cock-eyed general. Butler not only understood; he was putting the final touches to the preliminary details, laying a pontoon bridge near Broadway Landing, where Smith would cross the Appomattox tonight for a quick descent on Petersburg next morning, and preparing to sink five stone-laden vessels in the channel of the James at Trent's Reach, within cannon range of his bottled-up right, to block the descent below that point of rebel gunboats which might otherwise make a suicidal attempt to disrupt the main crossing, some thirty winding miles downstream. Satisfied that no hitch was likely to develop in this direction, either from neglect or misconception, Grant prepared to return to Wilcox Landing for a follow-up meeting with Meade, but before he left he got off a wire to Halleck, who had opposed the movement from the outset in the belief that the scattered segments of both armies, Meade's and Butler's, would be exposed to piecemeal destruction by Lee while it was in progress. "Our forces will commence crossing the James today," Grant informed him. "The enemy show no signs yet of having brought troops to the south side of Richmond. I will have Petersburg secured, if possible, before they get there in much force. Our movement from Cold Harbor to the James River has been made with great celerity and so far without loss or accident."

The answer came next morning, not from Old Brains, who was not to be dissuaded from taking counsel of his fears, but from the highest authority of all:

> Have just read your dispatch of 1 p.m. yesterday. I begin to see it. You will succeed. God bless you all.
>
> A. Lincoln

By that time Smith was over the Appomattox and moving directly on Petersburg, whose outer defenses lay within six miles of Broadway Landing. He had 16,000 men in his three infantry divisions, including one that joined him from City Point at daybreak — a Negro outfit under Brigadier General Edward Hincks, which had been left behind when the rest of the corps shifted northside for a share in the Cold Harbor

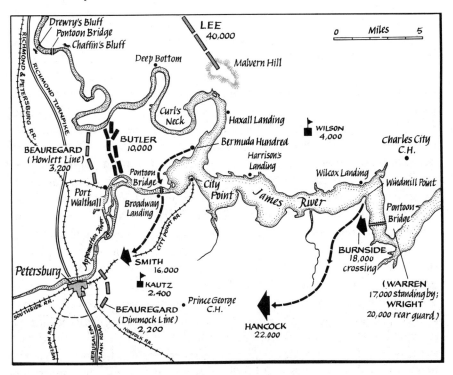

nightmare — plus Kautz's 2400 wide-ranging troopers, over toward the City Point Railroad, where they covered the exposed southeast flank of the column on the march. Four miles from the river, after receiving long-range shots from rebel vedettes who scampered when threatened, the marchers came upon a fast-firing section of artillery posted atop an outlying hill with butternut infantry in support. Hincks, on the left, sent his unblooded soldiers forward at a run. One gun got away, but they took the other, along with its crew, and staged a jubilation around the captured piece, elated at having made the most of a chance to discredit the doubts that had denied them a role in the heavy fighting two weeks ago. Baldy too was delighted, despite the delay, as he got the celebrants back into column, left and right, and resumed the march; for this was the route by which he believed Petersburg could have been taken in the first place, back in early May, and he had said as much, repeatedly though without avail, to Butler at the time. Another mile down the road, however, he came upon a sobering view, spirit-chilling despite the noonday heat, and called a halt for study and deployment.

What he saw, dead ahead down the tracks of the railroad, might well have given anyone pause, let alone a man who had just returned from playing a leading role in Grant's (and Lee's) Cold Harbor demonstration of what could happen to troops, whatever their numerical advantage, who delivered a hair-trigger all-out attack on a prepared position, however scantly it might be defended. Moreover, this one had been under construction and improvement not for two days, as had been the

case beyond the Chickahominy, but for nearly two years, ever since
August 1862, when Richmond's defenders learned that McClellan had
wanted to make just such a southside thrust, as a sequel to *his* Peninsular
"change of base," only to be overruled by Halleck, who had favored
the maneuver no more then, when he had the veto, than he did now
that he lacked any final say-so in the matter. Called the "Dimmock
Line" for Captain Charles H. Dimmock, the engineer who laid them out,
the Petersburg fortifications were ten miles in length, a half oval tied at
its ends to the Appomattox above and below the town, and contained
in all some 55 redans, square forts bristling with batteries and connected
by six-foot breastworks, twenty feet thick at the base and rimmed by a
continuous ditch, another six feet deep and fifteen wide. In front of this
dusty moat, trees had been felled, their branches sharpened and interlaced to discourage attackers, and on beyond a line of rifle pits for
skirmishers, who could fall back through narrow gaps in the abatis, the
ground had been cleared for half a mile to afford the defenders an
unobstructed field of fire that would have to be crossed, naked to whatever lead might fly, by whatever moved against them. Confronting the
eastward bulge of this bristly, hard-shelled oval, Smith gulped and then
got down to figuring how to crack it. First there was reconnoitering to
be done; a risky business, and he did much of it himself, drawing sniper
fire whenever he ventured out of the woods in which he concealed his
three divisions while he searched for some apparently nonexistent weak
point to assault.

Despite a superfluity of guns frowning from all those embrasures,
there seemed to be a scarcity of infantry in the connecting works. Accordingly, he decided to try for a breakthrough with a succession of
reinforced skirmish lines, strong enough to overwhelm the defenders
when they came to grips, yet not so thickly massed as to suffer unbearable losses in the course of their naked advance across the slashings. All
this took time, however. It was past 4 o'clock when Smith wound up his
reconnaissance and completed the formulation of his plan. Aware that
the defenders were in telegraphic contact with Richmond, from which
reinforcements could be rushed by rail — the track distance was only
twenty-three miles — he set 5 o'clock as the jump-off hour for a coördinated attack by elements from all three divisions, with every piece of
Federal artillery firing its fastest to keep the heads of the defenders
down while his troops were making their half-mile sprint from the
woods, where they now were masked, to the long slow curve of breastworks in their front.

It was then that the first organic hitch developed. Unaware that
an attack was pending (for the simple reason that no one had thought to
inform him) the corps artillery chief had just sent all the horses off for
water; which meant that there could be no support fire for the attackers
until the teams returned to haul the guns into position along the western

fringe of the woods. Angered, Baldy delayed the jump-off until 7. While he and his 18,000 waited, and the sun drew near the landline, word came that Hancock, after a similar hitch on Windmill Point this morning, was on the way but would not arrive till after dark. For a moment Smith considered another postponement; Hancock's was the largest corps in Meade's army, and the notion of more than doubling the Petersburg attack force to 40,000 was attractive. But the thought of Confederate reinforcements, perhaps racing southward in untold thousands even now, jam-packed into and onto every railway car available in this section of Virginia — plus the companion thought that Hancock outranked him and might therefore hog the glory — provoked a rejection of any further delay. The revised order stood, and at 7 o'clock the blue skirmishers stepped from the woods, supported by fire from the just-arrived guns, and started forward to where friendly shells were bursting over and around the rebel fortifications, half a mile ahead.

Once more Hincks and his green black troops showed the veterans how to do the thing in style. Swarming over the cleared ground and into the red after-glory of the sunset, they pursued the grayback skirmishers through the tangled abatis, across the ditch, and up and over the breastworks just beyond. Formidable as they had been to the eye, the fortifications collapsed at a touch; no less than seven of the individual bastions fell within the hour, five of them to the jubilant Negro soldiers, who took twelve of the sixteen captured guns and better than half of the 300 prisoners. Astride and south of the railroad, the blue attackers occupied more than a mile of intrenchments, and Hincks, elated at the ease with which his men had bashed in the eastern nose of the rebel oval, wanted to continue the drive right into the streets of Petersburg, asking only that the other two divisions support him in the effort. Smith demurred. It was night now, crowding 9 o'clock, and his mind was on Lee, who was reported to have detached a considerable portion of his army for a crossing of the James that afternoon; they had probably arrived by now, in which case the Federals might be counterattacked at any moment by superior numbers of hornet-mad Confederate veterans. The thing to do, he told Hincks, was brace for the shock and prepare to hold the captured works until Hancock arrived to even or perhaps reverse the odds. Then they would see.

Hancock arrived something over an hour later; two of his three divisions, he said, were a mile behind him on the road from Prince George Courthouse. This had been a trying day for him and his dusty marchers, beginning at dawn, when he received orders to wait on Windmill Point for 60,000 rations supposedly on the way from Butler. He had no use for them, having brought his own, but he waited as ordered until 10.30 and then set out without them. That was the cause of the first delay, a matter of some five hours. The second, equally wasteful of time, was caused by an inadequate map, which misled him badly — with the result that the distance to Petersburg by the direct route, sixteen miles, was nearly doubled by the various countermarches he was obliged to make when he found that the roads on the ground ran in different directions from those inked on paper — and faulty instructions, which identified as his destination a point that later turned out to lie within the enemy lines. "I spent the best hours of the day," he would complain in his report, "marching by an incorrect map in search of a designated position which, as described, was not in existence."

Nor was that the worst of the oversights and errors that developed in the course of this long hot June 15, from which so much had been expected and of which some ten critical hours thus were thrown away. Approaching Prince George Courthouse about sunset, Hancock met a courier from Baldy Smith, who gave him a dispatch headed 4 p.m. and including the words: "If the II Corps can come up in time to make an assault tonight after dark, in the vicinity of Norfolk & Petersburg Railroad, I think we can be successful." This was the first he had heard that he and his 22,000 were intended to have any part in today's action; no one on Grant's staff had thought to tell Meade, who could scarcely be expected to pass along orders he himself had not received. Hancock hastened his march and rode ahead to join Smith at about 10.30, two miles east of Petersburg, only to find that the Vermonter had changed his mind about a night attack. He requested, rather, that Hancock relieve Hincks's troops — whether as a restful reward for all they had done today, or out of a continuing mistrust of their fighting qualities, he did not say — in occupation of the solid mile of rebel works they had taken when they charged into the sunset.

It was done, though Hincks continued to insist that he could march into Petersburg if his chief would only unleash and support him. Hancock rather agreed, though he declined to assume command, being unfamiliar with the ground and partly incapacitated by his Gettysburg wound, which had reopened under the strain of the fretful march. Smith — suffering too, as he said, "from the effects of bad water, and malaria brought from Cold Harbor" — was willing, even glad, to bide his time; his mind was still on all those probable grayback reinforcements coming down from Richmond in multi-thousand-man relays. The 40,000 Federals on hand would be about doubled tomorrow by the arrival of Burnside, who was over the James by now, and Warren, who had just begun to cross. Wilson and Wright would bring the total to roughly 100,000 the following morning; which would surely be enough for practically anything, Smith figured, especially since they had only to expand the gains already made today.

"Unless I misapprehend the topography," he wired Butler before turning in at midnight, "I hold the key to Petersburg."

Beauregard agreed that Baldy held the key. What was more, he also agreed with Hincks that the key was in the lock, that all the blue-coats had to do at this point was give the thing a turn and the gate would swing ajar. "Petersburg was clearly at the mercy of the Federal commander, who had all but captured it," he said later, looking back on that time of strain and near despair.

He had in all, this June 15, some 5400 troops in his department: 3200 with Bushrod Johnson, corking the bottle in which Butler was confined on Bermuda Hundred, and 2200 with Brigadier General Henry A. Wise at Petersburg. The rest — Hoke's division and the brigades of Ransom and Gracie; about 9000 in all — were beyond the James, detached to Lee or posted in the Richmond fortifications. Wise, it was true, had held his own last week in the "Battle of the Patients and the Penitents," which turned back a similar southside thrust, but the Creole identified this recent probe by Butler as no more than "a reconnaissance connected with Grant's future operations." Heavier blows were being prepared by a sterner commander, and he had been doing all he could for the past five days to persuade the War Department to return the rest of his little army to him before they landed. Smith had no sooner been spotted moving in transports up the James the day before, June 14, than Beauregard redoubled his efforts, insisting, now that the crisis he had predicted was at hand, that Hoke and the others be sent without delay. Next morning — today — with Smith bearing ponderously down on him from Broadway Landing and his detached units still unreleased by Richmond, he warned Bragg that even when these were returned, as he was at last assured they would be, he probably would have to choose which of his two critical southside positions to abandon, the Howlett Line above the Appomattox or the Dimmock Line below, if he was to scrape together enough defenders to make a fight for the other. While Wise shifted his few troops into the eastern nose of the intrenchments ringing Petersburg, thus to confront the enemy approaching down the City Point Railroad, Beauregard put the case bluntly in a wire to Richmond: "We must now elect between lines of Bermuda Hundred and Petersburg. We can not hold both. Please answer at once." Evading the question, Bragg merely replied that Hoke was on the way and should be used to the best advantage. Old Bory lost patience entirely. "I did not ask your advice with regard to the movement of troops," he wired back, "but wished to know preference between Petersburg and lines across Bermuda Hundred Neck, for my guidance, as I fear my present force may prove unequal to hold both."

Bragg made no reply at all to this, and while Wise and his 2200, outnumbered eight-to-one by the blue host assembling in front of their works, made enough of a false show of strength to delay through the long afternoon an assault that could scarcely fail, the Creole general fumed and fretted.

Smith's sunset attack was about as successful as had been expected,

though fortunately it was not pressed home; Hoke came up in time to
assist in work on the secondary defenses, to which Wise and his survivors had fallen back when more than a mile of the main line caved in.
Beauregard's strength was now about 8000 for the close-up defense
of the town, but this growth was inconsiderable in the light of information that a second Federal column, as large as the first, was approaching from Prince George Courthouse. Dawn would no doubt bring a
repetition of the sunset assault, which was sure to be as crumpling since
it could be made with twice the strength. Alone in the darkness, ignored
by his superiors, and convinced that Wise and Hoke were about to be
swamped unless they could be reinforced, the southside commander,
who had joined them by then from his headquarters north of the
Appomattox, notified Richmond that he had decided to risk uncorking
Butler so as to reinforce Petersburg, even though this was likely to
mean the loss of its vital rail and telegraph connections with the
capital beyond the James. "I shall order Johnson to this point," he
wired Bragg. "General Lee must look to the defenses of Drewry's
Bluff and Bermuda Hundred, if practicable."

     Notified of this development two hours past midnight, Lee reacted
promptly. He had suspected from the outset that Grant would do as
he had done; "I think the enemy must be preparing to move south of
James River," he warned Davis at noon on June 14, before the first
blue soldier crossed to Windmill Point. Still, that did not mean that
he could act on the supposition. Responsible for the security of Richmond, he had his two remaining corps disposed along a north-south
line from White Oak Swamp to Malvern Hill, where he covered the
direct approach to the capital twelve miles in his rear, and he could not
abandon or even weaken this line until he was certain that the Federals
did not intend to come this way. Information that Smith was back at
Bermuda Hundred, and then that he had crossed the Appomattox for
an attack on Petersburg, was no real indication of what *Meade* would
do; Smith was only returning to the command from which he had
been detached two weeks ago. Nor was the report that a corps from the
Army of the Potomac was on the march beyond the James conclusive
evidence of what Grant had in mind for the rest of that army. Butler
had reinforced Meade for the northside strike at Lee: so might Meade
be reinforcing Butler for the southside strike at Beauregard — who, in
point of fact, had yet to identify or take prisoners from any unit except
Smith's; all he had really said, so far, was that he had an awesome
number of bluecoats in his front, and that was by no means an unusual
claim for any general to make, let alone the histrionic Creole.

     However, when Lee was wakened at 2 o'clock in the morning to
learn that the Howlett Line had been stripped of all but a skeleton
force of skirmishers ("Cannot these lines be occupied by your troops?"
Beauregard inquired. "The safety of our communications requires it")

he no longer had any choice about what to do if he was to save the capital in his rear. A breakout by Butler, westward from Bermuda Hundred, would give the Federals control of the one railroad leading north from Petersburg, and that would have the same effect as if the three railroads leading south had been cut; Richmond would totter, for lack of food, and fall. Accordingly, Lee had Pickett's division on the march by 3 a.m. and told Anderson to follow promptly with one of his other two divisions, Field's, and direct the action against Butler, who almost certainly would have overrun the Howlett Line by the time he got there. Moreover, leaving instructions for A. P. Hill to continue shielding Richmond from a northside attack by Meade — whose army, even with one corps detached, was still better than twice as large as the Army of Northern Virginia, depleted by Early's departure three days ago — Lee struck his tent at Riddell's Shop, while it still was dark, and mounted Traveller for the headquarters shift to Chaffin's Bluff, where Anderson's troops would cross by a pontoon bridge to recover the critical southside works Beauregard had abandoned the night before.

Sure enough, when Lee reached Chaffin's around 9.30 this June 16 and crossed the James behind Pickett, just ahead of Field, the nearby popping of rifles and the distant rumble of guns informed him, simultaneously, that Butler had indeed overrun the scantly manned Bermuda works, whose northern anchor was six miles downriver, and that Beauregard was fighting to hang onto Petersburg, a dozen miles to the south. Presently word came from Anderson that Butler's uncorked troops had advanced westward to Port Walthall Junction, where they were tearing up track and digging in to prevent the movement of reinforcements beyond that point, either by rail or turnpike. Lee replied that they must be driven off, and by nightfall they were, though only as far as the abandoned Howlett Line, which they held in reverse, firing west. All this time, Beauregard's guns had kept growling and messages from him ranged in tone from urgent to laconic, beginning with a cry for help — to which Lee replied, pointedly, that he could not strip the north bank of the James without evidence that more than one of Meade's corps had crossed — and winding up proudly, yet rather mild withal: "We may have force sufficient to hold Petersburg." In response to queries about Grant, whose whereabouts might indicate his intentions, Old Bory could only say at the end of the long day's fight: "No satisfactory information yet received of Grant's crossing James River. Hancock's and Smith's corps are however in our front."

Lee already knew this last. What he did not know, because Beauregard did not know it to pass it along to him, was that Burnside had been in front of Petersburg since midmorning (in fact, his was the corps responsible for such limited gains as the Federals made today) and that Warren was arriving even then, bringing the blue total to more than 75,000, with still another 25,000 on the way. Wilson, who had served Grant well in Sheridan's absence with the other two mounted divisions, was riding hard through the twilight from Windmill Point, and Wright would finish crossing the pontoon bridge by midnight with the final elements of Meade's army. Beauregard, whose strength had been raised in the course of the day to just over 14,000 by the arrival of Johnson from Bermuda Hundred and Ransom and Gracie from Richmond, might find the odds he had faced yesterday and today stretched unbearably tomorrow, despite the various oversights and hitches that had disrupted the Union effort south of the James for the past two days.

In all that time, hamstrung by conflicting orders and inadequate maps — and rendered cautious, moreover, by remembrance of Cold Harbor, fought two weeks ago tomorrow — the attackers had not managed to bring their preponderance of numbers to bear in a single concerted assault on the cracked and creaking Dimmock Line. Yet Grant, for one, was not inclined to be critical at this juncture. As he prepared for bed tonight in his tent at City Point, where he had transferred his headquarters the day before, he said with a smile, sitting half undressed on the edge of his cot: "I think it is pretty well, to get across a great river and come up here and attack Lee in the rear before he is ready for us."

So he said, and so it was; "pretty well," indeed. But June 17, even though all of Meade's army was over the James before it dawned and had been committed to some kind of action before it ended, turned out to be little different. Today, as yesterday, the pressure built numerically beyond what should have been the rebel breaking point — better than 80,000 opposed by fewer than 15,000 — yet was never brought decisively to bear. From the outset, things again went wrong: beginning with Warren, who came up the previous night. Instructed to extend the left beyond the Jerusalem Plank Road for a sunrise attack up that well-defined thoroughfare, he encountered skirmishers on the approach march and turned astride the Norfolk Railroad to drive them back, thus missing a chance (which neither he nor his superiors knew existed) to strike beyond the occupied portion of the Dimmock Line. If this had not happened, if Warren had brushed the skirmishers aside and continued his march as instructed, Beauregard later said, "I would have been compelled to evacuate Petersburg without much resistance." As it was, the conflict here at the south end of the line amounted to little more than an all-day long-range demonstration.

Northward along the center, where Burnside's and Hancock's corps were posted, the fighting was a good deal bloodier, although not much more productive in the end. One of Burnside's divisions started things off by seizing a critical hill, yet could not exploit the advantage because he failed to alert his other two divisions to move up quickly in support. The Confederates had time to shore up their crumbling defenses, both here and just to the north where Hancock's three divisions were lying idle; Hancock having been obliged by his reopened wound to turn the command over to Birney — a good man, but no Hancock — they too had failed to get the word, with the result that they were about as much out of things as were Wright's three divisions, one of which was used to bolster the fought-out Smith, inactive on the right, while the other two were sent in response to Butler's urgent plea for reinforcements to keep Lee from driving him back into the bottle he had popped out of yesterday. Wright went, but failed to arrive in time to do anything more than join the Bermuda Hundred soldiers in captivity. By midafternoon, Pickett and Field had retaken the Howlett

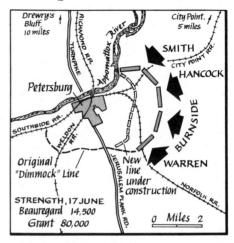

Line from end to end; Butler was recorked, this time for good, and still more troops were reported to be on the march from Lee's position east of Richmond.

If they got there, if Petersburg was heavily reinforced, the Army of the Potomac would simply have exchanged one stalemate for another, twice the distance from the rebel capital and on the far side of a major river. There still was time to avoid this, however. None of Lee's veterans was yet across the Appomattox, and most of them were still beyond the James. With the railroad severed at Walthall Junction, even the closest were unlikely to reach the field by first light tomorrow; which left plenty of time for delivering the coördinated attack the Federals had been trying for all along, without success.

Happily, near sunset, at least a portion of the army recovered a measure of its old élan. Burnside and Birney, suddenly meshing gears, surged forward to seize another mile of works along the enemy center, together with a dozen guns and about 500 prisoners. A savage counterattack (by Gracie's brigade, it later developed, though at the time the force had seemed considerably larger) forestalled any rapid enlargement of the breakthrough, either in width or depth. Dusk deepened into darkness, and though the moon, only two nights short of the full, soon came out to flood the landscape with its golden light, Meade — 'ike Smith before him, two dusks ago — declined to follow through by continuing the advance. Instead, he issued orders for a mass assault to be launched all along the line at the first wink of dawn.

Beauregard said afterwards that at this point, with his center pierced and Petersburg once more up for grabs, it seemed to him that "the last hour of the Confederacy had arrived." In fact, he had been ex-

pecting his patched-up line to crack all day, and he had begun at noon
the laying out of a new defensive position, the better part of a mile in
rear of the present one, to fall back on when the time came. He had no
engineers, and indeed no reserves of any kind for digging; all he could
do was mark the proposed line with white stakes, easily seen at night,
and hope the old intrenchments would hold long enough for darkness
to cover the withdrawal of his soldiers, who would do the digging when
they got there. The old works, or what was left of them, did hold; or
anyhow they nearly did, and Gracie's desperate counterattack delayed
a farther blue advance until nightfall stopped the fighting. Old Bory
ordered campfires lighted all along the front and sentinels posted well
forward; then at midnight, behind this curtain of light and the fitful spatter
of picket fire, the rest of his weary men fell back through the moon-
drenched gloom to the site of their new line, which they then began to
dig, using bayonets and tin cans for tools and getting what little sleep
they could between shifts.

At 12.40 a.m. their commander got off his final dispatch of the
day to Lee. "All quiet at present. I expect renewal of attack in morning. My troops are becoming much exhausted. Without immediate
and strong reinforcements results may be unfavorable. Prisoners report
Grant on the field with his whole army."

Lee now had a definite statement, the first in five days, not only
that Meade's army was no longer in his front, but also that it was in
Beauregard's, and he reacted accordingly. In point of fact, he had
begun to act on this premise in response to a dispatch written six hours
earlier, in which the southside commander informed him that increasing
pressure along his "already much extended lines" would compel him
to retire to a shorter line, midway between his original works and the
vital rail hub in his rear. "This I shall hold as long as practicable," he
added, "but without reinforcements I may have to evacuate the city
very shortly." Petersburg's fate was Richmond's; Lee moved, as he had
done two nights ago when the Creole stripped the Howlett Line, to
forestall disaster — or anyhow to be in a better position to forestall it —
by ordering Anderson's third division to proceed to Bermuda Neck
and A. P. Hill to cross the James at Chaffin's Bluff and await instructions for a march in either direction, back north or farther south down
the Petersburg Turnpike, depending on developments.

So much he had done already, and now that Beauregard's 12.40
message was at hand, stating flatly that Grant was "on the field with
his whole army," he followed through by telling Anderson to send his
third division on to Petersburg at once and follow with the second.
A. P. Hill would go as well, leaving one of his three divisions north
of the Appomattox in case Richmond came under attack. This last
seemed highly unlikely, however; for a report came in, about this time,
that cavalry had ridden down the Peninsula the previous afternoon, as

far as Wilcox Landing, and found that all four of Meade's corps had crossed to Windmill Point in the course of the past three days. Beauregard's information, gathered from prisoners, thus was confirmed beyond all doubt. It was now past 3.30 in the morning, June 18; Lee's whole army, except for one division left holding the Howlett Line against Butler — and of course Early, who made contact with Hunter at Lynchburg that same day — would be on the march for Petersburg within the hour.

Two staff officers arrived just then from beyond the Appomattox, sent by their chief to lend verbal weight to his written pleas for help. "Unless reinforcements are sent before forty-eight hours," one of them told Lee he had heard Old Bory declare, "God Almighty alone can save Petersburg and Richmond." Normally, Lee did not approve of such talk; it seemed to him tinged with irreverence. But this was no normal time. "I hope God Almighty will," he said.

For the first time since the crossing of the James, Meade's army gave him on schedule all he asked for. In line before dawn, the troops went forward before sunrise, under orders to take the Confederate works "at all costs." They took them, in fact, at practically no cost at all; for they were deserted, covered only by a handful of pickets who got off a shot or two, then scampered rearward or surrendered.

The result was about as disruptive to the attackers, however, as if they had met the stiffest kind of resistance. First, there was the confusion of calling a halt in the abandoned trenches, which had to be occupied for defense against a tricky counterstroke, and then there followed the testy business of groping about to locate the vanished rebels. All this took time. It was midmorning before they found them, nearly a mile to the west, and presently they had cause to wish they hadn't. Beauregard had established a new and shorter line, due south from the Appomattox to a connection with the old works beyond the Jerusalem Plank Road, and was dug in all along it, guns clustered thicker than ever. A noon assault, spearheaded by Birney, was bloodily repulsed: so bloodily and decisively, indeed, that old-timers among the survivors — who had encountered this kind of fire only too often throughout six weeks of crablike sidling from the Rapidan to the Chickahominy — sent back word that Old Bory had been reinforced: by Lee.

It was true. Anderson's lead division had arrived at 7.30 and the second marched in two hours later, followed at 11 o'clock by Lee himself, who rode out to confer with Beauregard, now second-in-command, his lonely ordeal ended. As fast as the lean, dusty marchers came up they were put into line alongside the nearly fought-out defenders, some of whom tried to raise a feeble cheer of welcome, while others wept from exhaustion at the sudden release from tension. They were pleased to hear that A. P. Hill would also be up by nightfall to reduce the all-but-unbearable odds to the accustomed two-to-one, but as far as they were concerned the situation was stabilized already; they had considered their line unbreakable from the time the first of the First Corps veterans arrived to slide their rifles across the newly dug earth of the parapets and sight down them in the direction from which the Yankees would have to come when they attacked.

Across the way, the men who would be expected to do the coming flatly agreed. Remembering one Cold Harbor, they saw here the makings of another, and they wanted no part of it. The result, after the costly noon repulse, was a breakdown of the command system, so complete that Meade got hopping mad and retired, in effect, from any further participation in the effort. "I find it useless to appoint an hour to effect coöperation.... What additional orders to attack you require I cannot imagine," he complained in a message sent to all corps commanders. His solution, if it could be called such, was for them "to attack at all hazards and without reference to each other."

Under these circumstances, the army was spared another Cold Harbor only because its members, for the most part, declined to obey such orders as would have brought on a restaging of that fiasco. Hancock's troops had come up in high spirits, three days ago; "We knew that we had outmarched Lee's veterans and that our reward was at hand," one would recall. These expectations had died since then, however, along with a great many of the men who shared them. "Are you going to charge those works?" a cannoneer asked as a column of infantry passed his battery, headed for the front, and was told by a foot soldier: "No, we are not going to charge. We are going to run toward the Confederate earthworks and then we are going to run back. We have had enough of assaulting earthworks."

As the afternoon wore on, many declined to do even that much. Around 4 o'clock, for example, Birney massed a brigade for an all-out attack on the rebel center. He formed the troops in four lines, the front two made up of half a dozen veteran units, the rear two of a pair of outsized heavy-artillery regiments, 1st Massachusetts and 1st Maine. All four lines were under instructions to remain prone until the order came to rise and charge; but when it was given, the men in the front ranks continued to hug the ground, paying no attention to the shouts and exhortations of their saber-waving officers. They looked back and saw that the rear-rank heavies had risen and were preparing to go forward. "Lay down, you damn fools! You can't take them works!" they cried over their shoulders. For all their greenness, the Bay State troops knew sound advice when they heard it. They lay back down. But the Maine men were rugged. They stepped through and over the prone ranks of veterans and moved at the double against the enemy intrenchments, which broke into flame at their approach. None of them made it up to the clattering rebel line, and few of them made it back to their own. Of the 850 who went forward, 632 fell in less than half an hour. That was just over 74 percent, the severest loss suffered in a single engagement by any Union regiment in the whole course of the war.

This could not continue, nor did it. Before sunset Meade wired Grant that he believed nothing more could be accomplished here today. "Our men are tired," he informed his chief, "and the attacks have not been made with the vigor and force which characterized our fighting in the Wilderness; if they had been," he added, "I think we should have been more successful." Grant — who had maintained a curious hands-off attitude throughout the southside contest, even as he watched his well-laid plan being frustrated by inept staff work and the bone-deep disconsolation of the troops — invoked no ifs and leveled no reproaches. Declaring that he was "perfectly satisfied that all has been done that could be done," he agreed that the time had come to call a halt. "Now we will rest the men," he said, "and use the spade for their protection until a new vein can be struck."

A new vein might be struck, in time, but not by the old army, which had suffered a further subtraction of 11,386 killed, wounded, or captured from its ranks since it crossed the James. That brought the grand total of Grant's losses, including Butler's, to nearly 75,000 men — more than Lee and Beauregard had had in both their armies at the start of the campaign. Of these, a precisely tabulated 66,315 were from the five corps under Meade (including Smith's, such time as it was with him) and that was only part of the basis for the statement by its historian, William Swinton, that at this juncture "the Army of the Potomac, shaken in its structure, its valor quenched in blood, and thousands of its ablest officers killed and wounded, was the Army of the Potomac no more."

Much the same thing could be said of the army in the Petersburg intrenchments. Though its valor was by no means "quenched," it was no longer the Army of Northern Virginia in the old aggressive sense, ready to lash out at the first glimpse of a chance to strike an unwary adversary; nor would it see again that part of the Old Dominion where its proudest victories had been won and from which it took its name. When Lee arrived that morning, hard on the heels of one corps and a few hours in advance of the other, Beauregard was in such a state of elation ("He was at last where I had, for the past three days, so anxiously hoped to see him," the Creole later wrote) that he proposed an all-out attack on the Union flank and rear, as soon as A. P. Hill came up. Lee rejected the notion out of hand, in the conviction that his troops were far too weary for any such exertion and that Hill's corps would be needed to extend the present line westward to cover the two remaining railroads, the Weldon and the Southside, upon which Richmond — and perhaps, for that matter, the Confederacy itself — depended for survival. He did not add, as he might have done, that he foresaw the need for conserving, not expending in futile counterstrokes, the life of every soldier he could muster if he was to maintain, through the months ahead, the stalemate he had achieved at the price of his old mobility. "We must destroy this army of Grant's before he gets to James River," he had told Early three weeks ago, in the course of the shift from the Totopotomoy. "If he gets there it will become a siege, and then it will be a mere question of time." It was not that yet; Richmond was not under direct pressure, north of the James, and Petersburg was no more than semi-beleaguered; but that too, he knew, was only a "question of time."

Grant agreed, knowing that the length of time in question would depend on the rate of his success in reaching around Lee's right for control of the two railroads in his rear. First, though, there was the need for making the hastily occupied Federal line secure against dislodgment. The following day, June 19, was a Sunday (it was also the summer solstice; *Kearsarge* and *Alabama* were engaged off Cherbourg, firing at each other across the narrowing circles they described in the choppy waters of the Channel, and Sherman was maneuvering, down in Georgia, for ground from which to launch his Kennesaw assault); Meade's troops kept busy constructing bombproofs and hauling up heavy guns and mortars that would make life edgy, not only for the grayback soldiers just across the way, but also for the civilians in Petersburg, whose downtown streets were so little distance away that the blue gun crews could hear its public clocks strike the hours when all but the pickets of both armies were rolled in blankets. Grant had it in mind, however, to try one more sudden lunge — a two-corps strike beyond the Jerusalem Plank Road — before settling down to "gradual approaches."

Warning orders went out Monday to Wright, whose three divisions would be reunited by bringing the detached two from Bermuda Hundred, and to Birney, whose corps would pull back out of line for the westward march, and on Tuesday, June 21, the movement got under way. Simultaneously, while still waiting for Sheridan to return from his failure to link up with Hunter near the Blue Ridge, Wilson, reinforced by Kautz, was sent on a wide-ranging strike at both the Petersburg & Weldon and the Southside railroads, with instructions to rip up sizeable stretches of both before returning. Grant had settled down at his City Point headquarters that afternoon to await the outcome of this double effort by half of Meade's infantry and all of the cavalry on hand, when "there appeared very suddenly before us," a staff colonel wrote his wife, "a long, lank-looking personage, dressed all in black and looking very much like a boss undertaker."

It was Lincoln. After sending his "I begin to see it" telegram to Grant on the 15th, he had gone up to Philadelphia for his speech next day at the Sanitary Fair; after which he returned to Washington, fidgeted through another three days while the Petersburg struggle mounted to climax, and finally, this morning, boarded a steamer for a cruise down the Potomac and a first-hand look at the war up the James. "I just thought I would jump aboard a boat and come down and see you," he said, after shaking hands all round. "I don't expect I can do any good, and in fact I'm afraid I may do harm, but I'll just put myself under your orders and if you find me doing anything wrong just send me right away."

Grant replied, not altogether jokingly, that he would do that, and the group settled down for talk. By way of reassurance as to the outcome of the campaign, which now had entered a new phase — one that opened with his army twice as far from the rebel capital as it had been the week before — the general took occasion to remark that his present course was certain to lead to victory. "You will never hear of me farther from Richmond than now, till I have taken it," he declared. "I am just as sure of going into Richmond as I am of any future event. It may take a long summer day, as they say in the rebel papers, but I will do it."

Lincoln was glad to hear that; but he had been watching the casualty lists, along with the public reaction they provoked. "I cannot pretend to advise," he said, somewhat hesitantly, "but I do sincerely hope that all may be accomplished with as little bloodshed as possible."

Aside from this, which was as close to an admonition as he came, he kept the conversation light. "The old fellow remained with us till the next day, and told stories all the time," the staff colonel informed his wife, adding: "On the whole he behaved very well."

One feature of the holiday was a horseback visit to Hincks's division, where news of Lincoln's coming gathered around him a throng of black soldiers ("grinning from ear to ear," the staffer wrote, "and displaying an amount of ivory terrible to behold") anxious for a chance to touch the Great Emancipator or his horse in passing. Tears in his eyes, he took off his hat in salute to them, and his voice broke when he thanked them for their cheers. This done, he rode back to City Point for the night, then reboarded the steamer next morning for an extension of his trip upriver to pay a courtesy call on Ben Butler, whose views on politics were as helpful, in their way, as were Grant's on army matters. He returned to Washington overnight, refreshed in spirit and apparently reinforced in the determination he had expressed a week ago at the Sanitary Fair: "We accepted this war for an object, a worthy object, and the war will end when that object is attained. Under God, I hope it never will until that time."

Helpful though the two-day outing was for Lincoln, by way of providing relaxation and lifting his morale, the events of that brief span around Petersburg had an altogether different effect on Grant, or at any rate on the troops involved in his intended probe around Lee's right. After moving up, as ordered, on the night of June 21, Wright and Birney (Hancock was still incapacitated, sloughing fragments of bone from the reopened wound in his thigh) lost contact as they advanced next morning through the woods just west of the Jerusalem Plank Road, under instructions to extend the Federal left to the Weldon Railroad. Suddenly, without warning, both were struck from within the gap created by their loss of contact. Lee had unleashed A. P. Hill, who attacked with his old fire and savagery, using one division to hold Wright's three in check while mauling Birney's three with the other two. The result was not only a repulse; it was also a humiliation. Though his loss in killed and wounded was comparatively light, no fewer than 1700 of Birney's men — including those in a six-gun battery of field artillery, who then stood by and watched their former weapons being used against their former comrades — surrendered rather than risk their lives in what he called "this most unfortunate and disgraceful affair." Hardest hit of all was Gibbon's division, which had crossed the Rapidan seven weeks ago with 6799 men and had suffered, including heavy reinforcements, a total of 7970 casualties, forty of them regimental commanders. Such losses, Gibbon declared in his formal report, "show why it is that troops, which at the commencement of the campaign were equal to almost any undertaking, became toward the end of it unfit for almost any."

Wilson, after a heartening beginning, fared even worse than the infantry in the end. Reinforced by Kautz to a strength of about 5000 horsemen and twelve guns, he struck and wrecked a section of the Weldon Railroad above Reams Station, nine miles south of Petersburg, then plunged on to administer the same treatment to the Southside and the Richmond & Danville, which crossed at Burkeville, fifty miles to the west. Near the Staunton River, eighty miles southwest of Petersburg, with close to sixty miles of track ripped up on the three roads, he turned and started back for his own lines, having been informed that they would have been extended by then to the Petersburg & Weldon. On the way there, he was harried by ever-increasing numbers of gray cavalry, and when he approached Reams Station he found it held, not by Wright or Birney, who he had been told would be there, but by A. P. Hill. Moreover, the mounted rebels, pressing him by now from all directions, turned out to be members of Hampton's other two divisions, returned ahead of Sheridan from the fight at Trevilian Station. Outnumbered and all but surrounded, Wilson set fire to his wagons, spiked his artillery, and fled southward in considerable disorder to the Nottoway River, which he succeeded in putting between him and his pursuers for a getaway east and north. He had accomplished most of what he was sent out to do, but at a cruel cost, including 1500 of his troopers killed or captured, his entire train burned, and all twelve of his guns abandoned.

Grant had the news of these two near fiascos to absorb, and simultaneously there came word of still a third, one hundred air-line miles to the west, potentially far graver than anything that had happened close at hand. Wright and Birney at least had extended the Federal left beyond the Jerusalem Road, and Wilson and Kautz had played at least temporary havoc with no less than three of Lee's critical rail supply lines. But David Hunter, aside from his easy victory two weeks ago at Piedmont and a good deal of incidental burning of civilian property since, accomplished little more, in the end, than the creation of just such a military vacuum as Lee specialized in filling.

Descending on Lynchburg late in the day, June 17, Hunter found Breckinridge drawn up to meet him with less than half as many troops. He paused overnight, preparing to stage another Piedmont in the morning, only to find, when it broke, that Jubal Early had arrived by rail from Charlottesville to even the odds with three veteran divisions: whereupon Hunter (for lack of ammunition, he later explained) went over to the defensive and fell back that night, under cover of darkness, to the shelter of the Blue Ridge. Early came on after him, and Hunter decided that, under the circumstances, his best course would be to return to West Virginia without delay. For three days Early pursued him, with small profit, then gave it up and on June 22 — while A. P. Hill was mauling Birney, south of Petersburg — marched for Staunton and the head of the Shenandoah Valley, that classic route for Confederate invasion which Lee had used so effectively in the past to play on Halleck's and Lincoln's fears.

These last were likely to be enlarged just now, and not without cause. With Hunter removed from all tactical calculations, nothing blue stood between Early and the Potomac, and with the capital defenses stripped of their garrisons to provide reinforcements and replacements for Meade, little remained with which to contest a gray advance from the Potomac into Washington itself. Lincoln had come up the James this week for a first-hand look at the war, but now it began to appear that he needed only to have waited a few days in the White House for the war to come to him.

So much was possible; Halleck's worst fears as to the consequences of the southside shift for the failed assault might now be proved only too valid. But Grant was not given to intensive speculation on possible future disasters; he preferred to meet them when they came, having long since discovered that few of them ever did. Instead, in writing to Old Brains on June 23 he stressed his need for still more soldiers, as a way of forestalling requests (or, in Lincoln's case, orders) for detachments northward from those he had on hand. "The siege of Richmond bids fair to be tedious," he informed him, "and in consequence of the very extended lines we must have, a much larger force will be necessary than would be required in ordinary sieges against the same force that now opposes us." Two days later, in passing along the news that Hunter was indeed in full retreat, he added that Sheridan had at last returned, though with his horses too worn down to be of any help to Wilson, who was fighting his way back east against lengthening odds. "I shall try to give the army a few days' rest, which they now stand much in need of," Grant concluded, rather blandly.

★   ★   ★

After frightening Hunter's 18,000 away from Lynchburg, westward beyond the Blue Ridge, and enjoying a day's rest from the three-day Allegheny chase that followed, the 14,000 Confederates took up the march for Staunton via Lexington, where on June 25 part of the column filed past Stonewall Jackson's grave, heads uncovered, arms reversed, bands intoning a dirge with muted horns and muffled drums. This salute to the fallen hero was altogether fitting as an invocation of the spirit it was hoped would guide the resurrected Army of the Valley through the campaign about to be undertaken by his old Second Corps, now led by Jubal Early. "Strike as quick as you can," Lee had telegraphed a week ago, as soon as he learned that Meade's whole army was south of the James, "and, if circumstances authorize, carry out the original plan, or move upon Petersburg without delay."

The original plan, explained to Early on the eve of his departure from Cold Harbor, June 13, was for him to follow the slash at Hunter with a fast march down the Valley, then cross the Potomac near Harpers Ferry and head east and south, through western Maryland, for a menacing descent on the Federal capital itself. Lee's hope was that this would produce one of two highly desirable results. Either it would alarm Lincoln into ordering heavy detachments northward from the Army of the Potomac, which might give Richmond's defenders a chance to lash out at the weakened attackers and drive them back from the city's gates, or else it would provoke Grant into staging a desperate assault, Cold Harbor style, that would serve even better to bleed him down for being disposed of by the counterattack that would follow his repulse. Given his choice, Early stuck to the original plan. After driving Hunter beyond the mountains, which removed him from all immediate tactical calculations, the gray pursuers rested briefly, then passed for the last time in review by their great captain's grave in battered Lexington and continued on to Staunton, where their hike down the Valley Turnpike would begin.

Early got there next day, ahead of his troops, and reorganized the 10,000 foot soldiers into two corps while awaiting their arrival. By assigning Gordon's division to Breckinridge, who coupled it with his own, he gave the former Vice President a post befitting his dignity and put thirty-five-year-old Robert Rodes — a native of Lynchburg, which he had just helped to save from Hunter's firebrands, and a graduate and one-time professor at V.M.I., whose scorched ruins he viewed sadly, and no doubt angrily as well, after marching his veterans past that other V.M.I. professor's grave — in charge of the remaining corps, composed of his own and Dodson Ramseur's divisions; Ramseur, a North Carolinian, promoted to major general the day after his twenty-seventh birthday early this month, was the youngest West Pointer to achieve that rank in Lee's army. The remaining 4000 effectives were cavalry and artillery, and these too were included in the shakeup designed to promote efficiency in battle and on the march. Robert Ransom, sent from Richmond for the purpose, was given command of the three mounted brigades ("buttermilk rangers," Early disaffectionately styled these horsemen, riled by their failure to bring Hunter to bay the week before) along with instructions to infuse some badly needed discipline into their ranks. As for the long arm, it was not so much reshuffled as it was stripped by weeding out the less serviceable guns and using only the best of teams to draw the surviving forty, supplemented by ten lighter pieces the cavalry would bring along. Recalling his predecessor Ewell's dictum, "The road to glory cannot be followed with much baggage," Early stipulated that one four-horse "skillet wagon" would have to suffice for transporting the cooking utensils for each 500 men, and he even warned that "regimental and company officers must carry for themselves such underclothing as they need for the present expedition." One major problem remained unsolved: a lack of shoes for half the army. This would not matter greatly in Virginia, but experience had shown that barefoot men suffered cruelly on the stony Maryland roads. Assured by the Quartermaster General that a shipment of shoes would overtake him before he crossed the Potomac, Early put the column in motion at first light June 28. Already beyond New Market two days later, some fifty miles down the turnpike, he informed Lee that his troops were "in fine condition and spirits, their health greatly improved. . . . If you can continue to threaten Grant," he added, "I hope to be able to do something for your relief and the success of our cause shortly. I shall lose no time."

True to his word, he reached Winchester on July 2, the Gettysburg anniversary, and there divided his army, sending one corps north, through Martinsburg, and the other east toward Harpers Ferry, where they were to converge two days later; Franz Sigel was at the former place with a force of about 5,000, while the latter contained a garrison roughly half that size, and Early wanted them both, if possible, together with all their equipment and supplies. It was not possible. Sigel — who by now had been dubbed "The Flying Dutchman" — was too nimble for him, scuttling eastward to join the Ferry garrison before the rebel

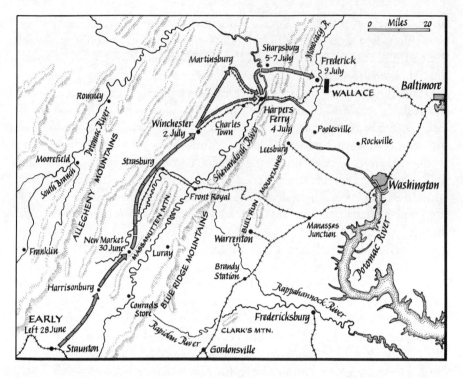

jaws could close and then taking sanctuary on Maryland Heights, which Early found too stout for storming when he came up on Independence Day. While one brigade maneuvered on Bolivar Heights to keep up the scare across the way, the rest of the Valley army settled down to feasting on the good things the Federals had left behind, here and at Martinsburg as well. Two days were spent preparing to cross the Potomac at Boteler's Ford, just upstream near Shepherdstown, and distributing the shipment of shoes that arrived on schedule from Richmond. On July 6 the crossing began in earnest; a third gray invasion was under way. No bands played "My Maryland," as before, but there was a chance for some of the veterans to revisit Sharpsburg, where they had fought McClellan, two Septembers back, from dawn to dusk along Antietam Creek. On they trudged, across South Mountain on July 8, breaking in their new shoes, and entered Frederick next morning in brilliant sunlight. East and southeast, beyond the glittering Monocacy River, the highway forked toward Baltimore and Washington, their goal.

Certain adjunctive matters had been or were being attended to by the time the infantry cleared Frederick. Coincident with the Potomac crossing, Imboden's cavalry had been sent westward, out the Baltimore & Ohio, to wreck a considerable stretch of that line and thus prevent a rapid return by Hunter's numerically superior force from beyond the Alleghenies, and simultaneously, by way of securing reparation for Hunter's recent excesses in the Old Dominion, a second mounted brigade, under Brigadier General John McCausland — another V.M.I.

graduate and professor — was sent to Hagerstown with instructions to exact an assessment of $200,000, cash down, under penalty of otherwise having the torch put to its business district. En route, McCausland somehow dropped a digit, and the Hagerstown merchants, knowing a bargain when they saw one, were prompt in their payment of $20,000 for deliverance from the flames. No such arithmetical error was made at Frederick, where McCausland rejoined in time to see the full $200,000 demanded and paid in retaliation for what had been done, four weeks ago in Lexington, to Washington College and his alma mater. No sooner had he returned than the third brigade of horsemen, under Colonel Bradley Johnson, was detached. Hearing from Lee, in a sealed dispatch brought north by his son Robert, that a combined operation by naval elements and undercover agents was planned for the liberation of 17,000 Confederate prisoners at Point Lookout, down Chesapeake Bay at the mouth of the Potomac, Early sent for Johnson — a native of Frederick, familiar with the region to be traversed — and told him to take his troopers eastward, cut telegraph wires and burn railroad bridges north and south of Baltimore in order to prevent the flow of information and reinforcements through that city when the gray main body closed on Washington, and then be at or near Point Lookout on the night of July 12, in time to assist in setting free what would amount to a full new corps for the Army of Northern Virginia. If things worked out just right, for them and for Early, the uncaged veterans might even return south armed with weapons taken from various arsenals, ordnance shops, and armories in the Federal capital, just over forty miles from Frederick, at the end of a two-day march down the broad turnpike.

Two days, that is, provided there was no delay en route: a battle, say, or even a sizeable skirmish, anything that would oblige a major portion of the army to deploy, engage, and then get back into march formation on the pike — always a time-consuming business, even for veterans such as these. And sure enough, Early had no sooner ridden southeast out of Frederick, down the spur track of the B. & O. toward its junction with the main line near the Monocacy, than he saw, drawn up to meet him on the far side of the river, with bridgeheads occupied to defend the crossings — the railroad itself and the two macadamized turnpikes, upstream and down — a considerable enemy force, perhaps as large as his own, with sunlight glinting from the polished tubes of guns emplaced from point to point along the line. Its disposition looked professional (which might signify that Grant had hurried reinforcements north from the Army of the Potomac, under orders from Lincoln to cover the threatened capital) but Early's first task, in any case, was to find out how to come to grips with this new blue assemblage and thereby learn its identity and size, preferably without a costly assault on one of the bridgeheads. McCausland promptly gave him the answer by plunging across a shallow ford, half a mile to the right of the Washington road, and launching a dismounted charge that overran a Federal battery. Counterattacked in force, the troopers withdrew, remounted, and splashed back across the river. Though they were unable to hold the guns they had seized, they brought with them something far more valuable: the key to the enemy's undoing. So Early thought at any rate.

By now it was noon, and he wasted no time in fitting the key to the lock. Rodes and Ramseur would feint respectively down the Baltimore pike and the railroad, while the main effort was being made downstream by Gordon, who would cross by the newly discovered ford for a flank assault, with Breckinridge in support. "No buttermilk rangers after you now, damn you!" Old Jube had shouted three weeks ago at Lynchburg, shaking his fist at the bluecoats as they backpedaled under pressure from his infantry, just off the cars from Charlottesville. He repeated this gesture today on the Monocacy, confident that victory was within his grasp whether the troops across the way were veterans, up from Petersburg, or hundred-day militia, hastily assembled from roundabout the Yankee capital and dropped in his path as a tub to the invading rebel whale.

They were both, but mostly they were veterans detached from the Army of the Potomac three days ago, on July 6, just as Early began crossing into Maryland. Warned by Halleck that Hunter had skittered westward, off the tactical margin of the map, and that Sigel too had removed his troops from contention with the 20,000 to 30,000 Confederates reported to be about to descend on Washington — which had nothing to defend it but militia, and not much of that — Grant loaded Ricketts' 4700-man VI Corps division onto transports bound for Baltimore, along with some 3000 of Sheridan's troopers, dismounted by the breakdown of their horses on the recent grueling raids beyond Burkeville and Louisa. Three days later, with Early across South Mountain and Washington approaching a state of panic, if not of siege, he not only followed through by ordering Wright to steam north in the wake of Ricketts with his other two divisions; he also informed Old Brains that he would be sending the XIX Corps, whose leading elements were due about now at Fortress Monroe, en route from New Orleans and the fiasco up Red River. This last came hard, badly needed as these far-western reinforcements were as a transfusion for Meade's bled-down army, straining to keep up the pressure south of the James. Yet Grant was willing to do even more, if need be, to meet the rapidly developing crisis north of the Potomac.

"If the President thinks it advisable that I should go to Washington in person," he wired Halleck that evening from City Point, while the last of Wright's men were filing aboard transports for the trip up Chesapeake Bay, "I can start in an hour after receiving notice, leaving everything here on the defensive."

Meantime Ricketts had landed at Baltimore, headquarters of Major

General Lew Wallace's Middle Department, including Maryland, Delaware, and the Eastern Shore of Virginia. Wallace was not there, however. He had left two days ago, on July 5, after learning that the rebels were at Harpers Ferry in considerable strength, their outriders already on the loose in western Maryland as an indication of where they would be headed next. A former Illinois lawyer, now thirty-seven years old, he had been at the time of Shiloh the youngest major general in the Union army, but his showing there had soured Grant on him; the brilliant future predicted for him was blighted; he was shifted, in time, to this quiet backwater of the war. Quiet, that is, until an estimated 30,000 graybacks appeared this week on the banks of the Potomac, with nothing substantially blue between them and the national capital. Wallace said later that when he pondered the consequences of such a move by Early, "they grouped themselves into a kind of horrible schedule." If Washington fell, even temporarily, he foresaw the torch being put in rapid sequence to the Navy Yard, the Treasury, and the Quartermaster Depot, whose six acres of warehouses were stocked with $11,000,000 in equipment and supplies; "the war must halt, if not stop for good and all." Accordingly, having decided to meet the danger near the rim of his department — though at considerable personal risk, for while he knew that Halleck was keeping tabs on him for Grant, watching sharply for some infraction that would justify dismissal, he could not inform his superiors of what he was about to do, since he was convinced that they would forbid it as too risky — he got aboard a train for Monocacy Junction, where the roads from nearby Frederick branched toward Baltimore and Washington. There he would assemble whatever troops he could lay hands on, from all quarters, and thus cover, from that one position, the approaches to both cities: not so much in hope of winning the resultant battle, he afterwards explained, as in hope of slowing the rebel advance by fighting the battle at all. Whatever the outcome, the delaying action on the Monocacy would perhaps afford the authorities time to brace for the approaching shock, not only by assembling all the available militia from roundabout states, but also by summoning from Grant, down in Virginia, a substantial number of battle-seasoned veterans to throw in the path of the invaders.

Sure enough, after managing to scrape together in two days, July 6–7, a piecemeal force of 2300 of all arms, he learned that this last had in fact been done, or at least was in the process of being done. Troops from the Army of the Potomac were debarking at Baltimore even then, hard-handed men in weathered blue who had taken the measure of Lee's touted veterans down the country and were no doubt willing and able to do the same up here. Greatly encouraged, Wallace sent for Ricketts to bring his division to Monocacy Junction without delay, leaving Sheridan's unhorsed troopers — more than a third of whom lacked arms as well as mounts — to man the Baltimore or Washington defenses, and thereby help, perhaps, to reduce the civilian panic reported to be swelling in both places. Ricketts arrived by rail next day, and none too soon; Early came over South Mountain that afternoon, July 8, and on into Frederick next morning. By noon he had his army moving by all the available roads down to the Monocacy, where Wallace had disposed his now 7000-man force to contest a crossing, posting Ricketts on the left, astride the Washington pike, where he figured the rebels would launch their main attack.

He figured right, but not right enough to forestall an end-on blow that soon resulted in a rout. Gordon struck from beyond the capital pike, not astride it, coming up from the ford downstream for an attack that Ricketts saw would roll up his line unless he effected a rapid change of front. He tried and nearly succeeded in getting his soldiers parallel to the turnpike, facing south, before they were hit. They gave ground, uncovering the unburnable iron railroad bridge for a crossing by Ramseur, who together with Breckinridge added the pressure that ended all resistance on this flank. Rickett's two brigades, or what was left of them by now — the second, made up of veterans long known as "Milroy's weary boys," had been through this kind of thing before — scrambled northward for the Baltimore road, the designated avenue of retreat, and there lost all semblance of order in their haste to get out of range of the whooping rebels, one of whom afterwards called this hot little Battle of the Monocacy "the most exciting time I witnessed during the war."

By 4 o'clock it was over, and though Wallace (with 1880 casualties, including more than a thousand captured or otherwise missing, as compared to fewer than 700 killed or wounded on the other side) managed to piece together a rear guard not far east of the lost field, there was no real pursuit; Early did not want to be encumbered with more prisoners than he had already taken, more or less against his will. Nor did he want to move eastward, in the direction of Baltimore. His route was southeast, down the Washington pike, which Gordon's attack had cleared for his use in continuing the march begun that morning out of Frederick.

In any case he knew now, from interrogating captives with the canted VI Corps cross on the flat tops of their caps, that troops had arrived from the Army of the Potomac, and though he had whipped them rather easily — as well he might have expected to do, with the odds at two-to-one — he knew only too well that others were probably on the way, if indeed they were not already on hand in the capital defenses. If this was a source of satisfaction, knowing that he had fulfilled a considerable measure of Lee's purpose by obliging Grant to reduce the pressure on Petersburg and Richmond, it also recommended caution. Additional blue detachments might have arrived or be arriving from down the country in such numbers that his small army, cut off from the few available fords across the Potomac as he advanced, would be swamped and abolished. As it was, he had only to turn southwest, down the B. & O. to Point of Rocks, for a crossing that would gain him the security of the Virginia Piedmont, after which he could move south or west, unmolested, for a return to Lee or the Shenandoah Valley. Either course had its attractions, but Early dwelt on neither. He would move as he had intended from the outset, against Washington itself, and deal with events as they developed, knowing from past service under Jackson that audacity often brought its own rewards. Today was too far gone for resumption of the march, but he passed the word for his men to bed down for a good night's rest, here on the field where they had fought today, and be ready to move at "early dawn."

Sunday, July 10, was hot and dusty. By noon, the cumulative effect of all those twenty-mile hikes since the army left Staunton twelve days ago had begun to tell. Straggling increased as the day wore on, until finally the head of the column went into bivouac short of Rockville, just over twenty miles from the Monocacy and less than ten from the District of Columbia. Rear elements did not come up till after midnight, barely three hours before Early, hopeful of storming the Washington defenses before sundown, ordered the march resumed in the predawn darkness. Aware that he might be engaged in a race with reinforcements on the way there, he could afford to show his weary men no mercy, though he sought to encourage them, as he doubled the column on his lathered horse, with promises of rest and a high feast when the prize was won. Beyond Rockville, he had McCausland's troopers hold to the main pike for a feint along the Tenallytown approaches, while the infantry forked left for Silver Spring, half a dozen miles from the heart of the city by way of the main-traveled Seventh Street Road.

Heat and dust continued to take their toll; "Our division was stretched out almost like skirmishers," one of Gordon's veterans, tottering white-faced with fatigue near the tail of the column, would recall. Then, close to 1 o'clock, the heavy, ground-thumping boom-bam-*boom* of loud explosions — guns: siege guns! — carried back from the front, where the head of the column had come within range of the outlying capital works.

Early rode fast toward the sound of firing, beyond the District line, and drew rein in time to watch his advance cavalry elements dismount and fan out to confront a large earthwork on rising ground to the right of the road, two miles below Silver Spring. Identified on the map as Fort Stevens, a major installation, it lay just over a thousand yards away, and when he studied it through his binoculars he saw a few figures on the parapet; by no means enough, it seemed to him, to indicate that the work was heavily, even adequately, manned. He had won his race with Grant. All he had to do, apparently, was bring up his men and put them in attack formation, then move forward and take it, along with much that lay beyond, including the Capitol itself, whose new dome he could see plainly in the distance, six miles south of where he stood.

Just now, though, his troops were in no condition for even the slightest exertion, whatever prize gleamed on the horizon. Diminished by cavalry detachments, by their losses in battle two days ago, and by stragglers who had fallen out of the column yesterday and today, they scarcely totaled 10,000 now, and of these no more than a third were fit for offensive action without a rest. All the same, he told Rodes, whose division was in the lead, to see what he could accomplish along those lines, and while Rodes did his best — which wasn't much; his men were leaden-legged, short of wind and spitting cotton — Early continued to study the objective just ahead. Beyond it, around 1.30, he saw a long low cloud of dust approaching from the rear, up the Seventh Street Road. Reinforcements, most likely; but how many? and what kind? Then he spotted them in his glass, the ones at the head of the fast-stepping column at any rate, and saw that they were dressed not in linen dusters and high-crowned hats, after the manner of home guardsmen or militia, but in the weathered blue tunics and kepis he had last encountered two days ago, when he found Ricketts' VI Corps veterans drawn up to meet him on the Monocacy.

Veterans they were, all right, and VI Corps veterans at that; Wright and the first of his other two divisions, the second relay of reinforcements ordered north from the Army of the Potomac, had begun debarking at the Sixth Street docks a little after noon and were summoned at once to the point of danger, out the Seventh Street Road. Grant himself might be on the way by now, moreover, for Lincoln — under increasing pressure as the rebel column, having knocked Wallace out of its path, drew closer to Washington hour by hour — had responded approvingly to the general's offer to come up and take charge "in person," adding that it might be well if he brought still more of his soldiers along with him. "What I think," he told Grant, "is that you should provide to retain your hold where you are, certainly, and bring the rest with you personally and make a vigorous effort to destroy the enemy's force in this vicinity. I think there is really a fair chance to do this if the movement is prompt." In other words, hurry. But then, mindful once more of his resolution not to interfere in military matters, even with the graybacks practically at the gate, he closed by saying: "This is what I think, upon your suggestion, and it is not an order."

If he was jarred momentarily from his purpose — and, after all, the notion was Grant's in the first place; Lincoln merely concurred —

it was small wonder, what with Hunter fled beyond recall up the Kanawah, Sigel holed up at Harpers Ferry, out of touch since July 4, and Washington panicked by rumors of Armageddon. Wallace, falling back down the Baltimore pike from his sudden drubbing on July 9, reported that Early had hit him with 20,000 of all arms, and though this was 10,000 fewer than Sigel had reported before the wire went dead in his direction, it still was 10,000 more than had been mustered, including War Department clerks and green militia, to man the capital defenses. Sheridan's dismounted troopers arrived about that time, a rather straggly lot who did less to bolster confidence here than their removal from Baltimore had done to provoke resentment there. When a group of that city's leading citizens telegraphed Lincoln that Sunday evening, July 10, protesting that they had been abandoned to their fate, he did what he could to reassure them. "Let us be vigilant, but keep cool," he replied. "I hope neither Baltimore nor Washington will be taken."

They remained disgruntled, wanting something more substantial. By next morning things looked better, however, at least in their direction. Returning with Ricketts, Wallace assured them that Early was headed for Washington, not Baltimore just yet. And even in the capital there was encouraging news to balance against reports that the rebel column had cleared Rockville soon after sunrise; Wright was expected hourly from Virginia with his other two divisions, and an advance detachment of 600 troops was already on hand from the XIX Corps, fine-looking men with skin tanned to mahogany by the Louisiana sun. Even Henry Halleck — who, according to an associate, had spent the past week "in a perfect maze, bewildered, without intelligent decision or self-reliance" — recovered his spirits enough to reply with acid humor to a telegram from an unattached brigadier at the Fifth Avenue Hotel, New York City, offering his services in the crisis now at hand. "We have five times as many generals here as we want," Old Brains informed him, "but are greatly in need of privates. Anyone volunteering in that capacity will be thankfully received." Then at noon the transports arrived at the Sixth Street docks (near which the Navy had a warship berthed with steam up, ready to whisk the President downriver in case the city fell); Wright's lead division came ashore and marched smartly through the heart of town to meet Early, who was reported to be approaching by way of Silver Spring. Presently the boom of guns from that direction made it clear how close the race had been, and was.

Lincoln, having ridden down to the docks to greet them from his carriage, also rode out the Seventh Street Road to watch them reinforce Fort Stevens; he may have been one of the figures — surely, if so, the tallest — Early saw etched against the sky when he focussed his binoculars on the parapet of the works just over a thousand yards ahead. Watching the dusty blue stream of veterans flow into position in the course of the next hour, Old Jube — or "Jubilee," as soldiers often styled him — knew there could be no successful assault by his weary men today. A good night's rest might make a difference, though, depending on how heavily the defenses had been reinforced by morning, either here or elsewhere along the thirty-seven miles of interconnected redans, forts, and palisades ringing the city and bristling with heavy guns at every point. What remained of daylight could be used for reconnaissance (and was; "Examination showed what might have been expected," Early would report, "that every application of science and unlimited means had been used to render the fortifications around Washington as strong as possible") but the thing to do now, he saw, was put the troops into bivouac, then feed and get them bedded down, while he and his chief lieutenants planned for tomorrow. He and they had come too far, and Lee had risked too much, he felt, for the Army of the Valley to retire from the gates of the enemy capital without testing to see how stoutly they were hung.

Accordingly, he turned his horse and rode back toward Silver Spring, where his staff had set up headquarters, just beyond the District line, in the handsome country house of Francis P. Blair, who had decamped to avoid an awkward meeting with one-time friends among the invaders. A member of Andrew Jackson's "kitchen cabinet" and an adviser to most of the Presidents since, Old Man Blair had two sons in high Union places: Montgomery, Lincoln's Postmaster General, whose own home was only a short walk up the road, and Frank Junior, the former Missouri congressman, now a corps commander with Sherman.

Guards had been posted to protect the property; especially the wine cellar, which contributed to the festive spirit that opened the council of war with recollections by Breckinridge, as the toasts went round, of the good times he had had here in the days when he was Vice President under Buchanan. Someone remarked that tomorrow might give him the chance to revisit other scenes of former glory, such as the U.S. Senate, where he had presided until Lincoln's inauguration and then had sat as a member until he left, eight months later, to throw in with other Confederate-minded Kentuckians for secession. This brought up the question Early had called his lieutenants together to consider: Was an attack on Washington tomorrow worth the risk? Time was short and getting shorter; Hunter and Sigel could be expected to come up from the rear, eventually, and Grant was known to have sent what seemed to be most of a corps already. Doubtless other reinforcements were on the way, from other directions, and though the prize itself was the richest of all — perhaps even yielding foreign recognition, at long last, not to mention supplying the final straw that might break the Federal home-front camel's back — was it worth the risk of losing one fourth of Lee's army in the effort?

Early considered, with the help of his four division commanders, and decided that it was. He would launch an assault at dawn, he told them, "unless some information should be received before that time showing its impracticability."

Such information was not long in coming. The council of war had scarcely ended when a courier arrived from Bradley Johnson, whose brigade was still on its way to Point Lookout. After wrecking railroad bridges and tearing down telegraph lines around Baltimore he had sent scouts into the city to confer with Confederate agents, and from these he learned that not one but *two* Federal corps, the VI and the XIX, were steaming up Chesapeake Bay and the Potomac to bolster the Washington defenses. In the light of this intelligence that tomorrow might find him outnumbered better than two to one by the bluecoats in the capital intrenchments, Early countermanded his orders for a dawn assault. This came hard. Just thirty days ago tomorrow he had received instructions from Lee to attempt what he was on the verge of doing. Now though — as a result, he perceived, of the victory Wallace had obliged him to win on the Monocacy, at the cost of a twenty-hour delay — it began to appear that the verge was as close as he was likely to get. Daylight would give him the chance to reconnoiter the Union works and thus determine the weight of this new unwelcome information, but he could see already that an attack was probably beyond his means and a good deal worse than risky.

Dawn broke, July 12, over a Washington in some ways even more distraught than it had been the morning before, with the rebels bearing down on its undermanned defenses. Overnight the shortage had been considerably repaired; Wright's third division followed the second out the Seventh Street Road at dusk, and soon after dark the first of the two XIX Corps divisions landed. But as these 20,000 stalwarts arrived to join about the same number of militiamen, galvanized clerks, and dismounted cavalry in the outworks, so did a host of rumors, given unlimited opportunity for expansion by the fact that the city was cut off from all communication northward, either by rail or wire, newspapers or telegrams, speech or letters. Known secessionists did not trouble to mask broad smiles, implying that they knew secrets they weren't sharing. One that leaked out by hearsay was that Lee had given Meade the slip, down around Richmond, and was crossing the Potomac, close at hand, with an army of 100,000 firebrands yelling for vengeance for what had been done, these past three years, in the way of destruction to their homeland.

Lincoln rose early, despite a warning from Stanton that an assassination plot was afoot, and rode with Seward to visit several of the fortifications out on the rim of town, believing that the sight of him and the Secretary of State, unfled and on hand to face the crisis unperturbed, would help to reduce the panic in the streets through which their carriage passed. His main hope, now that he knew Grant would not be coming — "I think, on reflection, it would have a bad effect for me to leave here," the general had replied from City Point to the suggestion that he come north without delay — was in Horatio Wright, who had helped to drive these same gray veterans southward, down in Virginia, throughout the forty days of battle in May and June. Lincoln's belief was that the Connecticut general, now that he had the means, could do the same up here.

Wright rather thought so too. Taking Early's failure to attack this morning as a sign that the rebels were preparing to withdraw, probably after nightfall, he wanted to hit them before they got away unscathed. In particular he wanted to drive off their skirmishers, who had crept to within rifle range of Fort Stevens and were sniping at whatever showed above the parapet. However, when he requested permission, first of the fort commander and then of the district commander, Major Generals Alexander McCook and C. C. Augur — both of whom outranked him, although neither had seen any action for nearly a year, having been retired from field service as a result of their poor showings, respectively, at Chickamauga and Port Hudson — they declined, saying that they did not "consider it advisable to make any advance until our lines are better established."

By midafternoon this objection no longer applied; McCook, bearded in his command post deep in the bowels of the fort, agreed at last to permit a sortie by units from one of the VI Corps divisions. Wright started topside for a last-minute study of the terrain, and as he stepped out of the underground office he nearly bumped into Abraham Lincoln, who had returned from a cabinet meeting at the White House to continue his tour of the fortifications. Informed of what was about to be done, he expressed approval, and when the general asked, rather casually, whether he would care to take a look at the field — "without for a moment supposing he would accept," Wright later explained — Lincoln replied that he would indeed. Six feet four, conspicuous in his frock coat and a stovepipe hat that added another eight inches to his height, he presently stood on the parapet, gazing intently at puffs of smoke from the rifles of snipers across the way. Horrified, wishing fervently that he could revoke his thoughtless invitation, Wright tried to persuade the President to retire; but Lincoln seemed not to hear him amid the twittering bullets, one of which struck and dropped an officer within three feet of him. From down below, a young staff captain — twenty-three-year-old Oliver Wendell Holmes, Junior, whose combat experience had long since taught him to take shelter whenever possible under fire — looked up at the lanky top-hatted civilian and called out to him, without recognition: "Get down, you damn fool, before you get shot!"

This got through. Lincoln not only heard and reacted with amusement to the irreverent admonition, he also obeyed it by climbing down and taking a seat in the shade, his back to the parapet, safe at last from the bullets that continued to twang and nicker overhead.

Relieved of the worst of his concerns, Wright turned now to the interrupted business of clearing his front. Deployment of the brigade assigned the task required more time than had been thought, however, with the result that it was close to 6 o'clock before the signal could be given to move out. The firing swelled, and Lincoln, popping up from time to time to peer over the parapet, had his first look at men reeling and falling in combat and being brought past him on stretchers, groaning or screaming from pain, leaking blood and calling on God or Mamma, in shock and out of fear. Presently the racket stepped up tremendously, and the brigade commander sent back for reinforcements, explaining that he had encountered, beyond the retiring screen of pickets, a full-fledged rebel line of battle. Supporting regiments moved up in the twilight and the attack resumed, though with small success against stiffened resistance. Gunflashes winked and twinkled along the slope ahead until about 10 o'clock, when they diminished fitfully and finally died away. The cost to Wright had been 280 killed and wounded in what one of his veterans called "a pretty and well-conducted little fight."

Across the way, the Confederates considered it something worse: especially at the outset, when it erupted in the midst of their preparations to depart. Early had needed no more than a cursory look at the enemy works that morning to confirm last night's report that they would be substantially reinforced by dawn. Permanently canceling the deferred assault, he ordered skirmishers deployed along a line that stretched for a mile to the left and a mile to the right of the Seventh Street Road to confront Forts Reno, Stevens, and De Russy, while behind this he had Rodes and Gordon form their divisions, in case the Federals tried a sortie, and sent word for McCausland to keep up the feint on the far right, astride the Georgetown pike. Here they would stay, bristling as if about to strike, until night came down to cover the withdrawal, back through Silver Spring to Rockville, then due west for a recrossing of the Potomac. Fortunately, the Yankees seemed content to remain within their works, and Early, having learned that the amphibious raid on Point Lookout had been called off because the prison authorities had been warned of it, had time to send a courier after Johnson, whose horsemen were beyond Baltimore by then, instructing him to turn back for the Confederate lines by whatever route seemed best now that the capture of Washington was no longer a part of the invasion plan. Preparations for the retirement were complete — were, in fact, about to be placed in execution — when Wright's attack exploded northward from Fort Stevens, flinging butternut skirmishers back on the main body, which then was struck by the rapid-firing Federals coming up in apparently endless numbers through the gathering dusk. The thing had the look of an all-out battle that would hold the Army of the Valley in position for slaughter tomorrow by preventing it from taking up its planned retreat tonight. Major Kyd Douglas, formerly of Jackson's staff and now of Early's, said quite frankly that he thought "we were gone up."

Presently though, to everyone's relief, the fireworks sputtered into darkness; the field grew still, except for the occasional jarring explosion of a shell from one of the outsized siege guns in the forts, and Early, resuming his preparations for withdrawal, summoned to headquarters Breckinridge and Gordon, whose divisions would respectively head and tail the column, for last-minute orders on the conduct of the march. They arrived to find him instructing Douglas to take charge of a rear-guard detail of 200 men and with them hold the present position until midnight, at which time he too was to pull out for Rockville: provided, of course, the bluecoats had not gotten wind of what was up, beforehand, and obliterated him. When the handsome young Marylander left to assume this forlorn assignment, Early called after him, apparently in an attempt to lift his spirits: "Major, we haven't taken Washington, but we've scared Abe Lincoln like hell!"

Douglas stopped and turned. "Yes, General," he said, as if to set the record straight, "but this afternoon when that Yankee line moved out against us, I think some other people were scared blue as hell's brimstone."

"How about that, General?" Breckinridge broke in, smiling broadly beneath his broad mustache.

"That's true. But it won't appear in history," Early replied, thereby assuring the exchange a place in all the accounts that were to follow down the years.

It turned out there were no further losses, even for the rear-guard handful under Douglas, who took up the march on schedule without a parting shot being fired in his direction. He saw, as he went past it after midnight, that except for the depletion of its wine cellar and linen closets — all the bedclothes had been ripped into strips for bandages — Old Man Blair's mansion had suffered no damage from the occupation, but that his son Montgomery's house, just up the road, had been reduced to bricks and ashes by some vengeance-minded incendiary. Although the act perhaps was justified by Hunter's burning of Former Governor Letcher's home the month before, Early's regret that this had been done was increased when he learned that Bradley Johnson, off on his own, had also indulged in retaliation by setting fire to Governor A. W. Bradford's house near Baltimore. Such exactions, he knew, were unlikely to encourage pro-Confederate feelings, either here in Maryland or elsewhere. In any case, dawn of July 13 — thirty days, to the hour, since the re-created Army of the Valley pulled out of Cold Harbor, bound for Lynchburg and points north — found the column slogging through Rockville, where it turned left for Poolesville and the Potomac. At White's Ford by midnight, just upstream from Ball's Bluff and thirty miles from its starting point on the outskirts of Washington, the army crossed the river in good order next morning, still unmolested, to make camp near Leesburg for a much needed two-day rest; after which it shifted west, July 16, beyond the Blue Ridge. Back once more in the Lower Valley, within an easy day's march of Harpers Ferry, Early began preparing for further adventures designed to disrupt the plans of the Union high command.

This recent thirty-day excursion had accomplished a great deal in that direction, as well as much else of a positive nature, including the recovery of the grain-rich Shenandoah region from Hunter and Sigel, just in time for the harvesting of its richest crop in years, and the return from beyond the Potomac with a large supply of commandeered horses and cattle, not to mention $220,000 in greenbacks for the hard-up Treasury and close to a thousand prisoners, most of them captured on the Monocacy, the one full-scale battle of the campaign. In fact, aside from his two main hopes — and hopes were all they were — that he could occupy Washington, even for a day, and that he could provoke Grant into making a suicidal assault on Lee's intrenchments, Early had accomplished everything that could have been expected of him. Best of all, he had obliged Grant to ease the pressure on Petersburg by sending large detachments north, and still had managed, despite the smallness of his force, if not to reverse the tide of the war, then anyhow to strike fear in the hearts of the citizens of Washington and Baltimore, both of which saw gray-clad infantry at closer range than any Federal had come, so far, to Richmond. This was much; yet there was more. For in the process Early had won the admiration not only of his fellow countrymen, whose spirits were lifted by the raid, but also of foreign observers, who still might somehow determine the outcome of this apparently otherwise endless conflict.

"The Confederacy is more formidable than ever," the London *Times* remarked when news of this latest rebel exploit crossed the ocean the following week. And closer at hand, on July 12 — even as Early and his veterans bristled along the rim of the northern capital, quite as if they were about to assail and overrun the ramparts in a screaming rush — the *New York World* asked its readers: "Who shall revive the withered hopes that bloomed on the opening of Grant's campaign?"

★ ★ ★

Who indeed. The task was Lincoln's, as the national leader, but evidence piled higher every day that it would be his no longer than early March, when the outcome of the presidential election, less than four months off, was confirmed on the steps of the lately threatened Capitol. Despite setbacks, such as Cold Harbor, Petersburg, and this recent gray eruption on the near bank of the Potomac, he was convinced that he had found in U. S. Grant the man to win the war. But that was somewhat beside the point, which was whether or not the people could be persuaded, between now and November, to believe it, too — and whether or not, believing it, they would agree that the prize was worth the additional blood, the additional money, the additional drawn-out anguish it was clearly going to cost. They, like Grant, would have to "face the arithmetic," and keep on facing it, to the indeterminate end.

One of the things that made this difficult was that the arithmetic kept changing, not only in the lengthening casualty lists, but also in the value fluctuations of what men carried in their wallets, a region where their threshold of pain was notoriously low. Gold opened the year at 152 on the New York market. By April it had risen to 175, by mid-June to 197, and by the end of that month to an astronomical 250. Reassurances from money men that the dollar was "settling down" brought the wry response that it was "settling down out of sight." Sure enough, on July 11, as Early descended on Washington, gold soared to 285, reducing the value of the paper dollar to forty cents. Moreover, Lincoln faced this crisis without the help of the man who had advised him in such matters from the outset: Salmon Chase.

In late June, with the office of assistant treasurer of New York about to be vacated, the Secretary recommended a successor unacceptable to Senator Edwin D. Morgan of that state, who suggested three alternates for the post. "It will really oblige me if you will make a choice among these three," Lincoln wrote Chase, explaining the political ramifications of a tiff with Morgan at this time. Chase then requested a personal interview, which Lincoln refused "because the difficulty does not, in the main part, lie within the range of a conversation between you and me." In reaction to this snub, the Secretary went home and, as was his custom in such matters, "endeavored to seek God in prayer." So he wrote in his diary that night, adding: "Oh, for more faith and clearer sight! How stable is the City of God! How disordered the City of Man!" Mulling it over he reached a decision. His resignation was on the presidential desk next morning. "I shall regard it as a real relief if you think proper to accept it," he declared in a covering letter.

Lincoln read this fourth of the Ohioan's petulant resignations, and accepted it forthwith. "Of all I have said in commendation of your ability and fidelity, I have nothing to unsay," he replied, "and yet you and I have reached a point of mutual embarrassment in our official relationship which it seems cannot be overcome or longer sustained consistently with the public service." Ohio's Governor John Brough, who happened to be in town, went to the White House in an attempt to "close the breach," as he had done in one of the other instances of a threatened resignation, only to find that he could perform no such healing service here today. "You doctored the business up once," Lincoln told him, "but on the whole, Brough, I reckon you had better let it alone this time." Chase departed, still in something of a state of shock from the unexpected thunderclap, and retired to think things over, for a time, in the hills of his native New Hampshire.

A replacement was not far to seek. Next morning, July 1, when William Pitt Fessenden of Maine, chairman of the Senate Finance Committee, called on the President to recommend someone else for the Treasury post, Lincoln smiled and informed him that his nomination had just been sent for approval by his colleagues on the Hill. Fessenden's dismay was plain. "You must withdraw it. I cannot accept," he protested. His health was poor; Congress was to adjourn tomorrow, and he looked forward to a vacation away from the heat and bustle of the capital. "If you decline, you must do it in open day," Lincoln told him, "for I shall not recall the nomination." Fessenden hurried over to the Senate in an attempt to block the move, only to find that he had been unanimously confirmed in about one minute. Regretfully, with congratulations pouring in from all quarters — even Chase's — he agreed to serve, at least through the adjournment. A soft-money man like his predecessor, he was sworn in on July 5, and it was observed that no appointment by the President, except perhaps the elevation of Grant four months before, had met with such widespread approval by the public and the press. "Men went about with smiling faces at the news," one paper noted.

Lincoln himself was not smiling by then. His trouble with Chase — whom he described as a man "never perfectly happy unless he is thoroughly miserable, and able to make everyone else just as uncomfortable as he is" — had been personal; Chase irked him and he got rid of him. But on the day after Fessenden's appointment he found himself in an even more irksome predicament, one that was susceptible to no such resolution because the men involved were not subject to dismissal; not by him, at any rate. On the morning of July 2, last day of the congressional session that was scheduled to adjourn at noon, Lincoln sat in the President's room at the Capitol, signing last-minute bills, including one that repealed the Fugitive Slave Law and another that struck the $300 commutation clause from the Draft Act. Both of these he signed gladly, along with others, but as he did so there was thrust upon him the so-called Wade-Davis bill, passed two months ago by the House and by the Senate within the hour. He set it aside to go on with the rest, and when an interested observer asked if he intended to sign it, he replied that the bill was "a matter of too much importance to be swallowed in that way."

He found it hard, in fact, to swallow the bill in any way at all, since what it represented was an attempt by Congress — more specifically, by the radicals in his party — to establish the premise that the legislative, not the executive, branch of government had the right and duty to define the terms for readmission to the Union by states now claiming to have left it; in other words, to set the tone of Reconstruction. Sponsored by Benjamin Wade in the Senate and Henry Winter Davis in the House, the bill proceeded from Senator Charles Sumner's thesis that secession, though of course not legally valid, nonetheless amounted to "State suicide," and it set forth certain requirements that would have to be met before the resurrected corpse could be readmitted to the family it had disgraced by putting a bullet through its head. Lincoln had done much the same thing in his Proclamation of Amnesty and Reconstruction, back in December, but this new bill, designed not so much to pave as to bar the path to reunion, was considerably more stringent. Where he had required that ten percent of the qualified voters take a loyalty oath, the Wade-Davis measure required a majority. In addition, all persons who had held state or Confederate offices, or who had voluntarily borne arms against the United States, were forbidden to vote for or serve as delegates to state constitutional conventions; the rebel debt was to be repudiated, and slavery outlawed, in each instance. Moreover, this was no more than a precedent-setting first step; harsher requirements would come later, once the bill had established the fact that Congress, not the President, was the rightful agency to handle all matters pertaining to reconstruction of the South. Sumner and Zachariah Chandler in the Senate, Thaddeus Stevens and George W. Julian in the House — Jacobins all and accomplished haters, out for vengeance at any price — were strong in their support of the measure and were instrumental in ramming it through on this final day of the session.

Gideon Welles saw clearly enough what they were after, and put what he saw in his diary. "In getting up this law, it was as much an object of Mr. Henry Winter Davis and some others to pull down the Administration as to reconstruct the Union. I think they had the former more directly in view than the latter." Lincoln thought so, too, and was determined to keep it from happening, if he could only find a way to do so without bringing on the bitterest kind of fight inside his party.

The fact was, he had already found what he perceived might be the beginning of a way when he set the bill aside to go on signing others. Zachariah Chandler, who had asked him whether he intended to endorse it and had then been told that it was "too important to be swallowed in that way," warned him sternly, in reference to the pending election: "If it is vetoed, it will damage us fearfully in the Northwest. The important point is the one prohibiting slavery in the reconstructed states." "That is the point on which I doubt the authority of Congress to act." "It is no more than you have done yourself." "I conceive that I may, in an emergency, do things on military grounds which cannot be done constitutionally by Congress," Lincoln replied, and Chandler stalked out, deeply chagrined.

His chagrin, and that of his fellow radicals, was converted to pure rage the following week — July 8; Early was crossing South Mountain to descend on Frederick — when Lincoln, having declined either to sign or to veto the bill, issued a public proclamation defending his action (or nonaction) on grounds that, while he was "fully satisfied" with some portions of the bill, he was "unprepared" to give his approval of certain others. "What an infamous proclamation!" Thaddeus Stevens protested. "The idea of pocketing a bill and then issuing a proclamation as to how far he will conform to it!"

By means of the "pocket veto," as the maneuver came to be called, Lincoln managed to avoid, at least for a season, being removed from all connection with setting the guidelines for Reconstruction; but he had not managed to avoid a fight. Indeed, according to proponents of the bill now lodged in limbo, he had precipitated one. Convinced, as one of them declared, that his proposed course was "timid and almost pro-slavery," they took up the challenge of his proclamation, which they defined as "a grave Executive usurpation," and responded in more than kind, early the following month in the New York *Tribune*, with what became known as the Wade-Davis Manifesto. Seeking "to check the encroachments of the Executive on the authority of Congress, and to require it to confine itself to its proper sphere," bluff Ben Wade and vehement Henry Davis charged that "a more studied outrage on the legislative authority of the people has never been perpetrated," and they warned that Lincoln "must understand that our support is of a cause and not of a man," especially not of a man who would connive to procure electoral votes at the cost of his country's welfare.

All this the manifesto set forth, along with much else of a highly personal nature from the pens of these Republican leaders, just three months before the presidential election. Lincoln declined to read or discuss it, not wanting to be provoked any worse than he was already, but he remarked in this connection: "To be wounded in the house of one's friends is perhaps the most grievous affliction that can befall a man."

Horace Greeley, editor of the paper in which the radical manifesto made its appearance, had been involved for the past month in an affair that added to Lincoln's difficulties in presenting himself as a man of war who longed for peace. Hearing privately in early July that Confederate emissaries were waiting on the Canadian side of Niagara Falls with full authority to arrange an armistice, Greeley referred the matter to the President and urged in a long, high-strung letter that he seize the opportunity this presented to end the fighting. "Confederates everywhere [are] for peace. So much is beyond doubt," he declared. "And therefore I venture to remind you that our bleeding, bankrupt, almost dying country also longs for peace — shudders at the prospect of fresh conscription, of further wholesale devastations, and of new rivers of human blood." Placed thus in the position of having to investigate this reported gleam of sunlight (which he suspected would prove to be moonshine) Lincoln was prompt with an answer. "If you can find any person anywhere professing to have any proposition of Jefferson Davis in writing, for peace, embracing the restoration of the Union and the abandonment of slavery, whatever else it embraces, say to him he may come to me with you." The editor, aware of the risk of ridicule, had not counted on being personally involved. He responded with a protest that the rebel agents "would decline to exhibit their credentials to me, much more to open their budget and give me their best terms." Lincoln replied: "I was not expecting you to send me a letter, but to bring me a man, or men." He also told Greeley, in a message carried by John Hay, who was to accompany him on the mission, "I not only intend a sincere effort for peace, but I intend that you shall be a personal witness that it is made."

Being thus coerced, Greeley went with Hay to Niagara, where he discovered, amid the thunder and through the mist, what Lincoln had suspected from the start: that the "emissaries" not only had no authority to negotiate, either with him or with anyone else, but seemed to be in Canada for the purpose of influencing, by the rejection of their empty overtures, the upcoming elections in the North. He retreated hastily, though not in time to prevent a rash of Copperhead rumors that the President, through him, had scorned to entertain decent proposals for ending the bloodshed. Lincoln wanted to offset the effect of this by publishing his and Greeley's correspondence, omitting of course the editor's references to "our bleeding, bankrupt, almost dying country," as well as his gloomy prediction of a Democratic victory in November. Greeley said no; he would consent to no suppression; either print their exchange in full or not at all. Obliged thereby to let the matter drop, Lincoln explained to his cabinet that it was better to withhold the letters, and abide the damaging propaganda, than "to subject the country to the consequences of their discouraging and injurious parts."

Simultaneously, in the opposite direction — down in Richmond itself — another peace feeler was in progress, put forth by Federal emissaries who had no more official sanction than their Confederate counterparts in Canada. Still, Lincoln had better hopes for this one, not so much because he believed that it would end the conflict, but rather, as he remarked, because he felt that it would "show the country I didn't fight shy of Greeley's Niagara business without a reason." What he wanted was for the northern public to become acquainted with Jefferson Davis's terms for an armistice, which he was sure would prove unacceptable to many voters who had been lured, in the absence of specifics, by the siren song of orators claiming that peace could be his for the asking, practically without rebel strings. Moreover, he got what he wanted, and he got it expressed in words as strong and specific as any he himself might have chosen for his purpose.

Colonel James F. Jaquess, a Methodist minister who had raised and led a regiment of Illinois volunteers, had become so increasingly shocked by the sight of fellow Christians killing each other wholesale — especially at Chickamauga, where he lost more than two hundred of his officers and men — that he obtained an extended leave of absence to see what he could do, on his own, to prepare the groundwork for negotiations. He had no success until he was joined in the effort by J. R. Gilmore, who enjoyed important Washington connections. A New York businessman, Gilmore had traveled widely in the South before the war, writing of his experiences under the pen name Edmund Kirke, and he managed to secure Lincoln's approval of an unofficial visit to Richmond by Jaquess and himself, under a flag of truce, for the purpose of talking with southern leaders about the possibility of arriving at terms that might lead to a formal armistice. On Saturday, July 16, the two men were conducted past one of Ben Butler's outposts and were met between the lines by Judge Robert Ould, head of the Confederate commission for prisoner exchange. By nightfall they were lodged in the Spotswood Hotel, in the heart of the rebel capital, Jaquess wearing a long linen duster over his blue uniform. Next morning, amid the pealing of church bells, they conferred with Judah Benjamin, who promised to arrange a meeting for them that evening, here in his State Department office, with the President himself. They returned at the appointed time, and there — as Gilmore later described the encounter — at the table, alongside the plump and smiling Benjamin, "sat a spare, thin-featured man with iron-gray hair and beard, and a clear, gray eye full of life and vigor." Jefferson Davis rose and extended his hand. "I am glad to see you, gentlemen," he said. "You are very welcome to Richmond."

Although he neither mentioned the fact nor showed the strain it cost him, he had not been able to receive them earlier this Sunday because of the lengthy cabinet meeting that had resulted in the dismissal telegram Joe Johnston was reading now, on the outskirts of Atlanta. "His face was emaciated, and much wrinkled," Gilmore observed from across the table, "but his features were good, especially his eyes, though one of them bore a scar, apparently made by some sharp instrument. He wore a suit of grayish brown, evidently of foreign manufacture. . . . His manners were simple, easy and quite fascinating, and he threw an indescribable charm into his voice."

Jaquess opened the interview by saying that he had sought it in the hope that Davis, wanting peace as much as he did, might suggest some way to stop the fighting. "In a very simple way," the Mississippian replied. "Withdraw your armies from our territory, and peace will come of itself." When the colonel remarked that Lincoln's recent Proclamation of Amnesty perhaps afforded a basis for proceeding, Davis cut him short. "Amnesty, Sir, applies to criminals. We have committed no crime." Gilmore suggested that both sides lay down their arms, then let the issue be decided by a popular referendum. But Davis, thinking no doubt of the North's more than twenty millions and the South's less than ten, was having no part of that either. "That the *majority* shall decide it, you mean. We seceded to rid ourselves of the rule of the majority, and this would subject us to it again." It seemed to Gilmore that the dispute narrowed down to "Union or Disunion," and the Confederate President agreed, though he added that he preferred the terms "Independence or Subjugation." Despairing of semantics and the profitless exchange of opposite views that had brought on the war in the first place, the New Yorker made an appeal on personal grounds. "Can you, Mr Davis, as a Christian man, leave untried any means that may lead to peace?" Davis shook his head. "No, I cannot," he replied. "I desire peace as much as you do; I deplore bloodshed as much as you do." He spoke with fervor, but seemed to choose his words with care. "I tried in all my power to avert this war. I saw it coming, and for twelve years I worked night and day to prevent it, but I could not. And now it must go on till the last man of this generation falls in his tracks, and his children seize his musket and fight his battle, *unless you acknowledge our right to self-government.* . . . We are fighting for Independence — and that, or extermination, we will have."

Additional matters were discussed or mentioned, including the military situation, which Davis saw as favorable to the South, and slavery, which he maintained was never "an essential element" in the contest, "only a means of bringing other conflicting elements to an earlier culmination." But always the talk came back to that one prerequisite. Whether it was called Self-Government or Disunion, all future discussion between the two parties would have to proceed from that beginning if there was to be any hope of ending the carnage they both deplored. The Confederate leader made this clear as he rose to see his visitors to the door, shook their hands, and spoke his final words. "Say to Mr Lincoln, from me, that I shall at any time be pleased to receive proposals for peace on the basis of our Independence. It will be useless to approach me with any other."

Whatever sadness he felt on hearing this evidence that the war was unlikely to end through negotiation, Lincoln perceived that the closing message, along with much that preceded it, would serve quite well to further his other purpose, which was to demonstrate his adversary's intransigence in the face of an earnest search for peace. He asked Gilmore, who had stopped by Washington on his return journey from Richmond, what he proposed to do with the transcript he had made of the interview. "Put a beginning and an end to it, Sir, on my way home," the New Yorker said, "and hand it to the *Tribune*." Lincoln demurred. He had had enough of Horace Greeley for a while. "Can't you get it into the *Atlantic Monthly*? It would have less of a partisan look there." Gilmore was sure he could; but first, by way of counteracting what Lincoln called "Greeley's Niagara business," it was decided to release a shorter version in the Boston *Evening Transcript* the following week, while the full *Atlantic* text was being set in type and proofed for review by Lincoln. "Don't let it appear till I return the proof," he cautioned. "Some day all this will come out, but just now we must use discretion." The *Transcript* piece appeared July 22, followed a month later by the one in the *Atlantic*, from which the President had deleted a few hundred words mainly having to do with terms he had found acceptable off the record. Both received much attention, especially the longer version. Indeed, so widely was it reprinted, at home and abroad, that another distinguished contributor — Oliver Wendell Holmes, whose son had lately cursed Lincoln off the parapet at Fort Stevens — soon told Gilmore that it had attracted more readers than any magazine article ever written.

Meantime (as always) Lincoln had kept busy with other problems, military as well as political. Often they overlapped, as in the case of facing up to the need for replacing the troops whose fall or discharge left gaps in the ranks of the two main armies: especially Meade's, which had a lower reënlistment quotient and had been further reduced, moreover, by detachments northward to shield Washington from attack by Early, still hovering nearby. On Sunday, July 17, while Jaquess and Gilmore talked in Richmond with Jefferson Davis — who had just put a message on the wire to Atlanta that presaged a step-up in the fighting there — Lincoln telegraphed Grant: "In your dispatch of yesterday to General Sherman I find the following, to wit: 'I shall make a desperate effort to get a position here which will hold the enemy without the necessity of so many men.' Pressed as we are by lapse of time, I am glad to hear you say this; and yet I do hope you may find a way that the effort shall not be desperate in the sense of a great loss of life." He sent this by way of preparation for a proclamation, issued next day, calling for 500,000 volunteers and ordering a draft to take place immediately after September 5 for any unfilled quotas.

This must surely be the last before November, he was saying, although there were already those who believed, despite the recent removal of the $300 exemption clause, that the results would not suffice even for the present. "We are not now receiving one half as many [troops] as we are discharging," Halleck complained to Grant the following day. "Volunteering has virtually ceased, and I do not anticipate much from the President's new call, which has the disadvantage of again postponing the draft for fifty days. Unless our government and people will come square up to the adoption of an efficient and thorough draft, we cannot supply the waste of our army."

Coming square up was easily said, but it left out factors that could not be ignored, including the reaction to this latest call for volunteers, which was seen as a velvet glove encasing the iron hand of a new draft. "Only half a million more! Oh that is nothing," one angry Wisconsin editor fumed, and followed through by saying: "Continue this Administration in power and we can all go to war, Canada, or to hell before 1868."

Now that the year moved into the dog days, with the fall elections looming just beyond, there was need for caution, if not in the military, then certainly in the political arena. Yet even caution might not serve, so portentous were the signs that a defeat was in the making. Frémont was something of a joke as an opponent, though not as a siphon for drawing off the Radical votes that would be needed if Lincoln was to prevail against the Democrats, who were scheduled to convene in Chicago in late August to adopt a platform and select a candidate for November. The platform would be strong for peace, and the candidate, it was believed, would be George McClellan: a formidable combination, one that might well snare both the anti-war and the soldier vote, not to mention the votes of the disaffected, likely to go to almost any rival of the present national leader. Indeed, the prospect so thoroughly alarmed a number of members of the Republican hierarchy that a secret call went out for a convention to meet in Cincinnati in September "to consider the state of the nation and to concentrate the Union strength on some one candidate who commands the confidence of the country, even by a new nomination if necessary."

For the present this was circulated privately, with the intention of bringing it out in the open when the time was ripe. In point of fact, however, the time seemed ripe enough already, to judge by the immediate response. Dissatisfaction with Lincoln had grown by now to include even close friends: Orville Browning, for example, who confessed he had long suspected that his fellow Illinoisan could not measure up to the task required. "I thought he might get through, as many a boy has got through college, without disgrace; but I fear he is a failure." Others agreeing were the eminent lawyer David Dudley Field, whose brother Lincoln had recently appointed to the Supreme Court, and

Schuyler Colfax, Speaker of the House. Chase expressed interest in the supersession, of course, and Ben Butler lent encouragement from down on Bermuda Hundred. Henry Davis was vehemently for it, but Wade and Sumner remained aloof for the time being, the former because he preferred to wait till after the Democratic convention, the latter because he thought it would make less trouble for the party if they gave Lincoln a chance to withdraw voluntarily. Many prominent editors favored the maneuver, including Parke Godwin of the New York *Evening Post* and Whitelaw Reid of the *Cincinnati Gazette*. But the most vociferous of them all was Horace Greeley, whose expression was cherubic but whose spirit had lately been strained beyond forbearance. "Mr Lincoln is already beaten," he declared. "He cannot be elected. And we must have another ticket to save us from overthrow."

Lincoln knew little or nothing yet of this plan by his friends and associates for a midstream swap, but he saw as clearly as they did that the drift was toward defeat and was likely to remain so unless some way could be found, between now and November, to turn the tide. A military victory would help, even one on a fairly modest scale — the more modest the better, in fact, so far as bloodshed was concerned — just so it encouraged the belief that things were looking up for one or another of the armies. But that was mainly up to Grant, locked in a stalemate below Richmond, and Sherman, apparently no better off in front of Atlanta. The other possibility was politics, Lincoln's field, and he was prepared to do all he could in that direction. His native Kentucky would be the first state to hold an election since his nomination; August 1 was the balloting date, and though only some county offices and an appellate judgeship were at stake, the contest was certain to be regarded as a bellwether for the rest, which were to follow in September. Consequently, he took off the gloves for this one. Declaring martial law, he suspended the writ of habeas corpus on July 5, continued the suspension through election day, and gave a free rein to Stephen Burbridge, who, having recently disposed of John Morgan at Cynthiana, proposed to move in a similar aggressive manner against all foes of the Administration throughout his Department of Kentucky. As a result, prominent Democrats were arrested wholesale for "disloyalty," and the name of their candidate for the judgeship was ordered stricken from the ballot on the same vague charge, obliging the survivors to make a last-minute substitute nomination for the post. Lincoln awaited the outcome with much interest, only to find on August 1 that all his pains had gone for nothing. The Democratic candidates swept the state.

There would be other contests; Maine, for instance, was coming up next, to be followed by Vermont. Although the snub just given him in his native state did not augur well for the result, he had no intention of doing anything less than his best to win in all of them, with the help of whatever devices he thought might help and despite the clamor of his critics, left and right, in his own party or the other. "The pilots on our western rivers steer from point to point, as they call it," he told a caller one of these days, "setting the course of the boat no farther than they can see. And that is all I propose to do in the great problems that are before us." One such point now was Atlanta; or anyhow it seemed to him it might be. Events that followed hard on the rebel change of commanders there had brought the fighting to a pitch of intensity, throughout the last two weeks in July, that matched the savagery of the struggle here in the East before it subsided into stalemate. The same thing might happen there — for that seemed to be the pattern: alternate fury and exhaustion — but Lincoln kept peering in that direction, seeking a point to steer by in his effort to land the boat in his charge before it split and sank.

✗   2   ✗

"The appointment has but one meaning," the Richmond *Examiner* declared on July 19, in reference to Johnston's supersession down in Georgia the day before, "and that is to give battle to the foe." Because John Bell Hood, in contrast to his predecessor, was "young, dashing, and lucky," the rival *Whig* informed its readers that same day, "the army and the people all have confidence in his ability and inclination to fight, and will look to him to drive back Sherman and save Atlanta." Thus the two papers were in agreement on the matter, not only with each other, but also, for once, with the new western leader's red-haired adversary, who rarely subscribed to any journalist's opinion, North or South. "I inferred that the change of commanders meant fight," Sherman remarked after conferring with subordinates who had known Hood in the days before the war. But he added, in contrast to the inference the two Confederate editors drew, five hundred miles away: "This was just what we wanted, viz., to fight in open ground, on anything like equal terms, instead of being forced to run up against prepared intrenchments."

He was about to get what he said he wanted. Hood — whose recent association with Johnston, he later explained, had made him "a still more ardent advocate of the Lee and Jackson school" — needed only one full day at his post before he resolved to go over to the offensive. By then, moreover, though he had had to spend a good part of the time discovering where his own troops were, he not only had decided to lash out at the encircling Federal host; he also had determined just when and where and how he would do so, with a minimal adjustment of the lines now held by his three corps. Accordingly, on the evening of July 19, he summoned Hardee and Stewart to headquarters along with Ben Cheatham, his temporary successor as corps commander, and gave them face-to-face instructions for an attack to be launched soon after midday tomorrow in order to take advantage of an opportunity Sherman was affording them, apparently out of overweening contempt or unconcern, to accomplish his piecemeal destruction. In the execution of what he termed "a general right wheel" from the near bank of the Chattahoochee, with Thomas inching the pivot forward across Peachtree Creek to close down on Atlanta from the north, and McPherson and Schofield swinging wide to come in from the east along the Georgia Railroad, the Ohioan had in effect divided his army and developed a better than two-mile gap between the inner edges of its widespread wings. It was Hood's intention, expressed in detail at his first council of war tonight on the outskirts of the city in his charge, not to plunge into but rather to preserve this gap, and thus keep the two blue wings divided while he crushed them in furious sequence, left and right.

Cheatham, with the help of Wheeler's troopers and some 5000 Georgia militia, would confront McPherson and Schofield from his present intrenchments east of Atlanta, taking care to mass artillery on his left and thus prevent the bluecoats in front from crossing the gap between them and Thomas, who meantime would be receiving the full attention of the other two corps. The Union-loyal Virginian's infantry strength was just above 50,000 — about the number Hood had in all — but the intention was to catch him half over Peachtree Creek, which he had begun to bridge today, and hit him before he could intrench or bring up reinforcements. Hardee on the right and Stewart on the left, disposed along a jump-off line roughly four miles north of the city, were to attack in echelon, east to west, each holding a division in reserve for immediate exploitation of any advantage that developed, "the effort to be to drive the enemy back to the creek, and then toward the river, into the narrow space formed by the river and creek." Once Thomas had been tamped into that watery pocket and ground up, the two gray corps would shift rapidly eastward to assist Cheatham in mangling Schofield and McPherson, with Wheeler's free-swinging horsemen standing by to carry out the roundup that would follow. Hood explained all this to his chief lieutenants "by direct interrogatory," having long since learned "that no measure is more important, upon the eve of battle, than to make certain in the presence of commanders that each thoroughly comprehends his orders."

His concern in this regard was not unfounded. Remembering, as he must have done, the Army of Tennessee's latest — and indeed, under Johnston, only — contemplated full-scale offensive at Cassville two months ago today, midway down the doleful road from Tunnel Hill to Atlanta, Hood knew only too well the dangers that lurked in tactical iotas. Nothing had come of the Cassville design, largely because of his own reaction to finding a misplaced blue column approaching his flank,

and presently on July 20, with all his troops in position and the 1 o'clock jump-off hour at hand, there were signs that a repetition was in the making. Cheatham sent word before noon that he would have to shift his line southward to keep McPherson from overlapping his right, beyond the railroad. Hood could only approve, and issue simultaneous instructions for Hardee and Stewart to conform by side-stepping half a division-front to their right, thus to prevent too wide an interval from developing between them and Cheatham, through which Schofield might plunge when he came up alongside McPherson. Hardee then had a difficult choice to make. Sidestepping as ordered, he found the interval wider than Hood had supposed, which left him with the decision whether to continue the sidling movement, at the cost of delaying his jump-off, or go forward on schedule — it was 1 o'clock by now — with a mile-wide gap yawning empty on his right. He chose the former course, Stewart conforming on his left, and thus delayed the attack for better than two hours. Shortly after 3 o'clock he sent three of his four divisions plunging northward into the valley of Peachtree Creek.

George Thomas was there, in strength and largely braced. Though the attack achieved the desired surprise, those extra two hours had given him time, not only to get nearly all of his combat elements over the creek, but also to get started on the construction of intrenchments. Hardee struck them and rebounded as if from contact with a red-hot stove, followed by Stewart, who drove harder against the enemy right with no better luck. The Federals either stood firm or hurried reinforcements to shore up threatened portions of their line. Moreover, in the unexpected emergency, Thomas abandoned his accustomed role of Old Slow Trot. Urging his guns forward to "relieve the hitch," he used the point of his sword on the rumps of laggard battery horses, then crossed the stream to direct in person the close-up defense of the bridgehead. An Indiana officer judged the progress of the fighting by the way Old Tom fiddled with his short, thick, gray-shot whiskers. "When satisfied he smoothes them down; when troubled he works them all out of shape." They were badly tousled now, and presently, when he saw the attackers falling back from the blast of fire that met them, he moved even further out of character in the opposite direction. "Hurrah!" he shouted, and took off his hat and slammed it on the ground in pure exuberance. "His whiskers were soon in good shape again," the Hoosier captain noted.

They might have been worse ruffled shortly thereafter; Hardee was about to throw Cleburne's reserve division into the melee, and in fact had just summoned him forward, when an urgent dispatch from Hood directed that troops be sent at once to the far right, where Cheatham's flank was under heavy pressure from McPherson. Cleburne arrived after nightfall, in time to confront a piece of high, cleared ground known as Bald Hill, two miles east of Atlanta and a mile south of the Georgia Railroad; Wheeler's dismounted troopers, after being pushed back all morning, had managed to hang on there through most of the afternoon. Northward, the battle raged along Peachtree Creek, but with decreasing fury, until about 6 o'clock, when it sputtered out. At a cost of 2500 casualties suffered, and 1600 inflicted, Hood's plan for crushing first Thomas, then the other two Union armies, had failed because the Rock of Chickamauga declined, as usual, to be budged or flustered. The southern commander had only praise for Cheatham and Wheeler, who fought hard all day against long odds, and especially for Stewart, who, though his losses were close to two thirds of the Confederate total, "carried out his instructions to the letter." He put the blame for his lack of success on Hardee — his former senior, known since Shiloh as Old Reliable — whose corps, "although composed of the best troops in the army, virtually accomplished nothing" and in fact, as a comparison of casualties would show, "did nothing more than skirmish with the enemy."

So Hood would report afterwards, when he got around to distributing blame for the failure of his first offensive action; the Battle of Peachtree Creek, it was called, or "Hood's First Sortie." But that did not keep him from choosing Hardee to deliver the main effort, two days later, in what would be referred to as "Hood's Second Sortie" or the Battle of Atlanta.

While Cleburne struggled the following day to prevent a blue advance past Bald Hill — the fighting on this third anniversary of First Manassas, he said, was "the bitterest" of his life — Wheeler moved still farther to the right, another mile beyond the railroad, to forestall another Federal flanking effort. What he found instead was an invitation for just such a movement by the Confederate defenders. McPherson, apparently with his full attention drawn to the day-long contest with Cleburne, had his left flank "in the air," unprotected by cavalry and wide open to assault. Informed of the situation early that morning, Hood grasped eagerly at this chance to turn the tables on the attackers. It was one of the chief regrets of his career that he had missed Chancellorsville, having been on detached service with Longstreet around

Suffolk while the Lee-Jackson masterpiece was being forged in the smoky, vine-choked Wilderness a hundred miles away. Now here was a God-given once-in-a-lifetime opportunity to stage a Chancellorsville of his own, down in the piny woods of Georgia, within a scant five days of his appointment to command the hard-luck Army of Tennessee.

In preparation for exploiting this advantage — and also because both ends of his present line were gravely threatened, Thomas having begun to build up pressure against the left about as heavy as McPherson had been exerting on the right — Hood directed that all three corps begin a withdrawal at nightfall to the works rimming the city in their rear, already laid out by Johnston the month before. These were to be held by Stewart and Cheatham, on the north and east, while Hardee marched south, then southeast, six miles down the McDonough Road to Cobb's Mill, where he would turn northeast and continue for the same distance up the Fayetteville Road to the Widow Parker's farm, south of the railroad about midway between Atlanta and Decatur. This would put his four divisions (including Cleburne's, which would join him on his way through town) in position for an all-out assault on McPherson's left rear. Though the route was as circuitous and long as Stonewall's flanking march had been, fourteen months ago in Virginia, an early start this evening should enable Old Reliable to launch a dawn

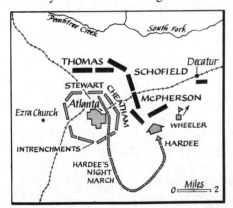

attack, and a dawn attack would give him a full day in which to accomplish McPherson's destruction, whereas Jackson had had only the few hours between sunset and dusk to serve Hooker in that fashion. Moreover, by way of increasing the blue confusion and distress, Wheeler's troopers, after serving as guides and outriders for the infantry column, would continue eastward to Decatur for a strike at McPherson's wagon train, known to be parked in the town square with all his reserve supplies and munitions. Hood explained further that once the flank attack got rolling he would send Cheatham forward to assail McPherson's front and keep Schofield from sending reinforcements to the hardpressed Union left, while Stewart, around to the north, engaged Thomas for the same purpose. Now, as before the Peachtree venture, he assembled a council of war to make certain that each of his lieutenants understood exactly what was required of him, and why. This was all the more advisable here, because of the greater complexity of what he was asking them to do. "To transfer after dark our entire line from the immediate presence of the enemy to another line around Atlanta, and to throw Hardee, the same night, entirely to the rear and flank of McPherson — as Jackson was thrown, in a similar movement, at Chancellorsville and Second Manassas — and to initiate the offensive at daylight, required no small effort on the part of the men and officers. I hoped, however, that the assault would result not only in a general battle, but in a signal victory to our arms."

Such hope was furthered by the secrecy and speed of the nighttime withdrawal to Atlanta's "inner line," which Stewart and Cheatham then began improving with picks and shovels while Hardee set out on his march around the Federal south flank. Almost at once the first hitch developed. Two miles to the east, confronting the enemy on Bald Hill, Cleburne had trouble breaking contact without giving away the movement or inviting an attack; it was crowding midnight before Hardee solved the problem by instructing him to leave his skirmishers in position and fall in behind W. H. T. Walker's men, marking time in rear of the other two divisions under Bate and George Maney, Cheatham's senior brigadier. Cleburne managed this by 1 a.m. of the projected day of battle — Friday, July 22 — but it was 3 o'clock in the morning before the final elements of the corps filed out of the unoccupied intrenchments south of town.

That was the first delay. Another was caused by the weariness of the marchers, still unrested from Wednesday's bloody work and Thursday's fitful skirmishing under the burning summer sun. Strung out on the single, narrow road, which had to be cleared from time to time when Wheeler's dusty horsemen clattered up or down it, the head of the column did not reach Cobb's Mill until dawn, the supposed jump-off hour. Disgruntled, Hardee turned northeast for the Widow Parker's, another half dozen miles up the troop-choked road. It was close to noon by the time he got there, evidently unsuspected by the enemy in the woods across the way, and 12.30 before the corps was formed for assault, Maney and Cleburne on the left, astride the Flat Shoals Road, which ran northwest past Bald Hill, where McPherson's flank was anchored — Cleburne thus had nearly come full circle — and Walker and Bate on the right, on opposite sides of Sugar Creek, which also led northwest, directly into McPherson's rear. Old Reliable could take pride in being just where he was meant to be, in position to duplicate Jackson's famous end-on strike at Hooker, but he was also uncomfortably aware that he was more than six hours behind schedule.

This made him testy: as anyone near him could see in these final minutes before he gave the order to go forward. When Wheeler sent word that a sizeable column of blue troopers had passed this way a while ago, apparently headed southward on a raid, and requested permission to take out after them, Hardee was quick to say no; "We must attack, as we arranged, with all our force." So Wheeler, disappointed at being denied the chance to cross sabers with the intruders, set out eastward for Decatur and McPherson's unsuspecting and perhaps unguarded wagon

train. Then Walker came to headquarters to report that he had discovered in his immediate front a giant brier patch, which he asked to
be allowed to skirt when he advanced, despite the probable derangement of his line and the loss of still more time. Normally courteous,
Hardee was emphatic in refusal. "No, sir!" he said roughly, not bother-
ing to disguise his anger. "This movement has been delayed too long
already. Go and obey my orders!"

    Walker, a year younger at forty-seven than his chief, who had
finished a year behind him at West Point—a veteran of the Seminole
and Mexican wars, heavily bearded, with stern eyes, he was one of
three West Pointers among the eight Confederate generals named
Walker—then demonstrated a difficulty commanders risked with
high-strung subordinates in this war, particularly on the southern side.
He took offense at his fellow Georgian's tone, and he said as much to an
aide who rode with him on the way back to his division. "Major, did
you hear that?" he asked, fuming. The staffer admitted he had; "General
Hardee forgot himself," he suggested. Walker was not to be put off,
however. "I shall make him remember this insult. If I survive this battle,
he shall answer me for it." Just then an officer from Hardee's staff
overtook them with the corps commander's regrets for "his hasty and
discourteous language" and assurance that he would have "come in
person to apologize, but that his presence was required elsewhere, and
would do so at the first opportunity." So the envoy informed Walker,
whose companion remarked soothingly, after they had ridden on: "Now
that makes it all right." But Walker's blood was up. He was by no
means satisfied. "No, it does not," he said hotly. "He must answer
me for this."

    As it turned out, no one on this earth was going to answer to
W. H. T. Walker for anything. Ordered forward shortly thereafter,
he and his three brigades clawed their way through the brier patch,
hearing Maney's and Cleburne's attack explode on the left as it struck
McPherson's flank, and then emerged from a stand of pines into what
was to have been the Union rear, only to find a nearly mile-long triple
line of bluecoats confronting them on ground that had been empty
when it was reconnoitered, half an hour before. Walker had little chance
to react to this discovery, however, for as he and his men emerged from
the trees, sunlight glinting on his drawn saber and their rifles, a Federal
picket took careful aim and shot him off his horse.

    Hood, who had waited and watched impatiently for the past six
hours in a high-sited observation post on the outskirts of Atlanta, was
dismayed by what he saw no more than a mile away across the treetops.
Plunging northwest, on the far left of the Confederate assault, Maney
overlapped the Union flank and had to swing hard right as he went past
it, which threw his division head-on against the enemy intrenchments
facing west. This caused Hood to assume — and later charge — that

Hardee's attack had been launched, not into the rear of the blue left flank, as directed, but against its front, with predictable results; Maney rebounded, then lunged forward again, and again rebounded. Beyond him, out of sight from Hood's lookout tower, Cleburne was doing better, having struck the Federals endwise, and was driving them headlong up the Flat Shoals Road, which ran just in rear of their works below Bald Hill. Still farther to the east, however, Bate and Walker's successor, Brigadier General Hugh Mercer, were having the hardest time of all. In this direction, the element of surprise was with the defenders, whose presence was as unexpected, here on the right, as the appearance of the attackers had been at the opposite end of the line.

Advancing westward yesterday and this morning, under instructions "not to extend any farther to the left" beyond the railroad, lest his troops be spread too thin, McPherson's front had contracted so much that he could detach one of his three corps, led by Major General Grenville M. Dodge, to carry out an order from Sherman to "destroy every rail and tie of the railroad, from Decatur up to your skirmish line." Dodge completed this assignment before midday and was moving up to take a position in support of Blair, whose corps was on the left, when he learned that a heavy force of graybacks was approaching from the southeast, up both banks of Sugar Creek. Under the circumstances, all he had to do was halt and face his two divisions to the left, still in march formation on an east-west road, to establish the triple line of defense whose existence Walker and Bate had not suspected until they emerged from the screen of pines and found it bristling in their front. If they had come up half an hour earlier they would have stepped into a military vacuum, with little or nothing between them and the rear of Blair and Logan, whose corps was on Blair's right, connecting McPherson and Schofield. Now, instead, Walker was dead and Bate and Mercer were involved in a desperate fight that stopped them in their tracks, much as Maney had been stopped on the left, under different circumstances. Thus, of the four gray divisions involved in the attack from which so much had been expected, only Cleburne's was performing as intended. Yet he and his fellow Arkansans made the most of their advantage, including the killing of the commander of the Army of the Tennessee.

McPherson was not with his troops when Hardee's attack exploded on his flank. He was up in rear of Schofield's left, just over half a mile north of the railroad, conferring with Sherman in the yard of a two-story frame house that had been taken over for general headquarters, about midway of the line confronting Atlanta from the east. What he wanted was permission to open fire with a battery of long-range 32-pounders on a foundry whose tall smokestack he could see beyond the rebel works from a gun position he had selected and already had under construction on Bald Hill — or Leggett's Hill, as it was called

on the Federal side, for Brigadier General Mortimer Leggett, whose
division of Blair's corps occupied it. McPherson's notion was that if
he could "knock down that foundry," along with other buildings inside
Atlanta, he would hasten the fall of the city. Moreover, he had personal
reasons for wanting to accomplish this in the shortest possible time,
since what he was counting on, in the way of reward, was a leave of
absence that would permit him to go to Baltimore and marry a young
lady to whom he had been engaged since his last leave, just after the
fall of Vicksburg. He had tried his best to get away in March and April,
but Sherman had been unwilling, protesting that there was too much
to be done before the drive through Georgia opened in early May. So
the thirty-five-year-old Ohioan had had to bide his time; though only
by the hardest. Just last week he had asked his friend Schofield when he
supposed his prayers would be answered. "After the capture of Atlanta,
I guess," Schofield replied, and McPherson had taken that as his preliminary objective, immediately preceding the real objective, which was
Baltimore and a union that had little to do with the one he and more
than a hundred thousand others would die fighting to preserve.

Sherman readily assented to the shelling of the city, and ordered
it to begin as soon as the guns were in position. His first impression, on
finding the rebel trenches empty in his front this morning, had been
that Hood had evacuated Atlanta overnight; but that had lasted only until he relocated the enemy in occupation of the city's inner line, as
bristly as ever, if not more so, and now he took the occasion of Mc-
Pherson's midday visit to show him, on the headquarters map, his plan
for shifting all three armies around to the west for the purpose of cutting Hood's remaining rail connections with Macon and Mobile, which
would surely bring on the fall of Atlanta if the proposed bombardment
failed. It was by then around 12.30, and as they talked, bent over the
map, the sound of conflict suddenly swelled to a roar: particularly
southward, where things had been quiet all morning. Sherman whipped
out his pocket compass, trained it by earshot, and "became satisfied that
the firing was too far to our left rear to be explained by known facts."
McPherson quickly called for his horse and rode off to investigate,
trailed by members of his staff. Sherman stood and watched him go,
curly bearded, six feet tall, with lights of laughter often twinkling in his
eyes; "a very handsome man in every way," according to his chief,
who thought of his fellow Ohioan as something more than a protégé or
younger brother. He thought of him in fact as a successor — and not
only to himself, as he would tell another friend that night. "I expected
something to happen to Grant and me; either the rebels or the newspapers would kill us both, and I looked to McPherson as the man to
follow us and finish the war."

From a ridge in rear of the road on which Dodge had been marching until he stopped and faced his two divisions left to meet the assault

by Bate and Walker, McPherson could see that the situation here was less desperate than he had feared; Dodge was plainly holding his own, although the boom of guns from the east gave warning that a brigade he had posted at Decatur to guard the train in the cavalry's absence was also under attack. Sending the available members of his staff in both directions, with instructions for all units to stand firm at whatever cost, the army commander turned his attention westward to Blair's position, where the threat seemed gravest.

In point of fact it was graver than he knew. Cleburne by now had driven Blair's flank division back on Leggett, whose troops were fighting to hold the hill that bore his name, and numbers of enemy skirmishers had already worked their way around in its rear to seize the wooded ground between there and Dodge's position. That was how it happened that McPherson, who had sent away all of his staff except an orderly, encountered graybacks while trotting along a road that led across to Leggett's Hill. Indeed, he was practically on top of one group of Confederates before he suspected they were there. An Arkansas captain, raising his sword as a signal for the two riders to surrender, was surprised by the young general's response ("He checked his horse slightly, raised his hat as politely as if he were saluting a lady, wheeled his horse's head directly to the right, and dashed off to the rear in a full gallop") but not for long. "Shoot him," the gray-clad officer told a corporal standing by, and the corporal did.

McPherson was bent over his mount's withers to keep from being swept from the saddle by the drooping limbs of trees along the road. He fell heavily to the ground, struck low in the back by a bullet that ranged upward through or near his heart. His companion, unhorsed and momentarily stunned by a low-hanging branch, recovered consciousness to find the general lying beside him, clutching his breast in pain, and the butternut soldiers hurrying toward them. He bent over him and asked if he was hurt. "Oh, orderly, I am," McPherson said, and with that he put his face in the dust of the road, quivered briefly, and died. The orderly felt himself being snatched back and up by his revolver belt; "Git to the rear, you Yankee son of a bitch," he heard the rebel who had grabbed him say. Then the captain got there and stood looking down at the polished boots and buff gauntlets, the ornate sash about the waist, and the stars of a major general on both dead shoulders. "Who is this lying here?" he asked. The orderly had trouble answering. Sudden grief had constricted his throat and tears stood in his eyes. "Sir, it is General McPherson," he said. "You have killed the best man in our army."

Sherman's grief was as great, and a good deal more effusive. "I yield to no one but yourself the right to exceed me in lamentations for our dead hero," he presently wrote the Baltimore fiancée. "Though the cannon booms now, and the angry rattle of musketry tells me that

I also will likely pay the same penalty, yet while life lasts I will delight in the memory of that bright particular star which has gone before to prepare the way for us more hardened sinners who must struggle to the end."

But that was later, when he could spare the time. Just now he responded to the news that McPherson's horse had come riderless out of the woods in back of Leggett's Hill by ordering John Logan, the senior corps commander, to take charge of the army and counterattack at once to recover the ground on which his chief might be lying wounded. Logan did so, and within the hour McPherson's body was brought to headquarters in an ambulance. Someone wrenched a door off its hinges and propped it on two chairs for a catafalque, and Sherman went on directing the battle from the room where his fellow Ohioan was laid out. Already he had sent a brigade from Schofield to support the one Dodge had defending Decatur from Wheeler's attack, but aside from this he sent no reinforcements to help resist the assault on his left flank and rear. "I purposely allowed the Army of the Tennessee to fight this battle almost unaided," he later explained, partly because he wanted to leave to McPherson's veterans the honor of avenging his fall, and also because he believed that "if any assistance were rendered by either of the other armies, the Army of the Tennessee would be jealous."

His confidence in his old army — it had also once been Grant's, and had yet to come out loser when the smoke of battle cleared — was justified largely today because of Logan, who exercised his new command in style. Dubbed "Black Jack" by his soldiers, the former Illinois politician knew how to translate stump oratory into rousing military terms. Clutching his flop-brim hat in one hand so that his long raven hair streamed behind him in the wind, he spurred from point to embattled point and bellowed: "Will you hold this line with me? Will you hold this line?" The veterans showed they would. "Black Jack! Black Jack!" they chanted as they beat off attacks that soon were coming from all directions: particularly on Leggett's Hill, which Hood by now had ordered Cheatham to assault from the west while Cleburne kept up pressure from the south and east. Brigadier General Manning Force's brigade, menaced front and rear, was obliged at times to fight on alternate sides of its breastworks. At one critical point he called for a flag, and a young lieutenant, assuming from the look of things that the time had come to surrender, began a frantic search for a white handkerchief or shirt. "Damn you, sir!" Force shouted. "I don't want a flag of truce; I want the *American* flag!" Shot in the face shortly thereafter, he lost the use of his voice and fell back on conducting the hilltop defense with gestures, which were no less flamboyant and seemed to work as well. The hill was held, though at a cost of ten guns — including the four McPherson had planned to use against Atlanta at long range — fifteen stands of colors, and better than a thousand prisoners, mostly from Blair's other division under Brigadier General Giles A. Smith (one of an even dozen Federal generals with that name, including one who spelled it Smyth) which had given way at the outset, badly rattled by Cleburne's unexpected flank-and-rear assault.

Although there were no other outright surprises, the issue continued to swing in doubt from time to time and place to place. Sherman watched with interest from his headquarters on the central ridge, and when Cheatham scored a breakthrough around 4 o'clock, just north of the railroad, he had Schofield mass the fire of several batteries to help restore Logan's punctured right. Word came then from Decatur that the two brigades of infantry had managed to keep Wheeler's troopers out of the town square, where the train was parked, and from Dodge that he was confident of holding against weakening attacks on the left rear. Mercurial as always, despite the tears that trickled into his stub red beard whenever he thought of McPherson laid out on his improvised bier inside the house, Sherman was in high spirits as a result of these reports, which reached him as he paced about the yard and watched the progress of the fighting in all directions. Presently the headquarters came under long-range fire, obliging him and his attendants to take cover in an adjoining grove of trees. Sheltered behind one of these, he noticed a terrified soldier crouched nearby in back of another, moaning: "Lord, Lord, if I once get home," and: "Oh, I'll be killed!" Sherman grinned and picked up a handful of stones, which he then began to toss in that direction. Every pebble that struck the tree brought a howl or a groan from behind it. "That's hard firing, my man," he called to the unstrung soldier, who replied without opening his tight-shut eyes: "Hard? It's fearful! I think thirty shells have hit this tree while I was here." The fire subsided, and the general stepped into the open. "It's all over now; come out," he told the man, who emerged trembling. When he saw who had been taunting him, he took off running through the woods, pursued by the sound of Sherman's laughter.

From end to end, the Federal line was held or restored, except where Smith's unfortunates had been driven back across the lower slopes of Leggett's Hill, and though the fighting was sometimes hand-to-hand and desperate, on past sundown into twilight, there was by then no doubt that Hood's Second Sortie — aside, that is, from the capture of a dozen guns and an assortment of Union colors — had been no less a failure than his First, two days ago. It was, however, considerably more expensive; for this time the Confederate leader held almost nothing back, including the Georgia militia, which he used in a fruitless attack on Schofield that had no effect on the battle except to swell the list of southern casualties. In the end, Hood's loss was around 8000 killed, wounded, and missing, as compared to Sherman's 3700.

All next day the contending armies remained in position, licking their wounds, until Hardee withdrew unimpeded the following night into the Atlanta works. Saddened by the loss of Walker, who had called at headquarters on the eve of battle to assure him of his understanding and support, as well as by the news about McPherson — "No soldier fell in the enemy's ranks whose death caused me equal regret," he later said of his West Point friend and classmate — Hood was profoundly disappointed by the failure of his two sorties to accomplish the end for which they had been designed; but he was by no means so discouraged that he did not intend to attempt a third, if his adversary presented him with still another opportunity. He knew only too well how close he had come, except for the unlucky appearance of Dodge's corps in exactly the wrong place at the wrong time, to wrecking the encircling Union host entirely.

Frank Blair, for one, concurred in this belief. Hood's flanking movement, he afterwards declared, "was a very bold and a very brilliant one, and was very near being successful. The position taken up accidentally by [Dodge's] corps prevented the full force of the blow from falling where it was intended to fall. If my command had been driven from its position at the time that [Logan's] corps was forced back from its intrenchments, there must have been a general rout of all the troops of the Army of the Tennessee . . . and, possibly, the panic might have been communicated to the balance of the army."

Sherman was not much given to speculation on the might-have-beens of combat, and in any case he no more agreed with this assessment than he did with subsequent criticism that, in leaving Schofield and Thomas standing comparatively idle on the sidelines while Logan battled for survival, he had missed a prime chance to break Atlanta's inner line, weakened as it was by the withdrawal of a major portion of its defenders for the attack on his south flank. What he mainly concluded, once the smoke had cleared, was that in staging two all-out sorties in as many days — both of them not only unsuccessful but also highly expensive in energy, blood, and ingenuity — Hood had shot his wad. And from this Sherman concluded further that he was unlikely to be molested in his execution of the maneuver he had described to McPherson at their final interview; that is, "to withdraw from the left flank and add to the right," thereby shifting his whole force counterclockwise, around to the west of the city, in order to probe for its rail supply lines to the south.

First, though, there was the problem of finding a permanent replacement for his fallen star, McPherson. On the face of it, Logan having performed spectacularly under worse than trying conditions, the solution should have been simple. But it turned out to be extremely complicated, involving the exacerbation of some tender feelings and, in the end, nothing less than the reorganization of the command structure of two of the three armies in his charge.

Thomas came promptly to headquarters to advise against keeping

Logan at his temporary post. Although there was bad blood between them, dating back to Chattanooga, basically his objection was that Black Jack, like all the other corps and division leaders in the Army of the Tennessee — not one of them was a West Pointer, whereas two thirds of his own and half of Schofield's were Academy graduates — was a nonprofessional. "He is brave enough and a good officer," the Virginian admitted, "but if he had an army I am afraid he would edge over on both sides and annoy Schofield and me. Even as a corps commander he is given to edging out beyond his jurisdiction." Sherman agreed in principle that volunteers from civilian life, especially politicians, "looked to personal fame and glory as auxiliary and secondary to their political ambition. . . . I wanted to succeed in taking Atlanta," he later explained, "and needed commanders who were purely and technically soldiers, men who would obey orders and execute them promptly and on time." That ruled out Logan, along with Blair. Who then? he asked Thomas, who replied: "You cannot do better than put Howard in command of that army." Sherman protested that this would make Logan "terribly mad" and might also create "a rumpus among those volunteers," but then agreed. One-armed and two years younger even than McPherson, O. O. Howard, West Point '54, a Maine-born recent eastern import to the western theater, was then announced as the new commander of the army that had once been Sherman's own.

Returned to his corps, Logan managed to live with the burning aroused in his breast by this disappointment. But the same could not be said for Old Tom's ranking corps commander, the altogether professional Joe Hooker. Outraged at having been passed over in favor of the man he largely blamed for his defeat at Chancellorsville, Fighting Joe characterized the action as "an insult to my rank and services" and submitted at once a request to be relieved of his present duties. Thomas "approved and *heartily* recommended" acceptance of this application, which Sherman was quick to grant, remarking incidentally that the former commander of the Army of the Potomac had not even been considered for the post that now was Howard's, since "we on the spot did not rate his fighting qualities as high as he did." Hooker departed for an inactive assignment in the Northern Department, where he spent the rest of the war, further embittered by the news that his successor was Major General Henry W. Slocum, another enemy, who had been sent to Vicksburg on the eve of the present campaign to avoid personality clashes between them. Pending Slocum's arrival from Mississippi, Alpheus Williams would lead the corps as senior division commander, much as Major General David S. Stanley had succeeded to the command of Howard's corps, though on a permanent basis.

By July 25, within five days of the Peachtree crossing, when work on it began, the railroad bridge over the Chattahoochee — 760 feet long and 90 high — was completed and track relaid to a forward base im-

mediately in Thomas's rear. Sherman, his supplies replenished and generals reshuffled, was ready within another two days to begin the counterclockwise western slide designed to bring on the fall of Atlanta by
severing its rail connection with the world outside. Already this had
been accomplished up to the final step; for of the four lines in and out
of the city all but one had been seized or wrecked by now, beginning
with the Western & Atlantic, down which the Federals had been moving ever since they chevied Johnston out of Dalton. Then Schofield and
McPherson had put the Georgia Railroad out of commission by dismantling it as they moved westward from Stone Mountain and Decatur.
Of the remaining two — the Atlanta & West Point and the Macon &
Western, which shared the same track until they branched southwest
and southeast at East Point, five miles south of the city — the former,
connecting with Montgomery and Mobile, had been severely damaged
the week before by Major General Lovell Rousseau, who raided southward through Alabama with 2500 troopers, practically unopposed, and
tore up close to thirty miles of the line between Montgomery and
Opelika, where it branched northeast for West Point and Atlanta. That
left only the Macon road, connecting eastward with Savannah, for
Hood's use in supplying his army and for Sherman to destroy. He began
his large-scale semicircular maneuver to accomplish this on July 27,
ordering Howard to swing north, then west — in rear of Schofield and
Thomas, who would follow him in turn — for a southward march
down the near bank of the Chattahoochee, which would serve as an
artery for supplies, to descend as soon as possible on that one railroad still
in operation out of a place that once had boasted of being "the turntable of
the Confederacy."

　　Simultaneously, by way of putting two strings to his bow, he
turned 10,000 horsemen loose on the same objective in an all-out double
strike around both rebel flanks. Brigadier General Edward McCook, his
division reinforced to a strength of 3500 by the addition of a brigade
from Rousseau — who, it was hoped, had established the model for the
current operation, over in Alabama the week before — would ride down
the north bank of the Chattahoochee for a crossing at Campbelltown,
under orders to proceed eastward and hit the Macon & Western at or
below Jonesboro, just under twenty miles on the far side of Atlanta. This
was also the goal of the second mounted column, 6500 strong, which
would set out from Decatur under Stoneman, who had Garrard's division attached to his own for a southward lunge around the enemy
right. Both columns were to start on July 27, the day the infantry slide
began; Sherman expected them back within three days at the most. But
when Stoneman asked permission to press on, once the railroad had been
wrecked, to Macon and Andersonville for the purpose of freeing the
prisoners held in their thousands at both places, he readily agreed to this
hundred-mile extension of the raid, on condition that Garrard head back

as soon as the Macon road was smashed, to work with McCook in covering the infantry's left wheel around Atlanta. The redhead's hopes were high, but not for long: mainly because of Joe Wheeler, who, though outnumbered three-to-two by the blue troopers, did not neglect this opportunity to deal with them in detail.

Right and left, at Campbelltown and Decatur, both of them closer to Jonesboro than they were to each other at the outset, the two columns took off on schedule, though not altogether in the manner Sherman intended. Stoneman's mind was fixed so firmly on his ultimate goal — Andersonville and its 30,000 inmates, whose liberation would be nothing less than the top cavalry exploit of the war — that he no longer had any discernible interest in the limited purpose for which the two-pronged strike had been conceived. Accordingly, without notifying anyone above him, he sent Garrard's 4300 troopers pounding due south to draw off the enemy horsemen while he and his 2200 rode east for Covington, which Garrard had raided five days ago during the Battle of Atlanta. In this he was successful; he reached Covington undetected and turned south, down the east bank of the Ocmulgee River, for Macon, the first of his two prison-camp objectives. Garrard meantime had been no less successful in carrying out his part of the revised design, which was to attract the attention of the rebels in his direction. On Snapfinger Creek that afternoon, barely ten miles out of Decatur, he ran into mounted graybacks whose number increased so rapidly overnight that at Flatrock Bridge next morning, another five miles down the road, he had to turn and ride hard, back to Decatur, to keep from losing everything he had. His nimbleness kept down his losses; yet even so these would have been much heavier if Wheeler, about to give chase with eight brigades — just over 6000 sabers in all — had not received word that McCook had crossed the Chattahoochee, en route for the Macon & Western, and that Stoneman was beyond the Ocmulgee, apparently headed for Macon itself. The Georgia-born Alabamian, two months short of his twenty-eighth birthday, left one brigade to keep up the pressure on Garrard and turned with the other seven to meet these rearward threats, sending three brigades to deal with Stoneman while he himself set out with the rest to intercept McCook.

As it turned out, the interception came after, not before, McCook struck the railroad at Lovejoy Station, seven miles beyond Jonesboro. He got there four hours ahead of Wheeler, which gave him time to burn the depot, tear up a mile and a half of track, and destroy a sizeable wagon train, along with its 800 mules, before the graybacks arrived to drive him off and pursue him all the way to the Chattahoochee. Overtaken at Newnan, due west on the West Point road, McCook lost 950 troopers killed and captured, along with his pack train and two guns, between there and the river, which he crossed to safety on July 30, reduced in strength by nearly a third and much the worse for wear.

By that time Stoneman had reached the outskirts of Macon, only to find it defended by local militia. While he engaged in a long-range duel across the Ocmulgee with these part-time soldiers, hoping to cover his search for a downstream ford, the three brigades sent after him by Wheeler came up in his rear. He tried for a getaway, back the way he had come, then found himself involved in a running fight that ended next day near Hillsboro, twenty-five miles to the north, when he was all but surrounded at a place called Sunshine Church. He chose one brigade to make a stand and told the other two to escape as best they could; which they did, while he and his chosen 700 were being overrun and rounded up. One of the two surviving brigades made it back to Decatur two days later, but the other, unable to turn west because of the swarm of rebels on that flank, was wrecked at Jug Tavern on August 3, thirty miles north of Covington. Stoneman and his captured fellow officers were in Macon by then, locked up with the unfortunates they had set out to liberate, and the enlisted men were in much the same position, though considerably worse off so far as the creature comforts were concerned, sixty miles to the southwest at Andersonville.

"On the whole," Sherman reported to Washington in one of the prize understatements of the war, "the cavalry raid is not deemed a success."

In plain fact, aside from McCook's fortuitous interception of the 800-mule train — the break in the track at Lovejoy's, for example, amounted to nothing worse than a two-day inconvenience, after which the Macon & Western was back in use from end to end — the raid not only failed to achieve its purpose, it was also a good deal harder on the raiders than on the raided. Sherman's true assessment was shown by what he did, on the return of his badly cut up horsemen, rather than by what he wrote in his report. Garrard's division, which had suffered least, was dismounted and used to occupy the intrenchments Schofield vacated when he began his swing around the city in Howard's wake, and the other two were reorganized, after a period of sorely needed rest and refitment, into units roughly half their former size. Not that Sherman expected much from them, offensively speaking, in the critical days ahead. "I now became satisfied," he said later, "that cavalry could not, or would not, make a sufficient lodgment on the railroad below Atlanta, and that nothing would suffice but for us to reach it with the main army."

But that turned out to be about as difficult an undertaking as the one assigned to Stoneman and McCook. For one thing — against all his expectations, which were founded on the belief that Hood by now had shot his wad — he had no sooner begun his counterclockwise wheel, shifting Howard around in rear of Schofield and Thomas to a position west of the city so that his right could be extended to reach the vital railway junction at East Point, than he was confronted with still a third

sortie by his Confederate opponent, quite as savage as the other
two.

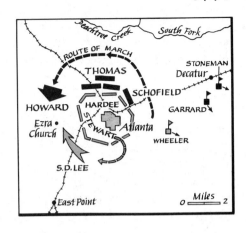

All had gone well on the
first day, July 27; Howard
pulled out undeterred and took
up the march, first north, then
west along the near bank of
Peachtree Creek. Riding south
next morning in rear of Logan,
whose corps was in the lead,
Sherman and the new army commander came under fire from a
masked battery as they approached the Lickskillet Road, which ran due
east into Atlanta, three miles off. Howard did not like the look of things,
and said so. "General Hood will attack me here," he told his companion,
who scoffed at the notion: "I guess not. He will hardly try it again." But
Howard remained persuaded that he was about to be struck, explaining
later that he based his conviction on previous acquaintance with the man
who would do the striking; "I said that I had known Hood at West Point,
and that he was indomitable."

Indomitable. Presented thus with a third chance to destroy an
isolated portion of the enemy host, Hood had designed still another
combined assault, once more after the manner of Lee and Jackson, to
forestall this massive probe around his left. His old corps, now under
Stephen D. Lee — the South Carolinian had been promoted to lieutenant
general and brought from Alabama to take over from Cheatham —
would march out the Lickskillet Road on the morning of July 28 to
occupy a position from which it could block Howard's extension of
the Union right and set him up for a flank attack by Stewart, who
would bring his corps out the Sandtown Road that evening, a mile in
Lee's rear, to circle the head of the stalled blue column and strike from
the southwest at Howard's unguarded outer flank next morning. Hardee,
reduced to three divisions, each of which received a brigade from the
fallen Walker's broken-up division, would hold Atlanta's inner line
against whatever pressure Schofield and Thomas might exert. Lee, who
had assumed command only the day before, moved as ordered, determined to prove his mettle in this first test at his new post — two
months short of his thirty-first birthday, he was six years younger than
anyone else of his rank in the whole Confederacy — but found himself
involved by midday, three miles out the Lickskillet Road, near a rural
chapel known as Ezra Church, in a furious meeting engagement that
left him no time for digging in or even getting set. So instead he took
the offensive with all three of his divisions.

They were not enough: not nearly enough, as the thing developed. Howard, who was only two years older than Lee and no less anxious to prove his mettle, having also assumed command the day before, had foreseen the attack (or anyhow forefelt it, despite Sherman's scoff) and though there was no time for intrenching, once he had called a halt he had his lead corps throw up a rudimentary breastwork of logs and rails; so that when Lee's men charged — "with a terrifying yell," the one-armed commander would recall — they were "met steadily and repulsed." They fell back, then charged again, with the same result. Busily strengthening their improvised works between attacks, Logan's four divisions stood their ground, reinforced in the course of the struggle by others from Dodge and Blair, while Sherman rode back and alerted Thomas to be ready to send more. These last were unneeded, even though Hood by then had abandoned his plan for a double envelopment and instead told Stewart to go at once out the Lickskillet Road to Lee's assistance. Stewart added the weight of one division to the contest before sundown, without appreciable effect. "Each attack was less vigorous and had less chance than the one before it," a Union veteran was to note.

Alarmed by reports coming in all afternoon from west of Atlanta, Hood had Hardee turn his corps over to Cheatham, who had returned to his division, and proceed without delay to Ezra Church to take charge of the other two. Old Reliable arrived to find that the battle had sputtered out, and made no effort to revive it. Lee and Stewart between them had lost some 2500 killed and wounded — about the same number that had fallen along Peachtree Creek eight days ago — as compared to Howard's loss of a scant 700. Nor was that the worst of it, according to Hardee, who afterwards declared: "No action of the campaign probably did so much to demoralize and dishearten the troops engaged in it."

Sherman knew now that he had been wrong, these past five days, in thinking that Hood had shot his wad in the Battle of Atlanta. He would have been considerably closer to the truth, however, if he had reverted to this belief on the night that followed the Battle of Ezra Church. Moreover, there were Confederates in the still smoky woods, out beyond Howard's unbroken lines, who would have agreed with him; almost.

"Say, Johnny," one of Logan's soldiers called across the breastworks, into the outer darkness. "How many of you are there left?"

"Oh, about enough for another killing," some butternut replied.

This attitude on both sides, now that another month drew to a close, was reflected in their respective casualty lists. Including his cavalry subtractions, which were heavy, Sherman had lost in July about 8000 killed, wounded, and missing — roughly the number that fell in June, and better than a thousand fewer than fell in May. The over-all Federal total, from the outset back at Tunnel Hill, came to just under 25,000.

Hood, on the other hand, had suffered 13,000 casualties in the course of his three sorties, which brought the Confederate total, including Johnston's, to 27,500. That was about the number Lee had lost during the same three-month span in Virginia, whereas Sherman had lost considerably fewer than half as many as Meade. Grant could well be proud of his western lieutenant, if and when he got around to comparing the cost, in men per mile, of the campaigns in Georgia and the Old Dominion, West and East.

Still, there was a good deal more to war than mere killing and maiming. "Lee's army will be your objective point," he had instructed Meade before the jump-off, only to have the eastern offensive wind up in a stalemate, a digging contest outside Petersburg. Similarly, he had told Sherman to "move against Johnston's army," and the red-haired Ohioan had done just that — so long as the army was Johnston's. But now that it was Hood's, and had come out swinging, a change set in: particularly after Ezra Church, the third of Hood's three roaring sorties. Lopsided as that victory had been for Sherman, it served warning that, in reaching for the railroad in his adversary's rear, his infantry might do no better than his cavalry had done, and indeed might suffer as severely in the process.

Inching southward all the following week he found rebel intrenchments bristling in his path. On August 5, having brought Schofield around in the wake of Howard, he reinforced him with a corps from Thomas and ordered the drive on the railroad resumed. Schofield tried, the following morning, but was soon involved in the toils of Utoy Creek and suffered a bloody repulse. It was then that the change in Sherman — or, rather, in his definition of his goal — became complete. Formerly the Gate City had been no more than the anvil on which he intended to hammer the insurgent force to pieces. Now it became the end-all objective of his campaign. He would simply pound the anvil.

"I do not deem it prudent to extend any more to the right," he wired Halleck next day, "but will push forward daily by parallels, and make the inside of Atlanta too hot to be endured."

In line with McPherson's proposal at their farewell interview, he sent to Chattanooga for siege guns and began a long-range shelling of the city, firing over the heads of its defenders and into its business and residential districts. "Most of the people are gone; it is now simply a big fort," he informed his wife that week, and while this was by no means true at the time, it became increasingly the case with every passing day of the bombardment. "I can give you no idea of the excitement in Atlanta," a southern correspondent wrote. "Everybody seems to be hurrying off, especially the women. Wagons loaded with household furniture and everything else that can be packed upon them crowd every street, and women old and young and children innumerable are hurrying to and fro. Every train of cars is loaded to its utmost capacity.

The excitement beats everything I ever saw, and I hope I may never witness such again." Presently, though the destruction of property was great and the shelling continued day and night, the citizens learned to take shelter in underground bombproofs, as at Vicksburg the year before, and Hood said later that he never heard "one word from their lips expressive of dissatisfaction or willingness to surrender." Sherman's reaction was to step up the rate of fire. "We can pick out almost any house in town," he boasted to Halleck. He was by nature "too impatient for a siege," he added, but "One thing is certain. Whether we get inside of Atlanta or not, it will be a used-up community when we are done with it."

His troops shared his ebullience, if not his impatience, finding much to admire in this notion of bloodless engagement at long range. "There goes the Atlanta Express!" they cheered as the big shells took off at fifteen-minute intervals over their and the rebel trenches. When one of the outsized guns developed the habit of dropping its projectiles short, they turned and shouted rearward through cupped hands: "Take her away! She slobbers at the mouth." Sherman moved among them, a reporter noted, with "no symptoms of heavy cares — his nose high, thin, and planted with a curve as vehement as the curl of a Malay cutlass — tall, slender, his quick movements denoting good muscle added to absolute leanness, not thinness." Uncle Billy, they called him, with an affection no blue-clad soldiers had shown for a commander, West or East, since Little Mac's departure from the war. What was more, unlike McClellan, he shared their life as well as their rations, though a staffer recorded that he was mostly "too busy to eat much. He ate hardtack, sweet potatoes, bacon, black coffee off a rough table, sitting on a cracker box, wearing a gray flannel shirt, a faded old blue blouse, and trousers he had worn since long before Chattanooga. He talked and smoked cigars incessantly, giving orders, dictating telegrams, bright and chipper."

Partly this was exuberance. Partly it was fret, which he often expressed or covered in such a manner. Either way, it was deadly: as was shown in a message he sent Howard, August 10, amid the roar of long-range guns. "Let us destroy Atlanta," he said, "and make it a desolation."

★　★　★

Sherman's ebullience was heightened by news that arrived next day, roundabout from Washington, of a great naval victory scored the week before by Farragut down in Mobile Bay. Long the target of various plans that had come to nothing until now — including Grant's, which went badly awry up the Red that spring with the near destruction of Banks's army and Porter's fleet — this last of the South's major Gulf of Mexico ports, second only to Wilmington as a haven for blockade runners, had been uppermost in Farragut's mind ever since the fall of New Orleans, more than two years ago. He then solicited the Department for permission to steam booming into the bay before its defenses could be strengthened, only to be told that he and his sea-going vessels would continue to prowl the Mississippi until the big river was open from source to mouth. By the time this was accomplished, a year later at Port Hudson, both the admiral and his flagship *Hartford* were sorely in need of rest and repairs. However urgent its priority, the reduction of Mobile would have to await their return, respectively, from Hastings-on-Hudson, the Tennessee-born sailor's adoptive home, and the Brooklyn Navy Yard.

A Christmas visit to New York City was disrupted by an intelligence report that reached him amid the splendors of the Astor House, confirming his worst fears. Not only had Mobile's defenders greatly strengthened the forts guarding the entrance to the harbor; refugees now declared that they also were building a monster ironclad up the Alabama River, more formidable in armament and armor than any warship since the *Merrimac*. Farragut knew, from a study of what the latter had done in Hampton Roads before the *Monitor*'s arrival — as well as from his own experience, near Vicksburg, when the *Arkansas* steamed murderously through the blue flotilla — just what damage one such vessel could do to any number of wooden ships. The answer, he saw, was to get back down there fast and, if possible, go up the river and destroy her before she was ready to engage; or else acquire some ironclads of his own, able to fight her on a give-and-take basis. In any case, after four months of rest and relaxation, he was galvanized into action. He went straight to Brooklyn and served notice that he expected the workmen to have the *Hartford* ready for sea by the evening of January 3. She was, and he dropped anchor at Pensacola two weeks later.

Off Mobile next day, January 18, he learned at first hand, not only that the rebel ironclad existed, as rumored, but also that she was now in the mouth of Dog River, up at the head of the bay. C.S.S. *Tennessee* was her name, and Admiral Franklin Buchanan, former commander of the *Merrimac-Virginia* and ranking man in the Confederate navy, was in charge; "Old Buck," Farragut called him, though at sixty-four Buchanan was only a year his senior and in fact had five years less service, having waited till he was fifteen to become a midshipman, which Farragut had done at the age of nine. Informed of a rumor that the ram was about to come down and attack the nine blockaders on station outside the bay, the Federal admiral braced his captains for the shock, and though he had small personal use for the new-fangled weapons ("If a shell strikes the side of the *Hartford*," he explained, "it goes clean through. Unless somebody happens to be directly in the path, there is no damage excepting a couple of easily plugged holes. But when a shell makes its way into one of those damned tea-kettles, it can't get out again") he submitted an urgent request for at least a pair of monitors. "If I had them," he told Washington, "I should not hesitate to become the assailant instead of awaiting the attack."

Actually, though she had just completed the 150-mile downriver run from Selma, where she was built, there was little danger that the *Tennessee* would steam out into the Gulf. At this point, indeed, there was doubt that she could even make it into the bay, since she drew fourteen feet of water and the depth over Dog River Bar was barely ten. Ingenuity, plus three months of hard labor, solved the problem by installing "camels" — large floats attached to the hull below the water line — which lifted her enough to clear the bar with a good tide. By mid-May she was in Mobile Bay, and Farragut got his first distant glimpse of her from a gunboat cruising Mississippi Sound; "a formidable-looking thing," he pronounced her, though to one of his lieutenants "she looked like a great turtle."

More than 200 feet in length and just under 50 in the beam, she wore six-inch armor, backed by two solid feet of oak and pine, and carried six hard-hitting 6.4- and 7-inch Brooke rifles, one forward and one aft, mounted on pivots to fire through alternative ports, and two in each broadside. Her captain was Commander J. D. Johnston, an Alabama regular who had spent the past two years on duty in the bay, and her skeleton crew was filled out with volunteers from a Tennessee infantry regiment, inexperienced as sailors but proud to serve aboard a vessel named for their native state. Two drawbacks she had, both grave. One was that her engines, salvaged from a river steamboat, gave her a top speed of only six knots, which detracted from her maneuverability and greatly reduced her effectiveness as a ram. The other was that her steering chains led over, rather than under, her armored rear deck, and thus would be exposed to enemy fire. However, she also had one awesome feature new to warfare, described by her designer as "a hot water attachment to her boilers for repelling boarders, throwing one stream forward of the casemate and one abaft." What was more, with Buchanan directing events, there was every likelihood that the device would be brought into play; for he was a proud, determined man, with a fondness for close-quarter fighting and no stomach for avoiding dares.

"Everybody has taken it into their heads that one ship can whip a dozen," he wrote a friend while the ironclad was being readied for action, "and if the trial is not made, we who are in her are damned for life; consequently, the trial must be made. So goes the world."

Mobile's reliance was by no means all on the iron ram, however. In addition to three small paddle-wheel gunboats that completed the gray squadron — *Morgan* and *Gaines*, with six guns each, and *Selma* with four, all unarmored except for strips of plate around their boilers — three dry-land installations guarded the two entrances down at the far end of the thirty-mile-long bay. The first and least of these, Fort Powell, a six-gun earthwork on speck-sized Tower Island, a mile off Cedar Point, covered the approach from Mississippi Sound, off to the west, through Grant's Pass. Another was Fort Gaines, a pentagonal structure on the eastern tip of Dauphin Island, crowned with sixteen guns that commanded the western half of the main entrance, three miles wide, between there and Mobile Point, a long narrow spit of sand at whose extremity — the site of old Fort Bowyer, whose smoothbores had repelled the British fifty years ago — Fort Morgan, the stoutest and most elaborate of the three defensive works, reared its mass of dark red brick. This too was a five-sided structure, double-tiered and mounting no less than forty heavy guns in barbette and casemates, together with seven more in an exterior water battery on the beach in front of its northwest curtain. Both entrances had been narrowed by rebel contrivance, the one from the Sound by driving pilings from Cedar Point to Tower Island and from the northern end of Dauphin Island to within about half a mile of Fort Powell, the one from the Gulf by sinking others southeastward from Fort Gaines to within a mile of Mobile Point, while just in rear of the remaining gap a triple line of mines (called "torpedoes") had been strewn and anchored, barely out of sight below the surface, to within about two hundred yards of the western tip of the spit of land across the way. The eastern limit of this deadly underwater field was marked by a red buoy, fixed there for the guidance of blockade runners whose pilots could avoid sudden destruction by keeping to the right of it and steaming directly under the high-sited guns of Fort Morgan, almost within pistol range of those in the water battery on the beach.

Farragut planned to take that route, mainly because there seemed to be no other. Grant's Pass was too shallow for all but the lightest of his vessels, which would be no match for the iron ram once they entered the bay, and the combination of piles and mines denied him the use of any part of the main Gulf channel except that scant, gun-dominated 200-yard stretch just off the tip of Mobile Point. He was willing to take his chances there, as he had done in similar runs past Forts Jackson and St Philip and the towering bluffs at Vicksburg and Port Hudson, yet he did not enjoy the notion of getting inside the bay with the forts alive in his rear, his wooden ships crippled, and the *Tennessee* likely to pound or butt them into flotsam. Contemplating this, he saw more clearly than ever the need for ironclads of his own, and though four of these had been promised him by now, two from the Atlantic squadron and two from the Mississippi, none had arrived by the time the squat metallic rebel monster steamed down the bay and dropped anchor behind Fort Morgan on May 20, intending either to await the entrance of the Union fleet or else run out and smash it in the Gulf. Farragut stormed at the delay, his patience stretched thin by the nonarrival of the monitors.

"I am tired of watching Buchanan," he wrote home in June, "and

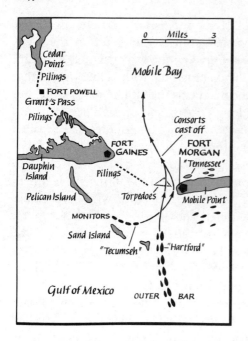

wish from the bottom of my heart that Buck would come out and try his hand upon us. The question has to be settled, iron versus wood, and there never was a better chance.... We are today ready to try anything that comes along, be it wood or iron, in reasonable quantities."

His plan was for the monitors to lead the way, holding to the right of the red buoy and providing an iron screen for the wooden ships as the two columns made their parallel runs past Fort Morgan, then going on to engage the ram in an all-out fight inside the bay, with such help as the multi-gunned sloops could provide. He would more or less ignore Fort Gaines while steaming in, not only because it was more than two miles off, but also because he planned to distract the attention of its gunners by having the army make a landing on the other end of Dauphin Island, then move east to invest the work from the landward side; after which Morgan would be served in the same fashion. But here too was a rub. The army, like the monitors, though promised, did not come. First there was Banks's drawn-out involvement up the Red, then a delay while Canby got the survivors back to New Orleans and in shape for the march to Mobile — which finally was cancelled when Grant was obliged to summon all but a handful to Virginia in late June, as replacements for Meade's heavy casualties. Canby visited the fleet in early July and agreed to send Major General Gordon Granger with 2000 men in transports, admittedly a small force but quite as large as he felt he could afford.

Farragut had to be satisfied, and in any case his impatience was mainly with the monitors, which still had not arrived. By way of diversion from the heat and boredom, both of which were oppressive, he rehearsed the run past Fort Morgan, and the fight that was to follow inside the bay, on a wardroom table grooved with the points of the compass, maneuvering little boat-shaped wooden blocks carved for him by the *Hartford*'s carpenter. Meanwhile, Buchanan's inactivity puzzled and irked him more and more. "Now is the time," he declared in mid-July. "The sea is as calm as possible and everything propitious.... Still he remains behind the fort, and I suppose it will be the old story over again. If he won't visit me, I will have to visit him. I am all ready as soon as the soldiers arrive to stop up the back door of each fort."

He was not, of course, "all ready," nor would he be so until the monitors were on hand, the *Albemarle* having redemonstrated in April and May, at Plymouth and in the North Carolina Sound from which she took her name, what was likely to happen to his wooden ships if he had no ironclads of his own to stand between them and the *Tennessee.* Then on July 20 the first of the promised four arrived from the Atlantic coast; *Manhattan* she was called, wearing ten inches of armor on her revolving turret, which carried two 15-inch guns. Ten days later the *Chickasaw* put in from New Orleans, double turreted with a pair of 11-inch guns in each, followed next day by her sister ship *Winnebago.* All were on hand by August 1 except the *Tecumseh,* en route from the Atlantic in the wake of her twin *Manhattan.* Farragut found the waiting even harder now that it was about to end; he improved the time by instructing his skippers in their duties, using the tabletop wooden blocks to show just where he expected their ships to be put in all eventualities. Meantime, as he had been doing for the past ten days, he continued to send out nightly boat crews, under cover of darkness and with muffled oars, to grapple for or sink as many as possible of the torpedoes anchored between the end of the line of pilings southeast of Dauphin Island and the red buoy just off Mobile Point. A number were so removed or destroyed, and the admiral was pleased to learn that many were found to be duds, their firing mechanisms having long been exposed to the corrosive effect of salt water.

Granger's 2000 soldiers arrived on August 2. They were taken around into Mississippi Sound the following night for a landing on the west end of Dauphin Island, and from there began working their way through heavy sand toward the back door of Fort Gaines. *Tecumseh* still had not appeared, but Farragut now was committed. "I can lose no more days," he declared. "I must go in day after tomorrow morning at daylight or a little later. It is a bad time, but when you do not take fortune at her offer you must take her as you can find her." Despite a heavy squall that evening, the grapplers went about their work in the mine field, undetected, and early next morning, August 4, the admiral took his fleet captains aboard the tender *Cowslip* for a closer look at the objective, cruising under the lee of Sand Island where the three monitors were anchored, ready to move out. Returning he went to his cabin, took out pen and paper, and composed a provisional farewell. "My dearest Wife: I write and leave this letter for you. I am going into Mobile Bay in the morning, if God is my leader, as I hope He is, and in Him I place my trust. . . . The Army landed last night, and are in full view of us this morning. The *Tecumseh* has not yet arrived."

Just then she did, steaming in from Pensacola to take position at the head of the iron column on the far side of Sand Island. The Union line of battle was complete. Asked at bedtime if he would consent to giving the men a glass of grog to nerve them up for the fight next morning, Farragut replied: "No, sir. I never found that I needed rum to enable me to do my duty. I will order two cups of good coffee to each man at 2 o'clock, and at 8 o'clock I will pipe all hands to breakfast in Mobile Bay."

Fog delayed the forming of the line past daybreak, the prearranged time for the start of the run, but a dawn breeze cleared the mist away by sunup, which came at 5.30 this Friday morning, August 5. As the four monitors began their movement eastward off the lee shore of Sand Island, in preparation for turning north beyond the line of pilings and the mine field — at which point the wooden column of seven heavy ships, each with a gunboat lashed to its port side for reserve power in case its boilers or engines were knocked out, would come up in their left rear for the dash past Mobile Point and the brick pentagon looming huge and black against the sunrise — Farragut was pleased to see that fortune had given him the two things he prayed for: a westerly wind to blow the smoke of battle away from the fleet and toward the fort, and a flood tide that would carry any pair of vessels on into the bay, even if both were disabled. Captain James Alden's 2000-ton 24-gun *Brooklyn* led the way, given the honor because she was equipped with chase guns and an antitorpedo device called a cowcatcher. Then came Flag Captain Percival Drayton's *Hartford* with the admiral aboard, followed by the remaining five, *Richmond, Lackawanna, Monongahela, Ossipee,* and *Oneida,* each with its gunboat consort attached to the flank away from the fort and otherwise readied for action in accordance with instructions issued as far back as mid-July: "Strip your vessels and prepare for the conflict. Send down all superfluous spars and rigging. Trice up or remove the whiskers. Put up the splinter nets on the starboard side, and barricade the wheel and steersmen with sails and hammocks. Lay chains or sandbags on the deck over the machinery to resist a plunging fire. Hang the sheet chains over the side, or make any other arrangements for security that your ingenuity may suggest." As a result, according to a Confederate who studied the uncluttered ships from Mobile Point, "They appeared like prize fighters ready for the ring."

Buchanan, aboard the *Tennessee,* got word that they were coming at 5.45, shortly after they started his way. He hurried on deck in his drawers for a look at the Yankee vessels, iron and wood, and while he dressed passed orders for the ram and its three attendant gunboats to move westward and take up a position athwart the main channel, just in rear of the inner line of torpedoes, for crossing the Union T if the enemy warships — eighteen of them, mounting 199 guns, as compared to his own four with 22 — passed Fort Morgan in an attempt to enter the bay. Balding, clean-shaven like Farragut, with bright blue eyes and a hawk nose, the Marylander assembled the *Tennessee*'s officers and crew on her gun deck and made them a speech that managed to be at once brief and rambling. "Now, men, the enemy is coming, and I want you to do your duty," he began, and ended: "You shall not have it said when you leave this vessel that you were not near enough to the enemy, for I will meet them, and you can fight them alongside of their own ships. And if I fall, lay me on the side and go on with the fight."

Farragut came on deliberately in accordance with his plan, the flagship crossing the outer bar at 6.10 while the iron column up ahead was making its turn north into the channel. Ten minutes later the lead monitor *Tecumseh* fired the opening shot, a 15-inch shell packed with sixty pounds of powder and half a bushel of cylindrical flathead bolts. It burst squarely over the fort, which did not reply until shortly after 7 o'clock, when the range to *Brooklyn*, leading the wooden column, had been closed to about a mile. Morgan's heaviest weapon was a 10-inch Columbiad, throwing a projectile less than half the weight of the one from *Tecumseh*, but the effect was altogether memorable for a young surgeon on the *Lackawanna*, midway down the line of high-masted vessels. "It is a curious sight to catch a single shot from so heavy a piece of ordnance," he later wrote. "First you see the puff of white smoke upon the distant ramparts, and then you see the shot coming, looking exactly as if some gigantic hand has thrown in play a ball toward you. By the time it is half way, you get the boom of the report, and then the howl of the missile, which apparently grows so rapidly in size that every green hand on board who can see it is certain that it will hit him between the eyes. Then, as it goes past with a shriek like a thousand devils, the inclination to do reverence is so strong that it is almost impossible to resist it."

Now the action became general, and by 7.30 the leading sloops, closing fast on the sluggish monitors, had their broadsides bearing fairly on the fort, whose gun crews were distracted by flying masonry, clouds of brickdust, and an avalanche of shells. Then two things happened, one in each of the tandem columns, for which Farragut had not planned while rehearsing the operation on the table in his cabin. Directly ahead of the flagship, *Brooklyn* had to slow to keep from overtaking the rear monitor *Chickasaw*. Presently, to the consternation of all astern, Alden stopped and began making signals: "The monitors are right ahead. We cannot go on without passing them. What shall we do?" While Farragut was testily replying, "Go ahead!" — and the guns of the fort and water battery, less than half a mile away, were stepping up their fire — Commander Tunis Craven of the *Tecumseh*, at the head of the iron column, reacted to a similar crisis in quite a different way, though it too involved a departure from instructions. Approaching the red buoy that marked the eastern limit of the mine field, he saw the breakers off Mobile Point, just off his starboard bow, and said to his pilot, out of fear of running aground: "It is impossible that the admiral means us to go inside that buoy." He ordered a hard turn to port, which carried the *Tecumseh* to the left, not right, of the red marker. But not for long. A

sudden, horrendous explosion against her bottom, square amidships —
whether of one or more torpedoes was later disputed — shook and
stopped the iron vessel, set her lurching from side to side, and sent water
pouring down her turret as she wallowed in the waves.

All aboard her must have known the hurt was mortal, though no
one guessed how short her agony would be. Craven and his pilot, for
example, standing face to face at the foot of the ladder that led to the
only escape hatch, staged a brief, courtly debate.

"Go ahead, Captain."

"After you, Pilot."

So they said; "But there was nothing after me," the pilot later
testified. As he put his foot on the top rung of the ladder, *Tecumseh* and
her captain dropped from under him.

Through a sight slit in the turret of *Manhattan*, next in line, an
engineer watched the lead monitor vanish almost too abruptly for belief.
"Her stern lifted high in the air with the propeller still revolving, and
the ship pitched out of sight like an arrow twanged from the bow."
With her went all but a score of her 114-man crew, including four who
swam to Mobile Point and were taken captive, while the others who
managed to wriggle out before she hit bottom were picked up by a
boat from the *Hartford*'s consort, *Metacomet*.

Farragut sent the boat, though the fact was he had problems
enough on his hands by then, including the apparent likelihood that such
rescue work was about to be required in his own direction. *Brooklyn*'s
untimely halt, practically under Morgan's guns, had thrown the wooden
column into confusion; for when she stopped her bow yawed off to starboard, subtracting her broadside from the pounding the fort was taking,
and what was worse she lay nearly athwart the channel, blocking the
path of the other ships. Nor was that the end of the trouble she and her
captain made. Alarmed by the sudden dive of the *Tecumseh* ("Sunk by
a torpedo! Assassination in its worst form!" he would protest in his
report) Alden spotted, just under his vessel's prow, "a row of suspicious-
looking buoys" which he took to be floats attached to mines. He reacted
by ordering *Brooklyn*'s engines reversed, and this brought her bearing
down, stern foremost, on the *Hartford*. Farragut, who had climbed the
mainmast rigging as far as the futtock shrouds for a view above the
smoke — he was tied there with a rope passed round his body by a
sailor, sent aloft by Drayton, lest a collision or a chance shot bring
him crashing to the deck some twenty feet below — angrily hailed the
approaching sloop, demanding to know the cause for such behavior, and
got the reply: "Torpedoes ahead."

Like the *Brooklyn*, which took 59 hits in the course of the fight,
Hartford was absorbing cruel punishment from the guns on Mobile
Point: particularly from those in the water battery, whose fire was point-
blank and deadly. Men were falling fast, their mangled bodies placed in

a row on one side of the deck, while the wounded were sent below in numbers too great for the surgeons to handle. A rifled solid tore a gunner's head off; another took both legs off a sailor who threw up his arms as he fell, only to have them carried away by still another. Farragut looked back down the line, where the rest of his stalled vessels were being served in much the same fashion, and saw that it would not do. He either had to go forward or turn back. In his extremity, he said later, he called on God: "Shall I go on?" and received the answer from a commanding voice inside his head: "Go on." *Brooklyn* blocked the channel on the right, so he asked the pilot, directly above him in the maintop, whether there was enough water for the *Hartford* to pass her on the left. The pilot said there was, and the admiral, exultant, shouted down to Drayton on the quarterdeck: "I will take the lead!" Signaling "close order" to the ships astern, he had the *Metacomet* back her engines and the flagship go all forward. This turned her westward, clear of *Brooklyn*, which she passed as she moved out. Someone called up a re-minder of Alden's warning, but Farragut, lashed to the rigging high above the smoke of battle, with Mobile Bay in full view before him, had no time or mind for caution. "Damn the torpedoes!" he cried. "Full speed ahead!"

Ahead he went, followed by the others, west of where the *Brooklyn* lay until she rejoined the column — and west, too, of the red buoy marking the eastern limit of the mine field. Though Farragut had been encouraged by the work of his nighttime grapplers, who not only had removed a considerable number of mines in the course of the past two weeks, but also reported a high percentage of duds among them, *Tecumseh* had just given an only-too-graphic demonstration of what might await him and all his warships, iron or wood, as a result of this sudden departure from his plan to avoid the doom-infested stretch of water the *Hartford* now was crossing. And sure enough, while she steamed ahead with all the speed her engines could provide, the men on deck — and, even worse, the ones cooped up below — could hear the knock and scrape of torpedo cases against her hull and the snap of primers designed to ignite the charges that would blast her to the bottom. None did, either under the *Hartford* or any of the vessels in her wake, but the passage of Morgan became progressively more difficult as the lead sloops steamed out of range and left the tail of the column, along with the slow-moving monitors, to the less-divided attention of the cannoneers in the fort and on the beach. *Oneida*, which brought up the rear, took a 7-inch shell in the starboard boiler, scalding her firemen with escaping steam, and another that burst in the cabin, cutting both wheel ropes. Powerless and out of control, she too made it past, tugged along by her consort, only to emerge upon a scene of even worse destruction, just inside the bay.

Buchanan had succeeded in his design to cross the Union T; with the result that when Farragut ended his sprint across the mine field he found the *Tennessee* and the three rebel gunboats drawn up to receive him in line ahead, presenting their broadsides to the approaching column, whose return fire was limited to the vessels in the lead, and even these could bring only their bow guns into play. *Hartford*'s was promptly knocked out by a shot from *Selma*, smallest of the three, and this was followed by another that passed through the chain armor on the flag-ship's starboard bow, killing ten men, wounding five, and hurling bodies, or parts of bodies, aft and onto the decks of the *Metacomet*, lashed alongside. Farragut kept coming, with *Brooklyn* and *Richmond* close astern, and managed to avoid an attempt by Buchanan to ram and sink him, meantime bringing his big Dahlgrens to bear on the gunboats, one of which then retired lamely toward Fort Morgan, taking water through a hole punched in her hull. This was the *Gaines*; she was out of the fight, and presently so were the others, *Morgan* and *Selma*; for *Hartford* and *Richmond* cast off their consorts to engage them and they fled. *Metacomet* led the chase, yawing twice to fire her bow gun, but then stopped firing to concentrate on speed. While *Morgan* made it to safety under the lee of Mobile Point, *Selma* kept running eastward across the shallows beyond the channel, still pursued despite the *Metacomet*'s deeper draft. Out on the bow of the northern vessel, a leadsman was already calling one foot less than the ship drew, but her captain, feeling the soft ooze of the bottom under her keel, refused to abandon the chase. "Call the man in," he told his exec. "He is only intimidating me with his soundings."

Persistence paid. Overtaken, *Selma* lost eight killed and seven wounded before she hauled down her flag. Westward, the *Gaines* burned briskly, set afire by her crew, who escaped in boats as she sank in shallow water. Only *Morgan* survived, anchored under the frown of the fort's guns to wait for nightfall, when she would steal around the margin of the bay to gain the greater safety of Mobile, inside Dog River Bar.

Left to fight alone, Buchanan steamed after the *Hartford* for a time, still hoping to ram and sink her, despite the agility she had shown in avoiding his first attempt, but soon perceived that her speed made the chase a waste of effort; whereupon he turned back and made for the other half-dozen sloops, advancing in closer order. *Tennessee* passed down the line of high-walled wooden men-of-war, mauling and being mauled. Two shots went through and through the *Brooklyn*, increasing her toll of killed and wounded to 54, but another pair flew high to miss the *Richmond*. Both ships delivered point-blank broadsides that had no effect whatever on the armored vessel as she bore down on *Lackawanna*, next in line, and *Monongahela*, which she struck a glancing blow, then swung round to send two shells crashing into the *Ossipee*. That left *Oneida*, whose bad luck now turned good, at least for the moment.

Aboard the ram, defective primers spared the crippled ship a pounding; then one gun fired a delayed shot that cost the northern skipper an arm and the use of his 11-inch after pivot, which was raked. *Tennessee* turned hard aport in time to meet the three surviving monitors, just arriving, and exchanged volleys in passing that did no harm on either side. Then she proceeded to Fort Morgan and pulled up, out of range on the far side of the channel.

Farragut dropped anchor four miles inside the bay, and the rest of the blue flotilla, wood and iron, steamed up to join him, their crews already at work clearing away debris and swabbing the blood from decks, while belowdecks surgeons continued to ply their scalpels and cooks got busy in the galleys. It was 8.35; he was only a bit over half an hour behind schedule on last night's promise to "pipe all hands to breakfast in Mobile Bay" by 8 o'clock. All the same, despite the general elation at having completed another spectacular run past formidable works, rivaling those below New Orleans and at Vicksburg and Port Hudson, there was also a tempering sorrow over the loss of the *Tecumseh* and considerable apprehension, as well, from the fact that the murderous rebel iron ram was still afloat across the way.

Drayton promptly expressed this reservation to the admiral, who by now had come down from the flagship's rigging and stood on the poop. "What we have done has been well done, sir," he told him. "But it all counts for nothing so long as the *Tennessee* is there under the guns of Morgan." Farragut nodded. "I know it," he said, "and as soon as the people have had their breakfasts I am going for her."

As it turned out, there was no need for that, and no time for breakfast. At 8.50, fifteen minutes after *Hartford* anchored, there was a startled cry from aloft. "The ram is coming!" So she was, and presently those on deck saw her steaming directly for the fleet, apparently too impatient to wait for a fight in which she would have the help of the guns ashore. Farragut prepared for battle, remarking as he did so: "I did not think Old Buck was such a fool."

Fool or not, throughout the pause Buchanan had been unwilling to admit the fight was over, whatever the odds and no matter how far he had to go from Fort Morgan to renew it. Instrumental in the founding of the academy at Annapolis, he had served as its first superintendent and thought too highly of naval tradition to accept even tacit defeat while his ship remained in any condition to engage the enemy. "If he won't visit me, I will have to visit him," his adversary had remarked three weeks ago, and Buchanan felt much the same about the matter now as he gazed across three miles of water at the Yankee warships riding at anchor in the bay — *his* bay — quite as if there was no longer any question of their right to be there. Gazing, he drew the corners of his mouth down in a frown of disapproval, then turned to the *Tennessee*'s captain. "Follow them up, Johnston. We can't let them off that way." With that, the ram started forward: one six-gun vessel against a total of seventeen, three of them wearing armor heavier than her own, mounting 157 guns, practically all of them larger than any weapon in her casemate. That Buchanan was in no mood for advice was demonstrated, however, when one of his officers tried to call his attention to the odds. "Now I am in the humor, I will have it out," he said, and that was that. The ram continued on her way.

The monitors having proved unwieldy, Farragut's main reliance was on his wooden sloops, particularly the *Monongahela* and the *Lackawanna*, which were equipped with iron prows for ramming. Their orders were to run the ram down, while the others pitched in to do her whatever damage they could manage with their guns. Accordingly, when the *Tennessee* came within range about 9.20, making hard for the flagship, *Monongahela* moved ahead at full speed and struck her amidships, a heavy blow that had no effect at all on the rebel vessel but cost the sloop her iron beak, torn off along with her cutwater. *Lackawanna* rammed in turn, with the result that an eight-foot section of her stem was crushed above and below the waterline. *Tennessee* lurched but held her course, and the two flagships collided nearly head on. "The port bow of the *Hartford* met the port bow of the ram," an officer aboard the Federal vessel later wrote, "and the ships grated against each other as they passed. The *Hartford* poured her whole port broadside against the ram, but the solid shot merely dented the side and bounded into the air. The ram tried to return the salute, but owing to defective primers only one gun was discharged. This sent a shell through the berth-deck, killing five men and wounding eight. The muzzle of the gun was so close to the *Hartford* that the powder blackened her side."

When the two ships parted Farragut jumped to the port quarter rail and held to the mizzen rigging while he leaned out to assess the damage, which was by no means as great as he had feared. Finding the perch to his liking he remained there, lashed to the rigging by friendly hands for the second time that day, and called for Drayton to give the *Tennessee* another thump as soon as possible. As the *Hartford* came about, however, she was struck on the starboard flank by the *Lackawanna*, which was also trying to get in position, crushing her planking on that side and upsetting one of the Dahlgrens. "Save the admiral! Save the admiral!" the cry went up, for it was thought at first that the flagship was sinking, so great was the confusion on her decks. Farragut untied himself, leaped down, and crossed to the starboard mizzen rigging, where he again leaned out to inspect the damage, which though severe did not extend to within two feet of the water. Again he ordered full speed ahead, only to find the *Lakawanna* once more looming on his starboard quarter. At this, one witness later said, "the admiral became a trifle excited." Forgetting that he had given the offending ship instructions to lead the ram attack, he turned to the communications officer on the bridge.

"Can you say 'For God's sake' by signal?"

"Yes, sir."

"Then say to the *Lackawanna*, 'For God's sake, get out of our way and anchor.' "

By now the ironclad had become the target for every ship that could get in position to give her a shot or a shove, including the double-turreted *Chickasaw*, which "hung close under our stern," the *Tennessee*'s pilot afterwards declared, "firing the two 11-inch guns in her forward turret like pocket pistols." Such punishment began to tell. Her flag-staff went and then her stack, giving the ram what one attacker called "a particularly shorn, stubby look" and greatly reducing the draft to her fires. Her steam went down, and then, as a sort of climax to her disablement, the monitor hard astern succeeded in cutting her rudder chain, exposed on the afterdeck, so that she would no longer mind her helm. Still she kept up the fight, exploiting her one advantage, which was that she could fire in any direction, surrounded as she was, without fear of hitting a friend or missing a foe. Presently, though, this too was reduced by shots that jammed half of her gunport shutters against the shield, thereby removing them from use. When this happened to the stern port, Buchanan sent for a machinist to unjam it, and while the man was at work on the cramped bolt, an 11-inch shell from the *Chickasaw* exploded against the edge of the cover just above him. "His remains had to be taken up with a shovel, placed in a bucket, and thrown overboard," a shipmate would recall. One of the steel splinters that flew inside the casemate struck Buchanan, breaking his left leg below the knee. "Well, Johnston," he said to the *Tennessee*'s captain as he was taken up to be carried down to the berth deck, "they've got me. You'll have to look out for her now. This is your fight, you know."

Johnston did what he could to sustain the contest with the rudder-less, nearly steamless vessel, blind in most of her ports and taking heavy-caliber punches from two big sloops on each quarter and the monitor astern. Finally he went below and reported the situation to Buchanan. "Do the best you can, sir," the admiral told him, teeth gritted against the pain from the compound fracture of his leg, "and when all is done, surrender." Returning topside, the Alabamian found the battle going even worse. Unable to maneuver, the ram could not bring a single gun to bear on her tormentors; moreover, Johnston afterwards reported, "Shots were fairly raining upon the after end of the shield, which was now so thoroughly shattered that in a few moments it would have fallen and exposed the gun deck to a raking fire of shell and grape." He lowered the *Tennessee*'s ensign, in token of her capitulation, and when this did not slacken the encircling fire — it had been shot down before, then raised again on the handle of a rammer staff poked through the overhead grille of the smoky casemate — "I then decided, although with an almost bursting heart, to hoist the white flag."

At 10 o'clock the firing stopped, and presently Farragut sent an officer to demand the wounded admiral's sword, which then was handed over. *Tennessee*'s loss of two men killed and nine wounded brought the Confederate total for all four ships to 12 killed and 20 wounded. Union losses were 172 killed, more than half in the *Tecumseh*, and 170 wounded. Their respective totals, 32 and 342, were thus about in ratio of the strength of the two fleets, though in addition 243 rebel sailors were captured aboard *Selma* and the ironclad.

"The Almighty has smiled upon me once more. I am in Mobile Bay," Farragut wrote his wife that night, adding: "It was a hard fight, but Buck met his fate manfully. After we passed the forts, he came up in the ram to attack me. I made at him and ran him down, making all the others do the same. We butted and shot at him until he surrendered."

Westward across the bay, as he wrote, there was a burst of flame and a loud explosion off Cedar Point. The garrison of Fort Powell, taken under bombardment from the rear that afternoon by one of the big-gunned monitors at a range of 400 yards, had evacuated the place under cover of darkness and set a slow match to the magazine. Next morning the fleet dropped down and began shelling the eastern end of Dauphin Island, where Fort Gaines was under pressure from the landward side by Granger and his soldiers. This continued past nightfall, and the fort's commander asked for terms the following day, August 7. Told they were unconditional, he accepted and promptly surrendered his 818 men, together with all guns and stores. That left Fort Morgan; a much tougher proposition, as it turned out.

While the troops were being taken aboard transports for the shift to Mobile Point and a similar rear approach to the fortifications there, Farragut submitted under a flag of truce a note signed by himself and Granger, demanding the unconditional surrender of Fort Morgan "to prevent the unnecessary sacrifice of human life which must follow the opening of our batteries." The reply was brief and negative. "Sirs: I am prepared to sacrifice life, and will only surrender when I have no means of defense. . . . Respectfully, etc. *R. L. Page*, Brigadier General."

Approaching fifty-seven, Richard Page was a Virginian, a forty-year veteran of the Union and Confederate navies, who had transferred to the army five months ago when he assumed command of the outer defenses of Mobile Bay. His beard was white, his manner fiery; "Old Ramrod" and "Bombast Page" were two of his prewar nicknames, and if he bore a resemblance to R. E. Lee (both were born in 1807) it was no wonder. His mother had been Lee's father's sister.

Farragut's run past Morgan had come as a shock to its defenders, who fired close to 500 shots at the slow-moving Yankee column. "I do not see how I failed to sink the *Hartford*," Page said ruefully, shaking his head as the smoke cleared; "I do not see how I failed to sink her." Fort Powell's evacuation and the unresistant capitulation of Fort Gaines, neither of which had been done with his permission, angered and made him all the more determined to resist to the utmost the amphibious seige that got under way on August 9, shortly after he rejected unconditional surrender. Granger's men had been put ashore that morning on the bay side of Mobile Point, just over a mile to the east of the fort, and by nightfall — after they had performed the back-breaking labor of hauling guns and ammunition through shin-deep sand, which one of them said was "hot enough during the day for roasting potatoes" — took the east curtain and ramparts under fire with their batteries, while the sloops and ironclads, including the captured *Tennessee*, poured in shells and hotshot from the bay and Gulf. The fort shook under this combined pounding, but Page was no more of a mind to surrender now than he had been when he first declined the combined demand at midday.

For two weeks this continued, and throughout that time the pressure grew. Daily the troops drew closer on the landward side, increasing the number of weapons they brought to bear until at last there were 25 guns and 16 heavy mortars, their discharges echoed by those from the ships beyond and on both sides of the point. The climax came on August 22, when 3000 rounds were flung at the fort in the course of a twelve-hour bombardment, under whose cover the blue infantry extended its parallels to within reach of the glacis. All but two of the fort's guns were silenced and the citadel was burning; sharpshooters drew beads on anything that showed above the ramparts, and 80,000 pounds of powder had to be removed from the magazine and flooded, so close were the flames. Practically all that remained by now was wreckage and scorched debris. At 5 o'clock next morning two last shots were fired by the defenders, and one hour later the white flag went up. Farragut sent Drayton to arrange the formal surrender, which took place that afternoon amid the rubble. He had Buchanan's sword for a trophy, but he did not get Page's. The general and all his officers, displaying what Farragut called "childish spitefulness," had broken or thrown away their side arms just before the ceremony.

The admiral did get another 546 prisoners, however, which brought the total to better than 1700 on land and water — and he did get Mobile Bay, which after all was what he had come for. Blockade running might continue on the Atlantic coast, where Wilmington and Charleston still held out, but it was ended on the Gulf except for the sealed-off region west of the Mississippi, which in any case lay outside the constricting Anaconda coils. Mobile itself, thirty miles away at the head of the bay, was no part of Farragut's objective. Except as a port, it contributed little to the South's defense, and it was a port no longer. Moreover, Canby not only lacked the strength to expel the town's defenders; he could not have afforded to garrison it afterwards, so urgent were the calls for replacements for the men who had fallen in Georgia and, above all, in Virginia.

Best of all the immediate gains obtained from the naval battle, though, was the elation that followed, throughout the North, the announcement of the first substantial victory that had been scored, East or West, in the three months since the opening of Grant's spring offensive. Lincoln and his political supporters were pleased above all, perhaps, with the lift it seemed to give his chances for survival in the presidential contest, which by then was less than three months off.

As usual, there was bad news with the good, and in this case the bad was double-barreled, concerning as it did a pair of highly spectacular reverses, one afloat and one ashore. In Washington on August 12, while the celebration of Farragut's week-old triumph over the *Tennessee* was still in progress at the Navy Department — word had come belatedly by wire from Ben Butler, who read of the bay battle in a Richmond paper smuggled through his Bermuda Hundred lines the day before — the telegraph line from coastal New Jersey began to chatter about a mysterious rebel cruiser at work off Sandy Hook. Yesterday she had taken seven prizes, and today she was adding six more to her list, which would reach a total of thirty U.S. merchant vessels within the week. It was as if the *Alabama*, eight weeks in her watery grave outside Cherbourg, had been raised, pumped out, and sped across the Atlantic to lay about her in a manner even more destructive than when she was in her prime. Quickly, all the available Federal warships within reach were ordered out to find and sink her at all costs. But who, or what, was she? Where had she come from? Who was her captain?

She was the *Tallahassee*, a former blockade runner, built up the Thames the year before and purchased that summer by the Confederates, who converted her into a raider by installing three guns and sent her out from Wilmington under Commander John T. Wood, a onetime Annapolis instructor, grandson of Zachary Taylor, aide to Jefferson Davis, and participant in a number of naval exploits, including the *Merrimac-Monitor* fight, New Bern, and the retaking of Plymouth. Setting out on the night of August 6 he showed the blockaders a clean pair of heels; for that was the ship's main virtue, speed. Twin stacked, with a 100-horsepower engine driving each of her two screws, she was 220 feet in length and only 24 in the beam, a combination that gave her a top speed of seventeen knots and had enabled her, on her shakedown cruise, to make the Dover-Calais crossing in seventy-seven minutes. Five mornings later, 500 miles up the Atlantic coast, *Tallahassee* encountered her first prize, the schooner *Sarah Boyce*, and before the day was over she ran down six more Union merchant vessels, ransoming

the last to put all prisoners ashore. That was Thursday, August 11;
"Pirate off Sandy Hook capturing and burning," the commandant of
the Brooklyn Navy Yard wired Washington. Friday, off Long Island,
she took six prizes, Saturday two, and Sunday — as if by way of resting
on the Sabbath — one. By now she was cruising the New England coast,
and on Monday she took six ships, Tuesday five, and Wednesday three,
rounding out a week that netted her thirty prizes, all burned or scuttled
except seven that were ransomed to clear her crowded decks of captured
passengers and crews. On August 18, running low on coal, she put into
the neutral port of Halifax to refuel.

Under instructions from the Queen, and over ardent protests
from the American consul, the Nova Scotia authorities gave Wood
twenty-four hours to fill his bunkers, and when this did not suffice they
granted him a twelve-hour extension. *Tallahassee* steamed out the following night in time to avoid half a dozen enemy warships that arrived
next day, the vanguard of a fleet of thirteen ordered to Halifax as
soon as the consul telegraphed word of the raider's presence in the
harbor. She headed straight for Wilmington, taking so little chance on
running out of coal that she only paused to seize one prize along the
way, and arrived on the night of August 26 to speed and shoot her way
through the blockade flotilla and drop anchor up the Cape Fear River,
whose entrance was guarded by Fort Fisher. Her twenty-day cruise
had cost the enemy 31 merchant vessels and had given Wood's fellow
countrymen some welcome news to offset the bad from Mobile Bay,
where Fort Morgan had fallen three days ago. They took pride in the
fact that "this extemporaneous man-of-war," as Jefferson Davis called
the *Tallahassee*, had "lit up the New England coast with her captures,"
and they could tell themselves, as well, that no matter what misfortunes
befell their regular navy, outnumbered as it invariably was in combat,
their irregular navy (so to speak) had won them the admiration of the
world and was rapidly scouring the seas of Yankee shipping.

That was the first Federal reverse. The second, which occurred
simultaneously ashore, was quite as spectacular and, if anything, even
more "irregular" — as was often the case in operations involving Bedford Forrest. He had been given a free rein to conduct the defense of
North Mississippi by Major General Dabney Maury, who succeeded to
command of the Department of Alabama, Mississippi, and East Louisiana in late July, when Stephen Lee left to join Hood at Atlanta. "We
must do the best we can with the little we have," Maury wrote from
Meridian in early August, "and it is with no small satisfaction I reflect
that of all the commanders of the Confederacy you are accustomed to
accomplish the very greatest results with small means when left to
your own untrammeled judgment. Upon that judgment I now rely."

Forrest took him at his word. "All that can be done shall be
done," he replied, adding that since he lacked "the force to risk a general

engagement" in resisting the next blue incursion, he would "resort to all other means." Other means, in this case, included a raid on Memphis, the enemy's main base, under occupation for better than two years. Tactically, such a strike would be likely to disrupt the plans of the Federals for extending their conquest deep into Mississippi. Moreover, Forrest himself — a former alderman — would not only derive considerable personal satisfaction from returning to his home town, which no Confederate had entered, except as a spy or prisoner, since its fall in June of 1862; he would also be exacting vengeance for a battle fought the month before, near Tupelo, which was as close to a defeat as he had come so far in his career. Lee had been in command of the field, one week before his departure for Atlanta, but the memory rankled and Forrest was anxious to wipe it out or anyhow counterbalance it.

Hard on the heels of Brice's Crossroads in mid-June, when he received orders from Sherman "to make up a force and go out and follow Forrest to the death, if it costs 10,000 lives and breaks the Treasury," C. C. Washburn, the Memphis commander, assigned the task to A. J. Smith, reinforcing two of his divisions, just returned from their excursion up and down Red River, with Bouton's brigade of Negro infantry and Grierson's cavalry division, both of them recent graduates of the hard-knocks school the Wizard of the Saddle was conducting for his would-be conquerers down in Mississippi. On July 5 this column of 14,200 effectives, mounted and afoot, supported by six batteries of artillery and supplied with twenty days of rations — "a force ample to whip anything this side of Georgia," Washburn declared — set out southward from La Grange, fifty miles east of Memphis. Sherman's orders by then had been expanded; Smith and his gorilla-guerillas, who had polished their hard-handed skills in Louisiana under Banks, were to "pursue Forrest on foot, devastating the land over which he passed or may pass, and make him and the people of Tennessee and Mississippi realize that, although [he is] a bold, daring, and successful leader, he will bring ruin and misery on any country where he may pause or tarry. If we do not punish Forrest and the people now," the red-haired Ohioan wound up, "the whole effect of our past conquests will be lost."

Three days out, and just over fifty miles down the road, Smith showed that he took this admonition to heart by burning much of the town of Ripley, including the courthouse, two churches, the Odd Fellows Hall, and a number of homes. Next day, July 9, still mindful of his instructions to "punish Forrest and the people," he pressed on across the Tallahatchie and through New Albany, trailed by a swath of desolation ten miles wide.

Ahead lay Pontotoc, and beyond it Okolona, where Sooy Smith had come to grief five months before, checked almost as disastrously as Sturgis had been at nearby Brice's Crossroads, a month ago tomorrow. So far, only token opposition to the current march had developed, but at

Pontotoc, which he cleared on July 11, this new Smith began to encounter stiffer resistance. Butternut troopers hung on the flanks of the column, as if to slow it down before it made contact with whatever was waiting to receive it up ahead, perhaps at Okolona. Smith would never know; for at dawn on July 13, well short of any ambush being laid for him there or south of there, he abruptly changed direction and struck out instead for Tupelo, fifteen miles to the east on the Mobile & Ohio, "his column well closed up, his wagon train well protected, and his flanks covered in an admirable manner."

So Forrest's scouts informed him at Okolona, where he was waiting — it was his forty-third birthday — for both Smith and Stephen Lee, who was on the way with 2000 troops and had ordered him not to commit his present force of about 6000 until these reinforcements got there to reduce the odds. Arriving from the south to find that the blue column had veered east, Lee took charge of pressing the pursuit. His urgency was based on reports from Dabney Maury, at Mobile, that Canby was preparing to march from New Orleans and attack the city from the landward side; Lee wanted Smith dealt with quickly so that the men he had brought to reinforce Forrest could be sent to Maury. "As soon as I fight I can send him 2000, possibly 3000," he explained in a dispatch to Bragg, though he added that this depended on whether the Mississippi invaders did or did not "succeed in delaying the battle." Smith was capable and canny, halting from time to time to beat off rearward threats while Grierson's horsemen rode on into Tupelo and began tearing up track above and below the town. All day the Federal infantry marched, then called a halt soon after nightfall at Harrisburg, two miles west of Tupelo, which had grown with the railroad and swallowed the older settlement as a suburb. Forrest came up presently in the darkness and "discovered the enemy strongly posted and prepared to give battle the next day."

Smith was at bay, and though his position was a stout one, nearly two miles long and skillfully laid out — flanks refused, rear well covered by cavalry, the line itself strengthened with fence rails, logs, timbers from torn-down houses, and bales of cotton — Forrest counted this a happy ending to an otherwise disappointing birthday. "One thing is certain," he told Lee; "the enemy cannot remain long where he is. He must come out, and when he does, all I ask or wish is to be turned loose with my command." No matter which way Smith headed when he emerged fretful and hungry, Forrest said, "I will be on all sides of him, attacking day and night. He shall not cook a meal or have a night's sleep, and I will wear his army to a frazzle before he gets out of the country."

Lee could see the beauty of that; but he had Mobile and Canby on his mind, together with the promises he had made to Bragg and Maury, and did not feel that he could afford the time it would take to deal with the penned-up bluecoats in this manner. There were better that 14,000 of them, veterans to a man, and though he had only about 8000 troops on hand he issued orders for an all-out assault next morning. Forrest would take the right and he the left. Together they would storm the Union works, making up for the disparity in numbers by the suddenness and ardor of their charge.

Ardor there was, and suddenness too, but these turned out to be the qualities that robbed Lee of what little chance he had for success in the first place. July 14 dawned hot and still, and the troops on line were vexed by delays in bringing several late-arriving units into position for the attack. Around 7.30, a Kentucky brigade near the center jumped the gun and started forward ahead of the others, who followed piecemeal, left and right, with the result that what was to have been a single, determined effort, all along the line, broke down from the outset into a series of individual lunges. Smith's veterans, snug behind their improvised breastworks, blasted each rebel unit as it advanced. "It was all gallantry and useless sacrifice," one Confederate was to say. To Smith, the disjointed attack "seemed to be a foot race to see who should reach us first. They were allowed to approach, yelling and howling like Comanches, to within canister range. . . . They would come forward and fall back, rally and forward again, with the like result. Their determination may be seen from the fact that their dead were found within thirty yards of our batteries." None got any closer, and after two hours of this Lee called a halt. He had lost 1326 killed and wounded and missing, Smith barely half that many, 674.

Skirmishing resumed next morning, but so fitfully and cautiously that it seemed to invite a counterattack. Smith instead clung fast to his position. He did, that is, until midday, when he was informed that much of the food in his train had spoiled in the Mississippi heat, leaving only one day's rations fit to eat, and that his reserve supply of artillery ammunition was down to about a hundred rounds per gun: whereupon he decided to withdraw northward, back in the direction he had set out from ten days ago, even though this meant leaving his more grievously wounded men behind in Tupelo. There followed the curious spectacle of a superior force retreating from a field on which it had inflicted nearly twice as many casualties as it suffered and being harassed on the march by a loser reduced to less than half the strength of the victor it was pursuing. In any case, after setting fire to what was left of Harrisburg, the Federals not only withdrew in good order and made excellent time on the dusty roads; they also succeeded, when they made camp at sunset on Town Creek, five miles north, in beating off a rebel attack and inflicting on Bedford Forrest, whom Lee had put in charge of the pursuit — and whom Smith had been told to "follow to the death" — his third serious gunshot wound of the war. The bullet struck him in the foot (the base of his right big toe, to be explicit) causing him so much pain that he had to relinquish the command, temporarily at least, and retire to a dressing station.

Smith kept going, unaware of this highly fortunate development, back through New Albany and across the Tallahatchie. Midway between there and La Grange he encountered a supply train sent to meet him. He kept going, despite this relief, and returned to his starting point on July 21, after sixteen round-trip days of marching and fighting. "I bring back everything in good order; nothing lost," he informed Washburn, who found the message so welcome a contrast to those received from other generals sent out after Forrest that he passed it along with pride to Sherman.

Far from proud, Sherman was downright critical, especially of the resultant fact that Forrest had been left to his own devices, which might well include a raid into Middle Tennessee and a strike against the blue supply lines running down into North Georgia. Engaged at the time in the Battle of Atlanta, Sherman replied that Smith was "to pursue and continue to follow Forrest. He must keep after him till recalled. . . . It is of vital importance that Forrest does not go to Tennessee." Smith returned to Memphis on July 23, miffed at this unappreciative reaction to his campaign, and began at once to prepare for a second outing, one that he hoped to improve beyond reproach.

This time the invasion column would number 18,000 of all arms, one quarter larger than before, and he would proceed by a different rout — down the Mississippi Central, which he would repair as he advanced, thus solving the problem of supplies whose lack had obliged his recent withdrawal in mid-career. By August 2 the railroad was in running order down to the Tallahatchie, and Washburn notified Sherman that Smith's reorganized command, which he assured him could "whip the combined force of the enemy this side of Georgia and east of the Mississippi," would set out "as soon as possible. . . . Forrest's forces were near Okolona a week since," he added, saving the best news for last; "Chalmers in command. Forrest [has] not been able to resume command by reason of wound in fight with Smith. I have a report today that he died of lockjaw some days ago."

It was true that Chalmers was in nominal command, but not that Forrest was dead, either of lockjaw or of any other ailment, although a look at him was enough to show how the rumor got started. Troubled by a siege of boils even before he was wounded, "sick-looking, thin as a rail, cheekbones that stuck out like they were trying to come through the skin, skin so yellow it looked greenish, eyes blazing" — one witness saw him thus at Tupelo that week — he rode about the camps in a buggy, his injured foot propped on a rack atop the dashboard, waiting impatiently for it to heal enough for him to mount a horse and resume command of his two divisions. They were all that were left him now, about 5000 horsemen, after his casualties at Harrisburg and the departure of Stephen Lee, first for Mobile (where the reinforcements he took with him turned out not to be needed, Grant having ruled out Canby's attack by diverting his troops to Virginia) and then for Atlanta, to join Hood. Partly, too, Forrest's haggard appearance was a result of the recent bloody repulse he had suffered in the assault on Smith. Even though he had advised against the attack, and was thereby absolved from blame for its failure, he was unaccustomed to sharing in a defeat and he burned with resentment over the useless loss of a thousand of his men, just at a time when they seemed likely to be needed most. Smith, he knew, was refitting in Memphis and would soon be returning to North Mississippi, stronger than before and with a better knowledge of the pitfalls. Sure enough, by early August the new blue column of 18,000 effectives had moved out to Grand Junction and begun its advance down the Mississippi Central to Holly Springs, a day's march from the Tallahatchie. "We knew we couldn't fight General Smith's big fine army," a butternut artillery lieutenant would recall, "and we knew that we couldn't get any reinforcements anywhere, and we boys speculated about what Old Bedford was going to do."

Old Bedford wondered too, for a time. At first he thought Smith's movement down the railroad was a feint, designed to "draw my forces west and give him the start toward the prairies." Back in command — and in the saddle, though he only used one stirrup — he sent Chalmers's division over to cover the Mississippi Central, but kept Buford's around Okolona to oppose what he believed would be the main blue effort. He soon learned better. On August 8 Smith moved in strength from Holly Springs and forced a crossing of the Tallahatchie, sending his cavalry ahead next day to occupy Oxford, twelve miles down the line. Forrest wired Chalmers to "contest every inch of ground," and set out at once for Oxford with Buford's division. Grierson fell back when he learned of this on August 10, and Smith remained at the river crossing, constructing a bridge to ensure the rapid delivery of supplies when he continued his march south. It was then, in this driest season of the Mississippi year, that the rain began to fall. It fell and kept falling for a week, marking what became known thereafter in these parts as "the wet August."

Both sides were nearly immobilized by the deepening mud and washouts, but they sparred as best they could, in slow motion, and planned for the time ahead. On August 18, though the weather still was rainy, Smith began inching southward; muddy or not, he had made up his mind to move, however slowly.

So by then had Forrest. At 5 o'clock that afternoon he assembled on the courthouse square at Oxford, after a rigorous "weeding out of sick men and sore-back and lame horses," close to 2000 troopers from two brigades and Morton's four-gun battery. In pelting rain and under a sky already dark with low-hanging clouds, the head of the column took up the march westward; Chalmers, left behind with the remaining 3000, had been told to put up such a show of resistance to the advancing Federals, who outnumbered him six to one, that Smith would not suspect for at least two days that nearly half of Forrest's command had left his front and was moving off to the west — in preparation for turning north around his flank, some were saying up and down the long gray column. "It got abroad in camp that we were going to Memphis," one rider later wrote. "That looked radical, but pleased us."

They knew they were right next morning, after a night march of twenty-five miles across swollen creeks and up and down long slippery hills, when they reached Panola and crossed the Tallahatchie, taking the route of the Mississippi & Tennessee Railroad, which ran north some sixty bee-line miles to Memphis. Four separate invasions they had repulsed in the past six months, three by pitched battle, one by sheer bluff, and now they were out to try their hand at turning back the fifth with a strike at the enemy's main base, close to a hundred miles in his rear. Radical, indeed. But Forrest knew what he would find when he got there; home-town operatives had kept him well informed. Washburn, under repeated urgings from Sherman to strengthen Smith to his utmost, had stripped the city's defense force to a minimum, and Fort Pickering, whose blufftop guns bore on the river and the city, but not on its landward approaches, offered little in the way of deterrent to an operation of this kind; Forrest did not intend to stay there any longer than it took his raiders to spread confusion among the defenders and alarm them into recalling Smith, who by now was skirmishing with Chalmers around Oxford, unaware that the man he was charged with following "to the death" had already rounded his flank and was about to set off an explosion deep in his rear.

Twenty miles the butternut column made that day, north from Panola to Senatobia, lighter by about two hundred troopers whose mounts had broken down before they reached the Tallahatchie and turned back, along with all but two of Morton's guns, whose teams were increased to ten horses each to haul them. The rain had stopped, as if on signal from the Wizard. All day the sun beamed down on roads and fields, but only enough, after eight days of saturation, to change the mud from slippery to sticky.

One mile north of Senatobia, which he cleared at first light, August 20, Forrest came upon Hickahala Creek, swollen to a width of sixty feet between its flooded banks; a formidable obstacle, but one for which he had planned by sending ahead a detachment to select a crossing point and chop down two trees on each bank, properly spaced, the stumps to be used for the support of a pair of cables woven from muscadine vines, which grew to unusual size and in great profusion in the bottoms. By the time the main body came up, the suspension cables had been stretched and were supported in midstream by an abandoned flatboat, which in turn was buoyed up by bundles of poles lashed to its sides. All that remained was for the span to be floored, and this was done with planks the troopers had ripped from gins and cabins on the approach march. In all, the crossing took less than an hour; but six miles north lay the Coldwater River, twice as wide. That took three, the work party having hurried ahead to construct another such grapevine bridge with the skill acquired while improvising the first. The heaviest loads it had to bear were the two guns, which were rolled across by hand, and several wagons loaded with unshucked corn for the horses, which were unloaded, trundled empty over the swaying rig, and then reloaded on the opposite bank. Forrest set the example by carrying the first armload, limping across on his injured foot, much to the admiration and amusement of his soldiers. "I never saw a command more like it was out for a holiday," one later wrote, while the general himself was to say: "I had to continually caution the men to keep quiet. They were making a regular corn shucking out of it."

Many of them, like him, were on their way home for the first time in years, and it was hard to contain the exuberance they were feeling at the prospect. Eight miles beyond the Coldwater by dark, Forrest called a rest halt at Hernando, where he had spent most of his young manhood, twenty-five miles from downtown Memphis. Near midnight the column pushed on, reduced to about 1500 sabers (so called, though for the most part they preferred shotguns and navy sixes) by the breakdown of another 200-odd horses, and stopped at 3 a.m. just short of the city limits, there to receive final instructions for the work ahead — work that was based on detailed information smuggled out by spies. One detachment under the general's brother, Captain William Forrest, would lead the way over Cane Creek Bridge and ride straight for the Gayoso House on Main Street, where Washburn's predecessor Stephen Hurlbut was quartered while awaiting reassignment; two other detachments, one of them under another brother, Lieutenant Colonel Jesse Forrest, would proceed similarly to capture Brigadier General R. P. Buckland, commander of the garrison, and Washburn himself, both of whom were living with their staffs in commandeered private residences. Two major generals and a brigadier would make a splendid haul and Forrest intended to have them, along with much else in the way of spoils assigned to still other detachments. Half an hour before dawn of this foggy Sunday morning, August 21, the head of the column entered the sleeping city whose papers had carried yesterday a special order from the department commander, prohibiting all "crying or selling of newspapers on Sunday between the hours of 9 a.m. and 5 p.m.," the better to preserve the peace and dignity of the Sabbath.

In some ways, the raid — the penetration itself — was anticlimactic. For example, all three Federal generals escaped capture, one because he slept elsewhere that night (just *where* became the subject of much scurrilous conjecture) and the other two because they were alerted in time to make a dash for safety under Fort Pickering's 97 guns, which Forrest had no intention of storming. Buckland woke to a hammering, a spattering of gunfire some blocks off, and leaned out of his upstairs bed-room window to find a sentry knocking at the locked door of the house. He called down, still half asleep, to ask what was the matter.

"General, they are after you."

"Who are after me?"

"The rebels," he was told.

He had time to dress before hurrying to the fort. Not so Wash-burn, who had to make a run for it in his nightshirt through back alleys; so sudden was the appearance of the raiders at his gate, he barely had time to leave by the rear door as they entered by the front. By way of consolation, Jesse Forrest captured two of his staff officers, along with his dress uniform and accouterments. Bill Forrest got even less when he clattered up Main Street to the Gayoso and, without pausing to dis-mount, rode his horse through the hotel doorway and into the lobby; Hurlbut, as aforesaid, had slept elsewhere and had only to lie low, wherever he was, to avoid capture. This he did, and survived to deliver himself of the best-remembered comment anyone made on either side in reference to the raid. "They removed me from command because I couldn't keep Forrest out of West Tennessee," he declared afterwards, "and now Washburn can't keep him out of his own bedroom."

By then enough blue units had rallied to bring on a number of vicious little skirmishes and fire-fights, resulting in a total of 35 Con-federates and 80 Federals being killed or wounded, in addition to 116 defenders captured — many of them officers, rounded up in their night clothes at the Gayoso and elsewhere — along with some 200 horses. All this time, surprise reunions were in progress around town, despite the fact that recognition was not always easy: as, for example, in the case of a young raider who hailed his mother and sister from the gate of the family home, only to find that they had trouble identifying a tattered mud-spattered veteran as the boy they had kissed goodbye when he left three years ago, neatly turned out in well-pressed clothes for a war that would soon be won. At 9 o'clock, satisfied that he had created enough disturbance to produce the effect he wanted, Forrest had the recall sounded and began the prearranged withdrawal. Beyond Cane Creek he paused to return, under a flag of truce, Washburn's uniform, which his brother Jesse proudly displayed as a trophy of the raid. (Whatever de-ficiencies he might show in other respects, Washburn knew how to re-turn a courtesy. Some weeks later he sent Forrest, also under a flag of truce, a fine gray uniform made to measure by the cavalryman's own prewar Memphis tailor.) The column then took up the southward march, clearing Hernando that afternoon to ride back across the Tallahatchie and into Panola, late the following day. "If the enemy is falling back, pursue them hard," Forrest instructed Chalmers in a message taken cross-country by a courier who found him just below Oxford, still resisting Smith's advance.

That admonition — "pursue them hard" — was presently translated into action. Smith had entered Oxford that morning, but had no sooner done so than he began to backpedal in response to the news, brought forward under armed escort, that Forrest had raided Memphis the day before. Withdrawing, the Federals set fire to the courthouse, along with other public buildings and a number of private residences. "Where once stood a handsome little country town," an Illinois correspondent wrote, "now only remain the blackened skeletons of houses, and smouldering ruins." Smith's retrograde movement was hastened by a follow-up report next day, August 23, that the raiders were returning to Memphis for a second and heavier strike. The report was false (Forrest was still at Panola, a hard two-day march to the south, resting his troopers from their 150-mile excursion through the Mississippi bottoms) but was almost as disruptive, in its effect, as if it had been true. Alarm bells rang; regulars and militiamen turned out — "eager for the fray," one of the latter said — and Washburn asked the naval commander to have a gunboat steam downriver, below Fort Pickering, to shell the southern approaches to the city. This was done, but with no more than pyrotechnical effect, since the raiders were only there by rumor, not in fact. "The whole town was stampeded," Washburn's inspector general declared, calling the reaction "the most disgraceful affair I have ever seen." This too had its influence. Within another two days no part of A. J. Smith's command remained below the Tallahatchie, and so closely did Chalmers press him, in accordance with Forrest's instructions, that he soon abandoned close to a hundred miles of telegraph wire along the route from the river-crossing, all the way back to the outskirts of Memphis.

Washburn put the best possible interpretation on the outcome of the visit paid him by the raiders. "The whole Expedition was barren of spoils," he wrote his congressman brother Elihu. "They were in so great a hurry to get away that they carried off hardly anything. I lost two fine horses, which is about the biggest loss of anybody." So did Sherman tend to look on the bright side of the event. "If you get the chance," he wired Washburn on August 24, the day after the big stampede, "send word to Forrest that I admire his dash but not his judgment. The oftener he runs his head against Memphis the better."

There was much in that; Forrest's activities, these past four months, had been limited to North Mississippi and the southwest corner of Tennessee, with the result that he had been kept off Sherman's all-important supply line throughout this critical span. But it also rather missed the point that, with Memphis under cower and afflicted with a bad case of the shakes, the Wizard now was free to ride in practically any direction he or his superiors might choose: including Middle Tennessee, a region that nurtured a vital part of that supply line. The question was whether there was time enough, even if he were given his head at last, for Forrest's movement to be of much help to Hood in besieged Atlanta.

★   ★   ★

Encouraged by Wheeler's recent victories over Stoneman and McCook, which he believed more or less disposed of the blue cavalry as a threat, Hood by then had thrown his own cavalry deep into the Union rear in North Georgia and East Tennessee, hoping, as he explained in a wire requesting the President's approval, that by severing Sherman's life line he would provoke him into rashness or oblige him to retreat. Davis readily concurred, having urged such a strike on Johnston, without success, from the outset to the time of his removal. He replied that he shared Hood's hope that this would "compel the enemy to attack you in position," but added, rather pointedly, and in a tone not unlike Lincoln's when cautioning Grant, down near Richmond the month before, on the heels of repulses even more costly than Hood had just suffered around Atlanta: "The loss consequent upon attacking him in his intrenchments requires you to avoid that if practicable."

Wheeler set out on August 10, taking with him some 4500 effectives from his eight brigades and leaving about the same number behind, including William Jackson's three-brigade division, to patrol and protect Hood's flanks and rear while he was gone. His itinerary for the following week, northward along the Western & Atlantic, resembled a synopsis, in reverse, of the Johnston-Sherman contest back in May. Marietta, Cassville, Calhoun, Resaca: all were hit on a five-day ride that saw the destruction of some thirty miles of track and the rebuilt bridge across the Etowah. On August 14, after detaching one brigade to escort his prisoners and captured livestock back to Atlanta, he began a two-day demonstration against Dalton, then continued north, around and beyond Chattanooga, to Loudon. He intended to cross the Tennessee River there, but found it in flood and had to continue upstream nearly to Knoxville, where he detached two more brigades to wreck the railway bridge at Strawberry Plains, then turned southwest, beyond the Holston and the Clinch, to descend on the Nashville & Chattanooga Railroad, which he broke in several places before he recrossed the Tennessee at Tuscumbia, Alabama, on September 10, his twenty-eighth birthday. At a total cost of 150 casualties on this month-long raid, in the course of which he "averaged 25 miles a day [and] swam or forded 27 rivers," Wheeler reported the seizure of "1000 horses and mules, 200 wagons, 600 prisoners, and 1700 head of beef cattle," and claimed that his command had "captured, killed, or wounded three times the greatest effective strength it has ever been able to carry into action."

As an exploit, even after allowing for the exaggeration common to most cavalry reports, this was much. In other respects, however, it amounted to little more than a prime example of how events could transform a tactical triumph into a strategic cipher. Although Wheeler accomplished practically everything he was sent out to do, and on a grander scale than had been intended, the only real effect of the raid was not on Sherman — whose work gangs were about as quick to repair damage to the railroads as the gray troopers had been to inflict it — but on Hood, who was deprived thereby of half his cavalry during the critical final stage of the contest for Atlanta; which, in point of fact, had ended before Wheeler recrossed the Tennessee. One further result of the raid, also negative, was that Hood at last was convinced, as he said later, "that no sufficiently effective number of cavalry could be assembled in the Confederacy to interrupt the enemy's line of supplies to an extent to compel him to retreat."

Sherman was no more provoked into rashness than he was into retreat, but Wheeler's absence did encourage him, despite the recent failure of such efforts, to venture still another cavalry strike at the Macon & Western, Hood's only remaining rail connection, whose rupture would oblige him to evacuate Atlanta for lack of supplies. Another persuasive factor was Judson Kilpatrick. Back in the saddle after a ten-week convalescence from the wound he had taken at Resaca, he seemed to Sherman just the man to lead the raid. Unlike Garrard — who, in Sherman's words, would flinch if he spotted "a horseman in the distance with a spyglass" — Little Kil had a reputation as a fighter, and though in the present instance he was advised "not to fight but to work," only boldness would assure success. Reinforced by two brigades from Garrard, the bandy-legged New Jerseyite took his division southeast out of Sandtown on the night of August 18, under instructions to "break up the Macon [rail]road about Jonesboro," twenty miles below Atlanta. He got there late the following day, unimpeded, and began at once to carry out Sherman's orders, passed on by Schofield: "Tell Kilpatrick he cannot tear up too much track nor twist too much iron. It may save this army the necessity of making a long, hazardous flank march."

First he set fire to the depot, then turned his attention to the road itself. But before he had ripped up more than a couple of miles of track he was attacked from the rear by a brigade of Texans from Jackson's division. Kilpatrick pressed on south, pursued by this and Jackson's other two brigades, but ran into infantry intrenched near Lovejoy Station and veered east, then north to reënter his own lines at Decatur. That was on August 22, and he proudly reported that he had done enough damage to Hood's life line to remove it from use for the next ten days. Sherman was delighted: but only overnight. Next morning, heavy-laden supply trains came puffing into Atlanta over tracks he had been assured were demolished. Told "not to fight but to work," Kilpatrick apparently had not done much of either, or else the rebel crews were as adept at repairs as their Union counterparts north of the city. In any case, Sherman said later, "I became more than ever convinced that cavalry could not or would not work hard enough to disable a railroad properly, and therefore resolved at once to proceed to the execution of my original plan."

This was the massive counterclockwise slide, the "grand left wheel around Atlanta," which he had designed to bring on the fall of the city by transferring all but one of his seven infantry corps around to the south, astride its only rail connection with the outside world. Interrupted at Ezra Church in late July, the maneuver had been resumed only to stall again in the toils of Utoy Creek in early August. Since then, Sherman had sought by continuous long-range shelling, if not to convert the Gate City into "a desolation," as he had proposed two weeks ago, then in any case to reduce it to "a used-up community," and in this he had succeeded to a considerable extent, though not at a rate that matched his impatience, which was quickened by the spirit-lifting news of Farragut's triumph down in Mobile Bay. Now — Kilpatrick having failed, in Wheeler's absence, to spare him "the necessity of making a long, hazardous flank march" — he was ready to resume his ponderous shift. Leaving Slocum's corps (formerly Hooker's) north of Atlanta, securely intrenched in a position from which to observe the reaction there and also protect the railway bridge across the Chattahoochee, he pulled all three armies rearward out the Sandtown Road on August 26 and started them south the following day in three wide-sweeping arcs, Howard and Schofield on the left and right, Thomas as usual in the center. Their respective objectives, all on the Macon Railroad, were Rough & Ready Station, four miles below East Point; Jonesboro, ten miles farther down the line; and a point about midway between the two. Thomas and Howard took off first, having longer routes to travel, and reached the inactive West Point Railroad next day at Red Oak and Fairburn, where

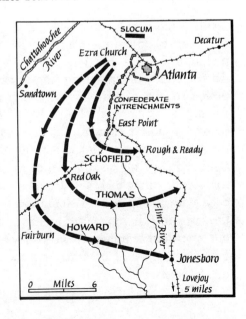

they were to swing east. Then Schofield set out on his march, which was shorter but was presumably much riskier, since he would be a good deal closer to the rebels massed in and around Atlanta. As it turned out, however, he met with no more resistance than Howard and Thomas had done in the course of their wider sweeps; which was practically none at all. Welcome as this nonintervention was, Sherman also found it strange, particularly in contrast to his opponent's previous violent reaction to any attempt to move across his front or round his flank.

Hood's reaction, or nonaction, was stranger than any Federal supposed, being founded on a total misconception of what his adversary was up to. Not that his error had been illogically arrived at; it had not; but the logic, such as it was, was based insubstantially on hope. Suddenly, on August 26, after weeks of intensive shelling, the bombardment of Atlanta stopped as abruptly as a dropped watch, and when patrols went out at midday to investigate this unexpected silence — which somehow was even heavier with tension than the diurnal uproar that preceded it — they found the Union trenches empty and skirmishers posted rear-guard-fashion along and on both sides of the road leading west to Sandtown and the Chattahoochee. Apparently a mass movement was in progress in that direction. Only on the north side of the city, in position to defend the indispensable railroad crossing and forward base, were the old works still occupied in strength. Hood's spirits took a leap at the news; for the brigade detached by Wheeler the week before, up near Calhoun, had returned that morning with its haul of prisoners and cattle and a first-hand account of the extensive damage so far done to the Western & Atlantic, including the burning of the vital span across the Etowah. Wheeler himself, according to a report just in, was beyond Chattanooga with the rest of his command, preparing by now to cross the Tennessee River and descend on the blue supply line below Nashville. All this was bound to have its effect; Sherman must already be hurting for lack of food and ammunition. Indeed, there was testimony on hand that this was so. Six days ago, a woman whose home was inside Schofield's lines had appealed to one of his division commanders for rations, only to be refused. "No," she was told; "I would like to draw, myself. I have been living on short rations for seven days, and now that your people have torn up our railroad and stolen our beef cattle, we must live a damned sight shorter." On such evidence as this, and out of his own sore need for a near miracle, Hood based his conclusion that Sherman, threatened with the specter of starvation by Wheeler's disruption of his life line, was in full retreat across the Chattahoochee with all of his corps but one, left temporarily in position north of the city to cover the withdrawal by rail of what remained of his sorely depleted stockpile of provisions.

Orders went out for Jackson to bring his overworked troopers in from the flanks and take up the pursuit toward Sandtown. Jackson did, beginning next day, but reported that the bluecoats seemed to him to be regrouping, not retreating. Hood rejected this assessment, preferring to believe that his cavalry simply lacked the strength to penetrate the Federal rear guard. So near the end of his military tether that he had nothing to fall back on but delusion, he held his three corps in the Atlanta intrenchments, which had been extended down to East Point, awaiting developments.

They were not long in coming. Sherman had Howard and Thomas spend a day astride the West Point Railroad, "breaking it up thoroughly," as he said, lest the rebels someday try to put it back in commission. His veterans were highly skilled at such work by now, and he later described how they went about it. "The track was heaved up in sections the length of a regiment, then separated rail by rail; bonfires were made of the ties and of fence rails on which the rails were heated, carried to trees or telegraph poles, wrapped around and left to cool." Not content with converting the rails into scrap iron — "Sherman neckties," the twisted loops were called — he then proceeded against the roadbed itself. "To be still more certain, we filled up many deep cuts with trees, brush, and earth, and commingled with them loaded shells, so arranged that they would explode on an attempt to haul out the bushes. The explosion of one such shell would have demoralized a gang of negroes, and thus would have prevented even the attempt to clear the road." Next morning, August 30, he started both armies east toward the headwaters of Flint River, which flowed south between the two converging railroads, the one he had just undone in his rear and the one ahead, whose loss would undo Hood.

Elated at the prospect of achieving this objective, he accompanied Thomas on the march, and as they approached the Flint that afternoon — still without encountering serious opposition, though the Macon road lay only a scant two miles beyond the river — he exulted to the Virginian riding beside him: "I have Atlanta as certainly as if it were in my hand!"

Hood by now had begun to emerge from his wishful three-day dream. Reports that Union infantry had appeared in strength on the West Point road the day before, above and below Fairburn and Red Oak, obliged him to concede that part at least of Sherman's host was headed for something other than the Chattahoochee River, and when follow-up dispatches informed him this morning that the same blue wrecking force was moving eastward, in the direction of the Macon road, he knew he had to act. All surplus goods were ordered packed for shipment out of the nearly beleaguered city, by whatever routes might be available when the time came, and Hardee was told to shift to Rough & Ready, bracing his corps for the defense of the rail supply line, there or farther down, while Lee moved out to take his place at East Point, under instructions to be ready for a march in either direction, southward to reinforce Hardee or back north to assist Stewart in the close-up defense of Atlanta, depending on which turned out to need him worst. Old Straight remained in the works that rimmed the city, not only because of Slocum's hovering menace, but also because Hood had revised — indeed, reversed — his estimate of the enemy's intentions. It seemed to him that Sherman was trying to draw him out of Atlanta with a strike at his supply line, say by half the Federal force, so that when he moved to meet this threat, the other half, concealed till then near the Chattahoochee, could swoop down and take the city. Hood's job, as he assessed it, was to avoid being lured out in such numbers that Atlanta would fall in their absence, its scantly manned intrenchments overrun, and yet at the same time to prevent the seizure or destruction of the Macon Railroad, whose loss would require him to give up the city for lack of subsistence.

Caught thus between the blue devil and the deep blue sea, Hood saw no choice, now that he had been shaken out of the dream that transformed his red-haired opponent from a destroyer into a deliverer, except to try to meet these separate dangers as they developed. All in all, outnumbered as he was, the situation was pretty much as Sherman was describing it to Thomas even now, a dozen-odd miles to the south: "I have Atlanta as certainly as if it were in my hand." What had the earmarks of a frothy boast — of a kind all too common in a war whose multi-thumbed commanders were often in need of reassurance, even if they had to express it themselves — was in fact merely a tactical assessment, somewhat florid but still a good deal more accurate than most.

Or maybe not. When Hood heard from Hardee, around midday, that the blue march seemed to be aimed at both Rough & Ready and Jonesboro, ten miles apart, he saw once more a chance to strike the enemy in detail. And having perceived this he was no less willing to undertake it than he had been three times before, in as many costly sorties. Now as then he improvised a slashing assault designed to subject a major portion of the Union host to destruction. His plan — refined to deal with a later, more specific report that Logan's corps had crossed the Flint that afternoon and gone into camp within cannon range of Jonesboro, supported only by Kilpatrick's horsemen, while the other two corps of the Army of the Tennessee remained on the west bank of the stream — was for Hardee to fall upon this exposed segment early next morning and "drive the enemy, at all hazards, into Flint River, in their rear." Moreover, when the rest of Howard's troops attempted to come to Logan's assistance they could be whipped in detail with help from Lee, whose corps would set out down the railroad from East Point at the same time Hardee's moved from Rough & Ready on a night march that would put them in position for attack at first light, August 31. To make certain that his plan was understood, Hood wired both generals to leave their senior division commanders in charge of the march to Jonesboro and report to him in Atlanta, by rail, for the usual face-to-face instructions, which experience had shown were even more necessary than he had thought when he first took charge of the Army of Tennessee.

In Atlanta that night, at the council of war preceding this Fourth Sortie, Hood expanded his plan to include a follow-up attack September 1. After sharing in tomorrow's assault, which would drive the Federals away from the Macon road and back across the Flint, Lee was to return to Rough & Ready Station, where he would be joined by Stewart for an advance next morning, down the west bank of the river, that would strike the flank of the crippled bluecoats, held in position overnight by Hardee, and thus complete their destruction. This was in some ways less risky and in others riskier than Hood knew, believing as he did that only Howard's army was south of the city, which thus would be scantly protected from an assault by Thomas and Schofield. For that reason, Hood took what he believed was the post of gravest responsibility: Atlanta, whose defenses would be manned, through this critical time, only by Jackson's dismounted troopers and units of the Georgia militia. It was late when the council broke up and Hardee, who was put in charge of the attack, boarded a switch engine for a fast ride to Jonesboro. He arrived before dawn, expecting to find his and Lee's corps being posted for the assault at daybreak. Neither was there; nor could he find anyone who could tell him where they were — Lee's, which that general must have rejoined by now, or his own, which had set out southward from Rough & Ready the night before.

Howard remained all morning in what he called a "saucy position," content to reinforce Logan's corps, intrenched on the east bank of the Flint, with a single division from Dodge, who was away recuperating from being struck on the forehead by a bullet the week before. He expected to be attacked by a rebel force that seemed to be gathering in Jonesboro, less than a mile across the way; that was why he kept most of his troops out of sight on the west side of the river, hoping, now that Logan's men had had plenty of time to strengthen their intrenchments, that the graybacks would come to him, rather than wait for him to storm their works along the railroad. But when nothing had come of this by the time the sun swung past the overhead, he decided he would have to prod them. He told Logan to move out at 3 o'clock. At 2.45, just as Black Jack's veterans were preparing to leave their trenches, long lines of butternut infantry came surging out of Jonesboro in far greater numbers than Howard had expected while trying to provoke them into making an attack.

Hardee was even tardier in launching Hood's Fourth Sortie than he had been in either of the other two committed to his charge, the first having opened two hours behind schedule, the second nearly seven, and this one more than nine. Yet here again the blame was hard to fix. Cleburne, left in corps command when Old Reliable went to Atlanta the night before, had found enemy units blocking his line of march and had had to detour widely around them, which delayed his arrival in Jonesboro until an hour after sunrise; while Lee, whose longer route was even worse obstructed, did not come up till well past noon. As a result, it was 2 o'clock before Hardee could get the two road-worn corps into jump-off positions and issue orders for the attack. These were for Cleburne to turn the enemy's right and for Lee to move against their front as soon as he heard Cleburne's batteries open. Such a signal had often failed in the past, and now it did so here. Mistaking the clatter of skirmishers' rifles for the roar of battle, Lee started forward on his own and thus exposed his corps to the concentrated fire of the whole Union line, with demoralizing results. Cleburne then moved out, driving Kilpatrick's troopers promptly across the Flint, but found Logan's works too stoutly held for him to effect a lodgment without assistance. Hardee urged Lee to renew his stalled advance, only to be told that it was impossible; Howard was bringing reserves across the river to menace the shaken right. In reaction, Hardee called off the attack and ordered both Cleburne and Lee to take up defensive positions, saying later: "I now consider this a fortunate circumstance, for success against such odds could at best have only been partial and bloody, while defeat would have [meant] almost inevitable destruction to the army."

That ended the brief, disjointed Battle of Jonesboro; or half ended it, depending on what Howard would do now. Lee and Cleburne had suffered more than 1700 casualties between them, Logan and Kilpatrick less than a fourth as many, and these were the totals for this last day of August, as it turned out, since Howard did not press the issue. Late that night, in response to Hood's repeated summons, Hardee detached Lee's three divisions for the return march north, tomorrow's scheduled follow-up offensive down the west bank of the Flint having been ruled out by the failure of today's attempt to set up Howard for the kill.

What Hood now wanted Lee for, though, was to help Stewart hold Atlanta against the assault he expected Sherman to make next morning with the other two Federal armies, which he still thought were lurking northwest of the city. He presently learned better. Soon after dark, reports came in that bluecoats were across the Macon road in strength at Rough & Ready, as well as at several other points between there and Jonesboro. Lee not only confirmed this when he reached East Point at daylight, having managed to slip between the enemy columns in the darkness; he also identified them as belonging to Schofield and Thomas. This was a shock, and its meaning was all too clear. Atlanta was doomed. The only remaining question, now that Sherman had the bulk of his command astride the city's last rail supply line, squarely between Hardee and the other two corps, was whether the Army of

Tennessee was doomed as well. Hood and his staff got to work at once on plans for the evacuation of Atlanta and the reunion, if possible, of his divided army, so that it could be saved to fight another day.

Such a reunion was not going to include Hardee's third of that army if Sherman had his way. Primarily he had undertaken this six-corps grand left wheel as a railroad-wrecking expedition, designed to bring on the fall of Atlanta by severing its life line, but now that he saw in Hardee's isolation an opportunity to annihilate him, he extended its scope to achieve just that. Both Schofield and Thomas were told to move on Jonesboro without delay, there to combine their three corps with Howard's three — a total of more than 60,000, excluding cavalry — for an assault on Hardee's 12,500, still licking the wounds they had suffered in their repulse the day before. While this convergence was in progress Howard put the rest of Dodge's corps across the Flint, where Logan confronted the rebels in their works, and sent Blair to cut the railroad south of town and stand in the path of any escape in that direction. Noon came and went, this hot September 1, still with no word from Thomas or Schofield, who were to attack the Confederates on their right while Howard clamped them in position from the front. Sherman fumed at the delay, knowing the graybacks were hard at work improving their intrenchments, and kept fuming right up to 3 o'clock, when the first of Slow Trot Thomas's two corps arrived, formerly John Palmer's but now under Jeff C. Davis, Palmer having departed in a huff after a squabble with Schofield, who he claimed had mishandled his troops in the Utoy Creek fiasco. The other Cumberland corps, David Stanley's, was nowhere in sight, and in fact did not turn up till after sundown, having got lost on its cross-country march, and Schofield moved so slowly from Rough & Ready, tearing up track as he went, that he arrived even later than Stanley. Combined with the detachment of Blair to close the southward escape hatch, the nonappearance of these two corps reduced the size of the attacking force by half. But that still left Sherman with considerably better than twice the number he faced, and he also enjoyed the advantage of having Davis come down unexpectedly on the enemy right, which was bent back across the railroad north of town.

Davis was a driver, a hard-mannered regular who had come up through the ranks, thirty-six years old, with wavy hair and a bushy chin-beard, a long thin nose and the pale, flat eyes of a killer; which he was. Still a brigadier despite his lofty post and a war record dating back to Sumter, he had been denied promotion for the past two years because of the scandal attending his pistol slaying of Bull Nelson in Kentucky, long ago in '62, and he welcomed such assignments as this present one at Jonesboro, seeing in them opportunities to demonstrate a worth beyond the grade at which he had been stopped in his climb up the military ladder. He put his men in line astride the railroad — three divisions, containing as many troops as Hardee had in all — and sent them roaring down against the rebel flank at 4 o'clock. Cleburne's division was posted there, in trenches Lee had occupied the day before. Repulsed, Davis dropped back, regrouped quickly, and then came on again in a mass assault that went up and over the barricade to land in the midst of Brigadier General Dan Govan's veteran Arkansas brigade. Two batteries were overrun and Govan himself captured, along with more than half his men. "They're rolling them up like a sheet of paper!" Sherman cried, watching from an observation post on Howard's front.

But Granbury's Texans were next in line, and there the rolling stopped. Cleburne shored up his redrawn flank, massing fire on the lost salient, and Davis had all he could do to hold what he had won. Unwilling to risk a frontal assault by Howard, Sherman saw that what he needed now was added pressure on the weakened enemy right by Stanley, who was supposed to be coming up in rear of Davis. Angrily he turned to Thomas, demanding to know where Stanley was, and the heavy-set Virginian, who already had sent courier after courier in search of the errant corps, not only rode off in person to join the hunt, but also did so in a manner that later caused his red-haired superior to remark that this was "the only time during the campaign I can recall seeing General Thomas urge his horse into a gallop." Even so, the sun had set by the time Stanley turned up, and night fell before he could put his three divisions in attack formation. Darkness ended this second day of the Battle of Jonesboro, which cost Sherman 1275 casualties, mostly from Davis's corps, and Hardee just under 1000, two thirds of them captured in the assault that cracked his flank.

Disgruntled, Sherman bedded down, hopeful that tomorrow, with Schofield up alongside Stanley, he would complete the fate he planned for Hardee. He had trouble sleeping, he would recall, and soon after midnight, to add to his fret, "there arose toward Atlanta sounds of shells exploding, and other sounds like that of musketry." This was disturbing; Hood might well be doing to Slocum what he himself intended to do to Hardee. Yesterday he had instructed Thomas to have Slocum "feel forward to Atlanta, as boldly as he can," adding: "Assure him that we will fully occupy the attention of the rebel army outside of Atlanta." This last he had failed to do, except in part, and it seemed to him likely, from those rumblings twenty miles to the north, that he had thereby exposed Slocum to destruction by two thirds of Hood's command. Other listeners about the campfire disagreed, interpreting the muffled clatter as something other than battle, and Sherman decided to settle the issue by visiting a nearby farmhouse, where he had seen lights burning earlier in the evening. Shouts brought the farmer out into the yard in his nightshirt. Had he lived here long? He had. Had he heard such rumblings before? Indeed he had. That was the way it sounded when there was heavy fighting up around Atlanta.

The noise faded, then died away; which might have an even more gruesome meaning. Sherman returned to his campfire, still unable to sleep. Then at 4 o'clock it rose again, with the thump and crump and muttering finality of a massive coup de grâce. Again it died, this time for good. Dawn came, and with the dawn a new enigma. Thomas and Schofield moved as ordered, the latter on the left to sweep across the rebel rear — "We want to destroy the enemy," Sherman told them, anxious to be done with the work at hand — but found that Hardee had departed under cover of darkness and the distractive far-off rumblings from the north. Sherman took up the pursuit, southward down the railroad, still wondering what had happened deep in his rear. This was the hundred and twentieth day of the campaign, and while he was at Jonesboro another month had slipped into the past, costing him 7000 casualties and his adversary 7500: a total to date of 31,500 Federals and 35,000 Confederates, rough figures later precisely tabulated at 31,687 and 34,979 respectively. Close to 20,000 of the latter had been suffered by Hood in the nearly seven weeks since he took over from Johnston, while Sherman had lost just under 15,000 in that span.

Presently, as the six blue corps toiled southward down the railroad in search of Hardee's three vanished divisions, Schofield sent word that he took last night's drumfire rumblings from the direction of Atlanta to be the sound of Hood blowing up his unremovable stores, in preparation for evacuation. Two hours later, at 10.25, he followed this with a report that a Negro had just come into his lines declaring that the rebs were departing the city "in great confusion and disorder." Unconvinced, still troubled about "whether General Slocum had felt forward and become engaged in a real battle," Sherman kept up his pursuit of Hardee until he came upon him near Lovejoy Station, six miles down the line, his corps posted in newly dug intrenchments "as well constructed and as strong as if these Confederates had a week to prepare them." Such was his assessment after a tentative 4 o'clock probe was savagely repulsed. "I do not wish to waste lives by an assault," he warned Howard, explaining more fully to Thomas: "Until we hear from Atlanta the exact truth, I do not care about your pushing your men against breastworks." Still fretted by doubts about Slocum, he maintained his position of cautious observation through sunset into darkness. "Nothing positive from Atlanta," he informed Schofield within half an hour of midnight, "and that bothers me."

Finally, between then and sunup, September 3, a courier arrived with a dispatch from Slocum, who was not only safe but was safe inside Atlanta. Alerted by last night's racket, just across the way — it turned out to be the explosion of 81 carloads of ammunition, together with five locomotives, blown up in relays when they were found to be cut off from escape by the loss of the Macon road — he had felt his way forward at daylight to the city limits, where the commander of his lead division encountered a delegation of civilians. "Sir," their leader said with a formal bow. His name, it developed, was James M. Calhoun, and that was strangely fitting, even though no kinship connected him with the South Carolina original, John C. "The fortunes of war have placed the city of Atlanta in your hands. As mayor of the city I ask protection for noncombatants and private property." Slocum telegraphed the news to Washington: "General Sherman has taken Atlanta," and passed the word to his chief, approaching Lovejoy by then, that Hood had begun his withdrawal at 5 p.m. the day before, southward down the Mc-Donough Road and well to the east of the Macon & Western, down which Howard and Thomas and Schofield were marching.

This meant that Hood had crossed their front and flank with Stewart and Lee and the Georgia militia, last night and yesterday, and by now had reunited his army in the intrenchments hard ahead at Love-joy Station. Wise by hindsight, Sherman began to see that he had erred in going for Hardee, snug in his Jonesboro works, when he might have struck for the larger and more vulnerable prize in retreat on the Mc-Donough Road beyond. Moreover, if he had been unable to pound the graybacks to pieces while he had them on the Atlanta anvil, there seemed little chance for success in such an effort now that they were free to maneuver as they chose. Such at last was the price he paid for having redefined his objective, not as the Army of Tennessee — "Break it up," Grant had charged him at the outset, before Dalton — but rather as the city that army had been tied to, until now.

In any case, he had it, and he was ready and anxious to take possession in person. "Atlanta is ours, and fairly won," he wired Halleck. "I shall not push much farther in this raid, but in a day or so will move to Atlanta and give my men some rest."

✕ 3 ✕

Slocum's wire, received in Washington on the night of the day it was sent — "General Sherman has taken Atlanta" — ended a hot-weather span of anxiety even sorer than those that followed the two Bull Runs, back in the first two summers of the war. The prospect of stalemate, at this late stage, brought on a despondency as deep as outright defeat had done in those earlier times, when the national spirit displayed a resilience it had lost in the course of a summer that not only was bloody beyond all past imagining, but also saw Early within plain view of the Capitol dome and Democrats across the land anticipating a November sweep. Farragut's coup, down in Mobile Bay, provided no more than a glimmer of light, perfunctorily discerned before it guttered out in the gloom invoked by Sherman's reproduction, on the outskirts of Atlanta, of Grant's failure to take Richmond when he reached it the month before. Both wound up, apparently stalled, some twenty miles beyond their respective objectives, and by the end of August it had begun to appear that neither of them, having overshot the mark, was going to get back where he had been headed at the outset.

Nowhere, East or West or in between, was the disenchantment so complete as it was on the outskirts of Petersburg by then. Partly this was because of the high price paid to get there (Meade's casualties, exclusive of Butler's, were more than twice as heavy as Sherman's, though the latter had traveled nearly twice as far by his zigzag route) and partly too because, time and again, the public's and the army's expectations had been lifted only to be dashed, more often than not amid charges of incredible blundering, all up and down the weak-linked chain of command. A case in point, supplementing the fiasco that attended the original attack from across the James, was an operation that came to be called "The Crater," which occurred in late July and marked a new high (or low) for mismanagement at or near the top, surpassing even Cold Harbor in that regard, if not in bloodshed.

Early that month, after the failure of his probe for the Weldon Railroad in late June, Grant asked Meade how he felt about undertaking a new offensive against Lee's center or around his flank. Faced as he was with the loss of Wright, whose corps was being detached just then to counter Early's drive on Washington, Meade replied that he was doubtful about the result of either a flank or a frontal effort, citing "the facility with which the enemy can interpose to check an onward movement." However, lest his chief suppose that he was altogether without aggressive instincts or intentions — which, in point of fact, he very nearly was by now — Meade did let fall that he had in progress a work designed to permit a thrust, not through or around, but *under* the Confederate intrenchments. Burnside was digging a mine.

The proposal had come from a regimental commander, Lieutenant Colonel Henry Pleasants, whose 48th Pennsylvania was made up largely of volunteers from the anthracite fields of Schuylkill County, one of whom he happened to hear remark, while peering through a firing slit at a rebel bastion some 150 uphill yards across the way: "We could blow that damned fort out of existence if we could run a mine shaft under it." Formerly a civil engineer engaged in railroad tunneling, Pleasants liked the notion and took a sketch of it to his division commander, Brigadier General Robert Potter, who passed it along to corps. Burnside told Pleasants to start digging, then went himself to Meade for approval and assistance. He got Meade's nod, apparently because the work at least would keep some bored men busy for a time, but not his help, his staff having advised that the project was impractical from the engineering point of view. No such tunnel could exceed 400 feet in length, the experts said, that being the limit at which fresh air could be provided without ventilation shafts, and this one was projected to extend for

more than 500 feet from the gallery entrance to the powder chamber
at its end.

Pleasants had been hard at work since June 25, the day Burnside
told him to start burrowing into the steep west bank of an abandoned
railway cut, directly in rear of his picket line and well hidden from
enemy lookouts. By assigning his men to shifts so that the digging went
forward round the clock, he managed to complete the tunnel within a
month — though his miners later claimed they could have done the
job in less than half that time, if they had been given the proper tools.
Not that Pleasants hadn't done his best in that regard. Denied any issue
of special implements, such as picks, he contrived his own with the help
of regimental blacksmiths, converted hardtack boxes into barrows for
moving dirt, took over a wrecked sawmill to cut timbers and planks
for shoring up the gallery walls and roof, and even borrowed a theodo-
lite, all the way from Washington, when Meade's engineers declined to
lend him one of theirs. Technical problems he solved in much the same
improvisatory fashion, including some which these same close-fisted
experts defined as prohibitive; ventilation, for example. Just inside the
entrance he installed an airtight canvas door and beneath it ran a square
wooden pipe along the floor of the shaft to the diggers at the end, extending it as they progressed. A fireplace near the sealed door sent heated
air up its brush-masked chimney, creating a draft that drew the stale
air from the far end of the tunnel and pulled in fresh air through the
pipe, whose mouth was beyond the door. Working in the comparative
comfort of a gallery five feet high, four feet wide at the bottom and two
feet at the top — they had sweated and strained and wheezed and
shivered through longer hours, with considerably less headroom and
under far worse breathing conditions, back home in the Pennsylvania
coal fields — the miners completed 511 feet of shaft by July 17.

This put them directly under the rebel outwork, whose defenders
they could hear walking about, twenty feet above their heads, apparently unmindful of the malevolent, mole-like activity some half-
dozen yards below the ground they stood on. Next day the soldier
miners began digging laterally, right and left, to provide a powder
chamber, 75 feet long, under the enemy bastion and the trenches on
both flanks. By July 23 the pick and shovel work was done. After a
four-day rest, Pleasants brought in 320 kegs of black powder, weighing
25 pounds each, and distributed this gritty four-ton mass among eight
connected magazines, sandbagged to direct the explosion upward. When
his requisition for insulated wire and a galvanic battery did not come
through, he got hold of two fifty-foot fuzes, spliced them together, then
secured one end to the monster charge and ran the other back down the
gallery as far as it would reach; after which he replaced the earth of the
final forty feet of tunnel, firmly tamped to provide a certain backstop.

That was on July 28. All that remained was to put a match to the fuze, and get out before the boom.

Next afternoon, with the mine scheduled to be exploded early the following morning, Burnside assembled his division commanders to give them last-minute instructions for the assault that was to be launched through the resultant gap in the rebel works. Of these there were four, though only three of their divisions had done front-line duty so far in the campaign; the fourth, led by Brigadier General Edward Ferrero, was composed of two all-Negro brigades whose service up to now had been confined to guarding trains and rearward installations, largely because of the continuing supposition — despite conflicting evidence, West and East — that black men simply were not up to combat. "Is not a Negro as good as a white man to stop a bullet?" someone asked Sherman about this time, over in Georgia. "Yes; and a sandbag is better," he replied. Like many eastern generals he believed that former slaves had their uses in war, but not as soldiers. Burnside felt otherwise, and what was more he backed up his contention by directing that Ferrero's division, which was not only the freshest but was also by now the largest of the four, would lead tomorrow's predawn charge. By way of preparation, he had had the two brigades spend the past week rehearsing the attack until every member knew just what he was to do, and how; that is, rush promptly forward, as soon as the mine was sprung, and expand the gap so that the other three divisions, coming up behind, could move un-opposed across the Jerusalem Plank Road and onto the high ground im-mediately in rear of the blasted enemy intrenchments, which would give them a clear shot at Petersburg itself.

He was in high spirits, partly because the digging had gone so well and partly because Meade and Grant, catching a measure of his enthusiasm as the tunnel neared completion, had expanded the operation. Not only were Warren's and Baldy Smith's corps ordered to stand by for a share in exploiting the breakthrough — which was to be given close-up support by no less than 144 field pieces, mortars, and siege guns: more artillery, pound for pound, than had been massed by either side at Gettysburg — but Grant also sent Hancock's corps, along with two of Sheridan's divisions, to create a diversion, and if possible score an accompanying breakthrough, on the far side of the James. Hancock, who had returned to duty the week before, found the Confederates heavily reinforced in front of Richmond: as did Sheridan, who was worsted in a four-hour fight with Hampton on the day the fuze was laid to Pleasants's mine. Still, the feint served its purpose by drawing large numbers of graybacks away from the intended scene of the main effort, about mid-way down the five-mile rebel line below the Appomattox. Intelligence reported that five of Lee's eight infantry divisions were now at Bermuda Hundred or north of the James, leaving Beauregard with only three divisions, some 18,000 men in all, for the defense of the Petersburg rail hub. Moreover, there still was time for Hancock to return tomorrow — the day of Burnside's last-minute council of war — to lend still greater weight to the assault that would accompany the blasting of the under-manned enemy works before daylight next morning.

Burnside was happily passing this latest news along to his lieu-tenants when he was interrupted by a courier from army headquarters, bearing a message that had an effect not unlike the one expected, across the way, when the mine was sprung tomorrow. It contained an order from Meade, approved by Grant, for the assault to be spearheaded not by Ferrero's well-rehearsed Negroes, but by one of the white divisions. This change, which landed like a bomb in the council chamber, was provoked by racism; racism in reverse. "If we put the colored troops in front and [the attack] should prove a failure," Grant would testify at the subsequent investigation, "it would then be said, and very properly, that we were shoving those people ahead to get killed because we did not care anything about them."

Stunned, Burnside tried to get the order rescinded, only to be told that it would stand; Meade was not about to give his Abolitionist critics this chance to bring him down with charges that he had exposed black recruits to slaughter in the forefront of a long-shot operation. By now the scheduled assault was less than twelve hours off, all but four of them hours of darkness, and the ruff-whiskered general, too shaken to decide which of his three unrehearsed white divisions should take the lead, had their commanders draw straws for the assignment. It fell to Brigadier General James H. Ledlie, a former heavy artilleryman, least experienced of the three. Potter and Brigadier General Orlando Willcox would attack in turn, behind Ledlie; Ferrero would bring up the rear.

As they departed to alert their troops, Burnside could find con-solation only in reports that the Confederates — two South Carolina regiments, posted in support of the four-gun battery poised above the sealed-off powder chamber — seemed to have abandoned their former suspicion that they were about to be blown skyward. For a time last week they had tried countermining, without success, and when the underground digging stopped, July 23, so did their attempts at inter-section. Apparently they too had experts who advised them that such a tunnel was impracticable; with the result that when the sound of picks and shovels stopped, down below, they decided that the Yanks had given up, probably after a disastrous cave-in or mounting losses from asphyxiation.

Eventually the troops were brought up in the darkness, groping their way over unfamiliar terrain to take up assigned positions for the jump-off: Ledlie's division out front, just in back of the ridge where the pickets were dug in, Potter's and Willcox's along the slope of the rail-way cut, and Ferrero's along its bottom, aggrieved at having been shunted to the rear. Elsewhere along the Union line the other corps stood by, including Hancock's, which had returned from its demonstration beyond the James. Shortly after 3 o'clock Pleasants entered the tunnel to light the fuze. The guns and mortars were laid, ammunition stacked and cannoneers at the ready, lanyards taut. Burnside had his watch out, observing the creep of its hands toward 3.30, the specified time for the springing of the mine. 3.30 finally came; but not the explosion. Half an hour went by, and still the night was black, unsplit by flame. Another half hour ticked past, bringing the first gray hint of dawn to the rearward sky, and though Pleasants had accepted his mine-boss sergeant's offer to go back into the tunnel and investigate the delay, there still was no blast. Grant, losing patience, considered telling Burnside to forget the explosion and get on with his 15,000-man assault. Daylight grew, much faster now, and the flat eastern rim of earth was tinted rose, anticipating the bulge of the rising sun, by the time the sergeant and a lieutenant who had volunteered to join him — Harry Reese and Jacob Douty were their names — found that the fuze had burned out at the splice. They cut and relit it and scrambled for the tunnel entrance, a long 150 yards away, emerging just before 4.44, when the 8000-pound charge, twenty feet below the rebel works, erupted.

"A slight tremor of the earth for a second, then the rocking as of an earthquake," an awed captain would recall, "and, with a tremendous blast which rent the sleeping hills beyond, a vast column of earth and smoke shoots upward to a great height, its dark sides flashing out sparks of fire, hangs poised for a moment in mid-air, and then, hurtling down with a roaring sound, showers of stones, broken timbers and blackened human limbs, subsides — the gloomy pall of darkening smoke flushing to an angry crimson as it floats away to meet the morning sun." Another watcher of that burgeoning man-made cloud of dust and turmoil, a brigadier with Hancock, left an impression he never suspected would be repeated at the dawn of a far deadlier age of warfare, just over eighty years away: "Without form or shape, full of red flames and carried on a bed of lightning flashes, it mounted toward heaven with a detonation of thunder [and] spread out like an immense mushroom whose stem seemed to be of fire and its head of smoke."

Added to the uproar was the simultaneous crash of many cannon, fired by tense gunners as soon as they saw the ground begin to heave from the overdue explosion. Ledlie's men, caught thus between two shock waves, looked out and saw the rising mass of earth, torn from the hillside hard ahead, mount up and up until it seemed to hover directly above them, its topmost reaches glittering in the full light of the not-yet-risen sun. As the huge cluster started down, they recovered at least in part from their shock and reacted by breaking in panic for the rear. This was not too serious; their officers got them back in line within ten minutes and started them forward before the dust and smoke had cleared.

But what happened next was serious indeed. In his dismay over the last-minute change in orders, Burnside had neglected to have the defensive tangle of obstacles cleared from in front of the parapets, with the result that the attack formation was broken up as soon as the troops set out. Instead of advancing on a broad front, as intended — a brigade in width, with the second brigade coming up in close support — they went forward through a hastily improvised ten-foot passway that not only delayed their start but also confined them to a meager file of wary individuals who advanced a scant one hundred yards, then stopped in awe of what they saw before them. Where the Confederate fort had stood there now was a monstrous crater, sixty feet across and nearly two hundred feet wide, ranging in depth from ten to thirty feet. All was silent down there on its rubbled floor except for the thin cries of the wounded — who, together with the killed, turned out to number 278 — mangled by the blast and buried to various depths by the debris.

As Ledlie's soldiers stood and gazed at this lurid moonscape, strewn with clods that ranged in size up to that of a small house, they not only forgot their instructions to fan out right and left in order to widen the breakthrough for the follow-up attack; they even forgot to keep moving. At last they did move, but not far. For more than a month their fighting had been confined to rifle pits and trenches, and now here at their feet was the biggest rifle pit in all the world. They leaped into it and busied themselves with helping the Carolinian survivors, many of whom, though badly dazed, had interesting things to say when they were uprooted and revived. Ledlie might have gotten his division back in motion by exhortation or example, but he was not available just now. He was immured in a bombproof well behind the lines, swigging away at a bottle of rum he had cadged from a staff surgeon. It later developed that this had been his custom all along, in times of strain. In any case, there he remained throughout what was to have been a fast-moving go-for-broke assault on Petersburg, by way of the gap Henry Pleasants had blown in the rebel line.

That gap was already larger than any Federal knew. When the mine was sprung, the reaction of the graybacks right and left of the hoisted battery was the same as that of the intended attackers across the way. They too bolted rearward, panicked by the fury of the blast, and thus broadened the unmanned portion of their line to about 400 yards. What was more, it remained so for some time. The second and third blue waves rolled forward, paused in turn on the near rim of the crater, much as the first had done, and then, like it, swept down in search of cover amid the rubble at the bottom. By then, most of the bolted Confederates had returned to their posts on the flanks of the excavation, and Beauregard was bringing up reinforcements, along with all the artillery he could lay hands on.

They arrived, men and guns, at about the time Burnside's fourth wave started forward. Loosed at last (but without Ferrero; he had joined Ledlie in the bombproof, nearly a quarter-mile away) the Negro soldiers advanced in good order. "We looks like men a-marching on, We looks like men of war," they sang as they came up in the wake of the other three divisions, which were scarcely to be seen, having vanished quite literally into the earth. Disdaining the crater, they swung around it, in accordance with the maneuver they had rehearsed, and drove for the high ground beyond. However, now that the defenders had rallied and been reinforced, they not only failed to get there; they also lost a solid third of their number in the attempt — 1327 out of just under 4000. "Unsupported, subjected to a galling fire from batteries on the flanks, and from infantry fire in front and partly on the flank," a witness later wrote, "they broke up in disorder and fell back to the crater."

Conditions there were not much better. In some ways they were worse. Presently they were much worse in every way. More than 10,000 men, crowded hip to hip in a steep-walled pen less than a quarter-acre in extent, presented the gray cannoneers with a compact target they did not neglect. Counterbattery work by the massed Union guns was excellent, but the surviving rebel pieces, including hard-to-locate mortars, still delivered what one occupant of the crater termed "as heavy a fire of canister as was ever poured continuously upon a single objective point." The result was bedlam, a Bedlam in flames, and this got worse as the enemy infantry grew bolder, inching closer to the rim of the pit, where marksmanship would be about as superfluous as if the shots were directed into a barrel of paralyzed fish. Anticipating this, some bluecoats chose to run the gauntlet back to their own lines, while others preferred to remain and risk the prospect: which was soon at hand. Around 9.30, with Grant's disgusted approval, Meade had cancelled the follow-up attack and told Burnside to withdraw his corps.

But that was easier said than carried out. Burnside by then had fallen into a state of euphoric despair, much as he had done at Fredericksburg twenty months ago, under similar circumstances, and delayed transmission of the order till after midday, apparently in hope of some miraculous deliverance. Shortly after noon, two brigades from Mahone's division — they had slipped away from Warren's front unseen — gained the lip of the crater, where they added rapid-fire rifle volleys to the horror down below, then followed up with a bayonet charge that shattered what little remained of blue resistance. Hundreds surrendered, thousands fled, more hundreds fell, and the so-called Battle of the Crater was soon over. It had cost Burnside 3828 men, nearly half of them captured or missing, and losses elsewhere along Meade's line raised the Union total above 4000 for the day; Confederate casualties, mostly wounded, came to about one third that number. By nightfall, all that remained as evidence of this latest bizarre attempt to break Lee's line was a raw scar, about midway down its length below the Appomattox, which in time would green over and loose its jagged look, but would never really heal.

Nor would a new bitterness Southerners felt as a result of this affair. Not only had they been blown up while sleeping — "a mean trick," they declared — but for the first time, here in the Old Dominion, black soldiers had been thrown into the thick of a large-scale fight. That was something far worse than a trick; that was infamy, to Lee's men's way of thinking. And for this they cursed their enemy in cold blood. "Eyes gleamed, teeth clenched," a nurse who tended Mahone's wounded would recall, "as they showed me the locks of their muskets, to which blood and hair still clung, when, after firing, without waiting to reload, they had clenched the barrels and fought hand to hand." Privately — like the troopers who stormed Fort Pillow, out in the wilder West — they admitted to having bayoneted men in the act of surrender, and they were by no means ashamed of the act, considering their view of the provocation. It was noted that from this time forward there were no informal truces in the vicinity of the Crater. Sniping was venomous and continuous, dawn to dusk, along that portion of the line.

Ledlie (but not Ferrero, who was somehow overlooked in the caterwaul that followed) presently departed, condemned by a Court of Inquiry for his part in the mismanagement of what Grant pronounced "the saddest affair I have witnessed in this war." Burnside left even sooner, hard on the heels of a violent argument with Meade, an exchange of recriminations which a staff observer said "went far toward confirming one's belief in the wealth and flexibility of the English language as a medium of personal dispute." Meade wanted the ruff-whiskered general court martialed for incompetence, but Grant, preferring a quieter procedure, sent him home on leave. "He will never return whilst *I* am here," Meade fumed.

Nor did he. Resigning from the service, Ambrose Everett Burnside, forty years old, returned to his business pursuits in Rhode Island, where he not only prospered but also recovered the geniality he had lost in the course of a military career that required him to occupy positions he himself had testified he was unqualified to fill. In time he went into politics, serving three terms as governor, and would die well into his second term as a U.S. senator, twenty years after the war began.

Tactically speaking, Lee no doubt regretted Burnside's departure. He would miss him, much as he missed McClellan, now in retirement, and John Pope and Joe Hooker, who had been shunted to outlying regions where their ineptitudes would be less costly to the cause they served. This was not to say that mistakes came cheap from those commanders who remained near the violent center. Meade's losses for July, swollen by the botched attempt to score an explosive breakthrough near its end, totaled 6367, and he had scarcely an inch of ground to show for their subtraction. Yet Lee could take small comfort in the knowledge that his own were barely half that. In contrast to his custom in the old aggressive days, when a battle was generally followed by a Federal retreat, he now not only derived no positive gain for his losses; he was also far less able to replace them, so near was the Confederacy to the bottom of its manpower barrel. "There is the chill of murder about the casualties of this month," one of his brigadiers reported from the Petersburg intrenchments. Even such one-sided triumphs as the Crater were getting beyond his means, and much the same thing could be said of Early's recent foray to the gates of Washington, which, for all its success in frightening the authorities there, had failed to lure the Army of the Potomac into staging another Cold Harbor south of the James.

That was what Lee had wanted, and even expected. "It is so repugnant to Grant's principles and practice to send troops from him," he wrote Davis, "that I had hoped before resorting to it he would have preferred attacking me." Instead, Grant had detached two corps whose partial arrival discouraged Early from storming the capital defenses and obliged him to fall back across the Potomac. After a brief rest at Leesburg, in defiance of the superior blue force charged with pressing his pursuit, Old Jube returned to the lower Shenandoah Valley and continued to maneuver between Winchester and Harpers Ferry, Jackson style, as if about to move on Washington again. Before his adversaries managed to combine against him — they were drawn from four separate departments, with desk-bound Halleck more or less in charge by telegraph — he lashed out at George Crook near Kernstown, July 24, and after inflicting close to 1200 casualties, drove him all the way north across the Potomac. Following this, in specific retaliation for Hunter's burning of the homes of three prominent Virginians, Early sent two brigades of cavalry under John McCausland to Chambersburg, Pennsylvania, to demand of its merchants, under penalty of its destruction, $100,000 in gold or a cool half-million in greenbacks. When they refused, McCausland evacuated the 3000 inhabitants and set fire to the business district. That was on July 30, the day of the Crater, and by midnight two thirds of the town was in ashes, another casualty of a war that was growing harsher by the month.

Lee's acute concern for Early — whose foot-loose corps, though badly outnumbered, not only continued to disrupt the plans of the Union high command by bristling aggressively on both banks of the Potomac just upstream from Washington, but also served through this critical stretch of time as a covering force for the grain-rich Shenandoah region and the Virginia Central Railroad — was increased on August 4, five days after the Crater, by reports that Grant was loading another large detachment of troops aboard transports at City Point. "I fear that this force is intended to operate against General Early," Lee told Davis, "and when added to that already opposed to him, may be more than he can manage. Their object may be to drive him out of the Valley and complete the devastation they [had] commenced when they were ejected from it." In point of fact, next to provoking his adversary into making a headlong assault on his intrenchments, there was nothing Lee wanted more than just such a weakening of the pressure against them. However, there were limits beyond which a precarious balance would be lost; Early's defeat would mean the loss, as well, of the Shenandoah Valley and the Virginia Central, both necessary for the survival of the rest of the army, immobilized at Petersburg and Richmond. Lee conferred next day with the President and reached the conclusion that, whatever the risk to his thinly held works beyond the James, he would have to strengthen Early. Accordingly, on August 6 he ordered Richard Anderson to leave at once, with Kershaw's division of infantry and Fitz Lee's of cavalry, for Culpeper, where he would be in a position either to speed back to Richmond by rail, in case of an emergency there, or else to fall on the flank and rear of the Federals, just beyond the Blue Ridge, in case they advanced up the Valley.

As usual, Lee was right about Grant's intentions, though in this case they were more drastic than he knew. Not only did the Federal commander plan to "complete the destruction" begun by Hunter before Early drove him off; he already had directed that this was to be accomplished by a process of omnivorous consumption. When Early fell back in turn from Washington in mid-July, Grant told Halleck to see to it that he was pursued by "veterans, militiamen, men on horseback, and everything that can be got to follow," with specific instructions to "eat out Virginia clean and clear as far as they go, so that crows flying over it for the balance of this season will have to carry their own provender with them."

Nothing much had come of that, so far. The crows waxed fat on the Valley harvest, deep in Early's rear, while Halleck, convinced that all his doubts about Grant's movements since Cold Harbor had been confirmed by the events of the past month, fumbled his way through a pretense of directing the "pursuit" from his desk in Washington. "*Entre nous*," he wrote Sherman on July 16, "I fear Grant has made a fatal mistake in putting himself south of James River. He cannot now reach Richmond without taking Petersburg, which is strongly fortified, crossing the Appomattox, and recrossing the James. Moreover, by placing his army south of Richmond he opens the capital and the whole North to rebel raids. Lee can at any time detach 30,000 to 40,000 men without our knowing it till we are actually threatened. I hope we may yet have full success, but I find that many of Grant's general officers think the campaign already a failure." Old Brains was determined to play no active role in what he saw as a discredited operation, and Grant soon found there was little he himself could do from an even greater distance. One answer might be for him to go up the Potomac and take charge of the stalled pursuit, but the fact was he had problems enough on his hands at Petersburg just then, including Meade's immovability, Burnside's mine, and the presence of Ben Butler, who by virtue of his rank would assume command of all the forces south of the James if Grant went up the country.

Unable to get Butler transferred (though he tried — only to find that this was no time to risk offending a prominent hard-war Democrat who might retaliate by taking the stump against the Administration) Grant turned on his one-time favorite Baldy Smith, who by now, mainly because of what Rawlins called "his disposition to scatter the seeds of discontent throughout the army," had become as much of a thorn in Grant's side as he had been in his cock-eyed superior's all along. On July 19 he was relieved and Major General Edward Ord, in temporary command at Baltimore, was brought down to take charge of his three divisions. Similarly, when the dust of the Crater settled, Burnside was superseded by his long-time chief of staff, Major General John G. Parke. Both of these new corps commanders — Ord was forty-five, a West Pointer like Parke, who was thirty-six — had fought under Grant at Vicksburg, and he was pleased to have them with him, here in front of Petersburg, to help conduct another siege.

None of this improved conditions northwest of Washington, however, and on the last day of July, with the ashes of Chambersburg still warm in that direction, Grant went down the James to Fortress Monroe for a conference with Lincoln about the situation Early had created up the Potomac.

For weeks he had favored merging the separate departments around the capital under a single field commander, though when he suggested his classmate William Franklin for the post — Franklin was conveniently at hand in Philadelphia, home on leave from Louisiana — he was told that the Pennsylvanian "would not give satisfaction," apparently because of his old association with McClellan, which still rankled in certain congressional minds. Rebuffed, Grant then considered giving Meade the job, with Hancock as his successor in command of the Army of the Potomac, but then thought better of it and decided that David Hunter, with his demonstrated talent for destruction, was perhaps the best man for the assignment after all. By the time he got to Fort Monroe on July 31, however, he had changed his mind again, and with the President's concurrence announced his decision next day in a telegram to Halleck: "I want Sheridan put in command of all the troops in the field, with instructions to put himself south of the enemy and follow him to the death."

Back in Washington, Lincoln saw the order two days later, and though he already had approved the policy announced, he was so taken with the message that he felt called upon to wire its author his congratulations — together with a warning. "This, I think, is exactly right as to how our forces should move," he replied, "but please look over the dispatches you may have received from here, even since you made that order, and discover, if you can, [whether] there is any idea in the head of anyone here of 'putting our army south of the enemy' or of 'following him to the death' in any direction. I repeat to you it will neither be done nor attempted unless you watch it every day and hour and force it."

This last was sound advice, and Grant reacted promptly despite his previous reluctance to leave the scene of his main effort. Delaying only long enough to compose a carefully worded note for Butler — "In my absence remain on the defensive," he told him, adding: "Please communicate with me by telegraph if anything occurs where you may wish my orders" — he was on his way down the James within two hours of reading Lincoln's message. In Washington next morning he visited neither the White House nor the War Department, but went instead to the railway station and caught a train for Monocacy Junction, where Hunter had gathered the better part of the 32,500-man force supposed to be in hot pursuit of Early. Grant arrived on August 5 to find him in a state of shock, brought on by having been harassed for more than a month by the rebels and his superiors, who had confused him with conflicting orders and unstrung his nerves with alarmist and misleading information. In any case, his jangled state facilitated the process of removal. Displaying what Grant later called "a patriotism none too common in the army," Hunter readily agreed not only to stand aside for Sheridan, whom he outranked, but also to step down for Crook, who took over his three divisions when he presently departed for more congenial duty in the capital.

Sheridan arrived on August 6, in time for a brief interview with Grant, who also gave him a letter of instructions. Two of his three cavalry divisions had been ordered up from Petersburg, and these, combined with the troops on hand, the Harpers Ferry garrison, and the rest of Emory's corps en route from Louisiana, would give him a total of just over 48,000 effectives: enough, Grant thought, to enable him to handle Jubal Early and any other problem likely to arise as he pressed south toward a reunion with Meade near Richmond, wrecking as he went. He would have to take preliminary time, of course, to acquaint himself with his new duties in an unfamiliar region, as well as to restore some tone to Hunter's winded, footsore men, now under Crook, and to Wright's disgruntled veterans, who had little patience with the mismanagement they had recently undergone. But Grant made it clear — despite protests from Stanton and Halleck, being registered in Washington even now, that the thirty-three-year-old cavalryman was too young for the command of three full corps of infantry — that he looked forward to hearing great things from this direction before long, when Sheridan began to carry out what was set forth in his instructions. "In pushing up the Shenandoah Valley, as it is expected you will have to do first or last," the letter read, "it is desirable that nothing should be left to invite the enemy to return. Take all provisions, forage, and stock wanted for the use of your command. Such as cannot be consumed, destroy. . . . Bear in mind, the object is to drive the enemy south, and to do this you want to keep him always in sight. Be guided in your course by the course he takes."

The interview was brief because Grant was in a hurry to get back down the coast before Lee reached into his bag of tricks and dangled something disastrously attractive in front of Butler's nose. Returning to Washington, he boarded the dispatch steamer that had brought him up Chesapeake Bay four days ago, and stepped ashore at City Point before sunrise, August 9.

His haste came close to costing him his life before the morning ended. Around noon he was sitting in front of his headquarters tent, which was pitched in the yard of a high-sited mansion overlooking the wharves and warehouses of the ordnance supply depot he had established near the confluence of the James and the Appomattox, when suddenly there was the roar of an explosion louder than anything heard in the region since the springing of Pleasants's mine, ten days back. "Such a rain of shot, shell, bullets, pieces of wood, iron bars and bolts, chains and missiles of every kind was never before witnessed. It was terrible — awful — terrific," a staffer wrote home. Grant agreed. "Every part of the yard used as my headquarters is filled with splinters and fragments of shell," he telegraphed Halleck before the smoke had cleared.

By then it was known that an ammunition barge had exploded, along with an undeterminable number of the 20,000 artillery projectiles on its deck and in its hold, though whether by accident or by sabotage was difficult to say, all aboard having died in the blast, which scattered parts of their bodies over a quarter-mile radius and flung more substantial chunks of wreckage twice that far. A canal boat moored alongside, for example, was loaded with cavalry saddles that went flying in every direction, one startled observer said, "like so many big-winged bats." These were nearly as deadly in their flight as the unexploded shells, and contributed to the loss of 43 dead and 126 injured along the docks, while others, killed or wounded on the periphery — including a head-quarters orderly and three members of Grant's staff — nearly doubled both those figures. "The total number killed will never be known," an investigator admitted, though he guessed at "over 200," and it was not until the war ended that the cause of the disaster was established by the discovery of a report by a rebel agent named John Maxwell.

He had stolen through the Union lines the night before, bringing with him a "horological torpedo," as he called the device, a candle box packed with twelve pounds of black powder, a percussion cap, and a clockwork mechanism to set it off. Reaching City Point at daybreak — about the same time Grant arrived — he went down to the wharves to watch for a chance to plant his bomb. It came when he saw the captain of a low-riding ammunition vessel step ashore, apparently intent on business: whereupon the agent set the timer, sealed the box, and delivered it to a member of the crew, with a request from the skipper to "put it down below" till he returned. "The man took it without question," Maxwell declared, "while I went off a little distance." His luck held; for though, as he said, he was "terribly shocked by the explosion," which soon followed, he not only was uninjured by falling debris, he also made it back in safety to the Confederate lines, having accomplished overnight, with a dozen pounds of powder, more damage, both in lives and property, than the Federals had done ten days ago with four tons of the stuff, after a solid month of digging.

Fearful though the damage was — estimates ran to $2,000,000 and beyond — wrecked equipment could be repaired and lost supplies replaced. More alarming, in a different way, was an intelligence report, just in, that Lee had detached Anderson's entire First Corps three days ago, along with Fitz Lee's cavalry, to reinforce Early out in the Valley. If true (which it was not, except in part; Anderson had been detached, but only with Kershaw's, not all three of his infantry divisions) this would give Early close to 40,000 soldiers, veterans to a man; enough, in short, to enable him to overrun Sheridan's disaffected conglomeration for a second crossing of the Potomac, this time with better than twice the strength of the one that had wound up at the gates of Washington last month. As things stood now, Lincoln might or might not survive the November election, but with 40,000 graybacks on the outskirts of the capital, let alone inside it, there was little doubt which way the votes would go. And as the votes went, so went Grant — a hard-war man, unlikely to survive the inauguration of a soft-war President. Promptly he got off a warning to Little Phil that his adversary was being reinforced to an extent that would "put him nearer on an equality with you in numbers than I want to see." What was called for, under the circumstances, was caution: particularly on the part of a young general less than a week in command, whose total strategy up to now could be summarized in his watchword, "Smash 'em up!"

Caution he recommended; caution he got. Sheridan had begun an advance from Halltown, near Harpers Ferry, and had pressed on through Winchester, almost to Strasburg — just beyond which, after cannily fading back, Early had taken up a strong position at Fisher's Hill, inviting attack — when word came on August 14, via Washington, that Anderson was on the way from Richmond, if indeed he had not come up already, with reinforcements that would enable Early to go over to the offensive with close to twice his estimated present strength of better than 20,000 veterans. Little Phil, experiencing for the first time the loneliness of independent command, reacted with a discretion unsuspected in his makeup until now. "I should like very much to have your advice," he wrote Grant, rather plaintively, as he began a withdrawal that presently saw him back at Halltown, within comforting range of the big guns at Harpers Ferry.

Early too returned to his starting point in the Lower Valley, skirmishing with such enemy units as he could persuade to venture beyond reach of the heavy batteries in their rear, and resumed his harassment of the Baltimore & Ohio, threatening all the while to recross the Potomac for another march on the Yankee capital. He had 16,500 men, including detached cavalry, and when Kershaw and Fitz Lee joined him the total came to 23,000: about half the number his adversary enjoyed while backing away from a confrontation. The result was a scathing contempt which Old Jube did not bother to conceal, remarking then and later that Sheridan was not only "without enterprise" but also "possessed an excessive caution which amounted to timidity." As the stand-off continued, on through August and beyond, Early's confidence grew to overconfident proportions. "If it was his policy to produce the impression that he was too weak to fight me, he did not succeed," he said of Little Phil, "but if it was to convince me that he was not an energetic commander, his strategy was a complete success."

Grant meantime had not been long in finding that only one of Anderson's divisions had left the Richmond-Petersburg front; yet he still thought it best for Sheridan to delay his drive up the Valley until pressure from Meade obliged Lee to recall the reinforcements now with Early. Accordingly, he began at once to exert that pressure, first on one bank of the James, pulling the few Confederate reserves in that direction, then the other. Hancock, with his own and one of Butler's corps, plus the remaining cavalry division, was ordered to repeat the northside maneuver he had attempted on the eve of the Crater. This began on August 14, the day Sheridan started to backtrack, and continued on the morrow, but with heavier casualties than before and even less success. Attacking at Deep Bottom Run with hopes of turning the Chaffin's Bluff defenses, Hancock found veterans, not reserves, in occupation of Richmond's outer works, and suffered a repulse. A renewal of the assault next day, just up the line, brought similar results until he called it off, confessing in his report that his men had not behaved well in the affair. His losses were just under 3000, more than three times Lee's, but Grant had him remain in position to distract his opponent's attention from a second offensive, off at the far end of the line.

Warren had the assignment, which was basically to repeat the late-June effort to get astride the Weldon Railroad a couple of miles southwest of where the present Union left overlapped the Jerusalem Plank Road. This time he succeeded. Moving with four divisions on the morning of August 18 he struck the railroad at Globe Tavern, four miles south of Petersburg, and quickly dispossessed the single brigade of cavalry posted in defense of the place while most of the gray infantry

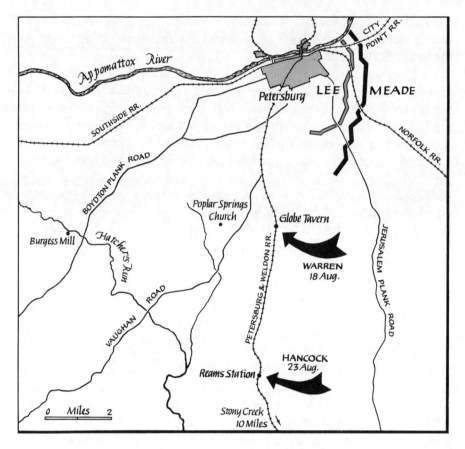

confronted Hancock on the far side of the James. Elated by their success, the attackers pushed north from the tavern, but soon found that holding the road was a good deal harder than breaking it had been. Beauregard counterattacked that afternoon, using such troops as he could scrape together, then more savagely next morning, when A. P. Hill came down with two of his divisions. Warren lost 2700 of his 16,000 men, captured in mass when two brigades were caught off balance in poorly aligned intrenchments, but managed to recover the ground by sundown. That night he fell back to a better position, just over a mile down the line, where he was reinforced for two more days of fighting before the Confederates were willing to admit that they could not dislodge him. His casualties for all four days came to 4500, while the rebel loss was only 1600 — plus of course the Weldon Railroad; or anyhow the final stretch of track. Lee at once put teamsters to work hauling supplies in wagons by a roundabout route from the new terminus at Stony Creek, twenty miles below Petersburg and about half that distance beyond the limits of Federal destruction.

Grant was determined to lengthen this mule-drawn interval, if only to keep up the pressure he hoped would bring Anderson back from the Valley, and when Hancock recrossed the James on August 21 —

the day Lee gave up trying to drive Warren off the railroad — he received orders to proceed south with two of his divisions, plus Gregg's troopers, for a follow-up strike at the vital supply line near Reams Station, about five miles below Globe Tavern and ten above Stony Creek. He reached his objective on August 23, and by the close of the following day had torn up three miles of track beyond it. That night, while resting his wreckers for an extension of their work tomorrow, he learned that A. P. Hill was moving in his direction. Arriving at noon, Little Powell drove in the blue cavalry so fast that the infantry had little time to get set. The main blow fell on three New York regiments, green troops lately assigned to Gibbon's division, some of whom fled, while most surrendered, and to Hancock's further outrage a reserve brigade, ordered into the resultant gap, "could neither be made to go forward nor fire." Before darkness ended the fighting, better than 2000 men here and elsewhere along the Union line chose prison over combat. Two more divisions were on the way as reinforcements, but Hancock decided not to wait for them and instead pulled out that night. He had lost 2750 killed or wounded or missing, along with nine guns, a dozen battle flags, and well over 3000 rifles abandoned on the field. Hill's loss was 720.

This came hard for Hancock — "Hancock the Superb," newsmen had called him ever since the Seven Days; *Hancock*, who had broken Pickett's Charge, stood firm amid the chaos of the Wilderness, and cracked the Bloody Angle at Spotsylvania — as well as for his veteran lieutenants, especially John Gibbon, former commander of the Iron Brigade, whose division had been considered one of the best in the whole army until it was bled down to skeleton proportions and then fleshed out with skulkers finally netted by the draft. Ashamed and angered, Gibbon submitted his resignation, then was persuaded to withdraw it, though he presently left both his division and the corps: the hard-driving II Corps, which had taken more than forty enemy colors before it lost one of its own, and then abandoned or surrendered twelve of these in a single day at Reams Station, August 25. After that, even Grant was obliged to admit that its three divisions were unfit for use on the offensive, now and for some time to come, and Hancock's adjutant later said of his chief's reaction to the blow: "The agony of that day never passed from that proud soldier, who for the first time, in spite of superhuman exertions and reckless exposure on his part, saw his lines broken and his guns taken."

Back at Petersburg next day, Hill was pleased but not correspondingly elated, having done this sort of thing many times before, under happier circumstances. Moreover, it was much the same for Lee, who saw deeper into the matter. A month ago, in a letter to one of his sons, he had said of Grant, with a touch of aspersion: "His talent and strategy consists in accumulating overwhelming numbers." Now he was faced with the product of that blunt, inelegant strategy — that "talent" — which included not only the loss of the final stretch of the Weldon Railroad, but also the necessity for extending his undermanned Petersburg works another two miles westward to match the resultant Federal extension beyond Globe Tavern.

Of the two problems thus posed for him, the first might seem more irksome at the moment, coming as it did at a time when the army's reserve supply of corn was near exhaustion; but the second was potentially the graver. For while there were other railroads to bring grain from coastal Georgia and the Carolinas — the Southside line, on this bank of the Appomattox, and the Richmond & Danville, coming down from beyond the James for an intersection at Burkeville — the accustomed influx of recruits from those and other regions had dwindled to a trickle. Lee could scarcely replace his losses, let alone avoid the thinning of a line already stretched just short of snapping. "Without some increase of our strength," he warned Seddon, even as Hill was moving against Hancock, "I cannot see how we are to escape the natural military consequences of the enemy's numerical superiority." Ten days later he reviewed the situation in a letter to the President, stressing "the importance of immediate and vigorous measures to increase the strength of our armies. . . . The necessity is now great," he said, "and will soon be augmented by the results of the coming draft in the United States. As matters now stand, we have no troops disposable to meet movements of the enemy or to strike where opportunity presents, without taking them from the trenches and exposing some important point. The enemy's position enables him to move his troops to the right or left without our knowledge, until he has reached the point at which he aims, and we are then compelled to hurry our men to meet him, incurring the risk of being too late to check his progress and the additional risk of the advantage he may derive from their absence. This was fully illustrated in the late demonstration north of James River, which called troops from our lines here, who if present might have prevented the occupation of the Weldon Railroad."

Across the way, at City Point, admonitions flowed in the opposite direction. Halleck warned Grant in mid-August that draft riots were likely to occur at any time in New York and Pennsylvania, as well as in Indiana and Kentucky: in which case he would be called upon, as Meade had been last summer, to furnish troops to put them down. Anticipating such troubles between now and the election in November, Old Brains suggested it might be well for the army to avoid commitment to any operation it could not discontinue on short notice. "Are not the appearances such that we ought to take in sail and prepare the ship for a storm?" he asked.

Grant thought not, and said so. Such police work should be left for the various governors to handle with militia, which should be called out now for the purpose. "If we are to draw troops from the field to keep the loyal states in harness," he declared, "it will prove difficult to suppress the rebellion in the disloyal states." Besides, he added, to ease the pressure on Lee at Petersburg and Richmond would be to allow him to reinforce Hood at Atlanta, just as he had reinforced Bragg at Chickamauga a year ago this month, and that "would insure the defeat of Sherman." In short, Grant had no intention of relaxing his effort on either bank of the James, whatever civilian troubles might develop up the country in his rear.

Lincoln read this reply on August 17 and promptly telegraphed approval. "I have seen your dispatch expressing your unwillingness to break your hold where you are. Neither am I willing. Hold on with a bulldog grip, and chew and choke as much as possible."

Scanning the words at his headquarters overlooking City Point, Grant laughed aloud — a thing he seldom did — and when staffers came over to see what had amused him so, passed them the message to read. "The President has more nerve than any of his advisers," he said.

Nerve was one thing, hope another, and Lincoln was fast running out of that: not so much because of the current military situation — though in point of fact this was glum enough, on the face of it, with Meade and Sherman apparently stalled outside Petersburg and Atlanta, Forrest rampant in Memphis, and the *Tallahassee* about to light up the New England coast with burning merchantmen — as in regard to his own political survival, which was seen on all sides as unlikely, especially in view of what had happened this month in his native Kentucky despite some highly irregular efforts to forestall defeat for a party that soon was still worse split by the Wade-Davis Manifesto. Six days after his chew-and-choke message to Grant, and six days before the Democrats were scheduled to convene in Chicago to nominate his November opponent — a time, he would say, "when as yet we had no adversary, and seemed to have no friends" — Lincoln sat in his office reading the morning mail. Thurlow Weed, an expert on such matters, recently had informed him that his reëlection was impossible, the electorate being "wild for peace." Now there came a letter from Henry J. Raymond, editor of the friendly *New York Times* and chairman of the Republican National Executive Committee, who said much the same thing.

"I feel compelled to drop you a line," he wrote, "concerning the political condition of the country as it strikes me. I am in active correspondence with your staunchest friends in every state, and from them all I hear but one report. The tide is setting strongly against us." Oliver Morton, Simon Cameron, and Elihu Washburne had respectively warned the New Yorker that Indiana, Pennsylvania, and Illinois were probably lost by now. Moreover, he told Lincoln, he was convinced that his own state "would go 50,000 against us tomorrow. And so of the rest. Nothing but the most resolute action on the part of the government and its friends can save the country from falling into hostile hands. . . . In some way or other the suspicion is widely diffused that we can have peace with Union if we would. It is idle to reason with this belief — still more idle to denounce it. It can only be expelled by some authoritative act, at once bold enough to fix attention and distinct enough to defy incredulity and challenge respect."

What Raymond had in mind was another peace commission, armed with terms whose rejection by Richmond would "unite the North as nothing since the firing on Fort Sumter has hitherto done." Lincoln knew only too well how little was apt to come of this, having tried it twice in the past month, and was correspondingly depressed. If this was all that could save the election he was whipped already. Sadly he took a sheet of paper from his desk and composed a memorandum.

> Executive Mansion
> Washington, Aug. 23, 1864
> This morning, as for some days past, it seems exceedingly probable that this Administration will not be reëlected. Then it will be my duty to so coöperate with the President-elect as to save the Union between the election and the inauguration; as he will have secured his election on such ground that he cannot possibly save it afterwards.
> A. LINCOLN

He folded the sheet, glued it shut, and took it with him to the midday cabinet meeting, where, without so much as a hint as to the subject covered, he had each member sign it on the back, in blind attestation to whatever it might contain — a strange procedure but a necessary precaution, since to tell them what was in the memorandum would be to risk increasing the odds against his reëlection by having it spread all over Washington, by sundown, that he himself had predicted his defeat. "In this peculiar fashion," his two secretaries later explained, "he pledged himself and the Administration" (so far, at least, as the pledge was binding: which was mainly on himself, since he alone knew the words behind the seal) "to accept loyally the anticipated verdict of the people against him, and to do their utmost to save the Union in the brief remainder of his term of office."

Not that he did not intend to do all he could, despite the odds, in the eleven weeks between now and the day the issue would be settled. Treading softly where he felt he must, and firmly where he didn't, he attended to such iotas as recommending in advance to field commanders that Indiana soldiers, who were required by law to be present to cast their ballots, be given furloughs in October to go home and offset the pacifist vote in their state election, considered important as a forecast of what to expect across the nation in November and as an influence on those whose main concern was that their choice be a winner. Besides, he foresaw trouble for his opponents once they came out in the open, where he had spent the past four years, a target for whatever mud was flung. The old Democratic rift, which had made him President in the first place, was even wider than it had been four years ago, except that now the burning issue was the war itself, not just slavery, which many said had caused it, and Lincoln expected the rift to widen further when a platform was adopted and a candidate named to stand on it. The front runner was Major General George B. McClellan, who was expected to attract the soldier vote, although numbers of Democrats were saying they would accept no candidate "with the smell of war on his garments." Either way, as Lincoln saw the outcome, platform and man were likely to be mismatched, with the result that half the opposition would be disappointed with one or the other, perhaps to the extent of bolting or abstaining when Election Day came round. "They must nominate a Peace Democrat on a war platform, or a War Democrat on a peace platform," he told a friend who left that weekend for the convention in his home state, "and I personally can't say I care much which they do."

He was right. Convening in Chicago on August 29, in a new pine Wigwam like the one set up for the Republicans in 1860, the Democrats heard New York's Governor Horatio Seymour establish the tone in a keynote speech delivered on taking the gavel as permanent chairman. "The Administration cannot save the Union. We can. Mr Lincoln views many things above the Union. We put the Union first of all. He thinks a proclamation more than peace. We think the blood of our people more precious than edicts of the President." After this, the assembly got down to adopting a platform framed in part by Clement L. Vallandigham, the nation's leading Copperhead and chairman of the Resolutions Committee, who had returned last year from presidential banishment, first beyond the rebel lines, then back by way of Canada, to run unsuccessfully for governor of Ohio. The former congressman's hand was most apparent in the peace plank, which resolved: "That this convention does explicitly declare, as the sense of the American people, that after four years of failure to restore the Union by the experiment of war . . . justice, humanity, liberty, and the public welfare demand that immediate efforts be made for a cessation of hostilities, with a view to an ultimate convention of the States, or other peaceable means, to the end that at the earliest practicable moment peace may be restored on the basis of the Federal Union of the States."

The stress here, as in Seymour's keynote speech, was on achieving peace through restoration of the Union, not "at any price," as was claimed by hostile critics. Vallandigham had emphasized this on the eve of the convention, saying: "Whoever charges that I want to stop this war in order that there may be Southern independence charges that which is false, and lies in his teeth, and lies in his throat!" But presently the nominee himself lent strength to the charge by repudiating the plank in question. It was McClellan, as expected; he was chosen by acclaim on the first ballot, with Congressman George H. Pendleton of Ohio, long an advocate of negotiated peace, as his running mate. Ten days after his nomination — a delay that prompted a Republican wit to remark in the interim that Little Mac was "about as slow in getting up on the platform as he was in taking Richmond" — he tendered the notification committee his letter of acceptance. "I could not look in the face of my gallant comrades of the army and navy who have survived so many bloody battles," he declared, "and tell them that their labors and the sacrifices of so many of our slain and wounded brethren have been in vain, that we had abandoned that Union for which we have so often periled our lives. A vast majority of our people, whether in the army and navy or at home, would, as I would, hail with unbounded joy the permanent restoration of peace, on the basis of the Union under the Constitution, without the effusion of another drop of blood. But no peace can be permanent without Union."

Thus McClellan sought to deal with the dilemma Lincoln had foreseen, and wound up infuriating the faction that admired what he rejected: as Lincoln also had foreseen. But that was not as important by then as it had seemed the week before, when the charge that the "experiment of war" had been a failure, East and West, was one that could perhaps be contested but could scarcely be refuted in the face of evidence from practically every front. Aside from Farragut's coup in Mobile Bay — seen now as rather a one-man show, with the credit all his own — incredible casualties had produced only stalemates or reverses, whether out in North Mississippi, down around Richmond and Atlanta, or up in the Shenandoah Valley. United in their anticipation of victory at the polls in November, whatever internal troubles racked the party, the Democrats adjourned on August 31, having wound up their business in jig time. Then two days later fate intervened, or seemed to. Slocum's wire reached Washington on September 2, followed next day by Sherman's own: "Atlanta is ours, and fairly won."

Church bells rang across the land as they had not rung since the fall of Vicksburg, fourteen months ago. "Sherman and Farragut have knocked the bottom out of the Chicago platform," Seward exulted, and Lincoln promptly tendered "national thanks" to the general and the admiral, issuing at the same time a Proclamation of Thanksgiving and Prayer, to be offered in all churches the following Sunday, for "the glorious achievements" of the army and the navy at Atlanta and in Mobile Bay. Grant too rejoiced, and telegraphed Sherman next day: "In honor of your great victory, I have ordered a salute to be fired with *shotted* guns from every battery bearing upon the enemy." Within earshot of that cannonade, the editor of the Richmond *Examiner* spoke of "disaster at Atlanta in the very nick of time when a victory alone could save the party of Lincoln from irretrievable ruin.... It will obscure the prospect of peace, late so bright. It will also diffuse gloom over the South."

Gladdened by congratulations from all sides, including some from political associates who he knew had been about to desert what they had thought was a sinking ship, Lincoln enjoyed the taste of victory so well that it made him hungry for still more. "Sheridan and Early are facing each other at a deadlock," he wired Grant on September 12. "Could we not pick up a regiment here and there, to the number of say ten thousand men, and quietly but suddenly concentrate them at Sheridan's camp and enable him to make a strike? This is but a suggestion." A suggestion was enough. Grant replied next day that he had been intending for a week "to see Sheridan and arrange what was necessary to enable him to start Early out of the Valley. It seems to me it can successfully be done." Content to have Meade in charge while he was gone — Butler was conveniently on leave — he set out the following day on his second trip up the Potomac in six weeks. Once more without stopping in Washington, he reached Sheridan's headquarters near Harpers Ferry on September 16.

"That's Grant," a veteran sergeant told a comrade, pointing him out. "I hate to see that old cuss around. When that old cuss is around there's sure to be a big fight on hand."

This applied even more to the present visit than to most, since Grant had in his pocket a plan for a campaign to drive Early all the way to Richmond, destroying first the Shenandoah Valley and then the Virginia Central Railroad in his wake. However, he was not long in finding that Little Phil had plans of his own which he was anxious to place in execution, having received from a spy in Winchester, just that morning, word that the time was ripe for an advance. A Quaker schoolteacher, Rebecca Wright by name, had smuggled out a note, wrapped in tinfoil and cached in the mouth of a Negro messenger, informing him that Anderson had left the Valley two days ago, with Kershaw's division and three batteries of artillery, recalled by Lee to help meet the stepped-up pressure from Meade on both sides of the James. What was more, Early — encouraged, as Lee had been in withdrawing the reinforcements, by his opponent's apparent quiescence under cover of the guns on Bolivar Heights for the past month — had posted three of his four infantry divisions in scattered positions above Winchester, toward the Potomac, to promote the fear that he was about to take the offensive with many more troops than the 18,000 or so which Sheridan now knew were all he had. Sheridan's plan was to use his field force of 40,000 not merely to drive Early from the Valley but to annihilate him by attacking his lone division at Winchester, then moving over or around it to cut off the escape of the rest up the Valley Turnpike.

Grant heard the ebullient young general out, and finding him "so

clear and so positive in his views, and so confident of success," said nothing about the plan that remained in his pocket. Instead — today was
Friday — he asked if the whole blue force could be ready to move by
Tuesday. Sheridan replied that, subject to Grant's approval, he intended
to take up the march before daybreak Monday, September 19. Grant
thought this over, then nodded and issued his briefest order of the war:
"Go in."

He left next morning, and though he still avoided Washington he
managed a side excursion to Burlington, New Jersey, where his wife had
taken a house after coming East. That night and part of Sunday he spent
with her and the children, then returned to City Point on Monday, hoping for news of the Valley offensive, which had been scheduled to open
that morning. Delayed by breakdowns, Sheridan's wire did not arrive
till the following day, but when it did it more than justified the buildup
of suspense. Headed "Winchester, 7.30 p.m." — itself a confirmation of
success — the telegram read: "I have the honor to report that I attacked
the forces of General Early on the Berryville pike at the crossing of

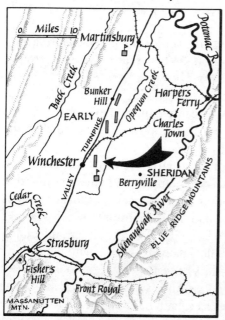

Opequon Creek, and after a
most stubborn and sanguinary
engagement, which lasted from
early in the morning until 5
o'clock in the evening, completely defeated him." There
followed a list of their losses,
including "2500 prisoners, five
pieces of artillery, nine army
flags, and most of their
wounded," but a companion
message, written in greater heat
by his chief of staff, better caught
the public's fancy, being quoted
in all the papers: "We have just
sent them whirling through
Winchester, and we are after
them tomorrow. This army behaved splendidly."

Actually, there had been a good deal more to it than that. For one
thing, Sheridan's loss was considerably heavier than Early's — just over
5000 killed, wounded, or missing, as compared to just under 4000 — and
for another, despite his achievement of surprise at the outset, he had
come close to getting whipped before he got rolling. On the approach
march, against orders, Wright brought his corps train along, old-army
style, which so clogged the Berryville Pike in his rear that Emory was
unable to cross Opequon Creek in time to join the dawn assault on
Ramseur's division and Fitz Lee's troopers, posted three miles east of

Winchester. Ramseur alternately held his position and withdrew slowly, in good order, and thus not only gave Early time to call in his other three infantry divisions, six to ten miles north of town, but also enabled him to launch a counterattack by Gordon and Rodes when Emory came up around midmorning, led onto the field by Sheridan himself, who, in a rage at the delay, had ordered Wright's wagons flung into ditches to clear the pike. Here fell Robert Rodes, the tall blond Virginia-born Alabamian who had led Jackson's flank attack at Chancellorsville, thirty-five years old and a veteran of all the army's major battles, from First Manassas on. Shot from his horse while directing the charge into the breach between Emory and Wright, he did not live to see it healed by the latter's reserves when they arrived. Emory, badly shaken — he had finished at West Point in 1831, the year Sheridan was born — had to be reinforced by Crook, whose two divisions had been intended for use in a flanking effort to block the path of a Confederate escape. Still, as the fight continued the weight of numbers told. Early, with some 14,000 men on hand, gave ground steadily all afternoon, under pressure from Sheridan's 38,000, and finally, about 5 o'clock, fell back through the streets of the town and retreated up the Valley Turnpike, which Fitz Lee's horsemen managed to keep open although Fitz himself had had to retire from the conflict, pinked in the thigh by a stray bullet. The battle — called Third Winchester by the defenders and Opequon Creek by the attackers — was over. Early did not stop till he reached Fisher's Hill, beyond Strasburg, twenty miles to the south, where Sheridan had ended his advance the month before, preceding his with-drawal to Harpers Ferry.

Grant's response next day was threefold. Wiring Stanton a rec-ommendation that Sheridan be rewarded with a promotion to regular-army brigadier (which was promptly conferred) he also ordered the firing of a hundred-gun celebration salute in front of Richmond, just as he had done two weeks ago in Sherman's honor, and telegraphed Sheridan his congratulations for "your great victory," adding: "If practicable, push your success and make all you can of it."

Sheridan — whose 5018 casualties, though more than a thousand heavier than Early's 3921, had cost him only an eighth of his command, whereas Early had lost a solid fourth — intended to do just that. Late next day, with a force that was now three times the size of the one he was pursuing, he called a halt near Strasburg, advancing two corps across Cedar Creek and holding the third in reserve while he went for-ward to study the rebel position, two miles beyond the town. He found it quite as formidable as it had been six weeks ago, when he had de-clined to test its strength.

Massanutton Mountain, looming dead ahead between the sun-glinted forks of the Shenandoah, divided the Valley into two smaller valleys: Luray on the left, beyond Front Royal, and what remained of the main valley on the right, narrowed at this point to a width of about four miles between the North Fork of the Shenandoah River and Little North Mountain, a spur of the Alleghenies. His flanks anchored east and west on the river and the mountain, Early also enjoyed the advantage of high ground overlooking a boggy stream called Tumbling Run, which the Federals would have to cross, under fire from massed artillery and small arms, if they were to attack him from the front. Down to fewer than 10,000 effectives as a result of his battle losses and the need for detaching two of Fitz Lee's three brigades to hold the midway notch in Massanutton (lest Sheridan send part of his superior force up the Luray Valley for a crossing there to get astride the turnpike at New Market, twenty miles in the Confederate rear) Early had to dismount troops from his other cavalry division, under Lunsford Lomax — most of whom had arrived too late for yesterday's fight, having been involved in railroad wrecking around Martinsburg, some fifty miles to the north — to man the western extension of his four-mile line to the lower slopes of Little North Mountain. Although the Winchester defeat had gone far toward disabusing him of the notion that his opponent "possessed an excessive caution which amounted to timidity," he had confidence in the natural strength of his position on Fisher's Hill, as well as in the veterans who held it, and believed that the bluecoats had little choice except to come at him head-on, in which case they were sure to be repulsed.

He was mistaken: grievously mistaken, as it turned out. Sheridan intended to approach him only in part from the front, using Wright's three and Emory's two divisions to fix him in place while Crook's two, kept hidden in reserve, made a flanking march, under cover of Little North Mountain, for a surprise descent on the Confederate left — where Early, expecting an assault on his right center, had posted his least dependable troops. All next day this misconception was encouraged by the sight of heavy blue columns filing through Strasburg, down toward Tumbling Run. Moreover, here as at Winchester two days ago, Little Phil intended to do more than merely whip or wreck his adversary; he planned to bag him entirely, and with this in mind he detached two of his three cavalry divisions, under Torbert, for a fast ride up Luray Valley and across Massanutton Mountain, through the midway notch in its knife-edge crest, to get control of the Valley Turnpike at New Market and thus prevent the escape of such gray fugitives as managed to slip through the net he would fling over Fisher's Hill tomorrow.

Crook set out before dawn, September 22, marching with flags and guidons trailed to keep them from being spotted by butternut lookouts while he rounded the wooded upper slopes of Little North Mountain, beyond the rebel left. Wright and Emory began their frontal demonstration after sunup, banging away with all their guns and bristling along Tumbling Run, as if about to splash across at any moment. This was a drawn-out business, continuing well past midday, since Crook's West Virginians — so-called because that was where they had done most of their fighting until now, though in fact they were in large part from Ohio, with a sprinkling of Pennsylvanians and New Yorkers thrown in to leaven or "easternize" the lump — had a long hard way to travel, much of it uphill. Finally at 4 o'clock, twelve hours after they set out, they struck.

"Flanked! Outflanked!" the cry went up on Early's left as the dismounted horsemen he had scorned from the outset, calling them buttermilk rangers and worse, fled before the onslaught of Crook, whose two divisions came whooping down the mountainside to strike them flank and rear. Eastward along Fisher's Hill, where the defenders had begun to remark that Sheridan must have lost his nerve and called off the attack he had been threatening all day, the confusion spread when Wright's corps joined the melee, advancing division by division across Tumbling Run as the gray line crumbled unit by unit from the shattered left. Fearful of being trapped in the angle between river and run, they too bolted, leaving the teamless cannoneers to slow the blue advance while they themselves took off, first down the rearward slope, then southward up the turnpike.

"Forward! Forward everything!" Sheridan yelled, coursing the field on his black charger and gesturing with his flat-topped hat for emphasis. "Don't stop! Go on!" he shouted as his infantry overran and captured twelve of the guns on Fisher's Hill.

Anticipating "results still more pregnant," he counted on Averell, whose division he presently launched in pursuit of the rebels fleeing through the twilight, to complete the Cannae he had had in mind when he sent Torbert with two divisions up the Luray Valley for a crossing of Massanutton to cut off Early's retreat at New Market. Alas, both cavalry generals failed him utterly in the crunch. Torbert came upon Fitz Lee's two brigades, posted in defense of a narrow gorge twelve miles beyond Front Royal, and decided there was nothing to be gained from being reckless. He withdrew without attempting a dislodgment. Sheridan was "astonished and chagrined" when he heard of this next morning. But his anger at Torbert was mild compared to what came over him when he learned that Averell had put his troopers into bivouac the night before to spare them the risk of attacking Early's rear guard in the darkness. Enraged, Little Phil fired off a message informing the cavalryman that he expected "resolution and actual fighting, with necessary casualties, before you retire. There must be no more backing and filling," he fumed, and when Averell did no better today, despite this blistering, he relieved him of command and sent him forthwith back to West Virginia, "there to await orders from these headquarters or higher authority."

By that time Early had cleared New Market, and though Sheridan kept up the pursuit beyond Harrisonburg, where the graybacks turned off eastward around the head of Massanutton to find shelter near one of the Blue Ridge passes a dozen miles southeast of Staunton, he had to be content with what he had won at Fisher's Hill and picked up along the turnpike afterwards. This included four additional guns, which brought the total to sixteen, and more than a thousand prisoners. Early's over-all loss, in the battle and on the retreat, was about 1400 killed, wounded, and missing; Sheridan's came to 528.

Gratifying as the comparison was, another was even more so. When Sheridan took over Hunter's frazzled command at Monocacy eight weeks ago, the rebs were bristling along the upper Potomac, as if their descent on Washington the month before had been no more than a rehearsal for a heavier blow. Now they were a hundred miles from that river, and it seemed doubtful they would ever return to its banks, so complete had been his triumph this past week, first near Winchester and then, three days later, at Fisher's Hill. "Better still," Grant replied to his protégé's announcement of the second of these victories, "it wipes out much of the stain upon our arms by previous disasters in that locality. May your good work continue is now the prayer of all loyal men."

Exultation flared among Lincoln supporters, whose number had grown considerably in the course of the three-week September span that opened with news of Atlanta's fall and closed with this pair of Shenandoah victories to balance the tally East and West. The candidate himself was in "a more gleeful humor," friends testified after visits to the White House. "Jordan has been a hard road to travel," he told one caller, "but I feel now that, notwithstanding the enemies I have made and the faults I have committed, I'll be dumped on the right side of that stream."

Abrupt though it was, he had cause for this change in mood from gloom to glee. Within two weeks of his August 23 pledge-prediction, countersigned blindly by the cabinet as a prelude to defeat, the news from Sherman down in Georgia produced a scurry by disaffected Jacobins to get back aboard the bandwagon: especially after the mid-September elections in Maine and Vermont showed the party not only holding its own, contrary to pre-Atlanta expectations, but also registering a slight gain. These straws in the wind grew more substantial with the announcement of Sheridan's triumphal march up the Valley. Salmon Chase paid his respects at the White House, then left to take the stump in Ohio, Vallandigham's stamping ground, while Horace Greeley, privately declaring that he intended to "fight like a savage in this campaign — I hate McClellan," he explained — announced that the *Tribune* would "henceforth fly the banner of Abraham Lincoln for President." Even Ben Wade and Henry Davis, whose early-August manifesto had sought to check what they called his "encroachments," took to the stump, like Chase, in support of the very monster they had spent the past two months attacking, though they maintained a measure of consistency by spending so much of their time excoriating the Democratic nominee that they had little left for praise in the other direction. "To save the nation," Wade told a colleague in explanation of his support for a leader he despised, "I am doing all for *him* that I could possibly do for a better man."

Meantime Lincoln, no doubt as amused as he was gratified by these political somersaults, did not neglect the particulars incident to victory and available to the candidate in office. Patronage and contracts were awarded to those who could do most for the party, and a binding promise went to James Gordon Bennett that he would be appointed Minister to France in exchange for his support in the New York *Herald.* There remained the thorny problem of Frémont, whose continuation in the race threatened to siphon off a critical number of die-hard radical voters. These had long been calling for the removal of Montgomery Blair, whose presence in the cabinet they considered an affront, and though Lincoln, aware that his compliance would be interpreted as an act of desperation, had resisted their demand for the Postmaster General's removal, now that Atlanta had turned the tide he felt willing to be persuaded: provided, that is, he got something commensurate in exchange.

The something in this case was Frémont's withdrawal, and he got it without having to drop the pretense of unwillingness he had kept up all along. "The President was most reluctant to come to terms, *but came,*" Zachariah Chandler informed his wife after serving as go-between in the bargain. On September 22 — by coincidence, the day Sheridan hustled Early off Fisher's Hill — Frémont renounced his candidacy. "The union of the Republican Party has become a paramount necessity," he explained in his announcement of withdrawal, but he added, by way of a backhand lick in parting: "In respect to Mr Lincoln I continue to hold exactly the sentiments contained in my letter of acceptance. I consider that his administration has been politically, militarily, and financially a failure, and that its necessary continuance is a cause of regret for the country."

Blair's head rolled next day. "My dear Sir," Lincoln wrote him: "You have generously said to me more than once that whenever your resignation could be a relief to me it was at my disposal. The time has come." There followed compliments and thanks, if not regrets. Blair saw clearly enough that he was in fact "a peace offering to Frémont and his friends." The thought rankled. "The President has, I think, given himself, and me too, an unnecessary mortification in this matter," he wrote his wife before clearing out his desk, "but then I am not the best judge and I am sure he acts from the best motives." A good party man, like all the Blairs, he soon was out wooing voters for the chief who had let him go when bargain time came round.

While this high-level politicking was in progress up the country, Grant tried another pendulum strike at opposite ends of Lee's line, first north then south of the James. Encouraged by news from the Valley, which seemed to show what determination could accomplish, he was also provoked by a mid-September coup the rebel cavalry scored at his expense. On Coggins Point, six miles downriver from his head-quarters, a large herd of cattle awaited slaughter for Meade's army; or so it was thought until a rustling operation, dubbed "Hampton's Cattle Raid," caused the beef to wind up in stomachs unaccustomed to such fare. Hampton set out with three brigades on a wide swing around the Union left, September 14, and reached his objective before dawn two days later. Two brigades fought a holding action, hard in the Federal rear, while the third rounded up the animals on Coggins Point; then all three turned drovers and rode back into their own lines next day with just over 300 prisoners and just under 2500 beeves, at a cost of fewer than 60 casualties. Lee's veterans were feasting on Yankee beef by the time Grant returned from his Harpers Ferry conference with Sheridan to find that in his absence, and to his outrage, the graybacks had foraged profitably half a dozen miles in rear of City Point. Determined to avenge this indignity — and aware, as well, that the year was about to move into the final month before the national election, still without the main eastern army having chalked up a gain to compare with those scored recently in Georgia and the nearby Shenandoah Valley — he told Meade to pro-ceed with another of those sequential right-left strikes, such as he had attempted twice in the past month, designed to throw Lee off balance and overrun at least a portion of his works.

Both times before, the initial attack north of the James had been made by Hancock, but his corps by now was practically *hors de combat* as a result of these and other efforts there and elsewhere. So this time the assignment went to Butler. Presumably refreshed by his recent leave, the Massachusetts general drew up a plan whereby 20,000 men from Kautz's cavalry and the two corps of infantry under Ord and David Birney — successors to the disgruntled and departed Baldy Smith and Quincy Gillmore — crossed the river on the night of September 28 for a double-pronged assault on Forts Harrison and Gilmer, works that were part of Richmond's outer line, down near the James, and covered Lee's critical Chaffin's Bluff defenses. Ord, coming up on schedule through a heavy morning fog, launched an all-out attack which quickly overran the first of these, a mile beyond the river, along with its surprised and meager garrison, though at the cost of a crippling wound that caused him to be carried off the field. Alerted by the racket, just over a mile away, the defenders of Fort Gilmer were ready when Birney struck. Repulsed, he drew back and struck again, with help from Ord, only to find that the place had been reinforced from Richmond, where the tocsin still was sounding. Grant arrived that afternoon to order still a third assault, which was also unsuccessful, and the effort here was abandoned in favor of bracing Fort Harrison against Lee's expected attempt to retake it. This came next day, September 30, when two gray divisions and part of a third, 10,000 men in all, came over from Petersburg under Richard Anderson to make three desperate attacks, all of which failed. Butler's loss for the two days was 3327 of all arms. Lee's was about 2000; plus the fort.

This last was no great deprivation. Lee promptly drew a retrenchment in rear of Fort Harrison, still beyond small-arms range of Chaffin's Bluff, that resulted in a stronger line than the one laid out before. Still, Ben Butler had provided northern journalists with an item fit for crowing over, and best of all — potentially at least — Lee once more had been decoyed into stripping that portion of his defenses where the main blue effort was about to land, off beyond the far end of the long curve of intrenchments south of the James.

Warren and Parke, with two divisions each and Gregg's cavalry in support, set out westward from Globe Tavern while Butler's assault on the forts was in progress. Their mission was to cut, and if possible hold, both the Boydton Plank Road and the Southside Railroad, the two remaining arteries whose severance would bring on the collapse of Petersburg. They were stopped next day along Vaughan Road, less than halfway to the first of these objectives, by Hampton, who skirmished with Warren's column at Poplar Springs Church. Moving west to meet the threat with two divisions from the Petersburg defenses — already weakened by the detachment of Anderson for the attempt to retake Fort Harrison that same day — A. P. Hill encountered Parke at nearby Peebles Farm. Badly shot up, Parke managed to hang on until Warren sent reinforcements to help him hold his ground along Squirrel Level Road, where both corps dug in at nightfall. That was the limit of their lateral advance, and it cost them 2889 casualties, all told, as compared to about 900 for Hill and Hampton. With scarcely a pause for rest, the Federals got busy with picks and shovels, constructing a line of intrenchments from their new position, back east to Globe Tavern, two miles away on the Weldon Railroad. Lee, of course, was obliged to conform, extending once more the length of line his dwindling army had to cover to keep its flank from being turned.

By ordinary standards, Grant's gain in this third of his pendulum strikes at the Richmond-Petersburg defenses — a rather useless rebel earthwork, one mile north of the James, plus a brief stretch of country road, two miles beyond the previous western limit of his line — was incommensurate with his loss of just over 6000 men, a solid half of them captives already on their way to finish out the struggle in Deep

South prison camps, as compared to just under 3000 for Lee, most of them wounded and soon to return to the gray ranks. But with the presidential contest barely five weeks off, this was no ordinary juncture. Ordinary standards did not apply. What did apply was that Lincoln supporters now had something they could point to, down around the Confederate seat of government itself, which seemed to indicate, along with recent developments in Atlanta and the Shenandoah Valley, that the war was by no means the failure it had been pronounced by the opposition in Chicago, five weeks back.

In recognition of this, Democrats lately had shifted their emphasis from the conduct to the nature of the war; "The Constitution as it is, the Union as it was," was now their cry. How effective this would prove was not yet known, for all its satisfying ring. But the evidence from Pennsylvania, Ohio, and Indiana, all of which held their state and congressional elections on October 11, was far from encouraging to those who were out of power and wanted in. With help from Sherman, who at Lincoln's urging not only granted furloughs wholesale to members of the twenty-nine Hoosier regiments in his army down in Georgia, but also sent John A. Logan and Frank Blair with them on electioneering duty, all three states registered gains for the Union ticket, both in Congress and at home.

"There is not, now, the slightest uncertainty about the reëlection of Mr Lincoln. The only question is, by what popular and what electoral majority?" Chase had told a friend in Ohio the week before, and once the ballots were tallied in these three states — all considered spheres of Copperhead influence — *Harper's Weekly* was quick to agree with the former Treasury head's assessment: "The October elections show that unless all human foresight fails, the election of Abraham Lincoln and Andrew Johnson is assured."

Neither of these nominees campaigned openly, any more than McClellan or Pendleton did, but their supporters around the country — men of various and sometimes awesome talents, such as the stout-lunged New Orleans orator, who "when he got fairly warmed up," one listener declared, "spoke so loud it was quite impossible to hear him" — more than made up for this traditional inactivity, which was designed to match the dignity of offices too lofty to be sought. Behind the scenes, other friends were active, too; especially those on the Union executive committee, responsible for funding the campaign. Cabinet members were assessed $250 each for the party coffers, and a levy of five percent was taken from the salaries of underlings in the War, Treasury, and Post Office departments. Gideon Welles alone refused to go along with this, pronouncing the collectors "a set of harpies and adventurers [who] pocket a large portion of the money extorted," and though workers in the Brooklyn Navy Yard "walked the plank in scores" for demonstrating support or sympathy for the opposition, Welles was by no means as active in this regard as Edwin Stanton, who at a swoop fired thirty War Department clerks for the same cause, including one whose sole offense was that he let it be known he had placed a bet on Little Mac. Such methods had produced excellent results in the recent state elections, held four weeks, to the day, before the national finale, scheduled for November 8, when still better returns were not only hoped for but expected, as the result of yet a third Sheridan-Early confrontation, providentially staged within three weeks of that all-important first Tuesday following the first Monday in November.

After Fisher's Hill, Sheridan's progress southward up the Valley — described by a VI Corps veteran as "a grand triumphal pursuit of a routed enemy" — ended at Mount Crawford, beyond the loom of Massanutton, where he gave his three infantry corps some rest while the cavalry raided Staunton and Waynesboro, a day's march ahead on the Virginia Central. Grant wanted the whole force, horse and foot, to move in that direction and down that railroad for a junction with Meade, wrecking Lee's northside supply lines as it went. "Keep on," he wired, "and your good work will cause the fall of Richmond." But Sheridan, with Hunter's unhappy example before him — not to mention that of bluff John Pope, who had tried such a movement two years ago, only to wind up riding herd on Indians out in Minnesota — replied that, even though Early had been eliminated as a deterrent, this was "impracticable with my present means of transportation. . . . I think that the best policy will be to let the burning of the crops in the Valley be the end of this campaign, and let some of this army go elsewhere." Lured by the notion of bringing Wright's hard-hitting corps back down the coast to Petersburg, Grant agreed that Sheridan would do well to make a return march down the Valley, scorching and smashing left and right to ensure that this classic "avenue of invasion" would no longer furnish subsistence even for those who lived there, let alone for Lee's army around Richmond. "Carry off stock of all descriptions, and negroes, so as to prevent further planting," he reminded Little Phil, elaborating on previous instructions. "If this war is to last another year we want the Shenandoah Valley to remain a barren waste."

He knew his man. Beginning the countermarch October 6, Sheridan reported the following night from Woodstock, forty miles away, that he had "destroyed over 2000 barns filled with wheat, hay, and farming implements; over 70 mills filled with flour and wheat; have driven in front of the army over 4000 head of stock, and have killed and issued to the troops not less than 3000 sheep. . . . Tomorrow I will continue the destruction of wheat, forage, &c. down to Fisher's Hill. When this is completed the Valley, from Winchester up to Staunton,

92 miles, will have but little in it for man or beast." Others attested to his proficiency in destruction, which continued round the clock. "The atmosphere, from horizon to horizon, has been black with the smoke of a hundred conflagrations," a correspondent wrote, "and at night a gleam brighter and more lurid than sunset has shot from every verge.... The completeness of the devastation is awful. Hundreds of nearly starving people are going north. Our trains are crowded with them. They line the wayside. Hundreds more are coming." They had little choice, a staff captain noted, having been "left so stripped of food that I cannot imagine how they escaped starvation."

To hurt the people, the land itself was hurt, and the resultant exodus was both heavy and long-lasting. A full year later, an English traveler found the Valley standing empty as a moor.

By now, although Early was being careful to maintain a respectful distance with his twice-defeated, twice-diminished infantry, butternut cavalry was snapping at the heels of the blue column, and Sheridan took this as continuing evidence of the timidity his own cavalry had shown, just over two weeks ago, after Fisher's Hill. Approaching that place from the opposite direction, October 9, he gave Torbert a specific order: "Either whip the enemy or get whipped yourself," then climbed nearby Round Hill for a panoramic view of the result. It was not long in coming. After crossing Tom's Brook, five miles short of Strasburg, Torbert had Merritt and Custer whirl their divisions around and charge the two pressing close in their rear under Lomax and Tom Rosser, who had recently arrived from Richmond with his brigade. Startled, the gray troopers stood for a time, exchanging saber slashes till their flanks gave way, then panicked and fled southward up the pike, pursued by the whooping Federals, who captured eleven of the dozen rebel guns in the course of a ten-mile chase to Woodstock and beyond, along with some 300 graybacks on fagged horses. "The Woodstock Races," the victors dubbed the affair, taking their cue from the Buckland Races, staged at Custer's expense by Jeb Stuart, a year ago this month, on the far side of the Blue Ridge. His temper cooled, his spirits lifted, Sheridan passed through Strasburg and crossed Cedar Creek next morning to put Crook's and Emory's corps in bivouac on the high ground, while Wright prepared his three divisions for an eastward march through Ashby's Gap, as agreed upon beforehand, to rejoin Grant at Petersburg.

They set out two days later, on October 12: only hours, as it developed, before Early reappeared on Fisher's Hill, five miles to the south. He had been reinforced from Richmond, not only by Rosser's cavalry brigade, but also by Kershaw's infantry division, which had been with him last month until it was recalled by Lee on the eve of the Federal strike at Winchester. Aware of these acquisitions, Sheridan was not disturbed, knowing as he did that they barely lifted Early's strength to half his own. If Old Jubal was in search of a third drubbing, he would be happy to oblige him when the time came.

All the same, he recalled the three VI Corps divisions from Ashby's Gap next day, deferring their departure until the situation cleared, and set about making his Cedar Creek position secure against attack while he determined his next move. Amid these labors, which included preparations for a horseback raid to break up the railroad around Charlottesville, he was summoned to Washington by Halleck for a strategy conference, October 16. He left that morning to catch a train at Front Royal, and when he got there he was handed a telegram from Wright, whom he had left in command on Cedar Creek, quoting a message just intercepted from a rebel signal station on Massanutton Mountain: "Be ready to move as soon as my forces join you, and we will crush Sheridan." The signature was *Longstreet*; which was news in itself, if the message was valid. Little Phil considered it "a ruse," however, designed to frighten him out of the Valley, and he declined to be frightened. Besides, he had confidence in Wright, who assured him: "I shall hold on here until the enemy's movements are developed, and shall only fear an attack on my right, which I shall make every preparation for guarding against and resisting." Aside from calling off the Charlottesville raid, Sheridan did not change his plans. Boarding the train for Washington, he advised Wright: "Look well to your ground and be well prepared. Get up everything that can be spared," he added, and promised to return within two days, "if not sooner."

He was right in assuming the intercepted dispatch was a plant, and right as well about its purpose. But he was altogether wrong if he thought his twice-whipped adversary did not intend to try something far more drastic if the invoked ghost of Old Peter failed to frighten him away. In point of fact, so thoroughly had the bluecoats scorched the country in his rear, Early believed he had no choice except "to move back for want of provisions and forage, or attack the enemy in his position with the hope of driving him from it." Another reason, despite his usual crusty disregard for the opinions of others in or out of the army, was that he had a reputation to retrieve; "To General Sheridan, care of General Early," cynics had chalked on the tubes of guns sent from Richmond to replace the 21 pieces he had lost in battle this past month, exclusive of the eleven abandoned by the cavalry last week in its panicky flight from Tom's Brook to Woodstock. Admittedly, with the blue force nearly twice his size, securely in position on high ground, its front covered by a boggy creek and one flank anchored on the Shenandoah, the odds against a successful assault were long. But his predecessor Jackson, in command of these same troops, had taught him how far audacity could go toward evening such odds, and Lee himself, in a letter that followed the sending of reinforcements, had just told him: "I have weakened myself very much to strengthen you. It was done with the expectation of enabling you to gain such success that you could return the troops if not rejoin me yourself. I know you have endeavored to gain that success, and believe you have done all in your power to assure it. You must not be discouraged, but continue to try. I rely upon your judgment and ability, and the hearty coöperation of your officers and men still to secure it. With your united force it can be accomplished."

Sustained and appealed to thus, Early was "determined to attack." But how, against such odds, could he do so with any real hope of success? Crippled as he was by arthritis, which aged him beyond his not quite forty-eight years and prohibited mountain climbing, he sent John Gordon, his senior division commander since the fall of Rodes, and Major Jedediah Hotchkiss, a staff cartographer inherited from Jackson, atop Massanutton to study the enemy position, which lay spread out below them, facing southwest along Cedar Creek. Crook's two divisions were nearest, on the Federal left, then Emory's two, beyond the turnpike, and finally Wright's three, on the distant right, where most of the blue cavalry was posted, obviously in expectation that if an attack was made it would come from that direction. Hotchkiss had discovered and recommended the route for the movement around Hooker's flank at Chancellorsville, but what he and Gordon saw from their high perch this bright fall morning, October 18, was an opportunity for an end-on strike that might outdo even Stonewall's masterpiece. A night march around the steep north face of Massanutton, following a crossing of the Shenandoah near Fisher's Hill, would permit a recrossing of the river beyond its confluence with Cedar Creek, and this in turn would place the flanking column in direct confrontation with the unsuspecting Union left, which could be assaulted at first light in preparation for further assaults on Emory and Wright, once Crook's position had been overrun. Gordon, in fact, was so confident of success that when he came down off the mountain to urge the adoption of the plan, he offered to take all responsibility for any failure that occurred.

Early had never been one to avoid responsibility, nor did

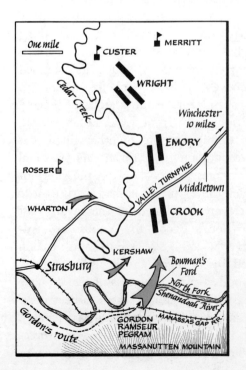

he delay approval of the plan. He would march tonight and strike at dawn, he announced at a council of war called that afternoon. Gordon would be in charge of the turning column made up of his own and the divisions of Ramseur and Rodes, the latter now commanded by its senior brigadier John Pegram, recently recovered from the leg wound he had taken in the Wilderness. Kershaw would move through Strasburg, also under cover of darkness, and attack on the right of the Valley pike, crossing lower Cedar Creek to join the flanking effort as soon as he heard Gordon open fire, and Brigadier General Gabriel Wharton — successor to Breckinridge, who had been recalled to eastern Virginia on the eve of Fisher's Hill — would advance along and to the left of the turnpike, accompanied by Rosser's troopers, to menace and fix the Federals in position on the far side of the creek while the massed Second Corps, with Kershaw's help, struck their flank and drove them north across his front. Rosser then would take up the pursuit, as would Lomax, whose horsemen were to come upon the field by a roundabout march through Front Royal in order to cut off the blue retreat this side of Winchester, fifteen miles beyond Middletown, which was close in the Union rear. The plan was elaborate, involving a convergence by three columns, but it seemed pat enough to Early and his lieutenants, who went straight from the meeting to prepare for the various night marches designed to yield revenge for the two defeats they had recently suffered, here in the Valley from which their army took its name. The first of these — Third Winchester — had occurred exactly a month ago tomorrow, and this made them and their butter-nut veterans all the more eager to get started on the observance of that anniversary.

Aided by the light of a moon only three nights past the full, Gordon's column set out shortly after dark, the men of all three divisions having left their cooking utensils and even their canteens behind to avoid any give-away clink of unnecessary metal, and was in position in the shadows close to Bowman's Ford before daybreak, half a mile beyond the confluence of Cedar Creek and the river, prepared to splash across on signal. Similarly, accompanied by Early and his staff, as well as by most of the army's guns, Kershaw moved undetected around Strasburg to the near bank of the creek, across which he could see low-burnt campfires glowing in the darkness. Wharton followed, turning off to the left of the macadamized pike, preceded by Rosser, whose troopers rode at a walk to muffle the sound of hoofbeats on the stony ground. At 4.30, after an hour's wait on the creekbank, Early told Kershaw to go ahead and cross. He did, and while he was getting his men back into column on the other side, the boom of Rosser's horse artillery came from well upstream, along with the rattling clatter of picket fire nearby on the right, where Gordon was fording the Shenandoah just off the unalerted Union flank. The surprise was complete, if not quite overwhelming at the outset. "As we emerged from a thicket into the open," one of Kershaw's South Carolinians later wrote, "we could see the enemy in great commotion. But soon the works were filled with half-dressed troops, and they opened a galling fire upon us."

Kershaw charged, and as he did so, racing uphill through the spreading dawn, Gordon struck the left rear of the hastily formed blue line, which promptly broke. Elated (for these were Crook's men, the so-called West Virginians who had flanked them unceremoniously off Fisher's Hill four weeks ago) the Confederates surged forward on a broad front across the turnpike, pursuing and taking prisoners by the hundreds. With only a bit more time for getting set, Emory's corps fared little better, its unbraced ranks plowed by shells from rebel batteries massed on a hill beyond the creek. Fugitives from the four routed divisions fled northward through Wright's camps, in rear of which his Potomac veterans were falling in for battle. By now the sun was rising, alternately bright and pale as drifts of smoke blew past it, and the graybacks — joined at this stage by Wharton, who had been left with nothing in his front — came on yelling as they drove Wright's troops northeast across the open fields, first to a second and then to still a third position nearly two miles in rear of Middletown, where Jackson had captured Banks's wagon train in May of '62. This seemed to some a comparable achievement, while others went further afield in search of a parallel triumph. "The sun of Middletown! The sun of Middletown!" Early kept exclaiming, as if to say he had found his Austerlitz.

It was now past 9 o'clock, and he was delighted that within a scant four hours he had driven seven infantry divisions from the field with only five of his own, taking in the process more than 1300 prisoners, 18 guns, and an uncounted number of flags.

He was delighted; but he was also satisfied, it seemed. "Well, Gordon, this is glory enough for one day," he declared on meeting the Georgian near the front soon afterward. They stood looking across the fields at the Yankees reduced to stick men in the distance. "This is the 19th," he went on. "Precisely one month ago today we were going in the opposite direction." Gordon too was happy, but his thoughts were on the immediate future, not the past. "It is very well so far, General," he replied, "but we have one more blow to strike, and then there will not be left an organized company of infantry in Sheridan's army." His chief demurred. "No use in that. They will all go, directly." The Georgian was doubtful, and said so, indicating the bluecoats on the horizon. "This is the VI Corps, General. It will not go unless we drive it from the field." Once more Early shook his head. "Yes, it will go directly," he insisted as he continued to wait for the whipped Federals to withdraw.

Gordon said no more just then, but he later wrote: "My heart went into my boots." He was remembering "that fatal halt on the first day at Gettysburg," as well as Old Jube's daylong refusal, back in May, to let him strike Grant's unguarded flank in the Wilderness, which he believed had cost the Army of Northern Virginia the greatest of all its victories.

His heart might have sunk still deeper if he had known what was happening, across the way, while he and his chief stood talking. Sheridan had just arrived and was reassembling his scattered army for an all-out counterattack. True to his promise to return from the capital in two days, "if not sooner," he had slept last night in Winchester and had heard the guns of Cedar Creek, some fifteen miles away, while still in bed this morning. Dismissing the cannonade as "irregular and fitful" — most likely a reconnaissance-in-force by one of Wright's brigades — he tried to get back to sleep, without success. At breakfast, the guns still were muttering in the distance, faint but insistent, and he ordered his staff and cavalry escort to saddle up without delay. On the way out of town, he noticed "many women at the doors and windows of the houses, who kept shaking their skirts at us and who were otherwise markedly insolent in their demeanor." It occurred to him that they "were in rapture over some good news," mysteriously received, "while I as yet was utterly in ignorance of the actual situation." What was more, the sound of firing seemed to be moving to meet him; an ominous development. But it was not until he crossed Mill Creek, beyond Kernstown, and reached the crest of a low hill on the far side, that he and his staff and escort saw their worst fears confirmed by "the appalling spectacle of a panic-stricken army."

His first notion was to rally what was left of his command, here if not still farther back toward Winchester, for a last-ditch stand against the rebel force, which might or might not include Longstreet and his famed First Corps. With this in mind, Little Phil ordered his staff and escort to form a straggler line along the crest of the hill: all, that is, except two aides and a score of troopers, who would proceed with him toward Cedar Creek to find out what had happened.

In the course of the twelve-mile ride — "Sheridan's Ride," it came to be called — his purpose changed. Partly this was because of his aggressive nature, which reasserted itself, and partly it was the result of encountering groups of men along the roadside boiling coffee. That did not seem to indicate demoralization; nor did the cheers they gave when they saw him coming up the turnpike. "As he galloped on," one of the two aides later wrote, "his features gradually grew set, as though carved in stone, and the same dull red glint I had seen in his piercing black eyes when, on other occasions, the battle was going against us, was there now." Grimness then gave way to animation. He began to lift his little flat-topped hat in jaunty salute, rather as if in congratulation for a victory, despite the contradictory evidence. "The army's whipped!" an unstrung infantry colonel informed him, only to be told: "You are, but the army isn't." He put the spurs to Rienzi — an under-sized, bandy-legged man, perched high on the pounding big black horse he had named for the town in Mississippi where he acquired him two years ago — and called out to the retreaters, "About face, boys! We are going back to our camps. We are going to lick them out of their boots!" He kept saying that, shouting the words at the upturned faces along the pike. "We are going to get a twist on those fellows. We are going to lick them out of their boots!"

And did just that: but not with the haste his breakneck manner had implied. Arriving about 10.30 he found Crook's corps disintegrated and Emory's not much better off, though most of it at least was still on hand. Wright's, however, was holding firm in its third position, a couple of miles northwest of Middletown, its line extended southeast across the turnpike by Merritt's and Custer's horsemen. Sheridan got to work at once, concentrating on getting Emory's troops, together with a trickle of retreaters who were returning in response to the exhorta-tions he had shouted as he passed them on the pike, regrouped to sup-port Wright in his resistance to the expected third assault by Early's whooping graybacks. Nor was he unmindful, even at this stage, of the fruits a sudden counterstroke might yield. "Tell General Emory if they attack him again to go after them, and to follow them up, and to sock it to them, and to give them the devil. We'll have all those camps and cannon back again." Emory got the message, and reacted with a sort of fervid resignation. "We might as well whip them today," he said. "If we don't, we shall have to do it tomorrow. Sheridan will get it out of us sometime."

Noon came and went, then 1 o'clock, then 2, and Little Phil continued to withhold his hand: as did Early, across the way.

At 3 o'clock, having at last persuaded his chief to let him under-take a limited attack, Gordon probed the Federal position beyond Middletown, but was easily repulsed. Still Sheridan held back, his numbers growing rapidly as more and more blue fugitives returned from their flight down the turnpike. Finally, after interrogating prisoners to make certain Longstreet was not there, he gave orders for a general advance at 4 o'clock. At first, though their ranks were thinned by looters prowling the Yankee camps in search of food and booty, the graybacks refused to budge. But then one of Emory's brigades found a weak spot in the rebel line, and before it could be reinforced Custer struck with his whole division, launching an all-out mounted charge that sundered the Confederate force and sent the two parts reeling back on Cedar Creek. "Run! Go after them!" Sheridan cried. "We've got the God-damnedest twist on them you ever saw!"

Early did what he could; which, at that stage, wasn't much. For the past four hours — hearing nothing from Lomax, whose roundabout march with half the cavalry later turned out to have been blocked near Front Royal by Torbert's third division — he had watched the steady buildup across the way, aware that this, combined with the rearward leakage from his idle ranks, restored the odds to about what they had been at daybreak, when he enjoyed the lost advantage of surprise. Increasingly apprehensive, he withdrew his captured guns beyond Cedar Creek for quick removal in a crisis, and started his nearly two thousand prisoners on their long trek south to Staunton. All this time, the vaunted "sun of Middletown" was declining, and the nearer it drew to the peaks of the Alleghenies the clearer he saw that the Federals not only had no intention of quitting their third position, in which they had little trouble fending off a belated feeling-out by Gordon, but were in fact preparing to launch a massive counterstroke. When it came, as it did at straight-up 4 o'clock, Early managed to withstand the pressure, left and center, until Emory drove a wedge between two of Gordon's brigades, opening a gap into which Custer flung his rapid-firing troopers; whereupon the Georgian's veterans, foreseeing disaster, began a scurry for the crossings in their rear. Rapidly the panic spread to the divisions of Kershaw and Ramseur, next in line. Dodson Ramseur — a major general at twenty-seven, the youngest West Point graduate to attain that rank in the Confederate army — tried his best to stay the rout, appealing from horseback to his men, but took a bullet through both lungs and was left to die in enemy hands next day, near Sheridan's reclaimed Belle Grove headquarters, where he fell.

By then there would be no uncaptured rebels within twenty miles; Sheridan, having spared his hand until he felt that victory was clearly within reach, exploited the break for all he was worth. "It took less time to drive the enemy from the field than it had for them to take it," according to Merritt, whose division clashed with Rosser's and overran the Confederate far left. Early pulled in Wharton and Pegram to brace the center, under assault from the VI Corps, but only succeeded in delaying Wright's advance. Rearward, meantime, a flying column of Union cavalry wrecked the bridge at Spangler's Mill, just west of Strasburg, with the result that the three miles of turnpike between there and the crossing at Cedar Creek were crowded with artillery and vehicles of all kinds, trapped and at the mercy of the pursuers. Little Phil thus recovered all the guns lost that morning, together with 25 of his adversary's, which enabled him to report that he had taken no less than 43 pieces at one swoop, though he neglected to mention that 18 of them were his own, recaptured in the confusion of the gray retreat.

Early fell back to Fisher's Hill in the twilight, intending to make a stand there in the morning, but soon saw that it would not do. Though his casualties were only a bit over half as heavy as Sheridan's this day —

2910, as compared to 5665 — his army, routed for the third time in thirty days, was in no condition for further resistance to an enemy twice its size. He took up the march for New Market before daylight, fighting off Custer's and Merritt's horsemen, who snapped at his heels all the way. Summing it up afterwards, Old Jube remarked sadly: "The Yankees got whipped. We got scared."

No explanation could shield him now, however, from the blame about to be heaped upon his head by his own people; blame that outweighed the praise that had come his way, three months ago, when he hovered defiantly on the outskirts of the northern capital. Indeed, the brightness of that midsummer exploit only served to deepen, by contrast, the shadows that gathered in this dark autumn of the Confederacy, which some were already saying would be its last. In the past thirty days Early had fought three full-scale battles, and all three had turned out to be full-scale routs. It mattered little to his critics that he had obliged Grant to lessen the pressure on Lee by detaching a veteran corps from Meade and rerouting another, on its way by sea to reinforce him, in order to meet Jubal's threat, first on the far and then on the near side of the Potomac. Nor did it matter that in the course of his follow-up campaign in the Valley, where he was out-numbered roughly three-to-one from start to finish, he inflicted a total of 16,592 casualties on his adversary — the equivalent of still another blue corps, by Sheridan's own count, and about as many combat troops as he himself had been able to scrape together for any one of those several confrontations — at a cost of less than 10,000 of his own. What mattered in the public's estimation was that, here on the field of Stone-wall Jackson's glory, Early had been whipped three times running, each time more soundly than before. Tart of tongue, intolerant of the shortcomings of others since the outset of the war, the former Commonwealth's Attorney of Franklin County now found himself accused of ineptness, inefficiency, incompetence, even drunkenness and coward-ice, in the journals and in public and private talk, here in his native Virginia as well as elsewhere in the South.

It was otherwise for Sheridan, whose praises now were being sung throughout the North. "With great pleasure," Lincoln wrote him, three days after Cedar Creek, "I tender to you and your brave army the thanks of the nation and my own personal admiration and gratitude for the month's operations in the Shenandoah Valley, and especially for the splendid work of October 19." The following evening, shortly before midnight, he was awakened by Assistant Secretary of War Charles A. Dana, who had just arrived from Washington to present him with the most prized of all rewards: his commission as a major general in the regular army, together with a commendation from the Adjutant General's office citing him "for the personal gallantry, military skill, and just confidence in the courage and patriotism of his troops . . .

whereby, under the blessing of Providence, his routed army was re-organized, a great national disaster averted, and a brilliant victory achieved." Riding through the camps with Little Phil next morning, October 25, Dana thought he had never seen a general so popular with all ranks: not even Sherman or Pap Thomas — maybe not even Mc-Clellan in his heyday.

Grant by then was ready to try still another of his pendulum swings at Lee. After ordering a second hundred-gun salute fired with shotted guns in honor of his protégé's third victory in the Valley, he wrote his wife: "I hope we will have one here before a great while to celebrate," and put his staff to work at once on plans for the heaviest strike, so far, at the Richmond-Petersburg defenses. Butler would feint north of the James, with the same number as before, but this time the lunge around the enemy right would be made by no less than 43,000 troops from Hancock, Warren, and Parke, on the theory that what two corps had failed to achieve, just under a month ago, might be accomplished now by three.

On October 27, with Butler already over the river, demonstrating for all he was worth at Fair Oaks, the companion blow was launched. As a further diversion, Parke was to hit the western end of the gray line, just east of Hatcher's Run, while Hancock and Warren swung wide around that stream to cross the Boydton Plank Road and then press north to get astride the Southside Railroad. Alas, no part of this flanking effort went well, and most parts went very badly indeed. Parke encountered stiff resistance and was stalled, and though Hancock made it to his initial objective on schedule, he had to stop and wait for Warren, who was delayed by difficult terrain. While Hancock waited Hill and Hampton struck him flank and front, attacking with about half of the 23,000 effectives Lee had kept south of the river, and forced him to withdraw that night, nearly out of ammunition and altogether out of patience. Meantime Warren turned east, under orders from Grant to help Parke envelop the Hatcher's Run defenses, but was unable to cross the creek; so he too withdrew. None of the three corps in this direction, Parke's or Hancock's or Warren's, had carried out its part of a plan whose only tangible result was the loss of 1758 men — plus the confirmation of Hancock's resolution to seek duty elsewhere; which he would do the following month, suffering as much from recent damage to his pride as from the continuing discomfort of his Gettysburg wound. North of the James, where Lee was not deceived by his gyrations around Fair Oaks, Butler lost 1103 killed, wounded, and missing, as compared to a Confederate loss of 451 there and perhaps twice that number in the opposite direction, along the Boydton Road and Hatcher's Run.

All lines remained the same, north and south of the river, as both armies prepared to go into winter quarters. No more discouraged by this latest failure than he had been by those others outside Petersburg and Richmond, Grant maintained what Lincoln called his "bulldog grip," prepared to "chew and choke" as long as need be. He could fail practically any number of times, and only needed to succeed but once. "I will work this thing out all right yet," he told his wife in a home letter.

In any case, this late-October affair down around Richmond went practically unnoticed by a public still absorbed in the recent Shenandoah drama, finding it restorative of the romantic, picture-book aspect so long missing from the war. "The nation rings with praises of Phil Sheridan," the Chicago *Tribune* noted, three days after the famous ride that saved the day at Cedar Creek and prompted black Rienzi's master to change his name to Winchester in commemoration of the exploit. Various poets tried their hand at the subject, including Herman Melville, but the one who caught the public's fancy best was T. Buchanan Read in a ballad titled "Sheridan's Ride."

> *Hurrah! Hurrah for Sher-i-dan!*
> *Hurrah! Hurrah for horse and man!*

its refrain went. Availing himself of a poetic license which the general he praised sometimes employed in his reports, Read doubled the distance of the gallop, eliminated all stops along the way, and had Rienzi himself announce the nick-of-time arrival to the troops:

> *"I have brought you Sheridan, all the way*
> *From Winchester, down to save the day."*

Widely read and recited, the piece made a fine recruiting and electioneering appeal, especially when delivered by professionals such as James E. Murdoch, a retired actor and celebrated "reader," whose declamation of the poem at a theater in Cincinnati on November 1, just one week before the presidential contest was to be settled at the polls, threw the crowd into a frenzy of approval for the war and for the men who fought and ran it.

χ 4 χ

Elsewhere — not only in the embattled heartland of the South, but also in places as far afield as Kansas, Vermont, and Brazil — both sides undertook desperate measures, throughout the critical two-month span that opened with the fall of Atlanta, in attempts to influence militarily the early-November political decision that perhaps would begin to end the war itself, come Inauguration Day. For example:

Aside from an abortive Union gunboat probe down White River in late June, which was turned back at Clarendon before the flotilla could enter the Arkansas to help patrol that line of Federal occupation, there had been no significant clash of arms in the Transmississippi since Frederick Steele retired from Camden in late April and Banks and Porter abandoned in May their effort to ascend the Red. Since then, Kirby Smith had seemed content to rest on his laurels, clinging precariously to what was left of Texas, Louisiana, Arkansas, and the Indian Territory — "Kirby-Smithdom," this vast but empty stretch of the continent was called — and resisted all efforts by Richmond and homesick subordinates to persuade him to go over to the offensive, either toward New Orleans or Saint Louis. Discontent to have so many good troops standing idle, even against such odds as here obtained, the authorities instructed him in mid-July to prepare Richard Taylor's corps, along with "such other infantry as can be spared," for a prompt movement across the Mississippi to assist in the defense of Atlanta and Mobile. Smith passed the order to Taylor, who had been sulking in Natchitoches for the past six weeks, his hurt feelings, if not his animosity toward his chief, somewhat relieved by a promotion to lieutenant general as a reward for his repulse of Banks. Eager to shake the dust of Kirby-Smithdom from his feet, Taylor looked into the possibility of a crossing, either by ferries or by the employment of what would have been the longest pontoon bridge in history, but replied in the end that it couldn't be done, since the Federals, getting wind of the project, had stationed ironclads at twelve-mile intervals all the way from Vicksburg past the mouth of the Red, with gunboats on constant patrol between them, day and night. "A bird, if dressed in Confederate gray, would find it difficult to fly across the river," a reconnoitering cavalryman declared.

Regretfully, for he was as anxious to get rid of Taylor as Taylor was to be quits with him, Smith informed his superiors in Virginia that the shift could not be made. By then the year had moved into August, and Richmond's answer solved at least a part of his problem by dusting the gadfly Taylor off his back. Stephen Lee having been sent to Georgia to head a corps under Hood, the Kentucky-born Louisianian (and presidential brother-in-law) was ordered to replace him in command of the Department of Alabama, Mississippi, and Eastern Louisiana, temporarily under Maury at Mobile. On a moonless night, within a week of receiving the order on August 22, Taylor crossed the river in a dugout canoe, swimming his mare alongside, and set out eastward for his new headquarters in Meridian. Before he reached it, Smith — or, more specifically, Sterling Price — had placed an alternate plan in execution, back in the Transmississipi, by launching 12,000 horsemen northward into Missouri.

Originally designed to draw attention away from the downriver crossing, the operation was now to be undertaken for its own sake: first against St Louis, where government warehouses bulged with the goods of war, then westward along the near bank of the Missouri River to the capital, Jefferson City — whose occupation, however brief, would refurbish the somewhat tarnished star representing the state on the Confederate battle flag — then finally back south "through Kansas and the Indian Territory, sweeping that country of its mules, horses, cattle, and military supplies." So Price was told by Smith in his instructions for the raid, which was also to serve the double-barreled purpose of discouraging the departure of still more bluecoats to lengthen the odds against Hood and Lee, east of the Mississippi, and of attracting recruits to the gray column as it swept through regions whose voters were about to get their chance, as the case was being put to them in the campaign already under way, to "throw off the yoke of oppression." Mounted on Bucephalus, a warhorse as gray as its rider and stockily built to withstand his two hundred and ninety dead-weight pounds, Old Pap left Camden on August 28 and was joined next day at Princeton by the divisions of Marmaduke and Fagan, who rode with him across the Arkansas River at Dardanelle on September 2, midway between Little Rock and Fort Smith, neither of whose blue garrisons ventured out to challenge the invaders. At Pocahontas on the 13th, up near the Missouri line, Jo Shelby added his division to the column, now 12,000 strong, with fourteen guns, though only about two thirds of the troopers were adequately armed — a deficiency Price intended to repair when he encountered opposition. On September 19, the day before his fifty-fifth birthday, he crossed into his home state, headed for Ironton, eighty miles to the north, terminus of the railroad running south out of St Louis, another eighty miles away. At nearby Pilot Knob there was a Union fort, Fort Davidson, with a garrison of about one thousand men and seven guns, and he had chosen this as his first prize of the campaign, to be followed by those other, larger prizes, north and west.

Assembling his three divisions at Fredericktown on the 25th — a day's ride east of Pilot Knob, which he intended to move against tomorrow — he received news from St Louis that was both good and bad, from different points of view. Department Commander William Rosecrans, on learning in early September that the graybacks had crossed the Arkansas in strength, wired Halleck a request that A. J. Smith's two veteran divisions, then aboard transports at Cairo on their way to rejoin Sherman after service up the Red and in North Mississippi, be sent instead to help defend Missouri against this new incursion. Old Brains complied by ordering Smith upriver at once to "operate against Price & Co." This meant that one purpose of the raid had been achieved before the first blow landed; Price not only had discouraged the sending of more troops east across the Mississippi, he had even provoked a drain in the opposite direction, though at the cost of lengthening the odds against fulfilling his other objectives, including the strike at goods-rich St Louis, whose defenses now were manned by Smith's 8000 gorilla-guerillas, in addition to its regular complement. In any case, after sending a brigade to rip up track on the railroad above Ironton and thus prevent the sudden arrival of reinforcements, he completed his plans for the reduction of Fort Davidson, twenty miles west of Fredericktown, and had it invested by nightfall the following day. He badly wanted its thousand-man garrison and their arms: especially those seven guns, whose addition would increase by half the firepower of the artillery he had brought along for blasting a path through his beloved Missouri.

Brigadier General Thomas Ewing, commander of the District of St Louis — Sherman's brother-in-law and author, too, of last year's infamous Order 11, which emptied Missouri's western counties of civilians in an attempt to ferret out guerillas whose bloody work grew bloodier in reaction to the hardships thus imposed on their women and children — had come down to the fort on an inspection trip, only to have the railroad cut in his rear, and decided not to abandon the place under threat from ten times the number he had for its defense. Accordingly, when a rebel delegation came forward under a flag of truce that night, demanding surrender, he sent it back with a defiant challenge, and when the demand was repeated a few hours later he did the same thing, adding that he would fire on the next white flag that approached his works. These were extremely stout, heptagonal in shape, with earthen walls nine feet tall and ten feet thick, surrounded by a dry moat as deep as the walls were high. Next day, September 27, they were tested in a furious six-hour fight that cost the attackers 1500 casualties, half again more than the total number of defenders, who lost 200. Falling back at dark, Old Pap's troopers began the construction of scaling ladders to use when they renewed the assault at dawn, and Ewing, knowing the fort could not hold out past then — and that he himself, as the author of Order 11, was unlikely to survive capture — assembled a council of war to decide whether to surrender or risk attempting a getaway. The vote was for the latter; which succeeded. Under cover of darkness the blue garrison built a drawbridge, draped it with canvas to muffle the sound of boots and hoofs, and withdrew undetected through a gap in the gray lines, leaving behind a slow fuze laid to the powder magazine. Slogging along in a column of twos, Ewing and his 800 survivors were well out the road to Rolla, seventy miles northwest, when the magazine blew with a great eruption of flame that gave the investors their first hint the fort was empty.

Marmaduke and Shelby, furious over their losses and fairly itching to fit Ewing for a noose, wanted to take out after him at once, but their fellow Missourian Price, already regretting a fruitless three-day interlude which had deprived him of more than a tenth of his command and netted him nothing but rubble and spiked guns, was unwilling to use up still more time on a project that he suspected had already cost him whatever chance there had been for surprising Rosecrans in St Louis.

Sure enough, after following the Iron Mountain Railroad to within thirty miles of the city, he found its garrison reinforced to a strength reportedly greater than his own. So he turned west, as planned — though he had not intended to do so empty-handed — up the south bank of the Missouri, wrecking bridges and culverts along the Pacific Railroad as he proceeded, first across the Gasconade River and then the Osage, which he cleared on October 6 to put his raiders within easy reach of Jefferson City.

But this too was untakable, he decided upon learning that its defenses were manned by bluecoats drawn from beyond the river despite a flurry of apprehension caused there the week before by a ruthless attack on Centralia, fifty miles north of the capital, by a force of about 200 butternut guerillas under William Anderson, who bore and lived up to the nickname "Bloody Bill." A former lieutenant in William C. Quantrill's gang, of Lawrence and Fort Baxter fame, he had quarreled with his chief in Texas and returned to his old stomping ground, near the Missouri-Kansas border, along with other disaffected members of the band, including George Todd and David Pool, as well as Frank James and his seventeen-year-old brother Jesse. Clattering into Centralia at midday, September 27 — the day of the Fort Davidson assault, one hundred and fifty miles southeast at Pilot Knob — they held up a stagecoach and an arriving train, killed two dozen unarmed soldiers aboard on furlough, along with two civilians who tried to hide valuables in their boots, and left hurriedly, with $3000 in greenbacks from the express car, when three troops of Union cavalry unexpectedly appeared and gave chase. Three miles out of town, the guerillas turned on their pursuers, who numbered 147, and shot dead or cut the throats of all but 23 who managed to escape on fast horses. "From this time forward I ask no quarter and give none," Anderson had announced on the square in Centralia, and then proceeded to prove he meant it, first in town and then out on the prairie.

Price's decision to forgo a strike at Jefferson City, the main political objective of his raid, was based on more than information that the capital had been reinforced, not only from beyond the Missouri, but also from scattered posts on this side of the river, including Springfield and Rolla. He learned too, while skirmishing on the outskirts after crossing the Moreau, that Rosecrans, supposedly left holding the bag in St. Louis, had sent Smith's 8000 infantry westward in his wake, along with 7000 troopers under Major General Alfred Pleasonton, who had served the better part of a year as cavalry commander in the Army of the Potomac until Grant replaced him with Sheridan, back in March, and sent him west to share Old Rosy's exile. Price was aware that any prolonged attempt to break through the capital defenses was likely to be interrupted by the arrival of Pleasonton and Smith, now toiling along the demolished Pacific Railroad with a combined strength greater than his own. Moreover, scouts coming in from the Kansas border, a hundred and forty miles in the opposite direction, reported that more than 20,000 regulars and militia were being assembled there for his reception by the department commander, Major General Samuel R. Curtis, his old Pea Ridge adversary. The thing to do, he reasoned, was get there fast, before Curtis got organized or Smith and Pleasonton came up in his rear to make the fight for Kansas City a two-front affair. Accordingly, he turned his back on the state capitol, plainly visible on its hill beyond the treetops, and continued his march another forty miles upriver to Boonville, which he reached October 9. Riding due west for Lexington, sixty-odd miles away — the scene of his one unassisted victory, back in the first September of the war, hard on the heels of the triumph he had shared with Ben McCulloch at Wilson's

Creek — he put Marmaduke's division in the lead and had Shelby strike out left and right at Sedalia and Glasgow, both of which were taken on the 15th, together with their garrisons, while Fagan covered the rear, on the lookout for Pleasonton's horsemen, who were known to have reached Jefferson City four days ago. Four days later at Waverly, his home town on the south bank of the Missouri, twenty miles short of Lexington, Shelby encountered a force of Coloradans and Kansans under Major General James Blunt, brought in from the plains by Curtis and sent forward to delay the approach of the raiders. Here were fired the opening shots of what turned out to be a week-long running skirmish, covering more than a hundred miles of the border region, with several pauses for full-scale engagements along the way.

Shelby drove Blunt back through Lexington, October 20, and on across the Little Blue next day, fighting house-to-house through Independence to the Big Blue, just beyond. Curtis had established a line of works along the opposite bank, manned by 4000 regulars and an equal number of Kansas militia, some 16,000 of whom had come forward in the current emergency, though only about one fourth of them were willing to cross into Missouri, the remainder having called a halt at the state line, half a dozen miles to the west. His plan was to hang on there, securely intrenched, till Pleasonton came up in Price's rear, then go over to the offensive, east and west, against the graybacks trapped between the Big and Little Blues. It did not work out quite that way: partly because of the timid militia, skulking rearward on home ground, but mainly because of black-plumed Jo Shelby. While Marmaduke and Fagan took the bluecoats under fire from across the river on the morning of the 22d, Shelby splashed his three brigades across an upstream ford to flank the defenders out of their works and throw them into retreat on Westport, immediately south of Kansas City and within two miles of the state line. As a result, when Pleasonton arrived that night he found Curtis's intrenchments bristling in his path, occupied by the butternut invaders he had been trailing ever since he left St Louis, three weeks back.

Confronted east and west by forces that totaled three times his own, Old Pap took stock and pondered his next move. Staffers advised that this be south without delay, while the long road home lay open for a withdrawal in good order. But he was urged by Shelby, whose blood was up, to take advantage of a position which, though not without obvious dangers, fairly glittered with Napoleonic possibilities. Using one division to hold Pleasonton in check on the far side of the Big Blue, he could move with the other two against Curtis at nearby Westport, then turn, having disposed of the Kansan and his green militia, to crush Pleasonton and thus cap the raid with a stunning double victory; after which, according to Shelby, he could proceed at his leisure, rounding up Federal garrisons and Confederate recruits, as intended from the outset, on the final leg of his march back across the Arkansas. Price liked the notion, partly for its own glittering sake, partly because of the chance it gave him to put a gainful end to a campaign that so far had profited his country and his reputation next to nothing. Accordingly, after lodging Marmaduke's two brigades in the Union intrenchments overlooking the Big Blue, he ordered Fagan and Shelby to prepare their six for the attack on Curtis, whose troops were deployed along Brush Creek below Westport, at daybreak tomorrow, October 23.

Pleasonton, having posted his four brigades for a dawn assault on the former Union works across the river west of town, spent the night in Independence. A graduate of West Point and the hard-knocks school of combat in the East — including Brandy Station, where he had taken Jeb Stuart's measure on the eve of Gettysburg — he intended to do to Price tomorrow what Price had done to Curtis today; that is, dispossess him of those works. Even though no blue infantry was at hand (A. J. Smith's two divisions had turned south at Lexington, under orders from Rosecrans to head off a rebel swerve in that direction, and thus were removed from all possible contact with the raiders, now or later) the forty-year-old cavalryman was satisfied he could do the job on his own, and with this in mind had his cannoneers keep heaving shells across the Blue to discourage the intrenched defenders from getting much sleep till after midnight, a scant five hours before he planned to strike them.

By that time Curtis was planning to strike them too, despite his mistrust of the balky militia that comprised about four fifths of his command. Persuaded by Blunt — as Price had been by Shelby — that a victory was within his reach if he would only grasp it, the fifty-nine-year-old department head reversed his previous decision to fall back on Fort Leavenworth, twenty-five miles north on the Missouri, and agreed instead, under pressure from Blunt and others at a council of war in the Gillis House that night in Kansas City, to go over to the offensive in the morning. Down along Brush Creek all this while, his green recruits were kept awake by the boom of Pleasonton's guns on the far side of the river and by the nerve-jarring crump of shells on the near bank, close in their rear. "I'd rather hear the baby cry," one married volunteer remarked. Presently the guns left off, but he continued to fret, confiding in a friend that he expected to be killed in tomorrow's contest, and found small comfort in assurances that the future life was superior to this one. "Well, I don't know about that," he said, still worried.

His chances for survival were better than he knew. Next day's battle, though numerically the largest ever fought in the Transmississippi — out of 40,000 Federals and Confederates on the field, close to 30,000 were engaged, as compared to just under 27,000 at Pea Ridge, the next largest, and only about half that many at Wilson's Creek —

was neither as hotly contested nor as bloody as both sides had expected when they lay down to sleep the night before. Fagan and Shelby went forward as ordered, shortly after daybreak, and threw Curtis's green-horns into skittery retreat, much as Shelby had predicted and Curtis, who watched the action through a spyglass from the roof of a convenient farmhouse, had feared. But not for long. Thrown back on Westport and the Kansas line, the militiamen and regulars, outnumbering the attackers better than two to one, not only rallied and held their own against renewed assaults by the yelling graybacks, but even, in response to a horseback appeal from their commander, who came down off his roof to ride among them, began massing for a counterattack to recover the lost ground along the creek. Whereupon, in this moment of crisis — it was now about midmorning — Price was informed that Pleasonton had broken Marmaduke's line on the near bank of the Big Blue and was approaching his right rear, threatening to come between the raiders and their train, parked southward on the road he had been persuaded not to take the night before.

Enraged to find the dawn attack deferred to await his arrival from Independence, Pleasonton had begun his day with on-the-spot dismissals of two brigade commanders — "You're an ambulance soldier and belong in the rear," he told one of the brigadiers, shaking a cowhide whip in his face quite as if he meant to use it — and peremptory orders for their successors to throw everything they had against Byram's Ford, a strongly defended crossing on the rebel right. He did this on the theory that the enemy would least expect a major effort there, and the result was all he hoped for. When the dismounted horsemen splashed across the ford, through the abatis on the opposite bank, then up and over the intrenchments on the ridge beyond, he followed with a third brigade to deepen and widen the breakthrough, while the fourth came on behind. Marmaduke's rattled defenders, turned suddenly out of their works by twice their number, fled rearward across the prairie that stretched to the Kansas line, unobstructed except by the trees along Brush Creek, where Price's effort against Curtis was in crisis.

Pleasonton reined in his horse to watch them flee, and as he did he stabbed the air with one hand, pointing at the sticklike figures, running or wavering, near and far. "Rebels! Rebels! Rebels!" he shouted at his troopers, who had stopped, much as he himself had done, to watch this flight across the rolling tableland. "Fire! Fire, you damned asses!" he kept shouting.

There was not much time for that, however. Faced with the threat of annihilation on the open prairie, Price disengaged Fagan, pulled him back alongside Marmaduke's reassembled fugitives, and used them both to cover the withdrawal of his train, southward down the road on which it had been parked for ready accessibility or a sudden getaway. Shelby — as was only fair, since he was the one who had talked his chief into this predicament in the first place — was charged with stalling the blue pursuit, at least until the wagons and guns and the other two divisions, remounted to make the best possible time, escaped the closing jaws of the trap and got a decent head start down the road to Little Santa Fe, a dozen miles below on the Kansas border. Hemmed in as he was on three sides (and grievously outnumbered; Curtis and Pleasonton had just over 20,000 infantry and cavalry engaged from first to last — less than three quarters of their total force — while Price had only about 9000 — all that he had arms for) this was no easy task; but Shelby managed it in style, cutting his way out with a mounted charge in the final stage, near sunset, to join the gray column grinding its way south in the darkness. Too ponderous for even heavy-hocked Bucephalus to bear his weight for long, Price rode in a carriage on the retreat, depressed by the knowledge that Westport — sometimes disproportionately referred to as "the Gettysburg of the Transmississippi," though in point of fact it was fought for no real purpose and settled nothing — had merely added another repulse to his long list of reverses, east and west of the Mississippi River. Fortunately it was not a costly one, however. Neither commander filed a casualty report, but their losses seem not to have reached a thousand men on either side.

A heavier defeat, with heavier losses, came two days later, fifty miles beyond Little Santa Fe, soon after the raiders crossed the Marais des Cygnes, which flowed eastward into Missouri and the Osage. They had made good time, marching day and night through wet and blustery weather, but Pleasonton and Curtis dogged their heels, eager to close in for the kill. Swinging west to take advantage of better roads leading south beyond the Kansas line, Price halted Marmaduke on the far bank of the tributary river — mostly referred to hereabouts as the Mary Dayson — in hope of delaying his pursuers at that point. This the Missouri West Pointer did, briefly at least, and then fell back to a similar position on Mine Creek, three miles below, where Fagan had been deployed to support the rear-guard effort with ten of the column's fourteen pieces of artillery. Here on that same morning, October 25, occurred the first and last full-scale engagement between regulars, Federal and Confederate, to be fought on Kansas soil. The first Price knew of its outcome was when he saw troops from both divisions come stumbling toward him in disorder, pursued by whooping bluecoats, mounted and afoot. All ten guns were lost in the rout, along with close to a thousand prisoners, including Marmaduke himself, Brigadier General William Cabell — Old Pap's only other West Pointer, in charge of one of Fagan's Arkansas brigades — and four colonels. Hit in the arm and thrown from his horse, Marmaduke was taken single-handedly by James Dunlavy, an Iowa private, who marched his muddy, dejected captive directly to army headquarters. "How much longer have you to serve?" the department commander asked. Told, "Eight months, sir," Curtis turned to his adjutant: "Give Private Dunlavy a furlough for eight months." The Iowa soldier left for home next day, taking with him the long-haired rebel general's saber for a souvenir of the war that was now behind him, and Marmaduke and Cabell were soon on their way to northern prison camps, the war behind them too.

Once more Price called Shelby back to contest a further advance by the exultant Federals, who were delayed in following up their victory by an argument that broke out between Curtis and Pleasonton as to whether the latter's prisoners were to be sent to Leavenworth or St Louis and thus be credited to Curtis or to Rosecrans. While Shelby fought successive rear-guard actions on the Little Osage and the Marmiton, Price reassembled the other two divisions and pressed on south with the train. Beyond the Little Osage the road forked, one branch leading to Fort Scott, six miles south across the Marmiton, the other back southeast into Missouri. Formerly the fort had been on Old Pap's list of trophies to be picked up on this final leg of the raid, but now he had neither the time nor the strength to move against it. After pausing to lighten the train by burning some 400 wagons, together with the excess artillery ammunition — excess because only one four-gun battery remained — he took the left-hand fork and set out on a forced march of just over sixty miles to Carthage, down near the southwest corner of his home state. Although most of the blue pursuers stopped for food and a night's sleep at Fort Scott, and though Shelby managed to keep the rest from overtaking the train and its escort, still the night-long day-long night-long trek, ending at Carthage on the morning of the 27th, was an experience not soon forgotten by those who made it. "I don't know that a longer march graces history; a fatal day for horse flesh," one weary raider noted in his journal at its close.

Price rewarded their efforts with a full day's rest, then resumed the march next morning, hoping to reach and cross the Arkansas River, still more than a hundred miles away, without having to stop for another time- and man-killing fight for survival. His hope was not fulfilled. At Newtonia that afternoon, twenty-odd miles beyond Carthage, the Federals came up in his rear and obliged him to turn and form ranks for a battle no one knew was to be the last ever fought between regular forces west of the Mississippi. Back at Fort Scott two days ago, the Kansas militia and two of the Missouri cavalry brigades had retired from the chase — as had Pleasonton himself, after falling sick — but Curtis, with his regulars and Blunt's plainsmen still on hand, as well as Pleasonton's other two brigades, was determined to overtake the still-outnumbered raiders before they escaped. Here at Newtonia he got his chance; along with cause to regret it. Spotting dust clouds south of town, Blunt thought Price was attempting a getaway and galloped hard around his flank to cut him off, only to be cut off himself by Shelby, who handled him roughly until other blue units broke through to cover his withdrawal. The fighting sputtered out at sundown, with little or no advantage on either side, and Price took up his march southward, unpursued, while Curtis waited for Blunt to lick his wounds. "I must be permitted to say that I consider him the best cavalry officer I ever saw," Old Pap wrote gratefully of Shelby in his report of the campaign: an opinion echoed and enlarged upon by Pleasonton years later, when he said flatly that the Missourian was "the best cavalry general of the South."

Curtis rested briefly, then proceeded, no longer in direct pursuit of Price, who veered southwest beyond Newtonia, but rather by a shorter route, due south across the Arkansas line, in hope of intercepting the raiders when they swung back east to recross the Arkansas River between Fort Smith and Little Rock; probably at Dardanelle, he figured, where they had crossed on their way north eight weeks ago. Hurrying from Pea Ridge to the relief of Fayetteville, which was reported under attack by a detachment from the rebel main body at Cane Hill, just under twenty miles southwest, the Kansan supposed that his cut-off tactics had succeeded. When he reached Fayetteville on November 4, however, he not only found the attackers gone, he also learned that his adversary was moving en masse in the opposite direction, away from the trap contrived for his destruction. Reduced by casualties and desertions, badly worn by a thousand miles of marching, and even lower in spirits than he was on food and ammunition — which was low indeed — Price was in no condition to risk another heavy engagement, and to avoid one he had decided not to attempt a march east of Fort Smith, whose garrison would be added to the force that would surely intercept him before he made it across the river in that direction. Instead, he would move on west, toward Tahlequah in the Indian Territory, for an upstream crossing of the Arkansas twenty-odd miles beyond the border. Curtis followed as far as a north-bank settlement called Webber's Falls, November 8, only to find that the raiders, assisted by friendly Choctaws, had destroyed all the available boats on reaching the south bank the day before. So he pronounced the campaign at an end, fired a 24-gun salute in celebration, the booms reverberating hollowly across the empty plains, and turned back toward Kansas, glad to be done with an opponent who, as he declared in closing his report, had "entered Missouri feasting and furnishing his troops on the rich products and abundant spoils of the Missouri Valley, but crossed the Arkansas destitute, disarmed, disorganized, and avoiding starvation by eating raw corn and slippery-elm bark."

Worse things were said of Price by his own soldiers in the course of their detour through the wintry territorial wilds. "God damn Old Pap!" was among the milder exclamations on the march, and afterwards there was to be a formal inquiry into charges of "glaring mismanagement and distressing mental and physical military incapacity." One trooper wrote that his unit subsisted for four days on parched acorns, while another told how he and his comrades butchered and devoured a fat pony along the way. A cold wind cut through their rags, freezing the water in their canteens, and coyotes laughed from the darkness beyond their campfires, a terrifying sound to men too weak from hunger or dysentery to keep up with the column. Even so, hundreds fell out in the course of this last long stage of the raid, south through Indian country, down across the Red into Texas, and finally back east to Laynesport, Arkansas, which they reached on December 2, still a hundred miles west of Camden, which Price had left just over three months ago. Though he put the case as best he could in his report — "I marched 1434 miles; fought 43 battles and skirmishes; captured and paroled over 3000 Federal officers and men . . . [and] do not think I go beyond the truth when I state that I destroyed in the late expedition to Missouri property to the amount of $10,000,000 in value" — his claim that his own losses totaled fewer than a thousand men, in and out of combat, scarcely tallied with the fact that he returned with only 6000, including recruits, or barely half the number who had ridden northward with him in September.

Whatever the true figures were, in men or money, and however great the disruption had been along the Missouri River and the Kansas border, this last campaign in the Transmississippi had no more effect on the outcome of the national conflict than did a much smaller, briefer effort made at the same time, up near the Canadian border, against St Albans, a Vermont town of about 5000 souls. This too was a raid designed to bring home to voters remote from the cockpit of war — Westport and St Albans were both just under a thousand miles from Charleston — some first-hand notion of the hardships involved in a struggle they were about to decide whether to continue or conclude: with the difference that the New England blow was struck primarily at what was reputed to be a New Englander's tenderest spot, his wallet.

First Lieutenant Bennett Young, a twenty-one-year-old Kentuckian who had ridden with Morgan, reconnoitered St Albans on a visit from Canada, fifteen miles away, and returned on the evening of October 18 with twenty followers, most of them escaped or exchanged prisoners like himself. Arriving in twos and threes to avoid suspicion, they checked into various hotels and boarding houses, then assembled at 3 o'clock the following afternoon in the town square, where they removed their overcoats to reveal that each wore a gray uniform and a pair of navy sixes. At first, when Young announced that the place was under formal occupation and ordered all inhabitants to gather in the square, the townspeople thought they were being treated to some kind of joke or masquerade, but when the raiders began discharging pistols in the direction of those who were slow to obey the lieutenant's order, they knew better. Meantime, three-man details proceeded to the three banks and gathered up all the cash on hand, though not before outraged citizens began to shoot at them from second-story windows. In the skirmish that ensued, one townsman was killed, three invaders were wounded, and several buildings around the square were set aflame with four-ounce bottles of Greek fire, brought along to be flung as incendiary grenades.

Back in Canada not long after nightfall, once more in civilian dress, Young and his men counted the take from this farthest north of all Confederate army operations. It came to just over $200,000; none of which ever found its way to Richmond, as originally intended, being used instead to finance other disruptions in other Federal regions that had not felt the hand of war till now.

Afloat as ashore, throughout this critical span of politics and war, there were desperate acts by desperate men intent on winning a reputation before it was too late. Commander Napoleon Collins, for example, a fifty-year-old Pennsylvanian with thirty years of arduous but undistinguished service, learned while coaling at Santa Cruz de Tenerife in mid-September that the rebel cruiser *Florida* had been there for the same purpose the month before; reports attending her departure, August 4, were that her next intended port of call was Bahia, just around the eastern hump of South America, some 1500 nautical miles away. His orders, as captain of the U.S.S. *Wachusett* — a sister ship of the *Kearsarge* — were to intercept and sink her, much as Winslow had sunk the *Alabama* three months ago off Cherbourg, and he wasted no time in clearing the Canaries for Brazil. Arriving in early October he did not find the prize he sought in Bahia harbor; nor, despite her six-week head start and her reputed greater speed, had she been there. Apparently the Santa Cruz report was false, or else she had been terribly busy on the way. Then two days later, shortly after dark, October 4, a trim, low-lying sloop of war put into All Saints Bay, and when Collins dispatched a longboat to look her over he found to his delight that the report had been true after all. The twin-stacked handsome vessel, riding at anchor no more than a long stone's throw off his starboard flank, was indeed the *Florida*, one of the first and now the last of the famed Confederate raiders that had practically driven Federal shipping from the Atlantic.

Since her escape from Mobile Bay in January of the previous year, *Florida* had burned or ransomed 37 prizes, and to these could be added 23 more, taken by merchantmen she had captured and converted into privateers, thereby raising her total to within half a dozen of the *Alabama*'s record 66. Most of the time she had been in Commander John Maffitt's charge, but since the beginning of the current year, Maffitt having fallen ill, she had been under her present skipper, Lieutenant

Charles M. Morris. Her most recent prize was taken a week ago, and Collins had it very much in mind to see that she took no more. Employing Winslow's tactics, he sent Morris next day, through the U.S. consul at Bahia, a formal invitation to a duel outside the three-mile limit. But Morris not only declined the challenge, he even declined to receive the message, addressed as it was to "the sloop *Florida*," quite as if he and his ship were nationless. He would leave when he saw fit, he said, having been granted an extension of the two-day layover allowed by international law, and would be pleased to engage the *Wachusett* if he chanced to meet her on the open sea. Collins absorbed the failure of this appeal to "honor," which had worked so well for Winslow against Semmes, then fell back on a secondary plan, rasher than the first and having nothing whatever to do with honor. Tomorrow night would be the *Florida*'s third in Bahia harbor, and he was determined, regardless of the security guaranteed by her presence in a neutral port, that it would be her last.

Suspecting nothing, Morris coöperated fully in the execution of the plan now being laid for his undoing. He had had the shot withdrawn from his guns, as required by law before entering the harbor, and assured the port authorities — who seemed disturbed by the thought of what he (not Collins, with whose government their own had long-standing diplomatic relations) might do in the present edgy situation — that he would commit no hostile act, in violation of their neutrality, against the enemy vessel anchored off his flank. This done, he let his steam go down, hauled his fires, and gave the port and starboard watches turnabout shore leave while off duty. On the night of October 6 he went ashore himself, with several of his officers, to attend the opera and get a good night's sleep in a hotel, leaving his first lieutenant aboard in charge of half the crew. Long before dawn next morning he was awakened by the concierge, who informed him that his ship was under attack by the *Wachusett* in the harbor down below.

Collins had planned carefully and with all the boldness his given name implied. Slipping his cables in the deadest hour of night, he backed quietly to give himself space in which to pick up speed for a ram that would send the raider to the bottom, then paused to build up a full head of steam before starting his run on the stroke of 3 o'clock. His intention was to bear straight down on the sitting vessel and thus inflict a wound that would leave her smashed beyond repair; but *Wachusett* went a bit off course and struck instead a glancing blow that crushed the bulwarks along the rebel's starboard quarter and carried away her mizzenmast and main yard. Convinced that he had inflicted mortal damage, Collins was backing out to let his adversary sink, when there was a spatter of small arms fire from the wreckage on her deck. He replied in kind and added the boom of two big Dahlgrens for emphasis, later saying:

"The *Florida* fired first." As he withdrew, however, he saw that the raider was by no means as badly hurt as he had thought. Accordingly, he changed his plan in mid-career and decided to take her alive. Guns reloaded, he stopped engines at a range of one hundred yards and called out a demand for the sloop's immediate surrender before he blew her out of the water.

Aboard the crippled *Florida,* with no steam in her boilers, no shot in her guns, and only a leave-blown skeleton crew on hand, the lieutenant left in charge had little choice except to yield, though he did so under protest at this hostile action in a neutral port. Collins promptly attached a hawser to the captive vessel and proceeded to tow her out to sea, fired on ineffectively by the guns of a harbor fort and pursued by a Brazilian corvette which he soon outdistanced. Morris arrived from the hotel in time to see the two sloops leave the bay in this tandem fashion, *Wachusett* in front and his own battered *Florida* in ignominious tow, and though he too protested this "barbarous and piratical act," they were by then beyond recall on the high seas, bound for Norfolk.

After a stopover in the West Indies, Napoleon Collins brought the two warships into Hampton Roads on November 12, both under their own power. There he received a welcome as enthusiastic as the one that had greeted his former squadron commander, Captain Charles Wilkes — also at one time skipper of the *Wachusett* — following his removal, three years ago, of Mason and Slidell from the British steamer *Trent.* Seward, on learning of what had happened in Bahia harbor, was only too aware that the two cases were uncomfortably similar, except that this was an even more flagrant violation of international law. Like the two Confederate envoys, the *Florida* was likely to prove an elephant on the State Department's hands, and he began to regret that Collins had not sunk her outright instead of bringing her in, since there could be little doubt that the courts would order her returned intact to the neutral port where he had seized her. "I wish she was at the bottom of the sea," the Secretary was afterwards reported to have remarked in discussing the affair with David Porter, recently transferred from duty on the Mississippi to command the North Atlantic Blockading Squadron. "Do you mean it?" Porter asked, and Seward replied: "I do, from my soul." The admiral returned to his headquarters in Hampton Roads and ordered the captive sloop moved to Newport News and anchored, as an act of poetic justice, near the spot where the *Merrimac* had sunk the *Cumberland.* In the course of the shift, the raider collided with a transport, losing her jibboom and figurehead and being severely raked along one side. She began leaking rather badly, and though her pumps were put to work, suddenly and mysteriously in the early-morning hours of November 28 she foundered and went to the bottom, nine fathoms down. Or maybe not so mysteriously after all; Porter subsequently confided that he had put an engineer aboard with orders to "open her sea cock before midnight, and do not leave that engine room until the water is up to your chin."

This might or might not account for her loss (for with Porter as an unsupported witness, no set of facts was ever certain) but in any case Seward's task in responding to the formal Brazilian protest, which arrived next month, was greatly simplified. "You have justly expected that the President would disavow and regret the proceedings at Bahia," he replied, adding that the captain of the *Wachusett* would be suspended from duty and court-martialed. As for the rebel sloop, there could be no question of returning her, due to "an unforeseen accident which casts no responsibility upon the United States." All the same, a U.S. gunboat was to put into All Saints Bay on the Emperor's birthday, two years later, and fire a 21-gun salute as the *amende honorable* for this offense against the peace and dignity of Brazil. Collins himself was tried within six months, as Seward promised, and despite his plea that "the capture of the *Florida* was for the public good," was sentenced to be dismissed from the service. Gideon Welles, much pleased with the commander's response to a situation that had worked out well in the end, promptly set the verdict aside, restored the Pennsylvanian to duty, and afterwards promoted him to captain. Like Charles Wilkes, he would be a rear admiral before he died, a decade later.

Welles's pleasure was considerably diminished, however, by reports that followed hard on the heels of Collins's exploit, indicating that this was by no means the end of rebel depredations against Federal shipping on the sea lanes of the world. By coincidence, on October 8 — the day after the *Florida* was taken under tow in Bahia harbor — the Clyde-built steamer *Sea King*, a fast sailer with a lifting screw, an iron frame, and six-inch planking of East India teak, left London bound for Madeira, which she reached ten days later to rendezvous with a Liverpool-based tender bearing guns and ammunition and James I. Waddell, a forty-year-old former U.S. Navy lieutenant who had gone over to the Confederacy, with equal rank in its infant navy, when his native North Carolina left the Union. He took over at once as captain of the *Sea King*, supervised the transfer and installation of her armament, formally commissioned her as the C.S.S. *Shenandoah*, and set out two days later, October 20, on a cruise designed to continue the *Alabama-Florida* tradition. In point of fact, his mission was to extend that tradition into regions where his country's flag had never flown. Like the raid on St Albans, staged the day before he left Madeira, and the recent 31-prize sortie by the *Tallahassee*, to Halifax and back, *Shenandoah*'s maiden effort was designed as a blow at the pocketbooks of New England, although Waddell had no intention of sailing her anywhere near that rocky shore. "The enemy's distant whaling grounds have not been visited by us," Secretary Mallory had noted in an August letter of instructions. "This commerce constitutes one of his reliable sources of national wealth no less than one of his best schools for seamen, and we must strike it, if possible."

Nothing in the new captain's orders precluded the taking of prizes en route to the field of his prime endeavor. He took six — two brigs, two barks, a schooner, and a clipper — between the day he left Madeira and November 12, the day the captive *Florida* steamed into Hampton Roads. Three more he took — another schooner and two barks, bringing the total to nine in as many weeks — in the course of a stormy year-end voyage around the Cape of Good Hope to Hobson's Bay, Australia, where the *Shenandoah* stopped to refit before setting out again, northward through the Sea of Japan and into the North Pacific, to take up a position for intercepting Yankee whaling fleets bound for Oahu with the product of their labors in the Arctic Ocean and the Bering Sea. A whaler filled with sperm oil, Waddell had been told, would give a lovely light when set afire.

Cruisers were and would remain a high-seas problem, mainly viewed through a murk of inaccurate reports. But there were other problems the Union navy considered far more pressing, especially through this critical season of decision, because they were closer to home and the November voters. One was blockade-runners; or, more strictly speaking, the discontent they fostered. Although by now only three out of four were getting through the cordon off the Carolina coast, as compared to twice that ratio two years back, there was general agreement that they could never really be stopped until their remaining ports were sealed from the landward side. Meantime, sleek and sneaky, they kept weary captains and their crews on station in all weathers, remote from combat and promotion and contributing for the most part nothing but their boredom to a war they felt could be quickly won if only they were free to bring their guns to bear where they would count. Another problem was rebel ironclads, built and building, which threatened not only to upset plans for future amphibious gains, but also to undo gains already made.

A prime example of this last, now that the *Merrimac-Virginia*, the *Arkansas*, and the *Tennessee* had been disposed of, was the achievement of the *Albemarle* in reclaiming the region around the Sound whose name she bore. Since mid-April, when she retook Plymouth and blocked ascent of the Roanoke toward Petersburg and Richmond, a stalemate advantageous to the Confederacy had obtained there, and though the commander of the half-dozen Federal vessels lying off the mouth of the river had devised a number of highly imaginative plans for her discomfort — including one that involved the use of stretchers for lugging hundred-pound torpedoes across the intervening swamps, to be planted and exploded alongside the Plymouth dock where she was moored —

none had worked, so vigilant were the graybacks in protecting this one weapon whose loss would mean the loss of everything within range of her hard-hitting rifles, all up and down the river she patrolled. Not since early May, when she tried it and came uncomfortably close to being sunk or captured for her pains, had the ironclad ventured out to engage the fleet, but neither could the Union ships invite destruction by steaming up to engage her at close quarters within the confines of that narrow stream. It was clear, however, that something had to be done about her before long: for there were reports that two more rams were under construction up the river, one of them in the very cornfield where she herself had taken shape. One *Albemarle* was fearful enough to contemplate, even from a respectful distance. A flotilla of three, churning down into the Sound, was quite unthinkable.

The answer came from Lieutenant William B. Cushing, who presented two plans for getting rid of the iron menace. One involved the use of India-rubber boats, to be packed across the swamps to within easy reach of the objective, then inflated for use by a hundred-man assault force that would board the ram under cover of darkness, overpower her crew, and take her down to join the fleet at the mouth of the river, eight miles off. Plan Two, also a night operation, called for the boarding party to move all the way by water in a pair of light-draft steamers, each armed with a bow howitzer and a long spar tipped with a torpedo, to be used to sink the rebel warship if the attempt to seize her failed. He submitted his proposal in July, and when the Hampton Roads authorities chose the second plan and passed it on to Washington — where Welles approved it too, though with misgivings, since it seemed likely to cost the service one of its most promising young officers, not to mention the volunteers he proposed to take along — he left at once for New York, his home state, to purchase "suitable vessels" for the undertaking up the Roanoke.

No one who knew or knew of Cushing, and he was well known by now on both sides of the line, would have been surprised, once they learned that he was the author of the plan, at the amount of risk and verve its execution would require. Wisconsin-born, the son of a widowed schoolteacher, and not yet twenty-two — the age at which his brother Alonzo had died on Cemetery Ridge the year before, a West Pointer commanding one of the badly shot-up batteries that helped turn Pickett's Charge — he already had won four official commendations for similar exploits he had devised and carried out in the course of the past three years. Perhaps this was compensatory daring; he had been at Annapolis until midway through his senior year in 1861, when he was permitted to resign and thus avoid dismissal for unruly conduct and a lack of what the authorities called "aptitude for the naval service." He volunteered as an acting master's mate, in reaction to Sumter, and was restored to the rank of midshipman within six months. "Where there

is danger in the battle, there will I be," he informed a kinsman at the
time, "for I will gain a name in this war." By now he had done so, and
had won promotion to lieutenant, first junior, then senior grade, as well
as those four commendations signed by Welles. None of this was
enough; he wanted more; nothing less, indeed, than the highest of all
military honors. "Cousin George," he wrote as he left New York in
mid-October to keep his appointment with the *Albemarle* near Plymouth, "I am going to have a vote of thanks from Congress, or six feet
of pine box by the next time you hear from me."

He had secured two open launches originally built for picket
duty, screw-propelled vessels thirty feet long and narrow in the beam,
of shallow draft and with low-pressure engines for quiet running, his
notion being that one could stand by to provide covering fire and to
pick up survivors if the other was sunk in the assault. As it turned out,
this duplication was useful much sooner than he had expected; for one
was lost in a Chesapeake storm on the way down, and he decided to go
ahead with a single boat rather than wait for a replacement. Steaming in
through Hatteras Inlet — whose bar no Union monitor could cross to
ascend the Roanoke and engage the homemade iron ram — he joined
the fleet riding at anchor fifty miles up Albemarle Sound. Two days he
spent reconnoitering and drilling his volunteer crew, including fourteen
men in the launch with him and another twelve in a towed cutter, the
latter group to be used to silence rebel lookouts posted aboard the wreck
of the *Southfield*, sunk in April a mile downstream from the dock where
the *Albemarle* was moored. Soon after moonset, October 26, Cushing
began his eight-mile run, the cutter in tow, only to be challenged just
beyond the mouth of the river by Federal pickets who nearly opened
fire when they heard the launch approaching. He turned back, warned
by this apparent mishap that the expedition would have failed, and next
day had a carpenter box-in the engine to muffle its sound, then set out
again the following night, having added a tarpaulin to reduce the noise
still more.

This time all went well on the run upriver. A rainstorm afforded
such good additional cover that the launch chugged past the grounded
Southfield undetected, thus enabling Cushing to keep the cutter with him
in hope of using its dozen occupants to help overpower the crew of the
ram when he went aboard. But that was not to be. Challenged by a
sentry as he drew within hailing distance of the wharf, he changed
his plan in mid-career; "Ahead fast!" he called out, and cast the cutter
loose with orders to return downriver and deal with the pickets on the
Southfield. As he approached the ram, a signal fire blazed up ashore and
he saw by its light that the ironclad was surrounded by a pen of logs
chained in position to shield her from just such an attack as he was
about to make. Hailed by a sailor on her deck, he replied with a shot
from his howitzer and ran within pistol range for a better look at the

problem. The logs were placed too far out for him to reach the ram with the torpedo attached to the tip of its fourteen-foot spar, although closer inspection showed that they perhaps were slimy enough for the launch to slide onto or even over them if it struck hard, at a direct angle. (Getting off or out was of course another matter, but that was no part of the plan as he had revised it.) He came about, under heavy fire from the enemy ship and shore, and picked up speed for the attempt. The launch struck and mounted and slithered across the encircling pen of logs, and Cushing found himself looking into the muzzle of one of the big rifles on the *Albemarle*, which he later described as looming before him like a "dark mountain of iron."

Then came the hardest part. To control and produce the explosion he had three lines tied to his wrists: one to raise or lower the long spar goose-necked to the bow of the launch, another to arm the torpedo by dropping it into a vertical position, and a third to activate the firing mechanism. All three required the coolness and precision of a surgeon performing a delicate operation, since too sudden a pull on any one of the lines would result in a malfunction. In this case, moreover, the surgeon was grievously distracted, having lost the tail of his coat to a blast of buckshot and the sole of one shoe to a bullet. Working as calmly under fire as he had done while rehearsing the performance in the quiet of his quarters, Cushing maneuvered the spar and swung the torpedo under the overhang of the ram's iron deck to probe for a vital spot before he released the firing pin. As he did so, the big rifle boomed, ten feet ahead, and hurled its charge of grape across the bow and into the stern of the stranded launch, which then was swamped by the descent of a mass of water raised by the explosion, nearly strangling all aboard. "Abandon ship!" the lieutenant cried, removing his shoes and shucking off his coat to go over the side.

The river was cold, its surface lashed by fire from the shore and the now rapidly sinking ram, whose captain would later testify that the hole blown in her hull was "big enough to drive a wagon through." Cushing struck out for the opposite bank, intent on escape, and as he did, heard one of his crew, close behind him, give "a great gurgling yell" as he went down. Ceasing fire, the Confederates came out in boats to look for survivors; Cushing heard them call his name, but continued to go with the current, paddling hard to keep afloat until he made it to shallow water, half a mile below. Exhausted, he lay in the mud till daylight, then crept ashore to take cover in the swamp. Later he found an unguarded bateau, and at nightfall began a stealthy trip downstream.

"Ship ahoy! Send a boat!" the crew of a Union patrol ship heard someone call from the darkness of the mouth of the river before dawn. An armed detail sent to investigate presently returned with Cushing and the news that he had sunk the *Albemarle*. Cheers went up, as did rockets, fired to inform the other ships of the triumph scored two nights ago, and before long the weary lieutenant, who had been reported lost with all his crew, was sipping brandy in the captain's cabin. A few days later he was with Porter at Hampton Roads. "I have the honor to report, sir, that the rebel ironclad is at the bottom of the Roanoke River."

By then Plymouth, untenable without the protection of the ram, was back in Federal hands, having been evacuated after its works were taken under bombardment by the fleet on October 31. Upriver, the two unfinished ironclads were burned in their stocks when the whole region passed from rebel occupation. Cushing was promptly rewarded with a promotion to lieutenant commander, along with the thanks of Congress, upon Lincoln's recommendation, for having displayed what Porter called "heroic enterprise seldom equaled and never excelled." Much was expected of him in his future career, and he gave every sign of fulfilling those expectations. Before he was thirty, six years after the conflict ended, he would become the youngest full commander in the U.S. Navy. But that was as far as he went. He died at the age of thirty-two in a government asylum for the insane, thereby provoking much discussion as to whether heroism and madness, like genius and tuberculosis, were related — and, if so, had insanity been at the root of his exploits? or had the strain of performing them, or even of having performed them, been more than a sane man could bear? In any case Farragut himself, in a subsequent conversation with Welles, stated flatly that "young Cushing was the hero of the war."

Westward to the Mississippi and north to the Ohio, Confederates did what they could to offset the loss of Atlanta by harassing the supply lines that sustained its Federal occupation. John Morgan was not one of these, for two sufficient reasons. One was that his command had by no means recovered from its unauthorized early-summer excursion into Kentucky, which had cost him half of his "terrible men," along with at least as great a portion of what remained of a reputation already diminished by the collapse of his Ohio raid the year before. The other was that he was dead — shot down in a less-than-minor skirmish on September 4, two days after Atlanta fell and nine months short of his fortieth birthday.

Informed that a blue column had set out from Knoxville for a strike at Saltville and the Southwest Virginia lead mines, he left Abingdon on September 1 and two days later reached Greeneville, Tennessee, where he prepared to confront the raiders when they emerged from Bull's Gap tomorrow or the next day. Down to about 2000 men, he deployed them fanwise to the west, covering three of the four roads in that direction, and retired for the night in the finest house in town, which as usual meant that its owner had Confederate sympathies. Greeneville, like many such places in East Tennessee, was a town with divided loyalties; Longstreet had wintered here, awaiting orders to rejoin Lee, and Andrew Johnson had been its mayor in the course of his rise from tailor to Lincoln's running mate in the campaign now in progress. Around sunup, after a rainy night, Morgan was wakened this Sunday morning by rifle fire, spattering in the streets below his bedroom window, and by a staff captain who brought word that the Union advance guard had arrived by the untended road. He pulled on his trousers and boots and went out by a rear door in an attempt to reach the stable and his horse, but was cut off and had to turn back, taking shelter in a scuppernong arbor that screened the walkway from the house.

"That's him! That's Morgan, over there among the grape vines!" a woman called from across the street to the soldiers pressing their search for the raider.

"Don't shoot; I surrender," Morgan cried.

"Surrender and be God damned — I know you," a blue trooper replied as he raised and fired his carbine at a range of twenty feet.

"Oh God," Morgan groaned, shot through the breast, and collapsed among the rain-wet vines, too soon dead to hear what followed.

"I've killed the damned horse thief!" the trooper shouted, and he and his friends tore down an intervening fence in their haste to get at Morgan's body, which they threw across a horse for a jubilant parade around the town before they flung it, stripped to a pair of drawers, into a muddy roadside ditch. Two captured members of the general's staff were allowed to wash and dress the corpse in the house where he had slept the night before, and others, returning after the enemy withdrew, reclaimed the body and sent it back to Abingdon, where his widow — the former Mattie Ready, pregnant with the daughter he would never see — had it removed to a vault in Richmond, to await the time when it could be returned in peace to the Bluegrass region he had loved and raided. That was the end of John Hunt Morgan.

It was otherwise with Forrest. Not only was he still very much alive, he now also had a department commander who would use him for something more than repelling Memphis-based raids into North Mississippi; would use him, indeed, on raids of his own against Sherman's life line up in Middle Tennessee. One of Richard Taylor's first acts, on assuming command at Meridian in early September, was to notify his presidential brother-in-law of this intention, while summoning the cavalryman to headquarters for instructions. Davis approved, and Forrest arrived by rail on September 5, "a tall, stalwart man, with grayish hair, mild countenance, and slow and homely of speech."

Taylor saw him thus for the first time, two weeks after his Memphis strike — three days after Atlanta fell and the day after Morgan died — though he knew him, of course, by reputation: nothing in which had prepared him for the Wizard's initial reaction to the news that he was to be sent at last "to worry Sherman's communications north of the

Tennessee River." Forrest responded more with caution than with elation, inquiring about the route prescribed, the problem of subsistence, his possible lines of retreat in case of a check, and much else of that nature. "I began to think he had no stomach for the work," Taylor later wrote. But this was in fact his introduction to the Forrest method; for presently, he noted, "having isolated the chances of success from causes of failure with the care of a chemist experimenting in his laboratory," the Tennessean rose and brought the conference to an end with an abrupt transformation of manner. "In a dozen sharp sentences he told his wants, said he would leave a staff officer to bring up his supplies, asked for an engine to take him back north to meet his troops, informed me he would march with the dawn, and hoped to give an account of himself in Tennessee."

That was how Taylor would recall the parting, but here again he misconstrued the method. Far from marching "with the dawn," Forrest took ten days to get ready before he set out from below Tupelo with everything in order, plans all laid and instructions clearly understood by subordinates charged with carrying them out. Chief among these was Abraham Buford, in command of his own two brigades and one from Chalmers, who would remain behind to patrol the region around Memphis. Eight guns rolled with the column, which left on September 16 with just over 3500 effectives, anticipating a meeting near the Tennessee River with nearly a thousand Alabama troopers under William Johnson, who had shown his mettle at Brice's Crossroads back in June. At Tuscumbia on the 20th Forrest also met someone he had not expected: Joe Wheeler. The diminutive Georgian was recrossing the river to wind up his long raid through East and Middle Tennessee, begun on August 10. Although the destruction he had wrought was about as extensive as he claimed to Hood, he neglected to add that Sherman's road gangs had repaired the damage about as fast as it was inflicted, often appearing on the scene before the twisted rails were cool. Moreover, there was something else the young West Pointer did not include in his report, and this was the condition of his command. Grievously diminished (for he tallied only his combat losses, which were barely a twentieth of the total suffered in the course of his six-week ride from Atlanta, up to Strawberry Plains near Knoxville, then back into North Alabama) the survivors were scarecrow examples of what could happen to troopers off on their own behind enemy lines. Originally 4500 strong — the number Forrest would have when Johnson joined tomorrow — they now counted fewer than 2000. A good many of the missing were stragglers whose mounts had broken down, and Forrest wrote Taylor that night, amid preparations for crossing the river next day: "I hope to be instrumental in gathering them up."

Fording his horsemen and floating his guns and wagons across on flatboats, he camped the following night on the north bank of the river, five miles west of Florence, which he passed through next morning,

September 22, on the way to his main objective, the Tennessee & Alabama Railroad, just over forty miles to the east. One of Sherman's two main supply lines, running from Nashville through Columbia and Pulaski to Decatur, where it joined the Memphis & Charleston to connect with Chattanooga and Atlanta, its nearest point was Athens, and that was where Forrest was headed. He got there after sunset on the 23d to begin his investment of the town and its adjoining fort, a ditched and palisaded work a quarter-mile in circumference, occupied by a force of 600 infantry and considered impregnable to assault: as indeed perhaps it was, although no one would ever know. Soon after daybreak John Morton opened fire with his eight guns, "casting almost every shell inside the works," according to the garrison commander. Before long, Forrest halted fire to send in a white-flag note demanding "immediate and unconditional surrender." The Federal declined, but then unwisely consented to a parley, in the course of which Forrest pulled his customary trick of exposing troops and guns in triplicate, thereby convincing his adversary that he was besieged by a host of 15,000 of all arms, with no less than two dozen cannon. Capitulation came in time for the graybacks to give their full attention to a relief column that arrived from Decatur to take part in a brief skirmish before joining the surrender. Reduction of two nearby railway blockhouses raised the day's bag to 1300 prisoners, two pieces of artillery, 300 horses, and a mountain of supplies and equipment, including two locomotives captured with their cars in Athens. Forrest put the torch to the stores and installations, issued the horses to those of his men who needed them, smashed the rolling stock, and sent the prisoners back through Florence for removal south. Then he took up the march northward along the railroad, wrecking as he went.

Halfway to the Tennessee line next morning, September 25, he came upon the Sulphur Branch railway trestle, 72 feet high and 300 long, guarded by a double-casemated blockhouse at each end and a large fortress-stockade with a garrison of about one thousand men. Surrender declined, Morton opened fire and kept it up for two cruel hours, slamming in 800 rounds that left the fort's interior "perforated with shell, and the dead lying thick along the works." So Forrest would report, adding that a repeated demand for surrender was promptly accepted. This time the yield was 973 bluecoats, two more guns, another 300 horses, and a quantity of stores. Again he sent his prisoners rearward, together with the captured guns and four of his own, so greatly had the bombardment reduced his supply of artillery ammunition, and after setting fire to the two blockhouses, the buildings in the fort, and the long trestle they had been designed to shield, rode on north to the Elk River, which he reached next day, about midway between Athens and Pulaski. Here too there was a blockhouse at each end of a bridge even longer than the trestle at Sulphur Branch; but they were unmanned, abandoned by a commander who had heard from below how little protection they afforded, either to the installations they overlooked or to the garrisons they contained. Forrest burned them, along with the Elk River span, and pushed on to Richland Creek, seven miles beyond the Tennessee line and the same distance from Pulaski. Here there was a 200-foot-long truss bridge, stoutly built to take the weight of heavy-laden supply trains. The raiders crossed and sent it up in flames.

Now the character of the expedition changed. "Enemy concentrating heavily against me," Forrest notified Taylor the following night, September 27, from the vicinity of Pulaski. Touched where he was tender, Sherman had reacted hard and fast, sending George Thomas himself from Atlanta with two divisions to take charge in Middle Tennessee, with instructions for "the whole resources" of the region, including Kentucky and North Alabama, to be "turned against Forrest ... until he is disposed of." Other divisions were on the way by rail and river from Memphis and Chattanooga, and Rosecrans had been urged to return A. J. Smith's gorillas from Missouri. As a result, fully 30,000 reinforcements were converging by now from all directions upon Pulaski, where Lovell Rousseau, arriving from Nashville to meet the threat, already had more men in its fortifications than were in the gray column on its outskirts. "Press Forrest to the death," Thomas wired ahead, "keeping your troops well in hand and holding them to the work. I do not think that we shall ever have a better chance than this."

The chance was not as good as the blue Virginian thought: not yet at any rate. Though he kept his Pulaski defenders "well in hand," Rousseau found the raiders gone from his front next morning. Forrest had built up his campfires the night before, and leaving them burning had pulled out. Having done what he could, at least for the present, to cripple the Tennessee & Alabama, he now was moving toward that other, more vital supply line, the Nashville & Chattanooga, fifty miles to the east. He was obliged, however, to do it no more than superficial damage, learning from scouts when he got beyond Fayetteville on the 29th that the Chattanooga road was heavily protected by reinforcements hurried up it from Georgia and down it from Kentucky. He contented himself with detaching a fifty-man detail to tear up wires and track around Tullahoma, then confused the regathering Federals still more by splitting his force in two. Buford turned south with his division and Morton's four remaining guns, under orders to return to the Tennessee River by way of Huntsville, which he was to capture if possible, and tear up track on the Memphis & Charleston, between there and Decatur, before recrossing. Forrest himself, with the other two brigades, turned northwest through Lewisburg, then north across Duck River, passing near his Chapel Hill birthplace on the last day of September to descend once more, at high noon of the following day, on the already hard-hit Tennessee & Alabama near Spring Hill, ten miles north of Columbia and about

four times that distance above Pulaski, which he had left four days ago.

He turned south, ripping up track, capturing three more blockhouses — mainly by bluff, since Buford had the guns — firing bridges, and smashing culverts all the way to Columbia, which he bypassed on October 2 to avoid the delay of a gunless fight with the bluecoats in its works. The time had come to get out, and Forrest, as one of his troopers said, was "pretty good on a git." Taking off southwest away from what remained of the Tennessee & Alabama, he moved by country roads through Lawrence-burg, where he camped on the night of the 3d, and crossed the Alabama line the next day to return to Florence on October 5, one day less than two weeks after he left it. Buford was there ahead of him, having found Huntsville too stoutly garrisoned to be taken, and though the Tennessee was swollen past fording he had managed to get his men and guns across in relays on three rickety ferries, swimming the horses alongside. Now it was Forrest's turn.

A slow and risky business, with the enemy reported close astern, the piecemeal crossing took two full days, and was only accomplished, a veteran would recall, with "considerable disregard of the third commandment." Fretted and tired, the general was in the last boat to leave. While helping to pole against the swift-running current he noticed a lieutenant standing in the bow and taking no part in the work. "Why don't you take hold of an oar or pole and help get this boat across?" The lieutenant replied that, as an officer, he did not feel "called on to do that kind of work" while private soldiers were available to perform it. Astounded by this implied reproach — for he himself was as hard at work as anyone aboard — Forrest slapped the young man sprawling into the river, then held out the long pole and hauled him back over the gunwale, saying: "Now, damn you, get hold of the oars and go to work! If I knock you out of the boat again I'll let you drown." Another passenger observed that the douched lieutenant "made an excellent hand for the balance of the trip."

In the two weeks spent south of Nashville, within the great bend of the Tennessee, Forrest had captured 2360 of the enemy and killed or wounded an estimated thousand more, at a cost to himself of 340 casualties, only 47 of whom were killed. He had destroyed eleven block-houses, together with the extensive trestles and bridges they were meant to guard, and had taken seven U.S. guns, 800 horses, and more than 2000 rifles, all of which he brought out with him, in addition to fifty captured wagons loaded with spoils too valuable for burning. Best of all, he had wrecked the Tennessee & Alabama so thoroughly that even the skilled blue work crews would need six full weeks to put it back in operation. Indeed, Taylor was so encouraged by this Middle Tennessee expedition that he promptly authorized another, to be aimed this time at Johnsonville, terminus of the newly extended Nashville & Northwestern Railroad, by which supplies, unloaded from steamboats and barges on the Tennessee, were sent to Sherman by way of Nashville, seventy-five miles due east. A blow at this riverport depot, whose yards and warehouses were crowded with stores awaiting transfer, would go far toward increasing the Union supply problem down in Georgia, and Forrest spent only a week resting and refitting his weary troopers, summoning Chalmers to join him en route, and adding a pair of long-range Parrotts to Morton's two batteries, before he took off again for Johnsonville, a hundred miles north of Corinth, to which he had returned on October 9.

Much was expected of this follow-up strike, even though the first — successful as it had been, within its geographic limitations — had failed to achieve its major purpose, which was to make Sherman turn loose of Atlanta for lack of subsistence for his army of occupation. Not only did the red-haired Ohioan by then have ample stockpiles of supplies, he also had the scarcely interrupted use of the Nashville & Chattanooga line, having repaired within twelve hours the limited damage inflicted near Tullahoma by the fifty-man detail Forrest had detached when he turned north beyond Fayetteville. If the raid had been made a month or six weeks earlier, while the Federals were fighting outside Atlanta, opposed by an aggressive foe and with both overworked railroads barely able to meet their daily subsistence needs, the result might have been different. Even so, Forrest with only 4500 troopers had managed to disrupt Sherman's supply arrangements, as well as the troop dispositions in his rear, and had brought him to the exasperated conclusion, expressed to Grant on October 9, that it would be "a physical impossibility to protect the roads, now that Hood, Forrest, Wheeler, and the whole batch of devils are turned loose without home or habitation."

✕ 5 ✕

First there had been the fret of verbal contention. Drawing back from Jonesboro, as he said, "to enjoy a short period of rest and to think well over the next step required in the progress of events," Sherman announced on September 8 that "the city of Atlanta, being exclusively required for warlike purposes, will at once be evacuated by all except the armies of the United States." He foresaw charges of inhumanity, perhaps from friends as well as foes, but he was determined neither to feed the citizens nor to "see them starve under our eyes. . . . If the people raise a howl against my barbarity or cruelty," he told Halleck, "I will answer that war is war and not popularity-seeking."

Sure enough, when Mayor Calhoun protested that the suffering of the sick and aged, turned out homeless with winter coming on, would be "appalling and heart-rending," Sherman replied that while he gave "full credit to your statement of the distress that will be occasioned," he would not revoke his orders for immediate resettlement. "They were not designed to meet the humanities of the case, but to prepare for the future struggle. . . . You cannot qualify war in harsher terms than I will. War is cruelty, and you cannot refine it. . . . You might as well appeal against the thunder storm as against these terrible hardships of war. . . . Now you must go," he said in closing, "and take with you your old and feeble, feed and nurse them, and build for them, in more quiet places, proper habitations to shield them against the weather until the mad passions of men cool down and allow the Union and peace once more to settle over your old homes at Atlanta. Yours in haste."

Hood attacked as usual, head down and full tilt, in response to a suggestion for a truce to permit the removal southward, through the lines, of the unhappy remnant of the city's population. He had, he said, no choice except to accede, but he added: "Permit me to say that the unprecedented measure you propose transcends, in studied and ingenious cruelty, all acts ever brought to my attention in the dark history of war. In the name of God and humanity, I protest."

"In the name of common sense," Sherman fired back, "I ask you not to appeal to a just God in such a sacrilegious manner. You who, in the midst of peace and prosperity, have plunged a nation into war — dark and cruel war — who dared and badgered us to battle, insulted our flag, seized our arsenals and forts." There followed an arm-long list of Confederate outrages, ending: "Talk thus to the marines, but not to me, who have seen these things. . . . If we must be enemies, let us be men and fight it out as we propose to do, and not deal in such hypocritical appeals to God and humanity. God will judge us in due time, and he will pronounce whether it be more humane to fight with a town full of women and the families of a brave people at our backs, or to remove them to places of safety among their own friends."

For two more days, though both agreed that "this discussion by two soldiers is out of place and profitless," the exchange continued, breathy but bloodless, before a ten-day truce was agreed on and the exodus began. Union troops escorted the refugees, with such clothes and bedding as they could carry, as far as Rough & Ready, where Hood's men took them in charge and saw them south across the fifteen-mile railroad gap to Lovejoy Station, within the rebel lines. Sherman was glad

to see them go, and truth to tell had rather enjoyed the preceding alter-
cation, which he saw as a sort of literary exercise, beneficial to his spleen,
and in which he was convinced he had once more gotten the best of
his opponent. But in other respects, having little or nothing to do with
verbal fencing, he was far less satisfied, and a good deal more perturbed.

On September 8, the day he ordered Calhoun and his people to
depart, he also issued a congratulatory order proclaiming to his soldiers
that their capture of Atlanta "completed the grand task which has been
assigned us by our Government." This was untrue. Welcome as the fall
of the city was at this critical time — he was convinced, for one thing,
that it assured Lincoln's reëlection, and for another he could present it,
quite literally, to his troops as a crowning reward for four solid months
of combat — his real objective, agreed on beforehand and identified
by Grant in specific instructions, was the Army of Tennessee; he had
been told to "break it up," and Atlanta had been intended merely to
serve as the anvil upon which the rebel force was to be fixed and
pounded till it shattered. That had been, and was, his true "grand task."
Not only was Hood's army still in existence, it was relatively intact,
containing close to 35,000 effectives, even with Wheeler gone for the
past month; whereas Sherman's own, though twice as strong as Hood's at
the time of occupation, started dwindling from the wholesale loss of
veterans whose three-year enlistments ran out about the time the truce
began. Subtractions from the top were even heavier in proportion.
Schofield had to return for a time to Knoxville to attend to neglected
administrative matters in his department, and Dodge, wounded soon after
he received a promotion to major general, took off on sick leave, never
to return; his corps was broken up to help fill the gaps in Howard's other
two, whose commanders, Logan and Blair — "political soldiers," Sherman scornfully styled them — had been given leaves of absence to
stump for Lincoln in their critical home states. Presently even George
Thomas was gone, along with two of his nine infantry divisions, sent
back to Tennessee when the news came down that Forrest was on the
rampage there, scooping up rear-guard detachments and providing the
rail repair gangs with more work than they could handle in a hurry.

Various possibilities obtained, even so, including a march on
Macon, Selma, or Mobile; but what the army needed most just now was
rest and refitment, a brief period in which to digest its gains and shake
its diminished self together, while its leader pondered in tranquillity his
next move. Fortified Atlanta seemed an excellent place for this, although the situation afforded little room for error. "I've got my wedge
pretty deep," Sherman remarked in this connection, "and must look
out I don't get my fingers pinched." One drawback was that the interlude surrendered the initiative to Hood, who had shown in the past that
he would be quick to grasp it, however stunned his troops might be as
a result of their recent failures, including the loss of the city in their

charge. Wheeler's damage to the supply line running back to Chattanooga had long since been repaired, but it seemed likely that his chief would strike there again, this time in heavier force; perhaps, indeed, with all he had.

This was in fact what Hood intended, if only because he felt he had no other choice. Determined to do *some*thing, yet lacking the strength to mount a siege or risk another large-scale confrontation on the outskirts of Atlanta, he had begun to prepare for a rearward strike while exchanging verbal shafts with his opponent inside the city. First he asked Richmond for reinforcements, and was told: "Every effort [has been] made to bring forward reserves, militia, and detailed men for the purpose.... No other resource remains." This denial had been expected, but it was promptly followed by another that had not. By gubernatorial proclamation on September 10, one week after Atlanta's fall, Joe Brown withdrew the Georgia militia beyond Confederate reach, granting blanket furloughs for his "pets," as they were called, "to return to their homes and look for a time after other important interests," by which he meant the tending of their farms. Discouraged but not dissuaded by this lengthening of the numerical odds, Hood held to his plan for a move northward, requesting of the government that the 30,000 Andersonville inmates, ninety miles in his rear, be transferred beyond reach of the Federals in his front and thus permit him to shift his base from Lovejoy Station, on the Macon & Western, to Palmetto on the Atlanta & West Point; that is, from south of the city to southwest. This, he explained in outlining his proposed campaign, would open the way for him to recross the Chattahoochee, west of Marietta, for a descent on the blue supply line north of the river. Sherman most likely would follow to protect his communications, leaving a strong garrison to hold Atlanta; in which event Hood would be able to fight him with a far better chance of winning than if he tried to engage him hereabouts, with the odds at two-to-one. If, on the other hand, Sherman responded to the shift by moving against Augusta, Mobile, or some other point to the east or south, Hood would return and attack his rear. In any case, whatever risk was involved in his proposal, he was convinced that this was the time to act, since "Sherman is weaker now than he will be in the future, and I as strong as I can expect to be."

Richmond, approving this conditional raid-in-force, ordered the transfer of all able-bodied prisoners from Andersonville, near Americus, to stockades down in Florida. This began on September 21, by which time Hood had completed his twenty-mile shift due west to Palmetto, about the same distance southwest of Atlanta, and had his subordinates hard at work on preparations for the march north around Sherman's flank. They were still at it, four days later — September 25, a rainy Sunday that turned the red dust of their camps to mire — when Jefferson Davis arrived for a council of war.

He came for other purposes as well, including the need — even direr now than at the time of his other western trips, in early winter and late fall of the past two years, when Bragg had been the general in trouble — "to arouse all classes to united and desperate resistance." Outwardly at least, Davis himself never quailed or wavered under adversity, Stephen Mallory would testify after working close to him throughout the war. "He could listen to the announcement of defeat while expecting victory, or to a foreign dispatch destructive to hopes widely cherished, or to whispers that old friends were becoming cold or hostile, without exhibiting the slightest evidence of feeling beyond a change of color. Under such circumstances, his language temperate and bland, his voice calm and gentle, and his whole person at rest, he presented rather the appearance of a man, wearied and worn by care and labor, listening to something he knew all about, than of one receiving ruinous disclosures." But this reaction was by no means characteristic of the high-strung people, in or out of uniform, to and for whom he was responsible as Commander in Chief and Chief Executive: and it was especially uncharacteristic now that the Federal penetration of the heartland had regional leaders of the caliber of Brown and Aleck Stephens crying havoc and talking of calling the dogs of war to kennel. Leaving Richmond five days ago, the day after Early's defeat at Winchester provided a companion setback in the eastern theater, Davis remarked to a friend: "The first effect of disaster is always to spread a deeper gloom than is due to the occasion." Then he set out for Georgia, as he had done twice before, in an attempt to dispel or at any rate lighten the gloom that had gathered and deepened there since the fall of Atlanta, three weeks back.

Army morale was a linked concern. Addressing himself to this on the day of his arrival at Palmetto, he attempted to lift the spirits of the troops with a speech delivered extemporaneously to Cheatham's Tennesseans, who flocked to meet him at the station. "Be of good cheer," he told them, "for within a short while your faces will be turned homeward and your feet pressing the soil of Tennessee."

Shouts of approval greeted this extension of the plan Hood had proposed; but other responses had a different tone. "Johnston! Give us Johnston!" Davis heard men cry or mutter from the ranks, and though he made no reply to this, it pointed up another problem he had come west to examine at first hand — the question of possible changes in the structure of command. Hardee, for example, had recently repeated his request for a transfer that would free him from further service under Hood, who blamed him for the collapse of two of his three Atlanta sorties, as well as for his failure to whip the enemy at Jonesboro, which had brought on the fall of the city. So Hood said, at any rate, wiring Richmond: "It is of the utmost importance that Hardee should be relieved at once. He commands the best troops in this army. I must have another commander." One or the other clearly had to go. Now at Palmetto, in tandem interviews, Davis heard the two generals out, recriminations abounding, and arrived at a decision that pleased them both: Hood by replacing Hardee with Cheatham, his senior division commander, and Hardee by ordering him to proceed at once to Charleston, where he would head the Department of South Carolina, Georgia, and Florida.

That was Beauregard's old bailiwick, and he was there even now, conducting a rather superfluous inspection of the coastal defenses. But there would be no overlapping of duties when Hardee arrived, since Davis planned for the Creole to be gone by then, summoned west as the solution to another command problem in the Army of Tennessee, this one at the very top. In mid-September, just before he left Richmond, he had received from Samuel French, who led a division in Stewart's corps, a private communication reminiscent of the famous round-robin letter that reached him after Chickamauga. This one was signed only by French, though it was written, he said, at the request of several high-ranking friends "in regard to a feeling of depression more or less apparent in parts of this army." His suggestion — or theirs, for the tone of the letter was strangely indirect — was that the President "send one or two intelligent officers here to visit the different divisions and brigades to ascertain if that spirit of confidence so necessary for success has or has not been impaired within the past month or two." Hood was not mentioned by name or position, as Bragg had been in the earlier document, but he was clearly responsible for conditions in a command which he had assumed "within the past month or two" and from which, the letter implied, he ought to be removed. This, combined with the public outcry over the loss of Atlanta, was part of what prompted the President's visit, and even before he set out he had arrived at a tentative solution to the problem by inviting Beauregard to go along. Old Bory was down in Charleston at the time, and Davis could not wait for him. He did, however, ask R. E. Lee to find out whether the Louisianian would be willing to return to duty in the West. Frustrated by subservience to Lee for the three months since Petersburg came under formal siege, Beauregard replied that he would "obey with alacrity" any such order for a transfer, and Davis wired from Palmetto for the Creole to meet him in Augusta on his way back in early October.

Beauregard, receiving the summons, assumed that he was about to return, as Hood's successor, to command of the army that had been taken from him more than two years ago, after Shiloh and the evacuation of Corinth. In this he was mistaken: though not entirely. Davis had it in mind to put him in charge not only of Hood's but also of Taylor's department, the whole to be known as the Military Division of the West, containing all of Alabama and Mississippi, together with major parts of Georgia and Louisiana and most of Tennessee. Assigned primarily in an advisory capacity, he would exercise direct control of troops only when he was actually with them — and only then, in Davis's words, "whenever in your judgment the interests of your command render it expedient." This was the position in which Johnston had fretted so fearfully last year; "a political device," a later observer was to term its creation, "designed to silence the critics of Hood, satisfy the friends of Beauregard, and save face for the Administration." That was accurate enough, as far as it went, but for Davis the arrangement had two other pragmatic virtues. One was that Hood's accustomed rashness might be tempered, if not controlled, by the presence of an experienced superior close at hand, and the other was that there was no room left for Joe Johnston, whose return Davis was convinced would result in a retreat down the length of the Florida peninsula. In any case, Beauregard was highly acceptable to the generals Davis talked with at Palmetto, including Hood, and he was determined to offer him the post when they met in Augusta the following week.

Mainly, though, the presidential visit was concerned with the strategy Hood had evolved for drawing the blue army north by striking at its supply line beyond the Chattahoochee, where he would take up a strong defensive position inviting a disadvantageous attack. Now in discussion this was expanded and improved. If Sherman appeared too strong even then, or if Hood, as Davis put it, "should not find the spirit of his army such as to justify him in offering battle" at that point, he was to fall back down the Coosa River and through the mountains to Gadsden, Alabama, where he would establish a new base, supplied by the railroad from Selma to Blue Mountain, and there "fight a conclusive battle" on terrain even more advantageous to the defender; Sherman, drawn far from his own base back in Georgia, might then be annihilated. If, on the other hand, the Ohioan declined battle on those terms and returned to Atlanta, Hood would follow, and when Sherman, his supply line cut, moved from there, Hood would still pursue: either northward, across the Tennessee — which would undo the Federal gains of the past four months and open the way for a Confederate march on Nashville — or south or east, through Selma or Montgomery to the Gulf or through Macon or Augusta to the Atlantic, in which case the Union rear could be assaulted. That was the expanded plan, designed to cover all contingencies, as Hood and the Commander in Chief developed it over the course of the three-day visit. Then on the evening of September 27 Davis took his leave.

In Macon next morning, at a benefit for the impoverished Atlanta refugees, he took up the spirit-lifting task he had begun at Palmetto when he told the Tennessee soldiers their faces would soon turn homeward. "What though misfortune has befallen our arms from Decatur to Jonesboro," he declared, "our cause is not lost. Sherman cannot keep up his long line of communications; retreat sooner or later he must. And when that day comes, the fate that befell the army of the French Empire in its retreat from Moscow will be re-enacted. Our cavalry and our people will harass and destroy his army, as did the Cossacks that of Napoleon, and the Yankee general, like him, will escape with only a bodyguard. . . .

"Let no one despond," he said in closing, and repeated the words the following day in Montgomery, speaking at the Capitol where he had been inaugurated forty-three months ago. "There be some men," he told the Alabamians, in support of his advice against despondence, "who when they look at the sun can only see a speck upon it. I am of a more sanguine temperament perhaps, but I have striven to behold our affairs with a cool and candid temperance of heart, and, applying to them the most rigid test, am more confident the longer I behold the progress of the war. . . . We should marvel and thank God for the great achievements which have crowned our efforts."

Closeted that night with Richard Taylor, who had transferred his headquarters from Meridian to Selma, he was glad to learn the particulars of Forrest's current raid into Middle Tennessee, but disappointed to be told that any hopes he retained for securing reinforcements from beyond the Mississippi were quite groundless, not only because the situation there would not permit it, but also because of the gunboats Taylor had had to dodge, even at night in a small boat, when he returned. Davis was able to counter this with news that Hood had begun today a crossing of the Chattahoochee near Campbelltown, twenty miles southwest of Atlanta, for his strike at the Federal life line. Taylor was pleased to hear it, remarking that the maneuver would no doubt "cripple [Sherman] for a time and delay his projected movements." Whatever enthusiasm surged up in him on hearing of this new offensive was certainly well contained. Moreover: "At the same time," he later wrote of the exchange, "I did not disguise my conviction that the best we could hope for was to protract the struggle until spring. It was for statesmen, not soldiers, to deal with the future."

This was chilling in its implications, coming as it did from a friend and kinsman whose opinion he respected and whose experience covered all three major theaters of the war, but Davis refused to be daunted; like Nelson off Copenhagen, putting the telescope to his blind eye, he declined to see these specks upon the Confederate sun. The two men parted to meet no more in the course of a conflict Taylor believed was drawing to a close, and Davis resumed his journey eastward from Montgomery next day, joined en route by Hardee for the scheduled meeting with Beauregard in Augusta on October 2, the President's second Sunday away from Richmond. Old Bory's spirits took a drop when he learned that he was to occupy an advisory rather than a fighting post, but they soon revived at the prospect of conferring with Hood on plans for reversing the western tide of battle. In the end, he was as pleased as

Hardee was with his new assignment, and both generals sat on the rostrum with their chief the following day at a patriotic rally. "We must beat Sherman; we must march into Tennessee," Davis told the Augustans. "There we will draw from 20,000 to 30,000 to our standard, and, so strengthened, we must push the enemy back to the banks of the Ohio and thus give the peace party of the North an accretion no puny editorial can give." Such was the high point of his last speech in Georgia, and having made it he presented the two generals to the crowd. Beauregard, who had fired the first gun of the war, was cheered for saying that he "hoped to live to fire the last," and Hardee, a native son, drew loud applause when he reported that Hood had recently told him "he intended to lay his claws upon the state road in rear of Sherman, and, having once fixed them there, it was not his intention to let them loose their hold."

Next day, October 4 — by which time the three speakers had reached or were moving toward their separate destinations: Beauregard west, Hardee east, and Davis north to the South Carolina capital — Hood had carried out at least the first part of this program. Completing his crossing of the Chattahoochee before September ended, he struck the Western & Atlantic at Big Shanty and Acworth, capturing their garrisons, and now was on the march for Allatoona, the principal Union supply base near the Etowah. Best of all, Sherman had taken the bait and was hurrying northward from Atlanta with most of his army, apparently eager for the showdown battle this gray maneuver had been fashioned to provoke. While the opening stage of the raid was in progress, and even as Hood's troops were tearing up some nine miles of track around Big Shanty, Davis delivered in Columbia the last in his current series of addresses designed to lift the spirits of a citizenry depressed by the events of the past two months.

"South Carolina has struggled nobly in the war, and suffered many sacrifices," he declared, beginning as usual with praise for the people of the state in which he spoke. "But if there be any who feel that our cause is in danger, that final success may not crown our efforts, that we are not stronger today than when we began this struggle, that we are not able to continue the supplies to our armies and our people, let all such read a contradiction in the smiling face of our land and in the teeming evidences of plenty which everywhere greet the eye. Let them go to those places where brave men are standing in front of the foe, and there receive the assurance that we shall have final success and that every man who does not live to see his country free will see a freeman's grave." He himself was on his way back from such a visit, and he had been reassured by what he saw. "I have just returned from that army from which we have had the saddest accounts — the Army of Tennessee — and I am able to bear you words of good cheer. That army has increased in strength since the fall of Atlanta. It has risen in tone; its march is onward, its face looking to the front. So far as I am able to judge, General Hood's strategy has been good and his conduct has been gallant. His eye is now fixed upon a point far beyond that where he was assailed by the enemy. He hopes soon to have his hand upon Sherman's line of communications, and to fix it where he can hold it. And if but a half — nay, one fourth — of the men to whom the service has a right will give him their strength, I see no chance for Sherman to escape from a defeat or a disgraceful retreat. I therefore hope, in view of all the contingencies of the war, that within thirty days that army which has so boastfully taken up its winter quarters in the heart of the Confederacy will be in search of a crossing of the Tennessee River." Having claimed as much, he pressed on and claimed more. "I believe it is in the power of the men of the Confederacy to plant our banners on the banks of the Ohio, where we shall say to the Yankee: 'Be quiet, or we shall teach you another lesson.' "

So he said, bowing low to the applause that followed, and after a day's rest — badly needed, since two weeks of travel on the buckled strap-iron of a variety of railroads amounted to a form of torture rivaling the rack — ended his fifteen-day absence from Richmond on the morning of October 6. The warm bright pleasant weather of Virginia's early fall belied the strain its capital was under; Fort Harrison had toppled just one week ago, creating a dent in the city's defenses north of the James, and the fight next day at Peebles Farm, though tactically a victory, had obliged Lee to extend his already thin-stretched Petersburg lines another two miles west. For Davis, however, any day that brought him back to his family was an occasion for rejoicing. And rejoice he did: especially over its newest member, three-month-old Varina Anne. Born in late June, while the guns were roaring on Kennesaw and Jubal Early was heading north from Lynchburg, she would in time be referred to as the "Daughter of the Confederacy," but to her father she was "Winnie," already his pet name for her mother, or "Pie-Cake," which her sister and brothers presently shortened to "Pie." He was glad to be back with her and the others, Maggie, Little Jeff, Billy, and his wife, who was pleased, despite her distress at the wear he showed, to hear how well the trip had gone in regard to his efforts to lift the flagging morale of the people with predictions of great success for Hood — whose troops were moving northward even now — and "defeat or a disgraceful retreat" for Sherman.

Grant, for one, disagreed with this assessment of the situation in North Georgia. Informed of Davis's late-September prediction that the fate that crumpled Napoleon in Russia now awaited Sherman outside Atlanta, he thought it over briefly, then inquired: "Who is to furnish the snow for this Moscow retreat?"

Afterwards, Sherman took this one step further, professing to have been delighted that the rebel leader's "vainglorious boasts" had in effect presented "the full key to his future designs" to those whom they were intended to undo; "To be forewarned was to be forearmed," he explained. But that was written later, when he seemed to have taken what he called "full advantage of the occasion." Davis in fact had said very little more in his recent impromptu speeches, including his proposal "to plant our banners on the banks of the Ohio," than he (and, indeed, many other Confederate spokesmen) had expressed on previous tours undertaken to lift spirits that had sagged under the burden of defeat. As for Hood's reported promise to "lay his claws" on the railroad north of Atlanta, they were already fixed there by the time Sherman heard from his spies or read in the papers of what Davis or Hardee was supposed to have said — days after Hood's whole army was across the Chattahoochee in his rear. Besides, the red-haired Ohioan was far too busy by then, attempting to deal with this newly developed threat to his life line, to conjecture much about what Hood might or might not have in mind as a next step.

Leaving Slocum's corps to hold Atlanta, he began recrossing the Chattahoochee with the other five — some 65,000 of all arms, exclusive of the two divisions sent back to Tennessee with Thomas the week before — when he discovered on October 3 that Hood, after crossing in force near Campbelltown, was moving north through Powder Springs, apparently with the intention of getting astride the Western & Atlantic somewhere around or beyond Marietta. Sherman rushed a division from Howard north by rail, under Brigadier General John M. Corse, to cover Rome in case the graybacks veered in that direction, but by the time he got the last of his men over the river next day he learned that the rebs had taken Big Shanty and Acworth, along with their garrisons, and had torn up nine miles of track on their way to seize his main supply base at Allatoona, which they would reach tomorrow. He got a message through for Corse to shift his troops by rail from Rome to Allatoona, reinforcing its defenders, and to hang on there till the rest of the army joined him.

Corse complied, but only by the hardest. When Sherman climbed Kennesaw next morning, October 5, he could see the Confederate main body encamped to the west around Lost Mountain, his own men at work repairing the railroad past Big Shanty, just ahead, and gunsmoke lazing up from Allatoona Pass, a dozen air-line miles to the north, where Corse was making his fight. Hood had detached Stewart's corps for the Acworth strike, and Stewart, before heading back to rejoin Hood last night, had in turn detached French's division to extend the destruction to the Etowah. "General Sherman says hold fast; we are coming," the Kennesaw signal station wigwagged Allatoona over the heads of the attackers. Corse — a twenty-nine-year-old Iowan who had spent two years at West Point before returning home to study law and run for public office, only to lose the election and enter the army, as was said, "to relieve the pain of political defeat" — had arrived, although with less than half of his division, in time to receive a white-flag note in which French allowed him five minutes "to avoid a needless effusion of blood" by surrendering unconditionally. He declined, replying: "We are prepared for the 'needless effusion of blood' whenever it is agreeable to you." The engagement that followed was as savage as might have been expected from this exchange. Corse had just under 2000 men, French just over 3000, and their respective losses were 706 and 799 killed, wounded, or captured. After two of the three redoubts had fallen, Corse withdrew his survivors to the third, near the head of the pass, and kept up the resistance, despite a painful face wound and the loss of more than a third of his command. By 4 o'clock, having intercepted wigwag messages that help was on the way from the 60,000 Federals in his rear, French decided to pull out before darkness and Sherman overtook him. Corse was exultant: so much so that when Sherman, still on Kennesaw, inquired by flag as to his condition the following day, he signaled back: "I am short a cheekbone and an ear, but am able to whip all hell yet."

Such was the stuff of which legends were made, including this one of the so-called Battle of Allatoona Pass. "Hold the fort, for I am coming," journalists quoted Sherman as having wigwagged from the top of Kennesaw, and that became the title of P. P. Bliss's revival hymn, inspired by the resolute valor Corse and his chief had shown in defending a position of such great natural strength that the latter had chosen not to risk an attack when he found it looming across his southward path in May. French, moreover, got clean away, long before any blue relief arrived, and when Sherman encountered the high-strung young Iowa brigadier a few days later he was surprised to find on his cheek only a small bandage, removal of which revealed no more than a scratch where the bullet had nicked him in passing, and no apparent damage to the ear he had claimed was lost. Sherman laughed. "Corse, they came damned near missing you, didn't they?" he said.

He laughed, yet the fact was he found small occasion for humor in the present situation. Hood withdrew his reunited army westward beyond Lost Mountain to New Hope Church and Dallas. There he stopped, or anyhow paused. Sherman, however, had no intention of re-entering that tangled wasteland, even though this meant leaving the initiative to an adversary who had just shown that he would use it to full advantage and now seemed about to do as much again. Sure enough, when the sun came up on October 7 the graybacks had disappeared. Wiring Slocum that they had "gone off south," Sherman warned that they might be doubling back for a surprise attack on Atlanta, and when he discovered later in the day that they were actually headed north, he charged that Hood was an eccentric: "I cannot guess his movements as

I could those of Johnston, who was a sensible man and only did sensible things."

Delayed by an all-day rain next day, he did not reach Allatoona until October 9, when he heard from scouts that the butternut column was on the march for Rome. But that was not true either, it turned out. Crossing the Coosa River west of Rome, then moving fast up the right bank of the Oostanaula, Hood struck Resaca on October 12 and wrecked a dozen miles of railroad between there and Dalton, where he captured the thousand-man garrison next day and then ripped up another five miles of track on his way to Tunnel Hill, where the contest for North Georgia had begun five months ago. When Sherman moved against him from Rome and Kingston, he fell back through Snake Creek Gap to a position near LaFayette, some twenty miles south of where Bragg and Rosecrans had clashed about this time last year at Chickamauga, and there took up a defensive stance, both flanks stoutly anchored and a clear field of fire to his front. Sherman came on after him from Resaca, reaching LaFayette on October 17. By the time he got his troops arrayed for battle, however, Hood was gone again — vanished westward, across the Alabama line, into even more rugged terrain where Sherman would be obliged to risk defeat a long way from his base. Exasperated, the red-head complained bitterly that everything his adversary had done for the past three weeks was "inexplicable by any common-sense theory." Recalling Jefferson Davis's boast of Hood's intentions: "Damn him," he said testily of the latter. "If he will go to the Ohio River I will give him rations. . . . Let him go north. My business is down South."

Whether this last was to be the case or not was strictly up to the general-in-chief, and that was the main cause of Sherman's irritability through this difficult and uncertain time, even more than the loss of much of the railroad in his rear. The railroad could be rebuilt — would in fact be back in use within ten days — but Hood's evident ability to smash it, more or less at will, might have an adverse influence on the decision Grant had been pondering for the past month, ever since Sherman first made it clear what he meant when he said that his business was "down South."

Back in early May, at the start of his campaign to "knock Jos. Johnston," a staffer had asked what he planned to do at its end; "Salt water," he replied, flicking the ash from his cigar. Mobile and the Gulf had been what he meant, but thanks to Farragut there was not much left in that direction worth the march. He now had a different body of water in mind, rimming a different coast. In brief, his proposal — first made on September 20, while the refugee truce was still in effect below Atlanta — was that the navy secure and provision a base for him on the Atlantic seaboard — probably Savannah, since that was the closest port — and his army would "sweep the whole state of Georgia" on its way there. Such a march, he told Grant, would be "more than fatal to the possibility of Southern independence. They may stand the fall of Richmond, but not of all Georgia," he declared, and added a jocular, upbeat flourish to close his plea: "If you can whip Lee and I can march to the Atlantic, I think Uncle Abe will give us a twenty days' leave of absence to see the young folks."

Grant had doubts. With its attention fixed on Wilmington, the last major port still open to blockade runners, the navy would not willingly divert its strength to a secondary target more than two hundred miles down the coast; besides which, the mounting of such an effort would take months, and previous attempts against Charleston had shown there was little assurance of success, even if every ironclad in the fleet was employed in the attack. His main objection, however, was the continued existence of Hood's army. Speaking in Georgia, Alabama, and South Carolina, hard on the heels of Sherman's proposal, Jefferson Davis announced plans for a northward campaign that might well succeed if Sherman marched eastward and thus removed from Hood's path the one force that could stop him. Grant said as much, opposing the expedition on both counts, but Sherman replied that he did not really need for the navy to take Savannah before he got there; all he wanted was for supply ships to be standing by, ready to steam in after he reduced the city from the landward side. As for Hood, Thomas was on the way to Nashville even now with two divisions which he would combine with troops already there and others on the way; "Why will it not do to leave Tennessee to the forces which Thomas has, and the reserves soon to come to Nashville, and for me to destroy Atlanta and march across Georgia to Savannah or Charleston, breaking roads and doing irreparable damage? We cannot remain on the defensive."

That was written October 1. By the time the message reached City Point, Forrest had rampaged through Middle Tennessee, smashing installations within thirty miles of Nashville, and Hood was across the Chattahoochee, ripping up track on the Western & Atlantic thirty miles north of Atlanta. Grant saw these strikes as confirmation of his objection to Sherman's departure, but Sherman took them as proof of his contention that he was wasting time by remaining where he was; that it was, in fact, as he insisted on October 9, "a physical impossibility to protect the roads, now that Hood, Forrest, Wheeler, and the whole batch of devils are turned loose.... By attempting to hold the roads, we will lose a thousand men each month and will gain no result." Having said as much, he returned to his plea that he himself be "turned loose" to make for the coast. This time, noting that he had some 8000 head of cattle on hand, as well as 3,000,000 rations of bread, and expected to find "plenty of forage in the interior of the state," he went into logistical details of the expedition. "I propose that we break up the railroad from Chattanooga forward, and that we strike out with our wagons for Milledgeville, Millen, and Savannah. Until we can repopulate Georgia, it is useless for us to occupy it; but the utter destruction of its roads, houses, and people will cripple their military resources.... I can make this march, and make Georgia howl!"

Hood by then had retired westward, but soon he was on the go again, about to throw another punch at the railroad forty miles farther north. Even before it landed, Sherman predicted that it would be successful and renewed his appeal to be spared the patchwork soldiering that would follow, urging Grant to let him "send back all my wounded and unserviceable men, and with my effective army move through Georgia, smashing things to the sea. Hood may turn into Tennessee and Kentucky," he admitted, "but I believe he will be forced to follow me." In any case, Thomas could handle him, he said, and best of all, "instead of being on the defensive, I will be on the offensive. Instead of my guessing at what he means to do, he will have to guess at my plans. The difference in war would be fully 25 percent.... Answer quick, as I know we will not have the telegraph long."

Grant's reply next day, October 12 — the day Hood landed astride the railroad at Resaca — was encouraging. "On reflection I think better of your proposition," he wired back. "It will be much better to go south than to be forced to come north." He suggested that the move be made with "every wagon, horse, mule, and hoof of stock, as well as the Negroes," and that plenty of spare weapons be taken along to "put them in the hands of Negro men," who could serve as otherwise unobtainable reinforcements on the march. All the same, his approval was only tentative, not final, and Sherman continued to fume, irked in front by Hood and from the rear by Grant.

The former got away westward again, through Snake Creek and Ship's gaps, to a position just below LaFayette, which he abandoned at the approach of the blue army, and fell back down the valley of the Chattooga River, across the Alabama line. "It was clear to me that he had no intention to meet us in open battle," Sherman later wrote, "and the lightness and celerity of his army convinced me that I could not possibly catch him on a stern-chase." Angry at being drawn in the direction he least wanted to go — and resentful, above all, at the mounting proof of his error in having turned back to Atlanta, when the city fell to Slocum in his rear, instead of pressing after Hood to achieve the true purpose of his campaign — the red-head called a halt at Gaylesville, thirty miles short of Gadsden, and there continued to fret and fume as October wore away, still with no definite go-ahead from the general-in-chief. Evidence of his snappishness appeared in a telegram he sent a cavalry brigadier, posted at Calhoun on rear-guard duty, when he heard that a sniper had taken pot shots at cars along the newly repaired Western & Atlantic: "Cannot you send over about Fairmont and Adairsville, burn ten or twelve houses of known secessionists, kill a few at random, and let them know that it will be repeated every time a train is fired on from Resaca to Kingston?"

Across the way at Gadsden, while Sherman thus was breathing fire and threatening random slaughter, Hood's troubles were not so much with his superior, Beauregard, as they were with his subordinates, who he felt had let him down. Drawn up for combat near LaFayette the week before, he had "expected that a forward movement of one hundred miles would reinspirit the officers and men to a degree to impart to them confidence, enthusiasm, and hope of victory," but when he took a vote at a council of war, assembled on the eve of what he intended as an all-out effort to whip Sherman, "the opinion was unanimous that although the army was much improved in spirit, it was not in a condition to risk battle against the numbers reported." Disappointed, he withdrew down the Chattooga Valley and the Coosa River to Gadsden for a meeting on October 21 with Beauregard, who had formally assumed command of the new Military Division of the West only four days ago. To the Creole's great surprise, Hood presented for his approval a broad-scale plan, conceived en route, for "marching into Tennessee, with a hope to establish our line eventually in Kentucky."

'Broad-scale' was perhaps not word enough; spread-eagle was more like it. But knowing as he did that time was on the side of the Union — that delay would enable Thomas to complete his buildup in Tennessee and combine with Sherman to corner and crush the fugitive gray army, wherever it might turn — Hood was determined to extend and enlarge the flea-bite offensive by which he had managed, ever since he left Palmetto three weeks back, to keep his adversaries edgy and off-balance. A northward march, into or past the mouth of the Federal lion, was admittedly a risky undertaking, but he was of the Lee-Jackson school, whose primary tenet was that the smaller force must take the longest chances, and moreover he had before him the example of Bragg, who by just such a maneuver after the fall of Corinth, two years ago, had reversed the gloomy situation in this same theater by dispersing the superior enemy combinations then being assembled to bring on his destruction.

His plan, he said, was to cross the Tennessee River at Guntersville, which would place him within reach of Sherman's single-strand rail supply line in the delicate Stevenson-Bridgeport area, and move promptly on Nashville, smashing Thomas's scattered detachments on the way. Possessed of the Tennessee capital, he would resupply his army from its stores, thicken his ranks with volunteers drawn to his banner, and move on through Kentucky to the Ohio, where he would be in a position to threaten Cincinnati and receive still more recruits from the Bluegrass. If Sherman followed, as expected, Hood would then be strong enough

to whip him; after which he would either send reinforcements to beleaguered Richmond or else take his whole command across the Cumberlands to come up in rear of the blue host outside Petersburg. Or if
Sherman did not follow, but instead took off southward for the Gulf
or eastward for the Atlantic, Hood explained that he would move by
the interior lines for an attack on Grant "at least two weeks before he,
Sherman, could render him assistance." Such a shift, he said, winding
up in a blaze of glory, "would defeat Grant and allow General Lee, in
command of our combined armies, to march upon Washington or turn
upon and annihilate Sherman."

Old Bory was amazed, partly by the bold sweep of the plan, which
seemed to him as practicable as it was entrancing, and partly by the
shock of recognition, occasioned by its resemblance to the half-dozen
or so which he himself had submitted to friends and superiors over the
course of the past three years, invariably without their being adopted.
One difference was that he had always insisted on heavy reinforcement at the outset, whereas Hood proposed to strike with what he had.
If this seemed rash, Beauregard could see that it might well be a virtue
in the present crisis, not only because no reinforcements were available,
but also because it would save time, and time was of the essence in a
situation depending largely on how rapidly the invaders moved —
especially against Thomas, who must not be given a chance to pull his
scattered forces together for the protection of the capital in his care. In
any case, approval was little more than a formality; Hood had informed
the government two days ago that he intended to cross the Tennessee,
and only yesterday had wired ahead to Richard Taylor, whose department he had entered for the crossing: "I will move tomorrow for
Guntersville." Beauregard did not withhold his blessing, though after
much discussion he insisted that Wheeler's cavalry, which had rejoined
the army near Rome ten days ago, be left behind to operate against
Sherman's communications and attack his rear if he set out south or
east, through otherwise undefended regions between Atlanta and the
Gulf or the Atlantic. Hood readily agreed to this subtraction when the
Creole added that Forrest would join him on the march, replacing
Wheeler, as soon as he and his troopers returned from their current
raid on Johnsonville; which, incidentally, would add to the Federal
confusion Hood hoped to provoke when he moved on Nashville.

Word went out to the camps that the shift northward would begin at daylight, and their commander later recalled that the news was
greeted with "that genuine Confederate shout so familiar to every
Southern soldier." By this he meant the rebel yell, the loudest of
which no doubt came from the bivouacs of the Tennesseans. Davis had
told them four weeks ago that their feet would soon be pressing native
soil, and now they whooped with delight at finding the promise about to
be kept.

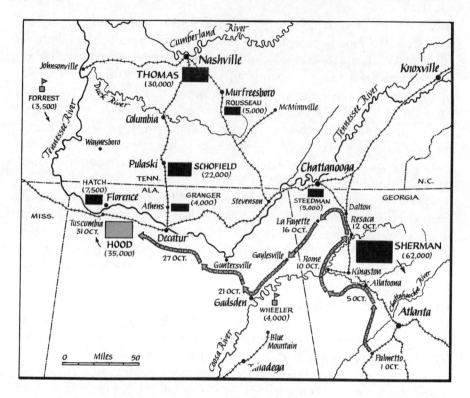

It was kept, although by no means as promptly as they and
Beauregard expected when they parted at Gadsden next morning.
Guntersville, thirty-odd miles northwest, turned out to be crowded
with bluecoats, and Hood decided to veer west for a crossing at Decatur,
just over forty miles downriver. However, when he drew close to there
on October 26, after four days on the march, he found that it, like
Guntersville, was too stoutly garrisoned to be stormed without heavier
losses than he felt he could afford; so he pressed on for Courtland,
twenty miles beyond Decatur, which he bypassed the following day.
It was not until then that Beauregard, who had been off making supply
arrangements and was miffed at not having been informed of the change
in route, caught up with the column some fifty miles west of its original
objective. He was aggrieved not only because the detour had ruled out
the disruptive strike at Stevenson, now clearly beyond range of the
butternut marchers, but also because of the loss of time, which Sherman
and Thomas would surely use to their advantage. He had said from the
start that celerity was Hood's best hope for success in this long-odds
undertaking; yet five whole days had already been spent in search of a
crossing that still had not been reached. Nor was that the worst of it.
Informed by his engineers that they did not have enough pontoons to
bridge the rain-swollen Tennessee at Courtland, Hood decided to push
on and use the partly demolished railway span at Tuscumbia, another
twenty-five miles downstream and well over eighty from Guntersville,

where he had intended to ford the river a week ago. At Tuscumbia on the last day of October, he further alarmed his superior by announcing that he lacked sufficient provisions for the march that would follow the crossing, as well as shoes for his men and the horses in Jackson's two slim brigades, which were all the cavalry he would have until Forrest returned from Johnsonville, more than a hundred miles downriver to the north.

Taylor had unwelcome news for them in that regard as well. Unmindful of the need for haste, he had waited till Hood drew near Decatur on the 26th to send a courier summoning Forrest, who had left five days ago, and even then had told him to complete his mission before heading back. Hood took this, then and later, as evidence that he had done well to shift his infantry westward in search of a crossing, since this reduced the gap between it and the cavalry he was obliged to wait for anyhow. Moreover, while he marked time at Tuscumbia, doing what he could to repair his supply deficiencies and giving his men some well-earned rest through the first fine days of November, word came back that the delay had perhaps been worth the vexation after all, adding as it did a highly colorful chapter to the legend surrounding the Wizard of the Saddle.

After reaching the Tennessee River near the Kentucky line on October 28, thirty miles north of Johnsonville, Forrest converted a portion of his 3500 troopers into literal horse marines and put them aboard two Union vessels, the gunboat *Undine* and the transport *Venus*, which he captured by posting batteries at both ends of a five-mile stretch of river to prevent their escape when he took them under fire with other guns along the bank. For three days, November 1–3, while this improvised two-boat navy molested traffic and drew attention northward, he led his horsemen south, up the west bank of the swollen Tennessee, to carry out the devastation that was the purpose of his raid. Well before midday November 4, after losing the *Venus* in an engagement with two gunboats and burning the eight-gun *Undine* to prevent her recapture, the two divisions were directly opposite Johnsonville, masked from view by trees and brush. While Morton was sneaking his guns into position, under orders to open fire at 2 o'clock, Forrest examined with his binoculars the unsuspecting target on the far side of the half-mile-wide river. Three gunboats, eleven transports, and eighteen barges were moored at the wharves, aswarm with workers unloading stores, and beyond them, spread out around a stockade fortress on high ground, warehouses bulged with supplies and acres of open storage were piled ten feet high with goods of every description, covered with tarpaulins to protect them from the weather. Two freight trains were being made up for the run to Nashville, just under eighty miles away, and neither the soldiers at work nor the officers scattered among them seemed aware that they were in any more danger now than they had been at any time since the base — named for the military governor who was Lincoln's running mate in the election only four days off — was put in operation, six months back.

Promptly at 2 o'clock they found out better. Morton having synchronized the watches of his chiefs of section, all ten pieces went off with an enormous bang that seemed to come from a single heavy cannon. For nearly an hour, after this introductory clap of thunder out of a cloudless sky, their fire was concentrated on the gunboats, the most dangerous enemy weapon, and when these were abandoned by their crews, who left them to burn and sink with the transports and barges they had been ordered to protect, the rebel artillerists shifted their attention to the landward installations, including the hilltop fortress whose unpracticed cannoneers replied wildly, blinded by smoke from riverside sheds and warehouses that had been set afire by sparks from the burning wharves and exploding vessels down below. Soon all those acres of high-piled stores were a mass of flames, and the exultant rebel gunners chose individual targets of opportunity, neglected until now. Perhaps the most spectacular of these was a warehouse on high ground, which, when struck and set afire, turned out to be stocked with several hundred barrels of whiskey that burst from the heat and sent a crackling blue-flame river of bourbon pouring down the hillside. Tantalized by the combined aroma of burnt liquor, roasting coffee beans, and frizzled bacon, wafted to them through a reek of gunsmoke, Morton's hungry veterans howled with delight and regret as they kept heaving shells into the holocaust they had created across the way. Forrest himself took a hand in the fun, directing the fire of one piece. "Elevate the breech of that gun a little lower!" he shouted, and the crew had little trouble understanding this unorthodox correction of the range. Within two hours all of Johnsonville was ablaze, resulting in a scene that "beggared description," according to one Federal who confined himself to the comment that it was "awfully sublime."

It was also awfully expensive. The base commander later put his loss at $2,200,000, taking the burned-out steamers and barges into account, but not the three sunken gunboats — four, including the *Undine*, subtracted during the naval phase of the raid, along with three more transports and three barges, mounting a total of 32 guns. Forrest's estimate of $6,700,000 included all of these, and probably came closer to the truth. His own loss, over-all, was two men killed and nine wounded, plus two guns lost when the *Venus* was recaptured. Retiring southward by the glare of flames still visible when he made camp six miles away, he encountered in the course of the next few days a series of couriers from Beauregard, all bearing orders for him to report at once to Hood, who was waiting at Tuscumbia for the outriders he would need on his march north. Forrest did what he could to hurry, but the going was slow through the muddy Tennessee bottoms, especially for the artillery. Even with sixteen horses to each piece, spelled by oxen impressed from farms adjoining the worst stretches along the way, he could see that he would need more than a week to reach Hood in Northwest Alabama.

Beauregard's distress at this development was matched by opposite reactions up the Coosa and beyond the Tennessee. Not only did the delay give Thomas added time to prepare for the blow Hood's drawn-out march had warned him was about to land; it also prompted Sherman to send still more reinforcements to Nashville, even while putting the final touches to his plan for making Georgia howl by slogging rough-shod across it to the sea.

Grant by now had assented unconditionally to the expedition, though not until he recovered from a last-minute fit of qualms brought on by the news that Hood was headed north. Sherman at Gaylesville had not known that the gray army had left Gadsden, thirty miles away, until it turned up near Decatur, ninety miles to the west, on October 26. His reaction, once Hood's departure had ruled out a confrontation near the Alabama-Georgia line, was to send Stanley's corps to strengthen Thomas, and when he learned that Hood was still in motion westward, apparently intending to force a crossing at Tuscumbia, he also detached Schofield's one-corps Army of the Ohio and directed that A. J. Smith's divisions return at once from Missouri to join in the defense of Middle Tennessee. Between them, Stanley, Schofield, and Smith had close to 40,000 men, and these, added to those already on hand — including more than half of Sherman's cavalry, sent back earlier; sizeable garrisons at Murfreesboro, Chattanooga, Athens, and Florence; and recruits coming down from Kentucky and Ohio, in response to Forrest's early-October penetration of the region below Nashville — would give Thomas about twice as many troops as Hood could bring against him. Surely that was ample, even though most of them were badly scattered, others were green, and some had not arrived. Best of all, however, from Sherman's point of view, this new arrangement provided a massive antidote for dealing with Grant's reawakened fears as to what might happen if Old Pap was left to face the invasion threat alone. "Do you not think it advisable, now that Hood has gone so far north, to entirely ruin him before starting on your proposed campaign?" Grant inquired on November 1, and added, rather more firmly: "If you see a chance of destroying Hood's army, attend to that first, and make your other move secondary."

This, of all things, was the one Sherman wanted least to hear, and in his reply he marshaled his previous arguments in redoubled opposition. "No single army can catch Hood," he declared, "and I am convinced that the best results will follow from our defeating Jeff. Davis's cherished plan of making me leave Georgia by maneuvering." Edgy and appre-hensive, fearing a negative reaction, he followed this with a second, more emphatic plea, before there was time for an answer to the first. "If I turn back, the whole effect of my campaign will be lost. By my movements I have thrown Beauregard (Hood) well to the west, and Thomas will have ample time and sufficient troops to hold him. . . . I am clearly of opinion that the best results will follow my contemplated movement through Georgia."

To his great relief, Grant wired back on November 2 that he was finally persuaded that Thomas would "be able to take care of Hood and destroy him." Moreover, he added, echoing his lieutenant's words in closing, "I really do not see that you can withdraw from where you are to follow Hood without giving up all we have gained in territory. I say, then, go as you propose."

Here at last was the go-ahead Sherman had been seeking all along, and now that he had it he moved fast, as if in fear that it might be revoked. Trains that had been shuttling between Chattanooga and Atlanta for the past two months, heavy-laden coming down and empty going back, now made their runs the other way around, returning all but the supplies he would take along in wagons when he set out for the sea with his four remaining corps, two from what was left of the Army of the Cumberland, under Slocum, and two from his old Army of the Tennessee, under Howard. They numbered better than 60,000 of all arms, including a single division of cavalry under Kilpatrick. He saw this mainly as an infantry operation, much like the one against Meridian last year, and had ordered the rest of his troopers back to Nashville for reorganization under James Wilson, who had recently been promoted to major general and sent by Grant to see what he could do about the poor showing western horsemen had been making ever since the start of the campaign. Sherman might have taken him along, a welcome addition on a march into the unknown, except that Thomas would most likely need him worse. Besides, he said, "I know that Kilpatrick is a hell of a damned fool, but I want just that sort of a man to command my cavalry on this expedition."

In "high feather," as he nearly always was when he was busy, he reëstablished headquarters at Kingston, the main-line railroad junction on the Etowah east of Rome, and there, with trains grinding north and rattling south at all hours of the day and night, supervised the final runs before the Western & Atlantic was closed down and its several depot garrisons withdrawn to become part of Major General J. B. Steedman's command at Chattanooga, on call for service under Thomas against Hood. His own army seemed to Sherman in splendid condition, fattened by veterans returning from thirty-day reënlistment furloughs, yet trimmed for hard use by evacuating all who were judged by surgeons not to be in shape for the 300-mile cross-Georgia march. On Sunday, November 6, he took time out to compose a farewell letter to Grant, a general statement of his intention, as he put it, "to act in such a manner against the material resources of the South as utterly to negative Davis' boasted threat." While he wrote, paymasters were active in all the camps, seeing to it that the soldiers would be in an appreciative frame of mind to support the Administration in the election two days off. "If we can march a well-appointed army right through his territory, it is a demonstration to the world, foreign and domestic, that we have a power which Davis cannot resist. This may not be war, but rather statesmanship. Nevertheless it is overwhelming to my mind that there are thousands of people abroad and in the South who reason thus: If the North can march an army right through the South, it is proof positive that the North can prevail."

He would set out, he told his chief, hard on the heels of Lincoln's reëlection — "which is assured" — and would thereby have the advantage of the confusion, not to say consternation, that event would provoke in the breasts of secessionists whose heartland he would be despoiling. What he would do after he reached Savannah he would decide when he got there and got back in touch with City Point. Meantime, he said, "I will not attempt to send couriers back, but trust to the Richmond papers to keep you well advised."

Grant — observing with hard-won equanimity the unusual spectacle of the two main western armies, blue and gray, already more than two hundred miles apart, about to take off in opposite directions — replied next day: "Great good luck go with you. I believe you will be eminently successful, and at worst can only make a march less fruitful than is hoped for."

★ ★ ★

In Richmond that same day, November 7 — election eve beyond the Potomac — Congress was welcomed back into session by a message from the Chief Executive, who had continued in Virginia the efforts made on his Georgia trip to lift spirits depressed by the outcome of the Hood-Sherman contest for Atlanta. Indeed, Davis went further here today in his denial that the South could be defeated, no matter what calamities attended her resistance to the force that would deny her independence.

After speaking of "the delusion fondly cherished [by the enemy] that the capture of Atlanta and Richmond would, if effected, end the war by the overthrow of our government and the submission of our people," he said flatly: "If the campaign against Richmond had resulted in success instead of failure, if the valor of [Lee's] army, under the leadership of its accomplished commander, had resisted in vain the overwhelming masses which were, on the contrary, decisively repulsed — if we had been compelled to evacuate Richmond as well as Atlanta — the Confederacy would have remained as erect and defiant as ever. Nothing could have been changed in the purpose of its government, in the indomitable valor of its troops, or in the unquenchable spirit of its people. The baffled and disappointed foe would in vain have scanned the reports of your proceedings, at some new legislative seat, for any indication that progress had been made in his gigantic task of conquering a free people." And having said as much he said still more in that regard. "There are no vital points on the preservation of which the continued existence of the Confederacy depends. There is no military success of the enemy which can accomplish its destruction. Not the fall of Richmond, nor Wilmington, nor Charleston, nor Savannah, nor Mobile, nor of all combined, can save the enemy from the constant and exhaustive drain of blood and treasure which must continue until he shall discover that no peace is attainable unless based on the recognition of our indefeasible rights."

He spoke at length of other matters, including foreign relations and finances — neither of them a pleasant subject for any Confederate — and referred, near the end, to the unlikelihood of being able to treat for peace with enemy leaders "until the delusion of their ability to conquer us is dispelled." Only then did he expect to encounter "that willingness to negotiate which is now confined to our side." Meantime, he told the assembled representatives, the South's one recourse lay in self-reliance. "Let us, then, resolutely continue to devote our united and unimpaired energies to the defense of our homes, our lives, and our liberties. This is the true path to peace. Let us tread it with confidence in the assured result."

Nowhere in the course of the long message did he mention tomorrow's election in the North, although the outcome was no less vital in the South — where still more battles would be fought if the hard-war Union party won — than it was throughout the region where the ballots would be cast. For one thing, any favorable reference to McClellan by Jefferson Davis would cost the Pennsylvanian votes he could ill afford now that Atlanta's fall and Frémont's withdrawal had transformed him, practically overnight, from odds-on favorite to underdog in the presidential race. In point of fact, much of the suspense had gone out of the contest, it being generally conceded by all but the most partisan of Democrats, caught up in the hypnotic fury of the campaign, that Little Mac had only the slimmest of chances.

Lincoln himself seemed gravely doubtful the following evening, however, when he crossed the White House grounds, soggy from a day-long wintry rain, to a side door of the War Department and climbed the stairs to the telegraph office, where returns were beginning to come in from around the country. These showed him leading in Massachusetts and Indiana, as well as in Baltimore and Philadelphia, and the trend continued despite some other dispatches that had McClellan ahead in Delaware and New Jersey. By midnight, though the storm delayed results from distant states, it was fairly clear that the turbulent campagin would end in Lincoln's reëlection.

Earlier he had said, "It is strange that I, who am not a vindictive man, should always, except once, have been before the people in canvasses marked by great bitterness. When I came to Congress it was a quiet time, but always, except that, the contests in which I have been prominent have been marked with great rancor." Now he lapsed into a darkly reminiscent mood, telling of that other election night, four years ago in Springfield, and a strange experience he had when he came home, utterly worn out, to rest for a time on a horsehair sofa in the parlor before going up to bed. Across the room, he saw himself reflected in a mirror hung on the wall above a bureau, almost at full length, murky, and with two faces, one nearly superimposed upon the other. Perplexed, somewhat alarmed, he got up to study the illusion at close range, only to have it vanish. When he lay down again it reappeared, plainer than before, and he could see that one face was paler than the other. Again he rose; again the double image disappeared. Later he told his wife about the phenomenon, and almost at once had cause — for both their sakes — to wish he hadn't. She took it as a sign, she said, that he would be reëlected four years later, but that the pallor of the second face indicated that he would not live through the second term.

The gloom this cast was presently dispelled by further reports that put all of New England and most of the Middle West firmly in his column. Around 2 o'clock, word came that serenaders, complete with a band, had assembled on the White House lawn to celebrate a victory whose incidentals would not be known for days. These would show that, out of some four million votes cast this Tuesday, Lincoln received 2,203,831 — just over 55 percent — as compared to his opponent's 1,797,019. Including those of Nevada, whose admission to the Union had been hurried through, eight days ago, so that its three votes could tip the scales if needed, he would receive 212 electoral votes and McClellan only the 21 from Delaware, New Jersey, and Kentucky. Yet the contest had been a good deal closer than these figures indicated. Connecticut, for example, was carried by a mere 2000 votes and New York by fewer than 7000, both as a result of military ballots, which went overwhelmingly for Lincoln, here as elsewhere. Without these two states, plus four others whose soldier voters swung the balance — Pennsylvania, Illinois, Maryland, and Indiana — he would have lost the election. Moreover, even in victory there were disappointments. New York City and Detroit went Democratic by majorities that ran close to three to one, and McClellan not only won the President's native state, Kentucky, he also carried Sangamon County, Illinois, and all the counties on its border. Lincoln could say to his serenaders before turning in that night, "I give thanks to the Almighty for this evidence of the people's resolution to stand by free government and the rights of humanity," but there was also the sobering realization, which would come with the full returns, that only five percent less than half the voters in the nation had opposed with their ballots his continuance as their leader.

Still, regardless of its outcome, he found consolation in two aspects of the bitter political struggle through which the country had just passed, and he mentioned both, two nights later, in responding to another group of serenaders. One was that the contest, for all "its incidental and undesirable strife," had demonstrated to the world "that a people's government can sustain a national election in the midst of a great civil war." This was much, but the other aspect was more complex, involving as it did the providence of an example distant generations could look back on when they came to be tested in their turn. "The strife of the election is but human nature practically applied to the facts of the case," he told the upturned faces on the lawn below the window from which he spoke. "What has occurred in this case must ever recur in similar cases. Human nature will not change. In any future great national trial, compared with the men of this, we shall have as weak and as strong, as silly and as wise, as bad and as good. Let us therefore study the incidents of this, as philosophy to learn wisdom from, and none of them as wrongs to be revenged."

Even so, a cruel paradox obtained. McClellan the loser was soon off on a European tour, a vacation that would keep him out of the country for six months, whereas Lincoln now more than ever, despite the stimulus of victory at the polls, could repeat what he had said two years before, in another time of trial: "I am like the starling in Sterne's story. 'I can't get out.'"

He had this to live with, as well as the memory of that double-image reflection in the mirror back in Springfield: both of which no doubt contributed, along with much else, to the nighttime restlessness a member of the White House guard observed as he walked the long second-story corridor, to and fro, past the door of the bedroom where the President lay sleeping. "I could hear his deep breathing," the sentry would recall. "Sometimes, after a day of unusual anxiety, I have heard him moan in his sleep. It gave me a curious sensation. While the expression of Mr Lincoln's face was always sad when he was quiet, it gave one the assurance of calm. He never seemed to doubt the wisdom of an action when he had once decided on it. And so when he was in a way defenseless in his sleep, it made me feel the pity that would almost have been an impertinence when he was awake. I would stand there and listen until a sort of panic stole over me. If he felt the weight of things so heavily, how much worse the situation of the country must be than any of us realized! At last I would walk softly away, feeling as if I had been listening at a keyhole."

You Cannot Refine It

★ ✗ ☆

INDIAN SUMMER HAD COME TO VIRGINIA
while Northerners were going to the polls, muting with its smoky haze
the vivid yellow vivid scarlet flare of maples and dogwoods on the
Peninsula and down along the sunlit reaches of the James, where close
to a hundred thousand blue-clad soldiers, in camps and trenches curving
past the mouth of the Appomattox, celebrated or shook their heads at
the news that they and more than half the men back home had voted
to sustain a war that lacked only a winter of being four years old.
Across the way, in the rebel works, the reaction was less mixed — and
less intense. Partly this was because of distractions, including hunger and
the likelihood of being hoisted by a mine or overrun; partly it proceeded
from a sense of contrast between the present molelike state of existence
and the old free-swinging foot cavalry days when the Army of Northern Virginia ranged the region from which it took its name but now
would range no more.

"We thought we had before seen men with the marks of hard
service upon them," an artillery major was to write, recalling his impression of the scarecrow infantry his battalion had been ordered to
support on arriving from beyond the river back in June, "but the appearance of this division made us realize for the first time what our
comrades in the hottest Petersburg lines were undergoing. We were
shocked at the condition, the complexion, the expression of the men
. . . even the field officers. Indeed, we could scarcely realize that the un-
washed, uncombed, unfed, and almost unclad creatures were officers
of rank and reputation in the army." Thus he had reacted and reflected
in early summer. Now in November he knew that he too looked like
that, if not more so, with an added five hard months of wear and tear.

Richmond and Petersburg, semi-beleaguered at opposite ends of
the line, were barely twenty crow-flight miles apart, but the intrenchments covering and connecting them had stretched by now to nearly

twice that length. From White Oak Swamp on the far left, due east
of the capital, these outer works (as distinguished from the 'inner'
works, two miles in their rear) ran nine miles south, in a shielding curve,
to Chaffin's Bluff on the James; there they crossed and continued for
four gun-studded miles along the river's dominant right bank to a westward loop where the Howlett Line — Beauregard's cork in Butler's
bottle — began its five-mile run across Bermuda Neck to the Appomattox, then jogged another four miles south, up the left bank of that
stream, to connect with the trenches covering Petersburg at such close
range that its citizens had grown adept at dodging Yankee shells. The first
four miles of these trans-Appomattox installations — disfigured about
midway by the red yawn of the Crater — defined the limits of the
original blue assault as far south as the Jerusalem Plank Road, where
both sides had thrown up imposing and opposing fortifications. Officially
dubbed Forts Sedgwick and Mahone, but known respectively by their
occupants as Fort Hell and Fort Damnation, these were designed to
serve as south-flank anchors, back in June, for the two systems winding
northward out of sight. Since that time, however, as a result of Grant's

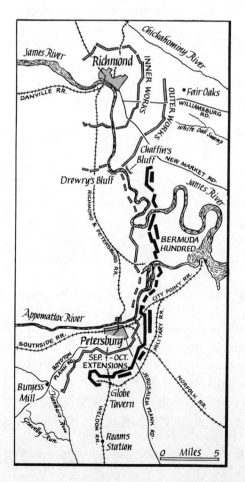

four all-out pendulum strikes
(staged one a month, July
through October, and costing
him some 25,000 casualties, all
told, as compared to Lee's
10,000) the gray line had been
extended nine miles to the west
and southwest, covering the
Boydton Plank Road down to
Hatcher's Run. All these segments brought the Confederate
total to thirty-five miles of
earthworks, not including cavalry extensions reaching up to
the Chickahominy on the left
and down past Burgess Mill to
Gravelly Run on the right. Lee's
basic problem, with only about
half as many troops as he opposed, was that his line was not
only longer, it was also more
continuous than Grant's, who,
having no national capital or
indispensable railroad junction
close in his rear, had less to fear
from a breakthrough at any
given point.

Another problem was food; or rather the lack of it. Badly as Lee needed men — and the need was so stringent he could not give his Jewish soldiers a day out of the trenches for Rosh Hashana or Yom Kippur — he saw no way of feeding substantial reinforcements even if they had been available, which they were not. As it was, he barely managed to sustain the troops on hand by reducing their daily ration to a pint of cornmeal, baked into pones when there was time, and an ounce or two of bacon. Moreover, with the Shenandoah Valley put to the torch and only two rail lines open to Georgia and the Carolinas — the Southside out of Petersburg, the Danville out of Richmond — there was little hope that the fare could be improved, despite the fact that the trench-bound men were losing weight and strength at an alarming rate. They looked fit enough, to a casual eye, but would "pant and grow faint" at the slightest exertion, a staffer noted. "General, I'm hongry," some would reply when Lee rode out and asked them how they were. All through this grim time, a veteran would say, "I thanked God I had a backbone for my stomach to lean up against."

Others remarked that the quality of such food as they received was even lower than its quantity; which was low indeed. The meal was unbolted, generally with much of the cob ground in, and alive with weevils. But the bacon remained longest in their memories and night-mares. Nassau bacon, it was called, though one memorialist was to testify that "Nausea with a capital would have been better. It came through the blockade, and we believed it was made from the hog of the tropics and cured in the brine of the ocean. More likely it was dis-carded ship's pork, or 'salt junk.'.... It was a peculiarly scaly color, spotted like a half-well case of smallpox, full of rancid odor, and utterly devoid of grease. When hung up it would double its length. It could not be eaten raw, and imparted a stinking smell when boiled. It had one redeeming quality: elasticity. You could put a piece in your mouth and chew it for a long time, and the longer you chewed it the bigger it got. Then, by a desperate effort, you would gulp it down. Out of sight, out of mind."

Nor was the outer man, in his butternut rags, any better served than the inner. Shoes, for example, had always been a scarce requisition item, and now that the once bounteous yield of well-shod Union corpses had diminished as a dividend of battle, the shortage was acute. Even so, and with cold weather coming on, many soldiers preferred going barefoot to wearing the "pitiable specimens" of footgear issued by the government as a substitute for shoes. "Generally made of green, or at best half-cured leather," one who suffered from them later wrote, "they soon took to roaming. After a week's wear, the heel would be on one side, at an angle to the foot, and the vamp in turn would try to do duty as a sole.... While hot and dry, they would shrink like parchment, and when wet they just slopped all over your feet."

Crippling as this was, other shortages cramped the army's style still more. Chief among these, despite the sacrifice of most of the South's stills, was the scarcity of copper, indispensable in the manufacture of percussion caps, without which not a shot could be fired. Riflemen in the critical outer pits were limited to eighteen caps a day, while their Federal counterparts across the way complained of bruised shoulders from being required to expend no less than a hundred rounds in the same span. Other metals not only were less rare, they also could be salvaged from incoming projectiles, much as boots and overcoats had been scavenged from incoming infantry, back in the days of mobile warfare. "As an inducement to collecting scrap iron for our cannon foundries," a line officer would recall, "furloughs were offered, a day for so many pounds collected. Thus, gathering fragments of shells became an active industry among the troops. So keen was their quest that sometimes they would start toward the point where a mortar shell fell, even before it exploded." Similarly, the loose dirt of the parapets was periodically sifted for spent lead, but only under cover of darkness, when snipers were inactive. Twice each day, an hour before dawn and half an hour before dusk, every regiment mounted the fire step along its portion of the trenches and remained there, on the alert, until full daylight spread or night came down. Between times, round the clock, half the men kept watch, while the other half slept or rested on their arms, ready to assist in repelling an attack whenever their on-duty comrades sounded the alarm.

Outnumbered and outgunned, ill-clad, ill-shod, and invariably hungry, running after fragments of shell as they once had run after rabbits — except that now they were not in direct pursuit of food, for there was none at the scene of the chase, but rather of the chance to win a day out of the trenches, on the roam where a few mouthfuls could be scrounged from roadside gardens ("They stole more from us than the Yankees did; poor things," a farmwife was to say long afterwards) — Lee's veterans fought less by now for a cause than they did for a tradition. And if, in the past six months, this had become a tradition not so much of victory as of undefeat, it had nonetheless been strengthened by the recent overland campaign and now was being sustained by the current stalemate, which was all that Grant's hundred thousand casualties had earned him in this latest On-to-Richmond effort, launched in May. Mainly, though, Lee's veterans fought for Lee, or at any rate for the pride they felt when they watched him ride among them. He had "a fearless look of self-possession, without a trace of arrogance," a Tarheel captain noted, and though a fellow Virginian observed that "he had aged somewhat in appearance," it was also evident that he "had rather gained than lost in physical vigor, from the severe life he had led. His hair had grown gray, but his face had the ruddy hue of health and his eyes were as clear and bright as ever."

Partly this appearance of well-being derived from the extended spell of golden weather, which continued through November into December; Lee had always been responsive to climatic fluctuations, good and bad, even before the onset of what doctors called his rheumatism. A staff cavalryman, however, looking back on this hale, autumnal time — when the general, as he said, "seldom, if ever, exhibited the least trace of anxiety, but was firm, hopeful, and encouraged those around him in the belief that he was still confident of success" — believed he saw deeper into the matter. "It must have been the sense of having done his whole duty, and expended upon the cause every energy of his being, which enabled him to meet the approaching catastrophe with a calmness which seemed to those around him almost sublime."

Perceptive as this was by hindsight, there were other, more evident causes for the confidence he displayed. One was the return of Longstreet in mid-October, on the day of Early's defeat at Cedar Creek. His right arm partly paralyzed by the effects of his Wilderness wound, Old Peter had learned to write with his left hand, and he gladly accepted full responsibility for the defense of that part of the line above the James, where he soon demonstrated that he had lost none of his cool, hard-handed skill in conducting a battle. Lee's wisdom in leaving the fighting there to his "old war horse" was confirmed within eight days of the Georgian's return to duty; no northside drive on Richmond was ever so easily shattered, at such low cost to the defenders, as the one that made up part of Grant's fourth and final pendulum strike, October 27. What was more, the confidence this inspired was enlarged by Hill's and Hampton's canny resistance along Hatcher's Run, where three Federal corps were turned back in confusion the following day, after suffering even heavier losses than had been inflicted on the other two corps, at the far end of the line.

Small wonder, then, that Lee gave an impression of vigor and well-being as he rode north or south, through the flare and haze of Indian Summer, to inspect his nearly forty miles of unbroken line from the Chickahominy down past Burgess Mill. Even Grant, who was slow to learn negative lessons, had apparently been convinced by this latest failure that he would never take the Confederate capital by storm, and this estimate was strengthened in mid-November by the recall of Kershaw's division from Early to join Longstreet, whose reunited First Corps now occupied all the defenses north of the Appomattox, including those across Bermuda Neck. A. P. Hill's Third Corps held the Petersburg intrenchments, supported by Hampton's cavalry on the right, and a new Fourth Corps was improvised by combining the divisions of Hoke and Bushrod Johnson (but only on paper; Hoke remained north and Johnson south of the James) to provide a command for Richard Anderson, commensurate with his rank, after Old Peter's return. With Dick Ewell in charge of the reserves in Richmond, on call for manning the city's inner works, Lee felt that his army was not only back under his immediate control — aside, that is, from Early's three Second Corps divisions, still licking their wounds out on the near rim of the Shenandoah Valley — but also, in the light of its performance against four all-out assaults in as many months by twice its numbers, that it had recovered a considerable measure of the responsive, agile quality that made it like a rapier in his hand.

Still, for all its delicate balance and true temper, the rapier had become an exclusively defensive weapon, swift in parry and effective in occasional riposte, but not employed for months now to deliver a bold, original thrust or slash, as in the days when Lee's aggressive use of it, whether to pink or maim, had dazzled admirers all over the world. Moreover, he knew that in time, without proper care or refurbishment, the fine-honed instrument would wear out (or the fencer would, which came to the same thing) under the constant hammering of the Union broadsword, any one of whose strokes would end the duel if his arm wearied and let it past. "Without some increase of strength," he had warned Seddon more than two months ago, "I cannot see how we can escape the natural military consequences of the enemy's numerical superiority." Nothing much had come of this, nor of a follow-up protest to Bragg one month later: "I get no additions. The men coming in do not supply the vacancies caused by sickness, desertions, and other casualties." Now in November he appealed to the President himself. "Grant will get every man he can. . . . Unless we obtain a reasonable approximation to his force I fear a great calamity will befall us."

Nothing came of that either; Davis could only reply, as he had done to similar pleas from Hood, "No other resource remains." And now that Lincoln's reëlection had dashed Confederate hopes for an early end to the war by negotiation, Lee saw clearly enough that all his skilled resistance had really gained him, north and south of the James, was time — time with which, lacking substantial reinforcements, he could do little except continue to resist; until time ran out, as it finally must, and broke the vicious, tightening circle. His belief that Grant was at last convinced of the folly involved in prolonging a series of bungled attempts to overrun him was encouraged, if not confirmed, when November drew to a close without a major assault having been launched against any part of his works from start to finish, the first such month since the siege began. But he also knew this did not mean there would be a let-up in Grant's efforts to accomplish by attrition what he had failed to achieve by overwhelming force. Expecting renewed strikes at his overworked supply lines, west and south of Petersburg and Richmond, Lee told Davis in early December: "All we want to resist them is men."

Subsequently, looking back on his close association as the general's aide, a staff colonel declared that the two- or three-week span from late November into December was "the most anxious period of Grant's entire military career." Although Horace Porter, who made the statement, had not shared his chief's times of trial out West — after Donelson, when Halleck tried to sack him: after Shiloh, when Sherman persuaded him not to quit the service in dejection: after Vicksburg, when he spent a fretful month watching his army be dismembered, while he hobbled about on crutches from his New Orleans horseback fall — the young West Pointer had practical as well as psychological grounds for his contention that this latest tribulation was the hardest. Those previous afflictions of the spirit had followed significant battlefield successes, two of them even resulting in rebel surrenders, whereas this one came at a time when the best Grant could claim, at any rate for the army under his hand, was a stalemate achieved at a cost in casualties roughly twice as great as the number he inflicted. Victory was a future, not a present thing, as in two of those other three cases, and its nearness — within his reach, as he believed, but not within his grasp, as Lee had shown — was one source of his frustration. Another, which raised this reaction to the pitch of true anxiety, was a growing apprehension that things might go dreadfully awry in Tennessee (or, what was worse, Kentucky) on the very eve of triumph in Virginia. He had never been one to take counsel of his fears, but there were plenty of veteran officers around — including Porter, who had served on McClellan's staff — to remind him that Little Mac once had stood about where he was standing now, close enough to hear the tocsin clang in Richmond, and yet had wound up confronting a Maryland invasion fifty miles northwest of his own capital, which lay more than a hundred miles in rear of Harrison's Landing, just across the way from City Point.

First there was the unavoidable admission that the headlong approach, which by now had cost Meade and Butler some 36,000 casualties between them — 11,000 in the initial June assault, plus 25,000 since — provided no quick solution to the Petersburg dilemma. That came hard for Grant, who seldom acknowledged failure, especially in large-scale undertakings, and in fact declined to do so now; except tacitly, by desisting. Hancock did it for him, though, in a ceremony staged at his headquarters on November 26, when he bid farewell to the once-proud II Corps. Ostensibly, he was returning to Washington under War Department orders to recruit and organize a new I Corps of reënlisted veterans for service in the spring. Nothing was to come of that, however. Nor was there much validity in the claim that he was leaving because of his unhealed Gettysburg wound. The real damage was to his soldier's pride, which had suffered cruelly in the series of dispiriting reverses he and his troops had undergone in the course of the past five months, north of the James and south of the Appomattox. His departure was a measure of the extent to which Grant's breakthrough concept had broken down in the fire of Lee's resistance, and it was clear that the men of the three divisions Hancock left behind would need a great deal of rest and recuperation before they were fit for any such use by his successor, Major General A. A. Humphreys, a fellow Pennsylvanian and West Pointer, who had served as Meade's chief of staff for the past year and was fifty-four years old.

Sharpest of the stings involved in the stalling of Grant's offensive was the fact that he could almost never get his orders carried out as he intended; Baldy Smith had been the first, after the passage of the James, but he was by no means the last offender in this regard. "Three different times has Richmond or Petersburg been virutally in his hands," a military visitor wrote home about this time, "and by some inexcusable neglect or slowness each time his plans were ruined and the opportunity lost. How Grant stands it I do not see." Moreover, there seemed to be no cure for this condition: not even the removal of Baldy and Burnside, along with such lesser lights as Ledlie and Ferrero. These, after all, were only four among the many — including Butler, who could not be dealt with in that fashion, though he was at times, because of his lofty rank and large command, a greater trial than all the rest combined.

Just now, for example, he was at work on a plan for cracking Wilmington's seaward defenses, obviously a top-priority assignment, not only because it would close the South's last major port and thus increase Lee's problem of subsistence, but also because it would divert attention, as well as possible rebel reinforcements, away from Sherman's destination on the Georgia coast, 250 miles below. Yet Butler kept delaying the start of the movement, which he was to make with two of his divisions and the support of David Porter's fleet, by thinking up ways to ensure that the amphibious assault would be brief and successful, without too great a cost in ships and men. His latest notion was to pack an expendable ocean-going steamer with 350 tons of powder and run it under the walls of Fort Fisher, which would be reduced to rubble by the timed explosion, leaving the attackers little to do but move in and take over when the smoke cleared. Grant liked the plan and approved it, though he did not like or approve of the delays. He kept prodding the cock-eyed general, urging him to be off before the Carolinians got word of what was in store for them; but Butler, still "as visionary as an opium eater in council," refused to be hurried, insisting that a close attention to details provided the only guarantee of success. Then on November 27 — the day after Hancock's farewell ceremony — an enemy agent came close to solving Grant's problem by removing the former Bay State politician not only from his command but from the earth.

Butler and Porter were conferring aboard the former's headquarters steamer *Greyhound*, a short distance up the James from Bermuda Landing, "when suddenly an explosion forward startled us, and in a

moment large volumes of smoke poured out of the engine room." So
Porter later described the mishap, which fortunately was no worse
because the explosion set off no others and the flames were soon extinguished, but he marveled at an ingenuity rivaling his companion's
in such matters. What was thought at first to have been a boiler accident
turned out to have been caused by a "coal torpedo," a blackened piece
of cast iron, machined to resemble a lump of coal and loaded with
ten pounds of powder, which the rebel agent had somehow placed in
the steamer's bunker and a stoker had shoveled into the furnace. "In
devices for blowing up vessels the Confederates were far ahead of us,
putting Yankee ingenuity to shame," the admiral declared.

Three days later, on the last day of November, Grant learned that
part of the Wilmington garrison was being withdrawn to intercept
Sherman at Augusta, Georgia, on the theory that he would pass that
way en route to Charleston. Not only was this no immediate threat to
Sherman, whose true destination was almost a hundred miles farther
down the coast, it also simplified Butler's task by reducing, at least
for the present, the resistance he would encounter when he struck
Wilmington's defenses. Informed of this, the Massachusetts general
replied that he was delighted; he would proceed as soon as his floating
bomb was ready for use, a further delay having been required by his
notion of altering the steamer's lines to make her resemble a blockade
runner, which he figured would cause the rebel cannoneers to cheer
her, rather than shoot at her, right up to the moment she blew. Grant
could see the humor in this, but he was losing patience. Aware that the
Confederates would soon have the choice of returning to Wilmington
or ganging up on Sherman, he told Butler on December 4 to start for
North Carolina at once, "with or without your powder boat." But that
did not work either. For ten more days the squint-eyed Butler, unruffled by his superior's apprehensions or his own near brush with death
aboard the *Greyhound*, continued to balk and tinker before he got his
two divisions onto transports at Hampton Roads and headed down
the coast.

Grant's concern for Sherman's welfare, even his survival, off on
his own and due to pop up any day now, more than four hundred
miles down the seaboard — a ready target for whatever combination
of forces the rebels were able to throw in that direction — was real
enough, but it was by no means as grievous a source of anxiety as were
several others, over which — at least in theory, since he was in direct
communication with the subordinates in charge — he could exercise
some measure of control. For one thing, as he had told Stanton at the
outset, seeking to reassure the Secretary as to the degree of risk involved in cutting loose from Atlanta for the march through Georgia to
the coast, "Such an army as Sherman has (and with such a commander)
is hard to corner or capture." For another, his over-all design for the

Confederacy's defeat by strangulation did not hinge on the outcome of the current maneuver by his red-haired friend, whose success could shorten but whose defeat would not lengthen the war by so much as a day. Besides, his reliance on Sherman and Sherman's army — once his own — was unmatched by any such feeling of confidence in George Thomas and the scratch collection of recruits, dismounted cavalrymen, and culled veterans Old Tom had been attempting to put together in Middle Tennessee ever since Sherman set out for the sea, leaving Hood and Hood's hard-hitting army alive in his rear, poised for a strike at the critical Union center.

There was the rub. The Rock of Chickamauga was superb on the defensive, and at Chattanooga he had shown what he could do in an assault on a fixed position. But how would Old Slow Trot perform in a fluid situation requiring him to deal with an enemy in motion around his flank? So far the signs were unpromising, and that was the chief source of Grant's anxiety: that Hood would bypass Nashville, where Thomas was intrenched, and cross the Cumberland River unmolested, perhaps on a march all the way to the Ohio. If that happened, all Grant's well-laid plans might come undone in a sudden reversal of the tide of war. Even the siege of Richmond might have to be lifted, in order to furnish troops for the protection of Kentucky, and Sherman's march through Georgia might as well have occurred in a vacuum, ending as it would in nothing more than a long ride north aboard transports, then west by rail to resume the contest with his old adversary in a region two hundred miles in rear of the one through which he had fought his way in May and June.

Lincoln saw it, too, and abandoned for the time, at least by proxy, his hands-off policy with regard to military operations. "The President feels solicitous about the disposition of General Thomas to lay in fortifications for an indefinite period," Stanton wired on December 2. "This looks like the McClellan and Rosecrans strategy of do nothing and let the rebels raid the country. The President wishes you to consider the matter."

Grant did consider the matter and stepped up the pressure, warning Thomas that he would "suffer incalculable injury . . . if Hood is not speedily disposed of. Put forth therefore every possible exertion to gain this end," he told him, but with no more success than he was having at the same time in getting Butler on the go for Wilmington. Stanton returned to the charge, protesting that the Virginian seemed "unwilling to attack because it is hazardous — as if war was anything but hazardous," he sneered — which drew from Grant the admission that, for all of Thomas's reputed bulldog qualities, "I fear he is too cautious to take the initiative." All the same, he tried again, this time with a direct order: "Attack Hood at once and wait no longer. . . . There is great danger of delay resulting in a campaign back to the Ohio River."

This was clear enough, but it only caused the Tennessee commander to shift his ground under prodding from the rear. He had been on the verge of launching an all-out attack, he replied, but "a terrible storm of freezing rain has come on today, which will make it impossible for our men to fight to any advantage."

Thwarted thus at every turn in his efforts to get Butler and Thomas moving, stalled on the outskirts of Richmond by a resistance so discouraging that it had just cost Meade the best of his corps commanders, deprived of any reliable information as to Sherman's progress or misfortune in the Georgia hinterland, and harried as he was beginning to be by superiors who had been altogether forbearing up till now, Grant was determined to do what he personally could at City Point, through this "most anxious period," if only by way of relieving the strain that came with finding how much there was that he could not do elsewhere. One thing he could do, despite his recent abandonment of headlong tactics against Petersburg's intrenchments, was keep up the pressure on its overtaxed supply lines. That would not only add to Lee's subsistence problem, in direct ratio to the degree of success achieved; it would also prevent the old fox from sending reinforcements to Tennessee or Georgia, as he had done the year before, in the absence of such pressure. Accordingly, Grant planned another strike at the Weldon Railroad, this time down near the Carolina line, its purpose being to lengthen the twenty-mile wagon haul the rebels now were obliged to make from Stony Creek, the terminus of the road since August, when Hancock wrecked it that far south. The assignment went to Warren, whose three divisions would be reinforced by one from Humphreys, and Gregg's troopers would go along to screen the march.

First, though, Grant decided to lengthen the numerical odds against his adversary by returning Wright's long-absent corps from the Shenandoah Valley, where all it had been doing for the past six weeks was assist Sheridan in the destruction being visited on that much-fought-over region, once the classic avenue for invasions that played on northern fears, but now not even a source of grain or cattle, practically all of which had been put to the torch or gone under the Union knife. Wright's leading elements began unloading from transports at City Point on December 4; three days later Warren set out on his march to strike the Petersburg & Weldon at the crossing of the Meherrin River, twenty miles beyond Stony Creek.

When Lee discovered that Wright was en route from the Valley to rejoin Meade, he countered by ordering Early to send back two of his divisions, Gordon's and Ramseur's, the latter now under its senior brigadier, John Pegram. Neither arrived in time to help fend off Warren's threat to the railroad, which began on December 7, but the southern commander, gambling on his belief that Grant would attempt no more frontal assaults this year, risked pulling most of Hill's corps out of the Petersburg works to undertake, along with Hampton's cavalry, an interception of what he thought was a drive on Weldon. Next day, however, the weather turned intensely cold. Pelted by sleet, the butternut marchers shivered in their rags, and many fell out of the slow-moving column after slogging barefoot over miles of frozen ground. When those who managed to keep going reached the railroad below Stony Creek, December 9, they found sixteen miles of track ripped up, piles of ties still smoking, heat-twisted rails warm to the touch, and the Federals gone, turned back by home-guard batteries at Hicksford, firing at them from just beyond the Meherrin, as well as by the miserable weather and the near exhaustion of their three-day rations. Hampton overtook and slashed at the flanks of the blue column trudging north, but only managed to kill or capture about a hundred stragglers; the rest got away into their own lines the following day. If there was some criticism of Hill for not having engaged the marauders before they escaped, there was also a feeling of relief that they had not inflicted heavier damage on the already crippled supply line, whose railhead now was forty miles south of Petersburg's hungry defenders.

Winter came with mid-December vengeance, and though the advantage had to be weighed against the suffering of his thinly clad men in the trenches astride the James, Lee knew that the Federals too, for all their sturdy boots, snug overcoats, and rations that warmed them inside as well as out, would be restricted by ice and mud and frozen rain if they continued their efforts to move around his flanks. Moreover, the rough weather afforded him one last chance — however slight, in comparison with what Wright's return brought Grant — to increase the number of troops he could post along his thirty-odd miles of line between White Oak Swamp and Hatcher's Run. When he got word that a six-inch snow had clogged the roads in the upper Valley, he told Early to send the third of his divisions to Richmond in the wake of the other two (which had just arrived) but to remain out there himself, as district commander, with a force reduced to Wharton's undersized infantry division and Rosser's two slim cavalry brigades, in necessarily long-range observation of Sheridan's continuing depredations. Presently the old Second Corps, down to a skeleton strength of fewer than 9000 effectives — the result of its six-month excursion down and up the Valley and its brief side trip to the outskirts of Washington and back — was again an integral, on-hand part of the Army of Northern Virginia.

Lee named Gordon acting corps commander, the first nonprofessional to occupy so high a post. This was an indication of what inroads attrition had made at the upper levels, as was the fact that two of the three divisions were similarly led by their senior brigadiers. Clement Evans, a former Georgia lawyer like his chief, succeeded Gordon, and Bryan Grimes, once a North Carolina planter, had taken over from the fallen Rodes. Only Pegram, a Virginia-born West Pointer, had seen military service before the war. And of the four, including the major general in charge of all three divisions, only Grimes had reached his middle thirties. He was thirty-six; Gordon and Pegram were thirty-two, and Evans was thirty-one.

Glad as Lee was at the reassembling of his army, however shrunken it might be at all its levels, he was also saddened by the knowledge that this had been accomplished at the price of abandoning hope of going over to the offensive. Not since Chancellorsville and the death of Jackson, close to twenty months ago, had he won the kind of brilliant, large-scale victory that brought him and his lean, caterwauling veterans the admiration of the world, and now that the Valley was irretrievably lost, along with Stonewall, his recall of the Second Corps to join the others huddled in the trenches around Petersburg and Richmond set the seal on his admission, however tacit, that the war, however much or little of it was left to fight, was for him and them no longer a pursuit of glory on the road to national independence, but rather a grim struggle for survival, which would take them down a quite different road to the same goal — if they could reach its end. Yet here was where a paradox came in. While Grant reacted to the prospect of ultimate victory by growing jumpy at the thought of having the prize snatched from him just as it seemed about to come within his grasp, Lee faced the ultimate prospect of defeat with "a fearless look of self-possession" and "a calmness which seemed to those around him almost sublime."

Or perhaps there was no paradox in that. Perhaps the two reactions were quite natural, considering the two quite different kinds of strain imposed on these two quite different kinds of men. In some ways, since nothing worse could happen to him than what seemed foreordained, Lee's was the easier role to play. Expectation braced him for the shocks: even the loss, before the month was out, of more than a tenth of the force he had been at such pains to assemble for Richmond's protection in mid-December. Warned that Wilmington was about to be hit, three hundred miles down the coast, he was obliged to send Hoke's division to its defense — a detachment that cost him the equivalent of a solid two thirds of all he had gained by the return of Early's survivors from the Valley. His year-end strength, including 5358 reservists under Ewell, came to 57,134. Across the way, Meade had 83,846 and Butler 40,452: a total of 124,278 for Grant.

Outnumbered two to one, the gaps in their ranks only partly chinked with conscripts, the defenders saw clearly enough that time, which they were being told was on their side, could only lengthen the odds against survival. Good men had fallen and were falling every day, picked off by snipers or dropped by mortars in a roughly man-for-man exchange that worked to the considerable disadvantage of the smaller force, not only because its proportionate loss was twice as heavy on that basis, but also because the replacements being scraped from the bottom of the Confederate barrel did not "supply the vacancies," as Lee had complained to Bragg three months before. Moreover, some who fell could scarcely have been replaced in the best of times: Rodes and Ramseur, for example, or John Gregg and Archibald Gracie, both of whom had won distinction at Chickamauga. Gregg was cut down at the head of his Texas brigade, in a skirmish east of Richmond in October, and Gracie was killed in early December by a shell that burst over a normally quiet stretch of Petersburg intrenchments while he was training a telescope on the works across the way. Such losses, suffered without the compensating stimulus of victory, came hard for the survivors, whose spirits drooped as their numbers dwindled. "Living cannot be called a fever here," a butternut artillerist declared, "but rather a long catalepsy." Desertions rose with the rising proportion of conscripts, many of them netted after years of avoiding the draft, and even the stalwarts who stood by their banners looked forward to furling them — whatever arrangements might have to be made to bring that end about.

"As we lay there watching the bright stars," one veteran lieutenant was to say, "many a soldier asked himself the question: What is this all about? Why is it that 200,000 men of one blood and one tongue, believing as one man in the fatherhood of God and the universal brotherhood of man, should in the nineteenth century of the Christian era be thus armed with all the improved appliances of modern warfare and seeking one another's lives? We could settle our differences by compromising, and all be at home in ten days."

✗ 2 ✗

Early morning, November 16; Sherman sat his horse on Bald Hill, where the worst of the fighting had raged in July, and looked down on the copse where McPherson had fallen, shot through the back while opposing the second of Hood's three all-out sorties. "Behind us lay Atlanta, smouldering and in ruins," he would recall, "the black smoke rising high in air and hanging like a pall over the ruined city. Away off in the distance, on the McDonough Road, was the rear of Howard's column, the gun barrels glistening in the sun, the white-topped wagons stretching away to the south, and right before us the XIV Corps [of Slocum's column] marching steadily and rapidly, with a cheery look and swinging pace that made light of the thousand miles that lay between us and Richmond."

Leading elements of both columns having stepped off the day before, east and southeast down the railroads, Atlanta had been set afire last night, partly by rear-guard arsonists, who stole away from, then rejoined their units passing through, and partly by design, in accordance with orders that nothing be left intact that might be of use to the rebs when they returned. In any case, the results were spectacular. "All the pictures and verbal descriptions of hell I have ever seen never gave me half so vivid an idea of it as did this flame-wrapped city tonight," a staff major wrote in his journal after dodging sparks and debris from explosions as he picked his way through the streets. Dawn showed more than a third of the town in ashes, with smoke still rising thick and slow from the longer-lasting fires. While Sherman watched from his hilltop, a mile beyond the eastward bend of Hood's abandoned fortifications, a band in the blue column below struck up the John Brown song, and presently the marchers joined in, roaring the words as they slogged along. "Never before or since have I heard the chorus of 'Glory, glory, hallelujah!' done with more spirit or in better harmony of time and place," their red-haired commander was to say.

He twitched his horse's head to the east and came down off the hill, trailed by his staff. "Uncle Billy," a weathered veteran hailed him near the bottom, "I guess Grant is waiting for us at Richmond!" Sherman grinned and rode on, doubling the column. "Atlanta was soon lost behind the screen of trees, and became a thing of the past. Around it clings many a thought of desperate battle, of hope and fear, that now seem like the memory of a dream. . . . I have never seen the place since."

Orders governing the expedition had been issued the week before, to afford all ranks plenty of time for study before moving out. They made no mention of route or destination, being mainly concerned with logistics and rules of conduct for the 62,000 participants, just over 5000 of whom were cavalry, under Kilpatrick, and just under 2000 were artillery, with 64 guns. Each of the four infantry corps — two in each of two "wings," both of which were equipped with 900-foot collapsible pontoon bridges transported in special trains — would move by a separate road, where practicable, and be independent for supplies. "The army will forage liberally on the country during the march," Sherman directed, though he specified that the foraging was to be done only by authorized personnel; "Soldiers must not enter the dwellings of inhabitants or commit any trespass." He hoped to keep nonmilitary damage to a minimum, but he made it clear that if guerillas or other civilians attempted to interfere with his progress, say by damaging bridges or obstructing roads, "then army commanders should order and enforce a devastation more or less relentless, according to the measure of such hostility." Privately, he expanded this admonition and directed that word of it be spread wherever the army went, in hopes that it would be carried ahead by the rebel grapevine, if not by the rebel papers. "If the enemy burn forage and corn in our route," he said, "houses, barns, and cotton gins must also be burned to keep them company."

Every man carried forty rounds of small-arms ammunition on his person, and another 200 followed in the wagons, along with a twenty-day supply of hardtack and coffee. Only a five-day reserve of grain went along for the horses, but he figured that was enough to get them clear of the clean-picked region around Atlanta; "I knew that within that time we would reach a country well stocked with corn, which had been gathered and stored in cribs, seemingly for our use, by Governor Brown's militia." The same went for foodstuffs for the men. Pigs and turkeys squealed and gobbled in farmyards all along the 300 miles of unspoiled hinterland his veterans would traverse, and sweet potatoes were waiting to be roasted in the ashes of a thousand campfires every night of the three or four weeks he expected it would take him to reach Savannah, where the navy would be standing by with supply ships.

That the march was made in two divergent columns, each about 30,000 strong and with half the guns, served a triple purpose: first, to avoid the crowding and delays that would result from trying to move all four corps along a single route: second, to broaden not only the foraging area but also the swath of destruction, which thus would be twice as horrendous: and third, to confuse and mislead the enemy as to Sherman's objective or objectives, on the Atlantic and on the way there. Howard's right wing, made up of his two-corps Army of the Tennessee — Blair was back from his electioneering duties, but Major General Peter Oster-haus, Logan's senior division commander, had charge of the XV Corps in the continued absence of his chief, who remained North after stumping for Lincoln — tramped south down the Macon & Western, as if bound for Macon, while Slocum's left wing, containing the corps under Davis and Williams — formerly part of Thomas's Army of the Cumberland, now styled the Army of Georgia — followed the line of the

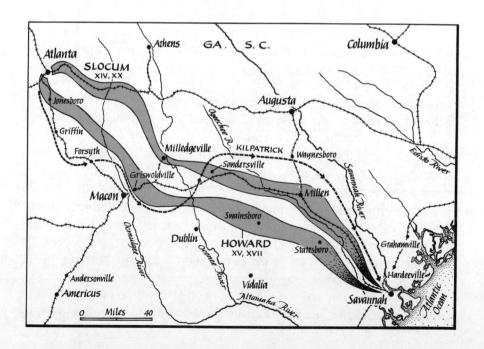

Georgia Railroad, which ran due east to Augusta. By now, most likely, the Confederates must be rushing all available reserves to the defense of both population centers. At any rate that was what Sherman hoped they would do; for he intended to move through neither, but rather through Milledgeville, the state capital, which lay between them.

This began to be fairly obvious to the right-wing marchers on their second day out of Atlanta, when Howard veered southeast from Jonesboro, leaving Kilpatrick to keep up the feint down the railroad nearly to Forsyth, twenty miles short of Macon, where he too turned off to rejoin the infantry column beyond the bypassed town. Slocum continued eastward from Atlanta for three days, ripping up track as he went, and then on the fourth — by which time the two wings were close to fifty miles apart — turned south along the near bank of the Oconee River toward Milledgeville, some forty miles downstream. "God has put a ring in Sherman's nose and is leading him to destruction," a Richmond clergyman had remarked when the widespread march began. But now, as a result of conflicting reports by his adversaries, which in turn were the result of careful planning on his part, scarcely anyone but God and the farmers whose crops he was consuming as he progressed knew where he was.

If the march had its rigors, mainly proceeding from the great distance to be covered and the occasional hard work of bridging creeks and corduroying roads, it also had its attendant compensations derived from the fatness of the land and the skylark attitude of the men fanned out across it in two columns, foraging along a front that varied from thirty to sixty miles in width. "This is probably the most gigantic pleasure excursion ever planned," one of Howard's veterans declared after swinging eastward on the second day out of Atlanta. "It already beats everything I ever saw soldiering, and promises to prove much richer yet." Expectations were as high, and as amply rewarded, in the column to the north. Riding with Slocum past Stone Mountain that same day, Sherman pulled off on the side of the road to review the passing troops and found them unneglectful of such opportunities as had come their way. One marcher who drew his attention had a ham slung from his rifle, a jug of molasses cradled under one arm, and a big piece of honeycomb clutched in the other hand, from which he was eating as he slogged along. Catching the general's eye, he quoted him *sotto voce* to a comrade as they swung past: "Forage liberally on the country."

Sherman afterwards told how he "reproved the man, explaining that foraging must be limited to the regular parties properly detailed," but he was not long in showing that despoilment had a place in his calculations, quite as much as it did in theirs. Four days later, after turning south toward Milledgeville just short of the Oconee, he came upon a well-stocked plantation which he happened to learn belonged to Major General Howell Cobb. A leading secessionist and one-time speaker of the U.S. House and Treasury Secretary under Buchanan, Cobb had been appointed by Joe Brown to command the state reserves in the present crisis; in which capacity — though it turned out there were no "reserves" for him to command — he had been exhorting his fellow Georgians to resist the blue invasion by the destruction of everything edible in its path. "Of course, we confiscated his property," Sherman would recall, "and found it rich in corn, beans, peanuts, and sorghum molasses. . . . I sent back word to General Davis to explain whose plantation it was, and instructed him to spare nothing. That night huge bonfires consumed the fence rails, kept our soldiers warm, and the teamsters and men, as well as the slaves, carried off an immense quantity of corn and provisions of all sorts."

His aim, he said, in thus enforcing "a devastation more or less relentless," was to convince the planters roundabout "that it is in their interest not to impede our movements." Simultaneously, however, this conclusion was discouraged by the activities of his foragers — "bummers," they were called, and called themselves, although the term had been one of opprobrium at the start — who worked along the fringes of the march, sometimes as "regular parties properly detailed," sometimes not. Isolated plantation owners, mostly wives and mothers whose sons and husbands were with Hood or Lee in Tennessee or Virginia, buried their silver and jewels on hearing of Sherman's approach, and the search for these provided fun, as well as the possibility of profit, for the blue-clad visitors. Out would come the ramrods for a vigorous probing of lawns and flowerbeds. "It was comical to see a group of these red-bearded, barefooted, ragged veterans punching the unoffending earth in an apparently idiotic but certainly most energetic way," an officer who observed them was to write. "A woman standing upon the porch of a house, watching their proceedings, instantly became an object of suspicion, and she was watched until some movement betrayed a place of concealment. Fresh earth thrown up, a bed of flowers just set out, the slightest indication of a change in appearance or position, all attracted the gaze of these military agriculturists. If they 'struck a vein' a spade was instantly put in requisition and the coveted wealth was speedily unearthed. It was all fair spoil of war, and the search made one of the excitements of the march." Other diversions included the shooting of bloodhounds, hated for their use in tracking runaway slaves and convicts through the swamps. Sometimes, by way of a joke, the definition was expanded to cover less offensive breeds. For example, when a poodle's mistress appealed for her lap dog to be spared, the soldier who had caught up the pet and was bearing it off to execution replied: "Madam, our orders are to kill every bloodhound." "But this is not a bloodhound!" she protested, only to be told: "Well, madam, we cannot tell what it will grow into if we leave it behind."

If there was a core of cruelty to such humor, it was precisely in such cruelty that the humor had its source. In time Sherman would concede that "many acts of pillage, robbery, and violence were committed by these parties of foragers." He had also "heard of jewelry taken from women and the plunder of articles that never reached our commissary," though he insisted that such depredations were "exceptional and incidental." In any case, whatever factors contributed to the total, he would report at the end of the march across Georgia that the damage inflicted came to no less than $100,000,000: "at least twenty millions of which has inured to our advantage, and the remainder is simple waste and destruction. This may seem a hard species of warfare," he declared, "but it brings the sad realities of war home to those who have been directly or indirectly instrumental in involving us in its attendant calamities." Such, after all, was one of the main purposes of the expedition, and if, in its course, southern women had been subjected to certain discourtesies in their homes, there was a measure of justice in that as well, since they were among the fieriest proponents of a war that might have ended by now except for their insistence that it be fought to the last ditch. Many of the soldiers believed as much, at any rate. "You urge young men to the battlefield where men are being killed by the thousands, while you stay home and sing *The Bonnie Blue Flag*," an Ohio colonel heard one of his troopers lecture a resentful housewife, "but you set up a howl when you see the Yankees down here getting your chickens. Many of your young men have told us they are tired of war, and would quit, but you women would shame them and drive them back." This applied only to white women, of course. Black ones were far more sympathetic to the invaders, especially on visits to their roadside bivouacs at night. "And they didn't charge us a cent," one grateful infantryman recorded.

So far, except for skittery detachments of butternut cavalry, not so much opposing as observing Kilpatrick's movement down the Macon & Western, neither Union column had encountered any organized resistance. One reason for this, in addition to their confusion as to Sherman's whereabouts or goal, was that the Confederates had little or nothing with which to confront him except Wheeler's 3500 scattered horsemen and an overload of brass. Within a week of his departure from Atlanta, both Hardee and Richard Taylor were at Macon, ordered there from Charleston and Selma by Beauregard — who himself was on the way from North Alabama — to confer with the Governor and his two chief military advisers, Howell Cobb and Major General G. W. Smith. Of these four high-ranking commanders, only the last brought any troops along, and all he had was 3000 Georgia militia summoned back into service by Brown to help meet the impending crisis. Learning that the blue infantry had left the railroad at Jonesboro, Hardee decided that Milledgeville, not Macon, was Howard's intermediary objective on a march that would continue southeast, through Millen to Savannah, and that Slocum would most likely push on eastward, through Augusta, to reach Charleston. He therefore advised that the militia be shifted northward to stand in Slocum's path, while he himself returned by rail to Savannah to prepare for its defense. Brown approving, the four makeshift brigades — so called, though none was much larger than a standard regiment — were ordered to set out at once, commanded by a militia brigadier named P. J. Phillips; Smith remained behind to make arrangements for supplies. That was on November 22, the day Sherman had one of Slocum's divisions clean out Cobb's plantation, ten miles north of Milledgeville, and that was how it came about that a brigade from one of Howard's divisions, ten miles east of Macon, fought that afternoon the only sizeable infantry action of the campaign between Atlanta and the Atlantic.

Aside from the high rate of casualties on one side, in contrast to the low rate on the other, there was little to distinguish the engagement from other such exercises in futility, staged for the most part in the early, picture-book days of the war, when blue and gray were green alike. Howard had bypassed Macon the day before, quarter-circling it clockwise from the north, and today, while Brown and the four generals were conferring, had posted a rear guard beyond Griswoldville, nine miles out the Central Georgia Railroad, which he crossed at that point on his way toward the Oconee for a crossing about midway between Milledgeville and Dublin. This rear guard, a single brigade from the tail division of Osterhaus's corps, had taken position along the crest of a hill one mile east of the station, its flanks protected by swampy ground and with open fields in front. So far, there had been no threat except from rebel troopers, who were easily kept off, but late that afternoon the 1500 defenders saw a heavy column of infantry moving toward them through the town. To their surprise, the marchers formed for attack and came straight at them across the stubble of the fields, displaying what one Federal called "more courage than discretion." With accustomed ease, the XV Corps veterans leveled their rifles and blasted the attackers back, only to see them reassemble and come on again, in much the same style and with similar results. Three times they charged uphill in close formation, and three times they were blown rearward by heavy volleys from the breastworks on the crest; until at last they gave it up and limped away, back through Griswoldville, toward Macon. Whooping, the victors moved out into the field to gather up the booty. Soon, however, the cheers froze in their throats at the sight of what lay before them in the stubble. They saw for the first time, to their horror, that they had been fighting mostly old men and young boys, who lay about in attitudes of death and agony — more than 600 of them in all, as compared to their own loss of 62.

"I was never so affected at the sight of dead and wounded before," an Illinois infantryman afterwards wrote home. "I hope we will never have to shoot at such men again. They knew nothing at all about fighting and I think their officers knew as little." A comrade, reacting not only to this but also to the pillage he had seen and shared in, put his thoughts in stronger words. "There is no God in war," he fumed. "It is merciless, cruel, vindictive, un-Christian, savage, relentless. It is all that devils could wish for."

Slocum's lead corps entered Milledgeville that same afternoon, twenty miles northeast of this scene of innocent valor, and the other arrived the following morning, accompanied by Sherman, who slept that night in the mansion vacated two days ago by Joe Brown, the fifth Confederate governor to be routed from his bed or desk by the approach of blue invaders. Unlike Nashville, Baton Rouge, Jackson, and Little Rock, all firmly in the Federal grip, the Georgia capital underwent only a temporary occupation; Slocum crossed the Oconee next morning, November 24, slogging eastward along the Central Georgia through Sandersville, toward Millen, while Howard took up a parallel route, some twenty miles to the south, toward Swainsboro. Brief as it was, the Milledgeville layover had been welcome, not only as a chance to get some rest after hiking the hundred miles from Atlanta, but also as a diversion from the workaday grind of converting more than sixty miles of railroad into a trail of twisted iron. Ebullient young officers, under the influence of what Sherman called "the spirit of mischief," assembled in the abandoned Hall of Representatives, and there, after a rousing debate, repealed the ordinance of secession and appointed committees to call forthwith on Governor Brown and President Davis for the purpose of landing official kicks on their official rumps. While this parliamentary business was in progress, soldiers ransacked the State House and amused themselves by heaving out of its windows all the books and papers they could find. A New Englander on Osterhaus's staff took private exception to such conduct, which seemed to him to go beyond a line that could not be crossed without a loss, if not of honor, then anyhow of due propriety. "I don't object to stealing horses, mules, niggers, and all such little things," he recorded in his journal, "but I will not engage in plundering and destroying public libraries."

Sherman, wearing low-quarter shoes and only one spur — "a general without boots," an admirer marveled — rode with Slocum, as before, except that Kilpatrick had been shifted from the right wing to provide cover for the flank that would be threatened if Richmond sent reinforcements from Virginia or the Carolinas. Apparently there were none of these; but there was something far more shocking, the red-haired Ohioan discovered when he came upon a division toiling across muddy fields because a young lieutenant had just had a foot blown off by an eight-inch shell that had been fuzed with matches and planted in the road. "This was not war, but murder," Sherman later wrote, "and it made me very angry. I immediately ordered a lot of rebel prisoners to be brought from the provost guard, armed with picks and spades, and made them march in close order along the road, so as to explode their own torpedoes or to discover and dig them up. They begged hard, but I reiterated the order, and could hardly help laughing at their stepping so gingerly along the road, where it was supposed sunken torpedoes might explode at each step."

There was no more trouble with torpedoes on the march after that; nor, indeed, from any other source. "No enemy opposed us," Sherman noted, "and we could only occasionally hear the faint reverberation of a gun to our left rear, where we knew that Kilpatrick was skirmishing with Wheeler's cavalry." In point of fact, though the scheduled rate of march had been reduced from fifteen to ten miles a day, thus assuring an unhurried and therefore thorough job of destruction across a front that varied in width from thirty to fifty miles, there was so little for Howard's wing to do that Blair's corps was summoned north to get in on the demolition of the Central Georgia. Up ahead was Millen, an important railroad junction on the far side of the Ogeechee, where a branch line ran north to Augusta to connect in turn with Wilmington and Richmond; Sherman sent word for Kilpatrick to take the lead and try his hand at effecting a "most complete and perfect break" in the installations there. "Let it be more devilish than can be dreamed of," he told the man he had called "a hell of a damned fool." Meantime both infantry wings kept slogging eastward unmolested, twisting iron and burning as they went. He was pleased to see that his "general orders of devastation" were being heeded by the Georgians in his path. Evidently the grapevine was in operation; "The people did not destroy food, for they saw clearly that it would be ruin to themselves."

At Millen, a hundred miles beyond Milledgeville and Macon, he paused for another one-day rest, two thirds of the way to his goal. Then he was off again, with his two now unequal wings on opposite banks of the Ogeechee, on the final lap of his march to the sea. It was early December now, and here on the left, beyond the river, marchers observed a change in the manner of the citizens whose crops they were despoiling; a change not so much in their attitude toward the invaders, as toward their neighbors across the Savannah River and toward the war itself. "All I ask is that when you get to South Carolina you will treat them the same way," one farmer said, and was echoed by another: "Why don't you go over to South Carolina and serve them this way? They started it." Sherman was encouraged by such talk. At the outset he had retained the option of switching his objective — including a tangential sprint for Pensacola, down on the Gulf — in case he encountered serious resistance. But no such shift was even considered, since there had been no resistance worth the name, either from regulars or guerillas. "Pierce the shell of the Confederacy and it's all hollow inside!" he exulted as he set out from Millen for Savannah, less than a hundred miles to the southeast.

One trouble there was, of increasing concern, despite his efforts to guard against it from the start. In the course of the march now approaching its end, an estimated 25,000 blacks of both sexes and all ages joined the various infantry columns at one time or another, and though at least three fourths of these turned back, either from weariness or homesickness, a considerable number managed to tag along, a growing encumbrance. Sherman tried to discourage this by explaining to their spokesmen — gray-haired preachers, for the most part — that he "wanted the slaves to remain where they were, and not load us down with useless mouths which would eat up the food needed for our fighting men." They nodded agreement, but continued to throng in the wake of each blue column, preferring instant liberty to the promise of eventual freedom, once the war was over. Beyond the Ogeechee the problem became acute, or seemed about to, not only because the land was less fruitful toward the seaboard, but also because of reports that Bragg had reached Augusta with reinforcements; Sherman decided to rid himself, in one way or another, of what might prove a military embarrassment in the event of a clash on that congested flank. He had not followed Grant's suggestion that he recruit able-bodied slaves as reinforcements, in part because he lacked missionary zeal and in part because he considered this a practice that would lead to future ills, both for the army and the country. "The South deserves all she has got from her injustice to the Negro," he would presently tell Halleck, "but that is no reason why we should go to the other extreme." In any case, he was determined to do what he could to disencumber his threatened left of these "useless mouths."

At Ebenezer Creek, which lay between the Ogeechee and the Savannah, about two thirds of the way from Millen to the coast, he found his chance — or, more strictly speaking, had it found for him, and acted upon, by one of his chief lieutenants. Davis's corps brought up the rear of Slocum's wing, and as soon as the last of his infantry cleared the unfordable stream he had his engineers hurriedly take up the pontoon bridge, leaving the refugees who were tailing the column stranded on the opposite bank. Whatever glee Davis and his soldiers felt at the success of this stratagem, which accomplished in short order all that weeks of exhortation and admonition had failed to achieve, was changed to sudden dismay when they saw what followed, first across the way and then in Ebenezer Creek itself. Wailing to find their march toward freedom halted thus in midstride and themselves abandoned to the mercy of Confederate horsemen, who soon would be upon them, the Negroes hesitated briefly, impacted by the surge of pressure from the rear, then stampeded with a rush into the icy water, old and young alike, men and women and children, swimmers and nonswimmers, determined not to be left behind by the deliverers they supposed had come to lead them out of bondage. Many drowned, despite the efforts of the engineers, who, horrified by the sight of the disaster their action had brought on, waded into the muddy creek to rescue as many of the unfortunates as they could reach. "As soon as the character of the unthinking rush and panic was seen," a Federal observer wrote, "all was done that could be done to save them from the water; but the loss of life was still great enough to prove that there were many ignorant, simple souls to whom it was literally preferable to die freemen rather than to live slaves."

In far-off City Point and Washington, all this time, nothing was known except at second hand — and rebel hand, at that — of what had occurred between the western army's high-spirited departure from Atlanta, three weeks back, and the tragic crossing of Ebenezer Creek, within thirty miles of Savannah. Mindful of its commander's plan to alter his route if serious opposition loomed, Grant drew an analogy that was apt: "Sherman's army is now somewhat in the condition of a ground-mole when he disappears under a lawn. You can here and there trace his track, but you are not quite certain where he will come out until you see his head." The President used much the same metaphor when John Sherman came to the White House to ask if there was any news of his brother down in Georgia. Lincoln replied that there was no word of the general's whereabouts or even his destination. "I know the hole he went in at, but I can't tell you the hole he will come out of."

In his December message that week he told Congress, "The most remarkable feature of the military operations of the year is General Sherman's attempted march of three hundred miles directly through the insurgent region. It tends to show a great increase of our relative strength that our General-in-Chief should feel able to confront and hold in check every active force of the enemy, and yet to detach a well-appointed large army to move on such an expedition." In the original draft, a sentence followed: "We must conclude that he feels our cause could, if need be, survive the loss of the whole detached force, while by the risk he takes a chance for the great advantages which would follow success." But this was dropped from the delivered text, on the grounds that it might be thought to show a lack of concern for the lives of 60,000 soldiers being risked on a long-odds gamble, hundreds of miles from the possibility of assistance. No one who was near Lincoln during this critical period would have made that error: least of all a friend who attended a reception at which the Chief Executive stood shaking hands with guests as they arrived. He seemed preoccupied, strangely perfunctory in his greetings, and the friend, refusing to be shuttled along like the others, stood his ground until the tall, sad-faced man emerged from his abstracted mood with a smile of recognition. "How do you do? How do you do?" he said warmly. "Excuse me for not noting you. I was thinking of a man down South."

Understandable as this was at that remove, events were soon to show that such concern had been unwarranted. By now Lincoln's "man down South" was approaching the goal of his trans-Georgia expedition, and those who were with him exulted in the damage they had inflicted and avoided. From first to last, barely two percent of their number, including the wounded, were judged unfit for duty in the course of a nearly four-week march that saw more than two hundred miles of railroad "utterly abolished" and the Confederacy riven. "The destruction could hardly have been worse," a veteran declared, "if Atlanta had been a volcano in eruption and the molten lava had flowed in a stream sixty miles wide and five times as long." Mostly they were young men, even those of highest rank; the twenty commanders of armies, corps, and divisions averaged forty years of age, while the volunteers from civilian life outnumbered the West Pointers, twelve to eight. Close to half their 218 regiments were from Ohio and Illinois, and all but 33 of the rest were from other western states. Their exuberance undiminished by strain or combat — aside, that is, from some momentary sadness after Griswoldville — the marchers treated the whole campaign, one soldier commentator said, as "a vast holiday frolic" and livened their nights, when they might have been sleeping, with occasional sham battles in which the principal weapon was lighted pine knots, flung whirling through the darkness with an effect as gaudy as anything seen in contests whose losses ran into the thousands. Cheering, they closed down upon Savannah's outer defenses on December 9 and 10.

Chief among these was Fort McAllister, a dozen miles to the south, on the right bank of the Ogeechee just above Ossabaw Sound. Sherman decided to reduce it first, thus clearing the way for the navy to steam upriver — if in fact the ships were waiting off the coast, as prearranged — before he moved against the city proper.

The navy was there all right, he discovered when he climbed to the roof of a rice mill, December 13, for a view of the fort and, beyond it, the blue waters of the sound; Howard had set up a signal station atop the mill to study the terrain and report on the progress of the attack by Brigadier General William Hazen's division. This had been Sherman's old Shiloh outfit, and concern for the survivors of those days — when Hazen, a thirty-year-old West Pointer, commanded an Ohio regiment — increased his impatience at finding the assault delayed far into the afternoon. However, while he waited and chafed, a lookout peering eastward spotted what Sherman later described as "a faint cloud of smoke and an object gliding, as it were, along the horizon above the tops of the sedge toward the sea, which little by little grew till it was pronounced to be the smokestack of a steamer." Soon, as the ship drew closer, the watchers identified the U.S. flag at her peak and a signalman asking in wigwag from her deck: "Who are you?" "Gen-

eral Sherman," the answer went back, and when this was followed by
another question: "Is Fort McAllister taken?" Sherman replied: "Not
yet, but it will be in a minute."

And it was, very nearly within that span. Hazen's division
swarmed out of the woods, across flats that had been thickly sown with
torpedoes, through the abatis, over the palisade, and into the fort itself,
where, as Sherman watched from his distant perch on the rice mill roof,
"the smoke cleared away and the parapets were blue with our men,
who fired their muskets in the air and shouted so that we actually heard
them, or felt that we did." The attack had lasted barely fifteen minutes;
Hazen lost 134 killed and wounded, many of them victims of exploding
torpedoes, and inflicted 48 casualties on the 250-man garrison, the rest
of whom were captured along with fifteen guns. "It's my old division;
I knew they'd do it!" Sherman crowed, and had an aide get off a message to Slocum at the far end of the line. "Dear General. Take a good
big drink, a long breath, and then yell like the devil. The fort was
carried at 4.30 p.m."

That night the ship steamed in through Ossabaw Sound and up the
Ogeechee River unopposed. Others followed, next day and the next,
bringing 600,000 rations and, best of all -- for, as Sherman said, "This
prompt receipt of letters had an excellent effect, making us feel that
home was near" — the mail that had been piling up for the troops ever
since they left Atlanta, four weeks, to the day, before the fall of Fort
McAllister.

There was also news, both good and bad, of recent developments
in Virginia and Tennessee, as well as of an effort, less than thirty miles
from Savannah, to break the railroad between there and Charleston.
That had been two weeks ago, on the last day of November, and
practically everything about the operation was unsatisfactory from the
Union point of view. From his headquarters up the South Carolina coast
at Hilton Head, Major General John G. Foster, successor to Quincy
Gillmore as commander of the Department of the South, sent a 5500-
man force inland to get astride the railroad near Grahamville Station
and thus prevent the Confederates from opposing Sherman with reinforcements sent by rail, in advance of his arrival, from points along the
seaboard between there and Richmond. As luck would have it — rebel
luck, that is — G. W. Smith reached Savannah that same day with the
Georgia militia; Joe Brown's Pets had come roundabout through Albany
and Thomasville after their savage treatment, eight days ago, by
Howard's rear guard east of Macon. Down to about 1400 effectives as
a result of that and other mishaps, they were sent by Hardee to meet
Foster's threat to the Charleston & Savannah. Meet it they did, and
with such élan, although the odds were as heavy against them here as
they had been in their favor back at Griswoldville, that they not only
wiped out the stain of that encounter, they also reversed the ratio of

casualties suffered. Encountering the invaders at Honey Hill, three miles south of Grahamville, they took up a position confronting a swamp-bound causeway, flung them back, frustrated a flank attack by setting fire to a field of broomsedge, and finally drove them out of range of the railroad, much as had been done two years ago at nearby Pocotaligo, where a similar blue force attempted the same maneuver with no better luck. Smith's loss was 8 killed, 42 wounded. The Federals lost 755, including 88 killed, 623 wounded, and 44 missing.

The newly arrived Westerners professed no great surprise at this defeat, having come to expect such ineptness from their allies in the paper-collar East, even against militia they themselves had trounced so roundly such a short time before. Besides, for all his success in keeping the railroad open northward, Hardee still had fewer than 15,000 inexperienced troops for the defense of Savannah against four times that number of hardened veterans. As for Sherman, he was far more interested in developments back in Middle Tennessee, where part of Thomas's scratch command had already fought one battle, more or less against his wishes, and seemed about to have to fight another, despite his apparent reluctance to do anything but sit tight. In a two-week-old letter, delivered to his red-haired friend at Fort McAllister by the navy, Grant sounded rather put out by the Tennessee situation and the way Old Pap was meeting it, but he expressed no discontent with his own lack of progress around Petersburg and Richmond. In fact, he was looking forward to a shipboard holiday. "After all becomes quiet, and the roads become so bad up here that there is likely to be a week or two when nothing can be done, I will run down the coast to see you," he wrote, adding the happy afterthought: "If you desire it, I will ask Mrs. Sherman to go with me."

Perhaps in part because even those who had wives back home could expect no such reunion by special delivery, most of this had little interest for soldiers who had just completed what was being hailed as one of the great marches of all time. By and large, their feeling was that now that they had reached the East the war would soon be over; but even this they were willing to leave to Uncle Billy, knowing that he would use them to that end when the time was right. They were more concerned with their own letters, reading and rereading them while improving their investment of Savannah and waiting for the siege guns their commander had requisitioned to reduce not only the city's defenses but also their own losses when the hour came for launching the assault. Except for coffee, which ran low at last, not even the delivery of those 600,000 rations provided much of a diversion. The fact was they had never eaten better than they had done for the past month, and Sherman even now was informing Grant that, after setting out from Atlanta with a herd of 5000 cattle and feeding beef to all who wanted it along the way, he had wound up on the coast with twice as many cows as when he started. For some time now a steady diet of sweet potatoes, corn, and pork had palled on northern palates. What they mainly looked forward to, throughout the final week of the march, was oysters, and now that they had reached salt water they had all of them they wanted. Just outside Savannah, over toward Ossabaw Sound, one soldier recorded a sample menu in a letter home: "Oyster soup, oysters on the half shell, roast goose, fried oysters, rice, raisins, and roast oysters."

★ ★ ★

Hood at last issued orders for the march north from the Tennessee River on November 16, the day Sherman drew rein on Bald Hill, two hundred air-line miles to the southeast, for a farewell look at smouldering Atlanta. Now as before, however — although Forrest, the ostensible cause of the army's marking time ever since it reached the northwest corner of Alabama in late October, had returned from his Johnsonville raid two days ago — there were further delays, occasioned by last-minute supply arrangements and a fierce storm that grew still worse throughout the next four days, converting the rain to sleet and the roads to hub-deep troughs of icy mud. But Hood would wait no longer. Just last week, in a message so characteristic that it was practically superfluous, he had told Jefferson Davis: "You may rely upon my striking the enemy whenever a suitable opportunity presents itself, and that I will spare no effort to make that opportunity." On November 20, a Sunday, he set out, and by the following morning — three weeks, to the day, since his arrival in Tuscumbia, just across the river — the last of his troops filed out of Florence, bound for Nashville and, it might be, the Ohio.

Preceded by Forrest, whose 6000 horsemen swept the front and covered the right flank, the march was in three columns, a three-division corps of just over 10,000 men in each: Stewart by way of Lawrenceburg, Cheatham by way of Waynesboro, thirty miles to the west, and Lee by way of country roads between. All three would converge on Mount Pleasant, seventy miles away by the nearest route, and move together — 38,000 strong, including the three cavalry divisions and the artillery with 108 guns — to Columbia, twelve miles northeast on Duck River, whose crossings at that point were the objective in this first stage of the advance through Middle Tennessee. Hood's purpose was to interpose his army between Thomas, who had been gathering troops at Nashville for the past month, and Schofield, posted eighty miles south at Pulaski with his own and Stanley's corps, detached by Sherman before he set out from Atlanta. Schofield had roughly 30,000 of all arms, Thomas about the same number, and if Hood got between them, in control of the Duck crossings with a force superior to either, he could deal with them individually, in whatever order he chose, and thus score a crowning double victory that would give him the Ten-

nessee capital, together with all
its stores, and clear the way for
his drive to the Ohio; which in
turn — or so ran the dream unfolded for Beauregard, now departed — would provoke the recall of Sherman, at the end of
his race through the Georgia
vacuum to the sea, and perhaps
free Hood to work the deliverance of Richmond by crossing
the Cumberlands into Virginia
to rejoin his beleaguered hero,
R. E. Lee.

Despite the unseasonably
bitter weather, which alternately
froze the roads iron hard, with ankle-twisting ruts, or thawed them into
quagmires that made every step a wrenching effort, the butternut veterans
clocked good time on their march beyond the Tennessee line. Indeed, so
successful was Forrest in driving Brigadier General Edward Hatch's reinforced cavalry division "from one position to another," thereby preventing any penetration of the screen, that Stewart's corps reached
Lawrenceburg, more than halfway to Columbia, before Schofield,
twenty miles due east at Pulaski, even knew that Hood was not only
on the way around his flank but was also not much farther by now
than he himself was from Duck River, which he would have to cross
if he was to avoid being cut off from Nashville and the other half of
the army Thomas had spent the past month assembling for the defense
of Middle Tennessee. That was on the night of November 22; Schofield began his withdrawal at first light next morning, prodding his five
divisions, 62 guns, and 800 wagons northward up the turnpike. He
knew he was involved in a race whose stakes were life or death, and
thanks to a faster, somewhat shorter track he won it handily by getting
his lead division to Columbia on the 24th, in time to keep the fast-riding
rebel troopers from seizing either of the two bridges across the Duck.
Moreover, he had his entire force dug in along the outskirts of the
south-bank town, guns emplaced, when Hood's infantry arrived from
Mount Pleasant on the 26th and took up a position, that day and the
next, confronting the newly erected breastworks anchored right and
left on the river above and below.

Hood was not discouraged by this loss of a long-odds race in
which some of his troops covered more than a hundred miles on inferior
roads while Schofield's did less than thirty-five on the turnpike. Nor
was he provoked into launching a headlong assault, which in fact was
no longer practicable — let alone judicious — by the morning of No-

vember 28, when he discovered that his one-time West Point room-mate and mathematics coach had withdrawn in the night to the north bank, destroying the two bridges over the river now in his front. What Hood had in mind instead, his lieutenants found when they reported as ordered to his headquarters beside the Pulaski pike that afternoon, was a flanking movement similar to the one he had just attempted, except that this time the odds were by no means long and he once more enjoyed the confidence that came with employing the tactics he had so much admired in Virginia, back in the days when he had both of his legs and the vigorous use of both his arms. As he saw it, later describing the frame of mind that led to the formulation of his plan, "The situation presented an occasion for one of those interesting and beautiful moves upon the chessboard of war, to perform which I had often desired an opportunity.... I had beheld with admiration the noble deeds and grand results achieved by the immortal Jackson in similar maneuvers; I had seen his corps made equal to ten times its number by a sudden attack on the enemy's rear, and I hoped in this instance to be able to profit by the teachings of my illustrious countryman."

The plan itself was as simple as it was bold. James Wilson having joined Schofield beyond the Duck with another 4000 horsemen, Forrest would cross the river today, ten miles upstream at Huey's Mill, and drive the blue cavalry northward, away from possible interference with Hood's infantry, which would cross at dawn at Davis Ford, three miles above the town. Cheatham would lead, his corps being posted on the right, and Stewart would follow, reinforced by one of Lee's divisions. Each would take along a single battery, for emergencies, and leave the rest of the guns behind — an even hundred, as it turned out — for use by Lee, who would demonstrate with them and his two remaining divisions in order to fix the Federals in position on the opposite bank of the river, while the bulk of the superior gray army moved around their left and into their rear at Spring Hill, a dozen miles up the turnpike from Columbia and about the same distance from Franklin, whose seizure would give the flankers control of the Harpeth River crossings, less than twenty miles from Nashville. In other words, another race would start at dawn, and this one too would be a matter of life or death for Schofield, though Hood did not intend for him to know — any more than he had known before — that a contest was in progress until it was at least half over; by which time, in contrast to the previous maneuver, there would be little he could do except look for a round-about avenue of escape. At that point Hood would be free either to turn on his former roommate or, having eliminated him as a factor by holding the rail and turnpike bridges across the Harpeth, plunge straight ahead for the Tennessee capital without delay. He seemed to favor the latter course just now, for he spoke that night, soon after the council of war broke up and the participants went out into the falling snow to alert their commands for tomorrow's march, of "calling for volunteers to storm the key of the works about the city." Next morning, while Cheatham's men were moving through the predawn darkness toward the pontoons thrown for them at Davis Ford the night before, he made this even more emphatic. "The enemy must give me a fight," he told a friend — Chaplain-Doctor, later Bishop, Charles Quintard — "or I'll be in Nashville before tomorrow night."

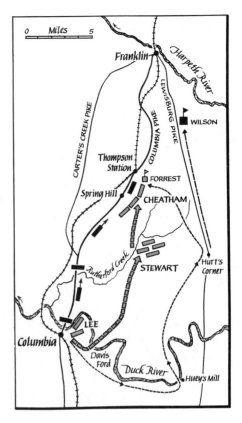

Mindful of the failure of a similar maneuver four months ago, which brought on the lost Battle of Atlanta, he went along this time in person, as he had not done before, riding with Cheatham near the head of the flanking column to see for himself that his Jacksonian plan was carried out as he intended. The result, throughout the opening phase, was all he could have hoped for. Both the crossing and the march north beyond the river, parallel to the turnpike three miles west, were unimpeded, thanks to Schofield's apparent lack of vigilance and to Forrest, whose three divisions clashed with Wilson's two at Hurt's Corner around midday, six miles out, and drove them headlong up the Lewisburg Pike toward Franklin; Forrest detached a brigade to keep up the pressure on the fleeing bluecoats and turned northwest with the rest of his troopers, as ordered, for a strike at Spring Hill in advance of the infantry. Moving up, Hood halted Stewart's reinforced corps at Rutherford Creek — presumably to protect his rear in case Schofield took alarm and moved against him from Columbia, though the steady booming of Lee's one hundred guns beyond the Duck gave assurance that the two Union corps were still in position on the north bank, unmindful of the fact that Hood had all his cavalry and all but two of his nine infantry divisions on their flank or in their rear. Elated, he told Cheatham, as he rode with him beyond the creek to within three miles of Spring Hill, to commit his lead division without delay, alongside Forrest's horsemen, and follow with the other two as soon as they came up. Meantime, Hood himself rode back to check on Stewart, whose four divisions could also be committed if they were needed; which seemed unlikely.

By then it was just after 3 o'clock. Behind him, over toward the turnpike in the direction of Spring Hill, a spatter of gunfire presumably announced that Forrest even now was overriding such resistance as the blue garrison could offer, surprised as its few members must be, midway between Columbia and Franklin, to find a host of graybacks bearing down on the little country town a dozen miles in Schofield's rear.

But that was by no means the case: mainly due to the vigilance of James Wilson. Though he lacked the time needed to whip Thomas's defeat-prone horsemen into any shape for standing up even briefly to a superior force of veterans under the Wizard of the Saddle, the young Illinois-born West Pointer had not forgotten the primary cavalry assignment of furnishing his chief with information. In fact he had sent a warning the night before, when, impressed by Forrest's aggressiveness, he notified headquarters that a heavy Confederate movement seemed to be in progress across the Duck, ten miles upstream. Schofield telegraphed word of this to Nashville, and Thomas promptly ordered a further withdrawal to Franklin. Accordingly, while Hood's infantry was passing unobserved over Davis Ford, Schofield started his 800 wagons and most of his guns up the turnpike with a train guard of two divisions under David Stanley, who was told to drop one of them off at Rutherford Creek, to secure the crossing there, and proceed with the other to Spring Hill, which he would cover for the rest of the army, soon to follow. By midmorning Stanley had cleared the creek, about one third of the distance between Columbia and Spring Hill, and learning as he drew near the latter place that rebel troopers were approaching in strength — it was by now past 2 o'clock — he double-timed Brigadier General George Wagner's division into position, just east of the town and the pike, in time to help the two-regiment garrison ward off an all-out mounted attack.

It was a near thing, and a bloody one as well, according to a Wisconsin infantryman who watched the charge get broken up, for the most part by artillery. "You could see a rebel's head falling off his horse on one side and his body on the other, and the horse running and nickering and looking for its rider. Others you could see fall off with their feet caught in the stirrup, and the horse dragging and trampling them, dead or alive. Others, the horse would get shot and the rider tumble head over heels, or maybe get caught by the horse falling on him."

Having repulsed the rebel troopers, who returned piecemeal to probe warily at his defenses, Stanley — Howard's successor as IV Corps commander, thirty-six years old, an Ohio-born West Pointer and peacetime Indian fighter, chief of cavalry under Rosecrans during the

last campaign in this region, back in the summer of '63 — proceeded
to align his force of just over 5000 for the protection of Spring Hill.
Resolute as he was in making his preparations for defense, he was
fortunate not to have his resolution strained by awareness that this
might have to be attempted against twice that number of gray infantry
now crossing Rutherford Creek with Cheatham, less than three miles
southeast across the fields, and an even larger number close in their rear
with Stewart. In any case, he parked the train between the turnpike and
the railroad, west of town, and unlimbered his 34 guns in close support of
Wagner's three brigades, disposed along a convex line to the east,
both flanks withdrawn to touch the pike above and below. Here, under
cover of breastworks hastily improvised by dismantling snake-rail
fences, they settled down to their task of keeping Schofield's escape
route open in their rear. Around 4 o'clock, half an hour before sundown, the first concerted assault struck their right, driving the flank
brigade from its fence-rail works and back on its support, three
batteries massed on the southern outskirts of the town for just such
an emergency as was now upon them. These eighteen pieces roared and
plowed the ranks of the attackers, who stumbled rearward in confusion,
having no guns of their own. In the red light of the setting sun, when
Stanley saw that their regimental flags bore the full-moon device of
Cleburne's division — by common consent, Federal and Confederate,
the hardest-hitting in Hood's army — he warned Wagner to brace
his men for their return, probably with substantial reinforcements.

They did return, their number doubled by the arrival of another
gray division; but little or nothing came of this menace in the end. After
milling about in the twilight, apparently with the intention of launching a swamping assault, they paused for a time, as if bemused, and then
— incredibly, for they presently were joined by still a third division
— went into bivouac, more or less where they were, their cookfires
twinkling in the frosty outer darkness, just beyond easy musket range of
Spring Hill and the turnpike close in rear of the makeshift breastworks
Stanley had feared were about to be rushed and overrun. Meantime
Schofield put two more divisions in motion north, leaving one at
Columbia to discourage Lee from crossing the Duck, and another at
Rutherford Creek, where it had been posted that morning. By midnight the first two had cleared Spring Hill, subjected to nothing worse
along the way than sporadic fire from the roadside and the loss of a few
stragglers, although there was a clash with some late-roaming butternut
troopers at Thompson Station, three miles up the pike. These were
soon brushed aside, and the two divisions that followed close behind,
from Rutherford Creek and Columbia, encountered even less trouble.
As a result, Wagner's division, which formerly had led the march but
now brought up the rear, was able to follow the unmolested train and

guns out of Spring Hill before dawn. By that time the lead division was at Franklin and had secured the crossings of the Harpeth, within twenty miles of heavily-fortified Nashville.

Just what had happened, out in the cookfire-twinkling darkness beyond the now abandoned Union breastworks east of Spring Hill and the turnpike, was not too hard to establish from such reports as were later made, both on and off the record. *Why* it happened was far more difficult to determine, though many tried in the course of the heated controversy that followed down the years. Still, whatever their persuasion as to a rightful distribution of the guilt — of which, in all conscience, there was enough to go around — a Texas lieutenant in Cleburne's division, after noting that Hood, Cheatham, "and others in high places have said a good deal in trying to fix the blame for this disgraceful failure," arrived at an assessment with which few could disagree: "The most charitable explanation is that the gods of war injected confusion into the heads of our leaders."

After Cleburne's 18-gun repulse he was joined by Bate, who came up on his left. Just as they were about to go forward together, shortly after sunset — Forrest had pulled back for lack of ammunition, the supply train having been left with Lee to disencumber the flanking column — an order came from Cheatham for the attack to be delayed until the third division arrived under Major General John C. Brown, who would give the signal to advance as soon as he got in position on Cleburne's right. Brown came up about 5.30, but finding his own right overlapped by the blue defenders, informed Cheatham that any advance by him "must meet with inevitable disaster." While he waited, obliging Cleburne and Bate to wait as well, Cheatham reported the problem to Hood, who authorized a suspension of the gunless night attack until Stewart arrived from Rutherford Creek. Stewart did not get there at all, however, having been misguided up a country road that paralleled the turnpike. Only his fourth division, detached from Stephen Lee, under Edward Johnson — Old Clubby, captured six months ago in the Spotsylvania Mule Shoe, had recently been exchanged and transferred West — was stopped in time to move into position on the left of Bate, adjoining the turnpike south of town. Stewart by then had received permission to put his other three divisions into bivouac where they were, two miles to the north and well back from the pike. By that time, practically everyone else — Cleburne and Bate and Brown and all their men, stalled on the verge of their twilight assault — had begun to bed down, too: including Hood, who had spent a long day strapped in the saddle, with considerable irritation to the stump of the leg he had lost at Chickamauga. He was close to exhaustion, and there still had been no report that Schofield had begun a rearward movement. In fact, Lee's guns were still growling beyond Duck River, strong evidence that the Federals were still on its north bank, when Hood retired for the night. Before he did so, he told Cheatham (as Cheatham later testified) that he "had concluded to wait until the morning, and directed me to hold my command in readiness to attack at daylight."

Not quite everyone was sleeping, he discovered when a barefoot private came to his farmhouse headquarters some time after midnight to report that he had seen Union infantry in motion on the turnpike in large numbers. Hood roused himself and told his adjutant to send Cheatham orders "to advance a line of skirmishers and confuse the enemy by firing into his columns." Cheatham passed the word to Johnson, whose division was nearby, but when the Virginian reconnoitered westward, two miles south of Spring Hill, he found the road lying empty in the moonlight, with nothing moving on it in either direction. Most likely he had encountered a gap between segments of the blue army on the march; in any case, like Hood and Cheatham before him, he too returned to the warmth of his blankets while Schofield's troops continued to slog north along the turnpike, just beyond earshot of the rebels sleeping eastward in the fields. Not all the marchers made it. "We were actually so close to the pike," a butternut lieutenant later wrote, "that many Federal soldiers came out to our fires to light their pipes and were captured." Not even all of these were gathered up, however. For example, two Confederates were munching cornbread beside a low fire when a man strolled up; "What troops are you?" he asked, and on being told, "Cleburne's division," turned and walked off in the darkness. "Say, wasn't that a Yank? Let's go get him," one grayback said, only to have his companion reply: "Ah, let him go. If you're looking for Yankees go down the pike and get all you want."

Amid all this confusion, high and low, one thing at least was clear with the dawn of the last day in November. Schofield had gotten clean away, undeterred after darkness fell, except for a brief clash at Thompson Station with one of Forrest's divisions which had managed to capture a meager supply of ammunition. If Hood was saddened by this Spring Hill fiasco — "The best move in my career as a soldier," he said later, "I was thus destined to behold come to naught" — he was also furious, mainly with Cheatham, but also with almost everyone in sight, including the ragged, barefoot men themselves. In his anger he renewed the charge that Joe Johnston had spoiled them for use in the offensive. "The discovery that the army, after a forward march of 180 miles, was still, seemingly, unwilling to accept battle unless under the protection of breastworks, caused me to experience grave concern. In my inmost heart I questioned whether or not I would ever succeed in eradicating this evil."

This he would say long afterward, not stopping then, any more than now, to consider what he asked of them in designing still another of those swift Jacksonian movements that had worked so well two years ago in Virginia; whereas the fact was, not even Lee's army was

"Lee's army" any longer; let alone Hood's. All the same, he believed he saw a corrective for the fault. If a flanking maneuver was beyond the army's capacity, perhaps a headlong assault was not only within its means but might also provide a cure for its lamentable habit of flinching at Yankee breastworks and depending so much on its own. In any case he was determined now to give the thing a disciplinary try — and he said as much, years later, looking back. "I hereupon decided, before the enemy would be able to reach his stronghold at Nashville, to make that same afternoon another and final effort to overtake and rout him, and drive him into the Harpeth River at Franklin."

✗ 3 ✗

So he said, anticipating vengeance. But when the Army of Tennessee set out from its camps around Spring Hill that morning — three fourths of it, at any rate; Stephen Lee was marching from Columbia, a dozen miles to the south, with his other two divisions and the artillery and trains — its commander, nearly beside himself with rage at last night's bungling, seemed "wrathy as a rattlesnake" to one of his subordinates, who were themselves engaged in a hot-tempered flurry of charges and countercharges as a result of Schofield's escape from the trap so carefully laid for his destruction. Down in the ranks, where mutual recrimination afforded less relief, the soldiers "felt chagrined and mortified," one afterwards remarked, "at the occurrence of the preceding day."

Yet this soon passed, at least as the dominant reaction, partly because of the weather, which had faired. "The weather was clear and beautiful," another infantryman wrote; "the cool air was warmed by the bright sunshine, and our forces were in fine condition." By way of added encouragement, the band from a Louisiana brigade, reported to be the army's best, fell out beside the turnpike and cut loose with a few rollicking numbers to cheer the marchers tramping past. "Each man felt a pride in wiping out the stain," the first soldier would recall, while the second added: "Their spirits were animated by encouraging orders from General Hood, who held out to them the prospect that at any moment he might call on them to deal the enemy a decisive blow."

This was as he had done before, on the march north from Florence, and the spirit now was much as it had been then, when the promise was that the Federals were about to be outflanked. For the Tennesseans the campaign was literally a homecoming, but for all the army's veterans it was a glad return to fields of anticipated glory, when they and the war were young and hopes were high. Once more patriot-volunteers of a Second American Revolution, many of them barefoot in the snow, as their forebears had been at Valley Forge, they were hailed along the way as returned deliverers, fulfillers of the faded dream that victory waited on the banks of the Ohio, which was once again their goal. Gladdest of all these scenes of welcome had been the march from Mount Pleasant to Columbia, a region of old families whose mansions lined the pike and whose place of worship — tiny, high-roofed St John's Church, ivy-clad and Gothic, where Bishop-General Polk had preached and his Episcopal kinsmen had their graves amid flowers and shrubbery fresh and green in bleak November — had so impressed Pat Cleburne, for one, that he checked his horse in passing and remarked that it was "almost worth dying for, to be buried in such a beautiful spot." Impromptu receptions and serenades greeted the returning heroes, and prayers of thanksgiving were offered in this and other churches along the way, especially in Pulaski and Columbia, where the Yankees had been thrown into retreat by the gray army's passage round their flank. Spring Hill too had been delivered, though at a heavy cost in Confederate mortification, which soon was transmuted into determination that the bluecoats, having escaped their pursuers twice, would not manage it still a third time unscathed. Accordingly, the seven gray divisions stepped out smartly up the Franklin Turnpike, preceded by Forrest's troopers. Hood was pleased, he later said, to find his army "metamorphosed, as it were, in one night. . . . The feeling existed which sometimes induces men who have long been wedded to but one policy to look beyond the sphere of their own convictions, and, at least, be willing to make trial of another course of action." In other words, they now seemed ready to charge breastworks, if need be, and he was prepared to take them up on that.

Stewart led the march today, having overshot the mark the night before, and Cheatham followed, accompanied by Johnson's division from Lee's corps, which was three hours in the rear. A dozen miles to the north by 2 o'clock, the vanguard approached Winstead Hill, three miles short of Franklin. On its crest, astride the turnpike, a Union brigade was posted with a battery, apparently under instructions to delay the gray pursuit; but Hood, unwilling to waste time on a pre-liminary skirmish — perhaps designed by Schofield to give the rest of his army a chance to get away unharmed — swung Stewart's three divisions to the right, along Henpeck Lane, and kept the other four marching straight on up the pike. To avoid being outflanked, the blue-coats limbered their guns and fell back out of sight beyond the rim of the slope up which the head of Cheatham's column now was toiling. When the Tennesseans topped the rise they gave a roaring cheer at the sight of the Harpeth Valley spread before them, with the town of Franklin nestled in a northeastward bend of the river and the Federals intrenched in a bulging curve along its southern and western outskirts. Beyond the crest, on the forward slope of Winstead Hill, Hood turned off to the left of the road, and while his staff got busy setting up a command post, the one-legged general dismounted — painfully, as always, with the help of an orderly who passed him his crutches once he was afoot — and there, in the shade of an isolated linn tree, removed his binoculars from their case for a careful study of the position his adversary had chosen for making a stand.

Schofield had been there since dawn, nine hours ago, and by now had completed the organization of an all-round defense of his Franklin bridgehead, on the off chance that the Confederates would attempt to interfere with the crossing or the follow-up sprint for the Tennessee capital, eighteen miles away. He would have been well on his way there already, safely over the river and hard on the march up the Nash-ville Pike, except that when he arrived with his two lead divisions, under Jacob Cox and Brigadier General Thomas Ruger, he found that the turnpike bridge had been wrecked by the rising Harpeth and Thomas had failed to send the pontoons he had so urgently requested, two days ago at Columbia, after burning his own for lack of trans-portation. Placing Cox in charge, he told him to have the two XXIII Corps divisions dig in astride the Columbia Pike, his own on the left and Ruger's on the right, half a mile south of the town in their rear, while awaiting the arrival of the three IV Corps divisions, still on the march from Rutherford Creek and Spring Hill. By the time Stanley got there with Thomas Wood's and Brigadier General Nathan Kimball's divisions, around midmorning, the engineers had floored the railroad bridge with planks ripped from nearby houses and the wagon train had started crossing. Schofield ordered Kimball to dig in on a line to the right of Ruger, extending the works northward so that they touched the river below as well as above the town, and passed Wood's division, along with most of Stanley's artillery, across the clattering, newly-planked railway span to take position on the high far bank of the Harpeth, overlooking Franklin and the fields lying south of the long curve of intrenchments thrown up by the other three divisions. That way, Wood could move fast to assist Wilson's horsemen in dealing with rebel flankers on that side of the river, upstream or down, and Cox was braced for confronting a headlong assault, if that was what developed.

This last seemed highly unlikely, however, since Hood — with two of his nine divisions far in the rear, together with all but eight of his guns — had fewer than 30,000 troops on hand, including cavalry, while Schofield had well above that number — 34,000 of all arms — stoutly intrenched for the most part and supported by 60-odd guns, nearly all of them able to pound anything that tried to cross the two-mile-deep plain that lay between the bristling outskirts of Franklin and the foot of Winstead Hill. Moreover, that deadly stretch of ground was not only about as level as a tabletop, it was also unobstructed. Originally there had been a small grove of locusts in front of Ruger's part of the line, but these had been felled for use as headlogs and abatis. Similarly, on the left, a thick-set hedge of Osage orange had been thinned to clear a field of fire for Cox, leaving only enough of the growth to provide a thorny palisade. There was one obstacle out front: two brigades from Wagner's division, intrenched in an advance position, half a mile down and astride the Columbia Pike, with instructions to remain in observation there unless Hood, when he came up, "showed a disposition to advance in force," in which case they were to retire within the lines and serve as a reserve for the three divisions now in their rear. Otherwise, one defender said, there was "not so much as a mullein stalk" to obstruct the aim of the infantry in the trenches or the cannoneers in emplacements they had selected and dug at their leisure, not yet knowing there could be little or no counterbattery fire, even if the rebels were so foolish as to provoke battle on a field so disadvantageous to them.

Wagner had arrived at noon with the last of the five divisions, weary from yesterday's Spring Hill fight, the all-night vigil behind his fence-rail breastworks, and this morning's hurried march as rear guard of the army. Leaving one brigade on Winstead Hill to serve as a lookout force, he put the other two in position as instructed, half a mile in front of the main line, and set them digging. While they dug, the rest of the troops, snug in their completed works, did what they could to make up for their loss of sleep on last night's march. From across the river, at high-sited Fort Granger — a bastioned earthwork, constructed more than a year ago for the protection of the two critical bridges over the Harpeth — Schofield looked south, beyond the bulge of his semi-circular line, and saw the brigade Wagner had left on lookout withdraw in good order down the hill and up the turnpike. He knew from this that the rebels must be close behind, for the brigade commander was Colonel Emerson Opdycke, a thirty-four-year-old Ohioan with a fiery reputation earned in most of the theater's major battles, from Shiloh, where he had been a captain, to Resaca, where he had been badly wounded, back in May, but recovered in time to lead the charge up Kennesaw six weeks later. Sure enough, soon after Opdycke's displacement, the first graybacks appeared on Winstead Hill. They gathered faster and began to flow, rather like lava, in heavy columns down the forward slope and around the east flank of the hill. Schofield watched with mounting excitement. It was now about 3 o'clock; all but the last of his 700 wagons had clattered across the railroad bridge and he had just issued orders for the rest of his men and guns to follow at 6 o'clock, shortly after dark, unless Hood attacked before sunset; which Schofield did not believe he would do, once he had seen what lay before him there along the northern margin of that naked plain.

He was mistaken. Three miles away, under the linn tree on the hillside to the south, Hood completed his study of the Federal dispositions, lowered his glasses, and announced to the subordinates who by now had clustered round him: "We will make the fight."

When he explained what he meant by "make the fight" — an all-out frontal assault, within the hour — consternation followed hard upon doubt by his lieutenants that they had heard aright. They too had looked out over the proposed arena, and could scarcely believe their ears. Attack? here? headlong and practically gunless, against a foe not only superior in numbers but also intrenched on chosen ground and backed by the frown of more than sixty pieces of artillery? ... For a time, only too aware of their commander's repeated scornful charge that they invariably flinched at Yankee breastworks, they held their tongues. Then Ben Cheatham broke the silence. "I do not like the looks of this fight," he said. "The enemy has an excellent position and is well fortified." Leaning on his crutches, his blond beard glinting in the sunlight, Hood replied that he preferred to strike the Federals here, where they had had only a short time to organize their defenses, rather than at Nashville, "where they have been strengthening themselves for three years."

Cheatham protested no more, having been reproached quite enough for one day. But Bedford Forrest — who was familiar with the region, including the location of usable fords over the Harpeth well this side of the enemy position, and who moreover had Hood's respect for his aggressive instincts — spoke out in support of his fellow Tennessean's assessment of the situation, though with a different application. He favored an attack, yet not a frontal one. "Give me one strong division of infantry with my cavalry," he urged, "and within two hours I can flank the Federals from their works." Hood afterwards reported that "the nature of the position was such as to render it inexpedient to attempt any further flanking movement." Just now, however, he expressed doubt that, for all their apparent confidence, the bluecoats would "stand strong pressure from the front. The show of force they are making is a feint in order to hold me back from a more vigorous pursuit."

This put an end to such unasked-for opposition as had been voiced. Hood's fame had begun when he broke Fitz-John Porter's center at Gaines Mill, back in Virginia thirty months ago, and he intended to do the same to Schofield here today. His final order, dismissing the informal council of war, was explicit as to how this was to be accomplished: "Drive the enemy from his position into the river at all hazards."

Stewart, who had rounded Winstead Hill on the approach march, would attack on the right, up the railroad and the Lewisburg Pike, which ran northwest along the near bank of the Harpeth; Loring's division was on that flank of the corps front, French's on the other, over toward the Columbia Pike, and Major General Edward Walthall's was posted astride the railroad in the center. Cleburne and Brown, of Cheatham's corps, would advance due north up both sides of the Columbia Pike, Cleburne on the right, adjoining French, with Bate on Brown's left, extending the line westward to the Carter's Creek Pike, which ran northeast. All three turnpikes converged on the outskirts of Franklin, half a mile in rear of the southward bulge of the Union works; Hood assumed that this configuration would serve to compact the mass, like a hand clenched gradually into a fist, by the time the attackers reached and struck the main blue line. Johnson's division remained in reserve behind the center, for rapid exploitation of any breakthrough right or left, and Forrest's horsemen would go forward on the flanks, near the river in both directions. At 3.45, one hour before sundown, Stewart and Cheatham sent word that their lines were formed and they were ready.

Hood could see them in panorama from his command post, the two corps in an attack formation well over a mile in width, their star-crossed flags hanging limp in the windless air of this last day in November, which was also to be the last in the lives of many who were about to follow those tattered symbols across the fields now in their front: six divisions, twenty brigades, just over one hundred regiments, containing in all some 18,000 infantry, with another 3500 in the four reserve brigades. Promptly Hood's order came down from Winstead Hill for them to go forward, and they did, stepping out as smartly as if they were passing in review; "a grand sight, such as would make a lifelong impression on the mind of any man who could see such a resistless, well-conducted charge," a Federal officer discerned from his post near the blue center, just under two miles across the way. "For the moment we were spellbound with admiration, although we knew that in a few brief moments, as soon as they reached firing distance, all that orderly grandeur would be changed to bleeding, writhing confusion."

It did not work out quite that way just yet. Opdycke, when he retired from the crest of Winstead Hill, had not stopped alongside the other two brigades of Wagner's division, intrenched half a mile in front of the main works, but continued his withdrawal up the turnpike to the designated reserve position in rear of a one-story brick residence owned by a family named Carter, less than a hundred yards inside the lines. Wagner had set up headquarters in a grove of trees beside the pike and just beyond the house, anticipating the arrival of the rest of his troops as soon as the gray host, now gathering two miles to the south, showed what his orders termed "a disposition to advance." Apparently he doubted that Hood would do so at all, after studying the field, or else he believed the preparations would take a lot more time than they actually did. In any case, the mass advance was well under way before the Ohio-born former Hoosier politician, whose view in that direction was blocked by the house and trees, even knew that it had begun. As a result, the two colonels left in charge out front not only delayed their withdrawal, they also chose to stand fast in their shallow works long enough to get off a couple of short-range volleys before retiring. This was to cost Wagner his command within the week, but it cost the men of those two brigades a great deal more today.

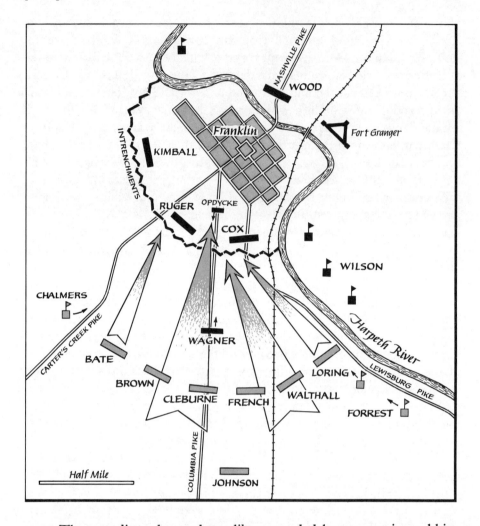

The gray line advanced steadily, preceded by scampering rabbits
and whirring coveys of quail, flushed from the brush by the approach
of close to 20,000 pairs of tramping feet. When they got within range,
the outpost Federals gave them a rattling fusillade that served to check
them for a moment; but not for long. Absorbing the shock, the men
under Cleburne and Brown — old rivals, from the days when the latter's
division was under Cheatham — came on with a rush and a yell, directly
against the front and around the flanks of the two unfortunate brigades,
both of which gave way in a sudden bolt for the security of the intrenchments half a mile in their rear. Too late; "Let's go into the works
with them!" the attackers cried, and pressed the pursuit up the turnpike,
clubbing and shooting the terrified bluecoats as they fled. "It seemed
bullets never before hissed with such diabolical venom," a Union captain
was to say, recalling too that the cries of the wounded, left to the mercy
of the screaming graybacks when they fell, "had a pathetic note of
despair I had never heard before." More than 700 were captured, hurt

or unhurt, and the main-line defenders, dead ahead, were kept from firing at the pursuers by fear of hitting their comrades in the lead. A staff colonel observed, however, that there was little time for thought at this critical juncture. "The triumphant Confederates, now more like a wild, howling mob than an organized army, swept on to the very works, with hardly a check from any quarter. So fierce was the rush that a number of the fleeing soldiers — officers and men — dropped exhausted into the ditch, and lay there while the terrific contest raged over their heads." Of these, the captain who had outrun the hissing bullets noted, "some were found [afterwards] with their thumbs chewed to a pulp. Their agony had been so great that they had stuck their thumbs in their mouths and bit on them to keep from bleating like calves."

That was the kind of battle it was, first for one side, then the other, combining the grisliest features of Pickett's Charge and Spotsylvania's Bloody Angle. Because they had sprinted the last half mile, and had a shorter distance to cover in reaching the southward bulge of the enemy line, Cleburne's and Brown's divisions struck and penetrated the Federal works before the units on their left or right came up to add weight to the effort. In close pursuit of the two fugitive brigades, they not only broke through along the turnpike, they also widened the gap by knocking a regiment loose from the intrenchments on each side and seized four guns still loaded with canister, which they turned on the enemy but could not fire because the battery horses had bolted with the primers in the ammunition chests. Suddenly then it was too late; the blue reserves were upon them, advancing through the smoke with bayonets flashing, and they were too blown from their race up the pike, too confused by their abrupt success, to stand long under the pounding of most of the two dozen guns Cox and Ruger had posted along this part of the line. They yielded sullenly, under savage attack from Opdycke, who had brought his brigade on the run from north of the Carter house, and fell back to find cover in front of the works they had crossed when they broke through. There they stayed, exchanging point-blank fire with the bluecoats on the other side of the ditch.

Stewart by then had come up on the right, where French made contact with Cleburne, but the other two divisions were roughly handled in their attempt to get to grips with the Union left. Approaching a deep railroad cut near the northward bend of the Harpeth, they found it under plunging fire from the guns massed in Fort Granger, and when they changed front to move around this trap they were struck on the flank by other batteries masked on the east bank of the river. Forrest drove these last away by sending Jackson's division across a nearby ford, but Wilson met this threat to Schofield's rear by throwing the rebel troopers back on the crossing and holding them there, under pressure from three times their number. Walthall and Loring meantime had rounded the railway cut and clawed their way through the Osage hedge, only to find themselves confronting an intrenched brigade equipped with repeating rifles that seemed to one observer "to blaze out a continuous sheet of destruction." Here the attackers had all they could do to hang on where they were, though some among them continued to try for a breakthrough: Brigadier General John Adams, for example, who was killed while attempting a mounted leap over the enemy works and whose body was found next morning alongside his horse, dead too, with its forefeet over the Federal palisade. Another of Loring's three brigade commanders, Brigadier General T. M. Scott, was gravely wounded, as was Brigadier General William Quarles of Walthall's division; both were out of the war for good, and in Quarles's brigade, so heavy was the toll of successive commanders, there presently was no surviving officer above the rank of captain. French's division, fighting near the center, also lost two of its three brigade leaders — Colonel William Witherspoon, killed outright, and Brigadier General Francis Cockrell, severely wounded — bringing Stewart's loss to five of the nine brigade commanders in his corps, along with more than half of the colonels and majors who began the attack at the head of his nearly fifty regiments.

Cheatham's losses were heavier still, though they were comparatively light in Bate's division, which only had one of its three brigades engaged when it struck the enemy trenches at an angle; the other two drifted northward to mingle with Chalmers' horsemen beyond the Carter's Creek Pike, where they remained in observation, dodging long-range shots from guns on the Union right. Cleburne and Brown, however, still holding the works astride the Columbia Turnpike in the center, more than made up for any shortage of bloodshed on the Confederate left. The sun by now was behind the rim of Winstead Hill, and in point of fact, so far as its outcome was concerned, the battle was over: had been over, at least in that respect, ever since Opdycke's furious counter-assault stopped and shattered the initial penetration. All that remained was additional killing and maiming, which continued well into the night. "I never saw the dead lay near so thick. I saw them upon each other, dead and ghastly in the powder-dimmed starlight," Opdycke would report. Brown himself was out of the action, badly crippled by a shell, and so were all four of his brigadiers, beginning with G. W. Gordon, who had been captured in the side yard of the Carter house just as the breakthrough was turned back. John C. Carter, who succeeded Brown in command of the division, was mortally wounded shortly afterwards (he would die within ten days) and States Rights Gist and Otho Strahl were killed in the close-quarters struggle that ensued. "Boys, this will be short but desperate," Strahl had told his Tennesseans as they prepared to charge; which was half right. After the repulse he stood in the Federal ditch, passing loaded rifles up to the men on top, and when one of them asked if it might not be wise to withdraw, he replied: "Keep on firing." Then he fell.

The resultant desperation, unrelieved by the saving grace of brevity, was quite as bad as he had predicted for Brown's division, but the strain was even worse for the Arkansans, Mississippians, Alabamians, and Texans next in line, heightened as it was by dread uncertainty as to the fate of their commander. "I never saw men put in such a terrible position as Cleburne's division was," an opposing bluecoat was to say. "The wonder is that any of them escaped death or capture." All too many of them did not; Hiram Granbury had been killed at the head of his Texas brigade in the first assault, and fourteen of the twenty regimental commanders were to fall before the conflict slacked and died away. Meantime a disheartening rumor spread through the ranks that Cleburne was missing — Irish Pat Cleburne, of whom it was said: "Men seemed to be afraid to *be* afraid where he was." He had last been seen going forward in the attack, dismounted because two horses had been shot from under him in the course of the advance. "If we are to die, let us die like men," he told a subordinate, speaking with the brogue that came on him at such times and thickened as the excitement rose. When his second horse was killed by a shot from a cannon, he went ahead on foot through the smoke and din, waving his cap. The hope of his veterans, who idolized him, was that he had been wounded for the third time in the war, or even captured; but this hope collapsed next morning, when his body was found beside the Columbia Pike just short of the enemy works. A single bullet had gone through his heart. His boots had been stolen, along with his sword and watch and everything else of value on him. He was buried first near Franklin, then in St John's churchyard, whose beauty he had admired on the march to his last fight, and finally, years later, back in Arkansas on a ridge overlooking Helena, his home town. His epitaph, as well as that of his division, was pronounced by his old corps commander, William Hardee, who wrote when he learned of his death: "Where this division defended, no odds broke its line; where it attacked, no numbers resisted its onslaught, save only once; and there is the grave of Cleburne."

High on his hillside two miles to the south, Hood knew even less about the progress of the battle than did the troops involved in the moiling, flame-stabbed confusion down below; which was little indeed. He had seen Cleburne and Brown go storming into the Union center, hard on the heels of Wagner's unfortunates, but what happened next was blanketed in smoke that hung heavy in the windless air and thickened as the firing mounted to a sustained crescendo. At 7 o'clock, an hour after full darkness cloaked the field, he committed his reserve division, and though Old Clubby's men attacked with desperation, stumbling over Cheatham's dead and wounded in the gloom, they only succeeded in adding Brigadier General Arthur Manigault's name to the list of a dozen brigade and division commanders who had fallen in the past three hours, as well as nine more regimental commanders, bringing the total to fifty-four; roughly half the number present. Of the twelve generals lost to the army here today, six were dead or dying, one was captured, and three of the remaining five were out of the war for good, while the other two, Brown and Cockrell, would not return for months. Down in the ranks, moreover, this dreadful ratio was approximated; 6252 Confederate veterans were casualties, including 1750 killed in action — as many as had died on either side in the two days of Shiloh or under McClellan throughout the Seven Days: more than had died under Rosecrans at Stones River, under Burnside at Fredericksburg, or under Hood himself in any of his three Atlanta sorties: almost as many, indeed, as Grant had had killed outright when he assaulted at Cold Harbor with three times as many men. Hood had wrecked his army, top to bottom, and the army knew it; or soon would. In the judgment of a Tennessee private who survived the wrecking, he had done so in the manner of a clumsy blacksmith, thinking "he would strike while the iron was hot, and while it could be hammered into shape.... But he was like the fellow who took a piece of iron to the shop, intending to make him an ax. After working for some time, and failing, he concluded he would make him a wedge, and, failing in this, said: 'I'll make a skeow.' So he heats the iron red-hot and drops it in the slack tub, and it went s-k-e-o-w, bubble, bubble, s-k-e-o-w, bust."

Hood did not know this yet, however — and would not have been likely to admit it if he had; Howard's word 'indomitable' still fit. He watched unseeing while the battle continued to rage with the same fury, even though all the combatants had to aim at now was the flash of each other's weapons. "Time after time they came up to the very works," a Union colonel afterwards said of the attackers, "but they never crossed them except as prisoners." Around 9 o'clock the uproar slacked. "Don't shoot, Yanks; for God Amighty's sake, don't shoot!" defenders heard pinned-down rebels implore from the smoky darkness just beyond their parapets. Within two more hours the contest sputtered into silence. Stephen Lee was up by then with his other two divisions and the army's guns, and Hood ordered the attack renewed at daybreak, preceded this time by a hundred-round bombardment. The batteries opened at first light, as directed, then ceased fire when word came back that there was nothing in the works ahead but Federal dead and wounded. Schofield had departed in the night.

That was really all the northern commander had wanted from the outset: a chance to get away, if Hood would only let him. Soon after his arrival the previous morning, on finding the turnpike bridge washed out and no pontoons on hand, he wired Nashville for instructions, and was told to defend the Harpeth crossing unless such an effort would require him "to risk too much." He responded: "I am satisfied that I have heretofore run too much risk in trying to hold Hood in check. . . . Possibly I may be able to hold him here, but do not expect to be able to do so long." Thomas, busy gathering troops to man the capital defenses, then put a limit to his request, in hope that this would serve to stiffen his lieutenant's resistance to the scarcely deterred advance of the rebel column up through Middle Tennessee. "Do you think you can hold Hood at Franklin for three days longer? Answer, giving your views," he wired, and Schofield replied: "I do not believe I can." In point of fact, both question and answer by then were academic. He had already ordered a nighttime withdrawal and Hood had just appeared on Winstead Hill. "I think he can effect a crossing tomorrow, in spite of all my efforts," Schofield added, "and probably tonight, if he attempts it. A worse position than this for an inferior force can hardly be found. . . . I have no doubt Forrest will be in my rear tomorrow, or doing some greater mischief. It appears to me that I ought to take position at Brentwood at once."

Nevertheless — having no choice — he stayed and fought, and won. His casualties totaled 2326, about one third the number he inflicted, and of these more than half were from Wagner's division: just under a thousand killed or captured in the two-brigade rearward sprint up the pike and just over two hundred killed and wounded in the other brigade, when Opdycke saved the day with a counterassault that cost him five of his seven regimental commanders but netted him 394 prisoners and nine Confederate flags. Except for David Stanley, who took a bullet through the nape of his neck and had to be lugged off the field at the height of the melee, no Federal above the rank of colonel was on the list of casualties when Schofield evacuated Franklin between 11 o'clock and midnight, leaving his dead and his nonwalking wounded behind as he crossed the river and set fire to the planked-over bridge in his rear. The blue column reached Brentwood by daylight, halfway to Nashville, and by noon all five divisions were safe in the capital works, alongside the others Thomas had been assembling all this time.

Hood sent Forrest to snap at the heels of the retreating victors, but deferred pursuit by his infantry now in occupation of the field. "Today spent in burying the dead, caring for the wounded, and reorganizing the remains of our corps," a diarist on Cheatham's staff recorded. Never before had even these veterans looked on horror so compacted. In places, hard against the abandoned works, the slain lay in windrows, seven deep; so thick, indeed, that often there was no room for those on top to touch the ground. One of Strahl's four successors was so tightly wedged by corpses, it was noted, that "when he at last received the fatal shot, he did not wholly fall, but was found stiffened in death and partly upright, seeming still to command the ghastly line of his comrades lying beneath the parapet." Blue and gray, in a ratio of about one to five, the wounded soon filled all the houses in the town, as well as every room in the courthouse, schools, and churches. Meantime the burial details were at work, digging long shallow ditches into which the perforated ragdoll shapes were tossed and covered over with the spoil. Federals and Confederates were lodged in separate trenches, and the even greater disparity in their numbers — roughly one to eight — imparted a hollow sound to Hood's congratulatory order, read at the head of what was left of each regiment that afternoon. "While we lament the fall of many gallant officers and brave men," its final sentence ran, "we have shown to our countrymen that we can carry any position occupied by our enemy."

Perhaps the battle did show that; perhaps it also settled in Hood's mind, at last, the question of whether the Army of Tennessee would charge breastworks. But, if so, the demonstration had been made at so high a cost that, when it was over, the army was in no condition, either in body or in spirit, to repeat it. Paradoxically, in refuting the disparagement, the troops who fell confirmed it for the future. Nor was the horror limited to those who had been actively involved; Franklin's citizens now knew, almost as well as did the few survivors among the men they had sent away three years ago, the suffering that ensued once the issue swung to war. This was especially true of the Carter family, an old man and his two daughters who took shelter in their cellar, just in rear of the initial breakthrough point, while the fighting raged outside and overhead. Emerging next morning from their night of terror, they found the body of their son and brother, Captain Tod Carter of Brown's division, Cheatham's corps, lying almost on the doorstep he had come home to when he died.

Nothing daunted — though his 7500 casualties over the past week, including more than 6000 the day before, had reduced his infantry strength to a scant 22,000 — Hood took up the march north that afternoon. Lee's corps was in the lead, only one of its three divisions having been exposed to the Franklin holocaust, and Stewart and Cheatham followed in that order, so severely bled down at all levels that Brown's division, for example, was under a colonel who had never commanded anything larger than a regiment, while several brigades in both these corps were led by officers with even less experience. Hood might have turned back and taken up a defensive position along Duck River, as Bragg had done two years ago under similar circumstances, or even along the Tennessee, which he had left ten days before. That would doubtless have been the most prudent course to follow, especially since one main purpose of the campaign — to provoke a countermarch by Sherman down in Georgia — had clearly failed already; the Ohioan was more than halfway to the Atlantic Ocean by now, and apparently had not given so much as a backward glance at the threat to Thomas, far in his rear. But it was not in the Kentucky-born Texan's nature to take counsel of his fears, if indeed he felt them in the first place, and prudence was by no means an integral part of his makeup. His concern was with quite different factors. One was time, which was running out, and the other was honor. "In truth," he said afterwards, "our army was in that condition which rendered it more judicious the men should face a decisive issue rather than retreat — in other words, rather than renounce the honor of their cause without having made a last and manful effort to lift up the sinking fortunes of the Confederacy. I therefore determined to move upon Nashville."

Moving upon it was no great task; Forrest's troopers by now had called a halt in sight of the Capitol tower and within plain view of the long curve of earthworks behind which Schofield had already taken shelter by the time the gray infantry forded the Harpeth. What Hood would do once he got there was a different matter, however, involving a choice between two highly unpromising alternatives. The first, to launch an immediate all-out assault, was rejected out of hand. No one wanted another Franklin, not even John Bell Hood, and Nashville — similarly cradled in the northward bend of a still wider river, with far stouter intrenchments ready-dug across its face — was Franklin magnified. Besides, after yesterday's grim Confederate subtractions, Schofield alone had more troops than Hood could bring against the place, and Thomas most likely had as many more gathered inside it, raising the numerical odds against the attacker to two, maybe three, to one. Assault was out. Yet so, Hood saw, was the alternative of crossing the Cumberland above or below, as originally envisioned, for a march to the Ohio. This would land him in Thomas's rear, true enough, but so would it put Thomas in Hood's own rear, undiminished and able to summon reinforcements from all over the North, while Hood himself, under the circumstances which now obtained, would scarcely be able to add a single recruit to the rolls of his Franklin-ravaged command. "In the absence of the prestige of complete victory," he later explained in answer to those who had urged the adoption of such a course, "I felt convinced that the Tennesseans and Kentuckians would not join our forces, since we had failed in the first instance to defeat the Federal army and capture Nashville."

Having rejected the notion of retiring southward as an admission of defeat, and having decided to forgo his previous intention of assaulting or bypassing Nashville, which he saw now as an invitation to disaster, he then — either in ignorance or defiance of Napoleon's definition of the passive defensive as "a form of deferred suicide" — settled on a plan that combined, simultaneously or in sequence, the worst features of all three of these dismissed or postponed alternatives. He would march to the outskirts of the Tennessee capital, intrench his army in direct confrontation with the outsized garrison lodged there, and await the inevitable attack, "which, if handsomely repulsed, might afford us an opportunity to follow up our advantage on the spot and enter the city on the heels of our enemy." So he said, apparently remembering the ease with which his troops had followed Wagner's into the Franklin works, but apparently not considering what had happened to them as soon as they achieved the penetration. In any case that was his plan, as he evolved it after the long march north and the frustrations he had encountered, first at Tuscumbia and Florence, where he waited three weeks before setting out, and then at Columbia, Spring Hill, and Franklin, where he not only failed to destroy a sizeable part of his opponent's army, but also came close to destroying his own. Still the old dream held for Hood: perhaps because he had no other to fall back on. "Should [Thomas] attack me in position," he subsequently reported, "I felt that I could defeat him and thus gain possession of Nashville with abundant supplies. . . . Having possession of the state, we should have gained largely in recruits and could at an early date have moved forward to the Ohio, which would have frustrated the plans of the enemy, as developed in his campaign toward the Atlantic coast." There was that, and there was still the pressure of knowing that this might well be the last chance, either for him or for the Confederacy itself. What better way was there to go down, or out, than in a blaze of glory? He seemed to ask that, later adding: "The troops would, I believed, return better satisfied even after defeat if, in grasping at the last straw, they felt that a brave and vigorous effort had been made to save the country from disaster."

So he went on, making camp that night at Brentwood, and pulled up in front of Nashville the following day, December 2. Lee took position astride the Franklin Pike, with Stewart and Cheatham respectively on his left and right, directly confronting the Union works, which extended northeast and northwest, as far as the eye could follow, from the bend of the river below to the bend above. Disposed along high ground in a ten-mile arc, some three miles from the marble Capitol in plain view on its hill in the heart of town, these required no more than a cursory look to confirm the claim that Nashville, along with Washington and Richmond, was among the three most heavily fortified cities in the land.

That was one part of Hood's problem, and almost at once another became apparent. "The entire line of the army will curve forward from General Lee's center," he directed on arrival, "so that General Cheatham's right may come as near the Cumberland as possible above Nashville, and General Stewart's left as near the Cumberland as possible below Nashville. Each position will be strengthened as soon as taken, and extended as fast as strengthened." But when the three corps settled in, plying spades and picks, it developed that the widest front they could cover with any measure of security was four miles — a good deal less than half the distance required if the line was to stretch to the near bank of the Cumberland in both directions; whereas in fact it did not reach the river in either direction, but left a vacancy of two miles beyond

Cheatham's outer flank and four beyond Stewart's. Of the eight turn-pikes converging spokelike on the capital hub to cross by the single bridge in its rear, four were covered and four remained uncovered, two on the left and two on the right, except by cavalry patrols. Both Confederate flanks thus were exposed to possible turning movements by the greatly superior force in the works ahead.

Hood had little fear of such a threat, however; at least for now. Familiar with his adversary's ponderous manner and lethargic nature, not only over the past six months of confrontation, stalemate, and maneuver, but also from old army days before the war — one had been a lieutenant, the other a major in Sidney Johnston's Texas-based 2d Cavalry — he counted on having as much time as he needed to prepare and improve his position in front of the Tennessee capital. Indeed, so confident was he of this, despite the long numerical odds, that he risked a further re-duction of force, as great as the one he had suffered at Franklin, for the sake of a sideline operation which seemed to offer a chance to make up for the prize he had failed to grasp at Spring Hill, where a sizeable part of the blue host now confronting him slipped through his fingers. Now another isolated segment, though only about one fourth as large, had come within his reach — provided, that is, he was willing to do a little stretching; which he was. When Hood set out from Florence to outflank Schofield at Pulaski, ten days back, Thomas had pulled Granger's 4000 troops out of the region below Athens, directly across the Tennessee River from Decatur, and combined them with Rousseau's 5000 at Murfreesboro, thirty-odd miles down the Chattanooga & Nash-ville from his capital headquarters, in case the gray invasion column veered west to approach or bypass him from that direction. These 9000 bluecoats were still there, and Hood had a mind to gather them up, or at any rate smash the railroad between there and Nashville, before Thomas called them in. Accordingly, while still on the approach march, he detached Bate, whose division had suffered least of the seven en-gaged at Franklin, and sent him crosscountry, reinforced by a brigade from each of the other two corps, for a strike at Murfreesboro and its garrison. Forrest meantime, on Hood's arrival at Nashville, would move down the Chattanooga Railroad with two of his divisions, breaking it up as he went, for a combined attack which he would direct by virtue of his rank.

Although the maneuver served its purpose of keeping Rousseau and Granger from reinforcing Thomas, it failed to achieve the larger design for bagging them entirely. Forrest left with Buford's and Jackson's divisions as soon as Hood came up, and after three days of reducing blockhouses, burning bridges, and wrecking several miles of track, combined with Bate on December 5, some ten miles north of the ob-jective. Next day's reconnaissance disclosed that Murfreesboro was almost as stoutly fortified as Nashville; Fortress Rosecrans, mounting

57 guns and enclosing 200 acres of the field where Bragg had come to grief two years ago this month, was practically unassailable; especially with 9000 defenders on hand to resist the 6500 graybacks moving against it, mounted and afoot. Forrest called a halt and decided instead to lure the garrison out for a fight in the open. In this he was partly successful the following day, December 7, when a 3500-man Union column staged a sally. He posted his infantry in the path of the attackers, with orders to stand firm while he brought his cavalry down on their flank. Everything went as planned, up to the critical moment when Bate's division — spooked no doubt by remembrance of Franklin, where its performance had been less than standard, eight days back — gave way in a panic, unspringing the trap. Forrest rode among the rattled soldiers, appealing to them to stand and fight, then cursing them for refusing to do so. He stood in the stirrups, eyes blazing, face gone red with rage, and began to lay about him with the flat of his saber, whacking the backs of the fleeing troops; to small avail. Ignoring the Wizard as best they could, the retreaters scuttled rearward beyond his grasp, even when he seized a color-bearer's flag, whose staff afforded a longer reach, and swung it bludgeonlike until at last, perceiving that this was equally ineffective, he flung it from him in disgust. "Right comical, if it hadn't been so serious," one veteran was to say.

Fortunately, the Federals did not press the issue, having just been recalled by Rousseau, and Bate was summoned back to Nashville two days later by Hood, who sent another brigade from Cheatham's corps to replace the three that left. Down to about 4500 of all arms — half the number inside the works — Forrest had to be content with bristling to discourage sorties that might have swamped him. This he did with such success that within another two days he felt justified in sending Buford to Andrew Jackson's Hermitage, ten miles northeast of Nashville, with instructions to picket a nearby stretch of the Cumberland and thereby prevent the arrival of reinforcements by that route. Next day, December 12, with the enemy still tightly buttoned up in Fortress Rosecrans, he had the infantry begin completing the destruction of the railroad back to La Vergne, just under twenty miles away. Thus, by the employment of barely half as many troops, Hood was able to prevent an additional 9000 effectives from joining the Nashville garrison: though whether this was wise or not, under the circumstances, was quite another matter. For one thing, even longer odds obtained in the vicinity of the Tennessee capital, where he remained in confrontation with Thomas, and for another, in the showdown battle which now was imminent, it seemed likely to cost him the use of two sorely-needed cavalry divisions, together with the help of their commander, whose talents would be missed.

Reduced as he was, by casualties and detachments, to a strength of less than 24,000 of all arms, it was no wonder one apprehensive infantryman remarked that the Confederate main line of resistance, which

stretched and crooked for four miles under the frown of long-range
Union guns in permanent fortifications, looked "more like the skirmish
line of an investing army than of that army itself." To make matters
worse, there had not been time for the completion of such outlying installations as had been planned to strengthen the flanks of the position:
particularly on the left, where three redoubts were under construction
beyond the Hillsboro Pike, the western limit of Hood's line, to blunt the
force of an attack from that direction, whether end-on or oblique. Work
on these began, but on the night of December 8, after a spell of de-
ceptively mild weather, the mercury dropped to nearly twenty degrees
below freezing and a cold rain quickly turned to sleet and fine-grained
snow. By morning, all the trees wore glittering cut-glass armor, each
twig sheathed in ice, and the earth was frozen iron hard, unpierceable
even with a knife, let alone a shovel. Work stopped, perforce, and the
soldiers huddled in unfinished trenches, shivering in their rags. For four
days this continued. Then on the fifth — December 13, the winter
solstice; Sherman had reached Savannah by now, completing his march
across Georgia's midriff, and would capture Fort McAllister before sundown — a thaw set in, relieving the rigid misery in which the besiegers
had been locked, but bringing with it troubles of a different kind. The
army floundered in Napoleon's "fifth element," unable to move forward,
back, or sideways in a Sargasso Sea of mud; all transportation stalled,
guns and wagons bellied axle deep, even on main-traveled roads, and no
supplies arrived to relieve shortages that had developed during the four-
day storm.

It was midway through this doleful immobilized span, with his
men and horses frozen or stuck in their tracks by alternate ice and mud,
that Hood apparently first became aware, in the fullest sense, of the
peril to which he had exposed his troops when he took up his present
position in point-blank confrontation with Thomas, whose army was
not only superbly equipped and entrenched, but was also better than
twice the size of his own. Earlier, when Forrest departed for Murfreesboro with the other two cavalry divisions, Chalmers had been obliged to
send one of his two brigades to patrol the region between Cheatham's
right and the river, and when he reported that this reduced his strength
too much for him to be able to perform that duty adequately on the
left, where the distance was twice as great, Hood detached a brigade of
infantry from Stewart and posted it beyond the Harding Pike, about
midway between his western flank and the river below Nashville. This
was not much help, really, for the unit chosen — Brigadier General
Matthew Ector's brigade of French's division, now under its senior
colonel while Ector recovered from the loss of a leg at Atlanta — was
down to fewer than 700 effectives as a result of its heavy casualties at
Franklin. Clearly enough, Chalmers' horsemen had more than they could
handle in both directions, especially the left, and Hood's alarm was

intensified when the ice storm halted work on the outlying redoubts he
had ordered installed to provide at least a measure of security for that
vulnerable flank.

On December 8, the day the freeze set in, he issued a circular order
calling for "regular and frequent roll calls . . . as a preventive of straggling." He used the term as a euphemism for desertion, which had become a growing problem. Of 296 dismounted troopers reassigned to
the infantry, all but 42 protested the indignity by departing without
leave: a loss that far outweighed the total of 164 recruits who had joined
Hood since he entered Tennessee. All too conscious of the odds he
faced, the crippled leader of a crippled army implored Beauregard to
forward any stray units he could lay hands on, and even appealed to
the War Department to order Kirby Smith to send "two or more
divisions" from the Transmississippi. This was a forlorn hope if ever
there was one, and Seddon was prompt to tell him so. Besides, even if
all the reinforcements he requested had been started in his direction without delay, it was altogether unlikely that they could arrive — even from
North Alabama, let alone elsewhere — in time to help him meet the
crisis now at hand. Two days later, midway through the ice storm, a
follow-up circular warned that it was "highly probable that we will fight
a battle before the close of the present year." Corps commanders were
told to look to their defenses and line of retreat; Lee, who had the
center, was cautioned to "select all good points in rear of his right and
left flanks, and fortify them with strong self-supporting detached works,
so that, should it become necessary to withdraw either of the corps now
upon his flanks, the flank thus becoming the right or left flank of the
army may be in condition to be easily defended." Furthermore, so important did Hood consider resumption of work on the outlying strong-
holds, all three lieutenant generals were urged to supervise their construction in person, "not leaving them either to subordinate commanders or
engineer officers."

He did what he could, ice-bound as he was, and three days later,
while the thaw converted the sleet to slush and the frozen earth to slime,
word came that Thomas had crossed his cavalry from Edgefield, over
the Cumberland, to Nashville. He was massing behind his works there,
spies reported, for an all-out attack on the Confederate left, where dirty
and fair weather had combined to prevent completion of the vital redoubts. Hood warned Stewart to "give Chalmers such assistance as you
think necessary, keeping in communication." Next day, December 14,
with the roads beginning to dry a bit, corps commanders were able to
begin complying with orders to "send all their wagons, except artillery,
ordnance, and ambulances, to the vicinity of Brentwood," five miles in
their rear. At the same time, previous instructions regarding the hoard-
ing of ammunition — in limited supply because of the transportation

breakdown — still applied: "Not a cartridge of any kind will be burned until further orders, unless the enemy should advance upon us."

✗ 4 ✗

Thomas intended to do just that: advance: but he was determined not to do so, despite prods and threats from his Washington and City Point superiors, until he felt that his army was in condition to accomplish the annihilation Hood had been inviting ever since he took up his present position, in front of the Tennessee capital, two weeks back. Numerically, the blue force assembled to oppose him had reached that stage before the end of the first week; Thomas by then had gathered 71,842 soldiers under his command, "present for duty, equipped." Of these, 9000 were at Murfreesboro and about the same number were garrison troops, two thirds of them posted at Nashville and the other third at such outlying points as Johnsonville and Chattanooga, whose complements had been stripped to skeleton proportions. The rest — some 54,000 of all arms — were available as a striking force, and that was the use their commander had in mind to make of them as soon as he judged the time was ripe. A. J. Smith's 12,000 arrived by transport from Missouri while the battle raged at Franklin, and next morning Schofield marched in with his own 10,000 and Stanley's 14,000 survivors, now under Wood. Steedman came by rail from Chattanooga, that day and the next, with 6000 more, including a number of veterans who had returned from re-enlistment furloughs too late to march with Sherman to the sea. Finally there was the cavalry, 12,000 strong, though more than a third lacked horses and the others were badly frazzled after a week of contesting Hood's advance from Duck River to the Harpeth and beyond.

This necessity for resting and refitting his weary troopers, while trying to find mounts for the 4000 Wilson had had to leave behind when he rode out to join Schofield at Columbia, was the principal cause of delay, at least at the outset. In response to a pair of wires from Grant, December 2, urging him to "move out of Nashville with all your army and force the enemy to retire or fight upon ground of your own choosing," Thomas stressed his need for "a cavalry force sufficient to contend with Forrest," who had "at least 12,000" veteran horsemen. That was close to twice the Wizard's actual strength, and roughly six times the number he left with Hood when he departed for Murfreesboro next morning; but Thomas accepted the estimate as a figure to be matched, or at any rate approximated, before he undertook Hood's destruction. His main problem, even with all of Kentucky at his back, was the procurement of remounts, which were in short supply after more than three years of a war that had been about as hard on horses as it was on men, and broke them down at an even faster rate. Some measure of his difficulty was shown by the response George D. Prentice, the Union-loyal editor of the Louisville *Courier*, received when he complained to Military Governor Andrew Johnson about the use to which the army had put a $5000 investment he had made in cotton down in Nashville. The bales had been commandeered for installation as part of the capital fortifications; he wanted them back, he wrote Johnson, with something less expensive put in their place. But there was nothing the Vice President-elect could do for him in the matter, having himself just had a fine team of carriage horses seized for conversion to cavalry mounts. Others suffered similar deprivations, including a traveling circus, whose bareback riders were left poised in mid-air, so to speak, and the city's streetcar line, which had to suspend operations throughout the crisis for lack of mules to draw its cars. All within reach, of whatever crowbait description, were sent across the Cumberland to Edgefield, where Wilson was reorganizing and getting his troopers in shape for their share in the deferred offensive against the rebels intrenched southward, in plain view from Capitol Hill and the high-sited forts that rimmed the city in that direction.

All this required time, however, and time was the one thing his superiors did not consider he, or they, could afford at the present critical juncture; especially Grant. Halleck kept warning Thomas that their chief was losing patience, but the Virginian's files contained by then a sheaf of dispatches that made only too clear the City Point general's feelings in that regard. "You will now suffer incalculable injury upon your railroads if Hood is not speedily disposed of. Put forth, therefore, every possible exertion." "Hood should be attacked where he is. Time strengthens him, in all probability, as much as it does you." "Attack Hood at once, and wait no longer for a remount of your cavalry. There is great danger of delay resulting in a campaign back to the Ohio River." "Why not attack at once? By all means avoid the contingency of a foot race to see which, you or Hood, can beat to the Ohio." Thus Grant fumed through the first week of the Tennessee stalemate. Thomas's replies, over that same span — in which he spoke of his "crippled condition" and promised to move out, first, "in a few days," then within "less than a week," and finally by December 7, "if I can perfect my arrangements" — only goaded his chief into greater exasperation. Moreover, Halleck by now was warning that continued inaction might lead to his removal. Thomas replied that he regretted Grant's "dissatisfaction at my delay in attacking the enemy. I feel conscious that I have done everything in my power.... If he should order me to be relieved I will submit without a murmur." That was on December 9, and he closed with a weather report that seemed to him to rule out, at least for the present, any further talk of an advance. "A terrible storm of freezing rain has come on since daylight, which will render an attack impossible until it breaks."

He also passed news of this to Grant. "I had nearly completed my preparations to attack the enemy tomorrow morning, but a terrible storm of freezing rain has come on today, which will make it impossible for our men to fight to any advantage. I am, therefore, compelled to wait for the storm to break and make the attempt immediately after." And he added: "Major General Halleck informs me that you are very much dissatisfied with my delay in attacking. I can only say I have done all in my power to prepare, and if you should deem it necessary to relieve me I shall submit without a murmur." Alas, the reply he received that night was, if anything, even more chill and grudging than the others. "I have as much confidence in your conducting a battle rightly as I have in any other officer," Grant informed the Rock of Chickamauga, "but it has seemed to me that you have been slow, and I have had no explanation of affairs to convince me otherwise.... I telegraphed to suspend the order relieving you until we should hear further. I hope most sincerely that there will be no necessity for repeating the order, and that the facts will show that you have been right all the time."

Thomas was hard put to comprehend how Grant, five hundred miles away in front of Richmond — stalemated himself, not for a week but for the past six months — could presume to say what was practicable for a conglomerate army, so hastily and recently assembled under a man who was a stranger to more than half its members. However, his chief of staff, Brigadier General William Whipple, an old-line West Pointer, had a theory that someone hereabouts was "using the wires to undermine his commander" in Washington or City Point or both. At first he suspected Andrew Johnson, but on being informed that the governor was too brusque and aboveboard for such tactics, he shifted to Schofield as a likelier candidate for the Judas role. Sure enough, a prowling staffer picked up at the telegraph office the original of a recent message from the New Yorker to Grant: "Many officers here are of the opinion that General Thomas is certainly slow in his movements." Thomas read it with considerable surprise, then turned to James Steedman, who was with him at the time. "Steedman, can it be possible that Schofield would send such a telegram?" Steedman, whose share in the glory of Chickamauga had been second only to his chief's, replied that he must surely be familiar with his own general's writing. Thomas put on his glasses and examined the message carefully. "Yes, it is General Schofield's handwriting," he admitted, and asked, puzzled: "Why does he send such telegrams?" Steedman smiled at the Virginian's guileless nature, uncorrupted by twenty-four years of exposure to army politics. "General Thomas," he presently asked, "who is next in command to you in case of removal?" Thomas hung fire for a moment. "Oh, I see," he said at last, and shook his head at what he saw.

In point of fact, there was more behind Grant's exasperation, and a good deal more had come of it, than Thomas or anyone else in Tennessee had any way of knowing. Prodded by Stanton, who translated Lincoln's trepidation into sneers at "the McClellan and Rosecrans strategy of do nothing and let the rebels raid the country," Grant said later, in confirmation of earlier testimony by his aide: "I was never so anxious during the war as at that time." Indeed, under pressure of this anxiety, he lost his accustomed military balance. His fret, of course, was not only for Slow Trot Thomas, out in Nashville; it was also for Sherman, who had not yet emerged from his trans-Georgia tunnel, and for Butler, who continued to resist being hurried down the coast to Wilmington. Worst of all, he saw the possibility of the war being turned around just at the moment when he believed it was practically won. "If I had been in Hood's place," he afterwards declared, "I would have gone to Louisville and on north until I came to Chicago." Taking counsel of his fears, he had told Halleck on December 8: "If Thomas has not struck yet, he ought to be ordered to hand over the command to Schofield." Old Brains replied that if this was what Grant wanted he would have to issue orders to that effect. "The responsibility, however, will be yours, as no one here, so far as I am informed, wishes General Thomas's removal." Grant drew back: "I would not say relieve him until I hear further from him." But there was no let-up in the telegraphic goading. "If you delay attack longer," he wired the Virginian on December 11, three days into the ice storm, "the mortifying spectacle will be witnessed of a rebel army moving for the Ohio River, and you will be forced to act, accepting such weather as you find. . . . Delay no longer for weather or reinforcements."

Thomas's reply, delivered the following morning — "I will obey the order as promptly as possible, however much I may regret it, as the attack will have to be made under every disadvantage. The whole country is covered with a perfect sheet of ice and sleet, and it is with difficulty the troops are able to move about on level ground" — exhausted what little patience Grant had left. "As promptly as possible" was far from a commitment, and the rest of the message seemed to imply that the blame for any failure, when and if the attack was launched, could not properly be placed on a commander who had done his best to resist untimely orders. Grant reacted by concluding that the hour was at hand for a change in Middle Tennessee commanders.

As it happened, John A. Logan was visiting City Point headquarters at the time, on leave from his corps, which had reached the outskirts of Savannah two days ago; he was still celebrating the national election, which he had helped the Administration win, and he still was trying to digest the disappointment he felt at not having been appointed to succeed McPherson as permanent head of the Army of the Tennessee. George Thomas had been instrumental in keeping him from receiving that reward, so there was a certain poetic justice in what Grant now had in mind; which was to make Logan the Virginian's own successor. He told him so next day, December 13, when he gave him a written order to that effect, along with verbal instructions to proceed at once by rail to Nashville, going by way of Washington and Louisville. If by the time he reached the latter place Thomas had attacked, Logan was to remain there and get in touch with Grant by telegraph. Otherwise he would proceed to Nashville and take over, as directed in the order.

Logan had no sooner left than Grant began to fret anew. Black Jack was unquestionably a fighter; indeed, that was why he had been chosen; plus, of course, the fact that he was handy at the time. But perhaps, as Sherman had indicated by passing him over for Howard after the Battle of Atlanta, he lacked other qualities indispensable in the commander of an army and a department; in which case personal supervision was required. That day, that night, and most of the day that followed — December 14; Ben Butler had finally departed for Wilmington and the powder-boat explosion he believed would abolish Fort Fisher — Grant pondered his way to a decision he reached by sundown. "I am unexpectedly called away," he told Meade in a last-minute note, and got aboard a fast packet for Washington, where he expected to catch the first train west. Arriving next morning he read a telegram Thomas had sent Halleck the night before: "The ice having melted away today, the enemy will be attacked tomorrow morning." Grant decided the best thing to do was suspend his journey and await the outcome, which he would learn from Logan at Louisville or Nashville, or from Thomas himself, before the day was over.

Accordingly, he checked into Willard's to wait in comfort; but not for long. Presently there was word from Halleck that Old Slow Trot had advanced as promised, with conspicuous success, although the battle was still in progress. "Well, I guess we won't go to Nashville," Grant remarked, passing the message to an aide, and then composed for Thomas an order so characteristic that it scarcely needed a signature: "Push the enemy and give him no rest until he is entirely destroyed. ...Do not stop for trains or supplies, but take them from the country as the enemy has done. Much is now expected."

Much was expected. In downtown Nashville, five days ago, the Virginian had said more or less the same thing to his chief subordinates when they assembled in his quarters at the St Cloud Hotel on December 10, midway through the ice storm, to receive preliminary instructions for the attack they would launch as soon as the rebel-occupied hills to the south unfroze enough for climbing. Close to twenty miles of intricate Federal intrenchments stretched from bend to bend of the Cumberland, including seven that ran in a secondary line a mile behind the first-line right and center, manned by the 8000 garrison and service troops under Chief Quartermaster J. L. Donaldson, a fifty-year-old West Pointer who had been awarded the brevet rank of brigadier. When the jump-off came, these would move forward and take over the works in their front, simultaneously guarding against a counterstroke and freeing well over half the 54,000 combat soldiers now arrayed in a long arc, east to west, under Steedman, Schofield, Wood, A. J. Smith, and Wilson, for the assault and the pursuit that was to follow the dislodgment. First off, Steedman would feint against the enemy right, drawing Hood's attention away from the main effort, which would then be made against his left by Smith and Wood in a grand left wheel, with Wilson's troopers shielding the outer flank and Schofield's two divisions waiting in reserve to be committed in either direction. Thus, with Donaldson's and Steedman's men employed on the defensive and the remaining 48,000 available for offensive use against barely half their number, Thomas had been able to plan something more than the usual massing of troops for a breakthrough at a single point. Instead, his line of battle would be of practically equal strength throughout its length as it swung forward gatelike, south and southeast, inexorably crunching whatever it encountered. In this way, once a thaw set in, the ponderous Virginian intended not only to defeat Hood, there on the ground where he stood, but also to destroy him in the process.

West Pointers all, except the battle-tested Steedman, the six lieutenants gave full approval to the plan, although Schofield expressed some disappointment at the comparatively minor role assigned his corps in the attack. He had nothing to say, however, regarding another matter that came up when Thomas told of the pressure being exerted on him to advance before he judged his cavalry was ready or the ground was fit for maneuver. Speaking first, as was customary for the junior at such councils, Wilson quickly protested any suggestion of a commitment until the ice had melted from the pikes and hillsides. "If I were occupying such an intrenched line as Hood's with my dismounted cavalrymen, each armed with nothing more formidable than a basket of brickbats," he declared, "I would agree to defeat the whole Confederate army if it should advance to the attack under such circumstances." Four of the other five generals (Donaldson and Smith, fifty and forty-nine respectively, were older than their chief, while Steedman and Wood, at forty-seven and forty-one, were younger) were similarly outspoken on the subject of untimely haste, and Schofield, who was thirty-three, concurred at least to the extent of keeping silent. With that, the conference adjourned; whereupon Thomas, after asking Wilson to remain behind — ostensibly for further instructions, but actually to thank him for his exuberant support — confided sadly: "Wilson, the Washington authorities treat me as if I was a boy." Thus, for the first and only time, the stolid Virginian, reported to be as ponderous of mind as he was of body, demonstrated some measure of the resentment he felt at being

prodded and lectured by Grant and Halleck, neither of whom was
within five hundred miles of the scene of the action they kept insisting
was overdue. Having said as much, even if only in confidence to a subordinate barely three months past his twenty-seventh birthday, he
seemed to experience a certain lift of spirits. "If they will just let me
alone, I will show them what we can do. I am sure my plan of operations is correct, and that we shall lick the enemy if only he stays to
receive our attack."

There was little to fear on the last count, however, since the condition of the roads precluded a Confederate withdrawal quite as much
as it did a Federal advance. Thomas received confirmation of this when,
two days later — in partial compliance with Grant's telegraphic order
the day before: "Delay no longer for weather or reinforcements" —
he had Wilson begin the movement of his troopers across the river from
Edgefield. Rough-shod though they were for surer footing, a considerable number of horses slipped and fell on the icy bridge and cobbled
streets, injuring their riders as well as themselves in the course of the
crossing by the four divisions to take position in rear of A. J. Smith on
the far right. "The Yankees brought their weather as well as their army
with them," Nashvillians were saying, watching men and mounts
topple and thrash about on the sleety pavement, with much attendant
damage to knees and dispositions. Thomas was watching, too, as the
freeze continued into its fourth day. An aide told how the thick-set
army commander, glumly stroking his gray-shot whiskers and brooding
under his massive overhang of brow, "would sometimes sit by the
window for an hour or more, not speaking a word, gazing steadily out
upon the forbidding prospect, as if he were trying to will the storm
away."

He seemed to have succeeded the following day, December 13,
when a warm rain began melting the sleet that rimed the hills and
caked the hollows. Indeed, he seemed to have known he would succeed; for only last night he had passed out written orders for the attack,
explaining that it would be launched as soon as a thaw provided footing
for the troops. Each man was to be issued three days' rations and
sixty rounds of ammunition, while supply and ordnance wagons were to
be fully loaded and double-teamed, ready to roll at a moment's notice.
Next morning the sun came out, glittering on what little ice remained,
and even began to dry the roads a bit. At 3 o'clock that afternoon
Thomas reassembled the corps commanders in his quarters and discussed with them the details of his plan. By way of revision, Steedman
was told to convert his feint into a real attack, if he found reason to
believe one would succeed, and Schofield was placated with assurance
that his veterans were only being required to stay their hand for delivery of the knockout blow, which would be landed as soon as the
enemy had been set up for the kill. Reveille would sound at 4 a.m. in

all the camps, allowing time for the designated units to breakfast and be poised for the jump-off two hours later, at first light; "or as soon thereafter as practicable," the orders read.

That night, having sent a wire to Halleck announcing tomorrow's long-deferred attack, Thomas left a call at the St Cloud desk for 5 o'clock, and when it came — an hour before dawn, two hours before sunrise, December 15 — went down to the lobby, checked out, and after handing his packed suitcase to an orderly mounted his horse for the three-mile ride to the front: specifically to Lawrence Hill, a high salient jutting out from the left of Wood's position in the center. This was to be the pivot for the "grand left wheel," and it also would afford him a clear view of most of the field, including Montgomery Hill, a somewhat lower eminence directly opposite, where the rebels had established a matching salient less than half a mile away.

It would have afforded a view, that is, except for the fog that rose from the warming earth to hold back the dawn and obscure the sun when it came up beyond Steedman's position, an hour past the time originally scheduled for the attack to open there. Still another hour went by before the first shots broke the cotton-wrapped stillness on the left; but Thomas did not fret at the delay. He was convinced there would be time enough, despite the brevity of mid-December daylight, to accomplish all he had in mind. Besides, he did not need to see the field to know it, having studied it carefully in the past from this same observation post, as well as on maps in the small-hours quiet of his room. Four of the eight main thoroughfares, radiating spokelike from the city in his rear, were open or scantly obstructed; the Lebanon and Murfreesboro turnpikes on the left, the Charlotte and Harding turnpikes on the right, were available for use by the superior blue force in moving out to strike the flanks of Hood's four-mile line of intrenchments, which covered the other four main-traveled roads, the Nolensville Pike on his right, the Hillsboro Pike on his left, and the Franklin and Granny White pikes between, running nearly due south in his rear. If Thomas could sweep wide around the rebel flank to seize and hold the latter two, meantime pinning his adversary in position on the hills confronting the Union fortifications, he could then, with better than twice as many troops and something over three times as many guns, destroy him at his leisure. That was just what he intended to do, once the delays were overcome and the crunch got under way.

It seemed however, at least for a time, that there would be no end to the delays, caused first by the fog, which held up the advance on the left till 8 o'clock, two hours behind schedule, and then by the initial attack there, which stalled almost as soon as it got started. Cheatham's corps, posted on Rains Hill, beside the Nolensville Pike, and on to a steep-banked railway cut beyond, held firm against repeated assaults by Steedman's three brigades, each about the size of a Con-

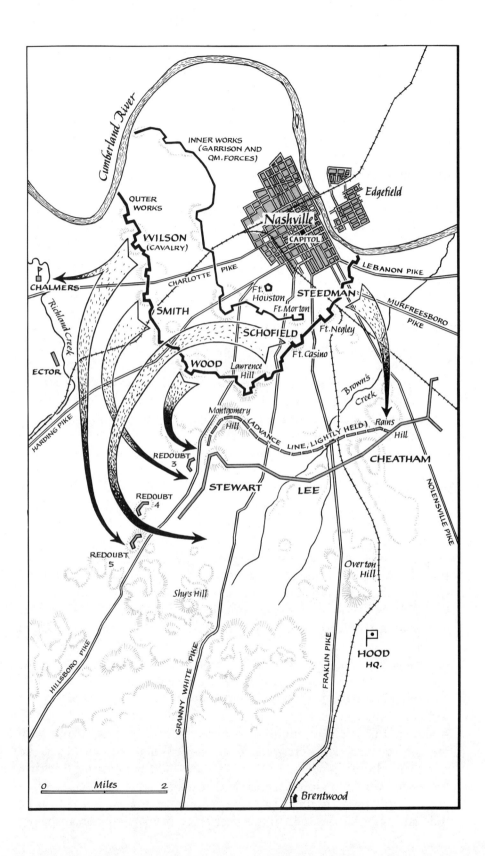

Cumberland River

INNER WORKS
(GARRISON AND
Q.M. FORCES)

Edgefield

OUTER
WORKS

WILSON
(CAVALRY)

Nashville
CAPITOL

LEBANON PIKE

CHALMERS

CHARLOTTE PIKE

STEEDMAN

MURFREESBORO PIKE

SMITH

Ft.
Houston

Ft. Morton

Richland Creek

SCHOFIELD

Ft. Negley

ECTOR

WOOD

Lawrence
Hill

Ft. Casino

Brown's
Creek

HARDING PIKE

Montgomery
Hill

(ADVANCE LINE, LIGHTLY HELD)

Rains
Hill

REDOUBT
3

CHEATHAM

STEWART

LEE

REDOUBT
4

NOLENSVILLE PIKE

REDOUBT
5

Overton
Hill

Shy's Hill

HILLSBORO PIKE

GRANNY WHITE PIKE

FRAKLIN PIKE

HOOD
HQ.

0   Miles   2

Brentwood

federate division. Two were composed of Negro troops, the first to be committed offensively in the western theater since the bloody repulse at Port Hudson, nearly twenty months ago — and the outcome here was much the same, as it turned out. Crossing Brown's Creek, whose banks were shoe-top deep in mud, they encountered the remnant of Granbury's Texas brigade of Cleburne's division, well dug in but numbering fewer than 500 survivors, and were badly cut up in a crossfire. They fell back "in a rather disorderly manner," one regimental commander admitted; then came on again. This continued, with much the same result, for two hours. Thomas, watching from his command post now that the mist had thinned and drifted off in tendrils, was not discouraged by the failure to gain ground with what had been intended as a feint in any case. Steedman apparently had not drawn Hood's reserves eastward to meet the threat, but at least he was keeping Cheatham occupied with only about an equal number of men — which helped to stretch the odds at the opposite end of the line, where the main effort was to be exerted. Hopefully, Thomas looked in that direction: only to find that, on the right as on the left, a snag had delayed the execution of his well-laid plan.

Beyond Wood's right, in rear of Smith and beyond his right in turn, Wilson's troopers awaited the signal to advance. A third of them, still without horses, would fight dismounted — supplementary infantry, so to speak — while the other 9000, armed to a man with the new seven-shot carbine repeater, comprised a highly mobile strike force. But Thomas no sooner ordered them forward, around 8.30, than the horsemen found both turnpikes blocked by one of Smith's divisions, which he was unexpectedly shifting eastward, across their front, for a closer link with Wood. For more than an hour Wilson fumed and fretted, champing at the bit until at last the slow-trudging foot soldiers cleared his path and let him get on with his task of rimming the "grand wheel." It was close to 10 o'clock by the time he moved out the Harding and Charlotte pikes to take position in Smith's front and on his outer flank.

The last wisps of fog had burned away by then, and well in rear of the advancing columns, along and behind the lofty fortress-studded double curve of intrenchments, spectators crowded the hilltops for a panoramic view of the show about to open on the right. Three years ago, before the occupation that followed hard on the fall of Donelson to Grant, Nashville had had a population of less than 30,000. Now it had better than three times that many residents: "nearly all of whom" — despite this triplicate influx of outsiders — "were in sympathy with the Confederacy," a Federal general observed. When he looked back and saw them clustered wherever the view was best, anticipating carnage, it crossed his mind that any applause that might come from those high-perched galleries was unlikely to be for him or the blue-clad men he rode among. "All the hills in our rear were black with human beings watching the battle, but silent. No army on the continent ever played on any field to so large and so sullen an audience."

What followed was still preliminary, for a time at any rate. Wilson and Smith, with a combined strength of 24,000 sabers and bayonets in their seven divisions, had small trouble driving Rucker's and Ector's outpost brigades — respectively from Chalmers' and French's divisions, and containing fewer than 2000 men between them, mounted and afoot — down the two pikes and over Richland Creek, where they could offer little or no resistance to the massive wheeling movement soon in progress across their front. By noon, so smoothly did the maneuver work once it got under way, the two blue corps were beyond the Harding Pike, confronting the mile-long extension of Hood's left down the Hillsboro Pike from the angle where his line bent sharply south in rear of Montgomery Hill. A low stone wall afforded cover for the division of graybacks crouched behind it on the east side of the road, and three unfinished redoubts bristled with guns on the side toward the Federals, who were massing to continue their advance across the remaining stretch of muddy, stump-pocked fields. Half the daylight had been used in getting set for the big push designed to bring on Hood's destruction. Now the other half remained for its execution.

Moreover, Thomas had another 24,000 standing by under Wood and Schofield, whose five divisions made up the other half of his right-wing strike force, awaiting orders to double the weight of the mass about to be thrown against Hood's left. These were the men who had stood fast at Franklin, and Wood, who had succeeded there to command of the army's largest corps when Stanley took a bullet through the neck, wanted nothing so much as he did an opportunity to wipe out the stain that had marred his record ever since he complied with instructions to "close up on Reynolds" at Chickamauga, thereby creating the gap through which Longstreet's troops had plunged. Still a brigadier, despite the mettle he had proved at Missionary Ridge and Lovejoy Station, he wanted above all a chance to show what he could do on his own. And here at Nashville he got it, just past noon, when word came down for him to execute his share of the grand wheel. All morning he had stood on Lawrence Hill, the pivotal center, obliged to contribute nothing more to the battle than long-range artillery fire, while Steedman and Wilson and Smith moved out, flags aflutter, on the left and on the right. Now that his turn had come, he was determined to make the most of it by storming the enemy works on Montgomery Hill, just opposite his command post.

This was by no means as difficult an undertaking as it appeared to be from where he stood. Five days ago, screened by the blinding fall of sleet, Hood had had Stewart withdraw his main line half a mile rearward, from the brow to the reverse slope of Montgomery Hill, leaving no more than a skeleton crew to man the works established on his arrival, two weeks back. Old Straight had only two full divisions on hand there anyhow, since one of French's three brigades was Ector's, on outpost duty two miles west, and another had been detached to guard the mouth of Duck River, lest Union gunboats penetrate the region in Hood's rear. French himself, a victim of failing eyesight, had departed just that morning, leaving only his third brigade, under Brigadier General Claudius Sears, posted between Walthall's division on the left and Loring's on the right. Stewart thus had barely 4800 men in the path of the 48,000 earmarked by Thomas for the execution of his grand left wheel.

Shortly after 12.30 Loring's pickets looked out from the all-but-abandoned trenches along the crest of the hill, midway between the two main lines of battle, and saw Wood's infantry coming toward them, out of the intervening valley and up the hillside. "The sharp rattle of fifty-caliber rifles sound[ed] like a canebrake on fire," one of the handful of defenders was to say. He and his fellows gave the advancing throng a couple of volleys, then scuttled rearward. Wood, peering intently from his command post on the far side of the valley, was impressed by what he saw. "When the grand array of troops began to move forward in unison," he would write in his report, "the pageant was magnificently grand and imposing. Far as the eye could reach, the lines and masses of blue, over which the national emblem flaunted proudly, moved forward in such perfect order that the heart of the patriot might easily draw from it the happy presage of the coming glorious victory." What pleased him most, apparently, was the progress made by the lead brigade of his old division, now under Brigadier General Samuel Beatty. Recalling its surge up the hillside in advance of all the rest, he waxed Homeric. "At the command, as sweeps the stiff gale over the ocean, driving every object before it, so swept the brigade up the wooded slope, over the enemy's intrenchments; and the hill was won."

What was won in fact was the crest of the hill and a line of empty trenches, not the new main line resistance, half a mile beyond, which held firm under the follow-up attack. Hood, having avoided being drawn off balance by the secondary effort against his right, saw clearly enough his adversary's true over-all intention, and on hearing from Stewart that his portion of the line — the critical left, already menaced by masses of bluecoats, north and west — was "stretched to its utmost tension," did what he could to reduce the lengthening odds in that direction. Stephen Lee, whose corps had scarcely fired a shot from its central position, was told to send Johnson's division to bolster the left, and similar orders went to Cheatham, who was having little trouble containing Steedman's effort on the right, to send Bate's division there as well. Whether they would arrive in time was another matter; Wood's assault had no sooner been launched against Stewart's front than Smith and Wilson resumed their combined advance upon his flank. Hard on the heels of this, moreover, Thomas passed the word for Schofield to join in the attack, bringing the total right-wheel commitment to just under 50,000 of all arms. That was better than twice the number Hood had on hand in his entire command, and roughly ten times as many as Stewart would have in his depleted corps until reinforcements reached him.

One unit had arrived by then as a reinforcement, albeit a small one: Ector's 700-man brigade, which came in from the west around 11 o'clock, after being driven back across Richland Creek by Smith and Wilson. Appealed to by the occupants of one of the redoubts short of the Hillsboro Pike, who urged them to join in its defense, the winded veterans replied: "It can't be done. There's a whole army in your front," and kept going, taking position on the left of Walthall, whose three brigades were strung out behind the stone wall running south along the far side of the pike. Such words were far from encouraging to the troops in the three redoubts, each of which was built on rising ground and contained a four-gun battery, manned by fifty cannoneers and supported by about twice that number of infantry lodged in shallow trenches alongside the uncompleted breastworks. These miniature garrisons had been told to hold out "at all hazards," and they were determined to do so, knowing they were all that stood between Hood's unshored left flank and the Federals who soon were massing to the west and northwest after completing the first stage of their grand wheel. Between noon and 1 o'clock, while Wood's attack exploded northward beyond the loom of Montgomery Hill, Wilson and Smith opened fire with their rifled batteries at a range of just under half a mile. The defenders replied as best they could with their dozen smoothbores, but hoarded their energy and ammunition for the close-up work that would follow when the dark blue mass, already in attack formation and biding its time through the bombardment, moved against them.

As it turned out, these three redoubts, numbered 3 and 4 and 5 — 1 and 2 lay northward, east of the pike, where Stewart's line bent south — held up the next stage of the wheeling movement, here on the Federal right, even longer than fog had delayed the jump-off on the left. For close to an hour the Union gunners made things hot for the clustered graybacks, who could do little more than hug their shell-jarred works and wait their turn. This came around 1.30 when the iron rain let up and the multiwaved assault rolled within range of their 12-pounders. Flailed ragged along its near edge by double-shotted canister, the blue flood paused in front of Redoubts 3 and 4, but not for long in front of Redoubt 5, which was unsupported on its outer flank, three quarters of a mile beyond the end of Walthall's line. Wilson's rapid-firing troopers, charging dismounted — somewhat awkwardly, it was true, for no one had thought to tell them to leave their low-slung cavalry

sabers behind — rushed past it on the left and right and swamped it
from the rear. They had no sooner done so, though, than they received
a high-angle salvo from Redoubt 4, next up the line, where Captain
Charles Lumsden's Alabama battery was supported by a hundred Alabama infantry. Lumsden, a V.M.I. graduate and one-time commandant
of cadets at the University of Alabama, had already notified Stewart
that he and his men, with a combined strength of 148, were likely to be
swept away in short order, once the enemy pressed the issue. Old
Straight's reply: "Hold on as long as you can," was followed to the
letter. Firing front and flank with their brass Napoleons and rifles,
the Alabamians held fast against the menace of a dozen regiments
from Smith and four from Wilson. In the end, nearly three hours past
the opening of the preliminary bombardment, the attackers came
tumbling between the fuming guns, bayonets flashing, carbines a-clatter.
"Take care of yourselves, boys!" Lumsden called out, and the survivors
trotted back to the main line, half a mile rearward, prepared to join
in its defense against the final stage of the blue assault.

Two of Johnson's brigades had arrived by then from Lee's corps
in the center, and Old Clubby was on the way with the other two,
while Bate hurried westward from the far right, sent by Cheatham on
orders from Hood to help shore up the hard-pressed left. Even if both
divisions arrived in time, however, they would do little to reduce the
odds; Schofield had come up, across the way, and was taking position on
Smith's right to overlap Stewart's extension of his line down the Hillsboro Pike. It was now past 3 o'clock. While the Federal batteries displaced forward, beyond fallen Redoubt 4, to try their hand at knocking
down the stone fence Walthall's men were crouched behind, Smith's
left division, commanded by Brigadier General John McArthur, advanced upon and captured Redoubt 3. Taken promptly under fire by
Redoubt 2, across the pike, McArthur — a Scotch-born former blacksmith who had prospered as the proprietor of a Chicago ironworks and
had served with bristly distinction in most of the western campaigns
— stormed and took the companion work as well, turning its guns on
nearby Redoubt 1, already under heavy pressure from two of Wood's
divisions.

If this went, all went: Stewart knew that, and so did Wood, who
had ordered two six-gun batteries advanced to bring converging, almost
point-blank fire to bear on the angle where Sears's brigade was posted,
hinge-like, between Walthall and Loring. Then at 4 o'clock, after a
good half hour's pounding by these dozen guns, Wood told Brigadier
General Washington Elliott — Wagner's replacement after Franklin
— to assault the rebel salient with his division "at all costs." At 4.30,
angered by the delay, which Elliott claimed was needed to give Smith's
corps time to come up on his right, Wood passed the word for Kimball
to make the strike instead. Kimball did so, promptly and with what his

superior later called "the most exalted enthusiasm." As his troops entered the works from the northeast, followed closely by the tardy Elliott's, McArthur's flank brigade came storming in from the west to assist in the reduction, together with the capture of four guns, four stands of colors, and "numerous prisoners."

Mainly these last were laggards or members of the forlorn hope, left behind to cover the withdrawal of the main body of defenders. Stewart, foreseeing disaster — both on his left, which was considerably overlapped by Schofield, and in his center, where the hinge was about to buckle under pressure from Wood and Smith — had just ordered a pull-back to a new position shielding the vital Granny White Pike, a mile in rear of the line that now was crumbling along the Hillsboro Pike and the near slope of Montgomery Hill. Despite the panic in certain units, what followed between sunset at 4.45 and full darkness, one hour later, was not a rout. Johnson's two advance brigades, posted in extension of Walthall's left before the fall of Redoubt 4, came unglued when the Federals charged them, and Ector's brigade was cut off from the rest of Stewart's corps, northward beyond the gap their flight created. Elsewhere, though, Walthall's and Loring's veterans responded in good order to instructions for disengagement. Up in the critical angle, under assault from two directions, Sears managed to pull most of his men out, avoiding capture, but as they fell back he turned to study the lost post with his binoculars and was struck in the right leg by a well-aimed solid, perhaps from one of his abandoned guns. He fell heavily, then was hustled off to an aid station, where surgeons removed his mangled leg that night. Meantime Stewart, reinforced at last by Bate and Johnson's other two brigades, got his two divisions realigned in a southward prolongation of Lee's unshaken left, helped by the jubilant confusion of the Federals, who were about as disorganized by their sudden twilight victory as his own troops were by their defeat.

Hood was there, too, intent on shoring up this battered third of his army. He had lost 16 guns today, along with some 2200 soldiers, more than half of them made prisoner in the collapse of his left wing, the rest killed or wounded here and on the right, which had stood firm. Meeting Ector's peripatetic brigade as it fell back from its second cut-off position, across the Hillsboro Pike from Redoubt 5, he spoke briefly to the men and led them nearly a mile eastward to a hill that loomed just short of the Granny White Pike. Four of the six regiments were one-time Texas cavalry outfits, long since dismounted for lack of horses and down to about a hundred men apiece.

"Texans," he said, "I want you to hold this hill regardless of what transpires around you."

They looked at the hill, then back at Hood, and nodded. "We'll do it, General," they told him.

★   ★   ★

Union and Confederate, the lines ran helter-skelter in the dusk. Still on Lawrence Hill, Thomas watched his army's campfires blossom where rebel fires had burned the night before. Except for unexpected delays — caused first by the fog, then by Smith's last-minute adjustment of his front, which held up the start of the grand wheel, and finally by the prolonged resistance of the flimsy enemy redoubts west of the Hillsboro Pike — he was convinced he would have achieved the Cannae he had planned for, and expected, until darkness caught up with the attackers before they could complete the massive turning movement he had designed to cut off Hood's retreat. In any case, not being much given to dwelling on regrets, he perceived that the best course now was for all units to bivouac where they were, in preparation for taking up their unfinished work tomorrow, well rested from the day-long exertions that had put them where they were tonight, practically within reach of the only two unseized turnpikes leading south. Just how far they would have to go, before the battle was resumed, would depend on what progress Hood's beaten troops could make on the muddy roads toward Franklin and the Harpeth — if, indeed, they were in any condition to move at all — before daylight and better than 50,000 Federals overtook them.

Returning to Nashville for a good night's sleep in a proper bed, Thomas got off to Halleck at 9 o'clock a telegram that somehow managed to be at once both ponderous and exuberant. "I attacked the enemy's left this morning and drove it from the river, below the city, very nearly to the Franklin Pike, a distance [of] about eight miles.... The troops behaved splendidly, all taking their share in assaulting and carrying the enemy's breastworks. I shall attack the enemy again tomorrow, if he stands to fight, and, if he retreats during the night, will pursue him, throwing a heavy cavalry force in his rear, to destroy his trains, if possible." A reply from Edwin Stanton himself, sent three hours later, hailed "the brilliant achievements of this day" as "the harbinger of a decisive victory that will crown you and your army with honor and do much toward closing the war. We shall give you a hundred guns in the morning." From Grant there came two wires, sent fifteen minutes apart, between 11.30 and midnight. "Much is now expected," the first ended, and the second had rather the nature of an afterthought — a brief correction of, if not quite an apology for, a lapse in manners. "I congratulate you and the army under your command for today's operations, and feel a conviction that tomorrow will add more fruits to your victory."

Closer at hand, there were those who did not share this conviction. Receiving after dark Thomas's order, "which was in substance to pursue the retreating enemy next morning," Schofield took alarm at the thought that such evident overconfidence, in addition to costing the army its half-won victory, might also expose it to defeat. He had supplied the crowning blow today, coming in hard around the crumpled rebel left at sunset, but he was by no means convinced that what had been delivered was a knockout punch, as his superior seemed to think. In fact he did not believe for a minute that Hood was in retreat. For all he knew, his former roommate was even then planning a first-light strike at one of the Union flanks: most likely his own, though both were more or less exposed. "He'll hit you like hell, now, before you know it," he had warned Sherman when Hood first took over, down around Atlanta five months ago, and it seemed to him, from the order just received, that Thomas needed reminding of that danger. Accordingly, he called for his horse and rode through the darkness to headquarters, back in Nashville, where he found the Virginian about to retire for the night. "You don't know Hood," he protested earnestly. "He'll be right there, ready to fight you in the morning."

Thomas knew Hood a good deal better than Schofield seemed to think; but even so this warning gave him pause. And having paused he acted in revision of his plans. Previously he had alerted his cavalry for a fast ride south at the first glimmer of the coming day, his purpose being to cut the retreating graybacks off, or anyhow bring them to a halt before they crossed the Harpeth, and thus expose them to slaughter without the protection of that river barrier, which might oblige the blue pursuers to fight a second Franklin, in reverse. Now instead he sent word for Wilson to "remain in your present position until it is satisfactorily known whether the enemy will fight or retreat." That would help cover his right, where the troopers had drawn rein at nightfall, and by way of further insurance he had A. J. Smith send one of his three divisions to reinforce Schofield on that flank, in case Hood really was planning the dawn assault his one-time roommate feared. This done, Thomas at last turned in for the good night's sleep he had prescribed for his whole army.

There was little or no rest, however, for the gray-clad troops across the way: not because they were on the march, as Thomas had presumed, but because they were digging — digging in. Schofield was right, at least in part: Hood had chosen to stay and fight, if only on the defensive. The crumpling of his left today, while the other two thirds of his army stood firm, had by no means convinced him that the enemy host, for all its heavy numerical advantage, was capable of driving him headlong from the field: whereas a Federal repulse, here at the capital gates, might still afford him an opening for the counterstroke on which his hopes were pinned. Moreover, the position he retired to, just under two miles south, was so much stronger than the first — especially in man-saving compactness, though it covered only two of the eight converging turnpikes — that the wonder was he had not occupied it at the outset, when he came within sight of Nashville, two weeks ago tomorrow.

Despite the confusion attending the sunset collapse of his defenses along the Hillsboro Pike and across Montgomery Hill, the nighttime withdrawal to this new line was accomplished in good order. Lee's
corps, which had scarcely been engaged today except for part of Johnson's division, simply fell back two miles down the Franklin Pike to
Overton Hill, east of the road, where the new right flank was anchored.
The left was just over two miles away, beyond the Granny White
Pike, and its main salient was the hill on which Hood had posted Ector's
brigade at twilight (Shy's Hill, it would afterwards be called for young
Lieutenant Colonel William Shy, who would die on its crown tomorrow
at the head of his Tennessee regiment); Cheatham, whose losses had also
been light today, occupied this critical height, his flank bent south
around its western slope. In the center, disposed along a range of hills
between the outer two, Stewart's diminished corps took position and
began to prepare for the resumption of the battle, as the others were
doing on the right and left, by scraping out shallow trenches and using
the spoil to pile up breastworks along that low range lying midway
between Brentwood, less than four miles south, and the Nashville fortifications. Like Ector's Texans, who by now had been joined by Bate's
division on its arrival from the right, they were determined to give Hood
all he asked of them, though they had trouble understanding why he
did so with two turnpikes leading unobstructed to the crossing of the
Harpeth, barely a dozen miles in their rear.

Dawn found them settled in, weary from their all-night toil but
confident, as one division commander said, that their improvised works
were "impervious to ordinary shots." Extraordinary shots presumably
would have to be taken as they came, but at any rate Chalmers had
combined his two brigades in Cheatham's rear, where his troopers were
in position to help fend off a repetition of yesterday's overlapping
assault upon that flank. Still, for all his determination not to be hustled
into disorderly retreat, Hood knew the odds he faced and was quite
aware of what they might portend. Accordingly, he ordered all wagons
to proceed at first light to the Harpeth, clearing the narrow gorges in his
rear, and soon afterwards, at 8 o'clock, sent warning notes to all three
corps commanders, specifying that "should any disaster happen to us
today," Lee would hold fast on the Franklin Pike, until Stewart had
moved down it, and Cheatham would take the Granny White Pike, his
withdrawal covered by Chalmers. Minor adjustments were made in the
line, which was only half as long as the one the day before, but most
of the morning was spent in idle waiting by the graybacks for the shock
that would come when Thomas resumed his effort to destroy them
where they stood.

The slowness of the Federals in getting back to grips with their
opponents was due to the scattered condition of the army when it
bedded down the night before. On the right, Wilson and Schofield

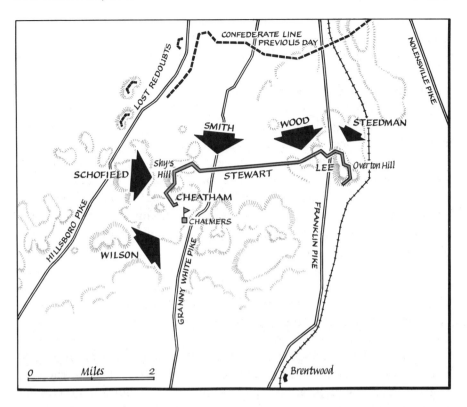

were in reasonable proximity to Cheatham on Shy's Hill, and so presently, on the left, was Steedman in relation to Lee, whose skirmishers he encountered as he approached Overton Hill, east of the Franklin Pike, around midmorning. It was in the center, in particular the right center, that the worst delays occurred; Smith and Wood were at right angles to each other, and neither knew, when the day began, whether the rebels had pulled out in the night, or, if not, what position Hood had chosen for another stand. By the time they found out, and got their troops aligned for the confrontation, noon had come and action had opened on the left. This was as it had been the day before, except that at no stage of the planning was Steedman's effort, reinforced by one of Wood's divisions, intended as a feint. His orders called for the Confederates to be "vigorously pressed and unceasingly harrassed," for if Hood's right could be turned and "his line of retreat along the Franklin Pike and the valley leading to Brentwood commanded effectually," Thomas would succeed today in bringing off the Cannae he had intended yesterday. The result, here on the Union left, was the bloodiest fighting of the two-day battle.

Two of Lee's divisions, under Major Generals Henry Clayton and Carter Stevenson, not only had scarcely been engaged the day before, they had not even taken part in the assault at Franklin, and their conduct here today, astride the Franklin Pike and on the crest of Overton

Hill, gave some notion of what Hood's whole army might have accomplished at the gates of Nashville, just over two weeks later, if it had been spared the late-November holocaust that cost it 6000 of its best men, including Pat Cleburne and a dozen other brigade and division commanders. At full strength, both in numbers and morale, these five brigades — reinforced by a sixth from Johnson, whose division was on their left, adjoining Stewart's corps in the center — stood off, between noon and 3 o'clock, a series of combined attacks by Wood and Steedman, whose persistence cost them dearly. Suffering little themselves, despite massed incoming artillery fire that Wood pronounced "uncommonly fine" and one defender said "was the most furious I ever witnessed," they inflicted such heavy punishment on the attackers that finally, after three hours of surging up and stumbling down the muddy slopes of the hill on the far Confederate right, the blue flood receded. Steedman's losses were especially cruel. One unit, the 13th U.S. Colored Infantry, suffered 221 casualties in all, the greatest regimental loss on either side. "After the repulse," Wood later reported, "our soldiers, white and colored, lay indiscriminately near the enemy works at the outer edge of the abatis."

When this attack first opened, threatening to turn his right and cut the Franklin Pike, Hood ordered Cheatham to send three of the four brigades from the division on his left — formerly Cleburne's, now under its senior brigadier, James A. Smith — to reinforce the opposite flank. As it turned out, this was a serious mistake. Lee not only needed no help, but by the time Smith's men reached him, around 3.30, the attack had been suspended. Worse, there wasn't time enough for them to return to their former position below Shy's Hill, which they had no sooner left than they were sorely missed. Stewart had been watching in both directions from his command post in the center, east of the Granny White Pike, and had seen trouble coming: not on the right, though the Overton Hill assault was even then approaching its climax, but on the left, where the situation was uncomfortably similar to the one he himself had faced the day before, when his had been the corps on that flank. "Should Bate fall back," he said in a hastily-written 2 o'clock note to Walthall, whose division adjoined Bate's on Cheatham's right, "keep your left connected with him, falling back from your left toward right and forming a new flank line extending to hills in rear."

There was more to this than a generally shared mistrust of Bate, whose three brigades had not done well in recent operations. All morning, though none of the five blue infantry divisions arrayed in a nearly semicircular line confronting Shy's Hill from the north and west had so far come to grips with the defenders, Wilson, fighting with two divisions dismounted while the other two ranged wide, had been pressing Chalmers' horsemen back on their supports. By noon, as a result, the Granny White Pike was firmly in Union possession to the south, no longer a possible rebel escape route, and Cheatham's left was bent in the shape of a fishhook. Hood pulled Ector's troops back from the crest of the hill to help Smith's remaining brigade hold off Wilson's at- tackers, whose repeaters gave them a firepower out of proportion to their already superior numbers. This caused Bate to have to extend his line still farther westward in taking over the works Ector's men had oc- cupied, and worst of all, now that the rapid-firing blue troopers had pushed within carbine range, this part of the line was taking close-up fire not only from its front and flank but also from its rear. "The Yankee bullets and shells were coming from all directions, passing one another in the air," a butternut private would recall.

By 3 o'clock, when the blue attack finally sputtered out on the Confederate right, a good part of the night-built breastworks on Shy's Hill had been flattened or knocked apart — small wonder; one of Scho- field's batteries, for example, pumped 560 rounds into the hill before the day was over — by well-aimed shots from artillery massed north and west and south. A cold rain had begun at midday, and the defenders could do little, under the fall of icy water and hot metal, but hug the earth and hope for a let-up that did not come, either of raindrops or of shells. It was more or less clear to everyone here, as it was to Stewart in the center, that the position now being pounded by close to a hundred guns could not be held much longer than it took the commanders of the three Union corps — one in its front, one on its flank, one in its rear — to stage the concerted push the situation called for.

Thomas, though he still declined to be hurried in his conduct of the battle — not even by a midday wire from the Commander in Chief, in which, after tendering "the nation's thanks for your good work of yesterday," Lincoln ended on a sterner note, as if on cue from Grant: "You made a magnificent beginning. A grand consummation is within your easy reach. Do not let it slip" — saw clearly enough what was called for, and was moving even now to bring it off. About the time the Overton Hill attack subsided he set out from his Franklin Pike command post and rode westward through the pelting rain in rear of the extension of Wood's line, on beyond the Granny White Pike, where A. J. Smith had his two remaining divisions in position, and then around the southward curve of front to Schofield's headquarters, due west of Shy's Hill. Wilson was there, remonstrating against Schofield's delay in giving the prearranged signal he and Smith had agreed would launch the converging assault by all three corps. The cavalryman had sent a series of couriers urging action for the past two hours, ever since he gained the rebel rear, and now at last — within an hour of sunset — had come in person to protest, although with small effect; Schofield wanted another division from Smith before advancing, on grounds that to attack high-sited intrenchments without a greater advantage in num- bers than he now enjoyed would be to risk paying more in blood for the hill than it was worth. Thomas heard him out, then said dryly: "The battle must be fought, if men *are* killed." He looked across the northwest slope of the fuming hill, where it seemed to him that McArthur, adjusting his line for a closer take-off, was about to slip the leash. "General Smith is attacking without waiting for you," he told Schofield. "Please advance your entire line."

Here at last was a direct order; Schofield had no choice but to obey. He did so, in fact, so promptly that Wilson, riding happily south to rejoin his troopers in rear of the blue-clamped rebel left, did not get back in time to direct their share of the three-sided push that drove the defenders from Shy's Hill. So sudden indeed was the gray collapse that Hood himself, watching from horseback in rear of his left center, said later that he could scarcely credit what he saw. "Our forces up to that moment had repulsed the Federals at every point, and were waving their colors in defiance, crying out to the enemy, 'Come on, come on.' " With the crisis weathered on his right and sunset barely an hour away, he planned to withdraw after nightfall for a dawn assault on the Union right, which he believed was exposed to being turned and shattered. Alas, it was his own flank that was shattered as he watched. "I beheld for the first and only time" — he had not been on Missionary Ridge with Bragg, just over a year ago — "a Confederate army abandon the field in confusion."

Old Straight had seen disaster coming two hours before, and it came as he had warned. Assailed by Smith and Schofield on both sides of the angle, all the while taking fire from Wilson's dismounted horsemen in their rear, Bate's three brigades gave back from their enfiladed works, fought briefly, and then for the most part fled, although some units — the Tennesseans under twenty-five-year-old William Shy, for instance, whose fall gave the lost hill its future name — resisted till they were overrun. By that time, the attack had widened and the panic had infected Stewart's corps, along with the rest of Cheatham's; "The breach once made, the lines lifted from either side as far as I could see," Bate would report. All three of his brigade commanders were captured, and so was Edward Johnson when the break extended beyond the center, under pressure from Smith and Wood, and spread to his division on Lee's left. Everywhere to the west of there, eastward across the rear of what had been the Confederate left and center, butternut veterans were in headlong flight for the Franklin Pike, the one remaining avenue of escape. They wanted to live: perhaps to fight another day, but certainly not here.

"It was more like a scene in a spectacular drama than a real incident in war," a colonel on Thomas's staff would note. "The hillside in front, still green, dotted with boys in blue swarming up the slope, the dark background of high hills beyond, the lowering clouds, the waving flags, the smoke rising slowly through the leafless treetops and drifting across the valleys, the wonderful outburst of musketry, the ecstatic cheers, the multitude racing for life down into the valley below — so exciting was it all that the lookers-on instinctively clapped their hands as at a brilliant and successful transformation scene; as indeed it was. For in those few moments an army was changed into a mob, and the whole structure of the rebellion in the Southwest, with all its possibilities, was utterly overthrown."

But that was to overstate the case, if not in regard to the eventualities, then at any rate in regard to the present dissolution of Hood's army. On Overton Hill, in the final moments before the opposite flank gave way, Stephen Lee observed that his troops were "in fine spirits and confident of success," congratulating themselves on their recent repulse of Wood and Steedman. Then out of nowhere came the collapse, first of Cheatham's corps, then Stewart's, and the blue attack rolled eastward to engulf them; Johnson's division wavered and broke, its commander taken, and Stevenson's, next in line, seemed about to follow. East of the Franklin Pike, in rear of Clayton's division, Lee spurred his horse westward, taking the fences on both sides of the turnpike, and drew rein amid the confusion behind his center, crowded now with graybacks who had bolted. He leaned down and snatched a stand of colors from a fugitive color bearer, then brandished it from horseback as he rode among the panicked veterans, shouting hoarsely at them: "Rally, men, rally! For God's sake, rally! This is the place for brave men to die!"

Some few stopped, then more. "The effect was electrical," one among them was to write. "They gathered in little knots of four or five, and he soon had around him three or four other stands of colors." They were not many, but they were enough, as it turned out, to cause the attackers — confused as much by their abrupt success today as they had been at the same late hour the day before — to hesitate before moving forward again through the smoky, rain-screened dusk that followed hard upon sunset. By that time Clayton, unmolested on the right, had managed to withdraw his division from Overton Hill and form it in some woods astride the Franklin Pike, half a mile below. When Lee fell back to there, the same observer noted, "he was joined by a few pieces of artillery and a little drummer boy who beat the long roll in perfect time." Stevenson's fugitives rallied too, in response to this steady drumming, and together the two divisions comprised a rear guard that kept open, well into darkness, the one escape route still available to the army.

This was of course no help to the men already rounded up in their thousands on the field of battle, including Johnson — he had just been exchanged in October, five months after his previous capture at Spotsylvania — and all three of Bate's brigade commanders, Brigadier Generals Henry Jackson and T. B. Smith and Major Jacob Lash. Old Clubby,

still crippled from the leg wound he had suffered at McDowell, two and
a half years ago, was taken while trying to limp away from his shattered
line, and it was much the same with Jackson, a forty-four-year-old
former Georgia lawyer-politician, who found the rearward going slow
because of the mud that weighted down his boots. He had stopped, and
was trying to get them off with the help of an aide, when a blue-clad
corporal and three privates came upon him by the roadside.

"You're a general," the corporal said accusatively, spotting the
wreathed stars on his prisoner's collar.

"That is my rank," Jackson admitted.

"Captured a general, by God!" the Federal whooped. He took
off his flat-topped forage cap and swung it round and round his head.
"I'll carry you to Nashville myself."

Smith and Lash on the other hand were taken on Shy's Hill itself, along with most of their men, when their lines were overrun. Imprisoned, Lash would not receive the promotion he had earned by
surviving his superiors, but Smith's was a crueler fate. A graduate of
the Nashville Military Institute and a veteran of all the western battles,
he had risen from second lieutenant, over the years, to become at twenty-
six the army's youngest brigadier; which perhaps, since his youth and
slim good looks implied a certain jauntiness in happier times, had something to do with what presently happened to him. While being conducted unarmed to the Union rear he was slashed three times across
the head with a saber by the colonel of the Ohio regiment that had
captured him, splitting his skull and exposing so much of his mangled
brain that the surgeon who examined his wounds pronounced them
fatal. He did not die, however. He survived a northern prison camp to
return to his native state when the conflict was over, then lived for
nearly another sixty years before he died at last in the Tennessee Hospital for the Insane, where he spent the last forty-seven of his eighty-
five years, a victim of the damage inflicted by the Ohio colonel. This
was another face of war, by no means unfamiliar on either side, but
one unseen when the talk was all of glory.

It was not the face Thomas saw when, completing a sunset ride
from the far right, he urged his horse up Overton Hill, which had
just been cleared, and looked out over the field where his troops were
hoicking long columns of butternut captives to the rear. He lifted his
hat in salute to the victors in the twilight down below, exclaiming as
he did so: "Oh, what a grand army I have! God bless each member
of it."

Such hilltop crowing was uncharacteristic of the Rock of Chickamauga, however well it might suit him in his new role as the Sledge
of Nashville, but in any case both salute and blessing were deserved.
His army captured here today an additional 3300 prisoners, bringing
its two-day haul, as a subsequent head-count would show, to 4462

rebels of all ranks. Moreover, another 37 pieces of artillery were taken, which made 53 in all, one more than R. E. Lee had captured throughout the Seven Days to set the previous battle record. Thomas's loss in killed, wounded, and missing, though twice heavier today than yesterday, barely raised his overall total above three thousand: 3061. Hood lost only half as many killed and wounded as he had done the day before, but his scant loss in those two categories — roughly 1500 for both days, or less than half the number his adversary suffered — only showed how readily his soldiers had surrendered under pressure, thereby lifting his loss to nearly 6000 casualties, almost twice as many as he inflicted. Thomas of course did not yet know these comparative figures. All he knew was that he had won decisively, more so tactically perhaps than any general in any large-scale battle in this war, and that was the cause of his exuberance on Overton Hill and afterwards, when he came down off the height and rode forward in the gathering darkness.

Normally mild of speech and manner, practically never profane or boastful, he continued to be quite unlike himself tonight: as was shown when he spotted his young cavalry commander riding back up the Granny White Pike to meet him. He recalled what he had told him in private on the eve of battle, and he greeted him now, the other would note, "with all the vehemence of an old dragoon" and in a voice that could be heard throughout this quarter of the rain-swept field. "Dang it to hell, Wilson!" he roared, "didn't I tell you we could lick 'em? Didn't I tell you we could lick 'em?"

Southward, the disorderly gray retreat continued. Lee's rear guard task was eased by having only Wood's corps to contend with; Steedman had stopped, apparently from exhaustion, and Smith and Schofield had been halted to prevent confusion when their two corps came together at right angles on Shy's Hill. Below there, Wilson's remounted troopers were opposed by Ector's surviving handful of infantry and Rucker's cavalry brigade, assigned by Chalmers to keep the bluecoats off the Franklin Pike, which was clogged with fugitives all the way to Brentwood. Rucker managed it, with the help of Ector's veterans and the rain and darkness, though at the cost of being captured — the fourth brigade commander in the past two hours — when he was shot from his horse in a hand-to-hand saber duel with two opponents. Lee meantime withdrew in good order, two miles beyond Brentwood to Hollow Tree Gap, where he set up a new rear-guard line by midnight, six miles short of Franklin and the Harpeth.

In this way, from sunset well into darkness, when they finally desisted, the Federals were kept from interfering with the retreat of the army they had routed. But neither could that army's own leaders interfere with its rearward movement, though they tried. "It was like trying to stop the current of Duck River with a fish net," one grayback was to say. Not even Ben Cheatham, for all the fondness his men had for him, could prevail on them to pause for longer that he could fix them with his eye. He would get one stopped, and then when he turned to appeal to another, the first would duck beneath the general's horse and continue on his way. Even so, he had better luck than did some younger staffers who tried their hand. One such, hailing a mud-spattered infantryman headed rearward down the turnpike, ordered him to face about and meet the foe. "You go to hell — I've been there," the man replied, and kept on trudging southward in the rain. None among them had any way of knowing that the war's last great battle had been fought. All they knew was they wanted no more of it; not for now, at any rate.

Hood was no better at organizing a rally short of Brentwood than the least of his subordinates had been. He tried for a time, then gave it up and went with the flow. A bandaged Tennessee private who had seen and pitied him earlier, just before the break — "How feeble and decrepit he looked, with an arm in a sling and a crutch in the other hand, trying to guide and control his horse" — felt even sorrier for him tonight when, seeking him out to secure "a wounded furlough," he came upon the one-legged general near Hollow Tree Gap, alone in his headquarters tent beside the Franklin Pike, "much agitated and affected" by the events of the past six hours "and crying like his heart would break." His left arm dangling useless at his side, he ran the fingers of his right hand through his hair in a distracted gesture as the tears ran down his cheeks into his beard, golden in the light of the lantern on the table by his chair. Unabashed — after the manner of Confederates of all ranks, who respected their superiors in large part for the respect they knew they would receive in turn if they approached them — the bullet-nicked private entered, asked for, and received his furlough paper, then went back out into the darkness and the rain, leaving Hood to resume his weeping if he chose. "I pitied him, poor fellow," the Tennessean wrote long afterward, remembering the scene. "I always loved and honored him, and will ever revere and cherish his memory. . . . As a soldier, he was brave, good, noble, and gallant, and fought with the ferociousness of the wounded tiger, and with the everlasting grit of the bulldog; but as a general he was a failure in every particular."

For all its harshness, Franklin and Nashville had confirmed and reconfirmed this assessment, so far at least as most of the Kentucky-born Texan's critics were concerned, before it was made: not only because he fought them with so little tactical skill, offensive or defensive, but also because he fought them at all. Within a span of just over two weeks, these two battles had cost him 12,000 casualties — better than twice the number he inflicted — and in the end produced a rout as complete as the one a year ago on Missionary Ridge. Pat Cleburne had saved Bragg's retreat then with his defense of Ringgold Gap, and though the Arkansan now was in his grave in St John's churchyard, Stephen Lee performed a similar service for Hood next morning at Hollow Tree Gap, which he held under pressure from Wilson and Wood while the rest of the graybacks crossed the Harpeth. Outflanked, he followed, burning the bridge in his wake, and took up a covering position on Winstead Hill, three miles south of Franklin, where Hood had had his command post for the attack that cost him the flower of his army. To-day's defense only cost him Lee, who was wounded there and had to turn his corps over to Stevenson when he fell back that evening to take up a new position near Spring Hill, another place of doleful memory.

By the following morning, December 18, Cheatham had reassembled enough of his corps to assume the duty of patrolling rain-swollen Rutherford Creek, which the pursuers could not cross, once the turnpike bridge was burned, until their pontoon train arrived. The resultant two-day respite from immediate blue pressure (for the train, having been missent toward Murfreesboro by a clerical error, then recalled, was obliged to creak and groan its way by a roundabout route over roads hub-deep in mud) was heartening to the graybacks plodding down the Columbia Pike. But the best of all news, especially for Chalmers' drooping horsemen, was the arrival last night of one of the four detached brigades of cavalry, followed today by another, which brought word that Forrest himself would soon be along with the other two. Sure enough, he rode in that night. Ordered by Hood to fall back from Murfreesboro through Shelbyville to Pulaski, he had decided instead to rejoin by a shorter route, through Triune, and had done so: much to his superior's relief. Hood's plan had been to call a halt along Duck River and winter in its lush valley, much as Bragg had done two years ago, but he saw now there could be no rest for his ground-down command short of the broader Tennessee, another seventy miles to the south. Accordingly, having begun his withdrawal across the Duck, he was all the more pleased by Forrest's early return, since it meant that the Wizard and his veteran troopers, lately conspicuous by their absence, would be there to hold off the Federals while the rest of the army went on with its dangerous task of crossing a major river in the presence of a foe not only superior in numbers, warmly clad, and amply fed, but also flushed with victory and clearly bent on completing the destruction begun three days ago at the gates of Nashville.

In taking over this rear-guard assignment — for which he had about 3000 cavalry whose mounts were still in condition for hard duty, plus 2000 infantry under Walthall, roughly a fourth of them bare-foot and all of them hungry, cold in their cotton tatters, and close to exhaustion from two days of battle and two of unrelieved retreat — Forrest combined his usual inventiveness with a highly practical application of the means at hand, however slight. Part of the problem was the weather, which changed next day from bad to worse. Alternate blasts of sleet and rain deepened the mud, stalled the supply train, and covered the roads and fields with a crust of ice that crunched and shattered under foot and made walking a torture for ill-shod men and horses. He solved the immobilized wagon dilemma by leaving half of them parked along the pike and using their teams to double those in the other half, which then proceeded. Because of the drawn-out Federal delay, first in clearing brim-full Rutherford Creek and then the more formidable Duck, four miles beyond, there was time for the doubled teams to haul the first relay far to the south and then return for the second before the pursuers bridged and crossed both streams. As for the infantry crippled for lack of shoes, Forrest solved that problem by commandeering empty wagons in which the barefoot troops could ride until they were called on to jump down and hobble back to their places in the firing line. "Not a man was brought in contact with him who did not feel strengthened and invigorated," one among them was to say of the general who thus converted shoeless cripples into horse-drawn infantry.

Not until the night of December 21, with their pontoons up and thrown at last, did the first Federals cross Duck River to begin next day at Warfield Station, three miles beyond Columbia, a week-long running fight that proceeded south across the frozen landscape in the earliest and coldest winter Tennesseans had known for years. Outflanked, Forrest fell back, skirmishing as he went, and at nightfall took up a new position at Lynnville, twelve miles down the line. Here he staged a surprise attack the following morning, using Walthall's men to block the pike while his troopers slashed at the Union flanks, then retired on the run before his pursuers recovered from the shock, bringing off a captured gun which he employed next day in a brisk Christmas Eve action on Richland Creek, eight miles north of Pulaski, where Buford suffered a leg wound to become the twenty-first Confederate brigade, division, or corps commander shot or captured in the course of the campaign. By then the main body, unmolested since Forrest took over the duty of guarding its rear, was well beyond the Alabama line, approaching the Tennessee River, and next day the head of the column pulled up on the near bank opposite Bainbridge, just below Muscle Shoals. It was Christmas, though scarcely a merry one, and a Sunday: five weeks, to the day, since Hood left Florence, four miles downstream, on the expedition that by now had cost him close to 20,000 veterans killed, wounded, or missing in and out of battle, including one lieutenant general, three major generals, and an even dozen brigadiers, together with five brigade commanders of lesser rank. Of these, moreover, only two — Lee and Buford — were alive, uncaptured, and had wounds that would permit an early return to the army that had set out for Middle Tennessee in such high spirits, five weeks back, with twice as many troops and guns as were now in its straggled ranks.

Forrest too was over the Alabama line by then, holding Wilson off while the gray main body bridged the river with the pontoons he had saved by doubling their teams. Gunboats, sent roundabout by Thomas from the Cumberland and the Ohio, tried their hand at shelling the rickety span, but were driven off by Stewart's artillery and Rear Admiral Samuel P. Lee's fear of getting stranded if he ventured within range of the white water at the foot of Muscle Shoals. Hood finished crossing on December 27; Forrest's cavalry followed, and Walthall's forlorn hope got over without further loss on the 28th, cutting the bridge loose from the northern bank. Thomas — whose own pontoons were still on the Duck, seventy miles away, and whose infantry had not cleared Pulaski — declared the pursuit at an end next day. Hood's army, he said, "had become a disheartened and disorganized rabble of half-naked and barefooted men, who sought every opportunity to fall out by the wayside and desert their cause to put an end to their sufferings. The rear guard, however, was undaunted and firm," he added, "and did its work bravely to the last."

Schofield was more generous in his estimate of the defeated army's fighting qualities, especially as he had observed them during the long-odds Battle of Nashville, where fewer than 25,000 graybacks held out for two days against better than 50,000 bluecoats massed for the most part of their flank. "I doubt if any soldiers in the world ever needed so much cumulative evidence to convince them they were beaten," he declared. This was not to say they weren't thoroughly convinced in the end. They were indeed, and they showed it through both stages of the long retreat: first, as one said, while "making tracks for the Tennessee River at a quickstep known to Confederate tactics as 'double distance on half rations,'" and then on the follow-up march beyond, after Hood decided his troops were no more in condition for a stand on the Tennessee than they had been when they crossed the Duck the week before. By way of reinforcing this assessment, Thomas would list in his report a total of 13,189 prisoners and 72 pieces of artillery captured on and off the field of battle in the course of the forty days between Hood's setting out, November 20, and his own calling of an end to the campaign, December 29. Moreover, weary as they were from their 120-mile trek over icy roads in the past two weeks, the butternut marchers themselves agreed that the better part of valor, at least for now, would be to find some place of refuge farther south, if any such existed. "Aint we in a hell of a fix?" one ragged Tennessean groaned as he picked himself up, slathered with mud from a fall on the slippery pike. "Aint we in a hell of a fix: a one-eyed President, a one-legged general, and a one-horse Confederacy!"

Their goal, they learned as they slogged west across North Alabama toward the Mississippi line, was Tupelo. There, just thirty months ago this week, Braxton Bragg had taken over from Beauregard after the retreat from Corinth, and there he had given them the name they made famous, the Army of Tennessee, first in Kentucky, then back again in Middle and East Tennessee and Georgia. Bragg's tenure had ended soon after Missionary Ridge, and so would Hood's after Nashville, a comparable rout; there was little doubt of that, either in or out of the army. "The citizens seemed to shrink and hide from us as we approached them," a soldier would recall, and the reaction of his comrades was shown in a song they sang as they trudged into Mississippi and the New Year. The tune was the banjo-twanging "Yellow Rose of Texas," but the words had been changed to match their regret, if not their scorn, for the quality of leadership that had cost them Pat Cleburne and so many others they had loved and followed down the years.

> So now I'm marching southward,
> My heart is full of woe;
> I'm going back to Georgia
> To see my Uncle Joe.
> You may talk about your Beauregard
> And sing of General Lee,
> But the gallant Hood of Texas
> Played hell in Tennessee.

✗ 5 ✗

Back at City Point after breaking off his intended western trip, Grant had the familiar hundred-gun victory salute fired twice in celebration of the Nashville triumph. "You have the congratulations of the public for the energy with which you are pushing Hood," he wired Thomas on December 22, adding: "If you succeed in destroying Hood's army, there will be but one army left to the so-called Confederacy capable of doing us harm. I will take care of that and try to draw the sting from it, so that in the spring we shall have easy sailing." He sounded happy. One week later, however, on learning that Hood's fugitives had crossed the Tennessee and Thomas had ordered his erstwhile pursuers into winter quarters to "recuperate for the spring campaign," Grant's petulance returned. "I have no idea of keeping idle troops in any place," he telegraphed Halleck, who passed the word to Thomas on the last day of the year: "General Grant does not intend that your army shall go into winter quarters. It must be ready for active operations in the field."

Grant's fear, throughout the two weeks leading up to the thunderous two-day conflict out in Tennessee, had been that Old Tom's balkiness would allow the rebels to prolong the war by scoring a central breakthrough all the way to the Ohio, thereby disrupting the combinations he had devised for their destruction. Yet this fear had no sooner been dispelled, along with the smoke from the mid-December battle, than another took its place; namely, that this same "sluggishness," as he called it during the two weeks following the clash at the gates of Nashville, would delay the over-all victory which now at last seemed practically within his grasp, not only because of the drubbing given Hood, whose survival hung in the balance until he crossed the Tennessee River, but also because of other successes registered elsewhere, at the same time, along and behind the butternut line stretching west from the Atlantic. A sizeable budget of good news reached City Point while Thomas was failing to overtake his defeated adversary, and every item in it only served to whet Grant's appetite for more. That had always been his way, but it was even more the case now that he saw the end he had worked so hard for in plain view, just up the road.

Chief among these simultaneous achievements was the occupation of Savannah, eleven days after Sherman's arrival before it at the end of his march from Atlanta. Having stormed and taken Fort McAllister on December 13, which enabled the waiting supply ships to steam up the Ogeechee, he proceeded with a leisurely investment — or near investment — of the city just over a dozen miles away. Within four days he had progressed so far with his preparations that he thought it only fair to give the defenders a chance to avoid bloodshed by surrendering. He was "prepared to grant liberal terms to the inhabitants and garrison," he said in a message sent across the lines; "but should I be forced to resort to assault, or to the slower and surer process of starvation, I shall then feel justified in resorting to the harshest measures, and shall make little effort to restrain my army, burning to avenge the national wrong which they attach to Savannah and other large cities which have been so prominent in dragging our country into civil war." The rebel commander replied in kind, declining to surrender, and in closing dealt in measured terms with Sherman's closing threat. "I have hitherto conducted the military operations intrusted to my direction in strict accordance with the rules of civilized warfare, and I should deeply regret the adoption of any course by you that may force me to deviate from them in the future. I have the honor to be, very respectively, your obedient servant, *W. J. Hardee*, Lieutenant General."

Hardee, with barely 15,000 regulars and militia — two thirds of them lodged in the city's defenses, the rest posted rearward across the Savannah River to cover his only escape route, still menaced by Foster near Honey Hill — had appealed to Richmond for reinforcements to help him resist the 60,000 newly arrived bluecoats closing in from the east and south. Davis conferred with Lee at Petersburg, then replied on December 17 — the day of Sherman's threat to unleash his burning veterans on Savannah when it fell — that none were available; he could only advise the Georgian to "provide for the safety of your communications and make the dispositions needful for the preservation of your army." This authorized the evacuation Beauregard had been urging from his headquarters in Charleston, a hundred miles up the coast. With a bridgeless river at his back and no pontoons on hand, that seemed about as difficult as staying to fight against six-to-one odds, but Old Reliable found the answer in the employment of some thirty 80-foot rice flats, lashed together endwise, then planked over to provide a three-section island-hopping span from the Georgia to the Carolina bank. It was finished too late for use on the night of December 19, as intended, so a circular was issued for the withdrawal to begin soon after dark next evening — by coincidence, the fourth anniversary of South Carolina's secession from the Union — preceded by daylong fire from all the guns, which would not only discourage enemy interference but would also reduce the amount of surplus ammunition to be destroyed, along with the unmovable heavy pieces, when the cannoneers fell back. Wagons and caissons would cross the river first, together with the light artillery, and the men themselves would follow, filing silently out of their trenches after moonset. "Though compelled to evacuate the city, there is no part of my military life to which I look back with so much satisfaction," Hardee was to say. And the fact was he had cause for pride. The operation went as planned from start to finish, despite some mixups and much sadness, especially for long-time members of the garrison, who thus were obliged to turn their backs on what had been their home for the past three years. "The constant tread of the troops and the rumblings of the artillery as they poured over those long floating bridges was a sad sound," one retreater would presently recall, "and by the glare of the large fires at the east of the bridge it seemed like an immense funeral procession stealing out of the city in the dead of night."

Sherman was not there for the formal occupation next morning, having gone up the coast to confer with Foster about bringing in more troops from Hilton Head to block the road to Charleston; the road over which, as it developed, Hardee marched to safety while the conference was in progress. When the Ohioan returned the following day, December 22 — chagrined if not abashed by the escape of 10,000 rebels he had thought were his for the taking — he found his army in possession of Savannah and quartermaster details busy tallying the spoils. These were considerable, including more than 200 heavy guns and something over 30,000 bales of cotton, negotiable on the world market at the highest prices ever known. Most of the guns had been spiked, but the rich haul of cotton was intact, not only because there had been no time or means to remove it, but also because, as Hardee explained to his superiors, it was "distributed throughout the city in cellars, garrets and warehouses, where it could not have been burnt without destroying the city." A U.S. Treasury agent was already on hand from Hilton Head, reckoning up the profit to the government, and when the red-haired commander bristled at him, as was his custom when he encountered money men, the agent turned his wrath aside with a suggestion that the general send a message, first by ship to Fort Monroe and then by wire to the White House, announcing the fall of Savannah as a Christmas present for Lincoln. "The President particularly enjoys such pleasantry," he pointed out. Sherman considered this a capital notion, and at once got off the following telegram, composed before the tally was complete.

> To his Excellency President Lincoln,
> Washington, D.C.
>
> I beg to present you, as a Christmas gift, the city of Savannah, with 150 heavy guns and plenty of ammunition; also about 25,000 bales of cotton.
>
> W. T. Sherman
> *Major General.*

He was, as usual, in high spirits after a colorful exploit — and this, which reached its climax with the taking of Savannah and would afterwards find its anthem in the rollicksome "Marching Through Georgia," had been the most colorful of all. Partly because of that scare-head aspect, lurid in its reproduction in the memory of participants, as well as in the imagination of watchers on the home front, the march achieved a significance beyond its considerable military value, and though the risk had turned out slight (103 killed, 428 wounded, 278 captured or otherwise missing: barely more, in all, than one percent of the force involved) even Sherman was somewhat awed in retrospect. "Like a man who has walked a narrow plank," he wrote his wife, "I look back and wonder if I really did it." In effect, after seven months of grinding combat at close quarters, he and his bummers had broken out of the apparent stalemate, East and West, to inject a new spirit of exuberance into the war. You could see the feeling reflected in the northern papers brought to headquarters by the navy, first up the Ogeechee, then the Savannah. "Tecumseh the Great," editors called him now, who had formerly judged him insane, and there was a report of a bill introduced in Congress to promote him to lieutenant general so that he and Grant could divide control of the armies of the Union. His reaction to this was similar to his reaction four months ago, at the time of the Democratic convention in Chicago, when there was talk of nominating him for President. "Some fool seems to have used my name," he wrote Halleck from his position in front of besieged Atlanta. "If forced to choose between the penitentiary and the White House . . . I would say the penitentiary, thank you." So it was now in regard to this latest proposal to elevate him. "I will accept no commission that would tend to create a rivalry with Grant," he informed his senator brother. "I want him to hold what he has earned and got. I have all the rank I want." As if to emphasize this conviction, he presently re-marked to a prying inquirer, in a tone at once jocular and forthright: "Grant is a great general. I know him well. He stood by me when I was crazy and I stood by him when he was drunk. And now, sir, we stand by each other always."

In point of fact, the general-in-chief was standing by him now, even to the extent of deferring to his military judgment: and that, too, was part of the cause for his red-haired exuberance. He had just made Georgia howl. Now he was about to make the Carolinas shriek.

Originally — that is, in orders he found waiting for him when he reached the coast — Grant had intended for Sherman and his Westerners to proceed by water "with all dispatch" to Virginia, where they would help Meade and Butler "close out Lee." He was to es-tablish and fortify a base near Savannah, garrison it with all his cavalry and artillery, together with enough infantry to protect them and "so threaten the interior that the militia of the South will have to be kept at home," then get the rest aboard transports for a fast ride north to the Old Dominion. "Select yourself the officer to leave in command, but you I want in person," Grant told him, adding: "Unless you see objections to this plan which I cannot see, use every vessel going to you for the purpose of transportation."

Sherman did have objections, despite the compliment implied in this invitation to be in on the kill of the old gray fox at Petersburg, and was prompt to express them. He much preferred a march by land to a boatride up the coast for the reunion, he replied, partly because of the damage he could inflict en route and the effect he believed an extension of his trans-Georgia swath would have on the outcome of the war. Besides, there was a certain poetic justice here involved. "We can punish South Carolina as she deserves, and as thousands of people in Georgia hoped we would do. I do sincerely believe that the whole United States, North and South, would rejoice to have this army turned loose on South Carolina, to devastate that state in the manner we have done in Georgia." He was convinced moreover, he said in closing, that the overland approach "would have a direct and im-mediate bearing upon the campaign in Virginia," and he went into more detail about this in a letter to Halleck, invoking his support. "I attach more importance to these deep incursions into the enemy's country," he declared, "because this war differs from European wars in this par-ticular: We are not only fighting hostile armies, but a hostile people, and must make old and young, rich and poor, feel the hard hand of war, as well as their organized armies. I know that this recent movement of mine through Georgia has had a wonderful effect in this respect. Thousands who have been deceived by their lying newspapers to be-lieve that we were being whipped all the time now realize the truth, and have no appetite for a repetition of the same experience." In short, he told Old Brains, "I think the time has come when we should attempt the boldest moves, and my experience is that they are easier of execution than more timid ones.... Our campaign of the last month, as well as every step I take from this point northward, is as much a direct attack upon Lee's army as though we were operating within the sound of his artillery."

To his surprised delight, Grant readily agreed: so readily, indeed, that it turned out he had done so even before his friend's objections reached him. In a letter written from Washington on the same date as Sherman's own — December 18: he was about to return to City Point: Fort McAllister had fallen five days ago, and Savannah itself would be taken in three more — the general-in-chief sent his congratulations "on the successful termination of your campaign" from Atlanta to the Atlantic. "I never had a doubt of the result," he said, though he "would not have intrusted the expedition to any other living commander." Then he added a few sentences that made Sherman's ears prick up. "I did think the best thing to do was to bring the greater part of your army here, and wipe out Lee. [But] the turn affairs now seem to be taking has shaken me in that opinion. I doubt whether you may not accomplish more toward that result where you are than if brought here, especially as I am informed, since my arrival in the city, that it would take about two months to get you here with all the other calls there are for ocean transportation. I want to get your views about what ought to be done, and what can be done.... My own opinion is that Lee is averse to going out of Virginia, and if the cause of the South is lost he wants Richmond to be the last place surrendered. If he has such views, it may be well to indulge him until we get everything else in our hands.... I subscribe myself, more than ever, if possible, your friend."

This reached Sherman on Christmas Eve, three days after the occupation of Savannah, and lifted his spirits even higher. Here, in effect, was the go-ahead he had sought for himself and his bummers, whom he described as being "in splendid flesh and condition." Promptly that same evening he replied to Grant at City Point, expressing his pleasure at the change in orders; "for I feared that the transportation by sea would very much disturb the unity and morale of my army, now so perfect.... In about ten days I expect to be ready to sally forth again. I feel no doubt whatever as to our future plans. I have thought them over so long and well that they appear as clear as daylight."

Chief among those "other calls ... for ocean transportation" were the ones that had secured for the Butler-Porter expedition, whose mission was the reduction of Fort Fisher, the largest number of naval vessels ever assembled under the American flag. Packed with 6500 troops in two divisions, Butler's transports cleared Hampton Roads on December 13, and five days later joined Porter's fleet of 57 ironclads,

frigates, and gunboats at Beaufort, North Carolina, ninety miles up the
coast from their objective. Next morning, December 19, they arrived
off Wilmington to find bad weather making up and the surf too rough
for a landing. This obliged the transports to return to Beaufort for
shelter, but the warships remained on station, riding out the storm while
the admiral studied the rebel stronghold through his telescope. Unlike
prewar forts, which mostly were of masonry construction, this one
had walls of sand, piled nine feet high and twenty-five thick, designed
to withstand by absorption the fire of the heaviest guns afloat, and was
laid out with two faces, one looking seaward, close to 2000 yards long,
and the other about one third that length, looking northward up the
narrow sand peninsula, formerly called Federal Point but renamed Confederate Point by the secessionists when they began work on the place
in 1861. Defended by a total of 47 guns and mortars, including a
battery posted atop a sixty-foot mound thrown up at the south end of
the seaward face to provide for delivering plunging fire if the enemy
ventured close, the fort seemed all but impossible to reduce by regular
methods; nor could the ships run past it, as had been done at New
Orleans and Mobile, since that would merely cram them into Cape
Fear River, sitting ducks for the rebel cannoneers, who would only
have to reverse their guns to blow the intruders out of the water. Porter
however had in mind a highly irregular method in which by now he
placed great faith. This was the ingenious Butler's powder ship, brought
along in tow from Norfolk and primed at Beaufort for the cataclysmic
explosion the squint-eyed general claimed would abolish Fort Fisher
between two ticks of his watch.

Porter was inclined to agree, though less emphatically, having
made a close inspection of the floating bomb. She was, or had been,
the U.S.S. *Louisiana*, an overaged iron gunboat of close to three hundred
tons, stripped of her battery and part of her deckhouse to lighten her
draft and make her resemble a blockade runner. In a canvas-roofed
framework built amidships, as well as in her bunkers and on her berth
deck — all above the water line, for maximum shock effect — 215
tons of powder had been stored and fuzed with three clockwork
devices, regulated to fire simultaneously an hour and a half after they
were activated. The plan was for a skeleton crew to run the vessel in
close to shore, anchor her as near as her eight-foot draft would allow
to the seaward face of the fort on the beach, set the timing mechanisms,
then pull hard away in a boat to an escort steamer that would take them
well offshore to await the explosion; after which the fleet, poised twelve
miles out for safety from the blast, would close in and subject what was
left of the place to a heavy-caliber pounding, while troops were being
landed two miles up the peninsula to close in from the north. Some said
the result of setting off that much powder — which, after all, was more
than fifty times the amount used near Petersburg, five months ago, to

create the still-yawning Crater — would be the utter destruction of everything on or adjoining Federal or Confederate Point. Others — mainly demolition "experts," who as usual were skeptical of anything they themselves had not conceived — discounted such predictions, maintaining that the shock would probably be no worse than mild. "I take a mean between the two," Porter declared judiciously, "and think the effect of the explosion will be simply very severe, stunning men at a distance of three or four hundred yards, demoralizing them completely, and making them unable to stand for any length of time a fire from the ship. I think that the concussion will tumble magazines that are built on framework, and that the famous Mound will be among the things that were, and the guns buried beneath the ruins. I think that houses in Wilmington [eighteen miles away] will tumble to the ground and much demoralize the people, and I think if the rebels fight after the explosion they have more in them than I gave them credit for."

In the fort meantime, during what turned out to be a three-day blow, the garrison prepared to resist the attack it had known was coming ever since the huge assembly of Union warships bulged over the curve of the eastern horizon. Determined to hold ajar what he termed "the last gateway between the Confederate States and the outside world," Fort Fisher's commander, Colonel William Lamb, had at first had only just over 500 men for its defense, half the regular complement having been sent to oppose Sherman down in Georgia. Blockade runners kept coming and going all this time, however, under cover of the storm, and on December 21 — when four of the swift vessels made outward runs after nightfall, all successful in slipping through the cordon of blockaders off the coast — some 400 North Carolina militia showed up, followed two days later by 450 Junior Reserves, sixteen to eighteen years of age. This total of 1371 effectives, most of them green and a third of them boys, were all Lamb would have until the arrival of Hoke's division, which had begun leaving Richmond two days ago, detached by Lee in the emergency, but was delayed by its necessarily roundabout rail route through Danville, Greensboro, and Raleigh.

The gale subsided on the day the Junior Reserves marched in, December 23, and though the wind remained brisk all afternoon, the night that followed was clear and cold. Despite the heightened visibility, which greatly lengthened the odds against blockade runners, the fast steamer *Little Hattie*, completing her second run that month, made it in through the mouth of the Cape Fear River, shortly before midnight, and soon was tied up at the dock in Wilmington, unloading the valuable war goods she had exchanged in Nassau a week ago for her outbound cargo of cotton.

Although no one aboard knew it, she had overtaken and passed the *Louisiana* coming in, and the signals flashed from Fort Fisher in response to those from the *Hattie* were of great help to the skeleton crew on the powder ship, groping its way through the darkness toward the beach. Encouraged by improvement in the weather, Porter had ordered the doomed vessel in at 11 o'clock that night, and had also sent word to Beaufort for the transports to return at once for the landing next day. Lightless and silent, the *Louisiana* dropped anchor 250 yards offshore, just north of the fort, and her skipper, Commander A. C. Rhind — told by the admiral, "You may lose your life in this adventure, but the risk is worth the running. . . . The names of those connected with the expedition will be famous for all time to come" — started all three clockwork fuzes ticking at precisely twelve minutes short of midnight. Finally, before abandoning ship, he set fire to half a cord of pine knots piled in the after cabin on instructions from Porter, who had little faith in mechanical devices; after which Rhind and his handful of volunteers rowed in a small boat to the escort steamer waiting nearby to take them (hopefully) out of range of the explosion, due by then within about an hour. Now there was nothing left to do but wait.

Twelve miles out, crews of the nearly sixty warships watched and waited too, training all available glasses on the starlit stretch of beach in front of the rebel earthwork. Started at 11.48, the ticking fuzes should do their job at 1.18 in what by now was the morning of Christmas Eve; or so the watchers thought, until the critical moment came and went and there was no eruption. By then, however, the pinpoint of light from Rhind's fire in the after cabin had grown to a flickering glow, and Porter felt certain all 215 tons of powder would go as soon as the flames reached the nearest keg. He was right, of course, though the wait was hard. 1.30: 1.35: 1.40: then it came — a huge instantaneous bloom of light, so quickly smothered in dust and smoke you could almost doubt you'd seen it. Just under one minute later the sound arrived; a low, heavy boom, a *New York Times* reporter was to say, "not unlike that produced by the discharge of a 100-pounder." Moreover, there seemed to be no accompanying shock wave, only the one deep cough or rumble, and a colleague aboard the press boat saw a gigantic cloud of thick black smoke appear on the landward horizon, sharply defined against the stars and the clear sky. "As it rose rapidly in the air, and came swiftly toward us on the wings of the wind," he later wrote, "[it] presented a most remarkable appearance, assuming the shape of a monstrous waterspout, its tapering base seemingly resting on the sea. In a very few minutes it passed us, filling the atmosphere with its sulphurous odor, as if a spirit from the infernal regions had swept by us."

If this was anticlimactic — which in fact was to put the measure of Porter's disappointment rather mildly — what followed, over the course of the next two days, was even more so. Subsequent testimony would show that, while there were those who claimed to have felt the shock as far away as Beaufort, the monster explosion had done the fort no damage whatever, producing no more than a gentle rocking motion, as if the earth had twitched briefly in its sleep. A sentinel on duty at the time made a guess to the man who relieved him that one of the Yankee ships offshore had blown her boiler. Many in the garrison, veterans and greenhorns alike, said later that they had not been awakened by the blast, though this was denied by one of the boy soldiers, captured next day in an outlying battery. "It was terrible," he said. "It woke up nearly everybody in the fort." Daylight showed no remaining vestige of the *Louisiana*, but Fort Fisher was unchanged, its flag rippling untattered in the breeze. Only in one respect did Butler's experiment work, even approximately, and that was in the disguise he had contrived for the vanished powder vessel. Lamb recorded in his diary that morning: "A blockader got aground near the fort, set fire to herself, and blew up."

Porter spent the morning absorbing the shock of failure, then steamed in at noon to begin the heaviest naval bombardment of the war to date. Capable of firing 115 shells a minute, his 627 guns heaved an estimated 10,000 heavy-caliber rounds at Fort Fisher in the course of the next five hours, to which the fort replied with 622, though neither seriously impaired the fighting efficiency of the other. Ashore, two guns were dismounted, one man killed, 22 injured, and most of the living quarters flattened, while the fleet lost 83 dead and wounded, more than half of them mangled by the explosion of five new hundred-pounder Parrotts on five of the sloops and frigates. Near sunset, Butler finally showed up with a few transports. The rest would soon be along, he said: much to Porter's disgust, for the day by then was too far gone for a landing. Disgruntled, the admiral signaled a cease fire.

As the ships withdrew, guns cooling, the fort boomed out a single defiant shot, the last. "Our Heavenly Father has protected my garrison this day," Lamb wrote in his diary that night, "and I feel that He will sustain us in defending our homes from the invader."

By 10.30 next morning — Christmas Day and a Sunday — the fleet was back on station, lobbing still more thousands of outsized projectiles into the sand fort. Three hours later, three miles up the way, just over 2000 soldiers were put ashore under Major General Godfrey Weitzel, second in command to Butler, who observed the landing from his flagship, a sea-going tug which he kept steaming back and forth in front of the beach while the troops were moving southward down it, capturing a one-gun outwork when they got within a mile of Fort Fisher's landward face. Porter maintained a methodical fire — mainly to make the defenders keep their heads down, since he believed he had done all necessary damage to their works the day before. Reports from Weitzel, however, showed that this was far from true. Approaching the fort, his men received volleys of canister full in their faces, and it soon developed that the final hundred yards of ground was planted thickly with torpedoes wired to detonator switches which rebel lookouts could throw whenever they judged an explosion would be most effective. Moreover, prisoners taken on the approach march bragged that Hoke's division, 6000 strong, was expected to arrive at any minute on the road from Wilmington, hard in the Federal rear. Butler weighed the evidence, along with signs that the rising wind would soon make it impossible for boats to return through the booming surf, and promptly ordered a withdrawal by all ashore. "In view of the threatening aspect of the weather," he signaled Porter when two thirds of Weitzel's men had been reloaded — the other third, some 700 wet and cold unfortunates for whom this holy day was anything but merry, were stranded when the breakers grew too rough for taking them off — "I caused the troops with their prisoners to re-embark." Seeing, as he said, "nothing further that can be done by the land forces," he announced: "I shall therefore sail for Hampton Roads as soon as the transport fleet can be got in order."

Fairly beside himself with rage at this unceremonious abandonment of the supposedly joint effort, Porter kept up a nightlong interdictory fire to protect "those poor devils of soldiers," whose rifles he could hear popping on the beach. Next afternoon, when the wind changed direction, he managed to get them off, thereby limiting the army's loss to one man drowned and 15 wounded — a total clearly indicative of something less than an all-out try for the fort's reduction. Butler by then was on his way to Norfolk, however, and the admiral had no choice except to retire as well, though only as far as Beaufort, withdrawing his ships a few at a time, that night and the following morning, so that Fort Fisher's defenders would not be able to claim a mass repulse.

Nevertheless: "This morning, December 27, the foiled and frightened enemy left our shore," Lamb wired Wilmington, where Hoke's veterans were at last unloading from their long train ride. The garrison had in fact had a harder time than Porter knew, losing 70 men in the second day's bombardment, which, though less intense, had been far more accurate than the first. "Never since the foundation of the world was there such a fire," a Confederate lieutenant testified. "The whole interior of the fort ... was one 11-inch shell bursting. You can now inspect the works and walk on nothing but iron." Lamb began repairing the damage without delay, knowing only too well that the Yankees would soon return, perhaps next time with an army commander willing to press the issue beyond pistol range of the sand walls.

That was just what Porter had in mind now that his fleet was reassembled at Beaufort, replenishing its stores and ammunition. Moreover, he could see at least one good proceeding from the abortive Yuletide expedition. "If this temporary failure succeeds in sending General Butler into private life, it is not to be regretted," he wrote

Welles, "for it cost only a certain amount of shells, which I expend in a month's target practice anyhow."

Grant was of the same opinion in regard to the need for a change when the effort against Fort Fisher was renewed, as he certainly intended it to be. "The Wilmington expedition has proven a gross and culpable failure," he informed Lincoln on December 28, adding: "Who is to blame I hope will be known." A wire to Porter, two days later, indicated that he had already decided on a cure. "Please hold on where you are for a few days," he requested, "and I will endeavor to be back again with an increased force and without the former commander."

His concern was based on a number of developments. First, because it had been determined that Sherman would march north through the Carolinas, Grant saw Wilmington as an ideal place of refuge, easily provisioned and protected by the navy, in case the rebels somehow managed to gang up on his red-haired friend. Second, he believed that a full report on the recent fiasco would provide him with excellent grounds for getting rid of Ben Butler, whose political heft was unlikely to stand him in nearly as good stead with the Administration now that the election had been won. Third — and no one who knew Grant would think it least — he was no more inclined than ever to accept a setback; especially now, when so many welcome reports were clicking off the wire at City Point from all directions, indicating that the end of the struggle was by no means as far off as it had seemed a short while back.

One of the most welcome of these came from George Stoneman, exchanged since his late-July capture down in Georgia and recently given command of all the cavalry in Northeast Tennessee. Anxious to retrieve his reputation, he set out from Knoxville on December 10 with 5500 troopers in an attempt to reach and wreck the salt and lead mines in Southwest Virginia, so long the object of raids that had come to nothing up to now. Beyond Kingsport, three days later, he brushed aside the remnant of Morgan's once-terrible men, still grieved by the loss of their leader three months before, and pressed on through Bristol, across the state line to Abingdon, where he drove off a small force of graybacks posted in observation by Breckinridge, whose main body, down to a strength of about 1200, was at Saltville, less than twenty miles ahead. Stoneman bypassed him for a lunge at Marion, twelve miles up the Virginia & Tennessee Railroad, obliging Breckinridge to back-pedal in an effort to save the vital lead works there and at Wytheville. This he did, by means of a fast march and a daylong skirmish on December 18; but while the fighting was in progress Stoneman sent half his horsemen back to undefended Saltville, with instructions to get started on the wreckage that was the true purpose of the expedition. Reuniting his raiders there next day, after giving Breckinridge the slip, he spent another two days completing the destruction of the salt works, then withdrew on December 21. Back in Knoxville by the end of the year, he could report complete success. Salt had been scarce in the Old Dominion for two years. Now it would be practically nonexistent, leaving the suppliers of Lee's army with no means of preserving what little meat they could lay hands on for shipment by rail or wagon to the hungry men in the trenches outside Petersburg and Richmond.

Sheridan too had not been idle during this period of stepped-up Federal activity, coincident with Thomas's pursuit of Hood and Sherman's occupation of Savannah. While the greater part of his army continued its impoverishment of the people in the Shenandoah region by the destruction of their property and goods — a scourging process he defined as "letting them know there is a God in Israel" — he launched a two-pronged strike, by three divisions of cavalry, at military targets beyond the rim of his immediate depredations. Torbert, with 5500 horsemen in two divisions, would aim for Gordonsville and the Virginia Central, east of the Blue Ridge, while Custer diverted attention from this main effort by taking his 2500-man division south up the Valley Pike for a raid on Staunton, which if successful could be continued to Lynchburg and the Orange & Alexandria. Both left their camps around Winchester on December 19, Torbert riding through Chester Gap next morning to cross the Rapidan two days later at Liberty Mills. Apparently Custer had decoyed Early's troopers westward from their position near Rockfish Gap, just east of Staunton, for there was no sign of them as the blue column approached Gordonsville after dark. There was, however, a barricade thrown up by local defenders to block a narrow pass within three miles of town, and Torbert chose to wait for daylight, December 23, before deciding whether to storm or outflank it. Alas, he then found it would be unwise to attempt either. Warned of his approach, Lee had detached a pair of veteran brigades from Longstreet, north of the James, and hurried them by rail to Gordonsville the night before. "After becoming fully satisfied of the presence of infantry," Torbert afterwards reported, "I concluded it was useless to make a further attempt to break the Central Railroad." Instead, he withdrew and made a roundabout return march, through Madison Courthouse and Warrenton, to Winchester on December 28.

Custer by then had been back five days, having done only too good a job of attracting Early's attention. In camp the second night, nine miles from Harrisonburg, he was attacked before reveille, December 21, by Rosser's cavalry division, which Early had sent to intercept him a day's march short of Staunton. Driven headlong, Custer kept going northward down the pike, abandoning the raid, and returned to his starting point next day. Between them, he and Torbert had lost about 150 killed or wounded or captured, exclusive of some 230 of Custer's men severely frostbitten during their fast rides out and back. He would have stayed and fought, he informed Sheridan — he would never be flat whipped till Little Big Horn, twelve years later — except for a shortage of rations and "my unprepared state to take charge of a large body of wounded, particularly under the inclement state of the weather. In addition," he said, straight-faced, "I was convinced that if it was decided to return, the sooner my return was accomplished the better it would be for my command."

Grant was not inclined to censure anyone involved: least of all Sheridan, who had exercised his aggressive proclivities in weather most generals would have considered fit for nothing but sitting around campfires, toasting their toes and swapping yarns. Moreover, hard as the two-pronged raid had been on Union horseflesh, not to mention the blue riders' frost-nipped hands and feet and noses — 258 of Torbert's mounts had broken down completely in the course of his ten-day outing — it had no doubt been even harder on the scantly clad Confederates and their crowbait nags, which would be that much worse off when spring unfroze the roads and northern troopers came pounding down them, rapid-fire carbines at the ready. That too was a gain, perhaps comparable in its future effect to Stoneman's descent on Saltville, and the two together fit nicely into the year-end victory pattern whose larger pieces were supplied by Thomas and Sherman, in Tennessee and Georgia, as well as by Pleasonton and Curtis out in the Transmississippi, where the last of Price's fugitive survivors came limping into Laynesport this week, in time for a far-from-Merry Christmas.

Now that all these pieces were coming together into a pattern, West and East, even those who had cried out loudest against Grant as "a bull-headed Suvarov" — a commander who relied on strength, and strength alone, to make up for his lack of military talent — could see the effects of the plan he had devised nine months ago, before launching the synchronized offensive that had re-split the South and was now about to go to work on the sundered halves.

With mounting excitement, though not without occasional stretches of doubt and fret at the lack of progress in front or back of Richmond, Atlanta, and Nashville, Lincoln had watched the pattern emerge with increasing clarity, until he saw at last in these year-end triumphs the fruits of the hands-off policy he had followed in all but the times of greatest strain. Sherman's wire — "I beg to present you, as a Christmas gift, the city of Savannah" — reached Washington on Christmas Eve, and the President released it for publication Christmas morning, pleased to share this gift with the whole country. Next day, when John Logan called at the White House, back from Louisville and on his way down the coast to resume command of his XV Corps, Lincoln gave him a letter for delivery to Sherman, expressing his thanks for the timely gift and restating his intention not to interfere with the actions or decisions of commanders in the field.

"When you were about leaving Atlanta for the Atlantic coast, I was anxious, if not fearful," he admitted, "but feeling that you were the better judge, and remembering that 'nothing risked, nothing gained,' I did not interfere. Now, the undertaking being a success, the honor is all yours; for I believe none of us went further than to acquiesce. And taking the work of General Thomas into the count, as it should be taken, it is indeed a great success. Not only does it afford the obvious and immediate military advantage, but in showing to the world that your army could be divided, putting the stronger part to an important new service, and yet leaving enough to vanquish the old opposing force of the whole — Hood's army — it brings those who sat in darkness to see a great light. But what next? I suppose it will be safer if I leave General Grant and yourself to decide."

Other duties, more clerkly in nature, had continued to require his attention as Commander in Chief throughout this final month of the year. One was the approval of a general order, December 2, removing Rosecrans from command of the Department of the Missouri and replacing him with Grenville Dodge, who had recovered by then from the head wound he had suffered near Atlanta in mid-August. Old Rosy had enjoyed no more success than his predecessors had done in reconciling the various "loyal" factions in that guerilla-torn region, and now he was gone from the war for good. Another departure, under happier circumstances, was made by Farragut, who left Mobile Bay aboard the *Hartford* about that same time, and dropped anchor December 13 in the Brooklyn Navy Yard. Like his flagship, soon to go into dry dock, the old man was in need of repairs, having declined command of the Fort Fisher expedition on a plea of failing health. "My flag [was] hauled down at sunset," he informed Welles a week later. As it turned out, he and the *Hartford* ended their war service together, though there was no end to the honors that came his way. Two days later, on December 22, Congress passed a bill creating the rank of vice admiral, and Lincoln promptly conferred it on the Tennessee-born sailor, who thus became the nation's first to hold that rank, just as he had been its first rear admiral. To crown his good with creature comforts, a group of New York merchants got up and presented to him, on the last day of the year, a gift of $50,000 in government bonds. "The citizens of New York can offer no tribute equal to your claims on their gratitude and affection," an accompanying letter read. "Their earnest desire is to receive you as one of their number, and to be permitted, as fellow citizens, to share in the renown you will bring to the Metropolitan City."

Two other events of a more or less military nature, widely separated in space but provoking simultaneous reactions, engaged the attention of the public and the President at this time. One was a late-

November attempt by a group of eight Confederate agents, operating out of Canada, to terrorize New York City by setting fire to a score of hotels with four-ounce bottles of Greek Fire, similar to those used at St Albans the month before. In the early evening of November 25, nineteen fires were started within a single hour, but they burned with nothing like the anticipated fury, apparently because the supposedly sympathetic local chemist had concocted a weak mixture, either to lengthen his profit or, as one agent later said, to "put up a job on us after it was found that we could not be dissuaded from our purpose." In any case, firemen doused the flames rather easily, except at Barnum's Museum, a target of opportunity, where bales of hay for the animals blazed spectacularly for a time. All the arsonists escaped save one, who was picked up afterwards in Michigan, trying to make it back to Toronto, and returned to Fort Lafayette for execution in the spring. Though the damage was minor, as it turned out, the possibilities were frightening enough. Federal authorities could see in the conspiracy a forecast of what might be expected in the months ahead, when the rebels grew still more desperate over increasing signs that their war could not be won on the field of battle.

The other semi-military event occurred four days later in the Colorado Territory, 1500 miles away. Indians throughout much of the West had been on the rampage for the past three years, seeing in the white man's preoccupation with his tribal war back East an opportunity for the red man to return to his old free life, roving the plains and prairies, and perhaps exact, as he did so, a measure of bloody satisfaction for the loss of his land in exchange for promises no sooner made than broken. When John Pope took over in Minnesota two years ago, hard on the heels of his Bull Run defeat, he put down one such uprising by the Santee Sioux, in which more than 400 soldiers and settlers had been killed, and had the survivors arraigned before a drumhead court that sentenced 303 of them to die for murder, rape, and arson. Reviewing the sentences, despite a warning from the governor that the people of Minnesota would take "private revenge" if there was any interference on his part, Lincoln cut the list to 38 of "the more guilty and influential of the culprits." Hanged at Mankato on the day after Christmas, 1862, wearing paint and feathers and singing their death song with the ropes about their necks, these 38 still comprised the largest mass execution the country had ever staged. Now two years later, farther west in Colorado, there was another — a good deal less formal, lacking even a scaffold, let alone a trial, but larger and far bloodier — in which the President had no chance to interfere, since it was over before he had any way of knowing it was in progress.

Colonel John M. Chivington, a former Methodist preacher and a veteran of the New Mexico campaign, rode out of Denver in mid-November with 600 Colorado Volunteers, raised for the sole purpose, as he said, of killing Indians "whenever and wherever found." The pickings were rather slim until he reached Fort Lyon, sixty miles from the Kansas border, and learned that 600 Cheyennes and Arapahoes were camped on Sand Creek, forty miles northeast. They had gathered there the month before, after a parley with the governor, and had been promised security by the fort commander on their word, truthful or not, that they had taken no part in recent depredations elsewhere in the territory. Chivington did not believe them, but it would not have mattered if he had. "I have come to kill Indians," he announced on arrival, "and believe it is right and honorable to use any means under God's heaven to kill Indians." Asked if this included women, he replied that it did. And children? "Nits make lice," he said.

He left Fort Lyon early the following evening, November 28, reinforced by a hundred troopers from the garrison, on a wintry all-night ride that brought the 700-man column and its four mountain howitzers within reach of the objective before dawn. Two thirds of them squaws and children — most of the braves of fighting age were off hunting buffalo, several miles to the east — the Indians lay sleeping in their lodges, pitched in a bend of the creek at their back. They knew nothing of the attack until it burst upon them, aimed first at the herd of ponies to make certain there would be no horseback escape in the confusion soon to follow. It did follow, and the slaughter was indiscriminate. The soldiers closed in from three sides of the camp, pressing toward the center where the terrified people gathered under a large American flag that flew from the lodgepole of a Cheyenne chief, Black Kettle, who had received it earlier that year, as a token of friendship and protection, from the Commissioner of Indian Affairs. He displayed it now, along with a white flag raised amid the smoke of the attack. Both were ignored. "It may perhaps be unnecessary for me to state that I captured no prisoners," Chivington would report. He claimed between four and five hundred killed, all warriors; but that was exaggeration. A body count showed 28 men dead, including three chiefs, and 105 women and children. The attackers lost 9 killed and 38 wounded, most of them hit in the crossfire. By way of retaliation, or perhaps out of sheer exuberance, the soldiers moved among the dead and dying with their knives, lifting scalps and removing private parts to display as trophies of the raid. Then they pulled out. Behind them, the surviving Indians scattered on the plains, some to die of their wounds and exposure, others to spend what remained of their lives killing white men.

This too — the Sand Creek Massacre — was part of America's Civil War, and as such, like so much else involved, would have its repercussions down the years. For one thing, Chivington's coup discredited every Cheyenne or Arapahoe chief (and, for that matter, every Sioux or Kiowa or Comanche) who had spoken for peace with the white man: including Black Kettle, who, in addition to the bright-striped flag, had been given a medal by Lincoln himself for his efforts in that direction. Moreover, when the buffalo-hunting braves returned and saw the mutilations practiced by the soldiers on their people — fathers and sons, mothers and daughters, wives and sisters — they swore to serve their enemy in the same fashion when the tables were turned, as they soon would be, in the wake of a hundred skirmishes and ambuscades. Nor was that the only emulation. There were those in and out of the region who approved of Chivington's tactics as the best, if not indeed the only, solution to the problem of clearing the way for the settlers and the railroads: Sheridan, for example, who took them as a guide, some four years later, in pursuing a policy summed up in the dictum: "The only good Indian is a dead Indian."

News of these and other late-November developments found Lincoln hard at work on the year-end message his secretary would deliver at a joint meeting of the House and Senate on December 6, the day after Congress began its second session. Otherwise, much of the month that followed his reëlection — the first ever won by a free-state President — was spent in putting his political house in order. In addition to paying off, as best he could with the limited number of posts at his disposal, the debts he had contracted in the course of the campaign, this meant a clearing up of administrative business that had hung fire while the outcome was in doubt, including the retirement and replacement of a long-time cabinet member, as well as the appointment of a new Chief Justice.

The cabinet member was Attorney General Edward Bates, a septuagenarian old-line Democrat of a type still fairly common in Washington, but getting rarer year by year as the new breed of office-holders settled in. For some time now the Missourian had been feeling out of step with the society around him, out of place among his radical cohorts, and out of touch with the leader who had summoned him here, four years ago, to play a role he found increasingly distasteful. Decrying the "pestilent doctrines" of the ultras, right and left, and complaining in a letter to a friend of "how, in times like these, the minds of men are made dizzy and their imaginations are wrought up to a frenzy by the whirl of events," Bates believed he saw the cause of the disruption: "When the public cauldron is heated into violent ebulition, it is sure to throw up from the bottom some of its dirtiest dregs, which, but for the heat and agitation, would have lain embedded in congenial filth in the lowest stratum of society. But once boiled up to the top they expand into foam and froth, [and] dance frantically before the gaping crowd, often concealing for a time the whole surface of the agitated mass." He was disillusioned, he was disillusioned and bitter; he was, in short, a casualty of this war. He had to go, and on December 1, the election safely over, he went. Lincoln found a replacement in another Border State lawyer-politician, James Speed of Kentucky. Now only

Seward and Welles remained of the original cabinet slate drawn up in Springfield.

Another source of disappointment for Bates, now on his way home to Missouri, was Lincoln's rejection of his application to succeed Roger Taney as Chief Justice, and it was no great consolation that others with the same ambition—Montgomery Blair and Edwin Stanton, for two— were similarly passed over in favor of still a fourth one-time cabinet member: Salmon Chase. The eighty-seven-year-old Taney—appointed as John Marshall's successor by Andrew Jackson in 1836, nine Presidents ago—died in mid-October, following a long illness. Hated as he was by abolitionists for his Dred Scott decision, and scorned by most liberals for several others since, when he fell sick and seemed about to pass from the scene ahead of James Buchanan, Ben Wade prayed hard that he would live long enough for Lincoln to name his successor. As a result, the Marylander not only survived Buchanan's term, he seemed likely to outlast Lincoln's. "Damned if I didn't overdo it," Wade exclaimed. Then in October, perhaps in answer to supplementary prayers sent up on the eve of what might be a victory for McClellan, the old man died. Chase was the party favorite for the vacant seat at the head of the Court, his views being sound on such issues as emancipation, summary arrests, and a number of controversial financial measures he had adopted as Treasury chief; but Lincoln took his time about naming a replacement. The election was less than four weeks off, and delay ensured Chase's continued fervent support—as well as Blair's. Moreover, here was one last chance to watch the Ohioan squirm, a prospect Lincoln had always enjoyed as retribution for unsuccessful backstairs politics. "I know meaner things about Mr Chase than any of these men can tell me," he remarked after talking to callers who objected to the appointment on personal grounds. One day his secretary brought in a letter from Chase. "What is it about?" Lincoln asked, having no time just then to read it. "Simply a kind and friendly letter," Nicolay replied. Lincoln smiled and made a brief gesture of dismissal, saying: "File it with his other recommendations." All the same, and with the uncertain hope (in vain, as it turned out) that this would cure at last the gnawing of the presidential grub in Chase's bosom, he sent to the Senate on December 6, four weeks after election, his nomination of "Salmon P. Chase of Ohio, to be Chief Justice of the Supreme Court of the United States vice Roger B. Taney, deceased." He wrote it out in his own hand, signing his name in full, as he only did for the most important documents, and the Senate confirmed the appointment promptly, without discussion or previous reference to committee.

On that same day, the President's fourth December message was read to the assembled Congress. Primarily a report on foreign relations and the national welfare, about which it went into considerable diplomatic and financial details furnished by Seward and Fessenden, the text made little mention of the war being fought in the field, except to state that "our arms have steadily advanced." But in it Lincoln spoke beyond the heads of his immediate listeners — albeit through the voice of Nicolay, who delivered it for him at the joint session — to the people of the South, much as he had done at his inauguration, just under four years ago, when he addressed them as "my dissatisfied countrymen." Now he had reason to believe that their dissatisfaction extended in quite a different direction, and he bore down on that, first by demonstrating statistically the emptiness of all hope for a Federal collapse or let-up. Pointing to the heavy vote in the recent election, state by northern state, as proof "that we have more men now than we had when the war began; that we are not exhausted, nor in process of exhaustion; that we are gaining strength, and may, if need be, maintain the contest indefinitely," he declared flatly that the national resources, in materials as in manpower, "are unexhausted, and, as we believe, inexhaustible." So, too, was the resolution of the northern people "unchanged, and, as we believe, unchangeable," to an extent that altogether ruled out a negotiated settlement. Previously he had avoided public reference to Jefferson Davis, making it his policy to pretend that the Mississippian was invisible at best. Now this changed. He spoke openly of his adversary, though still not by name, referring to him rather as "the insurgent leader," and pronounced him unapproachable except on his own inadmissable terms. "He would accept nothing short of severance of the Union," Lincoln pointed out: "precisely what we will not and cannot give. His declarations to this effect are explicit and oft repeated. He does not attempt to deceive us. He affords us no excuse to deceive ourselves. . . . Between him and us the issue is distinct, simple, and inflexible. It is an issue which can only be tried by war, and decided by victory. If we yield, we are beaten; if the Southern people fail him, he is beaten. Either way, it would be the victory and defeat following war." This did not mean, however, that those who followed Davis could not accept what he rejected. "Some of them, we know, already desire peace and reunion," Lincoln said. "The number of such may increase. They can, at any moment, have peace simply by laying down their arms and submitting to the national authority under the Constitution. After so much, the government could not, if it would, maintain war against them."

He spoke in this connection of "pardons and remissions of forfeiture," these being things within his right to grant, but he added frankly that there was much else "beyond the Executive power to adjust," including "the admission of members into Congress, and whatever might require the appropriation of money." Nor did he sugar his offer, or advice, with any concession on other matters: least of all on the slavery issue. Not only would the Emancipation Proclamation stand, he also urged in the course of his message the adoption of a proposed amendment to the Constitution abolishing slavery throughout the United States. It had nearly passed in the last session, and would surely pass in the next, whose Republican majority had been increased by last month's election; "And as it is to so go, at all events, may we not agree that the sooner the better?" Above all, he wanted to speak clearly, both to his friends and to his present foes, and he did so in a final one-sentence paragraph addressed to those beyond the wide-flung line of battle: "In stating a single condition of peace, I mean simply to say that the war will cease on the part of the government whenever it shall have ceased on the part of those who began it."

All this he said, or Nicolay said for him, on December 6. The next ten days were crowded with good news: first from Georgia, where Sherman reached the coast at last, so little worn by his long march that he scarcely paused before he stormed Fort McAllister to make contact with the navy waiting off the mouth of the Ogeechee: then from Middle Tennessee, where Thomas crushed Hood's left, in front of Nashville, and flung him into full retreat with the loss of more than fifty guns. Lincoln responded by tightening the screws. In late November the War Department had done its part by lowering the minimum standard height for recruits to "five feet, instead of five feet three as heretofore." Now the Commander in Chief followed through, December 19 — Sherman by then had closed in on Savannah, which Hardee would evacuate next day — by issuing another of his by now familiar calls for "300,000 more," this time presumably including men who were not much taller than the Springfields they would shoulder. Privately, moreover, Stanton assured Grant that still another 200,000 troops would be called up in March if those netted by the current proclamation did not suffice to "close out Lee."

Success, as usual, fostered impatience and evoked a sense of urgency: especially in Lincoln, who had read with pleasure a message Grant sent Sherman after the fall of Atlanta, just under four months ago: "We want to keep the enemy pressed to the end of the war. If we give him no peace whilst the war lasts, the end cannot be distant." Sherman then had marched to the sea, eastward across the Confederate heartland, and after taking Savannah, bloodlessly though at the cost of having its garrison escape, obtained approval for a follow-up march north through the Carolinas. He was preparing for it now. "I do not think I can employ better strategy than I have hitherto done," he wrote Halleck on the last day of the year: "namely, make a good ready and then move rapidly to my objective, avoiding a battle at points where I would be encumbered by my wounded, but striking boldly and quickly when my objective is reached." Lincoln liked the sound of that, much as he had enjoyed Grant's hustling tone in the Atlanta dispatch. But when Stanton set out the following week, on a trip down the coast to confer with the red-haired commander, it occurred to the impatient President that if the Westerners were to come up hard and fast to join in putting the final squeeze on Lee, there had perhaps not been enough stress on the advantage of an early start. Accordingly, he got off a reminding wire to that effect. "While General Sherman's 'get a good ready' is appreciated, and is not to be overlooked," he told the Secretary, "*Time,* now that the enemy is wavering, is more important than ever."

His advice to the southern people, tendered in the December message to Congress, had been more grim than conciliatory; they need only reject their "insurgent leader ... by laying down their arms," and he would do what he could for them in the way of "pardons and remissions." Since then, however, the news from Nashville and Savannah had encouraged him to believe that the hour was near when they would no longer have any choice in the matter, if only he could provoke in his generals the sense of urgency he was convinced would end the rebellion in short order, and he said as much in the wire that followed Stanton down the coast. Now that their adversary was "on the downhill, and somewhat confused," he wanted the Secretary to impress on Sherman the importance of "keeping him going."

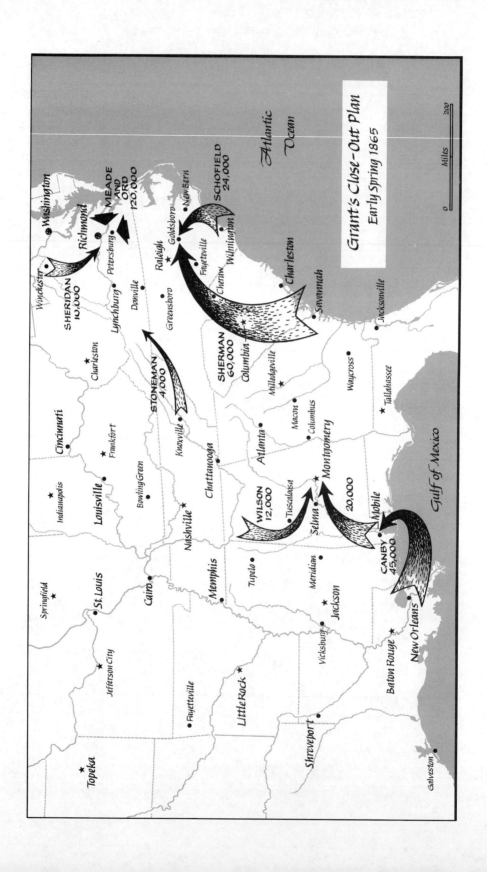

Grant's Close-Out Plan
Early Spring 1865

MEADE
AND
ORD
120,000

SCHOFIELD
24,000

SHERIDAN
10,000

SHERMAN
60,000

STONEMAN
4,000

WILSON
12,000

20,000

CANBY
45,000

Atlantic Ocean

Gulf of Mexico

Washington
Richmond
Petersburg
Winchester
Lynchburg
Danville
Greensboro
Raleigh
Goldsboro
New Bern
Fayetteville
Wilmington
Cheraw
Charleston
Columbia
Milledgeville
Savannah
Charleston
Jacksonville
Tallahassee
Waycross
Macon
Columbus
Montgomery
Atlanta
Knoxville
Chattanooga
Selma
Tuscaloosa
Mobile
Meridian
Jackson
Tupelo
Nashville
Memphis
Bowling Green
Frankfort
Cincinnati
Louisville
Indianapolis
Springfield
St. Louis
Cairo
Jefferson City
Fayetteville
Little Rock
Vicksburg
Shreveport
Baton Rouge
New Orleans
Galveston
Topeka

0   Miles   200

A Tightening Noose

★ ✗ ☆

TECUMSEH SHERMAN SHEATHED HIS CLAWS
for the occupation of Savannah. Not only did he retain the city's elected
officials at their posts, conducting business more or less as usual; he even
allowed Episcopal ministers to omit from their services the traditional
prayer for God to "behold and bless" the President of the United States.
"Jeff Davis and the devil both need it," he remarked, implying that
Abraham Lincoln didn't. Meantime he kept a restraining hand on the
veterans he had described, on the eve of their arrival, as "burning to
avenge the national wrong." Geary's division garrisoned the town —
milder-mannered Easterners for the most part, whose commander, ex-
ercising talents he had developed as mayor of San Francisco a decade
back, tempered discipline with compassion. He hauled in firewood to
warm the hearths and hearts of citizens, reopened markets for the sale
of farm goods, and encouraged public meetings at which, in time, a vote
of thanks was tendered "the noble Geary" and a resolution was adopted
urging Governor Brown to call a state convention for peace discussions.
Savannah's people knew that this was basically Sherman's doing, and all
in all the consensus was that the red-haired conqueror, whose coming
they had so greatly feared while he drew nearer mile by smoky mile,
had been maligned by editors whose views were printed in regions he
had not visited, so far. If not benign, he proved at any rate forbearing, and
certainly not the apocalyptic monster they had been told to expect before
he landed in their midst.

He himself was rather amused, seeing in all this a parallel to the
behavior in far-off Natchez, well over two years ago, of propertied
Confederates who found in coöperation a hope for the preservation, if
not of their treasured way of life, then in any case of their fine old
homes: an inducement altogether lacking, incidentally, in such new-
rich towns as Vicksburg and Atlanta, whose defiance was characterized
as an outgrowth of their war-boom attitude. He could chuckle over that,

referring to Savannah's mayor, Dr Richard D. Arnold, as "completely 'subjugated.' " But there was little of amusement in the reaction of those editors who had warned of his savage nature. "A dangerous bait to deaden the spirit of resistance in other places," the Richmond *Examiner* said of this pretended mildness down the coast, and the rival *Dispatch* was even more specific that same day, January 7, in exposing the duplicity being practiced. "Sherman seems to have changed his character as completely as the serpent changes his skin with the approach of spring," the Virginia editor observed, and then discerned a likeness in the general to an animal just as sneaky in its way, but considerably more voracious: "His repose, however, is the repose of the tiger. Let him taste blood once more and he will be as brutal as ever."

In point of fact, there were sounder grounds for this suppositional metaphor than anyone had any way of knowing without access to certain letters the Ohioan was sending and receiving through this period of rest and preparation. "Should you capture Charleston," Halleck wrote on learning that the Carolina march had been approved, "I hope that by *some accident* the place may be destroyed, and if a little salt should be sown upon its site it may prevent the growth of future crops of nullification and secession." Sherman's plan was not to move on Charleston, "a mere desolated wreck . . . hardly worth the time it would take to starve it out," but rather to feint simultaneously at that point and Augusta, respectively on the right and left of his true line of march, and strike instead at Columbia, the capital between. However, he told Halleck, "I will bear in mind your hint as to Charleston, and do not think 'salt' will be necessary. When I move, the XV Corps" — Logan's: the Illinois soldier-politician returned to duty January 8, bringing Lincoln's congratulatory thank-you note along — "will be on the right of the right wing, and their position will naturally bring them into Charleston first. . . . If you have watched the history of that corps, you will have remarked that they generally do their work pretty well."

Nor was that the worst of it, by far. For all the alarm rebel editors felt on contemplating the repose of the tiger in coastal Georgia, they would have been a great deal more disturbed, and with equal justification, if they had known what was in store for them throughout the rest of their country east of the Mississippi. Sherman's march to scourge the Carolinas on his way to gain Lee's rear, while altogether the heftiest, was by no means the only move Grant planned to make on the thousand-mile-wide chessboard he pored over in his tent at City Point. The time had come to close out the Confederacy entirely, he believed, and he proceeded accordingly. He did so, moreover, not without a measure of personal satisfaction, although this was incidental to his larger purpose. Benjamin Prentiss, John McClernand, Don Carlos Buell, William Rosecrans, all had incurred his displeasure in the course of his rise to the top of the military heap — with the result that, shelved or snubbed into retirement, they were all four out of the war. And so too now, to all effect, was George Thomas: or soon would be, so far at least as a share in the final victory was concerned. Idle since its mid-December triumph over Hood, his army was quite the largest force available for carrying out the peripheral work Grant had in mind, but the general-in-chief had no intention of exposing himself to another nerve-wracking span of trying to prod Old Slow Trot into motion. Instead he proposed to do to the Virginian, in the wake of the botched pursuit that followed Nashville, what Halleck had done to Grant himself after Shiloh and Vicksburg; to wit, dismember him. This he would do by dispersing his troops — some 46,000 of them, all told — leaving Thomas with barely a third of his present command to garrison Middle and East Tennessee and northern Alabama: a thankless assignment, unlikely to call for much fighting, if any, unless Lee somehow managed to get away westward, in which case Thomas would be expected to stand in his path while Meade and Sherman came up in his rear to accomplish his destruction.

Schofield was the first to be subtracted. In early January, expecting Fort Fisher to fall under renewed pressure from Porter and units already on the way back there from the Army of the James, Grant ordered the XXIII Corps detached from Thomas and hurried north and east, by boat and rail, to a point near Washington. There Schofield would put his 14,000 men aboard transports for a trip down the coast and a share in the follow-up drive on Wilmington, which then would be converted from a haven for blockade-runners to an intermediary refuge and supply base for Sherman, in case he ran into trouble slogging north. Otherwise, reinforced to a strength of 24,000 by troops from Foster and the Army of the James, Schofield was to move up the North Carolina littoral to occupied New Bern, where he would turn inland for a meeting with Sherman at Goldsboro, and from there the two columns would go on together — better than 80,000 strong — for the rest of the march, by way of Raleigh, into Virginia. Meade by then would have been joined by Sheridan from the Shenandoah Valley, and Grant would have well over 200,000 seasoned fighting men around Petersburg and Richmond: surely enough, and more than enough, as he put it, to "wipe out Lee." However, by way of encouraging further confusion in the region to be traversed, he also instructed Thomas to send Stoneman and 4000 troopers pounding eastward from Knoxville into North Carolina, where they would serve to distract the state's defenders while Sherman and Schofield were moving northward through it near the coast. This done, Stoneman too would cross into Virginia, where he would not only rip up Lee's supply lines west of Lynchburg, but would also perhaps be in position, when the time came, to get in on the kill.

That so much concerted havoc was about to be visited on the Carolinas and the Old Dominion did not mean that the Deep South was to be neglected or spared. No; Grant had plans for its disruption, too. In addition to Schofield's corps, shifted eastward in mid-January, he also ordered A. J. Smith's detached, along with a division of cavalry under Brigadier General Joseph Knipe, and sent by steamer down the Mississippi to New Orleans, where Edward Canby had gathered the survivors of last year's expedition up and down Red River. Smith's 16,000 veterans, most of whom had also had a share in that unfortunate adventure, would lift Canby's available strike force to a strength of 45,000 of all arms: enough, Grant thought, for him to undertake the long-deferred reduction of Mobile, which continued defiant, behind its outlying fortifications, despite the loss of its Bay and access to the Gulf. Moreover, that was only to be the first step in the campaign Grant proposed. Once the city fell (if not before; haste was to be the governing factor) Canby would move with a flying column of 20,000, mainly composed of Smith's free-swinging gorilla-guerillas, north and east into the heart of Alabama. Specifically he would proceed against Selma, the principal center for the production of munitions in that part of the country, where he would make contact — much as Sherman was to do with Schofield, six hundred miles to the northeast — with still another detachment from Thomas's fast-dwindling army up in Tennessee. In the weeks that followed the pursuit of Hood from Nashville, James Wilson had continued to mount, arm, and train incoming cavalry units at so rapid a rate that by the end of January he had no less than 22,000 troopers under his command. Knipe took 5000 of these to New Orleans with Smith, and Wilson presently was instructed to strike southward with 12,000 of the rest, sturdily mounted and armed to a man with repeaters that gave them more firepower than a corps of infantry. Forrest would no doubt attempt to interfere, as he had done before in such cases; Grant was willing to leave it to Wilson whether to avoid or run right over him, which he should be able to do rather easily, considering his advantage in numbers and equipment. In any case, his immediate objective would be Selma, where he would combine with Canby's flying column, after wrecking the manufactory installations there, to continue the heartland penetration eastward: first to Montgomery, the Confederacy's original capital, and then across the Georgia line to Columbus and Macon, all three of which had been spared till now the iron hand of war.

Such then was Grant's close-out plan. As he saw it, the Confederacy was already whipped and clinging groggily to the ring ropes; all that remained was for him to land what boxers called a one-two punch, delivered in rapid sequence to belly and jaw, except that this was to be thrown with both hands simultaneously. In broad outline, the design resembled the one he had worked out nearly a year ago, on taking command of all the armies of the Union, but this time he was not obliged to include any unwanted elements, such as the Red River venture, or any unwanted subordinates, such as Banks. For example, aside from maintaining garrisons within it to preserve the status quo, and gunboats on patrol along its watery flank to keep it cut off from all contact eastward, the Transmississippi had no share in his calculations; either it would wither on its own, from sheer neglect or folly such as Price's recent raid, or else he would attend to it in a similar undistracted fashion when the time came. Not only would this affordable neglect represent a considerable savings in troops who could be used where they were wanted, but the fact was he now had more of them than he had had when he began his forward movement, back in May. Despite heavy losses incurred in the past nine months — 100,000 in eastern Virginia alone, and about that number elsewhere — his total combat force, East and West, had grown to better than 600,000 effectives, exclusive of reserves amounting to half as many more; whereas the enemy's had dwindled to barely 160,000 of all arms. That too was part of his calculations, and part of his hope for an early end to the conflict which by now had cost the country — the two countries, Confederates insisted — close to a million casualties, on and off the field of battle, North and South.

Nowhere in all this was there any mention of an assignment for Ben Butler, and the reason was quite simple. He was no longer around. Grant had fired him; or at any rate — now that the election was safely over — had persuaded Lincoln to fire him. The one-time Democratic senator was out of the war for good.

Fort Fisher had been the final straw. Though Grant said nothing of the ineffectual powder-boat explosion or even of the precipitate withdrawal, when he had determined the facts in the case he wrote to Stanton requesting the Massachusetts general's removal. "I do this with reluctance," he declared, "but the good of the service requires it. In my absence General Butler necessarily commands, and there is a lack of confidence felt in his military ability, making him an unsafe commander for a large army. His administration of the affairs in his department is also objectionable." This was put aboard a fast packet at City Point on January 5, and when Grant found out next morning that Stanton was on his way to Savannah to visit Sherman, he followed it up with a telegram directly to the Commander in Chief. "I wrote a letter to the Secretary of War, which was mailed yesterday, asking to have General Butler removed from command. Learning that the Secretary left Washington yesterday, I telegraph asking you that prompt action may be taken in the matter."

Lincoln's response was prompt indeed. General Order Number 1, issued "by direction of the President of the United States," arrived by wire the following day. "Maj. Gen. B. F. Butler is relieved from command of the Department of North Carolina and Virginia. . . . [He] will repair to Lowell, Mass., and report by letter to the Adjutant General of the Army."

Grant passed the word to Butler next morning, January 8, and named Ord the new commander of the Army of the James, some 8000 of whose members had embarked — or reëmbarked for the most part, having only just returned from the fiasco down the coast — at Bermuda Hundred four days ago, under Brigadier General Alfred Terry, for another go at Fort Fisher. Butler, however, did not "repair to Lowell" as ordered; at least not yet. He went instead to Washington, where political connections assured him a sympathetic hearing before the Joint Congressional Committee on the Conduct of the War, which assembled just under ten days later to hear his complaint of unjust treatment by the Administration and its three-starred creature down at City Point. Grant had left the charges vague, presumably on grounds that they would be harder to refute that way, but Butler at once got down to specifics. He had been relieved, he said, for his failure to take Fort Fisher, and he brought along charts and duplicates of reports by subordinates to prove that he had been right to call off the attack in mid-career, not only because Porter had failed to give him adequate support, but also because a close-up study of the thick-walled fort and its outlying torpedo fields had shown it to be impregnable in the first place, both to naval bombardment and to infantry assault. While he spoke, referring assiduously to the documents at hand, a hubbub rose outside the room — cheers in the street, the muffled crump of shotless guns discharging a salute, and newsboys crying, "Extra! Extra! Read all about it!" Fort Fisher, it seemed, had fallen. "Impossible!" Butler protested, clutching his papers. "It's a mistake, Sir." But it turned out to be more than possible; it was a fact, confirmed by dispatches on hand from Porter. Laughter rippled, then roared through the room. After a moment of shock adjustment, the cock-eyed general joined in as heartily as anyone. Adjournment followed, and as the members and spectators began filing out, still laughing, Butler raised his hand and called pontifically for silence. "Thank God for victory," he intoned.

In time, the committee not only voted unanimously to exonerate the former Bay State senator — referred to affectionately by a colleague as "the smartest damned rascal that ever lived" — from all blame in connection with the failure of the earlier expedition; its members also commended him for having had the nerve, the presence of mind under pressure, to call off the assault at the last minute, thereby saving many lives. Such action, they ruled, "was clearly justified by the facts then known," including Porter's ragged gunnery, which had done little damage to the fort, and his inadequate support of the troops ashore. Not that their judgment affected either officer's future war career; Butler had none, and the admiral even now was receiving congratulations for his share in one of the best-conducted operations of the war, by land or sea or both.

Terry and his 8000 — Butler's force, plus two brigades of Negro troops for added heft — reached Beaufort on schedule, January 8, for the rendezvous with Porter and his sixty warships. Delayed there by another three-day blow, they planned carefully for this second amphibious strike at Fort Fisher, then set out down the coast and dropped anchor before nightfall, January 12, within sight of the objective. Porter was altogether pleased with his new partner, whom he pronounced "my beau ideal of a soldier and a general," adding: "Our coöperation has been most cordial." Partly this was the result of Grant's instructions, which were for Terry to get along harmoniously with his sea-going associate, and partly it was because of Terry's natural tact and training, in and out of the army, where, as the phrase went, he had "found a home." A thirty-seven-year-old former clerk of the New Haven County superior court, admitted to the Connecticut bar while still at Yale, he had fought as a militia colonel at First Bull Run and then stayed on to pick up much experience in coastal operations, including the expedition against Port Royal, the reduction of Fort Pulaski, and the siege of Battery Wagner, after which he was made a brigadier and put in charge of a division in the Army of the James. Now that he had command of a provisional corps, with a promotion to major general in the works, he was determined to justify the added star by disproving Butler's contention that Fort Fisher could not be taken by assault. Once ashore, he told Porter, he intended to stay there until Confederate Point was Federal Point again, by right of exclusive occupation, and blockade runners would no longer find a haven up Cape Fear River for the discharge of their cargoes.

Just how important those cargoes were to continued resistance by the rebels was shown by the fact that R. E. Lee himself had sent word to the fort commander, William Lamb, that he could not subsist his army without the supplies brought in there. More specifically, a government report of goods run into Wilmington and Charleston during the last nine weeks of the year — practically all into the North Carolina port, for Charleston was tightly blockaded — amounted to "8,632,000 pounds of meat, 1,507,000 pounds of lead, 1,933,000 pounds of saltpeter, 546,000 pairs of shoes, 316,000 pairs of blankets, 520,000 pounds of coffee, 69,000 rifles, 97 packages of revolvers, 2639 packages of medicine, 43 cannon," and much else. Lamb was back down to a garrison of 800 men, the Junior Reservists having departed, and though he had appealed to both the district and department commanders, W. H. C. Whiting and Braxton Bragg, no reinforcements had arrived by the time the outsized Union armada returned and dropped anchor, just out of range of his biggest guns, on the evening of January 12.

Two hours before dawn, Porter opened the action by committing all five ironclads at short range, his object being to provoke the defenders into disclosing the location of their guns by muzzle flashes. It worked, and he followed this up after sunrise by bringing the rest of his 627 pieces to bear on targets the lookouts had spotted. The result, according to one Confederate crouched beneath this deluge of better than a hundred shells a minute, was "beyond description. No language can describe that terrific bombardment." Moreover, the fire was not only heavy; it was highly accurate. Butler's complaint that the navy's gunnery had been ragged throughout the previous attempt was in large part true, and Porter, amid his denials, had taken pains to correct it. For one thing, his marksmen then had fired at the rebel flag, high on its staff above the fort, so that many of their shots plunged harmlessly into the river beyond the narrow sand peninsula. This time, he cautioned in his preliminary directive, "the object is to lodge the shell in the parapets, and tear away the traverses under which the bombproofs are located. A shell now and then exploding over a gun en barbette may have good effect, but there is nothing like lodging the shell before it explodes. . . . Commanders are directed to strictly enjoin their officers and men never to fire at the flag or pole, but to pick out the guns; the stray shots will knock the flagstaff down." And so it was. He saw through the smoke and flying debris that his instructions were being followed to the letter. One by one, sometimes two by two, rebel pieces winked out and fell silent in the boil of dust and flame. "Traverses began to disappear," he would report, "and the southern angle of Fort Fisher commenced to look very dilapidated."

Since 8 o'clock that morning, four hours into the bombardment, Terry had been landing troops on the stretch of beach Weitzel had selected in December. By 3 o'clock all 8000 were ashore. This time, in addition to the accustomed "forty rounds," each man carried three days' rations on his person, backed by a six-day reserve of hard bread and a 300,000-round bulk supply of rifle ammunition. He had come to stay, and he emphasized this by digging a stout defensive line across the peninsula, facing north in case Hoke's division, known to be camped this side of Wilmington, tried an attack from that direction. Out on the water all this time the fleet kept up its smothering fire on the fort two miles below. Porter was clearly having the better of the exchange, yet a number of his ships had taken cruel punishment; *Canonicus*, for example, a monitor from the James River squadron, took 36 hits in the course of the day, and though none of them pierced her armor she was badly cut up about her deck and wore out several relays of gunners, stunned by the jar of solids against their turret and unnerved by the ping and spatter of bullets aimed at their sight-slits by sharpshooters in the fort. Porter cared little or nothing for any of this, however. He kept banging away past sunset, using every gun that could be brought to bear, and only retired his wooden vessels after twilight. Even so, he held the ironclads on station all night long, with instructions to continue lobbing their 11- and 15-inch shells into the shoreward darkness and thus discourage the rebel repair crews from doing much about the damage the place had suffered from the unrelenting daylong pounding, much of it heavy caliber and most of it point-blank.

Friday the 13th had indeed been an unlucky day for Lamb and the fort in his charge. More than a hundred of its defenders had fallen, and less than half the guns on its seaward face were still in operation. Despite his pleas, no reinforcements had come downriver: only the district commander and his staff, who arrived at the height of the bombardment. Whiting had come unglued at Petersburg last spring, victim of a too vivid imagination, but he seemed resolute now, even jaunty, in contrast to the gloomy news he brought. "Lamb, my boy," he announced as he entered the works, "I have come to share your fate. You and your garrison are to be sacrificed." Startled, the young colonel replied: "Don't say so, General. We shall certainly whip the enemy again." But the Mississippian explained that when he left Wilmington that morning, the department commander — Bragg had returned by now from his failed attempt to intercept Sherman down in Georgia — "was hastily removing his stores and ammunition, and was looking for a place to fall back upon." In other words, so far as the survival of Fort Fisher was concerned, Hoke and his 6000 veterans might as well have remained with Lee in Virginia; Bragg was unlikely to order them within range of Porter's big-gunned warships for a fight with the superior force Terry had landed and intrenched just north of the doomed fort. Lamb hoped against hope that Whiting was wrong in this assessment, yet as the day wore on he came more and more to see that, under the rain of all that metal, there was little he could do about it, even in the way of repairing damages. Nightfall brought a slackening though by no means a cessation of the fire. Still at work beyond the surf, the five ironclads bowled their big projectiles "along the parapets, scattering shrapnel in the darkness" with such effect, Lamb said later, that "we could scarcely gather up and bury our dead without fresh casualties."

Dawn brought a resumption of the full-scale bombardment, with all the Federal warships back on station. In the December effort Porter had fired 20,271 projectiles weighing 1,275,000 pounds. This time, having called for a more deliberate rate of fire, he would expend several hundred fewer rounds — 19,682 all told — but greater reliance on his heavier weapons resulted in a total weight of 1,652,638 pounds, a new record for the amount of metal thrown in a single naval engagement. Lamb's casualties rose above two hundred before this second day was over, and though some 700 North Carolina soldiers and a detachment of 50 sailors arrived to lift the strength of the garrison to about 1550 — minus, of course, the sick and wounded and the dead — there was little the defenders could do but huddle in their bombproofs, awaiting word from lookouts that the land assault was under way, at which point they were to turn out and contest it, hand-to-hand if necessary.

It did not come today, as Lamb expected, but it would tomorrow. Porter and Terry met that evening aboard the flagship *Malvern,* and while the ironclads kept up their nightlong harassment, holding the rebel gunners in their burrows, the two commanders planned the timing for next day's climax to their joint effort. The fleet would resume its all-out pounding of the objective until 3 o'clock, then suddenly cease fire for the assault, which would be made by two separate columns driving down opposite sides of the peninsula, thus avoiding the field of torpedoes north of the fort. On the river flank, half of Terry's troops would attack the land face near its western end, leaving the other 4000 to hold the intrenchments against a possible attempt by Hoke to interfere at this critical moment. Simultaneously, a 2000-man all-navy column, recruited piecemeal from most of the vessels of the fleet — 1600 sailors, armed with cutlasses and revolvers, and 400 marines armed with rifles — would advance down the beach to strike the northeast salient of the fort, where the land and seaward faces joined. Both forces were to press the issue until Fort Fisher was secured.

Sunday, January 15, went much as Porter and Terry had planned it aboard the *Malvern.* A calm sea, after two days of intensive target practice, so improved the fleet's marksmanship that by noon only one gun remained in service on the seaward face and none at all on the other, whose palisade was swept away by the longitudinal fire. Around 2 o'clock a steamer put in at the wharf in rear and began unloading a brigade of South Carolinians sent downriver by Bragg in response to Whiting's telegraphic pleas. Only about a third of them made it ashore, however, before the boat was driven off by a storm of shells from the warships on the far side of the fort. These 350, exposed without preamble to this holocaust of screaming metal, barely replaced the casualties Lamb had suffered over the past three days, and by the time he got them into bombproofs, he said later, "they were out of breath, disorganized, and more or less demoralized." Just then a lookout shouted, "Colonel, the enemy are about to charge!" A heavy blue column was working its way down the beach, apparently with the intention of gaining a close-up position from which to launch an assault. While Lamb called out the garrison to meet the threat, Whiting got off a frantic wire to Bragg: "Enemy on the beach in front of us in very heavy force. ... Attack! Attack! It is all I can say and all you can do." By now the time was straight-up 3 o'clock, and the roar of guns hushed abruptly beyond the surf. There was a moment of eerie stillness, broken in turn by all the steam whistles of the fleet, shrieking and moaning in concert. Lamb wondered at this, then realized they were sounding the charge for the troops ashore. "A soul-stirring signal," he called it, "both to besiegers and besieged."

Cutlasses flashing in the wintry sunlight, the bluejackets made their dash along the beach, only to be stopped within 300 yards of the

objective by well-aimed volleys of musketry. There they held on for a
time, their losses mounting while they dug frantically in the loose sand
for cover, then turned, despite the pleas of their officers — who "in
their anxiety to be the first into the fort," a wounded ensign later said,
"had advanced to the heads of the columns, leaving no one to steady the
men behind" — and fled back up the low-tide-widened beach. One who
did what he could to stop them was William Cushing, recently promoted
for having sunk the *Albemarle*. He was weeping over the loss of a
friend, shot down along with some 300 others in the course of the attack,
and swearing at the retreaters in his frustration; to no avail. "We witnessed what we had never seen before," Lamb would report, "a disorderly rout of American sailors and marines."

Exultant, he looked down the line of blasted works and saw, to
his dismay, three Federal battle flags atop the ramparts near its western
end. Concealed by trees and brush along the river, the army column had
made its way up close to the fortifications undetected, then mounted
them in a rush.

Whiting too had seen the enemy flags, and while Lamb prepared to
follow with the rest of the main body, which had repulsed and been distracted by the attack on this end of the land face, the Mississippian led
a countercharge against the other. He retook one of two lost gun
chambers, but was wounded twice in quick succession. By the time Lamb
arrived with reinforcements, the general had been carried rearward on
a stretcher and a fierce struggle was raging for possession of the connecting traverse. With the penetration thus contained (though only by
the hardest; "The contestants were savagely firing into each other's faces,
and in some cases clubbing their guns, being too close to load and fire")
the attackers seemed to falter; Lamb believed that if he could hold on
until nightfall he would be able to drive them out. Just then, however,
the fleet steamed back into action, shelling the Confederates massed in
rear of the lost segment of their line. The result, combined with all that
had gone before, was "indescribably horrible," he said. "Great cannon
were broken in two, and over their ruins were lying the dead; others
were partly buried in graves dug by the shells which had slain them."
Up near the occupied portion of the works, where the warships could
not intervene for fear of hitting their own men, the fighting continued
at close quarters. "If there has ever been a longer or more stubborn
hand-to-hand encounter," Lamb declared, "I have failed to meet with it
in history."

Knocked sprawling by a bullet in the hip, he was put in a cot
alongside Whiting's in the hospital bombproof. Outside, the fighting
and shelling continued past sundown, on into darkness. At 8 o'clock an
aide reported the land face lost from end to end; the contest now was
for the interior, and he suggested that further resistance would be a useless sacrifice of life. Lamb replied that so long as he lived he would

never surrender. Whiting approved. "Lamb," he assured him from the adjoining cot, "when you die I will assume command, and I will not surrender the fort."

By now, however, Terry had four brigades inside the place. They did their work well, as indeed they had done from the outset, pressing the defenders southward down the sea face, traverse by traverse, until there was nothing left to fall back on. At 10 o'clock that night the flag came down. Something over 500 men had fallen in its defense, and now the survivors were prisoners, including Lamb and Whiting. (The former would survive his wound and a doleful stretch as a captive in Fort Columbus, New York Harbor, but Chase Whiting would die there in March, after nearly eight weeks of suffering from his wounds, complaining bitterly all the while of Bragg's failure to support the beleaguered garrison during a three-day resistance "unparalleled in the history of the war.") Terry lost 955 killed and wounded, Porter 386, ashore and afloat. "If hell is what it is said to be," a weary sailor wrote home next day, "then the interior of Fort Fisher is a fair comparison. Here and there you see great heaps of human beings laying just as they fell, one upon the other. Some groaning piteously, and asking for water. Others whose mortal career is over, still grasping the weapon they used to so good an effect in life."

For all the compacted horror of the scene, and despite the even steeper price the victors paid in blood for its creation, nothing deterred the gaudy all-night celebration that followed the announcement of surrender. "Cheer after cheer came from the fort," a Federal officer would recall, "and was answered by the ships with cheers, rockets, lights of all colors, ringing of bells, steam whistles, and all sorts of unearthly noises." To a watching sailor, "The rockets seemed to shoot higher and sparkle more brilliantly than usual," and even the shrieking whistles, whose shrillness had always hurt his ears, "seemed to discourse a sweet melody." Ashore, the informal distribution of whiskey found among the captured medical stores livened the rout for the jubilant soldiers, sailors, and marines, for whom the end of the fighting meant the end of discipline. Fort Fisher had been a hard go, and officers tended to overlook excesses, including the rapid-fire discharge of revolvers and a good deal of rowdy prowling after souvenirs in the wreckage. In the end, this resulted in tragedy. Guards had been posted at the entrances of some thirty underground powder magazines, but somehow the largest of these — a 20 by 60 foot chamber, roofed over with 18 feet of sand piled in a flat-topped mound sodded with grass to keep the rain from washing it away — was missed. Apparently no one suspected there were between six and seven tons of powder under the springy turf: certainly not the wearier members of a New York regiment, who found it too inviting a bed to be resisted this mild January night, and certainly not two drunken seamen who entered the magazine with lighted torches, shortly after dawn, in search of loot. The resultant explosion added 104 killed and wounded and missing to the Union casualty list, which thus was increased to just under 1500, or roughly three times the number the garrison suffered before it surrendered.

Confederates might find grim satisfaction in such a mishap, just as they did when news arrived that off Charleston this same day, 150 miles to the south, the monitor *Patapsco* struck a torpedo while searching for obstructions in the harbor channel. She went down fast, with the loss of more than half her crew of just over a hundred. Porter, however, was no more inclined to be daunted by this than he was by the explosion of the powder magazine. "Our success is so great that we should not complain," he informed Welles in the dispatch that broke up Butler's hearing before the Joint Committee. "Men, it seems, must die that this Union may live.... We regret our companions in arms and shed a tear over their remains, but if these rebels should succeed we would have nothing left us and our lives would be spent in terror and sorrow."

★ ★ ★

Fort Fisher's fall confirmed Butler's. Whatever his friends on the Washington committee might say as to his perspicacious conduct during the earlier attempt, he was gone for good. And so too now, to all effect, was Samuel Curtis; not at Grant's urging, but his own. Promoted to major general as a reward for his Pea Ridge victory nearly three years ago, he was disappointed to find little attention being paid to his recent Westport achievement or the rigorous follow-up southward, down the length of Missouri, into Arkansas and the Indian Territory. Apparently neither the newspapers nor the War Department had space or time for anything but Sherman's triumphal march across Georgia to the sea. Taken aback by this imbalance Curtis fell into a fit of pique. "Sherman's success was glorious," he wrote privately to his brother in early January, "but in justice to myself not equal to my pursuit of Price, in that I had a less force against a larger, won several victories, and had to go as far *through a desolate country*." Thinking it over, and finding it rankled, he applied to the War Department to be spared the strain of another campaign, and his request was promptly granted. Before the month was out he was transferred to command of the Department of the Northwest, with headquarters at Milwaukee, well removed from any possible clash of arms. Nor was there a commander appointed in his stead. As if to suggest that Curtis's role had been superfluous in the first place, Dodge's adjoining Department of the Missouri was simply enlarged to include Kansas and the Nebraska and Utah territories.

But this too went largely unnoticed. A peripheral shift having little to do with the close-out maneuver everyone could see was in the making on the seaboard, such a subtraction had no more bearing on the central issue than, say, the death of seventy-one-year-old Edward Everett, whose two-hour oration had preceded Lincoln's two-minute speech at Gettysburg just over a year ago. By now, with the end conceivably in sight, men looked beyond the cease-fire to insist with a new fervor that the victory be put to proper use. Slavery returned as the burning issue it had been at the outset.

Everett died on January 15, amid a congressional furor over the proposed adoption of a constitutional amendment — the first in more than sixty years — forbidding the existence of slavery "within the United States or any place subject to their jurisdiction." The Senate had approved it nine months earlier, but House proponents then had failed to secure the two-thirds vote required. Lincoln in his December message urged reconsideration during the present session, on grounds that approval would surely follow the seating of newly elected Republicans at the next. "As it is to so go, at all events, may we not agree that the sooner the better?" He asked that, yet he also did a good deal more than ask. He set out to get the necessary votes, mainly by logrolling. One opposed Democrat was promised a government job for his brother in New York; another was assured support in holding onto his contested seat; while a third, hired by a railroad to fight off adverse legislation, was guaranteed the threat would not mature. These three came over more or less gladly, and eight others, firmer in their resistance or more fearful of the home reaction to an outright shift, were similarly bargained into agreeing to abstain. Finally, on the last day of January — as soon as the Administration was reasonably certain of the outcome — House Speaker Schuyler Colfax put the resolution to a vote. Members and spectators alike followed the tally with mounting excitement. It came out 119 aye, 56 nay; passing thus with three switched votes to spare. Colfax's announcement of the result, according to the usually staid *Congressional Globe,* was greeted with an outburst of emotion. "The members on the Republican side of the House instantly sprang to their feet, and, regardless of parliamentary rules, applauded with cheers and clapping of hands. The example was followed by male spectators in the galleries, who waved their hats and cheered long and loud, while the ladies, hundreds of whom were present, rose in their seats and waved their handkerchiefs, participating in adding to the general excitement and intense interest of the scene. This lasted for several minutes."

Outside the chamber it lasted considerably longer. Three batteries of regular artillery, loaded and ready when the time came, began firing a hundred-gun salute from Capitol Hill, and men embraced on the streets in celebration. In addition to the realization that a goal had been reached, there was the feeling that a new road had been taken, even though by no means all were pleased to travel it, not being satisfied that they wanted to go where it led. All twelve amendments up to now, including the last in 1804, had dealt exclusively with governmental powers and functions; that is, they were "constitutional" in the strictest sense.

But this one — lucky or unlucky Thirteen — went beyond that to effect reform in an area recently considered outside the scope of the Constitution, overriding protests that no combination of parties to that contract, however sizeable their majority, could alter it to outlaw a domestic institution that existed before it was written. Pendleton of Ohio, McClellan's running mate in November, voiced his party's opposition in the debate leading up to the roll call. "Neither three-fourths of the states, nor all the states save one, can abolish slavery in that dissenting state," he told the House, "because it lies within the domain reserved entirely to each state for itself, and upon it the other states cannot enter." Such was the States Rights position, many of whose principal supporters had departed, just four years ago this month, to set up on their own. Then came the vote, and States Rights went by the board. Moreover, any last-ditch hope that the Supreme Court might overturn the measure was abandoned when it was noted, not only that five of the nine members — including Salmon Chase — were present for the vote, but also that their judicial gravity scarcely masked their satisfaction at the outcome.

Ironically, this Thirteenth Amendment abolished slavery, rather than assuring its continuance, as a direct result of secession. Six weeks before Sumter, both the Senate and the House had passed by a two-thirds vote a proposed Thirteenth Amendment stating flatly that Congress could never be given "the power to abolish or interfere within any State with the domestic institutions thereof, including that of persons held to labor or service by the laws of said State." Buchanan signed it on the eve of Lincoln's inauguration, but the measure was forgotten when the issue swung to war. On the other hand, if the departed Southerners had remained in Washington they and their northern friends, whose influence would have been for peace, could almost certainly have secured the requisite three-fourths ratification by their respective states. Charles Sumner, well aware of this, wasted no time in consolidating the victory he had worked so hard to win. He appeared before the Supreme Court next day, February 1, to move that a fellow lawyer, John S. Rock of Boston, be admitted to practice before it. Embraced by the Chief Justice, who had prepared his colleagues, the motion carried. Here indeed was a change; for Rock was a Negro, the first of his race to address that high tribunal, which less than a decade ago had denied that Dred Scott, a non-citizen, even had the right to be represented there.

Elated, a crowd with a brass band trooped onto the White House lawn that night and shouted for the President, who came out on a balcony to take the music and greet the serenaders. "Speech! Speech!" they called up, and he obliged them. He praised Congress's action yesterday as "the fitting if not indispensable adjunct to the consummation of the great game we are playing," and emphasized that his aim all along had been to root out this basic cause of national disturbance —

slavery — against the day when the states would be reunited. The Emancipation Proclamation had been issued with that in mind, he said, even though it freed only those slaves who came within the reach of blue-clad soldiers. Moreover, once the war had ended, it might be held invalid by the courts, leaving much of the evil uncorrected and still a subject for contention. "But this amendment is a King's cure for all the evils. It winds the whole thing up." Applauded, Lincoln paused and then remarked in closing that he could not but congratulate all present — himself, the country, and the world — "upon this great moral victory."

The victory claim was valid on other grounds as well, but only within problematical limitations. Ratification, once it came, would give the nation all that he maintained. Yet the dimensions of the victory depended altogether on the dimensions of the country when the amendment was adopted, and this in turn depended — more or less as had been the case, over the past two years, in the application of the Emancipation Proclamation — on the progress, between now and then, of Union arms. In short, it depended on whether Grant's close-out plan succeeded. Sherman's part was the critical one, at least in the early stages, and by coincidence he set out in earnest, this same February 1, on his march north through the Carolinas to gain Lee's rear.

Although he was thus some four weeks behind the schedule he had set for himself when he wrote Grant on Christmas Eve that he expected to start north "in about ten days," the delay was unavoidable. Heavy winter rains had swollen creeks and swamps along his projected route of march, while ice on the Potomac — their staging area, once they arrived from Nashville — prevented Schofield's men from steaming downriver aboard transports on their way to Wilmington. This last did not disturb the red-haired general, any more than had Butler's failure to clear the way by reducing Fort Fisher. "Fizzle; great fizzle!" he snorted when he heard of that yuletide fiasco. "I shall have to go up there and do that job myself. Eat 'em up as I go, and take 'em backside." In this connection he requested Dahlgren to keep up the scare along the South Carolina coast, maneuvering his warships as if to cover a series of landings by Foster, whose troops would go along. That would confuse the rebels throughout Sherman's period of preparation at Savannah. Later, when his march had pulled the defenders inland and cut the seaports off from reinforcements and supplies, such feints could be converted to actual landings, probably against nothing worse than token opposition, and possibly not even that. "I will shake the tree," he told Foster, "and you must be quick to pick up the apples."

He was feeling good, despite the delay, and he showed it. Pride in all his men had done was matched by pride in their conduct throughout the present span of comparative repose: as was demonstrated in a letter informing Grant that, "notwithstanding the habits begotten during our rather vandalic march," the behavior of his soldiers in Savannah had "excited the wonder and admiration of all." Not even a four-day visit by Stanton, January 11–15 — ostensibly for reasons of health, but actually to explore his fellow Ohioan's position on the Negro question — upset Sherman's feeling of well-being. He fancied he had set the Secretary straight as to his views on "Inevitable Sambo," alarming though they were to abolitionists up in Washington. "The South deserves all she has got for her injustice to the negro," he wrote Halleck at the time, "but that is no reason why we should go to the other extreme." Stanton heard him say such things, and seemed not to disapprove. As for the restoration of states now claiming to have departed from the Union, Sherman told Georgians who called on him in the course of the Secretary's visit: "My own opinion is that no negotiations are necessary, nor commissioners, nor conventions, nor anything of the kind.... Georgia is not out of the Union, and therefore talk of 'reconstruction' appears to me inappropriate." Meantime he kept busy, doing all he could to "make a good ready" for the expedition north. Dahlgren's loss of the *Patapsco* outside Charleston, along with 64 of her crew, was more than offset by the news that Porter and Terry had taken Fort Fisher that same day, preparing the way for Schofield, who wrote that he would be off down the coast as soon as the Potomac ice broke up. January was more than half gone by now, and Sherman stepped up the pace of his preparations.

His march would be due north in two columns, enabling him to feint simultaneously at Charleston and Augusta, on the right and left, while aiming in fact at Columbia, between and beyond them. North of the South Carolina capital he would feint again, this time at Chester and Charlotte, then turn east-northeast, through Cheraw and Fayetteville, for Goldsboro — chosen because two rail lines ran from there to Wilmington and New Bern, up which Schofield would be marching with supplies from those two ports. Refitted and reinforced to a strength of better than 80,000 Sherman then could drive on Raleigh, the North Carolina capital, en route to Petersburg and the combination with Meade. Now as before, Slocum would lead the two-corps left wing, Howard the two-corps right, while Kilpatrick's horsemen shielded the western flank. This time, though, they would stay closer together, cutting a narrower swath for readier mutual support, since an attack was considered far likelier here than in Georgia, where the outcome had been less obviously disastrous to the Confederate high command. "If Lee is a soldier of genius," the red-head explained to his staff, "he will seek to transfer his army from Richmond to Raleigh or Columbia. If he is a man simply of detail, he will remain where he is and his speedy defeat is sure. But I have little fear that he will be able to move; Grant holds him in a vise of iron."

In point of fact, so far as interference was concerned, there was

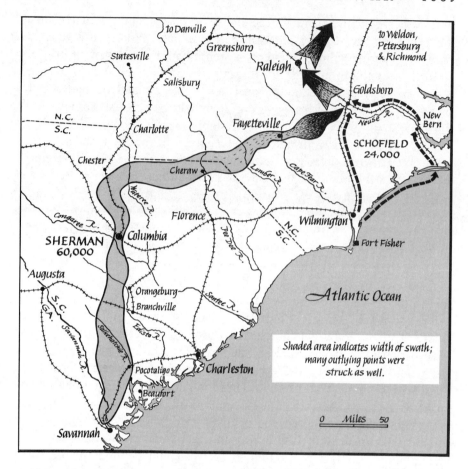

Shaded area indicates width of swath;
many outlying points were
struck as well.

0 　Miles　50

more to fear from rebel terrain than there was from rebel armies. Not
only would the Carolinas march — 425 miles, all told, from Savannah to
Goldsboro — be nearly half again longer than the one from Atlanta to
the sea; the difference in natural obstacles he would encounter, both in
kind and number, made the earlier expedition appear in retrospect as
something of a lark, a holiday outing in pleasant weather, through a
region of rich crops, ripe for harvest, and livestock waiting only to be
rounded up and butchered. Here the crops had already been gathered,
such as they were, and the cattle were few and scrubby at best, having
little to graze on but muck and palmetto. Moreover, luck had exposed
him to almost no rain on his way through Georgia, and it would not
have mattered a lot in any case; whereas he would be marching now in
the dead of winter, the rainiest in years, and it mattered a great deal.
Many rivers lay ahead, all reportedly brim full. After the Savannah,
there would be the Salkehatchie and the Edisto, the Congaree and the
Wateree, the Pee Dee and the Lumber, the Cape Fear and finally the
Neuse, all nine of them major streams, with creeks and bayous webbing
the swampy ground between, wet with all the rain that had fallen and
was falling between the seaboard and the near slopes of the Appalachi-

ans. Yet here too Sherman could prepare for trouble, much as he had done when he drilled repair crews for work on the railroads north of Atlanta and Chattanooga. Michigan lumbermen and rail-splitters from Indiana and Illinois were organized into a pioneer corps, 6600 strong, armed with axes for cutting, splitting, and laying saplings flat-side-down to corduroy roads for the 2500 wagons and 600 ambulances rolling northward in the wake of his 60,000 marchers. He did not intend to get bogged down, nor did he intend to be slowed down in avoiding it: in token of which he had already selected a rangy half-thoroughbred bay named Old Sam to serve as his accustomed mount on the campaign. Sam, a staff major noted ominously, was "a horribly fast-walking horse."

Beginning the feint, Sherman sent Howard's wing by boat to Beaufort, forty miles up the coast beyond Port Royal Sound, with instructions to move inland and occupy Pocotaligo, on the railroad about midway between Savannah and Charleston. By January 20 this had been done, and Slocum began slogging in the opposite direction, thirty miles up the drowned west bank of the Savannah River to Sister's Ferry, as if about to close upon Augusta. Unrelenting rain made the march a roundabout nine-day affair, with much discomfort for the troops. For them, however, as for their chief, "city life had become dull and tame, and we were anxious to get into the pine woods again." Moreover, they were sustained by anticipation of another kind. Ahead lay South Carolina, and they had been promised a free hand in visiting upon her the destruction she deserved for having led the Confederate exodus from the Union. "Here is where treason began, and by God here is where it shall end," they vowed, pleased with their role as avenging instruments and eager to put into sterner practice the talents they had acquired on the march through Georgia, accounts of which had reached and frightened the people in their new path northward. Sherman approved of the fear aroused. "This was a power, and I intended to utilize it," he said later, explaining: "My aim then was to whip the rebels, to humble their pride, to follow them to their inmost recesses, and make them fear and dread us. 'Fear of the Lord is the beginning of wisdom.'"

Already there were signs that the two-pronged feint was working in both directions. Augusta was in ferment over Slocum's approach, and in Charleston, menaced from the landward side by Howard and by Dahlgren from the sea, clerks were busy packing and shipping official records and historical mementos to Columbia for safe-keeping, never suspecting that the inland capital was not only high on Sherman's list of prime objectives, but was also to be dealt with as harshly as Atlanta had been served two months ago. "I look upon Columbia as quite as bad as Charleston," he wrote Halleck while cooling his army's heels in Savannah, "and I doubt if we shall spare the public buildings there as we did in Milledgeville." What was more, subordinates from private to major general took this prediction a step further when the march began in earnest, February 1. Blair and Logan cleared Pocotaligo and Davis and Williams crossed the Savannah in force that day. On the far left, at Sister's Ferry, Kilpatrick's troopers led the way, hoofs drumming on the planks of a pontoon bridge thrown there the day before. Soldiers of a Michigan infantry regiment, waiting their turn to cross, had heard that the bandy-legged cavalry commander had instructed his men to fill their saddlebags with matches for the work ahead, and now they believed it; for as he rode out onto the bridge he called back over his shoulder, "There'll be damned little for you infantrymen to destroy after I've passed through that hell-hole of secession!"

Here indeed was an end to what the Richmond editor termed "the repose of the tiger," in the course of which Sherman had told Old Brains: "The truth is the whole army is burning with an insatiable desire to wreak vengeance upon South Carolina. I almost tremble for her fate, but feel that she deserves all that seems in store for her."

✗ 2 ✗

A proposal that the women of the South cut off their hair for sale in Europe, thereby bringing an estimated 40,000,000-dollar windfall to the cause, had gained widespread approval by the turn of the year, despite some protests — chiefly from men, who viewed the suggested disfigurement with less favor than did their wives and sweethearts — that the project was impractical. After the fall of Fort Fisher, however, the Confederacy's last port east of the Mississippi was no longer open to blockade runners, coming or going, and the plan was abandoned. Even if the women sheared their heads there was no way now for the bulky cargo to be shipped, either to Europe or anywhere else; or if it could somehow be gotten out — from Charleston, say, in a sudden dash by a high-speed flotilla — the odds were even longer against a return with whatever the money would buy in the way of necessities, all of which were running low and lower now that the war was about to enter its fifth spring. Like so many other proposals, farfetched but by no means impossible if they had been adopted sooner, this one came too late.

Another was a return to the suggestion advanced informally by Pat Cleburne the previous winter, soon after Missionary Ridge, that the South free its slaves and enlist them in its armies. Hastily suppressed at the time as "revolting to Southern sentiment, Southern pride, and Southern honor," the proposition seemed far less "monstrous" now than it had a year ago, when Grant was not at the gates of Richmond and Sherman had not made his march through Georgia. Seddon, for one, had been for it ever since the fall of Atlanta, except that he believed emancipation should follow, not precede, a term of military service. In early January, Governor William Smith — "Extra Billy" to Old

Dominion voters — proposed that Virginia and the other states, not the central government, carry out the plan for black recruitment. Appealed to, R. E. Lee replied that he favored such a measure. "We must decide whether slavery shall be extinguished by our enemies and the slaves used against us, or use them ourselves at the risk of the effects which may be produced upon our social institutions. My own opinion is that we should employ them without delay. I believe that with proper regulation they can be made efficient soldiers." This was powerful support. If Lee wanted Negro troops, a once-oppugnant Richmond editor wrote soon afterward, "by all means let him have them." Westward, Richard Taylor agreed. In Mobile, when he congratulated a group of impressed slaves on their skill in building fortifications, their leader told him: "If you will give us guns we will fight for these works, too. We would rather fight for our own white folks than for strangers." Down in South Carolina, however, Mary Boykin Chesnut had her doubts. "Freeing Negroes is the latest Confederate Government craze," the mistress of Mulberry Plantation wrote in her diary. "We are a little slow about it; that is all. . . . I remember when Mr Chesnut spoke to his Negroes about it, his head men were keen to go in the army, to be free and get a bounty after the war. Now they say coolly that they don't want freedom if they have to fight for it. That means they are pretty sure of having it anyway."

Opinions differed: not so much along economic lines, as might have been expected — large slave-holders versus the slaveless majority of small farmers, merchants, and wage earners — but rather as a result of opposition from die-hard political leaders who contended that no government, state or central, whatever its desperation under the threat of imminent extinction, had the right to interfere in matters involving social institutions: especially slavery, which Aleck Stephens had called the "cornerstone" of the Confederacy, insisting that it made the nation's citizens truly free, presumably to establish a universal white aristocracy, by keeping the Negro in the inferior position God and nature intended for him to occupy down through time. As a result, after intense discussion, Virginia's General Assembly voted to permit the arming of slaves but included no provision for their emancipation, either before or after military service. Little or nothing came of that, as Mrs Chesnut had foreseen, but even less seemed likely to proceed from a similar bill introduced in the Confederate House and Senate in early February, only to run into virulent Impossiblist opposition. Despite Lee's earlier warning "that whatever measures are to be adopted should be adopted at once. Every day's delay increases the difficulty. Much time will be required to organize and discipline the men, and action may be deferred until too late," debate dragged on, week in, week out, as the legislators wrangled. Meanwhile, Federal enlistment teams kept busy in the wake of blue advances, signing up and swearing in black volunteers, many of them substitutes to help fill the draft quotas of northern states. In the end, of the nearly 180,000 Negroes who served in the Union ranks — 20,000 more than the "aggregate present" in all the armies of the South on New Year's Day — 134,111 were recruited in states that had stars in the Confederate battle flag, and the latter figure in turn was several thousand greater than the total of 125,994 gray-clad soldiers "present for duty" that same day; when the North had 959,460 and 620,924 in those respective categories.

It was by no means as great, however, as the total of 198,494 listed that day as absent from Confederate ranks. Moreover, this invisible army of the missing grew with every passing week, its membership swollen even by veterans from the Army of Northern Virginia, whose morale was said to be high despite short rations and the bone-numbing chill of the Petersburg trenches. Adversity had given them a pinched and scarecrow look, hard to connect with the caterwauling victors of so many long-odds battles in the past. A Connecticut soldier, peering through a Fort Hell sight-slit one cold morning to watch a detail of them straggle out to relieve their picket line, wrote home that he "could not help comparing them with so many women with cloaks, shawls, double-bustles and hoops, as they had thrown over their shoulders blankets and tents which flapped in the wind." Many by now had reached their limit of endurance; they came over into the Union lines in increasing numbers, especially from units posted where the rival works were close together and a quick sprint meant an end to shivering misery and hunger. A New England private told how he and his comrades would speculate each day on how many were likely to come in that night, depending on the darkness of the moon. "The boys talk about the Johnnies as at home we talk about suckers and eels. The boys will look around in the evening and guess that there will be a good run of Johnnies." Lee of course felt the drain, and knew only too well what the consequences must be if it continued. Before the end of January he warned Davis that if Grant was appreciably reinforced, either by Thomas from the west or by Sherman from the south — or, for that matter, by Lincoln from the north — "I do not see how in the present position he can be prevented from enveloping Richmond."

If in Virginia a sort of numbness obtained because of the military stalemate and the long-term deprivation of troops confined to earthworks, something approaching chaos prevailed at this time in the Carolinas while the various commanders — Bragg at Wilmington, Hardee at Charleston, G. W. Smith at Augusta, who between them mustered fewer than 25,000 effectives, including militia — engaged in a flurry of guesses as to where Sherman would strike next, and when, and how best to go about parrying the thrust, outnumbered and divided as they were. Yet the region in which conditions were by far the worst in regard to the physical state and morale of its defenders, even though there was no immediate enemy pressure on them, was Northeast Mississippi: specifically in the vicinity of Tupelo, where the Army of Tennessee made camp at last, January 8–10, on returning from its disastrous five-week excursion into the state from which it took its name. Its strength was down to 17,700 infantry and artillery, barely half the number answering roll-call when the long files set out north in mid-November. Most of the foot soldiers had no shoes, having worn them out on the icy roads, and an equal proportion of batteries had no guns; 72 pieces had been lost, along with a score of brigade and division commanders. Edward Walthall, whose division had shared with Forrest's horsemen the rear-guard duty that saved what remained of the army in the course of its ten-day retreat across the Tennessee, ended his official report on a sad and bitter note: "The remnant of my command, after this campaign of unprecedented peril and hardship, reduced by battles and exposure, worn and weary with its travel and its toil, numbered less when it reached its rest near Tupelo than one of its brigades had done eight months before."

Aside from a raft of scarehead accounts in northern papers, which told of a great conflict outside Nashville, of rebel prisoners taken in their thousands, and of victory salutes being fired in celebration all across the North, the authorities in Richmond heard nothing of what had occurred until more than two weeks after the battle, when a wire Hood sent on Christmas Day, via Corinth, reached the War Department on January 3. Headed Bainbridge, Alabama, it merely informed Seddon: "I am laying a pontoon here to cross the Tennessee River." That was all it said. But another, addressed to Beauregard at Montgomery, repeated this jot of information, then added: "Please come to Tuscumbia or Bainbridge."

The Creole was already on his way in that direction, not from Montgomery but from Charleston, whose defenses he had been attempting to bolster against expected pressure from occupied Savannah. His purpose in returning West was two-fold: first, to see for himself the condition of Hood's army, widely rumored to be dire, and second to draw troops from it, if possible, to help resist Sherman's pending drive through the Carolinas. He set out on the last day of the year, armed with authority from Davis to replace Hood with Richard Taylor if in his judgment a change in commanders was required. At Macon, three days later, he received two dispatches from Hood, both encouraging. One was nearly three weeks old, having been sent from Spring Hill on December 17, the morrow of the two-day fight at the gates of the Tennessee capital. In it Hood admitted the loss of "fifty pieces of artillery, with several ordnance wagons," but added flatly: "Our loss in killed and wounded is very small." The other message, dated January 3 and wired from Corinth, was quite as welcome. "The army has recrossed the Tennessee River without material loss since the battle in front of Nashville. It will be assembled in a few days in the vicinity of Tupelo, to be supplied with shoes and clothing, and to obtain forage for the animals." A few days later, still pressing westward by a roundabout route on the crippled railroads, Beauregard received a more detailed report, dated January 9, in which Hood not only repeated his claim that his loss in killed and wounded had been light, but also declared that few were missing from other causes. "Our exact loss in prisoners I have not been able to ascertain," he wrote, "but do not think it great."

Considerably reassured by what he had heard from Hood in the course of his balky two-week ride from Charleston, the Louisianan reached Tupelo on January 15 to find his worst fears confirmed by his first sight of the Army of Tennessee in the two months since he parted from it at Tuscumbia, about to set out in balmy weather on a march designed to carry the war to the Ohio. Now only about 15,000 infantry were on hand, huddled miserably in their camps, and of these fewer than half had shoes or blankets to help them withstand the coldest winter the Deep South had known for years. In shock from the sudden fall of the scales from his eyes, Beauregard saw in their faces the horror of Franklin and in their bearing the ravage of the long retreat that followed their rout on the near bank of the Cumberland. He looked at the tattered, shattered ranks, the shot-torn flags and gunless batteries, and could scarcely recognize what he himself had once commanded. "If not, in the strictest sense of the word, a disorganized mob," he later wrote, "it was no longer an army." Rage at Hood for having misled him so grievously these past three weeks, in slanted and delayed reports, gave way in part to sadness when he realized that the distortion had proceeded, not so much from deception, as from embarrassment; not so much from confusion, even, as from shame. Still, it was clear enough that the Kentucky-born Texan had to go, and the sooner the better for all concerned. Hood in fact had already spared him the unpleasant ritual of demanding his resignation. "I respectfully request to be relieved from the command of this army," he had wired Seddon two days ago, and by now the Secretary's answer was on the way: "Your request is complied with. . . . Report to the War Department in Richmond."

Beauregard now had seen for himself the all-too-wretched condition of the main western force, and this seemed on the face of it to preclude action on the second purpose of his trip — the reinforcement of Bragg and Hardee for the defense of the Carolinas against Sherman. "An attempt to move Hood's army at this time would complete its destruction," Dick Taylor wired Davis from Meridian as he prepared to set out for Tupelo to assume command of what one of its members described as "the shattered debris of an army." Old Bory was inclined to agree: the more so because he found it necessary to grant immediate furloughs to some 3500 of the worse broken-down troops, while another 4000 had to be sent to Mobile to help meet what the local commander said was an all-out threat from Canby in New Orleans. Taylor replaced Hood on January 23, and Forrest next day was put in charge of the Department of Mississippi, East Louisiana, and West Tennessee, which he would defend with his three cavalry divisions, now detached. Returning stragglers by then had brought the army's total strength to 18,742 of all arms, including the furloughed men and those on their way to Mobile, whose deduction left only about 11,000 so-called effectives. Not only was this fewer, in all, than the number Beauregard had hoped to send East, but the bedraggled state of this remnant was such that both he and Taylor doubted whether the troops could survive the move from Tupelo to the Carolinas, even if the crippled railroads could manage to get them there before Sherman took up, or indeed completed, his northward drive on Richmond.

Both generals were mistaken, at least in regard to the first of these assessments. Like so many others down the years, they underestimated the toughness of this most resilient of Confederate armies, whose ability to survive mistreatment and defeat was rivaled only by the Army of the Potomac. Even as Taylor assumed command, Stephen Lee's corps — now under Stevenson, pending Lee's recovery from the wound he had suffered on the retreat — was loading aboard the cars, 3078 strong, for its eastern journey over the bucking strap-iron and rotted crossties of a dozen railroads. Despite the Creole's telegraphed protest that "to divide this small army at this juncture to reinforce General Hardee would expose to capture Mobile, Demopolis, Selma, Montgomery, and all the rich valley of the Alabama River," the War Department would neither cancel nor delay the transfer. Cheatham's corps left two days later, and part of Stewart's followed before the month was out. Taylor thus lost practically his whole army within a week of taking over from Hood. Including Forrest's troopers, the furloughed men, the strengthened Mobile garrison, and detachments scattered at random from the Mississippi River to the Georgia line, he retained in all perhaps as many as 30,000 troops for use against greatly superior possible combinations by Thomas, Canby, Washburn, and others. Few as that was, it still was better than five times the number headed east with Beauregard, who was recalled simultaneously to organize and take charge of the defense of the Carolinas.

He reached Augusta on February 1, the day Sherman set out in earnest from Savannah. That was well in advance of the first relay of reinforcements from the Army of Tennessee, who had a more circuitous route to follow. Cheatham's men, for example, after leaving Tupelo on foot, trudged to West Point, where they boarded the cars for Meridian, then changed for Selma and a steamboat ride from there to Montgomery, after which they went by rail again to Columbus, Georgia. From Columbus they marched through Macon and Milledgeville to Mayfield, where they took the cars for Augusta — ten days after Beauregard passed that way — then marched again to Newberry, South Carolina, for a reunion with Stevenson's corps, which had preceded them by a no less roundabout route. Presently, sixty miles across the state, Mrs Chesnut watched them pass through the streets of Camden. In proof of their unquenchable spirit they were singing as they swung along, and the sound of it nearly broke her heart, combined as it was with the thought of all they had been through in the grim three years since Donelson. "So sad and so stirring," she wrote in her diary at nearby Mulberry that night. "I sat down as women have done before and wept. Oh, the bitterness of such weeping! There they go, the gay and gallant few, the last flower of Southern manhood. They march with as airy a tread as if they still believed the world was all on their side, and that there were no Yankee bullets for the unwary."

She had seen their former commander some weeks before, at the end of January, when Hood stopped off in Columbia on his way to Richmond. He no more considered his war career at an end now than he had done after losing a leg at Chickamauga. "I wish to cross the Mississippi River to bring to your aid 25,000 troops," he wired his friend the President on leaving Tupelo. "I know this can be accomplished, and earnestly desire this chance to do you so much good service. Will explain my plan on arrival." Breaking his journey at the South Carolina capital — which no one yet suspected lay in Sherman's path — he visited the family of Brigadier General John S. Preston, whose daughter Sally he was engaged to marry and whose son Willie had been killed fighting under him at Atlanta. "He can stand well enough without his crutch," Mrs Chesnut observed, "but he does very slow walking. How plainly he spoke out those dreadful words, 'My defeat and discomfiture. My army destroyed. My losses.' He said he had nobody to blame but himself."

She found him changed, remote, profoundly grieved, and so did Sally's younger brother Jack, who took her aside to ask: "Did you notice how he stared in the fire, and the livid spots which came out on his face, and the huge drops of perspiration that stood out on his forehead?"

"Yes, he is going over some bitter hours," Mrs Chesnut said. "He sees Willie Preston with his heart shot out. He feels the panic at Nashville, and its shame."

"And the dead on the battlefield at Franklin," Jack agreed. "That agony in his face comes again and again. I can't keep him out of those absent fits. . . . When he looks in the fire and forgets me, and seems going through in his own mind the torture of the damned, I get up and come out as I did just now."

In and around Richmond — where Hood was headed with a scheme no more farfetched, and considerably less expensive, than the one that put him in motion for the Ohio, ten weeks back — R. E. Lee and his troops had just endured their worst hunger crisis of the war to date. Heavy January rains washed out trestles on the Piedmont Railroad, completed last year as a link between Danville and the western Carolinas, and floods at the same time cut off supplies from the upper valley of the James, obliging the army to fall back on its meager food reserve. Within two days Commissary General Lucius Northrop's storehouses were as empty as the men's bellies. Lee's anger flared. "If some change is not made and the commissary department reorganized," he protested to Seddon, "I apprehend dire results. The physical strength of the men, if their courage survives, must fail under this treatment." Davis saw the letter and added his endorsement: "This is too sad to be patiently considered, and cannot have occurred without criminal neglect or gross incapacity." In early February he followed through by replacing the detested Northrop with Colonel Isaac St John, who had performed near miracles in charge of the Nitre and Mining Corps. Promoted to brigadier, St John reorganized the system for delivering supplies from outlying regions and instigated a plan whereby a local farmer undertook to ration an individual soldier for six months: all of which helped to some degree, though not enough. Hunger, even starvation, was a specter that stalked the camps of the Army of Northern Virginia.

Lee fretted and sometimes fumed. "Unless the men and animals can be subsisted," he informed the government, "the army cannot be kept together, and our present lines must be abandoned. Nor can it be moved to any other position where it can operate to advantage without provisions to enable it to move in a body." The implications were clear. There could be but one end for an army that could neither remain where it was nor shift its ground. "Everything, in my opinion, has depended and still depends upon the disposition and feelings of the people. Their representatives can best decide how they will respond to the demands which the public safety requires." Invited to Richmond for a meeting with Virginia congressmen, he told them of his army's plight and repeated what he had said in his report. They replied with professions of loyalty and devotion, expressing a willingness to make any sacrifice required; but that was as far as it went. They had nothing to propose, either to Lee or anyone else, as to what the sacrifice might be. That night after supper, which he took in town with his eldest son Custis, a major general serving under Ewell in the capital defenses, Lee paced up and down the room, gravely troubled. Suddenly he stopped and faced his son, who was seated reading a newspaper by the fire. "Well, Mr Custis," he said angrily, "I have been up to see the Congress and they do not seem able to do anything except eat peanuts and chew tobacco, while my army is starving. I told them the condition my men were in, and that something must be done at once, but I can't get them to do anything." He fell silent, resumed his pacing, then came back. "Mr Custis, when this war began I was opposed to it, bitterly opposed to it, and I told these people that unless every man should do his whole duty, they would repent it. And now" — he paused — "they will repent."

Hunger distressed him, but so did the dwindling number of the hungry. His strength was below 50,000 mainly because of recent detachments which left him with barely more than a man per yard of his long line, including Ewell's reserve militia and the three divisions of troopers, most of whom were posted a hard day's ride or more away, where forage was available for their mounts. Following Hoke's departure for Wilmington, Lee declined a request from the War Department that he send Bushrod Johnson's division as well. "It will necessitate the abandonment of Richmond," he told Davis, who deferred as usual to his judgment in such matters. In early January, however, with Sherman in occupation of Savannah and Governor Andrew G. Magrath calling urgently for troops to reinforce Hardee, Lee sent him a veteran South Carolina brigade from Kershaw's division of Longstreet's corps. That was little enough, considering the risk, not only to Charleston but also to his own rear, if Sherman marched northward unchecked for a link-up with Grant at Petersburg. Still, it was all he felt he could afford, at any rate until Wade Hampton approached him soon afterward with a proposal that Calbraith Butler's troopers be sent to South Carolina for what remained of the winter, leaving their horses behind and procuring new ones for the harassment of the invader once they reached their native state. Lee scarcely enjoyed the notion of losing a solid third of his cavalry, even temporarily, but he saw in this at least a partial solution to the growing remount problem. Accordingly, on January 19 — his fifty-eighth birthday — after a conference with the President, he authorized the horseless departure of Butler's division by rail for the Palmetto State, "with the understanding that it is to return to me in the spring in time for the opening of the campaign." Moreover, having thought the matter through ("If Charleston falls, Richmond follows," Magrath had written; "Richmond may fall and Charleston be saved, but Richmond cannot be saved if Charleston falls") he ordered Hampton himself to go along, explaining to Davis that the South Carolina grandee, badly needed as he was at his Virginia post, would "be of service in mounting his men and arousing the spirit and strength of the State and otherwise do good."

With his chief of cavalry gone far south, along with a third of his veteran troopers — gone for good, events would show, though he did not know that yet — Lee could find small solace elsewhere, least of all in any hope of distracting the host that hemmed him in at Petersburg and Richmond. Off in the opposite direction, conditions were tactically even worse for Jubal Early out on the fringes of the Shenandoah Valley. Discredited and unhappy, down in strength to a scratch collection of infantry under Wharton, called by courtesy a division though it numbered barely a thousand men, and two slim brigades of cavalry under Rosser, he could only observe from a distance Sheridan's continued depredations, which consisted by now of little more than a stirring of dead coals. In mid-January, however, Rosser struck with 300 horsemen across the Alleghenies at Beverly, West Virginia, a supply depot guarded by two Ohio regiments, one of infantry, one of cavalry. At scant cost to himself, he killed or wounded 30 of the enemy and captured 580, along with a considerable haul of rations. Welcome as these last were to his hungry troopers, the raid was no more than a reminder of the days when Jeb Stuart had done such things, not so much to obtain a square meal as to justify his plume. George Crook, the outraged commander of the blue department, secured the dismissal of a pair of lieutenant colonels, heads of the two regiments, "in order that worthy officers may fill their places, which they have proved themselves incompetent to hold," but otherwise the Federals suffered nothing they could not easily abide: certainly not Sheridan, who was chafing beyond the mountains for a return to the main theater. He soon would receive and execute the summons, despite Old Jube, who was charged with trying to hold him where he was.

Meantime Grant did not relax for a moment his close-up hug on Lee's thirty-odd miles of line from the Williamsburg Road to Hatcher's Run. Though he had attempted no movement that might bring him to grips with his opponent since the early-December strike down the Weldon Railroad, no day passed without its long-range casualties and the guns were never silent; not even at night, when the spark-trickling fuzes of mortar bombs described their gaudy parabolas above the rebel earthworks. Boredom provoked strange responses, as when some outdone soldier on either side would leap atop the parapet and defy the marksmen on the other. But a more common phenomenon was the "good run of Johnnies" who came over — "rejoining the Union," they called it — while, across the way, one grayback complained that "the enemy drank coffee, ate fat, fresh beef and good bread, and drank quantities of whiskey, as their roarings at night testified." Reactions varied, up and down the trenches. "There are a good many of us who believe this shooting match had been carried on long enough," one Maryland Confederate declared. "A government that has run out of rations can't expect to do much more fighting and to keep on in a reckless and wanton expenditure of human life. Our rations are all the way from a pint to a quart of corn-meal a day, and occasionally a piece of bacon large enough to grease your palate." On the other hand, a North Carolinian regretted to hear that people back home were in despair over the loss of Fort Fisher. "If some of them could come up here and catch the good spirits of the soldiers," he wrote his family, "I think they would feel better."

Lee himself was a military realist, and as such he had said nine months ago, a month before Grant maneuvered him into immobility south of the James, that a seige could only end in defeat for his penned-up army. He had also shown, however, that as a fighter he was perhaps most dangerous when cornered. Long odds encouraged his fondness for long chances, and not even the present gloom was deep enough to suppress an occasional flash of his old aggressive outlook. "Cheer up, General," a Virginia representative told him on the Richmond visit; "we have done a good work for you today. The legislature has passed a bill to raise an additional 15,000 men for you." Lee did not seem heartened by the news. "Passing resolutions is kindly meant," he replied with a bow, "but getting the men is another matter." He paused, and in that moment his eye brightened. "Yet if I had 15,000 fresh troops, things would look very different," he said. Hope died hard in Lee, whose resolution was shared by those around him. "My faith in this old Army is unshaken," a young staff colonel wrote his sweetheart at the time, adding: "Like a brave old lion brought to bay at last, it is determined to resist to the death and, if die it must, to die game. But we have not quite made up our minds to die, and if God will help us we shall yet prove equal to the emergency."

In essence, that was the view Jefferson Davis applied to the whole Confederacy. He had never embraced the notion that, without allies, the South could win an offensive war against the North; but this was not to say that her people could not confirm her independence for all time, provided they stood firm in the conviction that sustained their forebears in the original Revolution. What had worked for that other infant nation would work for this one. Moreover, once its enemy came to understand that defeat did not necessarily mean submission, that nothing much short of annihilation could translate conquest into victory, a nation willing to "die game" was unlikely to have to die at all. That had been at the root of his November claim that "not the fall of Richmond, nor Wilmington, nor Charleston, nor Savannah, nor Mobile, nor of all combined, can save the enemy from the constant and exhaustive drain of blood and treasure which must continue until he shall discover that no peace is attainable unless based on the recognition of our indefeasible rights." Since then, Savannah had fallen, and Wilmington and Charleston were directly threatened, as Mobile had been for the past six months and Richmond had been from the outset. Yet even here there was comfort for those who saw as Davis and Lee's young colonel did. As the odds lengthened, the margin for choice narrowed; the grimmer the prospect, the readier the people would be to accept their leader's view that resolution meant survival; or so he believed at any rate. After all, the only alternative was surrender, and he considered them no more ready for that than he was, now or ever.

Throughout January, while Sherman reposed in Savannah, letters and telegrams with the familiar signature *Jeff'n Davis* went out to Beauregard, Taylor, Bragg, and Hardee, as well as to the governors of North and South Carolina, Georgia, Alabama, and Mississippi, urging mutual support in the present crisis and vigorous preparation for the day when the tiger unsheathed his claws and started north. Not even Kirby Smith, remote and all but inaccessible, was overlooked as a possible source of borrowed strength. "Under these circumstances," Davis wrote him, stressing the massive Federal shift of troops from west to east, "I think it advisable that you should be charged with military operations on both banks of the Mississippi, and that you should endeavor as promptly as possible to cross that river with as large a force as may be prudently withdrawn." Nothing was likely to come of this; nor did it; yet when Hood showed up the following month, big with his plan for recruiting volunteers in his adoptive Texas, Davis gladly approved the mission and sent him on his Quixotic way, reduced to his previous rank of lieutenant general. Another defeated hero who returned at the same time, Raphael Semmes, was also welcomed and employed. Crossing the Atlantic in late October, four months after he fought and lost the famous channel duel off Cherbourg, he landed at Matamoros, Mexico, then worked his way on a wide swing east from Brownsville to his home in Mobile, where he rested before pushing on to Richmond, saddened by the devastation he saw had been visited on the land since his departure in the summer of '61. Promoted to rear admiral, he was given command of the James River squadron, though Davis in turn was saddened by his inability to award the former captain of the *Alabama* with anything more substantial than three small ironclads and five wooden gunboats, which collectively were no match for a single enemy monitor and in fact could do little more than support the forts and batteries charged with guarding the water approach to the capital in their rear.

Intent as he was on gathering and bracing his scattered and diminished armies for the shock of an eastern Armageddon, Davis had the still harder concomitant task of preparing the nation at large for survival after the defeat made probable by the odds. He too was a military realist, in his way, and as such he knew that, far more important than the loss of any battle — even one on such a promised cataclysmic scale as this — was the possible loss of the will to fight by those behind the lines. There was where wars were ultimately won or lost, and already there were signs that this will, though yet unbroken, was about to crumble. "It is not unwillingness to oppose the enemy," Governor Magrath informed him from threatened South Carolina, "but a chilling apprehension of the futility of doing so which affects the people." Just so: and Davis took as his chief responsibility, as the people's leader, the task of replacing this chill with the warmth of resolution. Whatever the odds, whatever the losses, he believed that so long as they had that, to anything like the degree that he possessed it, their desperate bid for membership in the family of nations could never be annulled.

His need to rally the public behind him had never been more

acute, but neither had it ever been more stringently opposed by his political adversaries, who saw in the current dilemma a fulfillment of all the woes they had predicted from the outset if Congress continued to let him have his way on such issues as conscription and the periodic suspension of the writ of habeas corpus, in violation of the rights not only of the states but also of individuals. Under the press of circumstance, Davis by now had gone beyond such preconceptions. "If the Confederacy falls," he told one congressman in a fruitless effort to bring him over, "there should be written on its tombstone, *Died of a Theory*."

That might be; still, the hard-line States Righters could not see it. Desist from such wicked practices, they were saying, and volunteers would flock again to the colors in numbers sufficient to fling the invader back across the Mason-Dixon line. Yet here was the Chief Executive, clearly seeking to move toward the arming of the slaves, with emancipation to follow as the worst of all possible violations of the rights they held dearest. "What did we go to war for, if not to protect our property?" R. M. T. Hunter wanted to know. A Virginian, he was president pro tempore of the Senate and one of its largest slave-holders, known privately to favor a return to the Union on terms likely to be gentler now than after the South's defeat, which the present crisis had convinced him was inevitable. Some colleagues agreed, while others believed the war could still be won if the Commander in Chief only had men around him who knew how to go about it. In mid-January, accordingly, Speaker of the House Thomas Bocock, after conferring with other Virginia members of that body, informed the President that his state desired a complete change in the Cabinet, all but Treasury Secretary George A. Trenholm, who had succeeded his fellow South Carolinian Christopher Memminger in July; otherwise they would put through a vote of censure that might bring the Government down. Davis had no intention of yielding to this unconstitutional threat, but the maneuver was partly successful anyhow, paradoxically costing him — and them — the only remaining member of his official family from the Old Dominion. Affronted by this slur from representatives of his native state, and wearied by two years and two months of almost constant tribulation, James Seddon promptly submitted his resignation and declined to withdraw it, only consenting to remain through the end of the month and thus give his successor, Kentuckian John C. Breckinridge, time to clear up matters in his Department of Southwest Virginia before coming to Richmond to take over as the Confederacy's fifth Secretary of War.

Under pressure, men responded in accordance with their lights. Some were convinced the time had come for one-man rule, not by Davis but by Lee, the one leader they believed could "guide the country through its present crisis." This went up in smoke, however, when Representative William C. Rives, a fellow Virginian and chairman of the

Committee on Foreign Affairs, went to the general with the proposal carefully worded to lessen the shock. Lee reacted as he might have done if presented with a gift-wrapped rattlesnake. Not only did he consider this man-on-horseback scheme a reflection on his loyalty as a soldier and a citizen, he also sent back word by Rives "that if the President could not save the country, no one could." Others were busy on their own. One-time U.S. Supreme Court Justice John A. Campbell of Alabama, for example, having failed to stave off war by his negotiations with Seward over Sumter, four years back, was in correspondence with a former associate, Supreme Court Justice Samuel Nelson of New York, "proposing to visit him [in Washington] and confer," a confidant noted, "with a view to ascertaining whether there is any way of putting an end to the war and suggesting conference, if Judge Nelson thinks it may lead to any good result, to be held by Judge Campbell with Mr Stanton or one or two other leading men." Supporters of Joe Johnston also stepped up their clamor for his reinstatement at this time, partly as a way of striking at the Administration, while some among them favored more drastic methods. "One solution which I have heard suggested," a War Department official confided in his diary, "is an entire change of the Executive by the resignation of the President and Vice President. This would make Hunter, as president of the Senate, the President, would really make Lee commander-in-chief, and would go far to restore lost confidence."

Davis was spared at least one measure of exacerbation through this period by the absence of his long-time stump opponent Henry Stuart Foote, who had defeated him in a Mississippi race for governor ten years before the war, but now represented a Tennessee district in Congress, where he fulminated alternately against the Yankees and the government. Arrested in early January while trying to cross the Potomac, he announced that he had been on his way to Washington to sue for peace and deliver his people from despotism. On his release, a vote to expel him from the House having failed for lack of a two-thirds majority, he struck out again. This time he made it all the way to Canada, only to find that no Federal authority would treat with him: whereupon he sailed for London, and there issued a manifesto calling on his constituents to secede from the Confederacy and again find freedom in the Union.

Good riddance, friends of the President said. But such relief as his departure brought was more than offset by the simultaneous reappearance of Alexander Stephens, who reacted in just the opposite way to a gloom as deep as Foote's. Instead of entering, he emerged from exile to lead a headlong attack on the Administration, not only for its failure to check Sherman's march through his beloved Georgia, but also for all its previous sins of omission and commission. Resuming his vice-presidential chore of presiding over the Senate, he arrived in time to cast the deciding vote restoring habeas corpus, then moved on to deliver a ringing speech in which he arraigned the government for incompetence, slack judgment, and despotic arrogance at all levels. The war having failed, he called for the removal of Davis or, short of impeachment, the opening of direct negotiations for peace with Washington, ignoring the Executive entirely, since there could be no end to the fighting so long as the present leader remained in control of the nation's destiny. Thus Stephens, whom Davis in friendlier days had referred to as "the little pale star from Georgia," and the Richmond *Examiner* took up the cry in its January 17 issue, urging the assembly of a convention to abolish the Constitution and remove the Chief Executive from office, both in preparation for a return to principles long since betrayed by those in whom the people, to their current dismay, had placed their trust.

On that same day Virginia's General Assembly passed and sent to the President a resolution calling for the appointment of R. E. Lee as commander of all the Confederate armies, on grounds that this would promote their efficiency, reanimate their spirit, and "inspire increased confidence in the final success of our arms." Though Davis saw the request as an attempt to infringe on his constitutional designation as Commander in Chief, he handled the matter tactfully in a letter to Lee, asking whether he wished to undertake this larger duty "while retaining command of the Army of Northern Virginia." Lee promptly replied that he did not. "If I had the ability I would not have the time. . . . I am willing to undertake any service to which you think proper to assign me, but I do not wish you to be misled as to the extent of my capacity." This was written on January 19, but Davis had known so well what Lee would say that he had not waited for an answer. His letter of response to the Assembly had gone out the day before. Thanking the members for their suggestion, as well as for "the uncalculating, unhesitating spirit with which Virginia has, from the moment when she first drew the sword, consecrated the blood of her children and all her natural resources to the achievement of the object of our struggle," he assured them "that whenever it shall be found practicable by General Lee to assume command of all the Armies of the Confederate States, without withdrawing from the direct command of the Army of Northern Virginia, I will deem it promotive of the public interest to place him in such command, and will be happy to know that by so doing I am responding to [your] expressed desire."

That more or less took care of that; or should have, except that the issue would not die. While the Virginians were framing their request, the Confederate Senate — by a 14–2 vote, January 16 — passed a resolution not only favoring Lee's elevation to general-in-chief, but also proposing that Beauregard take charge in South Carolina and that Johnston be restored to command of the Army of Tennessee. Varina Davis was indignant at this attempt to clip her husband's presidential wings. "If I were he," she told one cornered senator, "I would die or be hung before I would submit to the humiliation that Congress intended him." Davis himself had no intention of complying with the resolution, which landed on his desk a few days later. For one thing, he had just disposed of the Lee question, at least to his and the general's satisfaction, and Beauregard was already slated to assume the recommended post on his return from Mississippi, where he was busy turning Hood's army over to Richard Taylor. As for Johnston, Davis was presently engaged in composing a 5000-word survey of that other Virginian's war career from First Manassas to Peachtree Creek, a thorny indictment rounded off with a brief summation: "My opinion of General Johnston's unfitness for command has ripened slowly and against my inclination into a conviction so settled that it would be impossible for me again to feel confidence in him as the commander of an army in the field." Moreover, the lengthy document would close with a final cutting answer to those critics who sought to curtail the Chief Executive's military prerogatives. "The power to assign generals to appropriate duties is a function of the trust confided in me by my countrymen. That trust I have ever been ready to resign at my country's call; but, while I hold it, nothing shall induce me to shrink from its responsibilities or to violate the obligations it imposes."

He would not bow to the three-count resolution. However, now that Lee's deferential reply to the recent feeler had been received, he saw a chance for a compromise that would cost him nothing, either in principle or in practical application, yet would serve to placate his congressional foes, at least in part, and would also, as the Virginia members put it, "inspire increased confidence in the final success of our arms." Accordingly, on January 26 he gladly signed, apparently with no thought of the predicted veto, an act that had passed both houses three days ago, providing for the appointment of a Confederate general-in-chief. Congress of course had Lee in mind, and on the last day of the month Davis recommended his appointment, which the Senate quickly approved. Lee's response, addressed to Adjutant General Samuel Cooper, was something of a snub to the politicians who had worked for his elevation. "I am indebted alone to the kindness of His Excellency the President for my nomination to this high and arduous office," he declared, and a final sentence indicated how little he was likely to assert his independence at the post: "As I have received no instructions as to my duties, I do not know what he desires for me to undertake." To Davis himself, soon afterward, Lee expressed his thanks for "your indulgence and kind consideration. . . . I must beg you to continue these same feelings to me in the future and allow me to refer to you at all times for counsel and advice. I cannot otherwise hope to be of service to you or the country. If I can relieve you from a portion of the constant labor and anxiety which now presses upon you, and maintain a harmonious action between the great armies, I shall be more than compensated for the addition to my present burdens." This was no more and no less than Davis had expected. Not to be outdone in graciousness, he replied: "The honor designed to be bestowed has been so fully won, that the fact of conferring it can add nothing to your fame."

Greeted with enthusiasm, Lee's appointment encouraged many waverers to hope that his genius, which had transformed near-certain defeat into triumph in Virginia two and one half years ago, would now work a like miracle on a larger scale; the man who had saved beleaguered Richmond from McClellan, flinging him back in confusion, first on his gunboats and then on his own capital, would save the beleaguered Confederacy from Grant. But Davis knew only too well that the confirmed defeatists — men like Hunter, Campbell, and Stephens — were not converted by this stroke, which after all was of the pen and not the sword. They were for peace, peace *now*, and would not believe that anyone, even Robert E. Lee, could do anything more than stave off defeat and thus make the terms for surrender that much stiffer when it came. Above all, they and the Impossiblists, who wanted him removed for other reasons, mainly having to do with his overriding of States Rights, believed that Davis would never consent to the mildest compromise the Union authorities might offer, not only because of his known conviction that the loss of the war meant the loss of honor, but also because of his personal situation as the leader of a failed rebellion. "We'll hang Jeff Davis on a sour apple tree!" blue-clad troops were singing now, to the tune of *John Brown's Body*, and Republican politicians were saying much the same thing, in words as harsh and even more specific, from stumps all over the North, to wild applause.

Davis knew this, and knew as well that he had to find some way to answer and, if possible, discredit his domestic critics before he could unite the nation to meet the impending crisis. But how? He watched and waited. Then it came: from Lincoln, of all people — or, more specifically, Old Man Blair.

Blair, that long-time adviser to all the Presidents back through Jackson, wanted to add one more to his list in the person of Jefferson Davis, who had been his friend for more than twenty years, but was now beyond his reach. Or perhaps not. Approaching seventy-four, the distinguished Marylander hoped to crown a life of public service with a trip to Richmond for the purpose of persuading Davis to treat for peace and thereby end the war. In mid-December, shortly after Sherman reached the coast, Blair went to Lincoln and asked permission to make the trip. "Come to me after Savannah falls," the President told him; which he did, and on December 28 was handed a card inscribed, "Allow the bearer, F. P. Blair, Senr. to pass our lines, go South and return. A. Lincoln."

He left at once, and on December 30 sent Davis two letters from Grant's headquarters at City Point. One was brief, requesting admission to the Confederacy to search for some title papers missing since Jubal Early's July visit to his home in Silver Spring. The other, considerably longer, remarked that the first would serve as a cover for his true purpose, which was to "unbosom my heart frankly and without reserve" on matters regarding the "state of affairs of our country." He was "wholly unaccredited," he said, but he hoped to offer certain "suggestions" he believed would be of interest.

There were delays. Davis recognized another peace feeler, and though he did not expect to find anything advantageous in the exchange under present circumstances, he knew that a refusal to see the Washington emissary was apt to bring still heavier charges of intransigence on his head. Besides, his wife encouraged the visit for old times' sake. In the end he wrote the elder statesman to come on, and Blair did. Lodged unregistered at the Spotswood on January 12, he came that evening to the White House, where Mrs Davis met him with a hug.

Alone with Davis in the presidential study, he elaborated on what he had meant by "suggestions." In brief, his plan was for the North and South to observe a cessation of hostilities for such time as it might take to drive the French and their puppet Maximilian out of Mexico, possibly with none other than Jefferson Davis in command of the joint expeditionary force; after which the two former combatants, flushed with victory from their common vindication of the Monroe Doctrine, could sit down and discuss their various differences in calm and dignity. Davis did not think highly of the plan, mainly because it sounded to him like one of Seward's brainstorms, concocted for some devious purpose. Blair replied that the crafty New Yorker had had and would have no part in the matter. "The transaction is a military transaction, and depends entirely on the Commander in Chief." Whatever Seward's shortcomings, which admittedly were many, Lincoln was altogether trustworthy, Blair declared. Davis said he was glad to hear it. In point of fact, he added, he was willing now, and always had been, to enter into negotiations for ending the war by this or any other honorable method, and in demonstration of his sincerity he drafted a letter for Blair to take back and show Lincoln. "Notwithstanding the rejection of our former offers," the letter read in closing, "I would, if you could promise that a commission, minister, or other agent would be received, appoint one immediately, and renew the effort to enter into a conference with a view to secure peace to the two countries."

Back in Washington, Blair had a second interview with Lincoln on January 18. After giving him Davis's letter to read he reported that he had seen a number of prominent Confederates in the southern capital, many of them friends of long standing, and had found them for the most part despondent about the outcome of the war. Lincoln appeared more interested in this last than in the letter, which seemed to him to promise little in the way of progress, but in the end gave Blair a letter of his own, in indirect answer to the one from Davis. "You may say to him that I have constantly been, am now, and shall continue, ready to receive any agent whom he, or any other influential person now resisting the national authority, may informally send to me with the view of securing peace to the people of our one common country."

There in the final words of the paired notes — "the two countries": "our one common country" — the impasse was defined and, paradoxically, the maneuvering began in earnest: not so much between the two leaders, though there was of course that element in what followed, as between them and their respective home-front adversaries. Blair went back to Richmond four days later, then returned, his part complete, and newspapers North and South began to speculate frantically on what might come of the old man's go-between travels back and forth. Southern journalists accused Davis of near treason for having entertained a "foreign enemy" in the White House, while those who were for peace at almost any price expressed fears that he had rejected an offer to end the war on generous terms. Conversely, up in Washington, the Jacobins set up a hue and cry that Lincoln was about to stop the fighting just short of the point where they could begin to exact the vengeance they saw as their due from the rebellion. Each of the two Presidents thus had much to fret him while playing their game of high-stakes international poker, and they functioned in different styles: different not only from each other, but also different each from what he had been before. During this diplomatic interlude, Lincoln and Davis — fox and hedgehog — swapped roles. Lincoln remained prickly and unyielding, almost stolid, though always willing to engage on his own terms as he defined them. It was Davis who was foxy, secretive and shifty, quick to snap.

He began by inviting the Vice President to a consultation — their first since the government moved to Richmond, nearly four years ago — at which he showed him Lincoln's letter, reviewed its background, and requested an opinion. Stephens replied that he thought the matter should be pursued, "at least so far as to obtain if possible a conference upon the subject." Asked for recommendations on the makeup of the proposed commission, he suggested the Chief Executive as the most effective member, then added the names of several men who were known to be as strong for peace as he was, including John A. Campbell, the former Supreme Court Justice, now Assistant Secretary of War. Davis thanked him for his time and trouble, and next day, January 25, summoned the chosen three to his office. They were Campbell, Robert Hunter — who presided over the Senate, as president pro tem, in the Vice President's frequent absences — and Stephens himself. The frail Georgian protested but was overruled, and all three were handed their instructions: "In conformity with the letter of Mr Lincoln, of which the foregoing is a copy, you are requested to proceed to Washington City for an informal conference with him upon the issues involved in the existing war, and for the purpose of securing peace to the two countries."

There again were the critical words, "two countries." Judah Benjamin in the original draft had written, "for conference with him upon the subject to which it relates," but Davis had made the revision, not wanting to leave the trio of known "submissionists" any leeway when they reached the conference table. He knew well enough how little was likely to come of the effort with this stipulation attached, though he did not go into that at present. He merely informed the commissioners that they would set out four days from now, on Sunday the 29th, passing beyond the farthest Petersburg outworks under a flag of truce, presumably bound for Washington and a talk with Lincoln about the chances of ending the war without more bloodshed.

✗ 3 ✗

And so it was. Due east of Petersburg on that designated Sunday, near the frost-rimed scar of the Crater, a white flag appeared on the rebel parapet and a messenger came over with a letter addressed to Lieutenant General U. S. Grant. Word spread up and down the opposing lines that something was up; something important, from the look of things — something that maybe had to do with peace.

As it turned out, there was plenty of time for speculation. Grant was down the coast, looking over the Wilmington defenses with Schofield, who was to move against them as soon as his transports could descend the ice-jammed Potomac. By the time a fast packet got the flag-of-truce message to Fort Fisher, and word came back that the applicants were to be admitted and lodged at headquarters pending Grant's return, two days had passed. Then at last, on the final afternoon in January, a carriage bearing the three would-be commissioners came rolling out the Jerusalem Plank Road, which was lined with gray-clad soldiers and civilians, and on to an opening in the works, which were crowded left and right, as far as the eye could follow — northward to the Appomattox and south toward Fort Hell and Fort Damnation — with spectators who jammed the parapets for a look at what some were saying meant an end to all the killing. Across the way, the Union works were crowded too, and when the carriage turned and began to jolt eastward over the shell-pocked ground between the trenches, a roar of approval went up from opposite sides of the line of battle. "Our men cheered loudly," Meade would write his wife that night, "and the soldiers on both sides cried out lustily, 'Peace! Peace!'" Blue and gray alike, west and east of that no-man's land the carriage rocked across, spokes twinkling in the sunlight, men swung their hats and hollered for all they were worth. "Cheer upon cheer was given," a Federal artillerist would recall, "extending for some distance to the right and left of the lines, each side trying to cheer the loudest. 'Peace on the brain' appeared now to have spread like a contagion. Officers of all grades, from lieutenants to major generals, were to be seen flying in all directions to catch a glimpse of the gentlemen who were apparently to bring peace so unexpectedly."

Grant had returned by then, and though he saw to it that the three Confederates were made comfortable on a headquarters steamer tied up at the City Point wharf, he was careful not to discuss their mission with them. Which was just as well, since he received next morning a wire from the Commander in Chief, warning against any slackening of vigilance or effort on his part. "Let nothing which is transpiring change, hinder, or delay your military movements or plans," Lincoln told him, and Grant replied: "There will be no armistice in consequence of the presence of Mr Stephens and others within our lines. The troops are kept in readiness to move at the shortest notice if occasion should justify it." That afternoon Major Thomas Eckert, who normally had charge of the War Department telegraph office in Washington, arrived with instructions from the President to interview the proposed commissioners. Seward was on his way to Fort Monroe, and Eckert was to send them there to talk with him, provided they would state in writing that they had come for the purpose Lincoln had specified; that is, "with a view of securing peace to the people of our one common country."

Eckert saw them that evening. One look at their instructions quickly convinced him the main condition was unmet. At 9.30 he wired Washington, "I notified them that they could not proceed."

That seemed to be that; another peace effort no sooner launched than sunk. Lincoln inclined to that view next morning, February 2, when he received a somewhat puzzled telegram Seward had sent last night from Fort Monroe: "Richmond party not here." Eckert's followed, explaining the holdup. Lincoln was about to recall them both, ending the mission, when Stanton came in with a message just off the wire from Grant, a long and earnest plea that negotiations go forward despite Eckert's disapproval. In it, the general seemed to have come under the influence of the contagion that infected his soldiers, two days ago, while they watched the rebel carriage approach their lines. He had had a letter from and a brief talk with two of the Confederates, following Eckert's refusal to let them proceed, and he had been favorably impressed. "I will state confidentially, but not officially to become a matter of record," he wired Stanton, "that I am convinced, upon conversation with Messrs Stephens and Hunter, that their intentions are good and their desire sincere to restore peace and union.... I fear now their going back without any expression from anyone in authority will have a bad influence." He himself did not feel free to treat with them, of course; "I am sorry however that Mr Lincoln cannot have an interview with the two named in this dispatch, if not all three now within our lines. Their letter to me was all the President's instructions contemplated to secure their safe conduct if they had used the same language to Major Eckert."

For Lincoln, this put a different face on the matter. He got off two wires at once. One was to Seward, instructing him to remain where he was. The other was to Grant. "Say to the gentlemen I will meet them personally at Fortress Monroe as soon as I can get there."

He left within the hour, not even taking time to notify his secretary or any remaining member of his cabinet, and by nightfall was with Seward aboard the steamer *River Queen*, riding at anchor under the guns of Fort Monroe. The rebel commissioners were on a nearby vessel, also anchored in Hampton Roads; Seward had not seen them yet, and Lincoln sent word that he would receive them next morning in the *Queen*'s saloon. His instructions to the Secretary of State had been brief and to the point, listing three "indispensable" conditions for peace. One was "restoration of the national authority throughout all the states"; another was that there be no "receding" on the slavery question; while the third provided for "no cessation of hostilities short of the end of the war, and the disbanding of all forces hostile to the government." Lincoln considered himself bound by these terms as well, and had no intention of yielding on any of them, whatever else he might agree to.

The Confederates were punctual, coming aboard shortly after breakfast Friday morning, February 3. Handshakes and an exchange of amenities, as between old friends, preceded any serious discussion. "Governor, how is the Capitol? Is it finished?" Hunter asked. Seward described the new dome and the big brass door, much to the interest of the visitors, all three of whom had spent a good part of their lives in Washington, Campbell as a High Court justice, Hunter as a senator, and Stephens as a nine-term congressman. Lincoln was particularly drawn to the last of these, having admired him when they served together in the House at the time of the Mexican War, which they both opposed. "A little, slim, pale-faced, consumptive man," he called him then, writing home that his fellow Whig had "just concluded the very best speech of an hour's length I ever heard." Stephens, though still pale-faced, seemed to have put on a great deal of weight in the past few years; that is until he took off a voluminous floor-length overcoat fashioned from blanket-thick cloth, a long wool muffler, and several shawls wound round and round his waist and chest against the cold. Then it was clear that he had not added an ounce of flesh to his ninety-four pounds of skin and bones. "Never have I seen so small a nubbin come out of so much husk," Lincoln said with a smile as they shook hands.

That too helped to break the ice, and when the five took seats in the saloon, conversing still of minor things, the Union President and Confederate Vice President spoke of their days as colleagues, sixteen years ago. There had been a welcome harmony between the states and sections then, Stephens remarked, and followed with a question that went to the heart of the matter up for discussion: "Mr President, is there no way of putting an end to the present trouble?" Lincoln responded in kind, echoing the closing words of his recent message to Congress. "There is but one way," he said, "and that is for those who are resisting the laws of the Union to cease that resistance." Although this was plain enough, so far as it went, Stephens wanted to take it further. "But is there no other question," he persisted, "that might divert the attention of both parties for a time?" Lincoln saw that the Georgian was referring to the Mexico scheme, about which he himself had known nothing until Blair's return from Richmond, and declared that it had been proposed without the least authority from him. "The restoration of the Union is a *sine qua non* with me," he said; anything that was to follow had to follow that. Stephens took this to mean that a Confederate pledge for reunion must precede such action, and maintained that it was unneeded. "A settlement of the Mexican question in this way would necessarily lead to a peaceful settlement of our own." But that was not what Lincoln had meant — as he now made clear. He would make no agreement of any kind, he said, until the question of reunion was disposed of once and for all. That had to come first, if only because he could never agree to bargain with men in arms against the government in his care. Hunter, who had preceded Benjamin as Secretary of State and prided himself on a wide knowledge of international precedents, remarked at this point that Charles I of England had dealt with his domestic foes in just that way. Lincoln looked askance at the Virginian, then replied: "Upon questions of history I must refer you to Mr Seward, for he is posted in such things. My only distinct recollection of the matter is that Charles lost his head."

Hunter subsided, at least for a time, and the talk moved on to other concerns. Campbell, ever the jurist, wanted to know what the northern authorities had in mind to do, when and if the Union was restored, about southern representation in Congress, the two Virginias, and wartime confiscation of property, including slaves. Lincoln and Seward, between them, dealt with the problems one by one. Congress of course would rule on its own as to who would be admitted to a seat in either house. West Virginia was and would remain a separate state. As for compensation, both considered it likely that Congress would be lenient in its handling of property claims once the war fever cooled down, and Lincoln added that he would employ Executive clemency where he could, though he had no intention of revoking the Emancipation Proclamation, which was still to be tested in the courts. At this point Seward broke the news of the Thirteenth Amendment, approved while the commissioners were entering Grant's lines three days ago, and Lincoln remarked that he still favored some form of compensation by the government for the resultant loss in slaves — provided, of course, that Congress would go along, upon ratification, and vote the money for payment to former owners; which seemed unlikely, considering the present reported mood and makeup of that body.

All this came as a considerable shock to the three rebel listeners, but the shock was mild compared to what followed when Hunter, having recovered a measure of his aplomb, expressed their reaction in a question designed to demonstrate just how brutally intransigent such terms were. "Mr President, if we understand you correctly, you think that we of the Confederacy have committed treason; that we are traitors to your government; that we have forfeited our rights, and are proper subjects for the hangman. Is that not about what your words imply?" There was a pause while they waited for Lincoln's answer, and presently he gave it. "Yes," he said. "You have stated the proposition better than I did. That is about the size of it."

That remained about the size of it throughout the four-hour exchange in the *River Queen* saloon. He was unyielding, and though he told a couple of tension-easing stories — causing Hunter to observe with a wry smile, "Well, Mr Lincoln, we have about concluded that we shall not be hanged as long as you are President: if we behave ourselves" — the most he offered was a promise to use Executive clemency when the time came, so far at least as Congress would allow it. The Confederates, bound as they were by their own leader's "two countries" stipulation, could offer quite literally nothing at all, and so the conference wound down to a close.

Amid the flurry of parting handshakes, Lincoln said earnestly: "Well, Stephens, there has been nothing we could do for our country. Is there anything I can do for you personally?" Little Aleck, once more immured within his bulky overcoat and wrappers, shook his head. "Nothing," he said. But then he had a thought. "Unless you can send me my nephew who has been for twenty months a prisoner on Johnson's Island." Lincoln brightened at the chance. "I'll be glad to do it. Let me have his name." He wrote the name in a notebook, and that was how it came about that Lieutenant John A. Stephens, captured at Vicksburg in mid-'63, was removed from his Lake Erie island prison camp and brought to Washington the following week for a meeting with the President at the White House. Lincoln gave him a pass through the Union lines and a photograph of himself as well, saying of the latter: "You had better take that along. It is considered quite a curiosity down your way, I believe."

Young Stephens and the photograph were about all the South got out of the shipboard conference in Hampton Roads, except for an appended gift from the Secretary of State. Reaching their own steamer the commissioners looked back and saw a rowboat coming after them, its only occupant a Negro oarsman. He brought them a basket of champagne and a note with Seward's compliments. As they waved their handkerchiefs in acknowledgment and thanks, they saw the genial New Yorker standing on the deck of the *Queen*, a bosun's trumpet held to his mouth. "Keep the champagne," they heard him call to them across the water, "but return the Negro."

Stephens, Hunter, and Campbell spent another night tied up to the wharf at City Point, and then next day recrossed the Petersburg lines, their mission ended. "Today they returned to Richmond," Meade wrote his wife that evening, "but what was the result of their visit no one knows. At the present moment, 8 p.m., the artillery on our lines is in full blast, clearly proving that at this moment there is no peace."

★　★　★

A basket of wine, supplemented in time by a homesick Georgia lieutenant bearing a photograph of Lincoln, seemed a small return for the four-day effort by the three commissioners, who came back in something resembling a state of shock from having learned that negotiations were to follow, not precede, capitulation. Davis, however, was far from disappointed at the outcome. His double-barreled purpose — to discredit the submissionists and unite the country behind him by having them elicit the northern leader's terms for peace — had been fulfilled even beyond a prediction made in the local *Enquirer* while the conference was in progress down the James. "We think it likely to do much good," the editor wrote, "for our people to understand in an authoritative manner from men like Vice President Stephens, Senator Hunter, and Judge Campbell the exact degree of degradation to which the enemy would reduce us by reconstruction. We believe that the so-called mission of these gentlemen will teach our people that the terms of the enemy are nothing less than unconditional surrender." Now that this had been borne out, Davis used much the same words in a note attached to a formal report of the proceedings, submitted to Congress on the Monday after the Saturday the three envoys reappeared in Richmond: "The enemy refused to enter into negotiations with the Confederate States, or with any of them separately, or to give to our people any other terms or guaranties than those which the conqueror may grant, or to permit us to have [peace] on any other basis than our unconditional submission to their rule."

Wasting no time, he struck while the propaganda iron was hot. Amid the rush of indignation at the news from Hampton Roads, Virginia's redoubtable Extra Billy called a meeting at Metropolitan Hall that same evening, February 6, to afford the public a chance to adopt resolutions condemning the treatment its representatives had received three days ago, on board the *River Queen,* at the hands of the northern leader and his chief lieutenant. Robert Hunter was one of the speakers. "If anything was wanted to stir the blood," he informed the close-packed gathering, "it was furnished when we were told that the United States could not consent to entertain any proposition coming from us as a people. Lincoln might have offered *some*thing. . . . No treaty, no stipulation, no agreement, either with the Confederate States jointly or with them separately: what was this but unconditional submission to the mercy of the conquerors?"

The crowd rumbled its resentment, subsiding only to be aroused by other exhortations, then presently stirred with a different kind of excitement as a slim figure in worn gray homespun entered from Franklin Street, paused in the doorway, and started down the aisle. It was Davis. Governor Smith greeted the unexpected visitor warmly and escorted him to the platform, where he stood beside the lectern and looked out over the cheering throng. "A smile of strange sweetness came to his lips," one witness later wrote, "as if the welcome assured him that, decried as he was by the newspapers and pursued by the clamor of politicians, he had still a place in the hearts of his countrymen."

When the applause died down at last he launched into an hour-long oration which all who heard it agreed was the finest he ever delivered. Even Pollard of the *Examiner,* his bitterest critic south of the Potomac, noting "the shifting lights on the feeble, stricken face," declared afterwards that he had never "been so much moved by the power of words spoken for the same space of time." Others had a similar reaction, but no one outside the hall would ever know; Davis spoke from no text, not even notes, and the absence of a shorthand reporter caused this "appeal of surpassing eloquence" to be lost to all beyond range of his voice that night. Hearing and watching him, Pollard experienced "a strange pity, a strange doubt, that this 'old man eloquent' was the weak and unfit President" he had spent the past three years attacking. "Mr Davis frequently paused in his delivery; his broken health admonished him that he was attempting too much; but frequent cries of 'Go on' impelled him to speak at a length which he had not at first proposed. . . . He spoke with an even, tuneful flow of words, spare of gestures; his dilated form and a voice the lowest notes of which were distinctly audible, and which anon rose as a sound of a trumpet, were yet sufficient to convey the strongest emotions and to lift the hearts of his hearers to the level of his grand discourse."

Apparently the speech was in part a repetition of those he had made last fall, en route through Georgia and the Carolinas, in an attempt to whip up the flagging spirits of a people distressed by the loss of Atlanta. Now, as then, he praised the common soldier, decried the profiteer, and expressed the conviction that if half the absent troops would return to the ranks no force on earth could defeat the armies of the South. In any case, with or without these shirkers, he predicted that if the people would stand firm, the Confederacy would "compel the Yankees, in less than twelve months, to petition us for peace on our own terms." The darker the hour, the greater the honor for having survived it — and, above all, the deeper the discouragement of the enemy for his failure to bring a disadvantaged nation to its knees. As it was, he had nothing but scorn for those who spoke of surrender: especially now that Lincoln had unmasked himself at Hampton Roads, revealing the true nature of his plans for the postwar subjugation of all who had opposed him and his Jacobin cohorts in the North. The alternative to continued resistance was unthinkable. Not only did he prefer death "sooner than we should ever be united again" with such a foe; "What shall we say of the disgrace beneath which we should be buried if we surrender with an army in the field more numerous than that with which Napoleon achieved the glory of France — an army standing among its homesteads?" All this he said, and more, in response to enthusiastic urgings from the crowd, before he reached the ringing peroration. "Let us then unite our hands and hearts; lock our shields together, and we may well believe that before another summer solstice falls upon us, it will be the enemy who will be asking us for conferences and occasions in which to make known *our* demands."

There followed a series of patriotic rallies featuring speakers who took their cue from this lead-off address by the President in Metropolitan Hall. Three days later, at the African Church — requisitioned for the occasion because of its vast capacity — Hunter once more described how Lincoln had "turned from propositions of peace with cold insolence," and told his indignant listeners: "I will not attempt to draw a picture of subjugation. It would require a pencil dipped in blood." Benjamin, the next man up, came forward with his accustomed smile. "Hope beams in every countenance," he said. "We know in our hearts that this people must conquer its freedom or die." He brought up the touchy subject of arming the slaves, calling on Virginia to set the example by furnishing 20,000 black recruits within the next twenty days, and was pleased to find that the subject was not so touchy after all. The outsized crowd approved with scarcely a murmur of dissent. Davis spoke too, though briefly, again predicting a Confederate victory by the end of summer, then left the rostrum to other dignitaries who continued the daylong oratory into the evening. Judge Campbell, unstrung by his recent visit beyond the enemy lines, was not among them; nor was Stephens, who — though he was present, as Campbell was not —

was too disheartened to join the chorus of affirmation. Like all the rest, he was swept along by the President's address, which he praised for its "loftiness of sentiment and rare form of expression," as well as for the "magnetic influence in its delivery."

Even so, looking back on it later, he pronounced it "little short of demention." Asked by Davis after the meeting what his plans were, he replied that he intended "to go home and remain there." He would "neither make any speech, nor even make known to the public in any way of the general condition of affairs, but quietly abide the issue of fortune." Discredited, outmaneuvered, he threw in the sponge at last. He left Richmond next day, returning to Liberty Hall, his home near Crawfordville — a deserter, like some hundred thousand others — and there remained, in what he termed "perfect retirement," for the balance of the war.

Such defection was rather the exception through this time, even among the Vice President's fellow Georgians who lately had been exposed to the wrath or whim of Sherman's bummers. Howell Cobb, whose plantation had been gutted on specific orders from the red-haired destroyer himself, spoke fervently in Macon that same week, calling on the people to unite behind their government, which he said could never be conquered if they held firm. "Put me in my grave," he cried, "but never put on me the garments of a Submissionist!" Benjamin Hill followed Stephens back to their native state, but for a different purpose. Addressing crowds in Columbus, Forsyth, and La Grange, he declared that the Confederacy still had half a million men of military age, together with plenty of food and munitions; all it lacked was the will to win. "If we are conquered, subjugated, disgraced, ruined," the senator asserted with a figurative sidelong glance at Joe Brown in Milledgeville and Little Aleck in nearby Liberty Hall, "it will be the work of those enemies among us [who] will accomplish that work by destroying the faith of our people in their government." Robert Toombs, the fieriest Georgian of them all, emerged from his Achilles sulk to assume the guise of Nestor in reaction to the news from Hampton Roads. All that was needed was resolution, a recovery of the verve that had prevailed in the days when he himself was in the field, he told a wrought-up audience in Augusta. "We have resources enough to whip *forty* Yankee nations," he thundered, "if we could call back the spirit of our departed heroes." Similarly, in North Carolina, even so confirmed an obstructionist as Zeb Vance came over when he learned of Lincoln's "terms" for acceptance of the South's surrender. In response, the governor issued a mid-February proclamation calling for all Tarheels to "assemble in primary meetings in every county in the State, and let the whole world, and especially our enemies, see how a free people can meet a proposition for their absolute submission.... Great God! Is there a man in all this honorable, high spirited, and noble Commonwealth so steeped in every conceivable meanness, so blackened with all the guilt of treason, or so damned with all the leprosy of cowardice as to say: 'Yes, we will submit to this' . . . whilst there yet remains half a million men amongst us able to resist? . . . Should we willfully throw down an organized government, disband our still powerful armies, and invite all these fearful consequences upon our country, we would live to have our children curse our gray hairs for fastening our dishonor upon them."

Editors formerly critical of practically everything Davis did or stood for, especially during the twenty months since Gettysburg and the fall of Vicksburg, now swung abruptly to full support of his administration, as if in admission of their share in reducing public morale to so low a point that Lincoln felt he could afford to spurn all overtures for peace except on terms amounting to unconditional surrender. Formerly gloomy, they turned hopeful, claiming to find much that was encouraging in the current military situation. "Nil Desperandum," writing in the *Enquirer,* pointed out that less of the Confederacy was actually occupied by the enemy now than there had been two years ago; Sherman had marched through it, true enough, but had not garrisoned or held what he traversed, except for Savannah, where he had been obliged to stop and catch his breath. What was more, he had not really whipped anyone en route, according to the Georgia humorist Charles H. Smith, who signed himself Bill Arp: "Didn't the rebellyun klose rite up behind him, like shettin a pair of waful irons?" Pollard of the *Examiner* agreed. "His campaign comes to nought if he cannot reach Grant; nothing left of it but the brilliant zig-zag of a raid, vanishing as heat lightning in the skies."

Clergymen throughout the South, of varied denominations, prepared to undertake a new crusade designed to reunite their congregations, along with any number of strayed sheep, in resistance to the unholy fate it now was clear the enemy had in mind to impose in the wake of their defeat. Army units began sending home letters signed in mass, expressing confidence in victory if only those behind the lines would emulate the soldiers at the front. In response, a hundred Mobile citizens established the League of Loyal Confederates, dedicated to the promotion of such support, and vowed to expand the society to cover every section of the nation, whether occupied or still free of blue contamination. Congress too was caught up in the fervor of the occasion. Indignant over Lincoln's reported terms at Hampton Roads, both houses voted overwhelmingly for a set of resolutions asserting that "no alternative is left to the people of the Confederate States, but a continuance of the war or submission to terms of peace alike ruinous and dishonorable." The choice was plain, and Congress made it with no opposing vote in the Senate and only one in the House. Fighting would continue, the joint resolution declared, until "the independence of the Confederate States shall have been established."

Davis thus gained more than he had planned for when, at the urging of Old Man Blair, he first decided to send the trio of sub-missionists to confer with Lincoln on the prospect of "securing peace to the two countries." Not only had they returned discredited, as he had expected and assured in their instructions, but the nature of their failure — made evident by Hunter when he repeated at rallies the harsh terms laid out for them aboard the *River Queen* — united the clashing factions within the Confederacy more effectively than any single event had done since far-off Chancellorsville. Elation had been the causative reaction then. Now it was indignation, quite as heady an emotion and even more cohesive in effect, since not to feel it was to confess a lack of honor sensible to insult. And yet there was a measure of elation, too, this cold first week in February, based on the simul-taneous elevation of Lee as general-in-chief, the replacement of Nor-throp with Isaac St John as commissary general, and the appointment of Breckinridge — even more popular as the hero of New Market than he had been as the South's favorite candidate in the presidential election that brought on the current struggle for independence — to the post vacated by Seddon, who was associated with all the military disasters that had occurred since he took office, two long years ago. Men noted these administrative changes and found in them a cause for hope that the war, which Lincoln had just made clear would have to be fought to the finish, had taken a sharp turn for the better, at least in the way it would be run.

How deep the emotion went was another matter. It might be what Pollard, reverting to type, would call "a spasmodic revival, or short fever of the popular mind"; in which case not even the indignation, let alone the tentative elation, would outlast the march begun that week by Sherman, north through the Carolinas from Savannah. "The South's condition is pitiable," Seward had told his wife after talking with Blair on the eve of the Hampton Roads conference, "but it is not yet fully realized there." That too might be true; in which case, deep or shallow, the unifying reaction came too late. Davis had silenced his most vocifer-ous critics, driving them headlong from the public view; but he knew well enough, from hard experience, that they were only waiting in the wings. One bad turn of fortune, left or right, would bring them back, stage center and full-voiced.

✗ 4 ✗

Lee received formal notice of his appointment to command of all the armies on February 6, midway through a heavy three-day attack on his right flank at Hatcher's Run, word of which had reached him the day before, a Sunday, while he was at church in Petersburg. Contrary to his usual custom, though he waited out the service, he went with the first group to the chancel for Communion before he left to ride down the Boydton Plank Road, where guns were growling and infantry was engaged on the far side of the frozen stream. Some green recruits, exposed to their first large-scale action, were in a state of panic along one critical part of the line, and when the good gray general rode out to rally them — a heroic figure, accustomed to exciting worshipful fervor in veterans who then would set up a shout of "Lee to the rear! Lee to the rear!" — one badly rattled soldier flung both hands above his head in terror and exclaimed: "Great God, old man, get out of the way! You don't know nothing!"

Grant had made no serious effort to attack or flank the Petersburg defenses since his late-October drive to cut the Southside Railroad was turned back at Burgess Mill, where the Boydton Plank Road straddled Hatcher's Run. Mindful however of Lincoln's admonition on the eve of Hampton Roads — "Let nothing which is transpiring change, hinder, or delay your military movements or plans" — he considered it time, despite the bitterness of the weather, to give the thing another try, less ambitious both in size and scope, but profitable enough if it worked out. This time he would not attempt to seize the railroad; he would be content to reach and hold the Boydton pike, which ran northeast from Stony Creek and Dinwiddie Courthouse, believing that this was the route Lee's supply wagons took from the new Petersburg & Weldon railhead at Hicksford, just beyond the Meherrin River. Accordingly, on February 4 — the Saturday the three rebel envoys returned to their

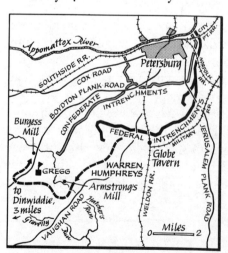

own lines from City Point — Warren and Humphreys were instructed to move out next morning, each with two of his three divisions, preceded by Gregg's troopers, who were to strike and patrol the objective from Dinwiddie to Burgess Mill, capturing whatever enemy trains were on it, until the infantry arrived to establish permanent occupation. So ordered: Gregg set out before dawn Sunday, and Warren followed from his position on the Union left, two miles west of Globe Tavern. Humphreys brought up the rear, his marchers breathing steam in the frosty air while their boots crunched ice in puddles along the way.

Hard as the weather was on men in the open, mounted or afoot, it had much to do with their success, first in reaching the Boydton Road unchallenged and then in holding their own through most of the three-day action which presently went into the books as the Battle of Hatcher's Run. Thinly clad and poorly fed, shivering in their trenches north of the stream, the Confederates apparently had not believed that any general, even Grant, would purposely expose his troops to the cutting wind, whistling over a bleak landscape frozen iron hard, for a prize of so little worth. As it turned out, Lee was scarcely using the Dinwiddie artery as a supply route at all, considering it too vulnerable to just such a strike as now was being made. Early on the scene, the blue troopers captured only a few wagons out on a foraging expedition, and when the infantry came up — Warren on the left, confronting Burgess Mill, and Humphreys opposite Armstrong's Mill, two miles below — there was little for them to do but dig in under long-range fire from guns in the rebel works beyond the run. Late that afternoon the graybacks tried a sortie against Humphreys, who rather easily turned it back. Reinforced that night by two divisions sent by Meade from the lines on the far side of Petersburg — one from Wright, the other from Parke — he was joined before daylight by Warren and Gregg, who gave up holding and patrolling the unused Boydton Plank Road in favor of a concentration of all available forces. Next morning (February 6; Lee was notified of his confirmation as general-in-chief, and Davis would speak that night in Metropolitan Hall) scouts reported the defenders hugging their works, but a probe by Warren that afternoon provoked a counterattack that drove him back in some disorder until he stiffened alongside Humphreys. Together they broke up the butternut effort, which turned out to have involved all three of Gordon's divisions, as well as one of Hill's. Despite this evidence of compacted danger and a total of 1474 casualties — most of them Warren's; Humphreys lost 155, all told — the Federals remained on the south bank of the creek well into the following day, then recrossed to take up a new position extending Grant's left to the Vaughan Road crossing of Hatcher's Run, three miles downstream from Burgess Mill and about the same distance southwest of where his flank had rested prior to this latest attempt to turn his adversary's right.

Militarily, the results of this latest flanking try were negligible except on two counts. One was that it required a corresponding three-mile extension of Lee's own line, now stretched to a length of more than 37 miles, exclusive of recurrent jogs and doublings, while the army that held it was reduced by casualties and desertion to a strength of 46,398, the number listed as "present for duty" although many among them were too weak for anything more rigorous than answering roll call from their widespread posts along the fire step. The other negative outcome was the loss of John Pegram, the only professional among Gordon's three division commanders. Shot through the heart, he fell leading the counterattack on the second day of battle, two weeks past

his thirty-third birthday, and was buried two days later from St Paul's
Church in Richmond, just three weeks after he was married there. Such
a loss came hard. But hardest of all, perhaps, was the feeling of what
the three-day fight portended, coming as it did at a time when the food
reserve was quite exhausted. Throughout the action, the troops received
no issue of meat, only a scant handful of meal per man. Lee protested
to the War Department about this and the absence of his cavalry, dispersed for lack of forage. "Taking these facts in connection with the
paucity of our numbers," he informed his superiors in the capital at his
back, "you must not be surprised if calamity befalls us."

     At the same time, he spoke to those below him not of calamity but
of fortitude and courage. On February 11, four days after the fighting
subsided along Hatcher's Run, he issued with the concurrence of the
President a final offer of pardon for all deserters who would return to
the colors within twenty days. Included in this general order, the first
since he took over as general-in-chief, was an address to all the nation's
soldiers, present and absent. The choice, he said, had been narrowed
"between war and abject submission," and "to such a proposal brave
men with arms in their hands can have but one answer. They cannot
barter manhood for peace, nor the right of self-government for life or
property.... Taking new resolution from the fate which our enemies
intend for us," Lee's appeal concluded, "let every man devote all his
energies to the common defense. Our resources, wisely and vigorously
employed, are ample, and with a brave army, sustained by a determined
and united people, success with God's assistance cannot be doubtful. The
advantages of the enemy will have but little value if we do not permit
them to impair our resolution. Let us then oppose constancy to adversity,
fortitude to suffering, and courage to danger, with the firm assurance that
He who gave freedom to our fathers will bless the efforts of their children
to preserve it."

     Sherman by then was eleven days out of Savannah, and though
all was confusion in his path and ruin in his rear, his purpose was becoming clearer with every northward mile he covered toward a link-up
with Schofield, moving inland from Fort Fisher against Wilmington and
Bragg. So too was Grant's purpose, which Lee believed was to act on
his own before the intended conjunction. Petersburg now had been
under seige for eight relentless months — five times the length of
Vicksburg's previous forty-eight-day record — but the chances were
that the blue commander wanted to avoid having it said that he could
never have taken the place without the help of the forces coming up
through the Carolinas. "I think Genl Grant will move against us soon,"
Lee wrote his wife some ten days later, "within a week if nothing pre-
vents, and no man can tell what may be the result."

★ ★ ★

"I want to see the long deferred chastisement begin. If we don't purify South Carolina it will be because we *can't get a light*," an Illinois major wrote home while awaiting orders to cross the Savannah River. Six weeks later, when he got his next chance to post a letter, he could look back on a job well done and satisfaction achieved. "The army burned everything it came near in the State of South Carolina," he informed his wife, "not under orders, but in spite of orders. The men 'had it in' for the state, and they took it out in their own way. Our track through the state is a desert waste."

In some commands — Judson Kilpatrick's, for one — there were at least informal orders for such destruction. "In after years," the cavalry leader told his staff at a dinner he gave on the eve of setting out, "when travelers passing through South Carolina shall see chimney stacks without houses, and the country desolate, and shall ask, 'Who did this?' some Yankee will answer, 'Kilpatrick's Cavalry.' " Moreover, he did what he could to fulfill this prophecy en route. Descending on Barnwell four days later, just beyond the Salkehatchie, his troopers left little behind them but ashes and the suggestion that the town be renamed Burnwell.

"It seems to be decreed that South Carolina, having sown the wind, shall reap the whirlwind," a veteran infantryman asserted, and was echoed by a comrade: "South Carolina has commenced to pay an installment, long overdue, on her debt to justice and humanity. With the help of God, we will have principal and interest before we leave her borders. There is a terrible gladness in the realization of so many hopes and wishes."

Sherman, having cast himself in the role of avenging angel, saw his long-striding western veterans as crusaders, outriders for the Union, charged with imparting to the heathen Carolinians a wisdom that began with fear, and they in turn were proud to view their service in that light; "Do Boys," they called themselves, happy to be at the bidding of a commander who did not intend to restrain his army unduly, "lest its vigor and energy should be impaired." Anticipating a two-way profit from such license — high spirits within the column, panic in its path — he was hard put to say which of these benefits he valued most. "It is impossible to conceive of a march involving more labor and exposure," he would say, "yet I cannot recall an instance of bad temper." Throughout what was known from the outset as the Smoky March, a free-swinging jocularity obtained, as if to demonstrate that the damage, however severe, was being inflicted in high good humor, not out of meanness or any such low motivation. "There goes your damned old gospel shop!" the soldiers crowed, by way of a warmup for the march, as they pulled down the steeple and walls of a church in Hardeeville. "Vandalism, though not encouraged, was seldom punished," according to an artillery captain who also served as an undercover reporter for the New York *Herald*. He noted that, while "in Georgia few houses were burned, here few escaped," with the result that "the middle of the finest day looked black and gloomy" because of the dense smoke rising on all sides. Here again the cavalry did its share, Kilpatrick being under instructions to signal his whereabouts out on the flank by setting fire to things along the way. "Make a smoke like Indians do on the plains," Sherman had told him.

By way of further protection against the pangs of conscience, in case any tried to creep in, the marchers developed a biding dislike for the natives, especially those who had anything to lose. "In Georgia we had to respect the high-toned feelings of the planters," the *Herald*'s artillerist explained, "for they yielded with a dignity that won our admiration. In Carolina, the inhabitants, with a fawning, cringing subserviency, hung around our camps, craving a bite to eat." Enlarging on this, a Massachusetts colonel declared that he felt no sympathy for these victims of the army's wrath or high jinks. "I might pity individual cases brought before me," he wrote home, "but I believe that this terrible example is needed in this country as a warning to those men in all time to come who may cherish rebellious thoughts; I believe it is necessary in order to show the strength of this Government and thoroughly to subdue these people."

For the most part, though, no matter how amusing all this was for the soldiers trudging northward, or painful for the victims in their path, such depredations had little more to do with the success or failure of the operation, at least at this stage, than did the marksmanship or battle skill of the invaders, who went unchallenged except by skittish bands of butternut horsemen on the flanks. What mattered now was endurance, the ability of the marchers to cover a dozen miles of icy calf-deep bog a day, and the dexterity of the road-laying pioneers, charged with getting the 3000-odd wagons and ambulances through, as well as the 68 guns. On the right, where Howard had taken a steam-propelled head start up Port Royal Sound, then overland to Pocotaligo, this was not so much of a problem; he had only the Salkehatchie to cross before he reached the railroad linking Charleston and Augusta, Sherman's initial tactical objective; whereas Slocum, on the left, had first the Savannah River and then the Coosawhatchie Swamp to get across before he even approached the Salkehatchie. Howard made it in seven days. The wonder was that Slocum took only two days longer, considering the obstacles he encountered — especially the Coosawhatchie, which was three rain-swollen miles across and belt-buckle-deep, or sometimes worse, for nearly a mile on either side of the main channel. "Uncle Billy seems to have struck this river end-ways," one floundering veteran complained, submerged to his armpits in liquid muck and crackling skim-ice.

In addition to a 300-foot bridge that spanned the deeper-bottomed channel, the pioneers had to corduroy both approaches, in and out of the morass, and pin down the split-sapling mats, laid crosswise two and three feet underwater, to keep them from floating away. All this was managed handily, using materials on the scene; the six divisions crossed with a minimum of delay, if not of discomfort. By February 9 Slocum had all his men and vehicles over the Salkehatchie and in camp along the railroad west of Blackville, alongside Howard, who had reached and begun wrecking it two days ago, east to Bamberg, within fifteen miles of Branchville. For two more days they stayed there, converting thirty miles of track into twisted scrap iron, and then both wings were off again, slogging northward for the Congaree and the capital on its opposite bank, some fifty miles away. In addition to the "terrible gladness" the marchers felt because of the destruction they had wrought, official and unofficial, along and on both sides of their line of march, they also felt considerable hindsight amazement at the speed they had made through the midwinter swamps.

Nor were they by any means the only ones to feel this. Up in western North Carolina, where he was awaiting the outcome of efforts by friends in Richmond to achieve his reinstatement to the command from which he had been removed just over half a year before, Joe Johnston was even more amazed than were the soldiers who had accomplished this near miracle of stamina and logistics. He had been told by experts that the South Carolina hinterland was impenetrable at this season of the year, all the roads being under water, and he had believed it. "But when I learned that Sherman's army was marching through the Salk swamps, making its own corduroy roads at the rate of a dozen miles a day and more," he said later, "I made up my mind that there had been no such army in existence since the days of Julius Caesar."

Sherman rather agreed with this assessment. He had ridden with Howard on the less-obstructed right, northwest from Pocotaligo across the Salkehatchie, and when Slocum came up on the left along the railroad, having also encountered little formal opposition, the red-haired general's enthusiasm flared. For one thing, it was evident that his strategy of striking at a central objective while feinting simultaneously at others beyond his flanks was still effective, and for another it was equally clear that his policy of giving his troops a freer hand, not only to forage but also to visit their frisky wrath on the property of aboriginal secessionists along both routes of march, was bearing fruit; soldiers and civilians alike, the Confederates seemed unstrung by indecision and alarm. So far, the only resistance had come from cavalry snapping ineffectively at his wingtips, and already he could see that Magrath's appeal for South Carolinians to ambuscade the bluecoats in their midst was even less productive than Joe Brown's had been, two months ago in Georgia — with the result that, in his attitude toward the enemy ahead, Sherman become more confident and high-handed than ever. "I had a species of contempt for these scattered and inconsiderable forces," he afterwards declared, and the record sustained his claim. Midway of the two-day pause for railroad twisting, for example, when he received a flag-of-truce note from Wheeler, offering to quit burning cotton in the path of the invaders if they in turn would "discontinue burning houses," he kept his answer brief and to the point. He was unwilling to waste time now in an argument over the propriety of gratuitous destruction, nor did he intend to fall into the fibrous trap that had snared Banks last spring up the Red River. In short, he declined to enter into any discussion of the matter, except to tell the rebel cavalryman: "I hope you will burn all cotton and save us the trouble. All you don't burn I will."

Next day — February 9 — he was off again, across the Edisto, hard on the go for the Congaree and Columbia, just beyond. The two wings marched in near conjunction now, and once more it was as if the friction match had replaced the rifle as the basic infantry weapon. Barns exploded in flame as soon as the foragers emptied them of stock and corn; deserted houses loosed heavy plumes of smoke on the horizon; even the split-rail fences crackled along roadsides, and Kilpatrick was complaining of how "the infernal bummers," outstripping his troopers in the race for booty, "managed to plunder every hamlet and town before the cavalry came up." Aware that their next prize was the state capital, the very cradle of secession, the veterans chanted as they swung along the roads converging northward on their goal:

> "Hail Columbia, happy land!
> If I don't burn you, I'll be damned."

Riding among them, his spirits as high as their own — "sandy-haired, sharp-featured," an associate described him; "his nose prominent, his lips thin, his gray eyes flashing fire as fast as lightning on a summer's day; his whole face mobile as an actor's, and revealing every shade of thought or emotion that flitters across his active mind" — Sherman would have been in even higher feather if he had known that Schofield's troops, long ice-bound up the Potomac, began unloading that same day at Fort Fisher, preparatory to moving against Wilmington and points inland, as agreed upon beforehand. Not only would this provide the northward marchers with supplies and reinforcements when the time came; it would create still more confusion for Beauregard, who was confused enough already by his instructions from Richmond to intercept the invaders with a force that was even more "scattered and inconsiderable" than his adversary knew.

The Creole had returned from Mississippi the week before, called back to conduct the defense of the Carolinas, where his name retained a measure of the magic it once evoked, first as the Hero of Sumter and then as the deliverer who turned back Du Pont's iron fleet. On February 2, the day after his arrival in Augusta, he assembled a council of war for discussion of how to go about intercepting Sherman's double-pronged advance, which had begun in earnest just the day before. Hardee was there, summoned by rail from Charleston, as were G. W. Smith, in command of the Georgia militia, and D. H. Hill, who had volunteered, as at Petersburg nine months before, for service under Beauregard in a time of national trial. Taking count, the council came up with a figure of 33,450 men available for the task. But this was a considerable over-estimate, since it included some 7500 veterans from the Army of Tennessee, only 3000 of whom were yet on hand, as well as Hoke's 6000, pinned down at Wilmington by the fall of Fort Fisher, and Smith's 1500 Georgians, forbidden by law to move outside their home state. The actual number available was just over 20,000, barely more than a third as many as Sherman had moving against them from Sister's Ferry and Pocotaligo. Moreover, they were grievously divided. Hardee had 12,500 in and around Charleston — 8000 in two divisions under Major Generals Lafayette McLaws and Ambrose Wright, 3000 South Carolina militia under Brigadier General William Taliaferro, and M. C. Butler's 1500 troopers, recently detached from the Army of Northern Virginia — while Harvey Hill had 9500 near Augusta, including Stevenson's 3000, just off the cars from Tupelo, and Wheeler's 6500 cavalry, already in motion to challenge the invaders in case they tried to cross the "impassable" Salkehatchie. Beauregard's decision, made in the absence of any information as to which blue wing was making the main effort, was to defend both cities, 120 miles apart, until such time as evidence of a feint allowed the troops in that direction to be shifted elsewhere. He himself would set up headquarters at Columbia, he said. If worse came to worse, both Hardee and Hill could fall back and join him there, evacuating Charleston and Augusta rather than suffer the loss of their commands to overwhelming numbers, and thus combine for an attack on one or another of the two blue columns toiling northward.

Poor as the plan was in the first place, mainly because of its necessary surrender of the initiative to the enemy, it was rendered even poorer — in fact inoperative — by the speed with which Sherman moved through the supposedly impenetrable swamps. By the time Beauregard set up headquarters in the capital on February 10, the invaders, having reached and wrecked the railroad between Charleston and Augusta, were over the Edisto and hard on the march for the Congaree, no longer by two routes but in a single unassailable column; Sherman, like a diving hawk, had closed his wings for a rapid descent on Columbia before either Hill or Hardee, outflanked on the left and right, had time to react as planned for the combined attack on some lesser segment of the Union host. Despondent, Beauregard wired Hill to leave Augusta and join him at once with Stevenson's men at Chester, fifty miles north of the South Carolina capital. Similar orders to Hardee struck a snag, however. Though he promptly detached Butler's remounted troopers to assist Wheeler in delaying the blue advance, Richmond had urged him not to abandon Charleston until it was absolutely necessary, and he wanted his chief to make that judgment in person, on the scene. Unable to end the Georgian's indecision by telegraph, Beauregard went to Charleston on February 14, convinced him there was no longer any choice in the matter, prepared written instructions for the evacuation, and returned that night to Columbia: only to learn next day that Hardee had suffered another change of heart, prompted by still another Richmond dispatch urging him to postpone the evacuation until it was certain that Beauregard could not stop the Federals on his own. Exasperated, the Creole wired peremptory orders for Hardee to get the endangered garrison aboard the cars for Chester while there still was time. Sherman by then was maneuvering for a crossing of the Congaree, upstream and down, and Columbia itself was being evacuated in hope of sparing the capital the destruction that would attend any attempt to defend it against the 60,000 bluecoats on its doorstep.

That was February 15. Beauregard stayed through the following day and set out north by rail for Chester after nightfall, leaving Wade Hampton, whose splendid peacetime mansion rivaled the new brick State House as the showplace of the capital, to conduct the final stage of the withdrawal before the Federals arrived. Placed in command of all the cavalry, the post he had filled in Virginia until Lee detached him for his present task, the South Carolina grandee was promoted to lieutenant general over Wheeler, who, though nearly two decades his junior in age — Hampton would be forty-seven next month; Wheeler was twenty-eight — had half a year's seniority on him as a major general. Like most evacuations under pressure, this one was attended with considerable disorder and a confusion enlarged by particular circumstances. Columbia, a neat, well-laid-out little city with a charm befitting its uplands heritage as a center for culture and commerce, had grown in the course of the past two years from a population of about 8000 to better than 20,000, largely as a result of the influx of people from threatened areas on the seacoast and, more recently and in even larger numbers, from regions along or near the Georgia border thought to lie in the path of Sherman's burners. Convinced that the capital was strategically unimportant, especially in comparison with directly menaced Charleston and Augusta, prominent landowners and businessmen sought refuge here for their families, as well as for their valuables and house slaves. Before the war, there had been three banks in Columbia; now there were fourteen, including all of bombarded Charleston's, shifted beyond reach of the heaviest naval guns. Moreover, this notion of inland security persisted well beyond the time that Sherman left Savannah. Just last week, on February 9, the editor of the local *South Carolinian* had assured his readers that there was "no real tangible cause" for supposing that the Yankees had Columbia in mind.

Then suddenly they knew better; Sherman was two days off, then one, then none, guns booming from the Congaree bottoms, just across the way; there was neither time nor means for removing their sequestered

goods beyond his reach. Offers as large as $500 hired no wagons, and
men and women competed testily for seats or standing room on every
northbound train. Earlier, the authorities had ordered all cotton transported from intown warehouses for burning in open fields beyond the
city limits, and the bales were trundled into the streets for rapid loading
when the time came. They sat there still, spilling their fluffy, highly
combustible fiber through rents in the jute bagging. Columbia thus was
a tinderbox, ready to burst into flame at the touch of a match or a
random spark, by the time the rear-guard handful of gray troopers pulled
out Friday morning, February 17, and Mayor T. J. Goodwyn set out
with three aldermen in a carriage flying a white flag, charged by Hampton with surrendering the capital to the bluecoats already entering its
outskirts.

Sherman rode in about midday, close on the heels of Howard's lead
brigade. Part of Logan's XV Corps, whose mere proximity he had said
would obviate the need for sowing any hated place with salt, its members
were given the customary privilege, as the first troops in, of policing
the captured town and enjoying all it had to offer in the way of food
and fun. A blustery wind had risen and was blowing the spilled cotton
about the streets in wisps and skeins. Asked later why, under these
explosive circumstances, he had not kept his veterans in formation and
under control while they were in occupation of the surrendered capital,
the red-haired Ohioan replied indignantly: "I would not have done such
a harshness to save the whole town. They were men, and I was not going
to treat them like slaves."

Liquor shops were among the first establishments to be looted
when the troops broke ranks and scattered. But this was more from
habit than from need, since friendly house slaves stood in front of many
residences, offering the soldiers drinks from bottles they had brought
up from abandoned cellers. "Lord bless you, Massa. Try some dis," a
genial white-haired butler said, extending a gourd dipper he kept filled
with fine old brandy from a bucket in his other hand. Breakfastless and
exuberant, a good part of the command was roaring drunk in short order.
Slocum, whose left wing crossed upstream and went into camp beyond
the city, saw in this the main cause for what would follow after
sundown. "A drunken soldier with a musket in one hand and a match
in the other is not a pleasant visitor to have about the house on a dark,
windy night," he afterwards remarked, "particularly when for a series
of years you have urged him to come so that you might have an opportunity of performing a surgical operation on him." Sherman apparently thought so, too. "Look out," he told Howard, observing the effect
of all this proffered whiskey, "or you'll have hell to pay. You'd better
go and see about it in person."

Howard did go and see about it. Alarmed, he stopped the informal
distribution of spirits and, after nightfall, ordered the drunken brigade

relieved by another from the same division, which had marched through
the city earlier to camp on the far side. But it was altogether too late by
then. The men of the first having scattered beyond recall, the practical
outcome was that a second XV Corps brigade was added to the milling
throng of celebrants and looters. By then, moreover, the frightened
citizens had learned what the soldiers meant when, passing through the
windy streets that afternoon, they told them: "You'll catch hell tonight."
Sherman could have interpreted for them, though as it happened he only
found out about the prophecy after it had been fulfilled. Weary, he
took an early supper and lay down to rest in a bedroom of the house
his staff had commandeered for headquarters. "Soon after dark," he
would remember, "I became conscious that a bright light was shining
on the walls."

Columbia was burning, and burning fiercely, in more than a dozen
places simultaneously. Hampton's mansion was one of the first to go,
along with Treasury Secretary Trenholm's, and lest it be thought that
these had been singled out because of their owners' wealth or politics,
the Gervais Street red-light district was put to the torch at the same
time, as well as Cotton Town, a section of poorer homes to the northwest, and stores and houses along the river front. One object of special
wrath was the Baptist church where the South Carolina secession convention had first assembled, but the burners were foiled by a Negro
they asked for directions. As it happened, he was the sexton of the
church they sought and he pointed out a rival Methodist establishment
just up the block, which soon was gushing flames from all its windows.
So presently was the nearby Ursuline convent, whose Mother Superior
was known to be the sister of Bishop Patrick N. Lynch, an outspoken
secessionist who had celebrated the breakup of the Union, back in '61,
with thanksgiving rites in his Charleston cathedral. Hardest hit of all
was the business district. Terrified pigeons flapped and wheeled in the
drifting smoke, unable to find a place to light, and the hysterical screams
of women combined strangely with the lowing of cattle trapped in their
stalls. "All around us were falling thickly showers of burning flakes," a
seventeen-year-old girl wrote in her diary next day. "Everywhere the
palpitating blaze walled the streets as far as the eye could reach, filling
the air with its terrible roar. On every side [was] the crackling and
devouring fire, while every instant came the crashing of timbers and the
thunder of falling buildings. A quivering molten ocean seemed to fill the
air and sky."

Mindful perhaps of a statement he had made to Mayor Goodwyn,
who served as his guide on an afternoon tour of inspection: "Go home
and rest assured that your city will be as safe in my hands as if you had
controlled it," Sherman himself turned out to fight the flames, along with
his staff, a number of unit commanders, and as many of their troops as
could be rounded up and persuaded to serve as firemen. Of the rest,

unwilling to end their fun or too drunk to follow orders, 370 were placed in arrest, two were shot and killed, and thirty wounded. That still left enough at large to defeat the efforts being made to confine the conflagration. Some among them hurried from block to block, carrying wads of turpentine-soaked cotton for setting fire to houses so far spared, while others used their rifles to bayonet hoses and cripple pumpers brought into play by the civilian fire department. Before the night was over, another whole division was summoned into the city to help subdue the arsonists and the flames, but even that did not suffice until about 4 o'clock in the morning, when the wind relented enough to let the flames die down and save the capital from annihilation. As it was, when the sun rose two hours later, blood red through the murk of heavy smoke, two thirds of Columbia lay in ashes. Fire had raged through 84 of its 124 blocks, with such effect that the girl diarist could see nothing from her position near the center "but heaps of rubbish, tall dreary chimneys, and shattered brick walls." Burned-out families gathered in the parks and on the common, huddled among such possessions as they had managed to save. Some of the women were weeping uncontrollably. Others were dry-eyed, either from shock or from a sharpened hatred of the Yankees. An Illinois surgeon moved among them for a time, then withdrew sadly. "I talked with some," he wrote in his diary that night, "but it made me feel too bad to be endured."

Sherman had a different reaction. "Though I never ordered it, and never wished it," he was to say of the burning, "I have never shed any tears over it, because I believe that it hastened what we all fought for — the end of the war." As for blame, he fixed that on Hampton for starting the fire and on God for enlarging it. He charged the rebel general with "ripping open bales of cotton, piling it in the streets, burning it, and then going away"; at which point "God Almighty started wind sufficient to carry that cotton wherever He would." Originally, while the fire was in progress, he had seen whiskey as the overriding cause of the catastrophe, available in quantity because the departed graybacks had foolishly made "an evacuated city a depot of liquor for an army to occupy." Under its influence, he admitted, his soldiers "may have assisted in spreading the fire after it once began, and may have indulged in unconcealed joy to see the ruin of the capital of South Carolina," but he did not dwell long on this aspect of the case, saying instead: "I disclaim on the part of my army any agency in this fire, but, on the contrary, claim that we saved what of Columbia remains unconsumed. And without hesitation I charge General Wade Hampton with having burned his own city of Columbia, not with malicious intent, or as the manifestation of a silly 'Roman stoicism,' but from folly and want of sense in filling it with lint, cotton, and tinder." So he declared in his formal report of the campaign, although he conceded in his memoirs, ten years later, that there had been method in his arraignment of his adversary for the burning. "I distinctly charged it to General Wade Hampton," he wrote then, "and confess I did so pointedly, to shake the faith of his people in him, for he was in my opinion a braggart, and professed to be the special champion of South Carolina."

For two more days the army remained in and around Columbia, probing the rubble for overlooked spoils and expanding the destruction by burning down the Confederate arsenal and a Treasury printing office, legitimate targets which somehow had survived the conflagration. The Preston mansion, where Hood had visited his fiancée on his way to Richmond two weeks back, escaped entirely: first, because John Logan occupied it during the three-day stay, and finally because Sherman gave permission for the homeless wards of the Ursuline convent to take up residence there on February 20, the day his troops moved out. Logan was supervising the placement of barrels of pitch in the cellar, intending to set them ablaze on his departure, when the white-clad pupils were herded in by the Mother Superior, armed with Sherman's order. Black Jack loosed a string of oaths at this sparing of a rebel general's ornate property, but had no choice except to let the house go unburned when he took up the march.

It was northward, as before. The feint now was at Chester, fifty miles away, and at Charlotte, about the same distance farther on, across the North Carolina line. Beyond Winnsboro, however — which the outriding bummers set afire next day, though not soon enough to keep the main body from coming up in time to save most of it from the flames — both infantry wings turned hard right for a crossing of the Wateree River, a dozen miles to the east, and a fast march on Cheraw, en route to Fayetteville and Goldsboro, where Sherman had arranged for Schofield to meet him with supplies brought inland from Wilmington and New Bern.

Alas, it was just at this critical stage, with by far the worst stretch of the march supposedly behind him, that the pace slowed to a crawl. Coming down to the Wateree on February 23, Howard's wing made it over the river in a driving rain, but only half of Slocum's crossed before the bridge collapsed under pressure from logs and driftwood swept downstream by the rush of rising water; Davis's XIV Corps was left stranded on the western bank, and the other three, having made it over, soon had cause to wish they hadn't. The mud, though thinner, was slick as grease on the high red ground beyond the river, and grew slicker and deeper throughout the record three-day rainfall, until at last — "slipping, stumbling, swearing, singing, and yelling" — the head of the column reached Hanging Rock Post Office on February 26, having covered barely twenty miles in the past four days; while the XIV Corps, still on the far side of the Wateree, had made no miles at all. Furious, Sherman called a halt and ordered Slocum to ride back and expedite a crossing. If necessary, he was to have Davis burn his wagons, spike his guns, shoot the mules, and ferry or swim his troops across; he was in fact to do anything, within reason or beyond, that would avoid prolonging the delay now that a solid half of the long trek to Goldsboro was behind the main body, slathered with mud and resting close to exhaustion at Hanging Rock, within twenty air-line miles of the North Carolina line.

No such drastic steps were needed. That afternoon the sun came out, beaming down on "bedraggled mules, toiling soldiers, and seas of mud," and by the next the river had fallen enough for Davis to improvise a bridge; his laggard corps got over that night with its guns and train, followed by the cavalry, which had kept up the feint against Chester after the infantry swung east. Sherman meanwhile improved the interim by sending a reinforced brigade to nearby Camden, with instructions to destroy all "government property, stores, and cotton." Reinspired despite their bone-deep weariness, the detached troops accomplished this and more, burning a large flour mill and both depots of the South Carolina Railroad, along with the Masonic Hall, and looting almost every private residence in town, then returned to Hanging Rock in time to take their place in column when the reunited army resumed its march on Cheraw, just under fifty miles away. They had recovered their high spirits, and so too, by now, had their commander. He had learned from newspapers gathered roundabout that Charleston, evacuated by Hardee on the night Columbia burned, had been occupied next morning by units from Foster's garrison at Savannah: a splendid example of what Sherman had meant when he told him to be ready to "pick up the apples." Symbolically, at any rate — for it was here, not quite two months under four long years ago, that the war began — this was the biggest apple of them all. Four days later, moreover, while the inland marchers were turning east to cross the Wateree, Schofield had captured Wilmington, freeing his and Terry's men for the appointed meeting in the interior next month.

One other piece of news there was, but Sherman was not sure, just yet, whether he was glad or sorry to receive it. Joe Johnston, he learned, had replaced Beauregard as commander of the "scattered and inconsiderable forces" assembling in his front.

★   ★   ★

Often, down the years, it would be said that Lee's first exercise of authority, following his confirmation as general-in-chief, had been to recall Johnston to active duty; whereas, in fact, one of his first acts at his new post was the denial of a petition, signed by the Vice President and seventeen prominent Senators, urging him to do just that by restoring his fellow Virginian to command of the Army of Tennessee. "The three corps of that army have been ordered to South Carolina and are now under the command of Genl Beauregard," he replied on February 13, one week after his elevation. "I entertain a high opinion of Genl

Johnston's capacity, but think a continual change of commanders is very injurious to any troops and tends greatly to their disorganization. At this time, as far as I understand the condition of affairs, an engagement with the enemy may be expected any day, and a change now would be particularly hazardous. Genl Beauregard is well known to the citizens of South Carolina, as well as to the troops of the Army of Tennessee, and I would recommend that it be certainly ascertained that a change was necessary before it was made." Besides, he told Stephens and the others, "I do not consider that my appointment . . . confers the right which you assume belongs to it, nor is it proper that it should. I can only employ such troops and officers as may be placed at my disposal by the War Department."

Old Joe it seemed would have to bide his time in the Carolina piedmont, awaiting the outcome of further efforts by his supporters. But developments over the course of the next week provoked a reassessment of the situation. For one thing, Beauregard's health was rumored to be "feeble and precarious," which might account for his apparent shakiness under pressure. Shifting his headquarters, formerly at Augusta, from Columbia to Chester, then to Charlotte, the Creole seemed confused and indecisive in the face of Sherman's "semi-amphibious" march through the boggy lowlands. "General Beauregard makes no mention of what he proposes or what he can do, or where his troops are," Lee complained to Davis. "He does not appear from his dispatches to be able to do much." Columbia by then had been abandoned, along with outflanked Charleston, and Wilmington was under heavy pressure from Schofield; at which point, on February 21, Davis received and passed on to Lee a wire just in from Beauregard, once more proposing a "grand strategy" designed to bring the Yankees to their knees. In the Louisianian's opinion, Sherman (who would not turn east, away from Chester, until the following day) was advancing upon Charlotte and Salisbury, North Carolina, on his way to a conjunction with Grant in rear of Richmond, and Old Bory saw in this — as he so often had done before, under drastic circumstances — the opportunity of a lifetime. "I earnestly urge a concentration of at least 35,000 infantry and artillery at [Salisbury], if possible, to give him battle there, and crush him, then to concentrate all forces against Grant, and then to march on Washington and dictate a peace. Hardee and myself can collect about 15,000 exclusive of Cheatham and Stewart, not likely to reach in time. If Lee and Bragg can furnish 20,000 more, the fate of the Confederacy would be secure."

Unknowingly, Beauregard had proposed his last air-castle strategy of the war. "The idea is good, but the means are lacking," Lee told Davis two days later. He had by then made up his mind that the Creole had to go, and by way of providing a successor he had already sounded out Breckinridge on the matter. "[Sherman] seems to have everything his own way," he informed the War Secretary on February 19, the day after Charleston fell, adding that he could get little useful information from the general charged with contesting the blue advance through the Carolinas. "I do not know where his troops are, or on what lines they are moving. His dispatches only give movements of the enemy. He has a difficult task to perform under present circumstances, and one of his best officers, Genl Hardee, is incapacitated by sickness. I have also heard that his own health is indifferent, though he has never so stated. Should his strength give way, there is no one on duty in the department that could replace him, nor have I anyone to send there. Genl J. E. Johnston is the only officer whom I know who has the confidence of the army and people, and if he was ordered to report to me I would place him there on duty. It is necessary to bring out all our strength. . . ."

Puzzled by Lee's indirectness, the Kentuckian asked just what it was he wanted, and when. Lee replied that he had intended "to apply for Genl J. E. Johnston, that I might assign him to duty, should circumstances permit." Understanding now that by "circumstances" Lee meant the President's objections, Breckinridge passed the request along, and Davis — despite his recent expression of "a conviction so settled that it would be impossible for me again to feel confidence in [Johnston] as the commander of an army in the field" — agreed, however reluctantly, to the recall and appointment, though he was careful to point out that he did so only "in the hope that General Johnston's soldierly qualities may be made serviceable to his country when acting under General Lee's orders, and that in his new position those defects which I found manifested by him when serving as an independent commander will be remedied by the control of the general-in-chief."

That was how it came about that Johnston received on February 23, the day after they were issued, simultaneous orders from the War Department and from Lee, recalling him to active duty and assigning him to command of the troops now under Beauregard, including the Army of Tennessee. He was then at Lincolnton, North Carolina — "I am in the regular line of strategic retreat," Mrs Chesnut, who preceded him there in her flight from threatened Mulberry, had remarked sarcastically when she learned that he was expected any day — thirty miles northwest of Charlotte, where Beauregard had established headquarters after falling back from Chester. Instructed to "concentrate all available forces and drive back Sherman," Johnston replied much as he had done on his arrival in Mississippi just under two years ago, preceding the fall of Vicksburg: "It is too late. . . . The remnant of the Army of Tennessee is much divided. So are the other troops. . . . Is any discretion allowed me? I have no staff."

Before taking over he went by rail to Charlotte to confer with his predecessor, now designated his second in command. Beauregard assured him of his support, having just wired Lee that he would "at all

times be happy to serve with or under so gallant and patriotic a soldier."
Privately, though, the Louisianian was bitterly disappointed at having
once more been relegated to a subordinate position, as at Manassas, Shiloh, and Petersburg. "My greatest desire has always been to
command a good army in the field," he had recently declared. "Will I
ever be gratified?" Now in the Carolinas — as in Mississippi nearly three
years before, following his canny withdrawal from Halleck's intended
trap at Corinth — another chance had come and gone, and he knew this
was the last; Fate and Davis had undone him, now as then.

Johnston was by no means correspondingly elated. Though he was
grateful for Beauregard's loyalty, he believed the post afforded little
opportunity for success or even survival. He had, as he informed one of
his Richmond supporters, "not exactly no hope, but only a faint hope,"
and even this was presently seen to have been an overstatement of the
case. He said later that he took over in Charlotte, February 25, "with a
full consciousness . . . that we could have no other object, in continuing
the war, than to obtain fair terms of peace; for the Southern cause must
have appeared hopeless then, to all intelligent and dispassionate Southern
men."

Sherman by now was astride Lynch's Creek, midway between the
Wateree and the Pee Dee, closing fast on Cheraw, his final intermediary
objective before he entered North Carolina. Moreover, the invaders by
then had still another powerful column in contention; Wilmington's fall,
on the day of Johnston's restoration by the War Department, freed
Schofield to join Sherman for a northward march across the Roanoke,
the last strong defensive line south of the Appomattox. Lee pointed out
that the only way to avoid the consequences of such a penetration
would be for him to combine with Johnston for a strike at Sherman before that final barrier was crossed, even though this would require him
not only to give up his present lines covering Petersburg and the national
capital, but also to manage the evacuation so stealthily that Grant would
not know he was gone until it was too late to overtake and crush him
on the march. How long the odds were against his achieving such a
deliverance Lee did not say, yet he did what he could to warn his superiors of the sacrifice involved in the attempt. On the day after Foster
occupied Charleston — February 18: the fourth anniversary of Davis's
provisional inauguration in Montgomery — he notified Breckinridge:
"I fear it may be necessary to abandon all our cities, and preparation
should be made for this contingency." Similarly, on the day after
Wilmington fell — February 22: the third anniversary of Davis's permanent inauguration in Richmond — he made it clear to Davis himself that
any attempt to "unite with [Johnston] in a blow against Sherman" would
"necessitate the abandonment of our position on James River, for which
contingency every preparation should be made." One other alternative
there was, and he mentioned it one week later in a different connection.

This was the acceptance of Lincoln's terms, as set forth aboard the *River Queen* four weeks ago in Hampton Roads. "Whether this will be acceptable to our people yet awhile," he told Davis, "I cannot say."

"Yet awhile" was as close as Lee had come, so far, to foreseeing surrender as the outcome of the present situation. As for himself, this detracted not a whit from the resolution he had expressed in a letter to his wife the week before: "Sherman and Schofield are both advancing and seem to have everything their own way. But trusting in a merciful God, who does not always give the battle to the strong, I pray we may not be overwhelmed. I shall however endeavor to do my duty and fight to the last."

Victory, and Defeat

★ ⚹ ☆

"EVERYTHING LOOKS LIKE DISSOLUTION in the South. A few more days of success with Sherman will put us where we can crow loud," Grant wrote his congressional guardian angel Elihu Washburne on the day after Schofield captured Wilmington, hard in the wake of Foster's occupation of Charleston and Sherman's burning of Columbia. By coincidence, this February 23 was also the day Lee warned Davis of the need for abandoning Richmond when the time came for him to combine with Johnston in a last-ditch effort to stop Sherman and Schofield before they crossed the Roanoke River, sixty miles in what had been his rear until he was cooped up in Petersburg. Far from being one of the things Grant looked forward to crowing about, however, such a move by his adversary, even though it would mean possession of the capital he had had under siege for eight long months, was now the Union commander's greatest fear. Looking back on still another of those "most anxious periods," he afterwards explained: "I was afraid, every morning, that I would awake from my sleep to hear that Lee had gone, and that nothing was left but a picket line. He had his railroad by the way of Danville south, and I was afraid that he was running off his men and all stores and ordnance except such as it would be necessary to carry with him for his immediate defense. I knew he could move much more lightly and more rapidly than I, and that, if he got the start, he would leave me behind so that we would have the same army to fight again farther south." In other words, he feared that Lee might do to him what he had done to Lee after Cold Harbor; that is, slip away some moonless night while the bluecoats, snug in their trenches across the way, engaged in lackadaisical speculation on "a good run of Johnnies." The result would be recovery by the old fox of his freedom to maneuver, a resumption of the kind of warfare at which he and his lean gray veterans had shown themselves to be past masters, back in May and early June; in which case, Grant summed it up, still shuddering at the prospect, "the war might be prolonged another year."

Three factors prevented or delayed effective Federal interference with either the preparation or execution of such a breakout plan. One was the weather, which had turned the roads into troughs of mud and the fields into quagmires, unfit for pursuit or maneuver if Lee, who had the use of the Danville and Southside lines for the removal of all he chose to put aboard them, was to be overtaken and overwhelmed before he achieved a link-up with Johnston in the Carolinas. Another was the strength of the Richmond-Petersburg defenses, which, combined with his skill in tactical anticipation, had withstood all efforts to penetrate or outflank them. The third was the prevailing cavalry imbalance, occasioned by Sheridan's protracted absence with two of his three divisions in the Shenandoah Valley, which made it highly inadvisable to attempt a strike at the tenuous rail supply lines deep in Lee's rear, vital though they were, not only to the subsistence of his army, but also to its breakout when the time came. There was little or nothing Grant could do about the first two of these three discouraging factors, except wait out a change in the weather and the continuous sapping effect of rebel desertions, neither of which was likely to prove decisive before Lee found a chance to slip away. However, the third factor was quite another matter, and Grant had already begun to do something about it three days ago, on February 20, in a letter assigning Sheridan the task of slamming shut Lee's escape route, west or southwest, through Lynchburg or Danville.

He had decided, as a result of his fear of the growing risk of a getaway by Lee, on an alteration in the bandy-legged cavalryman's role in the close-out plan devised to bring the Confederacy to its knees. Instead of awaiting a fair-weather summons, Sheridan was to leave the Valley "as soon as it is possible to travel," and instead of rejoining Meade by the shortest route, down the Virginia Central, he was to move with his two mounted divisions against Lynchburg, where the Southside Railroad and the Orange & Alexandria came together to continue west as the Virginia & Tennessee. A thorough wrecking of that important junction, together with an adjacent stretch of the James River Canal, would cut Lee off from supplies coming in from Southwest Virginia and would also end any hope he had for a flight beyond that point. "I think you will have no difficulty about reaching Lynchburg with a cavalry force alone," Grant wrote. "From there you could destroy the railroads and canal in every direction, so as to be of no further use to the rebellion." Then came the real surprise. "From Lynchburg, if information you might get there would justify it, you could strike south, heading the streams in Virginia to get to the westward of Danville, and push on and join Sherman."

Explaining this change — not only of route, in order to deny Lee both the Southside and the Richmond & Danville lines for use as all-weather avenues for escape, but also of destination — Grant tied what he called "this additional raid" in with those about to be launched by Canby and Wilson through Alabama and by Stoneman into North Carolina. Seen in that light, with these three on the rampage and Sherman "eating out the vitals of South Carolina," the proposed operation was "all that will be wanted to leave nothing for the rebellion to stand upon." There followed a final touch of the spur, applied as insurance against discouragement or delay. "I would advise you to overcome great obstacles to accomplish this. Charleston was evacuated on Tuesday last."

Sheridan seldom needed much urging on either count, and he did so less than ever now, having engaged in no large-scale fighting in the four months since his celebrated mid-October "ride" from Winchester to Cedar Creek, where he turned apparent defeat into a smashing victory and drove the shattered remnant of Early's army headlong out of the Valley. This was not to say that he had been idle all this time; far from it; but his activity was rather in the nature of common labor, directed more against enemy resources than against enemy soldiers, of which by now there were none on the scene; or almost none, if guerillas (or "rangers," as they preferred to call themselves) were taken into account. Such times as his troops were engaged in the devastation Grant had ordered, burning mills and barns, rounding up or butchering livestock, and removing or destroying all food and forage, they were in danger of being bushwhacked, and wagon trains also had to be heavily escorted, going and coming, to keep them from being captured. Not only did this interfere with the speedy conversion of the once-lush region into a wasteland, it was also hard on morale, requiring the blue troopers to turn out in freezing weather, at night and on days better spent in bed or round the campfire. Sometimes, indeed, the damage was far worse. For example, at 3 o'clock in the morning of the day Grant's letter arrived — February 21 — a small party of guerillas stole into Cumberland, Maryland, on the Potomac and the Baltimore & Ohio, fifty-odd miles above Harpers Ferry, and into the hotel room of George Crook himself, recently promoted to major general and put in charge of the Department of West Virginia as a reward for his performance as Sheridan's star corps commander at Winchester and Fisher's Hill. Undetected, they grabbed Crook and his ranking subordinate, Brigadier General B. F. Kelley, and got them onto waiting horses for a fast ride south, once more through the unsuspecting pickets, all the way to Libby Prison. Both generals were presently released by the terms of a special exchange worked out between Richmond and Washington, but the incident rankled badly as an example of what such brigands could accomplish without fear of personal reprisal.

That had not always been the case. At the outset, with the approval of Grant, Sheridan adopted a policy of reprisal that was personal indeed, especially against members of Colonel John S. Mosby's Partisan Rangers, two battalions with just under a hundred men in each, who claimed as their own a twenty-mile-square district containing most of Loudon and Fauquier counties; "Mosby's Confederacy," they dubbed it, cradled between the Bull Run Mountains and the Blue Ridge, through whose passes they raided westward across the Shenandoah River. Farmers by day, they rode mostly by night, and their commander, a former Virginia lawyer, thirty-three years old and sandy-haired, weighing less than 130 pounds in his thigh-high boots, red-lined cape, and ostrich plume, was utterly fearless, quite uncatchable, and altogether skillful in the conduct of operations which Lee himself, though he had small use for partisans in general, had praised as "highly creditable." In the past six months, in addition to keeping his superiors accurately informed of enemy activities in the Valley, he had killed, wounded, or captured more than a thousand Federals of all ranks, at a cost of barely twenty casualties of his own, and had taken nearly twice that many beeves and horses, along with a considerable haul of rations and equipment. Most of this came from Sheridan, who arrived on the scene in August. Appealing to Grant for permission to deal harshly with such guerillas as he was able to lay hands on, by way of deterring the rest, he was told: "When any of Mosby's men are caught, hang them without trial."

Promptly Sheridan passed the word to his subordinates, and in late September, having captured six of the rangers in a sudden descent on Front Royal, Custer shot four and hanged the other two, leaving their bodies dangling with a crudely lettered placard around the neck of one. "This will be the fate of Mosby and all his men," it read.

Mosby bided his time, even though another ranger was similarly captured, hanged, and placarded the following month in Rappahannock County. All this time, however, he was taking captives of his own, some 700 within a six-week span, and forwarding them to Richmond: unless, that is, they were from Custer's division, in which case they were set apart and kept under guard in an abandoned schoolhouse near Rectortown, just across the Blue Ridge from Front Royal. By early November he had 27 of Custer's men in custody, and he lined them up to draw folded slips of paper from a hat, informing them beforehand of his purpose. Twenty of the slips were blank; the rest, numbered 1 to 7, signified that those who drew them would be executed in retaliation for the postcapture death of his seven rangers. Harrowing as the lottery was for the participants, the game took an even crueler turn when it developed that one of the hard-luck seven was a beardless drummer, barely into his teens; Mosby had the delivered twenty draw again to determine who would take the boy's place. This done, a detail escorted the seven losers out into the night, under orders to hang them in proximity to Custer's headquarters at Winchester. One scampered off in the rainy darkness

as they approached the scene of execution near Berryville, where three
of the remaining six were hanged and the other three were lined up to be
shot. One of these also managed to get away in the confusion, but
Mosby later said that he was glad the two troopers escaped to "relate in
Sheridan's camps the experience they had with Mosby's men." Meantime,
under a flag of truce, a ranger scout — his safe conduct ensured by the
remaining hostages — was on his way to deliver in person a note to
Sheridan, informing him of what had been done, and why. "Hereafter,"
it concluded, "any prisoners falling into my hands will be treated with
the kindness due to their condition, unless some new act of barbarity shall
compel me reluctantly to adopt a line of policy repugnant to humanity.
Very respectfully, your obedient servant, John S. Mosby."

Deterred himself, Sheridan called off the hanging match and
agreed to deal henceforward with Mosby's men as he did with other
prisoners of war. It came hard for him just now, though, for the rangers
lately had wrecked and robbed a B. & O. express, dividing among themselves a $73,000 Federal payroll, and followed up this "Greenback
Raid," as they called it, by capturing Brigadier General Alfred Duffié,
out for a buggy ride near Bunker Hill, within ten miles of army headquarters. Besides, the Valley commander had more or less carried out
by then his instructions to "peel this land"; little remained to protect
or patrol except the trains bringing in rations for his troops, whose number had dwindled steadily as the infantry — first Wright's whole corps,
then most of Crook's, and finally part of Emory's — was detached, all
but a couple of rest-surfeited divisions, for transfer to more active
theaters. Grant's letter, outlining plans for an all-out cavalry strike at
Lynchburg and a subsequent link-up with Sherman, was greeted by
Sheridan as a reprieve from boredom, a deliverance from uncongenial
idleness in what had become a backwash of the war. He did not much
like the notion of a detour into Carolina, preferring to be in on the
smashing of Lee from the outset, but he was pleased to note that Grant
had left him room for discretion in the matter, just as he had done about
the date for setting out, saying merely that Sheridan could take off
southward "as soon as it is possible to travel."

Unleashed, he wasted no time in getting started, even though, as
he later reported, "the weather was very bad. . . . The spring thaw, with
heavy rains, had already come on, [and] the valley and surrounding
mountains were covered with snow which was fast disappearing, putting
all the streams nearly past fording." A more cautious man would have
waited; but not this one. Soon after sunrise, February 27 — one week
from the date on Grant's letter — he had 10,000 veteran troopers pounding south up the turnpike out of Winchester, leaving Mosby and boredom and other such problems to Hancock, who returned to active duty
to replace him in command of all he left behind in the lower Valley.
Thirty miles the two divisions made that day, and thirty the next, to

make camp at the end of the third day out — March 1 — within seven miles of Staunton, where Early had established headquarters after his rout at Cedar Creek. Next morning Sheridan rode into town to find Old Jube had departed eastward the day before, apparently headed for Charlottesville by way of Rockfish Gap. The question was whether to take out after him, in hope of completing his destruction, or press on south without delay to Lynchburg, leaving Early's remnant stranded in his wake; perhaps to bedevil Hancock. Sheridan chose the former course, and scored next day, as a result, a near Cannae that abolished what little remained of Stonewall Jackson's fabled Army of the Valley.

Twelve miles east out the Virginia Central almost to Waynesboro, a hamlet perched on the slope leading up to the snowy pass through the Blue Ridge in its rear, he came upon the thrice-whipped rebels posted in what he termed "a well chosen position" on the near side of a branch of the South Fork of the Shenandoah. They numbered about 1200 of all arms, all but a handful of Rosser's troopers being still en route from their rest camp forty miles west of Staunton. Early had stopped here in hope of delaying the bluecoats long enough to get his eleven guns across the mountain in double-teamed relays; otherwise, lacking horses enough to haul them up the slippery grade, he would have had to abandon five of them. "I did not intend making my final stand on this ground," he afterwards explained, "yet I was satisfied that if my men would fight, which I had no reason to doubt, I could hold the enemy in check until night, and then cross the river to take position in Rockfish Gap; for I had done more difficult things than that during the war."

He had indeed done more difficult things, but not with the disjointed skeleton of a command that had been trounced, three times running, by the general now closing fast upon his rear. As it turned out, holding his ground was not only difficult; it was impossible, mainly because Sheridan would not be denied even an outside chance at the total smash-up he had been seeking from the start. One division, under Brigadier General Thomas Devin — successor to Wesley Merritt, who had replaced Torbert as chief of cavalry — was delayed by orders to clean out a depot of supplies on the far side of Staunton, and though this left only Custer's division for the work at hand, Sheridan judged it would be enough, not only because he still enjoyed a better than four-to-one numerical advantage, but also because of Custer's nature, which he knew to be as aggressive as his own. He knew right. Told to move against the position, the yellow-haired Michigander — lately brevetted a major general on the eve of his twenty-fifth birthday — sent one brigade to strike the rebel left, which was somewhat advanced, and led the other two in a saber-swinging charge on the hastily thrown-up breastworks dead ahead. He had his favorite mount shot from under him in the assault, but that did not disrupt the breakthrough in either direction or slow down the lunge for the one bridge over the river in the Confederate rear. The result, according to the cartographer Jed Hotchkiss, posted by Early as a lookout, was "one of the most terrible panics and stampedes I have ever seen." Early himself agreed, though he caught no more than a tail-end glimpse of the rout. "I went to the top of a hill to reconnoiter," he later wrote, "and had the mortification of seeing the greater part of my command being carried off as prisoners, and a force of the enemy moving rapidly toward Rockfish Gap."

What was worse, "the greater part" was a considerable understatement. Merritt claimed "over 1000 prisoners"—a figure enlarged by Sheridan to 1600 and by Custer to 1800 in their reports, although the latter came to half again more than Early had on hand—along with 11 guns, close to 200 wagons, and 17 flags. Best of all, according to Sheridan, was the seizure of Rockfish Gap, "as the crossing of the Blue Ridge, covered with snow as it was, at any other point would have been difficult." The other division coming up next morning, March 3, he sent his captives and spoils back to Winchester under escort—all but the rebel battle flags, which he kept to flaunt in the faces of future opponents, if any—then moved on to make camp that night at Charlottesville, twenty miles away. For two days he rested his men and horses there, what time he did not have them ripping up track on the Virginia Central, before he set out southwest down the Orange & Alexandria on March 6, wrecking it too in his wake, bound for Lynchburg in accordance with the instructions in Grant's letter, written two weeks ago that day.

Old Jubilee had a harder road to travel. Escaping over the mountains with a few members of his staff—all that managed a getaway when Wharton's two brigades collapsed—he turned up at Lee's headquarters two weeks later. He had left with a corps, nine months ago; now he returned with nothing. Lee comforted him as best he could, but instead of restoring him to the post occupied by Gordon, ordered him back to the Valley. Although there was little to command there, Rosser's 1200 troopers having been summoned to Petersburg in partial replacement for the division still with Hampton in the Carolinas, Lee's hope was that he would be able to collect and attract such fugitives and under- or over-aged volunteers as remained in that burned-out region. Early departed on this mission, but before the month ended Lee rescinded the order, explaining to Breckinridge that he did so, despite his fellow Virginian's "great intelligence, good judgment, and undoubted bravery," because it was clear that his defeats in the lower Valley, capped by the recent final debacle at Waynesboro, had cost him the confidence of those he would be attempting to reassemble or recruit. To Early himself, at the same time, went a letter expressing Lee's "confidence in your ability, zeal, and devotion to the cause" and thanking him "for the fidelity and energy with which you have always supported my efforts, and for the courage and devotion you have ever manifested in the service."

This letter remained Old Jube's most treasured possession down the years, and did much to relieve the bitterness of the next few weeks — no doubt for him the hardest of the war — while he waited at home in Franklin County for orders to return to duty; orders that never came.

★　★　★

On March 3, about the time Sheridan's troopers were approaching Charlottesville, still jubilant over yesterday's lopsided victory at Waynesboro, Lincoln was up at the Capitol signing last-minute bills passed by Congress in preparation for adjournment tomorrow on Inauguration Day. He was interrupted by Stanton, who had just received a wire from Grant requesting instructions on how to reply to a formal query from Lee "as to the possibility of arriving at a satisfactory adjustment of the present unhappy difficulties, by means of a military convention."

There was more behind this than many people knew; Grant gave some of the details in his wire. Longstreet and Ord, it seemed, had met between the lines ten days ago, ostensibly to arrange a prisoner exchange, and Ord had advanced the notion that, the politicians having failed to agree on terms for peace at Hampton Roads, it might be well for the contestants themselves — the men, that is, who had been doing the actual bleeding all along — to "come together as former comrades and friends and talk a little." Grant and Lee could meet for an exchange of views, as could others, not excluding a number of their wives; Mrs Grant and Mrs Longstreet, for example, intimates before the war, could visit back and forth across the lines, along with their husbands, so that "while General Lee and General Grant were arranging for better feeling between the armies, they could be aided by intercourse between the ladies and officers until terms honorable to both sides could be found." Thus Ord spoke to his old army friend James Longstreet, who went to Lee with the proposal. Lee in turn conferred with Davis and Breckinridge. Both agreed the thing was worth a try: particularly the Kentuckian, who, as Old Peter later remarked, "expressed especial approval of the part assigned for the ladies." So Lee returned to Petersburg and sent his letter across the lines to Grant, suggesting "a military convention" as a means of ending the bloodshed, and Grant wired the War Department for instructions, saying: "I have not returned any reply, but promised to do so at noon tomorrow."

Noon tomorrow would be the hour at which Lincoln was scheduled to take the inaugural oath to "preserve, protect, and defend the Constitution of the United States" against what he conceived to be its domestic foes, and he did not intend to break — or, what might be worse, stand by while a clubby group of West Point professionals, North and South, broke for him — either that or another public oath he had taken just under nine months ago in Philadelphia: "We accepted this war for an object, a worthy object, and the war will end when that ob-

ject is attained. Under God, I hope it never will until that time." The
thing to do, as he saw it, was to nip this infringement in the bud. Accordingly, he wrote out in his own hand, for Stanton's signature, a carefully
worded reply to Grant's request for instructions. "The President directs
me to say to you that he wishes you to have no conference with General
Lee unless it be for the capitulation of Gen. Lee's army, or on some
minor and purely military matter. He instructs me to say that you are
not to decide, discuss, or confer upon any political question. Such questions the President holds in his own hands; and will submit them to no
military conferences or conventions. Meantime you are to press to the
utmost your military advantages."

That ended that; Grant informed Lee next day that he had "no
authority to accede to your proposition. . . . Such authority is vested in
the President of the United States alone." Lincoln meantime had wound
up his bill-signing chores and returned to the White House for the last
night of his first term in office, having received on February 12 — his
fifty-sixth birthday — formal notice from the Electoral College of his
victory over McClellan, back in November, by a vote of 212 to 21.

Inauguration Day broke cold and rainy. High on the dome of the
Capitol, unfinished on this occasion four years ago, Thomas Crawford's
posthumous bronze Freedom, a sword in one hand, a victory wreath in
the other, peered out through the mist on a scene of much confusion,
caused in part by deepening mud that hampered the movement of the
throng of visitors jammed into town for the show, and in part by Mrs
Lincoln, who, growing impatient at a long wait under the White House
portico, ordered her carriage to proceed up Pennsylvania Avenue at a
gallop, disrupting the schedule worked out by the marshals. Her husband
had already gone ahead to a room in the Senate wing, and was occupied
with signing another sheaf of bills rammed through to beat the deadline
now at hand. The rain let up before midmorning, though the sun did not
break through the scud of clouds, and around 11 o'clock a small, sharp-
pointed, blue-white diamond of a star — later identified as the planet
Venus — appeared at the zenith, directly over the Capitol dome, bright
in the murky daylight sky.

First the Senate would witness the swearing in of Andrew Johnson;
for which purpose, shortly before noon, all the members of both
houses and their distinguished guests fairly packed the Senate chamber. Diplomats in gold lace and feathers rivaled the crinolined finery of
the ladies in the gallery. Joe Hooker, hale and rosy in dress blues, represented the army, Farragut the navy; "The dear old Admiral," women
cooed as the latter entered, wearing all of his sixty-three years on his
balding head. Governors of most loyal states were there, together with
the nine Supreme Court justices, clad, as one observer noted, in "long
black silk nightgowns (so to speak) though it's all according to law."
These last — five of them of Lincoln's making, including the new Chief

Justice — were seated in the front row, to the right of the chair, while the Cabinet occupied the front row on the left. Lincoln sat between the two groups, looker trimmer than usual because of a shorter clip to his beard and hair.

As the clock struck 12, Vice President Hamlin entered, arm in arm with the man who would replace him. They had no sooner taken their seats than Hamlin rose and opened the ceremony by expressing his "heartfelt and undissembled thanks" to his colleagues for their kindness over the past four years. He paused, then asked: "Is the Vice President elect now ready to take and subscribe the oath of office?" Johnson got up. "I am," he said firmly, and launched without further preamble into an unscheduled oration. "Senators, I am here today as the chosen Vice President of the United States, and as such, by constitutional provision, I am made the presiding officer of this body." He wore his habitual scowl, as if to refute some expected challenge to his claim. "I therefore present myself here, in obedience to the high behests of the American people, to discharge a constitutional duty, and not presumptuously to thrust myself in a position so exalted." He spoke impromptu, without notes, and his words boomed loud against a hush more puzzled than shocked; just yet. "May I at this moment — it may not be irrelevant to the occasion — advert to the workings of our institutions under the Constitution which our fathers framed and George Washington approved, as exhibited by the position in which I stand before the American Senate, in the sight of the American people? Deem me not vain or arrogant; yet I should be less than man if under the circumstances I were not proud of being an American citizen, for today one who claims no high descent, one who comes from the ranks of the people, stands, by the choice of a free constituency, in the second place in this Government."

By now a buzz had begun in the chamber, spreading from point to point as his listeners gradually perceived that his near incoherence was not the result of faulty hearing or a lapse of comprehension on their part. "All this is in wretched bad taste," Speed whispered to Welles on his right. Welles agreed, saying to Stanton on his other side: "Johnson is either drunk or crazy." Stanton wagged his head. "There is evidently *some*thing wrong," he admitted. Then Welles had another thought. "I hope it is sickness," he said.

It was, in part. Six weeks ago, emerging shaky from a bout with typhoid and the strain of the campaign, the Tennessean had sought permission to stay in Nashville for the taking of the oath, but when Lincoln urged him to come to Washington he did so, though he still was far from well. "I am not fit to be here, and ought not to have left my home," he said that morning after he reached Hamlin's office in the Capitol. Someone brought him a tumbler of whiskey, which he drank to settle his nerves and get his strength up, then followed it with another just before he entered the overheated Senate chamber, saying: "I need all the strength for the occasion I can have." The result was the present diatribe, which continued despite tugs on his coattail from Hamlin, seated behind him, and unseen signals from his friends in front. He had stumped his way through a long campaign and he was stumping still. "Humble as I am, plebeian as I may be deemed," he went on, red-faced and unsteady, "permit me in the presence of this brilliant assemblage to enunciate the truth that courts and cabinets, the President and his advisers, derive their power and their greatness from the people." He wore on, croaking hoarsely toward the end, and when at last the oath had been administered he turned to the crowd with the Bible in both hands and kissed it fervently, saying as he did so: "I kiss this Book in the face of my nation of the United States."

Reactions varied. A reporter noted that, while Seward remained "bland and serene as a summer's day" and Charles Sumner "wore a saturnine and sarcastic smile," few others among those present managed to abide the harangue with such aplomb or enjoyment. Lincoln, for example, kept his head down throughout the blusterous display, apparently engaged in profound study of his shoe tips. Later he would discount the fears and rumors going round about the man who might replace him at any tragic moment. "I have known Andy for many years," he would say. "He made a bad slip the other day, but you need not be scared. Andy aint a drunkard." Just now, though, he had had enough embarrassment on so solemn an occasion. As he rose to join the procession filing out onto the inaugural platform set up along the east face of the building, he said pointedly to a marshal: "Do not let Johnson speak outside."

Emerging, he saw beneath the overcast of clouds what a journalist described as "a sea of heads in the great plaza in front of the Capitol, as far as the eye could reach, and breaking in waves along its outer edges." When he came out to take his seat a roar of applause went up from the crowd, which subsided only to rise again when the sergeant-at-arms, performing in dumb show, "arose and bowed, with his shining black hat in hand . . . and Abraham Lincoln, rising tall and gaunt among the groups about him, stepped forward." Just as he did so, the sun broke through and flooded the platform with its golden light. "Every heart beat quicker at the unexpected omen," the reporter declared. Certainly Lincoln's own did. "Did you notice that sunburst?" he later asked. "It made my heart jump." He moved to the lectern, unfolding a single large sheet of paper on which his speech was printed in two broad columns. "Fellow countrymen," he said.

There was, as he maintained, "less occasion for an extended address" than had been the case four years ago, when his concern had been to avoid the war that began soon afterward. Nor would he much con-

cern himself just now with purely military matters or venture a prediction as to the outcome, though his hope was high in that regard.
"Both parties deprecated war; but one of them would make war rather
than let the nation survive, and the other would accept war rather than
let it perish. And the war came.... Neither party expected for the
war the magnitude or the duration which it has already attained. Neither
anticipated that the cause of the conflict might cease with, or even before, the conflict itself should cease. Each looked for an easier triumph,
and a result less fundamental and astounding. Both read the same Bible
and pray to the same God, and each invokes His aid against the other.
It may seem strange that any men should dare to ask a just God's assistance in wringing their bread from the sweat of other men's faces;
but let us judge not, that we be not judged. The prayers of both could
not be answered; that of neither has been answered fully. The Almighty
has His own purposes. 'Woe unto the world because of offenses! for it
must needs be that offenses come; but woe to that man by whom the
offense cometh!' "

"Bless the Lord!" some down front cried up: Negroes mostly,
who took their tone from his, and responded as they would have done in
church. Lincoln kept on reading from the printed text in a voice one
hearer described as "ringing and somewhat shrill."

"If we shall suppose that American slavery is one of those offenses
which, in the providence of God, must needs come, but which, having
continued through His appointed time, He now wills to remove, and
that He gives to both North and South this terrible war, as the woe due
to those by whom the offense came, shall we discern therein any departure from those divine attributes which the believers in a living God
always ascribe to Him? Fondly do we hope — fervently do we pray —
that this mighty scourge of war may speedily pass away. Yet, if God
wills that it continue until all the wealth piled by the bondman's two
hundred and fifty years of unrequited toil shall be sunk, and until every
drop of blood drawn with the lash shall be paid by another drawn with
the sword, as was said three thousand years ago, so still it must be said:
'The judgments of the Lord are true and righteous altogether.' "

"Bless the Lord!" came up again through the thunder of applause,
but Lincoln passed at once to the peroration. He was beyond the war
now, into the peace which he himself would never see.

"With malice toward none; with charity for all; with firmness in
the right, as God gives us to see the right, let us strive on to finish the work
we are in; to bind up the nation's wounds; to care for him who shall have
borne the battle, and for his widow, and his orphan — to do all which
may achieve and cherish a just and a lasting peace, among ourselves and
with all nations."

Thus ended, as if on a long-held organ note, the shortest inaugural any President had delivered since George Washington was sworn in the second time. When the applause subsided, Chase signaled the clerk of the Supreme Court to come forward with the Bible held open-faced before him; Lincoln rested one hand on it while repeating the oath of office. "So help me God," he said, then bent and kissed the Book. Cheers went up as he rose once more to his full height and guns began thudding their shotless, flat-toned salutes in celebration. He turned to the crowd and bowed in several directions before he reëntered the Capitol and emerged again from a basement entrance, where a two-horse barouche waited to take him and Tad back to the White House in time for him to rest up for the reception scheduled there that evening. Between 8 and 11 o'clock, newsmen reckoned, he shook hands with no less than six thousand people, though these were by no means all who tried to get close enough to touch him. Walt Whitman, caught in the press of callers, was one of those who had to be content with watching from a distance. "I saw Mr Lincoln," the poet wrote in his notebook that night, "dressed all in black, with white kid gloves and a clawhammer coat, receiving, as in duty bound, shaking hands, looking very disconsolate . . . as if he would give anything to be somewhere else."

He was concerned about the reception of his speech that afternoon. "What did you think of it?" he asked friends as they passed down the line. He had heard and seen the cheers and tears of people near the platform, but tonight he was like a neglected author in wistful search of a discerning critic. Later, writing to Thurlow Weed, he said that he expected the address "to wear as well — perhaps better than — anything I have produced; but I believe it is not immediately popular. Men are not flattered by being shown that there has been a difference of purpose between the Almighty and them." Actually, the difficulty lay elsewhere. Some among his hearers and readers found his style as turgid, his syntax as knotty to unravel, as that of the new Vice President in the tirade staged indoors. "While the sentiments are noble," a disgruntled Pennsylvanian would complain this week in a private letter, "[Lincoln's inaugural] is one of the most awkwardly expressed documents I ever read — if it be correctly printed. When he knew it would be read by millions all over the world, why under the heavens did he not make it a little more creditable to American scholarship? Jackson was not too proud to get Van Buren to slick up his state papers. Why could not Mr Seward have prepared the Inaugural so as to save it from the ridicule of a sophomore in a British university?"

In point of fact, the British reaction was quite different from the one this Keystone critic apprehended. "It was a noble speech," the Duke of Argyll wrote his friend Sumner, "just and true, and solemn. I think it has produced a great effect in England." The London *Spectator* thought so, too, saying: "No statesman ever uttered words stamped at

once with the seal of so deep a wisdom and so true a simplicity." Even
the *Times*, pro-Confederate as it mostly was, had praise for the address.
Nor was approval lacking on this side of the Atlantic, even among those
with valid claims to membership in the New World aristocracy. "What
think you of the inaugural?" C. F. Adams Junior wrote his ambassador
father. "That rail-splitting lawyer is one of the wonders of the day.
Once at Gettysburg and now again on a greater occasion he has shown
a capacity for rising to the demands of the hour which we should not
expect from orators or men of the schools. This inaugural strikes me in
its grand simplicity and directness as being for all time the keynote of
this war; in it a people seemed to speak in the sublimely simple utterance of ruder times. What will Europe think of this utterance of the rude
ruler, of whom they have nourished so lofty a contempt? Not a prince
or minister in all Europe could have risen to such an equality with the
occasion."

Others besides Adams drew the Gettysburg comparison, being
similarly affected, and presently there was still another likeness in what
followed. Lincoln fell ill, much as he had done after the earlier address,
except then it had been varioloid, a mild form of smallpox, and this was
a different kind of ailment — noninfectious, nonspecific, yet if anything
rather more debilitating. In fact, that was at the root of his present indisposition. He was exhausted. "Nothing touches the tired spot," he
had begun to say within a year of taking office, and lately he had been
referring again to "the tired spot, which can't be got at," somewhere
deep inside him, trunk and limbs and brain. "I'm a tired man," he told
one caller. "Sometimes I think I'm the tiredest man on earth."

If so, he had cause. In the past five weeks — hard on the heels of
a bitter campaign for reëlection, which only added to the cumulative
strain of leadership through four bloody years of fratricidal conflict —
he had cajoled and logrolled Congress into passing the Thirteenth
Amendment, dealt with the Confederate commissioners aboard the
River Queen in Hampton Roads, and kept a watchful eye on Grant
while raising the troops and money required to fuel the war machine. All
this, plus the drafting and delivery of the second inaugural, was in addition to his usual daily tasks as Chief Executive, not the least of which
consisted of enduring the diurnal claims of office-seekers and their
sponsors, often men of political heft and high position. Two cabinet
changes followed within a week, both the result of his acceding to
Fessenden's plea that the time had come for him to leave the Treasury
and return to his seat in the Senate. Lincoln replaced him on March 7
with Hugh McCulloch, a Maine-born Hoosier banker, only to have
Interior Secretary John P. Usher resign on grounds that he too was
from Indiana. Iowa Senator James Harlan was named to take his place,

a felicitous choice, since he was a close family friend and the President's son Robert was courting the senator's daughter with the intention of marrying her as soon as he completed his military service.

This too was a problem for Lincoln — or, more specifically, for his wife; which came to the same thing. Just out of college, the young man wanted to enter the army despite strenuous objections by his mother, who grew sick with fear of what might happen to him there. As a result, Lincoln had worked out a compromise, back in January, that might satisfy them both, depending on Grant's response to a proposal made him at the time: "Please read and answer this letter as though I was not President, but only a friend. My son, now in his twenty-second year, having graduated from Harvard, wishes to see something of the war before it ends. I do not wish to put him in the ranks, nor yet to give him a commission to which those who have already served long are better entitled, and better qualified to hold. Could he, without embarrassment to you or detriment to the service, go into your military family with some nominal rank, I, and not the public, furnishing his necessary means? If no, say so without the least hesitation, because I am as anxious, and as deeply interested that you shall not be encumbered, as you can be yourself." Grant replied that he would be glad to have the young man on his staff as an assistant adjutant, his rank to be that of captain and his pay to come from the government, not his father. In mid-February the appointment came through. Soon after attending the inaugural ceremonies in the hard-galloping carriage with his mother and his prospective father-in-law, Robert set out down the coast for City Point. Lincoln was glad to have the difficult matter settled, but it came hard for him that he had had to settle it this way, knowing as he did that he had drafted into the shot-torn ranks of the nation's armies hundreds of thousands of other sons whose mothers loved and feared for them as much as Mary Lincoln did for hers.

As a result of all these pressures and concerns, or rather of his delayed reaction to them, what should have been for him a time of relieved tension — Congress, having adjourned, was not scheduled to reconvene until December, so that he had hope of ending the war in much the same way he had begun it; that is, without a host of frock-coated politicians breathing down his neck — turned out instead to be the one in which he looked and felt his worst. It was as if, like a spent swimmer who collapses only after he has reached the shore, he had had no chance till now, having been occupied with the struggle to keep afloat in a sea of administrative and domestic frets, to realize how close he was to absolute exhaustion. "His face was haggard with care and seamed with thought and trouble," Horace Greeley noted after a mid-March interview. "It looked care-ploughed, tempest-tossed and weather-beaten." One reporter diagnosed the ailment as "a severe attack of influenza," but another remarked more perceptively that the President was "suffering from the exhausting attentions of office hunters." In any case, on March 14 — ten days after the inauguration — Lincoln was obliged to hold the scheduled Tuesday cabinet meeting in his bedroom, prone beneath the covers but with his head and shoulders propped on pillows stacked against the headboard of his bed.

That day's rest did some good, and even more came from a new rule setting 3 o'clock as the close of office hours, so far at least as scheduled callers went. By the end of the week he felt well enough to go with his wife and guests to a performance of Mozart's *Magic Flute* at Grover's Theatre, enjoying it so much indeed that when Mrs Lincoln suggested leaving before the final curtain reunited the fire-tested lovers, he protested: "Oh, no. I want to see it out. It's best, when you undertake a job, to finish it." Much of his fascination was with one of the sopranos, whose feet were not only large but flat. "The beetles wouldn't have much of a chance there," he whispered, nodding toward the stage.

Here was at least one sign that he was better, though it was true he often joked in just this way to offset the melancholia that dogged him all his life. He still felt weary — "flabby," as he called it — and no amount of rest, by night or day, got through to the tired spot down somewhere deep inside him. He considered a trip, perhaps a visit to the army in Virginia, "immediately after the next rain." Then on March 20 a wire from Grant seemed to indicate that the general either had read his mind or else had spies in the White House. "Can you not visit City Point for a day or two? I would like very much to see you, and I think the rest would do you good."

Lincoln at once made plans to go. He would leave in the next day or two, aboard the fast, well-armed dispatch steamer *Bat.* "Will notify you of exact time, once it shall be fixed upon," he replied to Grant. But when he told his wife, she announced that she too would be going; it had been two weeks since Robert left for City Point, and she would see him there. So the expanded party shifted to the more commodious *River Queen*, retaining the *Bat* for escort. Tad would go, along with Mrs Lincoln's maid, a civilian bodyguard, and a military aide. Lincoln had heard from Grant on Monday, and on Thursday he was off down the Potomac, sailing from the Sixth Street wharf in the early afternoon.

X   2   X

That same Thursday — March 23 — Sherman reached Goldsboro, the goal of his 425-mile slog up the Carolinas, to find Schofield waiting for him with reinforcements enough to lift his over-all strength to just under 90,000 of all arms. Both had run into their first hard fighting of the double-pronged campaign, and both had come through it more or less intact, despite losses they would rather have avoided until they combined to inflict the utter destruction of whatever gray fragments presumed to stand in the path of their northward conjunction with Grant at the gates of Richmond.

What was more, for all the wretched weather and sporadic opposition, the two blue columns — themselves divided and out of touch, each with the other, until they arrived at their common objective — had made good time. Two weeks after Columbia went up in smoke, Sherman got both wings of his army up to the Pee Dee River and called a halt at Cheraw, March 3–5, to give his bedraggled troops a chance to dry their clothes and scrape away the mud they had floundered through while crossing the rain-bulged Wateree and soft-banked Lynch's Creek. Then he was off again, out of the Palmetto State at last. Reactions differed, up and down the long line of marchers; some looked back with cackling glee on the destruction, while others felt a softening effect. "South Carolina may have been the cause of the whole thing," a Michigan lieutenant wrote in a running letter home, "but she has had an awful punishment."

She had indeed, and now ahead lay the Old North State; a quite different prospect, Sherman believed, one that entailed a much higher degree of Union sentiment, which he intended to woo and play upon en route. "Deal as moderately and fairly by North Carolinians as possible," he told subordinates, "and fan the flame of discord already subsisting between them and their proud cousins of South Carolina. There never was much love lost between them. Touch upon the chivalry of running away, always leaving their families for us to feed and protect, and then on purpose accusing us of all sorts of rudeness."

Accordingly, guards were posted at the gates or on the steps of roadside houses, barring entrance to the marchers filing past, and the women, emboldened by this protection, came out on their porches to watch the invaders go by, shoulders hunched against the rain, feet made heavy with balled-up mud, and spirits considerably dampened. The women looked at the men, and the men looked back. "We glanced ruefully at them out of the shadow of our lowering, drenched hat rims," one soldier was to say, recalling freer times a week ago, when their red-haired commander had scorned to practice such restraint. Denied access to residences, they exercised their arsonist proclivities on the forests of pine through which they passed between the Pee Dee and Cape Fear rivers — and found the result even more spectacular than those produced when they set fire to barns and gins, back in Georgia and South Carolina. Notched for the drawing of sap, the trees burned like enormous torches, often hundreds at a time, when a match was put to them. Overhead, "the smoke could hardly escape through the green canopy, and hung like a pall," an Ohio colonel noted. "It looked like a fire in a cathedral." A New York private, highly conscious of being part of what he saw, found himself awed by the tableau, "all to be heard and seen only by glimpses under the smoke and muffled by the Niagara-like roar of the flames as they licked up turpentine and pitch. Now came rolling back from the depths of the pine forest the chorus of thousands singing 'John Brown's body lies a-moldering.' " He considered it "at once a prophecy and a fulfillment."

This final leg of the march, just over a fourth of the whole, would be covered in two sixty-mile jumps, with a rest halt in between: Cheraw to Fayetteville, a major Confederate supply base, and Fayetteville to Goldsboro, where Sherman had arranged to meet Schofield, barring serious complications. Driving rains and deepening mud, together with the washout of all bridges over the Wateree, had thrown him a bit off schedule by now, but he hoped to get back on it by making better time through the piny highlands. And so he did, despite the unrelenting downpour. "It was the damndest marching I ever saw," he said of an Illinois regiment's covering fifteen soggy miles in five hours. Delighted, he detached three enlisted volunteers — two of them disguised as rebel officers, the third as a civilian — to pick their way through enemy country, ninety-odd miles east to Wilmington, with a note for whoever Schofield had left in charge there: "If possible, send a boat up Cape Fear River.... We are well and have done finely. The rains make our roads difficult, and may delay us about Fayetteville, in which case I would like to have some bread, sugar, and coffee. We have abundance of all else. I expect to reach Goldsboro by the 20th instant." He kept going, crossing the Lumber River by the light of flaming pine knots, and made it into Fayetteville before midday, March 11, five days out of Cheraw; Hardee, he learned, had left the night before, and Hampton had come close to being captured by the first blue troopers riding in that morning. After running the national flag up over the market place and establishing headquarters in the handsome former U.S. arsenal — now U.S. again — his first concern was to find out whether anything had been heard from downriver in response to the note, written three days ago, which the three-man detail had been charged with getting through to Wilmington.

Nothing had. But at noon next day the Sabbath quiet was shattered by the scream of a steamboat whistle; Alfred Terry, in command at Wilmington, had sent the army tug *Davidson* upriver in response to Sherman's note, all three copies of which had reached him the day before. Armored with cotton bales to shield her crew from snipers, the boat's main cargo was not sugar, coffee, or hardtack, but news of the outside world, as set forth in dispatches and a bundle of the latest papers, North and South. "The effect was electric," Sherman was to say, "and no one can realize the feeling unless, like us, he has been for months cut off from all communication with friends and compelled to listen to the croakings and prognostications of open enemies." He ordered the tug to return downriver at sunset, passing the word that she would take with her all the letters anyone cared to write, and gave instructions for a larger vessel to be sent back up as soon as possible, this time with the hardtack, coffee, and sugar he had requested in the first place, plus all the shoes, stockings, and drawers that could be spared. Which done, he put his men back to work destroying rebel installations, including the Fayetteville arsenal itself, and spent much of the night and the following day studying the dispatches and perusing newspapers crammed with speculations as to his whereabouts and fate.

The best of the news was that Schofield, his strength increased above 30,000 by the addition of two new divisions, one made up of convalescents sent from Washington, the other of troops from coastal garrisons such as Beaufort, was hard on the go for Goldsboro and seemed likely to get there well within the time allotted. Leaving Terry to hold Wilmington with his X Corps, in case improbable rebel combinations obliged Sherman to veer in that direction at the last minute, he had sent Jacob Cox by sea to New Bern with his beefed-up XXIII Corps, under instructions to move west along the Atlantic & N.C. Railroad — which was not only shorter and more repairable than the Wilmington & Weldon, but was also provided with locomotives and cars, as the other was not — thus establishing a rapid-transit link between Goldsboro and the coast, not at the mouth of the Cape Fear River, as originally intended, but instead at the mouth of the Neuse in Pamlico Sound, which afforded the navy far better all-weather harbor facilities for unloading the mountain of supplies Sherman's 60,000 footsore, tattered veterans would need at the end of their long swing through the Carolinas. Cox had set out from New Bern on March 1, repairing the railroad as he went, and Schofield had left Wilmington to join him, wanting to be on hand in case he ran into serious opposition from Hoke, whose division, flung out of Wilmington two weeks before, was reported to have fallen back on Kinston, where the Atlantic & N.C. crossed the Neuse, about midway between Goldsboro and New Bern.

Sherman was pleased with this news of Schofield's progress across the way, promising as it did an early combination for the follow-up march into Virginia. He had grown more cautious since learning that Johnston, his wily Georgia adversary, was back in command of the forces in his front. So far, here inland, nothing had come of the shift, however, and Terry's report assured him that all was well in the other direction, too. "Jos. Johnston may try to interpose between me here and Schofield about New Bern," he had written Grant in a letter the *Davidson* carried downriver at sunset, March 12, "but I think he will not try that." His notion was that the Virginian would "concentrate his scattered armies at Raleigh": in which case, he told his friend the general-in-chief, "I will go straight at him as soon as I get our men reclothed and our wagons reloaded." Meantime, before he moved on, there was the arsenal to be disposed of, a handsome cluster of cream-colored brick structures whose well-kept grounds served Fayetteville as a municipal park. "The arsenal is in fine order, and has been much enlarged," he informed Stanton in a letter that went along with Grant's. "I cannot leave a detachment to hold it, therefore shall burn it, blow it up with gunpowder, and then with rams knock down its walls. I take it for granted the United States will never again trust North Carolina with an arsenal to appropriate at her leisure."

In point of fact, he had been right to suspect that Johnston was up to something, and wrong to think that all he was up to was a concentration at Raleigh. Terry's latest information about Schofield's other column, toiling westward out the Atlantic & N.C., was three days old; within which span, as a result of Johnston's caginess, Cox had had to fight a battle on disadvantageous ground. Schofield had reached New Bern by sea from Wilmington on March 7, and when he went forward next morning, beyond the spike-hammer din of rail repair crews, he found the head of the infantry column under fire from graybacks who had lain in wait along the high ground just this side of Southwest Creek, the western limit of Dover Swamp, a thirty-mile-wide marsh through which the railroad threaded its way to within three miles of Kinston and the Neuse. A sudden, unexpected attack had struck and scattered two blue regiments in advance, capturing three fourths of the men, and the attackers seemed determined to expand this opening setback into a full-scale defeat. What was more, they might be able to do just that, by the sheer weight of their numbers. Prisoners taken were found to be not only from Hoke's division, already suspected of lurking up ahead, but also from Stewart's and S. D. Lee's corps of the Army of Tennessee, a good five hundred miles from home.

It was Johnston, urged by R. E. Lee to strike before the Federals united in his front, who had made this possible by reinforcing the troops opposing Cox. Moreover, he had other such moves in mind, and was even now in the process of effecting them: not so much with the intention of actually defeating his red-haired antagonist — each of whose two wings, like Schofield's two-corps army over toward the coast, was nearly half again larger than his total force — but rather in the hope of delaying the blue combination until Lee could give Grant the slip and join him, here in Carolina, for an offensive combination of their own. Although by ordinary he was far from being the cut-and-slash sort of general who seized upon long chances as a means of redressing odds that were even longer, desperation had made him bold. Indeed, there was no better indication of the extent of Confederate desperation, at this stage, than Joseph E. Johnston's overnight conversion into the kind of commander he became, at least for a time, hard on the heels of having told Lee, while en route to take over from Beauregard at Charlotte: "It is too late," and following this with a letter in which, having studied the strength reports on hand, he said flatly: "In my opinion these troops form an army too weak to cope with Sherman."

He had at the time fewer than 20,000 men, considerably scattered. Hardee's 10,000 at Cheraw, the rail terminus he fell back on after evacuating Charleston, were joined by Hampton's 4000 cavalry, three fourths of them under Wheeler and the rest under Butler, while another 4000 infantry, on hand or still on the way from the Army of Tennessee, brought the total to 18,000 of all arms. Presently, on March 4, this figure was enlarged by Lee's extension of Johnston's authority to include Hoke's 5500, withdrawn by Bragg to Goldsboro after the fall of Wilmington. By then, however, Hardee had been obliged to evacuate Cheraw, under pressure from Howard and Slocum, and had fallen back on Fayetteville, reduced to about 8000 by desertions and the detachment of his South Carolina militia, who were forbidden by law to follow him out of the state. Sherman continued his march, obviously toward Fayetteville now, but Johnston was hard put to determine whether his adversary would be headed next for Goldsboro or for Raleigh. Splitting the difference, he decided to concentrate at Smithfield, on the railroad midway between the two, for a strike at one or another of Sherman's wings before they came together at whichever city was their goal. There was hope in this, but only by contrast with the surrounding gloom of the piecemeal and seemingly endless retreat. Desertions were heavy and getting heavier, particularly by Carolinians, South and North, whose homes lay in the path or wake of the blue despoilers tramping northward. Ambrose Wright, commanding one of Hardee's two divisions, took the occasion to return to his native Georgia, where he had been elected *in absentia* to the senate; Taliaferro took over his undersized division, adding the Sumter garrison to its roll — a disgruntled body in which tempers ran short among men unaccustomed to marching or going hungry. A sergeant, for example, on being reproved for advising comrades to desert, drew his pistol and attempted to use it on the lieutenant who had reproached him. Arrested, he was tried before a drumhead court and sentenced to be shot. He died without the consolation of religion. "Preacher, I never listened to you at Fort Sumter," he said bitterly to the chaplain who came to pray with him on the night before his execution, "and I won't listen to you now."

These were brave men; Wright had been one of the Army of Northern Virginia's hardest-hitting brigadiers, all the way from the Seven Days to the Siege of Petersburg, and the sergeant had stood up to everything the U.S. Navy had to throw at him in the rubble and brick dust of Sumter. What they mainly suffered from was despair, a discouragement verging into disgust as they were shuttled about, invariably rearward, to avoid being crushed by the compact masses of bluecoats in their front. Johnston knew well enough that the best correction for flagging morale lay in delivery of the blow he planned to throw as soon as he completed the concentration now in progress around Smithfield, although this was a necessarily slow procedure, scattered as his 21,500 soldiers were in their attempt to confront the 90,000 invaders moving against them from the south and east, unchecked so far, and scarcely even delayed. Then Bragg suggested an interim maneuver that might not only lift morale but also disrupt the Federal convergence. Schofield had divided his army, holding one corps at Wilmington while the other went to New Bern; Bragg's notion was for Johnston to reinforce him at Goldsboro for an attack, just east of Kinston, on the corps slogging westward along the Atlantic and N.C. Railroad; after which he would hurry back east by rail in time for a share in the strike at one of Sherman's wings before they closed on Raleigh or Goldsboro, whichever they headed for after reaching Fayetteville. "A few hours would suffice to unite the forces at Smithfield with mine and assure a victory," he telegraphed headquarters on March 6. Johnston thought it over, and then next day — uncharacteristically; for the shift involved a division of force in the presence of a greatly superior foe — decided to give the thing a try. All he had on hand just now were some 3000 men from the Army of Tennessee, forwarded by Beauregard, who had remained in Charlotte to expedite such movements; but he alerted them for the shift, and notified Bragg that they were at his disposal. "Send trains when fight is impending," he wired, "and send back troops as soon as it is over."

That was how it came about that Bragg was able to surprise and crumple the head of Cox's column next morning, March 8, just before it reached the western rim of Dover Swamp. Encouraged by this initial rout, which netted him close to a thousand prisoners, he pressed his assault on the main body. Schofield had arrived by then, however, and had ordered light intrenchments thrown up during the lull that followed the opening attack: with the result that Bragg rebounded to search elsewhere along Southwest Creek for a breakthrough point. He never found it, though he tried for the rest of that day and the next, when Cox brought up the remainder of his 15,000-man corps, including the railroad workers, to stand fast against the graybacks, whom he estimated at better than twice their actual number of 8500. On the third day, March 10, Bragg withdrew across the Neuse, burning the wagon and railway bridges in his rear, and got his troops aboard the cars for a fast ride west to Smithfield, as he had said he would do, in time for a share in the sequential attack on Sherman. The Battle of Kinston — or Wise's Forks, as the Federals sometimes called it — was a long way short of the triumph he had predicted, but the respective casualty lists went far toward sustaining his claim that he had scored a tactical success. He lost 134 men in all, while Cox lost 1257, most of them captured at the outset. What was more, the engagement had served its larger purpose as a check to Schofield's progress toward Goldsboro. It was March 14 before he got the bridges rebuilt across the Neuse, and still another week, after summoning Terry up from Wilmington, before he reached his appointed goal. Even so, he reached it well before Sherman, whom Johnston had struck not once but twice in the course of Schofield's final week of marching west along the railroad toward their common objective.

Old Joe was of course disappointed that Bragg had not been able to do Schofield all the damage promised in his plea for reinforcements, but he was grateful for the resultant easing of pressure from the east while he continued his efforts to pull his scattered units together for the projected strike at Sherman, about to move out of Fayetteville by now. Still uncertain whether this main blue force was headed for Raleigh or Goldsboro, he held Bragg and the Tennessee contingent near Smithfield, midway between them, and divided his cavalry to patrol the roads in both directions, Butler's troopers on the left and Wheeler's on the right, the latter covering Hardee's northward withdrawal from Fayetteville under instructions to slow down, if he could, the march of the Federals in his rear. For all his grave numerical disadvantage, Johnston at least had no shortage of brass in the corps-sized army he planned to unite and throw at one or another of Sherman's wings; Bragg was a full general, Hardee, Stewart, and Hampton lieutenant generals, and in addition he had fourteen major generals and innumerable brigadiers, not

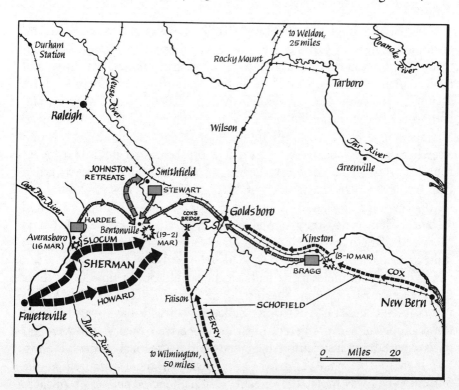

to mention another full general, Beauregard, expediting the movement
of troops through Charlotte, and still a fourth lieutenant general, S. D.
Lee, present but not yet recovered enough from his post-Nashville
wound to take the field. For all their various prickly characteristics —
including, in several paired cases, a stronger dislike for each other than
for anything in blue — they made a distinguished roster, one that
augured well for the conduct of the impending battle. Johnston took
much comfort from that, and also from something else he learned about
this time. Texas Senator Louis Wigfall, one of his most ardent supporters
in the capital, wrote that both the President and Mrs Davis appeared
to be in deep distress over the current situation. The Virginian replied
on March 14: "I have a most unchristian satisfaction in what you say
of the state of mind of the leading occupants of the Presidential Mansion. For me, it is very sufficient revenge."

      Sherman began his march out of Fayetteville that same day,
and by the next — having completed his demolition of the arsenal
by alternately blowing it up and battering it down — had both wings
over the Cape Fear River, trudging north for a feint at Raleigh before
he turned east to keep his March 20 appointment with Schofield at
Goldsboro, five days off. Terry had not been able to send shoes or
clothing on the *Davidson*'s return upriver, but he had sent coffee and
sugar, to the delight of the tattered, half-barefoot veterans, and he had
relieved the column of "twenty to thirty thousand useless mouths,"
started downriver by Sherman under escort, white and black, to be
herded into refugee camps at Wilmington; "They are a dead weight
to me and consume our supplies," the red-haired commander explained.
He was in higher spirits than ever, having learned that Sheridan would
likely be joining him in a week or two. Far from resenting the prospect
of sharing laurels with the man who next to himself was the chief hero
of the day, he looked forward to his fellow Ohioan's arrival as "a disturbing element in the grand and beautiful game of war.... If he
reaches me, I'll make all North Carolina howl," he told Terry, adding
the further inducement: "I will make him a deed of gift of every horse
in the state, to be settled for at the day of judgment."
      For all his lightness of heart as he set out on the final leg of his
march, he was thoroughly aware of possible last-minute dangers in his
path. Indeed, he was overaware of them, not only because of his great
respect for Johnston, who had shown in the past a capacity for reading
his mind as accurately as if he were reading his mail, but also because he
more than doubled his adversary's true numerical strength with an estimate of 45,000 of all arms; a not unreasonable error after all, since the
Virginian had been in command for better than two weeks, presumably
with every Confederate resource at his disposal for fending off this
ultimate strike through the Carolinas. Properly cautious now that he

was within a few days of his goal, Sherman ordered four divisions in each wing to travel light, ready for action, while the others — two in Slocum's case, three in Howard's — accompanied the train and guns to help them along through the mud, thereby assuring speed in case of breakdowns and alertness in case of attack. "I can whip Joe Johnston if he don't catch one of my corps in flank," he had written Terry from Fayetteville, "and I will see that my army marches hence to Goldsboro in compact form."

So he said. But compactness was no easy thing to achieve on roads that varied greatly in condition, especially under the pelting of rain, which now began to come down harder than ever. Besides, in the opening stage of this final leg of the march, while Howard's wing traveled a fairly direct route (a little north of east) toward Cox's Bridge, a dozen miles above Goldsboro on the Neuse, Slocum's followed a more circuitous route (a little east of north) up the Fayetteville-Raleigh road along the left bank of the Cape Fear River — a move designed to mislead Johnston into assembling all his troops for the defense of the state capital, in the belief that it was the Federal objective. If successful, this would remove the graybacks from contention; for Slocum meantime would have swung due east at Averasboro, twenty miles upriver from Fayetteville, to get back in touch with Howard near Bentonville, twelve miles short of Cox's Bridge, where both would cross for an on-schedule meeting with Schofield at Goldsboro and a brief pause for rest and refitment before turning to deal with Johnston, once and for all, preparatory to setting out for Virginia to join Grant. In any case, that was Sherman's plan, and he rode with Slocum to see that all went well.

All did, despite frequent clashes between Kilpatrick's horsemen, screening the outer flank, and Wheeler's. On the first night out, March 15, Slocum made camp about eight miles south of Averasboro, where he would swing east tomorrow to reunite the two blue columns before they reached the Neuse, ninth of the nine major rivers between Savannah and their goal. Or so Sherman thought until Slocum took up the march next morning, shortly after sunrise, only to run into heavy infantry fire from dead ahead.

It was Hardee. Instructed by Johnston to keep between Sherman and Raleigh for the double purpose of slowing the bluecoats down and determining their objective (if it was the capital, as seemed likely, he would be joined by Bragg and the Tennesseans for a strike before the Federals got there. If not, if instead they were marching somewhat roundabout on Goldsboro, he would move toward Smithfield, where Bragg and the Tennesseans were posted, for a combined attack somewhere short of the Neuse) he had decided the night before to make a stand, as he later explained, "to ascertain whether I was followed by Sherman's whole army, or part of it, and what was its destination." Half a dozen miles south of Averasboro, where the Cape Fear and

Black rivers were only four miles apart, he came upon suitable ground for such a delaying action. Adopting the tactics used by Daniel Morgan eighty-four years ago at Cowpens, just under two hundred miles away in northwest South Carolina, he placed Taliaferro's less experienced troops in a double line out front, astride the Fayetteville-Raleigh road and facing south between the rivers, with orders to fall back on Mc-Laws' veterans, dug in along another double line 600 yards to the north, as soon as the attackers pressed up close enough to overrun them. These six infantry brigades — Taliaferro's two were mostly converted artillerists from the Sumter garrison — together with Wheeler's two mounted brigades, gave Hardee an overall strength of about 11,000. How many the Federals had, except that they had a lot, the Georgian did not know. He expected to find out soon, however, since that was one of his three main reasons for stopping to fight them in the first place, the other two being to slow them down and find out for certain whether their march was a feint or a true drive on the North Carolina capital, thirty-odd miles in his rear.

They had about twice his number, as it turned out, immediately available under Kilpatrick and in the four divisions Sherman had ordered to travel light for ready use, plus half again as many more who could be called up from the train if they were needed; which they were not. Slocum advanced two divisions in support of the skirmishing troopers, and when at last around 10 o'clock, their progress badly hampered by muddy ravines and a driving rain, they encountered Taliaferro's makeshift force in position astride the road, they halted, pinned down by spattering fire, and sent back word that they had struck Hardee's main line of resistance, intrenched across the swampy neck of land between the rivers. Anxious to waste no more time, Sherman had Slocum commit a third division for an immediate assault. That burned still more daylight, however. It was 3 o'clock before the concerted push could be made, and though it was altogether successful in flinging the graybacks rearward with the loss of three guns and more than two hundred prisoners, the attackers pursued them less than a quarter of a mile before they were pinned down again by fire from a stronger line of works, some 600 yards in rear of the first. "It would have been worse than folly to have attempted a farther advance," one division commander would report, and Sherman and Slocum agreed. Long-range fire continued past sundown into dusk, then stopped. Hardee, who had suffered about 500 casualties, pulled back after nightfall, leaving Wheeler's horsemen to cover his rear, and issued next day a congratulatory order commending his troops, green and seasoned alike, for "giving the enemy the first check he has received since leaving Atlanta."

There was truth in that, and it was also true that Sherman wanted no more of it just now. Unlike Johnston, he was not seeking to fight his enemy piecemeal; he wanted him whole, for total destruction when the time came — after his and Schofield's forces were combined beyond the Neuse. Averasboro had gained him nothing more than control of the field next morning, and had cost him 682 casualties, 149 of them dead or missing, which left 533 wounded to fill the left-wing ambulances and hinder still further the train's hard-grinding progress through the mire. It had also cost him a day of critical time, both for Slocum and for Howard, who had to be told to slow his pace across the way, lest the space between them grow so great that mutual support would no longer be possible in a crisis. There seemed little likelihood of this last, however; Wheeler's troopers faded back up the Raleigh pike which Hardee's men had traveled the night before, apparently in delayed obedience to Johnston's orders for a concentration in front of the threatened capital. Satisfied that his feint had worked, Sherman turned the head of Slocum's column east for Bentonville and Cox's Bridge, as originally planned, when he came in sight of Averasboro at midday, March 17. The rain was pouring down harder than ever, and one officer later testified that St Patrick's Day and the two or three that followed were "among the most wearisome of the campaign. Incessant rain, deep mud, roads always wretched but now nearly impassable, seemed to cap the climax of tedious, laborious marching.... In spite of every exertion," he added, "the columns were a good deal drawn out, and long intervals separated the divisions."

In short, aside from the irreducible disparity in numbers, blue and gray, Johnston could scarcely have asked for a situation more favorable to his purpose than the one reported to him before daybreak, March 18. As a result — for the first time since Seven Pines, nearly three years ago, with his back to Richmond's eastern gates — he went over to the offensive. Informed by Hardee, who had fallen back not on Raleigh but to a point where the road forked east to Smithfield, and by Hampton, who was in touch with Butler and Wheeler, that both of Sherman's wings were across Black River, bound for Goldsboro in separate columns, a day's march apart and badly strung out on sodden, secondary roads, Old Joe called for a concentration at Bentonville that night and an all-out strike just south of there next morning, first at one and then the other of Slocum's corps toiling eastward through the mud. By the time Bragg and the Tennesseans left Smithfield, shortly after sunrise, he had matured his plan so far that he could direct Hardee, a day in advance, to take position "immediately on their right" when he arrived. Hampton, already with Butler on the chosen field, two miles beyond the town, would skirmish with Slocum's leading elements in an attempt to fix him in position for the execution Johnston had designed.

Sherman, having remained with the left wing so long as he supposed it was in graver danger than the other, set out crosscountry next morning — Sunday, March 19 — to join Howard for the crossing of the Neuse and the meeting with Schofield the following day, as scheduled. Soon after he started he heard what he called "some cannonading over about Slocum's head of column," but he kept going, on the assumption that it amounted to nothing more than another try by Hampton to divert and slow him down. Nine air-line miles to the south and east, after a wearing day spent doubling the right-wing column — as badly strung out, tail to head, as was Slocum's across the way — he came upon Howard at Falling Creek, where the roads from Fayetteville and Averasboro came together, four miles from Cox's Bridge; Howard had made camp there, less than twenty miles from Goldsboro, to give his two corps a chance to close up before crossing the river next day. All seemed well in this direction, and any worries Sherman might have had about the cannonade that erupted in his rear when he set out that morning, just short of Bentonville, had been allayed by a staff officer Slocum sent to overtake him with word that the clash was with butternut cavalry, which he was "driving nicely." Still, the rumble and thump of guns had continued from the northwest all day and even past sundown, when a courier reached Falling Creek with another left-wing message, altogether different from the first. Headed 1.30 p.m. and written under fire, it read: "I am convinced the enemy are in strong force to my front. Prisoners report Johnston, Hardee, Hoke and others present. They say their troops are just coming up. I shall strengthen my position and feel of their lines, but I hope you will come up on their left rear in strong force. Yours, truly, H. W. Slocum, Major General."

After reading the message in Howard's tent, where he had removed his boots and uniform to get some rest, Sherman rushed out to stand ankle-deep in the ashes of a campfire, hands clasped behind him — a lanky figure dressed informally, to say the least, in a red flannel undershirt and a pair of drawers. He seemed bemused, but not for long. Presently he was barking orders, and there was much of what one startled witness called "hurrying to and fro and mounting in hot haste." Once a courier was on the way with a note advising Slocum to fight a purely defensive action until the rest of the army joined him, Sherman told Logan, whose corps was in the lead today, to march for Bentonville on the road from Cox's Bridge, and sent word for Blair to follow by the same route; which hopefully would put them in the rebel rear, provided Slocum could hold his position until they got there. Whether this last was possible, however, in the light of subsequent dispatches from the field, was highly doubtful. "I deem it of the greatest importance that the Right Wing come up during the night," Slocum urged in a message written an hour after dark.

That could scarcely be; Bentonville was a good ten miles by road from Falling Creek. Moreover, by way of indicating the fury of the conflict up to now, he requested "all the ammunition and empty ambulances and wagons that can be spared," and added that he had positive information that "the corps and commands of Hardee, Stewart, Lee, Cheatham, Hill, and Hoke are here."

Which Lee? Which Hill? Sherman might have wondered as he stood amid the ashes, convinced as he had been till now that Old Joe would not risk fighting with the Neuse at his back. Still, as a roster — a Confederate order of battle — the list was not only accurate but complete: although it had not been the latter until past midday, when Hardee at last came up. Otherwise Slocum might not have survived the ambush Johnston had devised for his piecemeal destruction.

Bragg and the Tennesseans had reached Bentonville the night before, as ordered, and were deployed for combat by midmorning, two miles south of town. Hoke's 5500 were posted athwart the road on which Slocum was advancing, slowed by Hampton's skirmishing troopers, while the 4000 western veterans were disposed behind a dense screen of scrub oaks, north of the road and parallel to it, facing south. Johnston's plan was for Hoke to bring the bluecoats to a jumbled halt with a sudden blast of fire from dead ahead, at which point they would be struck in flank by the Tennesseans and Hardee, charging unexpectedly out of the brush. The trouble was that Old Reliable's 7500 — more than a third of the gray total, mounted and afoot — were not yet there to extend and give weight to the strike force stretching westward along the north side of the road. Misled by Johnston, who had himself been misled by a faulty map, Hardee had found yesterday's march twice its reckoned length; with the result that he had had to go into camp, long after dark, some six miles short of Bentonville. He notified his chief of this, but said that he hoped to make up for it by setting out again at 3 a.m. Even so, he did not reach the town until around 9 o'clock, and then found the single road leading south through the blackjack thickets badly clogged by rearward elements of the units already in position. It was well past noon before he approached the field, and by that time the trap had been sprung by pressure on Hampton, whose vedettes were driven back through the line of works Hoke's men had thrown across the road to block the Federal advance.

The trap snapped, but lacking Hardee it lacked power in the jaw that was intended to bite deeply into the flank of the startled Union column. Brigadier General William Carlin's division of Davis's corps had the lead today, and when the woods exploded in his front — a crash of rifles, with the roar of guns mixed in — he recoiled, then rallied and came on again, having called for help from Brigadier General James D. Morgan, whose other XIV Corps division was close behind. While Carlin pressed forward, as if to storm Hoke's light intrenchments, Morgan came up in time to help resist the rebel effort against the flank. They made a good team: Carlin, a thirty-five-year-old Illinois West

Pointer, and Morgan, twenty years his senior, an Illinoisian too, but born and raised in Massachusetts, a workhorse type who had risen by hard fighting. Holding in front, the Federals fell back south of the road and took up a new position facing north, where the graybacks were regrouping in the thickets for a follow-up assault. These were the three corps, so called, of the Army of Tennessee, though all three combined amounted to little more, numerically, than a single full division in the old days, and not one of the three was led today by its regular commander; Harvey Hill had replaced S. D. Lee, still out with his wound, while Bate had charge of his own and the remnant of Cleburne's division, Cheatham not having arrived with the third, and Loring had taken over from Stewart, whose rank gave him command of the whole. They lacked the strength for an overwhelming strike at the bluecoats intrenching rapidly in the woods, and not even Hardee's arrival from Bentonville at this critical juncture was of much help, as it turned out. From the left, dug in athwart the road, Bragg sent word that Hoke was on the verge of being overrun; whereupon Johnston — "most injudiciously," he later said — responded by ordering Hardee to send McLaws to his assistance. That left only Taliaferro's division to reinforce the effort on the right, and it was not enough.

It was especially not enough in light of the fact that Williams by now had his two available XX Corps divisions hurrying forward to close the gap between him and Davis, and the other two divisions, one from each corps, were presently summoned to move up from escort duty with the train. Methodical as always, Hardee extended Stewart's line with Taliaferro's Carolinians, hoping to overlap the enemy left, and then at last, soon after 3 o'clock, resumed the attack on the Federals intrenched by then in the woods to the south of the road. He suffered heavy losses in coming to grips with Morgan's men, and though he was successful in driving a good part of them from their hastily improvised works, taking three guns in the process — "We however showed to the Rebs as well as to our side some of the best running ever did," a Wolverine lieutenant would write home — it was only for a few hundred yards before they stiffened, and he had to call a halt again to realign his strike force in the tangled underbrush. While he did so, Williams' lead division came up and the Union right held firm against a belated attempt by Bragg to add to the confusion. Both commanders then had about 15,000 infantry on the field, and now that surprise was no longer a factor there was scant hope of an advantage for either side in any fighting that might ensue: barring, of course, the arrival of substantial reinforcements. In regard to this last, Slocum already had the other half of his two-corps wing moving up, and what was more he had hopes that Sherman, in response to repeated crosscountry pleas, would land Howard's wing in the Confederate rear tonight, or early tomorrow morning at the latest. But for Johnston there was no such hope and no such reassurance. He could expect no additional troops even in his own rear, let alone the enemy's; he could only try to make better use of those he had — including the solid fourth of his infantry under Mc-Laws, whose division, after groping blind around unmapped ponds and impenetrable thickets, finally reached the left to find that it was not only unneeded for the defense of Hoke's position, but was also too late for a share in the follow-up demonstration against Carlin. As a result of Hardee's miscalculated approach march and McLaws' futile detachment, Seven Pines now had a rival for the distinction of being at once the best-planned and worst-conducted battle of the war.

Still Hardee pressed on, as thorough as he was methodical. Cheered by the western veterans he had last commanded back in Georgia, he was also saddened by the thinness of their ranks. For example, the 1st, 13th, and 19th Tennessee, each of which had contained an average of 1250 effectives at the outset of the war, now had 65, 50, and 64 respectively present for duty; nor were these by any means the worst-off units in this gaunted aggregation, the ghost of the one-time Army of Tennessee, fighting southward now and farther from home than it had been even at Perryville, the northernmost of its lost victories. "It was a painful sight," one of Hoke's men wrote after watching these transplanted remnants of a departed host surge forward in their first charge since Franklin, "to see how close their battle flags were together, regiments being scarcely larger than companies and a division not much larger than a regiment should be." Blown as they were, their third attack — launched shortly after 5 o'clock, within an hour of sunset — was less successful than their second, two hours before; Morgan's men, stoutly dug in and reinforced by Williams' lead division, yielded nothing. The graybacks rebounded, then came on again, and the wierd halloo of the rebel yell rang out in the dusky Carolina woods, given with a fervor that seemed to signify a knowledge by the tattered Deep South veterans that this would be their last. "The assaults were repeated over and over again until a late hour," Slocum reported, "each assault finding us better prepared for resistance."

Convinced by now, if not sooner, that all had been done that could be done once his plan for exploiting the initial shock had gone awry, Johnston instructed Hardee to pull Stewart's and Taliaferro's men back in the darkness to their original position north of the road, confronting with Bragg the reunited half of Sherman's army under Slocum, while Wheeler's troopers, just arrived from their decoy work in front of Raleigh, proceeded east toward Cox's Bridge to delay the advance of the other half under Howard, who was no doubt hard on the way from that direction in response to the eight-hour boom and growl of guns near Bentonville today. (In point of fact, Old Joe would have had to do this, or something like it, in any case — preferably an outright skedaddle — since, even if he had succeeded in abolishing Slocum's wing entirely, despite its three-to-two preponderance in numbers, Sherman could then have brought Schofield across the Neuse to combine with Howard for a counterattack with the odds extended to three-to-one or worse.) Hardee managed the withdrawal before dawn, and when Wheeler sent word that he was in contact with Howard's advance, some half-dozen miles in rear of Hoke's division, Johnston had Bragg pull Hoke back, too, and place him in a newly intrenched position from which he would confront the blue right wing when it came up. Formerly concave, the gray line was now convex, a spraddled V, one arm opposing Slocum, the other Howard, whose first corps arrived by noon, followed shortly by the second. Before the day was over — March 20: the vernal equinox — Sherman thus had close to 60,000 soldiers on or near the field, while Johnston, bled down by his losses in yesterday's failed assault, had fewer than 20,000.

Here then for the red-haired Ohioan was a rare chance, not only to score the Cannae every general prayed for, but also to refute the charge leveled by scorners that he lacked the moral courage to commit his whole army in a single all-out effort. It was true he had never done so, yet it was also true he had never before had such an opportunity as this. Discouraged by their failure to snap shut the trap Old Joe had laid for Slocum, frazzled by hard fighting well into the previous night, confronted left and right today by three times their number, the Confederates clung to the spraddled V whose apex was three miles from the lone bridge over Mill Creek in their rear, and though their purpose was to afford the medical details time to evacuate the wounded, they knew well enough that in remaining within this snare of their own making they were also giving Sherman time to accomplish their destruction — provided, of course, he was willing to attempt it; which he was not. "I would rather avoid a general battle," he cautioned Slocum when the New Yorker concluded his report, "but if [Johnston] insists, we must accommodate him."

He stayed his hand, not so much from lack of moral courage as from mistrust of his own impulsive nature, which he only gave free rein in times of relaxation, while writing letters, say, or dealing with civilians, and almost never when men's lives were at stake. There was that deterrent, plus the fact that he knew little of Johnston's position, except that it was skillfully intrenched, or of his strength, except that it seemed great indeed, to judge by the number of units yielding prisoners from the Army of Tennessee; Sherman, unaware that most of its regiments had dwindled to company size, could assume that the whole army was in his front, as formidable in North Carolina as it had been in Georgia. Besides, his Bentonville casualties, though unreported yet, were clearly heavy; in fact, they would come to 1646 in all, and of these 1168 were wounded. Combined with the 533 from Averasboro, that gave him 1700 sufferers to find room for in his train. Any more

such — and who knew how many more there would be if he pressed
the issue here? — would overflow the ambulances and crowd the aid
stations far beyond the capacity of his surgeons to give them even minimal attention. At Goldsboro, on the other hand, he would be in touch
by rail with mountains of supplies, medical and otherwise, unloaded from
ships at New Bern and Wilmington, and that was where he wanted to
go, as soon as possible, for a combination with Schofield in the open
country beyond the Neuse, where he could deal with Johnston at his
leisure, fully rested and with half again more men than he had now. Ten
days ago, he had promised Schofield to meet him there today, and
though Averasboro and Bentonville had thrown him a couple of days
off schedule, he hoped to arrive without further delay. If Johnston
would only pull back, he himself would be free to go his way, and he
was somewhat puzzled by his opponent's apparent reluctance to co-
operate by retiring — as he plainly ought to do. "I cannot see why he
remains," Sherman complained, but added: "[I] still think he will avail
himself of night to get back to Smithfield."

In this he was mistaken, or at any rate premature. Night fell, ending the first day of spring, and the following dawn, March 21, showed
Old Joe still in occupation of the works across the way. His reason
for staying — concern for his wounded — was similar to Sherman's
for wanting to leave, except that in Johnston's case the problem was
evacuation, with heavier losses and even slimmer means of transportation. He suffered 2606 casualties in the battle, almost a thousand more
than his adversary, and of these 1694 were wounded, who, for lack of
enough wagons, had to be taken rearward across Mill Creek Bridge in
relays; all of which took time, and time was why he stayed, gambling
that the greatly superior enemy force would not overrun him while the
work was in progress.

As it turned out, that was nearly what happened: not by Sherman's orders, but rather by a flaunting of them by one of Blair's division commanders, Major General Joseph Mower. Vermont-born, a
Massachusetts carpenter in his youth, Mower had served as a private
in the Mexican War, and staying on in the army had been commissioned a second lieutenant by the time of Sumter. Since then, he had
risen steadily, always as an officer of the line; "the boldest young
soldier we have," Sherman had said of him the year before, when he
was a thirty-six-year-old brigadier, and here today, posted on the far
right, he demonstrated that such praise was deserved. Slipping the leash,
he committed his division in a headlong charge that broke through on
the rebel left, then drove hard for the single bridge in Johnston's rear.
Struck front and flank by a sudden counterattack, he paused and called
on Blair and Howard for reinforcements, certain that if he got them
nothing could prevent him from closing the only Confederate escape

hatch. What he got instead was a peremptory order from Sherman to return to his original position.

Hardee had stopped him with reinforcements brought over from the right, including the 8th Texas Cavalry, which sixteen-year-old Willie Hardee, the general's only son, had joined that morning after finally overcoming his father's objections that he was too young for army duty. "Swear him into service in your company, as nothing else will suffice," Old Reliable told the captain who reported to head-quarters with him. Then he kissed the boy and sent him on his way for what turned out to be a share in the critical job of checking Mower's penetration. Elated by the retirement of the bluecoats — which he did not know had been ordered by Sherman — Hardee grinned and said to Hampton, as they rode back from directing the counteraction: "Gen-eral, that was nip and tuck, and for a while I thought Tuck had it." Laughing, they continued across the field, only to encounter a pair of litter bearers bringing Willie from the front, badly wounded in his first charge. It was also his last; he would die three days later, with his father at his side, and be buried in a Hillsborough churchyard after the military funeral he would have wanted. For the present, Hardee could only dismount and spend a moment with him before rejoining Hamp-ton for deployment of their troops in case the Yankees tried for another breakthrough, somewhere else along the line.

There was no such attempt, and Johnston, having completed the evacuation of his wounded, pulled back that night across Mill Creek and took the road for Smithfield the next morning, unpursued. He had failed to carry out his plan for wrecking Slocum, but he had at least achieved the lesser purpose of delaying Sherman's march to the back door of Richmond, thereby gaining time for Lee to give Grant the slip and combine with him for another, more substantial lunge at the blue host slogging north. As for himself, now that all six Union corps were about to consolidate at Goldsboro, close to 90,000 strong — "I wonder if Minerva has stamped on the earth for our foes?" Beauregard marveled, contemplating their numbers in intelligence reports — Johnston was convinced that he could accomplish nothing further on his own, and he said as much in a wire to Lee when he crossed the Neuse the follow-ing day, March 23.

"Sherman's course cannot be hindered by the small force I have. I can do no more than annoy him," he told the general-in-chief. His only hope, slight as it was, lay in the proposed combination of the two gray armies for a sudden strike, here in the Old North State, and he con-tinued to urge the prompt adoption of such a course. "I respectfully suggest that it is no longer a question whether you leave present position; you have only to decide where to meet Sherman. I will be near him."

In point of fact he was near him now; Sherman by then was in

Goldsboro, barely twenty miles from Smithfield, a morning's boatride down the Neuse. Schofield had been there for two days, awaiting the arrival of his other corps under Terry, which Sherman had diverted from its direct route up the Wilmington & Weldon, with instructions to prepare a pontoon crossing for Slocum and Howard at the site of Cox's Bridge, burned by the rebels while the fighting raged a dozen miles to the west. As a result, there was no delay when the lead wing reached the river on March 22; Sherman rode into Goldsboro next morning, only three days off the time appointed. Fifty days out of Savannah, ten of which he had had his troops devote to halts for rest or intensive destruction, he had covered well over four hundred miles of rough terrain in wretched weather, crossing rivers and plunging full-tilt through "impenetrable" swamps, and now, after three battles of mounting intensity — Kinston, Averasboro, Bentonville — he combined his four corps with Schofield's two for a total of 88,948 effectives, half again more than he had had when he set out on what he called "one of the longest and most important marches ever made by an organized army in a civilized country." Best of all, from the tactical point of view, Goldsboro was within eighty miles of Weldon, and Weldon was more than halfway to Richmond, already under pressure from 128,046 Federal besiegers. Combined, as they soon could be, the two forces would give Grant 217,000 veterans for use in closing out R. E. Lee, whose own force had been ground down by combat and depleted by desertion to less than one fourth that number of all arms. Impatient for the outcome, which seemed to him foregone, Sherman said later, "I directed my special attention to replenishing the army for the next and last stage of the campaign."

First off, by way of preparation for the prospective meeting with the paper-collar Easterners, the outriding "bummers" were unhorsed and told to rejoin their units for reconversion into soldiers of the line. That came hard for them, accustomed as they had become to hard-handed, light-fingered living and the special pleasure of frightening civilians on their own, independent of the usual military restrictions. What might have been worse, their red-haired commander took it into his head to stage an impromptu review as they came striding into town, mud-spattered and ragged as they were. Oddly enough, the notion appealed to them about as much as it did to him; they saw that he was eager to show them off, and they were glad to please him. "They don't march very well, but they will fight," he told Schofield, who had ridden out to meet him. Half were shoeless, and their trousers were in tatters; "a sorry sight," one brigadier admitted, while a staff colonel noted that "nearly every soldier had some token of the march on his bayonet, from a pig to a potato." Uncle Billy was altogether delighted by their appearance, even their rags, which lent a rollicking touch to the column, and was amused by their unavailing efforts, as they swung past him, to close files that had not been closed in months. When Frank Blair remarked, "Look at those poor fellows with bare legs," Sherman scoffed at such misplaced sympathy.

"Splendid legs! Splendid legs!" he sputtered between puffs on his cigar. "I'd give both of mine for any one of them."

He had never cared for parades and such, and even in this case, for all his pride in the weathered marchers and his amusement at the show they made, he seemed to a reporter "to be wishing it was over. While the troops are going by he must be carrying on a conversation or smoking or fidgeting in some way or other." Self-distracted as he was, the approach of the colors nearly caught him unaware; "he looks up just in time to snatch off his hat. And the way he puts that hat on again! With a jerk and drag and jam, as if it were the most objectionable hat in the world and he was specially entitled to entertain an implacable grudge against it." So great was his impatience, indeed, that he cancelled the rest of the review as soon as the second regiment passed. However, there was more to this than the reporter knew. Sherman had just found out that neither railroad was in working order to the coast, and in his anger he fired off a wire to Schofield's chief quartermaster — now his own — demanding to know the whereabouts of "the vast store of supplies I hoped to meet here.... If you can expedite the movement of stores from the sea to the army, do so, and don't stand on expenses. There should always be three details of workers, of eight hours each, making twenty-four hours per day of work on every job, whether building a bridge, unloading vessels, loading cars, or what not. Draw everything you need from Savannah, Port Royal, Charleston, &c. for this emergency.... I must be off again in twenty days, with wagons full, men reclad, &c."

As a result of this round-the-clock prodding, the road to New Bern was in operation within two days, and Sherman himself was one of its first eastbound passengers, March 25. He was off on a trip: first to, then up, the coast. "If I get the troops all well placed, and the supplies working," he had written Grant when he entered Goldsboro, "I might run up to see you for a day or two before diving again into the bowels of the country." A year ago this week, he and the new general-in-chief had huddled over their maps in a Cincinnati hotel room, planning the vast campaign that was about to enter its final stage. He had not seen him since, and it occurred to him, now that his soldiers were at last in camp, idly awaiting delivery of their new clothes and other luxuries, that this would be a good time for him and his chief to get back in touch, to put their heads together again over plans for the close-out maneuver. Privately, in a jesting mood, he remarked to friends that he was going to see Grant in order to "stir him up," fearing that so long a time behind breastworks might have "fossilized" him. Actually, though, he saw the prospective conference as a means of saving time and lives by hastening the showdown operation and avoiding misunderstandings once it began. By way of preamble, he suggested in a follow-up letter, March 24, his notion of what could be done. "I think I see pretty clearly how, in one more move, we can checkmate Lee, forcing him to unite Johnston with him in the defense of Richmond, or, by leaving Richmond, to abandon the cause. I feel certain if he leaves Richmond, Virginia leaves the Confederacy."

Next day he was off. Leaving Schofield in command at Goldsboro, he took the cars for New Bern, where he spent the night before getting aboard the steamer *Russia* Sunday morning, March 26, for the trip to City Point. "I'm going up to see Grant for five minutes and have it all chalked out for me," he said, "and then come back and pitch in."

★   ★   ★

"How d'you do, Sherman."

"How are you, Grant."

Smiles broadened into laughter for them both as they shook hands on the wharf at City Point late Monday afternoon, then proceeded at once to headquarters for the reunion that ended their year-long separation. En route, the red-head launched into a description of his two marches, first across Georgia to the sea, then up through the Carolinas to within 150 miles of where they presently were sitting, Grant smoking quietly and Sherman talking, talking. He spoke for the better part of an hour, scarcely pausing — "Columbia; pretty much all burned, and burned *good*," a staffer heard him say — until his companion, jogged by a sudden recollection, interrupted to remark that the President too was there on a visit. Arriving late Friday he had spent the past three nights tied up to the City Point dock, aboard the *River Queen*. "I know he will be anxious to see you. Suppose we go and pay him a visit before supper?"

Lincoln was indeed on hand, and what was more, in leaving Washington four days ago for the double purpose of escaping the press of executive duties and seeing something of the war first-hand, he had arrived in time to have his first night's sleep disrupted before dawn, March 25, by what seemed to him a tremendous uproar over toward Petersburg, as if all the guns in this part of Virginia were being fired at once, barely half a dozen miles from his stateroom on the presidential yacht. They boomed and they kept booming; he thought surely a full-scale battle must be raging; that is until his son Robert, still proud of his untarnished captain's bars, came aboard for breakfast and informed him that there had been "a little rumpus up the line this morning, ending about where it began." There must have been more to it than that, however, because when Lincoln expressed a desire to visit the scene of the fight — or "rumpus," as Robert had it, affecting the jargon of the veterans whose life he had shared these past two weeks — Grant sent word that he couldn't permit the Commander in Chief to expose himself to the danger of being shot.

Presently, though, the general relented. Lincoln not only could view the scene of this morning's disturbance; he would also — along with Tad and Mrs Lincoln, as well as a number of visiting army wives — attend a review by a V Corps division, previously scheduled for noon, but postponed now till 3 o'clock, to be staged in rear of a sector adjoining the one where the predawn uproar had erupted.... Here, for those who could spot it in passing, was another of those unobtrusive but highly significant milestones on the long road to and through the war. This prompt rescheduling of the review, combined with young Robert's offhand reference to "a little rumpus up the line," was indicative of the extent to which the strength of the pent-up rebels had declined in the past few months. For what had awakened Lincoln before daylight was the last of the Army of Northern Virginia's all-out offensive strikes, so awesome in effect these past three years, but now more pitiful than savage. Despite casualties totaling close to 7000 on both sides — more, in fact, than had been suffered in all three battles down in North Carolina during the past two weeks — the only tangible result, once the smoke cleared, was a three-hour postponement of a formal review by part of a corps that had stood idle, within easy supporting distance, while another contained and repelled, unassisted, the heaviest assault the Confederates could manage at this late stage of the drawn-out siege of Petersburg and their national capital. Here indeed was a milestone worth remarking by those on the lookout, blue or gray, aboard the juggernaut fast approaching the end of its four-year grind across the landscape of the South.

No one knew better than Lee himself the odds against survival, by his army or his country — the two were all but synonymous by now, in most men's eyes — of the showdown that drew nearer as the lengthening days wore past. Early's defeat at Waynesboro not only had abolished his last conceivable infantry reserve, it had also cleared the way for a rapid descent on his westward supply lines by Sheridan's win-prone troopers; "against whom," Lee told a colleague, "I can oppose scarcely a vedette." At the same time he learned of this reverse, March 4, he received from Grant a reply to his proposal that ranking officers of their two armies meet to discuss a possible armistice. Declining, Grant informed him that all such matters were up to Lincoln, whose reinauguration day this was and who had said flatly, a month ago in Hampton Roads, that negotiations must follow, not precede, surrender. Lee perceived that his only remaining course, if he was to stave off disaster, was to set out southward for a combination with Johnston before Sherman overwhelmed or moved around him to combine with Grant and serve Petersburg's defenders in much the same fashion. Such a march, he had warned Davis nine days back, would "necessitate the abandonment of our position on James River, for which contingency every preparation should be made." Now he went in person to the capital, that same day, to notify the President that the time for such a shift — and such an abandonment — was closer at hand than he had presumed before Early's defeat and Grant's concomitant refusal to enter into negotiations that might have led to peace without more bloodshed.

In confirmation of what Lee called "his unconquerable will power," Davis did not flinch at the news that Richmond might have to be given up sooner than had been supposed till now. In fact, he countered by asking whether it wouldn't "be better to anticipate the necessity by withdrawing at once." Lee replied that his horses were too weak to haul his guns and wagons through the still-deep mud; he would set out when the roads had dried and hardened. What he had in mind for the interim, he went on, was a strike at Grant that might disrupt whatever plans he was making, either for a mass assault on the Confederate defenses or another westward extension of his line. The Mississippian approved that too, hoping, as he said later, that such a blow would "delay the impending disaster for the more convenient season for retreat." Nothing in his manner indicated that he viewed the loss of Richmond as anything worse than yet another shock to be absorbed in the course of resistance to forces that would deny him and his people the right to govern themselves as they saw fit, and Lee returned to Petersburg impressed and sustained by his chief's "remarkable faith in the possibility of still winning our independence."

That he termed such faith "remarkable" was a measure of his discouragement at this stage, as well as of his military realism in assessing the likely outcome of the problems he and his hungry soldiers faced. Yet in planning the strike just mentioned to Davis he demonstrated anew that none of his old aggressive fire was lacking. "His name might be Audacity. He will take more desperate chances, and take them quicker, than any other general in the country, North or South," a subordinate had said of him when he first assumed command of the army now clinging precariously to its 37 miles of works from White Oak Swamp to Hatcher's Run, and that this was as true now as the Seven Days had proved it to be then, nearly three years back, was shown by his reaction to a report from John Gordon, whom he instructed to study the works confronting his part of the line — due east of Petersburg and closer to the enemy defenses than either Hill's, winding off to the west, or Longstreet's, north of the James — with a view to recommending the point most likely to crumple under attack.

The Georgian chose Fort Stedman, a somewhat run-down Federal installation, midway between the Appomattox and the Crater, only 150 yards from the nose of a bulge in his own line known as Colquitt's Salient. His plan was to use all three of his divisions in a predawn assault, preceded by fifty axmen, whose job it would be to chop a path through the sharp-pointed abatis in front of the objective, and three groups of a hundred men each, who would make their way into the Union rear to seize three open-ended forts Gordon had spotted there, turning their captured guns on the works to the right and left of Stedman, so that the main body could widen the breach in both directions. One beauty in the choice of this location was that it lay in close proximity to the City Point Railroad, a vital supply route leading rearward to Grant's headquarters and main base; Grant would have little choice, if the operation went as planned, except to withdraw troops from his far left to meet the danger, thus shortening his line in just the direction Lee would be moving when the time came for him to set out on his march to join Joe Johnston.

Lee not only approved, he expanded the operation. Leaving the tactical details to Gordon, much as he had done in the old days with Jackson, he reinforced him with four brigades from Hill and two from Anderson — which lifted the total to about half of his southside infantry — as well as with Rooney Lee's cavalry division, summoned up from Stony Creek to be used in spreading havoc in the Union rear once the breakthrough had succeeded.

Although he thus would be stripping the Petersburg front practically bare of men except at the point of concentration, he was more than willing to accept the risk for the sake of the possible gain. For one thing, having told his wife some weeks ago that he intended to "fight to the last," he was going about it in his familiar style: all out. For another, in the nearly three weeks since his talk with Davis in Richmond, the over-all situation had worsened considerably. Sheridan, after disposing of Early, was reported to be moving toward a junction with Grant that would give the besiegers the rapid-fire mobility they had been needing for a raid-in-force around the Confederate right, which would not only menace the tenuous gray supply lines but would also block the intended escape route for the link-up down in Carolina. Moreover, things had gone from bad to worse in that direction too. On March 11 Johnston warned that if Sherman and Schofield combined, "their march into Virginia cannot be prevented by me." Twelve days and three lost battles later, on March 23, he sent word that the two blue armies had met at Goldsboro. "I can do no more than annoy him," he said of Sherman, whose 90,000 troops were closer to Grant at Globe Tavern, say — a ten-day march at worst — than Johnston, with scarcely one fifth that number around Smithfield, was to Lee at Petersburg.

Time had all but run out. Lee called Gordon in that night and told him to assemble his force next day for the strike at Fort Stedman before dawn, March 25. Gordon requested that Pickett's division be detached from Longstreet to strengthen the effort, and Lee agreed, though he doubted that it would arrive in time from beyond the Appomattox. "Still we will try," he said, adding by way of encouragement to the young corps commander, who at thirty-three was twenty-five years his junior: "I pray that a merciful God may grant us success and deliver us from our enemies."

Gordon cached his reinforced corps in Colquitt's Salient the following day, as ordered, and after nightfall had the obstructions quietly removed to clear the way for the attack. Exclusive of Pickett, who was not up, and the division of cavalry en route from Stony Creek, he had 12,000 infantry poised for the 4 o'clock jump-off, an hour before dawn and two hours before sunrise. Lee arrived on Traveller after moonset and took position on a hill just in rear of the trenches; he would share in the waiting, though he would of course be able to see nothing until daylight filtered through to reveal Fort Stedman, out ahead on Hare's Hill; by which time it should be in Gordon's possession, along with a considerable stretch of line in both directions. On schedule, the signal — a single rifle shot, loud against the bated silence — rang out, and the skirmishers overwhelmed the drowsy enemy pickets, followed by the fifty axmen and the 300-man assault force, all wearing strips of white cloth across their breasts and backs for ready identification in the darkness.

There was no alarm until the first wave started up the rising ground directly under the four guns in the fort. Then suddenly there was. All four guns began to roar, and the force of their muzzle blasts and the wind from passing shells tore at the hats of the attackers. "We went the balance of the way with hats and guns in hand," one would recall. At the moat, the axmen came forward to hack at the chevaux-de-frise, and the charging graybacks went up and over the parapet so quickly that the defenders, some 300 members of a New York heavy artillery outfit, had no time to brace themselves for hand-to-hand resistance. Stedman fell in that first rush, along with its guns, which were seized intact and turned on the adjacent works. Battery 10, on the immediate left, was promptly taken, as was Battery 11 on the right. Gordon was elated. A lean-faced man with a ramrod bearing, long dark hair, and glowing eyes — "as fierce and nearly cruel blue eyes as I ever looked into," a reporter was to note — he was much admired by his men, one of whom said of him: "He's most the prettiest thing you ever did see on a field of fight. It would put heart in a whipped chicken just to look at him." Happy and proud, he sent back word of his success and his intention to enlarge it, left and right and straight ahead.

Dawn had glimmered through by then, and the three 100-man assault teams pressed on beyond the captured works, toward the rim of sky tinted rose by the approaching sun. Trained artillerists were among them, assigned to serve the guns in the three backup forts, once they were taken, and thus bring them to bear on the rear of front-line redoubts north and south of fallen Stedman and its two companion batteries. This unexpected shelling from the rear, combined with pressure from the front and flanks, would assure enlargement of the gap

through which the waves of graybacks could push eastward, perhaps
within reach of City Point itself, where the wide-ranging cavalry would
take over the task of rounding up high-rank prisoners — conceivably including U. S. Grant himself, whose headquarters was known to be in
the yard of the Eppes mansion — while setting fire to the main enemy
supply base and disrupting the very nerve center of the encircling Union
host. Gordon saw that the pressure from the rear had better come soon,
though, for the bluecoats in Batteries 9 and 12 were standing firm,
resisting all efforts to widen the breach. Then at sunup he got the
worst possible news from runners sent back by officers in charge of the
assault teams. They could not locate the three open-ended forts on the
rearward ridge: for the simple reason, discovered later, that they did not
exist, being nothing more than the ruins of old Confederate works along
the Dimmock line, abandoned back in June by Beauregard. Meantime
the counterbattery fire was getting heavier and more accurate from
adjoining redoubts and Fort Haskell, within easy range to the south, as
well as from massed batteries of field artillery, brought forward to help
contain the penetration. Fort Stedman and its two flank installations were
subjected to converging fire from every Yankee gun along this portion
of the line; a fire so intense that the air seemed filled with shells whose
burning fuzes, one observer said, made them resemble "a flock of black-
birds with blazing tails beating about in a gale." Pinned down, the stalled
attackers huddled under what shelter they could find, waiting for the
metallic storm to lift.

Instead of lifting it grew heavier as the red ball of the sun bounced
clear of the landline. Gordon saw plainly that without help from the
nonexistent forts he not only could not deepen or widen the dent he
had made, he would not even be able to hold what he had won by the
predawn rush. Accordingly, he notified Lee of his predicament, and
word came back, shortly before 8 o'clock, for him to call off the attack
and withdraw. The Georgian was altogether willing to return to his own
lines, but the same could not be said for hundreds of his soldiers, who
preferred surrender to running the gauntlet of fire that boxed them in.
As a result, Confederate losses for this stage of the operation came to
about 3500 men, half of them captives, as compared to a Federal total
of 1044. Nor was that all. Convinced that Lee must have stripped the
rest of his southside line to provide troops for the strike at Stedman,
Grant ordered a follow-up assault to be launched against the rebel right,
where Hill's intrenched picket line was overrun near Hatcher's Run,
inflicting heavy casualties and taking close to a thousand additional
prisoners, not to mention securing a close-up hug on Hill's main line of
resistance. By the time a truce was called that afternoon for collecting
the dead and wounded on both sides, the casualty lists had grown to
4800 for Lee and 2080 for Grant. The bungled affair of the Crater —
which today's effort so much resembled, both in purpose and in out-

come — had been redressed, although with considerably heavier losses all around.

Another difference was that the southern commander could ill afford what his opponent had shrugged off, eight months ago and less than a mile down the line, with no more than a brief loss of temper. Riding rearward, Lee met Rooney coming forward in advance of his division. With him was his younger brother Robert, now a captain on his staff. Both greeted their father, who gave them the news that there would be no cavalry phase of the operation. The assault had failed, and badly, at great cost. "Since then," Robert declared long afterwards, "I have often recalled the sadness of his face, its careworn expression."

Lee's depression was well founded. On no single day since the Bloody Angle was overrun at Spotsylvania had he lost so many prisoners, and these combined with the killed and wounded had cost him a solid tenth of his command, as compared to Grant's loss of less than a sixtieth. "The greatest calamity that can befall us is the destruction of our armies," he had warned Davis eleven days ago, while Gordon was planning the Stedman operation. "If they can be maintained, we may recover from our reverses, but if lost we have no resource." Today marked a sizeable step toward the destruction of the first army of them all. Moreover, it had gained him nothing, while costing him Hill's outer defenses, now occupied by Grant, who could be expected to launch a swamping assault from this new close-up position — a sort of Stedman in reverse — in just the direction Lee would be obliged to move when he tried for a breakout west and south: no longer for the purpose of combining with Johnston for a lunge at Sherman before the red-head crossed the Roanoke, but simply as the only remaining long-shot chance of postponing the disaster he foresaw. Notifying Breckinridge of the failed attack, he made no complaint of Gordon's miscalculations; he merely remarked that the troops had "behaved most handsomely." But next day, in following this with a report to the President, he confessed himself at a loss as to his next move, except that he knew he had to get away, and soon. "I fear now it will be impossible to prevent a junction between Grant and Sherman," he frankly admitted, "nor do I deem it prudent that this army should maintain its position until the latter shall approach too near."

He was warning again that Richmond would have to be given up any day now, but what would follow that abandonment he did not say; perhaps because he did not know. All he seemed to have in mind was a combination with Johnston for the confrontation that was bound to ensue. "I have thought it proper to make the above statement to Your Excellency of the condition of affairs," he concluded, "knowing that you will do whatever may be in your power to give relief."

But the power was Grant's, and Grant knew it. When Lincoln

came to headquarters, shortly after the Confederates began their withdrawal from Fort Stedman — those of them, that is, who did not choose surrender over running the gauntlet of fire — the general observed that the assault had been less a threat to the integrity of the Union position than it was an indication of Lee's desperation in regard to the integrity of his own. Accordingly, he rescheduled the V Corps review, which would be staged in rear of a sector just south of the one where Gordon's attack had exploded before dawn, and decided as well that the President would be safe enough in taking a look at the ground where the struggle had raged between 4 and 8 o'clock that morning.

So it was that Lincoln, going forward on the railroad to the margin of that field, saw on a considerably larger scale what he had seen at Fort Stevens eight months earlier, just outside Washington. Mangled corpses were being carted rearward for burial in the army cemetery near City Point — which incidentally, like everything else in that vicinity, had been much expanded since his brief visit in June of the year before — and men were being jounced on stretchers, writhing in pain as they were lugged back for surgeons to probe their wounds or remove their shattered arms and legs. There was pride and exhilaration in statements that Parke, cut off from communication with Meade and Grant while the fighting was in progress, had used only his three IX Corps divisions to contain and repulse the rebels without outside help. But for Lincoln, interested though he always was in military matters, the pleasure he would ordinarily have taken in such reports was greatly diminished by the sight of what they had cost. He looked "worn and haggard," an officer who accompanied him declared; "He remarked that he had seen enough of the horrors of war, that he hoped this was the beginning of the end, and that there would be no more bloodshed."

Still another shock was in store for him before the day was over, this one involving his wife. For some time now, particularly since the death of her middle and favorite son, eleven-year-old Willie, Mary Lincoln had been displaying symptoms of the mental disturbance that would result, a decade later, in a medical judgment of her case as one of insanity. Her distress, though great, was scarcely greater than her family misfortunes — exclusive of the greatest, still to come. Four of her five Kentucky brothers had gone with the South, and three of them died at Shiloh, Baton Rouge, and Vicksburg. Similarly, three of her four sisters were married to Confederates, one of whom fell at Chickamauga. Such losses not only brought her grief, they also brought on a good deal of backhand whispering about "treason in the White House." All this, together with Lincoln's lack of time to soothe her hurts and calm her fears, combined to produce a state in which she was quick to imagine slights to her lofty station and threats to all she valued most, including her two surviving sons and her husband.

It was the latter who was in danger today, or so she conceived from something she heard as she rode with Mrs Grant and Lieutenant Colonel Adam Badeau, Grant's military secretary, in an ambulance on the way to the review that had been rescheduled for 3 o'clock. Badeau happened to remark that active operations could not be far off, since all army wives had recently been ordered to the rear: all, that is, but the wife of Warren's ranking division commander, Mrs Charles Griffin, who had been given special permission by the President to attend today's review. The First Lady flared up at this. "What do you mean by that, sir? Do you mean to say that she saw the President alone? Do you know that I never allow the President to see any woman alone?" Speechless with amazement at finding her "absolutely jealous of poor, ugly Abraham Lincoln," the colonel tried to assume a pleasant expression in order to show he meant no malice; but the effect was otherwise. "That's a very equivocal smile, sir," Mrs Lincoln exclaimed. "Let me out of this carriage at once! I will ask the President if he saw that woman alone."

Badeau and Mrs Grant managed to persuade her not to alight in the mud, but it was Meade who saved the day. Coming up to pay his respects on their arrival, he was taken aside by Mrs Lincoln for a hurried exchange from which she returned to fix the flustered staffer with a significant look. "General Meade is a gentleman, sir," she told him. "He says it was not the President who gave Mrs Griffin the permit, but the Secretary of War." Badeau afterwards remarked that Meade, the son of a diplomat, "had evidently inherited some of his father's skill."

Unfortunately, the Pennsylvanian was not on hand for a similar outburst the following day, when the troops reviewed were Ord's, beyond the James. Arriving late, again in an ambulance with the staff colonel and Mrs Grant, Mrs Lincoln found the review already in progress, and there on horseback beside her husband, who was mounted too — he wore his usual frock coat and top hat, though his shirt front was rumpled and his strapless trouser legs had worked up to display "some inches of white socks" — was Mrs Ord. She was neither as young nor as handsome as Mrs Griffin, but that was no mitigation in Mary Lincoln's eyes. "What does the woman mean by riding by the side of the President? And ahead of me! Does she suppose that *he* wants *her* by the side of *him*?" She was fairly launched, and when Mrs Grant ventured a few words of reassurance she turned on her as well, saying: "I suppose you think you'll get to the White House yourself, don't you?" Julia Grant's disclaimer, to the effect that her present position was higher than any she had hoped for, drew the reply: "Oh, you had better take it if you can get it. 'Tis very nice."

Mrs Ord, seeing the vehicle pull up, excused herself to the dignitaries around her. "There come Mrs Lincoln and Mrs Grant; I think I had better join them," she said, unaware of the tirade in progress across the way, and set out at a canter. It was not until she drew rein beside the ambulance that she perceived that she might have done better to ride in the opposite direction. "Our reception was not cordial," an aide who accompanied her later testified discreetly. Badeau, a former newsman, gave a fuller account of Mrs Ord's ordeal. "Mrs Lincoln positively insulted her, called her vile names in the presence of a crowd of officers, and asked what she meant by following up the President. The poor woman burst into tears and inquired what she had done, but Mrs Lincoln refused to be appeased, and stormed till she was tired. Mrs Grant tried to stand by her friend, and everybody was shocked and horrified. But all things come to an end, and after a while we returned to City Point."

Things were no better there, however: certainly not for Lincoln, who was host that night at a dinner given aboard the *Queen* for the Grants and Grant's staff. Mrs Lincoln, with the general seated on her right, spent a good part of the evening running down Ord, who she said was unfit for his post, "not to mention his wife." Making no headway here, she shifted her scorn toward her husband, up at the far end of the table, and reproached him for his attentions to Mrs Griffin and Mrs Ord. Lincoln "bore it," Badeau noted, "with an expression of pain and sadness that cut one to the heart, but with supreme calmness and dignity. He called her Mother, with old-time plainness; he pleaded with eyes and tones, and endeavored to explain or palliate the offenses." Nothing worked, either at table or in the saloon afterwards; "she turned on him like a tigress," until at last "he walked away, hiding that noble, ugly face that we might not catch the full expression of its misery." Yet that did not work either; she kept at him. After the guests had retired, she summoned the skipper of the *Bat*, Lieutenant Commander John S. Barnes, who had been present at today's review, and demanded that he corroborate her charge that the President had been overattentive to Mrs Ord. Barnes declined the role of "umpire," as he put it, and earned thereby her enmity forever. He left, and when he reported aboard next morning to inquire after the First Lady, Lincoln replied that "she was not at all well, and expressed the fear that the excitement of the surroundings was too great for her, or for any woman."

By then it was Monday, March 27. Sherman's courtesy call that evening, within an hour of his arrival from down the coast, was all the more welcome as a diversion: for Lincoln at any rate, if not for the red-haired Ohioan, who had accepted Grant's suggestion — "Suppose we pay him a visit before supper?" — with something less than delight at the prospect. "All right," he said. He had small use for politicians, including this one, whom he had met only once, four years ago this week, at the time when the Sumter crisis was heading up. Introduced at the White House by his senator brother as a first-hand witness of recent activities in the South, he testified that the people there were preparing for all-out conflict. "Oh, well," he heard the lanky Kentuckian say, "I guess we'll manage to keep house." Disgusted, he declined to resume his military career, and though he relented when the issue swung to war, he retained down the years that first impression of a lightweight President.

Now aboard the *Queen*, however — perhaps in part because he could later write, "He remembered me perfectly" — he found himself in the presence of a different man entirely, one who was "full of curiosity about the many incidents of our great march" and was flatteringly concerned "lest some accident might happen to the army in North Carolina in my absence." Sherman's interest, quickened no doubt by Lincoln's own, deepened into sympathy as the exchange continued through what he called "a good, long, social visit." He saw lights and shadows unsuspected till now in a figure that had been vague at best, off at the far end of the telegraph wire running back to Washington. "When at rest or listening," he would say of his host, now three weeks into a second term, "his arms and legs seemed to hang almost lifeless, and his face was careworn and haggard; but, the moment he began to talk, his face lighted up, his tall form, as it were, unfolded, and he was the very impersonation of good-humor and fellowship."

Taking their leave, the two generals returned to Grant's quarters, where Mrs Grant, laying out tea things, asked if they had seen the First Lady. They had not; nor had they thought to tender their respects. "Well, you are a pretty pair!" she scolded.

After some badinage about the risk of having Julia within earshot ("Know all men by these presents," he observed, might just as well read "Know one woman," if what you wanted was to spread the word) Grant brought his companion up to date on the progress of other forces involved in his plan for closing out the rebellion. Mainly it had been a vexing business, especially in regard to the strikes by Canby, Stoneman, and Wilson, from which so much had been expected, both on their own and by way of diversion, if they had been launched in conjunction with Sherman's march through the Carolinas; which they had not. Canby was the worst offender, delaying his movement against Mobile while he gathered materials and built up a construction corps for laying seventy miles of railroad supply line. Moreover, he had put Gordon Granger in charge of one wing of his army, despite Grant's known dislike of the New Yorker, and had wanted to give Baldy Smith the other, until Grant vetoed the notion and flatly told him to get moving with what he had. Finally he did. Two columns of two divisions each, one under Granger, the other under A. J. Smith, together with a division of cavalry and a siege train, were put in motion around the east side of Mobile Bay, while a third column, also of two divisions, set out from Pensacola under Frederick Steele, resurrected from Arkansas, where he had spent the past ten months recuperating from his share in the Red River expedition. This brought a total of 45,000 men converging on an estimated 10,000 defenders in the works that rimmed Mobile; surely enough to

assure reduction in short order. But it was March 17 by the time Canby
got started, more than a month behind schedule, and March 26 — just
yesterday — by the time Spanish Fort, an outwork up at the head of the
bay, nine miles east of the city, was taken under fire. How long it might
be at this rate before the Mobile garrison surrendered or skedaddled,
Grant did not try to guess, but he saw clearly enough that it would
not be in time to free any portion of Canby's army for the projected
march on Selma in coöperation with the mounted column Thomas had
been ordered to send against that vital munitions center, the loss of
which would go far toward ending Confederate resistance in the western
theater.

There was however another rub, no less vexing because it had
been more or less expected with Old Slow Trot in command. Late as
Canby was in setting out, Thomas was even later: not only in getting Wilson headed south for Selma, but also in launching Stoneman eastward into
the Carolinas, where he had been told to operate against the railroad between Charlotte and Columbia and thus disrupt the rebel effort to assemble troops in the path of Sherman's army slogging north. As it turned
out, Sherman had fought at Averasboro and was midway through the
Bentonville eruption, within a day's march of his Goldsboro objective,
by the time Stoneman left Knoxville on March 20, and it took him and
his 4000 horsemen a week, riding through Morristown, Bull's Gap, and
Jonesboro, before he crossed the Smokies to approach the western
North Carolina border. By then — today, March 27; Sherman would
reach City Point at sundown — there was little raiders could do in that
direction; so Grant wired Thomas to have Stoneman turn north into
Southwest Virginia instead, and there "repeat the raid of last fall, destroying the [Virginia & Tennessee] railroad as far toward Lynchburg
as he can." That way, at least he might be able to cripple Lee's supply
line and be on hand in case the old fox tried a getaway westward. Perhaps it would even work out better, Grant reasoned, now that Sherman
had managed to come through on his own. But it was vexing, in much
the same way Sigel's and Butler's ineptitudes had been vexing at the
outset of the previous campaign, back in May of the year before.

Wilson posed a somewhat different problem, in part because Grant
had a fondness for him dating back to their Vicksburg days, when the
young West Pointer had been a lieutenant colonel on his staff, and also
because real danger was involved. Danger was always an element in
military ventures, but in Wilson's case the danger was Bedford Forrest,
who could be depended on to try his hand at interfering with this as he
had done with other Deep South raids, all too often disastrously — as
Abel Streight, Sooy Smith, and Samuel Sturgis could testify, along with
Stephen Hurlbut, A. J. Smith, Cadwallader Washburn, and several others
who had encountered him at various removes, including Grant and
Sherman. However, his recent promotion to lieutenant general was no

measure of the number of soldiers he now had at his disposal; Wilson, with 12,500 troopers armed to a man with Spencer carbines, three batteries of horse artillery, and a supply train of 250 wagons (a command he described, on setting out, as being "in magnificent condition, splendidly mounted, perfectly clad and equipped") would outnumber his adversary two-to-one in any likely confrontation. Even without the distraction Canby would fail to supply, and even though the long delay had given Forrest and Richard Taylor an extra month to prepare for its reception, Grant believed the blue column would be able to ride right over anything they were able to throw in its path.

Still, this delay was as vexing as the others — and even longer, as it turned out. It was March 18 before Wilson, who had been having remount troubles, was able to start crossing the Tennessee, swollen by the worst floods the region had ever known. The steamboat landing at Eastport, his crossing point into Mississippi's northeast corner, was so far under water that he needed three whole days to get his horsemen over the river and reassembled on the southern bank. Finally, on March 22, he set out across the hilly barrens of Northwest Alabama, hard on the go for Selma, two hundred miles to the southeast. Five days later — March 27; Sherman was steaming up the James for a handshake with Grant, a visit with Lincoln, and later that night the present informal briefing by the general-in-chief — Wilson began to cross the upper forks of the Black Warrior River near Jasper, almost halfway to his goal. So far, he had encountered nothing he could not brush aside with a casual motion of one hand; but up ahead, somewhere between there and Selma, Forrest no doubt was gathering his gray riders for whatever deviltry he had in mind to visit on the invading column's front or flank or rear. Grant, conferring with Sherman that evening in his quarters, could only hope it was nothing his twenty-seven-year-old former staff engineer couldn't handle on his own.

By way of contrast with Canby, Stoneman, and Wilson — whose efforts, as Grant declared in his vexation, might turn out to be "eminently successful, but without any good results" because they were launched too near the end they had been designed to hasten — Phil Sheridan had demonstrated, here in the eastern theater, the virtue of promptness when striking deep into enemy territory. Leaving Winchester a month ago today, within a week of receiving orders to set out "as soon as it is possible to travel," he had caught Early unprepared at Waynesboro, his back to the Blue Ridge, and after wrecking him there moved on through Rockfish Gap to Charlottesville, where he tore up track on two vital rail supply lines, first the Virginia Central and then the Orange & Alexandria, the latter while proceeding south in accordance with his instructions to cross the James for a link-up with Sherman beyond the Carolina line. As he approached Lynchburg, however — the main objective of his raid, as defined by Grant, because it was there that the Orange & Alexandria and Lee's all-important Southside Railroad came together to continue west as the Virginia & Tennessee — he received reports from scouts that the place had been reinforced too heavily for him to move against it. What was more, the rebels had burned all the nearby bridges over the James, which was swollen to a depth past fording and a width beyond the span of his eight pontoons. Accordingly, he drew rein, thought the matter over briefly, and turned east, intending to move down the north bank of the river to the vicinity of Richmond, where he would rejoin Grant. This was not a difficult decision, since it led to what he had wanted in the first place. Regardless of orders, which required him either to cross the James or turn back to the Valley, he wanted to be where the action was. And in his eyes, the action — the real action: so much of it as remained, at any rate — was not with Sherman in North Carolina, opposing Johnston, but here in Virginia with Grant, opposing Lee. "Feeling that the war was approaching its end," he afterwards explained in fox-hunt terms, "I desired my cavalry to be in at the death."

At Columbia on March 10, fifty-odd miles upstream from the rebel capital, he gave his troopers a day's rest from their exertions, which included the smashing of locks on the James River Canal, and got off a crosscountry message to Grant, "notifying him of our success, position, and condition, and requesting supplies to be sent to White House." That was his goal now, McClellan's old supply base on the Pamunkey River, well within the Union lines on the far side of Richmond. To reach it, he turned away from the James next day at Goochland and rode north across the South Anna to Beaver Dam Station, which he had visited back in May on the raid that killed Jeb Stuart. From there he turned east and south again, down the Virginia Central to Hanover Courthouse, then crossed the North Anna to proceed down the opposite bank of the Pamunkey to White House, arriving on March 20 after three full weeks on the go. Though his loss in horses had been "considerable — almost entirely from hoof-rot," he noted — his loss in men "did not exceed 100," including some "left by the wayside, unable to bear the fatigues of the march." The rest, he said, "appeared buoyed up by the thought that we had completed our work in the Valley of the Shenandoah, and that we were on our way to help our brothers-in-arms in front of Petersburg in the final struggle."

Assurance that he and they would have a share in the close-out operation against Lee was contained in a dispatch the general-in-chief had waiting for him at White House, along with the supplies he had requested. Dated yesterday, the message instructed him to cull out his broken-down horses and men, give the others such rest and refitment as they needed to put them back in shape, and prepare to cross the James for a strike around Lee's right flank at Petersburg, in conjunction with some 40,000 infantry who would be shifted in that direction. "Start for this place as soon as you conveniently can," Grant told him. His assignment would be to wreck the Southside and Danville railroads, "and then either return to this army or go on to Sherman, as you may deem most practicable." Which of the two he chose, Grant said, "I care but little about, the principal thing being the destruction of the only two roads left to the enemy at Richmond."

Sheridan was delighted, knowing already which course he would "deem most practicable" when the time came. Next day, March 21, a follow-up message arrived. "I do not wish to hurry you," it began, and then proceeded to do just that, explaining: "There is now such a possibility, if not probability, of Lee and Johnston attempting to unite that I feel extremely desirous not only of cutting the lines of communication between them, but of having a large and properly commanded cavalry force ready to act with in case such an attempt is made." Elsewhere, Grant added, things were moving at last. "Stoneman started yesterday from Knoxville"; "Wilson started at the same time from Eastport"; "Canby is in motion, and I have reason to believe that Sherman and Schofield have formed a junction at Goldsboro." As for Sheridan, "I think that by Saturday next you had better start, even if you have to stop here to finish shoeing up."

Saturday next would be March 25. On Friday, still busy getting his horses and troopers reshod and equipped, the bandy-legged cavalryman received from Grant a letter — copies of which also went to Meade and Ord, as heads of armies: proof, in itself, of his rise in the military hierarchy since his departure for the Valley, back in August — giving details of the maneuver designed to accomplish Lee's undoing. "On the 29th instant the armies operating against Richmond will be moved by our left, for the double purpose of turning the enemy out of his present position around Petersburg and to insure the success of the cavalry under General Sheridan, which will start at the same time, in its efforts to reach and destroy the South Side and Danville railroads." That was the opening sentence; specific instructions followed. Ord was to cross the James with four of his seven divisions, including one of cavalry, and take over the works now occupied by Humphreys and Warren on the Federal left, thus freeing their two corps to move west beyond Hatcher's Run, where Sheridan's three mounted divisions — 13,500 strong — would plunge north, around Lee's right, to get astride the vital rail supply routes in his rear. Meantime, Ord's other three divisions under Weitzel, north of the James and across Bermuda Hundred, together with the two corps under Parke and Wright and Ord's four divisions south of the river, were to keep a sharp lookout and attack at once if they saw signs that Lee was drawing troops from the works in their front to meet the threat to his flank and rear.

In short, what Grant had devised was another leftward sidle, the maneuver he had employed all the way from the Rapidan to the James, with invariable success in obliging his adversary to give ground. Since then, in the nine months spent on this side of the James, the maneuver had been a good deal less successful, achieving little more in fact than a slow extension of the rebel earthworks, along with his own, more or less in ratio to his lengthening casualty lists. Much of that time, however, Sheridan had been on detached service up the country; whereas, this time, Little Phil and his hard-hitting troopers would not only be on hand — "the left-hand man of Grant the left-handed," someone dubbed him — but would also lead the strike intended to dispossess Lee, first of his tenuous rail supply lines and then of Petersburg itself, whose abandonment would mean the loss of his capital as well.

Presently it developed that Grant intended to dispossess him of even more than that, right here and now. Sheridan began crossing his horsemen on March 26, riding ahead for a talk with his chief at City Point. Pleased though he was at having been told he could do as he chose, "return to this army or go on to Sherman" once he and his troops had completed their share in the upcoming sidle, he still worried that Grant might change his mind and send him south against his will. And, indeed, further written instructions he found waiting for him at headquarters reinforced this fear by stressing the possibility of having him "cut loose from the Army of the Potomac" and continue his ride "by way of the Danville Railroad" into North Carolina. Watching him scowl as he read that part of the order, Grant took him aside, out of earshot of the staff, and quietly told him: "General, this portion of your instructions I have put in merely as a blind." He explained that if the sidle failed, as others had done in the course of the past nine months, he would be able to head off criticism by pointing to these orders as proof that it had been designed as nothing more than a sidelong slap at Lee by Sheridan, en route to a junction with Sherman. Actually, Grant assured him, he had no intention of sending him away. He wanted him with him, in the forefront of the strike about to be launched and the chase that would ensue. Little Phil began to see the light; a light that grew swiftly into a sunburst when he heard what his chief said next. "I mean to end the business here," Grant told him. The cavalryman's raid-weathered face brightened at the words; Lee was to be dispossessed, not only of Petersburg and Richmond, but also of his army — here and now. Sheridan grinned. "I am glad to hear it," he said. He slapped his thigh. "And we can do it!" he exclaimed.

Elated by this private assurance from the general-in-chief (and flattered by Lincoln, who told him later that morning, in the course of a boatride down the James: "General Sheridan, when this peculiar war began I thought a cavalryman should be at least six feet four inches high, but I have changed my mind. Five feet four will do in a pinch") he was alarmed the following afternoon by news that Sherman was expected at City Point that evening. His concern proceeded from awareness that his fellow Ohioan was not only badly in need of mounted reinforcements, still having only Kilpatrick's frazzled division on hand at Goldsboro, but was also an accomplished talker, possessed of considerable "zeal and powers of emphasis," which might well enable him to persuade his friend Grant to revise his plan for keeping Sheridan and all three of his divisions in Virginia. Disturbed by the threat, he got the last of his troopers over the James by nightfall — one month, to the day, since they left Winchester — then boarded a train and set out for headquarters. Breakdowns delayed his arrival till nearly midnight, just as Grant and Sherman were ending the conference that followed their meeting with Lincoln aboard the *River Queen.* So far as he could tell, the interloper had not changed their chief's mind about the use of cavalry in the pending operation against Lee, if indeed the subject had come up. Still the danger remained, and Sheridan continued to fret about it, even after all three of them had turned in for the night. His alarm increased next morning, March 28, when the red-head came to his room and woke him up, talking earnestly of "how he would come up through the Carolinas and hinting that I could join him." Sheridan responded so angrily, however, that Sherman dropped the subject and retired.

There was by now little time for argument, even if Sherman had thought it would do any good. He and Grant were scheduled to see Lincoln again this morning, and the President's concern for the safety of his army in his absence had led him to promise that he would start back for Goldsboro as soon as this second meeting aboard the *Queen* was over; in which connection David Porter, who was there to give advice on naval matters, had volunteered to substitute the converted blockade-runner *Bat* for the sluggish *Russia,* thus assuring the western general a faster voyage down the coast. This time, coming aboard the presidential yacht, Grant remembered to tender his and Sherman's respects to the First Lady, but when her husband went to her stateroom she sent word that she hoped they would excuse her; she was unwell. Whereupon the four men — Grant and Sherman, Porter and Lincoln — took their seats in the saloon, and the high-level conference began.

It was not, properly speaking, a council of war; "Grant never held one in his life," a staffer was to note; but it did begin with a discussion of the military situation here and in North Carolina. In regard to the former, Grant explained that Sheridan's horsemen had crossed the James in preparation for a strike at Lee's rail supply lines, which, if successful, would leave the old fox no choice except to surrender or (as he had done on a lesser scale three days ago at Fort Stedman, no doubt to his regret) come out and fight: unless, that is, he managed to slip away beforehand, in which case Meade and Ord would be close on his heels in pursuit. As for the danger to Sherman, in the event that Lee made it south to combine with Johnston, the red-head assured Lincoln that his army at Goldsboro was strong enough to hold its own against both rebel forces, "provided Grant could come up within a day or so." As for a matching attempt by Johnston to give him the slip, either on foot or by rail, he saw little chance of that; "I have him where he cannot move without breaking up his army, which, once disbanded, can never be got together."

Tactically, the Commander in Chief was satisfied that victory was at last within reach. But it seemed to him, from what had just been pointed out, that all this squeezing and maneuvering was leading to a high-loss confrontation, an Armageddon that would serve no purpose on either side except to set the seal on a foregone conclusion. "Must more blood be shed?" he asked. "Cannot this last bloody battle be avoided?" Both generals thought not. In any case, that was up to the enemy; Lee being Lee, there was likely to be "one more desperate and bloody battle." Lincoln groaned. "My God, my God," he said. "Can't you spare more effusions of blood? We have had so much of it."

In the pause that followed — for they had no answer, except to repeat that the choice was not with them — Sherman observed again, as he had done the night before, the effect four years of war had had on the leader charged with its conduct all that time. "When in lively conversation, his face brightened wonderfully, but if the conversation flagged his face assumed a sad and sorrowful expression." Presuming somewhat on his feeling of sympathy, and wanting to be prepared for what was coming, he then "inquired of the President if he was all ready for the end of the war" and, more specifically, "What was to be done with the rebel armies when defeated?" That was the question, as he recalled it a decade later, when he also set down Lincoln's answer. "He said he was all ready; all he wanted of us was to defeat the opposing armies, and to get the men composing the Confederate armies back to their homes, at work on their farms and in their shops." Warming to the subject, Lincoln went on to expand it. He was also ready, he declared, "for the civil reorganization of affairs in the South as soon as the war was over." In this connection, the general would remember, "he distinctly authorized me to assure Governor Vance and the people of North Carolina that, as soon as the rebel armies laid down their arms, and resumed their civil pursuits, they would at once be guaranteed all their rights as citizens of a common country," and he added that in order to avoid anarchy in the region, "the state governments then in existence, with their civil functionaries, would be recognized by him as the government *de facto* till Congress could provide others."

Sherman, "more than ever impressed by his kindly nature, his deep and earnest sympathy with the afflictions of the whole people, resulting from the war and the march of hostile armies through the South," perceived (or gathered) from these remarks, uttered offhand and in private, that Lincoln's "earnest desire seemed to be to end the war speedily, without more bloodshed or devastation, and to restore all the men of both sections to their homes." *All*, he said; but did he mean it? Did that apply to the fire-eaters who had engineered secession; to the stalwarts, in and out of uniform, who sustained the rebellion after the fire-eaters fell by the wayside? Coming down to the most extreme example, Sherman wanted to know: Did the hope for such restoration apply to Jefferson Davis?

Now it was Lincoln's turn to pause, though not for long. As Chief Executive, the possible reviewing authority for any future legal action taken in the matter, he was "hardly at liberty to speak his mind fully," he declared, yet he was willing to reply, as he had done so often down the years, with a story. "A man once had taken the total-abstinence pledge. When visiting a friend he was invited to take a drink, but declined, on the score of his pledge; when his friend suggested lemonade, which was accepted. In preparing the lemonade, the friend pointed to the brandy bottle, and said the lemonade would be more palatable if he were to pour in a little brandy; when his guest said, if he could do so 'unbeknown' to him, he would not object." Thus Sherman retold the story, no doubt tightening it up a bit in the transcription, from which he inferred that the northern President hoped his southern counterpart would "escape, 'unbeknown' to him" — clear out, leave the country — "only it would not do for him to say so openly."

By then it was close to leaving time; Barnes had steam up on the *Bat*, waiting for Sherman to come aboard, and Lincoln was no less anxious for him to get started down the coast, where he could look to the security of his army and prepare for the movement scheduled to begin on April 10, first on Raleigh to dispose of Johnston, then north across the Virginia line to Burkeville, chosen as his objective because it was there that the Southside and Danville railroads crossed, fifty miles west of Petersburg; which meant that, once he reached that point, he would not only have cut Lee's two remaining all-weather supply lines — if, indeed, they survived till then — but would also be in position to intercept him if he retreated in that direction. Before he left, however, he and Grant and the President took a walk along the river bank, glad of a chance to stretch their legs after confinement in cramped quarters on the *Queen* for the past three hours. A reporter saw and described them as they strolled. "Lincoln, tall, round-shouldered, loose-jointed, large-featured, deep-eyed, with a smile upon his face, is dressed in black and wears a fashionable silk hat. Grant is at Lincoln's right, shorter, stouter, more compact; wears a military hat with a stiff, broad brim, has his hands in his pantaloon pockets, and is puffing away at a cigar. Sherman, tall, with a high, commanding forehead, is almost as loosely built as Lincoln; has sandy whiskers, closely cropped, and sharp, twinkling eyes, long arms and legs, shabby coat, slouched hat, his pantaloons tucked into his boots." As usual, the red-head did most of the talking —

"gesticulating now to Lincoln, now to Grant," the newsman noted, "his eyes wandering everywhere" — but at one point the President broke in to ask: "Sherman, do you know why I took a shine to Grant and you?"

"I don't know, Mr Lincoln," he replied. "You have been extremely kind to me, far more than my deserts."

"Well, you never found fault with me," Lincoln said.

This was not true. Sherman had found a good deal of fault with the President over the past four years, beginning with the day he heard him say, almost blithely, "Oh, well, I guess we'll manage to keep house." But it was true from this day forward. For one thing, Lincoln had in fact managed to "keep house," though sometimes only by the hardest, and for another, now that Sherman knew him he admired him, perhaps beyond all the men he had ever known. Again at the wharf, he boarded the *Bat* and set out down the James. Afterwards, looking back, he said of Lincoln, who had walked him to the gangplank: "I never saw him again. Of all the men I ever met, he seemed to possess more of the elements of greatness, combined with goodness, than any other."

✗ 3 ✗

Grant began his close-out sidle in earnest the following day. Ord's four divisions, after crossing the James in the wake of Sheridan's troopers, had replaced the six under Humphreys and Warren at the far end of the line the night before, freeing them to move in support of the cavalry strike around Lee's right, and Grant was leapfrogging his headquarters twenty miles southwest down the Vaughan Road, beyond the western limit of his intrenchments at Hatcher's Run, so he could watch the progress of events and make, first hand, such last-minute adjustments as might be needed in that direction. After breakfast, around 8.30, while he and his staff waited beside the tracks at City Point for their horses and gear to be loaded onto boxcars, Lincoln joined them and stood talking with the general for a time. Finally, after handshakes with the President all round — including one for Robert, about to take the field in his first campaign — Grant and his military family got aboard the cars. As the engine began to strain they raised their hats in salute to Lincoln, who lifted his in turn to them, and the train chuffed off, south then west, behind the long slow curve of trenches the army had dug in the course of the past nine months of stalemate here in front of Petersburg, a type of warfare the present shift had been designed to end.

In Richmond, that same March 29, Brigadier General Josiah Gorgas received at his office in the Ordnance Department, which he headed, a hastily written note signed Jefferson Davis. "Will you do me the favor to have some cartridges prepared for a small Colt pistol, of which

I send the moulds?" Gorgas, a Pennsylvania-born West Pointer who had married south — and who, starting with next to nothing in the way of machinery, skilled labor, raw materials, or the means of producing them, in the past four years had turned out seventy million rounds of small-arms ammunition, along with so much else, including weapons, that no Confederate army, whatever it suffered from being deprived of food and clothing, ever lost a battle for lack of ordnance equipment or supplies — filled the requisition overnight. The cartridges were not for Davis himself, but for his wife. He gave her the pistol and showed her how to load, aim, and fire it, saying: "You can at least, if reduced to the last extremity, force your assailants to kill you."

Four days ago, at the time of Lee's latest warning that Richmond was to be given up, he had told her she must prepare to leave without him. "My headquarters for the future may be in the field, and your presence would embarrass and grieve me instead of giving comfort." Though she begged to stay and help relieve the tension, he was firm in refusal. "You can do this in but one way: by going yourself and taking the children to a place of safety. If I live, you can come to me when the struggle is ended," he said: adding, however, that he did not "expect to survive the destruction of constitutional liberty." Regretfully she began her preparations for departure, hampered by his insistence that she not ask friends to look after the family silver, lest they be "exposed to inconvenience or outrage" when the Yankees took the city. So she sent the silver, together with some of the furniture, to an auctioneer for sale under the hammer. Then she "made the mistake," as she later said, of telling her husband that she intended to take along several barrels of flour she had bought — at the going price of $1500 a barrel — to help withstand the expected siege. He forbad this, saying flatly: "You can't take anything in the shape of food from here. The people need it." Saddened, she turned to packing what little was left, mainly clothes for herself and the four children, who ranged in age from ten years to nine months.

Others had done what Varina Davis was doing now, though with less conscientious interference by their husbands with regard to such household items as flour and silver. Since early February, foreseeing that the end of winter meant the end of Richmond, men of substance had been sending their wives and children to outlying estates, north and west of the threatened capital, or to North Carolina towns and cities so far spared a visit from Sherman. All through March the railway stations were crowded with well-off "refugees" boarding trains to avoid the holocaust at hand. Having no choice, those with nowhere to go (and no money either to pay the fare or live on when they got there) remained, as did the heads of families whose government duties or business interests required their presence; with the result that by the time the First Lady started packing, alerted for a sudden removal to

Charlotte, where Davis had rented a house for her and the children, Richmond's population was predominantly black and poor and male. A sizeable group among these last had been composed of the 105 congressmen and 26 senators, most of them eager for adjournment so they too could get aboard the cars rattling westward, away from the seven-hilled capital and the blue flood lapping the earthworks east and south — muddy dikes buttressed only by the scarecrow infantry under Lee, who was rumored to have given the government notice that they would not be there long.

In any case, these 131 elected representatives of the people felt that they had done all they could by March 18, when they adjourned and scattered for their homes, those who still had them. And, indeed, they had done much this term: including the unthinkable. After long and sometimes acrimonious debate, the House on February 20 and the Senate on March 8 authorized the enlistment of Negroes for service in the armies of the Confederacy. On March 13 a joint bill to that effect was forwarded for approval by the Chief Executive, who promptly signed it despite objections that it fell considerably short of what he — and Pat Cleburne, fifteen months ago — had wanted. For one thing, the recruits must all be volunteers, and at second hand at that; only "such able-bodied slaves as might be patriotically rendered by their masters" were to be accepted, although the President was authorized to call on the states to fill their respective quotas, limited in each case to no more than one fourth of its male slaves between the ages of eighteen and forty-five. Moreover, while it was stipulated that Negro soldiers were to receive the same pay, rations, and clothing as other troops, no mention was made of emancipation as a reward for military service, and it was even stressed in a final rider that nothing in the act was "to be construed to authorize a change in the relation which the said slaves shall bear toward their owners, except by the consent of their owners and of the states in which they may reside." Mainly, though, Davis regretted the extended debate that had kept the bill so long from his desk. "Much benefit is anticipated from this measure," he remarked, "though far less than would have resulted from its adoption at an earlier date, so as to afford time for organization and instruction during the winter months."

Grim as the warnings leading up to passage of the act had been, the fulminations that followed were even grimmer. "If we are right in passing this measure," Robert Hunter told his fellow senators, "we were wrong in denying the old government the right to interfere with the institution of slavery and to emancipate slaves." Howell Cobb agreed, writing from Georgia: "Use all the Negroes you can get, for the purposes for which you need them" — cooking, digging, chopping, and such — "but don't arm them. The day you make soldiers of them is the beginning of the end of the revolution. If slaves will make good soldiers our whole theory of slavery is wrong." Even Robert Kean, head of the Bureau of War, who knew better than most the urgent need for men in the ranks of the nation's armies, saw nothing but evil proceeding from a measure which, he noted in his diary, "was passed by a panic in the Congress and the Virginia Legislature, under all the pressure the President indirectly, and General Lee directly, could bring to bear. My own judgment of the whole thing is that it is a colossal blunder, a dislocation of the foundations of society from which no practical results will be reaped by us." Robert Toombs, after his brief return to the service during Sherman's march through Georgia, was strongest of all in condemnation of this attempt to convert the Negro into a soldier; a Confederate soldier, anyhow. "In my opinion," he wrote from his plantation in Wilkes County, where he had put down a full crop of cotton last year in response to a Davis proclamation calling on planters to shift to food crops, "the worst calamity that could befall us would be to gain our independence by the valor of our slaves. ... The day that the army of Virginia allows a negro regiment to enter their lines as soldiers they will be degraded, ruined, and disgraced."

Toombs need not have fretted about the prospect of disgrace to his former comrades, either in Virginia or elsewhere. For though the army, by and large, had favored adoption of the measure (144 out of 200 men in an Alabama regiment, for example, signed a petition addressed to Congress in its favor, and the proportion was about the same in a Mississippi outfit) the legislation failed in application: not so much because of the shortness of "time for organization and instruction," of which Davis had complained, as because of a lack of support by the owners of prospective black recruits — and possibly by the slaves themselves, though of the latter there was little chance to judge. Some few came or were sent forward to Richmond before the end of March; new gray uniforms were somehow found for them, and there was even a drill ceremony in Capitol Square, performed to the shrill of fifes and throb of drums; but that was all. Small boys jeered and threw rocks at the paraders, not one of whom reached the firing line while there was still a firing line to reach.

Nor was it only on this side of the Atlantic that the proposal to invoke the assistance of the Negro in the struggle which so intimately concerned him failed to achieve its purpose. Judah Benjamin, ever willing to play any last card in his hand, had written to Mason and Slidell in late December, instructing them to sound out the British prime minister and the French emperor, respectively, as to what effect a Confederate program for emancipation — "not suddenly and all at once, but so far as to insure abolition in a fair and reasonable time" — might have on their views with regard to recognition of the Confederacy and possible intervention in the war. Napoleon rather blandly replied that slavery had never been an issue so far as France was concerned, and Lord Palmerston said much the same of England in an interview on March 14 with Mason, who wrote Benjamin that he was "satisfied that the most ample concessions on our part in the matter referred to would have produced no change in the course determined by the British government." Twelve days later, in conversation with the Earl of Donoughmore, a Tory leader friendly to the South, the Virginian's view was confirmed by a franker response to the same question. If the proposal had been made in midsummer of 1863, while Lee was on the march in Pennsylvania, the earl did not doubt that recognition would have followed promptly. But that was then. What about now? Mason asked, and afterwards informed the Secretary: "He replied that the time had gone by."

It would have been at best a deathbed conversion, and as such would have lacked the validity of conviction and free will. Meantime, opponents of the earlier and more limited proposal — to induct blacks into the army, even without the promise of freedom as a reward for any suffering short of death — were no doubt pleased that, in practical application, the Lost Cause was spared this ultimate "stain" on its record. In any case the Confederacy's chief opponent, Abraham Lincoln, professed not to care one way or another about the success or failure of the experiment. "There is one thing about the Negro's fighting for the rebels which we can know as well as they can," he remarked, "and that is that they cannot at the same time fight in their armies and stay home and make bread for them. And this being known and remembered, we can have but little concern whether they become soldiers or not." Something else he saw as well, and when news of the action by the Richmond lawmakers reached Washington he expressed it in an address to an Indiana regiment passing through the capital on March 17, six days before he set out down the coast for City Point. "I am rather in favor of the measure," he told the Hoosiers, "and would at any time, if I could, have loaned them a vote to carry it. We have to reach the bottom of the insurgent resources, and that they employ or seriously think of employing the slaves as soldiers gives us glimpses of the bottom. Therefore I am glad of what we learn on this subject."

Davis by now had caught more than "glimpses" of the scraped bottom. Yet for all his West Point training and his regular army background, both of which contributed to the military realism that had characterized his outlook as Commander in Chief — and paradoxically, because of his unblinking recognition of the odds, had made him a believer in long chances and a supporter of those generals who would take them — it was also in his nature, as the leader of his people, to deny, even to himself, the political consequences of whatever of this kind he saw, even with his own eyes. "I'd rather die than be whipped," Jeb Stuart had said at Yellow Tavern, ten months back. So would Davis, but he took this a step further in his conviction that no man was ever whipped until he admitted it; which he himself would never do. Earlier this month, writing to thank a Virginia congressman for support "in an hour when so many believed brave have faltered and so many esteemed true have fallen away," he declared his faith in survival as an act of national will. "In spite of the timidity and faithlessness of many who should give tone to the popular feeling and hope to the popular heart, I am satisfied that it is in the power of the good man and true patriots of the country to reanimate the wearied spirit of our people. The incredible sacrifices made by them in the cause will be surpassed by what they are still willing to endure in preference to abject sub- mission, if they are not deserted by their leaders. Relying upon the sublime fortitude and devotion of my countrymen, I expect the hour of deliverance."

His resolution was to be tested to the full before the month was out. Gordon's failure at Fort Stedman prompted Lee to state unequiv- ocally next day that he would have to give up Richmond before Sherman and Grant effected a junction he could do nothing to prevent, and two days later, March 28, in response to a query from Breckinridge as to how much notice the capital authorities could expect — "I have given the necessary orders in regard to commencing the removal of stores, &c.," the Secretary wrote, "but, if possible, would like to know whether we may probably count on a period of ten or twelve days" — Lee replied: "I know of no reason to prevent your counting upon the time suggested." So he said. But next morning he learned that Grant had begun another crablike sidle around his thin-stretched right. Both infantry and cavalry were involved, and the movement was across Monk's Neck Bridge, over Rowanty Creek just below the confluence of Hatcher's and Gravelly runs; their initial objective seemed to be Dinwiddie Courthouse, a scant half-dozen miles beyond, which would give them a clear shot north at Five Forks, a critical intersection out the White Oak Road, about the same distance west of Burgess Mill, the right-flank anchor of Lee's line. Five Forks, defended now by no more than a handful of gray vedettes, was within three miles of the Southside Railroad, whose loss would interfere grievously — perhaps disastrously — with the army's projected withdrawal, not only from its lines below the James but also from those above, since the Richmond & Danville would also be exposed beyond the Appomattox.

Informed of this, Davis requisitioned from Gorgas ammunition for the pistol he gave his wife next day, along with instructions on how to use it. By that time Lee had troops in motion westward to meet the threat, which further reports had identified as substantial; Sheridan was at Dinwiddie with his cavalry, and two blue corps had also crossed the Rowanty, apparently to lend heft to the roundhouse left Lee believed was about to be thrown at Five Forks. Unable to stretch his line that far, lest it snap, the gray commander detached Pickett from Longstreet, reinforcing his division to a strength of 6400, and posted him there, four miles beyond the farthest reach of the intrenchments on that side of Hatcher's Run. Fitzhugh and Rooney Lee's divisions, as well as Rosser's, lately arrived from the Valley — a total of 5400 troopers; all but a handful of all the army had — were called in from roundabout and sent to bolster Pickett. Nor was that all Lee did. Aggressive as always, he visited the outpost position the following morning, March 30, and ordered an advance toward Dinwiddie the following day, hoping thus to seize the initiative and throw the flankers into confusion, despite odds he knew were long. This done, he rode back to Petersburg. "Don't think he was in good humor," a young lieutenant entered in his diary.

Heavy rain had been falling with scarcely a let-up since the night before, and it continued through the final day of March, hampering last-minute preparations for the departure that evening of Mrs Davis, made urgent by the threat to the Danville line. Guns boomed daylong east of Richmond, mixed with peals of thunder; Grant no doubt was feeling the works in that direction, as well as elsewhere along the nearly forty random miles of their extent, for evidence that Lee had weakened them to confront the movement around his right. Soon after dark an over-loaded carriage set out from the White House for the railroad station, bearing Mrs Davis and her sister Margaret Howell, the four children and their nurse, a young midshipman assigned as escort, and Burton Harrison, the President's secretary, who was to help them get settled in Charlotte, then rejoin his chief — wherever he might be by then. They arrived well before leaving time, 8 o'clock, and boarded a passenger coach which, though dilapidated and "long a stranger to paint," was the best the Confederacy could provide for its First Lady at this late stage of its existence. She looked with dismay at the lumpy seats, with threadbare plush the color of dried blood, and made the children as comfortable as she could; Billy, three, and the baby Pie were stretched out asleep by the time their father arrived to see them off. He sat talking earnestly with his wife, ten-year-old Maggie clinging to him all the while and eight-year-old Jeff trying hard to keep from crying. When the whistle blew, an hour and a half past schedule, he rose, kissed the children, embraced Varina, and turned to go, still with an appearance of great calm, though he came close to giving way to his emotion when Maggie persisted in clinging to him, sobbing, and Little Jeff begged tearfully to remain with him in Richmond. "He thought he was looking his last upon us," Mrs Davis later wrote.

There was a further wait on the station platform; he walked up and down it, talking with Harrison until 10 o'clock, when the train gave a sudden lurch that left the secretary barely time to leap aboard. Davis stood and watched the tail light fade and vanish, then rode back to the big empty-seeming house at Clay and 12th streets, there to await word from Lee that he too must leave the city.

All the evidence was that it would not be long, and next morning — All Fools Day — a message from the general-in-chief served
notice that the time was shorter than he or anyone else had known.
Pickett's advance the day before, supported by Fitz Lee's troopers, had
driven the startled Federals back on Dinwiddie by sunset, but there
they rallied, pumping lead from their rapid-fire carbines, and Pickett
felt obliged to pull back in the rainy predawn darkness, leaving the
situation much as it had been when he set out from Five Forks yesterday morning. Sheridan still held Dinwiddie, cutting the Stony Creek
supply line, and had followed up Pickett's withdrawal so closely as
to deny him use of the critical White Oak Road leading east to Hatcher's
Run. Supported as it was by at least two corps of infantry, Lee told
Davis, this movement of Grant's "seriously threatens our position and
diminishes our ability to maintain our present lines in front of Richmond and Petersburg. . . . I fear he can cut both the South Side and the
Danville railroads, being far superior to us in cavalry. This in my
opinion obliges us to prepare for the necessity of evacuating our position on James River at once, and also to consider the best means of
accomplishing it, and our future course."

★   ★   ★

"Grant has the bear by the hind leg while Sherman takes off the
hide," Lincoln had told a White House caller some weeks back, explaining the situation as it then obtained. But now the holder-skinner
roles were to be reversed, and Sheridan — much to his delight — was
the catalytic agent injected by Grant to bring the change about. At
Dinwiddie on the 29th, just as the rain began to patter on the roof of
the tavern where he had set up for the night, he received a dispatch
that sent his spirits fairly soaring. "I feel now like ending the matter,
if it is possible to do so, before going back," his chief informed him.
"In the morning, push around the enemy, if you can, and get onto his
right rear. The movements of the enemy's cavalry may, of course,
modify your action, [but] we will all act together as one army until
it is seen what can be done."

"Onto," Grant said, not *into* Lee's rear: meaning that the strike
at the two railroads had become incidental to his main purpose, which
was to crush the rebel army where it stood. "My hope was that Sheridan would be able to carry Five Forks, get on the enemy's right flank
and rear, and force them to weaken their center to protect their right so
that an assault in the center might be successfully made." That was how
he put it later; Warren and Humphreys would support the cavalry effort
west of Hatcher's Run, and Wright was to lunge at Petersburg on
signal, supported on the left and right by Ord and Parke, while Weitzel
maintained pressure on Richmond's defenses beyond the James, partly
to hold Longstreet in position, but also to be ready to move in when

the breakthrough came, beyond the Appomattox. Glad to find his
superior following through on what he had told him in private, three
days back — "I mean to end the business here" — Sheridan briefed
his subordinates on their share in the operation. All during the conference, however, rain drummed hard and harder on the tavern roof;

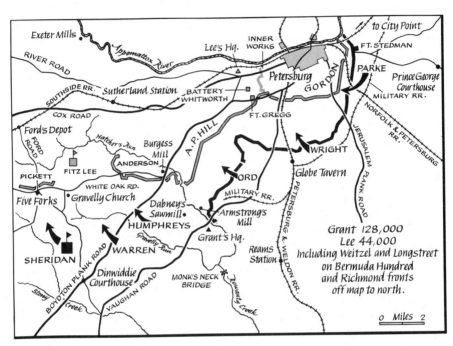

daylight showed a world in flood, with no sign of a let-up; roads were
practically bottomless, preventing the movement of supplies, and the
rain continued to fall in sheets, converting meadows into ponds. To
make things worse, a bogged observer noted, "the soil was a mixture
of clay and sand, partaking in some places of the nature of quicksand."
Grant could testify to this, his headquarters beside the Vaughan Road
being one such place. Formerly a cornfield, it now resembled a slough,
with effects at once comic and grim on men and mounts, coming and
going or even trying to stand still. "Sometimes a horse or mule would
be standing apparently on firm ground," he later wrote, "when all at
once one foot would sink, and as he commenced scrambling to catch
himself, all his feet would sink and he would have to be drawn by
hand out of the quicksands so common in that part of Virginia."

Veterans wagged their heads, remembering Burnside's Mud March,
and some declared the situation was no worse than might have been
expected, what with all the glib predictions that Bobby Lee was about
to be outfoxed. They had heard that kind of talk before, with results
that varied only in the extent of their discomfort when the smoke
cleared. "Four years of war, while it made the men brave and valorous,"
a Pennsylvania private would point out, "had entirely cured them

of imagining that each campaign would be the last." Still they were not dispirited; soggy crackers and soaked blankets often went with soldiering, especially on occasions like the present; "When are the gunboats coming up?" they called to one another as they slogged along the spongy roads or stood about in fields too wet for sitting.

Sheridan, on the other hand, fumed and fretted. He had scouting parties working northward out of Dinwiddie in accordance with his orders, but he feared the arrival of a dispatch changing those orders because of the weather. Sure enough, just such a message came from Grant around midmorning. "The heavy rain of today will make it impossible for you to do much until it dries up a little, or we get roads around our rear repaired." His suggestion was that Sheridan "leave what cavalry you deem necessary to protect the left" and return with the rest to a station on the military railroad, where he could draw rations and grain for his troopers and their mounts. Or, better yet: "Could not your cavalry go back by the way of Stony Creek Depot and destroy or capture the store of supplies there?"

Go back! Sheridan frowned as he read the words, then set out instead for Grant's command post, seven miles northeast, to argue for all he was worth against postponement of the forward movement. Hoping to save time — "a stumpy, quadrangular little man," a subsequent acquaintance was to say, "with a forehead of no promise and hair so short that it looks like a coat of black paint" — he rode a long-legged Kentucky pacer, much admired for its mile-eating gait. But the going was slow on the mud-slick roads, pelted by unrelenting rain, and slower still around midday when he turned off the Vaughan Road, a mile beyond Gravelly Run, and urged his mount across the drowned headquarters cornfield. "Instead of striking a pacing gait now," a staffer noted, "[the horse] was at every step driving its legs knee-deep into the quicksand with the regularity of a pile driver." Grant was in conference just then, but Little Phil, "water dripping from every angle of his face and clothes," launched forthwith into his protest to such listeners as were handy. Give him his head, he said, and Lee would be whipped in short order. How about forage? someone asked; to his disdain. "Forage?" he snorted. "I'll get all the forage I want. I'll haul it out if I have to set every man in the command to corduroying roads, and corduroy every mile of them from the railroad to Dinwiddie. I tell you I'm ready to strike out tomorrow and go to smashing things!"

Such enthusiasm was contagious. Twenty minutes alone with the general-in-chief, once he was free, resulted in agreement that the cavalry would "press the movement against the enemy with all vigor." Ord, Wright, and Parke were to remain on the alert for the signal to assault the rebel works in their front, and Sheridan would not only have the diversionary support of Humphreys and Warren, he would also be given direct command of the latter's corps at any time he requested it, thereby assuring full coöperation despite any difference of opinion that might arise. "Let me know, as early in the morning as you can, your judgment of the matter," Grant told him in parting, "and I will make the necessary orders." Elated, the bandy-legged Ohioan remounted and set out to rejoin his troopers around Dinwiddie, waving goodbye to the admiring group of staffers who came out into the still-driving rain to see him off, most of them as happy as he was over his success in getting their chief to cancel the postponement.

Still, a day had been lost to mud and indecision. And so, as it developed, was another — the last in March — not so much because of the weather, though rain continued to pelt the roads and sodden fields, as because of a double-pronged attack by Lee, who went over to the offensive in an attempt to disconcert the combinations moving against him west of Hatcher's Run. True to his word, Sheridan put Custer's whole division to work that morning, corduroying the Dinwiddie supply routes, while Devin probed northwest up the road to Five Forks, reinforced by a brigade from the third division, formerly Gregg's but now under George Crook; Gregg had resigned in February, exhausted or disheartened by a winter spent on the Petersburg front, and Crook was exchanged, one month after his capture up in Maryland, in time to take Gregg's place on the eve of the present maneuver, covering Dinwiddie today with his two remaining brigades while the other moved out with Devin for a share in what turned out to be a retreat in the face of heavy odds.

Approaching Five Forks around noon Devin encountered Pickett, who had been instructed by Lee to move out with his nearly 12,000 infantry and cavalry in order to beat the advancing Federals to the punch; which he did, emptying more than 400 U.S. saddles in the process. Outnumbered almost three to one, Devin had all he could do to make it back to Dinwiddie by sunset, still under heavy pressure. Crook's and Custer's troopers, called up and thrown dismounted into line alongside Devin's, managed to stop the graybacks in plain view of Sheridan's headquarters. Night came down, and with it came word of a similar repulse suffered by Warren across the way. Advancing in the direction of Lee's right, which he had been told to "feel," the New Yorker's corps was badly strung out on the muddy byroads, various units marking time while others ran heavy-footed to catch up; Brigadier General Romeyn Ayres' division, struck a sudden blow by a butternut host that came screaming out of the dripping woods ahead, took off rearward in such haste that Crawford's, next in line and with no chance to brace for the shock, was also overrun. The attack was delivered by veterans from Bushrod Johnson's division — all that remained of Anderson's improvised corps — reinforced by others brought over from A. P. Hill beyond the run, and was directed by Lee himself, who had no way of knowing that this would be his and the Army of Northern Virginia's last. In any case, the drive did not falter until it reached Griffin's division, posted in reserve, and even then was only contained with help from Humphreys, whose corps was advancing in better order on the right. After sundown, the attackers — some 5000 in all, of whom about 800 had fallen or been captured — withdrew to their works apparently satisfied with the infliction of just over 1400 casualties on Warren and just under 400 on Humphreys, both of whom testified that the call had been a close one, indicative of the need for caution while groping for contact with the rebel flank.

Sheridan did not agree. Nettled, but no more daunted by Devin's repulse than he was by Warren's, he was convinced that what had been learned from these two encounters far outweighed the loss of 2700 men on the Union left, today and yesterday. After all there still were some 50,000 blue-clad veterans west of Hatcher's Run, mounted and afoot, and he believed in using them all-out, with emphasis on getting the job done, rather than on caution. Lee had scarcely that many troops in his whole command, from White Oak Swamp to Five Forks, and if Little Phil had his way tonight the old fox would have a good many less before the sun went down tomorrow. What he had in mind was Pickett's detachment. Its movement against him today, while tactically successful, had increased its isolation and thereby exposed it to destruction, if only the right kind of pressure could be brought to bear. Even before sundown, with the issue still apparently in doubt, he said as much to a staff colonel sent over by Grant, who expressed alarm at finding Devin's troopers thrown back on the outskirts of Dinwiddie, skirmishing hotly within carbine range of the headquarters tavern. "This force is in more danger than I am," Sheridan told him. "If I am cut off from the Army of the Potomac, it is cut off from Lee's army, and not a man in it should ever be allowed to get back to Lee. We at last have drawn the enemy's infantry out of its fortifications, and this is our chance to attack it."

One doubt he had, which he also expressed. He would need a corps of infantry to help inflict Pickett's destruction, and today's encounter across the way had increased his mistrust of Warren as a fit partner, or even subordinate, in such an undertaking. Consequently, recalling how well he and Wright had worked together in the Valley, he urged the staffer to pass on to Grant his fervent request that the VI Corps be sent to him instead. Departing after nightfall, the colonel promised to support the plea, despite doubts that the change would be made this late, and presently these doubts were confirmed. Near midnight, word came from Grant — whose headquarters had been shifted that afternoon to Dabney's Sawmill, a mile northwest of the boggy Vaughan Road cornfield — that Wright could not be sent: first, because he was too far away to make the march tonight, and second because he would be needed where he was, to score the breakthrough scheduled to follow upon the smashing of Lee's right. In any case, Warren had been detached from Meade and ordered to proceed down the Boydton Plank Road to Dinwiddie, where he would report for such duty as Sheridan had in mind for him. He and his three divisions should arrive by midnight, Grant wrote, followed next morning by Brigadier General Ranald Mackenzie's troopers, one of the four divisions brought over from beyond the James two days ago. This would raise Sheridan's total to around 30,000 effectives, half cavalry, half infantry; quite enough, presumably, for the resumption of his stalled offensive. "You will assume command of the whole force sent to operate with you," the message ended, "and use it to the best of your ability to destroy the force which your command has fought so gallantly today."

More or less reconciled, Little Phil turned in for a few hours' sleep, only to have his wrath flare up again when he rose at dawn to find none of Warren's troops on hand. The rain had stopped at last, but even so their march had been a snarl of mud and confusion, including a four-hour jumbled wait for the washed-out bridge over Gravelly Run to be rebuilt. It was broad open daylight by the time the head of the 16,000-man column reached Dinwiddie, and crowding noon before Warren himself came up with his third division, eleven hours behind the schedule sent by Grant, but apparently satisfied that he and his men had done their best under difficult conditions. Sheridan took a less tolerant view. "Where's Warren?" he growled at a brigadier who arrived with the first of the mud-slathered infantry. Back toward the rear, attending to some tangle, the other replied. "That's where I expected to find him," the cavalryman snapped.

His impatience mounted with the fast-climbing sun, right up to midday, when he rode over to give the New Yorker instructions for his share in the attack. Pickett had withdrawn to Five Forks this morning and reoccupied breastworks along the White Oak Road, on both sides of the Ford Road crossing; Sheridan's plan was for his troopers, advancing northwest up the road from Dinwiddie — which bisected the southeast quadrant of the intersection and gave it the name Five Forks — to apply and maintain pressure in front, thus pinning the defenders in position while the infantry attacked their eastern flank in a turning movement whose main effort would be against the angle where their line bent north to confront a possible blue approach out the White Oak Road from Hatcher's Run, where Lee's intrenchments ended. By hitting this knuckle with one division and rounding the brief northward extension with the other two, Warren could throw two thirds of his corps — a force equal to everything Pickett had, mounted and dismounted — into their rear, and perhaps bag the lot when they gave way under double pressure, front and flank, in full flight for their lives. The important thing just now, the cavalryman stressed, was to get going before the rebs escaped or used still more of the time allowed them to improve their position. Warren nodded agreement, but it did not seem to Sheridan that much of his western enthusiasm had been communicated to the paper-collar Easterner, who left to rejoin his tired and sleepy men, muttering something about "Bobby Lee getting people into difficulties."

Actually, for all his chafing, Sheridan was to find that the delay had worked to his advantage by lulling the defenders into believing there would be no serious confrontation at Five Forks today: so much so, indeed, that when the attack did come — as it finally did, around 4 o'clock — neither the infantry nor the cavalry commander was even present to oppose him.

Reporting this morning on his two-day movement to Dinwiddie and back, Pickett was somewhat miffed by the tone of Lee's reply. "Hold Five Forks at all hazards," he was told. "Protect road to Ford's Depot and prevent Union forces from striking the Southside Railroad. Regret exceedingly your forced withdrawal, and your inability to hold the advantage you had gained." Not only did this seem tinged with unaccustomed panic, it also seemed to the long-haired hero of Gettysburg inappreciative of his efforts yesterday, which he was convinced had shocked the Federals into deferring whatever maneuver they had intended before he struck and drove them back. At any rate, on his return he put his five brigades of infantry in line along the White Oak Road, astride the Ford Road intersection, and covered their flanks and rear with cavalry, Rooney Lee's division on the right, Fitz Lee's on the left, and Tom Rosser's on guard with the train beyond Hatcher's Run, two miles to the north. All seemed well; he had no doubt that he could maintain his position against Sheridan's horsemen, even if they ventured to attack, and there had been no word of a farther advance by the blue infantry whose reported presence west of Gravelly Run had provoked his withdrawal this morning. Consequently, when an invitation came from Rosser to join in an alfresco meal of shad caught in the Nottoway River on his way from Stony Creek, Pickett gladly accepted, as did Fitzhugh Lee, who turned his division over to Colonel T. T. Munford around 1 o'clock, then set out for the rear with his ringleted superior for a share in their fellow Virginian's feast. Neither told any subordinate where he was going or why, perhaps to keep from dividing the succulent fish too many ways; with the result that when the attack exploded — damped from their hearing, as it was, by a heavy stand of pines along Hatcher's Run — no one knew where to find them. Pickett only made it back to his division after half its members had been shot or captured, a sad last act for a man who gave his name to the most famous charge in a war whose end was hastened by his three-hour absence at a shad bake.

Nor was he the only Gettysburg hero whose reputation suffered from his participation — or, strictly speaking, nonparticipation — in the fight that raged at Five Forks during the final daylight hours of April 1. Sheridan's wrath had continued to mount as the sun declined past midday and the V Corps plodded wearily up the road past Gravelly Run Church to execute its share of the fix-and-shatter maneuver already begun by the dismounted troopers banging away with their rapid-fire weapons in front of the enemy right and center. "This battle must be fought and won before the sun goes down," he grumbled on being told that it would be 4 o'clock by the time the three infantry divisions were deployed. "All the conditions may be changed in the morning; we have but a few hours of daylight left us. My cavalry are rapidly exhausting their ammunition, and if the attack is delayed much longer they may have none left." Warren, however, "seemed gloomy and despondent," Little Phil said later, and "gave me the impression that he wished the sun to go down before dispositions for the attack could be completed." If so, the New Yorker was in graver danger than he knew. Another staff colonel had arrived from Grant with a message for Sheridan, authorizing Warren's removal "if in your judgment the V Corps would do better under one of its division commanders." Sheridan saw this not only as an authorization but also as a suggestion, knowing that his chief was as displeased as he was by Warren's performance these past two days, despite his aura as the savior of Little Round Top, twenty-one months ago in Pennsylvania. All the same, he stayed his hand, controlling his temper by the hardest, and finally, not long after 4 o'clock, all three divisions started forward on a thousand-yard front, Ayres on the left, Crawford on the right, and Griffin in support, intending to strike and turn the rebel left, preliminary to the combined assault that would sweep the graybacks from the field and net them as they fled northward.

Alas, it was just at this critical moment that the bill for the worst of the day's inadvertencies came due. Informed by Sheridan that the road past Gravelly Run Church entered the White Oak Road at the point where the enemy works bent north, Warren had aligned his left division on it as a guide for the attack. Emerging from the woods, however, Ayres saw that the rebel angle — his objective — was in fact about half a mile west of the junction he was approaching. Accordingly, he swung left as he crossed the White Oak Road, then lunged westward: only to find that he was charging on his own. Crawford, on the right, kept going north, followed by Griffin close in his rear, while Mackenzie, who had arrived that morning to support the turning movement, led his troopers eastward, as instructed, to block the path of any reinforcements Lee might send across the three-mile gap between him and Pickett. Alarmed at the widening breach in the ranks of his supposed attackers, Warren spurred after the two divisions trudging north. He overtook Griffin and ordered him to turn west, where Ayres was taking concentrated punishment from guns that bucked and fumed along that end of the gray line. Then he rode on after Crawford, who continued to drift into the northward vacuum, unaware of the battle raging ever farther in his rear.

Sheridan reacted fast. Over on the left and center, Custer and Devin surged forward on schedule, their clip-fed weapons raising a clatter that sounded to one observer "as if a couple of army corps had opened fire," while Crook stood by for the mounted pursuit that was to follow. Just now, however, their chief gave his attention to the infantry in trouble on the right. "Where's my battle flag?" he cried. Snatching the swallow-tailed guidon from its bearer, he spurred Rienzi into the confusion Ayres had encountered on his lonely approach to the fuming rebel flank. "Come on, men!" he shouted, brandishing his twin-starred banner along their cowered ranks, a prominent if diminutive target, high on his huge black horse amid twittering bullets. "Go at 'em with a will. Move on at a clean jump or you'll not catch one of them! They're all getting ready to run now, and if you don't get on to them in five minutes they'll every one get away from you." Converted by such assertiveness, the wavering troops responded by resuming their advance. It was as if he addressed them individually: as, indeed, he sometimes did. Just then a nearby skirmisher was struck in the throat, blood gushing from the severed jugular. "I'm killed," he moaned as his legs gave way. But Sheridan would not have it. "You're not hurt a bit," he told the fallen soldier. "Pick up your gun, man, and move right on to the front." Dazed but convinced, the skirmisher rose, clutching his rifle, and managed to take a dozen forward steps before he toppled over, dead beyond all doubt.

For all the certainty in his voice and manner while hoicking the laggards into line, Little Phil's assurance that the rebs were "ready to run" was based not on what he could discern beyond the flame-stabbed bank of smoke that boiled up from their breastworks (he could in fact see very little, even at close range) but rather on his conviction of what would happen once the blue machine got rolling in accordance with his orders. With close to three times as many troops, and well over half of them deployed as flankers, he had no doubt about the outcome — if only they could be brought to bear as he intended. Then suddenly they were. No sooner had Ayres resumed his stalled advance than the lead elements of Griffin's division, redirected west just now by Warren, began to come up on his right, overlapping the northward extension of the enemy works. "By God, that's what I want to see: general officers at the front!" Sheridan greeted a commander who rode at the head of his brigade. He put these late arrivers in line alongside Ayres, adding others as they came up in rapidly growing numbers, then ordered the attack pressed home, all out.

Still brandishing his red and white guidon, he was in the thick of the charge that shattered the rebel left, where more than a thousand prisoners were trapped within the confines of the angle. He leaped Rienzi over the works and landed amid a group of startled graybacks. Hands shot skyward in surrender all around him. "Whar do you want us-all to go to?" one asked, and he replied, suddenly conversational if not quite genial, grinning down at them: "Go right over there. Go right along now. Drop your guns; you'll never need them any more. You'll all be safe over there. Are there any more of you? We want every one of you fellows."

There were in fact a great many more such fellows to be gathered up. Devin — known as "Sheridan's hard hitter" — broke through in front, just west of the shattered angle, and Mackenzie, finding no reinforcements on the way from Lee, returned to assist in the round-up; Griffin was into the rebel rear, and so by now was Crawford, overtaken at last by Warren and hustled westward to arrive in time for a share in the butternut gleaning. All told, at a cost of 634 casualties, the V Corps took 3422 prisoners; while the dead, plus fugitives who slipped through the infantry dragnet only to be snagged by the wider-ranging Federal troopers, raised the Confederate total above 5000; more, even, than had been lost at Fort Stedman, a week ago today. Sheridan, though exhilarated, was far from satisfied. When a jubilant brigadier reported the capture of five rebel guns, he roared back at him: "I don't care a damn for their guns — or you either, sir! What I want is the Southside Railway." He said as much to the troops themselves as they crowded round him, cheering and waving their caps. "I want you men to understand we have a record to make before that sun goes down that will make hell tremble." He stood in his stirrups, pointing north toward the railroad three miles off. "I want you there!" he cried. Encountering Griffin beyond Five Forks, shortly after sunset at 6.20, he told him: "Get together all the men you can, and drive on while you can see your hand before you."

Griffin — crusty Griffin, whom Grant had advised Meade to place in arrest for insubordination on his second day over the Rapidan — now headed the V Corps. Warren, deep in the rebel rear with Crawford, corralling prisoners as they came streaming north across the fields and up Ford Road, had sent a staff colonel to inform headquarters of his whereabouts and his success in carrying out the flanking operation, only to have Sheridan scoff at the report. "By God, sir," he interrupted hotly, "tell General Warren he wasn't in that fight." Astonished, the colonel replied that he would dislike to deliver any such message verbally. Might he take it down in writing? "Take it down, sir!" Sheridan barked. "Tell him by God he was not at the front." Nor was that all. At their sundown meeting he formally notified Griffin that he was to take over in place of Warren, to whom a hastily scrawled field order soon was on its way: "Major General Warren, commanding the Fifth Army Corps, is relieved from duty, and will at once report for orders to Lieutenant General Grant, commanding Armies of the United States. By command of Major General Sheridan."

All the same, though he now felt he had an infantry chief he could depend on, he called off the pursuit he had been urging. In part this was because of the encumbrance of so many grayback prisoners that he used their discarded rifles to corduroy the worst stretches of road; but mainly it was because, on second thought — detached as he was from the rest of the army — he concentrated instead on bracing his victory-scattered troops for the counterattack Lee's opponents had long since learned to expect in such a crisis. Nightfall cooled his blood, and with it his temper, even to the point where he came close to a downright apology for some of the rough talk he had unloaded on subordinates today. "You know how it is," he told a group of V Corps officers gathered around a Five Forks campfire. "We had to carry this place, and I was fretted all day until it was done." None of this applied to their former chief, however, and he had said as much to Warren himself when the New Yorker rode up to headquarters in the gathering dusk and asked him to reconsider the order issued for his removal in the heat of battle. "Reconsider, hell," Sheridan snorted; "I don't reconsider my decisions. Obey the order."

Sedgwick, Burnside, Hancock, Warren: now all four of the men commanding infantry corps at the time of the Rapidan crossing had departed, the last under conditions not unlike those attending the removal of his predecessor Fitz-John Porter, with whom he had shared an admiration for George McClellan, rejected like them by the powers that were. Reporting as ordered to headquarters at Dabney's Mill about 10 o'clock that night, he found a celebration of Sheridan's victory in progress. Grant, he said later, "spoke very kindly of my past services and efforts," though the best he could do for him now, apparently, was put him in charge of the inactive City Point area, where he sat in the backwash while the guns boomed westward. . . . Warren began at once to press for a court of inquiry to right the hot-tempered wrong he believed had been done him today. He finally got it, fourteen years later, and after nearly three more years of hearings and deliberation he also received a measure of vindication by the court, which not only cleared him of Sheridan's charges that he had been negligent at Five Forks, but also criticized the manner of his relief. However, that came three months after Warren himself was in his grave. Buried, as he directed in his will, in civilian clothes and without military ceremony, he would in time stand fully accoutered in bronze on the crest of Little Round Top, where he had saved Meade and, some would say, the Union.

Back at Dabney's, before Warren's appearance put something of a damper on the scene, the victory celebration had been set off by Horace Porter's arrival from Five Forks about an hour after dark; he had sent couriers, but overtook the last and most joyously burdened of these in his haste to share the good news with his friends and fellow members of the staff. They were sitting around a blazing campfire — Grant among them, wrapped in a long blue overcoat and smoking his usual cigar — when the young colonel rode into the firelight, shouting from horseback of Sheridan's success. "For some minutes," he would recall, "there was a bewildering state of excitement, grasping of hands, tossing up of hats, and slapping of each other on the back. It meant the beginning of the end, the reaching of the 'last ditch.' It pointed to peace and home."

Only the general-in-chief remained seated, puffing stolidly at his cigar while Porter burbled of six guns captured along with thirteen rebel flags. "How many prisoners have been taken?" Grant asked. More than 5000, he was told. He rose, went into his tent, and began to write telegraphic dispatches by the flickering light of a candle. When these were done he gave them to an orderly for transmission, then came back out to resume his seat beside the fire. "I have ordered an immediate assault along the lines," he said.

Hearing before sunset of the reverse at Five Forks (though not of its extent, which would leave Pickett gunless by nightfall and unable to muster 2000 infantry in his shattered ranks next morning) Lee ordered Anderson to have Bushrod Johnson march his three remaining brigades at once to Sutherland Station, three miles north on the Southside Railroad, to combine with Pickett and Fitz Lee for the defense of that vital supply line and the even more vital Richmond & Danville, farther west. In partial compensation for this stripping of his right, and though the shift reduced by about 400 the number of defenders in A. P. Hill's two divisions east of Burgess Mill — already so thin-spread, one of them declared, that the pickets were "as far apart as telegraph poles" — he brought two of Heth's regiments across Hatcher's Run to patrol the empty works along the south bank of that stream. Still robbing Peter to pay Paul, when he returned to his headquarters near the Appomattox, two miles west of Petersburg, he wired Longstreet to bring Field's division south by rail tonight from beyond the James. That would leave only Kershaw's reduced division and Ewell's reservists to cover Richmond: a grave risk, but no graver than the one Lee ran in gambling that Grant would not launch an all-out southside attack before Old Peter arrived to help prevent the breaking of Hill's line. Situated as he was, his right flank turned and a deep river at his back, if he had known that Pickett's losses today, combined with those a week ago at Stedman, had cost him a solid fourth of his army, he probably would have evacuated Petersburg that night. Instead, he held on where he was, shifting and sidling his few troops to meet a crisis whose true dimensions were unknown to him, in hope of deferring his departure until such time — quite possibly tomorrow night — as would allow him to alert his subordinate commanders, not to mention the Richmond authorities, at least a few hours in advance.

In any case, having done what he could within his means to meet the problem caused by the loss of Five Forks, he turned in early, so weary that he only removed his boots and outer garments before lying down to sleep. It was as well; for he had no sooner rested his head on the pillow, shortly after 9 o'clock, than guns began to growl all up and down the long curve of Union works, possibly signifying that he would have to turn out in a hurry to meet what Grant had in mind to do when the bombardment lifted. Whatever it was, he hoped it would not come before Field arrived to chink the undermanned stretches of his line. At 1.45 (April 2 now, a Sunday, though dawn was three hours off) a sudden ripple of picket fire intensified the duller rumble of artillery. Awake or asleep, Lee may or may not have heard it, intermittent at first and then a rising clatter. Certainly A. P. Hill did, for he appeared at the Turnbull house, Lee's command post, about an hour before dawn. Disturbed by the weakness of his six-mile front along the Boydton Plank Road leading down to Burgess Mill — especially those portions of it whose outworks had been overrun by the Federals in reaction to Gordon's storming of Fort Stedman, eight days back — Little Powell had returned from sick leave yesterday, though he still was far from well. Unable to sleep tonight, what with the roar of cannons and the stutter of small-arms fire, he had ridden from his own headquarters, back on the outskirts of Petersburg, a mile and a half out Cox Road to the Turnbull house to inquire whether anyone there knew what the Yankees were up to in the rackety, flame-stabbed darkness out beyond his front.

Lee was awake, though still in bed, when Hill arrived, hazel eyes glittering feverishly above his auburn beard, high-set cheekbones hectic with the illness that had kept him from duty so much of the past year. Nearly two decades apart in age — one fifty-eight and looking it, prone beneath the bedclothes, the other eight months short of forty, slim and immaculately uniformed as always — the two generals began a discussion of what could be done if, as seemed likely from the step-up in the firing with the swift approach of dawn, a blue assault preceded Field's arrival from beyond the James. Then Longstreet entered, burly and imperturbable despite the persistent lameness of his sword arm from the bullet that had cut him down at the height of his Wilderness flank attack, just one month less than a year ago this week. His arrival, as commander of the reinforcements ordered southward in all haste, was encouraging until he explained that he and his staff had ridden ahead on horseback to save space on the crowded cars for Field's 4600 infantry. They were still on the way, so far as he knew,

though he could not say how long it would be before the first of them
reached Petersburg, let alone the front. Daylight was glimmering
through by now, and Lee was indicating on a map the route he wanted
these troops to take as soon as they detrained, when a staff colonel
rushed into the room exclaiming that panicked teamsters were dashing
their wagons "rather wildly" up the Cox Road past the Turnbull gate,
apparently in flight from a Federal breakthrough somewhere down near
Hatcher's Run. A wounded officer, hobbling back on crutches, had even
told of being driven from his quarters more than a mile behind the
center of Hill's line.

Alarmed — as well he might be, since this first word of a penetration also indicated the likelihood of a rout — Lee drew a wrapper
around him and went to the front door. Sure enough, though swirls of
ground fog obscured the color of their uniforms in the growing light,
long lines of men resembling skirmishers were moving toward him from
the southwest, the nearest of them not over half a mile away. Uncertain
whether they were retreating Confederates or advancing Federals, he sent
an aide to take a closer look. Just then, however, they halted as if in doubt,
and as they did the quickening daylight showed their clothes were blue.
Lee turned to Longstreet and told him to go at once to the Petersburg
station and hurry Field's men westward, relay by relay, as fast as they
unloaded from the cars. Then he turned to speak to Hill; but Hill was
already running toward his horse, intent on reaching and rallying the
troops in rear of his broken line. He mounted and rode south, accompanied by Sergeant G. W. Tucker, his favorite courier. Disturbed
by something desperate in his fellow Virginian's manner — or perhaps because he had heard that during the recently interrupted sick leave, spent
with kinsmen in a Richmond rife with rumors of impending evacuation,
Little Powell had said he had no wish to survive the fall of the capital —
Lee sent a staffer to caution Hill not to expose himself unduly.

Out front, across the open fields to the southwest, the line of bluecoats remained halted in a swale. Apparently made cautious by the
activity in the Turnbull yard, they seemed to be waiting for reinforcements to come up before they continued their advance. Lee studied
them briefly, then went into the house to finish dressing. When he reappeared, he wore his best gray uniform and had buckled on his sword.
This last was so unusual that it occurred to at least one member of his
staff that the general had decided to be in "full harness" in case he was
obliged to surrender before the rising sun went down. In any event, he
mounted Traveller and rode out for a closer examination of whatever
calamity was at hand.

Piecemeal, in the absence of reports from subordinates who were
too busy just then to do anything but fight to hang on where they were
or hurry rearward to avoid capture, he managed to gather at least a
notion of what had happened as a result of the massive three-corps blue

assault launched at daybreak, 60,000 strong, against nearly the whole twelve miles of works, defended by less than one fourth that number, from the Appomattox down to Burgess Mill. On the left, east and directly south of Petersburg, Gordon's front-line troops were driven back on their inner fortifications by the force of Parke's attack. There they rallied, supported by Pendleton's reserve artillery, which Lee had massed in their rear the day before, and not only resisted all further efforts to dislodge them, but were counterattacking even now to recover the outworks they had lost. Southwest along the thinly manned stretch of Hill's line, whose forward positions had been overrun the week before, events took a different turn. Attacking from close up, one of Wright's three divisions broke through a single line of works defended by two of Wilcox's brigades. Swept from their trenches, these veterans fell back north through the soggy woods, firing as they went. Beyond the Boydton Plank Road — within two miles of the Turnbull house, where Lee was conferring with A. P. Hill and Longstreet — their pursuers fanned out to the left, southwest down the plank road toward Hatcher's Run, in rear of that part of the gray line under assault by Ord. Heth's division and the other half of Wilcox's, pressed in front and threatened from the rear, gave way in turn, withdrawing northwest up the left bank of the run, and Ord's and Wright's men followed for a time, then veered northeast into the angle between the Boydton Plank Road and Cox Road. These were the bluecoats Lee discerned through wisps of fog when he came to the Turnbull front door in his wrapper, and this was the breakthrough — the two breakthroughs, really — that had more or less abolished Hill's half dozen miles of line between Gordon's right and Hatcher's Run.

Fortunately for him, at this stage the attackers were about as disorganized by their sudden gains as his own troops were by their retreat. Straggling was heavy among the pursuers, and various units were intermingled, shaken loose from their regular order of battle and strung out in long lines like skirmishers. Their pause for realignment and the ensuing wait for reinforcements, at a time when absolutely nothing stood between them and his headquarters, gave Lee the chance to dress and mount Traveller for a first-hand study of the situation. Westward there was scattered firing, and a heavier clatter rolled in from the east, where the sun by now was rising over Petersburg, obscured by smoke from Pendleton's guns supporting Gordon in his fight to hold back Parke. Southward, however, there was an ominous silence along the lines where Ord and Wright had undone Heth and Wilcox. Riding toward the Turnbull gate for a look across the fields in that direction, Lee saw a group of horsemen turn in from the road: members of Hill's staff, he observed as they drew nearer, and then noted with a pang of apprehension that the man astride the corps commander's handsome dapple-gray was Sergeant Tucker. This could only mean that Hill was dead or wounded.

He was dead; Tucker, who had been with him when he fell, told how it happened. Proceeding south from the Turnbull house before sunrise, just short of the Boydton Plank Road they found Union soldiers cavorting among the huts the men of Mahone's division had occupied, as the army's one reserve, until they were detached and shifted north of the Appomattox to take over Pickett's position on Bermuda Hundred. This in itself showed the depth of the breakthrough, but Hill, skirting the celebration being staged a mile behind his lines, was determined to continue the search for his missing troops, even though all that could be seen in any direction were random groups of blue-clad stragglers from the attack that had swept this way and then moved on. Beyond the plank road he turned right, explaining that he hoped to reach Heth on the far side of the break that seemed to have made a clean sweep of Wilcox and all four of his brigades. The two rode west about a mile along a screen- ing fringe of woods, through which from time to time they sighted still more clots of Federals on the prowl, but no Confederates at all. "Ser- geant," Hill said at last, for the sense of danger grew as they proceeded, "should anything happen to me, you must go back to General Lee and report it." Tucker responded by taking the lead, and removed his navy Colt from its holster to be prepared for whatever loomed. Pres- ently he drew rein, having spotted a squad-sized cluster of bluecoats in the woods directly ahead, the two closest of whom scuttled for shelter behind a large tree and extended their rifle barrels around its trunk, one above the other. "We must take them," Hill said, coming forward. But Tucker would not have it. "Stay there: I'll take them," he said, and shouted to the hidden pair, some twenty yards away: "If you fire you'll be swept to hell! Our men are here. Surrender." Beside him now, Hill too had drawn his pistol and held it at the ready. "Surrender!" he cried, his gauntleted left hand extended palm-out toward the two blue soldiers crouched behind their tree. "I can't see it," Tucker heard one of them say, and then: "Let's shoot them." One rifle had been lowered. Now it rose and both went off. A bullet whistled past the courier's head: but not past Little Powell's. Unhorsed, he lay sprawled and motionless on the ground, arms spread. Later, when his body was recovered, friends discovered that the bullet had passed through the gauntlet, cutting off his thumb, before it entered his heart and dropped him, dead perhaps before he struck the earth. Tucker dodged and grabbed the bridle of the riderless gray horse, spurring his own mount back the way they had come. Beyond range of the two soldiers — Corporal John W. Mauk and Private Daniel Wolford, stragglers from a Pennsylvania regiment in one of Wright's divisions — he changed to the faster horse and made good time, first to Hill's headquarters, then to Lee's, where he told and retold what had happened to his chief, back there amid the wreckage of what had been his rear until this morning.

Lee's eyes brimmed with tears. "He is at rest now, and we who are left are the ones to suffer," he said on learning thus of his loss of fiery, high-strung Little Powell, the hard-hitting embodiment of his army's offensive spirit and the one troop commander Stonewall Jackson had called on in his last delirium, back in the days when that spirit burned its brightest. "Go at once, Colonel, and get Mrs Hill and her children across the Appomattox," he told the Third Corps chief of staff, adding: "Break the news to her as gently as possible."

As it turned out, there was no gentle way to break such news. Hesitating at the front door of the cottage she and Hill and their two small daughters had shared on an estate near Petersburg, the staffer could hear the unsuspecting widow singing as she went about her housework. He entered without knocking, hoping to spare her so abrupt a summons. But when Mrs Hill — John Morgan's younger sister Kitty, auburn-haired like the husband she did not yet know had fallen, though she had learned to live with apprehension of such loss throughout the nearly four years of her marriage — heard his slow footsteps in the hall, then turned and saw him, the singing stopped. "The general is dead," she said in a strained voice, numbed by shock. "You would not be here unless he was dead."

Back at the Turnbull house by then, Lee had begun planning to do for his southside units what he had told the colonel to do for Hill's widow and children; that is, get them over the Appomattox before the victory-flustered Union host completed its mission of cutting them off from a crossing. Tucker's account of all that he and his chief had seen, en route to their encounter with the two blue stragglers in rear of the crumpled right, was enough to convince him that the time had come — if, indeed, it was not already past — for him to order the evacuation not only of Petersburg but also of Richmond. Beyond Burgess Mill, Humphreys by now had added a fourth corps to the general assault, and Sheridan was reported driving north and east with his and Griffin's men, lifting the total to six full corps, any one of which had more troops on its roster than Lee had in all on this side of Hatcher's Run, including those in flight. Moreover, this would continue to be the case until Field arrived: if, in fact, he did arrive in time to stop or hinder Wright and Ord, whose buildup southwest of headquarters had continued to the point where they seemed ready to resume their stalled advance, unopposed by anything more than Lee and his staff and a single battery of guns just unlimbered in the Turnbull yard.

Around 10 o'clock, firing over the heads of infantry massing for attack, Federal gunners ended the providential four-hour lull by opening on the battery and the house itself. Before disconnecting the telegraph for departure, Lee dictated a series of dispatches to the Secretary of

War, the President, and Ewell, who had taken over from Longstreet north of the James. "I see no prospect of doing more than holding our position here till night. I am not certain that I can do that. If I can I shall withdraw tonight north of the Appomattox, and if possible it will be better to withdraw the whole line tonight from James River." This was the message to Breckinridge, ending summarily: "I advise that all preparation be made for leaving Richmond tonight." The one to Davis added that he was sending "an officer to Your Excellency to explain the routes by which the troops will be moved," as well as "a guide and any assistance that you may require." Ewell in turn was cautioned to "make all preparations quietly and rapidly to abandon your position. . . . Have your field transportation ready and your troops prepared for battle or marching orders, as circumstances may require."

But the time was short. When Lee came out again into the yard, where the gray cannoneers were getting badly knocked about in the process of limbering their pieces for withdrawal, a shell tore over his head and into the house, starting fires that soon would leave only four tall chimneys standing where his headquarters had been. "This is a bad business," he remarked as he mounted for the ride to find shelter in the inner fortifications, which Field's troops were to man when they arrived. Still, he waited for the guns to complete their displacement before he set out eastward, trailed by his staff. He rode at a walk, not looking back until a shell exploded close behind him, disemboweling a horse. Others followed rapidly, now that the enemy gunners had the range, and an officer riding beside him watched as Lee reacted to what he evidently considered a highly personal affront. "He turned his head over his right shoulder, his cheeks became flushed, and a sudden flash of the eye showed with what reluctance he retired before the fire directed upon him." Rearward he saw blue infantry moving out ahead of the bucking guns, their rifle barrels gleaming in the sunlight. Suppressing his defiance, if not his anger, he gave Traveller the spur and rode on nearly a mile to the thinly-held works about the same distance west of Petersburg. "Well, Colonel," he said to one of his staff as he drew rein, "it has happened as I told them it would at Richmond. The line has been stretched until it has broken."

These inner fortifications, where he and his staff took refuge from the shells that pursued them on their ride, were the so-far unused western portion of the old Dimmock Line, other parts of whose original half-oval had been put to such good use in June. Beauregard then had been grievously outnumbered, but Lee's predicament now was even worse. East and south, on the far side of town, Gordon had all he could do to hold off Parke, and Field's veterans had not yet appeared. The few garrison troops available to man this empty stretch of works extending from Gordon's hard-pressed right, northward a mile and a half to the Appomattox, were scarcely enough to delay, let alone prevent, a breakthrough by Ord and Wright, whose renewed advance, if undeterred, would end the war in the streets of Petersburg before the midday sun went down. Lee's hope, pending Field's arrival, was in two small earthworks under construction out the Boydton Plank Road, half a mile in front of the main line; Fort Gregg and Battery Whitworth, they were called. Less than a quarter-mile apart and mutually supporting, they were occupied by four slim regiments from Nathaniel Harris's Mississippi brigade — some 400 men in all, left on line when the rest of Mahone's division was shifted north — together with about a hundred North Carolinians, fugitives cut off from Wilcox by the collapse of his left center. Harris put just under half his troops into Gregg, along with two of his five guns, and took the rest with him to Whitworth, 300 yards north of the plank road. A Natchez-born former Vicksburg lawyer, thirty years old, he passed Lee's orders to Gregg's defenders when he left. "Men," he told them, shouting above the uproar of the opening cannonade, "the salvation of the army is in your keep. Don't surrender this fort. If you can hold out for two hours, Longstreet will be up." Behind him, as he turned to go, he heard someone call out after him: "Tell them we'll not give up."

It was noon by now, and presently they showed that they meant what their spokesman said, and more. Given the reduction assignment, Ord passed it along to John Gibbon and the two 6000-man divisions he had brought southside from his XXIV Corps, one against each of the outworks, intending to overrun them in short order. The attack on Whitworth was delayed by a wait for some huts set afire by the rebels to burn out in its front, but the one on Gregg was launched promptly at 1 o'clock, as soon as the bombardment lifted. A brigade in each, the advance was in three columns, which converged as they drew near the objective. Hit by massed volleys, they fell back in some disorder to reform, and then came on again; only to have the same thing happen. "In these charges," a defender would recall, "there was no shooting but by us, and we did cruel and savage work with them." Between attempts, observers back on the Confederate main line, where Field's leading elements were at last beginning to file into the trenches, heard faint cheering from the fort, as well as from Battery Whitworth, still not under immediate pressure. Lee watched from a high vantage point: as did Longstreet, who thought he recognized his old friend Gibbon when he studied the close-packed attackers through his glasses. "[I] raised my hat," he later wrote, "but he was busy and did not see me."

Gibbon was indeed busy, having learned by now that the only way he was going to reduce the two-gun earthwork was by swamping it. Fortunately he had the men, and the men themselves were willing. He brought down a brigade from the division standing idle in front of Whitworth, thus increasing the assault force to 8000, and sent them forward, no longer in successive waves but in a single flood. Inside the place, wounded graybacks loaded rifles taken from the dead and dying, and passed them up to rapid-firing marksmen perched atop the walls. Still the attackers came on, taking their losses to sweep past the flanks and into the rear of the uncompleted installation. Near the end, a butternut captain noted, "The battle flags of the enemy made almost a solid line of bunting around the fort. The noise was fearful, frightful, indescribable. The curses and groaning of frenzied men could be heard over the din of our musketry. Savage men, ravenous beasts — we felt there was no hope for us unless we could keep them at bay. We were prepared for the worst, and expected no quarter." Tumbling over the parapets, sometimes onto the lifted bayonets of the defenders, the Federals gained the interior, and there the struggle continued, hand to hand. One gun was out by then, but the other, trained on the still-advancing bluecoats on the far side of the ditch, was double shotted with canister, its lanyard held taut by a single cannoneer. "Don't fire that gun! Drop the lanyard or we'll shoot!" the attackers yelled, their rifles leveled at him. "Shoot and be damned!" he shouted back, leaning on the lanyard. Canister plowed the ranks out front, and the cannoneer, riddled with bullets, sprawled dead across the trail of the smoking gun.

For another twenty minutes the fight continued at close quarters with clubbed muskets, rammer staffs, and any weapons that were handy, including brickbats from a toppled chimney. By the time it ended, Gibbon's loss of 122 killed and 592 wounded more than tripled the rebel garrison of 214 men, of whom 55 were dead, 129 wounded — 86 percent — and only 30 surrendered uninjured. Northward, their flank exposed by Gregg's collapse and the huts at last burned out in front, Whitworth's defenders scuttled rearward, losing about 60 captives in the final rush by Gibbon's other division's other two brigades. By then it was just after 3 o'clock. Harris's Mississippians and the Tarheel fugitives had given Lee the two hours he asked of them, plus still another for good measure.

Something else they gave as well: an example for Field's veterans, now on line, to follow when and if the Federals tried to continue their advance: which they did not. "The enemy, not finding us inclined to give way for him," Field afterwards reported, "contented himself with forming line in front of us, but out of range. We stood thus in plain view of each other till night, when the army began its retreat."

While the contest for Gregg was in progress Lee and his staff worked on plans for the removal that night of the divided army, northward over the Appomattox and southward over the James, and its subsequent concentration at Amelia Courthouse on the Richmond & Danville, forty miles west-northwest and west-southwest, respectively, of Petersburg and the capital. From there, reunited for the first time since Cold Harbor, ten months back, the command was to follow the line of

the railroad, via Burkeville, for a combination with Joe Johnston somewhere beyond Danville, which was just over a hundred miles from
Amelia. What Grant would do with his greatly superior force, by way
of interfering with this proposed march of a hundred and fifty miles
or more, depended in part on how much of a head start Lee managed
to gain between nightfall and daylight — at the latest — when the
Union lookouts woke to find him gone. Accordingly: "The movement
of all troops will commence at 8 o'clock," the evacuation order read,
"the artillery moving out quietly first, infantry following, except the
pickets, who will be withdrawn at 3 a.m." Copies went to Longstreet
and Gordon, close at hand, to Ewell in Richmond and Mahone on the
Bermuda Hundred line, and to Anderson, who was instructed to collect
the shattered remnants of Pickett's, Johnson's, Heth's, and Wilcox's
divisions beyond Hatcher's Run, cut off from Petersburg by the enemy
now astride the Southside Railroad east of Sutherland Station.

Except for his anger at the Federals for their shelling of the Turnbull house that morning, the southern commander kept his temper all
through this long and trying day; save once. This once was when he
received a wire from Davis in the capital, protesting that "to move
tonight will involve the loss of many valuables, both for the want of
time to pack and of transportation. Arrangements are progressing," the
President added, however, "and unless you otherwise advise, the start
will be made." Lee bristled at the implied rebuke — perhaps forgetting
that five days ago he had promised Breckinridge a ten- or twelve-day
warning — and ripped the telegram to pieces. "I am sure I gave him
sufficient notice," he said testily, and dictated a reply that left no doubt
whatever about his intentions: "I think it is absolutely necessary that
we should abandon our position tonight. I have given all necessary orders
on the subject to the troops, and the operation, though difficult, I hope
will be performed successfully."

It was, and on schedule. Less than an hour after dark, Pendleton,
close in rear of the Second Corps, began withdrawing the reserve artillery through the cobbled streets of Petersburg and then across the Appomattox bridges, followed by other batteries from all parts of the
line. Field's First Corps division led the infantry displacement under
Longstreet, who had also been put in charge of those Third Corps units
cut off east of this morning's breakthrough. Assigned the rear-guard
duty, Gordon pulled his three divisions back in good order, with little
need for stealth and none at all for silence, since any noise his departing
soldiers made was drowned by the nightlong roar of Union guns, firing
all-out in apparent preparation for another dawn assault; an assault
which, if made at all, would be made upon a vacuum. Beyond the river,
approaching a road junction whose left fork Longstreet had taken to
ease the crowding when his own corps took the right, Gordon came
upon Lee, dismounted and holding Traveller's rein in one gauntleted

hand. All the troops left in Petersburg at sundown — fewer than 15,000 of all arms — would pass this way, and the gray-bearded commander had chosen this as his post for supervising the final stage of the evacuation. About the same number of graybacks were in motion elsewhere, miles away in the chilly early-April darkness. Kershaw was with Ewell up in Richmond, withdrawing too by then, along with reservists from the capital fortifications, guncrews from the heavy batteries on James River, and even a battalion of sailors, homeless landsmen now that they had burned their ships to keep them out of enemy hands. Mahone was on the march from Bermuda Hundred, just to the north, and Anderson presumably was working his way west along the opposite bank of the Appomattox with the remnants of Johnson's and Pickett's divisions, as well as parts of Hill's two, driven in that direction by the collapse of his line at daybreak, and Fitz Lee's troopers. South of the river, from point to scattered point along the otherwise empty eight-mile curve of intrenchments, the pickets kept their shell-jarred vigil. Soon now they too would be summoned rearward and engineer details would carry out their work of demolition, first on the abandoned powder magazines and then on the bridges, which were to be fired when the last man crossed, leaving Petersburg to the bluecoats who, at a cost of well over 40,000 casualties, had been doing all they could to take it for the past two hundred and ninety-three days.

Lee did not wait for that. About an hour before midnight, having observed that both gray columns were well closed up as they slogged past him there in the fork of the two roads, he mounted and set out westward for Amelia Courthouse, just under forty miles away.

By that time, up in the capital, Davis and his cabinet were departing from the railway station where, two nights ago, he had seen his wife and children off for Charlotte, three hundred miles to the southwest. His own destination was Danville, half as far away, just short of the North Carolina line. That was to be the new seat of government at least until Lee and his army got there, en route to a combination with Johnston; at which time another shift would no doubt be required, though how far and in what direction — still within or else beyond the borders of the Old Dominion, every vestige of whose "sacred soil" would in the latter case be given over to the invader — no one could say at this stage of a crisis that had become acute some twelve hours earlier, when a War Department messenger brought to the presidential pew in St Paul's Church, midway through the morning service, Lee's telegram advising that "all preparation be made for leaving Richmond tonight."

Nearby worshipers saw "a sort of gray pallor creep over his face" as he read the dispatch, then watched him rise and stride back down the aisle "with stern set lips and his usual quick military tread." Some few rose to follow, knowing the summons must be urgent for him to leave before taking Communion this first-Sunday; but for the most part, he said later, "the congregation of St Paul's was too refined to make a scene at anticipated danger." He went directly to the War Office to confer with Breckinridge and other cabinet members available at short notice on the Sabbath. One such was Judah Benjamin, who strolled over from his quarters on North Main, apparently unperturbed, "his pleasant smile, his mild Havana, and the very twirl of his slender gold-headed cane contributing to give casual observers an expression of casual confidence."

Davis's manner was almost as calm, though by no means as debonair, as he told the assembled ministers of the breaking of Lee's line and the impending evacuation, then directed them to have their most valuable records packed for delivery to the Richmond & Danville Depot, where they would meet that evening for departure as a group. Special instructions for the Treasury Department covered the boxing of Confederate funds on hand — some $528,000 in double-eagle gold pieces, Mexican silver coins, gold and silver bricks and ingots — for shipment aboard a special train, with a guard of sixty midshipmen from their academy training vessel *Patrick Henry*. These last would of course be furnished by Mallory, who was also told to pass the word for Raphael Semmes to see to the destruction of this and all other ships of the James River Squadron, iron and wood; after which their crews would proceed to Danville for service under Lee.

Later that afternoon, his desk cleared and his office put in order for tomorrow's faceless blue-clad occupant — Grant himself, for all he knew, or whoever else would command the occupation force — Davis set out through Capitol Square for the last of his familiar homeward walks to the White House, where he still had to pack for the journey south. More people were abroad today than usual, but they were strangely quiet, shocked by rumors that they and their city were about to be abandoned to the foe. Asked if it was true, he replied that it was, adding however that he hoped to return under better auspices. Some wept at the news, while others replaced false hope with resolution. "If the success of the cause requires you to give up Richmond, we are content," one matron came out of her house to tell him as he walked by, and he afterwards declared that "the affection and confidence of this noble people in the hour of disaster were more distressing to me than complaint and unjust censure would have been."

At the mansion there was much to do, including the disposition of certain effects he could not take with him yet did not want to have fall into enemy hands: the family cow, for instance, lent by a neighbor and now returned: a favorite easy chair, which he had carted to Mrs R. E. Lee's home on Franklin Street with a message expressing hope that it would comfort her arthritis: an oil painting, "Heroes of the Valley," and a marble bust of Davis himself, both turned over to a friend who offered to put them where "they will never be found by a Yankee." While a servant packed his valise he gave final instructions to the housekeeper, emphasizing that everything must be in decent order, swept and dusted, when the Federals arrived to take possession tomorrow morning. This done, he dressed carefully — trousers and waistcoat of Confederate gray, a dark Prince Albert frock coat, polished Wellingtons, a full-brimmed planter's hat — brushed his hair and tuft of beard, and waited in his pale-rugged private office — long the terror of muddy-booted officers reporting from the field — for word that the special train was ready for boarding. Shortly after 8 o'clock it came. He went out the front door and down the steps, mounted his saddle horse Kentucky, and set out for the railway station beside the James on the far side of town.

The ride was just over half a mile through crowded streets, and his impressions now were very different from those he had received four hours ago, in the course of his walk home from Capitol Square. Numbed decorum had given way to panic, a hysteria that grew more evident as he drew near the river and the depot. Government warehouses stocked with rations for the anticipated siege were there, and word had spread that the food was to be distributed to the public, on a first-come first-served basis, before the buildings were destroyed along with whatever remained in them by the time the army left. Some among those gathered were marauders out for spoils in the business district, their number swollen by convicts who, deserted by their guards, had broken out of jail and were rifling shops for clothing to replace their prison garb; "a crowd of leaping, shouting demons," one observer called these last, "in parti-colored clothes and with heads half-shaven. . . . Many a heart which had kept its courage to this point quailed at the sight." All in all, another witness would declare, this was "the saddest of many of the sad sights of war — a city undergoing pillage at the hands of its own mob, while the standards of an empire were being taken from its capitol and the tramp of a victorious enemy could be heard at its gates." Davis rode on, forcing his way through the throng, and finally reached the station. There the cabinet awaited his arrival; all but Breckinridge, who would remain behind to supervise the final stages of the evacuation, then follow Lee to observe and report on the military situation before rejoining his colleagues at Danville, or wherever they might be by then.

All got aboard the waiting coach, but there was another long delay while the treasure train, preceding them with its cargo of precious metals and its sixty nattily-uniformed midshipmen, cleared the southbound track and the bridge across the James. Glum but resigned, the ministers took their seats on the dusty plush. Trenholm, down with neuralgia and attended by his wife, the only woman in the party, had brought along a demijohn of peach brandy, presumably for medicinal purposes though it helped to ease the tension all around: especially for Benjamin, who smiled in his curly beard as he spoke from his fund of historical examples of other national causes that had survived reverses even more dismal than the one at hand. Mallory however remained somber, aware that the flotilla he had improvised for the capital's defense — three small ironclads and half a dozen wooden vessels — would be abolished, by his own orders, before dawn. By contrast, Attorney General George Davis was limited to theoretical regrets, his department having existed only on paper from the outset: and paper, unlike ships, could be replaced. Finally, at 11 o'clock — as Lee headed Traveller west from the road-fork on the near side of the Appomattox, twenty miles to the south — the train creaked out of the station. While the gaslit flare of Richmond faded rearward beyond the river, the fleeing President could reflect on the contrast between his departure tonight and his arrival, four bright springs ago, when the city had been festooned with flowers to bid him welcome. Whatever he was thinking, though, he kept his thoughts to himself. So did John Reagan, the selfmade Texan who had kept the mail in motion, if not on time, throughout the shrinking Confederacy all those years. He chewed morosely at his habitual quid, a colleague would recall, "whittling a stick down to the little end of nothing without ever reaching a satisfactory point."

Behind them as the train crept southward, worn wheels clacking on worn track, Richmond trembled for the last time from the tramp of gray-clad soldiers through her streets; Ewell was leaving, and only a cavalry rear guard, a small brigade of South Carolina troopers, stood between the city and some 20,000 bluecoats confronting the unmanned fortifications north of the James. On their way through town, demolition squads set fire to tobacco warehouses near the river, while others stood by to put the torch to buildings stocked with munitions of all kinds. City officials protested, but to no avail; the army had its orders, and no ranking member of the government was available to appeal to, all having left by midnight except John A. Campbell, who was not available either; he had last been seen at sundown, talking rapidly to himself as he walked along 9th Street with two books under his arm. A south wind sprang up, spreading flames from the burning tobacco, and soon the great waterside flour mills were on fire. Around 2 o'clock, a huge explosion jolted the city with the blowing of a downstream magazine, followed presently by another, closer at hand, that shattered plate glass windows all over Shockoe Hill. This last was a sustained eruption, volcano-like in its violence, for its source was the national arsenal, reported to contain 750,000 loaded projectiles, which continued to go off for hours. "The earth seemed fairly to writhe as if in agony," a diarist recorded; "the house rocked like a ship at sea, while stupendous thunders roared around." When the three ironclads went, near Rocketts Landing shortly afterward, Semmes pronounced the spectacle "grand beyond description," especially the one produced by his flagship, C.S.S. *Virginia Number 2*. "The explosion of her magazine threw all the shells, with their fuses lighted, into the air. The fuses were of different lengths, and as the shells exploded by twos and threes, and by the dozen, the pyrotechnic effect was very fine." By then both railway bridges were long lines of fire, reflected in the water that ran beneath them. Only Mayo's Bridge remained, kept open for the rear guard, though barrels of tar were stacked at intervals along it, surrounded by pine knots for quick combustion when the time came. At last it did. Shortly after dawn, having seen the last of his troopers across, the South Carolina brigadier rode out onto the span and touched his hat to the engineer in charge. "All over. Goodbye. Blow her to hell," he said, and trotted on.

From where he stood, looking back across the river at the holo-caust in progress along Richmond's waterfront, a butternut horseman afterwards observed, "The old war-scarred city seemed to prefer an-nihilation to conquest." What was more, she appeared well on the way toward achieving it. Both the Haxall and Gallego mills, reportedly the largest in the world, were burning fiercely, gushing smoke and darting tongues of flame from their hundreds of windows, while beyond them, after spreading laterally the better part of a mile from 8th to 18th streets, the fire licked northward from Canal to Cary, then on to Main, dispossessing residents and driving looters from the shops. Within this "vista of desolation," known henceforward as "the burnt district," prac-tically everything was consumed, including two of the capital's three newspaper offices and plants. Only the *Richmond Whig* survived to continue the long-term verbal offensive against the departed govern-ment. "If there lingered in the hearts of our people one spark of affec-tion for the Davis dynasty," its editor would presently declare, "this ruthless, useless, wanton handing over to the flames [of] their fair city, their homes and altars, has extinguished it forever." But that was written later, under the once-dread Union occupation. Just now, with the Confederate army gone and the fire department unequal to even a fraction of the task at hand, the only hope of stopping or containing the spread of destruction lay with the besiegers out on the city's rim, who perhaps would restore order when they arrived: if, indeed, they arrived in time for there to be anything left to save.

They barely did, thanks to the lack of opposition and an urgent plea by the mayor himself that they not delay taking over. From near the crest of Chimborazo, easternmost of Richmond's seven hills, a hospital matron watched the first of the enemy infantry approach. "A single bluejacket rose over the hill, standing transfixed with astonishment at what he saw. Another and another sprang up, as if out of the earth, but still all remained quiet. About 7 o'clock there fell upon the ear the steady clatter of horses' hoofs, and winding around Rocketts came a small and compact body of Federal cavalry in splendid condition, riding closely and steadily along." At that distance she did not perceive that the enemy troopers were black, but she did see, moving out the road at the base of the hill to meet them, a rickety carriage flying a white flag. In it was eighty-year-old Mayor Joseph Mayo. Dressed meticulously, as another witness remarked, "in his white cravat and irrepressible ruffles, his spotless waistcoat and his blue, brass-buttoned coat," he had set out from Capitol Square with two companions to urge the invaders to hasten their march, which he hoped would end with their bringing the mob and the fire under control, and he took with him, by way of authentication, a small leather-bound box containing the seal of the city he intended to surrender.

About that time — already some eight hours behind schedule, with other delays to follow — the presidential special crossed the Roanoke River and rolled creakily into Clover Station, two thirds of the way to Danville. A young lieutenant posted there had watched the treasure train go through at daybreak, loaded with bullion and cadets, and now came the one with the Chief Executive and his ministers aboard, all obviously feeling the strain of a jerky, sleepless night. "Mr Davis sat at a car window. The crowd at the station cheered. He smiled and acknowledged their compliment, but his expression showed physical and mental exhaustion." Finally the engine chuffed on down the track and over Difficult Creek, drawing its brief string of coaches and boxcars. Others followed at various intervals. Increasingly as they went by, jammed to overflowing with the archives and employees of the Treasury Department, Post Office, and Bureau of War, the conviction grew in the young officer that all, or nearly all, was lost; "I saw a government on wheels." Moreover, as he watched the passage of car after car, burdened with "the marvelous and incongruous débris of the wreck of the Confederate capital," it seemed to him that each grew more bizarre in its contents than the one before — as if whoever was loading them was getting closer and closer to the bottom of some monstrous grab bag. "There were very few women on these trains, but among the last in the long procession were trains bearing indiscriminate cargoes of men and things. In one car was a cage with an African parrot, and a box of tame squirrels, and a hunchback! Everybody, not excepting the parrot, was wrought up to a pitch of intense excitement." Then at last, near midday, the final train passed through. "Richmond's burning. Gone; all gone!" a man called from the rear platform, and it occurred to the lieutenant that Clover Station, within forty miles of the Carolina line, "was now the northern outpost of the Confederacy."

This was to discount or overlook Lee, whose army was even then making its way west from Richmond and Petersburg to converge on Amelia Courthouse, sixty miles back up the track. Davis, when he reached Danville in the midafternoon, did not make that mistake. Weary though he was — the normal four-hour run had taken just four times that long, and sleep had been impossible, what with the cinders and vibration, not to mention the crowds at all the many stops along the way — he had no sooner established headquarters in a proffered residence on Main Street than he set out on an inspection tour of the nearly four-year-old intrenchments rimming the town. Finding them "as faulty in location as in construction," he said later, "I promptly proceeded to correct the one and improve the other." So far, despite anxious inquiries, he had heard nothing of or from the general-in-chief, yet he was determined to do all he could to prepare for his arrival, not only by strengthening the fortifications Lee's men were expected to occupy around Danville, but also by collecting food and supplies with which to feed and refit them when they got there. "The design, as previously arranged with General Lee," he afterwards explained, "was that, if he should be compelled to evacuate Petersburg, he would proceed to Danville, make a new defensive line of the Dan and Roanoke rivers, unite his army with the troops in North Carolina, and make a combined attack upon Sherman. If successful," Davis went on, "it was expected that reviving hope would bring reinforcements to the army, and Grant being then far removed from his base of supplies, and in the midst of a hostile population, it was thought we might return, drive him from the soil of Virginia, and restore to the people a government deriving its authority from their consent."

Although this was unquestionably a great deal to hope or even wish for, it was by no means out of proportion to his needs; that is, if he and the nation he represented were to survive the present crisis. He went to bed that night, still with no word from Lee or any segment of his army, and woke Tuesday morning, April 4, to find that none had come in, either by wire or by courier, while he slept. Around midday Raphael Semmes arrived with 400 crewmen from the scuttled James flotilla; Davis made him a brigadier, reorganized his sailors into an artillery brigade, and put him in charge of the Danville fortifications, with orders to defend and improve them pending Lee's arrival from Amelia, one hundred miles to the northeast. This done, he retired to his office to compose a proclamation addressed "To the People of the Confederate States of America," calling on them to rally for the last-ditch struggle now so obviously at hand.

"It would be unwise, even if it were possible, to conceal the great moral as well as material injury to our cause that must result from the occupation of Richmond by the enemy." He admitted as much from the outset, but promptly added: "It is equally unwise and unworthy of us, as patriots engaged in a most sacred cause, to allow our energies to falter, our spirits to grow faint, or our efforts to become relaxed under reverses, however calamitous. . . . It is for us, my countrymen, to show by our bearing under reverses how wretched has been the self-deception

of those who have believed us less able to endure misfortune with fortitude than to encounter danger with courage." Squaring his shoulders
for the test to come, he urged his compatriots to do likewise. "We have
now entered upon a new phase of the struggle, the memory of which is
to endure for all ages and to shed an increasing luster upon our country.
Relieved from the necessity of guarding cities and particular points, important but not vital to our defense; with an army free to move from point
to point and strike in detail the garrisons and detachments of the enemy;
operating in the interior of our own country, where supplies are more
accessible and where the foe will be far removed from his own base and
cut off from all succor in case of reverse, nothing is now needed to
render our triumph certain but the exhibition of our own unquenchable
resolve. Let us but will it, and we are free — and who, in the light of
the past, dare doubt your purpose in the future?" He asked that, then
continued. "Animated by that confidence in your spirit and fortitude
which never yet has failed me, I announce to you, fellow countrymen,
that it is my purpose to maintain your cause with my whole heart and
soul; that I will never consent to abandon to the enemy one foot of the
soil of any one of the States of the Confederacy. . . . If by stress of numbers we should ever be compelled to a temporary withdrawal from
[Virginia's] limits, or those of any other border State, again and again
will we return, until the baffled and exhausted enemy shall abandon in
despair his endless and impossible task of making slaves of a people
resolved to be free. Let us not then despond, my countrymen, but,
relying on the never-failing mercies and protecting care of our God, let
us meet the foe with fresh defiance, with unconquered and unconquerable hearts."

Davis himself said later that the appeal had been "over-sanguine"
in its expression of what he called his "hopes and wishes" for deliverance;
but to most who read it, South as well as North, the term was all too
mild. To speak of the present calamitous situation as "a new phase of the
struggle," which ultimately would result in the withdrawal of Grant's
"baffled and exhausted" armies, seemed now — far more than two
months ago, when Aleck Stephens applied the words to Davis's speech
in Metropolitan Hall — "little short of demention," if indeed it was
short at all. However, this was to ignore the alternative which to Davis
was unthinkable. He was no readier to submit, or even consider submission, than he had been when fortune's scowl was a broad smile. Now
as in the days when he played Hezekiah to Lincoln's Sennacherib, he
went about his duties as he saw them, his lips no less firmly set, his
backbone no less rigid.

Mainly, once the proclamation had been composed and issued,
those duties consisted of overseeing the pick-and-shovel work Brigadier
Admiral Semmes's landlocked sailors were doing on the fortifications
Lee and his men were to occupy when they arrived from Amelia. In the

two days since his and their abandonment of Petersburg and Richmond, there had been no news of them whatever. Davis could only wait, as he had done so often before, for some word of their progress or fate, which was also his.

★   ★   ★

Lincoln spent the better part of that Tuesday in the capital Davis had left two nights ago, and slept that night aboard a warship just off Rocketts Landing, where he had stepped ashore within thirty hours of the arrival of the first blue-clad troops to enter the city in four years. The two-mile walk that followed, from the landing to the abandoned presidential mansion — Weitzel had set up headquarters there, as chief of occupation, less than twelve hours after Davis's departure — was a fitting climax to three days of mounting excitement that began soon after sundown, April 1, when he learned of Sheridan's coup at Five Forks. "He has carried everything before him," Grant wired, exulting over the taking of "several batteries" and "several thousand" prisoners. Other trophies included a bundle of captured flags, which he sent to City Point that evening by a special messenger. Lincoln was delighted. "Here is something material," he said as he unfurled the shot-torn rebel colors; "something I can see, feel, and understand. This means victory. This *is* victory."

Mrs Lincoln had left for Washington that morning, frightened by a dream of her husband's that the White House was on fire, and Lincoln, perhaps feeling lonesome, had decided to sleep on board Porter's flag-ship *Malvern*, a converted blockade runner. As a result, having declined the admiral's offer of his own commodious quarters, he spent an uncomfortable night in a six- by four-foot cubicle whose built-in bunk was four inches shorter than he was. Asked next morning how he had slept, he replied somewhat ruefully: "You can't put a long blade into a short scabbard. I was too long for that berth." In the course of the day — Sunday, April 2 — Porter had the ship's carpenter take down the miniature stateroom and rebuild it, together with the bed and mattress, twice as wide and half a foot longer. Lincoln however knew nothing of this; he was up at the telegraph office, reading and passing along to Stanton in Washington a series of high-spirited messages from the general-in-chief. Lee's line had been shattered in several places; Grant was closing in on what remained; "All looks remarkably well," the general wired at 2 o'clock, and followed this with a 4.30 dispatch — Fort Gregg and Battery Whitworth had just been overrun — announcing that "captures since the army started out will not amount to less than 12,000 men and probably 50 pieces of artillery." He had no doubt he would take Petersburg next morning, and he urged the President to "come out and pay us a visit." Lincoln replied: "Allow me to tender to you, and all with you, the nation's grateful thanks for this additional and magnificent success. At your kind suggestion, I think I will visit you tomorrow."

Back aboard the *Malvern* after dark, he and Porter watched from her deck the flash of guns against the sky to the southwest, where Grant had ordered a dawn assault if Lee was still in Petersburg by then. "Can't the navy do something now to make history?" Lincoln asked, unsated by the daylong flow of good news from the front. The admiral pointed out that the fleet had quite enough to do in standing by to counter a downriver sally by the Richmond flotilla, but he did send instructions for all the ships above Dutch Gap to open on the rebel forts along both banks of the James. Presently the northwest sky was aglow with flashes too, and Lincoln, his impatience relieved to some degree, turned in for another presumably fitful sleep in the cramped quarters he did not yet know had been enlarged. Next morning, rising early and well rested, he announced that a miracle had happened in the night. "I shrunk six inches in length, and about a foot sideways," he told Porter, straight-faced.

Their laughter was interrupted by a dispatch Lincoln passed along to Stanton at 8 o'clock: "Grant reports Petersburg evacuated, and he is confident Richmond also is. He is pushing forward to cut off, if possible, the retreating army. I start to join him in a few minutes." Accompanied by Tad and a civilian White House guard, he also took Porter with him on the train ride to the outskirts of Petersburg, where Robert was waiting with an escort and horses for them to ride the rest of the way. Tightly shuttered, the town seemed deserted except for a few Negroes on the roam amid the wreckage; Robert explained that Meade had been told to leave only a single division in occupation while he pressed on after Lee with all the rest. Proceeding up Market Street, the riders came to a house where Grant was waiting on the porch. A staffer watched as the President "dismounted and came in through the gate with long and rapid strides, his face beaming." Grant rose and met him on the steps. When they had shaken hands and exchanged congratulations, Lincoln said with a smile: "Do you know, General, I have had a sort of a sneaking idea for some days that you intended to do something like this." Grant replied that, rather than wait for Sherman and his Westerners to come up from Goldsboro, he had thought it better to let the Armies of the Potomac and the James wind up, unassisted, their long-term struggle against Lee's Army of Northern Virginia. That way, he believed a good deal of sectional jealousy and discord, East and West, would be avoided. Lincoln nodded. He could see that now, he said, but his anxiety had been so great that he had not cared what help was given, or by whom, so long as the job got done.

They talked for more than an hour, not only of the pursuit in progress but also of the peace to come, and it seemed to the staffer, listening while the President spoke, that "thoughts of mercy and magnanimity were uppermost in his mind." Before long the yard was crowded with former slaves, drawn by reports that Lincoln was there in the flesh: proof, if proof was needed, of their sudden deliverance from bondage. Round-eyed, they looked at him, and he at them, intently, neither saying a word to the other. Grant was eager to be off, yet he lingered in hope of hearing that Richmond had been taken before he set out to join the long blue columns toiling westward on this side of the Appomattox, intent on intercepting Lee when he turned south, as Grant felt sure he would try to do, for a link-up with Johnston in North Carolina. Finally he could wait no longer. He and Lincoln shook hands and parted; Lincoln stood on the porch and watched him ride off down the street.

Near Sutherland Station, eight miles out the Southside Railroad, a courier overtook the general and handed him a message. He read it with no change of expression, then said quietly: "Weitzel entered Richmond this morning at half past eight." Word spread rapidly down the line of marchers, accompanied by cheers. "Stack muskets and go home!" some cried, although there was no slackening of the pace. At Sutherland, Grant stopped long enough to wire Sherman the news, adding that he was hard on the go for Burkeville, the railroad crossing where he would block the route to Danville. If Lee got there first, he told Sherman, "you will have to take care of him with the force you have for a while," but if Lee lost the race and was thus obliged to keep moving west toward Lynchburg, "there will be no special use in you going any farther into the interior." In other words, the Army of the Potomac would need no assistance in disposing of its four-year adversary, and two closing sentences reflected the pride Grant felt in what had been achieved these past two days. "This army has now won a most decisive victory and followed the enemy. This is all it ever wanted to make it as good an army as ever fought a battle."

Back at City Point by sundown, Lincoln found a telegram Stanton had sent that morning in response to the one informing him that the President intended to visit Grant in Petersburg. "Allow me respectfully to ask you to consider whether you ought to expose the nation to the consequences of any disaster to yourself in the pursuit of a treacherous and dangerous enemy like the rebel army. If it was a question concerning yourself only I should not presume to say a word. Commanding Generals are in the line of their duty running such risks. But is the political head of a nation in the same condition?" Amused by the Secretary's alarm, and no doubt even more amused by the thought of his reaction to what he now had in mind to do, Lincoln replied: "Yours received. Thanks for your caution, but I have already been to Petersburg, staid with Gen. Grant an hour & a half, and returned here. It is certain now that Richmond is in our hands, and I think I will go there tomorrow. I will take care of myself."

He did "go there tomorrow," Tuesday, April 4, but the added promise to "take care" went unkept — indeed, could scarcely *be* kept: partly because of the inherently dangerous nature of the expedition, which was risky in the extreme, and partly because of unforeseen developments, which included the subtraction of all but a handful of the men assigned to guard him on the trip upriver and into the fallen capital itself. Still he went, and apparently would not have it otherwise. Once he learned at breakfast that the fire and the mob had been brought under control by the force in occupation since about that time the day before, he was determined to be off. "Thank God I have lived to see this," he told Porter. "It seems to me that I have been dreaming a horrid dream for four years, and now the nightmare is gone. I want to see Richmond."

So they set out, Lincoln and Tad and the White House guard on board the flagship with Porter, escorted by the *Bat*, which brought along a complement of marines detailed to accompany the President ashore. Approaching Dutch Gap by noon, they cleared the farthest upstream Union installation within another hour and entered a more dangerous stretch of river. Swept by now of floating and underwater mines, which lay along the banks like stranded fish, the channel was littered with charred timbers, the bloated, stiff-legged carcasses of horses, and other wreckage that made for cautious navigation. Past Chaffin's Bluff, under the spiked guns of Fort Darling, the admiral found the unremoved Confederate obstructions afforded too narrow passage for either the *Malvern* or the *Bat*, both sidewheelers. Accordingly, unwilling to wait on the tedious clearance operations, he unloaded a twelve-oared barge, commandeered a naval tug to tow him and his guests the rest of the way to Richmond, and put thirty of the marines aboard her to serve as guards when they arrived. Near the city, however, the tug ran hard aground, and Porter decided to proceed under oars, leaving the stuck vessel and the marines behind. Amused by this diminution of the flotilla, Lincoln told a story about "a fellow [who] once came to ask for an appointment as a minister abroad. Finding he could not get that, he came down to some more modest position. Finally he asked to be made a tide-waiter. When he saw he could not get that, he asked for an old pair of trousers. It is well to be humble."

Porter was more amused by the joke than he was by a situation whose difficulty grew obvious when he put in at Rocketts, on the outskirts of the city, to find not a single Federal soldier anywhere in sight. Apparently the occupation did not extend this far from the hilltop Capitol, visible through rifts in the smoke from the burned-out district between the river and Capitol Square, an air-line mile and a half to the northwest. Perturbed — as well he might be, with who knew how many diehard rebels and wild-eyed fanatics on the prowl in the toppled citadel of secession, wanting nothing on earth so much as they did a shot or a swing at the hated Yankee leader in his charge — the admiral landed ten of the twelve oarsmen, leaving two to secure the barge, and armed them with carbines to serve as presidential escorts, six in front and four behind, during the uphill walk toward the heart of town, where he hoped to find more adequate protection. They comprised a strange group in that setting, ten sailors in short jackets and baggy trousers, clutching their stubby, unfamiliar weapons; tall Abraham Lincoln in his familiar long black tailcoat, made even taller by contrast with the stocky Porter, whose flat-topped seaman's cap was more than a foot lower than the crown of the high silk hat beside him; the civilian guard holding Tad by the hand, and Tad himself, twelve years old today and looking somewhat possessively around him, as if his father had just given him Richmond for a birthday present. Before they could start they were set upon by a dozen jubilant Negroes, including one old white-haired man who rushed toward Lincoln shouting, "Bless the Lord, the great Messiah! I knowed him as soon as I seed him. He's been in my heart four long years, and he come at last to free his children from their bondage. Glory, hallelujah!" With that, he threw himself at the President's feet, as did the rest, much to Lincoln's embarrassment. "Don't kneel to me," he said. "That is not right. You must kneel to God only, and thank Him for the liberty you will enjoy hereafter." They responded with a hymn, "All Ye People, Clap Your Hands," and Lincoln and the others waited through the singing before they set out on their climb toward Capitol Square.

Behind them, as they trudged, the dozen celebrants were joined by many dozens more, and up ahead, as news of the Emancipator's coming spread, still larger clusters of people began to gather, practically all of them Negroes. The White House guard, whose name was William Crook, grew more apprehensive by the minute. "Wherever it was possible for a human being to gain a foothold there was some man or woman or boy straining his eyes after the President," he would recall. "Every window was crowned with heads. Men were hanging from tree-boxes and telegraph poles. But it was a silent crowd. There was something oppressive in those thousands of watchers, without a sound either of welcome or of hatred. I think we would have welcomed a yell of defiance. I stole a sideways look at Mr Lincoln. His face was set. It had the calm in it that comes over the face of a brave man when he is ready for whatever may come." Within half an hour they passed Libby Prison, empty now, still with its old ship chandler's sign attached. "We'll pull it down!" someone offered, but Lincoln shook his head. "No; leave it as a monument," he said. Skirting the burned district just ahead, the group began climbing Capitol Hill, and it occurred to Crook that he and his companions "were more like prisoners than anything else." Presently they saw their first evidence of welcome from anyone not black. A young white woman stood on the gallery spanning the street in front of the Exchange Hotel, an American flag draped over her shoulders. But she was the exception. A few blocks farther on, "one lady in a large and elegant building looked a while, then turned away her head as if from a disgusting sight." For the most part, such houses were shuttered, curtains drawn across the windows; but there were watchers in them as well, peering out unseen. "I had a good look at Mr Lincoln," one young matron wrote a friend next day. "He seemed tired and old — and I must say, with due respect to the President of the United States, I thought him the ugliest man I had ever seen."

By now they had encountered their first Union soldier, a cavalryman idly sitting his horse and gawking like all the others in the crowd. "Is that Old Abe?" he asked Porter, who sent him to summon a mounted escort. Soon it came, and for the first time since the landing at Rocketts the group had adequate protection.

Lincoln continued to plod along with the shambling, flat-footed stride of a plowman, past the Governor's Mansion, then three more blocks out 12th Street to Weitzel's headquarters, the former Confederate White House. Sweaty and tired from his two-mile walk, he entered the study Davis had vacated two nights ago. Perhaps it was for this he had been willing to risk the danger — the likelihood, some would have said — of assassination in the just-fallen rebel capital: this moment of feeling, for the first time since his first inauguration, four years and one month ago today, that he now was President of the whole United States. One witness described him as "pale and haggard, utterly worn out," while another saw "a serious, dreamy expression" on his face. In any case, exhausted or bemused, he crossed the cream-colored rug and sank wearily into the chair behind his fugitive rival's desk. "I wonder if I could get a glass of water?" he inquired.

After a light midafternoon lunch, John A. Campbell, the only prominent member of the Confederate government remaining in Richmond, turned up to propose returning Virginia to the Union by means of an appeal to her elected officials, who knew as well as he did, he declared, that the war was lost and over. Lincoln had not been impressed by the Alabama jurist at Hampton Roads two months ago, but now that he came less as an envoy than as a supplicant, having reported his "submission to the military authorities," his acceptability was considerably improved. "I speak for Virginia what would be more appropriate for a Virginian," he said, and quoted: "When lenity and cruelty play for a kingdom, the gentler gamester is the soonest winner." Lincoln liked the sound of that, along with the notion of Old Dominion soldiers — including, presumably, R. E. Lee — being removed, by authority of their own state government, from those rebel forces still arrayed against him. He told the former Assistant Secretary of War that he would be staying overnight in Richmond and would confer with him next morning on the matter. Just now, though, he was joining Weitzel for a carriage tour of the fallen capital.

He sat up front with one of the three division commanders Ord had left behind; Tad and Porter sat in back with Brigadier General George F. Shepley, Weitzel's chief of staff and the newly appointed military governor of Richmond, a post for which he had been schooled by service as Ben Butler's right-hand man in Louisiana. Weitzel himself — another Butler trainee, from New Orleans to Fort Fisher — rode alongside the carriage with a cavalcade of some two dozen officers, line and staff, who comprised a guard of honor for the sightseeing expedition. Their first stop was Capitol Square, where they pulled up east of Thomas Crawford's equestrian statue of the first President, posed gazing west, with one bronze arm extended majestically southward. "Washington is looking at me and pointing at Jeff Davis," Lincoln said. Refugees huddled about the Square, guarding the few household possessions they had managed to save from yesterday's fire, and the Capitol had been looted by vandals and souvenir hunters, military and civilian. From there the carriage rolled through the burned district, whose streets were choked with toppled masonry and littered with broken glass, on down Cary Street to Libby Prison, which Lincoln had passed earlier on his way uptown. It held captive rebels now, and in fact had had no Federal inmates since last May, when they were transferred to a new prison down in Georgia; but the thought of what it once had been caused one horseman to remark that Jefferson Davis should be hanged. Lincoln turned and looked at him. "Judge not, that ye be not judged," he said quietly. Soon afterwards Weitzel took the opportunity to ask if the President had any suggestions as to treatment of the conquered people in his charge. Lincoln replied that, while he did not want to issue orders on the subject, "If I were in your place I'd let 'em up easy; let 'em up easy."

Suddenly there was the boom of guns a mile downriver, which to everyone's relief turned out to be the *Malvern*; she had made it through the rebel obstructions to drop anchor at last off Rocketts, and was firing a salute in celebration. Porter was especially relieved. He still considered the President's welfare his responsibility, and he was in a state of dread from the risk to which he had let him expose himself today. Refusing to take no for an answer, he insisted that Lincoln sleep that night aboard the flagship, where he could be isolated from all harm. Weary from the strain of a long, exciting day, his charge turned in shortly after an early dinner, and presumably got another good night's sleep in the refurbished stateroom, this time with a guard posted outside his door.

One hundred miles to the north, few citizens of his own capital got any such rest, either that night or the one before. Washington was a blaze of celebration, and had been so ever since midmorning yesterday, when a War Department telegrapher received from Fort Monroe, for the first time in four years, the alerting message: "Turn down for Richmond," meaning that he was to relieve the tension on the armature spring of his instrument so that it would respond to a weak signal. He did, and the dit-dahs came through, distant but distinct. "We took Richmond at 8.15 this morning." Church bells pealed; fire engines clattered and clanged through the streets. Locomotives in the yards and steamboats on the river added the scream of their whistles to the uproar. Schools dismissed; clerks spilled out of government buildings; extras hit the stands. "Glory!!! Hail Columbia!!! Hallelujah!!! Richmond Ours!!!" the *Star* exulted. Army batteries fired an 800-gun salute that went on forever, three hundred for Petersburg, five hundred more for the fall of the rebel capital, while the Navy added another hundred from its biggest Dahlgrens, rattling windows all over town. "From one end of Pennsylvania Avenue to the other," a reporter noted, "the air seemed to burn with the bright hues of the flag. . . . Almost by magic the streets were crowded with hosts of people, talking, laughing, hurrahing and shouting in the fullness of their joy. Men embraced one another, 'treated' one another, made up old quarrels, renewed old friendships, marched arm-in-arm singing and chatting in that happy sort of abandon which characterizes our people when under the influence of a great and universal happiness. The atmosphere was full of the intoxication of joy." Stanton gave a solemn, Seward a light-hearted speech, both wildly cheered by the celebrants outside their respective offices: especially when the former read a dispatch from Weitzel saying Richmond was on fire. What should he reply? "Burn it, burn it! Let her burn!" the cry came up. "A more liquorish crowd was never seen in Washington than on that night," the newsman declared, and told of seeing "one big, sedate Vermonter, chief of an executive bureau, standing on the corner of F and 14th streets, with owlish gravity giving fifty-cent 'shin plasters' to every colored person who came past him, brokenly saying with each gift, 'Babylon has fallen.' "

That was Monday. The formal celebration — or "grand illumination," as it was called — was set for the following evening. All day Tuesday, while Lincoln walked and rode through the cluttered streets of Richmond, workmen swarmed over Washington's public buildings, preparing them for the show that would start at dusk. When it came it was altogether worth the waiting. "This is the Lord's doing; it is marvellous in our eyes" was blazoned in huge letters on a gaslighted transparency over the western pediment of the Capitol, which glittered from its basement to its dome. City Hall, the Treasury, the Post Office, the Marine Barracks, the National Conservatory, the prisons along First Street, even the Insane Asylum, lonely on its hill, burned like beacons in the night.

All Washington turned out to cheer and marvel at the candle-light displays, but the largest crowd collected in front of the Patent Office, where flaring gas jets spelled out U N I O N across the top of its granite pillars. A speaker's stand had been erected at their foot; for this was the Republican mass rally, opened by Judge David Cartter of the district supreme court, who got things off to a rousing start by referring in racetrack terms to Jefferson Davis as "the flying rascal out of Richmond," by way of a warm-up for the principal speaker, Andrew Johnson. He had been lying rather low since the inauguration, yet he showed this evening that he had lost none of his talent for invective on short notice. He too mentioned Davis early on, and when his listeners shouted, "Hang him! Hang him!" the Vice President was quick to agree: "Yes, I say hang him twenty times." Nor was the rebel leader the only one deserving of such treatment. Others like him were "infamous in character, diabolical in motive," and Johnson had a similar prescription for them all, including confiscation of their property. "When you ask me what *I* would do, my reply is — I would arrest them, I would try them, I would convict them, and I would hang them.... Treason must be made odious," he declared; "traitors must be punished and impoverished."

Other remarks, public and private — all in heady contrast to Lincoln's "Let 'em up easy," spoken today in the other capital after the interview in which Campbell described "the gentler gamester" as "the soonest winner" — followed as the celebration went on into and through the night. Long after the candles had guttered out and the flares had been extinguished, serenaders continued to make the rounds and corks kept popping in homes and hotel bars all over town.

Headaches were the order of the day in Washington by 10 o'clock Wednesday morning, April 5; at which time, as agreed on yesterday, the President received the Alabama jurist aboard the *Malvern*, riding at anchor off Rocketts Landing. Campbell brought a Richmond lawyer with him, Gustavus Myers, a member of the Virginia legislature, and their suggestion was that this body, now adjourned and scattered about the state, be reassembled for a vote withdrawing the Old Dominion from the Confederacy and formally returning her to her old allegiance. Weitzel, who was present, later summarized their proposal. "Mr Campbell and the other gentleman assured Mr Lincoln that if he would allow the Virginia Legislature to meet, it would at once repeal the ordinance of secession, and that then General Robert E. Lee and every other Virginian would submit; that this would amount to virtual destruction of the Army of Northern Virginia, and eventually to the surrender of all the other rebel armies, and would assure perfect peace in the shortest possible time."

Lincoln liked the notion, in part because it provided a way to get local government back in operation, but mainly because it offered at least a chance of avoiding that "last bloody battle" Grant and Sherman had told him would have to be fought before the South surrendered. Accordingly, he gave Campbell a document repeating his three Hampton

Roads conditions —"restoration of the national authority throughout all the states"; "no receding by the Executive on the slavery question"; "no cessation of hostilities short of an end to the war and the disbanding of all forces hostile to the government" — in return for which, confiscations of property would be "remitted to the people of any state which shall now promptly and in good faith withdraw its troops and other support from further resistance." In addition, though he declined to offer a general amnesty, he promised to use his pardoning power to "save any repentant sinner from hanging." Finally he agreed to reach an early decision in regard to permitting the Virginia legislators to reassemble.

This last he did next day, informing Weitzel that "the gentlemen who have acted as the legislature of Virginia, in support of the rebellion, may now desire to assemble at Richmond and take measures to withdraw the Virginia troops and other support from resistance to the general government. If they attempt it, give them permission and protection, until, if at all, they attempt some action hostile to the United States, in which case you will notify them and give them reasonable time to leave. . . . Allow Judge Campbell to see this, but do not make it public." Sending word to Grant of his decision, he added: "I do not think it very probable that anything will come of this, but I have thought it best to notify you, so that if you should see signs you may understand them," then closed with the familiar tactical warning: "Nothing I have done, or probably shall do, is to delay, hinder, or interfere with you in your work."

He was back at City Point by then, having steamed downriver at Porter's insistence as soon as the meeting with Campbell ended. Today — Thursday — made two full weeks he had been gone from Washington, and in response to a wire from Seward the day before, offering to come down for a conference on several matters "important and urgent in conducting the government but not at all critical or serious," he had informed the Secretary: "I think there is no probability of my remaining here more than two days longer. If this is too long come down." For one thing, he was awaiting the arrival next day of Mrs Lincoln. Having found her husband's dream of a White House fire a false alarm, she was returning with a number of distinguished visitors, all eager for a look at fallen Richmond. This might prolong his stay; or so he thought until bedtime Wednesday, when he received news that threatened to cut his vacation even shorter than he had supposed. Seward, he learned, had been thrown from his carriage that afternoon and had been so seriously injured, it was feared, that Lincoln might have to return to Washington at once. A follow-up wire from Stanton next morning, however, informed him that while the New Yorker's injuries were painful they were almost certainly not fatal; Lincoln could stay away as long as he chose. So he went down to the wharf at noon, this April 6, to meet his wife and the party of sightseers she had brought along on the boatride down the coast.

Irked to find that her husband had already been to the rebel capital and would not be going there again, Mrs Lincoln decided to make the trip herself on the *River Queen*, which would afford overnight accommodations for her guests, Senator and Mrs Harlan, Attorney General Speed and his wife, Charles Sumner and a young French nobleman friend, the Marquis de Chambrun. They left that afternoon and reached Richmond in time for a cavalry-escorted tour of the city before returning to sleep aboard the *Queen*, anchored in the James. Sumner was especially gratified by all he had seen, including the looted Capitol, where he asked in particular to examine the ivory gavel of the Congress. When it was brought he put it in his pocket — as a souvenir, or perhaps as further recompense for the caning he had suffered at the hands of Preston Brooks, nine years ago this spring — and brought it back with him to City Point next morning. Once more Lincoln was waiting on the dock, this time with an offer to take them by rail to Petersburg for a look at what ten months of siege and shelling had accomplished.

He was in excellent spirits, Harlan noted. "His whole appearance, pose, and bearing had marvelously changed. He was, in fact, transfigured. That indescribable sadness which had previously seemed to be an adamantine element of his very being had been suddenly changed for an equally indescribable expression of serene joy, as if conscious that the great purpose of his life had been attained." Partly this was the salutary effect of being removed for two full weeks from Washington and the day-in day-out frets that hemmed his White House office there, but a more immediate cause was a series of dispatches from Grant, all of them so encouraging to Lincoln that, in telling the general of his decision to let the Virginia legislature assemble, he remarked that Grant seemed to be achieving on his own, by "pretty effectually withdrawing the Virginia troops from opposition to the government," what he had hoped the legislators would effect by legal action. Not only had the blue pursuers won the race for Burkeville, thereby preventing Lee from turning south to combine with Johnston; they had also netted some 1500 grayback captives in the process. "The country is full of stragglers," Grant reported, "the line of retreat marked with artillery, burned or charred wagons, caissons, ambulances, &c." Gratifying as this was, he capped the climax with a wire sent late the night before, telling of a victory scored that afternoon by Humphreys, Wright, and Sheridan, some eight miles beyond Burkeville. Five rebel generals had been taken, including Richard Ewell and Custis Lee, along with "several thousand prisoners, fourteen pieces of artillery with caissons, and a large number of wagons." Such were the spoils listed by Sheridan in a message Grant passed along to Lincoln. "If the thing is pressed," the cavalryman urged his chief in closing, "I think Lee will surrender." Lincoln's enthusiasm soared, and he replied at 11 o'clock this Friday morning, about the time his wife and her guests returned from their overnight cruise to Richmond: "Sheridan says, 'If the thing is pressed I think that Lee will surrender.' Let the *thing* be pressed."

Two distractions, one slight and rather easily dismissed, the other a good deal more poignant in effect, broke into this three-day span of high good feeling. The first was a note from Andrew Johnson, who had come down on an army packet, now anchored nearby, and wanted to pay the President a visit before proceeding upriver for a tour of the fallen capital. Lincoln frowned, having read in the Washington papers of the Tennessean's call for all-out vengeance in his speech at the Republican mass rally Tuesday night. "I guess he can get along without me," he said distastefully, and did not reply to the note. That had been yesterday afternoon, and the second distraction followed that evening. He was taking the air after supper on the top deck of the *Malvern*, once more in a happy frame of mind, when he looked down from the rail and saw a group of rebel prisoners being loaded for shipment north aboard a transport moored alongside. The guard Crook, with him as usual, watched them too. "They were in a pitiable condition, ragged and thin; they looked half starved. When they were on board they took out of their knapsacks the last rations that had been issued to them before capture. There was nothing but bread, which looked as if it had been mixed with tar. When they cut it we could see how hard it was and heavy. It was more like cheese than bread." He watched, and as he did so he heard Lincoln groan beside him: "Poor fellows. It's a hard lot. Poor fellows." Crook turned and looked at his companion. "His face was pitying and sorrowful. All the happiness had gone."

Next morning's dispatch from the general-in-chief revived his genial spirits. "Let the *thing* be pressed," he replied, echoing Sheridan, and looked forward to the brightest news of all, which would be that Lee had at last been run to earth. Once that happened, he believed, commanders of other gray armies were likely to see the folly of further resistance on their part — if, indeed, they managed to survive that long. Developments elsewhere finally seemed to be moving at a pace that matched the stepped-up progress of events here in Virginia: particularly in South and Central Alabama. Canby had a close-up grip on Mobile's outer defenses, Spanish Fort and Fort Blakely, whose fall would mean the fall of the city in their rear, and he was preparing to assault, with results that were practically foregone, considering his better than four-to-one numerical advantage. Similarly — and incredibly, in the light of what had happened to those who tried it in the past — James Wilson, after crossing the Black Warrior, then the Cahaba, had driven Bedford Forrest headlong in the course of a two-day running skirmish, fifty miles in length, to descend on Selma, April 2, the day Richmond itself was abandoned. By now the all-important manufactories there were a mass of smoking rubble, and Wilson had his troopers hard on the go for Montgomery, where the Confederacy began. Neither Canby nor Wilson had started in time to be of much help to each other, as originally intended; nor had Stoneman crossed the Smokies in time to strike in Johnston's rear for Sherman's benefit. But now, in accordance with Grant's revised instructions, he turned his raiders north for Lynchburg, where Lee was apparently headed too.

No wonder, then, that Harlan found Lincoln "transfigured" as he stood on the dock at City Point to welcome his wife and her guests back from Richmond, or that he took increased encouragement from what he saw on the trip to Petersburg that afternoon. "Animosity in the town is abating," he told Chambrun; "the inhabitants now accept accomplished facts, the final downfall of the Confederacy and the abolition of slavery. There still remains much for us to do, but every day brings new reason for confidence in the future."

Aboard the *River Queen* that night — April 7; Good Friday was a week away — Elihu Washburne, en route to the front for another visit with Grant, whose rise he had done so much to promote through the first three years of a war that now had stretched to nearly four, called on Lincoln and found him "in perfect health and exuberant spirits," voluble in recounting for his guests the events of the past week, including his walk through the streets of Richmond. "He never flagged during the whole evening," the Illinois congressman would recall. Chambrun, however — a liberal despite his privileged heritage and the conservative domination of his homeland under the Second Empire — observed in his host contrasting traits often remarked by others in the past: Crook for one, just the night before, and Sherman at the conference held on this same vessel, ten days back. "He willingly laughed either at what was being said to him, or at what he said himself," the Frenchman later wrote. "But all of a sudden he would retire within himself; then he would close his eyes, and all his features would bespeak a kind of sadness as indescribable as it was deep. After a while, as though it were by an effort of his will, he would shake off this mysterious weight under which he seemed bowed; his generous and open disposition would again reappear. In one evening I happened to count over twenty of these alternations and contrasts."

Part of this intermittent sadness no doubt came from realization that he was approaching the end of the only real vacation he had taken in the past four years. All day Saturday preparations went forward for departure of the *Queen* that night, including a thorough check on the records of her crew, ordered by Porter in reaction to the belated fright he felt at the risk he had run in taking the President to and through the rebel capital, all but unescorted. That evening a military band came on board for a farewell concert. After several numbers, Lincoln requested the "Marseillaise," which he liked so well that he had it repeated. "You must, however, come over to America to hear it," he said wryly to the young marquis, knowing the Emperor had banned the piece in France. Then he called for "Dixie," much to the surprise of his guests and the musicians, as well as to listeners in the outer darkness on the docks and blufftop. "That tune is now Federal property," he told Chambrun. An hour before midnight, the *Queen* cast off and began to steam down the winding moonlit river, escorted by the *Bat*. Reaching Hampton Roads before dawn, she stopped long enough to board a pilot at Fort Monroe and was off again by sunrise, up Chesapeake Bay toward the mouth of the Potomac.

It was April 9; Palm Sunday. Eastward the sky was a glory of red, but the rising sun was presently dimmed by clouds rolling in from the sea with a promise of rain. The President and his guests rose early, and after breakfast went on deck to watch the gliding tableau of the ʳ' oreline. Soon after they entered the Potomac, paddle wheels churning ₐgainst the current, they passed Stratford Hall, the birthplace of Robert Lee — presumably still in flight for his life, a hundred-odd miles to the southwest — and within the hour, on that same bank, saw the birth-sites too of Washington and James Monroe. Almost in view of the capital, as they steamed past Mount Vernon just at sundown, someone remarked that Springfield would someday be equally honored. Lincoln, who had been musing at the rail, came out of himself on hearing his home town mentioned. "Springfield!" he exclaimed. He smiled and said he would be happy to return there, "four years hence," and live in peace and tranquillity. Mainly though, according to Chambrun, "the conversation dwelt upon literary subjects." Lincoln read to the assembled group from what Sumner called "a beautiful quarto Shakespeare," mainly from *Macbeth*, perhaps his favorite, with emphasis on the scenes that followed the king's assassination.

> *"Duncan is in his grave;*
> *After life's fitful fever he sleeps well;*
> *Treason has done his worst: nor steel, nor poison,*
> *Malice domestic, foreign levy, nothing*
> *Can touch him further."*

He paused, then read the lines again, something in them responding to something in himself. After the reading he was again withdrawn, although presently when his wife spoke of Jefferson Davis—saying, as the staff officer had said five days ago in Richmond, "He must be hanged"—he replied, as he had then: "Judge not, that ye be not judged." Contradiction was risky in that direction, inviting "malice domestic" as it did, but he ventured to repeat it when they came within sight of the roofs of Washington and he heard her tell Chambrun, "That city is filled with our enemies." Lincoln made a gesture of impatience. "Enemies," he said, as if with the taste of something bitter on his tongue. "We must never speak of that."

Rain was coming down hard in the twilight by the time the steamer reached the wharf at the foot of Sixth Street. The President's carriage was waiting to take him to the White House, but he let Tad and Mrs Lincoln off there and went on alone to Seward's house, nearby on Franklin Square, where the Secretary lay recovering from the injuries he had suffered. They were extensive, the right shoulder badly dislocated, the jaw broken on both sides; the pain had been so great that he had been in delirium for three of the four days since his fall. Indeed, he was scarcely recognizable when his friend entered the upstairs bedroom to find him stretched along the far edge of the bed, his arm projected over the side to avoid pressure on the bruised socket, his face swathed in bandages, swollen and discolored, his jaw clamped in an iron frame for healing. "You are back from Richmond?" he said in a hoarse whisper, barely able to speak because of the damage and the pain. "Yes, and I think we are near the end at last," Lincoln told him. First he sat gingerly on the bed, then sprawled across it, resting on an elbow, his face close to Seward's while he described much that had happened down near City Point in the course of the past two weeks. He stayed half an hour, by which time the New Yorker had fallen into a feverish sleep. Then he came out, gesturing for silence in the hall, and tiptoed down the stairs to the front door, where his carriage was waiting to take him back to the White House.

Later that evening, undressing for sleep, he felt the familiar weariness all men feel on their first night home from a vacation. Then there came a knock, and he opened the bedroom door to find a War Department messenger in the hall with a telegram that made Lincoln forget that weariness had anything to do with living. It was from Grant and had been sent from a place called Appomattox Courthouse.

> April 9, 1865 — 4.30 p.m.
>
> Hon. E. M. Stanton,
> *Secretary of War:*
>
> General Lee surrendered the Army of Northern Virginia this afternoon upon terms proposed by myself. The accompanying additional correspondence will show the conditions fully.
>
> U. S. Grant,
> *Lieutenant General.*

✗ 4 ✗

What had begun as a retreat the previous Sunday night, when Lee abandoned Petersburg and Richmond with the intention of marching southwest beyond the Roanoke, developed all too soon into a race against Grant and starvation, which in turn became a harassed flight that narrowed the dwindling army's fate to slow or sudden death. For six days this continued, ever westward. Then on the seventh — April 9, Palm Sunday — Lee made his choice. The agony ended, as his opponent said in the bedtime telegram to Lincoln, "upon terms proposed by myself."

Few at the start, in the column he accompanied, apparently thought it would turn out so: least of all Lee himself, who told a companion when they took up the march on Monday morning: "I have got my army safely out of its breastworks, and in order to follow me, the enemy must abandon his lines and can derive no further benefit from his railroads or James River." Others felt a similar elation at their successful withdrawal across the Appomattox, unpursued, and the exchange of their cramped trenches for the spread-out landscape, where sunlight glittered on greening fields and new-fledged trees along the roadside. Whatever the odds, this was Chancellorsville weather, with its reminders of their old skill at maneuver. "A sense of relief seemed to pervade the ranks at their release from the lines where they had watched and worked for more than nine weary months," a staff brigadier would recall. "Once more in the open field, they were invigorated with hope, and felt better able to cope with their powerful adversary."

But that applied only to the central column, the 13,000 infantry under Longstreet and Gordon, Pendleton's 3000 cannoneers, and Mahone's 4000-man division on its way from Bermuda Hundred via Chesterfield Courthouse. Most of these 20,000 effectives had stood fast the day before, had conducted the nighttime withdrawal in good order, and had sustained their group identity in the process. It was different for the 6000 coming down from beyond the James with Ewell. Less than a third were veterans under Kershaw, while the rest — combined extemporaneously under Custis Lee, who had lately been promoted to major general though he had never led troops in action outside the capital defenses — were reservists, naval personnel, and heavy artillerymen, so unaccustomed to marching that the road in their rear was already littered with stragglers, footsore and blown from a single night on the go. Nor was their outlook improved by the view they had had, back over their shoulders the night before, of Richmond in flames on the far side of the river. Even so, they were in considerably better shape than the 3500 men with Anderson beyond the Appomattox, rattled fragments of the four divisions of Pickett, Johnson, Heth, and Wilcox, working their way west in the wake of Fitz Lee's 3500 jaded troopers on worse-than-jaded horses. Badly trounced at Five Forks, two days back, and scattered by yesterday's breakthrough on the right — which had now become the left — they had been whipped, and knew it. "There was an attempt to organize the various commands," a South

Carolina captain later said of this smallest and worst-off of the three infantry columns; "to no avail. The Confederacy was considered as 'gone up,' and every man felt it his duty, as well as his privilege, to save himself. I do not mean to say there was any insubordination whatever, but the whole left of the army was so crushed by the defeats of the past few days that it straggled along without strength and almost without thought. So we moved on in disorder, keeping no regular column, no regular pace. When a soldier became weary he fell out, ate his scanty rations — if, indeed, he had any to eat — rested, rose, and resumed the march when his inclination dictated. There were not many words spoken. An indescribable sadness weighed upon us. The men were very gentle toward each other, very liberal in bestowing the little of food that remained to them."

All that day, well into darkness, Anderson's fugitive survivors kept up their march northwest along the south bank of the Appomattox. Around midnight, when a halt was called at last, the weary captain watched as his men "fell about and slept heavily, or else wandered like persons in a dream. I remember, it all seemed to me like a troubled vision. I was consumed by fever, and when I attempted to walk I staggered about like a drunken man." A night's sleep helped, and Tuesday morning when they encountered Longstreet's veterans, crossing the river with Lee himself at the head of the central column, they were comforted to find that the rest of the army was by no means as badly off as they were. Small bodies of blue cavalry, attempting to probe their flank and interrupt the march, were driven off and kept at a respectful distance. "We revived rapidly from our forlorn and desolate feeling," the captain would recall.

Hunger was still a problem, to put it mildly, but there was also comfort for that; at any rate the comfort of anticipation. Amelia Courthouse lay just ahead on the Richmond & Danville, five miles west of the river, and Lee had arranged for meat and bread to be sent there from the 350,000 rations amassed in the capital in the course of the past two months. Or so he thought until he arrived, shortly before noon, to find a generous shipment of ordnance equipment — 96 loaded caissons, 200 crates of ammunition for his guns, and 164 boxes of artillery harness — waiting aboard a string of cars pulled onto a siding; but no food. His requisition had not been received, the commissary general afterwards explained, until "all railroad transportation had been taken up."

If Lee's face, as a cavalry staffer noted, took on "an anxious and haggard expression" at the news, it was no wonder. At the close of a march of nearly forty miles in about as many hours, with nothing to eat but what they happened to have with them at the outset or could scrounge along the way, he had 33,000 soldiers — the number to which his army, including reservists, had been reduced in the past ten days by

its losses at Fort Stedman and Five Forks and during the Sunday breakthrough, each of which had cost him just under or over 5000 men —
converging on a lonely trackside village where not a single ration could
be drawn. His only recourse was to call a halt while commissary details
scoured the countryside for such food as they could find. This they
soon began to do, armed with an appeal "To the Citizens of Amelia
County," signed *R. E. Lee* and calling on them "to supply as far as
each one is able the wants of the brave soldiers who have battled for
your liberty for four years."

In point of fact, there would have been a delay in any case, since
nothing had yet been heard from Ewell, and the rest of the army could
not push on down the railroad until this laggard column was on hand.
Meantime, Lee got off a telegram to Danville, directing the immediate
rail shipment of rations from the stores St John had waiting for him
there, though whether the requisition would get through was doubtful,
the wires having been cut near Jetersville, a hamlet six miles down the
track and twelve miles short of Burkeville. After supper, a message
came from Ewell announcing that he had been delayed by flooded
bridges; he expected to cross the Appomattox tonight and would arrive
next morning. Lee could do nothing but wait for him and the commissary wagons, hopefully loaded with whatever food had been volunteered or impressed. Even so, he was aware that he had lost a good part
of the head start he had gained when he slipped away from Grant
two nights ago, and knowledge of this, together with the anguish he felt
for the hungry troops still hobbling in, was reflected in his bearing.
"His face was still calm, as it always was," an artillery sergeant major
later wrote, "but his carriage was no longer erect, as his soldiers had
been used to see it. The troubles of these last days had already plowed
great furrows in his forehead. His eyes were red as if with weeping, his
cheeks sunken and haggard, his face colorless. No one who looked
upon him, as he stood there in full view of the disastrous end, can ever
forget the intense agony written upon his features."

Such distress was general that evening. While the wagon details
were out scouring the picked-over region for something the men or
animals could eat, the half-starved troops, bedded down in fields around
the rural county seat or still limping toward a concentration that should
have been completed before nightfall, evidenced a discouragement more
profound than any they had known in the darkest days of the siege
that now had ended. "Their strength was slowly drained from them," an
officer declared, "and despondency, like a black and poisonous mist,
began to invade the hearts before so tough and buoyant." Some were
taken with a restlessness, a sort of wanderlust that outweighed their
exhaustion: with the result that there were further subtractions from the
army's ranks. "Many of them wandered off in search of food, with no

thought of deserting at all. Many others followed the example of their government, and fled."

A hard shock followed next morning, April 5, when the foraging details came rattling back, their wagons all but empty. So thoroughly had Northrop's and St John's agents done their work these past ten months, impressing stock and grain to feed the trench-bound men at Petersburg, few of the farmers roundabout had anything left to give, even in response to a personal appeal from Robert Lee. Still, he had no choice except to keep moving. To stay where he was meant starvation, and every hour's delay was another hour's reduction of his head-start gain: if, indeed, there was any of it left. All the troops were up by now, and he had done what he could to ease the strain, including a culling of nearly one third of the 200 guns and 1000 wagons — which, fully spread out, covered more than twenty miles of road — to provide replacements for those draft animals exhaustion had subtracted from the teams needed to keep the other two thirds rolling; the culls were to be forwarded, if possible, by rail. A cold rain deepened the army's gloom when the fall-in sounded for still a third day of marching on empty stomachs. Longstreet took the lead, Gordon the rear-guard duty; Anderson and Ewell slogged between, while Fitz Lee's troopers ranged well to the front on their gaunt, weak-kneed horses, left and right of the railroad leading down to Danville, a hundred miles to the southwest.

Five of those miles from Amelia by early afternoon, the outriders came upon bluecoats intrenched in a well-chosen position just short of Jetersville, a dozen miles from Burkeville, where the Southside and the Danville railroads crossed. This was no surprise; enemy cavalry had been active in that direction yesterday. Longstreet shook out skirmishers, preparing to brush these vedettes from his path, but shortly before 2 o'clock, when Lee arrived, reports came back that the force in front amounted to a good deal more than cavalry. One corps of Union infantry was already on hand, in support of Sheridan's horsemen, and another was rapidly approaching. Lee's heart sank at the news. His adversary had won the race for the critical Burkeville crossing; he was blocked, and so were the rations he had ordered sent from Danville in hope of intercepting them en route. Regretfully he lowered his glasses from a study of the position, which he knew was too strong for an attack by his frazzled army, heavily outnumbered as it was by the three blue corps, with others doubtless hard on the way to join them. Rejecting the notion, if it crossed his mind, of going out in an Old Guard blaze of glory, he turned his thoughts to another plan of action — another route — still with the intention, or anyhow the hope, of combining with Joe Johnston somewhere to the south.

He would veer west, across the upper quadrant of the spraddled X described by the two railroads, to the vicinity of Farmville on the upper Appomattox, where rations could be sent to meet him, via the Southside line, from stores collected at Lynchburg by St John. Then, having fed his hungry men and horses, he would move south again, across the western quadrant of the X, bypassing the Burkeville inter- section — Grant's reported point of concentration — to resume his march down the Danville line for a combination with Johnston, beyond the Roanoke, before turning on his pursuers. Admittedly this was a long-odds venture, difficult at best. Farmville was five miles farther away than Burkeville, and he knew little of the roads he would have to travel, except that they were poor. Moreover, he was by no means sure that his half-starved troops and animals could manage a cross-country slog of perhaps twenty roundabout miles without food, especially since they would have to begin it with still another night march if he was to avoid being overtaken and overwhelmed, practically at the start. Here again, however, he had no choice but to attempt it or face the narrowed alternatives of surrender or annihilation. Accordingly, instructions for the westward trek went out; "the most cruel marching order the commanders had ever given the men in four years of fighting," a later observer was to say. As always, all that time, "Lee's miserables" re- sponded as best they could when the move began near sundown. "It is now a race for life or death," one wrote in his diary at the outset.

It was indeed. "Night was day. Day was night," a groggy can- noneer was to recall. "There was no stated time to sleep, eat, or rest, and the events of morning became strangely intermingled with the events of evening. Breakfast, dinner, and supper were merged into 'some- thing to eat,' whenever and wherever it could be found." Four miles out, a bridge collapsed into Flat Creek, stalling the guns and wagons for hours before it could be repaired, and though the infantry got over by fording, the discomfort of wet feet was added to those of hunger and exhaustion. Confusion and sleeplessness made the marchers edgy, quick to panic: as when a runaway stallion broke loose from a fence where he was tethered and came pounding down the road, the rail still tied to his rein. Abrupt and point-blank exchanges of fire by several units, in response to what they assumed was a night attack by Yankee cavalry, resulted in an undetermined number of casualties. Straggling was heavy, and many who kept going simply dropped their rifles as they hobbled along, too weak to carry them any farther, or else planted them by the roadside, bayonet down, each a small monument to determination and defeat.

Dawn showed the effects of this harrowing night, not only in the thinness of the army's ranks, but also in the faces of the survivors, the sullen lines of strain around their mouths, the red etchings of fatigue along their lower eyelids. Many staggered drunkenly, and some found, when they tried to talk, that their speech was incoherent. They had reached what later came to be called "poor old Dixie's bottom dollar," and for the most part they were satisfied that even that was spent. One of Longstreet's Deep South veterans put it strongest, dropping back toward the tail of the column as he struggled to keep up, tattered and barefoot, yet still with some vestige of the raucous sense of humor that had brought him this far along the four-year road he had traveled. "My shoes are gone; my clothes are almost gone. I'm weary, I'm sick, I'm hungry. My family has been killed or scattered, and may now be wandering helpless and unprotected." He shook his head. "I would die; yes, I would die willingly," he said, "because I love my country. But if this war is ever over, I'll be damned if I ever love another country!"

This was Grant's doing, the outcome of his steadiness and simplicity of purpose, designed to accomplish in short order the destruction of his opponent now that he had flushed him out of his burrow, into the open field, and had him on the run. He became again, in brief, the Grant of Vicksburg. "There was no pause, no hesitancy, no doubt what to do," a staff colonel afterwards declared. "He commanded Lee's army as much as he did ours; caused and knew beforehand every movement that Lee made, up to the actual surrender.... There was no let up; fighting and marching, and negotiating, all at once."

Mindful perhaps of Sherman's dictum, "A stern chase is a long one," the northern commander had decided at the outset that he stood to gain more from heading his adversary off than he did from pursuing him across the Appomattox. That way, once he was in his front, he could bag him entire, rather than engage in the doubtful and drawn-out process of attempting his piecemeal destruction by means of a series of attacks upon his rear, not to mention avoiding ambuscades at practically every step along the way. Moreover, a comparison of the two probable routes, Union and Confederate, showed clearly enough the advantage the former offered. Lee doubtless intended to assemble his army somewhere along the upper stretch of the Danville Railroad, with a march to follow down it, through Burkeville, for a combination with Johnston beyond the Carolina line. From all three of his starting points, Richmond, Bermuda Hundred, and Petersburg, the distance to Burkeville was just under sixty miles, and two of his three columns would have to make two time-consuming river crossings, one at the start and one near the end of the move toward concentration; whereas Grant's route, due west along the Southside Railroad, from Sutherland Station to Burkeville — blue chord of the gray arc — not only spanned no river, but was also twenty miles shorter; which in itself was enough to abrogate the head start Lee had gained by taking off at first-dark Sunday. Accordingly, before his meeting with Lincoln in Petersburg next morning, Grant issued orders for winning the race as he conceived it. Sheridan of course would lead, fanning out to the right to keep tabs on the graybacks still on the near side of the Appomattox, and

Griffin would press along in the wake of the troopers as fast as his men could manage afoot, under instructions to support them in any action that developed, whether defensive or offensive. Humphreys and Wright would follow Griffin, while Ord and Parke stuck to the railroad, the latter repairing track as he went, thereby providing an all-weather supply line that led directly into the moving army's rear.

Speed was the main requirement, and the blue-clad veterans gave it willingly. "We never endured such marching before," a footsore private later wrote. As a result, they won the Monday-Tuesday race with time to spare. By Wednesday morning, April 5, when Lee began his delayed movement down the railroad from Amelia, Griffin was in position athwart his path, in close support of Sheridan's dug-in troopers; Humphreys was coming up fast in his rear, and Wright was expected before sundown. Confronted thus by twice his dwindled number, Lee called a halt that afternoon, just short of Jetersville, and Meade — who had traveled by ambulance for the past two days, a victim of wrought-up nerves and indigestion — decided that the army's best course would be to get some food and rest, including a good night's sleep, then pitch into the rebel host next morning. Sheridan fumed at this imposed restraint; rest was the last thing on earth he wanted at that stage, either for his own soldiers or anyone else's, blue or gray. "I wish you were here," he protested in a message to Grant, who was with Ord, some twelve miles off at Nottoway Courthouse. "I feel confident of capturing the Army of Northern Virginia if we exert ourselves. I see no escape for Lee."

In response to the summons, Grant undertook a cross-country ride over unfamiliar ground, with no more escort than a quartet of staff officers and a squad of cavalry, but arrived too late to overrule Meade, if in fact that was what he had had in mind when he set out. In any case, next morning's dawn proved Little Phil's concern well founded; Lee was gone. He had swung westward on a night march, scouts reported, apparently headed for Farmville, eighteen miles away on the upper Appomattox and the Southside Railroad, down which he could draw supplies from Lynchburg, then continue his getaway toward the fastness of the Blue Ridge, or turn back south in a renewal of his effort to combine with Johnston. Such disappointment as Grant felt at this loss of contact, this postponement of the showdown that was to have been his reward for winning the race to Burkeville, was more than offset by another consideration, stated later: "We now had no other objective than the Confederate armies, and I was anxious to close the thing up at once." In other words, the race was now a chase — "a matter of legs," as the saying went — and he had confidence in the outcome, not only because he had had a chance to compare the legs of the two armies, these past three days on the march from Petersburg, but also because he understood the temper of his soldiers and the motive that impelled them. "They began to see the end of what they had been fighting four years for. Nothing seemed to fatigue them. They were ready to move without rations and travel without rest until the end. Straggling had entirely ceased, and every man was now a rival for the front."

Pursuit began without delay, and even before contact was reëstablished — first by Sheridan, whose horsemen lapped the rebel flank, probing for a gap, and then by Humphreys, whose lead division overtook the tail of the slow-grinding butternut column within a couple of hours of setting out — all the indications were that the course would not be long. Abandoned rifles and blanket rolls, cluttering the roadsides west of Amelia, testified to the weariness of the marchers who had carried them this far, while the roads themselves were clogged from point to point by broken-down or mud-stalled wagons, as well as by the creatures who had hauled them. "Dropped in the very middle of the road from utter exhaustion," one pursuer would recall, "old horses, literally skin and bones, [were] so weak as scarcely to be able to lift their heads when some soldier would touch them with his foot to see if they really had life." But the best, or worst, evidence in this regard was the condition of the stragglers encountered in increasing numbers as the chase wore on. Collapsed in ditches or staggering through the woods and sodden fields, near delirium from hunger and fatigue, they not only offered little resistance to being gathered up; they seemed to welcome capture as a comfort. For them at least the war was over, won or lost, and winning or losing made less difference than they had thought before they reached the end of their endurance. Not that all of them, even now, had abandoned the last vestige of that cackling sense of the ridiculous they had flaunted from the start, four years ago. A squad of well-clad, well-fed bluecoats, for example, descended on a tattered, barefoot North Carolina private who had wandered off, lone and famished, in search of food. "Surrender, surrender! We've got you!" they cried as they closed in with leveled weapons. "Yes, you've got me," the Tarheel scarecrow replied, dropping his rifle to raise his hands, "and a hell of a git you got."

Any army in this condition, more or less from top to bottom, was likely to stumble into some error that would cost it dearly, and that was what happened this April 6, known thereafter as the Black Thursday of the Confederacy. Longstreet, still in the lead, was under orders to march hard for Rice, a Southside station three miles short of the Appomattox, lest Ord's corps, reported to be on its way up the track from Burkeville, get there first and cut the hungry graybacks off from the rations St John had waiting for them at Farmville. Behind the First Corps train came Anderson, then Ewell, followed by the guns and wagons of the other three corps — so called, though none was larger than a division had been in the old days — including Gordon's, which had been fighting a rear-guard action against Humphreys since 8.30 that morning, west of the Flat Creek crossing where the march had been delayed. By then Old Peter had reached Rice at the head of his lead division, not only in advance of Ord but also in time to send Rosser's horsemen in pursuit of a flying column of 600 Federals who had just passed through on their way north to burn the bridges the army would need if it was to cross the river. This too was successful. Overtaken and surrounded, outnumbered two to one, the raiders — two regiments of infantry, sent forward by Ord with a squadron of cavalry — were killed or captured, to a man, before they reached their objective. The bridges were saved, along with the rations still awaiting the arrival of the half-starved troops approaching from the south and, presumably, the east.

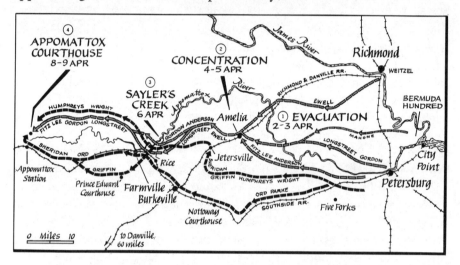

Lee's relief at this turn of events, which encouraged hope for a successful getaway, was soon replaced by tension from a new development, one that left him in the dark as to what might have happened to the other half of his army. Anderson, obliged to halt from time to time to fight off mounted attacks on his flank, had lost touch with Longstreet's rear; so that by noon, with three of the four First Corps divisions deployed near Rice to contest Ord's advance from the southeast, the gray commander could only guess at what might have occurred or be occurring rearward, beyond the gap Sheridan's troopers had created by delaying Anderson. There was mean ground in that direction, as Lee knew from just having crossed it: particularly between the forks of Sayler's Creek, which combined to flow into the Appomattox half a dozen miles below Farmville, athwart the westward march of all four corps. Riding north, then east in an attempt to find out for himself, he approached the point where the boggy little stream ran into the river, and saw beyond it a skirmish in progress between Gordon's rear-guard elements and heavy columns of blue infantry in pursuit. Not only was this dire in itself; it also deepened the mystery of the disappearance of Anderson and Ewell, supposedly on the march between Gordon and

Longstreet. Lee turned south and rode in search of them, only to encounter a staffer who informed him that enemy horsemen had struck
the unprotected train between the two branches of Sayler's Creek,
setting fire to wagons and creating panic among the teamsters. Eastward,
guns were booming in earnest now, and Lee still knew nothing as to the
fate or whereabouts of his two missing corps. "Where is Anderson?
Where is Ewell?" he said testily. "It is strange I can't hear from them."

It was worse than strange: far worse, he soon found out. Proceeding eastward with Mahone, whose division he summoned from its position in rear of Longstreet's other three near Rice, he topped a ridge
overlooking the valley of Sayler's Creek, and there he saw, spread out
below him and scrambling up the slope, the answer to his questions
about Anderson and Ewell. Union batteries were firing rapidly from a
companion ridge across the way, pounding the shattered remnant of
both gray corps as the fugitives streamed out of the bottoms where they
had met defeat; "a retiring herd," Mahone would later call them, made
up of "hurrying teamsters with their teams and dangling traces, infantry
without guns, many without hats — a harmless mob." Instinctively, Lee
straightened himself in the saddle at the sight. "My God!" he cried,
staring downhill at the worst Confederate rout he had seen in the thirty-
four months since Davis placed him in command amid the confusion
of Seven Pines. "Has the army been dissolved?"

That portion of it had at any rate, largely because of errors of
omission by the two corps commanders and the redoubled aggressiveness of the blue pursuers, mounted and afoot, once they became aware
of the resultant isolation of the graybacks slogging westward into the
toils of Sayler's Creek. Just as Anderson, in failing to notify Longstreet
of his need to stop and fight off cavalry attacks upon his flank, had
created the gap into which enemy troopers had plunged, so presently
had Ewell lost touch with Gordon through a similar oversight. Informed that the rear guard was heavily engaged, he too halted to let
part of the intervening train move on, then diverted the rest onto a
secondary road that led directly to High Bridge, where the railroad
crossed the Appomattox, three miles north of Rice, before looping back
to recross it at Farmville, four miles to the west. In resuming his march
to overtake Anderson, however, he neglected to tell Gordon of the
change: with the result that Gordon, still involved with the bluecoats
close in his rear, took the same route as the wagons he had been trailing
all along, unaware that he was alone, that his corps had become one of
three unequal segments into which Lee's army had been divided by this
double failure on the part of the two generals in charge of the central
segment. This was now the most gravely endangered of the three, though
neither of the two commanders knew it. Ewell, in fact, did not even
know that he had rear-guard duties until he came under fire from guns
of the VI Corps, which was coming up fast and massing for an assault

in conjunction with Sheridan's horsemen, still on Anderson's flank and cavorting among the burning wagons up ahead.

Sheridan had spotted the opportunity almost as soon as it developed. While Humphreys kept on after Gordon, pressing him back toward the crossing of the creek above the junction of its branches — this was the contest Lee had observed when he rode north from Rice in search of the missing half of his command — Little Phil sent word to Wright, whose corps was next in line, that together they could wipe out that portion of the rebel army stalled by his harassment of its flank and his probe of the resultant gap in front. Just then, about 2 o'clock, Anderson struck at Custer, who had made the penetration, and when Custer recoiled Sheridan threw in Devin to contain the drive. Then, hearing Wright's guns open against Ewell, a mile to the northeast, he committed Crook's division against Anderson's center, locked in position by Custer and Devin, front and rear. "Never mind your flanks," he shouted to his troopers as they dismounted for the assault. "Go through them! They're demoralized as hell."

He was right. Resistance by the jangled, road-worn survivors of the Petersburg breakthrough, four hungry days ago, was as brief and ineffectual as their commander later admitted when he reported that they "seemed wholly broken down and disheartened. After a feeble effort... they gave way in confusion." Only Wise's brigade of Virginians retired from the field as a military unit of any size. In all the rest it was more or less every man for himself, including those of highest rank; Anderson escaped on horseback, along with Pickett and Bushrod Johnson, but a solid half of the 3000 troops who had managed to stay with him this far on the retreat were killed or captured as they fled through the tangled brush and clumps of pine. Sheridan, leaving this roundup work to Custer, plunged on north with the other two divisions, intent on dealing with Ewell in much the same fashion. At Five Forks he had delivered the unhinging blow to Lee's army; now he was out to make Sayler's Creek the coup de grâce. And in fact that was what it came to, at least for that part of the bedraggled rebel host within his reach.

One-legged Ewell, strapped to the saddle to keep from falling off his horse, had his two undersized divisions facing east along the west side of the creek in an attempt to keep Wright from crossing before Anderson unblocked the road to Rice. Down to 3000 effectives as a result of the straggling by Custis Lee's reservists, he relied mainly on Kershaw's veterans in position on his right. Despite heavy shelling from the ridge across the way and mounting pressure from the three blue divisions in his front, he managed to hold his own until Kershaw's outer flank and rear were suddenly assailed by Sheridan's rapid-firing troopers, who had just overrun Anderson and came storming northward through the brush. "There's Phil! There's Phil!" the VI Corps infantrymen yelled as they splashed across the creek to join the attack being made by their old Valley comrades.

"On no battlefield of the war have I felt a juster pride in the conduct of my command," Joe Kershaw was to say, and Custis Lee was equally proud of what remained of his scratch division, though both saw clearly now that further resistance was useless. So did Ewell, who afterwards reported that "shells and even bullets were crossing each other from front and rear over my troops, and my right was completely enveloped. I surrendered myself and staff to a cavalry officer who came in by the same road General Anderson had gone out on." Some 200 of Kershaw's Georgians and Mississippians managed to escape in the confusion, but they were about all that got away. The rest were taken, along with their commanders at all levels. These 2800, combined with those lost earlier by Anderson, brought the total to 4300 graybacks snared in the fork of Sayler's Creek that afternoon. No wonder, then, that a Federal colonel visiting Sheridan's headquarters that evening found Richard Ewell "sitting on the ground hugging his knees, with his face bent down between his arms." Old Bald Head now bore little resemblance to the self he had been when he was Stonewall Jackson's mainstay, two years ago in the Shenandoah Valley. "Our cause is lost. Lee should surrender before more lives are wasted," he was reported to have told his captors. Watching him, the colonel remarked that "if anything could add force to his words, the utter despondency of his air would do it."

Sheridan provided a study in contrast. Elated, he got off a sundown message to Grant reporting the capture of one lieutenant general, two major generals, and three brigadiers, together with thousands of lesser prisoners, fourteen pieces of artillery, and an uncounted number of wagons. "I am still pressing on with both cavalry and infantry," he informed his chief, and added the flourish that would catch Lincoln's eye next morning: "If the thing is pressed I think Lee will surrender."

That might be, but Lee by then was in a better frame of mind than Sheridan supposed. Mahone, who was beside him on the western ridge when he exclaimed, in shock at what he saw in the valley down below, "My God! Has the army been dissolved?" replied stoutly, in reference to his division coming up behind: "No, General. Here are troops ready to do their duty." Lee at once recovered his composure, and turned his thoughts to preventing the enlargement of the disaster by the bluecoats in pursuit of the remnant of Anderson's corps streaming toward him up the hillside. "Yes, General," he said; "there are some true men left. Will you please keep those people back?"

Leaving Mahone to prepare a line of defense against "those people," he rode forward to meet and comfort his own. From somewhere, perhaps from the hand of a passing color bearer, or else from the ground where another had dropped it in flight, he secured a Confederate battle flag; with the result that Anderson's panicked fugitives, toiling uphill, saw him waiting astride Traveller near the crest, a gray general on a gray horse, over whose head the red folds of the star-crossed bunting caught the rays of the sun declining beyond the ridge. Some kept going, overcome by fear, while others stopped to cheer and cluster round him, though with more than a touch of delirium in their voices. "It's General Lee!" they cried. "Where's the man who won't follow Uncle Robert?" As at Gettysburg when they came limping back across the mile-wide valley from the carnage on Cemetery Hill, they found solace in his words and manner. Mahone's troops would cover their withdrawal, he said; they must go to the rear and form again. They did as he asked, most of them at any rate, and presently Mahone came forward to relieve him of the flag and escort him within the lines his veterans had drawn in case the Federals launched a follow-up assault.

No such attack ensued. Despite Sheridan's message assuring Grant that he was "pressing on," Custer had all he could handle in rounding up captives in the brush, as did Crook and Devin, a mile to the north; Wright went into bivouac, and Humphreys' clash with Gordon was still in progress near the Appomattox. Mahone remained in position till after dark, as Lee directed, then marched for High Bridge, four miles northeast, under instructions to cross and set it and an adjacent wagon span afire as soon as Gordon passed over with what remained of the three-corps train. Lee meantime had rejoined Longstreet at Rice for a night march to Farmville, where he too would cross the river and burn the bridges in his rear. A dispatch from Gordon, received soon after sundown, informed his chief that he was "fighting heavily" with Humphreys. "My loss is considerable," he reported, "and I am still closely pressed." By the time he was able to break contact, after nightfall, he had left some 1700 men behind as prisoners, together with a good part of the train. This brought the total to 6000 Confederates made captive today, with perhaps another 2000 killed, wounded, or otherwise knocked loose from their commands. Ewell's corps had been abolished, all but a couple of hundred survivors who made it through the lines that night. ("What regiment is that?" someone asked an officer at the head of the arriving column. "Kershaw's *division*," he replied.) Anderson's corps had been reduced by half, its units shattered except for one brigade, and Gordon's three divisions were cut to skeleton proportions, as Lee would see for himself when they came up next morning. "That half of our army is destroyed," he said of the troops engaged along Sayler's Creek this black Thursday.

Still, even though it was done at a cost of 8000 casualties — not half, but in any case a solid third of all that remained with the colors —

he had accomplished what he set out to do when he left Amelia the day before. Old Peter's corps was intact, having had little trouble holding off Ord's advance up the Southside Railroad. Moreover, rations in plenty were waiting ahead at Farmville, and once there, with the bridges burned behind him, he could put the swollen Appomattox between him and his pursuers, feed and rest his weary men, and perhaps, by moving westward on the north side of the river, get enough of a new head start to try again for a turn south to combine with Johnston in North Carolina. Or, failing that, he might press on to gain the fastness of the Blue Ridge Mountains, where he once had said he could hold out "for years."

The night was cold, with flurries of snow reported in nearby Burkeville next morning. Lee went ahead of Longstreet's men, who trudged on a poor cross-country road, and got a few hours' rest in a house at Farmville. When he rose at dawn, April 7, the First Corps troops were filing through the town, their step quickened by the promise of rations awaiting issue in boxcars parked on the northside tracks. Anxious for some first-hand word of the Sayler's Creek survivors, who were crossing downriver, with instructions to follow the railroad to the vicinity of Farmville, he again doubled Old Peter's column and proceeded eastward, beyond the Appomattox, until he encountered the first of his missing veterans in the person of Henry Wise, who had shared with him the rigors of his first campaign, out in western Virginia in the fall of '61. Arriving on foot at the head of his brigade — the only one to survive, as a unit more or less intact, Anderson's debacle of the day before — the former governor presented an outlandish picture of a soldier. He had lost not only his horse and baggage in yesterday's fight, but also much else in the hurried withdrawal, including his headgear and overcoat, which he had replaced with a jaunty Tyrolean hat, acquired en route, and a coarse gray blanket held together in front by a wire pin. His face, moreover, was streaked with red from having washed it in a puddle. This gave him, as he later said, the appearance of an aged Comanche brave. Lee thought so, too, and recovered a measure of his accustomed good humor at the sight. "I perceive that you, at any rate, have not given up the contest," he told his fellow Virginian, "as you are in your warpaint this morning." Wise drew himself up, shoulders back; he and Lee were of an age, just under two years short of sixty. "Ready for dress parade," he responded proudly to a question about the condition of his command.

Other good news he had as well. Mahone was over the river, too, in position to cover the downstream bridges; Gordon had crossed with all that remained of the train, preceded by a number of Anderson's stragglers, and Mahone was waiting for still others to get over before he gave the engineers word to fire both spans; that is, unless the Yankees came in sight beforehand, which they had not done by the time Wise left at sunup. Encouraged, Lee rode back to where his staff had set up headquarters opposite Farmville. Here he was visited presently by the Secretary of War, who had come on horseback by a different route from Richmond and was off again for Danville as soon as he had conferred with the general-in-chief. In a wire sent to the President next day, while moving roundabout to join him, Breckinridge reported that Lee had been "forced across the Appomattox" to find "temporary relief" from the heavy columns of Federals in pursuit, but that he would "still try to move around [them] toward North Carolina," once he resumed his westward march up the left bank of the river shielding his flank. So he had said at any rate. A military man himself, however, the Kentuckian added his own appraisal of Lee's chances as he saw them: "The straggling has been great, and the situation is not favorable."

In point of fact the situation was considerably less favorable than he had known when the brief conference ended. He had no sooner left, around midmorning, than a courier reached headquarters with news of a development that threatened to undo all Lee's plans for his next move, if indeed there was to be one. Bluecoats were over the Appomattox in strength at High Bridge, four miles east, and were closing even now upon the famished graybacks filing into the fields across from Farmville to draw their first issue of rations in five days. Mahone, it seemed, had pulled out behind Wise and Gordon without giving the engineers orders to fire the two bridges, and the resultant delay, while an officer spurred after him and returned, brought a heavy enemy column in sight before a match was struck. High Bridge itself, an open-deck affair on sixty-foot trusses of brick and pine, burned furiously at once, dropping four of its dozen spans into the water; but the low wagon bridge alongside, built of hardwood, caught fire so slowly that the whooping Federals arrived in time to stamp out the flames. By 9 o'clock Humphreys had his lead division over the river and a second arriving to reinforce the bridgehead to a strength too great for Mahone to retake it, though he counter-marched and tried. As for Lee, when he got word of what had happened he lost his temper entirely. "He spoke of the blunder," a staffer observed, "with a warmth and impatience which served to show how great a repression he ordinarily exercised over his feelings."

His rage at this sudden removal of the advantage of having the swollen river between him and his pursuers — not to mention the loss of the anticipated rest halt, which was to have given his road-worn soldiers time to cook and eat their rations and perhaps even get some badly needed sleep before setting out once more to regain the head start that would enable them to turn south for Danville, across the front of the blue column, or anyhow win the race for Lynchburg, where St John had still more rations waiting just over forty miles away — was subdued by the need for devising corrective defensive measures, lest his approximately 20,000 survivors, effective and noneffective, suffer destruction at the hands of more than 80,000 Federals converging upon them from the east and south, on both sides of the Appomattox. Because of a deep bend in the river above Farmville, the Lynchburg pike ran north for about three miles before it turned west near Cumberland Church, where a road from High Bridge joined it. Lee's orders were for Mahone, falling back under pressure from Humphreys, to take up a position there and hold the enemy off until Gordon and Longstreet cleared the junction. At the same time, he summoned Brigadier General E. P. Alexander, the First Corps chief of artillery, and gave him the double task of sending a battalion of guns to support Mahone and of destroying the two bridges at Farmville, as soon as Old Peter's men and wagons finished crossing, to prevent the bluecoats in their rear from joining Humphreys in his attempt to end the campaign, and with it the Army of Northern Virginia, here and now.

Alexander, a Georgia-born West Pointer, not quite thirty and a veteran of nearly all the army's major battles, got the guns off promptly to Cumberland Church, where they presently were in action against the Federals arriving from High Bridge, and prepared the railroad and wagon spans for burning as soon as the last of the gray infantry on the march from Rice were safely over. There was time for that, but not for the horsemen covering their rear; Alexander was taking no chances on a repetition of what had happened earlier, four miles downstream. Closely pursued by Crook, whose division had been sent over by Sheridan after a good night's rest, Fitz Lee was obliged to turn and fight on the outskirts of Farmville in order to give the tail of Longstreet's column a chance to clear the bridges. By the time he was able to break off the action and retire under fire through the streets of the town, both spans were ablaze from end to end; Fitz had to veer west in a race for an upstream ford, which he hoped would not prove too deep for his bone-tired horses to cross before Crook overtook them and used his guns to bloody the waters at that point. His uncle, watching from the opposite bank, took alarm at the thought of his cavalry being cut off, as well as at the sight of the hard-driving VI Corps, which arrived just then from Sayler's Creek and appeared on the hills overlooking the river from the south. Displaying the first real agitation he had shown on the retreat, Lee rode to where Longstreet's earliest arrivers had begun to frizzle bacon and boil cornmeal over newly kindled fires. In response to his urgent orders, and despite Old Peter's remonstrance that Fitz and his troopers could look out for themselves, the issue of rations was discontinued, amid groans from men still waiting to receive them, and those that had been partly cooked were dumped from skillets and kettles which then were flung over the tailgates of wagons whose drivers were in a panic to be off. In a state of torment from the smell of food they had not gotten to eat, the First Corps veterans fell in for the march beyond Cumberland Church, where Mahone was making his stand.

When they got there they found the road still open to the west, but they were unable to take it because Mahone, hard pressed by Humphreys' flankers, had to be reinforced if he was to continue holding out against bluecoats whose attacks grew harder to withstand as more and more of them arrived from downriver, eager to make the most of the opportunity their rapid, dry-shod crossing had afforded them, first to bring the fleeing rebs to bay — which they had done already — and then to overrun them, while the rest of the blue army effected a crossing in their rear to cut them off and help complete their destruction. Neither of these two last things happened, however. Supported by Gordon and Longstreet when they came up, Mahone not only held firm, he also counterattacked with a fury that went far toward making up for this morning's lapse at High Bridge, which had brought on the present crisis. Longstreet, informed that the enemy was menacing the left, detached a brigade from Field's division "with orders to get around the threatening force and break it up. Mahone so directed them through a woodland," he later wrote, "that they succeeded in over-reaching the threatened march and took in some 300 prisoners, the last of our troubles for the day."

The sun by then was going down. When it had set, and the fighting sputtered into a silence broken only by the mewls and groans of the wounded trapped between the lines, Old Peter rode through the twilight to a cottage where Lee had set up headquarters near Cumberland Church. He found him in a much better frame of mind than when he last saw him that morning, agitated by the news of Humphreys' easy coup, which voided his plans for a rest halt and a shielded march upriver, as well as by the threat of having his cavalry overwhelmed by the superior force of blue troopers in a race for the perhaps unusable ford northwest of the bridges on fire at Farmville. As it happened, though their best pace was no more than a shaky gallop, Fitz Lee's horsemen not only effected their escape across the Appomattox; they also managed to turn the tables on their pursuers once they reached the other side. Crossing by the ford, hard on the heels of the gray riders, Crook's lead brigade soon came in sight of Longstreet's train, grinding northward on a poor road near the river, and sought to repeat its successful foray at Sayler's Creek the day before. Fitz saw his chance and prepared to take it. Posting his own division to block the attack by receiving it head on, he sent Rosser against the Union flank, which crumpled when he struck it. Surprised and routed, the former aggressors scurried hard for the ford they had crossed when the pursuit was in the opposite direction, roles reversed.

Lee's spirits rose as he watched his nephew's rousing counterstroke, and lifted again when he learned of Mahone's success in keeping Humphreys' flankers off his line of retreat near Cumberland Church. There still was fight in his diminished army, fight in the style that had won it fame, and while he could not react as he once would have done by going over to the offensive against a divided foe, he was much encouraged by what had been achieved in the course of a day that opened with threats of disaster, left and right, and closed with his forces reunited after inflicting heavier casualties than they suffered. Although it was clear that another night march would have to be undertaken — the third in a row, and the fourth since leaving Petersburg and Richmond — by sundown his trains were rolling westward on the Lynchburg turnpike, unmolested, and his still-hungry soldiers were preparing to follow after moonrise. "Keep your command together and in good spirits, General," he had told his son Rooney that afternoon. "Don't let them think of surrender. I will get you out of this."

Surrender. Though the word was spoken in buoyant reaction to his nephew's savage counterslash at Crook, Lee's use of it showed that he knew his weary, half-starved troops were thinking of that contingency: as indeed he himself was, if only to counsel rejection. Grant, by contrast, was thinking of it quite purposely by then — in reverse, of course — as a proposal to end the drawn-out agony of his adversary's retreat, which he perceived was doomed in any case, and as a duty he presently said he felt "to shift from myself the responsibility of any further effusion of blood."

He had arrived from Burkeville around midday, shortly after Wright's infantry topped the hills overlooking Farmville from the south, and established headquarters in the local hotel, a rambling brick structure on the main street, two blocks short of where the still-burning wreckage of the town's two bridges released twin plumes of smoke above the swollen Appomattox, now a barrier to pursuit of the Confederates, who apparently were free at last to take some badly needed rest on the far side. Couriers soon were coming and going, however, back and forth across the broad hotel veranda, and all the news was good. Yesterday's forays along Sayler's Creek, which had netted some 6000 butternut prisoners, had cost the attackers fewer than 1200 casualties, only 166 of them killed. Best of all, though, was the news that Humphreys was over the river, four miles below, and moving westward to deny the rebels the rest they thought they had won when they fired the bridges in their rear. He was, as Grant said later, "in a very hazardous position," but the sound of his guns, roaring nearer and nearer from the northeast, gave evidence that his boldness was paying off. Besides, he would not stay unsupported long; Grant told Wright to throw a footbridge over the Appomattox, tied to the charred pilings of the railroad span, and use it to reinforce Humphreys as soon as possible with his whole corps. Including Crook's troopers, who would cross by an upstream ford, close to 40,000 Federals would then be on the north bank of the river. That was twice the strength to which Lee by now had dwindled or been cut: surely enough for Wright and Humphreys to perform the task of simultaneously driving and delaying him when he continued (as he would be obliged to do, if he could get away to try) his efforts to move westward to Lynchburg, where rations were known to be waiting in abundance.

For all its heft, this northside push involved no more than half Grant's army, and only half his plan for Lee's undoing. The other half — exclusive of Parke's corps, which had been given the laborious non-combat chore of shifting one track of the Southside Railroad an inch and a half inward, all the way from Petersburg to Burkeville, to accommodate the narrower-gauged Union cars and locomotives and thus provide a high-speed supply line running close in the moving army's rear from the high-piled docks at City Point — would move south of the Appomattox, and also westward, unimpeded, to outmarch and cut the old fox off before he reached his goal. Sheridan, in fact, after sending Crook to support the convergence on Farmville, had already set out in that direction from Sayler's Creek this morning with his other two divisions, riding hard for Prince Edward Courthouse, a dozen miles west of Rice, on the chance that Lee might succeed in giving his pursuers the slip and pass through there, en route to Danville and a combination with Johnston. Nothing came of that, but presently a wire reached headquarters from the bandy-legged cavalry commander, who had covered better than twenty miles of winding road by early afternoon. He was moving instead to Appomattox Station, twenty-five miles out the Southside line from Farmville, to intercept eight supply trains loaded with rations Lee had ordered shipped from Lynchburg to feed his troops when they rounded the nearby headwaters of the Appomattox River. Grant was quick to act on this; indeed, had begun to act on it before he received the information, by sending Griffin after Sheridan with instructions to do all he could to keep up with the fast-riding horsemen then on their way to Prince Edward. Now he added Ord's corps to this southside interception force, with the difference that Ord was to move by a more direct route, due west out the railroad. This too would be a 40,000-man effort, and Grant himself would go along to see that everything went as planned, leaving to Meade the supervision of the march beyond the river, until such time as the two halves, slogging westward along its opposite banks, came together near its source, like upper and nether millstones, to grind between them whatever remained by then of Lee's bedraggled army.

That should occur by tomorrow evening, or Sunday morning at the latest. Meantime he had little to do but wait for Wright to complete his footbridge, just up the street from the hotel, and Ord to get started out the railroad; Griffin was already west of Rice, slogging after Sheridan, and Humphreys' guns were still booming aggressively, two or three miles beyond the river. Despite his mud-spattered clothes, which he had not been able to change since getting separated from his baggage on the twilight ride to Jetersville two nights back, Grant was in a pleasant frame of mind. "Let the *thing* be pressed," Lincoln had wired him this morning, and he was proceeding to do just that, being similarly convinced that the iron was hot for striking. He saw the end in sight at last. What was more, he believed that Lee must see it, too, outnumbered two-to-one as he was by each half of the well-fed and superbly equipped army that soon would be driving him westward up the opposite bank of the dwindling Appomattox. According to Wright, who had talked with him yesterday after his capture, even so stout a fighter as Dick Ewell had confessed that the Confederate cause was lost "and it was the duty of the authorities to make the best terms they could while they still had a right to claim concessions." To continue the conflict under present conditions, he added, "would be but very little better than murder."

Grant rather thought so, too, and presently said as much. Shortly before 5 o'clock, Ord and Gibbon came by headquarters for a final check with him before setting out westward, and as the conference drew to a close he suddenly fell silent, musing, then looked up, and in what Gibbon called "his quiet way," remarked: "I have a great mind to summon Lee to surrender." He seemed to have surprised himself almost as much as he surprised his listeners, but there was no doubt that he meant what he said, for he called at once for ink and paper and began to write accordingly.

> Headquarters Armies of the United States,
> April 7, 1865 — 5 p.m.

General R. E. Lee,
Commanding C. S. Army.

General: The results of the last week must convince you of the hopelessness of further resistance on the part of the Army of Northern Virginia in this struggle. I feel that it is so, and regard it as my duty to shift from myself the responsibility of any further effusion of blood by asking of you the surrender of that portion of the C. S. Army known as the Army of Northern Virginia.

Very respectfully, your obedient servant,
> U. S. GRANT, Lieutenant General,
> Commanding Armies of the United States.

Brigadier General Seth Williams, Grant's inspector general, charged with delivery of the message under a flag of truce, set out at once for High Bridge to cross the river there and make his way through Humphreys' lines to Lee's. He would have saved time, and spared himself and his orderly and their mounts two thirds of the roundabout nine-mile ride, if he had waited for the VI Corps engineers to complete their footbridge over the Appomattox. They did so by sundown, and Wright's lead division began crossing shortly afterwards, marching three abreast up the street in front of headquarters, where Grant came out and took a seat on the veranda to watch the troops swing past "with a step that seemed as elastic," a staffer observed, "as on the first day of their toilsome tramp." On that day he had called them "as good an army as ever fought a battle," and now they returned the compliment in kind. Passing thus in review, they spotted their rather stumpy, dark-bearded commander on the hotel porch, his cigar a ruby point of light in the deepening shadows, and cheered him lustily to show that whatever reservations they had felt in the past were as gone as his own. He left his chair and came to the railing, still quietly smoking his cigar, and they cheered louder at this reduction of the distance between them. When night fell, bonfires were kindled for illumination along both sides of the street. The effect was one of a torchlight parade as the men broke ranks to snatch brands from the fires, then fell back in to flourish them over-head, roaring the John Brown song while they slogged on toward the river and Lee's army on the other side.

Grant did not wait for the last of Wright's cheering veterans to march past the hotel. After finishing his smoke he turned in early, re-tiring to a room in which the manager falsely assured him Lee had slept the night before.

Three miles to the north, where Mahone still held his position near Cumberland Church, Captain H. H. Perry, adjutant of the brigade sent by Longstreet to reinforce the left, went forward around 9 o'clock to investigate a report that a flag of truce had been advanced by the enemy in front. He proceeded with caution, for there had been a similar inci-dent about an hour earlier, which ended when the butternut pickets, suspecting a Yankee trick, opened fire at the first hail from the twilit woods across the way. Now here were the truce-seekers back again, if that was what they had been in the first place. The young Georgia cap-tain picked his way carefully to a point some fifty yards in front of the lines, where he stopped amid a scattering of blue-clad dead and wounded, hit in the last assault, and called for the flag: if that was what it was. It was: for now there appeared before him, resplendent in the light of the rising moon, what he later described as "a very handsomely dressed Federal officer" who introduced himself as Brigadier General Seth Williams of Grant's staff. Highly conscious of the contrast they presented, no less in looks than in rank — "The truth is, I had not eaten two ounces in two days, and I had my coattail then full of corn, waiting to parch it as soon as the opportunity might present itself" — Perry said later, "I drew myself up as proudly as I could, and put on the appearance as well as possible of being perfectly satisfied with my personal exterior."

Williams measured up to the occasion. Formerly the "efficient and favorite" prewar adjutant at West Point, including a time while R. E. Lee was superintendent, he had served McClellan, Burnside, Hooker, and Meade in the same capacity, with emphasis on his ability to celebrate the amenities. Now, as Grant's I.G. and special envoy — despite the loss, an hour ago, of his orderly in the fire that greeted his first attempt to open communications — he demonstrated that same ability in the moon-lit clearing between the lines of Humphreys and Mahone. Once the formal introductions were concluded, he produced a handsome silver flask and remarked, as Perry afterwards recalled, "that he hoped I would not think it an unsoldierly courtesy if he offered me some very fine brandy." The Georgian, who had nothing to offer in return but the unparched corn in the tail of his coat, found himself in a dilemma. "I wanted that drink awfully," he said later. "Worn down, hungry and dis-pirited as I was, it would have been a gracious godsend if some old Confederate and I could have emptied that flask between us in that dreadful hour of misfortune. But I raised myself about an inch higher, if possible, bowed and refused politely, trying to produce the ridiculous appearance of having feasted on champagne and pound cake not ten minutes before." Williams — "a true gentleman," his then companion would declare — returned the flask unopened to his pocket, and for this Perry was most grateful down the years. "If he had taken a drink, and my Confederate olfactories had obtained a whiff of the odor of it, it is possible that I should have caved." Spared this disgrace, he received from Williams the letter from Grant to Lee, together with a request for its prompt delivery; after which the ragged captain and the well-groomed brigadier "bowed profoundly to each other and turned away," each toward his own lines.

A courier soon reached Lee's headquarters in the cottage near Cumberland Church. Longstreet, still with his chief though the time by now was close to 10 o'clock, watched as he studied the message. There was no emotion in his face, and he passed it to his lieutenant with-out comment. Old Peter read the surrender request, then handed it back. "Not yet," he said.

Lee made no reply to that, but he did to Grant's letter; first, to refuse acceptance of the responsibility therein assigned him for such blood as might still be shed, and second, to explore the possibility — however remote — that his adversary might be willing to reopen the Ord-Longstreet peace discussions he had broken off so abruptly the month before, disclaiming any "authority" in such matters. As soon as Old Peter went out into the night, rejoining his troops for the march that had begun to get under way at moonrise, Lee wrote his answer on a single sheet of paper and gave it to the courier to be sent across the lines.

7th Apl '65

Genl

I have recd your note of this date. Though not entertaining the opinion you express of the hopelessness of further resistance on the

part of the Army of N. Va. I reciprocate your desire to avoid useless effusion of blood, & therefore before considering your proposition, ask the terms you will offer on condition of its surrender.

> Very respy your obt Svt
> R. E. LEE, Genl

Lt Genl U. S. Grant,
Commd Armies of the U States.

Old Peter cleared his camps well before midnight, but presently,
in accordance with instructions to assume the more rigorous task of
guarding the rear, halted to let Gordon take the lead on the westward
march up the left bank of the Appomattox. The army thus had a head
and a tail, but no middle now that the other two corps had been "dissolved" in battle and by Lee; Wise's still sizeable brigade — practically
all that remained of Johnson's division — was assigned to Gordon, in
partial compensation for his losses at Sayler's Creek, while skeletal fragments of the other three divisions, under Pickett, Heth, and Wilcox,
were attached to Longstreet, thereby rejoining comrades they had not
seen since the Petersburg breakthrough sundered them, six days back.
That left Richard Anderson and Bushrod Johnson troopless, and George
Pickett not much better off with only sixty armed survivors; Lee solved
the problem by formally relieving all three of duty, with authorization
to return to their homes before reporting to the War Department.
Anderson and Johnson left that afternoon, but Pickett's orders apparently went astray. In any case he was still around, that day and the
next, still nursing grievances over rejection of a report in which he had
sought to fix the blame on others for his Gettysburg repulse. Lee may or
may not have known about the Five Forks shad bake, a week ago today,
but subsequently, when he saw his fellow Virginian ride by headquarters, ringlets jouncing, air of command intact, he reacted with dark
surprise. "I thought that man was no longer with the army," he remarked.

Otherwise, aside from continuing hunger and fatigue, there was
much that was pleasant about this sixth day's march, especially by contrast with the five that had gone before. Not only had the weather improved, the plodding graybacks noted when the sun came up this
Saturday morning, but so had the terrain, barely touched by war till
now. It was a day, one pursuing Federal wrote, "of uneventful marching; hardly a human being was encountered along the way. The country
was enchanting, the peach orchards were blossoming in the southern
spring, the fields had been peacefully plowed for the coming crops, the
buds were beginning to swell, and a touch of verdure was perceptible
on the trees and along the hillsides. The atmosphere was balmy and
odorous; the hamlets were unburnt, the farms all tilled." Best of all,
no roar of guns disturbed what a South Carolinian called "the soft airs,

at once warm and invigorating, which blew to us along the high ridges we traversed." Fitz Lee, whose horsemen trailed the column at a distance of two miles, reported the enemy infantry no closer to him than he was to his own, while the blue cavalry seemed equally disinclined to press the issue. Still, there was a driving urgency about the march, an apprehension unrelieved by the lack of direct pressure, and the need for it was evident from even a brief study of the map. On the left, the dwindling Appomattox soon would cease to be a barrier to whatever Union forces were in motion on the other side. A dozen miles beyond that critical point, westward across a watershed traversed by the South-side Railroad, the James River flowed northeast to reënter the tactical picture as a new barrier — one that was likely to be controlled by whichever army rounded the headwaters of the Appomattox first. If it was Lee's, he could feed his men from the supply trains he had ordered sent to Appomattox Station, then press on next day to take shelter behind the James. If on the other hand the Federals got there in time to seize his provisions and in strength enough to block his path across the twelve-mile watershed, the campaign would be over. Alexander, the First Corps artillerist, saw this clearly. Examining on the map the "jug-shaped peninsula between the James and the Appomattox," he noted that "there was but one outlet, the neck of the jug at Appomattox Station." Both armies were headed there now, north and south of the river that had its source nearby — and "Grant had the shortest road."

What was likely to come of this was plain enough to a number of high-ranking officers who had conferred informally about it the previous evening while waiting to set out on what they judged might well be their last march. Concluding that surrender would soon be unavoidable, they requested William Pendleton, the senior of the group, to communicate their view to Lee and thus, as Alexander put it, "allow the odium of making the first proposition to be placed upon them," rather than on him. Neither Longstreet nor Gordon took part in the discussion, and when Pendleton told them of it next morning, seeking their endorsement, both declined. Old Peter, in fact — saying nothing of the message from Grant, which he had read the night before — was quick to point out that the Articles of War provided the death penalty for officers who urged capitulation on their commanders. As for himself, he said angrily, "If General Lee doesn't know when to surrender until *I* tell him, he will never know."

Pendleton, who had been at West Point with Lee before leaving the army to enter the ministry, bided his time until midday, when he found his fellow graybeard resting in the shade of a large pine beside the road. Like Longstreet, after hearing him out, Lee said nothing of Grant's message — or of his own reply, in which, by requesting terms, he had already begun the negotiations Pendleton was recommending

— but rather expressed surprise at the proposal. "I trust it has not come to that," he said sternly, even coldly. "We certainly have too many brave men to think of laying down our arms."

Snubbed and embarrassed, convinced, in Alexander's words, that Lee "preferred himself to take the whole responsibility of surrender, as he had always taken that of his battles," Pendleton rejoined the troops slogging past on the road beside the river, which narrowed with every westward mile through the long spring afternoon. The going was harder now that this morning's hunger and exertion had been added to those of the past five days. Tailing the march, Longstreet observed that "many weary soldiers were picked up, and many came to the column from the woodlands, some with, some without, arms — all asking for food." There were also those who were too far gone for rescue, sitting as Ewell had sat two days ago, his arms on his knees, his head down between them. Others were even worse undone, "lying prone on the ground along the roadside, too much exhausted to march farther, and only waiting for the enemy to come and pick them up as prisoners, while at short intervals there were wagons broken down, their teams of horses and mules lying in the mud, from which they had struggled to extricate themselves until complete exhaustion forced them to wait for death to glaze their wildly staring eyes." A Virginia trooper saw them thus, but added: "Through all this, a part of the army still trudged on, with their faith still strong, only waiting for General Lee to say whether they were to face about and fight."

Fortunately, no such turnabout action was required before nightfall ended the march with the head of the column approaching Appomattox Courthouse, some three miles short of Appomattox Station. Part of the train was already parked in the fields around the county seat, and the reserve batteries, which had also gone ahead, were in position over toward the railroad. Lee was just dismounting to make camp beside the pike, about midway between Gordon and Longstreet, when a courier overtook him at last with a sealed message that had come through the lines earlier in the day. By the light of a candle held by an aide, he saw that it was Grant's reply to last night's request for his terms of surrender. "Peace being my great desire," the Union commander wrote, "there is but one condition I would insist upon — namely, that the men and officers surrendered shall be disqualified for taking up arms against the Government of the United States until properly exchanged." Not only was this a far cry from the "unconditional" demand that had won him his nom-de-guerre three years ago at Donelson, but Grant considerately added: "I will meet you, or will designate officers to meet any officers you may name for the same purpose, at any point agreeable to you, for the purpose of arranging definitely the terms upon which the surrender of the Army of Northern Virginia will be received."

Nothing of Lee's reaction showed in his face. "How would you answer that?" he asked the aide, who read it and replied: "I would answer no such letter." Lee mused again, briefly. "Ah, but it must be answered," he said, and there by the roadside, still by the flickering light of the candle, he proceeded to do so. Parole was infinitely preferable to imprisonment, but he had to weigh his chances of getting away westward, beyond the James, against the advantage of negotiating while surrender remained a matter of choice. Moreover, he still clung to the notion of resuming more general peace discussions that might lead to something less than total capitulation. "In mine of yesterday," he now told Grant, "I did not intend to propose the surrender of the Army of N. Va., but to ask the terms of your proposition. To be frank, I do not think the emergency has arisen to call for surrender of this Army, but as the restoration of peace should be the sole object of all, I desired to know whether your proposals would lead to that end. I cannot therefore meet you with a view to surrender the Army of N. Va.; but as far as your proposal may affect the C. S. forces under my command, and tend to the restoration of peace, I shall be pleased to meet you at 10 a.m. tomorrow on the old stage road to Richmond, between the picket lines of the two armies."

Soon after the courier set out rearward with this reply, a roar of guns erupted from over near the railroad, three miles off. It swelled and held, then subsided, and after a time — around 9 o'clock — Pendleton arrived from that direction to explain that he had ridden forward, a couple of miles beyond the courthouse village just ahead, to check on the reserve artillery, which had left Farmville with the train the day before. Sixty pieces were in park, awaiting resumption of the march tomorrow; all seemed well, he said, until a sudden attack by Union cavalry exploded out of the twilight woods, full in the faces of the lounging cannoneers. Two batteries were ordered to hold off the blue troopers while the rest pulled back, and there ensued what a participant called "one of the closest artillery fights in the time it lasted that occurred during the war. The guns were fought literally up to the muzzles. It was dark by this time, and at every discharge the cannon were ablaze from touchhole to mouth. There must have been six or eight pieces at work, and the small arms of some three or four hundred men packed in among the guns in a very confined space. It seemed like the very jaws of the infernal regions." Pendleton by then had left to help withdraw such pieces as might be saved, but narrowly avoided capture himself by enemy horsemen who came swarming up the wagon-crowded road. He feared perhaps half the guns had been lost, he told Lee, including those in the two batteries left behind, which soon fell silent in the darkness, three miles to the southwest.

As it turned out, two dozen of them were taken, there and on the road. But that was by no means the worst of the news, or the worst of its implications. Just beyond the overrun gun park was Appomattox

Station, where the supply trains had been ordered to await the arrival
of the army. Most likely they had been captured too. If so, that meant
still another rationless march tomorrow: if, indeed, a march could be
made at all. No one could even guess at the number of Federals involved in the night attack across the way, and though they appeared to
be cavalry, to a man — so far at least as anyone had been able to tell
in the darkness and confusion — there was no way of knowing what
other forces were at hand, including division after division of blue infantry near the end of their unhindered daylong westward tramp up the
opposite bank of the river. One thing was certain in any case. If they
were there in any considerable strength, corking the James-Appomattox
jug, the way across the twelve-mile watershed was blocked and the
campaign was over, all but the formal surrender on whatever terms
Grant might require at the 10 o'clock meeting Lee had just requested.

Not even now, with the probable end in sight, did Lee show the
mounting tension he had been under since the collapse of his flank at
Five Forks, a week ago today. He did react swiftly to Pendleton's report, however, by summoning his two infantry corps commanders, as
well as his nephew Fitz, who was told to alert his troopers for a shift
from the tail of the column to its head. Before long, all three joined him
at his camp, pitched near a large white oak on the last low ridge overlooking the north branch of the Appomattox, and the council of war
began. Longstreet sat on a log, smoking his pipe; Gordon and Fitz
shared a blanket spread on the ground for a seat. The new-risen moon,
only two nights short of the full, lighted the scene while Lee, who
stood by a fire that had been kindled against the chill, explained the
tactical situation, so far as he knew it, and read them Grant's two
letters, together with his replies. Then he did something he had not
done, at least in this collective way, since the eve of the Seven Days,
shortly after he took over as their leader. He asked for their advice. "We
knew by our own aching hearts that his was breaking," Gordon was to
say. "Yet he commanded himself, and stood calmly facing and discussing the long-dreaded inevitable."

So did they, and the decision accordingly reached was that the
army would try for a breakout, a getaway westward beyond the glow
of enemy campfires rimming the horizon on all sides except the barren
north. While Fitz brought his horsemen forward to lead the attack out
the Lynchburg pike, Gordon would prepare to move in support of the
mounted effort. If successful in unblocking the road, they would then
wheel left to hold it open for the passage of the train, which would be
reduced to two battalions of artillery and the ammunition wagons, and
Longstreet would follow, guarding the rear in case the pursuing Federals
tried to interfere from that direction. It was a long-odds gamble at best;
moreover, Gordon pointed out, "The utmost that could be hoped for
was that we might reach the mountains of Virginia and Tennessee with

a remnant of the army, and ultimately join General Johnston." Still it was no more, or less, than could be expected of men determined to keep fighting so long as a spark of hope remained. If the bluecoats could not be budged, if more than cavalry had arrived to bar the way, there would be time enough then, as Fitz Lee put it, "to accede to the only alternative left us."

While his lieutenants rode off to issue instructions for their share in the predawn movement, Lee prepared to take his last sleep under the stars. Before he turned in, however, a member of Gordon's staff returned to ask where the head of the column was to make camp next night on its westward march. The question was put as if there could be no doubt that the breakthrough would succeed, and Lee's reply, though grim and not without a touch of irony, was in much the same vein. "Tell General Gordon I should be glad for him to halt just beyond the Tennessee line," he said, much to the staffer's chagrin; for the Tennessee line was nearly two hundred miles away.

Grant too was bedded down by then, some fifteen miles to the east in an upstairs room of a deserted house beside the pike; but not to sleep. He had a splitting headache — on this of all days, which had opened with a spirit-lifting message from Lee requesting terms in response to last night's suggestion that he surrender. After stating them in a note that was soon on its way through the lines, Grant changed his mind about riding with the southside column, and crossed the river instead to be where Lee's reply could reach him with the least delay. "Hello, old fellow!" he greeted Meade, to the shock of both their staffs, when he overtook the grizzled Pennsylvanian, still confined to his ambulance by dyspepsia and the added discomfort of chills and fever. All through the bright warm morning the march continued without incident; Grant's spirits continued to mount. At the midday halt, aware that Lincoln was on his way up the coast, he got off an exuberant telegram to Stanton, briefing him on the tactical situation and concluding: "I feel very confident of receiving the surrender of Lee and what remains of his army tomorrow." His terms in this morning's note, he felt, were too generous for his opponent to decline them in his present condition, which was evident from the dolorous state of the stragglers Humphreys and Wright were gleaning while they pressed on westward in the littered wake of the butternut throng. All the same, as the day wore on and there still was no response to his predawn offer, sent forward some eight hours before, he began to wonder at the delay and at the ability of the half-starved graybacks to keep beyond reach of their pursuers. Then out of nowhere, just as the rim of the declining sun glittered below the brim of his hat, the blinding headache struck.

It struck and it kept striking, even after he stopped for the night in a large frame house beside the pike, a dozen miles from Farmville.

The pain was by no means lessened by the banging some aide was giving a piano in the parlor directly below Grant's upstairs bedroom, nor by assurances from another staffer that his migraine attacks were usually followed by good news. Indeed, the arrival of just such a dispatch from Sheridan around 10 o'clock failed to bring relief, although the news was about as good as even he could have hoped for. The cavalryman reported that he had reached Appomattox Station at dusk, ahead of the leading elements of Lee's army. Not only had he captured four and chased off the rest of the supply trains waiting there for the hungry rebels to arrive from Cumberland Church; he had also followed through with a night attack by Custer toward Appomattox Courthouse, which had netted him some two dozen guns, a considerable haul of prisoners and wagons, and — best of all — a dug-in position athwart the Lynchburg road, blocking Lee's escape in the only direction that mattered. Moreover, by way of assuring that the road stayed blocked, he had urged Ord and Griffin to press on westward with their six divisions in a forced-march effort to join him before daylight. "If [they] can get up tonight we will perhaps finish the job in the morning," he told Grant, adding suggestively: "I do not think Lee means to surrender until compelled to do so."

Presently Grant had cause to agree with this closing assessment, and what was more he received it from Lee himself in a message that arrived soon after Sheridan's. Denying that he had intended to propose surrender in his previous response, or that an emergency had arisen which called for him to adopt so drastic a course, the southern commander said only that he would be willing to meet between the lines for a general discussion that might "tend to a restoration of peace." Grant studied the note, more saddened than angered by what he discerned, and shook his head. "It looks as if Lee meant to fight," he said.

He was disappointed. But that was mild compared to the reaction of his chief of staff, with whom he was sharing the bed in the upstairs room. "He did not propose to surrender!" Rawlins scoffed, indignant. "Diplomatic, but not true. He did propose, in his heart, to surrender. . . . He now wants to entrap us into making a treaty of peace. You said nothing about that. You asked him to surrender. He replied by asking what terms you would give. You answered by stating the terms. Now he wants to arrange for peace — something beyond and above the surrender of his army; something to embrace the whole Confederacy, if possible. No, sir. No, sir. Why, it is a positive insult — an attempt, in an underhanded way, to change the whole terms of the correspondence." Grant demurred. "It amounts to the same thing, Rawlins. He is only trying to be let down easy. I could meet him as requested, in the morning, and settle the whole business in an hour." But Rawlins would not have it so. Listeners downstairs heard him shout that Lee had purposely shifted his ground "to gain time and better terms." He saw the Virginian as a sharper, a wriggler trying to squirm from under the retribution about to descend on his guilty head. "He don't think 'the emergency has arisen'! That's cool, but another falsehood. That emergency has been staring him in the face for forty-eight hours. If he hasn't seen it yet, we will soon bring it to his comprehension! He has to surrender. He shall surrender. By the eternal, it shall be surrender or nothing else."

Grant continued to defend his year-long adversary, protesting that in his present "trying position," the old warrior was "compelled to defer somewhat to the wishes of his government. . . . But it all means precisely the same thing. If I meet Lee he will surrender before I leave." At this, Rawlins was quick to remind his chief of last month's wire from Stanton, forbidding him to treat with the enemy on such matters. "You have no right to meet Lee, or anyone else, to arrange terms of peace. That is the prerogative of the President, or the Senate. Your business is to capture or destroy Lee's army." Obliged to admit the force of this, Grant yielded; "Rawlins carried his point," one downstairs listener was to say, "as he always did, when resolutely set." Grant yielded; but he insisted that he still must do Lee the courtesy of answering his letter, if only to decline the suggested meeting. "I will reply in the morning," he said.

That ended the discussion, but not the throb in his head. Before daybreak, a staff colonel found him pacing about the yard of the house, both hands pressed to his aching temples. At the colonel's suggestion, he tried soaking his feet in hot water fortified with mustard, then placed mustard plasters on his wrists and the back of his neck; to no avail. When dawn began to glimmer through he went over to Meade's headquarters, just up the road, and had a cup of coffee. Feeling somewhat better, though not much, he composed a sort of open-ended refusal of Lee's request for a meeting between the lines this Sunday morning. "Your note of yesterday is received," he wrote. "I have no authority to treat on the subject of peace; the meeting proposed for 10 a.m. today could lead to no good. I will state, however, General, that I am equally anxious for peace with yourself, and the whole North entertains the same feeling. The terms upon which peace can be had are well understood. By the South laying down their arms they will hasten that most desirable event, save thousands of human lives, and hundreds of millions of property not yet destroyed. Seriously hoping that all our difficulties may be settled without the loss of another life, I subscribe myself, &c. *U. S. Grant*, Lieutenant General.

After a sunrise breakfast he went forward to find Humphreys and Wright again on the march. Meade was still in his ambulance, but Grant declined the offer of one for himself, despite the headache that made jogging along on horseback a constant torture, apparently having decided to put up with the pain, much as he was putting up with the rumpled and muddy uniform he had been wearing ever since his baggage went astray near Burkeville. Up ahead, though contact had not yet been established with the rebel rear, guns were thumping faintly in the distance. What this meant, or what might come of it, he did not know. He decided, however, that the best way to find out would be to approach the conflict not from this direction, with the column in pursuit, but from the front with Sheridan, who was in position over beyond Appomattox Courthouse. Accordingly, he told Meade goodbye and doubled back, accompanied by his staff, for a crossing of the river and a fast ride west on the far side. So he intended; but there were delays. "We had to make a wide detour to avoid running into Confederate pickets, flankers, and bummers," a reporter who went with him would recall. "It proved to be a long rough ride, much of the way without any well-defined road, often through fields and across farms, over hills, ravines, and 'turned out' plantations, across muddy brooks and bogs of quicksand." Once they even got lost in a pathless stretch of woods, narrowly avoiding capture by a band of rebel stragglers on the roam there. All this time, the rumble of guns up ahead had been swelling and sinking, swelling and sinking, until finally it hushed; a matter for wonder, indeed, though it might well flare up again, as it had before. The sun was nearing the overhead when the riders stopped at last to rest their horses in a roadside clearing whose timber had been cut and heaped for burning. While they dismounted to light cigars from the fuming logs, the reporter later wrote, "someone chanced to look back the way we had come, and saw a horseman coming at full speed, waving his hat above his head and shouting at every jump of his steed."

Soon recognized as one of Meade's lieutenants — a young man well acquainted with army protocol, and observant of it even under the excitement of his current mission — the rider drew rein in front of the chief of staff, saluted stiffly, and presented him with a sealed envelope. Rawlins tore one end open slowly, withdrew the message, and read it deliberately to himself. Nothing in his manner revealed his feelings as he passed the single sheet to Grant, who read it with no more expression on his face, the reporter noted, "than in a last year's bird's nest." Handing it back, he said quietly: "You had better read it aloud, General." Rawlins did so, in a deep voice that by now was a little shaky with emotion.

April 9th, 1865

General: I received your note of this morning on the picket line, whither I had come to meet you and ascertain definitely what terms were embraced in your proposal of yesterday with reference to the surrender of this army. I now request an interview, in accordance with the offer contained in your letter of yesterday, for that purpose.

Very respectfully, Your obt servt
R. E. Lee.

The celebration that followed was unexpectedly subdued. "No one looked his comrade in the face," the reporter would declare years later. One staffer hopped on a stump, waved his hat, and called for three cheers; but the hurrahs were few and feeble. Most throats were too constricted for speech, let alone cheers. "All felt that the war was over. Every heart was thinking of friends — family — home."

Grant was the first to recover his voice: perhaps in happy reaction to finding his headache cured, as he afterwards testified, "the instant I saw the contents of the note." This time Lee had said nothing about a broad-scale discussion that might "tend to the restoration of peace." He spoke rather of "the surrender of this army," and sought, as he said, an interview "for that purpose." Negotiations were back on the track, and the track was Grant's.

"How will that do, Rawlins?" he asked, smiling as he recalled his friend's tirade in their upstairs bedroom, late the night before.

"I think *that* will do," the other said.

★　★　★

Lee had foreseen the outcome from the start, and showed it when he joined his staff around the campfire that morning, a couple of hours before daylight, dressed in a splendid new gray uniform. His linen was snowy, his boots highly polished, and over a deep red silken sash, gathered about his waist, he had buckled on a sword with an ornate hilt and scabbard. When Pendleton expressed surprise at finding him turned out in such unaccustomed finery, he replied: "I have probably to be General Grant's prisoner, and thought I must make my best appearance."

No considerable insight was required for this assessment of what was likely to come of today's effort. Including 2000 cannoneers available to serve the remaining 61 guns, he had by now some 12,500 effectives in his ranks — fewer, in all, than Sheridan had in bivouac just to the west and south, their horses tethered athwart his one escape route, and only about one third of the skeleton force that began its withdrawal from Richmond, Bermuda Hundred, and Petersburg, a week ago tonight. Nearly as many more were present or scattered roundabout in various stages of collapse from hunger and exhaustion, but that was the number still fit for fight and still with weapons in their hands. Closing on Fitz, whose 2400 troopers were assembled in the yards and lanes of the little courthouse hamlet up ahead, Gordon was down to no more than 2000 infantry, while Longstreet, in motion behind the train of creaking wagons, had barely 6000 to cover the rear. Lee could hear them shuffling past in the darkness, along the road and in the woods surrounding the low glow of his headquarters fire, where the staff was breakfasting on gruel heated in a single metal cup and passed from hand to hand, more or less in the order of rank. He did not share in this, but when the meal was over, such as it was, and daylight began to glimmer through, he mounted Traveller and rode forward to watch his nephew and Gordon try for the breakout that at best would mean that the long retreat would continue beyond the dawn of this Palm Sunday.

Eastward the rim of sky was tinged with red by the time Fitz sent his horsemen forward on the right of Gordon, whose three-division corps — not much larger now than a single good-sized brigade had been when Grant first crossed the Rapidan, just one month less than a year ago this week — attacked due west out the Lynchburg pike, where the Federals had thrown up a gun-studded line of fieldworks in the night. The volume of fire was heavy, but because of a dense ground fog, which the growing light seemed to thicken, Lee could see little from his position on a hill overlooking the town and the fields beyond. If he could have observed the action, screened from his view by the mist that filled the valley, his heart would have lifted, as it had done so often at the start of one of his pulse-quickening offensives. Infantry and cavalry alike, the gray veterans reached and overran the enemy works in a single rush, taking two brass Napoleons and screaming with their old savage delight as the bluecoats scattered rearward to avoid the onslaught. Gordon, exultant, wheeled his cheering men hard left to hold the road open for the passage of the train. All the enemy dead and wounded had on spurs, and he took this for assurance that the breakthrough would be sustained. But then, as he watched the outdone troopers scuttle left and right, across the fields on both sides of the road, it was as if a theater curtain parted to show what he least wanted to see in all the world. There in rear of the gap, rank on rank and growing thicker by the minute, stood long lines of Union infantry, braced and ready, facing the risen sun, their blue flags snapping in the breeze that by now was beginning to waft the fog away.

It was Ord and it was Griffin, with close to 15,000 men apiece. They had arrived at dawn, after an all-night march undertaken in response to the summons from Sheridan, and each had two of his three divisions in position by sunup — in time to hear the high-throated caterwaul of the rebels bearing down on the dismounted cavalry up front. "The sweetest music I ever heard," Stonewall Jackson had called what the Federals themselves variously referred to as "that hellish yell," scarcely human either in pitch or duration, apparently with no hint of brain behind it, and "nothing like a hurrah, but rather a regular wildcat screech." A Wisconsin soldier put it best, perhaps, without even trying for a description. "There is nothing like it this side of the infernal region," he declared, "and the peculiar corkscrew sensation that it sends down your backbone under these circumstances can never be told. You have to *feel* it, and if you say you did not feel it, and heard the yell, then you have never *been* there." They heard it now, through the mist ahead, and for them too, as the cavalry scuttled rearward and sideways, the effect was one of a curtain parting on dread. There stood the butternut infantry, full in front, their regiments so diminished by attrition that their flags took the breeze not in intersticed rows, as in the old days, but in clusters of red, as if poppies or roses had suddenly burst into crowded bloom amid the smoke of their rapid-firing batteries. "We grew tired and prostrated," a blue veteran said of the hard six-day pursuit, "but we wanted to be there when the rebels found the last ditch of which they had talked so much." Now here it was, directly before them, and they were not so sure. Persuaded last night to press on westward out the railroad for the sake of getting a hot breakfast at Appomattox Station, they instead found graybacks in their front, scarecrow thin and scarecrow ragged, but still about as dangerous, pound for pound, as so many half-starved wolves or panthers. It might be the end, as some were saying, yet nobody wanted to be the last man to fall. "We were angry at ourselves," one candidate for that distinction later wrote, "to think that for the sake of drawing rations we had been foolish enough to keep up and, by doing so, get in such a scrape." It was not so much the booming guns they minded, he explained; "We dreaded the moment when the infantry should open on us."

Such dread was altogether mutual. Fitz Lee recoiled, and while the other two blue divisions came up to extend the triple Union line to a width of about three miles — 10,000 men to the mile, afoot — Sheridan remounted and alerted his troopers for an all-out strike at the rebel left as soon as the infantry started forward. "Now smash 'em, I tell you; smash 'em!" he was urging his subordinates, and Gordon knew only too well that, given the opportunity at hand, this was what Little Phil would be saying. Exposed to attack on both flanks and his center, the Georgian perceived that he had to pull back if he was to avoid being cut off and annihilated. He kept his sharpshooters active and stepped up the fire of his batteries, hoping at best to effect a piecemeal withdrawal that would discourage a swamping rush by the Federals in his front. Just then — about 8 o'clock — a staff colonel arrived from the fog-bound army command post to inquire how things were going. Gordon gave him a straight answer. "Tell General Lee I have fought my corps to a frazzle and I fear I can do nothing unless I am heavily supported by Longstreet."

Blind on his hilltop, Lee received the message without flinching, though he saw clearly enough what it meant. If so stalwart a fighter as Gordon could "do nothing" without the help of Longstreet, who had just been warned that Humphreys and Wright had resumed their advance and soon would pose as grave a threat to his rear as Ord and Griffin now presented in his front, he had lost all choice in the matter. What was more he admitted as much, however regretfully, in the presence of his staff. "Then there is nothing left me to do but go and see General Grant," he said, "and I would rather die a thousand deaths."

It was by now about 8.30. With more than an hour to wait before setting out for the meeting he had suggested in last night's letter across the lines, Lee returned to his headquarters beside the pike and sent for Longstreet. Leaving Field in charge of the rear guard, which had halted behind the stalled train and was digging in to confront the two blue corps reported to be advancing from the east, Longstreet brought Mahone and Alexander along, apparently in the belief that their advice would be helpful at the council of war he thought had been called to determine the army's next move. As it turned out, however, he had not been summoned for that purpose, but rather to give his opinion on the question of surrender. Countering with a question of his own, he asked whether the sacrifice of the Army of Northern Virginia would in any way help the cause elsewhere. Lee said he thought not. "Then your situation speaks for itself," Old Peter told him. Mahone felt the same. A slight, thin man in a long brown linen duster — so thin, indeed, that his wife, once informed that he had received a flesh wound, replied in alarm: "Now I know it is serious, for William has no flesh whatever" — he was shivering, and he wanted it understood that this was from the chill of the morning, not from fear. All the same, he too could recommend nothing but surrender under the present circumstances. Alexander disagreed. Ten years younger than Mahone, who was crowding forty, he proposed that the troops take to the woods, individually and in small groups, under orders to report to the governors of their respective states. That way, he believed, two thirds of the army would avoid capture by the Yankees; "We would be like rabbits or partridges in the bushes, and they could not scatter to follow us." Lee heard the young brigadier out, then replied in measured tones to his plan. "We must consider its effect on the country as a whole," he told him. "Already it is demoralized by the four years of war. If I took your advice, the men would be without rations and under no control of officers. They would be compelled to rob and steal in order to live. They would become mere bands of marauders, and the enemy's cavalry would pursue them and overrun many sections they may never have occasion to visit. We would bring on a state of affairs it would take the country years to recover from. And as for myself, you young fellows might go bushwhacking, but the only dignified course for me would be to go to General Grant and surrender myself and take the consequences of my acts." Alexander was silenced, then and down the years. "I had not a single word to say in reply," he wrote long afterwards. "He had answered my suggestion from a plane so far above it that I was ashamed of having made it."

Nothing much had been accomplished by all this, but at least Lee had managed to get through the better part of a hard hour: which had probably been his purpose in sending for Longstreet in the first place. Now the time was at hand, and he prepared to set out for the 10 o'clock meeting, rearward between the lines, with his young adjutant, Walter Taylor, and Lieutenant Colonel Charles Marshall, his military secretary; Sergeant George Tucker — Hill's courier, who had attached himself to Lee after the fall of his chief, a week ago this morning — would go along as bearer of the flag of truce. They rode eastward, the four of them, through the cheering ranks of First Corps troops waiting beside the road, and on beyond a stout log barricade under construction for reception of the enemy, due to arrive at any moment. Reaching the picket line, they paused for Tucker to break out the white flag — a soiled handkerchief, tied by one corner to a stick — then continued, half a mile or so, until they saw blue skirmishers approaching. They drew rein, and Marshall rode out front with Tucker, expecting to encounter Grant and his staff. Instead, a single Federal officer appeared, also a lieutenant colonel and also accompanied by an orderly with a flag of truce. He introduced himself as a member of Humphreys' staff, but said that he knew nothing about any meeting, here or elsewhere. All he knew was that he had been given a letter to deliver through the lines, together with instructions to wait for an answer, if one was made. Marshall took the envelope, which was addressed to Lee, and trotted back to hand it to him.

Lee broke it open and read the note Grant had written at Meade's headquarters before sunup, declining the proposed conference on grounds that he had "no authority to treat on the subject of peace," and declaring that hostilities could only be ended "by the South laying down their arms." It was, then, to be "unconditional" surrender; Grant had reverted to type, and Lee had no choice except to repeat his request for a meeting, this time in accordance with whatever preconditions were required. Accordingly, he dictated the message Rawlins would read aloud two hours later, on the far side of the Appomattox. Marshall took it back to the waiting colonel, told him of its contents, and asked that fighting be suspended on this front until it could be delivered and replied to. The Federal turned and rode back through the line of halted skirmishers. While waiting, Lee sent a note to Gordon, through Longstreet, authorizing him to request a similar truce of the enemy moving against him from the opposite direction.

A cease-fire, even a brief one, was likely to prove a good deal easier to ask for than to receive from either direction: especially westward, where Sheridan might have a voice in the matter. And so it was. "Damn them," the cavalryman said angrily on learning that a white flag had come out from Gordon, whose troops by then had fallen back through the town in their rear, "I wish they had held out an hour longer and I would have whipped hell out of them." Suspecting a trick, he wanted no let-up until he bagged the lot. "I've got 'em; I've got 'em like that!" he cried, and he brandished a clenched fist. But Ord outranked and overruled him, and the guns fell silent along the rebel front. Meade, however, reacted much as Sheridan did. Four miles to the east, coming up in the rear of the stalled gray army, he was for pressing the advantage he had worked so hard to gain, flat on his back though he was with chills and fever. "Hey! What?" he exclaimed, emerging from his ambulance when Humphreys' truce-flag colonel delivered Lee's request. "I have no authority to grant such a suspension. General Lee has already refused the terms of General Grant. Advance your skirmishers, Humphreys, and bring up your troops. We will pitch into them at once." He sent the colonel back to inform Lee that Grant had left that part of the field some hours ago; the letter could not reach him in time to stop the attack.

Marshall's reply was that if Meade would read Lee's note to Grant he would surely agree that a truce was in order, but even as the staffer rode back to deliver this suggestion the blue skirmishers resumed their advance. Lee held his ground, determined to do all he could to prevent unnecessary bloodshed, and when another white-flag officer emerged to warn him to withdraw, he responded — over Meade's head, so to speak — with a second message to Grant: "I ask a suspension of hostilities pending the adjustment of the terms of the surrender." Still the skirmishers came on, along and on both sides of the road where Lee and his three companions sat their horses. Only when the bluecoats were within one hundred yards, and he was peremptorily informed that their advance could not be halted, did he turn Traveller's head and ride back up the road, past his own pickets and beyond the now finished barricade. Longstreet was there, bracing his troops for the attack that seemed about to open. Instead — it was close to 11 o'clock by then — the Federal colonel reappeared with a note from Meade, agreeing to an informal one-hour truce and suggesting that Lee might be able to get in touch with Grant more quickly through some other part of the line. Lee accordingly rode on toward the front, which Gordon had established on the near side of the north fork of the Appomattox, and dismounted in a roadside apple orchard to compose his third message of the day to Grant, repeating his request for "an interview, at such time and place as you may designate, to discuss the terms of the surrender of this army."

He was weary from the strain of the long morning. After the messenger set out — this time through Gordon's lines, in accordance with Meade's suggestion — he lay down on a blanket-covered pile of fence rails in the shade of one of the trees. Longstreet presently joined him, and when Lee expressed concern that Grant was stiffening his terms, replied that he did not think so. Well acquainted with the northern commander for years before the war, he believed he would demand nothing that Lee would not demand if the roles were reversed. Lee still had doubts, however, and continued to express them until shortly after noon, when they saw riding toward them, from the direction of Gordon's lines, a well-mounted Federal officer under escort. Presuming that he had been sent by Grant to summon Lee to the meeting requested in one of his earlier notes, Old Peter told his chief: "Unless he offers us honorable terms, come back and let us fight it out." Lee sat up, squaring his shoulders, and Longstreet observed that "the thought of another round seemed to brace him."

Dismounting, the blue-clad emissary saluted and introduced himself as Lieutenant Colonel Orville Babcock of Grant's staff, then presented a note the Union commander had scribbled in his order book half an hour ago, five miles southeast of Appomattox Courthouse, in reply to Lee's first message that morning — the one that Rawlins had finally said would "do." Not mentioning terms or conditions, Grant merely wrote that he would "push forward to the front for the purpose of meeting you. Notice sent to me on this road where you wish the interview to take place will meet me."

Lee only delayed his departure to attend to two comparatively minor matters. One was to have Grant's aide send a dispatch to Meade, directing him to extend the truce until further orders, and the other was to grant a plea from his young adjutant, Walter Taylor, to be spared the heartbreak of attending the surrender. Then he set out, riding alongside Babcock and preceded by Marshall and Tucker, who led the way through Gordon's thin and silent line of battle, down the slope to the creek-sized north branch of the Appomattox. Here he paused to let Traveller drink, then continued his ride toward the courthouse village less than half a mile beyond the stream. Remembering at last that his adversary had left it to him to appoint a meeting place, he sent Marshall ahead, along with the flag-bearing sergeant, to select a proper house for the occasion.

By then it was close to 1 o'clock. Within half an hour Grant arrived from the southeast to find Sheridan waiting for him on the outskirts of town, still eager, as he said later, "to end the business by going in and forcing an absolute surrender by capture." Though this was the first time they had met since the start of the pursuit, a week ago tomorrow, the greetings exchanged were casual.

"How are you, Sheridan?"

"First rate, thank you. How are you?"

"Is Lee up there?"

"Yes, he is in that brick house."

"Very well. Let's go up."

The house Sheridan pointed out belonged to a man named Wilmer McLean, who had agreed to let it be used when Marshall rode in ahead of Lee in search of a place for the meeting with Grant. By the oddest of chances, McLean had owned a farm near Manassas Junction, stretching along the banks of Bull Run, at the time of the first of the two battles fought there. In fact, a shell had come crashing through one of his windows during the opening skirmish, and after that grim experience he had resolved to find a new home for his family, preferably back in the rural southside hill country, "where the sound of battle would never reach them." He found what he wanted at Appomattox Courthouse — a remote hamlet, better than two miles from the railroad and clearly of no military value to either side — only to discover, soon after midday on this fateful Palm Sunday, that the war he had fled was about to end on his doorstep; indeed in his very parlor, where Lee and Marshall waited a long half hour until Babcock, watching beside a window for his chief's arrival, saw him and his staff turn in at the gate, then crossed the room and opened the door into the hall.

Grant entered and went at once to Lee, who rose to meet him. They shook hands, one of middle height, slightly stooped, his hair and beard "nut-brown without a trace of gray," a little awkward and more than a little embarrassed, as he himself later said, mud-spattered trouser legs stuffed into muddy boots, tunic rumpled and dusty, wearing no side arms, not even spurs, and the other tall and patrician-looking, immaculately groomed and clad, with his red sash and ornate sword, fire-gilt buttons and polished brass, silver hair and beard, demonstrating withal, as one observer noted, "that happy blend of dignity and courtesy so difficult to describe." Fifteen years apart in age — the younger commander's forty-third birthday was just over two weeks off — they presented a contrast in more than appearance. Surprised at his own reaction to the encounter, Grant did not know what to make of Lee's at all. "As he was a man of much dignity, with an impassable face," he afterwards declared, "it was impossible to say whether he felt inwardly glad that the end had finally come, or felt sad over the result and was too manly to show it. Whatever his feelings they were entirely concealed from my observation; but my own feelings, which had been quite jubilant on the receipt of his letter, were sad and depressed. I felt like anything rather than rejoicing at the downfall of a foe who had fought so long and valiantly, and had suffered so much for a cause, though that cause was, I believe, one of the worst for which a people ever fought."

Lee resumed his seat, while Marshall remained standing beside him, leaning against the mantel over the unlighted fireplace. Grant took a chair near the middle of the room. Meantime his staff officers were filing in, as one would note, "very much as people enter a sick chamber where they expect to find the patient dangerously ill." Some found seats, but most stood ranged along one wall, looking intently at the old gray fox — the patient — cornered at last and seated across the room from them in his fine clothes. Grant tried to relieve the tension. "I met you once before, General Lee," he said, recalling a time in Mexico when the Virginian had visited his brigade. "I have always remembered your appearance and I think I should have recognized you anywhere." Lee nodded. "Yes, I know I met you on that occasion," he replied, "and I have often thought of it and tried to recollect how you looked. But I have never been able to recall a single feature." If this was a snub Grant did not realize it, or else he let it pass. He went on with his Mexican recollections, warming as he spoke, until Lee, feeling the strain of every dragging moment, broke in at the first pause to say: "I suppose, General Grant, that the object of our present meeting is fully understood. I asked to see you to ascertain upon what terms you would receive the surrender of my army." Grant's response was made with no change of expression, either on his face or in his voice. "The terms I propose are those stated substantially in my letter of yesterday — that is, the officers and men surrendered to be paroled and disqualified from taking up arms again until properly exchanged, and all arms, ammunition, and supplies to be delivered up as captured property." Inwardly, Lee breathed a sigh of vast relief: Longstreet had been right about Grant, and his own worst fears had been groundless. Now, though, it was his turn to mask his emotion, and he did so. "Those are about the conditions I expected would be proposed," he said quietly.

Grant spoke then of a possible "general suspension of hostilities," which he hoped would follow shortly throughout the land, but Lee, anxious to end the present surrender ordeal, once more cut him short, albeit courteously. "I would suggest that you commit to writing the terms you have proposed, so that they may be formally acted upon," he said, and the other replied: "Very well, I will write them out." He called for his order book, bound sheets of yellow flimsy with alternate carbons, and opened it flat on the small round marble-topped table before him. "When I put my pen to the paper," he later declared, "I did not know the first word I should make use of in writing the terms. I only knew what was in my mind, and I wished to express it clearly so that there could be no mistaking it." He succeeded in doing just that. Rapidly and in fewer than two hundred words, he stipulated that officers would "give their individual paroles not to take up arms against the Government of the United States until properly exchanged," that unit commanders would "sign a like parole for the men of their commands," and that "the arms, artillery and private property [were] to be parked and stacked and turned over to the officer appointed by me to receive them." He paused, looking briefly at Lee's dress sword, then added the two last sentences. "This will not embrace the side arms of the officers, nor their private horses or baggage. This done, each officer and man will be allowed to return to their homes, not to be disturbed by the United States authority so long as they observe their paroles and the laws in force where they may reside."

Lee made something of a ritual of examining the document now passed to him. No doubt in an effort to master his nerves, he placed the book on the table before him — small and marble-topped like Grant's, but square — took out his steel-rimmed spectacles, polished them very carefully with a handkerchief, crossed his legs, set the glasses deliberately astride his nose, and at last began to read. Nothing in his expression changed until he reached the closing sentences. Having read them he looked up at Grant and remarked in a warmer tone than he had used before: "This will have a very happy effect on my army." When his adversary said that he would have a fair copy made for signing, "unless you have some suggestions in regard to the form in which I have stated the terms," Lee hesitated before replying. "There is one thing I would like to mention. The cavalrymen and artillerists own their own horses in our army. Its organization in this respect differs from that of the United States. I would like to understand whether these men will be permitted to retain their horses." Grant overlooked what he later called "this implication that we were two countries," but said flatly: "You will find that the terms as written do not allow this." Lee perused again the two sheets of yellow flimsy. He was asking a favor, and he did not enjoy the role of supplicant. "No," he admitted regretfully, "I see the terms do not allow it. That is clear." Then Grant relented. Perhaps recalling his own years of hardscrabble farming near St Louis before the war — or Lincoln's remark at City Point, less than two weeks ago, that all he wanted, once the time came, was "to get the men composing the Confederate armies back to their homes, at work on their farms or in their shops" — he relieved Lee of the humiliation of having to plead for a modification of terms already generous. "Well, the subject is quite new to me," he mused, feeling his way as he spoke. "Of course I did not know that any private soldiers owned their animals, but I think this will be the last battle of the war — I sincerely hope so — and that the surrender of this army will be followed soon by all the others, and I take it that most of the men in the ranks are small farmers, and as the country has been so raided by the two armies it is doubtful whether they will be able to put in a crop to carry themselves and their families through the next winter without the aid of the horses they are now riding, I will arrange it this way; I will not change the terms as now written, but I will instruct the officers I shall appoint to receive the paroles to let all the men who claim to own a horse or mule take the animals home with them to work their little farms." Lee's relief and appreciation were expressed in his response. "This will have the best possible effect upon the men," he said. "It will be very gratifying, and will do much toward conciliating our people."

Grant passed the document to his adjutant for copying, and while this was in progress Lee had Marshall draft a letter of acceptance. In the wait that followed, the northern commander introduced his staff, together with Ord and Sheridan. Shaking hands with those who offered theirs, the Virginian bowed formally to the others, but spoke only to Seth Williams, his former West Point associate, and even then, for all his studied courtesy, could not manage a smile in response to a pleasantry of the old days. The introductions over, he informed Grant that he had a number of Federal prisoners he would like to return to their own lines as soon as it could be arranged, "for I have no provisions for them. I have, indeed, nothing for my own men. They have been living for the last few days principally on parched corn, and are badly in need of both rations and forage." Grant said he wanted his troops back as soon as possible, and would be glad to furnish whatever food the surrendered army needed. "Of about how many men does your present force consist?" Lee scarcely knew; casualties and straggling had been heavy, he admitted. "Suppose I send over 25,000 rations. Do you think that will be a sufficient supply?" "Plenty, plenty; an abundance," Lee replied.

Marshall having completed his draft of the brief acceptance, Lee made a few corrections — "Don't say, 'I have the honor to acknowledge receipt of your letter.' He is here. Just say, 'I accept the terms' " — and while he waited for the finished copy, Grant, whose appearance Marshall would charitably describe as "rather dusty and a little soiled" — in contrast to a quip by one of his own staffers, who remarked that he "looked like a fly on a shoulder of beef" — came over again and apologized for his rumpled clothes and lack of side arms. His baggage had gone astray, he said, "and I thought you would rather receive me as I was than be detained." Lee replied that he was much obliged; "I am very glad you did it that way." He signed the completed fair copy of his letter of acceptance, which Marshall then sealed and handed to Grant's adjutant, receiving in turn the signed and sealed terms of surrender. Lee broke the envelope open and read them through for the third time, but Grant did not bother with reading the letter to him just yet, later explaining that Lee's spoken acceptance of the terms was surety enough for him, without the formality of words set down on paper.

It was close to 4 o'clock by now, and all that protocol required had been performed. After nearly three hours in the McLean parlor — half of one spent waiting and the rest in what could scarcely be called negotiation, since his adversary had freely given all he asked and more than he had hoped for: including immunity, down the years, from prosecution on any charge whatever in connection with the war — Lee was free to go. He rose, shook hands with Grant again, bowed to the others, and passed from the room, followed by Marshall. Out on the porch, several blue-clad officers came to attention and saluted as he emerged. He put on his hat to return their salute, then crossed to the head of the steps leading down to the yard. There he drew on his gauntlets, distractedly striking the fist of one hand three times into the palm of the other as he looked out across the valley to where the men of his army were waiting to learn that they had been surrendered. "Orderly! Orderly!" he called hoarsely, not seeing Tucker close by with Traveller, whose bit had been slipped to let him graze. "Here, General, here," Tucker replied, and Lee came down the steps to stand by the horse's head while he was being bridled. A cavalry major, watching from the porch, noted that "as the orderly was buckling the throat latch, the general reached up and drew the forelock out from under the brow band, parted and smoothed it, and then gently patted the gray charger's forehead in an absent-minded way, as one who loves horses, but whose thoughts are far away, might all unwittingly do." Mounted, Lee waited for Marshall and Tucker, then started at a walk across the yard. Grant had come out of the house and down the steps by then, also on his way to the gate where his own horse was tethered. Stopping, he removed his hat in salute, as did the staff men with him. Lee raised his own hat briefly in return, and passed out through the gate and up the road. Presently, northward beyond the dwindled, tree-lined Appomattox, listeners on the porch heard cheers, and then a poignant silence.

Indoors behind them, as they watched him go and heard the choked-off yells subside beyond the tree line, scavengers were at work. "Relic-hunters charged down upon the manor house," a staff colonel would recall, "and began to bargain for the numerous pieces of furniture." Ord paid forty dollars for Lee's table, and Sheridan gave half as much for Grant's — though 'bargain' and 'paid' were scarcely words that applied to either transaction; Wilmer McLean, not wanting to sell his household possessions, threw the money on the floor or had it flung there when he declined to accept it. No matter; the rest of the furniture was quickly snapped up, beginning with the chairs the two commanders had sat in. Sheridan's brother Michael, a captain on his staff, made off with a stone inkstand, and an enterprising brigadier secured two brass candlesticks for ten dollars. Once these and other prize items were gone, mainly to persons whose rank had placed them early on the scene, what remained was up for grabs, and something close to pandemonium set in. "Cane-bottomed chairs were ruthlessly cut to pieces," a reporter was to write, "the cane splits broken into pieces a few inches long and parceled out among those who swarmed around. Haircloth upholstery, cut from chairs and sofas, was also cut into strips and patches and carried away." McLean was left surveying a Tacitean wilderness his enemies called peace. They made off with their spoils, exulting as they went, and a few years later — with still more rank, and again with the advantage of working close to the man in charge — some of them would try their hand at doing much the same thing to the country at large, with considerable success.

Grant knew nothing of this, of course, just as he would know little or nothing of their later endeavors along that line. He rode on toward his headquarters tent, which had been found at last, along with his baggage, and pitched nearby. He had not gone far before someone asked if he did not consider the news of Lee's surrender worth passing on to the War Department. Reining his horse in, he dismounted and sat on a large stone by the roadside to compose the telegram Lincoln would receive that night. By the time he remounted to ride on, salutes were beginning to roar from Union batteries roundabout, and he sent word to have them stopped, not only because he feared the warlike racket might cause trouble between the victors and the vanquished, both of them still with weapons in their hands, but also because he considered it unfitting. "The war is over," he told his staff. "The rebels are our countrymen again."

Lee by then was back in the apple orchard he had left four hours ago. The yells that greeted him as he reëntered Gordon's lines had come in part by force of custom; the troops, for all their cumulative numbness from hunger, weariness, and stress, cheered him as they had always done when he moved among them. Moreover, despite the grinding week-long retreat and its heavy losses, more from straggling than in combat — despite last night's red western glow of enemy campfires and this morning's breakout failure; despite the coming and going of couriers, blue and gray, and his own outward passage through their line of battle, accoutered for something more solemn even than church on this Palm Sunday — many of them were still not ready to believe the end had come. One look at his face as he drew near, however, confirmed what they had been unwilling to accept. They broke ranks and crowded round him. "General, are we surrendered? Are we surrendered?" they began asking.

Hemmed in, Lee removed his hat and spoke from horseback to a blurred expanse of upturned faces. "Men, we have fought the war together, and I have done the best I could for you. You will all be paroled and go to your homes until exchanged." Tears filled his eyes as he tried to say more; he could only manage an inaudible "Goodbye." Their first stunned reaction was disbelief. "General, we'll fight 'em yet," they told him. "Say the word and we'll go in and fight 'em yet." Then it came home to them, and though most responded with silence, one man threw his rifle down and cried in a loud voice: "Blow, Gabriel, blow! My God, let him blow, I am ready to die!"

Grief brought a sort of mass relaxation that let Traveller proceed, and as he moved through the press of soldiers, bearing the gray commander on his back, they reached out to touch both horse and rider, withers and knees, flanks and thighs, in expression of their affection. "I love you just as well as ever, General Lee!" a ragged veteran shouted, arms held wide above the crowd. At the orchard he drew rein, dismounted, and walked through the trees to one well back from the road, and there began pacing back and forth beneath its just-fledged branches, too restless to sit down on this morning's pile of fence rails. "He seemed to be in one of his savage moods," a headquarters engineer declared, "and when these moods were on him it was safer to keep out of his way." His own people knew to let him alone, but Federal officers kept arriving, "mostly in groups of four or five and some

of high rank. It was evident that they came from curiosity, or to see
General Lee as friends in the old army." He had small use for any of
them just now though, whether they were past acquaintances or strangers. Coming up to be presented, they removed their hats out of deference and politeness, but he did not respond in kind, and sometimes did
not even touch his hatbrim in return to their salutes. When he saw
one of his staff approach with another group of such visitors, "he
would halt in his pacing, stand at attention, and glare at them with a
look which few men but he could assume." Finally, near sundown,
when the promised rations began arriving from the Union lines, he
remounted and rode back to a less exposed position, under the white
oak tree on the ridge where he had slept the night before.

This second ride was through the ranks of the First Corps, and
Longstreet saw him coming. "The road was packed by standing troops
as he approached," Old Peter was to write, "the men with hats off,
heads and hearts bowed down. As he passed they raised their heads
and looked at him with swimming eyes. Those who could find voice
said goodbye; those who could not speak, and were near, passed their
hands gently over the sides of Traveller." From point to point there
were bursts of cheers, which the dark-maned gray acknowledged by
arching his neck and tossing his head, but Longstreet observed that
Lee had only "sufficient control to fix his eyes on a line between the
ears of Traveller and look neither to the right nor left." He too had
his hat off, and tears ran down his cheeks into his beard. Back on the
white oak ridge he stood for a time in front of his tent — "Let me
get in. Let me bid him farewell," the men were crying as they thronged
forward — then went inside, too choked for speech. Later he came
out and sat by the fire with his staff. He told Marshall to prepare an
order, a farewell to the army, but he had little heart for talk and
turned in early, weary from the strain of perhaps the longest and no
doubt the hardest day he had ever known.

A cold rain fell next morning. He kept mainly to his tent until
shortly after 9 o'clock, when word came that Grant, on the way to
see him, had been stopped by pickets who had been put out yesterday
to prevent the troops of the two armies from engaging in possible
squabbles. Embarrassed, Lee set out at a gallop and found his distinguished visitor waiting imperturbably on a little knoll beside the road,
just south of the north branch of the Appomattox. He lifted his hat
in greeting, as did the other; then they shook hands, sitting their horses
in the rain while their aides retired beyond earshot, and began to talk.
Grant had come to ask Lee to use his influence — "an influence that
was supreme," he later said — to help bring the war to an early end by
advising his subordinates, in command of the other armies of the South,
to lay down their arms under the terms he himself had received the
day before. Lee replied, in effect, that he agreed that further resistance

was useless, but that he felt obliged as a soldier to leave all such matters to his Commander in Chief; in any case, he could do nothing without conferring with him beforehand. Grant did not persist — "I knew there was no use to urge him to do anything against his ideas of what was right" — but he deeply regretted the refusal, he declared long afterward, because "I saw that the Confederacy had gone a long way beyond the reach of President Davis, and that there was nothing that could be done except what Lee could do to benefit the Southern people. I was anxious to get them home and have our armies go to their homes and fields."

He was also anxious to get himself to Burkeville, where, thanks to the hard-working IX Corps, he could take the cars for City Point and get aboard a fast packet for Washington. By now the war was costing four million dollars a day, and he wanted to get back to the capital and start cutting down on expenses. So the two parted, Grant to set out for Burkeville and Lee to return to his own lines. Within them, the latter encountered Meade, who had recovered from his indisposition and ridden over to see him. Lee at first did not recognize his old friend. Then he did, but with something of a shock. "What are you doing with all that gray in your beard?" he asked, and his Gettysburg opponent replied genially: "You have to answer for most of it." As they rode together toward headquarters, the soldiers camped along the road began to cheer, and Meade, not wanting to misrepresent himself, told his color bearer, who had the flag rolled up: "Unfurl that flag." The bearer did, and drew a sharp retort. "Damn your old rag!" a butternut veteran called from beside the road. "We are cheering General Lee."

Back in his tent Lee talked for a time with Meade, then turned to the writing of his report on the campaign that now was over. "It is with pain that I announce to Your Excellency the surrender of the Army of Northern Virginia," the document began. Walter Taylor did most of the work on this, as he had on all the others, but Lee also conferred with Charles Marshall, whom he had instructed to draw up an order bidding the troops farewell. Marshall, a former Baltimore lawyer and grandnephew of the illustrious Chief Justice, had delayed preparing the address — because all the coming and going around headquarters had left him no time, he said, but also because of a certain reluctance, a feeling of inadequacy for the task. "What can I say to those people?" he asked a friend this morning, still avoiding getting down to putting pen to paper. Lee settled this by ordering the colonel to get into his ambulance, parked nearby with a guard on duty to fend off intruders, and stay there until he finished the composition. Marshall, his writer's block effectively broken, soon emerged with a penciled draft. Lee looked it over and made a few changes, including the deletion of a paragraph he thought might "tend to keep alive the feel-

ing existing between the North and South"; after which the Marylander returned to the ambulance, wrote out the final version of the
order, and turned it over to a clerk for making inked copies which
Lee then signed for distribution to the corps commanders and ranking
members of his staff.

Having signed his parole he might have left then, as Grant had
done by noon on this rainy Monday; yet he did not. The formal surrender ceremony was set for Wednesday — the required turning over
of all "arms, artillery and public property," in accordance with the
terms accepted — and he stayed on, not to take an active role as a
participant, but simply to be on hand, if not in view, when his men
faced the sad ritual of laying down their shot-torn flags and weapons.
He continued to keep to his tent, however, through most of the waiting
time, while all around him, despite the pickets both sides had posted
to discourage fraternization, blue-clad visitors of all ranks drifted
through the camps for a look at their one-time enemies. For the most
part they were received without animosity; "Success had made them
good-natured," one grayback uncharitably observed. A Federal colonel
noted that the Confederates "behaved with more courtesy than cordiality," and it was true. "Affiliation was out of the question; we were
content with civility," one explained. Union troops, on the other hand,
were friendly and outgoing; "in fact almost oppressively so," a butternut declared. "We've been fighting one another for four years. Give
me a Confederate five-dollar bill to remember you by," a bluecoat
said, and his hearers found nothing offensive in his manner. Sometimes,
though, a discordant note would be struck and would bring on a fiery
answer — as when a Federal major, seeking a souvenir to take home,
asked a Confederate staff captain for the white towel he had carried
as a flag of truce on Sunday. "I'll see you in hell first!" the angered staffer
replied. "It is humiliating enough to have had to carry it and exhibit it;
I'm not going to let you preserve it as a monument of our defeat."
Similarly, when a visiting sergeant tried to open a friendly discussion
by remarking: "Well, Johnny, I guess you fellows will go home now
to stay," he found that he had touched a nerve. The rebel was in no
mood to be gloated over. "You *guess*, do you?" he said hotly. "Maybe
we are. But don't be giving us any of your impudence. If you do, we'll
come back and lick you again."

Much of Tuesday, with rain still murmurous on the canvas overhead, Lee spent working on his last report. He finished and signed it
next morning, April 12, while his veterans, in Longstreet's words,
"marched to the field in front of Appomattox Courthouse, and by
divisions and parts of divisions deployed into line, stacked their arms,
folded their colors, and walked empty-handed to find their distant,
blighted homes." The weather having faired, they made as brave a show
as their rags and sadness would permit; "worn, bright-eyed men," a

Federal brigadier would call them. They seemed to him "purged of the mortal, as if knowing pain or joy no more," and he asked himself as he watched them pass before him "in proud humiliation . . . thin, worn, and famished, but erect, and with eyes looking level into ours . . . Was not such manhood to be welcomed back into a Union so tested and assured?" They had been whipped about as thoroughly as any American force had ever been or ever would be, short of annihilation, but it was part of their particular pride that they would never admit it, even to themselves. "Goodbye, General; God bless you," a ragged private told his brigadier commander over a parting handshake at the close of the surrender ceremony. "We'll go home, make three more crops, and try them again."

They left in groups, dispersing by routes as varied as their desti-nations, and one of the smallest groups was Lee's. He rode with Taylor and Marshall northeast into Buckingham County, bound for Richmond, and stopped for the night, some twenty miles out, in a strip of woods beside the road. To his surprise he found Longstreet there before him, likewise headed for a reunion with his family. Once more they shared a campsite, then next morning diverged to meet no more. The burly Georgian was assailed by mixed emotions, partly as a result of having encountered his friend Grant on Monday, shortly before the blue com-mander's departure for Burkeville. "Pete, let's have another game of brag to recall the old days," Grant had said, and though there was no time for cards he gave him a cigar, which Longstreet said "was grate-fully received." Moved by the reunion, he later wondered: "Why do men fight who were born to be brothers?" and remarked, not without bitterness, that the next time he fought he would be sure it was necessary.

But that was by no means a reaction characteristic of the veterans now trudging the roads in all directions from the scene of their sur-render. They were content with "the satisfaction that proceeds from the consciousness of duty faithfully performed." The words were part of Lee's final behest they took with them from the farewell issued two days ago, near Appomattox Courthouse.

Headquarters Army of N. Va.
April 10, 1865

General Orders ⎱
    No. 9 ⎰

    After four years of arduous service marked by unsurpassed courage and fortitude, the Army of Northern Virginia has been compelled to yield to overwhelming numbers and resources.

    I need not tell the brave survivors of so many hard fought battles, who have remained steadfast to the last, that I have consented to this result from no distrust of them. But feeling that valor and devotion could accomplish nothing that could compensate for the loss that must have attended the continuance of the contest, I determined to avoid the useless sacrifice of those whose past services have endeared them to their countrymen.

By the terms of the agreement, officers and men can return to their homes and remain until exchanged. You will take with you the satisfaction that proceeds from the consciousness of duty faithfully performed, and I earnestly pray that a merciful God will extend to you His blessing and protection.

With an unceasing admiration of your constancy and devotion to your Country, and a grateful remembrance of your kind and generous consideration for myself, I bid you all an affectionate farewell.

R. E. LEE
General.

In addition to the copies made by Marshall's clerk for normal distribution, others were transcribed and taken to the general for his signature, and these remained for those who had them the possession they cherished most. One such was Henry Perry, the young infantry captain who had refused a drink from Seth Williams' silver flask three nights before, near Cumberland Church. Later he told how he got it and how he felt, then and down the years, about the man who signed it. "I sat down and copied it on a piece of Confederate paper," he recalled, "using a drumhead for a desk, the best I could do. I carried this copy to General Lee, and asked him to sign it for me. He signed it and I have it now. It is the best authority, along with my parole, that I can produce why after that day I no longer raised a soldier's hand for the South. There were tears in his eyes when he signed it for me, and when I turned to walk away there were tears in my own eyes. He was in all respects the greatest man who ever lived, and as a humble officer of the South, I thank heaven I had the honor of following him."

Lucifer in Starlight

★ ❁ ☆

GUNS BOOMED THE NEWS OF APPOMATTOX
as dawn broke over Washington next morning, April 10, one week
after a similar uproar hailed the fall of Richmond. If the reaction now
was less hysterical, if many loyal citizens were content to remain abed,
counting the five hundred separate thuds of the salute — as compared
to nine hundred the Monday before — that was not only because of the
earlier drain on their emotions, it was also because of rain drumming
hard on their bedroom windows and mud slathered more than shoetop-
deep outside. Still, a carousing journalist observed, the streets were
soon "alive with people singing and cheering, carrying flags and saluting
everybody, hungering and thirsting for speeches." They especially
wanted a speech from Lincoln, whose presence in town, after his return
from down the coast last evening, was in contrast to his absence during
the previous celebration. At the Treasury Department, for example,
when the clerks were told they had been given another holiday, the
same reporter noted that they "assembled in the great corridor of their
building and sang 'Old Hundredth' with thrilling, even tear-compelling
effect," then trooped across the grounds to the White House, where,
still in excellent voice, they serenaded the President with the national
anthem.

He was at breakfast and did not appear, but a night's sleep had
done nothing to diminish the excitement he felt on reading Grant's
wire at bedtime. "Let Master Tad have a Navy sword," he directed in
a note to Welles, and added in another to the Secretary of War (omitting
the question mark as superfluous on this day of celebration): "Tad
wants some flags. Can he be accommodated." Stanton evidently complied in short order, for when a procession arrived from the Navy
Yard a couple of hours later, dragging six boat howitzers which were
fired as they rolled up Pennsylvania Avenue, the boy stood at a second-
story window and flaunted a captured rebel flag, to the wild applause

of a crowd that quickly swelled to about three thousand. Presently Lincoln himself appeared at the window, and the yells redoubled. "Speech! Speech!" men cried from the lawn below. But he put them off. He would speak tonight, or more likely tomorrow, "and I shall have nothing to say if you dribble it all out of me before." As the laughter subsided he took up a notion that had struck him. "I see you have a band of music with you," he said, and when a voice called up: "We have two or three!" he proposed closing the interview by having the musicians play "a particular tune which I will name.... I have always thought 'Dixie' one of the best tunes I ever heard. Our adversaries over the way attempted to appropriate it, but I insisted yesterday that we fairly captured it. I presented the question to the Attorney General and he gave it as his legal opinion that it is now our lawful prize. I now request the band to favor me with its performance."

The band did, to roars of approval from the crowd, then followed the irreverent rebel anthem with a lively rendition of "Yankee Doodle," after which Lincoln called for "three good hearty cheers for General Grant and all under his command." These given, he requested "three more cheers for our gallant navy," and when they were over he retired, as did the rollicking crowd. Near sundown, a third crew of celebrants turned up, to be similarly put off on grounds that he had to be careful what he said at times like this. "Everything I say, you know, goes into print. If I make a mistake it doesn't merely affect me nor you, but the country. I therefore ought at least to try not to make mistakes. If, then, a general demonstration be made tomorrow evening, and it is agreeable, I will endeavor to say something and not make a mistake without at least trying carefully to avoid it."

Next night he was back, as promised, and they were there to hear him in their thousands, packed shoulder to shoulder on the White House lawn and looking up at the same window. Off in the drizzly distance, Arlington House — R. E. Lee's former home, long since commandeered by the government he had defied — glittered on its hillside beyond the Potomac, illuminated tonight along with all the other public buildings, while nearer at hand, gilded with light from torches and flares, the Capitol dome seemed to float like a captive balloon in a gauzy mist that verged on rain. To one observer yesterday, seeing him for the first time, Lincoln "appeared somewhat younger and more off-hand and vigorous than I should have expected. His gestures and countenance had something of the harmless satisfaction of a young politician at a ratification meeting after his first election to the Legislature. He was happy, and glad to see others happy." Tonight, though, he was different. Appearing after Tad had once more warmed the crowd by flourishing the Confederate banner, he seemed grave and thoughtful, and he had with him, by way of assuring that he would "not make a mistake without at least trying carefully to avoid it," a rolled-up manuscript he had spent most of the day preparing. What he had in mind to deliver tonight was not so much a speech as it was a closely written document, a state paper dealing less with the past, or even the present, than with the future; less with victory than with the problems victory brought. The crowd below did not know this yet, however, and Noah Brooks — a young newsman who was slated to replace one of his private secretaries — saw "something terrible in the enthusiasm with which the beloved Chief Magistrate was received. Cheers upon cheers, wave after wave of applause rolled up, the President patiently standing quiet until it was over."

"Fellow Citizens," he said at last. Holding a candle in his left hand to light the papers in his right, he waited for new cheers to subside, and then continued. "We are met this evening not in sorrow but in gladness of heart. The evacuation of Petersburg and Richmond, and the surrender of the principal insurgent army, give hope of a righteous and speedy peace whose joyous expression cannot be restrained." Cheered again, he sought relief from the difficulty of managing both the candle and his manuscript by signaling to Brooks, who stood behind one of the window drapes beside him, with what the journalist called "a comical motion of his left foot and elbow, which I construed to mean that I should hold his candle for him." With both hands free to grip the sheaf of papers, and Brooks extending the light from behind the curtain, he went on with his speech, dropping each read page as he began the next. Unseen by the crowd, Tad scrambled about on the balcony floor to catch the sheets as his father let them flutter down. "Another, another," he kept saying impatiently all through the reading, heard plainly because of a hush that soon descended on the celebrants on the lawn below.

Referred to afterwards by Brooks as "a silent, intent, and perhaps surprised multitude," they were in fact both silent and surprised, but they were more confused than they were intent. Until Lincoln began speaking they had not supposed tonight was any occasion for mentioning sadness, even to deny it, and as he continued along other lines, equally unexpected at a victory celebration, their confusion and discomfort grew. After this brief introduction, scarcely fitting in itself, he spoke not of triumphs, but rather of the problems that loomed with peace; in particular one problem. "By these recent successes," he read from the second of the sheets that fell fluttering to his feet, "the reinauguration of the national authority — reconstruction — which has had a large share of thought from the first, is pressed much more closely upon our attention. It is fraught with great difficulty. Unlike the case of a war between independent nations, there is no authorized organ for us to treat with — no one man has authority to give up the rebellion for any other man. We simply must begin with, and mold from, disorganized and discordant elements. Nor is it a small additional embarrassment that we, the loyal people, differ among ourselves as to the mode, manner, and means of reconstruction."

This then was his subject — "the mode, manner, and means of reconstruction" — and he stayed with it through Tad's retrieval of the last dropped sheet, addressing himself less to his listeners, it seemed, than to the knotty problem itself, and in language that was correspondingly knotty. For example, in dealing with the claim that secession, while plainly illegal, had in fact removed from the Union certain states which now would have to comply with some hard-line requirements before they could be granted readmission, he pronounced it "a merely pernicious abstraction," likely to "have no effect other than the mischievous one of dividing our friends" left and right of the stormy center. "We all agree that the seceded states, so called, are out of their proper practical relation with the Union, and that the sole object of the government, civil and military, in regard to those states, is to again get them into that proper practical relation. I believe it is not only possible, but in fact easier, to do this without deciding or even considering whether these states have even been out of the Union, than with it. Finding themselves safely at home, it would be utterly immaterial whether they had ever been abroad. Let us all join in doing the acts necessary to restoring the proper practical relations between these states and the Union, and each forever after innocently indulge his own opinion whether, in doing the acts, he brought the states from without into the Union, or only gave them proper assistance, they never having been out of it."

In regard to the new state government in Louisiana, which had the support of only ten percent of the electorate, he acknowledged the validity of criticism that it was scantly based and did not give the franchise to the Negro. All the same, though he himself wished its constituency "contained fifty, thirty, or even twenty thousand [voters] instead of only twelve thousand, as it does," and though he preferred to have the ballot extended to include the blacks — at least "the very intelligent" and "those who serve our cause as soldiers" — he did not believe these shortcomings invalidated the present arrangement, which in any case was better than no arrangement at all. "Concede that the new government of Louisiana is only to what it should be as the egg is to the fowl, we shall sooner have the fowl by hatching the egg than by smashing it." For one thing, the state legislature had already voted to ratify the 13th Amendment, and the sooner its authority was recognized by Congress, the sooner all men would be free throughout the land. He had thought long and hard about the problem, as well as about various proposals for its solution, "and yet so great peculiarities pertain to each state, and such important and sudden changes occur in the same state, and withal, so new and unprecedented is the whole case, that no exclusive and inflexible plan can safely be prescribed as to details and collaterals.... In the present 'situation,' as the phrase goes, it may be my duty to make some new announcement to the people of the South. I am considering, and shall not fail to act when satisfied that action will be proper."

That was the end, and he let it hang there, downbeat, enigmatic, inconclusive, as perfunctory and uncertain, even in its peroration, as the applause that followed when his listeners finally understood that the speech — if that was what it had been — was over. Tad gathered up the last sheet of manuscript, and as Lincoln stepped back into the room he said to Brooks, still holding the candle out from behind the window drape: "That was a pretty fair speech, I think, but you threw some light on it." Down on the lawn, the misty drizzle had turned to rain while he spoke, and the crowd began to disperse, their spirits nearly as dampened as their clothes. Some drifted off to bars in search of revival. Others walked over to Franklin Square to serenade Stanton, who might do better by them.

Not that there were no repercussions. There were, and they came fast — mostly from disaffected radicals who contended that secession had been a form of suicide from which no state could be resurrected except on conditions imposed by them at the end of the struggle now drawing rapidly to a close. Differing from Lincoln in this, or at any rate on what those terms should be, they believed they saw clearly enough what he was up to. Congress would not meet again until December, and he had it in mind to unite the people behind him, between now and then, and thus confront his congressional opponents with an overwhelming majority of voters whom he would attract to his lenient views by a series of public appeals, such as the one tonight from the high White House window or last month's inaugural, adorned with oratorical phrases as empty as they were vague. "Malice toward none" had no meaning for them, as here applied, and "charity for all" had even less; for where was the profit in winning a war if then you lost the peace? They asked that with a special urgency now that they had begun to suspect the Administration of planning to neglect the Negro, who was in fact what this war had been about from start to finish. Lincoln's reference tonight to a possible limited extension of the franchise to include those who were "very intelligent" only served to increase their apprehension that the cause of the blacks was about to be abandoned, possibly in exchange for the support of certain reactionary elements in the reunited country — not excluding former Confederates — in putting together a new and powerful coalition of moderates, unbeatable at the polls for decades to come. One among those perturbed was Chase, who had written this day to his former chief of his fears in regard to that neglect. The most acceptable solution, he said, was "the reorganization of state governments under constitutions securing suffrage to all citizens.... This way is recommended by its simplicity, facility, and, above all, justice," the Chief Justice wrote. "It will be hereafter counted equally a crime and a folly if the colored loyalists of the rebel states shall be left to the control of restored rebels, not likely in that case to be either wise or just, until taught both wisdom and justice by new calamities."

Lincoln found the letter on his desk when he came into the office next morning, and Chase followed it up with another, that same Wednesday, midway of Holy Week, suggesting an interview "to have the whole subject talked over." Others had the same notion; Charles Sumner, for example. He had not heard the speech last night, but his secretary reported that it was "not in keeping with what was in men's minds. The people had gathered, from an instructive impulse, to rejoice over a great and final victory, and they listened with respect, but with no expressions of enthusiasm, except that the quaint simile of 'the egg' drew applause. The more serious among them felt that the President's utterances on the subject were untimely, and that his insistence at such an hour on his favorite plan was not the harbinger of peace among the loyal supporters of the government." The Massachusetts senator felt this, too, and regretted it, his secretary noted; "for he saw at hand another painful controversy with a President whom he respected, on a question where he felt it his duty to stand firm." Already his mail was filled with urgings that he do just that. "Magnanimity is a great word with the disloyal who think to tickle the President's ear with it," a prominent New Yorker wrote. "Magnanimity is one thing. Weakness is another. I know you are near the throne, and you must guard its honor." A Boston constituent knew where to fix the blame: on Lincoln, whose reconstruction policy was "wicked and blasphemous" in its betrayal of the cause of freedom by his failure to take the obvious next step after emancipation. "No power but God ever has or could have forced him up to the work he has been instrumental of, and now we see the dregs of his backwardness."

Mainly these were old-line abolitionists, men with a great capacity for wrath. Ben Wade, for one, expressed the hope that such neglect would goad the southern blacks to insurrection. "If they could contrive to slay one half of their oppressors," he asserted, "the other half would hold them in the highest regard, and no doubt treat them with justice." But even this was mild compared to the reaction that followed disclosure that Lincoln had authorized John A. Campbell to reassemble the Virginia legislature, composed in part of the very men who had withdrawn the Old Dominion from the Union in the first place. As it happened, the Joint Committee on the Conduct of the War was down at Richmond now, aboard the steamer *Baltimore*, and one of its members went ashore this morning to get the daily papers. He came back, much excited, with a copy of the Richmond *Whig*, which carried an Address to the People of Virginia by some of the legislators then about to assemble. Moreover, Weitzel had indorsed it, and Wade went into a frenzy at this evidence of official sanction for the outrage. Fuming, he declared — "in substance, if not in exact words," a companion afterwards testified — "that there had been much talk of the assassination of Lincoln; that if he authorized the approval of that paper . . . by God, the sooner he was assassinated the better!" Others felt as strongly about this development, which seemed to them to undo all they had worked for all these years. Zachariah Chandler, according to the same report, "was also exceedingly harsh in his remarks," and none of the other members took offense at the denunciations.

In Washington, the Secretary of War was apparently the first to get the news. He went at once to Lincoln, then to Sumner, who wrote Chase: "I find Stanton much excited. He had a full and candid talk with the President last eve, and insisted that the proposed meeting at Richmond should be forbidden. He thinks we are in a crisis more trying than any before, with the chance of losing the fruits of our victory. He asks if it was not Grant who surrendered to Lee, instead of Lee to Grant. He is sure that Richmond is beginning to govern Washington."

But Lincoln by then had revoked his authorization for the Virginians to assemble. At a cabinet meeting the day before, he had found Stanton and Speed vehement in their opposition, and none of the rest in favor of creating a situation in which, as Welles pointed out, "the so-called legislature would be likely to propose terms which might seem reasonable, but which we could not accept." To these were added the protests of various other advisers, by no means all of them die-hard radicals. Lincoln considered the matter overnight — aside, that is, from the time he spent delivering his speech from the balconied window — and though, as he said, he rather fancied the notion of having the secessionists "come together and undo their own work," at 9 o'clock Wednesday morning he telegraphed Weitzel a question and a suggestion: "Is there any sign of the rebel legislature coming together on the basis of my letter to you? If there is any sign, inform me of what it is; if there is no such sign you may as [well] withdraw the offer."

Although it was true he had no wish just now for a knockdown drag-out fight with either wing of his party, his decision to revoke what he called his 'offer' was in fact less political than it was practical in nature. The conditions under which it had been extended no longer obtained; the gains sought in exchange had since been won. His purpose in approving Campbell's proposal, just under a week ago, had been to encourage Virginia's legislators, in return for certain "remissions" on his part, to withdraw her troops from the rebel armies and the state itself from the Confederacy. Grant had accomplished the first of these objectives on Palm Sunday — the formal surrender ceremony was getting under way at Appomattox Courthouse even as Lincoln's telegram went over the wire to Weitzel — and the second scarcely mattered, since there was no longer any sizeable body of armed graybacks within the borders of the Old Dominion. So much for that. As for the problem of keeping or breaking his promise to Campbell, that was merely personal; which was only another way of saying it didn't count. "Bad promises are better broken than kept," he had said in his speech the night before, with reference to assurances he had given those who set up the provisional Louisiana government. "I shall treat this as a bad promise, and break it, whenever I shall be convinced that keeping it is adverse to the public interest." And so it was in this case; he simply labeled the promise 'bad' — meaning profitless — and broke it.

When he heard from Weitzel that afternoon that "passports have gone out for the legislators, and it is common talk that they will come together," Lincoln wired back a definite order that their permission to assemble be revoked. He prefaced this, however, with some lawyerly explication of the events leading up to his decision, which he said was based on statements made by Campbell in a letter informing certain of the prospective legislators what their task would be in Richmond. He had talked the matter over with the President on two occasions, the Alabama jurist declared, and both conversations "had relation to the establishment of a government for Virginia, the requirement of oaths of allegiance from the citizens, and the terms of settlement with the United States." Lincoln flatly denied this in his sundown wire to Weitzel. "[Judge Campbell] assumes, as appears to me, that I have called the insurgent legislature of Virginia together, as the rightful legislature of the state, to settle all differences with the United States. I have done no such thing. I spoke of them not as a legislature, but as 'the gentlemen who have *acted* as the Legislature of Virginia in support of the rebellion.' I did this on purpose to exclude the assumption that I was recognizing them as a rightful body. I dealt with them as men having power *de facto* to do a specific thing; to wit, 'to withdraw the Virginia troops and other support from resistance to the general government.' . . . I meant this and no more. Inasmuch however as Judge Campbell misconstrues this, and is still pressing for an armistice, contrary to the explicit statement of the paper I gave him, and particularly as Gen. Grant has since captured the Virginia troops, so that giving a consideration for their withdrawal is no longer applicable, let my letter to you and the paper to Judge Campbell both be withdrawn, or countermanded, and he be notified of it. Do not allow them to assemble; but if any have come, allow them safe-return to their homes."

Word of this revocation spread rapidly over Washington and out across the land, to the high delight of those who lately had seethed with indignation: particularly the hard-war hard-peace Jacobins, who saw in the action near certain proof that, in a crunch, the President would always come over to their side of the question — provided, of course, the pressure was kept on him: which it would be. James Speed, who had no sooner been confirmed as Attorney General than he went over to the radicals all-out, presently wrote to Chase that Lincoln "never seemed so near our views" as he did now, with Holy Week drawing rapidly toward a close.

★ ★ ★

Davis by then was in Greensboro, North Carolina, just under fifty miles south of the Virginia line. Once more "a government on wheels," he and his cabinet had left Danville late Monday night in a driving rainstorm that only added to the depression and confusion brought on by the arrival of simultaneous reports, no less alarming for being unofficial and somewhat vague, that Lee had surrendered to Grant the day before, near Appomattox Courthouse, and that a heavy column of enemy cavalry was approaching from the west. Nothing more was heard for a time about the extent of Lee's removal from the war — that is, whether all or only part of his army had been surrendered — but the other report was soon confirmed by word that a detachment from the column of blue troopers, some 4000 strong under Stoneman, had burned the Dan River bridge a few hours after the fugitive President's train rattled across it and on into Carolina. Informed of his narrow escape from capture, Davis managed a smile of relief. "A miss is as good as a mile," he remarked, and his smile broadened.

Such pleasure as he took from this was soon dispelled by the coolness of his reception when the train crept into Greensboro next morning. Though news of his coming had been wired ahead, no welcoming group of citizens turned out to greet him or even acknowledge his presence, which made their town the Confederacy's third capital in ten days. For the most part, like many in this Piedmont region of the Old North State, they had never been enthusiastic about the war or its goals, and their pro-Union feeling had been considerably strengthened by reports, just in, that Stoneman's raiders were headed in their direction and that Sherman had begun his advance from Goldsboro the day before, first on Raleigh, with Johnston known to be falling back, and then on them. Fearing reprisal for any courtesy offered Davis and his party, they extended none — except to the wealthy and ailing Trenholm; he and Mrs Trenholm were taken in by a banker who, it was said, hoped to persuade the Secretary to exchange some gold from the treasure train for his Confederate bonds. Davis himself would have had no place to lay his head if an aide, John T. Wood — former skipper of the *Tallahassee* and the President's first wife's nephew — had not had his family refugeeing in half of a modest Greensboro house. Despite protests from the landlord, who feared that his property would go up in flames as soon as Stoneman or Sherman appeared, Wood's wife had prepared a small upstairs bedroom for the Chief Executive. While Trenholm was being made comfortable in the banker's mansion across town, the rest of the cabinet adapted themselves as best they could to living in the dilapidated coaches, which had been shunted onto a siding near the depot.

Beauregard and his staff were similarly lodged in three boxcars parked nearby. He had arrived the previous night, en route to Danville in response to a summons from the Commander in Chief, and now he crossed the tracks to report aboard the presidential coach. Davis greeted him cordially, eager for news of the situation around Raleigh. Dismayed, the Creole told of Johnston's hurried evacuation of Smithfield, under pressure from Sherman, and of his present withdrawal toward the state capital, which he did not plan to defend against a force three times his size. In short, Beauregard said, the situation was hopeless. Davis disagreed. Lee's surrender had not been confirmed; some portion of his army might have escaped and could soon be combined with Johnston's, as originally intended. The struggle would continue, whatever the odds, even if it had to be done on the far side of the Mississippi. Beauregard was amazed, but by no means converted from his gloom, when Davis got off a wire instructing Johnston to come at once to Greensboro for a strategy conference. "The important question first to be solved is what point of concentration should be made," the President declared. He had no intention of giving up the war, and he wanted the Virginian to be thinking of his next move before they met, though he was frank to admit that "your more intimate knowledge of the data for the solution of the problem deters me from making a specific suggestion on that point."

Johnston arrived next morning — Wednesday, April 12 — and took up quarters in one of Beauregard's boxcars. Yesterday in Raleigh, Zeb Vance had warned him that Davis, "a man of imperfectly constituted genius, . . . could absolutely *blind himself* to those things which his prejudices or hopes did not desire to see." Johnston readily agreed, having observed this quality often in the past. But he had never seen it demonstrated more forcefully than he did today, when he and his fellow general entered the presidential coach for the council of war to which he had been summoned from his duties in the field. "We had supposed that we were to be questioned concerning the military resources of our department in connection with the question of continuing or terminating the war," he later wrote. Instead, "the President's object seemed to be to give, not obtain information." Quite as amazed as his companion had been the day before, he listened while Davis spoke of raising a large army by rounding up deserters and conscripting men who previously had escaped the draft. Both generals protested that those who had avoided service in less critical times were unlikely to come forward now, and when Johnston took the occasion to advise that he be authorized to open a correspondence with Sherman regarding a truce that might lead to a successful conclusion of the conflict, this too was rejected out of hand. Any such effort was sure to fail, he was informed, and "its failure would have a demoralizing effect on both the troops and the people, neither of [whom]" — as Davis later summed up his reply — "had shown any disposition to surrender, or had any reason to suppose that their government contemplated abandoning its trust."

There was a pause. All three men sat tight-lipped, brooding on the impasse they had reached. Davis at last broke the silence by remarking that Breckinridge was expected to arrive at any moment from Virginia with definite information about the extent of Lee's disaster, and he suggested that they adjourn until the Secretary got there. The two generals were glad to retire from a situation they found awkward in the extreme — something like being closeted with a dreamy madman — although the encounter was not without its satisfactions for them both, convinced as they were, not only that they were right and he was wrong about the military outlook, but also that he would presently be obliged to admit it; if not to them, then in any case to Grant and Sherman.

In point of fact, they were righter than they would have any way of knowing until reports came in from close at hand and far afield. On this fourth anniversary of the day Beauregard opened fire on Sumter, Lee's men — not part: all — were formally laying down their arms at Appomattox Courthouse, just over a hundred miles away, and James Wilson, after visiting destruction upon Selma, even now was riding unopposed into Montgomery, the Confederacy's first capital, in bloodless celebration of the date the shooting war began. Nor was that all by any means. Canby marched this morning into Mobile, which Maury had abandoned in the night to avoid encirclement and capture; while here in North Carolina itself, some eighty miles to the east, Sherman was closing on Raleigh, whose occupation tomorrow would make it the ninth of the eleven seceded state capitals to feel the tread of the invader; all, that is, but Austin and Tallahassee, whose survival was less the result of their ability to resist than it was of Federal oversight or disinterest. Even nearer at hand — but unaware that Jefferson Davis was a prize within their reach — Stoneman's raiders had bypassed Greensboro to strike today at Salisbury, fifty of the ninety miles down the railroad to Charlotte, rounding up 1300 prisoners and putting the torch to supplies collected in expectation that Lee would move that way from Burkeville. Also taken were 10,000 stands of small arms and 14 pieces of artillery, the latter commanded by Lieutenant Colonel John C. Pemberton, who had surrendered Vicksburg, three months under two years ago, as a lieutenant general. Enlarging his destruction to include the railway bridges for miles in both directions before he swung west from Salisbury to return to Tennessee, Stoneman, though still uninformed of its proximity, ensured that when the fugitive rebel government resumed its flight — Meade and Ord hovered northward;

Sherman was advancing from the east — Davis and his ministers would no longer have the railroad as a means of transportation, swift and tireless and more or less free of the exigencies of weather, but would have to depend on horses for keeping ahead of the fast-riding bluecoats who soon would be hard on their trail.

Arriving that evening after his roundabout ride from Richmond by way of Farmville, Breckinridge knew even less of most of this than Johnston and Beauregard did. He did know, however, that Lee's surrender included the whole of his army, and this in itself was enough to convince the two generals that any further attempt to continue the conflict "would be the greatest of crimes." Johnston said as much to the Secretary when he called on him that night, adding that he wanted the opportunity to tell Davis the same thing, if Davis would only listen. Breckinridge assured him he would have his chance at the council of war, which he had been informed would be resumed next morning in the house John Wood had provided across town.

When the two generals entered the small upstairs room at 10 o'clock Thursday morning the atmosphere was grim. "Most solemnly funereal," Reagan later called it; for he and his fellow cabinet members, Benjamin, Mallory, and George Davis — Trenholm, still ailing, was absent — had just concluded a session during which Breckinridge presented his report, and "it was apparent that they had to consider the loss of the cause." Only the President and the imperturbable Benjamin seemed unconvinced that the end was at hand. Davis in fact not only did not believe that Lee's surrender meant the death of Confederate hopes for survival; he began at once, after welcoming Johnston and Beauregard, a further exposition of his views that resistance could and must continue until the northern people and their leaders grew weary enough to negotiate a peace that acknowledged southern independence. "Our late disasters are terrible," he admitted, "but I do not think we should regard them as fatal. I think we can whip the enemy yet, if our people will turn out." After a pause, which brought no response, he turned to the senior of the two field commanders. "We should like to hear your views, General Johnston."

The Virginian had been told he would have his chance, and now he took it. In a tone described by Mallory as "almost spiteful" he spoke directly to the man he had long considered his bitterest enemy, North or South. "My views are, sir, that our people are tired of the war, feel themselves whipped, and will not fight." Overrun by greatly superior Union forces, the Confederacy was "without money, or credit, or arms, or ammunition, or means of procuring them," he said flatly, driving home the words like nails in the lid of a coffin. "My men are daily deserting in large numbers. Since Lee's defeat they regard the war as at an end." There was, he declared in conclusion, no choice but surrender. "We may perhaps obtain terms which we ought to accept."

Davis heard him out with no change of expression, eyes fixed on a small piece of paper which he kept folding, unfolding, and folding. After the silence that followed Johnston's declaration of defeat, he asked in a low even tone: "What do you say, General Beauregard?" The Creole too had his moment of satisfaction. "I concur in all General Johnston has said," he replied quietly. Another silence followed. Then Davis, still holding his eyes down on the paper he kept folding and refolding, addressed Johnston in the same inflectionless voice as before: "You speak of obtaining terms...." The general said he would like to get in touch with Sherman to arrange a truce during which they could work out the details required for surrender. All those present except Benjamin agreed that this was the thing to do, and Davis accepted their judgment, but not without a reservation he considered overriding. "Well, sir, you can adopt this course," he told Johnston, "though I am not sanguine as to ultimate results." At the general's insistence, he dictated a letter to Sherman for Johnston's signature. "The results of the recent campaign in Virginia have changed the relative military condition of the belligerents," it read. "I am, therefore, induced to address you in this form the inquiry whether, to stop the further effusion of blood and devastation of property, you are willing to make a temporary suspension of active operations . . . the object being to permit the civil authorities to enter into the needful arrangements to terminate the existing war."

Tomorrow was Good Friday; Davis spent it preparing to continue his flight southward. Others might treat for peace, not he. Nor would he leave the country. He had, he said when urged to escape to Mexico or the West Indies by getting aboard a ship off the Florida coast, "no idea whatever of leaving Confederate soil as long as there are men in uniform to fight for the cause." Fortunately, the treasure train had been sent ahead to Charlotte before Stoneman wrecked the railroad above and below Salisbury, but Davis and his party would have to take their chances on the muddy roads and byways. Nothing in his manner showed that he had any doubt of getting through, however, any more than he doubted the survival of the nation he headed. Only in private, and only then in a note he wrote his wife that same Good Friday, did he show that he had anything less than total confidence in the outcome of a struggle that had continued unabated for four years and was moving even now into a fifth.

"Dear Winnie," he wrote to her in Charlotte, employing her pet name before signing with his own, "I will come to you if I can. Everything is dark. You should prepare for the worst by dividing your baggage so as to move in wagons.... I have lingered on the road to little purpose. My love to the children and Maggie. God bless, guide and preserve you, ever prays Your most affectionate Banny."

★ ★ ★

There was a ceremony that same holy day in Charleston Harbor, held in accordance with War Department instructions which Stanton himself had issued back in March. "*Ordered*. That at the hour of noon on the 14th day of April, 1865, Brevet Major General Anderson will raise and plant upon the ruins of Fort Sumter the same United States flag which floated over the battlements of that fort during the rebel assault, and which was lowered and saluted by him and the small force of his command when the works were evacuated on the 14th day of April, 1861."

At first there was only minor interest in the occasion, even when it was given out that Henry Ward Beecher, the popular Brooklyn minister, would be the principal speaker. Presently, however, the fall of Richmond, followed within the week by Lee's surrender, placed the affair in a new light, one in which it could be seen as commemorating not only the start but also the finish of the war, in the same place on the same date, with precisely four years intervening between the hauling down and running up of the same flag. People began to plan to attend from all directions, especially from Boston and Philadelphia, where abolitionist sentiment ran strong, as well as from the sea islands along the Georgia and Carolina coasts, where uplift programs had been in progress ever since their occupation. Prominent men were among them, and women too, who for decades had been active in the movement. "Only listen to that — in Charleston's streets!" William Lloyd Garrison marveled, tears of joy brimming his eyes as a regimental band played "John Brown's Body" amid the ruins created by the long bombardment, which another visitor noted "had left its marks everywhere, even on gravestones in the cemeteries." So many came that the navy was hard put, this mild Good Friday morning, to provide vessels enough to ferry them from the Battery wharves out to the fort. More than four thousand were on hand, including a number of blacks from nearby plantations, though it was observed that there were scarcely a dozen local whites in the throng pressed close about the platform where the dignitaries awaited the stroke of noon.

Except for the bunting draped about the rostrum, the polished brass of army and navy officers, and the colorful silks on some of the women, the scene was bleak enough. Sumter, a Union soldier declared at the time it was retaken, "was simply an irregular curved pile of pulverized masonry, which had with enormous labor been industriously shoveled back into place as fast as we knocked it out of shape, and was held up on the inside by gabions and timber work. So many tons of projectiles had been fired into it that the shot and shell seemed to be mixed through the mass as thick as plums in a pudding." Somewhere in the pudding mass of the central parade, where the crowd gathered, was the grave of Private Daniel Hough, who had died in a flare-back while firing the fifty-gun salute of departure, four years ago today, and thus had been the first to fall in a war that by now had cost well over 600,000 lives. What was more, the man generally credited with firing from nearby Cummings Point the first shot of that war — white-haired Edmund Ruffin, past seventy and still hating, as he said in a farewell note this week, "the perfidious, malignant and vile Yankee race" — was dead too now from a bullet he put through his head when he heard the news from Appomattox.

Few if any were thinking of either Hough or Ruffin, however, as noon approached and Robert Anderson arrived with Quincy Gillmore, the department commander. Two months short of sixty, Anderson looked much older; sickness had worn him down and deprived him, except for a brief period of command in his native Kentucky, of any part in the struggle that followed the bloodless two-day bombardment in Charleston Harbor, which had turned out to be the high point in his life. He carried himself with military erectness, but he appeared somewhat confused: perhaps because, as a journalist would report, he "could see nothing by which to recognize the Fort Sumter he had left four years ago."

Still, this was another high point, if not so high as the one before, and as such had its effect both on him and on those who watched from in front of the canopied platform, where a tall new flagstaff had been erected. After a short prayer by the chaplain who had accompanied the eighty-odd-man force into the fort on the night after Christmas, 1860 — six days after South Carolina left the Union — and a responsive reading of parts from several Psalms, selected for being appropriate to the occasion — "When the Lord turned again the captivity of Zion, we were like them that dream" — a sergeant who was also a veteran of the bombardment stepped forward, drew from a leather pouch the scorched and shot-ripped flag Anderson had kept for use as a winding sheet when the time came, and began to attach it to the rope that would run it up the pole.

"We all held our breath for a second," a young woman from Philadelphia was to write many years later, "and then we gave a queer cry, between a cheer and a yell; nobody started it and nobody led it; I never heard anything like it before or since, but I can hear it now." Then, as she watched, "General Anderson stood up, bareheaded, took the halyards in his hands, and began to speak. At first I could not hear him, for his voice came thickly, but in a moment he said clearly, 'I thank God that I have lived to see this day,' and after a few more words he began to hoist the flag. It went up slowly and hung limp against the staff, a weather-beaten, frayed, and shell-torn old flag, not fit for much more work, but when it had crept clear of the shelter of the walls a sudden breath of wind caught it, and it shook its folds and flew straight out above us, while every soldier and sailor instinctively saluted."

What happened next was confused in her memory by the emotion of the moment. "I think we stood up; somebody started 'The Star-Spangled Banner,' and we sang the first verse, which is all that most people know. But it did not make much difference, for a great gun was fired close to us from the fort itself, followed, in obedience to the President's order, 'by a national salute from every fort and battery that fired upon Fort Sumter.' The measured, solemn booming came from Fort Moultrie, from the batteries on Sullivan and Folly Islands, and from Fort Wagner. . . . When the forts were done it was the turn of the fleet, and all our warships, from the largest — which would look tiny today — down to the smallest monitor, fired and fired in regular order until the air was thick and black with smoke and one's ears ached with the overlapping vibrations."

All this was prelude, so to speak, to the main event, the address to be delivered by the reverend Mr Beecher, the fifty-two-year-old younger brother of the author of *Uncle Tom's Cabin*, whom Lincoln was said to have greeted once as "the little lady who started this great war." Beecher's specialty was flamboyance: as when, some years before, he staged in his church a mock auction of a shapely mulatto who stood draped in white beside the pulpit, her loosened hair streaming down her back. "How much am I bid? How much am I bid for this piece of human flesh?" he intoned, and men and women in their enthusiasm removed their jewelry and unhooked their watches for deposit in the collection baskets which then were passed. There was no such heady reaction here today, however, perhaps because, as another Philadelphia visitor noted, the Brooklyn pastor "spoke very much by note, and quite without fire. [He] *read* his entire oration." His performance was also cramped by the wind, which rose briskly, once the flag was aloft, and presented him with some of the problems Lincoln had had at the White House window, two nights back, in trying to manage a candle at the same time he delivered a quite different kind of speech. Beecher's problem, while the stiff breeze off the ocean whipped his hair and threatened to scatter his manuscript broadcast, was his hat. His solution was to clap it firmly on his head and jam it down tight against his ears, thus freeing both hands to grip the wind-fluttered leaves of his text.

Even so, a measure of the old fiery rhetoric came through the awkwardness of his disadvantaged performance. For though he predicted that the common people North and South would soon unite to rule the country, he entertained no notion of forgiveness for those "guiltiest and most remorseless traitors," the secessionist aristocrats. They were the villains; "polished, cultured, exceedingly capable and wholly unprincipled," they were the ones who had "shed this ocean of blood," and he foresaw eternal agony for them on the Day of Judgment, when they would be confronted by their victims. "Caught up in black clouds full of voices of vengeance and lurid with punishment,

[they] shall be whirled aloft and plunged downward forever and for-ever in endless retribution." He paused for a brief rest and a drink of water, then passed on to the subject of reconstruction, which he be-lieved posed no problems not easily solved. "*One nation, under one government, without slavery,* has been ordained, and shall stand.... On this base, reconstruction is easy, and needs neither architect nor engineer." In closing, though he had been one of Lincoln's harshest critics throughout the war — "Not a spark of genius has he; not an element for leadership. Not one particle of heroic enthusiasm" — Beecher wound up his address by offering the President "our solemn congratu-lations that God has sustained his life and health under the unparalleled burdens and sufferings of four bloody years, and permitted him to be-hold this auspicious confirmation of that national unity for which he has waited with so much patience and fortitude, and for which he has labored with such disinterested wisdom."

Robert Anderson, having performed what he called "perhaps the last act of my life, of duty to my country," had a somewhat let-down feeling as the ceremony ended and he and the rest got aboard boats to return to Charleston. At the outset he had urged Stanton to keep the program brief and quiet, but it had turned out to be neither. What was more, he faced still another speaking ordeal that night at a formal dinner Gillmore was giving for him and other guests of honor, includ-ing the old-line abolitionist Garrison, who had been hanged and burned in effigy on a nearby street corner, thirty-odd years before, in reaction to the Nat Turner uprising in Virginia. Garrison spoke, as did Beecher again — impromptu this time, and to better effect — and John Nicolay, who had been sent from Washington to deliver the Chief Executive's regrets that he himself was unable to attend. Others held forth at considerable length, interrupted from time to time by the crump and crackle of a fireworks display being staged in the harbor by Dahlgren's fleet, with Battery wharves and rooftops nearly as crowded as they had been for a grimmer show of pyrotechnics, four years ago this week. In the banquet hall of the Charleston Hotel the evening wore on as speaker after speaker, not sharing Anderson's aver-sion to exposure, had his say. At last, the various orators having sub-sided, the Kentuckian's turn came round.

He rose, glass in hand, and haltingly, with no mention of Union victory or Confederate defeat, of which so much had already been said by the others, proposed a toast to "the man who, when elected President of the United States, was compelled to reach the seat of government without an escort, but a man who now could travel all over our coun-try with millions of hands and hearts to sustain him. I give you the good, the great, the honest man, Abraham Lincoln."

★　★　★

The man to whom the celebrants raised their glasses down in Charleston this Good Friday evening was seated in a box at Ford's Theater, attentive to the forced chatter of a third-rate farce which by then was into its second act. Apparently he was enjoying himself, as he generally did at the theater, even though he had come with some reluctance, if not distaste, and more from a sense of obligation than by choice. "It has been advertised that we will be there," he had said that afternoon, "and I cannot disappoint the people. Otherwise I would not go. I do not want to go."

In part this was because of a last-minute withdrawal by Grant, who earlier had accepted an invitation for him and his wife to come along, and whose presence, as the hero of Appomattox, would have lent the presidential box a glitter that outdid anything under limelight on the stage. Besides, Lincoln had looked forward to the general's company as a diversion from the strain of the daily grind, which the advent of peace had not made any less daily or less grinding. Today, for example, he was in his office by 7 o'clock as usual, attending to administrative matters in advance of the flood of supplicants who would descend on him later. After issuing a call for a cabinet meeting at 11, he went back upstairs for breakfast with Mrs Lincoln and their two sons. Robert, just up from Virginia, brought with him a photograph of R. E. Lee which he presented to his father at the table, apparently as a joke. Lincoln did not take it so. He polished his glasses on a napkin, studied the portrait, then said quietly: "It's a good face. I am glad the war is over."

This last was repeated in varied phrasings through the day. Returning to his office he conferred first with Speaker Colfax, who was slated for a cabinet post — probably Stanton's, who more than anything wanted a seat on the Supreme Court as soon as one became vacant — and then with Senator John Creswell, who had done much to keep Maryland in the Union during the secession furor. "Creswell, old fellow," Lincoln hailed him, "everything is bright this morning. The war is over. It has been a tough time, but we have lived it out. Or some of us have." His face darkened, then lightened again. "But it is over. We are going to have good times now, and a united country." He approved a number of appointments, granted a military discharge, sent a messenger over to Ford's on 10th Street to reserve the State Box for the evening performance — not forgetting to inform the management that Grant would be a member of his party, which would help to increase the normally scant Good Friday audience — and wrote on a card for two Virginians requesting passes south: "No pass is necessary now to authorize anyone to go and return from Petersburg and Richmond. People go and return just as they did before the war." Presently, as the hour approached for the cabinet meeting he had called, he walked over to the War Department, hoping for news from Sherman of Johnston's surrender. There was nothing, but he was not discouraged. He said later at the meeting that he was convinced some such news was on the way, and soon would be clicking off the wire, because of a dream he had had the night before.

Grant was there by special invitation, having arrived from City Point just yesterday. Welcomed and applauded as he entered the cabinet room, he told of his pursuit of Lee and the closing scene at Appomattox, but added that no word had come from Carolina, where a similar campaign was being mounted against Joe Johnston, hopefully with similar results. The President said he was sure they would hear from Sherman soon, for he had had this dream the night before. What sort of dream? Welles asked. "It relates to your element, the water," Lincoln replied, and told how he had been aboard "some singular, indescribable vessel" which seemed to be "floating, floating away on some vast and indistinct expanse, toward an unknown shore." The dream was not so strange in itself, he declared, as in the fact that it was recurrent; that "each of its previous occurrences has been followed by some important event or disaster." He had had it before Sumter and Bull Run, he said, as well as before such victories as Antietam, Stones River, Gettysburg, Vicksburg, and Wilmington. Grant — who seldom passed up a chance to take a swipe at Rosecrans — remarked that Stones River was no victory; he knew of no great results it brought. In any case, Lincoln told him, he had had this dream on the eve of that battle, and it had come to him again last night. He took it as a sign that they would "have great news very soon," and "I think it must be from Sherman. My thoughts are in that direction."

After a brief discussion of dreams and their nature, the talk returned to Appomattox. Grant's terms there had assured that no member of the surrendered army, from Lee on down, would ever be prosecuted by the government for treason or any other crime, so long as he observed the conditions of his parole and the laws in force where he resided. Lincoln's ready approval of this assurance gave Postmaster General William Dennison the impression that he would like to have it extended to the civilian leaders — a number of whom by now were fugitives, in flight for their lives amid the ruins of the rebellion — if only some way could be found to avoid having them hauled into court. "I suppose, Mr President," he half-inquired, half-suggested, "that you would not be sorry to have them escape out of the country?" Lincoln thought it over. "Well, I should not be sorry to have them out of the country," he replied, "but I should be for following them up pretty close to make sure of their going." Having said as much he said still more to others around the table. "I think it is providential that this great rebellion is crushed just as Congress has adjourned and there are none of the disturbing elements of that body to hinder and embarrass us. If we are wise and discreet we shall reanimate the states and get their governments in successful operation, with order prevailing and the Union reëstablished before Congress comes together in December." Returning to the question of what should be done with the rebel leaders, he became more animated both in speech and gesture. "I hope there will be no persecution, no bloody work after the war is over. No one need expect me to take any part in hanging or killing these men, even the worst of them. Frighten them out of the country; open the gates; let down the bars." He put both hands out, fluttering the fingers as if to frighten sheep out of a lot. "Shoo; scare them off," he said; "enough lives have been sacrificed."

It was for this, the consideration of reconstruction matters and incidentals preliminary to them, that the cabinet had been assembled in the first place, midway between its regular Tuesday gatherings. In the absence of Seward — still on his bed of pain, he was represented at the meeting by his son Frederick — Stanton had come armed with a plan, drawn up at the President's request, for bringing the states that had been "abroad" back into what Lincoln, in his speech three nights ago, had called "their proper practical relation with the Union." The War Secretary's notion was that military occupation should precede readmission, and in this connection he proposed that Virginia and North Carolina be combined in a single district to simplify the army's task. Welles took exception, on grounds that this last would destroy the individuality of both states and thus be "in conflict with the principles of self-government which I deem essential." So did Lincoln. After some earnest discussion, back and forth across the green-topped table, he suggested that Stanton revise his plan in this regard and provide copies for the other cabinet members to study between now and their next meeting, four days off. Congress would no doubt have its say when it returned in December, but as for himself he had already reached certain bedrock conclusions. "We can't undertake to run state governments in all these southern states. Their own people must do that — though I reckon that at first some of them may do it badly."

By now it was close to 2 o'clock, and the meeting, nearly three hours long, adjourned. Grant however remained behind to talk with Lincoln: not about army matters, it turned out, but to beg off going to the theater that night. His wife, he said, was anxious to catch the late-afternoon train for Philadelphia, en route to a visit with their young sons in Burlington, New Jersey. Lincoln started to press him, but then refrained, perhaps realizing from the general's embarrassed manner that the real reason was Julia Grant, who was determined not to expose herself to another of Mary Lincoln's tirades, this time in full view of the audience at Ford's. Disappointed, Lincoln accepted the excuse — reinforced just then by a note from Mrs Grant, reminding her husband not to be late for their 6 o'clock departure — and went upstairs for lunch, faced with the unpleasant job of informing his wife that the social catch of the season would not be going with them to the theater that evening. If he also told her, as he would tell others between now and curtain time, that he too no longer wanted to go, it made no difference; Grant or no Grant, she was set on attending what the papers were calling the "last appearance of Miss Laura Keene in her celebrated comedy of *Our American Cousin.*"

He was back in his office by 3 o'clock, in time for an appointment with the Vice President, the first since the scandalous scene at his swearing in. They talked for twenty minutes or so, and though neither left any record of what was said, witnesses noted that Lincoln called him "Andy," shaking him vigorously by the hand, and that Johnson seemed greatly relieved to find himself greeted cordially after nearly six weeks of pointed neglect. This done, Lincoln attended to some paper work, including an appeal on behalf of a soldier convicted for desertion. So far in the war he had approved 267 death sentences for military offenses, but not this one. "Well, I think the boy can do us more good above ground than under ground," he drawled as he fixed his signature to a pardon. Before setting out on a 4.30 carriage ride with his wife — "Just ourselves," he had said at lunch when she asked if he wanted anyone else along — he walked over to the War Department, in hope that some word had come at last from Sherman. Again there was nothing, which served to weaken his conviction that the news of "some important event or disaster" would shake the capital before the day was over. Time was running out, and he was disappointed. It was then, on the way back from the telegraph office, that he told his bodyguard Crook that he did not want to go to the theater that night, and would not go, except for notices in the papers that he would be there. Crook was about to go off shift, and when they reached the White House door Lincoln paused for a moment and turned to face him. He seemed gloomy, depressed. "Goodbye, Crook," he said, to the guard's surprise. Always before, it had been "Good night, Crook," when they parted. Now suddenly it was goodbye; "Goodbye, Crook."

Still, by the time the carriage rolled out of the driveway a few minutes later, on through streets that glittered with bright gold April sunshine, he had recovered his spirits to such an extent that he informed his wife: "I never felt better in my life." What was more — even though, just one month ago today, he had been confined to his bed with what his doctor described as "exhaustion, complete exhaustion" — he looked as happy as he said he felt. The recent City Point excursion, his first extended vacation of the war, had done him so much good that various cabinet members, after observing him at the midday meeting — in contrast to the one a month ago, when they gathered about his sickbed — remarked on the "expression of visible relief and content upon his face." One said that he "never appeared to better advantage," while another declared that "the weary look which his face had so long worn... had disappeared. It was cheerful and happy." They were glad to see him so. But Mary Lincoln, whose moods were quite as variable as his own, had a different reaction when he told her he had never felt better in his life. "Don't you remember feeling just so before our little boy died?" she asked. He patted her hand to comfort her, and spoke of a trip to Europe as soon as his term was up. After that they would return to Springfield, where he would resume the practice of law and perhaps buy a farm along the Sangamon. "We must both be more cheerful in the future," he told her. "Between the war and the loss of our darling Willie, we have both been very miserable."

The good mood held. Seeing two old friends just leaving as the open barouche turned into the White House driveway an hour later, he stood up and called for them to wait. They were Richard Oglesby, the new governor of Illinois, and his adjutant general Isham Haynie, a combat brigadier who had left the army to work for him and Lincoln in the recent campaign. Lincoln led the way inside, where he read to them from the latest collection of "Letters" by Petroleum V. Nasby, a humorist he admired so much that he once said he would gladly swap his present office for the genius to compose such things. "Linkin rides into Richmond!" he read from the final letter. "A Illinois rale-splitter, a buffoon, a ape, a goriller, a smutty joker, sets hisself down in President Davis's cheer and rites dispatchis! . . . This ends the chapter. The Confederasy hez at last consentratid its last consentrate. It's ded. It's gathered up its feet, sed its last words, and deceest. . . . Farewell, vane world." The reading went on so long — four letters, with time out for laughter and thigh-slapping all around — that supper was delayed, as well as his departure for the theater. Even so, with the carriage waiting, he took time to see Colfax, who called again to ask if a special session of Congress was likely to interrupt a Rocky Mountain tour he was planning. The President said there would be no special session, and they went on talking until Mrs Lincoln appeared in the office doorway. She wore a low-necked evening dress and was pulling on her gloves, by way of warning her husband that 8 o'clock had struck.

He excused himself and they started out, only to be interrupted by two more men, a Massachusetts congressman and a former congressman from Illinois, both of whom had political favors to collect. One wanted a hearing for a client who had a sizeable cotton claim against the government; Lincoln gave him a card that put him first on tomorrow's list of callers. What the other wanted no one knew, for he whispered it into the presidential ear. Lincoln had entered and then backed out of the closed carriage, cocking his head to hear the request. "Excuse me now," he said as he climbed in again beside his wife. "I am going to the theater. Come and see me in the morning."

Stopping en route at the home of New York Senator Ira Harris to pick up their substitute guests, the senator's daughter Clara and her fiancé, Major Henry Rathbone, the carriage rolled and clopped through intersections whose streetlamps glimmered dimly through the mist. It was close to 8.30, twenty minutes past curtain time, when the coachman drew rein in front of Ford's, on 10th Street between E and F, and the two couples alighted to enter the theater. Inside, about midway of Act I, the performance stopped as the President and his party came down the side aisle, and the orchestra struck up "Hail to the Chief" as they entered the flag-draped box to the right front. A near-capacity crowd of about 1700 applauded politely, masking its disappointment at Grant's absence. Clara Harris and Rathbone took seats near the railing; the First Lady sat a little behind them, to their left, and Lincoln slumped into a roomy, upholstered rocker toward the rear. This last represented concern for his comfort and was also the management's way of expressing thanks for his having been here at least four times before, once to see Maggie Mitchell in *Fanchon the Cricket,* once to see John Wilkes Booth in *The Marble Heart* — "Rather tame than otherwise," John Hay had complained — and twice to see James Hackett play Falstaff in *Henry IV* and *The Merry Wives of Windsor.* Tonight's play resumed, and Lincoln, as was his habit, at once grew absorbed in the action down below: though not so absorbed that he failed to notice that the major was holding his fiancée's hand, for he reached out and took hold of his wife's. Pleased by the attention he had shown her on their carriage ride that afternoon, and now by this further expression of affection, Mary Lincoln reverted to her old role of Kentucky belle. "What will Miss Harris think of my hanging onto you so?" she whispered, leaning toward him. Lincoln's eyes, fixed on the stage, reflected the glow of the footlights. "Why, she will think nothing about it," he said, and he kept his grip on her hand.

Act I ended; Act II began. Down in Charleston the banqueters raised their glasses in response to Anderson's toast, and here at Ford's, in an equally festive mood, the audience enjoyed *Our American Cousin* with only occasional sidelong glances at the State Box to see whether Grant had arrived. He might have done so without their knowledge, for though they could see the young couple at the railing and Mrs Lincoln half in shadow behind them, the President was screened from view by the box curtains and draped flags. Act II ended; Act III began. Lincoln, having at last released his wife's hand and settled back in the horsehair rocker, seemed to be enjoying what was happening down below. In the second scene, which opened shortly after 10 o'clock, a three-way running dialogue revealed to Mrs Mountchessington that Asa Trenchard, for whom she had set her daughter's cap, was no millionaire after all.

— No heir to the fortune, Mr Trenchard?
— Oh, no.
— What! No fortune!
— Nary a red. . . .

Consternation. Indignation.

— Augusta, to your room.

— Yes, ma. The nasty beast!

— I am aware, Mr Trenchard, that you are not used to the manners of good society, and that alone will excuse the impertinence of which you have been guilty.

Exit Mrs Mountchessington, trailing daughter. Trenchard alone.

— Don't know the manners of good society, eh? Wal, I guess I know enough to turn you inside out, you sockdologizing old mantrap!

Then it came, a half-muffled explosion, somewhere between a boom and a thump, loud but by no means so loud as it sounded in the theater, then a boil and bulge of bluish smoke in the presidential box, an exhalation as of brimstone from the curtained mouth, and a man coming out through the bank and swirl of it, white-faced and dark-haired in a black sack suit and riding boots, eyes aglitter, brandishing a knife. He mounted the ledge, presented his back to the rows of people seated below, and let himself down by the handrail for the ten-foot drop to the stage. Falling he turned, and as he did so caught the spur of his right boot in the folds of a flag draped over the lower front of the high box. It ripped but offered enough resistance to bring all the weight of his fall on his left leg, which buckled and pitched him forward onto his hands. He rose, thrust the knife overhead in a broad theatrical gesture, and addressed the outward darkness of the pit. "Sic semper tyrannis," he said in a voice so low and projected with so little clarity that few recognized the state motto of Virginia or could later agree that he had spoken in Latin. "Revenge for the South!" or "The South is avenged!" some thought they heard him cry, while others said that he simply muttered "Freedom." In any case he then turned again, hobbled left across the stage past the lone actor standing astonished in its center, and vanished into the wings.

Barely half a minute had passed since the jolt of the explosion, and now a piercing scream came through the writhing tendrils of smoke — a full-voiced wail from Mary Lincoln. "Stop that man!" Rathbone shouted, nursing an arm slashed by the intruder, and Clara Harris, wringing her hands, called down from the railing in a tone made falsely calm by shock: "Water. Water." The audience began to emerge from its trance. "What is it? What happened?" "For God's sake, what is it?" "What has happened?" The answer came in a bellow of rage from the curtained orifice above the spur-torn flag: "He has shot the President!" Below, men leaped from their seats in a first reaction of disbelief and denial, not only of this but also of what they had seen with their own eyes. "No. For God's sake, no! It can't be true." But then, by way of reinforcement for the claim, the cry went up: "Surgeon! A surgeon! Is there a surgeon in the house?"

The young doctor who came forward — and at last gained admission to the box, after Rathbone removed a wooden bar the intruder had used to keep the hallway door from being opened while he went about his work — thought at first that he had been summoned to attend a dead man. Lincoln sat sprawled in the rocker as if asleep, knees relaxed, eyes closed, head dropped forward so that his chin was on his chest. He seemed to have no vital signs until a closer examination detected a weak pulse and shallow breathing. Assuming that he had been knifed, as Rathbone had been, the doctor had him taken from the chair and laid on the floor in a search for a stab wound. However, when he put his hands behind the patient's head to lift it, he found the back hair wet with blood from a half-inch hole where a bullet had entered, three inches to the right of the left ear. "The course of the ball was obliquely forward," a subsequent report would state, "toward the right eye, crossing the brain in an oblique manner and lodging a few inches behind that eye. In the track of the wound were found fragments of bone driven forward by the ball, which was embedded in the anterior lobe of the left hemisphere of the brain." The doctor — Charles A. Leale, assistant surgeon, U.S. Volunteers, twenty-three years old and highly familiar with gunshot wounds — did not know all this; yet he knew enough from what he had seen and felt, here in the crowded box for the past five minutes, as well as in casualty wards for the past year, to arrive at a prognosis. Everything was over for Abraham Lincoln but the end. "His wound is mortal," Leale pronounced. "It is impossible for him to recover."

Two other surgeons were in the box by then, both senior to Leale in rank and years, but he remained in charge and made the decision not to risk a removal to the White House, six cobblestone blocks away. "If it is attempted the President will die before we reach there," he replied to the suggestion. Instead, with the help of four soldier volunteers, the three doctors took up their patient and carried him feet first down the stairs and aisle, out onto 10th Street — packed nearly solid with the curious and grieving, so that an infantry captain had to draw his sword to clear a path for the seven bearers and their awkward burden, bawling excitedly: "Out of the way, you sons of bitches!" — up the front steps, down a narrow hall, and into a small back ground-floor bedroom in one of a row of modest houses across the way. Let by the night by its owner, a Swedish tailor, the room was mean and dingy, barely fifteen by nine feet in length and width, with a threadbare rug, once Turkey red, and oatmeal-colored paper on the walls. The bed itself was too short for the long form placed diagonally on the cornshuck mattress; Lincoln's booted feet protruded well beyond the footboard, his head propped on extra pillows so that his bearded chin was on his chest, as it had been when Leale first saw him in the horsehair rocker, back at

Ford's. By then the time was close to 11 o'clock, some forty-five minutes after the leaden ball first broke into his skull, and now began a
painful, drawn-out vigil, a death watch that would continue for another
eight hours and beyond.

Three more doctors soon arrived, Surgeon General Joseph Barnes,
his chief assistant, and the family physician, who did what he could for
Mary Lincoln in her distress. Barnes took charge, but Leale continued
his ministrations, including the removal of the patient's clothing in a
closer search for another wound and the application of mustard plasters
in an attempt to improve his respiration and heartbeat. One did as little
good as the other; for there was no additional wound and Lincoln's
condition remained about the same, with stertorous breathing, pulse a
feeble 44, hands and feet corpse-cold to the wrists and ankles, and both
eyes insensitive to light, the left pupil much contracted, the right dilated
widely. Gideon Welles came in at this point and wrote next day in his
diary of "the giant sufferer" as he saw him from his post beside the bed.
"He had been stripped of his clothes. His large arms, which were occasionally exposed, were of a size which one would scarce have expected
from his spare appearance. His slow, full respiration lifted the bedclothes with each breath that he took. His features were calm and
striking. I had never seen them appear to better advantage than for the
first hour, perhaps, that I was there." Presently, though, their calm
appearance changed. The left side of the face began to twitch, distorting
the mouth into a jeer. When this desisted, the upper right side of the
face began to darken, streaked with purple as from a blow, and the eye
with the ball of lead behind it began to bulge from its socket. Mary
Lincoln screamed at the sight and had to be led from the room, while a
journalist noted that Charles Sumner, "seated on the right of the President's couch, near the head, holding the right hand of the President in
his own," was about equally unstrung. "He was sobbing like a woman,
with his head bowed down almost on the pillow of the bed on which the
President was lying."

By midnight, close to fifty callers were in the house, all of
sufficient prominence to gain entrance past the guards and most of them
wedged shoulder to shoulder in the death chamber, at one time or
another, for a look at the final agony of the man laid diagonally on the
bed in one corner. Andrew Johnson was there — briefly, however,
because his presence was painful to Mrs Lincoln, who whimpered at
the sight of her husband's imminent successor — as were a number of
Sumner's colleagues from the House and Senate, Robert Lincoln and
John Hay, Oglesby and Haynie again, a pair of clergymen — one
fervent, the other unctuous — and Laura Keene, who claimed a star's
prerogative, first in the box at the theater, where she had held the
President's bleeding head in her lap, and now in the narrow brick house
across the street, where she helped Clara Harris comfort the distraught

widow-to-be in the tailor's front parlor, what time she was not with her in the crowded bedroom toward the rear. All members of the cabinet were on hand but the Secretary of State, and most of the talk that was not of Lincoln was of him. He too had been attacked and grievously wounded, along with four members of his household, by a lone assassin who struck at about the same time as the one at Ford's: unless, indeed, it was the same man in rapid motion from one place to the other, less than half a mile away. Seward had been slashed about the face and throat, and he was thought to be dying, too, except that the iron frame that bound his jaw had served to protect him to some extent from the knife. "I'm mad, I'm mad," the attacker had said as he ran out into the night to vanish as cleanly as the other — or he — had done when he — or the other — leaped from the box, crossed the stage, entered the wings, and exited into the alley behind Ford's, where he — whoever, whichever he was — mounted his waiting horse and rode off in the darkness.

In this, as in other accounts concerning other rumored victims — Grant, for one, and Andrew Johnson for another, until word came that the general was safe in Philadelphia and the Vice President himself showed up unhurt — there was much confusion. Edwin Stanton undertook on his own the task of sifting and setting the contradictions straight, in effect taking over as head of the headless government. "[He] instantly assumed charge of everything near and remote, civil and military," a subordinate observed, "and began issuing orders in that autocratic manner so superbly necessary to the occasion." Among other precautions, he stopped traffic on the Potomac and the railroads, warned the Washington Fire Brigade to be ready for mass arson, summoned Grant back to take charge of the capital defenses, and alerted guards along the Canadian border, as well as in all major eastern ports, to be on the lookout for suspicious persons attempting to leave the country. In short, "he continued throughout the night acting as president, secretary of war, secretary of state, commander in chief, comforter, and dictator," all from a small sitting room adjacent to the front parlor of the tailor's house on 10th Street, which he turned into an interrogation chamber for grilling witnesses to find out just what had happened in the theater across the street.

From the outset, numbers of people who knew him well, including members of his profession, had identified John Wilkes Booth as Lincoln's attacker, and by now the twenty-six-year-old matinee idol's one-shot pocket derringer had been found on the floor of the box where he had dropped it as he leaped for the railing to escape by way of the stage and the back alley. Identification was certain. Even so, and though a War Department description eventually went out by wire across the land — "height 5 feet 8 inches, weight 160 pounds, compact build; hair jet black, inclined to curl, medium length, parted behind; eyes black, heavy dark eyebrows; wears a large seal ring on little finger; when talking inclines head forward, looks down" — Stanton was intent on larger game. Apparently convinced that the President could not have been shot by anyone so insignificant as an actor acting on his own, he was out to expose a full-scale Confederate plot, a conspiracy hatched in Richmond "and set on foot by rebels under pretense of avenging the rebel cause."

So he believed at any rate, and though he gave most of his attention to exploring this assumption — proceeding with such misdirected and disjointed vigor that he later aroused revisionist suspicions that he must have wanted the assassin to escape: as, for instance, by his neglect in closing all city bridges except the one Booth used to cross into Maryland — he still had time for periodic visits to the small back room, filled with the turmoil of Lincoln's labored breathing, and to attend to such incidental administrative matters as the preparation of a message giving Johnson formal notice that the President had died. His purpose in this, with the hour of death left blank to be filled in later, was to avoid delay when the time came, but when he read the rough draft aloud for a stenographer to take down a fair copy he produced a premature effect he had not foreseen. Hearing a strangled cry behind him, he turned and found Mary Lincoln standing in the parlor doorway, hands clasped before her in entreaty, a stricken expression on her face. "Is he dead? Oh, is he dead?" she moaned. Stanton tried to explain that what she had heard was merely in preparation for a foreseen contingency, but she could not understand him through her sobbing and her grief. So he gave it up and had her led back into the parlor, out of his way; which was just as well, an associate declared, for "he was full of business, and knew, moreover, that in a few hours at most she must be a widow."

It was by then about 1.30; Good Friday was off the calendar at last, and Mary Lincoln was into what everyone in the house, doctors and laymen alike, could see would be the first day of her widowhood. At intervals, supported on either side by Clara Harris and Laura Keene, she would return to the crowded bedroom and sit or stand looking down at her husband until grief overcame her again and the two women would half-guide half-carry her back to the front parlor, where she would remain until enough strength returned for her to repeat the process. She made these trips about once an hour, and each was more grueling than the last, not only because of her own cumulative exhaustion, but also because of the deteriorating condition of the sufferer on the bed, which came as a greater shock to her each time she saw him. Earlier, there had been a certain calm and dignity about him, as if he were in fact aboard "some singular, indescribable vessel . . . floating, floating away on some vast and indistinct expanse, toward an unknown shore." Now this was gone, replaced by the effects of agony. The dream ship had become a rack, and the stertorous uproar of his breathing, interspersed with drawn-out groans, filled the house as it might have filled a torture chamber. "Doctor, save him!" she implored first one and then another of the attending physicians, and once she said in a calmer tone: "Bring Tad. He will speak to Tad, he loves him so." But all agreed that would not do, either for the boy or for his father, who was beyond all knowledgeable contact with anything on earth, even Tad, and indeed had been so ever since Booth's derringer crashed through the laughter in the theater at 10.15 last night. All the while, his condition worsened, especially his breathing, which not only became increasingly spasmodic, but would stop entirely from time to time, the narrow chest expanded between the big rail-splitter arms, and then resume with a sudden gusty roar through the fluttering lips. On one such occasion, with Mrs Lincoln leaning forward from a chair beside the bed, her cheek on her husband's cheek, her ear near his still, cyanotic mouth, the furious bray of his exhalation — louder than anything she had heard since the explosion in the box, five hours ago — startled and frightened her so badly that she shrieked and fell to the floor in a faint. Stanton, interrupted in his work by the piercing scream, came running down the hall from his improvised Acting President's office up front. When he saw what it was he lost patience entirely. "Take that woman out," he ordered sternly, thrusting both arms over his head in exasperation, "and do not let her in again."

He was obeyed in this as in all his other orders, and she remained in the front parlor until near the very end. Meantime dawn came through, paling the yellow flare of gas jets. A cold rain fell on the people still keeping their vigil on the street outside, while inside, in the dingy room made dingier by daylight, Lincoln entered the final stage of what one doctor called "the saddest and most pathetic deathbed scene I ever witnessed." Interruptions of his breathing were more frequent now, and longer, and whenever this happened some of the men about the bed would take out their watches to note the time of death, then return them to their pockets when the raucous sound resumed. Robert Lincoln — "only a boy for all his shoulder straps," the guard Crook had said — "bore himself well," according to one who watched him, "but on two occasions gave way to overpowering grief and sobbed aloud, turning his head and leaning on the shoulder of Senator Sumner." At 7 o'clock, with the end at hand, he went to bring his mother into the room for a last visit. She tottered in, looked at her husband in confusion, saying nothing, and was led back out again. Stanton was there full-time now, and strangely enough had brought his hat along, standing motionless with his chin on his left hand, his right hand holding the hat and supporting his left elbow, tears running down his face into his beard.

By this time Lincoln's breathing was fast and shallow, cheeks pulled inward behind the closed blue lips. His chest heaved up in a last deep breath, then subsided and did not rise again. It was 7.22; the nine-hour agony was over, and his face took on what John Hay described as "a look of unspeakable peace." Surgeon General Barnes leaned forward, listened carefully for a time to the silent chest, then straightened up, removed two silver half-dollars from his pocket, and placed them carefully on the closed eyes. Observing this ritual, Stanton then performed one of his own. He stretched his right arm out deliberately before him, clapped his hat for a long moment on his head, and then as deliberately removed it, as if in salute. "Now he belongs to the ages," he said, or anyhow later saw to it that he was quoted as having said. "Let us pray," one of the parsons intoned, and sank to his knees on the thin red carpet beside the bed.

Soon thereafter Mary Lincoln was brought back into the room. "Oh, why did you not tell me he was dying?" she exclaimed when she saw her husband lying there with coins on his eyes. Then it came home to her, and her grief was too great to be contained. "Oh my God," she wailed as she was led out, weeping bitterly, "I have given my husband to die!" Presently she was taken from the house, and the other mourner witnesses picked their way through the wet streets to their homes and hotels near and far.

Bells were tolling all over Washington by the time Lincoln's body, wrapped in a flag and placed in a closed hearse, was on its way back to the White House, escorted (as he had not been when he left, twelve hours before) by an honor guard of soldiers and preceded by a group of officers walking bareheaded in the rain. He would lie in state, first in the East Room, then afterwards in the Capitol rotunda, preparatory to the long train ride back to Springfield, where he would at last be laid to rest. "Nothing touches the tired spot," he had said often in the course of the past four years. Now Booth's derringer had reached it.

At 10 o'clock that Saturday morning, less than three hours after Lincoln died in the tailor's house two blocks away, Andrew Johnson took the oath of office in the parlor of his suite at the Kirkwood House, just down Pennsylvania Avenue from the mansion that was soon to be his home. After kissing the Bible held out to him by Chase, he turned and made a short speech, a sort of extemporaneous inaugural, to the dozen senators and cabinet members present, all with faces that showed the strain of their all-night vigil. "Gentlemen," he said, "I have been almost overwhelmed by the announcement of the sad event which has so recently occurred." Other than this he made no reference to his predecessor, and as for any policy he would adopt, "that must be left for development as the Administration progresses.... The only assurance I can now give of the future is reference to the past. Toil, and an honest advocacy of the great principles of free government, have been my lot. The duties have been mine; the consequences are God's."

If this sounded at once conventional and high-handed, if some among the new President's hearers resented his singular omission of any reference to the old one — "Johnson seemed willing to share the glory of his achievements with his Creator," a New Hampshire senator observed, "but utterly forgot that Mr Lincoln had any share of credit in the suppression of the rebellion" — there were those beyond reach of his voice just then who were altogether delighted with the change, as they saw it, from a soft- to a hard-peace Chief of State. Back from Richmond that same day, most of the members of the Joint Committee on the Conduct of the War spent the afternoon at a caucus held to consider "the necessity of a new cabinet and a line of policy less conciliatory than that of Mr Lincoln." They had been upset by a number of things, including his recent speech from the White House window, and Julian of Indiana complained that "aside from his known tenderness to the rebels, Lincoln's last public avowal, only three days before his death, of adherence to the plan of reconstruction he had announced in December 1863, was highly repugnant." All in all, "while everybody was shocked at his murder," Julian declared, "the feeling was nearly universal that the accession of Johnson to the Presidency would prove a godsend to the country."

Sure enough, when they requested through their chairman a meeting with the new President — himself a member of the committee until he left the Senate, three years ago, to take up his duties as military governor of Tennessee — he promptly agreed to see them the following day, not at the White House, which was in a turmoil of preparation for the funeral, but next door at the Treasury Department. It was Easter Sunday, and Ben Wade, as chairman, got things off to a rousing start. "Johnson, we have faith in you," he said. "By the gods, there will be no trouble *now* in running the government."

Lincoln's life had ended, so to speak, in a tailor shop; Johnson's could be said to have begun in one, plying needle and thread while his wife taught him to read. Since then, he had come far — indeed, all the way to the top — with much of his success attributable to his skill as a stump speaker whose specialty was invective. Nor did he disappoint his Jacobin callers now in that regard. One year older and half a foot shorter than his predecessor, he thanked Wade for the warmth of his greeting and launched at once into a statement of his position on the burning issue of the day, repeating, with some expansion and adjustment of the words, what he had said on the steps of the Patent Office, twelve days back. "I hold that robbery is a crime; rape is a crime; murder is a crime; *treason* is a crime — and crime must be punished. Treason must be made infamous, and traitors must be impoverished." The impression here was as strong as the one produced at the Republican rally, two days after the fall of Richmond, and it was also encouraging to learn that the text under his lips when he kissed the Bible held out to him by Chase the day before, open to the lurid and vengeful Book of Ezekiel, carried a similar burden of blame and retribution: *And I will give them one heart, and I will put a new spirit within you; and I will take the stony heart out of their flesh, and will give them an heart of flesh: That they may walk in my statutes, and keep mine ordinances, and do them: and they shall be my people, and I will be their God. But as for them whose heart walketh after the heart of their detestable things and their abominations, I will recompense their way upon their own heads, saith the Lord God.* Although he made them no commitment as to changes in the cabinet he had inherited — not even regarding dismissal of the twice-injured Seward, whom they detested — they did not expect that; not just yet. It was enough, for the present, that he was with them. They knew him of old; he was *of* them, a long-time colleague, and they counted on him to come down stronger on their enemies all the time. They knew, as their chairman had said at the outset, there would be no trouble in running the government now.

Anyhow they thought they knew, and when Johnson presently issued a proclamation offering rewards that ranged from $100,000 to $10,000 for the capture of Jefferson Davis and certain of his "agents," on charges of having conspired to incite the murder of Abraham Lincoln, their cup nearly ran over. Zachariah Chandler, for one, was pleased with the prospect brought about by the assassination, and he said as much in a letter he wrote his wife in Michigan, one week after the Easter meeting. "Had Mr Lincoln's policy been carried out, we should have had Jeff Davis, Toombs, etc. back in the Senate at the next session of Congress, but now their chances to stretch hemp are better. . . . So mote it be."

✗ 2 ✗

Escorted by a small band of Tennessee cavalry, Davis and his official family left Greensboro on the morning Lincoln died, April 15, all on horseback except the ailing Trenholm, accompanied in his ambulance by Adjutant General Samuel Cooper, crowding seventy years of age, and Judah Benjamin, for whom a saddle was an instrument of torture. While they toiled southwest over clay roads made slippery by recent heavy rains, Joe Johnston waited in his Hillsboro headquarters, forty miles northwest of Union-occupied Raleigh, for a reply to his request, sent through the lines the day before — Good Friday; Lincoln had been right, after all, about good news in the offing — for "a temporary suspension of active operations . . . to permit the civil authorities to enter into the needful arrangements to terminate the existing war." Reluctant to have the overture made, even though he himself, under pressure from his advisers, had written the message the Virginian signed, Davis had said he was not "sanguine" as to the outcome. But the response, received by Johnston on Easter Sunday, showed Sherman to be a good deal more receptive to the notion than the departed President had expected. "I am fully empowered," the Ohioan replied, "to arrange with you any terms for the suspension of further hostilities between the armies commanded by you and those commanded by myself, and will be willing to confer with you to that end." He proposed surrender on the same terms Grant had given Lee, a week ago today, and spoke in closing of his "desire to save the people of North Carolina the damage they would sustain by the march of this army through the central or western parts of the state."

In point of fact, Sherman was even more pleased than he sounded: not only because, as he later said, "the whole army dreaded the long march to Charlotte" and beyond, "back again over the thousand miles we had just accomplished," but also because of his own fear that Johnston, overtaken, might "allow his army to disperse into guerrilla bands" and thereby cause the war to be "prolonged indefinitely." Surrender of course would obviate both of these unwanted eventualities, and Sherman, with Grant's example before him — "Glory to God and our country," he had exclaimed in a field order passing the news of Appomattox along to his troops, "and all honor to our comrades in arms, toward whom we are marching! A little more labor, a little more toil on our part, the great race is won, and our Government stands regenerated after four long years of war" — fairly leaped at the invitation thus extended. Accordingly, after assuring Washington that he would "be careful not to complicate any points of civil policy" in the terms he planned to offer, he arranged with Johnston to meet at noon on Monday, April 17, midway between the picket lines of the two armies.

That would be somewhere between the Confederate rear at Hillsboro and his own advance at Durham Station, twenty-odd miles up the track from Raleigh. Monday morning, as he was boarding the train that would take him and his staff to the midday meeting, a telegrapher came hurrying down the depot stairs with word that a coded message from the War Department, sent by steamer down the coast, was just coming over the wire from Morehead City. Sherman waited nearly half an hour for it to be completed and decoded, then took it from the operator, who came running back much excited. It was from Stanton and it had been nearly two days in transit. "President Lincoln was murdered about 10 o'clock last night in his private box at Ford's Theatre in this city, by an assassin who shot him through the head by a pistol ball." Seward too had been gravely hurt, and Andrew Johnson was about to take over even as Stanton wrote the final words of the message: "I have no time to add more than to say that I find evidence that an assassin is also on your track, and I beseech you to be more heedful than Mr Lincoln was of such knowledge."

Sherman thrust the sheet of flimsy into his pocket and said nothing of it to anyone but the telegrapher, whom he swore to secrecy. Aboard the train as it chuffed along he sat tight-lipped all the way to Durham, where he and his staff changed to horses for the flag-of-truce ride toward Hillsboro to meet Johnston. They encountered him and his party about five miles out, also under a flag of truce, and here, midway between their lines of battle, the two generals met for the first time in person: although, as Sherman put it afterwards, looking back on the hundred-mile minuet they had danced together in North Georgia from early May through mid-July, "We knew enough of each other to be well acquainted at once." Riding side by side — forty-five-year-old "Uncle Billy," tall and angular, and his spruce, spare companion, thirteen years his senior, "dressed in a neat gray uniform," a blue staffer noted, "which harmonized gracefully with a full beard and mustache of silvery whiteness, partly concealing a genial and generous mouth" — they led the small blue-gray column to a roadside house owned by a farmer named James Bennett, whose permission they asked for its use, and then went in, leaving their two staffs in the yard. Once they were alone Sherman took the sheet of flimsy from his pocket and handed it over without comment. As Johnston read it, "perspiration came out in large drops on his forehead," his companion observed, and when he had finished he denounced the assassination as "the greatest possible calamity to the South," adding that he hoped Sherman did not connect the Confederate government with the crime. "I told him," the red-head would recall, "I could not believe that he or General Lee, or the officers of the Confederate army, could possibly be privy to acts of assassination; but I would not say as much for Jeff Davis . . . and men of that stripe."

Johnston made no reply to this, and the two proceeded at once to the subject arranged beforehand. Both agreed that any resumption of the fighting would be "the highest possible crime," the Virginian — outnumbered four to one by enemy troops in the immediate vicinity, and ten to one or worse by others who could be brought to bear within a week — even going so far as to define the crime as "murder." All the same, they soon reached an apparent impasse. For while Sherman rejected any proposal designed to lead to negotiations between the civil authorities, Davis had consented to the meeting only if it was to be conducted on that basis; which, incidentally, was why he had not been "sanguine as to ultimate results." Johnston, however, stepped over the barrier by proposing that he and Sherman "make one job of it," then and there, by settling "the fate of all armies to the Rio Grande." Taken aback, the Ohioan questioned whether his companion's authority was that broad. Johnston replied that it was, or anyhow could be made so by the Secretary of War, whose orders would be obeyed by Taylor, Forrest, Maury, and all the others with forces still under arms, including Kirby Smith beyond the Mississippi. In fact, he said, he could send a wire requesting Breckinridge to join them overnight. Sherman demurred; he could not deal with a member of the rebel cabinet, no matter how desirable the outcome. However, when Johnston pointed out that the

Kentuckian was also a major general, and could be received on that basis, Sherman agreed. They would meet tomorrow, same time, same place, soldier to soldier, and work out the details, all of which would of course be dependent on approval by his Washington superiors, civil as well as military.

They parted "in extreme cordiality," Johnston later declared, he to wait near Greensboro for Breckinridge to arrive from Salisbury, which Davis and his party had reached by then, and Sherman to face the problem of how to go about informing his troops of Lincoln's death. So far, the occupation of the North Carolina capital had been orderly and forbearing; "Discipline was now so good that the men didn't know themselves," an Illinois infantryman observed. But their commander, nursing his bombshell of news on the trainride back to Raleigh, was aware that "one single word by me would have laid the city in ashes and turned its whole population homeless upon the country, if not worse." Accordingly, he ordered all units back to their camps before releasing a bulletin in which he was careful to exonerate the Confederate army from complicity in the assassination. It seemed to work. At least there was no violent reaction within the guarded bivouacs. However: "The army is crazy for vengeance," a private wrote home, remarking that "if we make another campaign it will be an awful one." Some even went so far as to hope that Johnston would not surrender; in which case they planned to turn loose with both hands. "God pity this country if he retreats or fights us," the soldier closed his letter.

From what he had heard today in the roadside farmhouse Sherman believed there was little chance of that; Johnston, he knew, was eager to surrender, and he intended to give him every chance. He would do so in part because of his soldier's pride in being generous to a disadvantaged foe who asked for mercy. "The South is broken and ruined and appeals to our pity," he would tell Rawlins before the month was out. "To ride the people down with persecutions and military exactions would be like slashing away at the crew of a sinking ship." There was that, and there was also his reaction to the Good Friday assassination, which was quite the opposite of the angered private's hope that Old Joe would not surrender. Lincoln's death brought Lincoln himself into sharper focus in Sherman's memory: particularly as he had come to know him at City Point, three weeks ago. Remembering his concern for avoiding "this last bloody battle," his eagerness "to get the men composing the Confederate armies back to their homes, at work on their farms and in their shops," he was resolved, as he set out for the second meeting Tuesday morning, "to manifest real respect for his memory by following after his death that policy which, if living, I felt certain he would have approved." Grant had removed from the contest the most feared and admired of the rebel armies; now Sherman would remove all the rest by taking Johnston up on his soldier-to-soldier proposal that they "make one job of it," here and now in the Bennett farmhouse, and settle "the fate of all armies to the Rio Grande."

He arrived first and went in alone, his saddlebags over one arm. They contained writing materials, together with something else he mentioned when Johnston entered the room with Breckinridge. "Gentlemen, it occurred to me that perhaps you were not overstocked with liquor, and I procured some medical stores on my way over. Will you join me before we begin work?" Johnston afterwards described his companion's expression — till now "rather dull and heavy" — as "beatific" when he heard these words. For some days the Kentuckian had been deprived of his customary ration of bourbon and had had to make do with tobacco, which he was chewing vigorously with a steady sidewise thrust of his jaw beneath the outsized mustache of a Sicilian brigand. When the bottle appeared, along with a glass, he tossed his quid into the fireplace, rinsed his mouth with water, and "poured out a tremendous drink, which he swallowed with great satisfaction. With an air of content he stroked his mustache and took a fresh chew of tobacco," while Sherman returned the bottle to his saddlebags. Thus refreshed, the three generals then got down to business, and Johnston observed that the former Vice President "never shone more brilliantly than he did in the discussions which followed. He seemed to have at his tongue's end every rule and maxim of international and constitutional law." Indeed, he cited and discoursed with such effect that Sherman — "confronted by the authority, but not convinced by the eloquence" — pushed his chair back from the table and registered a complaint. "See here, gentlemen," he protested. "Who is doing this surrendering anyhow? If this thing goes on, you'll have me sending a letter of apology to Jeff Davis."

Certain of his superiors would presently accuse him of having done just about that in the "Memorandum, or Basis of Agreement" arrived at in the course of the discussion. He wrote it himself, after rejecting a draft of terms prepared that morning in Greensboro by John Reagan — who had also come up from Salisbury but was not admitted to the conference because of his nonmilitary status — as "too general and verbose." Having said as much, he settled down to composing one of his own, more soldierly and direct, based on Reagan's and the agreements reached with Johnston yesterday and the silver-tongued Kentuckian today. As he worked he grew increasingly absorbed, until at one point, pausing to arrange his thoughts, he stopped writing, rose from the table, walked over to his saddlebags, and fumbled absent-mindedly for the bottle. Seeing this, Breckinridge removed his quid in anticipation of another treat. But that, alas, was not to be. Still preoccupied, the Ohioan poured himself a couple of fingers of whiskey, recorked the bottle and returned it to the bag, then stood gazing abstractedly out of a window, sipping the drink while he got his thoughts in order; which done, he set the empty glass down, still without so much as a sidelong glance at his companions, and returned to his writing. In a state of near shock, his face taking on what Johnston called "an injured, sorrowful look," the Kentuckian solaced himself as best he could with a new chew of tobacco. Finally Sherman completed his draft of the terms and passed it across the table, saying: "That's the best I can do."

It was enough, perhaps indeed even more than enough from the rebel point of view. In seven numbered paragraphs, the memorandum provided that the present truce would remain in effect pending approval by superior authorities on both sides; that the troops in all Confederate armies still in existence would be "disbanded and conducted to their several state capitals, there to deposit their arms and public property in the state arsenals"; that federal courts would be reëstablished throughout the land; that the U.S. President would recognize existing state governments as soon as their officials took the required oath of loyalty, and would guarantee to all citizens "their political rights and franchises, as well as their rights of person and property, as defined by the Constitution," pledging in addition that neither he nor his subordinates would "disturb any of the people by reason of the late war, so long as they live in peace and quiet, abstain from acts of armed hostility, and obey the laws in force at the place of their residence." Such, in brief, were the terms set forth, and though Sherman knew that they went far beyond those given Lee, and knew too that he had violated his promise "not to complicate any points of civil policy," he felt more than justified by the assurance, received in return, that all the surviving gray armies — not one of which had been brought to bay, let alone hemmed in, as Lee's had been at Appomattox — would disband en masse, rather than fragment themselves into guerilla bands which might disrupt and bedevil the nation for years to come. In any case, nothing he had promised would be given until, and unless, it was approved by his superiors. Moreover, even if all he had written was rejected — which, on second thought, seemed possible, and on third thought seemed likely — he still would be the gainer by the provisional arrangements he had made. "In the few days it would take to send the papers to Washington, and receive an answer," he rather slyly pointed out, "I could finish the railroad up to Raleigh, and be the better prepared for a long chase."

Once he and Johnston had signed the copies then drawn up, Sherman shouldered his saddlebags and walked out into the gathering dusk, convinced that he had found a simple, forthright, soldierly solution to the multifarious problems of reconstruction by declaring, in effect, that there would be no reconstruction; at any rate none that would involve the politicians. They might not be willing to go along with the instrument which achieved this — the "Memorandum, or Basis of Agreement" — but he believed he knew a solution to that, too. "If you will get the President to simply indorse the copy and commission me to carry out the terms," he told Grant in a letter sent north by courier with the document next morning, "I will follow them to the conclusion."

Johnston too seemed in good spirits as he walked out of the Bennett house and across the yard with his fellow Confederate, who, on the other hand, had reverted to the "full and heavy" condition that preceded the one drink he had been offered before their host recorked the bottle and stuffed it back into his saddlebag. Hoping to divert him, and perhaps dispel the gloom, the Virginian asked his companion what he thought of Sherman. Breckinridge glowered. "He is a bright man, a man of great force," he replied. "But, General Johnston" — his voice rose; his face took on a look of intensity — "General Sherman is a hog. Yes, sir, a hog. Did you see him take that drink by himself?" Johnston suggested that the Ohioan had merely been absent-minded, but Breckinridge had been offended past endurance. He could overlook charges of pillage and arson; not this, which he found quite beyond the pale. "No Kentucky gentleman would ever have taken away that bottle," he said hotly. "He knew we needed it, and needed it badly."

There was a five-day wait, both armies remaining in position as agreed, and then on April 24 the staff courier sent to Washington returned, accompanied — much to Sherman's surprise — by Grant, who had come down the coast to say in person that the proposed "agreement" wouldn't do; wouldn't do at all, in fact, from several points of view.

He himself had seen as much in a single hurried reading when the document first reached him, late in the afternoon three days ago, and got in touch at once with Stanton to have the President call a meeting of the cabinet that night. This was done, and when he read them what Sherman had written, the reaction of the assembled dignitaries was even more vehement than he had expected. Lincoln's body, on display for the past three days in the East Room of the White House and the Capitol rotunda, had been put aboard a crepe-draped train that morning for the burial journey back to Illinois; now, hard in the wake of that emotional drain — that sense of loss which swept over them as they watched the train fade down the track, the smell of cinders fading too — came this documentary evidence that one of the nation's top generals wanted to end the war by reproducing the conditions that began it. Not only was there no mention of the Negro in any of the seven numbered paragraphs Grant read, but the provision for home-bound rebel soldiers to deposit their arms in state arsenals sounded suspiciously like a plan for keeping them ready-stacked for re-rebellion once the men who had carried them for the past four years grew rested enough to try their hand again at tearing the fabric of the Union. Hard to take, too, was the suggested exculpation of all Confederates from all blame, which contrasted strongly with the new President's post-inaugural statement lumping treason with rape and murder as a crime that "must be punished." Johnson was particularly angered by this attempt to override his bedrock pronouncement on the issue of guilt. Angriest of all, however, was the Secretary of War, who saw Sherman's so-called "memorandum" as a bid for the "Copperhead nomination for President" three years hence — if, indeed, he was willing to wait that long and was not planning a military coup when he marched north. Speed, "prompted by Stanton, who seemed frantic," according to Welles, "expressed fears that Sherman, at the head of his victorious legions, had designs upon the government" right now.

Grant defended his friend as best he could; defended his motives, that is, even though he agreed that what they had led to "could not possibly be approved." Nor was he displeased with instructions from his superiors to go in person down to Raleigh and inform his out-of-line subordinate that, his plan having been rejected, he was to "notify General Johnston immediately of the termination of the truce, and resume hostilities against his army at the earliest moment." Their notion was that he should be there in case the red-head attempted defiance of the order, whereas his own purpose was to be on hand to blunt the sting of the rebuke; which was also why he kept the trip a secret, thereby avoiding speculation and gossip about his mission, as well as embarrassment for the man he was going to see. He left at midnight, steaming away from the 6th Street wharf, and two mornings later, after a trainride from the coast, was with Sherman at his headquarters in the North Carolina capital.

Actually, when told of the disapproval of his plan for bringing peace "from the Potomac to the Rio Grande," the Ohioan was not as shocked as Grant expected him to be. Just yesterday he had received a bundle of newspapers reflecting anger throughout the North at the shock of Lincoln's murder, and he sent them along to Johnston with the comment: "I fear much the assassination of the President will give such a bias to the popular mind, which, in connection with the desires of the politicians, may thwart our purpose of recognizing 'existing local governments.'" This last, in fact, was what Grant chose to stress as the principal reason for disapproval of the terms proposed. Making no mention of Johnson's or Stanton's fulminations, he produced a copy of the War Department telegram he had received in early March while still in front of Petersburg. "You are not to decide, discuss, or confer upon any political question," he had been told. "Such questions the President holds in his own hands; and will submit them to no military conference or conventions." Sherman read the dispatch through, then remarked that he wished someone had thought to send him a copy at the time. "It would have saved a world of trouble," he said dryly, and promptly notified Johnston that Washington had called off their agreement. "I am instructed to limit my operations to your immediate command and not to attempt civil negotiations," he wrote, serving notice that hostilities would resume within forty-eight hours unless the Virginian surrendered before that time, "on the same terms as were given General Lee at Appomattox on April 9, instant, purely and simply."

This was plainly an ultimatum; events had taken the course predicted by Davis even as he approved the now repudiated "Basis of Agreement." Dismayed, Johnston wired Breckinridge for instructions, but when these turned out to be a suggestion that he fall back toward Georgia with his cavalry, light guns, and such infantry as could be mounted on spare horses, he replied that the plan was "impracticable," and instead got in touch with Sherman to arrange a third meeting and work out the details for surrender in accordance with the scaled-down terms. Two days later — April 26; Grant, still concerned with avoiding any show of interference, did not attend — they met again in the Bennett farmhouse and the matter was soon disposed of, including an issue of ten days' rations for 25,000 paroled graybacks, offered by Sherman "to facilitate what you and I and all good men desire, the return to their homes of the officers and men composing your army." Johnston replied that "the enlarged patriotism manifested in these papers reconciles me to what I previously regarded as the misfortune of my life — that of having had you to encounter in the field." On this high note of mutual esteem they parted to meet no more, though Johnston would die some twenty-six years later from the effects of a severe cold he contracted in New York while standing bareheaded in raw February weather alongside the other pallbearers at Sherman's funeral. "General, please put on your hat," a friend urged the eighty-four-year-old Virginian; "you might get sick." Johnston refused. "If I were in his place," he said, "and he were standing here in mine, he would not put on his hat."

But that would be a full generation later. Just now all the talk was of surrender, at any rate in the Federal camps; for though a Confederate staffer had remarked on "the eagerness of the men to get to their homes" through these past ten days of on-and-off negotiations, another observed that on the day when the actual news came down, "they scarcely had anything to say." Such dejection was offset by the elation of the bluecoats in their bivouacs around Raleigh. One wrote home of how the birds woke him that morning with their singing — four years and two weeks, to the day, since the first shot was fired in Charleston harbor. "I never heard them sing so sweetly, and never saw them flit about so merrily," he declared, adding that "the green groves in which we were camped had a peculiar beauty and freshness, and as the sun rose above the steeples, it seemed as if we could float right up with it."

Presently there was other news, to which reactions also varied. On that same April 26, about midway between Washington and Richmond, Lincoln's assassin, run to earth at last, was shot and killed by a platoon of New York cavalry. After a week spent hiding in the woods and swamps of southeast Maryland, suffering all the while from pain in the leg he had broken in his leap from the box at Ford's, Booth and an associate succeeded in crossing the Potomac near Port Tobacco on April 22, then two days later made it over the Rappahannock, some twenty miles below Fredericksburg, only to be overtaken the following night on a farm three miles from the river. Surrounded by their pursuers they took refuge in a tobacco shed, and though his companion surrendered when ordered out (and was carried back to the capital next day to stand trial along with seven other alleged conspirators, including one who had made the knife attack on Seward and another who had been slated to dispose of the Vice President but had lacked the nerve to try) Booth himself refused to emerge, even after the tinder-dry structure was set afire. The troopers could see him in there, a crippled figure with a crutch and a carbine, silhouetted against the flames. Then one fired and he fell, dropped by a bullet that passed through his neck, "perforating both sides of the collar." He was still breathing when they dragged him out of the burning shed and onto the porch of a nearby house, but he was paralyzed below the point where his spinal cord had been struck. Two weeks short of his twenty-seventh birthday, he was so much the worse for wear — and the loss of his mustache, which he had shaved off the week before — that he scarcely resembled the darkly handsome matinee idol he had been before his ordeal of the past eleven days. "I thought I did for the best," he managed to say. Just at sunup he asked to have his hands lifted so he could see them, and when this was done he stared at them in despair. "Useless, useless," he muttered. Then he died.

So tight a grip had been kept on official news of the assassination — particularly southward, where Stanton believed the plot had been hatched and where such information might be of use to the conspirators in their flight from justice — most citizens did not know of the murder, except as one more piece of gossip among many that were false, until the murderer himself had been dispatched. Down in rural Georgia, for example, a full week after Lincoln's death and four days before Booth's, a young woman wrote in her diary: "None of our people believe any of the rumors, thinking them as mythical as the surrender of General Lee's army." Presently though, when the truth came out, there were those who reacted with a bitterness nurtured by four long years of a war that now was lost. Another Georgian, an Augusta housewife, writing to her mother-in-law on the last day of April, saw the northern leader's violent fall as a "righteous retribution," a minor comfort in a time of shock. "One sweet drop among so much that is painful is that he at least cannot raise his howl of diabolical triumph over us," she declared. Some in Johnston's army, waiting around Greensboro for the details of their surrender to be worked out, reacted initially in much the same fashion; that is, until Beauregard heard them whooping outside his tent. An aide later testified that this was the only time he saw Old Bory lose his temper all the way. "Shut those men up," he said angrily. "If they won't shut up, have them arrested. Those are my orders."

For the most part, however, even those celebrations that went unchecked lasted only about as long as it took the celebrants to turn their thoughts to Andrew Johnson, who was now in a position to exact the vengeance he had been swearing all along. Jefferson Davis perceived this from the outset. In Charlotte on April 19, when he learned from Breckinridge of his war-long adversary's sudden removal from the scene, he saw in the Tennessean's elevation a portent of much woe. "Certainly I have no special regard for Mr Lincoln," he remarked, "but there are a great many men of whose end I would rather hear than his. I fear it will be disastrous to our people, and I regret it deeply."

That was his first reaction, and he held to it down the years. Though, like Beauregard, he was quick to silence those in his escort who cheered the news, he never engaged in pious homilies over the corpse of his chief foe, but rather stressed his preference for him over the "renegade" who replaced him. "For an enemy so relentless in the war for our subjugation, we could not be expected to mourn," he wrote afterwards; "yet, in view of its political consequences, [Lincoln's assassination] could not be regarded otherwise than as a great misfortune to the South. He had power over the Northern people, and was without personal malignity toward the people of the South; [whereas] his successor was without power in the North, and [was] the embodiment of malignity toward the Southern people, perhaps the more so because he had betrayed and deserted them in the hour of their need."

★   ★   ★

As long ago as late September, before Hood set out on the northward march that turned his fine-honed army into a skeow — "s-k-e-o-w, bubble, bubble, s-k-e-o-w, bust" — Richard Taylor had told Davis that "the best we could hope for was to protract the struggle until spring." Now spring had come, and all he had left for the defense of his Department of Alabama, Mississippi, and East Louisiana were some 10,000 troops under Forrest and Maury, recently flung out of Selma and Mobile, plus something under half that number in garrisons scattered about the three-state region west of the Chattahoochee. Clearly enough, the time was at hand "for statesmen, not soldiers, to deal with the future." Accordingly, when he learned of the week-old "Basis of Agreement" worked out by Sherman, Johnston, and Breckinridge near Durham Station on April 18, he got in touch at once with Canby to arrange a similar armistice here in the western theater, pending approval by the civil authorities of terms that would, in Sherman's words, "produce peace from the Potomac to the Rio Grande." Canby — who knew no more than Taylor did of Washington's quick rejection of those terms — was altogether willing, and a meeting was scheduled for the last day in April, twelve miles up the railroad from Mobile.

Magee's Farm, the place was called. Canby, waiting at the appointed hour beside the tracks, had a full brigade drawn up as a guard of honor, along with a band and a brassy array of staffers, all turned out in their best. The effect, when Taylor at last pulled in, was anticlimactic to say the least. Arriving from Meridian on a handcar — practically the only piece of rolling stock left unwrecked by Wilson's raiders — he had been "pumped" down the line by two Negroes and was accompanied by a single aide whose uniform was as weathered as his own. Nothing daunted, for all his awareness that "the appearance of the two parties contrasted the fortunes of our respective causes," he then retired with the Federal commander to a room prepared in a nearby house, where they promptly agreed to observe a truce while awaiting ratification by their two governments of the terms given Johnston twelve days ago by Sherman, copies of which had been forwarded to them both. This done, they came out into the yard to share an al fresco luncheon that included a number of bottles of champagne, the drawing of whose corks provided what the Louisianian said were "the first agreeable explosive sounds I had heard for years." Presently, when the musicians struck up "Hail, Columbia," Canby ordered a quick switch to "Dixie," but Taylor, not to be outdone, suggested that the original tune continue, the time having come when they could "hail Columbia" together, as in the old days.

Back in Meridian next day he heard from Canby that the Sherman-Johnston agreement had been disavowed; that fighting would resume within forty-eight hours unless he surrendered — as Johnston had done, five days ago — on the terms accorded Lee at Appomattox, three weeks back. Taylor had neither the means nor the inclination to continue the struggle on his own; his task as he saw it, now that the Confederacy had crumbled, was "to administer on the ruins as residuary legatee," and he said as much in his reply, May 2, accepting Canby's scaled-down offer. Two days later they met again, this time at Citronelle, also on the Mobile & Ohio, twenty miles north of Magee's Farm, where, as Taylor later put it, "I delivered the epilogue of the great drama in which I had played a humble part." In Alabama, Mississippi, and East Louisiana, as had already been done in Virginia, North and South Carolina, and Georgia, all butternut survivors were to lay down their arms in exchange for assurance by the victors that they were not to be "disturbed" by the U.S. government "so long as they continue to observe the conditions of their parole and the laws in force where they reside." Although Sherman's proposal for restoring peace "from the Potomac to the Rio Grande" had been rejected, more or less out of hand, the arrangement that replaced it — commander to individual army commander, blue and gray, after the pattern set by Grant and Lee — achieved as much, in any case, for all of that region east of the Mississippi.

Or did it? Would it? Some, indeed many, believed it would not: including Sherman. "I now apprehend that the rebel armies will disperse," he had written Grant the week before, "and instead of dealing with six or seven states, we will have to deal with numberless bands of desperadoes, headed by such men as Mosby, Forrest, Red Jackson, and others who know not and care not for danger and its consequences."

One at least of these, despite the Ohioan's assertion that "nothing is left for them but death or highway robbery," had already proved him wrong. On April 21, soon after learning of Lee's capitulation, John Mosby formally disbanded his Rangers and presently — remarking, as if in specific response to Sherman: "We are soldiers, not highwaymen" — made official application for parole in order to hang up his shingle and resume the life he had led before the war. So much then for baleful predictions as to the postsurrender activities of Virginia's leading partisan, who soon was practicing law in the region where he and his men had given the blue authorities so much trouble for the past two years. As for Forrest and his red-haired subordinate, W. H. Jackson, there was considerable doubt, even in their own minds, as to what course they would follow. Between Taylor's final meeting with Canby, May 4 at Citronelle, and the issuance of paroles four days later, a staff colonel would recall, "all was gloom, broken only by wild rumors." This was especially the case in Forrest's camps around Gainesville, Alabama, fifty miles northeast of Meridian. There was much talk of "going to Mexico" as an alternative to surrender, and the general himself was said to be turning the notion over in his mind.

He was in fact in a highly disgruntled state, one arm in a sling from his fourth combat wound, suffered during a horseback fight with a young Indiana captain at Ebenezer Church, just north of Selma on the day before Wilson overran him there. The Federal hacked away at the general's upraised arm until Forrest managed to draw his revolver and kill him. "If that boy had known enough to give me the point of his saber instead of the edge," he later said, "I should not have been here to tell about it." Instead the Hoosier captain became his thirtieth hand-to-hand victim within a four-year span of war that also saw twenty-nine horses shot from under him, thereby validating his claim that he was "a horse ahead at the close." What rankled worse, despite the mitigating odds, was the drubbing Wilson had given him in what turned out to be his last campaign. Unaccustomed to defeat, this only soldier on either side who rose from private to lieutenant general had no more fondness for surrender now than he had had when he rode out of Donelson, nearly forty months ago. Mexico seemed preferable — at any rate up to the day before the one on which he and his troopers were scheduled to lay down their arms. That evening he and his adjutant set out on a quiet, thoughtful ride. Neither spoke until they drew rein just short of a fork in the road. "Which way, General?" his companion asked, and Forrest replied glumly: "Either. If one road led to hell and the other to Mexico, I would be indifferent which to take." They sat their horses in the moonlight for a time, the adjutant doing most of the talking, which had to do with the duty they owed their native land, whether in victory or defeat: particularly Forrest, who could lead into the ways of peace the young men who had followed him in war. "That settles it," the general said, and turned back toward camp.

As usual, once he made up his mind to a course of action, he followed it all-out: as did his men, who dropped all talk of Mexico when they learned that he had done so before them. Whatever doubt they had of this was dispelled by the farewell he addressed to them at Gainesville on May 9, soon after they furled their star-crossed flags and gave their parole to fight no more against the Union he and they rejoined that day.

SOLDIERS:
By an agreement made between Lieutenant General Taylor, commanding the Department of Alabama, Mississippi, and East Louisiana, and Major General Canby, commanding U.S. forces, the troops of this department have been surrendered. I do not think it proper or necessary at this time to refer to the causes which have reduced us to this extremity, nor is it now a matter of material consequence as to how such results were brought about. That we are beaten is a self-evident fact, and any further resistance on our part would be justly regarded as the height of folly and rashness. . . . Reason dictates and humanity demands that no more blood be shed. Fully realizing and feeling that such is the case, it is your duty and mine to lay down our arms, submit to the "powers that be," and aid in restoring peace and establishing law and order throughout the land. The terms upon which you were surrendered are favorable, and should be satisfactory and acceptable to all. They manifest a spirit of magnanimity and liberality on the part of the Federal authorities which should be met on our part by a faithful compliance with all the stipulations and conditions therein expressed. . . .
Civil war, such as you have just passed through, naturally engenders feelings of animosity, hatred, and revenge. It is our duty to divest ourselves of all such feelings, and, so far as it is in our power to do so, to cultivate feelings toward those with whom we have so long contested and heretofore so widely but honestly differed. Neighborhood feuds, personal animosities, and private differences should be blotted out, and when you return home a manly, straightforward course of conduct will secure the respect even of your enemies. Whatever your responsibilities may be to government, to society, or to individuals, meet them like men. The attempt made to establish a separate and independent confederation has failed, but the conscious-

ness of having done your duty faithfully and to the end will in some measure repay for the hardships you have undergone. . . . I have never on the field of battle sent you where I was unwilling to go myself, nor would I now advise you to a course which I felt myself unwilling to pursue. You have been good soldiers, you can be good citizens. Obey the laws, preserve your honor, and the government to which you have surrendered can afford to be and will be magnanimous.

N. B. FORREST,
Lieutenant General.

★ ★ ★

On April 26, the day of Booth's death and Johnston's renegotiated surrender, Davis met for the last time with his full cabinet and decided to end his week-long stay in Charlotte by pressing on at once to the southwest. He had not been surprised at Washington's rejection of the Sherman-Johnston "Basis of Agreement," which he himself had approved two days before, since his opinion of the new northern leader and "his venomous Secretary of War," as he said afterwards, did not permit him to expect "that they would be less vindictive after a surrender of the army had been proposed than when it was regarded as a formidable body defiantly holding its position in the field." What did surprise and anger him, some time later, was the news that Johnston, ignoring the suggestion that he fall back with the mobile elements of his army to draw Sherman after him, had laid down his arms without so much as a warning note to superiors he knew were in flight for their lives. Davis's indignation was heightened all the more when he learned that the Virginian, in his last general order, had blamed "recent events in Virginia for breaking every hope of success by war." Lee had fought until he was virtually surrounded and a breakout attempt had failed; whereas Johnston not only had not tried for the getaway suggested and expected, but had also, by a stroke of the pen, ended all formal resistance in three of the states through which his fugitive superiors would be traveling in their attempt to reach Dick Taylor or Kirby Smith, on this or the far side of the Mississippi River.

Hope for escape by that route had been encouraged by a series of dispatches from Wade Hampton, who did not consider himself or his troopers bound by the surrender negotiations then in progress. "The military situation is very gloomy, I admit," he wrote Davis on the day after the Sherman-Johnston-Breckinridge meeting near Durham Station, "but it is by no means desperate, and endurance and determination will produce a change." His notion was that the struggle should continue wherever there was ground to stand on, in or out of the country, whatever the odds. "Give me a good force of cavalry and I will take them safely across the Mississippi, and if you desire to go in that direction it will give me great pleasure to escort you. . . . I can bring to your support many strong arms and brave hearts — men who will fight to Texas, and who, if forced from that state, will seek refuge in Mexico rather than in the Union." Hoping to confer with the President in Salisbury, he reached Greensboro three days later, April 22, and found that the government had been transferred to Charlotte. "My only object in seeing you," he declared in a follow-up message, "was to assure you that many of my officers and men agree with me in thinking that nothing can be as disastrous to us as a peace founded on the restoration of the Union. A return to the Union will bring all the horrors of war, coupled with all the degradation that can be inflicted on a conquered people. . . . If I can serve you or my country by any further fighting you have only to tell me so. My plan is to collect all the men who will stick to their colors, and to get to Texas. I can carry with me quite a number, *and I can get there.*"

Heartened by this stalwart reassurance from the South Carolina grandee, whose views — delusions, some would say — were in accordance with his own, Davis took time out next day for the first real letter he had had a chance to write his wife since he left Richmond, three weeks back. In it were mingled the hopes expressed by Hampton and the private doubts that surfaced when he shifted his attention from his duty to his country, as the symbol of its survival, to his concern for the welfare of his four children and their mother. Threatened by Stoneman's descent on Salisbury, they had left Charlotte ten days ago, six days before he got there, and were now in Abbeville, South Carolina, down near the Georgia line. He spoke first of the difficulty of his position in deciding whether to urge his people to continue their resistance to what he saw as subjugation. "The issue is one which it is very painful for me to meet," he told Varina. "On one hand is the long night of oppression which will follow the return of our people to the 'Union'; on the other, the suffering of the women and children, and carnage among the few brave patriots who would still oppose the invader, and who, unless the people would rise en masse to sustain them, would struggle but to die in vain. I think my judgment is undisturbed by any pride of opinion, [for] I have prayed to our Heavenly Father to give me wisdom and fortitude equal to the demands of the position in which Providence has placed me. I have sacrificed so much for the cause of the Confederacy that I can measure my ability to make any further sacrifice required, and am assured there is but one to which I am not equal — my wife and my children. . . . For myself," he added, "it may be that a devoted band of cavalry will cling to me and that I can force my way across the Mississippi, and if nothing can be done there which it will be proper to do, then I can go to Mexico, and have the world from which to choose a location." That such a choice would come hard for him was shown by the emotion that swept over him when, having faced the prospect of spending the rest of his life in exile, he closed his letter. "Dear Wife, this is not the fate to which I invited [you] when the future was rose-colored to us both; but I know you will bear it even better than myself, and that, of us two, I alone will ever look back reproachfully on my past career.... Farewell, my dear. There may be better things in store for us than are now in view, but my love is all I have to offer, and that has the value of a thing long possessed, and sure not to be lost."

Three days later, in reaction to the news that Sherman's terms had been rejected, Davis and his advisers — fugitives in a profounder sense now that the new enemy President had branded them as criminals not eligible for parole — concluded that the time had come to press on southward, out of the Old North State. This was the last full cabinet meeting, for it was no sooner over than George Davis submitted his resignation on grounds that his motherless children required his attention at Wilmington. Concerned as he was about his own homeless family up ahead, Jefferson Davis had sympathy for the North Carolinian's view as to where his duty lay, and the Confederacy — which had never had any courts anyhow, Supreme or otherwise — no longer had an Attorney General by the time its government pulled out of Charlotte that same afternoon. At Fort Mill two mornings later, just over the South Carolina line, Trenholm also resigned, too ill to continue the journey even by ambulance. Davis thanked the wealthy Charlestonian for his "lofty patriotism and personal sacrifice," then shifted John Reagan to the Treasury Department, leaving the postal service headless and the cabinet score at two down, four to go.

"I *cannot* feel like a beaten man," he had remarked before setting out, and now on the march his spirits rose. In part this was because of his return to the field, to the open-air soldier life he always fancied. Four more cavalry brigades — so called, though none was as large as an old-style regiment, and all five combined totaled only about 3000 men — had turned up at Charlotte, fugitive and unattached, in time to swell the departing column to respectable if not formidable proportions. Breckinridge took command of the whole, and Davis had for company three military aides, all colonels, John Wood, Preston Johnston — son of his dead hero, Albert Sidney Johnston — and Francis Lubbock, former governor of Texas. Like Judah Benjamin, who had an apparently inexhaustible supply of wit and prime Havanas, these were congenial traveling companions. Moreover, progress through this section of South Carolina, which had been spared the eastward Sherman torch, was like a return to happier times, the crowds turning out to cheer their President and wish him well. This was the homeland of John C. Calhoun, and invitations poured in for one-night stays at mansions along the way. Davis responded accordingly. "He talked very pleasantly of other days," Mallory would recall, "and forgot for a time the engrossing anxieties of the situation." He spoke of Scott and Byron, of hunting dogs and horses, in a manner his fellow travelers found "singularly equable and cheerful" throughout the six-day ride to Abbeville, which they reached on May 2.

Mrs Davis and the children were not there, having moved on into Georgia three days ago. "Washington will be the first point I shall 'unload' at," she informed her husband in a note brought by a courier who met him on the road. That was less than fifty miles off, the closest they had been to one another in more than a month, and though she planned to "wait a little until we hear something of you," she urged him not to risk capture by going out of his way to join her, saying: "Let me beseech you not to calculate upon seeing me unless I happen to cross your shortest path toward your bourne, be that what it may." Stragglers and parolees from Lee's and Johnston's armies had passed through in large numbers, she also cautioned, and "not one has talked fight. A stand cannot be made in this country; do not be induced to try it. As to the Trans-Mississippi, I doubt if at first things will be straight, but the spirit is there and the daily accretions will be great when the deluded on this side are crushed out between the upper and nether millstone."

Speed then was the watchword, lest he be gathered up by blue pursuers or victimized by butternut marauders, hungry alike for the millions in treasury bullion he was rumored to have brought with him out of Richmond. At 4 o'clock that afternoon he summoned Breckinridge and the brigade commanders to a large downstairs parlor in the house where his family had stayed while they were here. Through a large window opening westward the five could see a rose garden in full bloom, and one among them later remarked that he had "never seen Mr Davis look better or show to better advantage. He seemed in excellent spirits and humor, and the union of dignity, graceful affability, and decision, which made his manner usually so striking, was very marked in his reception of us." After welcoming and putting them at ease, as was his custom at such meetings — even when the participants were familiars, as these were not; at least not yet — he passed at once to his reason for having called them into council. "It is time that we adopt some definite plan upon which the further prosecution of our struggle shall be conducted. I have summoned you for consultation. I feel that I ought to do nothing now without the advice of my military chiefs." He smiled as he said this last: "rather archly," according to one hearer, who observed that while "such a term addressed to a handful of brigadiers, commanding altogether barely 3000 men, by one who so recently had been the master of legions, was a pleasantry; yet he said it in a way that made it a compliment." What followed, however, showed clearly enough how serious he was. "Even if the troops now with me be all that I can for the present rely on," he declared, "3000 brave men are enough for a nucleus around which the whole people will rally when the panic which now afflicts them has passed away."

A tense silence ensued; none of the five wanted to be the first to say what each of them knew the other four were thinking. Finally one spoke, and the rest chimed in. What the country was undergoing wasn't panic, they informed their chief, but exhaustion. Any attempt to prolong the war, now that the means of supporting it were gone, "would be a cruel injustice to the people of the South," while for the soldiers the consequences would be even worse; "for if they persisted in a conflict so hopeless they would be treated as brigands and would forfeit all chance of returning to their homes." Breaking a second silence, Davis asked why then, if all hope was exhausted, they still were in the field. To assist in his escape, they replied, adding that they "would ask our men to follow us until his safety was assured, and would risk them in battle for that purpose, but would not fire another shot in an effort to continue hostilities." Now a third silence descended, in which the gray leader sat looking as if he had been slapped across the face by a trusted friend. Recovering, he said he would hear no suggestion that had only to do with his own survival, and made one final plea wherein, as one listener said, "he appealed eloquently to every sentiment and reminiscence that might be supposed to move a Southern soldier." When he finished, the five merely looked at him in sorrow. "Then all is indeed lost," he muttered, and rose to leave the room, deathly pale and unsteady on his feet. He tottered, and as he did so Breckinridge stepped forward, hale and ruddy, and offered his arm, which Davis, aged suddenly far beyond his nearly fifty-seven years, was glad to take.

Now it was flight, pure and simple — flight for flight's sake, so to speak — with no further thought of a rally until and unless he reached the Transmississippi. That was still his goal, and all agreed that the lighter he traveled the better his chances were of getting there. One encumbrance was the treasury hoard, which had got this far by rail, outracing Stoneman, but could go no farther. Of this, $39,000 had been left in Greensboro for Johnston to distribute among his soldiers (which he did; all ranks drew $1.15 apiece to see them home) and now the balance was dispersed, including $108,000 in silver coins paid out to troopers of the five brigades, the cadet guards, and other members of the presidential party; officers and men alike drew $26.25 each. Transferred to wagons, $230,000 in securities was sent on to a bank in Washington, just beyond the Georgia line, for deposit pending its return to Richmond and the banks that owned it, while $86,000 in gold was concealed in the false bottom of a carriage and started on its way to Charleston, there to be shipped in secrecy to England and drawn on when the government reached Texas. That left $30,000 in silver bullion, packed in trunks and stored in a local warehouse, and $35,000 in gold specie, kept on hand to cover expenses on the journey south and west. Relieved at last of their burden and "detached," the cadets promptly scattered for their homes.

Before leaving-time, which was midnight that same May 2, others expressed their desire to be gone, and one of these was Stephen Mallory. Pleading "the dependent condition of a helpless family," he submitted his resignation as head of the all-but-nonexistent C. S. Navy. He would leave soon after they crossed the Savannah River into Georgia, he said, and join his refugee wife and children in La Grange. That would bring the cabinet tally to three down, three to go. Or rather, four down, two to go; for by then still another member had departed. Plump and chafed, Judah Benjamin took off informally the following night, after a private conversation with his chief. His goal was the Florida coast, then Bimini, and he set out disguised variously as a farmer and a Frenchman, with a ramshackle cart, a spavined horse, and a mismatched suit of homespun clothes. Davis wished him well, but again declined an offer from Mallory, when the Floridian parted from him in Washington on May 4, of a boat then waiting up the Indian River to take him to Cuba or the Bahamas. He said, as he had said before — unaware that, even as he spoke, Dick Taylor was meeting with Canby at Citronelle to surrender the last gray army east of the Mississippi — that he could not leave Confederate soil while a single Confederate regiment clung to its colors.

Here again, as at Abbeville two days ago, he found that his family, fearful of being waylaid by marauders, had moved on south. "I dread the Yankees getting news of you so much," his wife had written in a note she left behind. "You are the country's only hope, and the very best intentioned do not calculate upon a stand this side of the river. Why not cut loose from your escort? Go swiftly and alone, with the exception of two or three. ... May God keep you, my old and only love," the note ended.

He had it in mind to do just that, or anyhow something close, and accordingly instructed Breckinridge to peel off next day with the five brigades of cavalry, leaving him only an escort company of Kentucky horsemen; which, on second thought — for they were, as he said, "not strong enough to fight, and too large to pass without observation" — he ordered reduced to ten volunteers. He would have with him after that, in addition to a handful of servants and teamsters, only these men, his three military aides, and John Reagan. The Texan had been with him from the start and was determined to stick with him to the finish, which he hoped would not come before they reached his home beyond the Mississippi and the Sabine. Davis was touched by this fidelity, as he also was by a message received when he took up the march next morning. Robert Toombs lived in Washington, and though none of the party had called on him, or he on them, he sent word that all he had was at the fugitive President's disposal. "Mr Davis and I have had a quarrel, but we have none now," he said. "If he desires, I will call all my men around here to see him safely across the Chattahoochee at the risk of my life." Davis, told of this, replied: "That is like Bob Toombs. He always was a whole-souled man. If it were necessary, I should not hesitate to accept his offer."

No such thoughts of another Georgia antagonist prompted a side trip when he passed within half a dozen miles of Liberty Hall, the Vice President's estate near Crawfordville; nor did he consider getting in touch with Joe Brown at Milledgeville, twenty-five miles to the west, when he reached Sandersville, May 6. Pressing on — as if aware that James Wilson had issued that day in Macon, less than fifty miles away, a War Department circular announcing: "One hundred thousand dollars Reward in Gold will be paid to any person or persons who will apprehend and deliver JEFFERSON DAVIS to any of the military authorities of the United States. Several millions of specie reported to be with him will become the property of the captors" — the now fast-moving column of twenty men and three vehicles made camp that evening on the east side of the Oconee, near Ball's Ferry. Their intention was to continue southwest tomorrow for a crossing of the Chattahoochee "below the point where the enemy had garrisons," but something Preston Johnston learned when he walked down to the ferry before supper caused a sudden revision of those plans. Mrs Davis and the children, escorted by Burton Harrison, had crossed here that morning, headed south, and there was a report that a group of disbanded soldiers planned to attack and rob their camp that night. Hearing this, Davis remounted his horse. "I do not feel that you are bound to go with me," he told his companions, "but I must protect my family."

What followed turned out to be an exhausting all-night ride beyond the Oconee. Though the escort horses finally broke down, Davis and his better-mounted aides kept on through the moonlit bottoms until shortly before dawn, near Dublin, close to twenty miles downstream, they came upon a darkened camp beside the road. "Who's there?" someone called out in an alarmed, determined voice which Davis was greatly relieved to recognize as Harrison's. He and his wife and children were together again for the first time since he put them aboard the train in Richmond, five weeks back.

Having rested their mounts, the escort horsemen arrived in time for breakfast, and the two groups — with Davis so bone-tired that he agreed for the first time to ride in an ambulance — pushed on south together to bivouac that night some twenty miles east of Hawkinsville, where 3000 of Wilson's raiders were reported to be in camp. Alarmed, Mrs Davis persuaded her husband to proceed without her the following day, May 8. Once across the Ocmulgee at Poor Robin Bluff, however, he heard new rumors of marauders up ahead, and stopped on the outskirts of Abbeville to wait for her and the children, intending to see them through another day's march before turning off to the southwest. They arrived that night, and next morning the two groups, again combined, continued to move south. Lee had surrendered a month ago today; tomorrow would make a solid month that Davis had been on the go from Danville, a distance of just over four hundred miles, all but the first and last forty of which he had spent on horseback; he was understandably weary. Yet the arrangement, when they made camp at 5 o'clock that afternoon in a stand of pines beside a creek just north of Irwinville, was that he would take some rest in his wife's tent, then press on with his escort after dark, presumably to see her no more until she rejoined him in Texas.

Outside in the twilight, seated with their backs against the boles of trees around the campfire, his aides waited for word to mount up and resume the journey. They too were weary, and lately they had been doubtful — especially during the two days spent off-course because of Davis's concern for the safety of his wife and children — whether they would make it out of Georgia. But now, within seventy miles of the Florida border, they felt much better about their chances, having come to believe that Breckinridge, when he peeled off near Washington with the five brigades, had decoyed the Federals onto his track and off theirs. In any case, the President's horse was saddled and waiting, a brace of pistols holstered on its withers, and they were waiting, too, ready to move on. They sat up late, then finally, receiving no call, dozed off: unaware that, even as they slept and dawn began to glimmer through the pines, two regiments of Union cavalry — 4th Michigan and 1st Wisconsin, tipped off at Hawkinsville that the rebel leader and his party had left Abbeville that morning, headed for Irwinville, forty-odd miles away — were closing in from opposite sides of the camp, one having circled it in the darkness to come up from the south, while the other bore down from the northwest. The result, as the two mounted units converged, was the last armed clash east of the Mississippi. Moreover, by way of a further distinction, all the combatants wore blue, including the two killed and four wounded in the rapid-fire exchange. "A sharp fight ensued, both parties exhibiting the greatest determination," James Wilson presently would report, not without a touch of pride in his men's aggressiveness, even when they were matched against each other. "Fifteen minutes elapsed before the mistake was discovered."

All was confusion in the night-drowsed bivouac. Wakened like the others by the sudden uproar on the fringes of the camp — he had lain down, fully dressed, in expectation of leaving before midnight, but had slept through from exhaustion — Davis presumed the attackers were butternut marauders. "I will go out and see if I can't stop the firing," he told his wife. "Surely I will have some authority with Confederates." When he lifted the tent flap, however, he saw high-booted figures, their uniforms dark in the pearly glow before sunrise, dodging through the woods across the creek and along the road on this side. "Federal cavalry are upon us!" he exclaimed. Terrified, Varina urged him to flee while there was time. He hesitated, then took up a lightweight sleeveless rain-coat — which he supposed was his own but was his wife's, cut from the same material — and started out, drawing it on along with a shawl she threw over his head and shoulders. Before he had gone twenty paces a Union trooper rode up, carbine at the ready, and ordered him to halt. Davis paused, dropping the coat and shawl, and then came on again, directly toward the trooper in his path. "I expected, if he fired, he would miss me," he later explained, "and my intention was in that event to put my hand under his foot, tumble him off on the other side, spring into his saddle, and attempt to escape." It was a trick he had learned from the Indians, back in his early army days, and it might have worked except for his wife, who, seeing the soldier draw a deliberate bead on the slim gray form advancing point-blank on him, rushed forward with a cry and threw her arms around her husband's neck. With that, all chance for a getaway was gone; Davis now could not risk his life with-out also risking hers, and presently other blue-clad troopers came riding up, all with their carbines leveled at him and Varina, who still clung to him. "God's will be done," he said in a low voice as he turned away and walked slowly past the tent to take a seat on a fallen tree beside the campfire.

Elsewhere about the camp the struggle continued on various levels of resistance. Four days ago, a wagon had gone south from Sandersville with most of the $35,000 in gold coin; the remaining $10,000, kept for travel expenses between there and the Gulf, was distributed among the aides and Reagan, who carried it in their saddlebags; as the bluecoats now discovered. Reagan, with his own and the President's portion of the burden — some $3500 in all — turned it over with no more than a verbal protest, but his fellow Texan Lubbock hung onto his in a tussle with two of the soldiers, despite their threats to shoot him if he did not turn loose. "Shoot and be damned!" he told them. "You'll not rob me while I'm alive and looking on." They did, though, and Preston Johnston lost his share as well, along with the pistols his father had carried when he fell at Shiloh. Only John Wood was successful in his resistance, and that was by strategy rather than by force. Knowing that he would be charged with piracy for his work off the New England coast last August, the former skipper of the *Tallahassee* took one of his captors aside, slipped him two $20 gold pieces, and walked off unnoticed through the pines — eventually to make it all the way to Cuba with Breckinridge, whom he encountered down in Florida two weeks later, determined like himself to leave the country rather than stay and face charges brought against him by the victors in their courts.

But that was later. For the present, all Wood's friends knew was that he was missing, and only one of his foes knew even that much. Besides, both groups were distracted by the loud bang of a carbine, followed at once by a shriek of pain. Convinced that the reported millions in coin and bullion must be cached somewhere about the camp, one unfortunate trooper had used his loaded weapon in an attempt to pry open a locked trunk, and the piece had discharged, blowing off one of his hands. Others took over and got the lid up, only to find that all the trunk contained was a hoop skirt belonging to Mrs Davis. Despite their disappointment, the garment turned out to have its uses, being added to the cloak and shawl as evidence that the rebel chieftain had tried to escape in women's clothes. Three days later, Wilson would inform the War Department that Davis, surprised by the dawn attack, "hastily put on one of Mrs Davis' dresses and started for the woods, closely pursued by our men, who at first thought him a woman, but seeing his boots while running suspected his sex at once. The race was a short one, and the rebel President soon was brought to bay. He brandished a bowie knife of elegant pattern, and showed signs of battle, but yielded promptly to the persuasion of Colt revolvers without compelling our men to fire." This was far too good to let pass unexploited, providing as it did a counterpart to the story of Lincoln's passage through Baltimore four years ago, similarly clad in a Scotch-plaid garment borrowed from his wife, on the way to his first inauguration. "If Jefferson Davis was captured in his wife's clothes," Halleck recommended after reading Wilson's dispatch, "I respectfully suggest that he be sent North in the same habiliments."

That too would come later, along with the many jubilant cartoons and a tableau staged by Barnum to display the Confederate leader in flight through brush and briers, cavorting in hooped calico and brandishing a dagger. Just now his worst indignity came from having to look on powerless while the treasure-hungry bluecoats rifled his and Varina's personal luggage, tossing the contents about and only pausing to snatch from the fire and gulp down the children's half-cooked breakfast. "You are an expert set of thieves," he told one of them, who replied: "Think so?" and kept on rifling. Presently the Michigan colonel approached and stood looking down at the Mississippian, seated on his log beside the campfire. "Well, old Jeff, we've got you at last," he declared with a grin. Davis lost his temper at this and shouted: "The worst of it all is that I should be captured by a band of thieves and scoundrels!" Stiffening, the colonel drew himself up. "You're a prisoner and can afford to talk that way," he said.

Davis knew well enough that he was a prisoner. What was more, in case it slipped his memory during the three-day trip to Wilson's headquarters at Macon, the soldiers took pains to keep him well reminded of the fact. "Get a move on, Jeff," they taunted him from time to time. He rode in an ambulance with his wife and a pair of guards, while her sister Margaret followed in another with the children, all four of whom were upset by her weeping. The other captives were permitted to ride their own horses, which were "lent" them pending arrival. There was a carnival aspect to the procession, at least among the troopers riding point. "Hey, Johnny Reb," they greeted paroled Confederates by the roadside, "we've got your President!" That was good for a laugh each time save one, when an angered butternut replied: "Yes, and the devil's got yours." A supposed greater shock was reserved for Davis along the way, when he was shown the proclamation Andrew Johnson had issued charging him with complicity in Lincoln's assassination. He took it calmly, however, remarking that there was one man who knew the document to be false — "the one who signed it, for he at least knew that I preferred Lincoln to himself."

After a night spent in Macon, May 13, he and his wife, together with Margaret Howell and the children, Reagan, Lubbock, and Preston Johnston, were placed in a prison train for an all-day roundabout journey to Augusta, where they were driven across town to the river landing and put on a tug waiting to take them down the Savannah to the coast. Already aboard, to his surprise, were two distinguished Confederates, now prisoners like himself. One was Joe Wheeler, who had been captured five days ago at Conyer Station, just east of Atlanta, frustrated in his no-surrender attempt to reach the Transmississippi with three members of his staff and eleven privates. The other was Alexander Stephens, picked up last week at Liberty Hall after Davis passed nearby. Pale and shaken, the child-sized former Vice President looked forlorn in the greatcoat and several mufflers he wore despite the balmy late-spring weather. Davis gave him a remote but courteous bow, which was returned in kind. At Port Royal, on the morning of May 16, the enlarged party transferred to an ocean-going steamer, the side-wheeler *William P. Clyde*. Presumably, under escort by the multigunned warship *Tuscarora*, she would take them up the coast, into Chesapeake Bay, then up the Potomac to the northern capital.

So they thought. But three days later, after a stormy delay while rounding Hatteras, the *Clyde* dropped anchor off the eastern tip of the York-James peninsula, and there she lay for three more days, under the guns of Fort Monroe, "the Gibraltar of the Chesapeake," whose thirty-foot granite walls, close to a hundred feet thick at their base, had sheltered its Union garrison throughout the four years of the war. Next day, May 20, Stephens and Reagan were transferred to the *Tuscarora* for delivery to Fort Warren in Boston harbor. The day after that, Wheeler, Lubbock, and Johnston were sent on their way to Fort Delaware, downriver from Philadelphia. Then on May 22 came Davis's turn, though he had nothing like as far to go. His destination was there at hand, and the delay had been for the purpose of giving the fort's masons time to convert a subterranean gunroom into a prison cell: strong evidence that, for him as for the others gone before, the charges and the trial to follow would be military, not civil.

"In leaving his wife and children," a witness informed Stanton,

"Davis exhibited no great emotion, though he was violently affected." This last was clearly true, in spite of the prisoner's efforts to conceal what he was feeling. "Try not to cry. They will gloat over your grief," he told Varina as he prepared to board the tug that would take him ashore. She managed to do as he asked, but then, having watched him pass from sight across the water, rushed to her cabin and gave way to weeping. It was as if she had read what tomorrow's New York *Herald* would tell its readers: "At about 3 o'clock yesterday, 'all that is mortal' of Jeff'n Davis, late so-called 'President of the alleged Confederate States,' was duly, but quietly and effectively, committed to that living tomb prepared within the impregnable walls of Fortress Monroe.... No more will Jeff'n Davis be known among the masses of men. He is buried alive."

✗ 3 ✗

On May 10, unaware that the Confederate leader had been captured before sunup down in Georgia, Andrew Johnson issued a proclamation declaring that "armed resistance to the authority of this Government in the said insurrectionary States may be regarded as virtually at an end." This was subsequently taken by some, including the nine Supreme Court justices, to mark the close of the war, and it was followed twelve days later — the day Davis entered the granite bowels of Fort Monroe — by another presidential edict announcing that all the reunited nation's seaports would be open to commerce, with the exception of Galveston and three others along the Texas coast, and that civilian trade in all parts of the country east of the Mississippi would be resumed without restrictions.

That was May 22, and this second pronouncement, like the first, not only reflected the widespread public hope for a swift return to the ways of peace, but also served to clear the Washington stage for still another victory celebration, a two-day Grand Review planned for tomorrow and the next day, larger in scale, and above all in panoply, than the other two combined. Meade's and Sherman's armies had come north from Appomattox and Raleigh, and by then were bivouacked around the capital; which gave rise to a number of problems. In addition to the long-standing rivalry between paper-collar Easterners and roughneck Westerners, the latter now had a new burden of resentment to unload. Soon after the Administration's rejection of the original Durham Station terms, the papers had been full of Stanton's denunciation of the red-haired general who composed them, including charges that he was politically ambitious, with an eye on the Copperhead vote, and quite possibly had been seduced by Confederate gold, slipped to him out of the millions the fugitive rebel leader carried southward when Sherman obligingly called a halt to let him pass across his front. Angered by the slander of their chief, western officers no sooner reached the capital than they began leaping on saloon bars to call for "three groans for the Secretary of War," and the men in the ranks provoked fistfights with the Potomac veterans, whom they saw as allied with Stanton if only because of proximity. Eventually Grant solved the problem, in part at least, by having the two armies camp on opposite sides of the river; yet the bitterness continued.

The showdown would come tomorrow and the following day, not in a direct confrontation — though by now large numbers of men in the ranks of both might have welcomed such a test — but rather in a tandem display, whereby the public would judge their respective merits in accordance with their looks, their martial demeanor as they swung up Pennsylvania Avenue toward a covered stand erected in front of the White House for the President and his guests, including Grant and other dignitaries, civil as well as military. By prearrangement, the Army of the Potomac would parade on May 23 and the Westerners would take their turn next day. Sherman had qualms about the outcome: as well he might, for close-order marching was reported to be the chief skill of the bandbox Easterners, who moreover would be performing on home turf to long-term admirers, whereas his own gangling plowboys, though they had slogged a thousand roundabout miles through Georgia and the Carolinas, then north across Virginia, had done scarcely any drilling since they set out south from Chattanooga, a year ago this month. Then too there was the matter of clothes and equipment, another comparative disadvantage for members of the Armies of the Tennessee and the Cumberland. Their uniforms had weathered to "a cross between Regulation blue and Southern gray," a New England soldier observed, and the men inside were no less outlandish in his eyes. "Their hair and beards were uncut and uncombed; huge slouched hats, black and gray, adorned their heads; their boots were covered with the mud they had brought up from Georgia; their guns were of all designs, from the Springfield rifle to a cavalry carbine." That was how they looked to him on their arrival, three days before the start of the Grand Review. Sherman, with only that brief span for preparation, could only order such intensified drill instruction as there was time for, between hours of refurbishing dingy leather and dull brass, and hope meanwhile for the best; or in any case something better than the worst, which would be to have his veterans sneered or laughed at by people along the route of march or, least bearable of all, by those in the reviewing stand itself.

Washington — midtown Washington anyhow; the outlying sections were practically deserted — had never been so crowded as it was on the day when the first of more than 200,000 blue-clad victors, up from Virginia and the Carolinas, stepped out for the start of their last parade. In brilliant sunshine, under a cloudless sky, bleachers lining the avenue from the Capitol, where the march began, overflowed with citizens dressed this Tuesday in their Sunday best to watch the saviors of the Union swing past in cadence, twelve abreast. All the national flags were at full staff for the first time since April 15, and the crepe had been removed from public buildings as a sign that nearly six weeks of mourning for Lincoln were to be rounded off with two days of rejoicing for the victory he had done so much to win but had not lived to see completed. Meade led the column of march today, and after saluting Johnson and Grant, who stood together against a frock-coated backdrop of dignitaries massed in the stand before the White House, dismounted and joined them to watch his troops pass in review. Zouaves decked in gaudy clothes, Irish units with sprigs of greenery in their caps, engineers with ponderous equipment, artillerists riding caissons trailed by big-mouthed guns, all lent their particular touches to a show dominated in the main by close-packed throngs of infantry, polished bayonets glittering fiery in the sunlight, and seven unbroken miles of cavalry, steel-shod hoofs clopping for a solid hour past any given point. Spectators marveled at the youth of many commanders: especially Custer, whose "sunrise of golden hair" rippled to his shoulders as if in celebration of his latest promotion, one week after Appomattox. Barely four years out of West Point, not yet twenty-six and already a major general of volunteers, he came close to stealing the show when his horse, spooked by a wreath tossed from the curb, bolted just short of the White House. "Runaway!" the crowd shrieked, frightened and delighted. A reporter, watching the general's hat fly off and "his locks, unskeined, stream a foot behind him," was put in mind — more prophetically than he knew — of "the charge of a Sioux chieftain." The crowd cheered as Custer brought the animal under control, though by then he had passed the grandstand and, as Sherman said, "was not reviewed at all."

Wedged among the politicians, diplomats, and other honored guests, the red-haired Ohioan studied today's parade with all the intentness of an athletic coach scouting a rival team. His eye was peeled for shortcomings, and he found them. Observing for example that the Potomac soldiers "turned their heads around like country gawks to look at the big people on the stand," he would caution his ranking subordinates tonight not to let their men do that tomorrow. "I will give [them] plenty of time to go to the capital and see everything afterwards," he promised, "but let them keep their eyes fifteen feet to the front and march by in the old customary way." Still, for all his encouragement, he decided he would do well to register a disclaimer in advance, and accordingly, as today's review wore toward a close, he found occasion to remark to Meade: "I am afraid my poor tatterdemalion corps will make a poor appearance tomorrow when contrasted with yours." The Pennsylvanian, pleased with his army's performance today, was sympathetic in response. People would make allowances, he assured him.

Hopeful, but still deeply worried about what kind of showing his Westerners would manage now that their turn had come, Sherman rose early next morning to observe his six corps as they filed out of their Virginia camps — a march likened by one journalist to "the uncoiling of a tremendous python" — first across the Potomac, then on to the assembly area back of Capitol Hill. There they formed, not without a good deal of confusion, and there at 9 o'clock a cannon boomed the starting signal. He was out front on a handsome bay, hat in hand, sunlight glinting coppery in his close-cropped hair, and though the tramp of Logan's XV Corps marchers sounded solid and steady behind him during breaks in the cheers from the bleachers on both sides, he lacked the nerve to glance rearward until he topped the rise beside the Treasury Building, where a sharp right would bring into view the stand in front of the White House. Then at last he turned in the saddle and looked back. What he saw down the long vista, a full mile and a half to the Capitol shining on its hilltop, brought immeasurable relief. "The sight was simply magnificent. The column was compact, and the glittering muskets looked like a solid mass of steel, moving with the regularity of a pendulum." So he later wrote, adding: "I believe it was the happiest and most satisfactory moment of my life." Now, though, he was content to grin as he released his bated breath. "They have swung into it," he said.

They had indeed swung into it, and the crowd responded in kind. A reporter noted "something almost fierce in the fever of enthusiasm" roused by the sight of these lean, sunburnt marchers, all "bone and muscle and skin under their tattered battle flags." Risking fiasco, their commander had decided to go with their natural bent, rather than try for the kind of spit-and-polish show their rivals had staged the day before, and the gamble paid off from the moment the first of them set out, swinging along the avenue with a proud, rolling swagger, their stride a good two inches longer than the mincing twenty-two inches required by regulations, and springier as well. "They march like the lords of the world!" spectators exclaimed, finding them "hardier, knottier, weirder" than yesterday's prim, familiar paraders. Moreover, they provided additional marvels, reminders of their recent excursion across Georgia, some grim, others hilarious in effect. Hushes came at intervals when ambulances rolled past in the wake of each division, blood-stained stretchers strapped to their sides, and there was also laughter — rollicksome, however: not the kind Sherman had feared — when the crowd found each corps trailed by a contingent of camp followers, Negro men and women and children riding or leading mules alongside wagons filled with tents and kettles, live turkeys and smoked hams. Pet pigs trotted on leashes and gamecocks crowed from the breeches of cannon, responding to cheers. "The acclamation given Sherman was without precedent," the same reporter wrote. "The whole assemblage raised and waved and shouted as if he had been the personal friend of each and every one of them."

He had approached the White House stand by then, delivered his salute, dismounted, and walked over to take his guest-of-honor place among the reviewers, intent on securing a satisfaction only slightly less rewarding than the one he had experienced when he turned in the saddle, a few minutes ago, and thrilled at the compact, rhythmic beauty of the column stretching all the way back to the marble Capitol. The men who composed it had already protested, in their hard-handed way, the recent slanders directed at their chief — and so, now that the time had come, would Sherman himself, in person. He had Edwin Stanton in mind, up there in the stand, and he was resolved, as he said later, not only "to resent what I considered an insult," but also to do so "as publicly as it was made." Accordingly, after shaking hands with the President he moved on to Stanton, who was standing with his hand out, next in line. "Sherman's face was scarlet and his red hair seemed to stand on end," one among the startled watchers noted, as he drew himself up, glared at the Secretary for a couple of baleful seconds, then stepped deliberately past him to shake hands with the other cabinet members before returning to take his post on the left of Johnson. For more than six hours his long-striding troops surged by, applauded enthusiastically by everyone who saw them. "On the whole, the grand review was a splendid success," he afterwards declared, "and was a fitting conclusion to the campaign and the war."

It was also, in its way, a valedictory. "In a few weeks," another journalist was to write, "this army of two or three hundred thousand men melted back into the heart of the people from whence it came, and the great spectacle of the Grand Army of the Republic ... disappeared from sight." In point of fact, a considerable portion of that army had already disappeared — or "melted back," as the reporter put it — in the course of the four years leading up to this and other last parades at various assembly points throughout the beaten South. A total of just over 110,000 northern soldiers had died on the field of battle or from wounds received there; which meant that, for every two men who marched up Pennsylvania Avenue on both days of the Grand Review, the ghost of a third marched with them. There were indeed skeletons at that feast, at any rate for those along the route who remembered this army of the fallen, equal in number to the survivors who swung past the grandstand, twelve abreast, for six long hours on either day.

One among the last to have joined this ghostly throng — later, even, than Abraham Lincoln, and like him the victim of a northern bullet — was a young V Corps lieutenant, George H. Wood, a line officer in a regiment from Maine. On the march north from Appomattox, two weeks back, his unit made camp one night just outside Fredericksburg, surrounded by memories of corpses lying frozen where they had been dropped in trying to reach the rebel-held sunken road at the base of Marye's Heights, and next morning, while the lieutenant and his platoon were getting ready to depart, a teamster accidentally fired a round from a carbine he was handling. It passed through several tents, then struck Wood. He had seen too much of death these past three years, as a veteran of all the major battles of the Army of the Potomac within that span, to find anything exceptional in his own, which the surgeons now informed him was at hand. His regret was not so much that he was dying, but rather that he had spent the past three years as he had done. A devout young man, he doubted that what he had been engaged in was the work of the Lord, and in this connection, hoping fervently for mercy in the hereafter, he expressed a further wish to the minister who was with him when the end drew near. "Chaplain," he said, "do you suppose we shall be able to forget anything in heaven? I would like to forget those three years."

Another veteran, of considerably higher rank, also missed the Grand Review: not as the result of any mishap — no piece of flying metal ever so much as grazed him, though it had been his practice, throughout an even longer war career, to go where there was least room between bullets — but rather because of last-minute orders that took him elsewhere. This was Sheridan. Arriving in Washington on May 16, one week before he and his seven miles of horsemen were scheduled to clop up Pennsylvania Avenue, he was informed next day by Grant that he was to proceed without delay to the Transmississippi and take charge of operations designed to restore West Louisiana and Texas to the Union. Although he would command a force of better than 50,000 seasoned effectives — Canby's army from Mobile, already alerted for the move, plus one corps each from Ord and Thomas at City Point and Nashville — Little Phil did not covet an assignment that would deny him a role in next week's big parade and separate him, permanently perhaps, from his hard-riding troopers. Moreover, while the Transmississippi would be the scene of what little fighting there was left, it did not seem to him to offer much in the way of a chance for distinction, especially by contrast with all he had achieved in the past year. As he had done on the eve of the Appomattox campaign, when the plan had been to send him down to Sherman, he protested for all he was worth at being shifted from stage center, out of the limelight.

Now as then, Grant explained that there was more to these new orders than met the eye, "a motive not explained by the instructions themselves." In addition to the task of closing down Kirby-Smithdom, there was also the problem of ending defiance of the Monroe Doctrine by the French in Mexico, where their puppet Emperor had been on the throne for a full year, usurping the power of the elected leader, President Benito Juárez. Maximilian had been pro-Confederate from the outset, Juárez pro-Union, and the time had come to persuade or compel the French "to quit the territory of our sister republic." The State Department — meaning Seward, who by now was on the mend from the slashing he had received on assassination night, just over a month ago — was "much opposed to the use of our troops along the border in any active way that would involve us in a war with European powers." Grant however went on to say that he did not think it would come to that; the French would remain in Mexico no longer than it took them to find that he had sent his most aggressive troop commander to patrol the border with 50,000 of the hardest-handed soldiers the world had known since Napoleon's illustrious uncle retired to Saint Helena. Flattered, Sheridan was more amenable to the shift, which he now perceived might involve him in still another war, despite his superior's confidence that his presence would serve rather to prevent one. Though he complained that he could not see why his departure could not be delayed a couple of days, so he could ride up the avenue at the head of his column of troopers, he later declared that, "under the circumstances, my disappointment at not being permitted to participate in the review had to be submitted to, and I left Washington without an opportunity of seeing again in a body the grand Army of the Potomac."

Whatever might come of the projected border venture, he soon discovered that he had been right to suspect that little or no additional glory awaited him for subduing what remained of the Confederacy beyond the Mississippi. Leaving the capital on May 21, two days short of the start of the Grand Review, he learned before he reached New Orleans, where he planned to confer with Canby on the upcoming campaign, that Kirby Smith had already agreed to surrender on the terms accepted earlier by Taylor, Johnston, and Lee.

Smith in fact had had little choice in the matter. Credited with 36,000 troops on paper, he commanded practically none in the flesh, and even these few, as he complained, were "deaf alike to the dictates of duty, reason, and honor." Price's ill-starred Missouri raid, from August through November, had used up their hope along with their dash. Such things as they did now were done on their own, usually under enemy compulsion: for example, a two-day engagement at Palmito Ranch, May 12–13, on the east bank of the Rio Grande near Brownsville, down at the very tip of Texas. Andrew Johnson's May 10 declaration that armed resistance was "virtually at an end" had thus been premature, but only by three days; for this was the last sizeable clash of arms in the whole war. Two Union regiments of white and colored infantry, plus one of cavalry, marched upriver from Brazos Santiago to attack the rebel camp. At first they were successful. Then they were driven back. Next day they tried again, and again succeeded, only to be repulsed when the defenders once more rallied and drove them from the ranch with a loss of 115 killed, wounded, and missing. It was Wilson's Creek all over again, reproduced in miniature and stretched out over a period of two days. When it was done, the Federals withdrew downriver to the coast. They had gained nothing except the distinction of having made the last attack of the four-year conflict, as well as the last retreat.

Ironically, this last fight, like the first, was a Confederate victory; yet the news was scarcely noticed in the excitement over the outcome of a conference held at the opposite end of the state while the second day of battle was in progress. Responding to a call from the department commander, the exiled governors of Louisiana, Arkansas, and Missouri met that day in Marshall, forty miles west of Shreveport, to assess the current situation, political as well as military, so far as it affected the four Transmississippi states, including Texas, whose ailing chief executive sent a spokesman in his place. Lee's surrender had been known for about three weeks now, together with the southward flight of the government from Richmond. Kirby Smith informed the assembled heads of states that he considered himself duty bound to hold out "at least until President Davis reaches this department, or I receive some definite orders from him." The governors, for all their admiration of his soldierly commitment, did not agree. Speaking for their people, whose despair they understood and shared, they considered it "useless for the Trans-Mississippi Department to undertake to do what the Cis-Mississippi Department had failed to do," and accordingly recommended an early surrender — if liberal, or anyhow decent, terms could be secured. In line with this, they appointed one of their number, Governor Henry W. Allen of Louisiana, to go to Washington and confer with the Federal authorities to that end.

But there was nothing like time enough for that. Returning to Shreveport with the threats of bitter-enders ringing in his ears — Jo Shelby, for one, wanted to turn him out if he so much as thought of capitulation — Smith rejected on May 15 terms proposed by an emissary from John Pope in Missouri, who presented him with a choice between outright surrender and "all the horrors of violent subjugation." Pope, as usual, overplayed his hand. Speaking for himself as well as his country, Smith replied that he could not "purchase a certain degree of immunity from devastation at the expense of the honor of its army." So he said. Yet he had no sooner done so than news of a series of disasters began arriving from beyond the Mississippi: first, that Johnston and Sherman had come to terms, and then that Taylor and Canby had followed suit. He now commanded, such as it was, the Confederacy's only unsurrendered department, and in reaction he ordered his headquarters moved from Shreveport to Houston, where he would be less vulnerable to attack in the campaign he knew was about to be launched against him. Before he could make the shift, however, word came that Davis himself had been captured in South Georgia. That did it. Convinced at last that he no longer had anything left to hope for, let alone fight for, Smith decided to reopen negotiations: not with Pope, up in Missouri, but with Canby, who was en route from Mobile to New Orleans. Rather than go himself he sent his chief of staff, Lieutenant General Simon Buckner, with full authority to accept whatever terms were offered. That was fitting. At Donelson, three years and three months ago, the Kentuckian had surrendered the first Conferedate army to lay down its arms. Now he was charged with surrendering the last.

His mission was soon accomplished. Steaming under a flag of truce, first down the Red and then the Mississippi, he reached New Orleans on May 25, the same day Canby got there. They conferred, and next morning, having accepted the terms afforded Lee and Johnston and Taylor, Buckner signed the surrender agreement with Peter Osterhaus, Canby's own chief of staff. One week later, on June 2, Kirby Smith came down to Galveston, boarded the Federal steamer *Fort Jackson* out in the harbor, and fixed his signature to the document brought from New Orleans for that purpose. Before he left Houston he had already issued his farewell to such troops as were still with him, if only on paper. "Your present duty is plain," he told them. "Return to your families. Resume the occupations of peace. Yield obedience to the laws. Labor to restore order. Strive both by counsel and example to give security to life and property. And may God, in his mercy, direct you aright and heal the wounds of our distracted country."

Thus the final place of refuge within the vanished Confederate borders passed from being, no longer a goal for die-hards such as Wheeler, who had been trying to get there when he was taken near Atlanta, three weeks back. Similarly, four days ago at Natchez, unaware that Buckner had come to terms with Canby a couple of hundred winding miles downstream, John B. Hood and two aides were picked up by Federal patrollers before they could get across the river. He had stopped off in South Carolina long enough for Sally Preston to break her engagement to him, and then, aggrieved, had ridden on, intent on reaching his adoptive Texas. Paroled on May 31, the day after his capture, he continued his journey, no longer as a general in search of recruits for the army he had promised Jefferson Davis he would raise there, but rather as one more one-legged civilian who had to find some way to make a living.

Thousands of others in the region had that problem, too, and only a handful solved it without changing the life style they had known for the past four years. These exceptions came mainly from the ranks of the guerillas, some of whom enlisted in the Union army, thereby avoiding government prosecution, while others simply moved on west and resumed on the frontier such wartime activities as bank and stagecoach robbery, with cattle rustling thrown in for a sideline. One among them was W. C. Quantrill, except that he went east, not west, bent on bringing off a coup that would outdo in notoriety even his sacking of Lawrence, Kansas, late in the summer of '63. Back in Missouri after Price retreated, Quantrill assembled some two dozen followers, including Frank James and Jim Younger — but not George Todd or Bill Anderson, who had been killed within a month of the Centralia massacre — and set out for a crossing of the Mississippi on New Year's Day, just north of Memphis, at the head of a column of blue-clad horsemen he identified as a platoon from the nonexistent 4th Missouri Cavalry, U.S. His plan, announced at the outset, was to proceed by way of Kentucky and Maryland to Washington, and there revive Confederate hopes by killing Abraham Lincoln. He took up so much time en route, however, that he never got there. In the Bluegrass by mid-April he learned that J. Wilkes Booth had beat him to the act. Still in Kentucky three weeks later, he was wounded in a barnyard skirmish on May 10, thirty miles southeast of Louisville. Like Booth he was struck in the spine and paralyzed, though he lived for nearly a month in that condition. Recognizing one of the physicians at his bedside, he asked if he had not treated him previously, in another part of the state. "I am the man. I have moved here," the doctor replied. "So have I," Quantrill said, enigmatic to the end, which came on June 6.

By that time Kirby Smith had returned from Galveston; the last outlying remnants of organized resistance were submitting or departing. On June 23 at Doaksville, near Fort Towson in the Indian Territory, Brigadier General Stand Watie, a Cherokee chief who had held out with a third of his people when the other two thirds renewed their allegiance to the Union, surrendered and disbanded his battalion of Cherokees, Creeks, Seminoles, and Osages, all proscribed as tribal outlaws for refusing to repudiate the treaty made with Richmond in the early days of the war. Close to sixty, a veteran of Wilson's Creek, Elkhorn Tavern, Prairie Grove, and a hundred lesser fights — not to mention the long march out the "trail of tears" from Georgia, nearly thirty years ago — Watie, his gray-shot hair spread fanwise on his shoulders, was the last Confederate general to lay down his arms.

One who did not surrender was Jo Shelby, who had sworn he never would. When news of the Buckner-Smith capitulation reached him he assembled his division on the prairie near Corsicana, Texas, for a speech. "Boys, the war is over and you can go home. I for one will not go home. Across the Rio Grande lies Mexico. Who will follow me there?" Some two hundred of his veterans said they would, and next morning, after parting with comrades who chose to stay behind, set out southward. Proceeding through Waco, Austin, and San Antonio, they picked up recruits along the way, together with a number of dignitaries in and out of uniform: John Magruder and Sterling Price, for instance, as well as Henry Allen of Louisiana and Texas Governor Pendleton Murrah, who rose from his sickbed to join the horsemen riding through his capital, five hundred strong by then. Finally, beyond San Antonio, Kirby Smith himself caught up with the column. He was bound for Mexico, like all the rest, but not as a soldier, having discovered for the first time since he left West Point, twenty years ago this month, "the feeling of lightness and joy experienced by me when I felt myself to be plain Kirby Smith, relieved from all cares and responsible only for my own acts."

Clearing Eagle Pass by the last week in June, Shelby paused to weight his tattered battle flag with stones and sink it in the Rio Grande before crossing into Mexico. At Monterrey the column lost most of its distinguished civilian hangers-on, who scattered variously for Cuba, Brazil, and other regions where ex-Confederates were reported to be welcome. But Shelby and his body of troopers, grown by now to the size of a small brigade, kept on for Mexico City, having decided — such was their proclivity for lost causes — to throw in with Maximilian, rather than Juárez. The Emperor, whose subjects already were showing how much they resented his foreign support, knew better than to enlist the help of *gringo* mercenaries. Still, he was friendly enough to offer them a plot of land near Vera Cruz for colonization. Most declined and went their several ways, being far from ready to settle down to the farming life they had left four years ago, but Shelby and a few others accepted and even sent for their families to join them; which they did, though not for long. The settlement — dubbed Carlota, in honor of the Empress — scarcely outlasted Maximilian, who fell in front of a firing squad two Junes later, after the troops supporting Juárez rushed into the vacuum left by the departing French. Grant had been right about Napoleon's reaction, once Sheridan reached the Texas border and bristled along it, much as he had done in the old days up and down the Shenandoah Valley.

Afloat, whether on salt water or fresh, the wind-down of the rebellion seemed likely to prove a good deal more erratic and explosive than on land, depending as it would on the attitude and nature of the individual skipper operating on his own, as so many did in the Confederate navy, up lonely rivers or far out to sea. "Don't give up the ship" — a proud tradition sometimes taken to irrational extremes: as in duels to the death, with eight-inch guns at ranges of eight feet — might apply no less at the finish than at the start. A case in point was Lieutenant Charles W. Read, whose handling of the steam ram *William H. Webb* in a late-April dash for freedom down the Red and the Mississippi provided a possible forecast of instances to come.

A twenty-four-year-old Mississippian, Read had finished at Annapolis in 1860, one year ahead of his Union counterpart William Cushing, and like him had had a colorful war career. He fought with distinction against Farragut below New Orleans, then again at Vicksburg as a
gunnery officer on the *Arkansas*, and next aboard the *Florida* in her
great days, when Maffitt gave him a captured brig, along with a crew
of twenty and one boat howitzer, and set him up as an independent
raider. In twenty-one days, cruising the Atlantic coast from Norfolk
to New England, he took twenty-one prizes before he himself was taken,
off Portland, Maine, in June of 1863, and confined at Fort Warren. Exchanged in October of the following year, he was assigned to duty with
the James River squadron below Richmond until March of 1865, when
Mallory chose him to command the *Webb*, languishing in far-off
Louisiana for the past two years. Reported to be "the fastest thing
afloat," she had seen no substantial action since her sinking of the
monster ironclad *Indianola*, back in the early spring of '63, and it was
Mallory's belief that she could be put to highly effective use against
Yankee merchantmen and blockaders, if Read could only get her out
into the open waters of the Gulf of Mexico.

Arriving by the end of the month he found the 206-foot side-
wheel steamer tied up eighty miles below Shreveport, "without a single
gun on board, little or no crew, no fuel, and no small arms save a few
cutlasses." Undaunted, he took her up to department headquarters and
secured from the army a 30-pounder Parrott rifle, which he mounted on
her bow, and two 12-pounder smoothbores, one for each broadside, as
well as fifty-one soldier volunteers and sixteen officers. Back at Alexandria, while training his new green crew, he put carpenters to work
constructing a rough bulwark around the *Webb*'s forecastle and loaded
close to two hundred bales of cotton for use as a shield for her machinery
until he reached Cuba and could exchange them for a longer-burning
fuel than the pine knots he now had stacked about her decks. By that
time, news had come of Lee's surrender and the government's flight
south. He knew he would have to hurry, and on April 22, as he prepared to cast off down the Red, he learned of Lincoln's assassination,
which might or might not add to the confusion he hoped to encounter
during his run past Baton Rouge and New Orleans and the warships
on patrol above and below them both. "As I will have to stake everything upon speed and time," he wrote Mallory that day, "I will not
attack any vessel in the passage unless I perceive a possibility of her
arresting my progress. In this event I am prepared with five torpedoes . . .
one of which I hold shipped on its pole on the bows."

He left that evening and reached the mouth of the river about
8.30 the following night, the first Sunday after Easter. Displaying the
lights of a Federal transport and running slow to reduce the engine
noise, he hoped to sneak past the blue flotilla on patrol there, which in-

cluded two ironclads and a monitor. For a time it seemed the *Webb* was going to steam by undetected, but then a rocket swooshed up from the deck of one of the blockaders, giving the signal: "Strange vessel in sight, positively an enemy." Read shouted, "Let her go!" and the engineer opened the throttle all the way. As the ram shot forward, whistles screamed and drums rolled beat-to-quarters along the line of warships dead ahead. "Keep for the biggest opening between them," Read told the pilot. Out in the moonless night, the monitor *Manhattan* swung her big guns in their turret and hurled two 11-inch shells at the rebel churning past. Both missed, and the *Webb* was soon out of range, driving hard as she began her intended 300-mile run down the Mississippi to the Gulf. Unpursued by anything that had even an outside chance of overtaking him, Read tied up to the east bank and sent a detail ashore to cut the telegraph wires, then set out again, gliding past Baton Rouge in the darkness, unseen or unrecognized, and on to Donaldsonville by daylight, still carrying the signals of a Union transport. Here too the ram passed unchallenged, though some who saw her booming along with the midstream current later testified that she was making a good 25 knots as she went by. That may well have been; for by 1 o'clock that afternoon, April 24, the church spires of low-lying New Orleans came in view.

Read hoisted the U.S. flag at half mast, brought his boiler pressure up to maximum, and began his run past the Crescent City. No warning message had got through, thanks to the cutting of the wires the night before; lookouts here, like those at Donaldsonville that morning, took the *Webb* to be a friendly transport, mourning with her lowered colors the death of Abraham Lincoln. They did, that is, until about midway through the run, when a bluejacket who had fought against her, a couple of years ago upriver, recognized her and gave the alarm, setting off a din of bells and drums and whistles, soon punctuated by the roar of guns. Most of the shots went wild, but three struck the ram before she cleared the fleet, one through her chimney, one into a bale of cotton, and one just above the waterline at her bow, damaging the torpedo mechanism so badly that the explosive had to be jettisoned. Stopping to accomplish this, Read took down the half-staffed Union emblem, ran up to the peak his true Confederate colors, and continued downriver at full speed, bound for the open waters of the Gulf.

Behind him New Orleans was abuzz with rumors that Jeff Davis and John Wilkes Booth were aboard the ram, headed for South America with millions in gold bullion. Read knew nothing of this, of course, but he did know that the two fastest gunboats in the enemy flotilla, *Hollyhock* and *Florida*, were churning downstream after him. Confident that he could outrun them, the young Mississippian was alarmed only so far as their pursuit might interfere with his plan for not reaching Forts Jackson and St Philip, sixty winding miles away, before night came down to help screen him from the plunging crossfire of guns on both sides of the river. He considered stopping to dispose of them, despite their superior armament, but up ahead just then, twenty-five miles below the city, he saw something that commanded all his attention. It was the veteran screw sloop *Richmond*, mounting twenty-one guns, anchored for engine repairs and now being cleared for action. He studied her briefly, regretting the loss of his spar torpedo, then told the pilot: "Make straight for the *Richmond*'s bow, and ram." "I can't reach her bow because of a shoal," the pilot replied, "but I can come in under her broadside." Read shook his head at that suggestion. "I've been under the *Richmond*'s broadside before, and don't wish to try it again," he said. He assembled all hands on the foredeck and informed them of what he knew he had to do. "It's no use. The *Richmond* will drown us all — and if she doesn't, the forts below will, as they have a range of three miles each way up and down the river, and they know by this time that we are coming." He turned to the helmsman. "Head for shore," he told him.

Fifty yards from bank the *Webb* struck bottom, and while most of the crew began climbing down ropes thrown over the bow, others went about dousing the deck and cabins with turpentine before they too abandoned ship. Read started fires with a lighted match, then went over the side, the last to leave the flaming ram. He and his men lay in waiting in the brush till they heard her magazine explode, after which they broke into groups and scattered. By daybreak, half of them had been rounded up, including Read, who suffered the indignity of being placed on public display in New Orleans; but not for long. Presently he and the rest were paroled and allowed to return to their homes. At a cost of one man wounded, and of course the *Webb* herself, he had given the victors notice of what they might expect in the way of naval daring between now and the time the final curtain fell.

Whatever might come of such fears as this aroused, a river mishap of far bloodier proportions occurred six hundred miles upstream in the early morning hours of April 27, the day Read was put on display in New Orleans. En route for Cairo with an outsized cargo of surplus army mules and discharged soldiers who had crowded aboard at Vicksburg and Helena after their release from Deep South prison camps, the sidewheel steamer *Sultana*, one of the largest on the Mississippi, blew her boilers near Paddy's Hen and Chickens, north of Memphis two hours before dawn. Although her authorized capacity was less than 400 passengers, she had about six times that number packed about her decks and in her hold — mostly Ohio, Illinois, and Indiana veterans, men who had fought perhaps the hardest war of all, sweating out its finish in stockades beyond reach of the various columns of invasion. So sudden was the blast and the fire that followed, those who managed to make it over the side had to dive through flames into muddy water running swift and cold as any millstream. A body count put the official death toll at 1238, but there was really no way of telling how many troops had been aboard or were consumed by shrimp and gars before all those hundreds of other blue-clad corpses bobbed up downstream in the course of the next month. Estimates ran as high as 1800 dead and presumed dead, with 1585 as the figure most generally agreed on. That was more than the number killed on both sides at First Bull Run and Wilson's Creek combined, and even by the lowest count the loss of the *Sultana* went into the books as the greatest marine disaster of all time. Just under one month later, as if to emphasize the shock that came with sudden peace, on May 25 — the day after the Grand Review up Pennsylvania Avenue ended, and the day before Simon Buckner surrendered to Canby in New Orleans for his chief — a warehouse on the Mobile waterfront, stocked with some twenty tons of surrendered ammunition, blew up and "shook the foundations" of the city. An estimated 300 people were killed outright, and the property loss was reckoned at $5,000,000.

By way of consolation for these subtractions — unexpected and all the more tragic because they were self-inflicted, so to speak — fears regarding those other losses, anticipated because of the example set by Read in his abortive downstream dash, turned out to be quite groundless. Joe Johnston's capitulation, followed within two weeks by Richard Taylor's — the former on the day before the *Sultana* blew her boilers above Memphis — brought about the surrender of the few surviving rebel warships east of the Mississippi, bloodlessly and practically without fanfare. On May 10, four that had taken refuge up the Tombigbee almost a month ago, after the evacuation of Mobile, struck their colors in accordance with a commitment by the flotilla captain to hand over to the Federals "all public property yet afloat under his command." On May 27, down in West Florida, the gunboat *Spray* was the last to go. Stationed up the St Marks River to cover the water approaches to Tallahassee, her skipper agreed to surrender when he learned that the troops defending the capital in his rear had laid down their arms the week before. Then came Kirby Smith's formal capitulation at Galveston, and next day, June 3, the *Webb*'s one-time consorts up the Red hauled down their flags. One among them was the ironclad *Missouri*, completed at Shreveport in late March and taken down to Alexandria, not in time to fight, but at any rate in time to be handed over with the rest. "A most formidable vessel," one Union officer pronounced her, though after a closer look he added an assessment that might have served as an epitaph for all the improvised warships knocked together by backwoods carpenters and blacksmiths, here and elsewhere throughout the South: "She is badly built of green lumber, caulked with cotton, leaks badly, and is very slow."

By that time, too, the gravest of all the Union navy's current fears had been allayed. These concerned still another ironclad, a seagoing armored ram described by those who had seen her as the most powerful thing afloat. Built not by amateur shipwrights in the rebel hinterland, but rather by French craftsmen at Bordeaux, she was commissioned the C.S.S. *Stonewall* — "an appellation not inconsistent with her character," the purchasing agent proudly declared — and in mid-January set out down the European coast on the first leg of a voyage across the Atlantic, under instructions to lift the blockade at Wilmington and elsewhere by sinking the blockaders: an assignment considered by no means beyond her capability, since in addition to her defensive attributes, which reportedly made her unsinkable, she featured such dread offensive devices as a protruding underwater beak, heavy enough to drive through the flank and bottom of any rival, wood or metal, and a 300-pounder Armstrong rifle mounted on her bow. Damaged by rough weather, she put into Ferrol, Spain, for repairs. By the time these were made, two multigunned U.S. frigates were on station outside the harbor, apparently waiting to take her on when she emerged. When she did so, however, on March 24, both refrained and stood aside to let her go, one blue skipper afterwards explaining that "the odds in her favor were too great and too certain, in my humble judgment, to admit of the slightest hope of being able to inflict upon her even the most trifling injury."

As it turned out, that one negative triumph, achieved by a bluff for whose success the Federal commander was court-martialed, was the *Stonewall*'s only contribution to the struggle whose tide of victory her purchasers had hoped she would reverse. After filling with coal at Lisbon, down the coast, she set out across the ocean on March 28, still unchallenged. Obliged to make another refueling stop in the Canaries, she did not reach Nassau until May 6. Not only had she made poor time; her bunkers were nearly empty again, and her skipper, Captain T. J. Page, a Virginian in his middle fifties, was shaking his head at her lumbering performance and the sharpness of French salesmen. "You must not expect too much of me," he wrote his superiors; "I fear the power and effect of this vessel have been much exaggerated." On May 11 he dropped anchor at Havana. News had not yet arrived of the capture of Jefferson Davis the day before, but he soon learned that both Lee and Johnston had surrendered their armies. While he pondered what to do, word came that Taylor had followed suit, ending all possibility of resistance east of the Mississippi. By now, moreover, Union warships of all types were assembling outside the harbor from all directions, including the monitors *Canonicus* and *Monadnock*, veterans of Fort Fisher and the first of their type to leave home waters. "*Canonicus* would have crushed her, and the *Monadnock* could have taken her beyond a doubt," the admiral in command of the blue flotilla later said of the holed-up *Stonewall*. No one would ever know for sure, however. On May 19, having reached his decision, Page turned over to the Captain

General of Cuba, for a decision by Spain as to her eventual disposition, the only ironclad ever to fly the Confederate flag on the high seas.

That flag still flew on the high seas, but only at one ever-moving point, the peak of the cruiser *Shenandoah*. "An erratic ship, without country or destination," Gideon Welles quite accurately described her, urging his otherwise unemployed frigate captains to locate and run down this last Confederate raider, which lately had been reported raising havoc in the South Pacific. By now, though, she was elsewhere; Welles was warm, yet far from hot, in the game of hide-and-seek the rebel privateer was playing with his men-of-war. James Waddell had sailed her north from Melbourne in mid-February, intent on "visiting," as his instructions put it, "the enemy's distant whaling grounds." He had no luck in that regard until April 1, when he approached Ascension Island in the eastern Carolines and found a quartet of the blubber-laden vessels anchored in Lea Harbor like so many sitting ducks. After putting the crews ashore he set all four afire and continued northward, past Japan, into the northwest reaches of the Sea of Okhotsk, where he took one more prize during the final week in May. So far, the pickings had been rather slim, but now he had accurate, up-to-date whaling charts, as well as a number of volunteers from the captured ships, to show him where to go: south, then north, around the Kamchatka Peninsula, into the Bering Sea. There the forty-year-old North Carolinian found what he had been seeking all along.

Off Cape Navarin on June 22 he came upon two whalers, one of which — a fast bark out of New Bedford, aptly named the *Jerah Swift* — tried to make a run for it. *Shenandoah* gave chase, dodging ice floes as she went, and after a hard three-hour pursuit, drew close enough to put a round from a 32-pounder Whitworth rifle across her bow; whereupon her captain "saw the folly of exposing the crew to a destructive fire and yielded to his misfortunes with a manly and becoming dignity." So Waddell later wrote, unaware at the time — as, indeed, he would remain for weeks to come — that he had just fired the last shot of the American Civil War. He burned the two ships, then started after more. Next day he took a trading vessel, only two months out of San Francisco, and found aboard her a newspaper dated April 17, containing the latest dispatches from the eastern theater. Lee had surrendered: Richmond had fallen: the Government had fled. Shaken though he was by this spate of disasters, he also read that Johnston had won a victory over Sherman in North Carolina, back in March, and that the President, resettled with his cabinet in Danville, had issued a proclamation announcing "a new phase of the struggle," which he urged all Confederates to wage with "fresh defiance" and "unconquered and unconquerable hearts." Waddell took his cue from that, and was rewarded three days later when he steamed into a cluster of six whalers lying becalmed off St Lawrence Island. Five he burned; the sixth he ransomed to take on board the crews of all the rest. Two days later, on June 28, he made his largest haul near the narrows of Bering Strait, where he fell in with a rendezvous of eleven whalers. He put all the crews aboard two of these, bonded as before, and set the other nine ablaze in a single leaping conflagration, rivaling with its glow of burning oak and sperm oil, reflected for miles on the ice that glittered round-about, the brilliance of the Aurora Borealis. In nine months of sailing close to 40,000 miles, the *Shenandoah* now had taken an even two dozen whalers, along with 1053 prisoners and another 14 merchant vessels, destroying all but six of the 38, whose total value Waddell placed at $1,361,983. Wanting still more, he steamed next day into the Arctic Ocean.

But there were no more. He discovered, after searching, that he had abolished the whaling trade, so far at least as his one-time fellow countrymen were concerned. Narrowly escaping getting ice-bound, he turned back and passed once more between the outpost capes of Asia and North America. Propeller triced up to save coal, he crowded on all sail and set out for the coast of Baja California, intending to make prizes of the clippers plying between Panama and San Francisco. By July 4 he was clear of the chain of the Aleutians and back into the ice-free waters of the North Pacific. For a month he held his southward course, sailing well out of sight of land, and then on August 2 encountered the English bark *Barracouta*, less than two weeks out of Frisco. Newspapers on her told of Kirby Smith's capitulation, two months ago today; Jefferson Davis was in prison, and the Confederacy was no longer among the nations of earth. Despite earlier indications, the news came hard for those on board the *Shenandoah*. "We were bereft of ground for hope or aspiration," her executive officer wrote in his journal that night, "bereft of a cause for which to struggle and suffer." Waddell now was faced with the problem of what to do with his ship and his people: a decision, he said, "which involved not only our personal honor, but the honor of the flag entrusted to us which had walked the waters fearlessly and in triumph." Though he ordered the battery struck below and the crew disarmed, he was determined to avoid capture if possible. Accordingly, after rejecting the notion of surrendering at some port close at hand, where treatment might be neither fair nor unprejudiced, he decided to make a nonstop run, by way of Cape Horn, for England.

The distance was 17,000 miles, very little of it in sight of land, and required three full months of sailing, never speaking another vessel from start to finish lest the *Shenandoah*'s whereabouts became known to Federal skippers who by now were scouring the seas under orders to take or sink her. Rounding the Horn in mid-September, she was driven off course by a northeast gale and did not cross the equator until October 11. Then she took the trades, with smooth going all the way to the western coast of England. "I believe the Divine will directed and protected that ship in all her adventures," her captain was to say. On November 5 she reached St George's Channel and dropped anchor to wait for a pilot, then steamed next morning up the Mersey to Liverpool, the Stars and Bars flying proudly at her peak. She had covered better than 58,000 miles, circumnavigated the globe, visited all its oceans except the Antarctic, and taken in the course of her brief career more prizes than any other Confederate raider except the *Alabama*. Anchored beside a British ship-of-the-line, she lowered her abolished country's last official flag and was turned over to the port authorities for adjudication. Two days later, Waddell and his crew were unconditionally released to go ashore for the first time since they left Melbourne, almost nine months ago. Looking back with pride and satisfaction on all the *Shenandoah* had accomplished in her thirteen months at sea, he later wrote: "I claim for her officers and men a triumph over their enemies and over every obstacle.... For myself," he added, "I claim having done my duty."

By that time, no more than a handful of Confederates remained in Federal custody, locked up awaiting trial or other disposition of their cases. On May 27, the day after Canby's provisional acceptance of the surrender of the last armed grayback in the Transmississippi, Andrew Johnson had ordered the discharge, with but few exceptions, of all persons imprisoned by military authorities. Two days later a presidential Proclamation of Amnesty offered pardon to all who had participated, directly or indirectly, in "the existing rebellion," with full restitution of property rights — except of course slaves — on the taking of an oath by such people that they would "henceforth" support and defend the Constitution and abide by the laws of the reunited land. In this latter instance, however, so many exceptions were cited that the document was about as much a source of alarm as it was of solace. Among those excluded were all who held civil or diplomatic offices in the secessionist regime and the governors of its member states; former U.S. congressmen, senators, and judges; West Pointers, Annapolis men, and members of the armed forces who had resigned or deserted to join the South; those engaged in the destruction of commerce or mistreatment of prisoners, officers above the rank of army colonel or navy lieutenant, and finally all "voluntary" participants with taxable property worth more than $20,000. The list ran on, and though it was stated that even those ineligibles could apply directly to the President for pardon, with assurance that "such clemency will be liberally extended as may be consistent with the facts of the case and the peace and dignity of the United States," few took much consolation in that provision, knowing as they did the views of Johnson with regard to treason and its consequences, which he had proclaimed so often in the course of the past four years. Kirby Smith, for example, no sooner read the offer than he rode off after Jo Shelby, bound for Mexico, as he informed his wife, in order "to place the Rio Grande between myself and harm."

Some measure of his concern, and that of others in flight from northern justice, was aroused by the savagery with which the eight accused of complicity with Booth in his assassination plot were being prosecuted at the time. Shackled at their trial, as no prisoner had been in an English-speaking court for more than a hundred and fifty years, they were kept hooded in their cells, with thick cotton pads over eyes and ears, lest they see or hear each other or their guards, and two small slits in the canvas for the admission of food and air. The military trial, presided over by nine high-ranking army officers in Washington's Arsenal Penitentiary, began on May 10 and ended June 30, when verdicts were returned. Johnson approved them on July 5, and two days later they were carried out. All eight had been found guilty. Four were soon on their way to the Dry Tortugas, three with life sentences, including a Virginia doctor who had set Booth's broken leg, and one, a stagehand at Ford's, with a six-year term for having allegedly helped the actor leave the theater. The other four got death: Lewis Paine, an ex-Confederate soldier who had made the knife attack on Seward, George Atzerodt, an immigrant carriage-maker who had lacked the nerve to attempt his assignment of killing the Vice President, David Herald, a slow-witted Maryland youth who had served as a guide for the fugitive in his flight, and Mary E. Surratt, the widowed proprietor of a boarding house where Booth was said to have met with some of the others in planning the work only he carried out in full. All were in their twenties except Mrs Surratt, who was forty-five and whose principal offense appeared to be that her twenty-year-old son had escaped abroad before he could be arrested for involvement in the crime. Some objections arose to the execution of a woman, but not enough to prevent her being one of the four who were hanged and buried in the yard of the penitentiary where Booth had been buried in secret, under the dirt floor of a cell, ten weeks before.

Despite this evidence of how ruthless the government — mainly Stanton, who had engineered the trial — could be in pursuit and removal of those it was determined to lay hands on, Johnson proved quite as liberal in granting clemency as he had said he would be in his amnesty proclamation. By mid-October, not only had all the arrested secessionist governors been released on their application for pardon, but so too had such once high-placed rebels as John Reagan and George Trenholm, John A. Campbell, and even Alexander Stephens. In November there was one sharp reminder of the claws inside the velvet Federal glove, when Captain Henry Wirz, the Swiss-born commandant of Andersonville, was convicted on trumped-up testimony of deliberate cruelty to the prisoners in his care. He was tried in violation of his parole, as well as of other legal rights, but Stanton had more or less assured a guilty verdict by appointing Lew Wallace president of the court; Wallace had consistently voted against the accused in the trial of the Lincoln conspirators, and Wirz was duly hanged on November 10, four days after the *Shenandoah* lowered the last Confederate flag. Meantime, Johnson continued granting amnesty to ex-rebels. By April 2 of the following year, when he declared the insurrection officially "at an end," Stephen Mallory had been relieved of long-pending charges of having promoted the willful destruction of commerce. Two weeks later Raphael Semmes was similarly released, along with Clement C. Clay, another Alabamian, who had been detained all this time on suspicion of having "incited, concerted, and procured" Lincoln's assassination from his post as a special commissioner in Canada. Now only Jefferson Davis remained behind bars in his cell at Fort Monroe.

Clay's release on April 17 resulted in a good deal of speculation about his former chief, who was being held on the same charge. Nothing came of that, for the present, but just over two weeks later, on May 3 — one week less than a year after his capture down in Georgia — Varina Davis was permitted to see her husband for the first time since they parted aboard the vessel that brought them up the coast to Hampton Roads. She was conducted past three lines of sentries, each requiring a password, then through a guardroom, until at last she approached and saw him beyond the bars of his quarters, moving toward her. His "shrunken form and glassy eyes" nearly caused her to collapse from shock, she later said. "His cheek bones stood out like those of a skeleton. Merely crossing the room made his breath come in short gasps, and his voice was scarcely audible."

He had had a harder time than she or anyone else not in the fort with him for the past year could know. What was more, it had begun in deadly earnest before the end of his first full day of incarceration. Near sundown, he looked up from reading his small-print Bible, the only possession allowed him except the clothes he wore, and saw that a guard captain had entered the casemate, accompanied by two men who seemed to be blacksmiths. One of them held a length of chain with a shackle at each end, and suddenly he knew why they were there, though he still could not quite believe it. "My God," he said. "You don't intend to iron me?" When the captain replied that those were indeed his orders, the prisoner rose and protested for all he was worth. "But the war is over; the South is conquered. For the honor of America, you cannot commit this degradation!" Told again that the orders were peremptory, Davis met this as he had met other challenges in the past, whatever the odds. "I shall never submit to such an indignity," he exclaimed. "It is too monstrous. I demand that you let me see the commanding general."

Here a certain irony obtained, unknown as yet to the captive in his cell. For it was the fort commander, Brigadier General Nelson A. Miles, who, in prompt response to a War Department directive authorizing him "to place manacles and fetters upon the hands and feet of Jefferson Davis…whenever he may think it advisable in order to render [his] imprisonment more secure," had made the decision to shackle him forthwith, not for the reason stated, but rather because he was eager to give his superiors what they wanted. Miles was cruel, in this as in other instances to follow, not so much by nature as by design. Not yet twenty-six, a one-time Massachusetts farm boy who had left the farm to clerk in a Boston crockery shop, he had achieved a brilliant record in the war, suffering four wounds in the course of his rise from lieutenant to brigadier, with the prospect of still another promotion if he did well at his current post, to which he had been assigned in part because of his lack of such West Point and Old Army ties as were likely to make him stand in awe of the prisoner in his charge. That he felt no such awe he quickly demonstrated, beginning with Davis's first full day in his care, and his reward would follow. By October he would be a major general. In a couple of years he would marry a niece of Sherman's, and before the century was out he would succeed Grant, Sherman, and Sheridan as general-in-chief; William McKinley, himself a former sergeant, would make him a lieutenant general, and he would live until 1925, when he died at a Washington circus performance and was buried at Arlington in a mausoleum he had built some years before. His was an American success story—Horatio Alger in army braid and stars—and part of the story was the time he spent as Jefferson Davis's jailer, giving his superiors what he saw they wanted, including the fetters now about to be applied.

Davis subsided after registering his protest, and the guard captain supposed him resigned to being ironed. "Smith, do your work," he said. But when the man came forward, kneeling to attach the shackles, the prisoner unexpectedly grabbed and flung him across the room. Recovering, the smith charged back, hammer lifted, and would have struck his assailant if the captain had not stopped him. One of the two armed sentries present cocked and leveled his rifle, but the captain stopped him too, instructing the four men "to take Mr Davis with as little force as possible." The struggle was brief, though it took more force than they had thought would be required; Davis, the captain later reported, "showed unnatural strength." While his helper and the sentries pinned the frail gray captive to the cot, the blacksmith riveted one clasp in place and secured its mate around the other ankle with a large brass lock, "the same as is in use on freight cars." The struggle ceased with the snap of the lock; Davis lay motionless, flat on his back, as the smith and his helper retired, their job done. Looking over his shoulder as he left, the captain saw the prisoner sit up, turn sideways on the cot, and with a heavy effort drop both feet to the stone floor. The clank of the chain was followed by unrestrained weeping, and the departing captain thought it "anything but a pleasant sight to see a man like Jefferson Davis shedding tears."

Mercifully, this particular humiliation was brief. Within five days, vigorous private and public objections — first by the post surgeon, who protested that the captive was being denied even such limited exercise as he could get from pacing up and down his cell, and then by a number of northern civilians who, though willing to keep on hating the former Confederate leader, disapproved of tormenting him in this fashion — caused the removal of the shackles. Other hardships continued in force, however, including the constant presence of two sentries under orders to keep tramping back and forth at all hours, a lamp that burned day and night, even while he slept or tried to, and the invariable dampness resulting from the fact that the floor of his cell was below the level of the water in the adjacent moat. Davis's health declined and declined, from neuralgia, failing eyesight, insomnia, and a general loss of vitality. Passing his fifty-seventh birthday in early June, he had to wait until late July, more than two months after his arrival, to be permitted an hour's daily exercise on the ramparts, and still another month went by before he was allowed to read the first letter from his wife. In October he was moved from the casemate to a second-story room in the fort's northwest bastion, but it was mid-December, after nearly seven months of seeing no one but the surgeon and his guards — including Miles, who sneered at him and called him Jeff — before he received his first visitor, his wartime pastor, who came down from Richmond to give him Communion and found him changed in appearance by long confinement, but not in spirit. "His spirit could not be subdued," the minister later wrote, "and no indignity, angry as it made him at the time, could humiliate him."

By that time, prominent Northerners — especially those in the legal profession — had seen the weakness of the government's case against Davis and the handful of Confederates yet being held. One who saw it was the Chief Justice who would rule on their appeal in the event that one was needed, which he doubted. "If you bring these leaders to trial it will condemn the North," Chase had warned his former cabinet colleagues in July, "for by the Constitution secession is not rebellion." As for the rebel chieftain, the authorities would have done better not to apprehend him. "Lincoln wanted Jefferson Davis to escape, and he was right. His capture was a mistake. His trial will be a greater one. We cannot convict him of treason. Secession is settled. Let it stay settled." Charles O'Conor, the distinguished New York attorney who had volunteered his services in Davis's behalf, was convinced that he would eventually be freed. "No trial for treason on any like offense will be held in the civil courts," he predicted, and as for his client's chances of being railroaded by the army, as Wirz and Mrs Surratt had been, "the managers at Washington are not agreed as to the safety of employing military commissions to color a like outrage upon any eminent person." Horace Greeley had come over, early on, and was saying in the *Tribune* that Davis should either be tried or turned loose without delay. Even so stalwart an Abolitionist as the philanthropist Gerrit Smith, a backer of John Brown, was persuaded that an injustice was in progress and was willing to sign a petition to that effect, as were others who wanted liberty for all men, black and white, by due process of law.

Clement Clay's release in mid-April, 1866, showed clearly enough the government's abandonment of the charge that he and Davis had been instigators of the assassination, but it also permitted total concentration on what was left of the case against the one prisoner still held. Stanton and Judge Advocate General Joseph Holt were determined, as Schuyler Colfax put it, to see the Mississippian "hanging between heaven and earth as not fit for either." Despite the Chief Justice's opinion, given in private nine months ago, that no such accusation could be sustained, they fell back on a vague charge of "treason," and persisted in it even after the distinguished jurist Francis Lieber, handed all the War Department evidence to study for recommendations on procedure, told them flatly: "Davis will not be found guilty and we shall stand there completely beaten." All the same, in early May an indictment was handed down by the U.S. Circuit Court, District of Virginia. "Jefferson Davis, yeoman," it began, "not having fear of God before his eyes, nor weighing the duty of his said allegiance, but being moved and seduced by the institution of the devil, and wickedly devising against the peace and tranquillity of the United States to subvert and to stir, move, and incite insurrection, rebellion, and war — " There was more, much more, but this alone was enough to rally support all over the South for its fallen leader. "That such a creature should be allowed to dispense justice is a perfect farce," Mrs R. E. Lee remarked of the judge presiding. "I think his meanness and wickedness have affected his brain."

By then Varina Davis was with her husband and had even begun to get accustomed to the change in his looks and condition, which had shocked her at first sight. Given quarters in the fort, and allowed to visit with him once a day, she could tell him of the growth of affection in the hearts of many who had turned blameful while the war was on the down slope. Recently she had written from New Orleans: "It is impossible to tell you the love which has been expressed here for you — the tenderness of feeling for you. People sit and cry until I am almost choked with the effort to be quiet. But it is a great consolation to know that a nation is mourning your suffering with me, and to be told hourly how far above reproach you are — how fair your fame. I am overwhelmed by the love which everything of your name attracts." Now that feeling had been extended and enlarged by the harsh indictment and the passing of the anniversary of his capture. To many of his former fellow countrymen it seemed that he alone was undergoing punishment for them all, and presently still another measure was added to the debt they felt they owed him. In late May, Mrs Davis secured an appointment with the President in Washington to plead for her husband's release. To her surprise, Johnson informed her that he was on her side. "But we must wait," he said. "Our hope is to mollify the public to Mr Davis." Meantime, he suggested, the prisoner's best course would be to make application for a pardon. Varina replied that she felt certain he would never do so, and she was right. When she returned to Fort Monroe and told Davis of Johnson's advice, he declined it on grounds that to ask for pardon would be to confess a guilt he did not feel. In this he resembled Robert Toombs, who, having gone abroad to avoid arrest, was counseled by northern friends to apply for pardon. "Pardon for what?" he said with an unreconstructed glare. "I have not pardoned you-all yet." So it was with Davis, and when word got round of his refusal, the growing affection for him grew still more. So long as he declined to ask forgiveness, it was as if they too had never humbled their pride. It was even as if they had never been defeated — except in fact, which mattered less and less as time wore on.

Reassured by such reports from the home front, so to speak, as well as by his attorneys, with whom he now was permitted to confer, Davis suffered a legal setback on June 5, two days after his fifty-eighth birthday, when his plea for an early trial was declined by the Richmond court on grounds that he had never been in its custody, despite the indictment recently handed down, but rather was being held as a State Prisoner "under order of the President, signed by the Secretary of War." A follow-up motion for his release on bail was also disallowed, but it was more or less clear by then that Stanton and Holt were fighting a holding action, with scarcely a hope of securing a conviction. They scheduled a trial for early October, overriding O'Conor's protest at the delay.

All Davis could do was wait. He found this easier, however, now that he had his wife to comfort him, unrestricted access to his mail, and a steady stream of visitors, including ex-President Franklin Pierce, Richard Taylor, and Wade Hampton. August brought two encouraging developments. One was the petition signed by Gerrit Smith and other prominent Northerners, addressed to Johnson in his behalf, and the other was a presidential order removing Nelson Miles as fort commander, after fifteen months of personal abuse. Miles's replacement soon gave the State Prisoner freedom of the post and better quarters, which he and Varina shared. A second Christmas came and went, the trial having been postponed; New Year's 1867 was far different from the one before.

The plan now was to force his release by a writ of habeas corpus, and among those willing to put up $25,000 each for bail were Horace Greeley and Cornelius Vanderbilt.

Spring came on, greening the York-James peninsula from the Chickahominy bottoms to its tip at Old Point Comfort, where "the world's most famous prisoner" was lodged. On the first Monday in May, the trial having been postponed again, an aide left for Richmond to secure the signature of the District Court clerk, as required by law, to the writ O'Conor and his associates had prepared. He returned to Fort Monroe on Friday, May 10 — the second anniversary of the then President's capture in South Georgia — to deliver the authenticated document to the fort commander, who was directed "to present the body of Jefferson Davis" in court three days later. Packed and ready, the State Prisoner and his wife set out upriver the following day. Still under guard, but hopefully not for long now, he saw from the rail that clusters of people had gathered at plantation landings along the James to salute him as he passed, and when the boat approached the capital that Saturday afternoon the wharves and streets along the rebuilt waterfront were so jammed that it seemed all Richmond had assembled to pay him its respects. Men removed their hats as he came ashore, and women fluttered handkerchiefs from balconies and windows along the route his carriage followed toward the heart of town. At the Spotswood, he and Varina were given the same rooms he had occupied when he arrived from Montgomery, six years back, and some declared that a greater number of people turned out to greet him now than had done so when he first arrived to take up his duties in the new capital. "I have never seen this city in such a state of pleased excitement," a visitor wrote home, "except upon the news of a Confederate victory. Men and women in tears was a common sight, and the ladies say they are very much afraid they will have to love the Yankees a little."

On Sunday the Davises kept to their rooms except for a secret trip to Hollywood Cemetery to lay flowers on the grave where their son Joe had lain since his fall from the White House balcony in that other fateful spring, three years ago. After church, old friends came by the hotel, some bringing daughters and nieces who had emerged from girlhood during the past two years, and it was noted that while Davis kissed them all on arrival, "he kissed the prettiest again on their departure." Still, the tension was unmistakable. Tomorrow he would appear before Judge John C. Underwood, who had composed the scabrous charge under which he had been indicted the previous May, and it was feared that he would no sooner have escaped the clutches of the military than Underwood would have him jailed on some new civil pretext of his own.

Next morning, leaving his wife to wait and pray at the hotel, he rode down Main Street — heavily thronged, especially for a Monday, with townspeople and others who had come in hope of witnessing his deliverance — to the old Customs House, where the hearing would be held, and went inside to join his lawyers — six of them, three northern and three southern — seated at a table within the bar. After the first shock of recognition, those watching in the close-packed chamber were pleased to see that the change he had undergone was mainly on the surface. "He wears a full beard and mustache," a reporter had observed in the *Enquirer* the day before, "but his countenance, although haggard and careworn, still preserves the proud expression and the mingled look of sweetness and dignity for which it was ever remarkable. His hair is considerably silvered, but his eye still beams with all the fire that characterized it in the old time." Now one among the spectators, watching him enter the courtroom "with his proud step and lofty look," was convinced that "a stranger would have sworn that he was the judge and Underwood the culprit."

What followed was not only brief and to the point; it also proved yesterday's fears to be groundless. Presented with "the body of Jefferson Davis," as he had required in response to the writ, Underwood declared that the prisoner had passed from the control of martial law to the custody of the local U.S. marshal. O'Conor then requested a trial without delay, and when the district attorney replied that the case could not be heard at the present term, the judge received and granted a motion for bail, which he fixed at $100,000. Horace Greeley was there, along with other one-time enemies who had agreed to give their bond for that amount, and while they came forward to sign the necessary papers, one among the applauding spectators crossed to a window and shouted down to the crowd below on Main Street: "The President is bailed!" A roar came up in response to the news, and those inside the courtroom could hear the cry being passed from street to street, all over Richmond and its seven hills: "The President is bailed!"

They still called him that, and always would: thanks in part to Stanton and his subordinates, whose harshness had recovered for him an affection and devotion as profound as any he had received when the title was his in fact. Presently, when he came out of the Customs House and got into his carriage, the roar of approval grew shrill with the weird halloo of the rebel yell, loosed by veterans who had been waiting two years now to give it. This continued vociferously all the way to the Spotswood, where a crowd of about 5000 had gathered. Then a strange thing happened. When the coachman pulled up in front of the entrance a grave hush came down, as if everyone in the throng had suddenly felt too deeply moved for cheers. "Hats off, Virginians!" a voice rang out. All uncovered and stood in silence as Davis stepped from the carriage, free at last, and entered the hotel where his wife was waiting.

✗ 4 ✗

All things end, and by ending not only find continuance in the whole, but also assure continuance by contributing their droplets, clear or murky, to the stream of history. Anaximander said it best, some 2500 years ago: "It is necessary that things should pass away into that from which they are born. For things must pay one another the penalty and compensation for their injustice according to the ordinance of time." So it was with the Confederacy, and so one day will it be for the other nations of earth, if not for earth itself. Appomattox was one of several endings; Durham Station, Citronelle, Galveston were others; as were Johnson's mid-May proclamation and the ratification of the 13th Amendment, which seven months later freed the slaves not freed in the course of a four-year struggle that reunited the nation Lincoln's election had split asunder. But at what cost — if not in suffering, which was immeasurable, then at any rate in blood — had the war been won and lost?

In round numbers, two million blue-clad soldiers and sailors were diminished by 640,000 casualties — more than a fourth — while the 750,000 in gray, all told, lost 450,000 — well over half. Of the former, 110,000 had been killed in battle, as compared to 94,000 of the latter. Death from diseases (dysentery, typhus, malaria, pneumonia, smallpox, measles, tuberculosis) or mishaps out of combat (murder, suicide, drowning, sunstroke, execution, adjunctive to a host of unstated causes) raised these totals to 365,000 and 256,000 respectively, and the addition of the wounded — 275,000 Federals, 194,000 Confederates — yielded the figures quoted above. Minimal computations (deceptive in their specificity, for they too were little more than educated guesses, especially with regard to the southern forces) showed a North-South total of 623,026 dead and 471,427 wounded. The butcher's bill thus came to no less than 1,094,453 for both sides, in and out of more than 10,000 military actions, including 76 full-scale battles, 310 engagements, 6337 skirmishes, and numerous sieges, raids, expeditions, and the like. For the most part, having fewer troops on any given field, the rebels lost fewer in the fighting, but in at least one category the ratio was reversed and extended. Out of 583 Union generals, 47 were killed in action; whereas, of the 425 Confederate generals, 77 fell — roughly one out of twelve, as compared to one out of five. Moreover, much the same awesome ratios obtained when applied to the number slain or maimed out of the total number available for conscription on each side. Approximately one out of ten able-bodied Northerners was dead or incapacitated, while for the South it was one out of four, including her noncombatant Negroes. Some notion of the drain this represented, as well as of the poverty the surrendered men came home to, was shown by the fact that during the first year of peace the state of Mississippi allotted a solid fifth of its revenues for the purchase of artificial arms and legs for its returning veterans.

Few wars — western wars, that is; for in China the Tai-ping Rebellion, which began in 1850 and ended only a year before our own, cost an estimated twenty million lives — had been so proportionately expensive, either in money or in blood. And yet, for all the hard-earned cynicism that prompted them to echo Bill Arp, saying: "I've killed as many of them as they have of me. I'm going home," veterans on both sides knew that, even as they headed for their farms and shops and the girls they left behind, something momentous was passing from them, something that could never be recaptured. "I have no idea that many of them will ever see as happy times as they have had in the army," Rutherford Hayes wrote his wife from West Virginia as he watched his discharged troops depart. They would no doubt have hooted at this, eager for home as they were just then, although some among them already had experienced intimations of nostalgia. "None of us were fond of war," an Indiana infantryman would recall, looking back on the farewell review Thomas staged in Nashville, "but there had grown up between the boys an attachment for each other they never had nor ever will have for any other body of men." For others, there were doubts and fears about the future; a future now at hand. "I do feel so idle and lost to all business," an Iowa cavalryman told his diary on the eve of the Grand Review, "that I wonder what will become of me. Can I ever be contented again? *Can I work?* Ah! how doubtful — it's raining tonight."

Among the shocks awaiting homebound northern soldiers, especially those who had been gone the longest, was the fact that while wages had been rising 43 percent in the course of the war, the cost of living had gone up 117 percent. "Democracies are prone to war, and war consumes them," Seward had said, fifteen years before, and doubtless that was part of what he meant. In any case, demobilization proceeded apace. Within six months of Kirby Smith's surrender, the Union army had declined from just over a million men to 183,000. By the end of the following year it was down to 54,000, and would continue to decline for thirty years. For Southerners there was of course no waiting to be mustered out; a man's parole was his discharge, and he started home as soon as he received it. What awaited him there, particularly if home was a place Sherman or Wilson had given their passing attention, had little or nothing to do with wages. All too often there were no wages, and the cost of living was measured less in dollars than in sweat. Some notion of the waiting desolation was given by a former Georgia slave, who recalled his own departure: "The master had three boys to go to war, but there wasn't one come home. All the children he had was killed. Master, he lost all his money, and the house soon begun dropping away to nothing. Us niggers one by one left the old place, and the last time I seed the home plantation I was standing on a hill. I looked back on it for the last time through a patch of scrub pine, and it looked so lonely. There wasn't but one person in sight, the master. He was a-setting in a wicker chair in the yard looking out over a small field of cotton and corn. There was four crosses in the graveyard on the side lawn where he was setting. The fourth one was his wife."

Whatever else the veterans brought or failed to bring home with them, and whether they returned to snugness or dilapidation, with or without back pay, bonuses, and pensions, they had acquired a sense of nationhood, of nationality. From the outset Lincoln had had the problem of uniting what remained of his divided country if he was to recover by conquest the segment that had departed, and though he succeeded well enough in this to achieve his immediate purpose, true fulfillment came after his death, after the victory that brought the soldiers home. They knew now they had a nation, for they had seen it; they had been there, they had touched it, climbed its mountains, crossed its rivers, hiked its roads; their comrades lay buried in its soil, along with many thousands of their own arms and legs. Nor did this apply only to those whose return was northward, above the Mason-Dixon line. Below it, too, men who never before had been fifty miles from their places of birth now knew, from having slept and fought in its fields and woods and cane brakes, gawked at its cities, such as they were, and trudged homeward through its desolation, that they too had had a country. Not secession but the war itself, and above all the memories recurrent through the peace that followed — such as it was — created a Solid South, more firmly united in defeat than it had been during the brief span when it claimed independence. Voided, the claim was abandoned, but the pride remained: pride in the segment reabsorbed, as well as in the whole, which now for the first time was truly indivisible. This new unity was best defined, perhaps, by the change in number of a simple verb. In formal as in common speech, abroad as well as on this side of its oceans, once the nation emerged from the crucible of that war, "the United States *are*" became "the United States *is*."

It would continue so, but toward what goal? Walt Whitman, for one, believed he saw what was to come of this forged unity. "I chant the new empire, grander than before. I chant commerce opening!" he exulted. John Sherman was more specific, telling his soldier brother: "The truth is, the close of the war with our resources unimpaired gives an elevation, a scope to the ideas of leading capitalists, far higher than anything ever undertaken before. They talk of millions as confidently as formerly of thousands." Soon the nation was into a raucous era whose inheritors were Daniel Drew, Jay Gould, Jim Fisk, and others of that stripe, operating in "a riot of individual materialism, under which," as Theodore Roosevelt was to say, "complete freedom for the individual ...

turned out in practice to mean perfect freedom for the strong to wrong the weak." The big fish ate the little fish, and once the little fish got scarce or learned to hide among the rocks, the big fish ate each other. *Laissez faire* meant *laissez nous faire*, and free enterprise reached its symbolic apogee with the attempt by a gang of thieves, one night late in 1876, to steal and ransom for $200,000 the body of Abraham Lincoln. They made it into his Springfield tomb and had begun removing the casket from its sarcophagus when they were caught.

Freedom then was variously interpreted, and these differences of stance and opinion — especially as they applied to the Negro in the procedure for getting the seceded states back into what Lincoln had called "their proper practical relation with the Union" — lay at the knotty heart of Reconstruction, the four-year war's lurid twelve-year epilogue. It was in fact a sequel, a drama in three acts, of which the first was much the shortest and the mildest. Johnson, in the remaining six months of the 1865 congressional recess, put into operation his predecessor's lenient plan for allowing the defeated rebels to form their own state governments and return to their old allegiance, on condition that they pledge obedience to the national laws and promise to deal fairly with their former slaves. Summer and fall wore by; Johnson declared the process of reconstruction all but complete. Then in December Congress reassembled for Act Two, the longest and quite the rowdiest of the three. Indignant over what had been done in their absence — particularly southward, where ex-Confederates were demonstrating their notion that the black man's preparation for freedom, after two hundred years of bondage, should include an indefinite interlude of peonage — the Republican majority repudiated the new state governments and declined to seat their elected senators and representatives. Vengeance-minded, the hard-war men were out for blood. "As for Jeff Davis," George Julian told the House, "I would indict him, I would convict him and hang him in the name of God. As for Robert E. Lee, unmolested in Virginia, hang him too. And stop there? Not at all. I would hang liberally while I had my hand in."

They were above all out to get Johnson, who had jumped as it were from their pocket, where he himself had assured them he was lodged, and betrayed them while their backs were turned. The battle, promptly joined, raged through the year that followed, beginning with the passage, over the President's veto, of the first civil rights bill. That was on the anniversary of Appomattox, and two months later came the 14th Amendment, which, together with other legislation barreled through, assured full citizenship to former slaves and disqualified former Confederate leaders from holding office or casting ballots in local or national elections. Victory at the polls in November having increased the close-knit, radical-dominated Republican majority to better than two thirds in both houses, Congress then was ready to move in for the kill. Impeached by the House in February 1868 for "high crimes and misdemeanors," chief among which was his "usurpation of power," Johnson avoided conviction in May by one vote in the upper chamber. Disappointed at not having replaced him with one of their own — Ben Wade, president pro tempore of the Senate — the Jacobins concentrated on winning the fall election, and got something even better for their pains. They got U. S. Grant; which was another way of saying they got their way through most of the next eight years. Grant, with his profound mistrust of intellectuals and reformers — "narrow headed men," he called them, with eyes so close-set they could "look out of the same gimlet hole without winking" — provided the perfect foil by which the Vindictives could secure what they were after. He admired their forthrightness, as he did that of certain high-powered businessmen, who also profited from his trust; with the result that the country would wait more than fifty years for an administration as crooked in money matters, and a solid hundred for one as morally corrupt.

In the end it was the sum of these excesses that brought down the second-act curtain and moved the drama into Act Three. Shock and indignation paled to boredom as news of the scandals grew, and this, combined with the effects of the financial panic of 1873, alienated enough voters to give the Democratic candidate, Samuel J. Tilden of New York, a substantial majority of the ballots cast in the presidential election three years later. Tilden did not get into the White House, though. An engineered deal, whereby the Republicans agreed to withdraw the last Union troops from occupation of the South in exchange for the electoral votes of Louisiana and Florida, put Rutherford Hayes — three times governor of Ohio by then — into office by an electoral count of 185 to 184. All this time the play had been winding down anyhow, as state after state reëstablished "home rule": Tennessee in 1869, Virginia and North Carolina in 1870, Georgia in 1871, Arkansas, Alabama, and Texas in 1874, and Mississippi in 1875. Now with the departure in 1877 of the occupation forces, Louisiana, Florida, and South Carolina also threw off the Federal yoke, and the final curtain fell. Reconstruction, so called, was over.

Home rule, as both sides knew, meant white supremacy. The Negro, then, was bartered: or his gains were, which came to the same thing. "Bottom rail on top!" he had cried in 1870 when Hiram Revels of Mississippi, the first black man to become a member of the U.S. Senate, took Jefferson Davis's former seat. After Revels came Blanche K. Bruce, also of Mississippi. He was the second Negro senator, and the last for ninety years. In 1883 the Supreme Court would invalidate the Civil Rights Act of 1875, and would follow through, before the turn of the century, by approving racial segregation on condition that "separate" accommodations also be "equal," which they seldom were. Bottom rail was back on bottom. The 14th and 15th Amendments remained as legacies of Reconstruction, along with greatly expanded free school facilities for both races, but until the government and the courts were ready again to take the Constitution at its word, the Negro — locked in a caste system of "race etiquette" as rigid as any he had known in formal bondage — could repeat, with equal validity, what an Alabama slave had said in 1864 when asked what he thought of the Great Emancipator whose proclamation went into effect that year. "I don't know nothing bout Abraham Lincoln," he replied, "cep they say he sot us free. And I don't know nothing bout that neither."

It so happened that the year that marked the end of Reconstruction, 1877, was also the watershed year in which the United States, well on its way toward becoming a — and, ultimately, the — major industrial power, began regularly exporting more than it imported. Simultaneously, the invention of what seemed at first to be little more than toys, together with their eventual mass production, was about to change the way of life, first of its own people, then the world's. Just the year before, Alexander Bell had sent the first telephone message; this year Thomas Edison had a phonograph playing, and within another two years George B. Selden would apply for a patent for a "gasoline carriage." Change was at hand, and there were those who observed its coming with mingled approval and apprehension. "I tell you these are great times," young Henry Adams had written his brother from London during the war. "Man has mounted science, and is now run away with. I firmly believe that before many centuries more, science will be the master of man. The engines he will have invented will be beyond his strength to control. Some day science may have the existence of mankind in its power, and the human race commit suicide by blowing up the world. Not only shall we be able to cruise in space, but I see no reason why some future generation shouldn't walk off like a beetle with the world on its back, or give it another rotary motion so that every zone should receive in turn its due portion of heat and light."

North and South, the veterans were part of this, but mainly as observers rather than participants, and least of all as profiteers. Few or no tycoons had served in the northern armies, and southern talents seemed not to lie in that direction, except for a prominent few who lent their names for use on letterheads. Well into what passed for middle age by then, they had something of the studied indifference of men who had spent their lives in another world. Visiting regions where they had fought, ten, then twenty, then thirty years ago, they found the distances not as great as they remembered, but the hills a good deal steeper. Certain tags of poetry had a tendency to hang in their minds, whether from a dirge by Whitman:

> *Beautiful that war and all its deeds of carnage*
> *must in time be utterly lost,*
> *That the hands of the sisters Death and Night*

incessantly softly wash again,
and ever again, this soil'd world —

or, more likely, a snatch from a rollicking cavalry tune, sung in time
with hoofbeats pounding the moon-drenched highways of their youth:

He who has good buttermilk aplenty,
    And gives the soldiers none,
Shan't have any of our buttermilk
When his buttermilk is gone.

Time played its tricks, distorting and subtracting. The rebel yell, for
instance — "shrill, exultant, savage," a one-time blue infantryman recalled, "so different from the deep, manly, generous shout of the Union
soldiers" — would presently be lost to all who had never heard it on the
field of battle. Asked at the close of a U.D.C. banquet to reproduce it,
a Tennessee veteran explained that the yell was "impossible unless made
at a dead run in full charge against the enemy." Not only could it not
be given in cold blood while standing still; it was "worse than folly to
try to imitate it with a stomach full of food and a mouth full of false
teeth." So it perished from the sound waves. Wildcat screech, foxhunt
yip, banshee squall, whatever it had been, it survived only in the fading
memories and sometimes vivid dreams of old men sunning themselves on
public benches, grouped together in resentment of the boredom they
encountered when they spoke of the war to those who had not shared
it with them.

Once a year at least — aside, that is, from regimental banquets and
mass reunions, attended more and more sparsely by middle-aged, then
old, then incredibly ancient men who dwindled finally to a handful of
octogenarian drummer boys, still whiskered for the most part in a clean-
shaven world that had long since passed them by — these survivors got
together to honor their dead. Observed throughout the North on May
30, Memorial Day hopscotched the calendar in the South, where individual states made their choice between April 26, May 10, and June 3.
In any case, whenever it came, this day belonged to the veterans and
their fallen comrades, and they made the most of it, beginning with their
choice of a speaker, always with the hope that he would rival the "few
appropriate remarks" Lincoln had uttered at Gettysburg on a similar
occasion. None ever did, but one at least came close at Keene, New
Hampshire, in 1884, twenty years after that day on the outskirts of
Washington when he yelled at the since-martyred leader, high on the
parapet of Fort Stevens: "Get down, you damn fool!" Young Captain
Holmes, thrice gravely wounded in three years of service, was forty-
three by now, not halfway into a distinguished life that would continue
through more than a third of the approaching century. He would deliver,
in the course of his ninety-four years, many speeches highly admired for
their pith and felicity of expression, yet he never spoke more to the

point, or more to the satisfaction of his hearers, than he did on this Memorial Day in his native New England.

He began by expressing his respect, not only for the veterans gathered to hear him, but also for the men they had fought, and he told why he felt it. "You could not stand up day after day, in those indecisive contests where overwhelming victory was impossible because neither side would run as they ought when beaten, without getting at last something of the same brotherhood for the enemy that the north pole of a magnet has for the south, each working in an opposite sense to the other, but unable to get along without the other." Such scorn as he felt he reserved for those who had stood aside when the call came for commitment. "I think that, as life is action and passion, it is required of a man that he should share the passion and action of his time at peril of being judged not to have lived." Memorial Day was for him and his listeners "the most sacred of the year," and he believed it would continue to be observed with pride and reverence. "But even if I am wrong, even if those who are to come after us are to forget all that we hold dear, and the future is to teach and kindle its children in ways as yet unrevealed, it is enough for us that to us this day is dear and sacred. ... For one hour, twice a year at least — at the regimental dinner, where the ghosts sit at table more numerous than the living, and on this day when we decorate their graves — the dead come back and live with us. I see them now, more than I can number, as once I saw them on this earth." He saw them, and he saw what they stood for, even now in the midst of what Mark Twain had dubbed the Gilded Age. "The generation that carried on the war has been set aside by its experience. Through our great good fortune, in our youth our hearts were touched with fire. It was given to us to learn at the outset that life is a profound and passionate thing. While we are permitted to scorn nothing but indifference, and do not pretend to undervalue the worldly rewards of ambition, we have seen with our own eyes, beyond and above the gold fields, the snowy heights of honor, and it is for us to bear the report to those who come after us."

No wonder, then, if they looked back on that four-year holocaust — which in a sense was begun by one madman, John Brown, and ended by another, J. Wilkes Booth — with something of the feeling shared by men who have gone through, and survived, some cataclysmic phenomenon; a hurricane or an earthquake, say, or a horrendous railway accident. Memory smoothed the crumpled scroll, abolished fear, leached pain and grief, and removed the sting from death. "Well," a former hospital steward testified, recalling the moribund patients in his ward, "they would see that the doctor gave them up, and they would ask me about it. I would tell them the truth. I told one man that, and he asked how long? I said not over twenty minutes. He did not show any fear — they never do. He put his hand up, so, and closed his eyes with his own fingers, then stretched himself out and crossed his arms over his breast. 'Now, fix me,' he said. I pinned the toes of his stockings together; that was the way we laid corpses out; and he died in a few minutes. His face looked as pleasant as if he was asleep, and smiling. Many's the time the boys have fixed themselves that way before they died." In time, even death itself might be abolished. Sergeant Berry Benson, a South Carolina veteran from McGowan's brigade, Wilcox's division, A. P. Hill's corps, Army of Northern Virginia — he had enlisted three months before Sumter, aged eighteen, and served through Appomattox — saw it so when he got around to composing the Reminiscences he hoped would "go down amongst my descendants for a long time." Reliving the war in words, he began to wish he could relive it in fact, and he came to believe that he and his fellow soldiers, gray and blue, might one day be able to do just that: if not here on earth, then afterwards in Valhalla. "Who knows," he asked as his narrative drew toward its close, "but it may be given to us, after this life, to meet again in the old quarters, to play chess and draughts, to get up soon to answer the morning roll call, to fall in at the tap of the drum for drill and dress parade, and again to hastily don our war gear while the monotonous patter of the long roll summons to battle? Who knows but again the old flags, ragged and torn, snapping in the wind, may face each other and flutter, pursuing and pursued, while the cries of victory fill a summer day? And after the battle, then the slain and wounded will arise, and all will meet together under the two flags, all sound and well, and there will be talking and laughter and cheers, and all will say: Did it not seem real? Was it not as in the old days?"

★　★　★

By then they had nearly all come round, both sides having entered into a two-way concession whereby the victors acknowledged that the Confederates had fought bravely for a cause they believed was just and the losers agreed it was probably best for all concerned that the Union had been preserved. The first step lay in admission of defeat, and one of the first to take it publicly was Joe Johnston. Aboard a Chesapeake Bay steamer, not long after his surrender, the general heard a fellow passenger insisting that the South had been "conquered but not subdued." Asked in what command he had served, the bellicose young man — one of those stalwarts later classified as "invisible in war and invincible in peace" — replied that, unfortunately, circumstances had made it impossible for him to be in the army. "Well, sir, I was," Johnston told him. "You may not be subdued, but I am."

Similarly, R. E. Lee encouraged all who sought his advice to take the loyalty oath required by the President's amnesty proclamation as a prerequisite to recovery of their rights as citizens, and even did so himself, barely two months after Appomattox, though nothing came of it then or later; he would go to his grave disfranchised. However, news that he had "asked for pardon" spread rapidly through the South, producing consternation, which was followed for the most part, even among those who had been die-hards up till then, by prompt acceptance and emulation. "You have disgraced the family, sir!" Ex-Governor Henry Wise sputtered when he learned that one of his sons had taken the oath. "But, Father," the former captain said, "General Lee advised me to do it." Taken aback, Wise paused only a moment before he replied: "That alters the case. Whatever General Lee advises is right."

Neither of these attitudes or reactions — Johnston's admission that he had been "subdued," Lee's willingness to pledge loyalty to a government he had sought to overthrow — was acceptable to Jefferson Davis in his own right. He did not object intrinsically to their view, so long as they applied it to themselves, but as the symbolic leader of a nation, even one that had been abolished by force of arms, he had other factors to consider. For him, the very notion of subdual was something to be rejected out of hand, if acceptance, as he conceived it, meant abandoning the principles of constitutional government. The war had been lost beyond denial, but not the cause. Nothing would ever bend him from that. He clung to the views he had held in 1861, and indeed ever since he entered public life some twenty years before. As for anything resembling an apology — which he believed was what he would be offering if he took the oath required — he would say repeatedly, first and last: "I have no claim to pardon, not having in any wise repented." No wonder, then, that Andrew Johnson referred to him as Lucifer incarnate, "the head devil of them all."

To his own people he was something else, in part because of all he had suffered, first in the granite bowels of Fort Monroe — where Miles, acting on Stanton's orders, martyred him about as effectively as Booth had martyred Lincoln — and then through much of the decade following his release on bail, a time referred to by his wife as one spent "floating uprooted." From Richmond, his trial having been put off until November, he went to Canada, where the two older of his four children were in school, then came back by way of Cuba for his health's sake, his trial having been postponed again till March of 1868, then still again until the following February. Impeachment was heading up by now in Washington, and the danger loomed of Johnson's being replaced by bluff Ben Wade, who was not above Star Chamber proceedings. On the advice of his attorneys, Davis and his family planned to sail for Europe, and did so in July, though Wade by then had been kept from becoming President by one senatorial vote. In England the former State Prisoner was entertained by high-born sympathizers and had the pleasure of dining with his old companion Judah Benjamin, fast on the rise as a distinguished member of the bar. A visit to France at the end of the year also gave him the satisfaction of declining an audience with

Napoleon and Eugénie, who, he said, had "played us false" at a time
when the need for friends was sore.

He had by now had more than enough of "floating," and his pride
would not allow him to accept indefinitely from admirers the financial
help he was obliged to live on while his trial was pending. Then suddenly
it no longer was. Early in 1869, with the indictment quashed at last, he
was free to come home and accept employment as president of the
Carolina Life Insurance Company, headquartered in Memphis. He returned without his family, got settled in the business, and went back
to England in late summer, 1870, for his wife and children. Docking at
Baltimore in mid-October he learned that Robert Lee had died that
week. "Virginia has need of all her sons," the general had replied when
asked by veterans what he thought of their going elsewhere to escape
the strictures of poverty and Reconstruction, and he himself had set
them an example by serving, at a salary of $1500 a year, as president
of Washington College, a small, all but bankrupt institution out in the
Shenandoah Valley. He aged greatly in the five years left him after
Appomattox, suffering from the heart ailment which his doctors now
could see had been what plagued him through much of the war, when
the symptoms were diagnosed as rheumatism. Stricken in late September,
he lingered till October 12. Back in battle toward the end, like Stonewall
before him, he called in his delirium on A. P. Hill: "Tell Hill he must
come up." Then he quieted, as Jackson too had done before he crossed
the river. "Strike the tent," he said, and then he died.

"Of the man, how shall I speak? His moral qualities rose to the
height of genuis," Davis declared at a memorial service held in Richmond in early November. It was his first public address since the end of
the war, and though he was encouraged by the fervor of his reception
in the one-time national capital, the passing of the great Confederate
captain was the signal for the onset of a series of reversals for his former
chief, the heaviest of which came two years later with the death of one
of his two surviving sons. Eleven-year-old Billy, conceived in Montgomery during the secession furore and born after the removal of the
government to Virginia, fell victim to diphtheria in Memphis. Settled
in a house of his own for the first time in six years, and released at last,
as he thought, from the life his wife described as "floating uprooted,"
Davis suffered this sudden deprivation only to have it followed by still
another during the financial panic of '73, precipitated by the failure of
Jay Cooke & Company in New York, which had marketed the huge
war loans of the Federal government. Carolina Life went under, too, a
chip among the flotsam, taking with it his last $15,000 and the only
job he had ever had. Afloat again, he sought other ventures, some involving trips to Europe in search of backers, but nothing came of them.
Though he kept his home in Memphis, even managing the expense of a
wedding for his daughter Maggie in 1875, the result was that he again

found himself floating rootless, his life no longer a career, but rather an existence.

When at last he found the answer, a way out of this dilemma, it was neither in Memphis nor in business. Ever since his release from prison he had had it in mind to write a personal history of the war, and even as early as his stay in Canada he had begun to look through such papers as were then available for his purpose, including duplicates of messages sent commanders in the field. One of the first he examined, however — a telegram he had addressed to Lee from Danville on the day of Appomattox, unaware that the surrender was in progress — put an end to this preliminary effort. "You will realize the reluctance I feel to leave the soil of Virginia," he had wired, "and appreciate my anxiety to win success north of the Roanoke." Mrs Davis, who was there to help him sort the documents, saw a stricken look come on his face at the memories the words called up. He pushed the papers away. "Let us put them by for a while. I cannot speak of my dead so soon," he told her. That had been nearly ten years ago, and he had not returned to them since, despite the urging of such friends as Preston Johnston, who admonished him: "I do not believe any man ever lived who could dare to tell in the light more fully what was done in the dark, than you can. It seems to be a friendly duty to warn you not to forget your design." Davis did not forget, but he was fully occupied by the insurance business: until it vanished, that is, along with what little he had left in the way of funds. Failure freed him to return to his old design; failure and necessity, and something else as well. Recently, old comrades who had shared the glory and pain of battles won and lost — ex-Confederates for the most part, though the victors also had their differences in public — had begun to turn on each other, quarreling over what they considered a proper distribution of praise and blame, especially the latter. One of the hottest of these arguments had to do with Gettysburg; Fitzhugh Lee and Jubal Early crossed swords with Longstreet, who had compounded their enmity by going over to the Republicans and his old friend Grant. Davis stayed well out of it, reserving his ire for a long-time adversary, Joseph E. Johnston, who had brought out in 1874 his *Narrative of Military Operations Directed During the Late War Between the States*, much of it devoted to unburdening himself of grievances against his former superior. "The advance sheets exhibit his usual malignity and suppression of the truth when it would affect his side of the case unfavorably," Davis informed his wife by way of warming up for the counteroffensive he now had it in mind to launch. He would write his own account, quartering much of the same ground, of course, and accordingly signed a contract with Appleton's of New York, who agreed to cover such expenses as he required for secretarial assistance.

Bustling Memphis, hot in summer, cold in winter — the scene of his loss, moreover, of the third of his four sons — seemed unconducive to the peace he believed he needed for such work. Who could write anything there, let alone a full-fledged two- or three-volume history of the war? He had found the atmosphere he wanted on a trip to the Mississippi Coast the previous November, when he wrote his wife that "the moaning of the winds among the pines and the rolling waves of the Gulf on the beach gave me a sense of rest and peace which made me wish to lay me down and be at home." Midway between New Orleans and Mobile was "Beauvoir," an estate belonging to Sarah E. Dorsey, a wealthy, recently widowed childhood friend of Varina's; "a fine place," Davis called it, with a "large and beautiful house" set among spreading live oaks "and many orange trees yet full of fruit." Receiving him now as a visitor, Mrs Dorsey offered him the use of a cottage on the grounds, "a refuge without encumbrances" in which to write his book. He quickly accepted, on condition of paying board, and by February 1877 he and a body servant had moved in. Quarters were found nearby for Major W. T. Walthall, his research assistant, and work began at once, with the added help of Sarah Dorsey herself. She had written four novels under the nom de plume "Filia," and was delighted to serve as an amanuensis, having long admired her house guest as "the noblest man she had ever met on earth."

Varina, who had never enjoyed the notion of sharing Jefferson Davis with anyone — least of all another woman, childhood friend or not — was considerably less pleased with this outcome of his quest for domestic tranquillity. She had been in Germany most of the past eight months, getting twelve-year-old Winnie settled in a girls' school in Carlsruhe, and despite urgings from her husband and Mrs Dorsey that she join them on the Coast, she remained in Europe for another eight, determined not to be a party to any such *ménage à trois* arrangement. Finally in October she returned, not to Beauvoir but to Memphis, where twenty-year-old Jeff Junior, after an unsatisfactory year at V.M.I., had accepted a place in a bank with his sister Maggie's husband. Davis himself came up at once, hoping to take her back with him, but she refused. She was pleased, however, to see him looking well, absorbed in his work and eager to get back to it. A new urgency was on him, caused in part by the recent passing of some of the principal characters in the story he was attempting to retell. Braxton Bragg, for example, had dropped dead on the street in Galveston last year, and Raphael Semmes had been buried only the month before in Mobile. Another great raider, Bedford Forrest, was dying in Memphis even now, wasted by diabetes to a scant one hundred pounds. "I am completely broke up," he confessed to friends. "I am broke in fortune, broke in health, broke in spirit." Davis sat by his bedside the day before he died, then served as a pallbearer at his funeral on the last day of October. In the carriage, en route to Elmwood Cemetery, a companion remarked on Forrest's greatness as a soldier. "I agree with you," the former President said. "The trouble was that the generals commanding in the Southwest never appreciated him until it was too late. Their judgment was that he was a bold and enterprising raider and rider. I was misled by them, and never knew how to measure him until I read the reports of his campaign across the Tennessee River in 1864. This induced a study of his earlier reports, and after that I was prepared to adopt what you are pleased to name as the judgment of history." Someone mentioned Brice's Crossroads, and Davis replied as before: "That campaign was not understood in Richmond. The impression made upon those in authority was that Forrest had made another successful raid. . . . I saw it all after it was too late."

He returned alone to Beauvoir, Sarah Dorsey, and his work. Varina was willing to help by mail, amplifying his recollections with her own, but not in person. "Nothing on earth would pain me like living in that kind of community," she had written from Europe, and she still felt that way about it. At any rate she did for another eight months before she relented, in part because of the heat of a Memphis summer, but mainly because her husband by then had offered to give up his present living arrangement if she would join him elsewhere. Apparently it was this she had been waiting for all along, for he no sooner made the offer than she consented to join him where he was. She arrived in July, 1878, and at once took over the job of amanuensis. Indignant at the unrelenting vindictiveness of Washington in excluding Davis from the benefits of a pension bill for veterans of the Mexican War, they settled down to work amid reports of a yellow fever epidemic moving upriver from New Orleans. Memphis and other cities and towns were still under quarantine in October when a wire reached Beauvoir to inform them that Jeff Junior had come down with the disease. Then five days later another arrived to tell them he had rallied and then died. Davis had lost the fourth of his four sons; Samuel, Joseph, William, and now Jeff. "I presume not God to scorn," he wrote a kinsman, "but the many and humble prayers offered before my boy was taken from me are hushed in the despair of my bereavement."

Work was the answer, as much for Varina as for her husband, and they got on with it, sometimes into the small hours of the night. In February the domestic strain was relieved by Mrs Dorsey, who sold Beauvoir to Davis for $5500, to be paid in three installments, then went to New Orleans to consult a physician for what turned out to be cancer. By July she was dead. Childless, she left Beauvoir to Davis, absolving him from making the other two payments. Nor was that all. "I hereby give and bequeath all my property, wherever located and situated, wholly and entirely, without hindrance or qualification," her will read, "to my most honored and esteemed friend, Jefferson Davis, ex-President of the Confederate States, for his sole use and benefit, in fee simple forever. . . . I do not intend," she had said in closing, "to share in the ingratitude of my country towards the man who is in my eyes the highest and noblest in existence." He was now the master of Beauvoir, along with much else, including three plantations in Louisiana, and Varina was its mistress.

The work went on. Reconstruction was over, but Davis still fought the war, landing verbal blows where armed strokes had failed. Soon the first of what were to be two large volumes was ready for the printer. *Rise and Fall of the Confederate Government*, he would call it: not *Our Cause*, as he had originally intended. He moved into and steadily through the second volume. On an afternoon in April, 1881, he took a long nap, then at 8 o'clock that evening resumed dictation. Speaking slowly and distinctly, so that Varina would not miss a word, he tugged firmly on the drawstrings of his logic for a final explication of his thesis that the North, not the South, had been the revolutionary party in the struggle, malevolent in its effort to subvert, subjugate, and destroy, respectively, the states, the people, and the Union as it had been till then. "When the cause was lost, what cause was it?" he asked, and answered: "Not that of the South only, but the cause of constitutional government, of the supremacy of law, of the natural rights of man." It was by then well past midnight, and only the rhythmic plash of waves on the beach came through the stillness of the dark hours before dawn. He kept on, launched now onto the last of nearly 1500 pages, restating his conviction "that the war was, on the part of the United States Government, one of aggression and usurpation, and, on the part of the South, was for the defense of an inherent, unalienable right." He paused, then continued.

> In asserting the right of secession, it has not been my wish to incite to its exercise: I recognize the fact that the war showed it to be impracticable, but this did not prove it to be wrong. And now that it may not be again attempted, and that the Union may promote the general welfare, it is needful that the truth, the whole truth, should be known, so that crimination and recrimination may forever cease, and then, on the basis of fraternity and faithful regard for the rights of the States, there may be written on the arch of the Union, *Esto perpetua*.

He leaned back, sighed, and closed his eyes against the glare of lamplight. It was 4 o'clock in the morning and he was within two months of being seventy-three years old. Her pen poised above the paper, Varina looked up, ready for the next sentence. "I think I am done," he said with a tired smile.

He was done, and the book — already in type, except these final pages — came out in June. In the South it was hailed and praised. No home that could afford them was without the two thick volumes, often bound in calf, on a parlor table. The trouble was, so few could afford them, and in the North the book was largely ignored, save in a few grudging magazine reviews. Financially, it was a failure; Appleton's lost money, and Davis himself made little, despite a drawn-out lawsuit with the publisher which ensued. In August he and Varina sailed for Europe to get Winnie, and returned in late November. "The Daughter of the Confederacy," born in the Richmond White House while the guns of Kennesaw were booming, was tall and fair, with clear gray eyes and a quiet manner; she spoke, to her father's surprise, with traces of a German accent which she would never lose. Settled again at Beauvoir he looked forward to a peaceful life through whatever years were left him. Then in mid-December came news that Joe Johnston had wondered aloud to a reporter what had become of all the treasury gold Davis had taken along on his flight through Georgia. It came, he heard, to $2,500,000; yet "Mr Davis has never given any satisfactory account of it." In the hue and cry that followed, the general was obliged to run for cover, and letters poured into Beauvoir from all parts of the country, expressing outrage at the slander and admiration for its victim. Davis had won his last skirmish with Johnston, who perhaps was confirmed in his distaste for the offensive.

Still, no amount of adulation North or South could temper the former President's resolution not to ask for pardon; not even pleas from his home-state Legislature that he do so in order to be returned to his old seat in the U. S. Senate. He did however agree to come to Jackson in March, 1884, for a ceremony staged to honor him as "the embodied history of the South." Standing in the high-ceilinged Capitol chamber where he had stood just over two decades ago, near the midpoint of the war, and told the assembled dignitaries, "Our people have only to be true to themselves to behold the Confederate flag among the recognized nations of the earth," he spoke now much as he had then: "It has been said that I should apply to the United States for a pardon. But repentance must precede the right of pardon, and I have not repented. Remembering, as I must, all which has been suffered, all which has been lost — disappointed hopes and crushed aspirations — yet I deliberately say, if it were all to do over again, I would again do just as I did in 1861." His hearers caught their breath at this, then applauded with all their might the fallen leader who represented, almost alone, the undefeat of which they boasted from stumps across the land, now and for years to come. Unforgiving, he was unforgiven, and he preferred it so, for their sake and his own.

Late in the spring of the following year a Boston paper called on Davis for an expression of his views on U. S. Grant, who was dying at Mount McGregor, New York, of cancer of the throat. Bankrupt by a brokerage partner who turned out to be a swindler, the general had lost even his sword as security for an unpaid loan, and was now engaged in a race with death to complete his *Memoirs*, hoping the proceeds would provide for his family after he was gone. He won, but only by the hardest. Reduced by pain to communicating with his doctor on slips of paper — "A verb is anything that signifies to be; to do; to suffer," one read. "I signify all three" — he managed to finish the book within a week of his death in July, and royalties approaching half a million dollars went to Julia and his sons. Davis had declined to comment on the career of this man whose name, in the course of his two White House terms, had come to stand for plunder and repression. "General Grant is dying," he replied to the request from Boston. "Instead of seeking to disturb the quiet of his closing hours, I would, if it were in my power, contribute to the peace of his mind and the comfort of his body." Similarly, he had withheld comment on the passing of other former enemies, beginning with George Thomas, whose weight rose above three hundred pounds within five years of the end of the war, when he died on duty of a stroke in the same year as his fellow Virginian, R. E. Lee. Henry Halleck and George Meade, who also stayed in the army, followed him two years later. George McClellan, after serving three years as governor of New Jersey, died three months after Grant, and was followed in turn by Winfield Hancock, who had run against Garfield in the presidential election six years back, just over three months later.

By then it was 1886, the silver anniversary of Sumter. Memorial services and reunions were being planned throughout the South, and Davis was pressed to attend most of them as guest of honor. He declined, pleading frailty, until someone thought to point out that Winnie might never know how dear he was to the hearts of his people unless he gave them the chance to show their love in public. That persuaded him. "I'll go; I'll go," he said, and accepted invitations from Montgomery, Atlanta, and Savannah. In late April he sat on the portico of the Alabama capitol, where he had been inaugurated twenty-five years before, and heard a eulogy pronounced by John B. Gordon, former U. S. senator and now a candidate for governor of Georgia, who also presented Winnie to the crowd, to wild applause. Next day Davis spoke briefly at the laying of the cornerstone for a monument to the Confederate dead — repeating once more his contention that the seceded states had launched no revolution; "Sovereigns never rebel," he said — then set out for Atlanta, where 50,000 veterans were assembling for a May Day reunion. He was on the platform, receiving the cheers of all that host, when he looked out beyond its distant fringes and saw a man approaching on horseback, portly and white-haired, with cottony muttonchop whiskers, decked out in Confederate gray with the looped braid of a lieutenant general on his sleeves. It was Longstreet. Uninvited because of his postwar views — "The striking feature, the one the people should keep in view," he had said at the outset of Reconstruction, "is that we are a conquered people. Recognizing this fact, fairly and squarely, there is but one course left for wise men to pursue, and that is to accept the terms that now are offered by the conquerers" — Old Peter had risen that morning at his home in nearby Gainesville, put on his full uniform, come down by train, and ridden out to show the throng that he was of them, whether they wanted him there or not. Dismounting, he walked up the steps of the platform where Davis was seated, and everyone wondered what Davis would do. They soon found out, for he rose and hurried to meet Lee's old warhorse. "When the two came together," a witness declared, "Mr Davis threw his arms around General Longstreet's neck and the two leaders embraced with great emotion. The meaning of the reconciliation was clear and instantly had a profound effect upon the thousands of veterans who saw it. With a great shout they showed their joy."

One occasion of the Atlanta visit was the unveiling of a statue to the late Senator Benjamin Hill, always a loyal friend in times of crisis. "We shall conquer all enemies yet," he had assured his chief within two weeks of Appomattox, but admitted nine years later, looking back: "All physical advantages are insufficient to account for our failure. The truth is, we failed because too many of our people were not determined to win." Davis knew the basic validity of this view, yet he preferred to stress the staunchness of his people and the long odds they had faced. Northern journalists had begun to note the "inflammatory" effect of his appearances, and he tried next week in Savannah to offset this by remarking at a banquet given by the governor in his honor: "There are some who take it for granted that when I allude to State sovereignty I want to bring on another war. I am too old to fight again, and God knows I do not want you to have the necessity of fighting again." He paused to let the reporters take this down, but while he waited he saw the faces of those around him, many of them veterans like himself; with the result that he undid what had gone before. "However, if the necessity *should* arise," he said, "I know you will meet it, as you always have discharged every duty you felt called upon to perform."

Although he returned to Beauvoir near exhaustion, he recovered in time, the following year, to challenge the prohibition movement as still another "monstrous" attempt to limit individual freedom. His words were quoted by the liquor interests and he was denounced by a Methodist bishop for advocating "the barroom and the destruction of virtue." But the fact was he had mellowed, partly under the influence of strong nationalist feelings never far below the surface of his resistance. When he went back to Georgia in October, to meet "perhaps for the last time" with veterans at a reunion staged in Macon — where he had first been taken after his capture near Irwinville, more than twenty-two years ago —he spoke to them of the North and South as indivisibly united. "We are now at peace," he said, "and I trust will ever remain so. . . . In referring therefore to the days of the past and the glorious cause you have served . . . I seek but to revive a memory which should be dear to you and to your children, a memory which teaches the highest lessons of manhood, of truth and adherence to duty — duty to your State, duty to your principles, duty to your buried parents, and duty to your coming children." That was the burden of what he had to say through the time now left him, including his last speech of all, delivered the following spring at Mississippi City, only a six-mile buggy ride from Beauvoir.

Within three months of being eighty years old, he had not thought he would speak again in public; but he did, this once, for a particular reason. The occasion was a convention of young Southerners, and that was why — their youth. He did not mention the war at all, not even as "a memory which should be dear," though he did refer at the outset to the nation he had led. "Friends and fellow citizens," he began, and stopped. "Ah, pardon me," he said. "The laws of the United States no longer permit me to designate you as fellow citizens. I feel no regret that I stand before you a man without a country, for my ambition lies buried in the grave of the Confederacy." Then he went on to tell them what he had come to say. "The faces I see before me are those of young men; had I not known this I would not have appeared before you. Men in whose hands the destinies of our Southland lie, for love of her I break my silence to speak to you a few words of respectful admonition. The past is dead; let it bury its dead, its hopes and its aspirations. Before you lies the future, a future full of golden promise, a future of expanding national glory, before which all the world shall stand amazed. Let me beseech you to lay aside all rancor, all bitter sectional feeling, and to take your places in the ranks of those who will bring about a consummation devoutly to be wished — a reunited country."

Those were his last public words, and they seemed withal to have brought him a new peace, one that fulfilled a hope he had recently expressed to an old friend: "My downs have been so many, and the feeling of injustice so great, that I wish to hold on and see whether the better days may not come." A reporter who came to Beauvoir for his eightieth birthday, June 3, not only found him "immaculately dressed, straight and erect, with traces of his military service still showing in his carriage, and with the flush of health on his pale, refined face," but also observed that he retained "a keen interest in current topics, political, social, religious." He kept busy. In the course of the next year he wrote three magazine articles, a *Short History of the Confederate States*, and even got started on an autobiography, though he soon put this aside. In early November, 1889, he set out for New Orleans to catch a steamer upriver for his annual inspection trip to Brierfield, which he had lost and then recovered by a lawsuit. Usually his wife went along but this time she remained behind with guests. Exposed to a sleety rain, he came down with a cold and was so ill by the time the boat reached Brierfield Landing, late at night, that he continued on to Vicksburg. Going ashore next morning, he rode down to the plantation, only to spend the next four days in bed, sick with bronchitis and a recurrence of the malaria that had killed his bride and nearly killed him, more than fifty years before, at the same place.

Alarmed, for Davis by then was near delirium, the plantation manager got him back to Vicksburg and onto a steamer headed south. Downriver that night the boat was hailed by another coming up with Varina on board. Warned by telegraph of her husband's condition, she had set out to join him, and now she did so, transferring in midstream to claim her place at his bedside. New Orleans doctors pronounced him too ill to be taken to Beauvoir, so he was carried on a stretcher to a private home in the Garden District. He seemed to improve in the course of the next week. "It may seem strange to you," he told an attending physician, "that a man of my years should desire to live; but I do. There are still some things that I have to do in this world." He wanted above all to get back to the autobiography he had set aside. "I have not told what I wish to say of my college-mates Sidney Johnston and Polk. I have much more to say of them. I shall tell a great deal of West Point — and I seem to remember more every day." Presently, though, it was clear that he would do none of these things, including the desired return to Beauvoir. Another week passed; December came in. On December 5, within six months of being eighty-two years old, he woke to find Varina sitting beside him, and he let her know he knew the time was near. "I want to tell you I am not afraid to die," he said, although he seemed no worse than he had been the day before.

That afternoon he slept soundly, but woke at dusk with a violent chill. Frightened, Varina poured out a teaspoon of medicine, only to have him decline it with a meager smile and a faint shake of his head. When she insisted he refused again. "Pray excuse me. I cannot take it," he murmured. These were the last words of a man who had taken most of the knocks a hard world had to offer. He lapsed into a peaceful sleep that continued into the night. Once when his breathing grew labored the doctors turned him gently onto his right side, and he responded childlike by raising his arm to pillow his cheek on his hand, the other resting lightly on his heart. Midnight came and went, and less than an hour later he too obeyed Anaximander's dictum, breathing his last so imperceptibly that Varina and the others at his bedside could scarcely tell the moment of his going.

He died on Friday and was buried on Wednesday, time being needed to allow for the arrival of friends and relatives from distant points. Meanwhile, dressed in a civilian suit of Confederate gray, his body lay in state at City Hall, viewed in the course of the next four days by an estimated hundred thousand mourners. Then the day of the funeral came, December 11, and all the church bells of New Orleans tolled. Eight southern governors served as pallbearers, the Washington Artillery as guard of honor; interment would be at Metairie Cemetery in the tomb of the Army of Northern Virginia, which was crowned with a statue of Stonewall Jackson atop a fifty-foot marble shaft. "The end of a long and lofty life has come. The strange and sudden dignity of death has been added to the fine and resolute dignity of living," the Episcopal bishop of Louisiana declared on the steps of City Hall as the casket was brought out to begin the three-hour march to Metairie. After the service at the tomb, when Taps had sounded, he spoke again. "In the name of God, amen. We here consign the body of Jefferson Davis, a servant of his state and country and a soldier in their armies; sometime member of Congress, Senator from Mississippi, and Secretary of War of the United States; the first and only President of the Confederate States of America; born in Kentucky on the third day of June, 1808, died in Louisiana on the sixth day of December, 1889, and buried here by the reverent hands of his people."

Much else was said in the way of praise across the land that day, and still more would be said four years later, when his body would be removed to its permanent resting place in Hollywood Cemetery, Richmond, to join his son Joe and others who had died nearby in Virginia during the war. Lincoln by now had been a full generation in his Springfield tomb, and all he had said or written would be cherished as an imperishable legacy to the nation, including the words he had spoken in response to a White House serenade on the occasion of his reëlection: "What has occurred in this case must ever recur in similar cases. Human nature will not change. In any future great national trial, compared with the men of this, we shall have as weak and as strong, as silly and as wise, as bad and as good. Let us therefore study the incidents of this, as philosophy to learn wisdom from, and none of them as wrongs to be revenged." Davis could never match that music, or perhaps even catch its tone. His was a different style, though it too had its beauty and its uses: as in his response to a recent Beauvoir visitor, a reporter who hoped to leave with something that would help explain to readers the underlying motivation of those crucial years of bloodshed and division. Davis pondered briefly, then replied.

"Tell them — " He paused as if to sort the words. "Tell the world that I only loved America," he said.

List of Maps

Bibliographical Note

LIST OF MAPS

*Maps drawn by Rafael Palacios, from originals
by the author. All are oriented north.*

BIBLIOGRAPHICAL NOTE

So there now. Twenty years have come and gone and I can say with Chaucer, "Farwel my book and my devocion." All through the second of these two decades — the drawn-out time it took to write this third and final volume — my debt to those who went before me, dead and living, continued to mount even as the Centennial spate diminished to a trickle and then ran dry. Previous obligations were enlarged, and new ones acquired, on both sides of the line defining the limits of the original material: especially on the near side, where the evidence was assembled and presented in general studies, biographies, and secondary accounts of individual campaigns. Chief among these last, to take them in the order of their use, were the following: *Red River Campaign* by Ludwell H. Johnson, *Lee's Last Campaign* by Clifford Dowdey, *Autumn of Glory* by Thomas L. Connelly, *Jubal's Raid* by Frank E. Vandiver, *The Decisive Battle of Nashville* by Stanley F. Horn, *Sherman's March Through the Carolinas* by John G. Barrett, and two recitals of the Appomattox chase, *An End to Valor* by Philip Van Doren Stern and *Nine April Days* by Burke Davis. Similarly, my long-term obligation to works on naval matters was extended by Virgil Carrington Jones's *Civil War at Sea: The Final Effort* and Edward Boykin's *Ghost Ship of the Confederacy*.

No one who has read or even scanned these books can fail to see my debt to them, as well as to the biographies cited earlier, two of which had concluding volumes that came out just as the need for them was sorest: Hudson Strode's *Jefferson Davis: Tragic Hero* and Bruce Catton's *Grant Takes Command*. Having had them, I cannot see how I could have managed without them, and the same applies to J. G. Randall's *Lincoln the President*, completed after his death by Richard N. Current in *Last Full Measure*, and Jim Bishop's *Day Lincoln Was Shot*. Clifford Dowdey's *Lee* brought his subject into sharper focus, and T. Harry

Williams filled a sizeable gap with his *Hayes of the Twenty-third*, as E. B. Long did many others with *The Civil War Day by Day: An Almanac*. Nash K. Burger's and John K. Bettersworth's *South of Appomattox* helped get me down to the wire, and Kenneth M. Stampp, who was with me at the start in *And the War Came*, was also with me at the finish in *The Era of Reconstruction*, another old friend among the many I know only through their work.

To all these I am grateful, as I was and am to those mentioned in the end notes to the first two volumes of this iliad, most of whom continued their contribution through the third. Originally I intended to list my obligations in a complete bibliography here at the close of the whole, but even this chore has been spared me — along with a considerable added bulkiness for you — by Ralph G. Newman and E. B. Long, whose 1964 pamphlet, *A Basic Civil War Library*, first published in the *Journal of the Illinois State Historical Society*, enumerates by category the 350-odd books I owe most to, old and new and in and out of print. Other such compilations are readily available, including a much fuller one in Long's own *Almanac*, yet this one is to me the best in its inclusion of the works I mainly relied on, at any rate up to its date of issue. While I hope I have acknowledged my heaviest contemporary debts in this trio of notes, there are two I would like to stress in particular. One is to Bruce Catton, whose *Centennial History of the Civil War* was finished in time for its third volume, *Never Call Retreat*, to be available, together with his earlier *Stillness at Appomattox*, as a source and guide all through the writing of my own third volume. I was, as Stonewall Jackson said in another connection on his deathbed, "the infinite gainer" from having him thus meet his deadline even as I was failing to reach mine. My other chief debt is to the late Allan Nevins, whose close-packed *Organized War to Victory*, the last in his four-volume *War for the Union*, was similarly available during the past two years. Both gave me a wealth of useable material, but at least as valuable was their example of dedication and perseverance, double-barreled proof that such an undertaking could be carried to a finish. In that sense my debt to them is personal, though not as much so, nor as large, as the ones I owe my editor, Robert Loomis, and my wife, Gwyn Rainer Foote, both of whom bore with me all the way.

Perhaps in closing I might add that, although nowhere along the line have I had a "thesis" to argue or maintain — partly no doubt because I never saw one yet that could not be "proved," at least to the satisfaction of the writer who advanced it — I did have one thing I wanted to do, and that was to restore a balance I found lacking in nearly all the histories composed within a hundred years of Sumter. In all too many of these works, long and short, foreign and domestic, the notion prevailed that the War was fought in Virginia, while elsewhere — in an admittedly large but also rather empty region known vaguely as "the West" — a sort of running skirmish wobbled back and forth, presumably as a way for its participants, faceless men with unfamiliar names, to pass the time while waiting for the issue to be settled in the East. I do not claim that the opposite is true, but I do claim that it is perhaps a little closer to the truth; that Vicksburg, for example, was as "decisive" as Gettysburg, if not more so, and that Donelson, with its introduction of Grant and Forrest onto the national scene, may have had more to do with the outcome than either of the others had, for all their greater panoply, numbers, and documentation. In any case, it was my hope to provide what I considered a more fitting balance, East and West, in the course of attempting my aforesaid purpose of re-creating that war and making it live again in the world around us.

So, anyhow, "Farwel my book and my devocion," my rock and my companion through two decades. At the outset of this Gibbon span, plunk in what I hope will be the middle of my writing life, I was two years younger than Grant at Belmont, while at the end I was four months older than Lincoln at his assassination. By way of possible extenuation, in response to complaints that it took me five times longer to write the war than the participants took to fight it, I would point out that there were a good many more of them than there was of me. However that may be, the conflict is behind me now, as it is for you and it was a hundred-odd years ago for them.

—S.F.

Index

A

Catharpin Road, 148, 151, 152, 158, 165, 166, 174, 192, 199
Cedar Creek, 250, 302, 564, 565, 566–72, 574, 631, 804
    casualties, 571–72
    See also Fisher's Hill
Cedar Mountain, 20, 24
Cedar Point, 495, 506
Centerville, 122
Central Georgia Railroad, 646, 647
    demolition of, 648
Centralia, 578
Chaffin's Bluff, 254, 261, 304, 435, 438, 545, 560, 561, 628, 896
Chalmers, James R., 106–7, 108, 597, 601, 670
    Memphis patrol, 597
    Nashville battle, 679–80, 690, 698, 700, 705, 707
    in North Mississippi, 513, 514, 515, 518
Chambersburg, 451
    burning of, 539
Chambrun, Marquis de, 903, 905–6
Chancellorsville, 113, 134, 135, 142, 146, 147, 150, 174, 179, 188, 189, 190, 347, 475, 477, 485, 555, 566, 639, 783, 908
Chandler, Zachariah, 464–65, 559, 963, 988
Chantilly, 20
Charles I, King, 776
Charles City Courthouse, 313
Charleston, 17, 121, 256, 258, 427, 507, 586, 614, 624, 635, 645, 646, 736, 751, 753, 764, 799, 1006
    evacuated, 797, 804, 822
    expulsion of British consul, 99
    Fort Sumter ceremonies (April, 1865), 969–73, 979
    goods run into (1864), 741
    occupation of, 800
Charleston Convention of 1860, 19
Charleston & Savannah Railroad, 652–53
Charlotte, Empress, 376, 1023
Charlotte, North Carolina, 796, 798, 859, 863, 885, 967, 969, 989, 998
    Confederate government headquarters, 1002–4
Charlottesville, 270, 302, 306, 309, 311, 445, 450, 565, 807, 808, 850
Chase, Salmon P., 38, 462–63, 471, 558, 559, 562, 814, 963, 965, 987–88
    on reorganization of state governments, 961–62
    on secession, 1035
    Supreme Court appointment, 728
    swearing in of Johnson, 986
Chattahoochee River, 320, 321, 343, 344, 347, 353, 392, 394, 395, 399, 412, 413, 417, 418, 419, 473, 485–87, 521–23, 524, 604, 607–9, 611, 614, 998, 1007
    Federal crossing of, 402–10, 411, 415, 419

Chattanooga, 4, 13, 27, 112, 117, 135, 187, 319–21, 322, 323, 331, 337, 344, 347, 391, 395, 485, 491, 492, 519, 598, 599, 615, 621, 622, 636, 681, 1014
Chattanooga Railroad, *see* Nashville & Chattanooga Railroad
Chattooga River, 615
Cheatham, Benjamin F., 605, 606, 759, 798
    Atlanta battle, 473–76, 477, 482, 483, 490
    at Bentonville, 830, 831
    Franklin battle, 663, 667–70, 671, 673, 674
    and Hood's march north, 656, 657, 659, 660–61
    at Kennesaw Mountain, 396–97, 398, 399
    Nashville battle, 676–77, 678, 679, 690, 692, 694, 698–703, 706, 707
    and Peachtree Creek, 473–76
Cheraw, 751, 796, 800, 818, 819, 822
Cherbourg harbor, 508, 587, 765
Cherokee Indians, 1022
Chesapeake Bay, 127, 450, 457, 906, 1012
Chesnut, James, Jr., 755
Chesnut, Mary Boykin, 755, 760, 799
Chester, 791–92, 796, 798, 799
Chesterfield Bridge, 266, 268, 269, 270, 274
Chesterfield Courthouse, 908
Cheyenne Indians, 726
Chicago, Convention, 378–79, 470, 549, 551–52, 713
Chicago *Times*, 186
Chicago *Tribune*, 574
Chickahominy, 233, 260, 264, 275, 277, 279, 280, 281, 285, 286, 287, 292, 300, 303, 313, 315, 316, 430, 439, 628, 631
Chickamauga, 13–14, 16, 122, 171, 244, 257, 258, 330, 349, 350, 370, 399, 408, 458, 549, 606, 640, 660
Chickasaw (ship), 497, 499, 505
Chilesburg, 225, 307
Chillicothe (steamer), 83
China, 1041
Chivington, John M., 725–27
Choctaw Indians, 68, 69, 585
Churchill, Thomas J., 36–37, 42–44, 45, 47–49, 53, 54, 73, 75, 76
Cincinnati, 13, 21, 24, 108, 133, 616, 837
Cincinnati Convention, 470
Cincinnati Gazette, 471
Citronelle, 999, 1040
City Belle (transport), 79–80
City Point, 19, 127, 151–52, 251–53, 255, 256, 261, 263, 313, 436, 442, 443, 450, 458, 548, 554, 560, 614, 623, 637, 650, 710–11, 715, 739, 784, 853–54, 893, 895, 903, 926, 953, 975, 1018
City Point Railroad, 429, 433, 841
Civil Rights Act of 1875, 1044
Clark, John S., 41

Mobile & Ohio Railroad, 364, 365, 366, 511, 999

Monadnock (monitor), 1028

Monett's Ferry, 54, 57, 58

Monitor (ironclad), 493, 508, 591

Monk's Neck Bridge, 862

Monocacy Junction, 451, 542

Monocacy River, 448–50, 451, 452, 453, 457, 461, 558

Monongahela (sloop), 498, 502, 504

Monroe, James, 906

Monroe Doctrine, 376–77, 771, 1018–19

Montgomery, 326, 408, 486, 607, 608, 758, 759, 905, 967, 1038, 1050, 1056

Montgomery Hill, 688, 691, 693, 695, 698

Moreauville, 86, 87

Morgan, Daniel, 827

Morgan, Edwin D., 462

Morgan, James D., 830, 831, 832

Morgan, John H., 105, 113, 245–46, 247, 319, 412, 414–15, 471, 880

    death of, 595–96, 721

    East Tennessee raid, 595–96

    Kentucky raid, 358–62, 373, 374, 380, 593

Morgan, Mattie Ready, 596

Morgan (gunboat), 494, 502

Morris, Charles M., 587–88, 589

Morton, John W., 365, 366, 367, 369–70

    at Johnsonville, 619–20

    in Middle Tennessee, 598, 599, 601

    in North Mississippi, 514, 515

Morton, Oliver P., 549

Mosby, John S., 805–6, 1000

Mott, Gershom, 161–62, 177

    Spotsylvania battle, 209, 210, 212, 213

Moulton, Alfred, 42, 44, 49

Mound City (gunboat), 83

Mount Jackson, 248, 250

Mount Pleasant, 654, 655, 663

Mount Sterling, 361, 362

    Confederate looting of, 358–59

Mount Vernon, 906

Mower, Joseph A., 834, 835

Mozart, Wolfgang Amadeus, 817

Munford, Thomas T., 870

Murdoch, James E., 574

Murfreesboro, *see* Stones River

Murrah, Pendleton, 1023

Muscle Shoals, 708, 709

Myers, Gustavus A., 901

N

Nancy's Creek, 409–10

Napoleon I, 29, 157, 608, 610, 675, 679, 780, 1019

Napoleon III, 15, 25, 99, 860, 1019, 1023, 1050

    occupation of Mexico, 376–77

Nasby, Petroleum V., *see* Locke, D. R.

Nashville, 7, 13, 21, 31, 64, 92, 102, 108, 112, 117, 357, 365, 395, 522, 598, 600, 607, 614, 616, 617, 619, 621, 636, 647, 654–60, 662, 666, 672, 673, 750, 1018, 1041

Nashville, battle for, 674–710, 737, 738

    casualties, 678, 695, 700, 705, 706, 708

    city fortifications, 676

    first day, 688–95

    Murfreesboro strike, 677–78, 679, 681

    prisoners-of-war, 704–5, 709

    second day, 698–705

    withdrawal of Confederate army, 705–10, 757

Nashville & Chattanooga Railroad, 519, 599, 601, 677

Nashville Military Institute, 704

Nashville & Northwestern Railroad, 601

Nassau, 717, 1028

Nassau bacon, 629

Nat Turner uprising, 973

Natchez, 735

Natchitoches, 32, 34, 35, 38, 39, 40, 54, 56–57, 68, 85, 91, 92, 575

    burning of, 57

National Union party, 378

Naval operations, 14, 17, 30, 100, 109, 110, 309, 315, 317, 587–95, 614, 709

    at Bermuda Hundred, 251–54, 257–58

    blockade runners, 493, 507, 591, 614, 717, 737, 741, 754

    off Brazil, 587–90

    Butler-Porter expedition (to Wilmington), 715–21

        casualties, 715

        failure of, 721

    off Carolina coast, 113–17, 591–95

    off Cherbourg harbor, 380–90, 442, 587

    defense of Washington, 457

    on the high seas, 590–91, 1028–31

    James River Squadron, 765, 886, 888–89, 1024

    last shot of the Civil War, 1029

    late-April through November (1865), 1023–31

    in Mobile Bay, 492–508

    off New England coast, 508–9, 1010, 1024

    North Atlantic Blockading Squadron, 589

    Red River campaign, 26, 28, 30, 32–33, 38–39, 51, 52–56, 59–60, 61, 68, 73, 85, 88, 104

        casualties, 88–89

        cotton seizure policy, 38–39

        divergence from land forces, 39–40

COMPREHENSIVE TABLE OF CONTENTS

The Civil War: A Narrative

Volume I, *Fort Sumter to Perryville*

"A stunning book full of color, life, character and a new atmosphere of the Civil War, and at the same time a narrative of unflagging power. Eloquent proof that an historian should be a writer above all else." —BURKE DAVIS

"This is historical writing at its best....It can hardly be surpassed." —*Library Journal*

"Anyone who wants to relive the Civil War, as thousands of Americans apparently do, will go through this volume with pleasure....Years from now, Foote's monumental narrative most likely will continue to be read and remembered as a classic of its kind."
—*New York Herald Tribune Book Review*

"There is, of course, a majesty inherent in the subject. Some sense of that ineluctable fact, however reluctant its expression, is evident in every honest consideration of our history. But the credit for recovering such majesty to the attention of our skeptical and unheroic age will hereafter belong peculiarly to Mr. Foote." —M. E. BRADFORD, *The National Review*

The Civil War: A Narrative

Volume II, *Fredericksburg to Meridian*

"Gettysburg...is described with such meticulous attention to action, terrain, time, and the characters of the various commanders that I understand, at last, what happened in that battle. ...Mr. Foote has an acute sense of the relative importance of events and a novelist's skill in directing the reader's attention to the men and the episodes that will influence the course of the whole war, without omitting items which are of momentary interest. His organization of facts could hardly be bettered." —*Atlantic*

"Though the events of this middle year of the Civil War have been recounted hundreds of times, they have rarely been re-created with such vigor and such picturesque detail as in Mr. Foote's 'Civil War: A Narrative.' " —*New York Times Book Review*

"The lucidity of the battle narratives, the vigor of the prose, the strong feeling for the men from generals to privates who did the fighting are all controlled by a constant sense of how it happened and what it was all about. Foote has the novelist's feeling for character and situation, without losing the historian's scrupulous regard for recorded fact. *The Civil War* is likely to stand unequaled." —WALTER MILLS